A HISTORY OF WESTERN SOCIETY

A History of Western Society

FOURTH EDITION

John P. McKay

UNIVERSITY OF ILLINOIS AT URBANA–CHAMPAIGN

Bennett D. Hill

GEORGETOWN UNIVERSITY

John Buckler

UNIVERSITY OF ILLINOIS AT URBANA–CHAMPAIGN

HOUGHTON MIFFLIN COMPANY   BOSTON
DALLAS   GENEVA, ILLINOIS
PALO ALTO   PRINCETON, NEW JERSEY

About the Authors

John P. McKay Born in St. Louis, Missouri, John P. McKay received his B.A. from Wesleyan University (1961), his M.A. from the Fletcher School of Law and Diplomacy (1962), and his Ph.D. from the University of California, Berkeley (1968). He began teaching history at the University of Illinois in 1966 and became a professor there in 1976. John won the Herbert Baxter Adams Prize for his book *Pioneers for Profit: Foreign Entrepreneurship and Russian Industrialization, 1885–1913* (1970). He has also written *Tramways and Trolleys: The Rise of Urban Mass Transport in Europe* (1976) and has translated Jules Michelet's *The People* (1973). His research has been supported by fellowships from the Ford Foundation, the Guggenheim Foundation, the National Endowment for the Humanities, and IREX. His articles and reviews have appeared in numerous journals, including *The American Historical Review, Business History Review, The Journal of Economic History,* and *Slavic Review.* He edits *Industrial Development and the Social Fabric: An International Series of Historical Monographs.*

Bennett D. Hill A native of Philadelphia, Bennett D. Hill earned an A.B. at Princeton (1956) and advanced degrees from Harvard (A.M., 1958) and Princeton (Ph.D., 1963). He taught history at the University of Illinois at Urbana, where he was department chairman from 1978 to 1981. He has published *English Cistercian Monasteries and Their Patrons in the Twelfth Century (1968)* and *Church and State in the Middle Ages* (1970); and articles in *Analecta Cisterciensia, The New Catholic Encyclopaedia, The American Benedictine Review,* and *The Dictionary of the Middle Ages.* His reviews have appeared in *The American Historical Review, Speculum, The Historian, The Catholic Historical Review,* and *Library Journal.* He has been a fellow of the American Council of Learned Societies and has served on committees for the National Endowment for the Humanities. Now a Benedictine monk of St. Anselm's Abbey, Washington, D.C., he is also a Visiting Professor at Georgetown University.

John Buckler Born in Louisville, Kentucky, John Buckler received his B.A. from the University of Louisville in 1967. Harvard University awarded him the Ph.D. in 1973. From 1984 to 1986 he was the Alexander von Humboldt Fellow at Institut für Alte Geschichte, University of Munich. He is currently a professor at the University of Illinois. In 1980 Harvard University Press published his *The Theban Hegemony, 371–362 B.C.*. He has also published *Philip II and the Sacred War* (Leiden 1989), and co-edited *BOIOTIKA: Vorträge vom 5. International Böotien-Kolloquium* (Munich 1989). His articles have appeared in journals both here and abroad, like the *American Journal of Ancient History, Classical Philology, Rheinisches Museum für Philologie, Classical Quarterly, Wiener Studien,* and *Symbolae Osloenses.*

Contents in Brief

Contents

29

DICTATORSHIPS AND THE SECOND WORLD WAR

30

THE RECOVERY OF EUROPE AND THE AMERICAS

31

LIFE IN THE POSTWAR ERA

Maps

Timelines/Genealogies

Note: *Italics* indicate comparative tables.

Preface

A HISTORY OF WESTERN SOCIETY grew out of the authors' desire to infuse new life into the study of Western civilization. We knew full well that historians were using imaginative questions and innovative research to open up vast new areas of historical interest and knowledge. We also recognized that these advances had dramatically affected the subject of European economic, intellectual, and, especially, social history, while new research and fresh interpretations were also revitalizing the study of the traditional mainstream of political, diplomatic, and religious development. Despite history's vitality as a discipline, however, it seemed to us that both the broad public and the intelligentsia were generally losing interest in the past. The mathematical economist of our acquaintance who smugly quipped "What's new in history?"—confident that the answer was nothing and that historians were as dead as the events they examine—was not alone.

It was our conviction, based on considerable experience introducing large numbers of students to the broad sweep of Western civilization, that a book reflecting current trends could excite readers and inspire a renewed interest in history and our Western heritage. Our strategy was twofold. First, we made social history the core element of our work. Not only did we incorporate recent research by social historians, but also we sought to recreate the life of ordinary people in appealing human terms. At the same time we were determined to give great economic, political, intellectual, and cultural developments the attention they unquestionably deserve. We wanted to give individual readers and instructors a balanced, integrated perspective, so that they could pursue on their own or in the classroom those themes and questions that they found particularly exciting and significant. In an effort to realize fully the potential of our fresh yet balanced approach, we made many changes, large and small, in the second and third editions.

Changes in the New Edition

In preparing the fourth edition we have worked hard to keep our book up-to-date and to make it still more effective. First, every chapter has been carefully revised to incorporate recent scholarship. Many of our revisions relate to the ongoing explosion in social history and once again important findings on such subjects as class relations, population, and the family have been integrated into the text. We have made a special effort to keep up with the rapidly growing and increasingly sophisticated scholarship being done in European women's history. Thus we have added or revised sections on women in early Jewish society and in classical Greece, in Christian evangelization and in the Crusades, as well as in the Renaissance, the Reformation, the Enlightenment, and the Industrial Revolution. The roots of modern feminism have been explored.

A major effort has also been made to improve the treatment of economic development and accompanying social changes in the modern period in the light of new research and fresh concepts. We are proud of the resulting changes, which include a new discussion of early modern crises in Chapter 16, a reconsideration of the eighteenth century in Chapters 19 and 20, and a fundamental rethinking of European industrialization in Chapter 22 and its global significance in Chapter 26. Other subjects incorporating new scholarship in this edition include early human evolution, Germanic tribes, the Inquisition, French industrialization, and utopian socialism. New topics designed to keep the work fresh and appealing include Greek federalism, the Vikings, anti-Semitism in the Middle Ages, and reform and revolution in the Soviet Union and eastern Europe in the 1980s.

Second, as in the third edition, we have carefully examined each chapter for organization and clarity. The book begins with a new section on the study of history and the meaning of civilization. There is expanded coverage of Islam and its impact on medieval Europe in Chapter 7, while discussion of the early baroque has been moved from the chapter on absolutism in eastern Europe to Chapter 15 for better thematic and chronological organization. Other organizational improvements include a more appropriate positioning of the story of the Irish famine in Chapter 23, a new section on the

Civil War in the United States in Chapter 25 to facilitate more continuous transatlantic comparisons, a revised discussion of intellectual trends in Chapter 28 that emphasizes the connection between these movements and subsequent political developments, and a unified account of the Second World War in Chapter 29. We have also taken special care to explain terms and concepts as soon as they are introduced.

Third, the addition of more problems of historical interpretation in the third edition was well received, and we have continued in that direction in this edition. We believe that the problematic element helps the reader develop the critical-thinking skills that are among the most precious benefits of studying history. New examples of this more open-ended, more interpretive approach include the debate over Alexander the Great and his achievements (Chapter 4), the controversy regarding the causes of Rome's decline (Chapter 6), the significance of abandoned children in the Middle Ages (Chapter 10), the social costs of English enclosure (Chapter 19), and the impact of industrialization on women and the standard of living (Chapter 22).

Finally, the illustrative component of our work has been completely revised. There are many new illustrations, including nearly two hundred color reproductions that let both great art and important events come alive. As in earlier editions, all illustrations have been carefully selected to complement the text, and all carry captions that enhance their value. Artwork remains an integral part of our book, for the past can speak in pictures as well as in words.

The use of full color throughout this edition also serves to clarify the maps and graphs and to enrich the textual material. Again for improved clarity, maps from the third edition have been completely redesigned to provide easily read and distinguished labels and prominent boundaries and topographical relief. We have also added new maps that illustrate social as well as political developments, including maps on Cistercian expansion and economic activity, seventeenth-century Dutch commerce, Europe at 1715, the ethnic and political boundaries of the Soviet republics, and the reform movements of 1989 in Eastern Europe.

In addition to the many maps that support text discussion, we offer a new, full-color map essay at the beginning of each volume. Our purpose is two-fold. First, by reproducing and describing such cartographic landmarks as the Babylonian world map, the medieval Ebstorf map, maps of the Americas, Africa, and the British Empire based on Ptolemy and Mercator, and contemporary global projections and satellite images, we hope to demonstrate for students the evolution of Western cartography and to guide them toward an understanding of the varied functions and uses of maps. Second, the map essay is intended to reveal the changing European world-view and its expansion from antiquity to the present. In this sense, the map essay may serve as an introduction to the course as well as to cartography.

Distinctive Features

Distinctive features from earlier editions remain in the fourth. To help guide the reader toward historical understanding we have posed specific historical questions at the beginning of each chapter. These questions are then answered in the course of the chapter, each of which concludes with a concise summary of the chapter's findings. The timelines added in the third edition have proved useful, and still more are found in this edition, including double-page timelines that allow students to compare simultaneous political, economic, religious, and cultural developments.

We have also tried to suggest how historians actually work and think. We have quoted extensively from a wide variety of primary sources and have demonstrated in our use of these quotations how historians sift and weigh evidence. We want the reader to think critically and to realize that history is neither a list of cut-and-dried facts nor a senseless jumble of conflicting opinions. It is our further hope that the primary quotations, so carefully fitted into their historical context, will give the reader a sense that even in the earliest and most remote periods of human experience, history has been shaped by individual men and women, some of them great aristocrats, others ordinary folk.

Each chapter concludes with carefully selected suggestions for further reading. These suggestions are briefly described to help readers know where to turn to continue thinking and learning about the Western world. The chapter bibliographies have been revised and expanded to keep them current with the vast and complex new work being done in many fields.

Western civilization courses differ widely in chronological structure from one campus to another. To accommodate the various divisions of historical time into intervals that fit a two-quarter, three-quarter, or two-semester period, *A History of Western Society* is being published in four versions, three of which embrace the complete work:

One-volume hardcover edition, A HISTORY OF WESTERN SOCIETY; two-volume paperback, A HISTORY OF WESTERN SOCIETY *Volume I: From Antiquity to the Enlightenment* (Chapters 1–17), *Volume II: From Absolutism to the Present* (Chapters 16–32); three-volume paperback, A HISTORY OF WESTERN SOCIETY *Volume A: From Antiquity to 1500* (Chapters 1–13), *Volume B: From the Renaissance to 1815* (Chapters 12–21), *Volume C: From the Revolutionary Era to the Present* (Chapters 21–32). For courses on Europe since the Renaissance, we are offering A HISTORY OF WESTERN SOCIETY *Since 1400* (Chapters 13–32) for the first time in the fourth edition.

Note that overlapping chapters in both the two- and the three-volume sets permit still wider flexibility in matching the appropriate volume with the opening and closing dates of a course term.

Ancillaries

Learning and teaching ancillaries, including a *Study Guide, MicroStudy Plus* (a computerized version of the *Study Guide*) *Instructor's Resource Manual, Test Items, MicroTest* (a computerized version of the *Test Items*), and *Map Transparencies,* also contribute to the usefulness of the text. The excellent *Study Guide* has been thoroughly revised by Professor James Schmiechen of Central Michigan University. Professor Schmiechen has been a tower of strength ever since he critiqued our initial prospectus, and he has continued to give us many valuable suggestions and his warmly appreciated support. His *Study Guide* contains chapter summaries, chapter outlines, review questions, extensive multiple-choice exercises, self-check lists of important concepts and events, and a variety of study aids and suggestions. New to the fourth edition are study-review exercises on the interpretation of visual sources and major political ideas as well as suggested issues for discussion and essay and chronology reviews. Another major addition is the section, Understanding the Past Through Primary Sources. Seven primary source documents widely used by

historians are included, each preceded by a description of the author and source and followed by questions for analysis. The *Study Guide* also retains the very successful sections on studying effectively. These sections take the student by ostensive example through reading and studying activities like underlining, summarizing, identifying main points, classifying information according to sequence, and making historical comparisons. To enable both students and instructors to use the *Study Guide* with the greatest possible flexibility, the guide is available in two volumes, with considerable overlapping of chapters. Instructors and students who use only Volumes A and B of the text have all the pertinent study materials in a single volume, *Study Guide, Volume I* (Chapters 1–21); likewise, those who use only Volumes B and C of the text also have all the necessary materials in one volume, *Study Guide, Volume 2* (Chapters 12–32). The multiple-choice sections of the *Study Guide* are also available as *MicroStudy Plus,* a computerized, tutorial version that tells students not only which response is correct but also why each of the other choices is wrong and provides the page numbers of the text where each question is discussed. These "rejoinders" to the multiple-choice questions also appear in printed form at the end of the *Study Guide. MicroStudy Plus* is available for both IBM and Macintosh computers.

The *Instructor's Resource Manual,* prepared by Professor John Marshall Carter of Oglethorpe University, contains learning objectives, chapter synopses, suggestions for lectures and discussion, paper and class activity topics, and lists of audio-visual resources. The accompanying *Test Items,* by Professor Charles Crouch of St. John's University in Collegeville, Minnesota offer identification, multiple-choice, and essay questions for a total of approximately 2000 test items. These test items are available to adopters in both IBM and Macintosh versions, both of which include editing capabilities. In addition, a set of full-color *Map Transparencies* of all the maps in the text is available on adoption.

JOHN P. MCKAY

BENNETT D. HILL

JOHN BUCKLER

Acknowledgments

It is a pleasure to thank the many instructors who have read and critiqued the manuscript through its development:

Ann Allen
University of Louisville

Alfred J. Bannan
University of Dayton

Martin Berger
Youngstown State University

Lenard R. Berlanstein
University of Virginia

Stephen Blumm
Montgomery County Community College

Rebecca L. Boehling
University of Maryland, Baltimore County

Jack Cargill
Rutgers University

Gregory D. Delf
Lane Community College

Helen C. Feng
College of Dupage

Robert Frakes
University of California, Santa Barbara

Frank J. Frost
University of California, Santa Barbara

Sally T. Gershman
Georgia Southern College

Richard M. Golden
Clemson University

Gerald H. Herman
Northeastern University

Michael Honhart
University of Rhode Island

Robert Janosov
Luzerne County Community College

Leslie Moch
University of Michigan—Flint

Jo Ann Moran
Georgetown University

Robert Mueller
University of California, Santa Barbara

Robert L. Munter
San Diego State University

Kathryn Norberg
University of California, Los Angeles

William J. Olejniczak
College of Charleston

Neal N. Pease
University of Wisconsin—Milwaukee

William A. Percy
University of Massachusetts—Boston

William M. Reddy
Duke University

Thomas Schlunz
University of New Orleans

Shapur Shahbazi
Eastern Oregon State College

Sherill Spaar
East Central University

Merry Wiesner
University of Wisconsin—Milwaukee

Many of our colleagues at the University of Illinois kindly provided information and stimulation for our book, often without even knowing it. N. Frederick Nash, Rare Book Librarian, gave freely of his time and made many helpful suggestions for illustrations. The World Heritage Museum at the University continued to allow us complete access to its sizable holdings. James Dengate kindly supplied information on objects from the museum's collection. Caroline Buckler took many excellent photographs of the museum's objects and generously helped us at crucial moments in production. Such wide-ranging expertise was a great asset for which we are very appreciative. Bennett Hill wishes to express his sincere appreciation to Ramón de la Fuente of Washington, D.C., for his support, encouragement, and research assistance in the preparation of this fourth edition.

Each of us has benefited from the generous criticism of his co-authors, although each of us assumes responsibility for what he has written. John Buckler has written the first six chapters; Bennett Hill has continued the narrative through Chapter 16; and John McKay has written Chapters 17 through 32. Finally, we continue to welcome from our readers comments and suggestions for improvements, for they have helped us greatly in this ongoing endeavor.

J.P.M.   B.D.H.   J.B.

Expanding Horizons: Mapmaking in the West

Today cartography, the art of making maps, is as widespread as typography, the process of printing. Maps are so much a part of daily life that people take them for granted. But people are not born with maps in their heads, as they are with fingers on their hands. The very concept of a map is a human invention of vast intellectual and practical importance. Like writing itself, cartography depends on people's use of visual and symbolic means to portray reality. Earth is not a flat table, devoid of physical features. Instead it is marked by mountains, valleys, rivers, oceans, and distances among them all. The knowledge of these features and the accurate portrayal of them allow people to understand their relationship to the planet on which they live. That is the basic reason for a map or an atlas.

The intellectual motivations of cartographers are easily overlooked, but they contribute something singular to the understanding of people. Human beings have a natural curiosity about their world and a joy in discovering new parts of it or learning more about regions not so well known. The Roman statesman and orator Cicero once asked, "*Ubinam gentium sumus?*" ("Where in the world are we?") Although he used this question as a figure of speech, many people were quite serious about finding an accurate answer to it. This curiosity and desire have led people to examine not only the earth but its relation to the cosmos of which it is a part. Early cartographers learned to use the stars as fixed points for the measurement of place and distance. Even today American nuclear submarines depend on celestial

MAP 1 Babylonian world map, ca 600 B.C. (*Source: Courtesy of the Trustees of the British Museum*)

navigation, transmitted by satellite, to determine their course and position. Once people looked to the stars, they began to wonder about the shape, nature, and content of the universe itself. Mapping of the earth was no longer enough; people now charted the cosmos. The Hubble Space Satellite, launched in May 1990, is a sign that the quest continues today.

For ordinary purposes cartography fills a host of practical needs. Maps were first used as a way to describe people's immediate environment—to illustrate the shape of villages and the boundaries of fields. As knowledge of the earth grew, maps became indispensable for travel, both on land and sea. People needed to know where their destination lay, how to reach it, and what to expect along the way. Mariners used the geographical knowledge provided by maps to sail from one port to another.

Other uses of early maps were economic. As people came into contact with one another, they saw new opportunities for barter and trade. It was no longer enough to know how to travel to different locations. Merchants needed to understand the geography of their markets and to know what foreign lands produced and what trading partners wanted in return for their goods. In short, economic contact itself increased knowledge of the face of the land, which could be preserved on maps by symbols to indicate the natural resources and products of various lands.

A third important function of early maps was military. Rulers and generals needed exact knowledge of distances and terrain through which their armies could move and fight. Their needs spurred interest in *topography,* the detailed description and representation of the natural and artificial features of a landscape. The military need for detail led to greater accuracy of maps and better definition of the physical environment.

The demands of empire were not only military but also administrative. The only effective way to govern an area is to know where each part of it is located and what its importance is. Rulers need precise maps to enforce their authority, dispatch commands, collect taxes, and maintain order. Thus the value to historians of some maps lies in their illustration of people's knowledge of the world in relation to the needs of government and the exercise of authority over broad distances.

These are only a few of the uses of cartography, but what of the maps themselves? How do people depict visually and accurately large sections of land or the entire face of the globe? The ways are numerous and some more exact than others. The earliest maps are only pictures of towns showing spatial relationships within a very limited context.

A more accurate way of making a map was derived from land surveys. Beginning about 1500 B.C., surveyors trained in geometry and trigonometry began to study the land in question and to divide its physical features into a series of measured angles and elevations. Cartographers then placed this information onto a grid, so that they could represent visually, according to a consistent and logical system, relations among areas. Although the method sounds simple, it presented early cartographers with a daunting problem, one that still exists today. Mapmakers must represent on a two-dimensional surface the face of a three-dimensional globe. To complicate matters even further, the earth is not a perfect sphere. How cartographers have grappled with these problems can best be seen from the maps illustrated here.

Since maps are basically visual, it is best to trace their evolution in their own context. People of other cultures also mapped their lands, but the Western tradition of cartography enjoyed its own singular path of development. The earliest known map of the Western world is the Babylonian world map, which dates to about 600 B.C. (Map 1). Babylon, with its neighbors around it, lies at the center of the world. Surrounding the land is the ocean, depicted as a circle. Quite interesting are the triangles beyond the ocean, which indicate that the Babylonians knew of peoples beyond the ocean. Here for the first time is evidence of a people who attempted to put themselves geographically into the context of their larger world.

The greatest geographer of the Greco-Roman period was unquestionably Claudius Ptolemaeus, better known as Ptolemy, who lived in Alexandria in the second century A.D. He advanced far beyond the schematic Babylonian world map to produce a scientific atlas based on data. He knew from previous scholars that the world was spherical, so he devised a way of using conic lines of *longitude,* angular distances east and west, and of *latitude,* angular distances north and south, to plot the positions and distances of the earth's features. Despite its distortions, Ptolemy's *Geographia* became the standard Western work on geography until the Age of Discovery (ca 1450–1650) in the early modern period.

The best illustration of his brilliant vision actually dates much later than its first representation to a manuscript produced in the German city of Ulm in 1482 (Map 2). Ptolemy put cartography on a scientific basis.

Some of the practical fruits of Ptolemy's labor can be seen in the series of maps known as the Peutinger Table, which probably dates to ca A.D. 500. The Table is a good example of how cartography served the Roman Empire. The section illustrated here is typical of the entire series: it indicates roads, rivers, mountains, cities, and towns in Greece (Map 3). In that respect it is an ancient road map, for its purpose was not to define the known world, as Ptolemy had done, but to inform the emperor and his bureaucracy how they could most easily administer and communicate with the provinces. Although alien to modern notions of the shape of Europe, the Peutinger Table is a remarkably accurate atlas of routes and distances and thus displays vividly and beautifully one of the most practical functions of cartography.

Europeans in the Middle Ages, like their predecessors, drew maps of the world, but now religion became an ingredient of cartography. Ptolemy's concepts of geography remained in force, but maps also served another and different purpose for society. The Ebstorf Map, drawn during the thirteenth century, shows the world surrounded by the ocean, a conception dating to antiquity (Map 4). Yet the

MAP 2 Map from Ptolemy's *Geographica (Source: Michael Holford)*

MAP 3 Section of the Peutinger Table illustrating Greece, ca A.D. 500 *(Source: Osterreichische Nationalbibliothek)*

MAP 4 Ebstorf map, thirteenth century *(Source: Niedersächsische Landesbibliothek Hannover)*

Map boasts several novel features. Its background is the crucifixion of Jesus, whose head stands at the top to indicate east with his arms pointing north and south. Jerusalem occupies the center of the map to represent the place of Jesus' death as the center of the Christian world. Thus the Ebstorf Map was intended to convey a religious message, a declaration of faith, unlike the practical maps of the Peutinger Table.

Islamic cartographers also drew heavily on Ptolemy's research, but they relied on exploration as well. The most famous of them was al-Idrisi, who lived in the twelfth century. His atlas depicted the entire known world and was accompanied by a written commentary of the places illustrated. The portion shown here represents North Africa at the straits of Gibraltar and Spain (Map 5). As in the Peutinger Table, physical features such as rivers and mountains are stylized, but Idrisi has made a serious effort to delineate the general features of the landmass. If the map looks odd, it is because Idrisi used south as his basic point of orientation, not north as do modern cartographers.

The people of the Middle Ages were not content to rely solely on Ptolemy for their understanding of the world. They explored the concept of triangula-

MAP 5 Portion of the map of al-Idrisi, showing North Africa and Spain *(Source: Reproduced by permission of Norman J. W. Thrower, Department of Geography, UCLA)*

MAP 6 Catalan Atlas of 1375 *(Source: Bibliothèque Nationale, Paris/Photo Hubert Josse)*

tion to survey the land and to navigate the seas. Cartographers chose several major points to serve as hubs of a series of lines extended to other major points. The face of the globe was thereby cut up into a pattern of triangles, rectangles, and occasionally squares. Although this system proved complicated and unwieldy, triangulation did improve the utility of maps for explorers. An excellent example of a triangulated map comes from the Catalan Atlas of 1375 (Map 6). To make the atlas even more functional, the cartographer has indicated orientation, so that users may locate their position according to a compass.

Only with the Age of Discovery did European explorers and cartographers make significant advances over Ptolemy's view of the world. Sailors and navigators who voyaged to find new lands or to become better acquainted with familiar places dealt in an aspect of reality that is essential to map-making: they had to be able to calculate where they were. They knew that the world was curved, and they used the stars as fixed points to guide them. It is thus ironic that one of the most important advances in geographical knowledge came by mistake. In 1492 Christopher Columbus discovered the New World by sailing westward from Europe, looking for a sea passage to India. Although Columbus himself did not immediately recognize the full significance of his achievement, his discovery revolutionized geographical thinking. There was more to the world than Ptolemy had known, and the basic features of the earth had to be explored, relationships rethought, and a new way of looking at the globe found.

Perhaps nothing better indicates the fluid state of geography and cartography at the time than the map of Juan de la Cosa of Columbus's second voyage to the Americas (Map 7). A navigator and an explorer, de la Cosa charted the newly found coast of Central America using the points of the compass to orient the fall of the land and triangulation to project his findings inland. Although he

MAP 7 Juan de la Cosa's map of Columbus's discoveries, 1493 *(Source: Museo Naval de Madrid)*

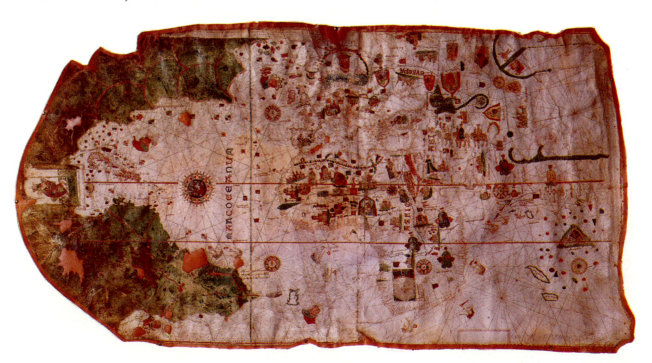

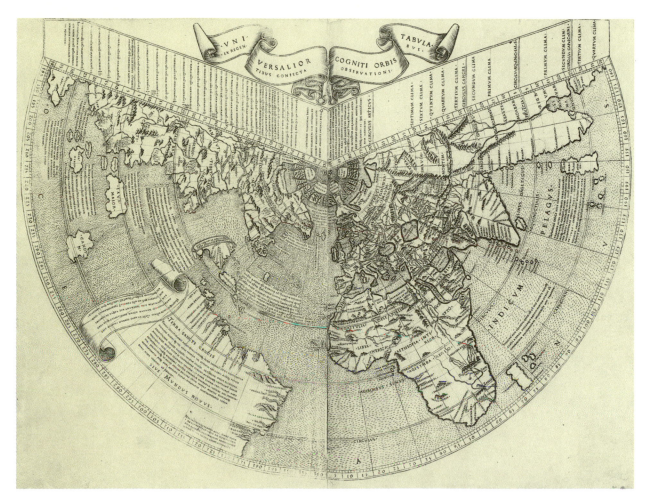

MAP 8 World map of Johannes Ruysch, 1507 and 1508 *(Source: British Library, Department of Maps)*

could depict the coastline accurately because of direct observation, de la Cosa could reveal little about the land beyond.

The discoveries of the European explorers opened a new era, both in how people thought of the world and in how to depict the new findings. The first person to apply effectively Ptolemaic geography to the discoveries of his age was perhaps Johannes Ruysch, who included material on the the New World in his editions of Ptolemy, printed in Rome in 1507 and 1508 (Map 8). Yet the real breakthrough came with Geradus Mercator (1512–1594). Mercator improved Ptolemy's system of latitude and longitude by substituting straight lines for Ptolemy's curved lines. He used this grid to incorporate the discoveries in a completely new atlas. Admittedly Mercator's method distorts the actual physical relations of the land masses over broad spaces. (A weakness of Mercator's system is that areas in the polar regions appear larger than lands near the equator. For instance, Greenland on Mercator's grid is larger than South America.) More important, however, his concept has proved that every portion of the world may be seen as possessing four right angles to orient users of his maps to every other portion of it. Mercator's grid, in one form or another, has endured as a cartographic staple to this day.

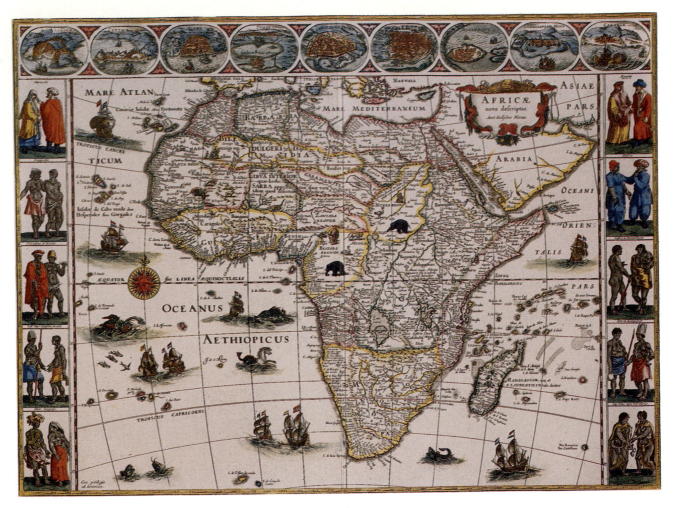

MAP 9 Blaeu's map of Africa, early seventeenth century *(Source: From* Grooten
Atlas, 1648–65. British Library, Department of Maps)

The cumulative effects of the advance of knowledge in geography and cartography can best be seen in the three maps that demonstrate an increasingly precise familiarity with Africa. The map of Blaeu, dating to the early seventeenth century, combines the concepts of scale maps and picture maps (Map 9). Obviously explorers had an accurate idea only of the shape of the continent. The inland was *terra incognita,* unknown territory where fabulous beasts and peoples dwelt. The amazing progress of human knowledge of the land and how to map it can immediately be seen by comparing Blaeu's map of Africa with that of d'Anville, which was published in 1747 (Map 10). D'Anville made excellent use of Mercator's system to produce a profile of Africa that could find its place in any modern atlas. Yet d'Anville was intellectually honest enough to leave the interior of Africa largely blank. True d'Anville's map is not so visually delightful as Blaeu's, but in terms of cartography it is far more important. It showed its users what was yet to be discovered and how to proceed with finding it.

MAP 10 D'Anville's map of Africa, 1747 *(Source: Library of Congress)*

MAP 11 Map of British possessions in the nineteenth century *(Source: Courtesy, David Nash)*

Modern research has put maps to new tasks. After the basic shape and distances of the earth's features were reasonably known, it became possible to plot information on maps that illustrated the findings of scholars and scientists. Thus maps assumed an additional importance because they could record novel aspects of human life and history. The map of the British Empire illustrates when and where the British extended their control of portions of the earth (Map 11). The use of color to indicate the extent of British rule is another application of symbols to convey information. The same is true of the nineteenth-century thematic map of the spread of disease throughout the world (Map 12). Such maps give cartography a new dimension. They show not only where people are on earth but also what they have done in time. In short, they are historical maps that have as much to do with people as with places.

Mapmakers today continue to grapple with the age-old problem of how accurately to portray landmasses, their shapes, and their spatial relationships on an earth that is not a perfect sphere. The problem has been that no matter what projection is used, some geographical areas will be distorted.

In struggling with this problem, cartographers

have used circles, ovals, and rectangles to portray maps on a flat surface. The orthographic projection (the circular maps at the four corners of Maps 13, 14, and 15) uses circles and is one of the oldest. Because it shows only one hemisphere at a time, distortion is minimized, especially at the center of the map where attention is focused. It is a realistic view of the globe, but it is not possible to display more than one hemisphere at a time. As you look at the other projections, it will be useful to compare them to the orthographic projection to see where they are distorted.

The greatest distortion occurs in world maps because of their greater geographical area. Not only are the sizes of regions distorted, but so are their shapes. Different projections are able to minimize some of these distortions. Both the Sinusoidal (Map 13) and the Mollweide (Map 14) map projections provide fairly accurate area representation; that is, the relative size of the continents is correct.

MAP 12 Map illustrating the spread of disease during the nineteenth century *(Source: British Library, Department of Maps)*

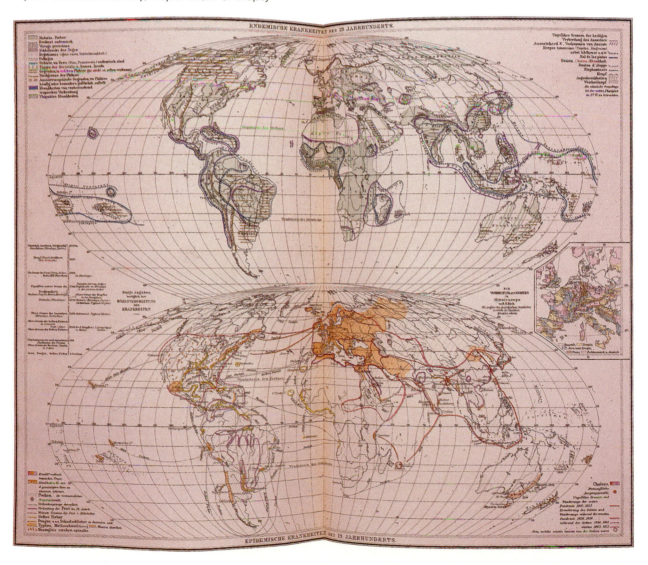

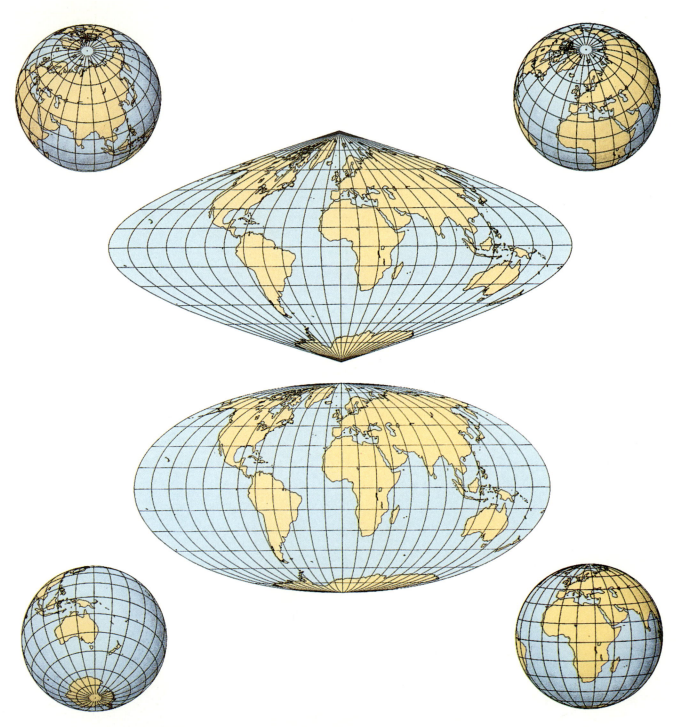

MAP 13 (top) The Sinusoidal projection. **MAP 14** (bottom) The Mollweide projection *(Source: Reproduced with permission from* Which Map is Best? © *1988, by the American Congress on Surveying and Mapping)*

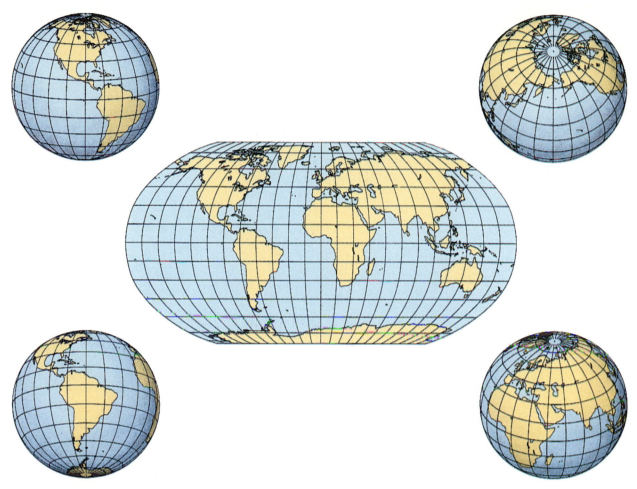

MAP 15 The Robinson projection *(Reproduced with permission from* Which Map is Best? © *1988, by the American Congress on Surveying and Mapping)*

But to accomplish this, they greatly distort the shapes of the continents, especially at the poles.

One way to minimize this distortion is to represent the tops of the poles as lines rather than as points, as shown in the Robinson projection (Map 15). There is still some distortion (note how large Antarctica is), but cutting off the poles diminishes it. The Robinson projection is a compromise because it sacrifices some accuracy in area to achieve less distortion in shape. These modern attempts to depict visually the round earth on flat maps remind people that the problems first perceived by Ptolemy and Mercator remain to be solved.

Yet contemporary cartographers enjoy the use of a new and unusual tool for mapping the globe and exploring the universe: the orbiting satellite. Technology has become so precise within the past ten years that parts of the earth difficult to enter or too remote and forbidding to explore can be examined with minute accuracy from space. The Landsat sat-

MAP 16 Landsat image of the Nile Delta *(Source: GEOPIC,™ Earth Satellite Corporation)*

ellite image of the Nile Delta (Map 16) gives an excellent idea of how much more there is to learn about the planet that we often take for granted, our home, the earth.

JOHN BUCKLER

SUGGESTED READING

Bagrow, Leo. *History of Cartography.* 2nd ed. Chicago: Precedent Publishing, Inc., 1985. Brown, Lloyd A. *The Story of Maps.* New York: Dover Publications, 1979. Dilke, O. A. W. *Greek and Roman Maps.* Ithaca: Cornell University Press, 1985. Harley, J. B., and D. Woodward, eds. *The History of Cartography,* Vol. 1: Cartography in Prehistoric, Ancient and Medieval Europe and the Mediterranean. Chicago and London: University of Chicago Press, 1967. Harvey, Paul D. A. *The History of Topographical Maps.* London: Thames & Hudson, 1980. Hodgkiss, Alan G. *Understanding Maps: A Systematic History of Their Use and Development.* Folkestone: Dawson, 1981. Skelton, Raleigh A. *Decorative Printed Maps of the Fifteenth to Eighteenth Centuries.* London: Staples Press, 1952. Reprinted by Spring Books, 1970. Skelton, Raleigh A. *Explorers' Maps: Chapters in the Cartographic Record of Geographical Discovery.* London: Routledge and Kegan Paul, 1958. Reprinted by Spring Books, 1970. Thrower, Norman J. W. *Maps & Man: An Examination of Cartography in Relation to Culture and Civilization.* Englewood Cliffs, N.J.: Prentice-Hall, 1978. Tooley, R. V., Cand Bricker, and G. R. Crone. *A History of Cartography: 2500 Years of Maps and Mapmakers.* London: Thames & Hudson, 1969.

1

Near Eastern Origins

The culture of the modern Western world has its origins in the ancient Near East, a region that includes the lands bordering the Mediterranean's eastern shore, the Arabian Peninsula, and parts of northeast Africa. In these areas human beings abandoned their life of roaming and hunting to settle in stable agricultural communities. From these communities grew cities and civilizations, societies that invented concepts and techniques that have become integral parts of contemporary life. Fundamental is the development of writing by the Sumerians in Mesopotamia, an invention that allows knowledge of the past to be preserved and facilitates the spread and accumulation of learning, lore, literature, and science. Mathematics, astronomy, and architecture were all innovations of the ancient Near Eastern civilizations. So, too, were the first law codes and religious concepts that still permeate daily life.

But how do people know and understand these things? Before embarking on the study of history, it is necessary to ask, "What is it?" Only then can anyone proceed to link the peoples and events of tens of thousands of years into a coherent whole. Once the nature of history is understood, further questions can be asked and reasonably answered. Specifically for this chapter,

- How did nomadic hunters become urban dwellers?

- How did Western culture originate in Mesopotamia, and what caused Mesopotamian culture to become predominant throughout most of the ancient Near East?

- What part did the Egyptians play in this vast story?

- Last, what did the arrival of the Hittites on the fringes of Mesopotamia and Egypt mean to the more advanced cultures of their new neighbors?

These are the questions we will explore in this chapter.

WHAT IS HISTORY AND WHY?

History is the effort to reconstruct the past to discover what people thought and did and how their beliefs and actions continue to influence human life. In order to appreciate the past fully, we must put it into perspective so that we can understand the factors that have helped to shape us as individuals, the society in which we live, and the nature of other peoples' societies. Why else should we study periods so separated from ours through time, distance, and culture as classical Greece, medieval Germany, and modern Russia? Although many of the people involved in these epochs are long dead, what they did has touched everyone alive today.

Historians begin to reconstruct the past by posing questions about it. How and why, for example, did cities emerge? How did the political system of a particular society evolve? How did people create an economic system to sustain a complex society? What were a society's religious beliefs, and how did they influence daily life? These are just a few of the kinds of questions that historians ask to guide their research and focus their approach to the past.

To answer these questions historians examine *primary sources,* the firsthand accounts of people who lived through the events, people who were in the best position to know what happened. Thus, historians most commonly rely on the written record of human experience because, no matter how extensive a civilization's physical remains may be, its history largely remains a mystery if it has not left us records that we can read. Until we are able to decipher the written texts left us by the ancient civilization of Minoan Crete, for example, we can draw only vague conclusions about its history. Nonetheless, it is the historian's responsibility to examine all of the evidence left by the past, and this includes visual evidence. Examined properly, visual sources provide a glimpse of the world as contemporaries saw it. Especially in conjunction with written documents, art can be a singularly valuable and striking means of understanding the past. Similarly, archeology has proved a valuable avenue to the past, whether the excavation uncovers an ancient Greek city, a medieval church, or a modern factory building. Things as dissimilar as beautiful paintings and ordinary machines tell historians much about the ways in which people have lived and worked.

In the fifth century B.C., a Greek named Herodotus wrote the first true history of people and events in an effort to understand a great conflict between the Persians and the Greeks. Herodotus, the "father of history," wrote that he was publishing his "inquiry" into the past. The Greek word that he used for "inquiry" was *historia,* from which we derive the word *history.* The two concepts of inquiry and history, first joined by Herodotus, became inseparable, and their connection is as valid today as when Herodotus wrote.

When studying sources—the most basic activity in research—historians must assess the validity and perspective of each account. They try to determine whether their sources are honest and accurate, generally by comparing and contrasting the testimony of several different observers. They criticize sources both externally—to attempt to uncover forgeries and errors—and internally—to find the author's motives for writing, inconsistencies within the document, biases, even cases of outright lying. In some instances, especially in ancient and medieval history, contemporary written accounts have been lost; they are known to posterity only through people who later read the originals and incorporated the information into their own writings. Although historians must analyze the viewpoints and accuracy of such derivative, or *secondary,* sources very carefully, these writings have preserved much history that otherwise would have been lost. For the modern period historians have a vast supply of contemporary accounts of events, memoirs, personal letters, economic statistics, and government reports, all of them useful for an understanding of the past.

Once historians have pieced together what happened and have determined the facts, they must interpret what they have found. Understanding the past does not necessarily come easily, which is one of the joys and frustrations of history. Unlike the exact physical sciences, history cannot reproduce experiments under controlled conditions, because no two historical events are precisely alike. People cannot be put into test tubes, and they are not as predictable as atoms or hydrocarbons. That is hardly surprising, for history is about people, the most complex organisms on this planet.

To complicate matters, for many epochs of history only the broad outlines are known, so interpretation is especially difficult. For example, historians know that the Hittite Empire collapsed at the height of its power, but interpretations of the causes of the catastrophe are still speculative. On the other end of the spectrum, some developments are so vast and complex that historians must master mountains of data before they can even begin to interpret them properly. Events as diverse as the end of the Roman Empire, the origins of the Industrial Revolution, and the causes of the French Revolution are very complicated because so many people brought so many different forces to bear for so many different reasons. In such cases, there can never be one simple explanation that will satisfy everyone, and this fact in itself testifies to the complexity of life in developed societies.

Still another matter complicates an accurate understanding of the past. The attempt to understand history is uniquely human. Interpretations of the past sometimes change because people's points of view change in the course of life. The values and attitudes of one generation may not be shared by another. Despite such differences in interpretation, the effort of historians to examine and understand the past can give them a perspective that is valuable to the present. It is through this process of analysis and interpretation of evidence that historians come to understand not only the past but its relation to life today.

Social history, an important subject of this book, is itself an example of the historian's reappraisal of the meaning of the past. For centuries people took the basic facts, details, and activities of life for granted. Obviously, people lived in certain types of houses, ate certain food that they either raised or bought, and reared families. These matters seemed so ordinary that few serious historians gave them much thought. Yet within this generation a growing number of scholars have demonstrated that studies of the ways in which people have lived over the years deserve as much attention as the reigns of monarchs, the careers of great political figures, and the outcomes of big battles.

The topics of history and human societies lead to the question, "What is civilization?" *Civilization* is a word easier to describe than to define. It comes from the Latin adjective *civilis,* which refers to a citizen. Citizens willingly and mutually bind themselves in political, economic, and social organizations in which individuals merge themselves, their energies, and their interests in a larger community. In the course of time, civilization has come to embrace not only a people's system of social and political organization but also its particular shared way of thinking and believing, its art, and other facets of its culture—the complex whole that sets one people apart from other peoples who have different shared values and practices. One way to understand this idea is to observe the origins and development of the chief Western civilizations, analyzing similarities and differences among them. At the fundamental level, the similarities are greater than the differences. Almost all people in Europe and the

Americas share some values, even though they may live far apart, speak different languages, and have different religions and political and social systems. These values are the bonds that hold a civilization together. By studying these shared cultural values, which stretch through time and across distance, we can see how the various events of the past have left their impression on the present and even how the present may influence the future.

THE FIRST HUMAN BEINGS

On December 27, 1831, young Charles Darwin stepped aboard the H.M.S. *Beagle* to begin a voyage to South America and the Pacific Ocean. In the course of that five-year voyage, he became convinced that species of animals and human beings had evolved from lower forms. At first Darwin was reluctant to publicize his theories because they ran counter to the biblical account of creation, which claimed that God had made Adam in one day. Finally, however, in 1859 he published *On the Origin of Species*. In 1871 he followed it with *The Descent of Man,* in which he argued that human beings and apes are descended from a common ancestor. Even before Darwin had proclaimed his theories, evidence to support them had come to light. In 1856 the fossilized bones of an early form of man were discovered in the Neander valley of Germany. Called "Neanderthal Man" after the place of his discovery, he was physically more primitive than modern man (*Homo sapiens,* or thinking man). But he was clearly a human being and not an ape. He offered proof of Darwin's theory that *Homo sapiens* had evolved from less developed forms.

The theories of Darwin, supported by the evidence of fossilized remains, ushered in a new scientific era in which scientists and scholars have reexamined the very nature of human beings and their history. Men and women of the twentieth century have made many discoveries, solved some old problems, but raised many new ones. Although the fossil remains of primitive unicellular organisms can be dated back roughly two and a half billion years, the fossil record is far from complete. Thus the whole story of evolution cannot yet be known.

Ideas of human evolution have changed dramatically, particularly in the past few years. Generations of paleoanthropologists—better remembered as fossil-hunters—have sought the "missing link." Ever since Darwin published his theories of evolution, scholars have tried to find the one fossil that would establish the point from which human beings and apes went their own different evolutionary ways. In 1974 an American team of scholars working in Africa discovered extensive remains of a skeleton that they named "Lucy." Lucy was an ape that had walked upright some three million years ago and had displayed human characteristics. Had the missing link finally been found? No. Lucy was an intriguing step along the road of development between human beings and apes, but she was only a step, not the missing link.

Since the discovery of Lucy, many other less spectacular but nonetheless instructive finds have caused scholars to question the very concept of the missing link and its implications. Fossil remains in China suggest that evolution was more complicated than paleoanthropologists previously thought and even that human beings may not have originated in Africa. It is not simply that paleoanthropologists, like historians, must interpret their data; they must rethink everything that they have discovered in the light of their latest findings.

Many contemporary paleoanthropologists working in widely separated parts of the world have proposed some startling ideas. Some suggest that the search for a missing link is itself a blind alley. They point out that the fossil record, extensive but incomplete, suggests that thousands of missing links may have existed, no one of them more important than the other. Given the small numbers of these primates and the extent of the globe, there is an almost infinitesimal chance of finding a skeleton that can be considered the missing link between other primates and human beings. Instead, contemporary scholars stress the need to study all of these fossil remains to open new vistas for the understanding of evolution. That conclusion should not be surprising. A number of years ago Loren Eiseley, a noted American anthropologist, offered the wisest and humblest observation: "The human interminglings of hundreds of thousands of years of prehistory are not to be clarified by a single generation of archeologists."[1]

Despite the enormous uncertainty surrounding human development, a reasonably clear picture can be drawn of two important early periods: the Paleolithic or Old Stone Age, and the Neolithic or New Stone Age. The immensely long Paleolithic Age, which lasted from about 400,000 to 7000 B.C., takes its name from the crude stone tools the earliest hunters chipped from flint and obsidian, a black volcanic rock. During the much shorter Neolithic Age, which lasted from about 7000 to 3000 B.C., human beings began using new types of stone tools and, more important, pursuing agriculture.

THE PALEOLITHIC AGE

Paleolithic peoples hunted a huge variety of animals, ranging from elephants in Spain to deer in China. The hunters were thoroughly familiar with the habits and migratory patterns of the animals on which they relied. But success in the hunt also depended on the quality and effectiveness of the hunters' social organization. Paleolithic hunters were organized—they hunted in groups. They used their knowledge of the animal world and their power of thinking to plan how to down their prey. The ability to think and act as an organized social group meant that Paleolithic hunters could successfully feed on animals that were bigger, faster, and stronger than themselves.

Paleolithic peoples also nourished themselves by gathering nuts, berries, and seeds. Just as they knew the habits of animals, so they had vast knowledge of the plant kingdom. Some Paleolithic peoples even knew how to plant wild seeds to supplement their food supply. Thus they relied on every part of the environment for survival.

The basic social unit of Paleolithic societies was probably the family, but family bonds were no doubt stronger and more extensive than those of families in modern, urban, and industrialized societies. It is likely that the bonds of kinship were strong not just within the nuclear family of father, mother, and children but throughout the extended family of uncles, aunts, cousins, nephews, and nieces. People in nomadic societies typically depend on the extended family for cooperative work and mutual protection. The ties of kinship probably also extended beyond the family to the tribe. A *tribe* was a group of families, led by a *patriarch,* a dominant male who governed the group. Tribe members considered themselves descendants of a common ancestor. Most tribes probably consisted of thirty to fifty people.

As in the hunt, so too in other aspects of life—group members had to cooperate to survive. The

Paleolithic Cave Painting   All Paleolithic peoples relied primarily on hunting for their survival. This scene, painted on the wall of a cave in southern France, depicts the animals that this group normally hunted. Paleolithic peoples may have hoped that by drawing these animals they gained a magical power over them. *(Source: Douglas Mazonowicz/Gallery of Prehistoric Art)*

adult males normally hunted and between hunts made stone weapons. The women's realm was probably the camp. There they made utensils and —as the likely inventors of weaving—fashioned skins into clothing, tents, and footwear. They left the camp to gather nuts, grains, and fruits to supplement the group's diet. The women's primary responsibility was the bearing of children, who were essential to the continuation of the group. Women also had to care for the children, especially the infants. Part of women's work, too, was tending the fire, which served for warmth, cooking, and protection against wild animals.

Some of the most striking accomplishments of Paleolithic peoples were intellectual. The development of the human brain made abstract concepts possible. Unlike animals, whose lives are conditioned by instinct and learned behavior, Paleolithic peoples also used reason to govern their actions. Thought and language permitted the lore and experience of the old to be passed on to the young. An invisible world also opened up to *Homo sapiens.* The Neanderthals developed the custom of burying their dead and leaving offerings with the body, perhaps in the belief that somehow life continued after death.

Paleolithic peoples produced the first art. They decorated cave walls with paintings of animals and scenes of the hunt. They also began to fashion clay models of pregnant women and of animals. Many of the surviving paintings, such as those at Altamira in Spain and Lascaux in France, are located deep in the caves, in areas not easily accessible. These areas were probably places of ritual and initiation, where young men were taken when they joined the ranks of the hunters. They were also places of magic. The animals depicted on the walls were those either hunted for food or feared as predators. Many are shown wounded by spears or arrows; others are pregnant. The early artists may have been expressing the hope that the hunt would be successful and game plentiful. By portraying the animals as realistically as possible, the artist-hunters may have hoped to gain power over them. The statuettes of pregnant women seem to express a wish for fertile women to have babies and thus ensure the group's survival. The wall paintings and clay statuettes of Paleolithic peoples represent the earliest yearnings of human beings to control their environment.

THE NEOLITHIC AGE

Hunting is at best a precarious way of life, even when the diet is supplemented with seeds and fruits. If the climate changed even slightly, the all-important herds might move to new areas. Paleolithic tribes either moved with the herds and adapted themselves to new circumstances or perished. Several long ice ages—periods when huge glaciers covered vast parts of Europe—subjected the small bands of Paleolithic hunters to extreme hardship.

Not long after the last ice age, around 7000 B.C., some hunters and gatherers began to rely chiefly on agriculture for their sustenance. This development has traditionally been called the "Agricultural Revolution." Yet the work of Jack R. Harlan, a leading scientist in the field of agronomy, has caused scholars to reappraise the origins of agriculture. He has argued from available evidence that agriculture evolved slowly over a long length of time.

Striking support for Harlan's view came in 1981 from an American archeological expedition to the Nile Valley in Egypt. Investigators found that for thousands of years nomads had planted wheat and barley in the silt left by the flooding of the Nile. These people, however, never shifted to a life of settled farming. Instead, the crops they grew were just another, though important, source of food. In short, hunters and gatherers apparently long knew how to grow crops but did not base their existence on them.

The real transformation of human life occurred when hunters and gatherers gave up their nomadic way of life to depend primarily on the grain they grew and the animals they domesticated. Agriculture made possible a more stable and secure life. Neolithic peoples flourished, fashioning an energetic, creative era. They were responsible for many fundamental inventions and innovations that the modern world takes for granted. First, obviously, is systematic agriculture—that is, the reliance of Neolithic peoples on agriculture as their primary, not merely subsidiary, source of food. Thus they developed the primary economic activity of the entire ancient world and the basis of all modern life. With the settled routine of Neolithic farmers went the evolution of towns and eventually cities. Neolithic farmers usually raised more food than they could consume, and their surpluses permitted larger, healthier populations. Population growth in turn created an even greater reliance on settled farming, as only systematic agriculture could sustain the increased numbers of people. Since surpluses of food could also be bartered for other commodities, the Neolithic era witnessed the beginnings of large-scale exchange of goods. In time the increasing complexity of Neolithic societies led to the development of writing, prompted by the need to keep records and later by the urge to chronicle experiences, learning, and beliefs.

The transition to settled life also had a profound impact on the family. The shared needs and pressures that encourage extended-family ties in nomadic societies are less prominent in settled societies. Bonds to the extended family weakened. In towns and cities, the nuclear family was more dependent on its immediate neighbors than on kinfolk.

Meanwhile, however, the nomadic way of life and the family relationships it nurtured continued to flourish alongside settled agriculture. Even nomadic life changed. Often farmers and nomads bartered peaceably with one another, each group trading its surpluses for those of the other. Although nomadic peoples continued to exist throughout the Neolithic period and into modern times, the future belonged to the Neolithic farmers and their descendants. While the development of systematic agriculture may not have been revolutionary, the changes that it ushered in certainly were.

Until recently, scholars thought that agriculture originated in the ancient Near East and gradually spread elsewhere. Contemporary work, however, points to a more complex pattern of development. For unknown reasons people in various parts of the world all seem to have begun domesticating plants and animals at roughly the same time, around 7000 B.C. Four main points of origin have been identified. In the Near East, the inhabitants of sites as far apart as Tepe Yahya in modern Iran, Jarmo in Iraq, Jericho in Palestine, and Hacilar in modern Turkey (Map 1.1) raised wheat, barley, peas, and lentils. They also kept herds of sheep, pigs, and possibly goats. In western Africa, Neolithic farmers domesticated many plants, including millet, sorghum, and yams. In northeastern China, peoples of the Yangshao culture developed techniques of field agriculture, animal husbandry, potterymak-

Tower at Jericho Photographed during excavation, this tower is a good example of the strong fortifications of Neolithic towns. The sheer size of the walls amply illustrates the huge amount of labor and central planning necessary to build them. *(Source: Consulate General of Israel)*

ing, and bronze metallurgy. Innovations in the New World were equally striking. Central and South American Indians domesticated a host of plants, among them corn, beans, and squash. From these far-flung areas, knowledge of farming techniques spread to other regions.

Once people began to rely on farming for their livelihood, they settled in permanent villages and built houses. The location of the village was crucial. Early farmers chose places where the water supply was constant and adequate for their crops and flocks. At first, villages were small, consisting of a few households. As the population expanded and prospered, villages usually developed into towns. Between 8000 and 7000 B.C., the community at Jericho grew to at least two thousand people. Jericho's inhabitants lived in mud-brick houses built on stone foundations, and they surrounded their town with a massive fortification wall. The

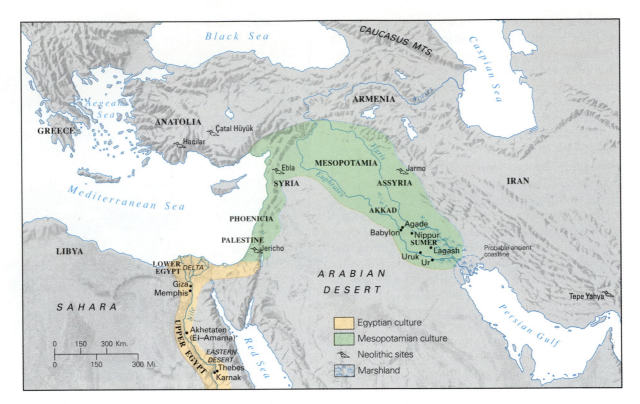

Map 1.1 Spread of Cultures   This map illustrates the spread of Mesopotamian and Egyptian culture through a semicircular stretch of land often called the "Fertile Crescent." From this area knowledge and use of agriculture spread throughout the western part of Asia Minor.

Neolithic site of Çatal Hüyük in Anatolia (modern Turkey) covered 32 acres. The outer houses of the settlement formed a solid wall of mud brick, which served as a bulwark against attack. At Tepe Yahya as well, the Neolithic farmers surrounded their town with a wall.

Walls offered protection and permitted a more secure, stable way of life than that of the nomad. They also prove that towns grew in size, population, and wealth, for these fortifications were so large that they could have been raised only by a large labor force. They indicate, moreover, that towns were developing social and political organization. The fortifications, the work of the whole community, would have been impossible without central planning.

One of the major effects of the advent of agriculture and settled life was a dramatic increase in population. No census figures exist for this period, but the number and size of the towns prove that Neo-

lithic society was expanding. Early farmers found that agriculture provided a larger and much more dependable food supply than hunting and gathering. No longer did the long winter months mean the threat of starvation. Farmers learned to store the surplus for the winter. Because the farming community was better fed than ever before, it was also more resistant to diseases that kill people suffering from malnutrition. Thus Neolithic farmers were healthier and longer-lived than their predecessors. All these factors explain the growth of towns like Jericho and Jarmo.

Agricultural surplus also made possible the division of labor. It freed some members of the community from the necessity of raising food. Artisans and craftsmen devoted their attention to making the new stone tools farming demanded—hoes and sickles for fieldwork and mortars and pestles for grinding the grain. Other artisans began to shape clay into pottery vessels, which were used to store grain, wine, and oil and to serve as kitchen utensils. Still others wove baskets and cloth. People who could specialize in particular crafts produced more and better goods than any single farmer could.

Until recently it was impossible to say much about these goods. But in April 1985 archeologists announced the discovery near the Dead Sea in modern Israel of a unique deposit of Neolithic artifacts. Found buried in a cave were fragments of the earliest cloth yet discovered, the oldest painted mask, remains of woven baskets and boxes, and jewelry. The textiles are surprisingly elaborate, some woven in eleven intricate designs. These artifacts give eloquent testimony to the sophistication and artistry of Neolithic craftsmen.

Prosperity and stable conditions nurtured other innovations and discoveries. Neolithic farmers improved their tools and agricultural techniques. They domesticated bigger, stronger animals, such as the bull and the horse, to work for them. To harness the power of these animals they invented tools such as the plow, which came into use by 3000 B.C. The first plows had wooden shares and could break only light soils, but they were far more efficient than stone hoes. By 3000 B.C., the wheel had been invented, and farmers devised ways of hitching bulls and horses to wagons. These developments enabled Neolithic farmers to raise more food more efficiently and easily than ever before, simply because animals and machines were doing a greater proportion of the work.

In arid regions such as Mesopotamia and Egypt, farmers learned to irrigate their land and later to drain it to prevent the buildup of salt in the soil. By diverting water from rivers, they were able to open new land to cultivation. River waters flooding the fields deposited layers of rich mud, which increased the fertility of the soil. Thus the rivers, together with the manure of domesticated animals, kept replenishing the land. The results included a further increase in population and wealth. Irrigation, especially on a large scale, demanded group effort. The entire community had to plan which land to irrigate and how to lay out the canals. Then everyone had to help dig the canals. The demands of irrigation underscored the need for strong central authority within the community. Successful irrigation projects in turn strengthened such central authority by proving it effective and beneficial. Thus corporate spirit and governments to which individuals were subordinate—the makings of urban life—began to evolve.

The development of systematic agriculture was a fundamental turning point in the history of civilization. Farming gave rise to stable settled societies, which enjoyed considerable prosperity. Farming also made possible an enormous increase in population. Some inhabitants of the budding towns turned their attention to the production of goods that made life more comfortable. Settled circumstances and a certain amount of leisure made the accumulation and spread of knowledge easier. Finally, sustained farming prepared the way for urban life.

MESOPOTAMIAN CIVILIZATION

Mesopotamia is the Greek name for the land between the Euphrates and Tigris rivers. Both rivers have their headwaters in the mountains of Armenia in modern Turkey. Both are fed by numerous tributaries, and the entire river system drains a vast mountainous region. Overland routes in Mesopotamia usually follow the Euphrates because the banks of the Tigris are frequently steep and difficult. North of the ancient city of Babylon the land levels out into a barren expanse. The desert continues south of Babylon, and in 1857 the English geologist and traveler W. K. Loftus depicted it in grim terms:

There is no life for miles around. No river glides in grandeur at the base of its [the ancient city of Uruk] mounds; no green date groves flourish near its ruins. The jackal and the hyena appear to shun the dull aspect of its tombs. The king of birds never hovers over the deserted waste. A blade of grass or an insect finds no existence there. The shrivelled lichen alone, clinging to the weathered surface of the broken brick, seems to glory in its universal dominion upon those barren walls.[2]

Farther south the desert gives way to a 6,000-square-mile region of marshes, lagoons, mud flats, and reed banks. At last, in the extreme south the Euphrates and the Tigris unite and empty into the Persian Gulf.

This forbidding area became the home of many folk and the land of the first cities. The region

Map of Nippur   The oldest map in the world, dating to ca 1500 B.C., shows the layout of the Mesopotamian city of Nippur. Inscribed on a clay tablet, the map has enabled archeologists to locate ruined buildings: (A) the ziggurat, (B) canal, (C) enclosure and gardens, (D) city gates, and (E) the Euphrates River. *(Source: The University Museum, University of Pennsylvania)*

around Akkad (or Agade, now modern Baghdad) was occupied by bands of Semitic nomads, people linked by the fact that their languages all belonged to the group of languages known as Semitic, a group that includes Hebrew and Arabic. Into the south came the Sumerians, a people of farmers and city builders who probably migrated from the east. By 3000 B.C. they had established a number of cities in the southernmost part of Mesopotamia, which became known as Sumer. As the Sumerians pushed north, they came into contact with the Semites, who readily adopted Sumerian culture and turned to urban life. The Sumerians soon changed the face of the land and made Mesopotamia the "cradle of civilization" (see Map 1.1).

Environment and Mesopotamian Culture

From the outset geography had a profound effect on the evolution of Mesopotamian civilization. In this region agriculture is possible only with irrigation and good drainage. Consequently, the Sumerians and later the Akkadians built their cities along the Tigris and Euphrates and the branches of these rivers. Some major cities, such as Ur and Uruk, took root on tributaries of the Euphrates, while others, notably Lagash, were built on branches of the Tigris. The rivers supplied fish, a major element of the city dwellers' diet. The rivers also provided reeds and clay for building materials. Since this entire area lacks stone, mud brick became the primary building block of Mesopotamian architecture.

Although the rivers sustained life, they also destroyed it by frequent floods that ravaged entire cities. Moreover, they restrained political development by making Sumer a geographical maze. Between the rivers, streams, and irrigation canals stretched open desert or swamp where nomadic tribes roamed. Communication among the isolated cities was difficult and at times dangerous. Thus each Sumerian city became a state, independent of the others and protective of its independence. Any city that tried to unify the country was resisted by the other cities. As a result, the political history of Sumer is one of almost constant warfare. Although Sumer was eventually unified, unification came late and was always tenuous.

Sumerian Society

The harsh environment fostered a grim, even pessimistic, spirit among the Mesopotamians. The Sumerians sought to please and calm the gods, especially the patron deity of the city. Encouraged and directed by the traditional priesthood, which was dedicated to understanding the ways of the gods, the people erected shrines in the center of each city and then built their houses around them. The best way to honor a god was to make the shrine as grand and as impressive as possible, for a god who had a splendid temple might think twice about sending floods to destroy the city.

The temple had to be worthy of the god, a symbol of his power, and it had to last. Special skills and materials were needed to build it. Only stone was suitable for its foundations and precious metals and colorful glazed tiles for its decoration. Since the Mesopotamians had to import both stone and metals, temple construction encouraged trade. Architects, engineers, craftsmen, and workers had to devote a great deal of thought, effort, and time to build the temple. By 2000 B.C. the result was Mesopotamia's first monumental architecture—the ziggurat, a massive stepped tower that dominated a city.

Once the ziggurat was built, the traditional priesthood assumed the additional duty of running it and performing the gods' rituals. The people of the city met the expenses of building and maintaining the temple and its priesthood by setting aside extensive tracts of land for that purpose. The priests took charge of the produce of the temple lands and the sacred flocks. Part of the yield went to feeding and clothing the priests and temple staff and for offerings to the gods. Part was sold or bartered to obtain goods needed for construction, maintenance, and ritual.

Until recently, the dominant position and wealth of the temple led historians to consider the Sumerian city-state an absolute *theocracy*, or government by an established priesthood. According to this view, the temple and its priests owned the city's land and controlled its economy. Newly discovered documents and recent work, however, have resulted in new ideas about the Sumerian city. It is now known that the temple owned a large fraction, but not all, of the city's territory and did not govern the city. A king (*lugal*) or local governor (*ensi*) exercised political power, and most of the city's land was the property of individual citizens.

Sumerian society was a complex arrangement of freedom and dependence, and its members were divided into four categories: nobles, free clients of the nobility, commoners, and slaves. The nobility consisted of the king and his family, the chief priests, and high palace officials. Generally, the king rose to power as a war leader, elected by the citizenry, who established a regular army, trained it, and led it into battle. The might of the king and the frequency of warfare quickly made him the supreme figure in the city, and kingship soon became hereditary. The symbol of royal status was the palace, which rivaled the temple in grandeur.

The king and the lesser nobility held extensive tracts of land that were, like the estates of the temple, worked by slaves and clients. Clients were free men and women who were dependent on the nobility. In return for their labor, the clients received small plots of land to work for themselves. Although this arrangement assured the clients of a livelihood, the land they worked remained the possession of the nobility or the temple. Thus, not only did the nobility control most—and probably the best—land, they also commanded the obedience of a huge segment of society. They were the dominant force in Mesopotamian society.

Commoners were free citizens. They were independent of the nobility; however, they could not rival the nobility in social status and political power. Commoners belonged to large patriarchal families who owned land in their own right. Commoners could sell their land, if the family approved, but even the king could not legally take their land without their approval. Commoners had a voice in the political affairs of the city and full protection under the law.

Until comparatively recent times, slavery has been a fact of life throughout the history of Western society. Some Sumerian slaves were foreigners and prisoners of war. Some were criminals who had lost their freedom as punishment for their crimes. Still others served as slaves to repay debts. These were more fortunate than the others, because the law required that they be freed after three years. But all slaves were subject to whatever treatment their owners might mete out. They could be beaten and even branded. Yet they were not considered dumb beasts. Slaves engaged in trade and made profits. Indeed, many slaves bought their freedom. They could borrow money and received at least some legal protection.

THE SPREAD OF MESOPOTAMIAN CULTURE

The Sumerians established the basic social, economic, and intellectual patterns of Mesopotamia, but the Semites played a large part in spreading Sumerian culture far beyond the boundaries of Mesopotamia. Despite the cultural ascendancy of the Sumerians, their unending wars wasted their strength. In 2331 B.C. the Semitic chieftain Sargon con-

Aerial View of Ur   This photograph gives a good idea of the size and complexity of Ur, one of the most powerful cities in Mesopotamia. In the lower right-hand corner stands the massive ziggurat of Urnammu. *(Source: Georg Gerster/Comstock)*

quered Sumer and created a new empire. The symbol of his triumph was a new capital, the city of Akkad. Sargon, the first "world conqueror," led his armies to the Mediterranean Sea. Although his empire lasted only a few generations, it spread Mesopotamian culture throughout the Fertile Crescent, the belt of rich farmland that extends from Mesopotamia in the east up through Syria in the north and down to Egypt in the west (see Map 1.1).

Sargon's impact and the extent of Mesopotamian influence even at this early period have been dramatically revealed at Ebla in modern Syria. In 1964 archeologists there unearthed a once-flourishing Semitic civilization that had assimilated political, intellectual, and artistic aspects of Mesopotamian culture. In 1975 the excavators uncovered thousands of clay tablets which proved that the people of Ebla had learned the art of writing from the Mesopotamians. Eblaite artists borrowed heavily from Mesopotamian art but developed their own style, which in turn influenced Mesopotamian artists. The Eblaites transmitted the heritage of Mesopotamia to other Semitic centers in Syria. In the process, a universal culture developed in the ancient Near East, a culture basically Mesopotamian but fertilized by the traditions, genius, and ways of many other peoples.

The Triumph of Babylon

Although the empire of Sargon was extensive, it was short-lived. The Akkadians, too, failed to solve the problems posed by Mesopotamia's geography and population pattern. It was left to the Babylonians to unite Mesopotamia politically and culturally. The Babylonians were Amorites, a Semitic people who had migrated from Arabia and settled on the site of Babylon along the middle Euphrates where that river runs close to the Tigris. Babylon enjoyed an excellent geographical position and was ideally suited to be the capital of Mesopotamia. It dominated trade on the Tigris and Euphrates rivers: all commerce to and from Sumer and Akkad had to pass by its walls. It also looked beyond Mesopotamia. Babylonian merchants followed the Tigris north to Assyria and Anatolia. The Euphrates led merchants to Syria, Palestine, and the Mediterranean. The city grew great because of its commercial importance and soundly based power.

Stele of Naramsin Naramsin, the grandson of Sargon, was one of the greatest of the Akkadian kings. The topmost figure on this stele, or commemorative tablet, he displays his power by defeating his enemies in battle. Naramsin's horned crown suggests that he considered himself divine. *(Source: Louvre/Cliché des Musées Nationaux, Paris)*

Babylon was also fortunate to have a far-seeing and able king, Hammurabi (r. 1792–1750 B.C.). Hammurabi set out to do three things: make Babylon secure, unify Mesopotamia, and win for the Babylonians a place in Mesopotamian civilization. The first two he accomplished by conquering

	Meaning	Pictograph	Ideogram	Phonetic sign
A	Star			
B	Woman			
C	Mountain			
D	Slave woman			
E	Water In			

Figure 1.1 Sumerian Writing *(Excerpted from S. N. Kramer,* The Sumerians: Their History, Culture and Character, *University of Chicago Press, Chicago, 1963. pp. 302–306)*

Assyria in the north and Sumer and Akkad in the south. Then he turned to his third goal.

Politically, Hammurabi joined in his kingship the Semitic concept of the tribal chieftain and the Sumerian idea of urban kingship. Culturally, he encouraged the spread of myths that explained how Marduk, the god of Babylon, had been elected king of the gods by the other Mesopotamian deities. Hammurabi's success in making Marduk the god of all Mesopotamians made Babylon the religious center of Mesopotamia. Through Hammurabi's genius the Babylonians made their own contribution to Mesopotamian culture—a culture vibrant enough to maintain its identity while assimilating new influences. Hammurabi's conquests and the activity of Babylonian merchants spread this enriched culture north to Anatolia and west to Syria and Palestine.

The Invention of Writing and the First Schools

The origins of writing probably go back to the ninth millennium B.C., when Near Eastern peoples used clay tokens as counters for record keeping. By the fourth millennium people had realized that drawing pictures of the tokens on clay was simpler than making tokens. This breakthrough in turn

suggested that more information could be conveyed by adding pictures of still other objects. The result was a complex system of *pictographs,* in which each sign pictured an object. These pictographs were the forerunners of a Sumerian form of writing known as *cuneiform,* from the Latin term for "wedge-shaped," used to describe the strokes of the stylus.

How did this pictographic system work, and how did it evolve into cuneiform writing? At first, if a scribe wanted to indicate a star, he simply drew a picture of it (line A of Figure 1.1) on a wet clay tablet, which became rock-hard when baked. Anyone looking at the picture would know what it meant and would think of the word for star. This complicated and laborious system had serious limitations. It could not represent abstract ideas or combinations of ideas. For instance, how could it depict a slave woman?

The solution appeared when the scribe discovered that signs could be combined to express meaning. To refer to a slave woman the scribe used the sign for woman (line B) and the sign for mountain (line C)—literally, "mountain woman" (line D). Because the Sumerians regularly obtained their slave women from the mountains, this combination of signs was easily understandable.

The next step was to simplify the system. Instead of drawing pictures, the scribe made conventionalized signs that were generally understood to represent ideas. Thus the signs became *ideograms:* they symbolized ideas. The sign for star could also be used to indicate heaven, sky, or even god.

The real breakthrough came when the scribe learned to use signs to represent sounds. For instance, the scribe drew two parallel wavy lines to indicate the word *a* or "water" (line E). Besides water, the word *a* in Sumerian also meant "in." The word *in* expresses a relationship that is very difficult to represent pictorially. Instead of trying to invent a sign to mean *in,* some clever scribe used the sign for water because the two words sounded alike. This phonetic use of signs made possible the combining of signs to convey abstract ideas.

The Sumerian system of writing was so complicated that only professional scribes mastered it, and even they had to study it for many years. By 2500 B.C. scribal schools flourished throughout Sumer. Most students came from wealthy families and were male. Each school had a master, teachers, and monitors. Discipline was strict, and students were caned for sloppy work and misbehavior. One graduate of a scribal school had few fond memories of the joy of learning:

My headmaster read my tablet, said:
"There is something missing," caned me.

. . . .

The fellow in charge of silence said:
"Why did you talk without permission," caned me.
The fellow in charge of the assembly said:
"Why did you stand at ease without permission," caned me.[3]

The Sumerian system of schooling set the educational standards for Mesopotamian culture, and the Akkadians and Babylonians adopted its practices and techniques. Students began by learning how to prepare clay tablets and make signs. They studied grammar and word lists and solved simple mathematical problems. Mesopotamian education always had a practical side because of the economic and administrative importance of scribes. Most scribes took administrative positions in the temple or palace, where they kept records of business transactions, accounts, and inventories. But scribal schools did not limit their curriculum to business affairs. They were also centers of culture and scholarship. Topics of study included mathematics, botany, and linguistics. Advanced students copied and studied the classics of Mesopotamian literature. Talented students and learned scribes wrote compositions of their own. As a result, many literary, mathematical, and religious texts survive today, giving a surprisingly full picture of Mesopotamian intellectual and spiritual life.

Mesopotamian Thought and Religion

The Mesopotamians made significant and sophisticated advances in mathematics using a numerical system based on units of sixty, ten, and six. They developed the concept of *place value*—that the value of a number depends on where it stands in relation to other numbers. Mesopotamian mathematical texts are of two kinds: tables and problems. Scribes compiled tables of squares and square roots, cubes and cube roots, and reciprocals. They wrote texts of problems, which dealt not only with equations and pure mathematics but also with concrete problems, such as how to plan irrigation

Sumerian Clay Tablet   This Sumerian clay tablet dating from about 3000 B.C. shows Sumerian writing in transition. The scribe has begun to use pictures of things to represent abstractions, which is an advance from pictographs to ideograms (see Figure 1.1). *(Source: Courtesy of the Trustees of the British Museum)*

ditches. The Mesopotamians did not consider mathematics a purely theoretical science. The building of cities, palaces, temples, and canals demanded practical knowledge of geometry and trigonometry.

Mesopotamian medicine was a combination of magic, prescriptions, and surgery. Mesopotamians believed that demons and evil spirits caused sickness and that magic spells could drive them out. Or, they believed, the physician could force the demon out by giving the patient a foul-tasting prescription. As medical knowledge grew, some prescriptions were found to work and thus were true medicines. Surgeons practiced a dangerous occupation, and the penalties for failure were severe. One section of Hammurabi's law code (see page 19) decreed: "If a physician performed a major operation on a seignior with a bronze lancet and has caused the seignior's death, or he opened up the eye-socket of a seignior and has destroyed the seignior's eye, they shall cut off his hand."[4] No wonder that one medical text warned physicians to have nothing to do with a dying person.

Mesopotamian thought had a very profound impact in theology and religion. The Sumerians originated many beliefs, and the Akkadians and

Babylonians added to them. The Mesopotamians believed that many gods run the world, but they did not consider all gods and goddesses equal. Some deities had very important jobs, taking care of music, law, sex, and victory, while others had lesser tasks, overseeing leatherworking and basket-weaving. The god in charge of metalworking was hardly the equal of the god of wisdom.

Mesopotamian gods lived their lives much as human beings lived theirs. The gods were *anthropomorphic,* or human in form. Unlike men and women, they were powerful and immortal and could make themselves invisible. Otherwise, Mesopotamian gods and goddesses were very human: they celebrated with food and drink, and they raised families. They enjoyed their own "Garden of Eden," a green and fertile place. They could be irritable, vindictive, and even irresponsible.

The Mesopotamians considered natural catastrophes the work of the gods. At times the Sumerians described their chief god, Enlil, as "the raging flood which has no rival." The gods, they believed, even used nature to punish the Mesopotamians. According to the myth of the Deluge, which gave rise to the biblical story of Noah, the god Enki warned Ziusudra, the Sumerian Noah:

A flood will sweep over the cult-centers;
To destroy the seed of mankind . . .
Is the decision, the word of the assembly of the gods.[5]

The Mesopotamians did not worship their deities because the gods were holy. Human beings were too insignificant to pass judgment on the conduct of the gods, and the gods were too superior to honor human morals. Rather, the Mesopotamians worshiped the gods because they were mighty. Likewise, it was not the place of men and women to understand the gods. The Sumerian equivalent to the biblical Job once complained to his god:

The man of deceit has conspired against me,
And you, my god, do not thwart him,
You carry off my understanding.[6]

The motives of the gods were not always clear. In times of affliction one could only pray and offer sacrifices to appease them.

The Mesopotamians had many myths to account for the creation of the universe. According to one Sumerian myth (echoed in Genesis, the first book of the Old Testament), only the primeval sea existed at first. The sea produced heaven and earth, which were united. Heaven and earth gave birth to Enlil, who separated them and made possible the creation of the other gods. Babylonian beliefs were similar. In the beginning was the primeval sea, the goddess Tiamat, who gave birth to the gods. When Tiamat tried to destroy the gods, Marduk proceeded to kill her and divide her body and thus created the sky and earth. These myths are the earliest known attempts to answer the question, "How did it all begin?" The Mesopotamians obviously thought about these matters, as about the gods, in human terms. They never organized their beliefs into a philosophy, but their myths offered understandable explanations of natural phenomena. The myths were emotionally satisfying, and that was their greatest appeal.

Mesopotamian myths also explained the origin of human beings. In one myth the gods decided to make their lives easier by creating servants, whom they wanted to have made in their own image. Nammu, the goddess of the watery deep, brought the matter to Enki. After some thought, Enki instructed Nammu and the others:

Mix the heart of the clay that is over the abyss.
The good and princely fashioners will thicken the clay.
You, do you bring the limbs into existence.[7]

In Mesopotamian myth, as in Genesis, men and women were made in the divine image but without godlike powers. The Mesopotamians believed it their duty to supply the gods with sacrifices of food and drink and to house them in fine temples. In return, they hoped that the gods would be kind.

In addition to myths, the Sumerians produced the first epic poem, the *Epic of Gilgamesh.* An epic poem is a narration of the achievements, labors, and sometimes the failures of heroes that embodies a people's or a nation's conception of its own past. Historians can use epic poems to learn about various aspects of a society, and to that extent epics can be used as historical sources. The Sumerian epic recounts the wanderings of Gilgamesh—the semihistorical king of Uruk—and his companion Enkidu, their fatal meeting with the goddess Ishtar after which Enkidu dies, and Gilgamesh's subsequent search for eternal life. Although Gilgamesh finds a miraculous plant that gives immortality to anyone who eats it, a great snake steals it from him.

Despite this loss, Gilgamesh visits the lower world to bring Enkidu back to life, thereby learning of life after death. The *Epic of Gilgamesh* is not only an excellent piece of literature but also an intellectual triumph. It shows the Sumerians grappling with such enduring questions as life and death, mankind and deity, and immortality. Despite its great antiquity, it addresses questions of importance to men and women today.

These ideas about the creation of the universe and of human beings are part of the Mesopotamian legacy to Western civilization. They spread throughout the ancient Near East and found a home among the Hebrews, who adopted much of Mesopotamian religious thought and made it part of their own beliefs. Biblical parallels to Mesopotamian literary and religious themes are many. Such stories as the creation of Adam, the Deluge, the Garden of Eden, and the tale of Job can be traced back to Mesopotamian origins. Through the Bible, Mesopotamian as well as Jewish religious concepts influenced Christianity and Islam. Thus these first attempts by women and men to understand themselves and their world are still alive today.

Gilgamesh   The epic hero Gilgamesh here holds two bulls with human faces. Gilgamesh is not being an animal lover. The scene probably depicts his epic battle with these monstrous and powerful enemies. *(Source: The University Museum, University of Pennsylvania)*

Daily Life in Mesopotamia

The law code of King Hammurabi offers a wealth of information about daily life in Mesopotamia. Hammurabi's was not the first law code in Mesopotamia; indeed, the earliest goes back to about 2100 B.C. Yet, like earlier lawgivers, Hammurabi proclaimed that he issued his laws on divine authority "to establish law and justice in the language of the land, thereby promoting the welfare of the people." Hammurabi's code inflicted such penalties as mutilation, whipping, and burning. Today in parts of the Islamic world these punishments are still in use. Despite its severity, a spirit of justice and a sense of responsibility pervade the code. Hammurabi genuinely felt that his duty was to govern the Mesopotamians as righteously as possible. He tried to regulate the relations of his people so that they could live together in harmony.

The Code of Hammurabi has two striking characteristics. First, the law differed according to the social status of the offender. Aristocrats were not punished as harshly as commoners, nor commoners as harshly as slaves. Second, the code demanded that the punishment fit the crime. Like the

Mosaic law of the Hebrews, it called for "an eye for an eye, and a tooth for a tooth," at least among equals. However, an aristocrat who destroyed the eye of a commoner or slave could pay a fine instead of losing his own eye. Otherwise, as long as criminal and victim shared the same social status, the victim could demand exact vengeance.

Hammurabi's code began with legal procedure. There were no public prosecutors or district attorneys, so individuals brought their own complaints before the court. Each side had to produce written documents or witnesses to support its case. In cases of murder, the accuser had to prove the defendant guilty; any accuser who failed to do so was put to death. This strict law was designed to prevent people from lodging groundless charges. The Mesopotamians were very worried about witchcraft and sorcery. Anyone accused of witchcraft, even if the charges were not proved, underwent an ordeal by water. The gods themselves would decide the case. The defendant was thrown into the Euphrates, which was considered the instrument of the gods. A defendant who sank was guilty; a defendant who floated was innocent. Another procedural regulation covered the conduct of judges. Once a judge had rendered a verdict, he could not change it. Any judge who did so was fined heavily and deposed. In

Law Code of Hammurabi Hammurabi ordered his code to be inscribed on a stone pillar and set up in public. At the top of the pillar Hammurabi is depicted receiving the scepter of authority from the god Shamash. *(Source: Louvre Clichés des Musées Nationaux, Paris)*

short, the code tried to guarantee a fair trial and a just verdict.

Consumer protection is not a modern idea; it goes back to Hammurabi's day. Merchants and businessmen had to guarantee the quality of their goods and services. A boatbuilder who did sloppy work had to repair the boat at his own expense. A boatman who lost the owner's boat or sank someone else's boat replaced it and its cargo. Housebuilders guaranteed their work with their lives. Careless work could result in the collapse of a house and the death of its inhabitants. If that happened, the builder was put to death. A merchant who tried to increase the interest rate on a loan forfeited the entire amount. Hammurabi's laws tried to ensure that consumers got what they paid for and paid a just price.

Crime was a feature of Mesopotamian urban life just as it is in modern cities. Burglary was a serious problem, hard to control. Because houses were built of mud brick, it was easy for an intruder to dig through the walls. Hammurabi's punishment for burglary matched the crime. A burglar caught in the act was put to death on the spot, and his body was walled into the breach the burglar had made. The penalty for looting was also grim: anyone caught looting a burning house was thrown into the fire.

Mesopotamian cities had breeding places of crime. Taverns were notorious haunts of criminals, who often met there to make their plans. Tavernkeepers were expected to keep order and arrest anyone overheard planning a crime. Taverns were normally run by women, and they also served as houses of prostitution. Prostitution was disreputable but neither illegal nor regulated by law. Despite their social stigma, taverns were popular places, for Mesopotamians were fond of beer and wine. Tavernkeepers made a nice profit, but if they were caught increasing their profits by watering drinks, they were drowned.

Because farming was essential to Mesopotamian life, Hammurabi's code dealt extensively with agriculture. Tenant farming was widespread, and tenants rented land on a yearly basis. Instead of money they paid a portion of their crops as rent. Unless the land was carefully cultivated, it quickly reverted to wasteland. Therefore tenants faced severe penalties for neglecting the land or not working it at all. Since irrigation was essential to grow crops, tenants had to keep the canals and ditches in good repair. Otherwise the land would be subject to floods and farmers to crippling losses. Anyone whose neglect of the canals resulted in damaged crops had to bear all the expense of the lost crops. Tenants who could not pay the costs were sold into slavery.

Sheep raising was very lucrative because textile production was a major Mesopotamian industry. The shepherd was a hired man with considerable responsibility. He was expected to protect the flock from wild animals, which were a constant problem, and to keep the sheep out of the crops. This strict regulation of agriculture paid rich dividends. The Mesopotamians often enjoyed bumper crops, which fostered a large and thriving population.

Hammurabi gave careful attention to marriage and the family. As elsewhere in the Near East, marriage had aspects of a business agreement. The prospective groom and the father of the future bride arranged everything. The man offered the father a bridal gift, usually money. If the man and his bridal gift were acceptable, the father provided his daughter with a dowry. After marriage the dowry belonged to the woman (although the husband normally administered it) and was a means of protecting her rights and status. Once the two men agreed on financial matters, they drew up a contract; no marriage was considered legal without one. Either party could break off the marriage, but not without paying a stiff penalty. Fathers often contracted marriages while their children were still young. The girl either continued to live in her father's house until she reached maturity or went to live in the house of her father-in-law. During this time she was legally considered a wife. Once she and her husband came of age, they set up their own house.

The wife was expected to be rigorously faithful. The penalty for adultery was death. According to Hammurabi's code: "If the wife of a man has been caught while lying with another man, they shall bind them and throw them into the water."[8] The husband had the power to spare his wife by obtaining a pardon for her from the king. He could, however, accuse his wife of adultery even if he had not caught her in the act. In such a case she could try to clear herself before the city council that investigated the charge. If she was found innocent, she could take her dowry and leave her husband. If a woman decided to take the direct approach and kill her husband, she was impaled.

The husband had virtually absolute power over his household. He could even sell his wife and children into slavery to pay debts. Sons did not lightly oppose their fathers, and any son who struck his fa-

ther could have his hand cut off. A father was free to adopt children and include them in his will. Artisans sometimes adopted children to teach them the family trade. Although the father's power was great, he could not disinherit a son without just cause. Cases of disinheritance became matters for the city to decide, and the code ordered the courts to forgive a son for his first offense. Only if a son wronged his father a second time could he be disinherited.

Law codes, preoccupied as they are with the problems of society, provide a bleak view of things. Other Mesopotamian documents give a happier glimpse of life. Although Hammurabi's code dealt with marriage shekel by shekel, a Mesopotamian poem tells of two people meeting secretly in the city. Their parting is delightfully modern:

Come now, set me free, I must go home,
Kuli-Enlil . . . set me free, I must go home.
What can I say to deceive my mother?[9]

Countless wills and testaments show that husbands habitually left their estates to their wives, who in turn willed the property to their children. All this suggests happy family life. Hammurabi's code restricted married women from commercial pursuits, but financial documents prove that many women engaged in business without hindrance. Some carried on the family business, while others became wealthy landowners in their own right. Mesopotamians found their lives lightened by holidays and religious festivals. Traveling merchants brought news of the outside world and swapped marvelous tales. Despite their pessimism, the Mesopotamians enjoyed a vibrant and creative culture, a culture that left its mark on the entire Near East.

EGYPT, THE LAND OF THE PHARAOHS (3100–1200 B.C.)

The Greek historian and traveler Herodotus in the fifth century B.C. called Egypt the "gift of the Nile." No other single geographical factor had such a fundamental and profound impact on the shaping of Egyptian life, society, and history as the Nile (Map 1.2). Unlike the rivers of Mesopotamia it rarely brought death and destruction by devastating entire cities. The river was primarily a creative

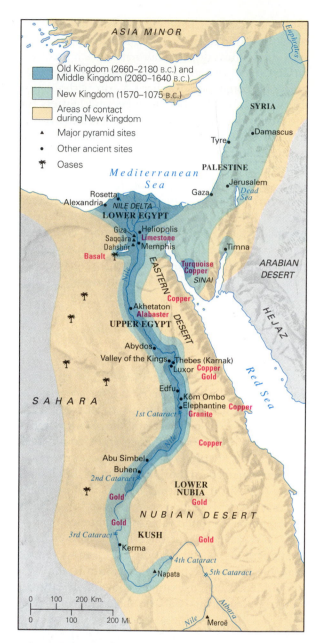

Map 1.2 Ancient Egypt   Geography and natural resources provided Egypt with centuries of peace and abundance.

He that makes to drink the desert . . .
He who makes barley and brings emmer [wheat] into
*   being . . .*
He who brings grass into being for the cattle . . .
He who makes every beloved tree to grow . . .
O Nile, verdant art thou, who makest man and cattle to
*   live.*[10]

In the mind of the Egyptians the Nile was the supreme fertilizer and renewer of the land. Each September the Nile floods its valley, transforming it into a huge area of marsh or lagoon. By the end of November the water retreats, leaving behind a thin covering of fertile mud ready to be planted with crops.

The annual flood made the growing of abundant crops almost effortless, especially in southern Egypt. Herodotus, used to the rigors of Greek agriculture, was amazed by the ease with which the Egyptians raised crops:

For indeed without trouble they obtain crops from the land more easily than all other men. . . . They do not labor to dig furrows with the plough or hoe or do the work which other men do to raise grain. But when the river by itself inundates the fields and the water recedes, then each man, having sown his field, sends pigs into it. When the pigs trample down the seed, he waits for the harvest. Then when the pigs thresh the grain, he gets his crop.[11]

As late at 1822, John Burckhardt, an English traveler, watched nomads sowing grain by digging large holes in the mud and throwing in seeds. The extraordinary fertility of the Nile valley made it easy to produce an annual agricultural surplus, which in turn sustained a growing and prosperous population.

Whereas the Tigris and Euphrates and their tributaries carved up Mesopotamia into isolated areas, areas, the Nile unified Egypt. The river was the region's principal highway, promoting easy communication throughout the valley. As individual bands of settlers moved into the Nile Valley, they created stable agricultural communities. By about 3100 B.C. there were some forty of these communities in constant contact with one another. This contact, encouraged and facilitated by the Nile, virtually ensured the early political unification of Egypt.

Egypt was fortunate in that it was nearly self-sufficient. Besides the fertility of its soil, Egypt possessed enormous quantities of stone, which served

force. The Egyptians never feared the relatively tame Nile in the way the Mesopotamians feared the Tigris. Instead, they sang its praises.

Hail to thee, O Nile, that issues from the earth and
*   comes to keep Egypt alive! . . .*
He that waters the meadows which Re created,

as the raw material of architecture and sculpture. Abundant clay was available for pottery, as was gold for jewelry and ornaments. The raw materials that Egypt lacked were close at hand. The Egyptians could obtain copper from Sinai and timber from Lebanon. They had little cause to look to the outside world for their essential needs, a fact that helps to explain the insular quality of Egyptian life.

Geography further encouraged isolation by closing Egypt off from the outside world. To the east and west of the Nile Valley stretch grim deserts. The Nubian Desert and the cataracts of the Nile discourage penetration from the south. Only in the north did the Mediterranean Sea leave Egypt exposed. Thus geography shielded Egypt from invasion and from extensive immigration. Unlike the Mesopotamians, the Egyptians enjoyed centuries of peace and tranquility during which they could devote most of their resources to peaceful development of their distinctive civilization.

Yet Egypt was not completely sealed off. As early as 3250 B.C., Mesopotamian influences, notably architectural techniques and materials and perhaps even writing, made themselves felt in Egyptian life. Still later, from 1680 to 1580 B.C., northern Egypt was ruled by foreign invaders, the Hyksos. Infrequent though they were, such periods of foreign influence fertilized Egyptian culture without changing it in any fundamental way.

The God-King of Egypt

The geographical unity of Egypt quickly gave rise to political unification of the country under the authority of a king whom the Egyptians called "phar-

Narmer Palette   This ceremonial object celebrates the deeds of Narmer, but it also illustrates several of the attributes of the pharaoh in general. On left at top, the conquering pharaoh views the decapitated corpse of an unknown enemy, showing his duty to defend Egypt by defeating its enemies. This same theme recurs on the right where the pharaoh—also represented by the falcon, symbol of Horus—is about to kill a captive. *(Source: Jean Vertut)*

aoh." The details of this process have been lost. The Egyptians themselves told of a great king, Menes, who united Egypt into a single kingdom around 3100 B.C. Thereafter the Egyptians divided their history into *dynasties,* or families of kings. For modern historical purposes, however, it is more useful to divide Egyptian history into periods (see page 27). The political unification of Egypt ushered in the period known as the Old Kingdom, an era remarkable for prosperity, artistic flowering, and the evolution of religious beliefs.

In religion, the Egyptians developed complex, often contradictory, ideas about an afterlife. These beliefs were all rooted in the environment itself. The climate of Egypt is so stable that change is cyclical and dependable: though the heat of summer bakes the land, the Nile always floods and replenishes it. The dry air preserves much that would decay in other climates. Thus there was an air of permanence about Egypt; the past was never far from the present.

This cyclical rhythm permeated Egyptian religious beliefs. According to the Egyptians, Osiris, a fertility god associated with the Nile, died each year, and each year his wife Isis brought him back to life. Osiris eventually became king of the dead, and he weighed human beings' hearts to determine whether they had lived justly enough to deserve everlasting life. Osiris's care of the dead was shared by Anubis, the jackal-headed god who annually helped Isis resuscitate Osiris. Anubis was the god of mummification, so essential to Egyptian funerary rites.

The focal point of religious and political life in the Old Kingdom was the pharaoh, who commanded the wealth, resources, and people of all Egypt. The pharaoh's power was such that the Egyptians considered him to be the falcon-god Horus in human form. The link between the pharaoh and the god Horus was doubly important. In Egyptian religion Horus was the son of Osiris (king of the dead), which meant that the pharaoh, a living god on earth, became one with Osiris after death. The pharaoh was not simply the mediator between the gods and the Egyptian people. Above all, he was the power that achieved the integration between gods and human beings, between nature and society, that ensured peace and prosperity for the land of the Nile. The pharaoh was thus a guarantee to his people, a pledge that the gods of Egypt (strikingly unlike those of Mesopotamia) cared for their people.

The king's surroundings had to be worthy of a god. Only a magnificent palace was suitable for his home; in fact, the very word *pharaoh* means "great house." The king's tomb also had to reflect his might and exalted status. To this day the great pyramids at Giza near Cairo bear silent but magnificent testimony to the god-kings of Egypt.

The religious significance of the pyramid is as awesome as the political. The pharaoh as a god was the earthly sun, and the pyramid, which towered to the sky, helped him ascend the heavens after death. The pyramid provided the dead king with everything that he would need in the afterlife. His body had to be preserved from decay if his *ka,* an invisible counterpart of the body, was to survive. So the Egyptians developed an elaborate process of embalming the dead pharaoh and wrapping his corpse in cloth. As an added precaution, they carved his statue out of hard stone; if anything happened to the fragile mummy, the pharaoh's statue would help keep his ka alive. The need for an authentic likeness accounts for the naturalism of Egyptian portraiture. Artistic renderings of the pharaohs combine accuracy and the abstract in the effort to capture the essence of the living person. This approach produced that haunting quality of Egyptian sculpture—portraits of lifelike people imbued with a solemn, ageless, serene spirit.

To survive in the spirit world the ka required everything that the pharaoh needed in life: food and drink, servants and armed retainers, costly ornaments, and animal herds. In Egypt's prehistoric period, the king's servants and herdsmen and their flocks were slaughtered at the tomb to provide for the ka. By the time of the Old Kingdom, artists had substituted statues of scribes, officials, soldiers, and servants for their living counterparts. To remind the ka of daily life, artists covered the walls of the tomb with scenes ranging from agricultural routines to banquets and religious festivities, from hunting parties to gardens and ponds. Designed to give joy to the ka, these paintings, models of furniture, and statuettes today provide an intimate glimpse of Egyptian life, 4,500 years ago.

The Pharaoh's People

Because the common folk stood at the bottom of the social and economic scale, they were always at the mercy of grasping officials. The arrival of the tax

The Pyramids at Giza Giza was the burial place of the pharaohs of the Old Kingdom and of their aristocracy, whose rectangular tombs are visible behind the middle pyramid. The small pyramids at the foot of the foremost pyramid probably belong to the pharaohs' wives. (Source: Geoffrey Clifford/Woodfin Camp & Associates)

collector was never a happy occasion. One Egyptian scribe described the worst that could happen:

And now the scribe lands on the river-bank and is about to register the harvest-tax. The janitors carry staves and the Nubians rods of palm, and they say, Hand over the corn, though there is none. The cultivator is beaten all over, he is bound and thrown into a well, soused and dipped head downwards. His wife has been bound in his presence and his children are in fetters.[12]

That was an extreme situation. Nonetheless, taxes might amount to 20 percent of the harvest, and tax collection could be brutal.

On the other hand, everyone, no matter how lowly, theoretically had the right of appeal, and the account of one such appeal, "The Tale of the Eloquent Peasant," was a favorite Egyptian story. The hero of the tale, Khunanup, was robbed by the servant of the high steward, and Khunanup had to bring his case before the steward himself. When the steward delayed his decision, Khunanup openly ac-

cused him of neglecting his duty, saying, "The arbitrator is a spoiler; the peace-maker is a creator of sorrow; the smoother over of differences is a creator of soreness."[13] The pharaoh himself ordered the steward to give Khunanup justice, and the case was decided in the peasant's favor.

Egyptian society seems to have been a curious mixture of freedom and constraint. Slavery did not become widespread until the New Kingdom. There was neither a caste system nor a color bar, and humble people could rise to the highest positions if they possessed talent. The most famous example of social mobility (which, however, dates to the New Kingdom) is the biblical story of Joseph, who came to Egypt as a slave and rose to be second only to the pharaoh. On the other hand, most ordinary folk were probably little more than serfs who could not easily leave the land of their own free will. Peasants were also subject to forced labor, including work on the pyramids and canals. Young men were drafted into the pharaoh's army, which served both as a fighting force and as a labor corps.

Hippopotamus Hunt   This wall painting depicts the success of two men in a small boat who have killed a hippopotamus, seen in the lower right-hand corner. Behind the hippopotamus swims a crocodile hoping for a snack. *(Source: Egyptian Museum SMPK, Berlin/Bildarchiv Preussischer Kulturbesitz)*

The vision of thousands of people straining to build the pyramids and countless artists adorning the pharaoh's tomb brings to the modern mind a distasteful picture of oriental despotism. Indeed, the Egyptian view of life and society is alien to those raised on the Western concepts of individual freedom and human rights. To ancient Egyptians

the pharaoh embodied justice and order—harmony among humans, nature, and the divine. If the pharaoh was weak or allowed anyone to challenge his unique position, he opened the way to chaos. Twice in Egyptian history the pharaoh failed to maintain rigid centralization. During those two eras, known as the First and Second Intermediate periods, Egypt was exposed to civil war and invasion. Yet the monarchy survived, and in each period a strong pharaoh arose to crush the rebels or expel the invaders and restore order.

The Hyksos in Egypt (1640–1570 B.C.)

While Egyptian civilization flourished behind its bulwark of sand and sea, momentous changes were taking place in the ancient Near East, changes that would leave their mark even on rich, insular Egypt. These changes involved enormous and remarkable movements, especially of peoples who spoke Semitic tongues.

The original home of the Semites was perhaps the Arabian peninsula. Some tribes moved into northern Mesopotamia, others into Syria and Palestine, and still others into Egypt. Shortly after 1800 B.C. people whom the Egyptians called *Hyksos,* which means "Rulers of the Uplands," began to settle in the Nile Delta. Egyptian tradition, as later recorded by the priest Manetho in the third century B.C., depicted the coming of the Hyksos as a brutal invasion:

In the reign of Toutimaios—I do not know why—the wind of god blew against us. Unexpectedly from the regions of the east men of obscure race, looking forward confidently to victory, invaded our land, and without a battle easily seized it all by sheer force. Having subdued those in authority in the land, they then barbarously burned our cities and razed to the ground the temples of the gods. They fell upon all the natives in an entirely hateful fashion, slaughtering them and leading both their children and wives into slavery. At last they made one of their people king, whose name was Salitis. This man resided at Memphis, leaving in Upper and Lower Egypt tax collectors and garrisons in strategic places.[14]

Although the Egyptians portrayed the Hyksos as a conquering horde, they were probably no more than nomads looking for good land. Their entry into the delta was probably gradual and generally peaceful. The Hyksos "invasion" was one of the

PERIODS OF EGYPTIAN HISTORY

Period	Dates	Significant Events
Archaic	3100–2660 B.C.	Unification of Egypt
Old Kingdom	2660–2180 B.C.	Construction of the pyramids
First Intermediate	2180–2080 B.C.	Political chaos
Middle Kingdom	2080–1640 B.C.	Recovery and political stability
Second Intermediate	1640–1570 B.C.	Hyksos "invasion"
New Kingdom	1570–1075 B.C.	Creation of an Egyptian empire
		Akhenaten's religious policy

fertilizing periods of Egyptian history; it introduced new ideas and techniques into Egyptian life. The Hyksos brought with them the method of making bronze and casting it into tools and weapons that became standard in Egypt. They thereby brought Egypt fully into the Bronze Age culture of the Mediterranean world, a culture in which the production and use of bronze implements became basic to society. Bronze tools made farming more efficient than ever before because they were sharper and more durable than the copper tools they replaced. The Hyksos' use of bronze armor and weapons as well as horse-drawn chariots and the composite bow, made of laminated wood and horn and far more powerful than the simple wooden bow, revolutionized Egyptian warfare. However much the Egyptians learned from the Hyksos, Egyptian culture eventually absorbed the newcomers. The Hyksos came to worship Egyptian gods and modeled their monarchy on the Pharaonic system.

The New Kingdom: Revival and Empire (1570–1200 B.C.)

Politically, Egypt was only in eclipse. The Egyptian sun shone again when a remarkable line of kings, the pharaohs of the Eighteenth Dynasty, arose to challenge the Hyksos. The pharaoh Ahmose (r. 1558–1533 B.C.) pushed the Hyksos out of the delta. Thutmose I (r. 1512–1500 B.C.) subdued Nubia in the south. Thutmose III (r. 1490–1436 B.C.) conquered Palestine and Syria and fought inconclusively with the Hurrians, who had migrated into the upper Euphrates from the north and created there the new Hurrian kingdom of Mitanni. In this way, Egyptian warrior-pharaohs inaugurated the New Kingdom—a period in Egyptian history characterized by enormous wealth and conscious imperialism. During this period, probably for the first time, widespread slavery became a feature of Egyptian life. The pharaoh's armies returned home leading hordes of slaves, who constituted a new labor force for imperial building projects.

The kings of the Eighteenth Dynasty created the first Egyptian empire. They ruled Palestine and Syria through their officers and incorporated into the kingdom of Egypt the African region of Nubia. Egyptian religion and customs flourished in Nubia, making a huge impact on African culture there and in neighboring areas. The warrior-kings celebrated their success with monuments on a scale unparalleled since the pharaohs of the Old Kingdom had built the pyramids. Even today the colossal granite statues of these pharaohs and the rich tomb objects of Tutankhamen ("King Tut") testify to the might and splendor of the New Kingdom.

Akhenaten and Monotheism

One of the most extraordinary of this unusual line of kings was Akhenaten (r. 1367–1350 B.C.), a pharaoh more concerned with religion than with conquest. Nefertiti, his wife and queen, encouraged his religious bent. The precise nature of Akhenaten's religious beliefs remains debatable. The problem began during his own lifetime. His religion was often unpopular among the people and the traditional priesthood, and its practice declined in the later years of his reign. After his death, it was condemned and denounced; consequently, not much is known about it. Most historians, however, agree that Akhenaten and Nefertiti were monotheists; that is, they believed that the sun-god Aton, whom they worshiped, was universal, the only god. They considered all other Egyptian gods and goddesses frauds and disregarded their worship.

The religious notions and actions of Akhenaten and Nefertiti were in direct opposition to traditional Egyptian beliefs. The Egyptians had long worshiped a host of gods, chief among whom was

The Goddess Selket   Selket appears in this statuette dressed as a queen. The goddess was originally a water scorpion who later assumed human form. She was the goddess who healed stings and bites. *(Source: Egyptian Museum, Cairo/Lee Boltin)*

Amon-Re. Originally Amon and Re had been two distinct sun-gods, but the Egyptians merged them and worshiped Amon-Re as the king of the gods. Egyptian religion had room for many gods and an easy tolerance for new gods. Furthermore, many Egyptians were sincerely devoted to their older gods, whom they thought had preserved Egypt and would grant them life after death.

To genuine religious sentiments were added the motives of the traditional priesthood. Although many priests were scandalized by Akhenaten's monotheism, many others were concerned more about their own welfare. By deposing the old gods Akhenaten destroyed the priests' livelihood and their reason for existence. On grounds of pure self-interest, the established priesthood opposed Akhenaten. Opposition in turn drove the pharaoh to intolerance and persecution. With a vengeance he tried to root out the old gods and their rituals.

Akhenaten's monotheism, imposed from above, failed to find a place among the people. The prime reason for Akhenaten's failure is that his god had no connection with the past of the Egyptian people, who trusted the old gods and felt comfortable praying to them. Average Egyptians were no doubt distressed and disheartened when their familiar gods were outlawed, for those gods were the heavenly powers that had made Egypt powerful and unique. The fanaticism and persecution that accompanied the new monotheism were in complete defiance of the Egyptian tradition of tolerant *polytheism,* or worship of several gods. Thus, when Akhenaten died, his religion died with him.

THE HITTITE EMPIRE

At about the time the Hyksos entered the Nile Delta, the Hittites, who had long been settled in Anatolia (modern Turkey), became a major power in that region and began to expand eastward (Map 1.3). The Hittites were an Indo-European people. The term *Indo-European* refers to a large family of languages that includes English, most of the languages of modern Europe, Greek, Latin, Persian, and Sanskrit, the sacred tongue of ancient India. During the eighteenth and nineteenth centuries, European scholars learned that peoples who spoke related languages had spread as far west as Ireland and as far east as central Asia. In the twentieth century, linguists deciphered the language of the Hit-

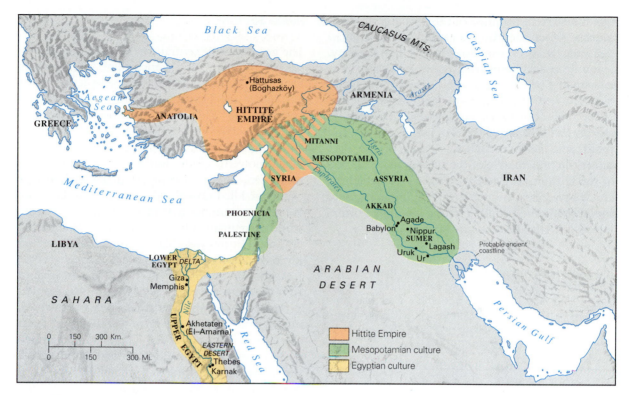

Map 1.3 Balance of Power in the Near East This map shows the regions controlled by the Hittites and Egyptians at the height of their power. As the striped area represents, the Hittites conquered part of Mesopotamia during their expansion eastward.

tites and the Linear B script of Mycenaean Greece. When both languages proved to be Indo-European, scholars were able to form a clearer picture of these vast movements. Archeologists were able to date the migrations roughly and put them into their historical context.

Around 2000 B.C., Indo-Europeans were on the move on a massive scale, perhaps from a starting point in central Europe. Peoples speaking the ancestor of Latin pushed into Italy, and Greek-speaking Mycenaeans settled in Greece. The Hittites rose to prominence in Anatolia, and other Indo-European folk thrust into Iran, India, and central Asia. Some Indo-Europeans, like the Hittites, came peacefully, but others disrupted existing states, only later helping to create stable new kingdoms.

The Rise of the Hittites

Until recently, scholars thought that as part of these vast movements the Hittites entered Anatolia around 1800 B.C. Current archeological work and

new documents, however, prove that Hittites had settled there at least as early as 2700 B.C. Nor did they overrun the country in a sweeping invasion, burning, looting, and destroying. Their arrival and diffusion seem in fact to have been rather peaceful, accompanied by intermarriage and alliance with the natives. So well did the Hittites integrate themselves into the local culture of central Anatolia that they even adopted the worship of several native deities.

The rise of the Hittites to prominence in Anatolia is reasonably clear. During the nineteenth century B.C. the native kingdoms in the area engaged in suicidal warfare that left most of Anatolia's once-flourishing towns in ashes and rubble. In this climate of exhaustion the Hittite king Hattusilis I built a hill citadel at Hattusas, the modern Boghazköy, from which he led his Hittites against neighboring kingdoms. Hattusilis's grandson and successor Mursilis I (ca 1595 B.C.) extended the Hittite conquests as far as Babylon. With help from the Kassites, a people who had newly settled along the upper reaches of the Euphrates River, Mursilis captured the city and snuffed out the dynasty of Hammurabi. While the Hittites carried off Babylonian loot, the Kassites took control of the territory. Upon his return home, the victorious Mursilis was assassinated by members of his own family, an act that plunged the kingdom into confusion and opened the door to foreign invasion. The Hittites quickly lost substantial tracts of land in the east and south, and Hattusas itself was attacked. Mursilis's career is representative of the success and weakness of the Hittites. They were extremely vulnerable to attack by vigilant and tenacious enemies. Yet, once they were united behind a strong king, the Hittites were a power to be reckoned with.

The Hittite God Atarluhas   This statue of the god Atarluhas, with two lions at his feet, was set up near the gateway of the Hittite city of Carchemish. A bird-headed demon holds the lions. In 1920 this statue was destroyed during a war between Turkey and Syria. *(Source: Courtesy of the Trustees of the British Museum)*

Hittite Society

The geography of central Anatolia encouraged the rise of self-contained agricultural communities. Each was probably originally ruled by a petty king, but under the Hittites a group of local officials known as the "Elders" handled community affairs. Besides the farming population, Hittite society included a well-defined group of artisans who fashioned pottery, cloth, leather goods, and metal tools. Documents also report that traveling merchants peddled goods and gossip, reminding individual communities that they were part of a larger world. Like many other societies, ancient and modern, the Hittites held slaves, who nonetheless enjoyed certain rights under the law.

At the top of Hittite society was the aristocracy, among whom the relatives of the king constituted a privileged group. The king's relations were a mighty and often unruly group who served as the chief royal administrators. The royal family was often a threat to the king, for some of them, such as the assassin of Mursilis I, readily resorted to murder as a method of seizing power. Hittite nobles often revolted against the king, a tendency that weakened central authority and left Hittite society open to outside attack. Below the nobles stood the warriors, who enjoyed the right to meet in their own assembly, the *pankus*. The pankus met to hear the will of the king, but it could not itself vote on policy. It was, however, a court of law, with the authority to punish criminals.

Just as the aristocracy stood at the head of society, so the king and queen stood above the aristocracy. The king was supreme commander of the army, chief judge, and supreme priest. He carried on all diplomatic dealings with foreign powers and in times of war personally led the Hittite army into the field. The queen, who was highly regarded, held a strong, independent position. She had important religious duties to perform, and some queens even engaged in diplomatic correspondence with foreign queens.

The Hittites are typical of many newcomers to the ancient Near East in that they readily assimilated the cultures that they found. Soon they fell under the powerful spell of the more advanced Mesopotamian culture. The Hittites adopted the cuneiform script for their own language. Hittite kings published law codes, just as Hammurabi had done. Royal correspondence followed Mesopotamian forms. The Hittites delighted in Mesopotamian myths, legends, epics, and art. To the credit of the Hittites, one must add that they used these Mesopotamian borrowings to create something of their own.

The Era of Hittite Greatness (ca 1475–ca 1200 B.C.)

The Hittites, like the Egyptians of the New Kingdom, eventually produced an energetic and capable line of kings who restored order and rebuilt Hittite power. Once Telepinus (r. 1525–1500 B.C.) had brought the aristocracy under control, Suppiluliumas I (r. 1380–1346 B.C.) secured central Anatolia, and Mursilis II (r. 1345–1315 B.C.) regained Syria. Around 1300 B.C. Mursilis's son stopped the Egyptian army of Rameses II at the battle of Kadesh in Syria. Having fought each other to a standstill, the Hittites and Egyptians first made peace, then an alliance. Alliance was followed by friendship, and friendship by active cooperation. The two greatest powers of the early Near East tried to make war between them impossible.

The Hittites exercised remarkable political wisdom and flexibility in the organization and administration of their empire. Some states they turned into vassal-kingdoms, ruled by the sons of the Hittite king; the king and his sons promised each other mutual support in times of crisis. Still other kingdoms were turned into protectorates whose native kings were allowed to rule with considerable freedom. The native kings swore obedience to the Hittite king and had to contribute military contingents to the Hittite army. Although they also sent tribute to the Hittites, the financial burden was moderate. The common people probably felt Hittite overlordship little if at all.

THE FALL OF EMPIRES (1200 B.C.)

Like the Hittite kings, Rameses II (ca 1290–1224 B.C.) used the peace after the battle of Kadesh to promote the prosperity of his own kingdom. Free from the expense and waste of warfare, he concentrated the income from the natural wealth and the foreign trade of Egypt on internal affairs. In the

Temple of Rameses II These colossal statues of Rameses II, carved literally out of the side of a hill, guard the entrance of a temple itself created by tunneling through rock. The statues of the last great pharaoh measure about 40 feet in height. *(Source: Geoffrey Clifford/Woodfin Camp)*

age-old tradition of the pharaohs, he began new building projects that brought both employment to his subjects and grandeur to Egypt. From Nubia to the delta of the Nile he bedecked his kingdom with grand, new monuments. Once again, Egypt was wealthy and secure within its natural boundaries. In many ways, he was the last great pharaoh of Egypt.

This stable and generally peaceful situation endured until the late thirteenth century B.C., when both the Hittite and the Egyptian empires were destroyed by invaders. The most famous of these marauders, called the "Sea Peoples" by the Egyptians, remain one of the puzzles of ancient history. Despite much new work, modern archeology is still unable to identify the Sea Peoples satisfactorily. It is known, however, that their incursions were part of a larger movement of peoples. Although there is serious doubt about whether the Sea Peoples alone overthrew the Hittites, they did deal both the Hittites and the Egyptians a hard blow, making the Hittites vulnerable to overland invasion from the north and driving the Egyptians back to the Nile Delta. The Hittites fell under the external blows, but the Egyptians, shaken and battered, retreated to the delta and held on.

SUMMARY

For thousands of years Paleolithic peoples roamed this planet seeking game. Although many groups of Paleolithic peoples relied partly on agriculture, they lived a largely nomadic life. Only in the Neolithic Age—with the invention of new stone tools, a reliance on sustained agriculture, and the domestication of animals—did peoples begin to live in permanent locations. These villages evolved into towns, where people began to create new social bonds and political organizations. The result was economic prosperity. The earliest area where these developments led to genuine urban societies is Mesopotamia. Here, the Sumerians and then other Mesopotamians developed writing, which enabled their culture to be passed on to others. The wealth of the Mesopotamians made it possible for them to devote time to history, astronomy, urban planning, medicine, and other arts and sciences. Mesopotamian culture was so rich and advanced that neighboring peoples eagerly adopted it, thereby spreading it through much of the Near East. Nor were the

Mesopotamians alone in advancing the civilization of the day. In Egypt another strong culture developed, one that made an impact more in Africa than in the Near East. The Egyptians too enjoyed such prosperity that they developed writing of their own, mathematical skills, and religious beliefs that influenced the lives of their neighbors. Into this world came the Hittites, an Indo-European people who were culturally less advanced than the Mesopotamians and Egyptians. The Hittites learned from their neighbors and rivals, but they also introduced their own sophisticated political system for administering their empire, a system that in some ways influenced both their contemporaries and later peoples.

NOTES

1. L. Eiseley, *The Unexpected Universe* (New York: Harcourt Brace Jovanovich, 1969), p. 102.
2. W. K. Loftus, *Travels and Researches in Chaldaea and Susiana* (New York: R. Carter & Brothers, 1857), p. 163.
3. Quoted in S. N. Kramer, *The Sumerians,* (Chicago: University of Chicago Press, 1964), p. 238. John Buckler is the translator of all uncited quotations from a foreign language in Chapters 1–6.
4. J. B. Pritchard, ed., *Ancient Near Eastern Texts,* 3d ed. (Princeton, N.J.: Princeton University Press, 1969), p. 175. Hereafter called *ANET.*
5. *ANET,* p. 44.
6. *ANET,* p. 590.
7. Kramer, p. 150.
8. *ANET,* p. 171.
9. Kramer, p. 251.
10. *ANET,* p. 372.
11. Herodotus, *The Histories* 2.14.
12. Quoted in A. H. Gardiner, "Ramesside Texts Relating to the Taxation and Transport of Corn," *Journal of Egyptian Archaeology* 27 (1941): 19–20.
13. A. H. Gardiner, "The Eloquent Peasant," *Journal of Egyptian Archaeology* 9 (1923): 17.
14. Manetho, *History of Egypt,* frag. 42.75–77.

SUGGESTED READING

Those interested in the tangled and incomplete story of human evolution will be rewarded by a good deal of new work, much of it difficult. C. E. Oxnard, *Fossils, Teeth and Sex* (1987), uses current information to conclude that the very search for the "missing link" is the wrong approach. R. Singer and J. K. Lundy, *Variation, Culture and Evolution in African Populations* (1986)—especially chap. 16—discusses recent developments in Africa. C. Gamble, *The Palaeolithic Settlement of Europe* (1986), covers both methodology and recent finds to offer a new interpretation of how early peoples spread through Europe. I. Rouse, *Migrations in Prehistory* (1989), studies population movements using information from cultural remains. A much broader book is T. C. Champion et al., *Prehistoric Europe* (1984). A fascinating study of Neolithic people in England is R. Castkeden, *The Stonehenge People* (1987), in which the author uses the famous monument as the starting point for a lively discussion of the society that built it. F. Dahlberg, *Woman the Gatherer* (1981), demonstrates the importance for primitive societies of women's role in gathering. A broader and newer study is M. Ehrenberg, *Women in Prehistory* (1989). A study of how primitive peoples depended on both hunting and gathering for survival is provided by T. D. Price and J. A. Brown, *Prehistoric Hunter-Gatherers* (1985), which also studies how hunting and gathering led to a more complex culture.

As the text suggests, the origins of agriculture and the Neolithic Age have recently received a great deal of attention. J. R. Harlan's conclusions are set out in a series of works including "Agricultural Origins: Centers and Noncenters," *Science* 174 (1971): 468–474; *Crops and Man* (1975); and "The Plants and Animals That Nourish Man," *Scientific American* 235 (September 1976): 89. The 1981 Egyptian expedition mentioned in the text is described by F. Wendorf and R. Schild, "The Earliest Food Producers." *Archaeology* 34 (September–October 1981): 30–36.

G. Barker, *Prehistoric Farming in Europe* (1984), and P. S. Wells, *Farms, Villages and Cities* (1984), treat the problem of commerce and urban origins in late prehistoric Europe. A very readable study, A. Ferrill, *The Origins of War* (1985), treats the topic of warfare from the Neolithic Age to Alexander the Great. Ferrill makes the interesting suggestion that more organized methods of warfare also influenced the trend toward urbanization.

For the societies of Mesopotamia, see A. Leo Oppenheim, *Ancient Mesopotamia,* rev. ed. (1977); M. E. L. Mallowan, *Early Mesopotamia and Iran* (1965); and H. W. F. Saggs, *The Greatness That Was Babylon* (1962). H. W. F. Saggs, *Everyday Life in Babylonia and Assyria* (1965), offers a delightful glimpse of Mesopotamian life.

C. B. Kemp, *Ancient Egypt: Anatomy of a Civilization* (1988), is a comprehensive reassessment of Egyptian society. D. B. Redford, *Akhenaten: The Heretic King* (1984), puts Akhenaten into his historical context, both political and religious. B. S. Lesko, *The Remarkable Women of Ancient Egypt,* 2d ed. (1987), a brief survey of aristocratic and ordinary women, concludes that Egyptian women led freer lives than the women of the Greco-Roman pe-

riod. The title of L. Manniche, *Sexual Life in Ancient Egypt* (1987), aptly describes the book's subject. J. M. White, *Everyday Life in Ancient Egypt* (1963), provides a broad survey of Egyptian society. M. Lichtheim, *Ancient Egyptian Literature,* 3 vols. (1975–1980), is a selection of readings covering the most important periods of Egyptian history. D. B. Redford, *Akhenaton* (1987), with illustrations, offers the most recent assessment of this complex pharaoh.

Introductions to problems and developments shared by several Near Eastern societies can be found in the studies edited by T. A. Wertime and J. D. Muhly, *The Coming of the Age of Iron* (1980), as well as in J. B. Pritchard, *The Ancient Near East,* 2 vols. (1958, 1976). The latter work is a fine synthesis by one of the world's leading Near Eastern specialists. A sweeping survey is C. Burney, *The Ancient Near East* (1977). Pioneering new work on the origins of writing appears in a series of pieces by D. Schmandt-Besserat, notably "An Archaic Recording System and the Origin of Writing," *Syro-Mesopotamian Studies* 1–2 (1977): 1–32, and "Reckoning Before Writing," *Archaeology* 32 (May–June 1979): 23–31.

O. R. Gurney, *The Hittites,* 2d ed. (1954), is still a fine introduction by an eminent scholar. Good also is J. G. MacQueen, *The Hittites and Their Contemporaries in Asia Minor,* 2d ed. (1986). J. P. Mallory, *In Search of the Indo-Europeans* (1989), uses language, archeology, and myth to study the Indo-Europeans. The 1960s were prolific years for archeology in Turkey. A brief survey by one of the masters of the field is J. Mellaart, *The Archaeology of Modern Turkey* (1978), which also tests a great number of widely held historical interpretations. The Sea Peoples have been the subject of two recent studies: A. Nibbi, *The Sea Peoples and Egypt* (1975), and N. K. Sandars, *The Sea Peoples* (1978).

A truly excellent study of ancient religions, from those of Sumer to those of the late Roman Empire, is M. Eliade, ed., *Religions of Antiquity* (1989), which treats concisely but amply all of the religions mentioned in Chapters 1 through 6. For Near Eastern religion and mythology, good introductions are E. O. James, *The Ancient Gods: The History and Diffusion of Religion in the Ancient Near East and the Eastern Mediterranean* (1960), and J. Gray, *Near Eastern Mythology* (1969). A survey of Mesopotamian religion by one of the foremost scholars in the field is T. Jacobsen, *The Treasures of Darkness: A History of Mesopotamian Religion* (1976).

Surveys of Near Eastern art include R. D. Barnett and D. J. Wiseman, *Fifty Masterpieces of Ancient Near Eastern Art* (1969); and J. B. Pritchard's delightful *The Ancient Near East in Pictures,* 2d ed. (1969). For literature, see S. Fiore, *Voices from the Clay: The Development of Assyro-Babylonian Literature* (1965); W. K. Simpson, ed., *The Literature of Ancient Egypt* (1973); and, above all, J. B. Pritchard, ed., *Ancient Near Eastern Texts,.* 3d ed. (1969).

2

Small Kingdoms and Mighty Empires in the Near East

The migratory invasions that brought down the Hittites and stunned the Egyptians in the late thirteenth century B.C. ushered in an era of confusion and weakness. Although much was lost in the chaos, the old cultures of the ancient Near East survived to nurture new societies. In the absence of powerful empires, the Phoenicians, Syrians, Hebrews, and many other peoples carved out small independent kingdoms, until the Near East was a patchwork of them. During this period Hebrew culture and religion evolved under the influence of urbanism, kings, and prophets.

In the ninth century B.C. this jumble of small states gave way to an empire that for the first time embraced the entire Near East. Yet the very ferocity of the Assyrian Empire led to its downfall only two hundred years later. In 550 B.C. the Persians and Medes, who had migrated into Iran, created a "world empire" stretching from Anatolia in the west to the Indus Valley in the east. For over two hundred years the Persians gave the ancient Near East peace and stability.

- How did Egypt, its political greatness behind it, pass on its cultural heritage to its African neighbors?

- How did the Hebrew state evolve, and what was daily life like in Hebrew society?

- What forces helped to shape Hebrew religious thought, still powerfully influential in today's world?

- What enabled the Assyrians to overrun their neighbors, and how did their cruelty finally cause their undoing?

- Last, how did Iranian nomads create the Persian Empire?

In this chapter we will seek answers to these questions.

EGYPT, A SHATTERED KINGDOM

The invasions of the Sea Peoples brought the great days of Egyptian power to an end. One scribe left behind a somber portrait of Egypt stunned and leaderless:

The land of Egypt was abandoned and every man was a law to himself. During many years there was no leader who could speak for others. Central government lapsed, small officials and headmen took over the whole land. Any man, great or small, might kill his neighbor. In the distress and vacuum that followed . . . men banded together to plunder one another. They treated the gods no better than men, and cut off the temple revenues.[1]

No longer able to dream of foreign conquests, Egypt looked to its own security from foreign invasion. Egyptians suffered a four-hundred-year period of political fragmentation, a new dark age known to Egyptian specialists as the Third Intermediate Period (eleventh–seventh centuries B.C.).

The decline of Egypt was especially sharp in foreign affairs. Whereas the pharaohs of the Eighteenth Dynasty had held sway as far abroad as Syria, their weak successors found it unsafe to venture far from home. In the wake of the Sea Peoples, numerous small kingdoms sprang up in the Near East, each fiercely protective of its own independence. To them Egypt was a memory, and foreign princes often greeted Egyptian officials with suspicion or downright contempt. In the days of Egypt's greatness, petty kings would never have dared to treat Egyptian officials in such a humiliating fashion.

Disrupted at home and powerless abroad, Egypt fell prey to invasion by its African neighbors. Libyans from North Africa filtered into the Nile Delta, where they established independent dynasties. Indeed, from 950 to 730 B.C. northern Egypt was ruled by Libyan pharaohs. The Libyans built cities, and for the first time a sturdy urban life grew up in the delta. Although the coming of the Libyans changed the face of the delta, the Libyans genuinely admired Egyptian culture and eagerly adopted Egypt's religion and way of life.

In southern Egypt, meanwhile, the pharaoh's decline opened the way to the energetic Africans of Nubia, who extended their authority northward throughout the Nile Valley. Nubian influence in these years, though pervasive, was not destructive. Since the imperial days of the Eighteenth Dynasty (see pages 27–28), the Nubians, too, had adopted many features of Egyptian culture. Now Nubian kings and aristocrats embraced Egyptian culture wholesale. The thought of destroying the heritage of the pharaohs would have struck them as stupid and barbaric. Thus the Nubians and the Libyans repeated an old Near Eastern phenomenon: new peoples conquered old centers of political and military power but were assimilated into the older culture.

The reunification of Egypt occurred late and unexpectedly. With Egypt distracted and disorganized by foreign invasions, an independent African state, the Kingdom of Kush, grew up in modern Sudan with its capital at Nepata. These Africans, too, worshiped Egyptian gods and used Egyptian hieroglyphs. In the eighth century B.C. their king Piankhy swept through the entire Nile Valley from Nepata in the south to the delta in the north. United once again, Egypt enjoyed a brief period of peace during which Egyptians continued to assimilate their conquerors. In the Kingdom of Kush, Egyptian methods of administration and bookkeeping, arts and crafts, and economic practices became common, especially among the aristocracy. Nonetheless, reunification of the realm did not lead to a new Egyptian empire. In the centuries between the fall of the New Kingdom and the recovery of Egypt, several small but vigorous kingdoms had taken root and grown to maturity in the ancient Near East. By 700 B.C. Egypt was once again a strong kingdom, but no longer a mighty empire.

Yet Egypt's legacy to its African neighbors remained vibrant and rich. By trading and exploring southward along the coast of the Red Sea, the Egyptians introduced their goods and ideas as far south as the land of Punt, probably a region on the Somali coast. As early as the New Kingdom, Egyptian pharaohs had exchanged gifts with the monarchs of Punt, and contact between the two areas persisted. Egypt was the primary civilizing force in Nubia, which became another version of the pharaoh's realm, complete with royal pyramids and Egyptian deities. Egyptian religion penetrated as far south as Ethiopia. Just as Mesopotamian culture enjoyed wide appeal throughout the Near East, so Egyptian culture had a massive impact on northeastern Africa.

THE CHILDREN OF ISRAEL

The fall of the Hittite Empire and Egypt's collapse created a vacuum of power in the western Near East that allowed for the rise of numerous small states. No longer crushed between the Hittites in the north and the Egyptians in the south, various peoples—some of them newcomers—created homes and petty kingdoms in Syria, Phoenicia, and Palestine. After the Sea Peoples had raided Egypt, a branch of them, known in the Bible as Philistines, settled along the coast of Palestine (Map 2.1). Establishing themselves in five cities somewhat inland from the sea, the Philistines set about farming and raising flocks.

Another sturdy new culture was that of the Phoenicians, a Semitic-speaking people who had long inhabited several cities along the coast of modern Lebanon. They had lived under the shadow of the Hittites and Egyptians, but in this period the Phoenicians enjoyed full independence. Unlike the Philistine newcomers, who turned from seafaring to farming, the Phoenicians took to the sea and became outstanding merchants and explorers. In

Map 2.1 Small Kingdoms in the Near East This map illustrates the political fragmentation of the Near East after the great wave of invasions that occurred during the thirteenth century B.C.

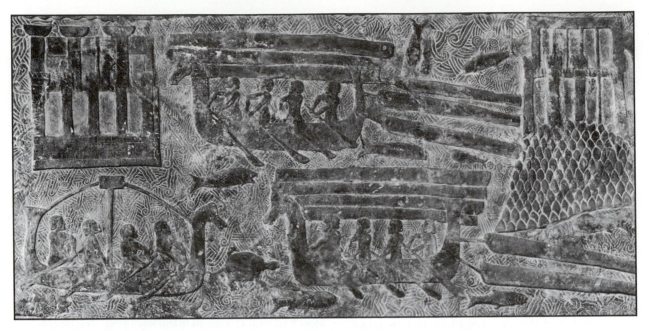

Phoenician Cargo Vessels   An Assyrian artist has captured all of the energy and vivacity of the seafaring Phoenicians. The sea is filled with Phoenician cargo ships, which ranged the entire Mediterranean. These ships are transporting cedar from Lebanon, some of it stowed on board, while other logs float in their wake. *(Source: Louvre/Giraudon/Art Resource)*

trading ventures they sailed as far west as modern Tunisia, where in 813 B.C. they founded the city of Carthage, which would one day struggle with Rome for domination of the western Mediterranean. Phoenician culture was urban, based on the prosperous commercial centers of Tyre, Sidon, and Byblos. The Phoenicians' overwhelming cultural achievement was the development of an alphabet: they, unlike other literate peoples, used one letter to designate one sound, a system that vastly simplified writing and reading. The Greeks modified this alphabet and then used it to write their own language.

South of Phoenicia arose another small kingdom, that of the Hebrews or ancient Jews. Although smaller, poorer, less important, and less powerful than neighboring kingdoms, the realm of the Hebrews was to nourish religious ideas that underlie all of Western civilization. Who were these people, and what brought them to this new land? Earlier Mesopotamian and Egyptian sources refer to people called "Habiru," or "Hapiru," which seems to mean a class of homeless, independent nomads. One such group of Habiru were the bibli-

cal Hebrews. Their original homeland was probably northern Mesopotamia, and the most crucial event in their historical development was enslavement in Egypt. According to the Old Testament, the Hebrews had followed their patriarch Abraham out of Mesopotamia into Canaan in modern Israel, where they became identified as the "Children of Israel" after the patriarch Jacob, who was also called "Israel."

The Old Testament, the first part of the Bible, is the major literary source for many events involving the early Hebrews. A mere reading of the Bible proves that the Old Testament was composed in various stages. Modern scholars have demonstrated that the origins of the earliest books go back to a time between 950 and 800 B.C. In this period literate people collected oral traditions of the Hebrew past, which included legends, myths, songs, proverbs, laws, and much else, and wove them into a narrative account of their past. Later prophets, priests, and historians added to the narrative until the Old Testament took its final form. Archeologists can help to clarify biblical events by trying to ascertain precisely what happened around the time of the Hebrew exodus from Egypt. The archeological record indicates that the thirteenth century B.C. was a time of warfare, disruption, and destruction and seems to confirm the biblical portrayal of the exodus as a long period of turmoil. It also shows that the situation in Palestine was far more complicated than the Bible suggests.

Many different peoples rubbed shoulders in Palestine in the thirteenth century B.C. Amorites, distant relatives of Hammurabi's Babylonians, had entered the area around 1800 B.C. They found there a Semitic-speaking people, the Canaanites, with whom they freely mingled. Hebrew tribes also arrived, an event about which there is great uncertainty as to time and detail. During the Eighteenth Dynasty of Egypt, some Hebrews were either taken to Egypt or migrated there voluntarily. Meanwhile, other Hebrews remained behind in Palestine. In Egypt the Hebrews were enslaved and forced to labor on building projects. During the thirteenth century B.C. Moses, who may be a mythical figure, led a group of Hebrews from Egypt. According to the biblical book of Exodus, this group consisted of twelve tribes, believed to be descended from the twelve great-grandsons of Abraham. Their wanderings took them to Palestine, where in a series of vicious wars and savage slaughters they slowly won a

place (see Map 2.1). Success was not automatic, and the Hebrews suffered defeats and setbacks; but gradually they spread their power northward. In some cases they assimilated themselves to the culture of the natives, even going so far as to worship Baal, an ancient Semitic fertility god. In other instances, they carved out little strongholds and enslaved the natives. Even after the conquest, nearly constant fighting was required to consolidate their position.

The greatest danger to the Hebrews came from the Philistines, whose superior technology and military organization at first made them invincible. In Saul (ca 1000 B.C.), a farmer of the tribe of Benjamin, the Hebrews found a champion and a spirited leader. In the biblical account, Saul carried the war to the Philistines, often without success. Yet in the meantime he established a monarchy over the twelve Hebrew tribes. Thus, under the peril of the Philistines, the Hebrew tribes evolved from scattered independent units into a centralized political organization in which the king directed the energies of the people.

Saul's work was carried on by David of Bethlehem, who in his youth had followed Saul into battle against the Philistines. Through courage and cunning, David hurled back the Philistines, and

Nomadic Semitic Tribe   This Egyptian fresco captures the essentials of nomadic life. These Semites have captured a gazelle and an ibex. The four men behind the leaders are portrayed with their weapons, a bow and spears, which were used for both hunting and defense. Bringing up the rear is a domesticated burro. *(Source: Erich Lessing Culture and Fine Arts Archive)*

waged war against his other neighbors. To give his kingdom a capital he captured the city of Jerusalem, which he enlarged, fortified, and made the religious and political center of his realm. David's military successes won the Hebrews unprecedented security, and his forty-year reign was a period of vitality and political consolidation. His work in consolidating the monarchy and enlarging the kingdom paved the way for his son Solomon.

Solomon (ca 965–925 B.C.) applied his energies to creating a nation out of a collection of tribes ruled by a king. He divided the kingdom, for purposes of effective administration, into twelve territorial districts cutting across the old tribal borders. To Solomon the twelve tribes of Israel were far less important than the Hebrew nation. To bring his kingdom up to the level of its more sophisticated neighbors, he set about a building program to make Israel a respectable Near Eastern state. Work was begun on a magnificent temple in Jerusalem, on cities, palaces, fortresses, and roads. Solomon worked to bring Israel into the commercial mainstream of the world around it and kept up good relations with Phoenician cities to the north. To finance all of the construction and other activities that he initiated, Solomon imposed taxes far greater than any levied before, much to the displeasure of his subjects.

Solomon dedicated the temple in grand style and made it the home of the Ark of the Covenant, the cherished chest that contained the holiest of Hebrew religious articles. The temple in Jerusalem was to be the religious heart of the kingdom and the symbol of Hebrew unity. It also became the stronghold of the priesthood, for a legion of priests was needed to conduct religious sacrifices, ceremonies, and prayers. Yet Solomon's efforts were hampered by strife. In the eyes of some people, he was too ready to unite other religions with the worship of the Hebrew god Yahweh, and the financial demands of his building program drained the resources of his people. His use of forced labor for building projects further fanned popular resentment. However, Solomon had turned a rude kingdom into a state with broad commercial horizons and greater knowledge of the outside world. At his death, the Hebrews broke into two political halves (see Map 2.1). The northern part of the kingdom of David and Solomon became Israel, with its capital at Samaria. The southern half was Judah, and Solomon's city of Jerusalem remained its center.

With political division went a religious rift: Israel, the northern kingdom, established rival sanctuaries for gods other than Yahweh. The Hebrew nation was divided, but at least it was divided into two far more sophisticated political units than before the time of Solomon. The Hebrews had taken their place in the increasingly cosmopolitan world of the Near East. Eventually, the northern kingdom of Israel was wiped out by the Assyrians, but the southern kingdom of Judah survived numerous calamities for several more centuries and kept the faith of the Children of Israel. The people of Judah came to be known as *Jews* and gave their name to *Judaism,* the worship of Yahweh.

The Evolution of Jewish Religion

Hand in hand with their political evolution from fierce nomads to urban dwellers, the Hebrews were evolving spiritual ideas that still permeate Western society. Their chief literary product, the Old Testament, has fundamentally influenced both Christianity and Islam and still exerts a compelling force on the modern world.

Fundamental to an understanding of Jewish religion is the concept of the *Covenant,* a formal agreement between Yahweh and the Hebrew people. According to the Bible, the god Yahweh, later often called "Jehovah," appeared to Moses on Mount Sinai. There Yahweh made a covenant with the Hebrews that was in fact a contract: if the Hebrews worshiped Yahweh as their only god, he would consider them his chosen people and protect them from their enemies. The Hebrews believed that Yahweh had led them out of bondage in Egypt and had helped them to conquer their new land, the promised land. In return, the Hebrews worshiped Yahweh and Yahweh alone. They also obeyed Yahweh's Ten Commandments, an ethical code of conduct revealed to them by Moses.

Yahweh was unique because he was a lone god. Unlike the gods of Mesopotamia and Egypt, Yahweh was not the son of another god, nor did he have a divine wife or family. Initially anthropomorphic, Yahweh gradually lost human form and became totally spiritual. Although Yahweh could assume human form, he was not to be depicted in any form. Thus the Hebrews considered graven images—statues and other physical representations—idolatrous.

Aerial View of Hazor   Hazor was a Jewish citadel built in the ninth century B.C. Organized on a rectangular plan, Hazor commanded the surrounding countryside and was well fortified. Nonetheless, the Assyrians destroyed the citadel in 732 B.C. *(Source: From HAZOR II, Y. Yadin, Pl. XIII.)*

At first Yahweh was probably viewed as no more than the god of the Hebrews, who sometimes faced competition from Baal and other gods in Palestine. Enlil, Marduk, Amon-Re, and the others sufficed for foreigners. In time, however, the Hebrews came to regard Yahweh as the only god. This was the beginning of true monotheism.

Yahweh was considered the creator of all things; his name means "he causes to be." He governed the cosmic forces of nature, including the movements of the sun, moon, and stars. His presence filled the universe. At the same time, Yahweh was a personal god. Despite his awesome power, he was neither too mighty nor too aloof to care for the individual. The Hebrews even believed that Yahweh intervened in human affairs.

Unlike Akhenaten's monotheism, Hebrew monotheism was not an unpopular religion. It became the religion of a whole people, deeply felt and cherished. Some might fall away from Yahweh's worship, and various holy men had to exhort the Hebrews to honor the Covenant, but on the whole the people clung to Yahweh. Yet the Hebrews did not consider it their duty to spread the belief in the one god. The Hebrews rarely proselytized, as later the Christians did. As the chosen people, their chief duty was to maintain the worship of Yahweh as he demanded. That worship was embodied in the Ten Commandments, which forbade the Hebrews to steal, murder, lie, or commit adultery. The Covenant was a constant force in Hebrew life, and the Old Testament records one occasion when the entire nation formally reaffirmed it:

And the king [of the Jews] stood by a pillar, and made a covenant before the lord, to walk after the lord, and to keep his commandments and his testimonies and his statutes with all their heart and all their soul, to perform the words of this covenant that were written in this book [Deuteronomy]. And all the people stood to the covenant.[2]

From the Ten Commandments evolved Hebrew law, a code of law and custom originating with Moses and built on by priests and prophets. The earliest part of this code, the Torah or Mosaic law, was often as harsh as Hammurabi's code, which had a powerful impact on it. Later tradition, largely the work of prophets who lived from the eleventh to the fifth centuries B.C., was more humanitarian. The work of the prophet Jeremiah (ca 626 B.C.) exemplifies this gentler spirit. According to Jeremiah, Yahweh demanded righteousness from his people and protection for the weak and helpless.

Jeremiah's emphasis is on mercy and justice, on avoiding wrongdoing to others because it is displeasing to Yahweh. These precepts replaced the old law's demand for "an eye for an eye." Jeremiah's message is thus representative of a subtle and positive shift in Hebrew thinking. Jeremiah proclaimed that the god of anger was also the god of forgiveness: "Return, thou backsliding Israel, saith the lord; and I will not cause mine anger to fall upon you; for I am merciful, saith the lord, and I will not keep anger forever."[3] Although Yahweh would punish wrongdoing, he would not destroy those who repented. One generation might be punished for its misdeeds, but Yahweh's mercy was a promise of hope for future generations.

The uniqueness of this phenomenon can be seen by comparing the essence of Hebrew monotheism with the religious outlook of the Mesopotamians. Whereas the Mesopotamians considered their gods capricious, the Hebrews knew what Yahweh expected. The Hebrews believed that their god would protect them and make them prosper if they obeyed his commandments. The Mesopotamians thought human beings insignificant compared to the gods, so insignificant that the gods might even be indifferent to them. The Hebrews, too, considered themselves puny in comparison to Yahweh. Yet they were Yahweh's chosen people, whom he had promised never to abandon. Finally, though the Mesopotamians believed that the gods generally preferred good to evil, their religion did not demand ethical conduct. The Hebrews could please their god only by living up to high moral standards as well as worshiping him.

Many parts of the Old Testament show obvious debts to Mesopotamian culture. Nonetheless, to the Hebrews goes the credit for developing a religion so emotionally satisfying and ethically grand that it has not only flourished but also profoundly influenced Christianity and Islam. Without Moses there could not have been Jesus or Muhammad. The religious standards of the modern West are deeply rooted in Judaism.

Daily Life in Israel

Historians generally know far more about the daily life of the aristocracy and the wealthy in ancient societies than about the conditions of the common people. Jewish society is an exception simply because the Old Testament, which lays down laws for all Jews, has much to say about peasants and princes alike. Comparisons with the social conditions of Israel's ancient neighbors and modern anthropological work among Palestinian Arabs shed additional light on biblical practices. Thus the life of the common people in ancient Israel is better known than, for instance, the lives of ordinary Romans or ancient Chinese.

The nomadic Hebrews first entered Palestine as tribes, numerous families who thought of themselves as all related to one another. As the Jews consolidated their hold on Palestine and as the concept of one Jewish nation took hold, the importance of the tribes declined.

At first good farmland, pastureland, and water spots were held in common by the tribe. Common use of land was—and still is—characteristic of nomadic peoples. Typically each family or group of families in the tribe drew lots every year to determine who worked which fields. But as formerly nomadic peoples turned increasingly to settled agriculture, communal use of land gave way to family ownership. In this respect the experience of the ancient Hebrews seems typical of that of many early peoples. Slowly the shift from nomad to farmer affected far more than just how people fed themselves. Family relationships reflected evolving circumstances. The extended family, organized in tribes, is even today typical of nomads. With the transition to settled agriculture, the tribe gradually becomes less important than the extended family. With the advent of village life and finally full-blown urban life, the extended family in turn gives way to the nuclear family.

The family—people related to one another, all living in the same place—was the primary social institution among the Jews. At its head stood the father who, like the Mesopotamian father, held great powers. The father was the master of his wife and children, with power of life and death over his family. By the eighth century B.C., with the advent of genuine urban life, the father's power and the overall strength of family ties relaxed. Much of the father's power, especially the power of life and death over his children, passed to the elders of the town. One result was the liberation of the individual from the tight control of the family.

For women, however, the evolution of Jewish society led to less freedom of action, especially in religious life. At first women served as priestesses in festivals and religious cults. Some were considered prophetesses of Yahweh, although they never conducted his official rituals. In the course of time, however, the worship of Yahweh became more male-oriented and male-dominated. Increasingly, he also became the god of holiness, and to worship him people must be pure in mind and body. Women were seen as ritually impure because of menstruation and childbirth. Because of these "impurities," women now played a much reduced role in religion. Even when they did participate in religious rites, they were segregated from the men. For the most part, women were largely confined to the home and the care of the family.

Marriage was one of the most important and joyous events in Hebrew family life. When the Hebrews were still nomads, a man could have only one lawful wife but any number of concubines. Settled life changed marriage customs, and later Jewish law allowed men to be polygamous. Not only did kings David and Solomon have harems, but rich men might also have several wives. The chief reason for this custom, as in Mesopotamia, was the desire for children. Given the absence of medical knowledge and the rough conditions of life, women faced barrenness, high infant mortality, and rapid aging.

The common man was too poor to afford the luxury of several women in the home. The typical marriage in ancient Israel was monogamous, and a virtuous wife was revered and honored. Perhaps the finest and most fervent song of praise to the good wife comes from the book of Proverbs in the Old Testament:

Who can find a virtuous woman? for her price is far above rubies. . . . Strength and honour are her clothing; and she shall rejoice in time to come. She openeth her mouth with wisdom; and in her tongue is the law of kindness. She look-

eth well to the ways of her household, and eateth not the bread of idleness. Her children arise up, and call her blessed; her husband also, and he praiseth her. . . . Favour is deceitful, and beauty is vain: but a woman that feareth the lord, she shall be praised.[4]

The commandment "honor thy father and thy mother" was fundamental to the Mosaic law. The wife was a pillar of the family, and her work and wisdom were respected and treasured.

Betrothal and marriage were serious matters in ancient Israel. As in Mesopotamia, they were left largely in parents' hands. Boys and girls were often married quite early, and the parents naturally made the arrangements. Rarely were the prospective bride and groom consulted. Marriages were often contracted within the extended family, commonly among first cousins—a custom still found among Palestinian Arabs today. Although early Jewish custom permitted marriage with foreigners, the fear of alien religions soon led to restrictions against mixed marriages.

The father of the groom offered a bridal gift to the bride's father. This custom, the marriage price, also existed among the Mesopotamians and still survives among modern Palestinian Arabs. The gift was ordinarily money, the amount depending on the social status and wealth of the two families. In other instances, the groom could work off the marriage price by performing manual labor. At the time of the wedding the man gave his bride and her family wedding presents; unlike Mesopotamian custom, the bride's father did not provide her with a dowry. A dowry is meant to protect the position of the wife, and the lack of it in Israel made it easier for the husband to divorce his wife without financial loss.

As in Mesopotamia, marriage was a legal contract, not a religious ceremony. At marriage a woman left her family and joined the family and clan of her husband. The occasion when the bride joined her husband's household was festive. The groom wore a crown and his best clothes. Accompanied by his friends, also dressed in their finest and carrying musical instruments, the bridegroom walked to the bride's house, where she awaited him in her richest clothes, jewels, and a veil that she removed only later when the couple were alone. The bride's friends joined the group, and together they all marched in procession to the groom's house, their way marked by music and songs honoring the newlyweds. Though the wedding feast might last for days, the couple consummated their marriage on the first night; the next day the bloody linen was displayed to prove the bride's virginity.

Divorce was available only to the husband. He could normally end the marriage very simply and for any of a number of reasons. The right to initiate a divorce was denied the wife. Even adultery by the husband was not necessarily grounds for divorce, although Jewish law, like the Code of Hammurabi, generally punished *women's* adultery with death. Overall, Jewish custom frowned on divorce, and the typical couple entered into marriage fully expecting to spend the rest of their lives together.

The newly married couple were expected to begin a family at once. Children, according to the book of Psalms, "are an heritage of the lord: and the fruit of the womb is his reward."[5] The desire for children to perpetuate the family was so strong that if a man died before he could sire a son, his brother was legally obliged to marry the widow. The son born of the brother was thereafter considered the offspring and heir of the dead man. If the brother refused, the widow had her revenge by denouncing him to the elders and publicly spitting in his face.

Sons were especially desired because they maintained the family bloodline and kept the ancestral property within the family. The first-born son had special rights, honor, and responsibilities. At his father's death he became the head of the household and received a larger inheritance than his younger brothers. Daughters were less highly valued because they would eventually marry and leave the family. Yet in Jewish society, unlike other cultures, infanticide was illegal; Yahweh had forbidden it.

The Old Testament often speaks of the pain of childbirth. Professional midwives frequently helped during deliveries. The newborn infant was washed, rubbed with salt, and wrapped in swaddling clothes—bands of cloth that were wrapped around the baby. Normally the mother nursed the baby herself and weaned the infant at about the age of three. The mother customarily named the baby immediately after birth, but children were free to change names after they grew up. Eight days after the birth of a son, the ceremony of circumcision— removal of the foreskin of the penis—took place. Circumcision signified that the boy belonged to the Jewish community; according to Genesis, it was the symbol of Yahweh's covenant with Abraham.

As in most other societies, in ancient Israel the early education of children was in the mother's hands. She taught her children right from wrong and gave them their first instruction in the moral values of society. As boys grew older, they received more education from their fathers. Fathers instructed their sons in religion and the history of their people. Many children were taught to read and write, and the head of each family was probably able to write. Fathers also taught sons the family craft or trade. Boys soon learned that inattention could be painful, for Jewish custom advised fathers to be strict: "He that spareth his rod hateth his son: but he that loveth him chasteneth him betimes."[6]

Once children grew to adulthood, they entered fully into economic and social life. For most that meant a life on the farm, whose demands and rhythm changed very little over time. Young people began with the lighter tasks. Girls traditionally tended flocks of sheep and drew water from the well for household use. The well was a popular meeting spot, where girls could meet other young people and even travelers passing through the country with camel caravans. After the harvest, young girls followed behind the reapers to glean the fields. Even this work was governed by law and custom. Once the girls had gone through the fields, they were not to return, for Yahweh had declared that anything the gleaners left behind belonged to the needy.

Boys also tended flocks, especially in wild areas. Like the young David, they practiced their marksmanship with slings and entertained themselves with music. They shared the lighter work, such as harvesting grapes and beating the limbs of olive trees to shake the fruit loose. Only when they grew to full strength did they perform the hard work of harrowing, plowing, and harvesting.

The land was precious to the family, not simply because it provided a living, but also because it was a link to the past. It was the land of the family's forebears and held their tombs. The family's feeling for its land was so strong that in times of hardship, when land had to be sold, the nearest kin had first right to buy it. Thus the land might at least remain within the extended family.

Ironically, the success of the first Hebrew kings endangered the future of many family farms. With peace, more settled conditions, and increasing prosperity, some Jews began to amass larger holdings by buying out poor and struggling farmers. Far from discouraging this development, the kings created their own huge estates. In many cases slaves, both Jewish and foreign, worked these large farms and estates shoulder to shoulder with paid free men. Although the Old Testament called on the royal and the rich to treat the slave and the laborer with justice and charity, there is no reason to think that Hebrew slavery was different from any other slavery. In still later times, rich landowners rented plots of land to poor, free families; the landowners provided the renters with seed and livestock and normally took half the yield as rent. Although many Old Testament prophets denounced the destruction of the family farm, the trend continued toward large estates that were worked by slaves and hired free men.

The development of urban life among the Jews created new economic opportunities, especially in crafts and trades. People specialized in certain occupations, such as milling flour, baking bread, making pottery, weaving, and carpentry. All these crafts were family trades. Sons worked with their father; daughters with their mother. If the business prospered, the family might be assisted by a few paid workers or slaves. The practitioners of a craft usually lived in a particular street or section of the town, a custom still prevalent in the Middle East today. By the sixth century B.C., craftsmen had joined together in associations known as guilds, intended like European guilds in the Middle Ages (see Chapter 9) to protect and aid their members. By banding together, craftsmen gained corporate status within the community.

Commerce and trade developed later than crafts. In the time of Solomon, foreign trade was the king's domain. Aided by the Phoenicians, Solomon built a fleet to trade with Red Sea ports. Solomon also participated in the overland caravan trade. Otherwise, trade with neighboring countries was handled by foreigners, usually Phoenicians. Jews dealt mainly in local trade, and in most instances craftsmen and farmers sold directly to their customers. Many of Israel's wise men disapproved of commerce and, like the ancient Chinese, considered it unseemly and immoral to profit from the work of others.

Between the eclipse of the Hittites and Egyptians and the rise of the Assyrians, the Hebrews moved from nomadism to urban life and full participation in the mainstream of ancient Near Eastern culture. Retaining their unique religion and customs, they drew from the practices of other peoples and contributed to the lives of their neighbors.

The Seasons of the Year The Hebrew agricultural year, like that of other peoples, was tied to the sun, seasons, and stars. The center of this mosaic floor shows the sun in its chariot, pulled by four horses. In the outer circle are the signs of the zodiac, while the four seasons of the year peer at the viewer from the corners of the panel. *(Source: Consulate General of Israel)*

ASSYRIA, THE MILITARY MONARCHY

Small kingdoms like those of the Phoenicians and the Hebrews could exist only in the absence of a major power. The beginning of the ninth century B.C. saw the rise of such a power: the Assyrians of northern Mesopotamia, whose chief capital was at Nineveh on the Tigris River. The Assyrians were a Semitic-speaking people heavily influenced, like so many other peoples of the Near East, by the Mesopotamian culture of Babylon to the south. They were also one of the most warlike peoples in history, largely because throughout their history they were threatened by neighboring folk. Living in an open, exposed land, the Assyrians experienced frequent and devastating attacks by the wild, warloving tribes to their north and east and by the Babylonians to the south. The constant threat to survival experienced by the Assyrians promoted political cohesion and military might.

For over two hundred years the Assyrians labored to dominate the Near East. In 859 B.C. the new Assyrian king Shalmaneser unleashed the first of a long series of attacks on the peoples of Syria and Palestine. Year after relentless year, Assyrian armies hammered at the peoples of the west. These ominous events inaugurated two turbulent centuries marked by Assyrian military campaigns, constant efforts by Syria and the two Jewish kingdoms to maintain or recover their independence, and eventual Assyrian conquest of Babylonia and northern Egypt. In addition, periodic political instability occurred in Assyria itself, which prompted stirrings of freedom throughout the Near East.

Under the Assyrian kings Tiglath-pileser III (774–727 B.C.) and Sargon II (r. 721–705 B.C.), both mighty warriors, the Near East trembled as never before under the blows of Assyrian armies. The Assyrians stepped up their attacks on Anatolia, Syria, and Palestine. The kingdom of Israel and many other states fell; others, like the kingdom of Judah, became subservient to the warriors from the Tigris. In 717 to 716 B.C. Sargon led his army in a sweeping attack along the Philistine coast into Egypt. He defeated the pharaoh, who suffered the further ignominy of paying tribute to the foreign conquerors. Sargon also lashed out at Assyria's traditional enemies to the north and then turned south against a renewed threat in Babylonia. By means of almost constant warfare, Tiglath-pileser III and Sargon carved out an Assyrian empire that stretched from east and north of the Tigris River to central Egypt (Map 2.2). Revolt against the Assyrians inevitably promised the rebels bloody battles, prolonged sieges accompanied by starvation, plague, and sometimes even cannibalism, and finally surrender followed by systematic torture and slaughter.

Though atrocity and terrorism struck unspeakable fear into Assyria's subjects, Assyria's success was actually due to sophisticated, far-sighted, and effective military organization. By Sargon's time the Assyrians had invented the mightiest military machine the ancient Near East had ever seen. The mainstay of the Assyrian army, the soldier who ordinarily decided the outcome of battles, was the infantryman armed with spear and sword and protected by helmet and armor. The Assyrian army also featured archers, some on foot, others on horseback, still others in chariots—the latter ready

Siege of a City Art here serves to glorify horror. The Assyrian king Tiglath-pileser III launches an assault on a fortified city. The impaled bodies shown at center demonstrate the cruelty of Assyrian warfare. Also noticeable are the various weapons and means of attack used against the city. *(Source: Courtesy of the Trustees of the British Museum)*

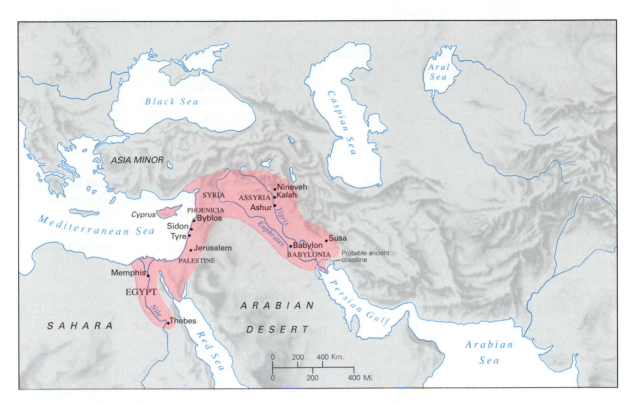

Map 2.2 The Assyrian Empire   The Assyrian Empire at its height (ca 650 B.C.) included almost all of the old centers of power in the ancient Near East. As Map 2.3 shows, however, its size was far smaller than that of the later Persian Empire.

to wield lances once they had expended their supply of arrows. Some infantry archers wore heavy armor, strikingly similar to the armor worn much later by William the Conqueror's Normans. These soldiers served as a primitive field artillery, whose job was to sweep the enemy's walls of defenders so that others could storm the defenses. Slingers also served as artillery in pitched battles. For mobility on the battlefield, the Assyrians organized a corps of chariots.

Assyrian military genius was remarkable for the development of a wide variety of siege machinery and techniques, including excavation to undermine city walls and battering-rams to knock down walls and gates. Never before in the Near East had anyone applied such technical knowledge to warfare. The Assyrians even invented the concept of a corps of engineers, who bridged rivers with pontoons or provided soldiers with inflatable skins for swimming. Furthermore, the Assyrians knew how to coordinate their efforts, both in open battle and in siege warfare. King Sennacherib's account of his

siege of Jerusalem in 701 B.C. is a vivid portrait of the Assyrian war machine in action:

As to Hezekiah, the Jew, he did not submit to my yoke, I laid siege to 46 of his strong cities, walled forts and to the countless small villages in their vicinity, and conquered them by means of well-stamped earth-ramps, and battering rams brought thus near to the walls combined with the attack by foot soldiers, using mines, breaches as well as sapper work. . . . Himself I made prisoner in Jerusalem, his royal residence, like a bird in a cage. I surrounded him with earthwork in order to molest those who were leaving his city's gate. . . . Hezekiah himself, whom the terror-inspiring splendor of my lordship had overwhelmed and whose irregular and elite troops which he had brought into Jerusalem, his royal residence, in order to strengthen it, had deserted him, did send me, later, to Nineveh, my lordly city, together with 30 talents of gold . . . and all kinds of valuable treasures.[7]

Hezekiah and Jerusalem shared the fate of many a rebellious king and capital and were indeed lucky to escape severe reprisals. The Assyrians were too powerful and well organized and far too tenacious to be turned back by isolated strongholds, no matter how well situated or defended.

Assyrian Rule and Culture

Not only did the Assyrians know how to win battles, they also knew how to use their victories. As early as the reign of Tiglath-pileser III, the Assyrian kings began to organize their conquered territories into an empire. The lands closest to Assyria became provinces governed by Assyrian officials. Kingdoms beyond the provinces were not annexed but became dependent states that followed Assyria's lead. The Assyrian king chose their rulers either by regulating the succession of native kings or by supporting native kings who appealed to him. Against more distant states the Assyrian kings waged frequent war in order to conquer them outright or make the dependent states secure.

Royal roads and swift mounted messengers linked the Assyrian Empire, and Assyrian records describe how these royal messengers brought the king immediate word of unrest or rebellion within the empire. Because of good communications, Assyrian kings could generally move against rebels at a moment's notice. Thus, though rebellion was common in the Assyrian Empire, it rarely got the opportunity to become serious before meeting with harsh retaliation from the king.

In the seventh century B.C. Assyrian power seemed secure. Yet the downfall of Assyria was swift and complete. Babylon finally won its independence in 626 B.C. and joined forces with a new people, the Medes, an Indo-European–speaking folk from Iran. Together the Babylonians and the Medes destroyed the Assyrian Empire in 612 B.C., paving the way for the rise of the Persians. The Hebrew prophet Nahum spoke for many when he asked: "Nineveh is laid waste: who will bemoan her?"[8] Their cities destroyed and their power shattered, the Assyrians disappeared from history, remembered only as a cruel people of the Old Testament who oppressed the Hebrews. Two hundred years later, when the Greek adventurer and historian Xenophon passed by the ruins of Nineveh, he marveled at the extent of the former city but knew nothing of the Assyrians. The glory of their empire was forgotten.

Yet modern archeology has brought the Assyrians out of obscurity. In 1839 the intrepid English archeologist and traveler A. H. Layard began to excavate Nineveh, then a mound of debris beside the Tigris. His findings electrified the world. In the course of a few years, Layard's discoveries shed remarkable new light on Assyrian history and had an equally stunning impact on the history of art. Layard's workers unearthed masterpieces, including monumental sculpted figures—huge winged bulls, human-headed lions, and sphinxes—as well as brilliantly sculpted friezes. Equally valuable were numerous Assyrian cuneiform documents, which ranged from royal accounts of mighty military campaigns to simple letters by common people.

Among the most renowned of Layard's finds were the Assyrian palace reliefs, whose number has been increased by the discoveries of twentieth-century archeologists. Assyrian kings delighted in scenes of war, which their artists depicted in graphic detail. By the time of Ashurbanipal (r. 668–633 B.C.), Assyrian artists had hit upon the idea of portraying a series of episodes—in fact, a visual narrative of events that had actually taken place. Scene followed scene in a continuous frieze, so that the viewer could follow the progress of a military campaign from the time the army marched out until the enemy was conquered. So, too, with another theme of the palace reliefs, the lion hunt. Hunting lions was probably a royal sport, although some scholars have suggested a magical significance. They argue that the hunting scenes depict the king as the protector of his people, the one who wards off evil. Here, too, the viewer proceeds in sequence, from preparations for the chase through the hunting itself to the killing of the lions.

Assyrian art, like much of Egyptian art, was realistic, but the warmth and humor of Egyptian scenes are absent from Assyrian reliefs. Assyrian art is stark and often brutal in subject matter, yet marked by an undeniable strength and sophistication of composition. Assyrian realism is well represented by the illustration on page 49, which portrays the climax of the royal lion hunt. The scene is like a photograph snapped at the height of the action. The king, mounted on horseback, has already fired arrows into two lions, who nonetheless are still full of fight. The wounded lion on the left has just pounced on a riderless horse, which in a moment will fall mortally wounded. Meanwhile, the king thrusts his spear into another lion, which has

Royal Lion Hunt   This relief from the palace of Ashurbanipal at Nineveh, which shows the king fighting two lions, is a typical representation of the energy and artistic brilliance of Assyrian sculptors. The lion hunt, portrayed in a series of episodes, was a favorite theme of Assyrian palace reliefs. *(Source: Courtesy of the Trustees of the British Museum)*

begun its spring. The artistic rendering of the figures is exciting and technically flawless. The figures are anatomically correct and in proper proportion and perspective. The whole composition conveys both action and tension. Assyrian art fared better than Assyrian military power. The techniques of Assyrian artists influenced the Persians, who adapted them to gentler scenes.

In fact, many Assyrian innovations, military and political as well as artistic, were taken over wholesale by the Persians. Although the memory of Assyria was hateful throughout the Near East, the fruits of Assyrian organizational genius helped enable the Persians to bring peace and stability to the same regions where Assyrian armies had spread terror.

THE EMPIRE OF THE PERSIAN KINGS

Like the Hittites before them, the Iranians were Indo-Europeans from central Europe and southern Russia. They migrated into the land to which they have given their name, the area between the Caspian Sea and the Persian Gulf. Like the Hittites, they then fell under the spell of the more sophisticated cultures of their Mesopotamian neighbors. Yet the Iranians went on to create one of the greatest empires of antiquity, one that encompassed scores of peoples and cultures. The Persians, the most important of the Iranian peoples, had a far-sighted conception of empire. Though as conquerors they willingly used force to accomplish their ends, they normally preferred to depend on diplomacy to rule. They usually respected their subjects and allowed them to practice their native customs and religions. Thus the Persians gave the Near East both political unity and cultural diversity. Never before had Near Eastern people viewed empire in such intelligent and humane terms.

The Land of Mountains and Plateau

Persia—the modern country of Iran—is a stark land of towering mountains and flaming deserts, with a broad central plateau in the heart of the country (see Map 2.3). Iran stretches from the Caspian Sea in the north to the Persian Gulf in the south. Between the Tigris-Euphrates Valley in the west and the Indus Valley in the east rises an immense plateau, surrounded on all sides by lofty mountains that cut off the interior from the sea.

The central plateau is very high, a landscape of broad plains, scattered oases, and two vast deserts. The high mountains, which catch the moisture coming from the sea, generate ample rainfall for the plateau. This semitropical area is very fertile, in marked contrast to the aridity of most of Iran. The mountains surrounding the central plateau are dotted with numerous oases, often very fertile, which have from time immemorial served as havens for small groups of people.

At the center of the plateau lies an enormous depression—a forbidding region devoid of water and vegetation, so glowing hot in summer that it is virtually impossible to cross. This depression forms two distinct grim and burning salt deserts, perhaps the most desolate spots on earth.

Iran's geographical position and topography explain its traditional role as the highway between East and West. Throughout history wild, nomadic peoples migrating from the broad steppes of Russia and central Asia have streamed into Iran. The very harshness of the geography urged them to continue in search of new and more hospitable lands. Confronting the uncrossable salt deserts, most have turned either eastward or westward, moving on until they reached the advanced and wealthy urban centers of Mesopotamia and India. When cities emerged along the natural lines of East-West communication, Iran became the area where nomads met urban dwellers, a meeting ground of unique significance for the civilizations of both East and West.

The Coming of the Medes and Persians

The Iranians entered this land around 1000 B.C. The most historically important of them were the Medes and the Persians, related peoples who settled in different areas. Both groups were part of the vast movement of Indo-European–speaking peoples whose wanderings led them into Europe, the Near East, and India in many successive waves (see page 29). These Iranians were nomads who migrated with their flocks and herds. Like their kinsmen the Aryans, who moved into India, they were also horse breeders, and the horse gave them a decisive military advantage over the prehistoric peoples of Iran. The Iranians rode into battle in horse-drawn chariots or on horseback and easily swept the natives before them. Yet, because the influx of Iranians went on for centuries, there continued to be constant cultural interchange between conquering newcomers and conquered natives.

Excavations at Siyalk, some 125 miles south of present-day Tehran, provide a valuable glimpse of the encounter of Iranian and native. The village of Siyalk had been inhabited since prehistoric times before falling to the Iranians. The new lords fought all comers: natives, rival Iranians, even the Assyrians, who often raided far east of the Tigris. Under the newly arrived Iranians, Siyalk became a fortified town with a palace and perhaps a temple, all enclosed by a circuit wall strengthened by towers and ramparts. The town was surrounded by fields and farms, for agriculture was the basis of this evolving society.

The Iranians initially created a patchwork of tiny kingdoms, of which Siyalk was one. The chieftain or petty king was basically a warlord who depended on fellow warriors for aid and support. This band of noble warriors, like the Greek heroes of the *Iliad,* formed the fighting strength of the army. The king owned estates that supported him and his nobles; for additional income the king levied taxes, which were paid in kind and not in cash. He also demanded labor services from the peasants. Below the king and his warrior nobles were free people who held land and others who owned nothing. Artisans produced the various goods needed to keep society running. At the bottom of the social scale were slaves—probably both natives and newcomers—to whom fell the drudgery of hard labor and household service to king and nobles.

This early period saw some significant economic developments. The use of iron increased. By the seventh century B.C., iron farm implements had become widespread, leading to increased productivity, greater overall prosperity, and higher standards of living. At the same time Iranian agriculture saw the development of the small estate. Farmers worked small plots of land, and the general prosperity of the period bred a sturdy peasantry, people who enjoyed greater freedom than their contemporaries in Egypt and Mesopotamia.

Kings exploited Iran's considerable mineral wealth, and Iranian iron, copper, and lapis lazuli attracted Assyrian raiding parties. Even more important, mineral wealth and Iranian horse breeding stimulated brisk trade with the outside world. Kings found that merchants, who were not usually Iranians, produced large profits to help fill the king's coffers. Overland trade also put the Iranians in direct contact with their Near Eastern neighbors.

Gradually two groups of Iranians began coalescing into larger units. The Persians had settled in Persis, the modern region of Fars, in southern Iran. Their kinsmen the Medes occupied Media, the modern area of Hamadan in the north, with their capital at Ecbatana. The Medes were exposed to attack by nomads from the north, but their greatest threat was the frequent raids of the Assyrian army. Even though distracted by grave pressures from their neighbors, the Medes united under one king around 710 B.C. and extended their control over the Persians in the south. In 612 B.C. the Medes were strong enough to join the Babylonians in overthrowing the Assyrian Empire. With the rise of the Medes, the balance of power in the Near East shifted for the first time east of Mesopotamia.

The Creation of the Persian Empire

In 550 B.C. Cyrus the Great (r. 559–530 B.C.), king of the Persians and one of the most remarkable statesmen of antiquity, threw off the yoke of the Medes by conquering them and turning their country into his first *satrapy,* or province. In the space of a single lifetime, Cyrus created one of the greatest empires of antiquity. Two characteristics lift Cyrus above the common level of warrior-kings. First, he

Jug of Siyalk   Though later the Persians derived their art primarily from their neighbors, this jug, which dates to ca 1000 B.C., demonstrates that the early settlers possessed a vigorous sense of art themselves. While some features of this jug were borrowed from neighboring artistic traditions, others are solely Persian. This jug was probably used to pour wine. *(Source: The Ancient Art and Architecture Collection)*

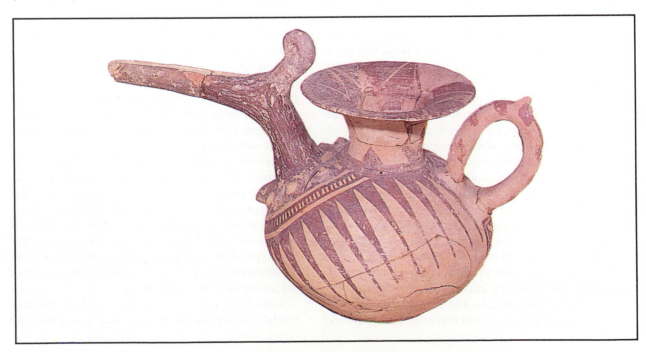

Tomb of Cyrus For all of his greatness Cyrus retained a sense of perspective. His tomb, though monumental in size, is rather simple and unostentatious. Greek writers reported that it bore the following epitaph: "O man, I am Cyrus the son of Cambyses. I established the Persian Empire and was king of Asia. Do not begrudge me my memorial." *(Source: The Oriental Institute, University of Chicago)*

thought of Iran, not just Persia and Media, as a state. His concept has survived a long, complex, and often turbulent history to play its part in the contemporary world.

Second, Cyrus held an enlightened view of empire. Many of the civilizations and cultures that fell to his armies were, he realized, far older, more advanced, and more sophisticated than his. Free of the narrow-minded snobbery of the Egyptians, the religious exclusiveness of the Hebrews, and the calculated cruelty of the Assyrians, Cyrus gave Near Eastern peoples and their cultures his respect, toleration, and protection. Conquered peoples continued to enjoy their institutions, religions, languages, and ways of life under the Persians. The Persian Empire, which Cyrus created, became a political organization sheltering many different civilizations. To rule such a vast area and so many diverse peoples demanded talent, intelligence, sensitivity, and

a cosmopolitan view of the world. These qualities Cyrus and many of his successors possessed in abundance. Though the Persians were sometimes harsh, especially with those who rebelled against them, they were for the most part enlightened rulers. Consequently, the Persians gave the ancient Near East over two hundred years of peace, prosperity, and security.

Cyrus showed his magnanimity at the outset of his career. Once the Medes had fallen to him, Cyrus united them with his Persians. Ecbatana, the Median capital, became a Persian seat of power. Medes were honored with important military and political posts and thenceforth helped the Persians to rule the expanding empire. Cyrus's conquest of the Medes resulted not in slavery and slaughter but in the union of Iranian peoples.

With Iran united, Cyrus looked at the broader world. He set out to achieve two goals. First he wanted to win control of the west and thus of the terminal ports of the great trade routes that crossed Iran and Anatolia. Second, Cyrus strove to secure eastern Iran from the pressure of nomadic invaders. In 550 B.C. neither goal was easy to accomplish. To the northwest was the young kingdom of Lydia in Anatolia, whose king Croesus was proverbial for his wealth. To the west was Babylonia, enjoying a new period of power now that the Assyrian Empire had been crushed. To the southwest was Egypt, still weak but sheltered behind its bulwark of sand and sea. To the east ranged tough, mobile nomads, capable of massive and destructive incursions deep into Iranian territory.

Cyrus turned first to Croesus's Lydian kingdom, which fell to him around 546 B.C. He established a garrison at Sardis, the capital of Lydia, and ordered his generals to subdue the Greek cities along the coast of Anatolia. Cyrus had thus gained the important ports that looked out to the Mediterranean world. In addition, for the first time the Persians came into direct contact with the Greeks, a people with whom their later history was to be intimately connected.

From Lydia, Cyrus next marched to the far eastern corners of Iran. In a brilliant campaign he conquered the regions of Parthia, Bactria, and even the most westerly part of India. All of Iran was now Persian, from Mesopotamia in the west to the western slopes of the Hindu Kush in the east. In 540 B.C. Cyrus moved against Babylonia, now isolated from outside help. When Persian soldiers marched quietly into Babylon the next year, the Babylonians welcomed Cyrus as a liberator. Cyrus won the hearts of the Babylonians with humane treatment, toleration of their religion, and support of their efforts to refurbish their capital.

Cyrus was equally generous toward the Jews. He allowed them to return to Palestine, from which they had been deported by the Babylonians. He protected them, gave them back the sacred items they used in worship, and rebuilt the temple of Yahweh in Jerusalem. The Old Testament sings the praises of Cyrus, whom the Jews considered the shepherd of Yahweh, the lord's anointed. Rarely have conquered peoples shown such gratitude to their conquerors. Cyrus's benevolent policy created a Persian Empire in which the cultures and religions of its members were respected and honored. Seldom have conquerors been as wise, sensitive, and far-sighted as Cyrus and his Persians.

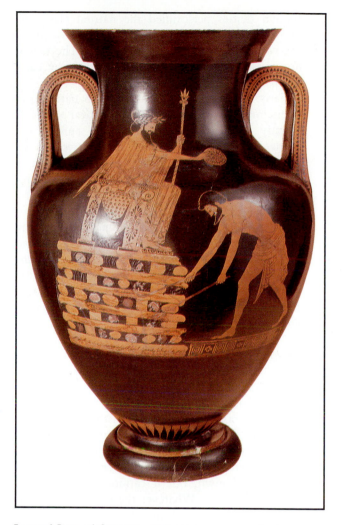

Funeral Pyre of Croesus This scene, an excellent example of the precision and charm of ancient Greek vase painting, depicts the Lydian king Croesus on his funeral pyre. He pours a libation to the gods while his slave lights the fire. Herodotus has a happier ending when he says that Cyrus the Great set fire to the pyre but that Apollo sent rain to put it out. *(Source: Louvre/Cliché des Musées Nationaux, Paris)*

Thus Spake Zarathustra

Iranian religion was originally simple and primitive. Ahuramazda, the chief god, was the creator and benefactor of all living creatures. Yet, unlike Yahweh, he was not a lone god. The Iranians were polytheistic. Mithra the sun-god, whose cult would later spread throughout the Roman Empire (see Chapter 6), saw to justice and redemption. Other

Iranian deities personified the natural elements: moon, earth, water, and wind. As in ancient India, fire was a particularly important god. The sacred fire consumed the blood sacrifices that the early Iranians offered to all of their deities.

Early Iranian religion was close to nature and unencumbered by ponderous theological beliefs. A priestly class, the Magi, developed among the Medes to officiate at sacrifices, chant prayers to the gods, and tend the sacred flame. A description of this early worship comes from the German historian Eduard Meyer:

Iranian religion knew neither divine images nor temples. On a hilltop one called upon god and his manifestations —sun and moon, earth and fire, water and wind—and erected altars with their eternal fire. But in other appropriate places one could, without further preparation, pray to the deity and bring him his offerings, with the assistance of the Magi.[9]

In time the Iranians built fire temples for these sacrifices. As late as the nineteenth century, fire was still worshiped in Baku, a major city on the Russian-Iranian border.

Around 600 B.C. the religious thinking of Zarathustra—Zoroaster, as he is better known— breathed new meaning into Iranian religion. So little is known of Zoroaster that even the date of his birth is unknown, but it cannot be earlier than around 1100 B.C. Whatever the exact dates of his life, his work endured long afterward. The most reliable information about Zoroaster comes from the *Zend Avesta,* a collection of hymns and poems, the earliest part of which treats Zoroaster and primitive Persian religion. Like Moses, Zoroaster preached a novel concept of divinity and human life. Life, he taught, is a constant battleground for two opposing forces, good and evil. Ahuramazda embodied good and truth but was opposed by Ahriman, a hateful spirit who stood for evil and falsehood. Ahuramazda and Ahriman were locked together in a cosmic battle for the human race, a battle that stretched over thousands of years. But, according to Zoroaster, people were not mere pawns in this struggle. Each person had to choose which side to join—whether to lead a life of good behavior and truthful dealings with others or one of wickedness and lies.

Zoroaster emphasized the individual's responsibility in this decision. He taught that people possessed the free will to decide between Ahuramazda and Ahriman and that they must rely on their own consciences to guide them through life. Their decisions were crucial, Zoroaster warned, for there would be a time of reckoning. He promised that Ahuramazda would eventually triumph over evil and lies, and that at death each person would stand before the tribunal of good. Ahuramazda, like the Egyptian god Osiris, would judge whether the dead had lived righteously and on that basis would weigh their lives in the balance. In short, Zoroaster taught the concept of a Last Judgment at which Ahuramazda would decide each person's eternal fate.

In Zoroaster's thought the Last Judgment was linked to the notion of a divine kingdom after death for those who had lived according to good and truth. They would accompany Ahuramazda to a life of eternal truth in what Zoroaster called the "House of Song" and the "Abode of Good Thought." There they would dwell with Ahuramazda forever. Liars and the wicked, denied this blessed immortality, would be condemned to eternal pain, darkness, and punishment. Thus Zoroaster preached a Last Judgment that led to a heaven or a hell.

Though tradition has it that Zoroaster's teachings originally met with opposition and coldness, his thought converted Darius (r. 521–486 B.C.), one of the most energetic men ever to sit on the Persian throne. The Persian royal family adopted Zoroastrianism but did not try to impose it on others. Under the protection of the Persian kings, Zoroastrianism swept through Iran, winning converts and sinking roots that sustained healthy growth for centuries. Zoroastrianism survived the fall of the Persian Empire to influence religious thought in the age of Jesus and to make a vital contribution to Manicheanism, a theology that was to spread through the Byzantine Empire and pose a significant challenge to Christianity. A handful of the faithful still follow the teachings of Zoroaster, whose vision of divinity and human life has transcended the centuries.

Persia's World Empire

Cyrus's successors rounded out the Persian conquest of the ancient Near East. In 525 B.C. Cyrus's son Cambyses (r. 530–522 B.C.) subdued Egypt.

Darius (r. 521–486 B.C.) and his son Xerxes (r. 486–464 B.C.) invaded Greece but were fought to a standstill and forced to retreat (see pages 78–79); the Persians never won a permanent foothold in Europe. Yet Darius carried Persian arms into India. Around 513 B.C. western India became the Persian satrapy of Hindush, which included the valley of the Indus River. Thus within thirty-seven years (550–513 B.C.) the Persians transformed themselves from a subject people to the rulers of an empire that included Anatolia, Egypt, Mesopotamia, Iran, and western India. They had created a "world empire" encompassing all of the oldest and most honored kingdoms and peoples of the ancient Near East. Never before had the Near East been united in one such vast political organization (Map 2.3).

The Persians knew how to use the peace they had won on the battlefield. Unlike the Assyrians, they did not resort to royal terrorism to keep order. Like the Assyrians, however, they employed a number of bureaucratic techniques to bind the empire together. The sheer size of the empire made it impossible for one man to rule it effectively. Consequently, the Persians divided the empire into some twenty huge satrapies measuring hundreds of square miles apiece, many of them kingdoms in themselves. Each satrapy had a governor, drawn from the Median and Persian nobility and often a relative of the king; the governor or *satrap* was directly responsible to the king. An army officer, also responsible to the king, commanded the military forces stationed in the satrapy. Still another official collected the taxes. Moreover, the king sent out royal inspectors to watch the satraps and other officials, a method of surveillance later used by the medieval king Charlemagne.

Effective rule of the empire demanded good communications. To meet this need the Persians established a network of roads. The main highway, known as the Royal Road, spanned some 1,677

Map 2.3 The Persian Empire   By 513 B.C. the Persian Empire not only included more of the ancient Near East than had the Assyrian Empire, but it also extended as far east as western India. With the rise of the Medes and Persians, the balance of power in the Near East shifted east of Mesopotamia for the first time.

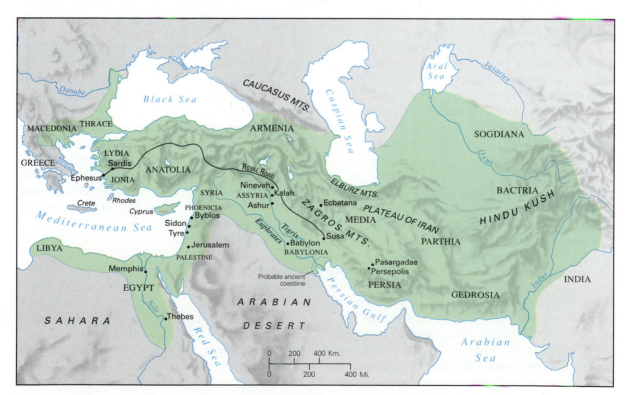

Darius and Xerxes   This relief from the Persian capital of Persepolis shows King Darius and Crown Prince Xerxes in state. Behind them the royal bodyguard stands at attention, as the royal pair receives the guard's commander. *(Source: The Oriental Institute, University of Chicago)*

miles from the Greek city of Ephesus on the coast of Asia Minor to Susa in western Iran. The distance was broken into 111 post stations, each equipped with fresh horses for the king's messengers. Other roads branched out to link all parts of the empire from the coast of Asia Minor to the valley of the Indus River. This system of communications enabled the Persian king to keep in intimate touch with his subjects and officials. He was able to rule efficiently, keep his ministers in line, and protect the rights of the peoples under his control. How effective Persian rule could be, even in small matters, is apparent in a letter from King Darius to the satrap of Ionia, the Greek region of Anatolia. The satrap had transplanted Syrian fruit trees in his province, an experiment Darius praised. Yet the governor had also infringed on the rights granted to the sanctuary of the Greek god Apollo, an act that provoked the king to anger:

The King of Kings, Darius the son of Hystaspes says this to Gadatas, his slave [satrap]. I learn that you are not obeying my command in every particular. Because you are tilling my land, transplanting fruit trees from across the Euphrates [Syria] to Asia Minor, I praise your project, and there will be laid up for you great favor in the king's house. But because you mar my dispositions towards the gods, I shall give you, unless you change your

ways, proof of my anger when wronged. For you exacted payment from the sacred gardeners of the temple of Apollo, and you ordered them to dig up secular land, failing to understand the attitude of my forefathers towards the god, who told the Persians the truth.[10]

Fruit trees and foreign gods—even such small matters as these were important to the man whom the world called "The Great King, King of Kings, King of Countries, containing all kinds of men, King in this great earth far and wide."[11] This document alone suggests the efficiency of Persian rule and the compassion of Persian kings. Conquered peoples, left free to enjoy their traditional ways of life, found in the Persian king a capable protector. No wonder that many Near Eastern peoples were, like the Jews, grateful for the long period of peace they enjoyed as the subjects of the Persian Empire.

SUMMARY

During the centuries following the Sea Peoples' invasions, Egypt was overrun by its African neighbors, but its long and rich traditions and culture, its firmly established religion, and its administrative techniques became the heritage of these conquerors. The defeat of Egypt also led to conditions that allowed the Hebrews to create their own state. A series of strong leaders fighting hard wars won the Hebrews independence and security. In this atmosphere Hebrew religion evolved and flourished, thanks to priests, prophets, and common piety among the people. Daily life involved the transition from nomad to farmer, and people's lives revolved around the religious and agricultural year. In the eighth century B.C. the Hebrews and others in the Near East fell to the onslaught of the Assyrians, a powerful Mesopotamian kingdom. The Assyrians combined administrative skills and wealth with military organization to create an aggressive military state. Yet the Assyrians' military ruthlessness and cruelty raised powerful enemies against them. The most important of these enemies were the Iranians, who created the Persian Empire. The Persians had migrated into Iran, settled the land, and entered the cultural orbit of the Near East. The result was rapid progress in culture, economic prosperity, and increase in population, which enabled them to create the largest empire yet seen in the Near East. Unlike the Assyrians, however, they ruled mildly and gave the Near East a long period of peace.

The Royal Palace at Persepolis   King Darius began and King Xerxes finished building a grand palace worthy of the glory of the Persian Empire. Pictured here is the monumental audience hall, where the king dealt with ministers of state and foreign envoys. *(Source: George Holton/Photo Researchers)*

The Ancient Near East

	Politics	Economics
3200 B.C.	Dominance of Sumerian cities in Mesopotamia, ca 3200–2340	Development of wheeled transport in Mesopotamia, by ca 3200
	Unification of Egypt; Archaic Period, ca 3100–2660	
	Old Kingdom in Egypt, ca 2660–2180	
	Dominance of Akkadian empire in Mesopotamia, ca 2331–2200	
	Middle Kingdom in Egypt, ca 2080–1640	
2000 B.C.	Babylonian empire in Mesopotamia, ca 2000–1595	First wave of Indo-European migrants, by ca 2000
	Hyksos "invasion" of Egypt, ca 1640–1570	Extended commerce in Egypt, by ca 2000
	Hittite empire in Asia Minor, ca 1600–1200	Horses introduced into western Asia, by ca 2000
	Kassites overthrow Babylonians, ca 1595	
	New Kingdom in Egypt, ca 1570–1075	
1500 B.C.	Third Intermediate Period in Egypt, ca 1100–700	Use of iron increases in western Asia, by ca 1300–1100
	Unified Hebrew kingdom under Saul, David, and Solomon, ca 1025–925	Second wave of Indo-European migrants, by ca 1200
1000 B.C.	Hebrew kingdom divided into Israel and Judah, 925	
	Rise and fall of Assyrian empire, ca 900–612	
	Phoenicians found Carthage, 813	
	Kingdom of Kush conquers and reunifies Egypt, 8th c.	
	Medes conquer Persians, 710	
	Babylon wins independence from Assyria, 626	
	Cyrus the Great conquers Medes, founds Persian Empire, 550	
	Persians complete conquest of ancient Near East, 521–464	

Religion	Culture
Growth of anthropomorphic religion in Mesopotamia, ca 3000–2000	Sumerian cuneiform writing, ca 3200
Emergence of Egyptian polytheism and belief in personal immortality, ca 2660	Sumerian temple architecture, ca 3200–2000
	Egyptian hieroglyphic writing, ca 3100
	Construction of first pyramid in Egypt, ca 2660
Covenant formed between Yahweh and the Hebrews; emergence of Hebrew monotheism, ca 1700	*Epic of Gilgamesh,* ca 1900
	Code of Hammurabi, ca 1790
Moses leads Exodus of the Hebrews from Egypt into Palestine, 13th c.	Phoenicians develop alphabet, ca 1400
Religious beliefs of Akhenaten, ca 1367	Naturalistic art in Egypt under Akhenaten, ca 1367
Era of the prophets in Israel, ca 1100–500	
Zoroaster revitalizes Persian religion, ca 600	Babylonian astronomical advances, ca 750–400
Babylonian Captivity of the Hebrews, 586–539	

NOTES

1. James H. Breasted, *Ancient Records of Egypt* (Chicago: University of Chicago Press, 1907), vol. 4, para. 398.
2. 2 Kings 23:3.
3. Jeremiah 3:12.
4. Proverbs 31:10, 25–30.
5. Psalms 128:3.
6. Proverbs 13:24.
7. J. B. Pritchard, ed., *Ancient Near Eastern Texts,* 3d ed. (Princeton, N.J.: Princeton University Press, 1969), p. 288.
8. Nahum 3:7.
9. E. Meyer, *Geschichte des Altertums,* 7th ed., vol. 4, pt. 1 (Darmstadt: Wissenschaftliche Buchgesellschaft, 1975), pp. 114–115.
10. R. Meiggs and D. M. Lewis, *A Selection of Greek Historical Inscriptions* (Oxford: Clarendon Press, 1969), no. 12.
11. R. G. Kent, trans., *Old Persian,* 2d ed. (New Haven: Yale University Press, 1953), p.138.

SUGGESTED READING

Although late Egyptian history is still largely a specialist's field, K. A. Kitchen, *The Third Intermediate Period in Egypt* (1973), is a good synthesis of the period from 1100 to 650 B.C. Valuable, too, is M. L. Bierbrier's monograph, *Late New Kingdom in Egypt, c. 1300–664 B.C.* (1975). More general is R. David, *The Egyptian Kingdoms* (1975). H. S. Smith, *A Visit to Ancient Egypt: Life at Memphis and Saqqara, c. 500–30 B.C.* (1974), gives a picture of life during the indicated period, and P. L. Shinnie, *Meroe: A Civilization of the Sudan* (1967), does the same for one of Egypt's most important southern neighbors. A. H. Gardiner, ed., *Late Egyptian Stories* (1973), contains other pieces of late Egyptian literature.

G. Herm, *The Phoenicians: The Purple Empire of the Ancient World* (1975), treats Phoenician seafaring and commercial enterprises. A more general treatment of the entire area is R. Fedden, *Syria and Lebanon,* 3d ed. (1965). Those interested in individual Phoenician cities should see N. Jidejian, *Byblos Through the Ages,* 2d ed. (1971), *Tyre Through the Ages* (1969), and *Sidon Through the Ages* (1971).

The Jews have been one of the best studied people in the ancient world; the reader can easily find many good treatments of Jewish history and society. A readable and balanced book is J. Bright, *A History of Israel,* 2d ed.

(1972). Other useful general books include G. W. Anderson, *The History and Religion of Israel* (1966), a solid, scholarly treatment of the subject. The archeological exploration of ancient Israel is so fast-paced that nearly any book is quickly outdated. Nonetheless, A. Negev, *Archaeological Encyclopedia of the Holy Land* (1973), which is illustrated, is still a good place to start.

S. Yeivin, *The Israelite Conquest of Canaan* (1971), though a bit dated, is a good survey of the Jewish entry into Palestine. M. R. de Vaux, *Ancient Israel, Its Life and Institutions,* 2d ed. (1965), which ranges across all eras of early Jewish history, is especially recommended because of its solid base in the ancient sources. The period of Jewish kingship has elicited a good deal of attention. B. Halpern, *The Constitution of the Monarchy in Israel* (1981), makes the significant point that the Jews are the only ancient Near Eastern people to have recorded the decision to adopt monarchy as a form of government. Also valuable in this connection is A. R. Johnson, *Sacral Kingship in Ancient Israel,* 2d ed. (1967). For an excellent discussion of the evolution of the Old Testament, see M. Smith, *Palestinian Parties and Politics That Shaped the Old Testament,* 2d ed. (1987). G. W. Ahlstrom, *Royal Administration and National Religion in Ancient Palestine* (1982), treats secular and religious aspects of Hebrew history. Last, W. D. Davis et al., *The Cambridge History of Judaism,* vol. 1 (1984), begins an important new synthesis with work on Judaism in the Persian period. R. Hachlili, *Ancient Jewish Art and Archaeology in the Land of Israel* (1988), attempts to trace the development and meaning of Jewish art in its archeological context.

Several new studies in the social history of the entire ancient world are so broad that they also bear on the topics treated in this chapter. Perhaps one of the most interesting is F. M. Snowden, Jr., *Before Color Prejudice* (1983), in which the author argues that the ancient world was largely free from racism against blacks. An ideal companion to Snowden's volume is L. Bugner, ed., *The Image of the Black in Western Art,* vol. 1 (1983), which covers the vast period from the pharaohs to the fall of the Roman Empire. Last, Averil Cameron and A. Kuhrt, *Images of Women in Antiquity* (1983), is a collection of essays dealing with women from early periods to Greco-Roman times.

The Assyrians, despite their achievements, have not attracted the scholarly attention that the ancient Jews and other Near Eastern peoples have. Even though outdated, A. T. Olmstead, *History of Assyria* (1928), has the merit of being soundly based in the original sources. More recent and more difficult is J. A. Brinkman, *A Political History of Post-Kassite Babylonia, 1158–722 B.C.* (1968), which treats the Babylonian response to the rise of Assyria. M. Cogan, *Imperialism and Religion: Assyria, Judah and Israel in the Eighth and Seventh Centuries B.C.E.* (1973), traces the various effects of Assyrian expansion on the two Jewish kingdoms.

A new edition of an earlier work, H. W. F. Skaggs, *Everyday Life in Babylonia and Assyria,* rev. ed. (1987), offers a general and well-illustrated survey of Mesopotamian history from 3000 to 300 B.C. Those who appreciate the vitality of Assyrian art should start with the masterful work of R. D. Barnett and W. Forman, *Assyrian Palace Reliefs,* 2d ed. (1970), an exemplary combination of fine photographs and learned, but not difficult, discussion.

In addition to the works on Iran cited in the notes, several new general works on ancient Iran have lately appeared. A comprehensive survey of Persian history is given by one of the leading scholars in the field, R. N. Frye, *History of Ancient Iran* (1984). I. Gershevitch, ed., *The Cambridge History of Iran,* vol. 2 (1985), offers the reader a full account of ancient Persian history, but many of the chapters are already out of date. E. E. Herzfeld, *Iran in the Ancient East* (1987), puts Persian history in a broad context. J. M. Cook, *The Persian Empire* (1983), presents a readable general account of the period. Lastly, S. A. Matheson, *Persia: An Archaeological Guide (1973),* is a good guide to Persian monuments.

J. H. Moulton, *Early Zoroastrianism: The Origins, the Prophet, and the Magi* (1972), is a sound treatment of the beginnings and early spread of Zoroastrianism. R. C. Zaehner, *The Dawn and Twilight of Zoroastrianism* (1961), discusses the whole course of Zoroastrianism's history. Zaehner also provides a good introduction to the basic teachings of Zoroastrianism in his *Teachings of the Magi: A Compendium of Zoroastrian Beliefs* (1975). Finally, M. Boyce, a leading scholar in the field, offers a sound and readable treatment in her *Zoroastrianism* (1979).

3

The Legacy of Greece

The rocky peninsula of Greece was the home of the civilization that fundamentally shaped Western civilization. The Greeks were the first to explore most of the questions that continue to concern Western thinkers to this day. Going beyond mythmaking and religion, the Greeks strove to understand, in logical, rational terms, both the universe and the position of men and women in it. The result was the birth of philosophy and science—subjects that were far more important to most Greek thinkers than religion. The Greeks speculated on human beings and society and created the very concept of politics.

While the scribes of the ancient Near East produced king lists, the Greeks invented history to record, and understand how people and states functioned in time and space. In poetry the Greeks spoke as individuals. In drama they dealt with the grandeur and weakness of humanity and with the demands of society on the individual. The greatest monuments of the Greeks were not temples, statues, or tombs, but profound thoughts set down in terms as fresh and immediate today as they were some 2,400 years ago.

The history of the Greeks is divided into two broad periods: the Hellenic period (the subject of this chapter), roughly the time between the arrival of the Greeks (approximately 2000 B.C.) and the victory over Greece in 338 B.C. of Philip of Macedon; and the Hellenistic period (the subject of Chapter 4), the age beginning with the remarkable reign of Philip's son Alexander the Great (336–323 B.C.) and ending with the Roman conquest of the Hellenistic East (200–148 B.C.).

- What geographical factors helped to mold the evolution of the city-state and to shape the course of the Greek experience?
- What was the nature of the early Greek experience, and how did the impact of the Minoans and Mycenaeans lead to the concept of a heroic past?

  How did the Greeks develop basic political forms, forms as different as democracy and tyranny, that have influenced all of later Western history?
- What did the Greek intellectual triumph entail, and what were its effects?
- Last, how and why did the Greeks eventually fail?

These profound questions, which can never be fully answered, are the themes of this chapter.

HELLAS: THE LAND

Hellas, as the ancient Greeks called their land, encompassed the Aegean Sea and its islands as well as the Greek peninsula (Map 3.1). The Greek peninsula itself, stretching in the direction of Egypt and the Near East, is an extension of the Balkan system of mountains. Perhaps the best and most eloquent description of Greece comes from the eminent German historian K. J. Beloch:

Greece is an alpine land, which rises from the waters of the Mediterranean Sea, scenically probably the most beautiful region in southern Europe. The noble contours of the mountains, the bare, rocky slopes, the dusty green of the conifer forests, the white cover of snow that envelops the higher summits for the greatest part of the year, added to which is the profound blue surface of the sea below, and above everything the diffused brightness of the southern sun; this gives a total picture, the charm of which impresses itself unforgettably on the soul of the observer.[1]

The rivers of Greece are never more than creeks, and most of them go dry in the summer. Greece is, however, a land blessed with good harbors, the most important of which look to the east. The islands of the Aegean serve as steppingstones between the peninsula and Asia Minor.

Despite the beauty of the region, geography acted as an enormously divisive force in Greek life. The mountains of Greece dominate the landscape, cutting the land into many small pockets and isolating areas of habitation. Innumerable small peninsulas open to the sea, which is dotted with islands, most of them small and many uninhabitable. The geographical fragmentation of Greece encouraged political fragmentation. Furthermore, communications were extraordinarily poor. Rocky tracks were far more common than roads, and the

MAP 3.1 Ancient Greece In antiquity the home of the Greeks included the islands of the Aegean and the western shore of Turkey as well as the Greek peninsula itself.

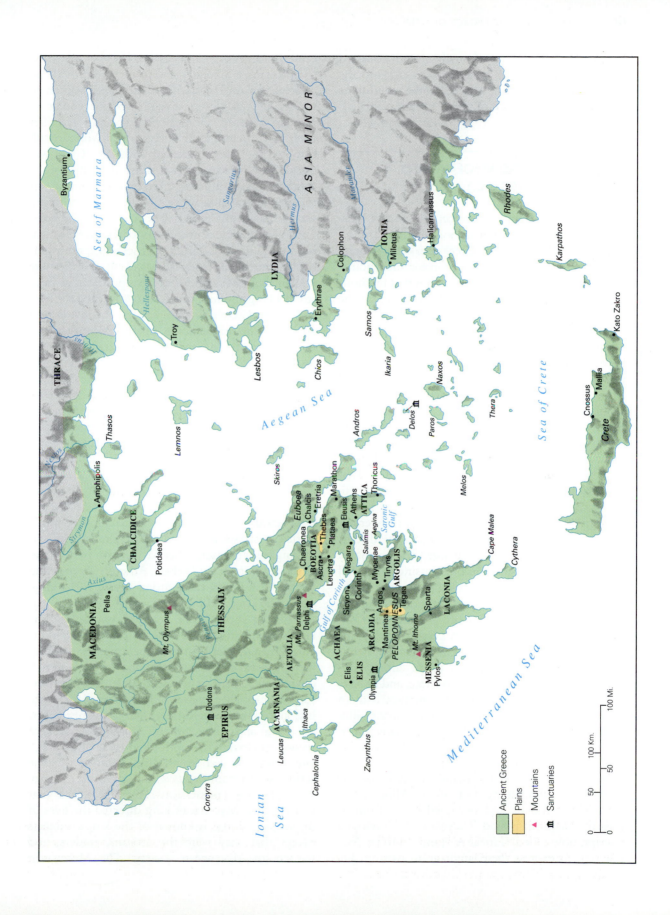

THRACE

Sea of Marmara

Byzantium•

ASIA MINOR

Hellespont

Sangarius

Hermus

Maeander

•Troy

LYDIA

•Colophon

IONIA

Halicarnassus•

•Erythrae

Miletus•

Rhodes

Thasos

Lesbos

Chios

Samos

Karpathos

Nestos

•Amphipolis

Skiros

Ikaria

Naxos

Delos ⚎

Kato Zakro

CHALCIDICE

Lemnos

Aegean Sea

Paros

Thera

Sea of Crete

Strymon

•Potidaea

Andros

Mallia

Axius

MACEDONIA

Pella•

Euboea

Marathon

Thoricus

Melos

Cnossus

Pella

THESSALY

Chaeronea •Chalcis

•Eretria

ATTICA

Crete

Mt. Olympus▲

BOEOTIA •Thebes

•Eleusis

•Athens

Peneus

Ascra•

Plataea ⚎

Megara•

Salamis

Aegina

Cape Malea

Leuctra•

Sicyon

•Corinth

Saronic

Gulf

Cythera

AETOLIA

Mt. Parnassus⚎

Mycenae•

Tiryns•

Delphi ▲⚎

Gulf of Corinth

•Argos

ARGOLIS

Mediterranean Sea

ACHAEA

ARCADIA

Sparta•

•Elis

Mantinea• •Tegea

LACONIA

ACARNANIA

ELIS

PELOPONNESUS

Mt. Ithome▲

Dodona⚎

Olympia ⚎

MESSENIA

EPIRUS

Ithaca

•Pylos

Leucas

Cephalonia

Zacynthus

Corcyra

Ionian

Sea

Ancient Greece

Plains

▲ Mountains

⚎ Sanctuaries

0   50   100 Mi.

0   50   100 Km.

few roads were unpaved. Usually a road consisted of nothing more than a pair of ruts cut into the rock to accommodate wheels. These conditions discouraged the growth of great empires.

THE MINOANS AND MYCENAEANS (ca 1650–ca 1100 B.C.)

The origins of Greek civilization are obscure. Neither historians, archeologists, nor linguists can confidently establish when Greek-speaking peoples made the Balkan peninsula of Greece their homeland. All that can now safely be said is that by about 1650 B.C. Greeks had established themselves at the great city of Mycenae in the Peloponnesus and elsewhere in Greece. Before then, the area from Thessaly in the north to Messenia in the south was inhabited by small farming communities. Quite probably the Greeks merged with these natives, and from that union emerged the society that modern scholars call "Mycenaean," after Mycenae, the most important site of this new Greek-speaking culture.

Of this epoch the ancient Greeks themselves remembered almost nothing. The *Iliad* and the *Odyssey,* Homer's magnificent epic poems (eighth century B.C.), retain some dim memory of this period but very little that is authentic. One of the sterling achievements of modern archeology is the discovery of this lost past. In the nineteenth century Heinrich Schliemann, a German businessman, fell in love with the *Iliad* and decided to find the sites it mentioned. He excavated Troy in modern Turkey, Mycenae, and several other sites in Greece to discover the lost past of the Greek people. At the turn of this century, the English archeologist Sir Arthur Evans uncovered the remains of an entirely unknown civilization at Cnossus in Crete, and he gave it the name "Minoan" after the mythical Cretan king Minos. Scholars since then have further illuminated this long-lost era, and despite many uncertainties a reasonably clear picture of the Minoans and Mycenaeans has begun to emerge.

By about 1650 B.C. the island of Crete was the home of the flourishing and vibrant Minoan culture. The Minoans had occupied Crete from at least the Neolithic period. They had also developed a script, now called "Linear A" (and yet to be deciphered), to express their language in writing. Because Linear A is still a riddle, it is as yet worthless to historians as a literary source and can provide no information on the status of men and women in society and politics or any idea of the course of Minoan History. Only archeology and art offer clues to Minoan life. The symbol of Minoan culture was the palace. Around 1650 B.C. Crete was dotted with palaces, such as those at Mallia on the northern coast and Kato Zakro on the eastern tip of the island. Towering above all others in importance was the palace at Cnossus. The palace was the political and economic center of Minoan society, which, like many ancient Near Eastern societies, was rigorously controlled from above. Few specifics are known about Minoan society except that at its head stood a king and his nobles, who governed the lives and toil of Crete's farmers, sailors, shepherds, and artisans. The implements of the Minoans, like those of the Mycenaeans, were bronze, so archeologists have named this period the "Bronze Age." Minoan society was wealthy and, to judge from the absence of fortifications on the island, peaceful. Enthusiastic sailors and merchants, the Minoans traded with Egypt and the cities of the Levant. Their ships also penetrated the Aegean Sea, throughout which they established trading posts. Their voyages in this direction brought them into contact with the Mycenaeans on the Greek peninsula.

By about 1650 B.C. Greek speakers were firmly settled at Mycenae, which became a major city and trading center. Later, other Mycenaean palaces and cities developed at Thebes, Athens, Tiryns, and Pylos. As in Crete, the political unit was the kingdom. The king and his warrior-aristocracy stood at the top of society. The seat and symbol of the king's power and wealth was his palace, which was also the economic center of the kingdom. Within its walls royal craftsmen fashioned jewelry and rich ornaments, made and decorated fine pottery, forged weapons, prepared hides and wool for clothing, and manufactured the other goods needed by the king and his retainers. Palace scribes kept records in Greek with a script known as "Linear B," which was derived from Minoan Linear A. The scribes kept account of taxes and drew up inventories of the king's possessions. From the palace, as at Cnossus, the Mycenaean king directed the lives of his subjects. Little is known of the king's subjects except that they were the artisans, traders, and farmers of Mycenaean society. The Mycenaean

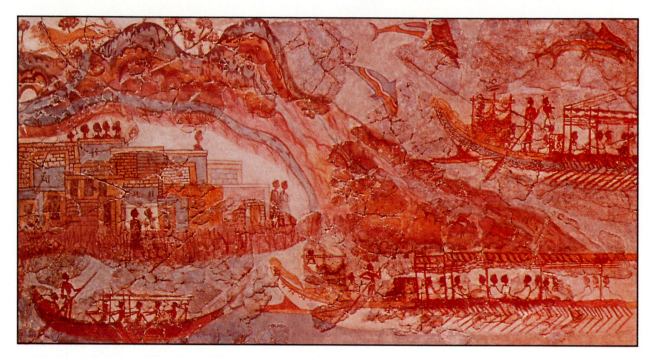

Minoan Naval Scene   This fresco, newly discovered at Thera, probably depicts the homecoming of a Minoan fleet of warships. Though later Greeks thought that the Minoans had ruled the sea, fleets such as the one pictured here probably protected Minoan maritime interests and suppressed piracy. Despite its military nature, the scene displays a general air of festivity, characteristic of Minoan art. (*Source: National Archaeological Museum, Athens/Ekdotike Athenon*)

economy was marked by an extensive division of labor, all tightly controlled from the palace. At the bottom of the social scale were the slaves, normally owned by the king and aristocrats, but who also worked for ordinary craftsmen.

Contacts between the Minoans and Mycenaeans were originally peaceful, and Minoan culture flooded the Greek mainland. But around 1450 B.C. the Mycenaeans attacked Crete, destroying many Minoan palaces and taking possession of the grand palace at Cnossus. For about the next fifty years the Mycenaeans ruled much of the island until a further wave of violence left Cnossus in ashes. These events are more disputed than understood, and the fate of Cnossus in particular has sparked controversy. Theories that Cnossus was destroyed by natural catastrophe have long since been disproved. Without doubt, human beings were responsible for the conflagration. Archeologists cannot, however, determine *who* was responsible—whether the My-

cenaeans at Cnossus were attacked by other Mycenaeans or whether the conquered Minoans rose in revolt.

Whatever the answer, the Mycenaean kingdoms in Greece benefited from the fall of Cnossus and the collapse of its trade. Mycenaean commerce quickly expanded throughout the Aegean, reaching as far abroad as Anatolia, Cyprus, and Egypt. Throughout central and southern Greece Mycenaean culture flourished as never before. Palaces became grander, and citadels were often protected by mammoth stone walls. Prosperity, however, did not bring peace, and between 1300 and 1000 B.C. kingdom after kingdom suffered attack and destruction.

Later Greeks accused the Dorians, who spoke a particular dialect of Greek, of overthrowing the Mycenaean kingdoms. Yet some modern linguists argue that the Dorians dwelt in Greece during the Mycenaean period. Archeologists generally conclude that the Dorians, if not already present, could have entered Greece only long after the era of destruction. Furthermore, not one alien artifact has been found on any of these sites; thus there is no archeological evidence for outside invaders. Normally, foreign invaders leave traces of themselves—for example, broken pottery and weapons—that are different from those of the attacked. We can conclude, therefore, that no outside intrusion destroyed the Mycenaean world. In fact, the legends preserved by later Greeks told of grim wars between Mycenaean kingdoms and of the fall of great royal families. Apparently Mycenaean Greece destroyed itself in a long series of internecine wars, a pattern that later Greeks would repeat.

The fall of the Mycenaean kingdoms ushered in a period of such poverty, disruption, and backwardness that historians usually call it the "Dark Age" of Greece (ca 1100–800 B.C.). Even literacy, which was not widespread in any case, was a casualty of the chaos. Yet even this period was important to the development of Greek civilization. It was a time of

Funeral Games At the end of the *Iliad* Homer describes the funeral games given in honor of Patroclus, the companion of Achilles. The main event was the chariot race. Here the race has begun, and the painter states in the Greek inscription that one of the chariots seen here belonged to Achilles. *(Source: National Archaeological Museum, Athens/Ekdotike Athenon)*

widespread movements of Greek-speaking peoples. Some Greeks sailed to Crete, where they established new communities. A great wave of Greeks spread eastward through the Aegean to the coast of Asia Minor. These immigrations turned the Aegean into a Greek lake. The people who stayed behind gradually rebuilt Greek society. They thus provided an element of continuity, a link between the Mycenaean period and the Greek culture that emerged from the Dark Age.

HOMER, HESIOD, AND THE HEROIC PAST (1100–800 B.C.)

The Greeks, unlike the Hebrews, had no sacred book that chronicled their past. Instead they had the *Iliad* and the *Odyssey* to describe a time when gods still walked the earth. And they learned the origin and descent of the gods from the *Theogony,* an epic poem by Hesiod (ca 700 B.C.). Instead of authentic history the poems of Homer and Hesiod offered the Greeks an ideal past, a largely legendary Heroic Age. In terms of pure history these poems contain scraps of information about the Bronze Age, much about the early Dark Age, and some about the poets' own era. Chronologically, then, the Heroic Age falls mainly in the period between the collapse of the Mycenaean world and the rebirth of literacy.

The *Iliad* recounts an expedition of Mycenaeans, whom Homer called "Achaeans," to besiege the city of Troy in Asia Minor. The heart of the *Iliad,* however, concerns the quarrel between Agamemnon, the king of Mycenae, and Achilles, the tragic hero of the poem, and how their quarrel brought suffering to the Achaeans. Only when Achilles put away his anger and pride did he consent to come forward, face, and kill the Trojan hero Hector. The *Odyssey,* probably composed later than the *Iliad,* narrates the adventures of Odysseus, one of the Achaean heroes who fought at Troy, during his voyage home from the fighting.

The splendor of these poems does not lie in their plots, although the *Odyssey* is a marvelous adventure story. Rather, both poems portray engaging but often flawed characters who are larger than life and yet typically human. Homer was also strikingly successful in depicting the great gods, who generally sit on Mount Olympus and watch the fighting at Troy like spectators at a baseball game, although they sometimes participate in the action. Homer's deities are reminiscent of Mesopotamian gods and goddesses. Hardly a decorous lot, the Olympians are raucous, petty, deceitful, and splendid. In short, they are human.

Homer at times portrayed the gods in a serious vein, but he never treated them in a systematic fashion, as did Hesiod, who lived somewhat later than Homer. Hesiod's epic poem, the *Theogony,* traces the descent of Zeus. Hesiod was influenced by Mesopotamian myths, which the Hittites had adopted and spread to the Aegean. Hesiod's poem claims that in the beginning there was chaos, the "yawning deep." From chaos came Gaea (Earth), who gave birth to Uranus (Heaven). Gaea and Uranus then gave birth to Cronus and Ocean (the deep-swelling waters). Cronus, the son of Earth and Heaven, like the Mesopotamian Enlil, separated the two and became king of the gods.

Like the Hebrews, Hesiod envisaged his *cosmogony*—his account of the way the universe developed—in moral terms. Zeus, the son of Cronus, defeated his evil father and took his place as king of the gods. He then sired Lawfulness, Right, Peace, and other powers of light and beauty. Thus, in Hesiod's conception, Zeus was the god of righteousness, who loved justice and hated wrongdoing.

In another epic poem, *Works and Days,* Hesiod wrote of his own time and his own village of Ascra in Boeotia, a scenic place set between beautiful mountains and fertile plains. In his will, Hesiod's father had divided his lands between Hesiod and his brother Perses. Perses bribed the aristocratic authorities to give him the larger part of the inheritance and then squandered his wealth. Undaunted by the injustice of the powerful, Hesiod thundered back in a voice reminiscent of Khunanup, the "Eloquent Peasant" (see page 25):

Bribe-devouring lords, make straight your decisions,
Forget entirely crooked judgments.
He who causes evil to another harms himself.
Evil designs are most evil to the plotter.[2]

The similarities are striking between the fictional Khunanup and Hesiod, both of whom were oppressed by the rich and powerful. Yet the differences are even more significant. Hesiod, unlike Khunanup, did not receive justice from the political au-

thorities of the day, but he fully expected divine vindication. Hesiod's call for justice has gone ringing through the centuries, its appeal as fresh today as when he first uttered it more than two millennia ago. Hesiod spoke of Zeus as Jeremiah had spoken of Yahweh, warning that Zeus would see that justice was done and injustice punished. He cautioned his readers that Zeus was angered by those who committed adultery, harmed orphans, and offended the aged. Hesiod's ethical concepts and faith in divine justice were the product of his belief that the world was governed by the power of good.

THE POLIS

After the upheavals that ended the Mycenaean period and the slow recovery of prosperity during the Dark Age, the Greeks developed their basic political and institutional unit, the *polis* or city-state. The details of this development are largely lost, but by the end of the Dark Age the polis was common throughout Greece. Rarely did there occur the combination of extensive territory and political unity that allowed one polis to rise above others. Only three city-states were able to muster the resources of an entire region behind them (see Map 3.1): Sparta, which dominated the regions of Laconia and Messenia; Athens, which united the large peninsula of Attica under its rule; and Thebes, which in several periods marshaled the resources of the fertile region of Boeotia. Otherwise, the political pattern of ancient Greece was one of many small city-states, few of which were much stronger or richer than their neighbors.

Physically the term *polis* designated a city or town and its surrounding countryside. The people of a typical polis lived in a compact group of houses within the city. The city's water supply came from public fountains and cisterns. By the fifth century B.C. the city was generally surrounded by a wall. The city contained a point, usually elevated, called the *acropolis,* and a public square or marketplace (*agora*). On the acropolis, which in the early period was a place of refuge, stood the temples, altars, public monuments, and various dedications to the gods of the polis. The agora was originally the place where the warrior assembly met, but it became the political center of the polis. In the agora were porticoes, shops, and public buildings and courts.

The Shape of the Athenian Polis This print of the Athenian acropolis shows clearly the geographical requirements of the polis. Early Greeks desired an elevated spot, or acropolis, for refuge; later it became the seat of the polis' temples. At the foot of the citadel spread the agora, public buildings, and private homes. *(Source: Caroline Buckler)*

The unsettled territory of the polis was typically its source of wealth. This territory consisted of arable land, pastureland, and wasteland. Farmers left the city each morning to work their fields or tend their flocks of sheep and goats, and they returned at night. On the wasteland men often quarried stone, mined for precious metals, and at certain times of the year obtained small amounts of fodder. Thus the polis encompassed a combination of urban and agrarian life.

The size of the polis varied according to geographical circumstances. Population figures for Greece are mostly guesswork, because most city-states were too small to need a census. The philosopher Plato thought that five thousand citizens constituted the ideal population of a polis. The intimacy of the polis was an important factor, one

hard for modern city dwellers to imagine. The small population enabled Greeks to see how the individual fitted into the overall system—how the human parts made up the social whole.

Regardless of its size or wealth, the polis was fundamental to Greek life. The polis was far more than a political institution. Above all, it was a community of citizens, and the affairs of the community were the concern of all. The customs of the community were at the same time the laws of the polis. Rome later created a single magnificent body of law, but the Greeks had as many law codes as they had city-states. Though the laws of one polis might be roughly similar to those of another, the law of any given polis was unique simply because the customs and the experience of each one had been unique.

The polis could be governed in any of several ways. First, it could be a *monarchy,* a term derived from the Greek for "the rule of one man." A king could represent the community, reigning according to law and respecting the rights of the citizens. Second, the *aristocracy* could govern the state. Third, the running of the polis could be the duty and prerogative of an *oligarchy,* which literally means "the rule of a few"—in this case a small group of wealthy citizens, regardless of their status at birth. Or the polis could be governed as a *democracy,* through the rule of the people, a concept which in Greece meant that all citizens, without respect to birth or wealth, administered the workings of government. How a polis was governed depended on who had the upper hand. When the wealthy held power, they usually instituted oligarchies; when the people could break the hold of the rich, they established democracies. In any case, no polis ever had an ironclad, unchangeable constitution. Still another form of Greek government was *tyranny.* Under tyranny the polis was ruled by a *tyrant,* a man who had seized power by unconstitutional means, generally by using his wealth to gain a political following that could topple the existing government.

Ironically, the very integration of the polis proved to be one of its weaknesses. Because the bonds that held the polis together were so intimate, Greeks were extremely reluctant to allow foreigners to share fully in its life. An alien, even someone Greek by birth, could almost never expect to be made a citizen. Nor could women play a political role. Women participated in the civic cults and served as priestesses, but the polis had no room for them in state affairs. Thus the exclusiveness of the polis doomed it to a limited horizon.

Although each polis was normally jealous of its independence, some Greeks banded together to create leagues of city-states. Here was the birth of Greek federalism, a political system in which several states formed a central government while remaining independent in their internal affairs. United in a league, a confederation of city-states was far stronger than any of its individual members and better able to withstand external attack.

Yet even federalism could not overcome the passionate individualism of the polis, which proved to be a serious weakness. The citizens of each polis were determined to remain free and autonomous.

Rarely were the Greeks willing to unite in larger political bodies. The political result in Greece, as in Sumer, was almost constant warfare. The polis could dominate, but unlike Rome it could not incorporate.

THE LYRIC AGE (800–500 B.C.)

The maturation of the polis coincided with one of the most vibrant periods of Greek history, an era of extraordinary expansion geographically, artistically, and politically. Greeks ventured as far east as the Black Sea and as far west as Spain (Map 3.2). With the rebirth of literacy, this period also witnessed a tremendous literary flowering as poets broke away from the heroic tradition and wrote about their own lives. Politically these were the years when Sparta and Athens—the two poles of the Greek experience—rose to prominence.

Overseas Expansion

During the years 1100–800 B.C., the Greeks not only recovered from the breakdown of the Mycenaean world, but also grew in wealth and numbers. This new prosperity brought with it new problems. Greece is a small and not especially fertile country. The increase in population meant that many men and their families had very little land or none at all. Land hunger and the resulting social and political tensions drove many Greeks to seek new homes outside of Greece. Other factors, largely intangible, played their part as well: the desire for a new start, a love of excitement and adventure, and natural curiosity about what lay beyond the horizon.

The Mediterranean offered the Greeks an escape valve, for they were always a seafaring people. To them the sea was a highway, not a barrier. Through their commercial ventures they had long been familiar with the rich areas of the western Mediterranean. Moreover, the geography of the Mediterranean basin favored colonization. The land and climate of the Mediterranean region are remarkably uniform. Greeks could travel to new areas, whether to Cyprus in the east or to Malta in the west, and establish the kind of settlement they had known in Greece. They could also raise the same crops they had raised in Greece. The move to a new home was not a plunge into totally unknown conditions. Once the colonists had established themselves in new homes, they continued life essentially as in Greece.

From about 750 to 550 B.C., Greeks from the mainland and from Asia Minor poured onto the coasts of the northern Aegean, the Ionian Sea, and the Black Sea and into North Africa, Sicily, southern Italy, southern France, and Spain (see Map 3.2). Just as the migrations of the Dark Age had turned the Aegean into a Greek lake, this later wave of colonization spread the Greeks and their culture throughout the Mediterranean.

Colonization presented the polis with a huge challenge, for it required organization and planning on an unprecedented scale. The colonizing city, called the *metropolis* or mother-city, first decided where to establish the colony, how to transport colonists to the site, and who would sail. Then the metropolis collected and stored the supplies that the colonists would need both to feed themselves and to plant their first crop. The metropolis must also provide adequate shipping for the voyage. All preparations ready, a leader, called an *oikist,* ordered the colonists to sail. From then the oikist was in full command of the band until the colony was established in its new site and capable of running its own affairs. A significant aspect of colonizing ventures is that colonists sailed as equals, and as equals they set about building a new life together.

Once the colonists landed, the oikist laid out the new polis, selected the sites of temples and public buildings, and established the government. Then he surrendered power to the new leaders. The colony was thereafter independent of the metropolis. For the Greeks, colonization had two important aspects. First, it demanded that the polis assume a much greater public function than ever before,

MAP 3.2 Colonization of the Mediterranean   Though the Greeks and Phoenicians colonized the Mediterranean basin at about the same time, the Greeks spread over far greater areas.

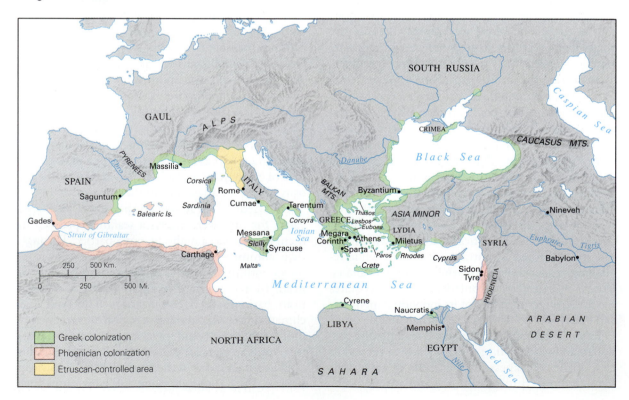

thus strengthening the city-state's institutional position. Second, colonization spread the polis and its values far beyond the shores of Greece. Even more important, colonization on this scale had a profound impact on the course of Western civilization. It meant that the prevailing culture of the Mediterranean basin would be Greek, the heritage to which Rome would later fall heir.

One man can in many ways stand as the symbol of the vital and robust era of colonization. Archilochus was born on the island of Paros, the bastard son of an aristocrat. He knew that because of his illegitimacy he would never inherit his father's land, and this knowledge seems to have made him self-reliant. He was also a poet of genius, the first of the lyric poets who left an indelible mark on this age. Unlike the epic poets, who portrayed the deeds of heroes, Archilochus sang of himself. He knew the sea, the dangers of sailing, and the price that the sea often exacted. He spoke of one shipwreck in grim terms and even treated the god of the sea with irony: "Of fifty men gentle Poseidon left one, Koiranos, to be saved from shipwreck."

Together with others from Paros he took part in the colonization of Thasos in the northern Aegean. He described the island in less than glowing terms: "Like the spine of an ass it stands, crowned to the brim with a wild forest." His opinion of his fellow colonists was hardly kinder: "So the misery of all Greece came together in Thasos." Yet at Thasos he fell in love with a woman named Neoboule. They did not marry because her father opposed the match. In revenge, Archilochus seduced Neoboule's younger sister, railed at the entire family, and left Thasos to live the life of a mercenary.

His hired lance took him to Euboea, and he left a striking picture of the fighting there:

Not many bows will be strung, nor slings be slung
When Ares begins battle in the plain.
There will be the mournful work of the sword:
For in this kind of battle are the spear-famed
Lords of Euboea experienced.[3]

Archilochus exemplifies the energy, restlessness, self-reliance, and sense of adventure that characterizes this epoch. People like him broke old ties, faced homelessness and danger, and built new homes for themselves. They made the Mediterranean Greek.

Mosaic Portrait of Sappho The Greek letters in the upper left corner identify this idealized portrait as that of Sappho. The mosaic, which was found at Sparta, dates to the late Roman Empire and testifies to Sappho's popularity in antiquity. *(Source: Caroline Buckler)*

Lyric Poets

Archilochus the colonist and adventurer is not nearly as important as Archilochus the lyric poet, whose individualism set a new tone in Greek literature. For the first time in Western civilization, men and women began to write of their own experiences. Their poetry reflected their belief that they had something precious to say about themselves. To them poetry did not belong only to the gods or to the great heroes on the plain of Troy. Some lyric poets used their literary talents for the good of their city-states. They stood forth as individuals and in their poetry urged their countrymen to be patriotic and just.

One of the most unforgettable of these writers is the poet Sappho. Unlike Archilochus, she neither braved the wilds nor pushed into the unknown, yet she was no less individual than he. Sappho was born in the seventh century B.C. on the island of Lesbos, a place of sun, sea, and rustic beauty. Her marriage produced a daughter, to whom she wrote some of her poems. Sappho's poetry is personal and intense. She delighted in her surroundings, which were those of aristocratic women, and celebrated the little things around her. Hers was a world of natural beauty, sacred groves, religious festivals, wedding celebrations, and noble companions. Sappho fondly remembered walks with a woman friend:

There was neither a hill nor a sanctuary
Nor a stream of running water
Which we failed to visit;
Nor when spring began any grove
Filled with the noise of nightingales.[4]

Sappho is best known for erotic poetry, for she expressed her love frankly and without shame. She was bisexual, and much of her poetry dealt with her homosexual love affairs. In one of her poems she remembered the words of her lover:

Sappho, if you don't come out,
Surely I will no longer love you.
O come to us and free your lovely
Strength from your bed.
Lifting off your Chian robe,
Bathe in the waters like a
Pure lily beside a spring.[5]

In antiquity Sappho's name became linked with female homosexual love. Today the English word *lesbian* is derived from Sappho's island home. The Greeks accepted bisexuality—that men and women could enjoy both homosexual and heterosexual lovemaking. Homosexual relationships normally carried no social stigma. In her mature years Sappho was courted by a younger man who wanted to marry her. By then she had already proclaimed her love for several girls, yet the young man was not troubled by these affairs. As it turned out, Sappho refused to marry because she was past childbearing age.

In their poetry Archilochus and Sappho reveal two sides of Greek life in this period. Archilochus exemplifies the energy and adventure of the age, while Sappho expresses the intensely personal side of life. The link connecting the two poets is their individualism, their faith in themselves, and their desire to reach out to other men and women in order to share their experiences, thoughts, and wisdom.

The Growth of Sparta

During the Lyric Age the Spartans expanded the boundaries of their polis and made it the leading power in Greece. Like other Greeks, the Spartans faced the problems of overpopulation and land hunger. Unlike other Greeks, the Spartans solved these problems by conquest, not by colonization. To gain more land the Spartans set out in about 735 B.C. to conquer Messenia, a rich, fertile region in the southwestern Peloponnesus. This conflict, the First Messenian War, lasted for twenty years and ended in a Spartan triumph. The Spartans appropriated Messenian land and turned the Messenians into *helots,* or state serfs.

In about 650 B.C., Spartan exploitation and oppression of the Messenian helots led to a helot revolt so massive and stubborn that it became known as the Second Messenian War. The Spartan poet Tyrtaeus, a contemporary of these events, vividly portrayed the ferocity of the fighting:

For it is a shameful thing indeed
When with the foremost fighters
An elder falling in front of the young men
Lies outstretched,
Having white hair and grey beard,
Breathing forth his stout soul in the dust,
Holding in his hands his genitals
stained with blood.[6]

Confronted with such horrors, Spartan enthusiasm for the war waned. Finally, after some thirty years of fighting, the Spartans put down the revolt. Nevertheless, the political and social strain it caused led to a transformation of the Spartan polis.

It took the full might of the Spartan people, aristocrat and commoner alike, to win the Second Messenian War. After the victory the non-nobles, who had done much of the fighting, demanded rights equal to those of the nobility. They had taken their place in the battle line next to their aristocratic neighbors but lacked the social prestige and political rights of their noble companions. The agitation of these non-nobles disrupted society until the aristocrats agreed to remodel the state.

Although the Spartans later claimed that the changes brought about by this compromise were the work of Lycurgus, a legendary, semidivine lawgiver, they were really the work of the entire Spar-

The Hoplite Phalanx   When the Greeks adopted heavy armor, weapons, and shields, their lack of mobility forced them to fight in several dense lines, each behind the other. Cohesion and order became as valuable as courage. To help the hoplites maintain their pace during the attack, a flute player here plays a marching tune. *(Source: Villa Giulia Museum/Ministero per i Beni Culturali e Ambientali, Rome)*

tan people. The "Lycurgan regimen," as these reforms were called, was a new political, economic, and social system. Political distinctions among the Spartans were eliminated, and all citizens became legally equal. In effect, the Lycurgan regimen abolished the aristocracy and made the government an oligarchy. Actual governance of the polis was in the hands of two kings, who were primarily military leaders. The kings and twenty-eight elders made up a council that deliberated on foreign and domestic matters and prepared legislation for the assembly, which consisted of all Spartan citizens. The real executive power of the polis was in the hands of five *ephors,* or overseers, elected from and by all the people.

To provide for their economic needs the Spartans divided the land of Messenia among all citizens. Helots worked the land, raised the crops, provided the Spartans with their living, and occasionally served in the army. The Spartans kept the helots in line by means of systematic terrorism, hoping to beat them down and keep them quiet. Spartan citizens were supposed to devote their time exclusively to military training.

In the Lycurgan system every citizen owed primary allegiance to Sparta. Suppression of the individual together with emphasis on military prowess led to a barracks state. Family life itself was sacrificed to the polis. Once Spartan boys reached the age of twelve, they were enrolled in separate companies with other boys of their age. They slept outside on reed mats and underwent rugged physical and military training until age twenty-four, when they became front-line soldiers. For the rest of their lives, Spartan men kept themselves prepared for combat. Their military training never ceased, and the older men were expected to be models of endurance, frugality, and sturdiness to the younger men. In battle Spartans were supposed to stand and die rather than retreat. An anecdote about one Spartan mother sums up Spartan military values. As her son was setting off to battle, the mother handed him his shield and advised him to come back either victorious, carrying the shield, or dead, being carried on it. In short, in the Lycurgan regimen Spartan men were expected to train vigorously, disdain luxury and wealth, do with little, and like it.

Similar rigorous requirements applied to Spartan women, who may have been unique in all of Greek society. They were prohibited from wearing jewelry or ornate clothes. They too exercised strenuously in the belief that hard physical training promoted the birth of healthy children. Yet they were hardly oppressed. They enjoyed a more active and open public life than most other Greek women, even though they could neither vote nor hold office. They were far more emancipated than many other Greek women in part because Spartan society felt that mothers and wives had to be as hardy as their sons and husbands. Sparta was not a place for weaklings, male or female. Spartan women saw it as their privilege to be the wives and mothers of victorious warriors, and on several occasions their own courage became legendary. They had a reputation for independent spirit and self-assertion. This position stemmed from their genuine patriotism, but also from their title to much Spartan land. For all of these reasons, they shared a footing with Spartan men that most other Greek women lacked in their own societies.

Along with the emphasis on military values for both sexes, the Lycurgan regimen had another purpose as well: it served to instill in society the civic virtues of dedication to the state and a code of moral conduct. These aspects of the Spartan system were generally admired throughout the Greek world.

The Evolution of Athens

Like Sparta, Athens faced pressing social and economic problems during the Lyric Age, but the Athenian response was far different from that of the Spartans. Instead of creating an oligarchy, the Athenians extended to all citizens the right and duty of governing the polis. Indeed, the Athenian democracy was one of the most thoroughgoing in Greece.

The late seventh century B.C. was for Athens a time of turmoil, the causes for which are virtually unknown. In either 632 or 636 B.C. Cylon, an Athenian aristocrat, seized the Acropolis in an effort to become tyrant. Rushing immediately into the city, peasants foiled Cylon's attempt. In 621 B.C. Draco, doubtless under pressure from the peasants, published the first law code of the Athenian polis. His code was thought harsh, but it nonetheless embodied the ideal that the law belonged to the citizens. Nevertheless, peasant unrest continued.

By the early sixth century B.C., social and economic conditions led to another explosive situation. The aristocracy still governed Athens as oppressively as the "bribe-devouring lords" of Boeotia against whom Hesiod had railed. The aristocrats owned the best land, met in an assembly to govern the polis, and interpreted the law. Noble landowners were forcing small farmers into economic dependence. Many families were sold into slavery; others were exiled and their land pledged to the rich. Poor farmers who had borrowed from their wealthy neighbors put up their land as collateral. If a farmer was unable to repay the loan, his creditor put a stone on the borrower's field to signify his indebtedness and thereafter took one-sixth of the annual yield until the debt was paid. If the farmer had to borrow again, he pledged himself and sometimes his family. If he was again unable to repay the loan, he became the slave of his creditor. Because the harvests of the poor farmer were generally small, he normally raised enough to live on but not enough to repay his loan.

In many other city-states conditions like those in Athens led to the rise of tyrants. One person who recognized these problems clearly was Solon, himself an aristocrat and poet, and a man opposed to tyrants. He was also the one man in Athens who enjoyed the respect of both aristocrats and peasants. Like Hesiod, Solon used his poetry to condemn the aristocrats for their greed and dishonesty. Solon recited his poems in the Athenian agora, where everyone could hear his relentless call for justice and fairness. The aristocrats realized that Solon was no crazed revolutionary, and the common people trusted him. Around 594 B.C. the nobles elected him *archon*, chief magistrate of the Athenian polis, and gave him extraordinary power to reform the state.

Solon immediately freed all people enslaved for debt, recalled all exiles, canceled all debts on land,

and made enslavement for debt illegal. He also divided society into four legal groups on the basis of wealth. In the most influential group were the wealthiest citizens, but even the poorest and least powerful group enjoyed certain rights. Solon allowed them into the old aristocratic assembly, where they could take part in the election of magistrates.

In all his work Solon gave thought to the rights of the poor as well as the rich. He gave the commoners a place in government and a voice in the political affairs of Athens. His work done, Solon insisted that all swear to uphold his reforms. Then, because many were clamoring for him to become tyrant, he left Athens.

Although Solon's reforms solved some immediate problems, they did not bring peace to Athens. Some artistocrats attempted to make themselves tyrants, while others banded together to oppose them. In 546 B.C. Pisistratus, an exiled aristocrat, returned to Athens, defeated his opponents, and became tyrant. Pisistratus reduced the power of the aristocracy while supporting the common people. Under his rule Athens prospered, and his building program began to transform the city into one of the splendors of Greece. His reign as tyrant promoted the growth of democratic ideas by arousing in the Athenians rudimentary feelings of equality.

Athenian acceptance of tyranny did not long outlive Pisistratus, for his son Hippias ruled harshly, committing excesses that led to his overthrow. After a brief period of turmoil between factions of the nobility, Cleisthenes, a wealthy and prominent aristocrat, emerged triumphant in 508 B.C., largely because he won the support of the people. Cleisthenes created the Athenian democracy with the full knowledge and approval of the Athenian people. He reorganized the state completely but presented every innovation to the assembly for discussion and ratification. All Athenian citizens had a voice in Cleisthenes' work.

Cleisthenes used the *deme,* a local unit, to serve as the basis of his political system. Citizenship was tightly linked to the deme, for each deme kept the roll of those within its jurisdiction who were admitted to citizenship. Cleisthenes also created ten new tribes as administrative units. All the demes were grouped in tribes, which thus formed the link between the demes and the central government. The central government included an assembly of all citizens and a new council of five hundred members.

The council prepared legislation for the assembly to consider, and it handled diplomatic affairs. Cleisthenes is often credited with the institution of *ostracism,* a vote of the Athenian people by which the man receiving the most votes went into exile. The goal of ostracism was to rid the state peacefully of a difficult or potentially dangerous politician. The result of Cleisthenes' work was to make Athens a democracy with a government efficient enough to permit effective popular rule.

Athenian democracy was to prove an inspiring ideal in Western civilization. It demonstrated that a large group of people, not just a few, could efficiently run the affairs of state. By heeding the opinions, suggestions, and wisdom of all its citizens, the polis enjoyed the maximum amount of good counsel. Because all citizens could speak their minds, they did not have to resort to rebellion or conspiracy to express their desires.

Athenian democracy must not, however, be thought of in modern terms. In Athens democracy meant a form of government in which poor men as well as rich enjoyed political power and responsibility. In practice, though, most important offices were held by aristocrats. Furthermore, Athenian democracy denied political rights to many people, including women and slaves. Foreigners were seldom admitted to citizenship. Unlike modern democracies, Athenian democracy did not mean that the citizen would vote for others who would then run the state. Instead, every citizen was expected to be able to perform the duties of most magistrates. In Athens citizens voted and served. The people were the government. They enjoyed equal rights under the law, and the voice of the majority determined law. It is this union of the individual and the state —the view that the state exists for the good of the citizen, whose duty it is to serve it well—that has made Athenian democracy so compelling an ideal.

THE CLASSICAL PERIOD (500–338 B.C.)

In the years 500 to 338 B.C., Greek civilization reached its highest peak in politics, thought, and art. In this period the Greeks beat back the armies of the Persian Empire. Then, turning their spears against one another, they destroyed their own political system in a century of warfare. Some thoughtful Greeks felt prompted to record and

Greek Family in Mourning   This funeral relief commemorates the death of a young girl. She stands on the right as though still living, bidding farewell to her mother, who is seated. Her father stands in the background. The scene is subdued but serene. Any Greek who saw this relief would know that parents and daughter were saying "XAIPE," which in Greek means "hello" as well as "goodbye." *(Source: Caroline Buckler)*

analyze these momentous events; the result was the creation of history. This era saw the flowering of philosophy, as thinkers in Ionia and on the Greek mainland began to ponder the nature and meaning of the universe and human experience; they used their intellects to explain the world around them and to determine humanity's place in it. The Greeks invented drama, and the Athenian tragedians Aeschylus, Sophocles, and Euripides explored themes that still inspire audiences today. Greek architects reached the zenith of their art and

created buildings whose very ruins still inspire awe. Because Greek intellectual and artistic efforts attained their fullest and finest expression in these years, this age is called the "Classical period." Few periods in the history of Western society can match it in sheer dynamism and achievement.

The Persian Wars (499–479 B.C.)

One of the hallmarks of the Classical period was warfare. In 499 B.C. the Ionian Greeks, with the feeble help of Athens, rebelled against the Persian Empire. In 490 B.C. the Persians struck back at Athens but were beaten off at the Battle of Marathon, a small plain in Attica (see Map 3.5). This failure only prompted the Persians to try again. In 480 B.C. the Persian king Xerxes led a mighty invasion force into Greece. In the face of this emergency, many of the Greeks united and pooled their resources to resist the invaders. The Spartans provided the overall leadership and commanded the Greek armies. The Athenians, led by the wily Themistocles, provided the heart of the naval forces.

The first confrontations between the Persians and the Greeks occurred at the pass of Thermopylae and in the waters off Artemisium, the northern tip of Euboea. At Thermopylae the Greek hoplites, heavily armed foot-soldiers, showed their mettle. Before the fighting began, a report came in that when the Persian archers shot their bows the arrows darkened the sky. One gruff Spartan replied merely, "Fine, then we'll fight in the shade." The Greeks at Thermopylae fought heroically, but the Persians took the position. In 480 B.C. the Greek fleet, inspired by the energetic Themistocles, met the Persian armada at Salamis, an island just south of Athens. Though outnumbered by the Persians, the Greek navy won an overwhelming victory. The remnants of the Persian fleet retired, and with them went all hope of Persian victory. In the following year, a coalition of Greek forces, commanded by the Spartan Pausanias with assistance from the Athenian Aristides, smashed the last Persian army at Plataea, a small polis in Boeotia. Greece remained free.

The significance of these Greek victories is nearly incalculable. By defeating the Persians, the Greeks ensured that oriental monarchy would not stifle the Greek achievement. The Greeks were thus able to develop their particular genius in freedom. These decisive victories meant that Greek political forms and intellectual concepts would be the heritage of the West.

Growth of the Athenian Empire (478–431 B.C.)

For the Greeks, who had just won the Persian wars, that conflict was a beginning, not an end. Before them was a novel situation: the defeat of the Persians had created a power vacuum in the Aegean. The state with the strongest navy could turn the Aegean into its lake. In 478 B.C., to take advantage of this situation, the Athenians and their allies, again led by Aristides, formed the Delian League, a grand naval alliance aimed at liberating Ionia from Persian rule. The league took its name from the small island of Delos, on which stood a religious center sacred to all parties. The Delian League was intended as a free alliance under the leadership of Athens. Athenians provided most of the warships and crews and determined how many ships or how much money each member of the league should contribute to the allied effort.

The Athenians, supported by the Delian League and led by the young aristocrat Cimon, carried the war against Persia. But Athenian success had a sinister side. While the Athenians drove the Persians out of the Aegean, they also became increasingly imperialistic, even to the point of turning the Delian League into an Athenian empire. Athens began reducing its allies to the status of subjects. The Athenians sternly put down dissident or rebellious governments, replacing them with trustworthy puppets. Tribute was often collected by force, and the Athenians placed the economic resources of the Delian League under tighter and tighter control.

Athens justified its conduct by its successful leadership. In about 467 B.C. Cimon defeated a new and huge Persian force at the Battle of the Eurymedon River in Asia Minor, once again removing the shadow of Persia from the Aegean. But as the threat from Persia waned and the Athenians treated their allies more harshly, major allies such as Thasos revolted (ca 465 B.C.), requiring the Delian League to use its forces against its own members. The expansion of Athenian power and the aggressiveness of

Athenian rule also alarmed Sparta and its allies. While relations between Athens and Sparta cooled, Pericles (ca 494–429 B.C.) became the leading statesman in Athens. Like the democracy he led, Pericles, an aristocrat of solid intellectual ability, was aggressive and imperialistic. At last, in 459 B.C. Sparta and Athens went to war over conflicts between Athens and some of Sparta's allies. Though the Athenians conquered Boeotia, Megara, and Aegina in the early stages of the war, they met defeat in Egypt and later in Boeotia. The war ended in 445 B.C. with no serious damage to either side and nothing settled. But this war divided the Greek world between the two great powers.

During the 440s and 430s Athens continued its severe policies toward its subject allies and came into conflict with Corinth, one of Sparta's leading supporters (Map 3.3). In 433 B.C. Athens sided with Corcyra against Corinth in a dispute between the two. Together with the Corcyraean fleet, an Athenian squadron defeated the Corinthian navy in open combat. The next year Corinth and Athens collided again, this time over the Corinthian colony of Potidaea, in a conflict the Athenians also won. In this climate of anger and escalation, Pericles took the next step. To punish Megara for alleged sacrilege, Pericles in 432 B.C. persuaded the Athenians to pass a law, the Megarian Decree, which excluded Megarians from trading with Athens and its empire. In response the Spartans convened a meeting of their allies, whose complaints of Athenian aggression ended with a demand that Athens be stopped. Reluctantly the Spartans agreed to declare war. The real reason for war, according to the Athenian historian Thucydides, was very simple: "The truest explanation, though the one least mentioned, was the great growth of Athenian power and the fear it caused the Lacedaemonians [Spartans], which drove them to war."[7]

The Peloponnesian War (431–404 B.C.)

At the outbreak of this conflict, the Peloponnesian War, the Spartan ambassador Melesippus warned the Athenians: "This day will be the beginning of great evil for the Greeks." Few men have ever prophesied more accurately. The Peloponnesian War lasted a generation and brought in its wake

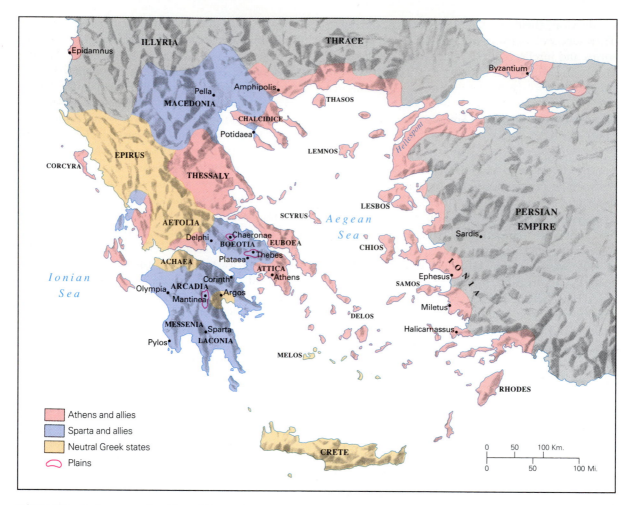

MAP 3.3 The Peloponnesian War   This map, which shows the alignment of states during the Peloponnesian War, vividly illustrates the large scale of the war and its divisive impact.

fearful plagues, famine, civil wars, widespread destruction, and huge loss of life.

After a Theban attack on the nearby polis of Plataea, the Peloponnesian War began in earnest. In the next seven years, the army of Sparta and its Peloponnesian allies invaded Attica five times. The Athenians stood behind their walls, but in 430 B.C. the cramped conditions nurtured a dreadful plague, which killed huge numbers, eventually claiming Pericles himself. The death of Pericles opened the door to a new breed of politicians, men who were rash, ambitious, and more dedicated to themselves than to Athens. One such was Cleon, a very daring and in some ways a very capable man. To divert the constant Spartan invasions of Attica,

Cleon proposed a counterattack at Pylos, a rocky peninsula in Messenia immediately opposite the Spartan-occupied island of Sphacteria. Spartan forces were defeated, yet the outcome failed to bring peace. Instead, the energetic Spartan commander Brasidas widened the war in 424 B.C. by capturing Amphipolis on the northern coast of the Aegean, one of Athens's most valuable subject states. Two years later, both Cleon and Brasidas were killed in a battle to recapture the city. Recognizing that ten years of war had resulted only in death, destruction, and stalemate, Sparta and Athens concluded the peace of Nicias in 421 B.C.

The Peace of Nicias resulted in a cold war. But even cold war, as the people of the twentieth century know so well, can bring horror and misery. Such was the case when in 416 B.C. the Athenians sent a fleet to the neutral island of Melos with an ultimatum: the Melians could surrender or perish. The motives of the Athenians were frankly and brutally imperialistic. The Melians resisted. The Athenians conquered them, killed the men of military age, and sold the women and children into slavery.

The cold war grew hotter, thanks to the ambitions of Alcibiades (ca 450–404 B.C.), an aristocrat, kinsman of Pericles, and student of the philosopher Socrates. A shameless opportunist, Alcibiades widened the war to further his own career and to increase the power of Athens. He convinced the Athenians to attack Syracuse, the leading polis in Sicily. The undertaking was vast, requiring an enormous fleet and thousands of sailors and soldiers. Trouble began at the outset. Alcibiades' political enemies indicted him, whereupon he fled to Sparta rather than stand trial. Meanwhile, in 414 B.C. the Athenians laid siege to Syracuse. The Syracusans fought back bravely, and even a huge Athenian relief force failed to conquer the city. Finally, in 413 B.C. the Syracusans counter-attacked, completely crushing the Athenians. Thucydides wrote the epitaph for the Athenians: "infantry, fleet, and everything else were utterly destroyed, and out of many few returned home."[8]

The disaster in Sicily ushered in the final phase of the war, which was marked by three major developments: the renewal of war between Athens and Sparta, Persia's intervention in the war, and the revolt of many Athenian subjects. The year 413 B.C. saw Sparta's declaration of war against Athens and widespread revolt within the Athenian empire. Yet Sparta still lacked a navy, the only instrument that could take advantage of the unrest of Athens's subjects, most of whom lived either on islands or in

Mosaic Portrait of Alcibiades   The artist has caught all the craftiness, intelligence, and quickness of Alcibiades, who became a romantic figure in antiquity. Besides the artistic merit of the portrait, the mosaic is interesting because Alcibiades' name in the upper right corner is misspelled. *(Source: Caroline Buckler)*

Ionia. The sly Alcibiades, now working for Sparta, provided a solution: he engineered an alliance between Sparta and Persia. The Persians agreed to build a fleet for Sparta. In return, the Spartans promised to give Ionia back to Persia. Now equipped with a fleet, the Spartans challenged the Athenians in the Aegean, the result being a long roll of inconclusive naval battles.

The strain of war prompted the Athenians in 407 B.C. to recall Alcibiades from exile. He cheerfully double-crossed the Spartans and Persians, but even he could not restore Athenian fortunes. In 405 B.C. Athens met its match in the Spartan commander Lysander, a man whose grasp of strategy, politics, and diplomacy easily rivaled Alcibiades'. Lysander destroyed the last Athenian fleet at the Battle of Aegospotami, after which the Spartans blockaded Athens until it was starved into submission. After twenty-seven years the Peloponnesian War was over, and the evils prophesied by the Spartan ambassador Melesippus in 431 B.C. had come true.

The Birth of Historical Awareness

One positive development grew out of the Persian and Peloponnesian wars: the beginnings of historical writing. Herodotus (ca 485–425 B.C.), known as the "father of history," was born at Halicarnassus in Asia Minor. As a young man he traveled widely, and later he migrated to Athens, which became his intellectual home.

In his book *The Histories,* Herodotus chronicled the rise of the Persian Empire, sketched the background of Athens and Sparta, and described the land and customs of the Egyptians and the Scythians, who lived in the region of the modern Crimea. The sheer scope of this work is awesome. Lacking newspapers, sophisticated communications, and easy means of travel, Herodotus nevertheless wrote a history that covered the major events of the Near East and Greece.

Perhaps Herodotus's most striking characteristic was his curiosity. He loved to travel, and like most travelers he accumulated a stock of fine stories. But tales and digressions never obscure the central theme of his work. Herodotus diligently questioned everyone who could tell him anything about the Persian wars. The confrontation between East and West unfolds relentlessly in *The Histories,* reach-

ing its climax in the great battles of Salamis and Plataea.

The outbreak of the Peloponnesian War prompted Thucydides (ca 460–ca 400 B.C.) to write a history of its course in the belief that it would be the greatest war in Greek history. An Athenian politician and general, Thucydides saw action in the war until he was exiled for a defeat. Exile gave him the time and opportunity to question eyewitnesses about the details of events and to visit battlefields. Since he was an aristocrat and a prominent man, he had access to the inner circles, the men who made the decisions.

Thucydides was intensely interested in human nature and how it manifested itself during the war. In 430 B.C. a terrible plague struck Athens. Thucydides described both the symptoms of the plague and the reactions of the Athenians in the same clinical terms. He portrayed the virtual breakdown of a society beset by war, disease, desperation, and despair. Similarly, he chronicled the bloody civil war on the island of Corcyra. Instead of condemning the injustice and inhumanity of the fighting, in which citizen turned on citizen and people ruthlessly betrayed their friends, he coolly observed that such things are normal, human nature being what it is.

Thucydides saw the Peloponnesian War as highly destructive to Greek character. He noted—with a visible touch of regret—that the old, the noble, and the simple fell before ambition and lust for power. He firmly rejected any notion that the gods intervened in human affairs. In his view the fate of men and women was, for good or ill, entirely in their own hands.

Athenian Arts in the Age of Pericles

In the last half of the fifth century B.C., Pericles turned Athens into the showplace of Greece. He appropriated Delian League funds to pay for a huge building program, planning temples and other buildings to honor Athena, the patron goddess of the city, and to display to all Greeks the glory of the Athenian polis. Pericles also pointed out that his program would employ a great many Athenians and bring economic prosperity to the city.

Thus began the undertaking that turned the Acropolis into a monument for all time. Construc-

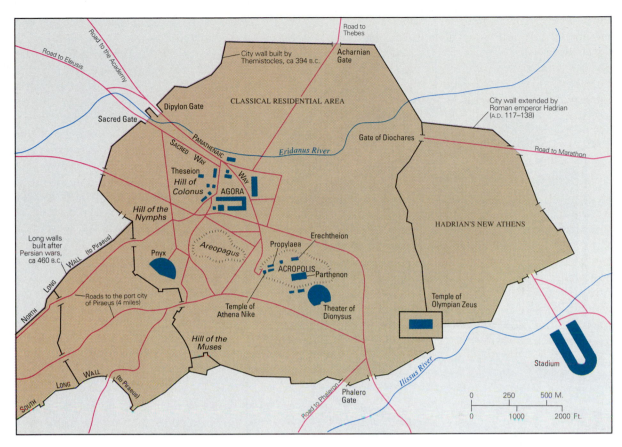

MAP 3.4 Ancient Athens   By modern standards the city of Athens was hardly more than a town, not much larger in size than one square mile. Yet this small area reflects the concentration of ancient Greek life in the polis.

tion of the Parthenon began in 447 B.C., followed by the Propylaea, the temple of Athena Nike (Athena the Victorious), and the Erechtheum (Map 3.4). Even today in their ruined state they still evoke awe. Even the pollution of modern Athens, although it is destroying the ancient buildings, cannot rob them of their splendor and charm.

The planning of the architects and the skill of the workmen who erected these buildings were both very sophisticated. Visitors approaching the Acropolis first saw the Propylaea, the ceremonial gateway, a building of complicated layout and grand design whose Doric columns seemed to hold up the sky. On the right was the small temple of Athena Nike, whose dimensions harmonized with those of the Propylaea. The temple was built to commemorate the victory over the Persians, and the Ionic frieze above its columns depicted the

struggle between the Greeks and the Persians. Here for all the world to see was a tribute to Athenian and Greek valor—and a reminder of Athens's part in the victory.

To the left of the visitors, as they passed through the Propylaea, stood the Erechtheum, an Ionic temple that housed several ancient shrines. On its southern side was the famous Portico of the Caryatids, a porch whose roof was supported by statues of Athenian maidens. The graceful Ionic columns of the Erechtheum provided a delicate relief from the prevailing Doric order of the massive Propylaea and Parthenon (see the illustration on page 84).

As visitors walked on, they obtained a full view of the Parthenon, thought by many to be the perfect Doric temple. The Parthenon was the chief monument to Athena and her city. The sculptures that adorned the temple portrayed the greatness of

FRIEZE COFFERS TYMPANUM

PEDIMENT

CYMATION

CORNICE
MUTULES
TRIGLYPHS
METOPES
GUTTAE
ARCHITRAVE

ABACUS
ECHINUS

STYLOBATE

Sectional View of the Parthenon   This figure both indicates what the Parthenon looked like in antiquity and explains the complex nature of Greek temple-building. As the illustration shows, the Parthenon's apparently simple façade is a work of great architectural sophistication. *(Source: Guide to Sculptures of the Parthenon, a British Museum publication)*

Athens and its goddess. The figures on the eastern pediment depicted Athena's birth, those on the west the victory of Athena over the god Poseidon in their struggle for the possession of Attica. Inside the Parthenon stood a huge statue of Athena, the masterpiece of Phidias, one of the greatest sculptors of all time.

In many ways the Athenian Acropolis is the epitome of Greek art and its spirit. Although the buildings were dedicated to the gods and most of the sculptures portrayed gods, these works nonetheless express the Greek fascination with the human and the rational. Greek deities were anthropomorphic, and Greek artists portrayed them as human beings. While honoring the gods, Greek artists were thus celebrating human beings. In the Parthenon sculp-

tures it is visually impossible to distinguish the men and women from the gods and goddesses. The Acropolis also exhibits the rational side of Greek art. Greek artists portrayed action in a balanced, restrained, and sometimes even serene fashion, capturing the noblest aspects of human beings: their reason, dignity, and promise.

Other aspects of Athenian cultural life were as rooted in the life of the polis as were the architecture and sculpture of the Acropolis. The development of drama was tied to the religious festivals of the city. The polis sponsored the production of plays and required that wealthy citizens pay the expenses of their production. At the beginning of the year, dramatists submitted their plays to the archon. He chose those he considered best and as-

The Parthenon   Stately and graceful, the Parthenon symbolizes the logic, order, and sense of beauty of Greek architecture. The Parthenon was also the centerpiece of Pericles' plan to make Athens the artistic showcase of the Greek world. *(Source: Caroline Buckler)*

signed a theatrical troupe to each playwright. Although most Athenian drama has perished, enough has survived to prove that the archons had superb taste. Many plays were highly controversial, but the archons neither suppressed nor censored them.

The Athenian dramatists were the first artists in Western society to examine such basic questions as the rights of the individual, the demands of society on the individual, and the nature of good and evil. Conflict is a constant element in Athenian drama. The dramatists used their art to portray, understand, and resolve life's basic conflicts.

Aeschylus (525–456 B.C.), the first of the great Athenian dramatists, was also the first to express the agony of the individual caught in conflict. In his trilogy of plays, *The Oresteia,* Aeschylus deals with the themes of betrayal, murder, and reconciliation. *The Agamemnon,* the first play, depicts Agamemnon's return from the Trojan War and his murder by his wife, Clytemnestra, and her lover, Aegisthus. In the second play, *The Libation Bearers,* Orestes, the son of Agamemnon and Clytemnestra, avenges his father's death by killing his mother and her lover. The last play of the trilogy, *The Eumenides,* works out the atonement and absolution of Orestes. The Furies, goddesses who avenged murder and unfilial conduct, demand Orestes' death. When the jury at Orestes' trial casts six votes to condemn and six to acquit him, Athena casts the deciding vote in favor of mercy and compassion. Aeschylus used *The Eumenides* to urge reason and justice to reconcile fundamental conflicts. The play concludes with a prayer that civil dissension never be allowed to destroy the city and that the life of the city be one of harmony and grace.

Sophocles (496–406 B.C.) also dealt with matters personal and political. In *Antigone* he examined the relationship between the individual and the state by exploring a conflict between the ties of kinship and the demands of the polis. In the play Polynices has attacked his own state, Thebes, and has fallen in battle. Creon, the Theban king, refuses to allow Polynices' body to be buried. Polynices' sister Antigone is appalled by Creon's action because custom demands that she bury her brother's corpse. Creon is right in refusing to allow Polynices' body to be buried in the polis but wrong to refuse any burial at all. He continues in his misguided and willful error. As the play progresses, Antigone comes to stand for the precedence of divine law over human defects. Sophocles touches on the need for recognition of the law and adherence to it as a prerequisite for a tranquil state.

A Greek God Few pieces of Greek art better illustrate the conception of the gods as greatly superior forms of human beings than this magnificent statue, over six feet, ten inches in height. Here, the god, who may be either Poseidon or Zeus, is portrayed as powerful and perfect but basically human in form. (Source: National Archaeological Museum, Athens)

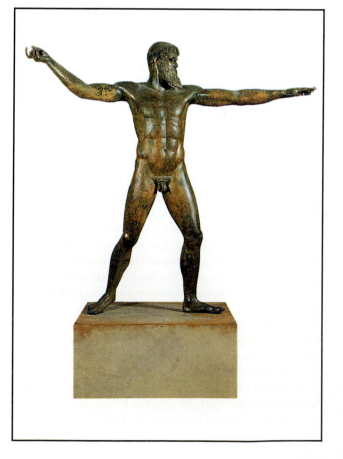

Sophocles' masterpieces have become classics of Western literature, and his themes have inspired generations of playwrights. Perhaps his most famous plays are *Oedipus the King* and its sequel, *Oedipus at Colonus. Oedipus the King* is the ironic story of a man doomed by the gods to kill his father and marry his mother. Try as he might to avoid his fate, Oedipus's every action brings him closer to its fulfillment. When at last he realizes that he has carried out the decree of the gods, Oedipus blinds himself and flees into exile. In *Oedipus at Colonus* Sophocles dramatizes the last days of the broken king, whose patient suffering and uncomplaining piety win him an exalted position. In the end the gods honor him for his virtue. The interpretation of these two plays has been hotly debated, but Sophocles seems to be saying that human beings should do the will of the gods, even without fully understanding it, for the gods stand for justice and order.

Euripides (ca 480–406 B.C.), the last of the three great Greek tragic dramatists, also explored the theme of personal conflict within the polis and sounded the depths of the individual. With Euripides drama entered a new, in many ways more personal, phase. To him the gods were far less important than human beings. Euripides viewed the human soul as a place where opposing forces struggle, where strong passions such as hatred and jealousy conflict with reason. The essence of Euripides' tragedy is the flawed character—men and women who bring disaster on themselves and their loved ones because their passions overwhelm reason. Although Euripides' plays were less popular in his lifetime than those of Aeschylus and Sophocles, Euripides was a dramatist of genius whose work later had a significant impact on Roman drama.

Writers of comedy treated the affairs of the polis bawdily and often coarsely. Even so, their plays, too, were performed at religious festivals. The comic playwrights dealt primarily with the political affairs of the polis and the conduct of its leading politicians. Best known are the comedies of Aristophanes (ca 445–386 B.C.), an ardent lover of his city and a merciless critic of cranks and quacks. He lampooned eminent generals, at times depicting them as morons. He commented snidely on Pericles, poked fun at Socrates, and hooted at Euripides. He saved some of his strongest venom for Cleon, a prominent politician. It is a tribute to the Athenians that such devastating attacks could openly and freely be made on the city's leaders and foreign policy. Even at the height of the Pelopon-

Theater at Delphi   This scene admirably illustrates the religious quality of Greek drama. The theater, in which the great plays of Aeschylus, Sophocles, and Euripides were performed, overlooks the rest of the sanctuary of Apollo of which it is a significant part. The theater stands as a monument to the importance of drama to Greek cultural life. *(Source: Ekdotike Athenon)*

nesian War, Aristophanes proclaimed that peace was preferable to the ravages of war. Like Aeschylus, Sophocles, and Euripides, Aristophanes used his art to dramatize his ideas on the right conduct of the citizen and the value of the polis.

Perhaps never were art and political life so intimately and congenially bound together as at Athens. Athenian art was the product of deep and genuine love of the polis. It aimed at bettering the lives of the citizens and the quality of life in the state.

Daily Life in Periclean Athens

In sharp contrast with the rich intellectual and cultural life of Periclean Athens stands the simplicity of its material life. The Athenians—and in this respect they were typical of Greeks in general—lived very happily with comparatively few material possessions. In the first place, there were very few material goods to own. The thousands of machines, tools, and gadgets considered essential for modern life had no counterparts in Athenian life. The inventory of Alcibiades' goods, which the Athenians confiscated after his desertion, is enlightening. His household possessions consisted of chests, beds, couches, tables, screens, stools, baskets, and mats. Other common items of the Greek home included pottery, metal utensils for cooking, tools, luxury goods such as jewelry, and a few other things. These items they had to buy from craftsmen. Whatever else they needed, such as clothes and blankets, they produced at home.

The Athenian house was rather simple. Whether large or small, the typical house consisted of a series of rooms built around a central courtyard, with doors opening onto the courtyard. Many houses had bedrooms on an upper floor. Artisans and craftsmen often set aside a room to use as a shop or work area. The two principal rooms were the men's dining room and the room where the women worked wool. Other rooms included the kitchen and bathroom. By modern standards there was not much furniture. In the men's dining room were couches, a sideboard, and small tables. Cups and other pottery were often hung on the wall from pegs. Other household furnishings included items such as those confiscated from Alcibiades after his desertion.

In the courtyard were the well, a small altar, and a washbasin. If the family lived in the country, the stalls of the animals faced the courtyard. Country dwellers kept oxen for plowing, pigs for slaughtering, sheep for wool, goats for cheese, and mules and donkeys for transportation. Even in the city, chickens and perhaps a goat or two roamed the courtyard together with dogs and cats.

Cooking, done over a hearth in the house, provided welcome warmth in the winter. Baking and roasting were done in ovens. Food consisted primarily of various grains, especially wheat and barley, as well as lentils, olives, figs, and grapes. Garlic and onion were popular garnishes, and wine was always on hand. These foods were stored at home in large jars; with them the Greek family sometimes ate fish, chicken, and vegetables. Women ground wheat into flour, baked it into bread, and on special occasions made honey or sesame cakes. The Greeks used olive oil for cooking, as families still do in modern Greece; they also used it as an unguent and as lamp fuel.

By American standards the Greeks did not eat much meat. On special occasions, such as important religious festivals, the family ate the animal sacrificed to the god and gave the god the exquisite delicacy of the thighbone wrapped in fat. The only Greeks who consistently ate meat were the Spartan warriors. They received a small portion of meat each day, together with the infamous Spartan black broth, a ghastly concoction of pork cooked in blood, vinegar, and salt. One Greek, after tasting the broth, commented that he could easily understand why the Spartans were so willing to die.

In the city a man might support himself as a craftsman—a potter, bronzesmith, sailmaker, or tanner—or he could contract with the polis to work on public buildings, such as the Parthenon and Erechtheum. Men without skills worked as paid laborers but competed with slaves for work. Slaves—usually foreigners, barbarian as well as Greek—were paid the same amount for their employment as were free men.

Slavery was commonplace in Greece, as it was throughout the ancient world. In its essentials Greek slavery resembled Mesopotamian slavery. Slaves received some protection under the law and could buy their freedom. On the other hand, masters could mistreat or neglect their slaves, although killing them was illegal. Most slaves in Athens served as domestics and performed light labor around the house. Nurses for children, teachers of reading and writing, and guardians for young men were often slaves. The lives of these slaves were much like those of their owners. Other slaves were skilled workers, who could be found working on public buildings or in small workshops.

The importance of slavery in Athens must not be exaggerated. Athenians did not own huge gangs of slaves as did Roman owners of large estates. Slave labor competed with free labor and kept wages down, but it never replaced the free labor that was the mainstay of the Athenian economy.

Most Athenians supported themselves by agriculture, but unless the family was fortunate enough to possess holdings in a plain more fertile than most of the land, they found it difficult to reap a good crop from the soil. Many people must have consumed nearly everything they raised. Attic farmers were free and, though hardly prosperous, by no means destitute. They could usually expect yields of five bushels of wheat and ten of barley per acre for every bushel of grain sown. A bad harvest meant a lean year. In many places farmers grew more barley than wheat because of the nature of the soil. Wherever possible, farmers also cultivated vines and olive trees.

For sport both countryman and city dweller often hunted for rabbits, deer, or wild boar. A successful hunt supplemented the family's regular diet. Wealthy men hunted on horseback; most others hunted on foot with their dogs. Hunting also allowed a man to display to his fellows his bravery and prowess in the chase. If wild boar were the prey, the sport could be dangerous, as Odysseus discovered when a charging boar slashed open his thigh.

The social condition of Athenian women has been the subject of much debate and little agreement. One of the difficulties is the fragmentary nature of the evidence. Women appear frequently in literature and art, often in idealized roles, but seldom in historical contexts of a wider and more realistic nature. This is due in part to the fact that most Greek historians of the time recounted primarily the political, diplomatic, and military events of the day, events in which women seldom played a notable part. Yet that does not mean that women were totally invisible in the life of the polis. It indicates instead that ancient sources provide only a glimpse of how women affected the society in which they lived. Greek wives, for example, played an important economic and social role by their management of the household. Perhaps the best way to describe the position of the free woman in Greek society is to use the anthropologist's term *liminal,* which means in this case that although women lacked official power, they nonetheless played a vital role in shaping the society in which they lived. The same situation had existed in Hammurabi's Babylonia, and it would later recur in the Hellenistic period. The mere fact that Athenian and other Greek women did not sit in the assembly does not mean that they did not influence public affairs.

The status of a free woman of the citizen class was strictly protected by law. Only her children, not those of foreigners or slaves, could be citizens. Only she was in charge of the household and the family's possessions. Yet the law protected her primarily to protect her husband's interests. Raping a free woman was a lesser crime than seducing her, because seduction involved the winning of her affections. This law was not concerned with the husband's feelings but with ensuring that he need not doubt the legitimacy of his children.

Women both in Athens and elsewhere in Greece received a certain amount of social and legal protection from their dowries. Upon marriage, the bride's father gave the couple a gift of land or money, which the husband administered. However, it was never his; and in the rare cases of divorce, it returned to the wife's domain. The same is often true in Greece today among the upper class.

Ideally, respectable women lived a secluded life in which the only men they saw were relatives. How far this ideal was actually put into practice is impossible to say. At least Athenian women seem to have enjoyed a social circle of other women of their own class. They also attended public festivals, sacrifices, and funerals. Nonetheless, prosperous and respectable women probably spent much of their time in the house. A white complexion—a sign that a woman did not have to work in the fields—was valued highly.

Courtesans lived the freest lives of all Athenian women. Although some courtesans were simply prostitutes, others added intellectual accomplishments to physical beauty. In constant demand, cultured courtesans moved freely in male society. Their artistic talents and intellectual abilities appealed to men who wanted more than sex. The most famous of all courtesans was Aspasia, mistress of Pericles and supposedly a friend of Socrates. Under Pericles' roof, she participated in intellectual discussions equally with some of the most stimulating thinkers of the day. Yet her position, like that of most other courtesans, was precarious. After Pericles' death, Aspasia fended for herself, ending her days as the madam of a house of prostitution.

A woman's main functions were to raise the children, oversee the domestic slaves and hired labor, and together with her maids work wool into cloth. The women washed the wool in the courtyard and then brought it into the women's room, where the loom stood. They spun the wool into thread and wove the thread into cloth. They also dyed wool at home and decorated the cloth by weaving in colors and designs. The woman of the household either did the cooking herself or directed her maids. In a sense, poor women lived freer lives than did wealthier women. They performed manual labor in the fields or sold goods in the agora, going about their affairs much as men did.

A distinctive feature of Athenian life and of Greek life in general was acceptance of homosexuality. The Greeks accepted the belief that both homosexual and heterosexual practices were normal parts of life. They did not think that these practices created any particular problems for those who engaged in them.

No one has satisfactorily explained how the Greek attitude toward homosexual love developed or determined how common homosexual behavior was. Homosexuality was probably far more common among the aristocracy than among the lower classes. Even among the aristocracy, attitudes toward homosexuality were complex and sometimes conflicting. Most people saw homosexual love affairs among the young as a stage in the development of a mature heterosexual life. Warrior-aristocracies generally emphasized the physical side of the relationship in the belief that warriors who were also lovers would fight all the harder to impress and to protect each other. Whatever their intellectual content, homosexual love affairs were also overtly sexual.

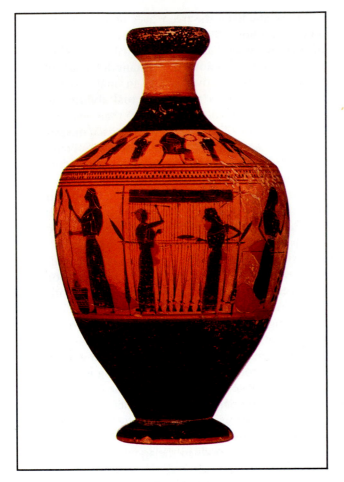

Women Working The scene on this vase represents the women of the household at work. It shows how they produced woolen cloth, from the spinning of yarn to the completion of the cloth itself, here held by two women. (Source: The Metropolitan Museum of Art, Fletcher Fund, 1931)

One particularly important aspect of social life in Athens and elsewhere in Greece was religion. Yet Greek religion is extremely difficult for modern people to understand, largely because of the great differences between Greek and modern cultures. In the first place, it is not even easy to talk about "Greek religion," since the Greeks had no uniform faith or creed. Although the Greeks usually worshiped the same deities—Zeus, Hera, Apollo, Athena, and others—the cults of these gods and goddesses varied from polis to polis. The Greeks had no sacred books such as the Bible, and Greek religion was often a matter more of ritual than of belief. Nor did cults impose an ethical code of conduct. Greeks did not have to follow any particular

rule of life, practice certain virtues, or even live decent lives in order to participate. Unlike the Egyptians and Hebrews, the Greeks lacked a priesthood as the modern world understands the term. In Greece priests and priestesses existed to care for temples and sacred property and to conduct the proper rituals, but not to make religious rules or doctrines, much less to enforce them. In short, there existed in Greece no central ecclesiastical authority and no organized creed.

Although temples to the gods were common, they were unlike modern churches or synagogues in that they were not normally places where a congregation met to worship as a spiritual community. Instead, the individual Greek either visited the temple occasionally on matters of private concern or walked in a procession to a particular temple to celebrate a particular festival. In Greek religion the altar, which stood outside the temple, was important; when the Greeks sought the favor of the gods, they offered them sacrifices. Greek religious observances were generally cheerful. Festivals and sacrifices were frequently times for people to meet together socially, times of high spirits and conviviality rather than of pious gloom. By offering the gods parts of the sacrifice while consuming the rest themselves, worshipers forged a bond with the gods.

Besides the Olympian gods, each polis had its own minor deities, each with his or her own local cult. In many instances Greek religion involved the official gods and goddesses of the polis and their cults. The polis administered the cults and festivals, and all were expected to participate in this civic religion, regardless of whether they even believed in the deities being worshiped. Participating unbelievers, who seem to have been a small minority, were not considered hypocrites. Rather, they were seen as patriotic, loyal citizens who in honoring the gods also honored the polis. If this attitude seems contradictory, an analogy may help. Before baseball games Americans stand at the playing of the national anthem, whether they are Democrats, Republicans, or neither, and whether they agree or disagree with the policies of the current administration. They honor their nation as represented by its flag, in somewhat the same way an ancient Greek honored the polis and demonstrated solidarity with it by participating in the state cults.

Though Greek religion in general was individual or related to the polis, the Greeks also shared some pan-Hellenic festivals, the chief of which were held at Olympia in honor of Zeus and at Delphi in honor of Apollo. The festivities at Olympia included the famous games, athletic contests that have inspired the modern Olympic games. Held every four years, these games were for the glory of Zeus. They attracted visitors from all over the Greek world and lasted well into Christian times. The Pythian games at Delphi were also held every four years, but these contests differed from the Olympic games by including musical and literary contests. Both the Olympic and the Pythian games were unifying factors in Greek life, bringing Greeks together culturally as well as religiously.

The Flowering of Philosophy

The myths and epics of the Mesopotamians are ample testimony that speculation about the origin of the universe and of mankind did not begin with the Greeks. The signal achievement of the Greeks was the willingness of some to treat these questions in rational rather than mythological terms. Although Greek philosophy did not fully flower until the Classical period, Ionian thinkers had already begun in the Lyric Age to ask what the universe was made of. These men are called the Pre-Socratics, for their work preceded the philosophical revolution begun by the Athenian Socrates. Though they were keen observers, the Pre-Socratics rarely undertook deliberate experimentation. Instead, they took individual facts and wove them into general theories. Despite appearances, they believed, the universe was actually simple and subject to natural laws. Drawing on their observations, they speculated about the basic building blocks of the universe.

The first of the Pre-Socratics, Thales (ca 600 B.C.), learned mathematics and astronomy from the Babylonians and geometry from the Egyptians. Yet there was an immense and fundamental difference between Near Eastern thought and the philosophy of Thales. The Near Eastern peoples considered such events as eclipses to be evil omens. Thales viewed them as natural phenomena that could be explained in natural terms. In short, he asked *why* things happened. He believed the basic element of the universe to be water. Although he was wrong, the way in which he had asked the question was momentous: it was the beginning of the scientific method.

Thales' follower Anaximander continued his work. Anaximander was the first of the Pre-Socratics to use general concepts, which are essential to abstract thought. One of the most brilliant of the Pre-Socratics, a man of striking originality, Anaximander theorized that the basic element of the universe is the "boundless" or "endless"—something infinite and indestructible. In his view, the earth floats in a void, held in balance by its distance from everything else in the universe. Anaximander even concluded that mankind had evolved naturally from lower organisms: "In water the first animal arose covered with spiny skin, and with the lapse of time some crawled onto dry land and breaking off their skins in a short time they survived."[9] This remarkable speculation corresponds crudely to Darwin's theory of evolution of species, although it predated Darwin by two and a half millennia.

Another Ionian, Heraclitus (ca 500 B.C.), declared the primal element to be fire. He also declared that the world had neither beginning nor end: "This world, the world of all things, neither any god nor man made, but it always was and it is and it will be: an everlasting fire, measures kindling and measures going out."[10] Although the universe was eternal, according to Heraclitus, it changed constantly. An outgrowth of this line of speculation was the theory of Democritus that the universe is made of invisible, indestructible atoms. The culmination of Pre-Socratic thought was the theory that four simple substances make up the universe: fire, air, earth, and water.

With this impressive heritage behind them, the philosophers of the Classical period ventured into new areas of speculation. This development was partly due to the work of Hippocrates (second half of the fifth century B.C.), the father of medicine. Like Thales, Hippocrates sought natural explanations for natural phenomena. Basing his opinions on empirical knowledge, not on religion or magic, he taught that natural means could be employed to fight disease. In his treatise *On Airs, Waters, and Places,* he noted the influence of climate and environment on health. Hippocrates and his followers put forward a theory that was to prevail in medical circles until the eighteenth century. The human body, they declared, contains four *humors,* or fluids: blood, phlegm, black bile, and yellow bile. In a healthy body the four humors are in perfect balance; too much or too little of any particular humor causes illness. But Hippocrates broke away from the mainstream of Ionian speculation by declaring that medicine was a separate craft—just as ironworking was—that had its own principles.

The distinction between natural science and philosophy, upon which Hippocrates insisted, was also promoted by the Sophists, who traveled the Greek world teaching young men. Despite differences of opinion on philosophical matters, the Sophists all agreed that human beings were the proper subject of study. They also believed that excellence could be taught, and they used philosophy and rhetoric to prepare young men for life in the

Socrates According to tradition, Socrates was homely at best. Yet this Roman copy of a fourth-century Greek statue has captured the simplicity and the thoughtfulness of the man. It also gives a sense of his intellectual exploration of basic human values. *(Source: Courtesy of the Trustees of the British Museum)*

polis. The Sophists laid great emphasis on logic and the meanings of words. They criticized traditional beliefs, religion, rituals, and myth and even questioned the laws of the polis. In essence, they argued that nothing is absolute, that everything is relative. Hence more traditional Greeks considered them wanton and harmful, men who were interested in "making the worse seem the better cause."

One of those whose contemporaries thought him a Sophist was Socrates (ca 470–399 B.C.), who sprang from the class of small artisans. Socrates spent his life in investigation and definition. Not strictly speaking a Sophist, because he never formally taught or collected fees from anyone, Socrates shared the Sophists' belief that human beings and their environment are the essential subjects of philosophical inquiry. Like the Sophists, Socrates thought that excellence could be learned and passed on to others. His approach when posing ethical questions and defining concepts was to start with a general topic or problem and to narrow the matter to its essentials. He did so by continuous questioning, a running dialogue. Never did he lecture. Socrates thought that by constantly pursuing excellence, an essential part of which was knowledge, human beings could approach the supreme good and thus find true happiness. Yet in 399 B.C. Socrates was brought to trial, convicted, and executed on charges of corrupting the youth of the city and introducing new gods.

Socrates' student Plato (427–347 B.C.) carried on his master's search for truth. Unlike Socrates, Plato wrote down his thoughts and theories and founded a philosophical school, the Academy. Plato developed the theory that all visible, tangible things are unreal and temporary, copies of "forms" or "ideas" that are constant and indestructible. Only the mind, not the senses, can perceive eternal forms. In Plato's view the highest form is the idea of good.

In *The Republic* Plato applied his theory of forms to politics in an effort to describe the ideal polis. His perfect polis was utopian; it aimed at providing the greatest good and happiness to all its members. Plato thought that the ideal polis could exist only if its rulers were philosophers. He divided society into rulers, guardians of the polis, and workers. The role of people in each category would be decided by the education, wisdom, and ability of the individual. In Plato's republic men and women would be equal to one another, and women could become rulers. The utopian polis would be a balance, with each individual doing what he or she could to support the state and with each receiving from the state his or her just due.

Aristotle (384–322 B.C.) carried on the philosophical tradition of Socrates and Plato. A student of Plato, Aristotle went far beyond him in striving to understand the universe. The range of Aristotle's thought is staggering. Everything in human experience was fit subject for his inquiry. In *Politics* Aristotle followed Plato's lead by writing about the ideal polis. Yet Aristotle approached the question more realistically than Plato and criticized *The Republic* and Plato's other writings on many points. In his *Politics* and elsewhere, Aristotle stressed moderation, concluding that the balance of his ideal state depended on people of talent and education who could avoid extremes.

Aristotle also tried to understand the changes of nature—what caused them and where they led. In *Physics* and *Metaphysics* he evolved a theory of nature that developed the notions of matter, form, and motion. He attempted to bridge the gap that Plato had created between abstract truth and concrete perception.

In *On the Heaven* Aristotle took up the thread of Ionian speculation. His theory of cosmology added ether to air, fire, water, and earth as building blocks of the universe. He concluded that the universe revolves and that it is spherical and eternal. He wrongly thought that the earth is the center of the universe, with the stars and planets revolving around it. The Hellenistic scientist Aristarchus of Samos later realized that the earth revolves around the sun, but Aristotle's view was accepted until the time of the sixteenth-century astronomer Nicolaus Copernicus.

Aristotle possessed one of the keenest and most curious philosophical minds of Western civilization. While rethinking the old topics explored by the Pre-Socratics, he also created whole new areas of study. In short, he tried to learn everything possible about the universe and everything in it. He did so in the belief that all knowledge could be synthesized to produce a simple explanation of the universe and of humanity.

The Final Act (404–338 B.C.)

When the Spartan commander Lysander defeated Athens in 404 B.C., he ordered the city's mighty walls torn down to the accompaniment of music provided by flute-girls. The Greeks thought "that day was the beginning of freedom for Greece."[11] The hopes of the Greeks were soon to be brutally dashed, for the aftermath of the Peloponnesian War brought more war until finally the Macedonian king Philip II conquered Greece in 338 B.C.

The turbulent period from 404 to 338 B.C. is sometimes mistakenly seen as a period of failure and decline. It was instead a vibrant era in which Plato and Aristotle thought and wrote, one in which literature, oratory, and historical writing flourished. The architects of the fourth century B.C. designed and built some of the finest buildings of the Classical period, and engineering made great strides. If the fourth century was a period of decline, this was so only in politics. The Peloponnesian War and its aftermath proved that the polis had reached the limits of its success as an effective political institution. The attempts of various city-states to dominate the others led only to incessant warfare. The polis system was committing suicide. Yet many practical and thoughtful Greeks recognized this problem and actively worked to solve it. They failed in the end, but many of their attempts proved useful to later generations.

The Greeks of the fourth century B.C. experimented seriously with two political concepts in the hope of preventing war. First was the "Common Peace," the idea that the states of Greece, whether large or small, should live together in peace and freedom, each enjoying its own laws and customs. In 386 B.C. this concept was a vital part of a peace treaty with the Persian Empire, in which the Greeks and Persians pledged themselves to live in harmony. The Common Peace thus tried to prevent one Greek state from dominating others and to enable them all to enjoy peaceful relations with Persia. Ultimately the Common Peace failed to end war among the Greeks, largely because of the unbridled rivalry of Sparta, Athens, and Thebes, but the Greeks kept trying to make it work, an attempt that war-weary people of the twentieth century can deeply respect and understand.

Federalism, the second concept to become prominent, already had a long history in some parts of Greece (see page 71). Strictly speaking, the new impetus toward federalism was intended more to gain security through numbers than to prevent war. Greek leagues had usually grown up in regions where geography shaped a well-defined area and where people shared a broad kinship. By banding together, the people in these leagues could marshal their resources, both human and material, to defend themselves from outside interference. For instance, the confederacy of the city-states of Boeotia dated back to the sixth century B.C., and by joining forces the members of this league became a major power in Greece. In the fourth century B.C. at least ten other federations of states either came into being or were revitalized (Map 3.5). Federalism never led to a United States of Greece, but the concept held great importance not only for fourth-century Greeks but also for the Hellenistic period and beyond. In 1787, when the Founding Fathers met in Philadelphia to frame the Constitution of the United States, they studied Greek federalism very seriously in the hope that the Greek past could help guide the American future.

The Struggle for Hegemony

If neither the Common Peace nor federalism put an end to inter-state rivalry, the principal reason was the stubborn desire of the principal states to dominate the others. The chief states, Sparta, Athens, and Thebes, each tried to create a *hegemony,* that is, a political ascendancy over other states, even though they sometimes paid lip service to the ideals of the Common Peace. In every instance, the ambition, jealousy, pride, and fear of the major powers doomed the effort to achieve genuine peace. In short, each major power wanted to be the leader, or *hegemon,* and refused to bow to the others who aspired to the same position.

The very defeat of Athens spawned several immediate problems both in Sparta and in the Aegean. The Spartans of 431 B.C. had proclaimed that they were fighting for the liberty of the Greeks. Yet the length of the struggle meant that by 404 B.C. a whole new generation of leaders had come to power who had never known anything but war. These people considered it hopelessly naive for Sparta to have fought for twenty-seven years only to dismantle the Athenian empire. Instead, Lysander persuaded Sparta to take the place of Athens as the head of a new empire. It was a cynical betrayal of Spartan ideals, but Lysander prevailed, and soon the Greeks learned that they had suffered the horrors of a long war only to exchange masters.

Their decision for empire quickly brought the Spartans into conflict with Persia, which now de-

manded the return of Ionia to its control (see page 82), and also with their own allies. The Spartan king Agesilaos, an impetuous man of mediocre ability, waged a fruitless war against the Persians in Ionia. From 400 to 396 B.C. the war dragged on, while relations between Sparta and its allies deteriorated. Finally, in 395 B.C. the war took a new twist when Thebes, Corinth, and Athens accepted Persian support for a war in Greece itself against Sparta. The result was the Corinthian War (395–386 B.C.), which saw Spartan hopes of empire thwarted. After years of indecisive fighting, the Spartans broke the stalemate by offering peace to the Persians if they dropped their support of Sparta's enemies. The Spartans promised not to attack Persia, to honor its right to rule Ionia, and to confine their ambitions to Greece alone. The result was the first formal Common Peace, the King's Peace of 386 B.C., which cost Sparta its empire but not its position of ascendancy in Greece.

Agesilaos was not intelligent enough to use the peace to consolidate Spartan power. Not content with Sparta's hegemony of Greece, he cynically betrayed the very concept of the Common Peace to punish cities that had opposed Sparta during the war. He turned first against some of his own allies who had lent Sparta half-hearted support, but who had done nothing to violate the Common Peace. He treacherously ordered Thebes to be seized and even condoned an unwarranted and unsuccessful attack on Athens. Agesilaos had gone too far. Even though it appeared that his naked use of force had made Sparta supreme in Greece, his imperialism was soon to lead to Sparta's downfall at the hands of the Thebans, the very people whom he sought to tyrannize.

The first sign of his failure, however, came from Athens in 378 B.C. Enraged by the unprovoked attack, the Athenians created the Second Athenian Confederacy—a federation of states, under the leadership of Athens, established to guarantee to the Greeks their rights under the Common Peace (see Map 3.5). Here, for the first time, a state had combined the three concepts of hegemony, federalism, and the Common Peace. Agesilaos's aggression also prompted the Thebans to regain their freedom and to re-establish the Boeotian Confederacy. The tide had turned against Sparta. Thebes and Athens united and fought Sparta so successfully that in 371 B.C. Agesilaos sought peace with Athens in order to destroy Thebes. The decision

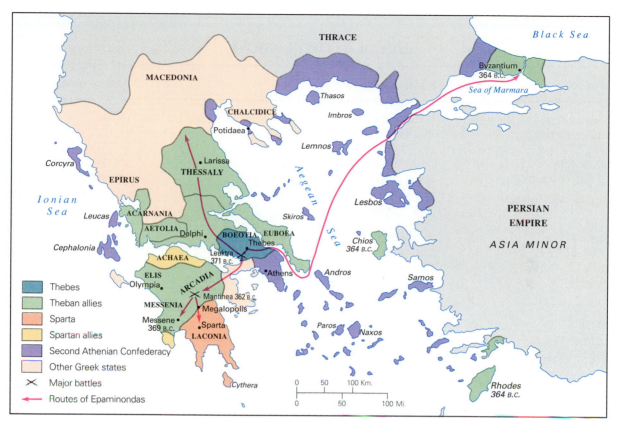

Map 3.5 Greece at 362 B.C. The fourth century B.C. witnessed the rapid growth of Greek federalism as states sought allies to gain security from rival powers.

proved fatal. The Thebans carried on the war alone, and in the summer of 371 B.C. their brilliant general Epaminondas decisively defeated a superior Spartan army at the battle of Leuctra. On one day the Spartans lost their hegemony in trying to reconquer Thebes; henceforth they would fight for their very homes.

The defeat of the once-invincible Spartans stunned the Greeks, who wondered how Thebes would use its victory. The architect of that victory, Epaminondas, was also a gifted statesman, who immediately grappled with the problem of how to translate military success into political reality. First, in a series of invasions he eliminated Sparta as a major power and liberated Messenia. He concluded alliances with many Peloponnesian states but made no effort to dominate them. Steadfastly refusing to create a Theban empire, he instead sponsored federalism in Greece. He also threw his support behind the Common Peace. Although he

made Thebes the leader of Greece from 371 to 362 B.C., other city-states and leagues were bound to Thebes only by voluntary alliances. By his insistence on the liberty of the Greeks, Epaminondas, more than any other person in Greek history, successfully blended the three concepts of hegemony, federalism, and the Common Peace. His premature death at the Battle of Mantinea in 362 B.C. put an end to his efforts, but not to these three political ideals. The question in 362 B.C. was whether anyone or any state could realize them all.

Philip and the Macedonian Conquest

While the Greek states exhausted one another in endless conflicts, a new and unlikely power rose in the north. In 359 B.C. Philip II, one of the most remarkable men in history, became king of Macedonia. Macedonia was by nature potentially strong.

PERIODS OF GREEK HISTORY

Period	Significant Events	Major Writers
Bronze Age 2000–1100 B.C.	Arrival of the Greeks in Greece Rise and fall of the Mycenaean kingdoms	
Dark Age 1100–800 B.C.	Greek migrations within the Aegean basin Social and political recovery Evolution of the polis Rebirth of literacy	Homer Hesiod
Lyric Age 800–500 B.C.	Rise of Sparta and Athens Colonization of the Mediterranean basin Flowering of lyric poetry Development of philosophy and science in Ionia	Archilochus Sappho Tyrtaeus Solon Anaximander Heraclitus
Classical Age 500–338 B.C.	Persian wars Growth of the Athenian Empire Peloponnesian War Rise of drama and historical writing Flowering of Greek philosophy Spartan and Theban hegemonies Conquest of Greece by Philip of Macedon	Herodotus Thucydides Aeschylus Sophocles Euripides Aristophanes Plato Aristotle

The land, extensive and generally fertile, bordered on the east by the Aegean Sea, nurtured a numerous and hardy population. Yet Macedonia was often distracted by foreign opportunists, the Athenians among them, and divided by internal dissension. Nevertheless, under a strong king Macedonia was a power to be reckoned with. Although the Greeks considered the Macedonians backward, Philip was a brilliant, cultured, and sometimes charming man. As a youth he spent several years in Thebes, when Epaminondas was at the height of his powers. In Thebes Philip learned about Greek politics and observed the military innovations of Epaminondas. He also fully understood the strengths and needs of the Macedonians, whose devotion he won virtually on the day that he ascended the throne.

The young Philip, already a master of diplomacy and warfare, quickly saw Athens as the principal threat to Macedonia. Once he had secured the borders of Macedonia against barbarian invaders,

he launched a series of military operations in the northwestern Aegean. Not only did he win rich territory, but he also slowly pushed the Athenians out of the region. Yet the Greeks themselves opened to him the road to ultimate victory in Greece. The opportunity came from still another internecine Greek conflict, the Sacred War of 356–346 B.C. The war broke out when the Phocians seized and plundered the sanctuary of Apollo at Delphi, their sacrilege openly condoned by Athens and Sparta. Although the Thebans and other Greeks struggled for ten years to liberate Delphi, failure and exhaustion finally compelled them to seek help from Philip. Thus invited to join a holy crusade, Philip and his Macedonians quickly crushed the Phocians in 346 B.C. and intimidated Athens and Sparta. Philip had entered the mainstream of Greek politics not as an invader but as a savior.

In 346 B.C. Philip seized the opportunity to make peace with Athens. Nonetheless, he pushed ever eastwards in the northern Aegean, a move that endangered vital Athenian interests there. One man in Athens, the orator and politician Demosthenes, realized the gravity of the Macedonian threat and tried vainly to warn his countrymen and the rest of Greece of Macedonian aggression. Others, too, saw Philip as a threat. A comic playwright used graveyard humor to depict one of Philip's ambassadors warning the Athenians:

Do you know that your battle will be with men
Who dine on sharpened swords,
And gulp burning firebrands for wine?
Then immediately after dinner the slave
Brings us dessert—Cretan arrows
Or pieces of broken spears.
We have shields and breastplates for
Cushions and at our feet slings and arrows,
And we are crowned with catapults.[12]

These dire predictions and the progress of Philip's military operations at last had their effect. Demosthenes persuaded the Athenians to make an alliance with Thebes, which also recognized the Macedonian threat. In 338 B.C. the armies of Thebes and Athens met Philip's veterans at the Boeotian city of Chaeronea. There on one summer's day Philip's army won a hard-fought victory that gave him command of Greece and put an end to classical Greek freedom. Because the Greeks could not put aside their quarrels, they fell to an invader. Yet Philip was wise enough to retain much of what the fourth-century Greeks had achieved. Not opposed to the concepts of peace and federalism, he sponsored a new Common Peace in which all of Greece, except Sparta, was united in one political body under his leadership. Philip thus used the concepts of hegemony, the Common Peace, and federalism as tools of Macedonian domination. The ironic result was the end of the age of Classical Greece.

SUMMARY

The mountainous geography of Greece divided the land into small pockets, so that at first small settlements were the natural pattern of human inhabitation. Never cut off from one another, these settlements evolved a common political and social institution, the polis. Although the causes for this common development are still unknown, the polis

The Lion of Chaeronea   This stylized lion marks the mass grave of nearly 300 elite Theban soldiers who valiantly died fighting the Macedonians at the Battle of Chaeronea. After the battle, when Philip viewed the bodies of these brave troops, he said: "May those who suppose that these men did or suffered anything dishonorable perish wretchedly." *(Source: Caroline Buckler)*

proved basic to Greek life. It was far different from the political institutions of the earlier Minoan and Mycenaean kingdoms, which did, however, leave all Greeks the heritage of a heroic past. Through the poetry of Homer and the monumental ruins of the Bronze Age, later Greeks remembered a time when great kings ruled the land. The polis, however, was a dramatic break with this past, and in this atmosphere the Greeks developed basic political forms that are still alive in the contemporary world. The Greeks gave serious thought to the relationship between society and the polis and the nature of political rights. From these thoughts, which they put into practice, developed concepts like democracy and tyranny. The Greek passion for open debates and exchange of ideas was also important to the intellectual explosion of Greek philosophy. Not bound to religions, Greek philosophy considered the human mind to be a sufficient tool to understand the cosmos. This very line of thinking underlies modern scientific thought. In view of all their great achievements, it seems incomprehensible that the Greeks and their polis could fail. Yet the desire of several powerful city-states to dominate the others led to years of warfare that eventually weakened them all and left them vulnerable to the successful invasion of the Macedonian king, Philip II.

NOTES

1. K. J. Beloch, *Griechische Geschichte,* vol. 1, pt. 1 (Strassburg: K. J. Trubner, 1912), p. 49. John Buckler is the translator of all uncited quotations from a foreign language in Chapters 1–6.
2. Hesiod, *Works and Days* 263–266.
3. F. Lasserre, *Archiloque* (Paris: Société d'Edition "Les Belles Lettres," 1958), frag. 9, p. 4.
4. W. Barnstable, *Sappho* (Garden City, N.Y.: Doubleday, 1965), frag. 24, p. 22.
5. Ibid., frag. 132, p. 106.
6. J. M. Edmonds, *Greek Elegy and Iambus* (Cambridge, Mass.: Harvard University Press, 1931), I.70, frag. 10.
7. Thucydides, *History of the Peloponnesian War* 1.23.
8. Ibid., 7.87.6.
9. E. Diels and W. Krantz, *Fragmente der Vorsokratiker,* 8th ed. (Berlin: Weidmannsche Verlagsbuchhandlung, 1960), Anaximander frag. A30.
10. Ibid., Heraclitus frag. B30.
11. Xenophon, *Hellenika* 2.2.23.
12. J. M. Edmonds, *The Fragments of Attic Comedy* (Leiden: E. J. Brill, 1957), 2.366–369, Mnesimachos frag. 7.

SUGGESTED READING

Translations of the most important writings of the Greeks and Romans can be found in the volumes of the Loeb Classical Library published by Harvard University Press. Paperback editions of the major Greek and Latin authors are available in the Penguin Classics. Recent translations of documents include the two volumes of *Translated Documents of Greece and Rome:* volume 1, by C. Fornara, *Archaic Times to the End of the Peloponnesian War* (1977); and volume 2, by P. Harding, *From the End of the Peloponnesian War to the Battle of Ipsus* (1985). M. Crawford and D. Whitehead, eds., *Archaic and Classical Greece: A Selection of Ancient Sources in Translation* (1983), is of uneven quality and inferior to the collections of Fornara and Harding.

Among the many general treatments of Greek history is that of H. Bengtson, *Griechische Geschichte,* 4th ed. (1969), which is now available in an English translation by E. F. Bloedow under the title *History of Greece* (1988); the translation is additionally valuable because of the added bibliography. Another sound general treatment is J. Fine, *The Ancient Greeks* (1984).

A number of books on early Greece are available in addition to those cited in the notes. A good, careful, and learned synthesis can be found in Lord W. Taylour, *The Mycenaeans,* rev. ed. (1983). More recent and wider in coverage is R. Drews, *The Coming of the Greeks* (1988), which puts the movements of the Greeks in the broader context of Indo-European migrations. M. Mueller, *The Iliad* (1984), discusses both the historical and the heroic aspects of one of the world's great poems. No finer introduction to the Lyric Age can be found than A. R. Burn's *The Lyric Age* (1960). Its sequel, *Persia and the Greeks,* 2d ed. (1984), which is still unsurpassed, carries the history of Greece to the defeat of the Persians in 479 B.C. More recent, however, is J. Boardman et al., *The Cambridge Ancient History,* 2d ed., vol. 4 (1988), which is profusely illustrated. It treats Greek and Mediterranean history from about 525 to 479 B.C., but the coverage is very uneven. C. Roebuck, *Economy and Society in the Early Greek World* (1984), treats several aspects of early Greek developments. A. J. Graham, *Colony and Mother City in Ancient Greece,* rev. ed. (1984), gives a good account of Greek colonization.

A good survey of work on Sparta is P. Cartledge, *Sparta and Lakonia* (1979), which can be warmly recommended. J. F. Lazenby, *The Spartan Army* (1985), studies the evolution and performance of the Spartan army somewhat apart from its social setting. The Athenian democracy and the society that produced it continue to attract scholarly attention. Interesting and important are two studies by R. Osborne. His *Demos* (1985) deals with many political and social aspects of early Athenian history. His *Classical Landscape with Figures* (1987) takes a new look at the relation of the polis to its surrounding territory, part of a growing trend in ancient history to blend archeological and literary evidence to understand ancient society. A series of new studies re-evaluates aspects of the Athenian democracy: M. Ostwald, *From Popular Sovereignty to the Sovereignty of Law* (1986); M. H. Hansen, *The Athenian Assembly* (1987); and J. Ober, *Mass and Elite in Democratic Athens* (1989). J. W. Roberts, *City of Socrates* (1987), is a recent and readable survey of Athens at its zenith.

The Athenian Empire and the outbreak of the Peloponnesian War are covered by R. Meiggs, *The Athenian Empire* (1972), and M. McGregor, *The Athenians and Their Empire* (1987). The best account of the outbreak of the Peloponnesian War, despite its defects, is G. E. M. de Ste. Croix, *The Origins of the Peloponnesian War* (1972). A concise treatment of the Peloponnesian War from a military point of view can be found in A. Ferrill, *The Origins of War* (1985), chap. 4. A. Forde, *The Ambition to Rule* (1989), places Thucydides' treatment of Alcibiades in the context of politics and imperialism.

The fourth century has been one of the most fertile fields of recent research. D. M. Lewis, *Sparta and Persia* (1977), is rich in information on the administration of the Persian Empire, Spartan diplomacy, and much else, but suffers from serious defects. G. Proietti, *Xenophon's Sparta* (1987), and P. Cartledge, *Agesilaos and the Crisis of Sparta* (1987), both treat Spartan government and society in its period of greatness and collapse. J. Buckler, *The Theban Hegemony, 371–362 BC* (1980), treats the period of Theban ascendancy, and his *Philip II and the Sacred War* (1989) studies the ways in which Philip of Macedonia used Greek politics to his own ends. J. Cargill, *The Second Athenian League* (1981), a significant study, traces Athenian policy during the fourth century. J. R. Ellis, *Philip II and Macedonian Imperialism* (1976), and G. Cawkwell, *Philip of Macedon* (1978), analyze the career of the great conqueror.

Greek social life has recently received a great deal of attention. R. Just, *Women in Athenian Law and Life* (1988), explores such topics as daily life, the family, and women's role in society. An ambitious study is D. M. Schaps, *Economic Rights of Women in Ancient Greece* (1981). W. K. Lacey, *The Family in Classical Greece* (1984), is the place to start for those who wish to learn more about ordinary family relations. A broader treatment of this topic is given in T. B. L. Webster, *Life in Classical Greece* (1969). D. Sansone, *Greek Athletics and the Genesis of Sport* (1988), well illustrated, provides a good and far-ranging treatment of what athletics meant to the classical Greek world. The topic of ancient Greek slavery is one of frequent interest, and two books address it in different but interesting ways: Y. Garlan, *Slavery in Ancient Greece* (1988), is sound; more adventurous is E. M. Wood, *Peasant-Citizen and Slave* (1988), which links the two groups to the founding of the Athenian democracy.

For Greek literature, culture, and science, see A. Lesky, *History of Greek Literature* (English translation, 1963); W. Jaeger, *Paideia,* 3 vols. (English translation, 1944–1945); H. C. Baldry, *The Greek Tragic Theater* (1971); J. Burnet, *Early Greek Philosophy,* 4th ed. (1930), and *Greek Philosophy, Thales to Plato* (1914); M. Clagett, *Greek Science in Antiquity* (1971); and E. R. Dodds, *The Greeks and the Irrational* (1951).

The classic treatment of Greek architecture is W. B. Dinsmoor, *The Architecture of the Ancient Greeks,* 3d ed. (1950). More recent (and perhaps more readable) is A. W. Lawrence, *Greek Architecture,* 3d ed. (1973). J. Boardman, *Greek Art,* rev. ed. (1973), is both perceptive and sound, as is J. J. Pollitt, *Art and Experience in Classical Greece* (1972). D. Haynes, *Greek Art and the Idea of Freedom* (1981), traces the evolving freedom of the human personality in Greek art.

J. Pinsent, *Greek Mythology* (1969), is a handy introduction. G. S. Kirk, *The Nature of Greek Myths* (1974), examines Greek religion and myth in the contemporary context. Newer treatments of Greek religion include E. Simon, *Festivals of Athens* (1983), which describes Athenian religious festivals in their archeological context; W. Burkert, *Greek Religion* (1987), which gives a masterful survey of ancient religious beliefs; and H. S. Versntel, *Faith, Hope and Worship* (1981), which examines many aspects of the religious mentality of the ancient world.

4

Hellenistic Diffusion

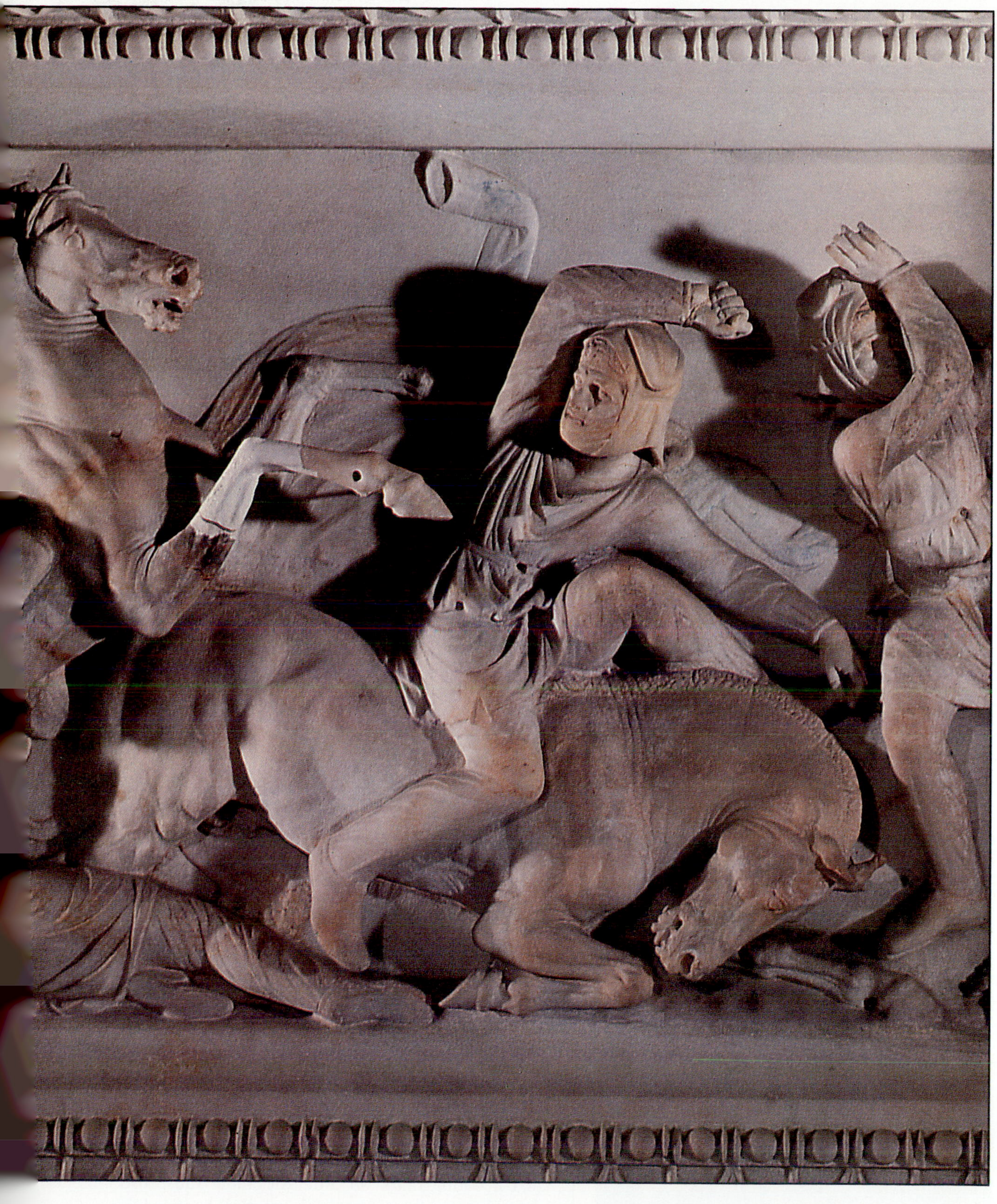

wo years after his conquest of Greece, Philip of Macedon fell victim to an assassin's dagger. Philip's twenty-year-old son, historically known as Alexander the Great (r. 336–323 B.C.), assumed the Macedonian throne. This young man, one of the most remarkable personalities of Western civilization, was to have a profound impact on history. By overthrowing the Persian Empire and by spreading *Hellenism*—Greek culture, language, thought, and the Greek way of life—as far as India, Alexander was instrumental in creating a new era, traditionally called "Hellenistic" to distinguish it from the Hellenic. As a result of Alexander's exploits, the individualistic and energetic culture of the Greeks came into intimate contact with the venerable older cultures of the Near East.

The impact of Philip and Alexander was so enormous that the great German historian Hermann Bengtson has commented:

Philip and his son Alexander were the ones who opened the door of the world to the Macedonians and Greeks. With Macedonian imperialism was joined the diffusion of the Greek spirit, which permeated the entire ancient world. Without the achievement of these two kings, neither the Roman Empire nor the diffusion of Christianity would have been conceivable.[1]

- Is this estimation correct, or is it mere rhetoric?
- What did the spread of Hellenism mean to the Greeks and the peoples of the Near East?
- What did the meeting of West and East hold for the development of economics, religion, philosophy, women's concerns, science, and medicine?

These are questions we will explore in this chapter.

Bust of Alexander This Roman portrait of Alexander the Great is a copy of a Greek original. Alexander's youth and self-confidence are immediately apparent. Yet the style is surprisingly simple for a bust of someone who had conquered the Persian Empire. The Greek inscription is equally simple: "Alexander, the son of Philip, Macedonian." *(Source: Louvre/Giraudon/Art Resource)*

ALEXANDER AND THE GREAT CRUSADE

In 336 B.C. Alexander inherited not only Philip's crown but also his policies. After his victory at Chaeronea, Philip had organized the states of Greece into a huge league under his leadership and announced to the Greeks his plan to lead them and his Macedonians against the Persian Empire. Fully intending to carry out Philip's designs, Alexander proclaimed to the Greek world that the invasion of Persia was to be a great crusade, a mighty act of revenge for the Persian invasion of Greece in 480 B.C. It would also be the means by which Alexander would create an empire of his own in the East.

Despite his youth, Alexander was well prepared to lead the attack. Philip had groomed his son to become king and given him the best education possible. In 343 B.C. Philip invited the philosopher Aristotle to tutor his son. From Aristotle, Alexander learned to appreciate Greek culture and literature, and the teachings of the great philosopher left a lasting mark on him. Alexander must also have profited from Aristotle's practical knowledge, but he never accepted Aristotle's political theories.

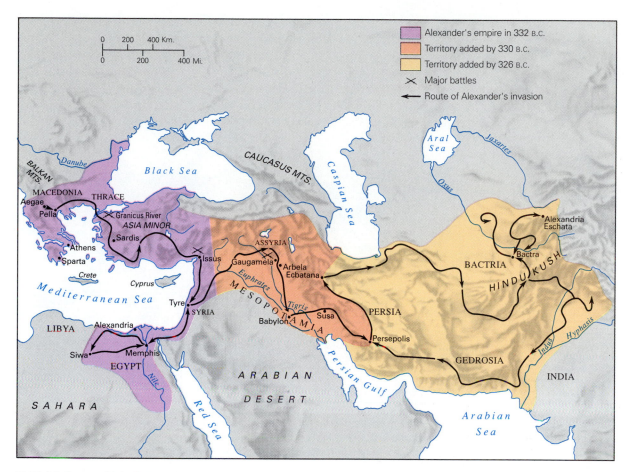

MAP 4.1 Alexander's Conqests   This map shows the course of Alexander's invasion of the Persian Empire and the speed of his progress. More important than the great success of his military campaigns was his founding of Hellenistic cities in the East.

Philip appointed Alexander regent of Macedonia at the age of sixteen, and two years later at the Battle of Chaeronea Alexander helped defeat the Greeks. By 336 B.C. Alexander had acquired both the theoretical and the practical knowledge to rule peoples and lead armies.

In 334 B.C. Alexander led an army of Macedonians and Greeks into Asia Minor. With him went a staff of philosophers and poets, scientists whose job was to map the country and study strange animals and plants, and the historian Callisthenes, who was to write an account of the campaign. Alexander intended not only a military campaign but also an expedition of discovery.

In the next three years Alexander won three major battles at the Granicus River, Issus, and Gaugamela. As Map 4.1 shows, these battle sites stand

almost as road signs marking his march to the East. After his victory at Gaugamela, Alexander captured the principal Persian capital of Persepolis, where he performed a symbolic act of retribution by burning the buildings of Xerxes, the invader of Greece. In 330 B.C. he took Ecbatana, the last Persian capital, and pursued the Persian king to his death.

The Persian Empire had fallen and the war of revenge was over, but Alexander had no intention of stopping. He dismissed his Greek troops but permitted many of them to serve on as mercenaries. Alexander then began his personal odyssey. With his Macedonian soldiers and Greek mercenaries, he set out to conquer the rest of Asia. He plunged deeper into the East, into lands completely unknown to the Greek world. Alexander's way was marked by bitter fighting and bloodshed. It took

Alexander at the Battle of Issus At left, Alexander the Great, bareheaded and wearing a breastplate, charges King Darius, who is standing in a chariot. The moment marks the turning point of the battle, as Darius turns to flee from the attack. *(Source: National Museum, Naples/Alinari/Scala/Art Resource)*

his soldiers four additional years to conquer Bactria and the easternmost parts of the now-defunct Persian Empire, but still Alexander was determined to continue his march.

In 326 B.C. Alexander crossed the Indus River and entered India. There, too, he saw hard fighting, and finally at the Hyphasis River his troops refused to go farther. Alexander was enraged by the mutiny, for he believed he was near the end of the world. Nonetheless, the army stood firm, and Alexander had to relent. Still eager to explore the limits of the world, Alexander turned south to the Arabian Sea. Though the tribes in the area did not oppose him, he waged a bloody, ruthless, and unnecessary war against them. After reaching the Arabian Sea and turning west, he led his army through the grim Gedrosian Desert. The army suffered fearfully, and many soldiers died along the way; nonetheless, in 324 B.C. Alexander reached his camp at

Susa. The great crusade was over, and Alexander himself died the next year in Babylon.

ALEXANDER'S LEGACY

Alexander so quickly became a legend in his lifetime that he still seems superhuman. That alone makes a reasoned interpretation of him very difficult. Some historians have seen him as a high-minded philosopher, and none can deny that he possessed genuine intellectual gifts. Others, however, have portrayed him as a bloody-minded autocrat, more interested in his own ambition than in any philosophical concept of the common good. Alexander, then, is the perfect example of the need for the historian carefully to interpret the known facts.

The historical record shows that Alexander in a drunken brawl murdered the friend who had saved his life at the Battle of the Granicus River. Alexander also used his power to have several other trusted officials, who had done nothing to offend him, assassinated. Other uglier and grimmer facts argue against the view that Alexander was a humane and tolerant man. In eastern Iran and India he savagely and unnecessarily slaughtered peoples whose only crime was their desire to be left in peace.

The only rationale to support those who see Alexander as a philosopher-king comes from a banquet held in 324 B.C. at the end of his career of carnage. This event is very important for a variety of reasons. It came immediately on the heels of a major Macedonian mutiny. The veteran and otherwise loyal Macedonians resented Alexander's new policy of giving high offices to Persians, people whom they had conquered after great suffering. Alexander realized that his Macedonians were too few to administer his new empire and that he needed the ability and experience of the Persians. As a gesture of reconciliation and to end the mutiny, Alexander named the entire Macedonian army his kinsmen and held a vast banquet to heal wounds. He reserved the place of honor for the Macedonians, giving the Persians and others positions of lesser status. At the banquet Alexander offered a public prayer for harmony and partnership between the Macedonians and the Persians, and this prayer has been interpreted as an expression of deep philosophical views. But far from representing an ideal desire for the brotherhood of man, the gesture was a blatant call for Macedonians and Persians to form a superior union for the purpose of ruling his new empire. It is undeniably true that the concepts of universal harmony and the brotherhood of man became common during the Hellenistic period, but they were the creations of talented philosophers, not the battle-hardened king of Macedonia.

Alexander was instrumental in changing the face of politics in the eastern Mediterranean. His campaign swept away the Persian Empire, which had ruled the East for over two hundred years. In its place he established a Macedonian monarchy. More important in the long run was his founding of new cities and military colonies, which scattered Greeks and Macedonians throughout the East.

Thus the practical result of Alexander's campaign was to open the East to the tide of Hellenism.

The Political Legacy

In 323 B.C. Alexander the Great died at the age of thirty-two. The main question at his death was whether his vast empire could be held together. The answer became obvious immediately. Within a week of Alexander's death, a round of fighting began that was to continue for forty years. No single Macedonian general was able to replace Alexander as emperor of his entire domain. By 275 B.C., as Map 4.2 shows, three officers had divided it into large monarchies. Antigonus Gonatas became king of Macedonia and established the Antigonid dynasty, which ruled until the Roman conquest in 168 B.C. Ptolemy, son of Lagus, made himself king of Egypt, and his descendants, the Ptolemies, assumed the powers and position of pharaohs. Seleucus, founder of the Seleucid dynasty, carved out a kingdom that stretched from the coast of Asia Minor to India. In 263 B.C. Eumenes, the Greek ruler of Pergamum, a city in western Asia Minor, won his independence from the Seleucids and created the Pergamene monarchy. Though the Seleucid kings soon lost control of their easternmost provinces, Greek influence in this area did not wane. In modern Turkestan and Afghanistan another line of Greek kings established the kingdom of Bactria and even managed to spread their power and culture into northern India.

The political face of Greece itself changed during the Hellenistic period. The day of the polis was over; in its place rose leagues of city-states. The two most powerful and extensive were the Aetolian League in western and central Greece and the Achaean League in the Peloponnesus. Once-powerful city-states like Athens and Sparta sank to the level of third-rate powers.

The political history of the Hellenistic period was dominated by the great monarchies and the Greek leagues. The political fragmentation and incessant warfare that marked the Hellenic period continued on an even wider and larger scale during the Hellenistic period. Never did the Hellenistic world achieve political stability or lasting peace. Hellenistic kings never forgot the vision of Alexander's empire, spanning Europe and Asia, secure under the rule of one man. Try though they did, they were never able to recreate it. In this respect, Alexander's legacy fell not to his generals but to the Romans of a later era.

The Cultural Legacy

As Alexander waded ever deeper into the East, distance alone presented him with a serious problem: how was he to retain contact with the Greek world behind him? Communications were vital, for he drew supplies and reinforcements from Greece and Macedonia. Alexander had to be sure that he was never cut off and stranded far from the Mediterranean world. His solution was to plant cities and military colonies in strategic places. In these settle-

ments Alexander left Greek mercenaries and Macedonian veterans who were no longer up to active campaigning. Besides keeping the road open to the West, these settlements served the purpose of dominating the countryside around them.

Their military significance apart, Alexander's cities and colonies became powerful instruments in the spread of Hellenism throughout the East. Plutarch described Alexander's achievement in glowing terms: "Having founded over 70 cities among barbarian peoples and having planted Greek magistracies in Asia, Alexander overcame its wild and savage way of life."[2] Alexander had indeed opened the East to an enormous wave of immigration, and his successors continued his policy by inviting Greek colonists to settle in their realms. For seventy-five years after Alexander's death, Greek im-

MAP 4.2 The Hellenistic World After Alexander's death, no single commander could hold his vast conquests together, resulting in the empire's breakup into several kingdoms and leagues.

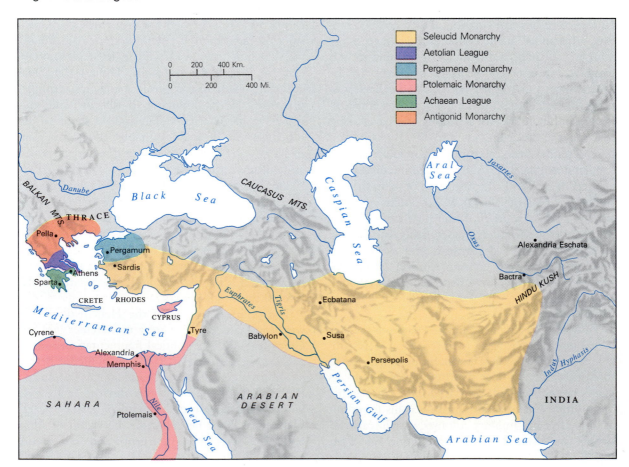

migrants poured into the East. At least 250 new Hellenistic colonies were established. The Mediterranean world had seen no comparable movement of peoples since the days of Archilochus (see page 72), when wave after wave of Greeks had turned the Mediterranean basin into a Greek-speaking region.

The overall result of Alexander's settlements and those of his successors was the spread of Hellenism as far east as India. Throughout the Hellenistic period, Greeks and Easterners became familiar with and adapted themselves to each other's customs, religions, and ways of life. Although Greek culture did not completely conquer the East, it gave the East a vehicle of expression that linked it to the West. Hellenism became a common bond among the East, peninsular Greece, and the western Mediterranean. This pre-existing cultural bond was later to prove supremely valuable to Rome—itself heavily influenced by Hellenism—in its efforts to impose a comparable political unity on the known world.

THE SPREAD OF HELLENISM

When the Greeks and Macedonians entered Asia Minor, Egypt, and the more remote East, they encountered civilizations older than their own. In some ways the Eastern cultures were more advanced than the Greek, in others less so. Thus this third great tide of Greek migration differed from preceding waves, which had spread over land that was uninhabited or inhabited by less-developed peoples.

What did the Hellenistic monarchies offer Greek immigrants politically and materially? More broadly, how did Hellenism and the cultures of the East affect one another? What did the meeting of East and West entail for the history of the world?

Cities and Kingdoms

Although Alexander's generals created huge kingdoms, the concept of monarchy never replaced the ideal of the polis. Consequently, the monarchies never won the deep emotional loyalty that Greeks had once felt for the polis. Hellenistic kings needed large numbers of Greeks to run their kingdoms. Otherwise royal business would grind to a halt, and

the conquerors would soon be swallowed up by the far more numerous conquered population. Obviously, then, the kings had to encourage Greeks to immigrate and build new homes. To these Greeks, monarchy was something out of the heroic past, something found in Homer's *Iliad* but not in daily life. The Hellenistic kings thus confronted the problem of making life in the new monarchies resemble the traditional Greek way of life. Since Greek civilization was urban, the kings continued Alexander's policy of establishing cities throughout their kingdoms in order to entice Greeks to immigrate. Yet the creation of these cities posed a serious political problem that the Hellenistic kings failed to solve.

To the Greeks civilized life was unthinkable without the polis, which was far more than a mere city. The Greek polis was by definition *sovereign*—an independent, autonomous state run by its citizens, free of any outside power or restraint. Hellenistic kings, however, refused to grant sovereignty to their cities. In effect, these kings willingly built cities but refused to build a polis.

Hellenistic monarchs gave their cities all the external trappings of a polis. Each had an assembly of citizens, a council to prepare legislation, and a board of magistrates to conduct the city's political business. Yet, however similar to the Greek polis they appeared, these cities could not engage in diplomatic dealings, make treaties, pursue their own foreign policy, or wage their own wars. None could govern its own affairs without interference from the king, who, even if he stood in the background, was the real sovereign. In the eyes of the king the cities were important parts of the kingdom, but the welfare of the whole kingdom came first. The cities had to follow royal orders, and the king often placed his own officials in the cities to see that his decrees were followed.

A new Hellenistic city differed from a Greek polis in other ways as well. The Greek polis had enjoyed political and social unity even though it was normally composed of citizens, slaves, and resident aliens. The polis had one body of law and one set of customs. In the Hellenistic city Greeks represented an elite citizen class. Natives and non-Greek foreigners who lived in Hellenistic cities usually possessed lesser rights than Greeks and often had their own laws. In some instances this disparity spurred natives to assimilate Greek culture in order to rise politically and socially. Other peoples, such as

Priene   The city of Priene in Asia Minor is an excellent example of the new Greek cities that sprang to life during the Hellenistic period. Greek architects designed the city of Priene to fit the slope of a hill that dominated the plain below. From the theater the spectator can see much of the city and the surrounding countryside. *(Source: Robert Harding)*

many Jews, firmly resisted the essence of Hellenism. The Hellenistic city was not homogeneous and could not spark the intensity of feeling that marked the polis.

In many respects the Hellenistic city resembled a modern city. It was a cultural center with theaters, temples, and libraries. It was a seat of learning, home of poets, writers, teachers, and artists. It was a place where people could find amusement. The Hellenistic city was also an economic center that provided a ready market for grain and produce raised in the surrounding countryside. The city was an emporium, scene of trade and manufacturing. In short, the Hellenistic city offered cultural and economic opportunities but did not foster a sense of united, integrated enterprise.

There were no constitutional links between city and king. The city was simply his possession. Its citizens had no voice in how the kingdom was run. The city had no rights except for those the king granted, and even those he could summarily take away. Ambassadors from the city could entreat the king for favors and petition him on such matters as taxes, boundary disputes, and legal cases. But the city had no right to advise the king on royal policy and enjoyed no political function in the kingdom.

Hellenistic kings tried to make the kingdom the political focus of citizens' allegiance. If the king could secure the frontiers of his kingdom, he could give it a geographical identity. He could then hope that his subjects would direct their primary loyalty to the kingdom rather than to a particular city.

However, the kings' efforts to fix their borders led only to sustained warfare. Boundaries were determined by military power, and rule by force became the chief political principle of the Hellenistic world.

Border wars were frequent and exhausting. The Seleucids and Ptolemies, for instance, waged five wars for the possession of southern Syria. Other kings refused to acknowledge boundaries at all. They followed Alexander's example and waged wars to reunify his empire under their own authority. By the third century B.C., a weary balance of power was reached, but only as the result of stalemate. It was not based on any political principle.

Though Hellenistic kings never built a true polis, that does not mean that their urban policy failed. Rather, the Hellenistic city was to remain the basic social and political unit in the Hellenistic East until the sixth century A.D. Cities were the chief agents of Hellenization, and their influence spread far beyond their walls. These cities formed a broader cultural network in which Greek language, customs, and values flourished. Roman rule in the Hellenistic East would later be based on this urban culture, which facilitated the rise and spread of Christianity. In broad terms, Hellenistic cities were remarkably successful.

The Greeks and the Opening of the East

If the Hellenistic kings failed to satisfy the Greeks' political yearnings, they nonetheless succeeded in giving them unequaled economic and social opportunities. The ruling dynasties of the Hellenistic world were Macedonian, and Greeks filled all important political, military, and diplomatic positions. They constituted an upper class that sustained Hellenism in the barbarian East. Besides building Greek cities, Hellenistic kings offered Greeks land and money as lures to further immigration.

The opening of the East offered ambitious Greeks opportunities for well-paying jobs and economic success. The Hellenistic monarchy, unlike the Greek polis, did not depend solely on its citizens to fulfill its political needs. Talented Greeks could expect to rise quickly in the governmental bureaucracy. Appointed by the king, these administrators did not have to stand for election each year,

as had many officials of a Greek polis. Since they held their jobs year after year, they had ample time to evolve new administrative techniques. Naturally they became more efficient than the amateur officials common in Hellenic Greek city-states. The needs of the Hellenistic monarchy and the opportunities it offered thus gave rise to a professional corps of Greek administrators.

Greeks and Macedonians also found ready employment in the armies and navies of the Hellenistic monarchies. Alexander had proved the Greco-Macedonian style of warfare to be far superior to that of the Easterners, and Alexander's successors, themselves experienced officers, realized the importance of trained Greek and Macedonian soldiers. Moreover, Hellenistic kings were extremely reluctant to arm the native populations or to allow them to serve in the army, fearing military rebellions among their conquered subjects. The result was the emergence of professional armies and navies consisting entirely of Greeks and Macedonians.

Greeks were able to dominate other professions as well. The kingdoms and cities recruited Greek writers and artists to create Greek literature, art, and culture on Asian soil. Architects, engineers, and skilled craftsmen found their services in great demand because of the building policies of the Hellenistic monarchs. If Hellenistic kingdoms were to have Greek cities, those cities needed Greek buildings—temples, porticoes, gymnasia, theaters, fountains, and houses. Architects and engineers were sometimes commissioned to design and build whole cities, which they laid out in checkerboard fashion and filled with typical Greek buildings. An enormous wave of construction took place during the Hellenistic period.

Despite the opportunities they offered, the Hellenistic monarchies were hampered by their artificial origins. Their failure to win the political loyalty of their Greek subjects and their policy of wooing Greeks with lucrative positions encouraged a feeling of uprootedness and self-serving individualism among Greek immigrants. Once a Greek had left home to take service with, for instance, the army or the bureaucracy of the Ptolemies, he had no incentive beyond his pay and the comforts of life in Egypt to keep him there. If the Seleucid king offered him more money or a promotion, he might well accept it and take his talents to Asia Minor. Why not? In the realm of the Seleucids he, a Greek, would find the same sort of life and environment that the kingdom of the Ptolemies had provided him. Thus professional Greek soldiers and administrators were very mobile and apt to look to their own interests, not their kingdom's.

As long as Greeks continued to replenish their professional ranks, the kingdoms remained strong. In the process they drew an immense amount of talent from the Greek peninsula, draining the vitality of the Greek homeland. However, the Hellenistic monarchies could not keep recruiting Greeks forever, in spite of their wealth and willingness to spend lavishly. In time, the huge surge of immigration slowed greatly. Even then, the Hellenistic monarchs were reluctant to recruit Easterners to fill posts normally held by Greeks. The result was at first the stagnation of the Hellenistic world and finally, after 202 B.C., its collapse in the face of the young and vigorous Roman republic.

Greeks and Easterners

The Greeks in the East were a minority, and Hellenistic cities were islands of Greek culture in an Eastern sea. But Hellenistic monarchies were remarkably successful in at least partially Hellenizing Easterners and spreading a uniform culture throughout the East, a culture to which Rome eventually fell heir. The prevailing institutions, laws, and language of the East became Greek. Indeed, the Near East had seen nothing comparable since the days when Mesopotamian culture had spread throughout the area.

Yet the spread of Greek culture was wider than it was deep. At best it was a veneer, thicker in some places than in others. Hellenistic kingdoms were never entirely unified in language, customs, and thought. Greek culture took firmest hold along the shores of the Mediterranean, but in the Far East, in Persia and Bactria, it eventually gave way to Eastern cultures.

The Ptolemies in Egypt made no effort to spread Greek culture, and unlike other Hellenistic kings they were not city builders. Indeed, they founded only the city of Ptolemais near Thebes. At first the native Egyptian population, the descendants of the pharaoh's people, retained their traditional language, outlook, religion, and way of life. Initially untouched by Hellenism, the natives continued to be the foundation of the state: they fed it by their

labor in the fields and financed its operations with their taxes.

Under the pharaohs, talented Egyptians had been able to rise to high office, but during the third century B.C. the Ptolemies cut off this avenue of advancement. They tied the natives to the land ever more tightly, making it nearly impossible for them to leave their villages. The bureaucracy of the Ptolemies was ruthlessly efficient, and the native population was viciously and cruelly exploited. Even in times of hardship the king's taxes came first, although payment might mean starvation for the natives. Their desperation was summed up by one Egyptian, who scrawled the warning: "We are worn out; we will run away."[3] To many Egyptians, revolt or a life of brigandage was certainly preferable to working the land under the harsh Ptolemies.

Throughout the third century B.C., the Greek upper class in Egypt had little to do with the native population. Many Greek bureaucrats established homes in Alexandria and Ptolemais, where they managed finances, served as magistrates, and administered the law. Other Greeks settled in military colonies and supplied the monarchy with fighting men. But in the second century B.C., Greeks and native Egyptians began to intermarry and mingle their cultures. The language of the native population influenced Greek, and many Greeks adopted Egyptian religion and ways of life. Simultaneously, natives adopted Greek customs and language and began to play a role in the administration of the kingdom and even to serve in the army. While many Greeks and Egyptians remained aloof from each other, the overall result was the evolution of a widespread Greco-Egyptian culture.

Meanwhile the Seleucid kings established many cities and military colonies in western Asia Minor and along the banks of the Tigris and Euphrates rivers in order to nurture a vigorous and large Greek population. Especially important to the Seleucids were the military colonies, for they needed Greeks to defend the kingdom. The Seleucids had no elaborate plan for Hellenizing the native population, but the arrival of so many Greeks was bound to have an impact. Seleucid military colonies were generally founded near native villages, thus exposing Easterners to all aspects of Greek life. Many Easterners found Greek political and cultural forms attractive and imitated them. In Asia Minor and Syria, for instance, numerous native villages and towns developed along Greek lines, and some of them became Hellenized cities. Farther east, the Greek kings who replaced the Seleucids in the third century B.C. spread Greek culture to their neighbors, even into the Indian subcontinent.

For Easterners the prime advantage of Greek culture was its very pervasiveness. The Greek language became the common speech of the East. A common dialect called *koine* even influenced the speech of peninsular Greece itself. Greek became the speech of the royal court, bureaucracy, and army. It was also the speech of commerce: any Easterner who wanted to compete in business had to learn it. As early as the third century B.C., some Greek cities were giving citizenship to Hellenized natives.

The vast majority of Hellenized Easterners, however, took only the externals of Greek culture while retaining the essentials of their own way of life. Though Greeks and Easterners adapted to each other's ways, there was never a true fusion of cultures. Nonetheless, each found useful things in the civilization of the other, and the two fertilized each other. This fertilization, this mingling of Greek and Eastern elements, is what makes Hellenistic culture unique and distinctive.

Hellenism and the Jews

A prime illustration of how the East took what it wanted from Hellenism while remaining true to itself is the impact of Greek culture on the Jews. At first, Jews in Hellenistic cities were treated as resident aliens. As they grew more numerous, they received permission to form a political corporation, a *politeuma,* which gave them a great deal of autonomy. The politeuma allowed Jews to attend to their religious and internal affairs without interference from the Greek municipal government. The Jewish politeuma had its own officials, the leaders of the synagogue. In time the Jewish politeuma gained the special right to be judged by its own law and its own officials, thus becoming in effect a Jewish city within a Hellenistic city.

The Jewish politeuma, like the Hellenistic city, obeyed the king's commands, but there was virtually no royal interference with the Jewish religion. Indeed, the Greeks were always reluctant to tamper with anyone's religion. Only the Seleucid king Antiochus Epiphanes (175–ca 164 B.C.) tried to suppress the Jewish religion in the Roman province of Judaea. He did so not because he hated the Jews (who were a small part of his kingdom), but because he was trying to unify his realm culturally to meet the threat of Rome. To the Jews he extended the same policy that he applied to all subjects. Apart from this instance, Hellenistic Jews suffered no official religious persecution. Some Jews were given the right to become full citizens of Hellenistic cities, but few exercised that right. Citizenship would have allowed them to vote in the assembly and serve as magistrates, but it would also have obliged them to worship the gods of the city—a practice few Jews chose to follow.

Jews living in Hellenistic cities often embraced a good deal of Hellenism. So many Jews learned Greek, especially in Alexandria, that the Old Testament was translated into Greek, and services in the synagogue came to be conducted in Greek. Jews often took Greek names, used Greek political forms, adopted Greek practice by forming their own trade associations, put inscriptions on graves as the Greeks did, and much else. Yet no matter how much of Greek culture or its externals Jews borrowed, they normally remained attached to their religion. Thus, in spite of Hellenistic trappings, Hellenized Jews remained Jews at heart. Their ideas and those of the Greeks were different. The exceptions were some Jews in Asia Minor and Syria who incorporated Greek or local Eastern cults into their worship. To some degree this development was due to the growing belief among Greeks and Easterners that all peoples, despite differences in cult and ritual, actually worshiped the same gods.

THE ECONOMIC SCOPE OF THE HELLENISTIC WORLD

Alexander's conquest of the Persian Empire not only changed the political face of the ancient world but also brought the East fully into the sphere of Greek economics. Yet the Hellenistic period did not see a revolution in the way people lived and worked. The material demands of Hellenistic society remained as simple as those of Athenian society in the fifth century B.C. Clothes and furniture were essentially unchanged, as were household goods, tools, and jewelry. The real achievement of Alexander and his successors was linking East and West in a broad commercial network. The spread of Greeks throughout the East created new markets and stimulated trade. The economic unity of the Hellenistic world, like its cultural bonds, would later prove valuable to the Romans.

Commerce

Alexander's conquest of the Persian Empire had immediate effects on trade. In the Persian capitals Alexander had found vast sums of gold, silver, and other treasure. This wealth financed the creation of new cities, the building of roads, and the development of harbors. Most of the great monarchies coined their money on the Attic standard, which meant that much of the money used in Hellenistic kingdoms had the same value. Traders were less in need of moneychangers than in the days when each major power coined money on a different standard. As a result of Alexander's conquests, geographical knowledge of the East increased dramatically, making the East far better known to the Greeks than previously. The Greeks spread their law and methods of transacting business throughout the East. Whole new fields lay open to Greek merchants, who eagerly took advantage of the new opportunities. Commerce itself was a leading area where Greeks and Easterners met on grounds of common interest. In bazaars, ports, and trading centers Greeks learned of Eastern customs and traditions while spreading knowledge of their own culture.

The Seleucid and Ptolemaic dynasties traded as far afield as India, Arabia, and sub-Saharan Africa. Overland trade with India and Arabia was conducted by caravan and was largely in the hands of Easterners. The caravan trade never dealt in bulk items or essential commodities; only luxury goods could be transported in this very expensive fashion. Once the goods reached the Hellenistic monarchies, Greek merchants took a hand in the trade.

In the early Hellenistic period, the Seleucids and Ptolemies ensured that the caravan trade proceeded efficiently. Later in the period—a time of increased war and confusion—they left the caravans unprotected. Taking advantage of this situation, Palmyra in the Syrian desert and Nabataean Petra in Arabia arose as caravan states. Such states protected the caravans from bandits and marauders and served as dispersal areas for caravan goods.

The Ptolemies discovered how to use monsoon winds to establish direct contact with India. One hardy merchant has left a firsthand account of sailing this important maritime route:

Hippalos, the pilot, observing the position of the ports and the conditions of the sea, first discovered how to sail across the ocean. Concerning the winds of the ocean in this region, when with us the Etesian winds begin, in India a wind between southwest and south, named for Hippalos, sets in from the open sea. From then until now some mariners set forth from Kanes and some from the Cape of Spices. Those sailing to Dimurikes [in southern India] throw the bow of the ship farther out to sea. Those bound for Barygaza and the realm of the Sakas [in northern India] hold to the land no more than three days; and if the wind remains favorable, they hold the same course through the outer sea, and they sail along past the previously mentioned gulfs.[4]

Although this sea route never replaced overland caravan traffic, it kept direct relations with eastern Europe alive, stimulating the exchange of ideas as well as goods.

More economically important than this exotic trade were commercial dealings in essential commodities like raw materials, grain, and industrial products. The Hellenistic monarchies usually raised enough grain for their own needs as well as a surplus for export. For the cities of Greece and the Aegean this trade in grain was essential, because many of them could not grow enough. Fortunately for them, abundant wheat supplies were available nearby in Egypt and in the Crimea in southern Russia.

The large-scale wars of the Hellenistic period often interrupted both the production and the distribution of grain. This was especially true when Alexander's successors were trying to carve out kingdoms. In addition, natural calamities, such as excessive rain or drought, frequently damaged harvests. Throughout the Hellenistic period, famine or severe food shortage remained a grim possibility.

Most trade in bulk commodities was seaborne, and the Hellenistic merchant ship was the workhorse of the day. The merchant ship had a broad beam and relied on sails for propulsion. It was far more seaworthy than the contemporary warship, which was long, narrow, and built for speed. A small crew of experienced sailors could handle the merchant vessel easily. Maritime trade provided opportunities for workers in other industries and trades: sailors, shipbuilders, dock workers, accountants, teamsters, and pirates. Piracy was always a factor in the Hellenistic world and remained so until Rome extended its power throughout the East.

The Greek cities paid for their grain by exporting olive oil and wine. When agriculture and oil production developed in Syria, Greek products began to encounter competition from the Seleucid monarchy. Later in the Hellenistic period, Greek oil and wine found a lucrative market in Italy. Another significant commodity was fish, which for export was either salted, pickled, or dried. This trade was doubly important because fish provided poor people with an essential element of their diet. Salt, too, was often imported, and there was some very slight trade in salted meat, which was a luxury item. Far more important was the trade in honey, dried fruit, nuts, and vegetables. Of raw materials, wood was high in demand, but little trade occurred in manufactured goods.

Slaves were a staple of Hellenistic trade. The wars provided prisoners for the slave market; to a lesser extent, so did kidnaping and capture by pirates. The number of slaves involved cannot be estimated, but there is no doubt that slavery flourished. Both old Greek states and new Hellenistic kingdoms were ready slave markets, as was Rome when it emerged triumphant from the Second Punic War (see Chapter 5).

Throughout the Mediterranean world slaves were almost always in demand. Only the Ptolemies discouraged both the trade and slavery itself, and they did so only for economic reasons. Their system had no room for slaves, who would only have competed with free labor. Otherwise, slave labor was to be found in the cities and temples of the Hellenistic world, in the factories and fields, and in the homes of wealthier people. In Italy and some parts of the East, slaves performed manual labor for large estates and worked the mines. They were vitally important to the Hellenistic economy.

Industry

Although demand for goods increased during the Hellenistic period, no new techniques of production appear to have developed. The discoveries of Hellenistic mathematicians and thinkers failed to produce any significant corresponding technologi-

Harbor and Warehouses at Delos During the Hellenistic period Delos became a thriving trading center. Shown here is the row of warehouses at water's edge. From Delos cargoes were shipped to virtually every part of the Mediterranean. *(Source: Adam Woolfitt/Woodfin Camp)*

cal development. Manual labor, not machinery, continued to turn out the raw materials and few manufactured goods the Hellenistic world used. Human labor was so cheap and so abundant that kings had no incentive to encourage the invention and manufacture of labor-saving machinery.

Perhaps only one noteworthy technological innovation dates to the Hellenistic period—the Archimedean screw, a device used to pump water into irrigation ditches and out of mines. At Thoricus in Attica miners dug ore by hand and hauled it from the mines for processing. This was grueling work; invariably miners were slaves, criminals, or forced laborers. The conditions under which they worked were frightful. The Ptolemies ran their gold mines along the same harsh lines. One historian gave a grim picture of the miners' lives:

The kings of Egypt condemn [to the mines] those found guilty of wrong-doing and those taken prisoner in war, those who were victims of false accusations and were put into jail because of royal anger. . . . The condemned— and they are very many—all of them are put in chains, and they work persistently and continually, both by day and throughout the night, getting no rest, and carefully cut off from escape.[5]

The Ptolemies even condemned women and children to work in the mines. The strongest men lived and died swinging iron sledgehammers to break up the gold-bearing quartz rock. Others worked underground following the seams of quartz; laboring with lamps bound to their foreheads, they were whipped by overseers if they slacked off. Once the diggers had cut out blocks of quartz, young boys

gathered up the blocks and carried them outside. All of them—men, women, and boys—worked until they died.

Apart from gold and silver, which were used primarily for coins and jewelry, iron was the most important metal and saw the most varied use. Even so, the method of its production never became very sophisticated. The Hellenistic Greeks did manage to produce a low-grade steel by adding carbon to iron.

Pottery remained an important commodity, and most of it was made locally. The pottery used in the kitchen, the coarse ware, did not change at all. Fancier pots and bowls, decorated with a shiny black glaze, came into use during the Hellenistic period. This ware originated in Athens, but potters in other places began to imitate its style, heavily cutting into the Athenian market. In the second century B.C. a red-glazed ware, often called Samian, burst on the market and soon dominated it. Athens still held its own, however, in the production of fine pottery. Despite the change in pottery styles, the method of production of all pottery, whether plain or fine, remained essentially unchanged.

Although new techniques of production and wider use of machinery did not develop, the volume of goods produced increased in the Hellenistic period. Small manufacturing establishments existed in nearly all parts of the Hellenistic world.

Agriculture

Hellenistic kings paid special attention to agriculture. Much of their revenue was derived from the produce of royal lands, rents paid by the tenants of royal land, and taxation of agricultural land. Some Hellenistic kings even sought out and supported agricultural experts. The Ptolemies, for instance, sponsored experiments on seed grain, selecting seeds that seemed hardy and productive and trying to improve their characteristics. Hellenistic authors wrote handbooks discussing how farms and large estates could most profitably be run. These handbooks described soil types, covered the proper times for planting and reaping, and discussed care of farm animals. Whether these efforts had any impact on the average farmer is difficult to determine.

The Ptolemies made the greatest strides in agriculture, and the reason for their success was largely political. Egypt had a strong tradition of central au-

Scene from Daily Life Art in the Hellenistic period often pursued two themes: increased realism and scenes from daily life. This statuette illustrates both. Here a peasant follows his donkey, which has fallen, to sell his grapes in the city. The peasant saves his grapes with one hand while trying to pull the donkey to its feet with the other. *(Source: National Archaeological Museum, Athens)*

thority dating back to the pharaohs, which the Ptolemies inherited and tightened. They could decree what crops Egyptian farmers would plant and what animals would be raised, and they had the power to carry out their commands. The Ptolemies recognized the need for well-planned and constant irrigation, and much native labor went into the digging and maintenance of canals and ditches. The Ptolemies also reclaimed a great deal of land from the desert, including the Fayum, a dried lake bed near the Nile.

The centralized authority of the Ptolemies explains how agricultural advances occurred at the local level in Egypt. But such progress was not possible in any other Hellenistic monarchy. Despite royal interest in agriculture and a more studied approach to it in the Hellenistic period, there is no evidence that agricultural productivity increased. Whether Hellenistic agricultural methods had any influence on Eastern practices is unknown.

RELIGION IN THE HELLENISTIC WORLD

In religion Hellenism gave Easterners far less than the East gave the Greeks. At first the Hellenistic period saw the spread of Greek religious cults throughout the East. When Hellenistic kings founded cities, they also built temples and established new cults and priesthoods for the old Olympian gods. The new cults enjoyed the prestige of being the religion of the conquerors, and they were supported by public money. The most attractive aspects of the Greek cults were their rituals and festivities. Greek cults sponsored literary, musical, and athletic contests, which were staged in beautiful surroundings among impressive Greek buildings. In short, the cults offered bright and lively entertainment, both intellectual and physical. They fostered Greek culture and traditional sports and thus were a splendid means of displaying Greek civilization in the East.

Despite various advantages, Greek cults suffered from some severe shortcomings. They were primarily concerned with ritual. Participation in the civic cults did not even require belief (see Chapter 3). On the whole, the civic cults neither appealed to religious emotions nor embraced matters such as sin and redemption. Greek mystery religions helped fill this gap, but the centers of these religions were in old Greece. Although the new civic cults were lavish in pomp and display, they could not satisfy deep religious feelings or spiritual yearnings.

Even though the Greeks participated in the new cults for cultural reasons, they felt little genuine religious attachment to them. In comparison with the emotional and sometimes passionate religions of the East, the Greek cults seemed sterile. Greeks increasingly sought solace from other sources. Educated and thoughtful people turned to philosophy as a guide to life, while others turned to superstition, magic, or astrology. Still others might shrug and speak of *Tyche,* which meant "Fate" or "Chance" or "Doom"—a capricious and sometimes malevolent force.

In view of the spiritual decline of Greek religion, it is surprising that Eastern religions did not make more immediate headway among the Greeks. Although Hellenistic Greeks clung to their own cults as expressions of their Greekness rather than for any ethical principles, they did not rush to embrace native religions. Only in the second century B.C., after a century of exposure to Eastern religions, did Greeks begin to adopt them.

Nor did Hellenistic kings make any effort to spread Greek religion among their Eastern subjects. The Greeks always considered religion a matter best left to the individual. Greek cults were attractive only to those socially aspiring Easterners who adopted Greek culture for personal advancement. Otherwise, Easterners were little affected by Greek religion. Nor did native religions suffer from the arrival of the Greeks. Some Hellenistic kings limited the power of native priesthoods, but they also subsidized some Eastern cults with public money. Alexander the Great actually reinstated several Eastern cults that the Persians had suppressed.

The only significant junction of Greek and Eastern religious traditions was the growth and spread of new "mystery religions," so called because they featured a body of ritual not to be divulged to anyone not initiated into the cult. The new mystery cults incorporated aspects of both Greek and Eastern religions and had broad appeal for both Greeks and Easterners who yearned for personal immortality. Since the Greeks were already familiar with old mystery cults, such as the Eleusinian mysteries in Attica, the new cults did not strike them as alien or barbarian. Familiar, too, was the concept of preparation for an initiation. Devotees of the Eleusinian mysteries and other such cults had to prepare them-

Religious Syncretism   This relief was found at the Greek outpost of Dura-Europus, located on the Euphrates. In the center sits Zeus Olympius-Baalshamin, a combination of a Greek god and a Semitic god. The Eastern priest at the right is burning incense on an altar, while the figure on the left in Macedonian dress crowns the god. Both the religious sentiments and the style of art show the meeting of East and West. *(Source: Yale University Art Gallery, Dura-Europos Collection)*

selves mentally and physically before entering the gods' presence. Thus the mystery cults fit well with Greek usage.

The new religions enjoyed one tremendous advantage over the old Greek mystery cults. Whereas old Greek mysteries were tied to particular places, such as Eleusis, the new religions spread throughout the Hellenistic world. People did not have to undertake long and expensive pilgrimages just to become members of the religion. In that sense the mystery religions came to the people, for temples of the new deities sprang up wherever Greeks lived.

The mystery religions all claimed to save their adherents from the worst that fate could do and promised life for the soul after death. They all had a single concept in common: the belief that by the rites of initiation devotees became united with the god, who had himself died and risen from the dead. The sacrifice of the god and his victory over death saved the devotee from eternal death. Similarly, all mystery religions demanded a period of preparation in which the convert strove to become holy, that is, to live by the religion's precepts. Once aspirants had prepared themselves, they went through an initiation in which they learned the secrets of the religion. The initiation was usually a ritual of great emotional intensity, symbolizing the entry into a new life.

The Eastern mystery religions that took the Hellenistic world by storm were the Egyptian cults of Serapis and Isis. Serapis, who was invented by King Ptolemy, combined elements of the Egyptian god Osiris with aspects of the Greek gods Zeus, Pluto (the prince of the underworld) and Asclepius. Serapis was believed to be the judge of souls, who rewarded virtuous and righteous people with eternal life. Like Asclepius, he was a god of healing. Serapis became an international god, and many Hellenistic Greeks thought of him as Zeus. Associated with Isis and Serapis was Anubis, the old Egyptian god who, like Charon in the Greek pantheon, guided the souls of initiates to the realm of eternal life.

The cult of Isis enjoyed even wider appeal than that of Serapis. Isis, wife of Osiris, claimed to have conquered Tyche and promised to save any mortal who came to her. She became the most important goddess of the Hellenistic world, and her worship was very popular among women. Her priests claimed that she had bestowed on humanity the gift of civilization and founded law and literature. She was the goddess of marriage, conception, and childbirth; and like Serapis she promised to save the souls of her believers.

There was neither conflict between Greek and Eastern religions nor wholesale acceptance of one or the other. Nonetheless, Greeks and Easterners noticed similarities among their respective deities and assumed that they were worshiping the same gods in different garb. These tendencies toward religious universalism and the desire for personal immortality would prove significant when the Hellenistic world came under the sway of Rome, for Hellenistic developments paved the way for the spread of Christianity.

PHILOSOPHY AND THE COMMON MAN

Philosophy during the Hellenic period was the exclusive province of the wealthy, for only they had leisure enough to pursue philosophical studies. During the Hellenistic period, however, philosophy reached out to touch the lives of more men and women than ever before. The reasons for this development were several. Since the ideal of the polis had declined, politics no longer offered people an intellectual outlet. Moreover, much of Hellenistic life, especially in the new cities of the East, seemed unstable and without venerable traditions. Greeks were far more mobile than they had ever been before, but their very mobility left them feeling uprooted. Many people in search of something permanent, something unchanging in a changing world, turned to philosophy. Another reason for the increased influence of philosophy was the decline of traditional religion and a growing belief in

Tyche This statue depicts Tyche as the city-goddess of Antioch, a new Hellenistic foundation of the Seleucid king Antiochus. Some Hellenistic Greeks worshiped Tyche in the hope that she would be kind to them. Philosophers tried to free people from her whimsies. Antiochus tried to win her favor by honoring her. *(Source: Photo Vatican Museums)*

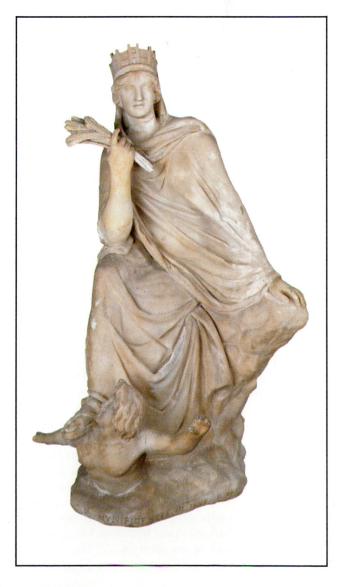

Tyche. To protect against the worst that Tyche could do, many Greeks looked to philosophy.

Philosophers themselves became much more numerous, and several new schools of philosophical thought emerged. The Cynics preached the joy of a simple life. The Epicureans taught that pleasure is the chief good. The Stoics emphasized the importance of deeds well done. There was a good deal of rivalry as philosophers tried to demonstrate the superiority of their views, but in spite of their differences the major branches of philosophy agreed on the necessity of making people self-sufficient. They all recognized the need to equip men and women to deal successfully with Tyche. The major schools of Hellenistic philosophy all taught that people could be truly happy only when they had turned their backs on the world and focused full attention on one enduring thing. They differed chiefly on what that enduring thing was.

Cynics

Undoubtedly the most unusual of the new philosophers were the Cynics, who urged a return to nature. They advised men and women to discard traditional customs and conventions (which were in decline anyway) and live simply. The Cynics believed that by rejecting material things people would become free and that nature would provide all necessities.

The founder of the Cynics was Antisthenes (b. ca 440 B.C.), but it was Diogenes of Sinope (ca 412–323 B.C.), one of the most colorful men of the period, who spread the philosophy. Diogenes came to Athens to study philosophy and soon evolved his own ideas on the ideal life. He hit on the solution that happiness was possible only by living according to nature and forgoing luxuries. He attacked social conventions because he considered them contrary to nature. Throughout Greece he gained fame for the rigorous way in which he put his beliefs into practice.

Diogenes' disdain for luxury and social pretense became legendary. Once, when he was living at Corinth, he was supposedly visited by Alexander the Great: "While Diogenes was sunning himself . . . Alexander stood over him and said: 'Ask me whatever gift you like.' In answer Diogenes said to him: 'Get out of my sunlight.' "[6] The story underlines the essence of Diogenes' teachings: even a

great, powerful, and wealthy conqueror such as Alexander could give people nothing of any real value. Nature had already provided them with everything essential.

Diogenes did not establish a philosophical school in the manner of Plato and Aristotle. Instead, he and his followers took their teaching to the streets and marketplaces. More than any other philosophical group, they tried to reach the common people. As part of their return to nature, they often did without warm clothing, sufficient food, or adequate housing, which they considered unnecessary. The Cynics also tried to break down political barriers by declaring that people owed no allegiance to any city or monarchy. Rather, they said, all people are cosmopolitan—that is, citizens of the world. The Cynics reached across political boundaries to create a community of people, all sharing their humanity and living as close to nature as humanly possible. The Cynics set a striking example of how people could turn away from materialism. Although comparatively few men and women could follow such rigorous precepts, the Cynics influenced all the other major schools of philosophy.

Epicureans

Epicurus (340–270 B.C.), who founded his own school of philosophy at Athens, based his view of life on scientific theories. Accepting Democritus's theory that the universe is composed of indestructible particles, Epicurus put forward a naturalistic theory of the universe. Although he did not deny the existence of the gods, he taught that they had no effect on human life. The essence of Epicurus's belief was that the principal good of human life is pleasure, which he defined as the absence of pain. He was not advocating drunken revels or sexual dissipation, which he thought actually caused pain. Instead, Epicurus concluded that any violent emotion is undesirable. Drawing on the teachings of the Cynics, he advocated mild self-discipline. Even poverty he considered good, as long as people had enough food, clothing, and shelter. Epicurus also taught that individuals can most easily attain peace and serenity by ignoring the outside world and looking into their personal feelings and reactions. Thus Epicureanism led to quietism.

Epicureanism taught its followers to ignore politics and issues, for politics led to tumult, which would disturb the soul. Although the Epicureans thought that the state originated through a social contract among individuals, they did not care about the political structure of the state. They were content to live in a democracy, oligarchy, monarchy, or any other form of government, and they never speculated about the ideal state. Their ideals stood outside all political forms.

Stoics

Opposed to the passivity of the Epicureans, Zeno (335–262 B.C.), a philosopher from Citium in Cyprus, advanced a different concept of human beings and the universe. When Zeno first came to Athens, he listened avidly to the Cynics. Concluding, however, that the Cynics were extreme, he stayed in Athens to form his own school, the Stoa, named after the building where he preferred to teach.

Stoicism became the most popular Hellenistic philosophy and the one that later captured the mind of Rome. Zeno and his followers considered nature an expression of divine will; in their view, people could be happy only when living in accordance with nature. They stressed the unity of man and the universe, stating that all men were brothers and obliged to help one another. Stoicism's science was derived from Heraclitus, but its broad and warm humanity was the work of Zeno and his followers.

Unlike the Epicureans, the Stoics taught that people should participate in politics and worldly affairs. Yet this idea never led to the belief that individuals should try to change the order of things. Time and again, the Stoics used the image of an actor in a play: the Stoic plays an assigned part but never tries to change the play. To the Stoics the important question was not whether they achieved anything, but whether they lived virtuous lives. In that way they could triumph over Tyche, for Tyche could destroy achievements but not the nobility of their lives.

Though the Stoics evolved the concept of a world order, they thought of it strictly in terms of the individual. Like the Epicureans, they were indifferent to specific political forms. They believed that people should do their duty to the state in which they found themselves. The universal state they preached about was ethical, not political. The Stoics' most significant practical achievement was the creation of the concept of natural law. The Stoics concluded that as all men were brothers, partook of divine reason, and were in harmony with the universe, one law—a part of the natural order of life—governed them all.

The Stoic concept of a universal state governed by natural law is one of the finest heirlooms the Hellenistic world passed on to Rome. The Stoic concept of natural law, of one law for all people, became a valuable tool when the Romans began to deal with many different peoples with different laws. The ideal of the universal state gave the Romans a rationale for extending their empire to the farthest reaches of the world. The duty of individuals to their fellows served the citizens of the Roman Empire as the philosophical justification for doing their duty. In this respect, too, the real fruit of Hellenism was to ripen only under the cultivation of Rome.

HELLENISTIC WOMEN

With the growth of monarchy in the Hellenistic period came a major new development: the importance of royal women, many of whom played an active part in political and diplomatic life. In the Hellenic period the polis had replaced kingship, except at Sparta, and queens were virtually unknown apart from myth and legend. Even in Sparta queens did not participate in politics. Hellenistic queens, however, did exercise political power, either in their own right or by manipulating their husbands. Many Hellenistic queens were depicted as willful or ruthless, especially in power struggles over the throne, and in some cases those charges are accurate. Other Hellenistic royal women, however, set an example of courage and nobility, for instance, Cratesiclea, mother of Cleomenes.

In 224 B.C. Cleomenes was trying to rebuild Sparta as a major power, but he needed money. King Ptolemy of Egypt promised to help the Spartans because doing so would further his own diplomatic ends. In return for his support, Ptolemy demanded that Cleomenes give him his mother, Cratesiclea, as a hostage. Ptolemy's demand was an insult and a grave dishonor to the Spartan lady, yet Cleomenes' plans could not succeed without Ptolemy's money. Reluctant to agree to Ptolemy's

Old Shepherdess Daily life for the poor and elderly was as hard in the Hellenistic period as in other times. Here a tough, old, scantily clothed shepherdess brings a sheep to market. Such scenes were common during the period; but art, not written sources, has preserved them for posterity. *(Source: Alinari/Art Resource)*

terms, Cleomenes was also reluctant to mention the matter to his mother. Plutarch related her reaction:

Finally, when Cleomenes worked up his courage to speak about the matter, Cratesiclea laughed aloud and said: "Is this what you often started to say but flinched from? Rather put me aboard a ship and send me away, wherever you think this body of mine will be most useful to Sparta, before sitting here it is destroyed by old age."[7]

Cratesiclea's selflessness and love of her state became legendary. Other royal Hellenistic women demonstrated similar self-sacrifice and sense of duty.

The example of the queens had a profound effect on Hellenistic attitudes toward women in general. In fact, the Hellenistic period saw a great expansion in social and economic opportunities for women. More women than ever before received educations that enabled them to enter medicine and other professions. Literacy among women increased dramatically, and their options expanded accordingly. Some won fame as poets, while others studied with philosophers and contributed to the intellectual life of the age. As a rule, however, these developments touched only wealthier women, and not all of them. Although some poor women were literate, most were not.

Women began to participate in politics on a limited basis. Often they served as priestesses, as they had in the Hellenic period, but they also began to serve in civil capacities. For their services to the state they received public acknowledgment. Women sometimes received honorary citizenship from foreign cities because of aid given in times of crisis. Few women achieved these honors, however, and those who did were from the upper classes.

This major development was not due to male enlightenment. Although Hellenistic philosophy addressed itself to many new questions, the position of women was not one of them. The Stoics, in spite of their theory of the brotherhood of man, thought of women as men's inferiors. Only the Cynics, who waged war on all accepted customs, treated women as men's equals. The Cynics were interested in women as individuals, not as members of a family or as citizens of the state. Their view did not make much headway. Like other aspects of Cynic philosophy, this attitude was more admired than followed.

The new prominence of women was largely due instead to their increased participation in economic affairs. During the Hellenistic period some women took part in commercial transactions. They still lived under legal handicaps; in Egypt, for example, a Greek woman needed a male guardian to buy, sell, or lease land, to borrow money, and to represent her in other transactions. Yet often such a guardian was present only to fulfill the letter of the law. The woman was the real agent and handled the business being transacted. In Hellenistic Sparta, women accumulated large fortunes and vast amounts of land. As early as the beginning of the Hellenistic period, women owned two-fifths of the land of Laconia. Spartan women, however, were exceptional. In most other areas, even women who were wealthy in their own right were formally under the protection of a male relative.

These changes do not amount to a social revolution. Although women had begun to participate in business, politics, and legal activities, such women were rare and labored under handicaps that men did not have. Even so, it was a start.

HELLENISTIC SCIENCE

The area in which Hellenistic culture achieved its greatest triumphs was science. Here, too, the ancient Near East made contributions to Greek thought. The patient observations of the Babylonians, who for generations had scanned the skies, had provided the raw materials for Thales' speculations, which were the foundation of Hellenistic astronomy. The most notable of the Hellenistic astronomers was Aristarchus of Samos (ca 310–230 B.C.), who was educated in Aristotle's school. Aristarchus concluded that the sun is far larger than the earth and that the stars are enormously distant from the earth. He argued against Aristotle's view that the earth is the center of the universe. Instead, Aristarchus propounded the *heliocentric theory*—that the earth and planets revolve around the sun. His work is all the more impressive because he lacked even a rudimentary telescope. Aristarchus had only the human eye and brain, but they were more than enough.

Unfortunately Aristarchus's theories did not persuade the ancient world. In the second century A.D. Claudius Ptolemy, a mathematician and astronomer in Alexandria, accepted Aristotle's theory of the earth as the center of the universe, and their view prevailed for 1,400 years. Aristarchus's heliocentric theory lay dormant until resurrected by the brilliant Polish astronomer Nicolaus Copernicus (1473–1543).

In geometry Hellenistic thinkers discovered little that was new, but Euclid (ca 300 B.C.), a mathematician who lived in Alexandria, compiled a valuable textbook of existing knowledge. His book *The Elements of Geometry* has exerted immense influence on Western civilization, for it rapidly became the standard introduction to geometry. Generations of students, from the Hellenistic period to the present, have learned the essentials of geometry from it.

The greatest thinker of the Hellenistic period was Archimedes (ca 287–212 B.C.), who was a clever inventor as well. He lived in Syracuse in Sicily and watched Rome emerge as a power in the Mediterranean. When the Romans laid siege to Syracuse in the Second Punic War, Archimedes invented a number of machines to thwart the Roman army. His catapults threw rocks large enough to sink ships and disrupt battle lines. His grappling devices lifted ships out of the water. Archimedes built such machines out of necessity, but they were of little real interest to him. In a more peaceful vein, he invented the Archimedean screw and the compound pulley. Plutarch described Archimedes' dramatic demonstration of how easily his pulley could move huge weights with little effort:

A three-masted merchant ship of the royal fleet had been hauled on land by hard work and many hands. Archimedes put aboard her many men and the usual freight. He sat far away from her; without haste, but gently working a compound pulley with his hand, he drew her towards him smoothly and without faltering, just as though she were running on the surface of the sea.[8]

Archimedes was far more interested in pure mathematics than in practical inventions. His mathematical research, covering many fields, was his greatest contribution to Western thought. In his book *On Plane Equilibriums* Archimedes dealt for the first time with the basic principles of mechanics, including the principle of the lever. He once said that if he were given a lever and a suitable place to stand, he could move the world. With his treatise *On Floating Bodies* Archimedes founded the science of hydrostatics. He concluded that whenever a solid floats in a liquid, the weight of the solid is equal to the weight of liquid displaced. The way he made his discovery has become famous:

When he was devoting his attention to this problem, he happened to go to a public bath. When he climbed down into the bathtub there, he noticed that water in the tub equal to the bulk of his body flowed out. Thus, when he observed this method of solving the problem, he did not wait. Instead, moved with joy, he sprang out of the tub, and rushing home naked he kept indicating in a loud voice that he had indeed discovered what he was seeking. For while running he was shouting repeatedly in Greek, "eureka, eureka" ("I have found it, I have found it.").[9]

Archimedes was willing to share his work with others, among them Eratosthenes (285–ca 204 B.C.), a man of almost universal interests. From his native Cyrene in North Africa, Eratosthenes traveled to Athens, where he studied philosophy and mathematics. He refused to join any of the philosophical schools, for he was interested in too many things to follow any particular dogma. Around 245 B.C. King Ptolemy invited Eratosthenes to Alexandria. The Ptolemies had done much to make Alexandria an intellectual, cultural, and scientific center. Eratosthenes came to Alexandria to become librarian of the royal library, a position of great prestige. While there, he continued his mathematical work and by letter struck up his friendship with Archimedes.

Unlike his friend Archimedes, Eratosthenes did not devote his life entirely to mathematics, although he never lost interest in it. He used mathematics to further the geographical studies for which he is most famous. He calculated the circumference of the earth geometrically, estimating it as about 24,675 miles. He was not wrong by much: the earth is actually 24,860 miles in circumference. Eratosthenes also concluded that the earth is a spherical globe, that the land mass is roughly four-sided, and that the land is surrounded by ocean. He discussed the shapes and sizes of land and ocean and the irregularities of the earth's surface. He drew a map of the earth and used his own system of explaining the divisions of the earth's land mass.

Using geographical information gained by Alexander the Great's scientists, Eratosthenes tried to fit the East into Greek geographical knowledge. Although for some reason he ignored the western

The Celestial Globe   In Greek mythology the god Atlas held the world on his strong shoulders, thereby preventing it from falling. Hellenistic scientists formed a very accurate idea of the shape and dimension of the earth. Here Atlas holds the globe, which rests on its axis and displays the skies, with figures representing constellations, as well as the equator, tropics, and polar circles. *(Source: National Museum, Naples/Alinari/Art Resource)*

Mediterranean and Europe, he declared that a ship could sail from Spain either around Africa to India or directly westward to India. Not until the great days of Western exploration did sailors such as Vasco da Gama and Magellan actually prove Eratosthenes' theories. Like Eratosthenes, other Greek geographers also turned their attention southward to Africa. During this period the people of the Mediterranean learned of the climate and customs of Ethiopia and gleaned some scant information about equatorial Africa.

In his life and work Eratosthenes exemplifies the range and vitality of Hellenistic science. His varied interests included the cultural and humanistic as well as the purely scientific. Although his chief interest was in the realm of speculative thought, he did not ignore the practical. He was quite willing to deal with old problems and to break new ground.

In the Hellenistic period the scientific study of botany had its origin. Aristotle's pupil Theophrastus (ca 372–288 B.C.), who became head of the Lyceum, the school established by Aristotle, studied the botanical information made available by Alexander's penetration of the East. Aristotle had devoted a good deal of his attention to zoology, and Theophrastus extended his work to plants. He wrote two books on the subject, *History of Plants* and *Causes of Plants*. He carefully observed phenomena and based his conclusions on what he had actually seen. Theophrastus classified plants and accurately described their parts. He detected the process of germination and realized the importance of climate and soil to plants. Some of Theophrastus's work found its way into agricultural handbooks, but for the most part Hellenistic science did not carry the study of botany further.

Despite its undeniable brilliance, Hellenistic science suffered from a remarkable weakness almost impossible for practical-minded Americans to understand. Although scientists of this period invented such machines as the air gun, the water organ, and even the steam engine, they never used their discoveries as labor-saving devices. No one has satisfactorily explained why these scientists were so impractical, but one answer is quite possible: they and the rest of society saw no real need for machines. Slave labor was especially abundant, a fact that made the use of labor-saving machinery superfluous. Science was applied only to war. Even though Hellenistic science did not lead the ancient

world to an industrial revolution, later Hellenistic thinkers preserved the knowledge of machines and the principles behind them. In so doing, they saved the discoveries of Hellenistic science for the modern age.

HELLENISTIC MEDICINE

The study of medicine flourished during the Hellenistic period, and Hellenistic physicians carried the work of Hippocrates into new areas. Herophilus, who lived in the first half of the third century B.C., worked at Alexandria and studied the writings of Hippocrates. He accepted Hippocrates' theory

Tower of the Four Winds This remarkable building, which still stands in Athens, was built by an astronomer to serve as a sundial, water-clock, and weather vane. It is one of the few examples of the application of Hellenistic science to daily life. (*Source: Ekdotike Athenon*)

Hellenistic Medicine During the Hellenistic period, the practice of medicine expanded greatly, and medical research made huge strides. Despite much harm done by quacks and dishonorable physicians, Hellenistic medicine made substantial progress in healing. In this relief, the physician at left treats a patient while other patients wait to the right. The invention of the waiting room also belongs to classical antiquity. *(Source: National Archaeological Museum, Athens)*

of the four humors and approached the study of medicine in a systematic, scientific fashion. He dissected dead bodies and measured what he observed. He discovered the nervous system and concluded that two types of nerves, motor and sensory, exist. Herophilus also studied the brain, which he considered the center of intelligence, and discerned the cerebrum and cerebellum. His other work dealt with the liver, lungs, and uterus. His younger contemporary, Erasistratus, also conducted research on the brain and nervous system and improved on Herophilus's work. He, too, followed in the tradition of Hippocrates and preferred to let the body heal itself by means of diet and air.

Both Herophilus and Erasistratus were members of the Dogmatic school of medicine at Alexandria. In this school speculation played an important part

in research. So, too, did the study of anatomy. To learn more about human anatomy, Herophilus and Erasistratus dissected corpses and even vivisected criminals whom King Ptolemy contributed for the purpose. The practice of vivisection seems to have been short-lived, although dissection continued. Better knowledge of anatomy led to improvements in surgery. These advances enabled the Dogmatists to invent new surgical instruments and techniques.

In about 280 B.C. Philinus and Serapion, pupils of Herophilus, led a reaction against the Dogmatists. Believing that the Dogmatists had become too speculative, they founded the Empiric school of medicine at Alexandria. Claiming that the Dogmatists' emphasis on anatomy and physiology was misplaced, they concentrated instead on the observation and cure of illnesses. They also laid heavier stress on the use of drugs and medicine to treat illnesses. Heraclides of Tarentum (perhaps first century B.C.) carried on the Empirical tradition and dedicated himself to observation and use of medicines. He discovered the benefits of opium and worked with other drugs that relieved pain. He also steadfastly rejected the relevance of magic to drugs and medicines.

Hellenistic medicine had its dark side, for many physicians were moneygrubbers, fools, and quacks. One of the angriest complaints comes from the days of the Roman Empire:

Of all men only a physician can kill a man with total impunity. Oh no, on the contrary, censure goes to him who dies and he is guilty of excess, and furthermore he is blamed. . . . Let me not accuse their [physicians'] avarice, their greedy deals with those whose fate hangs in the balance, their setting a price on pain, and their demands for down payment in case of death, and their secret doctrines.[10]

Abuses such as these existed already in the Hellenistic period. As is true today, many Hellenistic physicians did not take the Hippocratic oath very seriously.

Besides incompetent and greedy physicians, the Hellenistic world was plagued by people who claimed to cure illnesses through incantations and magic. Their potions included such concoctions as blood from the ear of an ass mixed with water to cure fever, or the liver of a cat killed when the moon was waning and preserved in salt. Broken bones could be cured by applying the ashes of a pig's jawbone to the break. The dung of a goat mixed with old wine was good for healing broken ribs. One charlatan claimed that he could cure epilepsy by making the patient drink spring water, drawn at night, from the skull of a man who had been killed but not cremated. These quacks even claimed that they could cure mental illness. The treatment for a person suffering from melancholy was calf dung boiled in wine. No doubt the patient became too sick to be depressed.

Quacks who prescribed such treatments were very popular but did untold harm to the sick and injured. They and greedy physicians also damaged the reputation of dedicated doctors who honestly and intelligently tried to heal and alleviate pain. The medical abuses that arose in the Hellenistic period were so flagrant that the Romans, who later entered the Hellenistic world, developed an intense dislike and distrust of physicians. The Romans considered the study of Hellenistic medicine beneath the dignity of a Roman; and even as late as the time of the Roman Empire, few Romans undertook the study of Greek medicine. Nonetheless, the work of men like Herophilus and Serapion made valuable contributions to the knowledge of medicine, and the fruits of their work were preserved and handed on to the West.

SUMMARY

It can safely be said that Philip and Alexander broadened Greek and Macedonian horizons, but not in ways that they had intended. Although Alexander established Macedonian and Greek colonies across western and central Asia for military reasons, they resulted in the spread of Hellenism as a side effect. In the Aegean and Near East the fusion of Greek and Eastern cultures laid the social, intellectual, and cultural foundations on which the Romans would later build. In the heart of the old Persian Empire, Hellenism was only another new influence that was absorbed by older ways of thought and life. Yet overall, in the exchange of ideas and the opportunity for different cultures to learn about one another, a new cosmopolitan society evolved. That society in turn made possible such diverse advances as a wider extent of trade and agriculture, the creation of religious and philosophical ideas that paved the way for Christianity, and greater freedom for women. People of the Hellenistic period also made remarkable advances in science and medicine. They not only built on the achievements of their predecessors, but they also produced one of the most creative intellectual eras of classical antiquity.

NOTES

1. H. Bengtson, *Philipp und Alexander der Grosse* (Munich: Callwey, 1985), p. 7. John Buckler is the translator of all uncited quotations from a foreign language in Chapters 1–6.
2. Plutarch, *Moralia* 328E.

3. Quoted in W. W. Tarn and G. T. Griffith, *Hellenistic Civilizations*, 3d ed. (Cleveland and New York: Meridian Books, 1961), p. 199.
4. *Periplous of the Erythraian Sea* 57.
5. Diodorus 3.12.2–3.
6. Diogenes, *Laertius* 6.38.
7. Plutarch, *Lives of Agis and Cleomenes* 22.5.
8. Ibid., 14.13
9. Vitruvius, *On Architecture* 9 Preface, 10.
10. Pliny the Elder, *Natural History* 29.8.18, 21.

SUGGESTED READING

General treatments of Hellenistic political, social, and economic history can be found in F. W. Walbank et al., *The Cambridge Ancient History*, 2d ed., vol. 7, pt. 1 (1984). Shorter is F. W. Walbank, *The Hellenistic World* (1981), a fresh appraisal by one of the foremost scholars in the field. The undisputed classic in this area is M. Rostovtzeff, *The Social and Economic History of the Hellenistic World*, 3 vols. (1941). A leading American scholar, E. S. Gruen, has recently chronicled the Roman expansion into the Hellenistic East in *The Hellenistic World and the Coming of Rome*, 2 vols. (1984). Good selections of primary sources in accurate and readable translation can be found in M. M. Austin, *The Hellenistic World from Alexander to the Roman Conquest* (1981), and S. M. Burstein, *The Hellenistic Age from the Battle of Ipsos to the Death of Kleopatra III* (1985).

Each year brings a new crop of biographies of Alexander the Great. Still the best, however, is J. R. Hamilton, *Alexander the Great* (1973). Old but still useful is U. Wilcken, *Alexander the Great* (English translation, 1967), which has had a considerable impact on scholars and students alike. Although many historians have idealized Alexander the Great, recent scholarship has provided a more realistic and unflattering view of him. The foremost expert on Alexander is E. Badian, who has reinterpreted Alexander's career in a variety of journal articles: *Historia* 7 (1958): 425–444; *Classical Quarterly* 52 (1958): 144–157; *Journal of Hellenic Studies* 81 (1961): 16–43; and *Greece and Rome* 12 (1965): 166–182. Badian's analysis of Alexander also appears in *The Cambridge History of Iran*, vol. 2 (1985), chap. 8. Recent political studies of the Hellenistic period include A. B. Bosworth, *Conquest and Empire* (1988), which sets Alexander's career in a broad context, and F. L. Holt, *Alexander the Great and Bactria* (1988), which discusses the formation of a Greco-Macedonian frontier in central Asia. A. K. Bowman, *Egypt After the Pharaohs* (1986), is a readable account of the impact of the Greeks and Macedonians on Egyptian society. The same topic is treated by N. Lewis, a major scholar in the field, in his *Greeks in Ptolemaic Egypt* (1986); and a brief, new study comes from the pen of another major scholar, A. E. Samuel, *The Shifting Sands of History: Interpretations of Ptolemaic Egypt* (1989), which deals with history and historiography. E. V. Hansen, *The Attalids of Pergamon*, 2d ed. (1971), though dated, is still the best treatment of that kingdom. B. Bar-Kochva, *Judas Maccabaeus* (1988), treats the Jewish struggle against the Seleucids and Hellenistic influences. A good portrait of one of the busiest ports in the Hellenistic world can be found in R. Garland, *The Piraeus* (1987).

Much new work has focused on the spread of Hellenism throughout the Near East. Very extensive is A. Kuhrt and S. Sherwin-White, eds., *Hellenism in the East* (1988), which touches on a broad range of topics, including biblical studies, Christianity, and Islam. A. E. Samuels, *The Promise of the West* (1988), studies the connections among Greek, Roman, and Jewish culture and thought and their significance for Western history. P. McKechnie, *Outsiders in the Greek Cities of the Fourth Century* (1989), provides an interesting study of the social dislocation of the Greeks in the time of Philip II and Alexander the Great.

No specific treatment of women in the Hellenistic world yet exists, but two recent studies shed light on certain aspects of the topic. The first, an illustrated collection of essays covering the whole of the ancient world, is I. van Sertima, ed., *Black Women in Antiquity*, 2d ed. (1985). S. B. Pomeroy, *Women in Hellenistic Egypt* (1984), studies women in the kingdom from which the most ancient evidence has survived.

Two general studies of religion in the Hellenistic world are F. Grant, *Hellenistic Religion: The Age of Syncretism* (1953), and H. J. Rose, *Religion in Greece and Rome* (1959). For the effects of Hellenistic religious developments on Christianity, see A. D. Nock, *Early Gentile Christianity and Its Hellenistic Background* (1964). R. van den Broek et al., eds., *Knowledge of God in the Graeco-Roman World* (1988), is a difficult but rewarding collection of essays that points out how similarly pagans, Hellenistic Jews, and Christians thought about human attempts to know god. R. E. Witt, *Isis in the Graeco-Roman World* (1971), an illustrated volume, studies the origins and growth of the Isis cult; and more specifically, S. K. Heyob, *The Cult of Isis Among Women in the Graeco-Roman World* (1975), explores its popularity among women. The cult of Isis's consort Osiris is the subject of J. G. Griffiths, *The Origins of Osiris and His Cult* (1980); and for the mystery cults in general, see W. Burkert, *Ancient Mystery Cults* (1987), written by one of the finest scholars in the field.

Hellenistic philosophy and science have attracted the attention of a number of scholars, and the various philosophical schools are especially well covered. A new general treatment can be recommended because it deals with the broader question of the role of the intellectual in the Classical and Hellenistic worlds: F. L. Vatai, *Intellectuals in Politics in the Greek World from Early Times to the Hellenistic Age* (1984). Broader is S. Blundell's *The Origin of Civilization in Greek and Roman Thought* (1986), a survey of classical political and social theories through a period of ten centuries, from Aristotle to the Stoics and their Roman successors. A convenient survey of Hellenistic philosophy is A. A. Long, *Hellenistic Philosophy* (1974). F. Sayre, *The Greek Cynics* (1948), focuses on Diogenes' thought and manners, while C. Bailey, *Epicureans* (1926), though decidedly dated, is still a useful study of the origins and nature of Epicureanism. Three treatments of Stoicism are J. Rist, *Stoic Philosophy* (1969), F. H. Sandbach, *The Stoics* (1975), and M. L. Colish, *The Stoic Tradition from Antiquity to the Early Middle Ages*, 2 vols. (1985), which devotes a great deal of attention to the impact of Stoicism on Christianity. A good survey of Hellenistic science is G. E. R. Lloyd, *Greek Science After Aristotle* (1963), and specific studies of major figures can be found in T. L. Heath's solid work, *Aristarchos of Samos* (1920), still unsurpassed, and E. J. Dijksterhuis, *Archimedes*, rev. ed. (1987).

5

The Rise of Rome

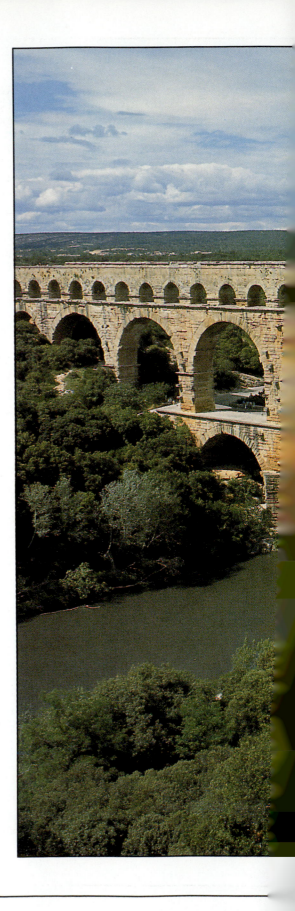

*W*ho is so thoughtless and lazy that he does not want to know in what way and with what kind of government the Romans in less than 53 years conquered nearly the entire inhabited world and brought it under their rule—an achievement previously unheard of?"[1] This question was first asked by Polybius, a Greek historian who lived in the second century B.C. With keen awareness Polybius realized that the Romans were achieving something unique in world history.

What was that achievement? Was it simply the creation of a huge empire? Hardly. The Persians had done the same thing. For that matter, Alexander the Great had conquered vast territories in a shorter time. Was it the creation of a superior culture? Even the Romans admitted that in matters of art, literature, philosophy, and culture they learned from the Greeks. Rome's achievement lay in the ability of the Romans not only to conquer peoples but to incorporate them into the Roman system. Rome succeeded where the Greek polis had failed. Unlike the Greeks, who refused to share citizenship, the Romans extended their citizenship first to the Italians and later to the peoples of the provinces. With that citizenship went Roman government and law. Rome created a world state that embraced the entire Mediterranean area.

Nor was Rome's achievement limited to the ancient world. Rome's law, language, and administrative practices were a precious heritage to medieval and modern Europe. London, Paris, Vienna, and many other modern European cities began as Roman colonies or military camps. When the Founding Fathers created the American republic, they looked to Rome as a model. On the darker side, Napoleon and Mussolini paid their own tribute to Rome by aping its forms. Whether Founding Father or modern autocrat, all were acknowledging admiration for the Roman achievement.

Roman history is usually divided into two periods: the Republic, the age in which Rome grew from a small city-state to ruler of an empire, and the Empire, the period when the republican constitution gave way to constitutional monarchy.

■ How did Rome rise to greatness?

■ What effects did the conquest of the Mediterranean have on the Romans themselves?

■ Finally, why did the republic collapse?

These are the questions we will attempt to answer in this chapter.

THE LAND AND THE SEA

To the west of Greece the boot-shaped peninsula of Italy, with Sicily at its toe, occupies the center of the Mediterranean basin. As Map 5.1 shows, Italy and Sicily thrust southward toward Africa: the distance between southwestern Sicily and the northern African coast is at one point only about a hundred miles. Italy and Sicily literally divide the Mediterranean into two basins and form the focal point between the halves.

Like Greece and other Mediterranean lands, Italy enjoys a genial, almost subtropical climate. The winters are rainy, but the summer months are dry. Because of the climate the rivers of Italy usually carry little water during the summer, and some go entirely dry. The low water level of the Arno, one of the principal rivers of Italy, once led Mark Twain to describe it as "a great historical creek with four feet in the channel and some scows floating around. It would be a very plausible river if they would pump some water into it."[2] The Arno at least is navigable. Most of Italy's other rivers are not. Clearly these small rivers were unsuitable for regular, large-scale shipping. Italian rivers, unlike Twain's beloved Mississippi, never became major thoroughfares for commerce and communications.

Geography encouraged Italy to look to the Mediterranean. In the north, Italy is protected by the Apennine Mountains, which break off from the Alps and form a natural barrier. The Apennines hindered but did not prevent peoples from penetrating Italy from the north. Throughout history, in modern times as well as ancient, various invaders have entered Italy by this route. North of the Apennines lies the Po Valley, an important part of modern Italy. In antiquity this valley did not become

MAP 5.1 Italy and the City of Rome The geographical configuration of the italian peninsula shows how Rome stood astride north-south communications and how the state that united Italy stood poised to move into Sicily and northern Africa.

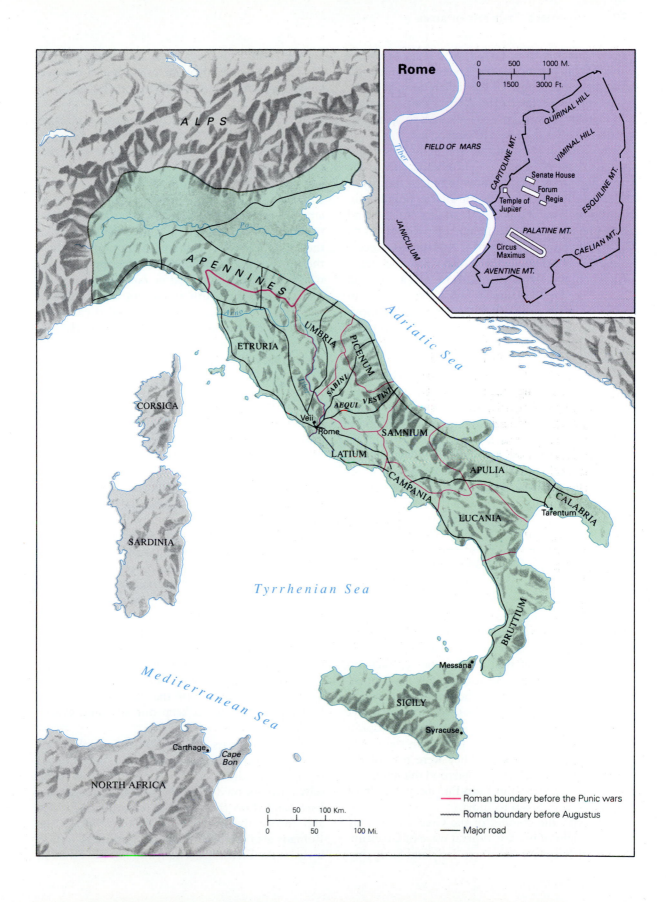

ALPS

Po

APENNINES

Arno

UMBRIA

ETRURIA

PICENUM

Tiber

SABINI

AEQUI VESTINI

Veii

Rome

SAMNIUM

LATIUM

CAMPANIA

APULIA

CALABRIA

Tarentum

LUCANIA

CORSICA

SARDINIA

BRUTTIUM

Tyrrhenian Sea

Adriatic Sea

Messana

SICILY

Syracuse

Mediterranean Sea

Carthage   *Cape Bon*

NORTH AFRICA

0	50	100 Km.
0	50	100 Mi.

—— Roman boundary before the Punic wars
—— Roman boundary before Augustus
—— Major road

Rome

0	500	1000 M.
0	1500	3000 Ft.

Tiber

FIELD OF MARS

QUIRINAL HILL

VIMINAL HILL

CAPITOLINE MT.

Senate House

Forum

Regia

ESQUILINE MT.

Temple of Jupiter

JANICULUM

PALATINE MT.

CAELIAN MT.

Circus Maximus

AVENTINE MT.

Roman territory until late in the history of the republic. From the north the Apennines run southward the entire length of the Italian boot; they virtually cut off access to the Adriatic Sea, a feature that further induced Italy to look west to Spain and Carthage rather than east to Greece.

Even though most of the land is mountainous, the hill country is not as inhospitable as are the Greek highlands. In antiquity the general fertility of the soil provided the basis for a large population. Nor did the mountains of Italy so carve up the land as to prevent the development of political unity. Geography proved kinder to Italy than to Greece.

In their southward course the Apennines leave two broad and fertile plains, those of Latium and Campania. These plains attracted settlers and invaders from the time when peoples began to move into Italy. Among these peoples were the Romans, who established their city on the Tiber River in Latium.

This site enjoyed several advantages. The Tiber provided Rome with a constant source of water. Located at an easy crossing point on the Tiber, Rome stood astride the main avenue of communications between northern and southern Italy. The famous seven hills of Rome were defensible and safe from the floods of the Tiber. Rome was in an excellent position to develop the resources of Latium and maintain contact with the rest of Italy.

THE ETRUSCANS AND ROME (750–509 B.C.)

In recent years archeologists have found traces of numerous early peoples in Italy. The origins of these cultures and their precise relations with one another are not yet well understood. In fact, no clear account of the prehistory of Italy is yet possible. Of the period before the appearance of the Etruscans (1200–750 B.C.), one fundamental fact is indisputable: peoples speaking Indo-European languages were moving into Italy from the north, probably in small groups. They were part of the awesome but imperfectly understood movement of peoples that spread the Indo-European family of languages from Spain to India.

Only with the coming of the Greeks does Italy enter the light of history. A great wave of Greek immigration swept into southern Italy and Sicily during the eighth century B.C., as described on pages 71–72. The Greeks brought urban life to these regions, spreading cultural influence far beyond their city-states.

In the north the Greeks encountered the Etruscans, one of the truly mysterious peoples of antiquity. Who the Etruscans were and where they came from are unknown. Nonetheless, this fascinating people was to leave an indelible mark on the Romans. Skillful metal workers, the Etruscans amassed extensive wealth by trading their manufactured goods in Italy and beyond. The strength of their political and military institutions enabled them to form a loosely organized league of cities whose dominion extended as far north as the Po Valley and as far south as Latium and Campania (see Map 5.1). In Latium they founded cities and took over control of Rome. Like the Greeks, the Etruscans promoted urban life, and one of the places that benefited from Etruscan influence was Rome.

The Etruscans found the Romans settled on three of Rome's seven hills. The site of the future Forum Romanum, the famous public square and center of political life, was originally the cemetery of the small community. According to Roman legend, Romulus and Remus had founded Rome in 753 B.C. Romulus built his settlement on the Palatine Hill, while Remus chose the Aventine (see inset, Map 5.1). Jealous of his brother's work, Remus ridiculed it by jumping over Romulus's unfinished wall. In a rage, Romulus killed his brother and vowed, "So will die whoever else shall leap over my walls." In this instance, legend preserves some facts. Archeological investigation has confirmed that the earliest settlement at Rome was situated on the Palatine Hill and that it dates to the first half of the eighth century B.C. The legend also shows traces of Etruscan influence on Roman customs. The inviolability of Romulus's walls recalls the Etruscan concept of the *pomerium,* a sacred boundary intended to keep out anything evil or unclean.

During the years 753 to 509 B.C. the Romans embraced many Etruscan customs. They adopted the Etruscan alphabet, which the Etruscans themselves had adopted from the Greeks. The Romans later handed on this alphabet to medieval Europe and thence to the modern Western world. The Romans also adopted symbols of political authority from the Etruscans. The symbol of the Etruscan king's right to execute or scourge his subjects was a bundle of rods and an ax, called in Latin the *fasces*, which the king's retainer carried before him on official occasions. When the Romans expelled the Etruscan kings, they created special attendants called "lictors" to carry the fasces before their new magistrates, the consuls. Even the *toga*, the white woolen robe worn by citizens, came from the Etruscans. In engineering and architecture the Romans adopted from the Etruscans the vault and the arch. Above all, it was thanks to the Etruscans that the Romans truly became urban dwellers.

Etruscan power and influence at Rome were so strong that Roman traditions preserved the memory of Etruscan kings who ruled the city. Under the Etruscans, Rome enjoyed contacts with the larger Mediterranean world, and the city began to grow. In the years 575 to 550 B.C. temples and public buildings began to grace the city. The Capitoline Hill became the religious center of the city when the temple of Jupiter Optimus Maximus (Jupiter the Best and Greatest) was built there. The Forum ceased to be a cemetery and began its history as a public meeting place, a development parallel to that of the Greek agora. Trade in metal work became common, and the wealthier Roman classes began to import large numbers of fine Greek vases. The Etruscans had found Rome a collection of villages and made it a city.

THE ROMAN CONQUEST OF ITALY (509–290 B.C.)

Early Roman history is an uneven mixture of fact and legend. Roman traditions often contain an important kernel of truth, but that does not make them history. In many cases they are significant because they illustrate the ethics, morals, and ideals that Roman society considered valuable. Rome's early history also presents the historian with another problem. Historical writing did not begin among the Romans until the third century B.C., hundreds of years after the founding of Rome. Much later still, around the time of Jesus, the historian Livy (59 B.C.–A.D. 17) gave final form to Roman legends.

How much genuine information about the early years did Romans such as Livy have? Did they simply take what they knew and try to make of it an

Etruscan Apollo A masterpiece of Etruscan art, this statue of Apollo testifies both to the artistic and the religious influence of the early Greeks. Yet Etruscan sculptors were not mere imitators, and they adapted Greek art to serve their own tastes. *(Source: Villa Giulia Museum, Rome/Art Resource)*

intelligible story? Livy gave his own answer to these questions: "Events before Rome was born or thought of have come down to us in old tales with more of the charm of poetry than of sound historical record, and such traditions I propose neither to affirm nor refute."[3] Livy also admitted that these legends and tales depicted men and women not necessarily as they were, but as Romans should be. For him the story of early Rome was an impressive moral tale. Today historians would say that Livy took these legends and made of them a sweeping epic. But they would also admit that the epic preserved the broad outlines of the Roman conquest of Italy and the development of Rome's internal affairs. Both parts of the epic—legend and fact—are worth examining for what they say about the Romans.

According to Roman tradition, the Romans expelled the Etruscan king Tarquin the Proud from Rome in 509 B.C. and founded the republic. In the years that followed, the Romans fought numerous wars with their neighbors on the Italian peninsula. They became soldiers, and the grim fighting bred tenacity, a prominent Roman trait. War also involved diplomacy, at which the Romans became masters. At an early date they learned the value of alliances and how to provide leadership for their allies. Alliances with the Latin towns around them provided them with a large reservoir of manpower. Their alliances involved the Romans in still other wars and took them farther afield in the Italian peninsula.

One of the earliest wars was with two nearby peoples, the Aequi and the Volsci. From this contest arose the legend of Cincinnatus. At one point, when the Aequi had launched a serious invasion, the Romans called on Cincinnatus to assume the office of dictator. In this period the Roman dictator, unlike modern dictators, was a legitimate magistrate given ultimate powers for a specified period of time. The Roman officials found Cincinnatus working his three-acre farm. Wiping the sweat from himself, he listened to the appeal of his countrymen and accepted the office. Fifteen days later, after he had defeated the Aequi, he returned to his farm. Cincinnatus personified the ideal Roman citizen—a man of simplicity, who put his duty to Rome before any consideration of personal interest or wealth.

The growth of Roman power was slow but steady. Not until roughly a century after the founding of the republic did the Romans try to drive the Etruscans entirely out of Latium. In 405 B.C. they laid siege to Veii, the last neighboring Etruscan city. Ten years later they captured it. The story of the siege of Veii is in some ways the Roman equivalent of the Greek siege of Troy. But once again tradition preserves a kernel of truth, confirmed now by archeological exploration of Veii. This was an important Roman victory, for the land of Veii went to the Romans and provided additional resources for Rome's growing population. Rome's concentrated landholdings formed a strong, unified core in central Italy. After the destruction of Veii, Rome overshadowed its Latin allies and enemies alike. Yet around 390 B.C. the Romans suffered a major setback when a new people, the Celts—or "Gauls," as the Romans called them—swept aside a Roman army and sacked Rome. More intent on loot than land, they agreed to abandon Rome in return for a thousand pounds of gold.

During the century from 390 B.C. to 290 B.C., Romans rebuilt their city and recouped their losses. They also reorganized their army to create the mobile legion, a flexible unit capable of fighting on either broken or open terrain. The Romans finally brought Latium and their Latin allies fully under their control and conquered Etruria. In 343 B.C. they grappled with the Samnites in a series of bitter wars for the possession of Campania and southern Italy. The Samnites were a formidable enemy and inflicted serious losses on the Romans. But the superior organization, institutions, and manpower of the Romans won out in the end. Although Rome had yet to subdue the whole peninsula, for the first time in history the city stood unchallenged in Italy.

Rome's success in diplomacy and politics was as important as its military victories. Unlike the Greeks, the Romans did not simply conquer and dominate. Instead, they shared with other Italians both political power and degrees of Roman citizenship. The Romans did not start out to build a system. They were always a practical people—that was one of their greatest strengths. When they found a treaty or a political arrangement that worked, they used it wherever possible. When it did not, they turned to something else. Consequently, Rome had a network of alliances and treaties with other peoples and states. With many of their oldest allies, such as the Latin cities, they shared full Roman citizenship. In other instances they granted citizenship without the franchise (*civitas sine suffragio*). Allies who held this status enjoyed all the rights of Roman citizenship except that they could not vote or hold Roman offices. They were subject to Roman taxes and calls for military service but ran their own local affairs. The Latin allies were able to acquire full Roman citizenship by moving to Rome.

By their willingness to extend their citizenship, the Romans took Italy into partnership. Here the political genius of Rome triumphed where Greece had failed. Rome proved itself superior to the Greek polis because it both conquered and shared the fruits of conquest with the conquered. Rome could consolidate where Greece could only dominate. The unwillingness of the Greek polis to share its citizenship condemned it to a limited horizon. Not so with Rome. The extension of Roman citizenship strengthened the state, gave it additional manpower and wealth, and laid the foundation of the Roman Empire.

THE ROMAN STATE

The Romans summed up their political existence in a single phrase: *senatus populusque Romanus,* "the Roman senate and the people." The real genius of the Romans lay in the fields of politics and law. Unlike the Greeks, they did not often speculate on the ideal state or on political forms. Instead, they realistically met actual challenges and created institutions, magistracies, and legal concepts to deal with practical problems. Change was consequently commonplace in Roman political life, and the constitution of 509 B.C. was far simpler than that of 27 B.C. Moreover, the Roman constitution, unlike the American, was not a single written document. Rather, it was a set of traditional beliefs, customs, and laws.

In the early republic, social divisions determined the shape of politics. Political power was in the hands of the aristocracy—the *patricians,* who were wealthy landowners. Patrician families formed clans, as did aristocrats in early Greece. They dominated the affairs of state, provided military leadership in time of war, and monopolized knowledge of law and legal procedure. The common people of Rome, the *plebeians,* had few of the patricians' advantages. Some plebeians formed their own clans and rivaled the patricians in wealth. Many plebeian merchants increased their wealth in the course of

Roman expansion, but most plebeians were poor. They were the artisans, small farmers, and landless urban dwellers. The plebeians, rich and poor alike, were free citizens with a voice in politics. Nonetheless, they were overshadowed by the patricians.

Perhaps the greatest institution of the republic was the senate, which had originated under the Etruscans as a council of noble elders who advised the king. During the republic the senate advised the consuls and other magistrates. Because the senate sat year after year, while magistrates changed annually, it provided stability and continuity. It also served as a reservoir of experience and knowledge. Technically, the senate could not pass legislation; it could only offer its advice. But increasingly, because of the senate's prestige, its advice came to have the force of law.

The Romans created several assemblies through which the people elected magistrates and passed legislation. The earliest was the *comitia curiata,* which had religious, political, and military functions. According to Roman tradition, King Servius Tullius (578–535 B.C.), who reorganized the state into 193 *centuries* for military purposes, created the *comitia centuriata* as a political body to decide Roman policy. The comitia centuriata voted in centuries, which in this instance means political blocks. The patricians possessed the majority of centuries because they shouldered most of the burden of defense. Thus they could easily outvote the plebeians. In 471 B.C. the plebeians won the right to meet in an assembly of their own, the *concilium plebis,* and to pass ordinances. In 287 B.C. the bills passed in the concilium plebis were recognized as binding on the entire population.

The chief magistrates of the republic were the two consuls, elected for one-year terms. At first the consulship was open only to patricians. The consuls commanded the army in battle, administered state business, convened the comitia centuriata, and supervised financial affairs. In effect, they and the senate ran the state. The consuls appointed *quaestors* to assist them in their duties, and in 421 B.C. the quaestorship became an elective office open to plebeians. The quaestors took charge of the public treasury and prosecuted criminals in the popular courts.

In 366 B.C. the Romans created a new office, that of *praetor,* and in 227 B.C. the number of praetors was increased to four. When the consuls were away from Rome, the praetors could act in their place.

The Roman Forum   The forum was the center of Roman political life. From simple beginnings it developed into the very symbol of Rome's imperial majesty. *(Source: Josephine Powell, Rome)*

The praetors dealt primarily with the administration of justice. When he took office, a praetor issued a proclamation declaring the principles by which he would interpret the law. These proclamations became very important because they usually covered areas where the law was vague and thus helped clarify the law.

Other officials included the powerful *censors,* created in 443 B.C., who had many responsibilities, the most important being supervision of public morals, the power to determine who lawfully could sit in the senate, the registration of citizens, and the leasing of public contracts. Later officials were the *aediles,* four in number, who supervised the streets and markets and presided over public festivals.

After the age of overseas conquest (see pages 138–141), the Romans divided the Mediterranean area into provinces governed by ex-consuls and ex-

praetors. Because of their experience in Roman politics, they were well suited to administer the affairs of the provincials and to fit Roman law and custom into new contexts.

One of the most splendid achievements of the Romans was their development of law. Roman law began as a set of rules that regulated the lives and relations of citizens. This civil law, or *ius civile,* consisted of statutes, customs, and forms of procedure. Roman assemblies added to the body of law, and praetors interpreted it. The spirit of the law aimed at protecting the property, lives, and reputations of citizens, redressing wrongs, and giving satisfaction to victims of injustice.

As the Romans came into more frequent contact with foreigners, they had to devise laws to deal with disputes between Romans and foreigners and between foreigners under Roman jurisdiction. In these instances, where there was no precedent to guide the Romans, the legal decisions of the praetors proved of immense importance. The praetors adopted aspects of other legal systems and resorted to the law of equity—what they thought was right and just to all parties. Free, in effect, to determine law, the praetors enjoyed a great deal of flexibility. This situation illustrates the practicality and the genius of the Romans. By addressing specific, actual circumstances the praetors developed a body of law, the *ius gentium,* "the law of peoples," that applied to Romans and foreigners and that laid the foundation for a universal conception of law. By the time of the late republic, Roman jurists were reaching decisions on the basis of the Stoic concept of *ius naturale,* "natural law," a universal law that could be applied to all societies.

SOCIAL CONFLICT IN ROME

Another important aspect of early Roman history was a great social conflict, usually known as the Struggle of the Orders, which developed between patricians and plebeians. What the plebeians wanted was real political representation and safeguards against patrician domination. The plebeians' efforts to obtain recognition of their rights is the crux of the Struggle of the Orders.

Rome's early wars gave the plebeians the leverage they needed: Rome's survival depended on the army, and the army needed the plebeians. The first showdown between plebeians and patricians came, according to tradition, in 494 B.C. To force the patricians to grant concessions, the plebeians seceded from the state; they literally walked out of Rome and refused to serve in the army. The plebeians' general strike worked. Because of it the patricians made important concessions. One of these was social. In 445 B.C. the patricians passed a law, the *lex Canuleia,* which for the first time allowed patricians and plebeians to marry one another. Furthermore, the patricians recognized the right of plebeians to elect their own officials, the *tribunes.* The tribunes in turn had the right to protect the plebeians from the arbitrary conduct of patrician magistrates. The tribunes brought plebeian grievances to the senate for resolution. The plebeians were not bent on undermining the state. Rather, they used their gains only to win full equality under the law.

The law itself was the plebeians' next target. Only the patricians knew what the law was, and only they could argue cases in court. All too often they had used the law for their own benefit. The plebeians wanted the law codified and published. The result of their agitation was the Law of the Twelve Tables, so called because the laws, which covered civil and criminal matters, were inscribed on twelve large bronze plaques. Later still, the plebeians forced the patricians to publish legal procedures as well. The plebeians had broken the patricians' legal monopoly and henceforth enjoyed full protection under the law.

The decisive plebeian victory came with the passage of the Licinian-Sextian rogations (or laws) in 367 B.C. Licinius and Sextus were plebeian tribunes who led a ten-year fight for further reform. Rich plebeians, such as Licinius and Sextus themselves, joined the poor to mount a sweeping assault on patrician privilege. Wealthy plebeians wanted the opportunity to provide political leadership for the state. They demanded that the patricians allow them access to all the magistracies of the state. If they could hold the consulship, they could also sit in the senate and advise the senate on policy. The two tribunes won approval from the senate for a law that stipulated that one of the two annual consuls had to be a plebeian. Though decisive, the Licinian-Sextian rogations did not automatically end the Struggle of the Orders. That happened only in 287 B.C. with the passage of a law, the *lex Hortensia,* that gave the resolutions of the concilium plebis the force of law for patricians and plebeians alike.

The Struggle of the Orders resulted in a Rome stronger and better united than before. It could have led to anarchy, but again certain Roman traits triumphed. The values fostered by their social structure predisposed the Romans to compromise, especially in the face of common danger. Resistance and confrontation in Rome never exploded into class warfare. Instead, both sides resorted to compromises to hammer out a realistic solution. Important, too, were Roman patience, tenacity, and a healthy sense of the practical. These qualities enabled both sides to keep working until they had resolved the crisis. The Struggle of the Orders ended in 287 B.C. with a new concept of Roman citizenship. All citizens shared equally under the law. Theoretically, all could aspire to the highest political offices. Patrician or plebeian, rich or poor, Roman citizenship was equal for all.

The Town of Terracina　The Romans founded numerous colonies, first in Italy and later throughout the Mediterranean. Roman colonies, which often grew into cities, were intended to be self-sufficient. This ancient drawing shows the colonia Axurnas, now Terracina, with its walls and towers for protection of the population sitting astride the Appian Way, the famous road to Rome. The lines to the left show how Roman surveyors had marked out the land for cultivation. *(Source: Bibliotheca Apostolica Vaticana)*

THE AGE OF OVERSEAS CONQUEST (282–146 B.C.)

In 282 B.C. Rome embarked on a series of wars that left it the ruler of the Mediterranean world. There was nothing ideological about these wars. Unlike Napoleon or Hitler, the Romans did not map out grandiose strategies for world conquest. They had no idea of what lay before them. If they could have looked into the future, they would have stood amazed. In many instances the Romans did not even initiate action; they simply responded to situations as they arose. Nineteenth-century Englishmen were fond of saying, "We got our empire in a fit of absence of mind." The Romans could not go quite that far. Though they sometimes declared war reluctantly, they nonetheless felt the need to dominate, to eliminate any state that could threaten them.

Rome was imperialistic, and its imperialism took two forms. In the barbarian West, the home of fierce tribes, Rome resorted to bald aggression to conquer new territory. In areas such as Spain and later Gaul, the fighting was fierce and savage, and gains came slowly. In the civilized East, the world of Hellenistic states, Rome tried to avoid annexing territory. The East was already heavily populated, and those people would have become Rome's responsibility. New responsibilities meant new problems, and such headaches the Romans shunned. In the East the Romans preferred to be patrons rather than masters. Only when that policy failed did they directly annex land. But in 282 B.C. all this lay in the future.

The Samnite wars had drawn the Romans into the political world of southern Italy. In 282 B.C., alarmed by the powerful newcomer, the Greek city of Tarentum in southern Italy called for help from Pyrrhus, king of Epirus in western Greece. A relative of Alexander the Great and an excellent general, Pyrrhus won two furious battles but suffered heavy casualties—thus the phrase "Pyrrhic victory" for a victory involving severe losses. Roman bravery and tenacity led him to comment: "If we win one more battle with the Romans, we'll be completely washed up." Against Pyrrhus's army the Romans threw new legions, and in the end manpower proved decisive. In 275 B.C. the Romans drove Pyrrhus from Italy and extended their sway over southern Italy. Once they did, the island of Sicily became a key for them to block Carthaginian expansion northward.

Pyrrhus once described Sicily as a future "wrestling ground for the Carthaginians and Romans." The Phoenician city of Carthage in North Africa (Map 5.2) had for centuries dominated the western Mediterranean. Sicily had long been a Carthaginian target. Since Sicily is the steppingstone to Italy, the Romans could not let it fall to an enemy. In 264 B.C. Carthage and Rome came to blows over the city of Messana, which commanded the strait between Sicily and Italy.

This conflict, the First Punic War, lasted for twenty-three years (264–241 B.C.). The Romans quickly learned that they could not conquer Sicily unless they controlled the sea. Yet they lacked a fleet and hated the sea as fervently as cats hate water. Nevertheless, with grim resolution the Romans built a navy and challenged the Carthaginians at sea. The Romans fought seven major naval battles with the Carthaginians and won six. Twice their fleet went down in gales. But finally the Romans wore down the Carthaginians. In 241 B.C. the Romans defeated their rivals and took possession of Sicily, which became their first real province. Once again Rome's resources, manpower, and determination proved decisive.

The peace treaty between the two powers brought no peace, in part because in 238 B.C. the Romans took advantage of Carthaginian weakness to seize Sardinia and Corsica. Although unable to resist, many Carthaginians concluded that genuine peace between Carthage and Rome was impossible. One such man was Hamilcar Barca, a Carthaginian commander who had come close to victory in Sicily. The only way Carthage could recoup its fortune was by success in Spain, where the Carthaginians already enjoyed a firm foothold. In 237 B.C. Hamilcar led an army to Spain in order to turn it into Carthaginian territory. With him he took his nineteen-year-old son, Hannibal, but not before he had led Hannibal to an altar and made him swear ever to be an enemy to Rome. In the following years Hamilcar and his son-in-law Hasdrubal subjugated much of southern Spain and in the process rebuilt Carthaginian power. Rome responded in

two ways: first, the Romans made a treaty with Hasdrubal in which the Ebro River formed the boundary between Carthaginian and Roman interests, and second, the Romans began to extend their own influence in Spain.

In 221 B.C. the young Hannibal became Carthaginian commander in Spain, and soon Roman and Carthaginian policies clashed at the city of Saguntum. When Hannibal laid siege to Saguntum, which lay within the sphere of Carthaginian interest, the Romans declared war, claiming that Carthage had attacked a friendly city. So began the Second Punic War, one of the most desperate wars ever fought by Rome. In 218 B.C. Hannibal struck first by marching more than a thousand miles over the Alps into Italy. Once there, he defeated one Roman army at the Battle of Trebia and later another at the Battle of Lake Trasimene in 217 B.C. In the following year, Hannibal won his greatest victory at the Battle of Cannae, in which he inflicted some forty thousand casualties on the Romans. He then spread devastation throughout Italy, and a number of cities in central and southern Italy rebelled

Coin of Hannibal   This Carthaginian coin bears one of the few profiles of Hannibal. The style of the profile is Roman, but the artist has captured the actual likeness of the archenemy of Rome. *(Source: Courtesy of the Trustees of the British Museum)*

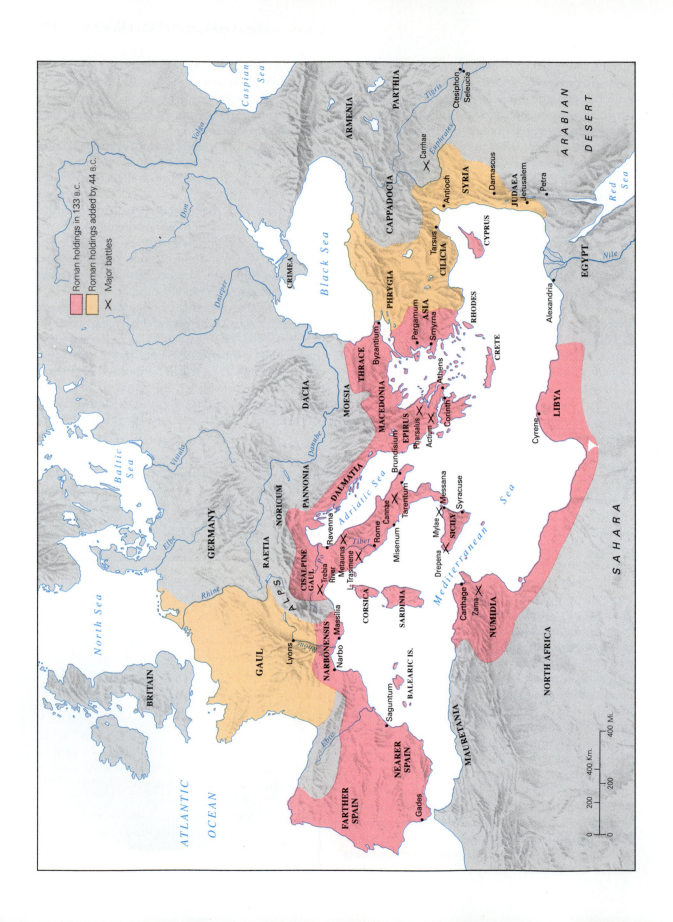

Roman holdings in 133 B.C.
Roman holdings added by 44 B.C.
X Major battles

ARABIAN   DESERT

Caspian Sea

PARTHIA

Tigris

Ctesiphon
Seleucia

Volga

ARMENIA

Carrhae ✕

Euphrates

Damascus

Antioch

SYRIA

Jerusalem
Petra

JUDAEA

Don

CAPPADOCIA

Red Sea

CRIMEA

Black Sea

Dnieper

Tarsus

CILICIA

CYPRUS

Nile

EGYPT

Alexandria

PHRYGIA

ASIA

RHODES

Pergamum
Smyrna

DACIA

Byzantium

THRACE

MOESIA

MACEDONIA

Athens

CRETE

LIBYA

Vistula

EPIRUS

Pharsalus ✕
Actium ✕

Corinth

Cyrene

Baltic Sea

PANNONIA

Brundisium

NORICUM

DALMATIA

Adriatic Sea

Elbe

GERMANY

RAETIA

A L P S

Ravenna

Cannae ✕

Tarentum

Messana ✕

Syracuse

Mediterranean Sea

SAHARA

Rhine

CISALPINE GAUL

Po

Rome

Tiber

Misenum

Mylae ✕

SICILY

Metaurus ✕

Trebia ✕
L. Trasimene ✕

Drepana ✕

North Sea

Rhône

CORSICA

SARDINIA

Carthage ✕
Zama ✕

NUMIDIA

NARBONENSIS

Massilia

GAUL

Lyons

Narbo

BALEARIC IS.

BRITAIN

Saguntum

Ebro

NORTH AFRICA

MAURETANIA

ATLANTIC OCEAN

NEARER SPAIN

FARTHER SPAIN

Gades

400 Mi.

400 Km.

200

200

0

0

against Rome. Syracuse, Rome's ally during the First Punic War, also went over to the Carthaginians. Yet Hannibal failed to crush Rome's iron circle of Latium, Etruria, and Samnium. The wisdom of Rome's political policy of extending rights and citizenship to its allies showed itself in these dark hours. And Rome fought back.

In 210 B.C. Rome found its answer to Hannibal in the young commander Scipio, later better known as Scipio Africanus. Scipio copied Hannibal's methods of mobile warfare, streamlining the legions by making their components capable of independent action and introducing new weapons. In the following years, Scipio operated in Spain, which in 207 B.C. he wrested from the Carthaginians. Also in 207 B.C. the Romans sealed Hannibal's fate in Italy. At the Battle of Metaurus, the Romans destroyed a major Carthaginian army coming to reinforce Hannibal. With Hannibal now bottled up in southern Italy, Scipio in 204 B.C. struck directly at Carthage itself. A Roman fleet landed his legions in North Africa, which prompted the Carthaginians to recall Hannibal from Italy to defend the homeland.

In 202 B.C., near the town of Zama (see Map 5.2), Scipio defeated Hannibal in one of the world's truly decisive battles. Scipio's victory meant that the world of the western Mediterranean would henceforth be Roman. Roman language, law, and culture, fertilized by Greek influences, would in time permeate this entire region. The victory at Zama meant that Rome's heritage would be passed on to the Western world.

The Second Punic War contained the seeds of still other wars. Unabated fear of Carthage led to the Third Punic War, a needless, unjust, and savage conflict that ended in 146 B.C. when Scipio Aemilianus, grandson of Scipio Africanus, destroyed the old hated rival. As the Roman conqueror watched the death pangs of that great city, he turned to his friend Polybius with the words: "I fear and foresee that someday someone will give the same order about my fatherland." It would, however, be centuries before an invader would stand before the gates of Rome.

During the war with Hannibal, the Romans had invaded Spain, a peninsula rich in material resources and the home of fierce warriors. When the Roman legions tried to reduce Spanish tribes, they met with bloody and determined resistance. Not until 133 B.C., after years of brutal and ruthless warfare, did Scipio Aemilianus finally conquer Spain.

During the dark days of the Second Punic War, the king of Macedonia made an alliance with Hannibal against Rome. Even while engaged in the West, the Romans turned east to settle accounts. When the Romans intervened in the Hellenistic East, they went from triumph to triumph. The kingdom of Macedonia fell to the Roman legions, as did Greece and the Seleucid monarchy. By 146 B.C. the Romans stood unchallenged in the eastern Mediterranean and had turned many states and kingdoms into provinces. In 133 B.C. the king of Pergamum in Asia Minor left his kingdom to the Romans in his will. The Ptolemies of Egypt meekly obeyed Roman wishes. The following years would bring the Romans new victories, and they would establish their system of provincial administration. But by 133 B.C. the work of conquest was largely done: the Mediterranean had become *mare nostrum,* "our sea."

OLD VALUES AND GREEK CULTURE

Rome had conquered the Mediterranean world, but some Romans considered that victory a misfortune. The historian Sallust (86–34 B.C.), writing from hindsight, complained that the acquisition of an empire was the beginning of Rome's troubles:

But when through labor and justice our Republic grew powerful, great kings defeated in war, fierce nations and mighty peoples subdued by force, when Carthage the rival of the Roman people was wiped out root and branch, all the seas and lands lay open, then fortune began to be harsh and to throw everything into confusion. The Romans had easily borne labor, danger, uncertainty, and hardship. To them leisure, riches—otherwise desirable— proved to be burdens and torments. So at first money, then desire for power grew great. These things were a sort of cause of all evils.[4]

MAP 5.2 Roman Expansion During the Republic The main spurt of Roman expansion occurred between 264 and 133 B.C., when most of the Mediterranean fell to Rome, followed by the conquest of Gaul and the eastern Mediterranean by 44 B.C.

Battle Between the Romans and Barbarians All of the brutality and fury of Rome's wars with the barbarians of western Europe come to life in this decoration for a horse's harness. Even the bravery and strength of the barbarians were no match for the steadiness and discipline of the Roman legions. *(Source: Museo Archeologico, Aosta)*

Sallust was not alone in his feelings. At the time, some senators had opposed the destruction of Carthage on the grounds that fear of their old rival would keep the Romans in check. In the second century B.C., Romans learned that they could not return to what they fondly considered a simple life. They were world rulers. The responsibilities they faced were complex and awesome. They had to change their institutions, social patterns, and way of thinking to meet the new era. They were in fact building the foundations of a great imperial system. It was an awesome challenge, and there were failures along the way. Roman generals and politicians would destroy each other. Even the republican constitution would eventually be discarded. But in the end Rome triumphed here just as it had on the battlefield, for out of the turmoil would come the *pax Romana*—"Roman peace."

How did the Romans of the day meet these challenges? How did they lead their lives and cope with these momentous changes? Obviously there are as

many answers to these questions as there were Romans. Yet two men represent the major trends of the second century B.C. Cato the Elder shared the mentality of those who longed for the good old days and idealized the traditional agrarian way of life. Scipio Aemilianus led those who embraced the new urban life, with its eager acceptance of Greek culture. Forty-nine years older than Scipio, Cato was a product of an earlier generation, one that confronted a rapidly changing world. Cato and Scipio were both aristocrats and neither of them was typical, even of the aristocracy. But they do exemplify opposing sets of attitudes that marked Roman society and politics in the age of conquest.

Cato and the Traditional Ideal

Marcus Cato (234–149 B.C.) was born a plebeian, but his talent and energy carried him to Rome's highest offices. He cherished the old virtues and consistently imitated the old ways. In Roman society ties within the family were very strong. In this sense Cato and his family were typical. Cato was *paterfamilias,* a term that meant far more than merely "father." The paterfamilias was the oldest dominant male of the family. He held nearly absolute power over the lives of his wife and children as long as he lived. He could legally kill his wife for adultery or divorce her at will. He could kill his children or sell them into slavery. He could force them to marry against their will. Until the paterfamilias died, his sons could not legally own property. At his death, the wife and children of the paterfamilias inherited his property.

Despite his immense power, the paterfamilias did not necessarily act alone or arbitrarily. To deal with important family matters he usually called a council of the adult males. In this way the leading members of the family aired their views. They had the opportunity to give their support to the paterfamilias or to dissuade him from harsh decisions. In these councils the women of the family had no formal part, but it can safely be assumed that they played an important role behind the scenes. Although the possibility of serious conflicts between a paterfamilias and his grown sons is obvious, no one in ancient Rome ever complained about the institution. Perhaps in practice the paterfamilias preferred to be lenient rather than absolute.

Like most Romans, Cato and his family began the day early in the morning. The Romans divided the period of daylight into twelve hours and the darkness into another twelve. The day might begin as early as half past four in summer, as late as half past seven in winter. Because Mediterranean summers are invariably hot, the farmer and his wife liked to take every advantage of the cool mornings. Cato and his family, like modern Italians, ordinarily started the morning with a light breakfast, usually nothing more than some bread and cheese. After breakfast the family went about its work.

Because of his political aspirations, Cato often used the mornings to plead law cases. He walked to the marketplace of the nearby town and defended anyone who wished his help. He received no fees for these services but did put his neighbors in his debt. In matters of law and politics Roman custom was very strong. It demanded that Cato's clients give him their political support or their votes in repayment whenever he asked for them. These clients knew and accepted their obligations to Cato for his help.

Cato's wife (whose name is unknown) was the matron of the family, a position of authority and respect. The virtues expected of a Roman matron were fidelity, chastity, modesty, and dedication to the family. Cato's wife also followed the old ways. While he was in town, she ran the household. She spent the morning spinning and weaving wool for the clothes the family wore. She supervised the domestic slaves, planned the meals, and devoted a good deal of attention to her son. In wealthy homes during this period, the matron had begun to employ a slave as a wet nurse. Cato's wife refused to delegate maternal duties. Like most ordinary Roman women, she nursed her son herself and bathed and swaddled him daily. Later the boy was allowed to play with toys and terra-cotta dolls. Roman children, like children everywhere, kept pets. Dogs were especially popular and valuable as house guards. Children played all sorts of games, and games of chance were very popular. Until the age of seven the child was under the matron's care. During this time the mother began to educate her daughter in the management of the household. After the age of seven, the son—and in many wealthy households the daughter, too—began to undertake formal education.

In the country, Romans like Cato continued to take their main meal at midday. This meal included either coarse bread made from the entire husk of wheat or porridge made with milk or water; it also included turnips, cabbage, olives, and beans. When Romans ate meat, they preferred pork. Unless they lived by the sea, the average farm family did not eat fish, an expensive delicacy. Cato once complained that Rome was a place where a fish could cost more than a cow. With the midday meal the family drank ordinary wine mixed with water. Afterward, any Roman who could took a nap. This was especially true in the summer, when the Mediterranean heat can be fierce. Slaves, artisans, and hired laborers, however, continued their work. In the evening, Romans ate a light meal and went to bed at nightfall.

The agricultural year followed the sun and the stars—the farmer's calendar. Like Hesiod in Boeotia, the Roman farmer looked to the sky to determine when to plant, weed, shear sheep, and perform other chores. Spring was the season for plowing. Roman farmers plowed their land at least twice and preferably three times. The third plowing was to cover the sown seed in ridges and to use the furrows to drain off excess water. The Romans used a variety of plows. Some had detachable shares. Some were heavy for thick soil, others light for thin, crumbly soil. Farmers used oxen and donkeys to pull the plow, collecting the dung of the animals for fertilizer. Besides spreading manure, some farmers fertilized their fields by planting lupines and beans; when they began to pod, farmers plowed them under. The main money crops, at least for rich soils, were wheat and flax. Forage

Manumission of Slaves   During the Republic some Roman masters began to free slaves in public ceremonies. Here two slaves come before their master or a magistrate, who is in the process of freeing the kneeling slave by touching him with a manumission-rod. The other slave shows his gratitude and his good faith with a handshake. *(Source: Collection Waroque, Mariemont, Belgium, © A.C.L. Brussels)*

crops included clover, vetch, and alfalfa. Prosperous farmers like Cato raised olive trees chiefly for the oil. They also raised grapevines for the production of wine. Cato and his neighbors harvested their cereal crops in summer and their grapes in autumn. Harvests varied depending on the soil, but farmers could usually expect yields of 5½ bushels of wheat or 10½ bushels of barley per acre.

An influx of slaves resulted from Rome's wars and conquests. Prisoners from Spain, Africa, and the Hellenistic East and even some blacks and other prisoners from Hannibal's army came to Rome as the spoils of war. The Roman attitude toward slaves and slavery had little in common with modern views. To the Romans slavery was a misfortune that befell some people, but it did not entail any racial theories. Races were not enslaved because the Romans thought them inferior. The black African slave was treated no worse—and no better—than the Spaniard. Indeed, some slaves were valued because of their physical distinctiveness: black Africans and blond Germans were particular favorites. For the talented slave, the Romans always held out the hope of eventual freedom. *Manumission*—the freeing of individual slaves by their masters—became so common that it had to be limited by law. Not even Christians questioned the institution of slavery. It was just a fact of life.

Slaves were entirely their master's property and might be treated with great cruelty. Many Romans were practical enough to realize that they got more out of their slaves by kindness than by severity. Yet in Sicily slaveowners treated their slaves viciously. They bought slaves in huge numbers, branded them for identification, put them in irons, and often made them go without food and clothing. In 135 B.C. these conditions gave rise to a major slave revolt, during which many of the most brutal masters died at their slaves' hands. Italy, too, had trouble with slave unrest, but conditions there were generally better than in Sicily.

For Cato and most other Romans, religion played an important part in life. Originally the Romans thought of the gods as invisible, shapeless natural forces. Only through Etruscan and Greek influence did Roman deities take on human form. Jupiter, the sky-god, and his wife, Juno, became equivalent to the Greek Zeus and Hera. Mars was the god of war but also guaranteed the fertility of the farm and protected it from danger. The gods of the Romans were not loving and personal. They were stern, powerful, and aloof. But as long as the Romans honored the cults of their gods, they could expect divine favor.

Along with the great gods the Romans believed in spirits who haunted fields, forests, crossroads, and even the home itself. Some of these deities were hostile; only magic could ward them off. The spirits of the dead, like ghosts in modern horror films, frequented places where they had lived. They, too, had to be placated but were ordinarily benign. As the poet Ovid (43 B.C.–A.D.17) put it:

The spirits of the dead ask for little.
They are more grateful for piety than for an expensive
*   gift—*
Not greedy are the gods who haunt the Styx below.
A rooftile covered with a sacrificial crown,
Scattered kernels, a few grains of salt,
Bread dipped in wine, and loose violets—
These are enough.
Put them in a potsherd and leave them in the middle of
*   the road.*[5]

A good deal of Roman religion consisted of rituals such as those Ovid describes. These practices lived on long after the Romans had lost interest in the great gods. Even Christianity could not entirely wipe them out. Instead, Christianity was to incorporate many of these rituals into its own style of worship.

Scipio Aemilianus: Greek Culture and Urban Life

The old-fashioned ideals that Cato represented came into conflict with a new spirit of wealth and leisure. The conquest of the Mediterranean world and the spoils of war made Rome a great city. Roman life, especially in the cities, was changing and becoming less austere. The spoils of war went to build baths, theaters, and other places of amusement. Romans and Italian townspeople began to spend more of their time in leisure pursuits. Simultaneously, the new responsibilities of governing the world produced in Rome a sophisticated society. Romans developed new tastes and a liking for Greek culture and literature. They began to learn the Greek language. It became common for an educated Roman to speak both Latin and Greek. Hellenism dominated the cultural life of Rome. Even

diehards like Cato found a knowledge of Greek essential for political and diplomatic affairs. The poet Horace (64–8 B.C.) summed it up well: "Captive Greece captured her rough conqueror and introduced the arts into rustic Latium."

One of the most avid devotees of Hellenism and the new was Scipio Aemilianus, the destroyer of Carthage. Scipio realized that broad and worldly views had to replace the old Roman narrowness. The new situation called for new ways. Rome was no longer a small city on the Tiber; it was the capital of the world, and Romans had to adapt themselves to that fact. Scipio was ready to become an innovator in both politics and culture. He broke with the past in the conduct of his political career, choosing a more personal style of politics, one that reflected his own views and one that looked unflinchingly at the broader problems that the success of Rome brought to its people. He embraced Hellenism wholeheartedly. Perhaps more than anyone else of his day, Scipio represented the new Roman —imperial, cultured, and independent.

In his education and interests, too, Scipio broke with the past. As a boy he had received the traditional Roman training, learning to read and write Latin and becoming acquainted with the law. He mastered the fundamentals of rhetoric and learned how to throw the javelin, fight in armor, and ride a horse. But later Scipio also learned Greek and became a fervent Hellenist. As a young man he formed a lasting friendship with the historian Polybius, who actively encouraged him in his study of Greek culture and in his intellectual pursuits. In later life Scipio's love of Greek learning, rhetoric, and philosophy became legendary. Scipio also promoted the spread of Hellenism in Roman society. He became the center of the Scipionic Circle, a small group of Greek and Roman artists, philosophers, historians, and poets. Conservatives like Cato tried to stem the rising tide of Hellenism, but men like Scipio carried the day and helped make the heritage of Greece an abiding factor in Roman life.

The new Hellenism profoundly stimulated the growth and development of Roman art and literature. The Roman conquest of the Hellenistic East resulted in wholesale confiscation of Greek paintings and sculpture to grace Roman temples, public buildings, and private homes. Roman artists copied many aspects of Greek art, but their emphasis on realistic portraiture carried on a native tradition.

Roman Baths Once introduced into the Roman world, social bathing became a passion. These baths, which date to the Roman Empire, are located in Bath, England, to which they gave their name. A triumph of sophisticated engineering, they also demonstrate how Roman culture and institutions influenced life even on the perimeters of the Roman Empire. *(Source: Michael Holford)*

Fabius Pictor (second half of the third century B.C.), a senator, wrote the first *History of Rome* in Greek. Other Romans translated Greek classics into Latin. Still others, such as the poet Ennius (239–169 B.C.), the father of Latin poetry, studied Greek philosophy, wrote comedies in Latin, and adapted many of Euripides' tragedies for the Roman stage. Ennius also wrote a history of Rome in Latin verse. Plautus (ca 254–184 B.C.) specialized in rough humor. He, too, decked out Greek plays in Roman dress but was no mere imitator. Indeed, his play *Amphitruo* was itself copied eighteen hundred years later by the French playwright Molière and the English poet John Dryden. The Roman dramatist Terence (ca 195–159 B.C.), a member of the Scipionic Circle, wrote comedies of refinement and

grace that owed their essentials to Greek models. His plays lacked the energy and the slapstick of Plautus's rowdy plays. All of early Roman literature was derived from the Greeks, but it managed in time to speak in its own voice and to flourish because it had something of its own to say.

The conquest of the Mediterranean world brought the Romans leisure, and Hellenism influenced how they spent their free time. During the second century B.C. the Greek custom of bathing became a Roman passion and an important part of the day. In the early republic Romans had bathed infrequently, especially in the winter. Now large buildings containing pools and exercise rooms went up in great numbers, and the baths became an essential part of the Roman city. Architects built intricate systems of aqueducts to supply the bathing establishments with water. Conservatives railed at this Greek custom, calling it a waste of time and an encouragement to idleness. They were correct in that bathing establishments were more than just places to take a bath. They included gymnasia, where men exercised and played ball. Women had places of their own to bathe, generally sections of the same baths used by men; for some reason, women's facilities lacked gymnasia. The baths contained hot-air rooms to induce a good sweat and pools of hot and cold water to finish the actual bathing. They also contained snack bars and halls where people chatted and read. The baths were socially important places where men and women went to see and be seen. Social climbers tried to talk to "the right people" and wangle invitations to dinner; politicians took advantage of the occasion to discuss the affairs of the day. Despite the protests of conservatives and moralists, the baths at least provided people—rich and poor—with places for clean and healthy relaxation.

This period also saw a change in the eating habits of urban dwellers. The main meal of the day shifted from midday to evening. Dinner became a more elaborate meal, and dinner parties became fashionable. Although Scipio Aemilianus detested fat people, more and more Romans began to eat excessively. Rich men and women displayed their wealth by serving exotic dishes and gourmet foods. After a course of vegetables and olives came the main course of meat, fish, or fowl. Pig was a favorite dish, and a whole suckling pig might be stuffed with sausage. A lucky guest might even dine on peacock and ostrich, each served with rich sauces. Dessert, as in Italy today, usually consisted of fruit. With the meal the Romans served wine, and during this period vintage wines became very popular.

Although the wealthy gorged themselves whenever they could, poor artisans and workers could rarely afford rich meals. Their dinners resembled Cato's. Yet they, too, occasionally spent generously on food, especially during major festivals. The Roman calendar was crowded with religious festivals, occasions not of dreary piety but of cheerful celebration. One was the festival of Anna Perenna, a festival of fertility, longevity, and prosperity. It was an occasion for fun and exuberant but harmless excess. The poet Ovid caught all the joy and charm of the event:

The ordinary people come [to the banks of the Tiber];
  And scattering themselves over the green grass,
They drink and lie down, each man with his woman.
Some remain under the open sky, a few put up tents,
  Others build leafy huts of twigs.
Some set up reeds instead of unbending columns,
  Over which they spread their togas.
Yet they grow warm with sun and wine, and pray
  For as many years as cups of wine they take, and they
    drink that many.

          . . . .

There also they sing the songs they have heard in the
    theaters,
  And they beat time to the words with lively hands.
Putting down the bowl, they join in rough ring dances,
  And the trim girlfriend dances with her hair flying.
As they return home, they stagger and are a spectacle to
    the vulgar.
  When meeting them, the crowd calls them blessed.
The procession came my way recently (a worthy sight in
    my opinion):
A drunk woman dragged along a drunk old man.[6]

Did Hellenism and new social customs corrupt the Romans? Perhaps the best answer is this: the Roman state and the empire it ruled continued to exist for six more centuries. Rome did not collapse; the state continued to prosper. The golden age of literature was still before it. The high tide of its prosperity still lay in the future. The Romans did not like change but took it in stride. That was part of their practical turn of mind and their strength.

THE LATE REPUBLIC (133–31 B.C.)

The wars of conquest created serious problems for the Romans, some of the most pressing of which were political. The republican constitution had suited the needs of a simple city-state but was inadequate to meet the requirements of Rome's new position in international affairs (see Map 5.2). Sweeping changes and reforms were necessary to make it serve the demands of empire. A system of

Roman Table Manners This mosaic is a floor that can never be swept clean. It whimsically suggests what a dining room floor looked like after a lavish dinner and also tells something about the menu: a chicken head, a wishbone, remains of various seafood, vegetables, and fruit are easily recognizable. *(Source: Museo Gregoria-Profano/Scala/Art Resource)*

provincial administration had to be established. Officials had to be appointed to govern the provinces and administer the law. These officials and administrative organs had to find places in the constitution. Armies had to be provided for defense, and a system of tax collection had to be created.

Other political problems were equally serious. During the wars Roman generals commanded huge numbers of troops for long periods of time. Men such as Scipio Aemilianus were on the point of becoming too mighty for the state to control. Although Rome's Italian allies had borne much of the burden of the fighting, they received fewer rewards than did Roman officers and soldiers. Italians began to agitate for full Roman citizenship and a voice in politics.

There were serious economic problems, too. Hannibal's operations and the warfare in Italy had left the countryside a shambles. The movements of numerous armies had disrupted agriculture. The prolonged fighting had also drawn untold numbers of Roman and Italian men away from their farms for long periods. The families of these soldiers could not keep the land under full cultivation. The people who defended Rome and conquered the world for Rome became impoverished for having done their duty.

These problems, complex and explosive, largely account for the turmoil of the closing years of the republic. The late Republic was one of the most dramatic eras in Roman history. It produced some of Rome's most famous figures: the Gracchi, Marius, Sulla, Cicero, Pompey, and Julius Caesar, among others. In one way or another, each of these men attempted to solve Rome's problems. Yet they were also striving for the glory and honor that were the supreme goals of the senatorial aristocracy. Personal ambition often clashed with patriotism to create political tension throughout the period.

When the legionaries returned to their farms in Italy, they encountered an appalling situation. All too often their farms looked like the farms of people they had conquered. Two courses of action were open to them. They could rebuild as their forefathers had done. Or they could take advantage of an alternative not open to their ancestors and sell their holdings. The wars of conquest had made some men astoundingly rich. These men wanted to invest their wealth in land. They bought up small farms to create huge estates, which the Romans called *latifundia*.

The purchase offers of the rich landowners appealed to the veterans for a variety of reasons. Many veterans had seen service in the East, where they had tasted the rich city life of the Hellenistic states. They were reluctant to return home and settle down to a dull life on the farm. Often their farms were so badly damaged that rebuilding hardly seemed worthwhile. Besides, it was hard to make big profits from small farms. Nor could the veterans supplement their income by working on the latifundia. Although the owners of the latifundia occasionally hired free men as day laborers, they preferred to use slaves. Slaves could not strike or be drafted into the army. Confronted by these conditions, veterans and their families opted to sell their land. They took what they could get for their broken farms and tried their luck elsewhere.

Most veterans migrated to the cities, especially to Rome. Although some found work, most did not. Industry and small manufacturing were generally in the hands of slaves. Even when there was work, slave labor kept the wages of free men low. Instead of a new start, veterans and their families encountered slum conditions that matched those of modern American cities.

This trend held ominous consequences for the strength of Rome's armies. The Romans had always believed that only landowners should serve in the army, for only they had something to fight for. Landless men, even if they were Romans and lived in Rome, could not be conscripted into the army. These landless men may have been veterans of major battles and numerous campaigns; they may have won distinction on the battlefield. But once they sold their land they became ineligible for further military service. A large pool of experienced manpower was going to waste. The landless ex-legionaries wanted a new start, and they were willing to support any leader who would provide it.

One man who recognized the plight of Rome's peasant farmers and urban poor was an aristocrat, Tiberius Gracchus (163–133 B.C.). Appalled by what he saw, Tiberius warned his countrymen that the legionaries were losing their land while fighting Rome's wars:

The wild beasts that roam over Italy have every one of them a cave or lair to lurk in. But the men who fight and die for Italy enjoy the common air and light, indeed, but nothing else. Houseless and homeless they wander about with their wives and children. And it is with lying lips that their generals exhort the soldiers in their battles to defend sepulchres and shrines from the enemy, for not a man of them has an hereditary altar, not one of all these many Romans an ancestral tomb, but they fight and die to support others in luxury, and though they are styled masters of the world, they have not a single clod of earth that is their own.[7]

Until his death Tiberius Gracchus sought a solution to the problems of the veterans and the urban poor.

After his election as tribune of the people in 133 B.C., Tiberius proposed that public land be given to the poor in small lots. Although his reform enjoyed the support of some very distinguished and popular aristocrats, he immediately ran into trouble for a number of reasons. First, his reform bill angered many wealthy aristocrats who had usurped large tracts of public land for their own use. They had no desire to give any of it back, so they bitterly resisted Tiberius's efforts. This was to be expected, yet he unquestionably made additional problems for himself. He introduced his land bill in the concilium plebis without consulting the senate. When King Attalus III left the kingdom of Pergamum to the Romans in his will, Tiberius had the money appropriated to finance his reforms—another slap at the senate. As tribune he acted totally within his rights. Yet the way in which he proceeded was unprecedented. Many powerful Romans became suspicious of Tiberius's growing influence with the people, some even thinking that he aimed at tyranny. Others opposed him because of his unparalleled methods. After all, there were proper ways to do things in Rome, and he had not followed them. As a result, violence broke out when a large body of senators, led by the pontifex maximus (the chief priest), killed Tiberius in cold blood. It was a black day in Roman history. The very people who directed the affairs of state and administered the law had taken the law into their own hands. The death of Tiberius was the beginning of an era of political violence. In the end that violence would bring down the republic.

Although Tiberius was dead, his land bill became law. Furthermore, Tiberius's brother Gaius Gracchus (153–121 B.C.) took up the cause of reform. Gaius was a veteran soldier with an enviable record, but this fiery orator made his mark in the political arena. Gaius also became tribune and demanded even more extensive reform than his brother. To help the urban poor, Gaius pushed legislation to provide them with cheap grain for bread. He defended his brother's land law and suggested other measures for helping the landless. He proposed that Rome send many of its poor and propertyless people out to form colonies in southern Italy. The poor would have a new start and lead productive lives. The city would immediately benefit because excess, nonproductive families would leave for new opportunities abroad. Rome would be less crowded, sordid, and dangerous.

Gaius went a step further and urged that all Italians be granted full rights of Roman citizenship. This measure provoked a storm of opposition, and it was not passed in Gaius's lifetime. Yet in the long run he proved wiser than his opponents. In 91 B.C. many Italians revolted against Rome over the issue of full citizenship, thus triggering the Social War, so named from the Latin word *socium,* or "ally." After a brief but hard-fought war (91–88 B.C.), the senate gave Roman citizenship to all Italians. Had the senate listened to Gaius earlier, it could have prevented a great deal of bloodshed. Yet Gaius himself was also at fault. Like his brother Tiberius, Gaius aroused a great deal of personal and factional opposition. To many he seemed too radical and too hasty to change things. Many political opponents considered him belligerent and headstrong. When Gaius failed in 121 B.C. to win the tribunate for the third time, he feared for his life. In desperation he armed his staunchest supporters, whereupon the senate ordered the consul Opimius to restore order. He did so by having Gaius killed, along with three thousand of Gaius's supporters who opposed the senate's order. Once again the cause of reform had met with violence.

The death of Gaius brought little peace, and trouble came from two sources: the outbreak of new wars in the Mediterranean basin and further political unrest in Rome. In 112 B.C. Rome declared war against the rebellious Jugurtha, king of Numidia in North Africa. Numidia had been one of Rome's *client kingdoms,* kingdoms still ruled by their own kings but subject to Rome. The Roman legions made little headway against Jugurtha until 107 B.C., when Gaius Marius, an Italian *new man* (a politician not from the traditional Roman aristocracy), became consul. Marius's values were those of the military camp. A man of fierce vigor and courage, Marius saw the army as the tool of his ambition. He took the unusual but not wholly unprecedented step of recruiting an army by permitting landless men to serve in the legions. Marius thus tapped Rome's vast reservoir of idle manpower. His volunteer army was a professional force, not a body of draftees. In 106 B.C. Marius and his new army handily defeated Jugurtha.

An unexpected war broke out in the following year when two German peoples, the Cimbri and Teutones, moved into Gaul and later into northern Italy. After the Germans had defeated Roman armies sent to repel them, Marius was again elected consul, even though he was legally ineligible. From 104 to 100 B.C. Marius annually held the consulship. Despite the military necessity, Marius's many consulships meant that a Roman commander repeatedly held unprecedented military power in his

Roman Legionary The backbone of the Roman army was the legionary, shown here in battle. His basic equipment—shield, sword, spear, and armor—is simple and allowed great flexibility of movement. *(Source: Laurie Platt Winfrey, Inc.)*

hands. This would later translate into a political problem that the Roman republic never solved.

Before engaging the Cimbri and Teutones, Marius reformed the Roman army. There was, however, a disturbing side to his reforms, one that would henceforth haunt the republic. To encourage enlistments, Marius promised land to his volunteers after the war. Poor and landless veterans flocked to him, and together they conquered the Germans by 101 B.C. When Marius proposed a bill to grant land to his veterans, the senate refused to act, in effect turning its back on the soldiers of Rome. It was a disastrous mistake. Henceforth the legionaries expected the commanders—not the senate or the state—to protect their interests. Through Marius's reforms the Roman army became a professional force, but it owed little allegiance to the state. By failing to reward the loyalty of Rome's troops, the senate set the stage for military rebellion and political anarchy.

The Social War brought Marius into conflict with Sulla, who was consul in 88 B.C. First Marius and later Sulla defeated the Italian rebels. In the final stages of the war, while putting down the last of the rebels, Sulla was deposed from his consulship because of factional chaos in Rome. He immediately marched on Rome and restored order, but it was an ominous sign of the deterioration of Roman politics and political ideals. With some semblance of order restored, Sulla in 88 B.C. led an army to the East, where King Mithridates of Pontus in Asia Minor challenged Roman rule. In Sulla's absence, rioting and political violence again exploded in Rome. Marius and his supporters marched on Rome and launched a reign of terror.

Although Marius died peacefully in 86 B.C., his supporters continued to hold Rome. Once Sulla had defeated Mithridates, he once again, this time in 82 B.C., marched on Rome. After a brief but intense civil war, Sulla entered Rome and ordered a ruthless butchery of his opponents. He also proclaimed himself dictator. He launched many political and judicial reforms, including strengthening the senate while weakening the tribunate; increasing the number of magistrates in order to administer Rome's provinces better; and restoring the courts.

In 79 B.C. Sulla voluntarily abdicated his dictatorship and permitted the republican constitution to function normally once again. Yet his dictatorship cast a long shadow over the late Republic. Sulla the political reformer proved far less influential than Sulla the successful general and dictator. Civil war was to be the constant lot of Rome for the next fifty years, until the republican constitution gave way to the empire of Augustus in 27 B.C. The history of the late Republic is the story of the power struggles of some of Rome's most famous figures: Julius Caesar and Pompey, Augustus and Marc Antony. One figure who stands apart is Cicero (106–43 B.C.), a practical politician whose greatest legacy to the Roman world and to Western civilization is his mass of political and oratorical writings.

Pompous, vain, and sometimes silly, Cicero was nonetheless one of the few men of the period to urge peace and public order. As consul in 63 B.C. he put down a conspiracy against the republic but refused to use force to win political power. Instead, he developed the idea of "concord of the orders," an idealistic, probably unattainable balance among the elements that constituted the Roman state. A truly brilliant master of Latin prose and undoubtedly Rome's finest orator, Cicero used his vast literary ability to promote political and social reforms and explore the underlying principles of statecraft. Cicero also wrote many letters to his political friends in which he commented on the events of the day, and these letters are an invaluable source of information to modern historians. Yet Cicero commanded no legions, and only legions commanded respect.

In the late Republic the Romans were grappling with the simple and inescapable fact that their old city-state constitution was unequal to the demands of overseas possessions and the governing of provinces. Thus even Sulla's efforts to put the constitution back together proved hollow. Once the senate and other institutions of the Roman state had failed to come to grips with the needs of empire, once the authorities had lost control of their own generals and soldiers, and once the armies put their faith in commanders instead of in Rome, the republic was doomed.

Sulla's real political heirs were Pompey and Julius Caesar, with at least Caesar realizing that the days of the old republican constitution were numbered. Pompey, a man of boundless ambition, began his career as one of Sulla's lieutenants. After his army put down a rebellion in Spain, he himself threatened to rebel unless the senate allowed him to run for consul. He and another ambitious politician, Crassus, pooled political resources, and both won the consulship. They dominated Roman poli-

Julius Caesar Both the majesty of empire and the way in which it was won shine forth from this statue of Julius Caesar. The famous conqueror wears the armor of the Roman legionary. His pose, however, is derived from that common among representations of Hellenistic kings. *(Source: Giraudon/Art Resource)*

tics until the rise of Julius Caesar, who became consul in 59 B.C. Together the three concluded a political alliance, the First Triumvirate, in which they agreed to advance one another's interests.

The man who cast the longest shadow over these troubled years was Julius Caesar (100–44 B.C.). More than a mere soldier, Caesar was a cultivated man. Born of a noble family, he received an excellent education, which he furthered by studying in Greece with some of the most eminent teachers of the day. He had serious intellectual interests, and his literary ability was immense. Caesar was a superb orator, and his affable personality and wit made him popular. He was also a shrewd politician of unbridled ambition. Since military service was an effective steppingstone to politics, Caesar launched his military career in Spain, where his courage won the respect and affection of his troops. Personally brave and tireless, Caesar was a military genius who knew how to win battles and turn victories into permanent gains.

In 58 B.C. Caesar became governor of Cisalpine Gaul, or modern northern Italy. By 50 B.C. he had conquered all of Gaul, or modern France. Caesar's account of his operations, his *Commentaries* on the Gallic wars, became a classic in Western literature and most schoolchildren's introduction to Latin. By 49 B.C. the First Triumvirate had fallen apart. Crassus had died in battle, and Caesar and Pompey, each suspecting the other of treachery, came to blows. The result was a long and bloody civil war that raged from Spain across northern Africa to Egypt. Although Pompey enjoyed the official support of the government, Caesar finally defeated Pompey's forces in 45 B.C. He had overthrown the republic and made himself dictator.

Julius Caesar was not merely another victorious general. Politically brilliant, he was determined to make basic reforms, even at the expense of the old constitution. He took the first long step to break down the barriers between Italy and the provinces, extending citizenship to many of the provincials who had supported him. Caesar also took measures to cope with Rome's burgeoning population. By Caesar's day perhaps 750,000 people lived in Rome. Caesar drew up plans to send his veterans and some 80,000 of the poor and unemployed to colonies throughout the Mediterranean. He founded at least twenty colonies, most of which were located in Gaul, Spain, and North Africa. These colonies were important agents in spreading Roman culture in the western Mediterranean. A Roman empire composed of citizens, not subjects, was the result.

In 44 B.C. a group of conspirators assassinated Caesar and set off another round of civil war. Caesar had named his eighteen-year-old grandnephew, Octavian—or Augustus, as he is better known to history—as his heir. Augustus joined forces with two of Caesar's lieutenants, Marc Antony and Lepidus, in a pact known as the Second Triumvirate, and together they hunted down and defeated Caesar's murderers. In the process, however, Augustus and Antony came into conflict. Antony, "boastful, arrogant, and full of empty exultation and capricious ambition," proved to be the major threat to Augustus's designs.[8] In 33 B.C. Augustus branded Antony a traitor and rebel. Augustus painted lurid pictures of Antony lingering in the eastern Mediterranean, a romantic and foolish captive of the seductive Cleopatra, queen of Egypt and bitter enemy of Rome. In 31 B.C., with the might of Rome at his back, Augustus met and defeated the army and navy of Antony and Cleopatra at the Battle of Actium in Greece. Augustus's victory put an end to an age of civil war that had lasted since the days of Sulla.

SUMMARY

The rise of Rome to greatness resulted from many factors. At the outset the geographical position of Rome put it on good, natural lines of communication within Italy. The Italian peninsula itself was generally fertile, and the mountains did not prevent political unification. The Etruscans transformed the Roman settlements into a city. Once free of the Etruscans, the Romans used their political organization, their prosperity, and their population to conquer their neighbors. Yet instead of enslaving them, the Romans extended citizenship to the conquered. Having united Italy under them, the Romans became a major power that looked to the broader Mediterranean world. In a succession of wars with Carthage, in Spain, and in the Hellenistic East, Rome won an empire. These conquests not only prompted the Romans to invent a system to administer the empire but also brought them into the mainstream of Hellenistic civilization. The wealth derived from the empire meant that life for many Romans became richer. But there was also a dark side to these developments. Personal ambition, as well as defects in the Roman system of government, led some ambitious leaders to seize unprecedented power. Others resisted, throwing the republic into a series of civil wars. Finally, Caesar and his grandnephew Augustus restored order, but in the process the Roman republic had become a monarchy.

NOTES

1. Polybius, *The Histories* 1.1.5. John Buckler is the translator of all uncited quotations from a foreign language in Chapters 1–6.
2. Mark Twain, *The Innocents Abroad* (New York: Signet Classics, 1966), p.176.
3. Livy, *History of Rome* Preface 6.
4. Sallust, *War with Catiline* 10.1–3.
5. Ovid, *Fasti* 2.535–539.
6. *Ibid.,* 3.525–542.
7. Plutarch, *Life of Tiberius Gracchus* 9.5–6.
8. Plutarch, *Life of Antony* 2.8.

SUGGESTED READING

H. H. Scullard covers much of Roman history in a series of books: *The Etruscan Cities and Rome* (1967), *A History of the Roman World, 753–146 B.C.,* 3d ed. (1961), and *From the Gracchi to Nero,* 5th ed. (1982). R. T. Ridley, *The History of Rome* (1989), is a new, undogmatic history of Rome, firmly based in the sources. A. E. Astin, ed., *The Cambridge Ancient History,* 2d ed., vol. 7 (1988), discusses the rise of Rome and its relations with other Mediterranean powers. The Etruscans have inspired a great deal of work, most notably M. Pallottino, *The Etruscans,* rev. ed. (1975); R. M. Ogilvie, *Early Rome and the Etruscans* (1976), an excellent account of Rome's early relations with those people from the north; and G. Dennis, *Cities and Cemeteries of Etruria,* rev. ed. (1985). K. Christ, *The Romans* (English translation, 1984), is a general treatment by one of Germany's finest historians. A very broad study, J. Ch. Meyer, *Pre-Republican Rome* (1983), treats the cultural relations of early Rome chronologically between 1000 and 500 B.C.

E. T. Salmon, *The Making of Roman Italy* (1982), analyzes Roman expansion and its implications for Italy. Roman expansion is also the subject of J. Heurgon, *The Rise of Rome to 264 B.C.* (English translation, 1973); R. M. Errington, *The Dawn of Empire* (1971); and W. V. Harris, *War and Imperialism in Republican Rome 327–70 B.C.* (1979). J. F. Lazenby, *Hannibal's War: A Military History of the Second Punic War* (1978), is a detailed treatment of one of Rome's greatest struggles. More general and encompassing is E. Gabba, *Republican Rome, the Army, and the Allies* (English translation, 1976). One of the best studies of Rome's political evolution is the classic by A. N. Sherwin-White, *The Roman Citizenship,* 2d ed. (1973), a work of enduring value. While S. L. Dyson, *The Creation of the Roman Frontier* (1985), deals with the process by which the Romans established their frontiers, two other works concentrate on Rome's penetration of the Hellenistic East: A. N. Sherwin-White, *Roman Foreign Policy in the Near East* (1984), and the far better but

longer book by E. S. Gruen, *The Hellenistic World and the Coming of Rome,* 2 vols. (1984). A. Keaveney, *Rome and the Unification of Italy* (1988), treats the way in which the Romans put down the revolt of their Italian allies and then integrated them into the Roman political system.

The great figures and events of the late Republic have been the object of much new work. E. S. Gruen, *The Last Generation of the Roman Republic* (1974), treats the period as a whole. Very important are the studies of E. Badian, *Roman Imperialism in the Late Republic* (1968) and *Publicans and Sinners* (1972). R. Syme, *The Roman Revolution,* rev. ed. (1952), is a classic. Valuable also are P. A. Brunt, *Social Conflicts in the Roman Republic* (1971); A. J. Toynbee, *Hannibal's Legacy,* 2 vols. (1965); and A. W. Lintott, *Violence in the Roman Republic* (1968).

Many new works deal with individual Romans who left their mark on this period. H. C. Boren, *The Gracchi* (1968), treats the work of the two brothers, and A. M. Eckstein's *Senate and Generals* (1987) discusses how the decisions of individual generals affected both the senate and Roman foreign relations. A. Keaveney, *Sulla: The Last Republican* (1983), is a new study of a man who thought of himself as a reformer. A. E. Astin has produced two works that are far more extensive than their titles indicate: *Scipio Aemilianus* (1967) and *Cato the Censor* (1978). J. Leach, *Pompey the Great* (1978), surveys the career of this politician, and B. Rawson, *The Politics of Friendship: Pompey and Cicero* (1978), treats both figures in their political environment. M. Gelzer, *Caesar, Politician and Statesman* (English translation, 1968), is easily the best study of one of history's most significant figures. E. G. Huzar, *Marc Antony* (1987), offers a new assessment of the career of the man who challenged Augustus for control of the Roman world. Caesar's one-time colleague Marcus Crassus is studied in B. A. Marshall, *Crassus: A Political Biography* (1976), and A. Ward, *Marcus Crassus and the Late Roman Republic* (1977).

K. D. White, *Roman Farming* (1970), deals with agriculture, and J. P. V. D. Balsdon covers social life in the Republic and the Empire in two works: *Life and Leisure in Ancient Rome* (1969) and *Roman Women,* rev. ed. (1974). Greek cultural influence on Roman life is the subject of A. Wardman, *Rome's Debt to Greece* (1976). F. Schulz, *Classical Roman Law* (1951), is a useful introduction to an important topic. H. H. Scullard, *Festivals and Ceremonies of the Roman Republic* (1981), gives a fresh look at religious practices. Work on Roman social history has advanced in several areas. G. Alfoeldy, a major scholar, has written *The Social History of Rome* (1985), an ambitious undertaking. R. M. Ogilvie, *Roman Literature and Society* (1980), uses literature to examine the development and achievements of Roman society. Work on Roman women, with emphasis on the aristocracy, includes J. P. Hallett, *Fathers and Daughters in Roman Society* (1984). S. Dixon, *The Roman Mother* (1988), focuses specifically on women's role as mothers within the Roman family.

Greece and Rome, ca 800 B.C.–A.D. 14

	Government and Law	Philosophy and Science
800 B.C.	Emergence of the Greek polis, ca 800 Founding of Rome, ca 750 Start of Lycurgan regimen in Sparta, ca 620 Solon's reforms in Athens, 594 Founding of Roman Republic, 509 Cleisthenes creates Athenian democracy, 508	Pre-Socratics in Greece, 6th c.: Thales, Anaximander, Heraclitus
500 B.C.	Persian wars, 499–479 Delian League, 478–404 Law of the Twelve Tables in Rome, 450 Peloponnesian War, 431–404 Expansion of Greek federalism, 4th c. Gauls sack Rome, 390 Rebuilding of Rome; Roman expansion in Italy, 390–290 Macedonian conquest of Greece, 338 Conquests of Alexander, 334–323 Division of Alexander's empire, 323	Socrates, ca 470–399 Hippocrates, ca 460–377 Sophists, ca 450–400 Plato, ca 427–347 Aristotle, 384–322 Euclid, ca 323–285
300 B.C.	Punic wars, 264–146 Reforms of the Gracchi, 133–121	Emergence of Cynicism, Epicureanism and Stoicism, ca 300 Hellenistic medical advances, ca 300–250
100 B.C.	Dictatorship of Sulla, 88–79 Civil war in Rome, 78–27 Dictatorship of Julius Caesar, 45–44 Principate of Augustus Caesar, 31 B.C.–A.D. 14	Seneca, 4 B.C.–A.D. 65

Economics	Religion	Arts and Letters
Concentration of landed wealth in Greece, ca 750–600 Greek overseas expansion, ca 750–600 Lydians invent coinage, ca 600	Zoroaster formulates Zoroastrian religion, ca 625	Lyric Age in Greece, ca 800–500: poetry of Archilochus, Sappho, Tyrtaeus
	Eleusinian mystery religions in Greece, ca 500–150	Classical Age in Greece, ca 500–338: Aeschylus, Sophocles, Euripides, Aristophanes, Herodotus, Thucydides, Phidias, the Parthenon
Growth of Hellenistic trade and cities, ca 300–100 Roman overseas expansion, ca 282–146 Growth of slavery, decline of small farmer in Rome, ca 250–100	Emergence of Mithraism, ca 300 Emergence of Eastern mystery religions in Rome, ca 250 Emergence of Eastern mystery religions in Greece, ca 150 Mithraism spreads to Rome, 27 B.C.–A.D. 270	"Golden Age" of Latin literature (Augustan age): Virgil, 70–19; Horace, 65–8; Livy, 59 B.C.–A.D. 17 Ovid, ca 43 B.C.–A.D. 17

6

The Pax Romana

*H*ad the Romans conquered the entire Mediterranean world only to turn it into their battlefield? Would they, like the Greeks before them, become their own worst enemies, destroying each other and wasting their strength until they perished? At Julius Caesar's death in 44 B.C. it must have seemed so to many. Yet finally, in 31 B.C., Augustus restored peace to a tortured world, and with peace came prosperity, new hope, and a new vision of Rome's destiny. The Roman poet Virgil expressed this vision most nobly:

You, Roman, remember—these are your arts:
To rule nations, and to impose the ways of peace,
To spare the humble and to war down the proud.[1]

In place of the republic, Augustus established what can be called a constitutional monarchy. He attempted to achieve lasting cooperation in government and balance among the people, magistrates, senate, and army. His efforts were not always successful. His settlement of Roman affairs did not permanently end civil war. Yet he carried on Caesar's work. It was Augustus who created the structure that the modern world calls the "Roman Empire." He did his work so well and his successors so capably added to it that Rome realized Virgil's hope. For the first and second centuries A.D. the lot of the Mediterranean world was the Roman peace—the *pax Romana*, a period of security, order, harmony, flourishing culture, and expanding economy. It was a period that saw the wilds of Gaul, Spain, Germany, and eastern Europe introduced to Greco-Roman culture. By the third century A.D., when the empire began to give way to the medieval world, the greatness of Rome and its culture had left an indelible mark on the ages to come.

- How did the Roman emperors govern the empire, and how did they spread Roman influence into northern Europe?

- What were the fruits of the pax Romana?

- Why did Christianity, originally a minor local religion, sweep across the Roman world to change it fundamentally?

- Finally, how did the Roman Empire meet the grim challenge of barbarian invasion and subsequent economic decline?

These are the main questions we will consider in this chapter.

AUGUSTUS'S SETTLEMENT (31 B.C.–A.D. 14)

When Augustus put an end to the civil wars that had raged since 83 B.C., he faced monumental problems of reconstruction. Sole ruler of the entire Mediterranean world as no Roman had ever been before, he had a rare opportunity to shape the future. But how?

Augustus could easily have declared himself dictator, as Caesar had, but the thought was repugnant to him. Augustus was neither an autocrat nor a revolutionary. His solution, as he put it, was to restore the republic. But was that possible? Some eighteen years of anarchy and civil war had shattered the republican constitution. It could not be rebuilt in a day. Augustus recognized these problems but did not let them stop him. From 29 to 23 B.C., he toiled to heal Rome's wounds. The first problem facing him was to rebuild the constitution and the organs of government. Next he had to demobilize much of the army and care for the welfare of the provinces. Then he had to meet the danger of barbarians at Rome's European frontiers. Augustus was highly successful in meeting these challenges. His gift of peace to a war-torn world sowed the seeds of a literary flowering that produced some of the finest fruits of the Roman mind.

The Principate and the Restored Republic

Augustus claimed that in restoring constitutional government he was also restoring the republic. Typically Roman, he preferred not to create anything new; he intended instead to modify republican forms and offices to meet new circumstances. Augustus planned for the senate to take on a serious burden of duty and responsibility. He expected it to administer some of the provinces, continue to be the chief deliberative body of the state, and act as a court of law. Yet he did not give the senate enough power to become his partner in government. As a result, the senate could not live up to the responsibilities that Augustus assigned. Many of its prerogatives shifted to Augustus and his successors by default.

Augustus's own position in the restored republic was something of an anomaly. He could not simply surrender the reins of power, for someone else would only have seized them. But how was he to fit into a republican constitution? Again Augustus had his own answer. He became *princeps civitatis*, the "First Citizen of the State." This prestigious title carried no power; it indicated only that Augustus was the most distinguished of all Roman citizens. In effect, it designated Augustus as the first among equals, a little "more equal" than anyone else in the state. His real power resided in the magistracies he held, in the powers granted him by the senate, and above all in his control of the army, which he turned into a permanent, standing organization. Clearly, much of the *principate*, as the position of First Citizen is known, was a legal fiction. Yet that need not imply that Augustus, like a modern dictator, tried to clothe himself with constitutional legitimacy. In an inscription known as *Res Gestae (The Deeds of Augustus)*, Augustus described his constitutional position:

In my sixth and seventh consulships [28–27 B.C.], I had ended the civil war, having obtained through universal consent total control of affairs. I transferred the Republic from my power to the authority of the Roman people and the senate. . . . After that time I stood before all in rank, but I had power no greater than those who were my colleagues in any magistracy.[2]

Augustus was not exactly being a hypocrite, but he carefully kept his real military power in the background. As consul he had no more constitutional and legal power than his fellow consul. Yet in addition to the consulship Augustus held many other magistracies, which his fellow consul did not. Constitutionally, his ascendancy within the state stemmed from the number of magistracies he held and the power granted him by the senate. At first he held the consulship annually; then the senate voted him proconsular power on a regular basis. The senate also voted him *tribunicia potestas*—the "full power of the tribunes." Tribunician power gave Augustus the right to call the senate into session, present legislation to the people, and defend their rights. He held either high office or the powers of chief magistrate year in and year out. No other magistrate could do the same. In 12 B.C. he became *pontifex maximus,* "chief priest of the state." By assuming this position of great honor, Augustus

Augustus   This statue portrays Augustus as the Pontifex Maximus, "chief priest of the state." The emperor thereby emphasized his peaceful role and his position as the intermediary between the Roman people and the gods. *(Source: Alinari/Art Resource)*

became chief religious official in the state. Without specifically saying so, he had created the office of emperor, which included many traditional powers separated from their traditional offices.

The main source of Augustus's power was his position as commander of the Roman army. His title *imperator,* with which Rome customarily honored a general after a major victory, came to mean "emperor" in the modern sense of the term. Augustus governed the provinces where troops were needed for defense. The frontiers were his special concern. There, Roman legionaries held the German barbarians at arm's length. The frontiers were also areas where fighting could be expected to break out. Augustus made sure that Rome went to war only at his command. He controlled deployment of the Roman army and paid its wages. He granted it bonuses and gave veterans retirement benefits. Thus he avoided the problems with the army that the old senate had created for itself. Augustus never shared control of the army, and no Roman found it easy to defy him militarily.

The very size of the army was a special problem for Augustus. Rome's legions numbered thousands of men, far more than were necessary to maintain

Roma et Augustus   The nature of the cult of Rome and Augustus is immediately obvious from this cameo. Seated to the left is Augustus, who holds a scepter, which symbolizes his right to reign. He speaks with Roma, who personified Rome and who holds in her lap a shield, a symbol of her protection of the city of Rome and its empire. *(Source: Kunsthistorisches Museum, Vienna)*

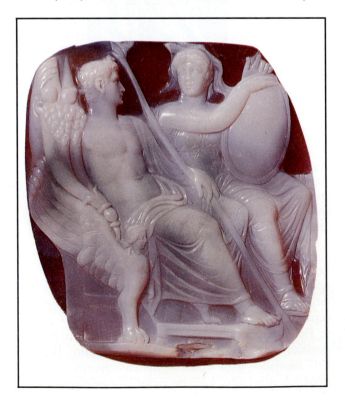

peace. What was Augustus to do with so many soldiers? This sort of problem had constantly plagued the late republic, whose leaders never found a solution. Augustus gave his own answer in the *Res Gestae:* "I founded colonies of soldiers in Africa, Sicily, Macedonia, Spain, Achaea, Gaul, and Pisidia. Moreover, Italy has 28 colonies under my auspices."[3] At least forty new colonies arose, most of them in the western Mediterranean. Augustus's veterans took abroad with them their Roman language and culture. His colonies, like Julius Caesar's, were a significant tool in the further spread of Roman culture throughout the West.

Roman colonies were very different from earlier Greek colonies. Greek colonies were independent. Once founded, they went their own way. Roman colonies were part of a system—the Roman Empire—that linked East with West in a mighty political, social, and economic network. The glory of the Roman Empire was its great success in uniting the Mediterranean world and spreading Greco-Roman culture throughout it. Roman colonies played a crucial part in that process, and deservedly Augustus boasted of the colonies he founded.

What is to be made of Augustus's constitutional settlement? Despite his claims to the contrary, Augustus had not restored the republic. Augustus had created a constitutional monarchy, something completely new in Roman history. The title *princeps,* "First Citizen," came to mean in Rome, as it does today, "prince" in the sense of a sovereign ruler.

Augustus also failed to solve a momentous problem. He never found a way to institutionalize his position with the army. The ties between the princeps and the army were always personal. The army was loyal to the princeps but not necessarily to the state. The Augustan principate worked well at first, but by the third century A.D. the army would make and break emperors at will. Nonetheless, it is a measure of Augustus's success that his settlement survived as long and as well as it did.

Augustus's Administration of the Provinces

To gain an accurate idea of the total population of the empire, Augustus ordered a census to be taken in 28 B.C. In Augustus's day the population of the Roman Empire was between 70 and 100 million people, fully 75 percent of whom lived in the provinces. In the areas under his immediate jurisdiction, Augustus put provincial administration on an ordered basis and improved its functioning. Believing that the cities of the empire should look after their own affairs, he encouraged local self-government and urbanism. Augustus respected local customs and ordered his governors to do the same.

As a spiritual bond between the provinces and Rome, Augustus encouraged the cult of Roma, goddess and guardian of the state. In the Hellenistic East, where king-worship was an established custom, the cult of *Roma et Augustus* grew and spread rapidly. Augustus then introduced it in the West. By the time of his death in A.D. 14, nearly every province in the empire could boast an altar or shrine to *Roma et Augustus*. In the West it was not the person of the emperor who was worshiped but his *genius*—his guardian spirit. In praying for the good health and welfare of the emperor, Romans and provincials were praying for the empire itself. The cult became a symbol of Roman unity.

Roman Expansion into Northern and Western Europe

For the history of Western civilization one of the most momentous aspects of Augustus's reign was Roman expansion into the wilderness of northern and western Europe (Map 6.1). In this respect Augustus was following in Julius Caesar's footsteps. Carrying on Ceasar's work, Augustus pushed Rome's frontier into the region of modern Germany.

Augustus began his work in the west and north by completing the conquest of Spain. In Gaul, apart from minor campaigns, most of his work was peaceful. He founded twelve new towns, and the Roman road system linked new settlements with one another and with Italy. But the German frontier, along the Rhine River, was the scene of hard fighting. In 12 B.C. Augustus ordered a major invasion of Germany beyond the Rhine. Roman legions advanced to the Elbe River, and a Roman fleet explored the North Sea and Jutland. The area north of the Main River and west of the Elbe was on the point of becoming Roman. But in 9 A.D. Augustus's general Varus lost some twenty thousand troops at the Battle of the Teutoburger Forest. Thereafter the Rhine remained the Roman frontier.

Meanwhile, more successful generals extended the Roman standards as far as the Danube. Roman legions penetrated the area of modern Austria, southern Bavaria, and western Hungary. The regions of modern Serbia, Bulgaria, and Romania fell. Within this area the legionaries built fortified camps. Roads linked these camps with one another, and settlements grew up around the camps. Traders began to frequent the frontier and to traffic with the barbarians. Thus Roman culture—the rough-and-ready kind found in military camps—gradually spread into the northern wilderness.

One excellent example of this process comes from the modern French city of Lyons. The site was originally the capital of a native tribe; and after his conquest of Gaul, Caesar made it a Roman military settlement. Augustus took an important step toward romanization and conciliation in 12 B.C., when he made it a political and religious center, with responsibilities for administering the area and for honoring the gods of the Romans and Gauls. Physical symbols of this fusion of two cultures can still be seen today. For instance, the extensive remains of the amphitheater and other buildings at Lyons testify to the fact that the Gallo-Roman city was prosperous enough to afford expensive Roman buildings and the style of life that they represented. Second, the buildings show that the local population appreciated Roman culture and did not find it alien. At Lyons, as at many other of these new cities, there emerged a culture that was both Roman and native.

Although Lyons is typical of the success of romanization in new areas, the arrival of the Romans often provoked resistance from barbarian tribes that simply wanted to be left alone. In other cases, the prosperity and wealth of the new Roman towns lured barbarians eager for plunder. The Romans maintained peaceful relations with the barbarians whenever possible, but Roman legions remained on the frontier to repel hostile barbarians. The result was the evolution of a consistent, systematic frontier policy.

Literary Flowering

The Augustan settlement's gift of peace inspired a literary flowering unparalleled in Roman history. With good reason this period is known as the golden age of Latin literature. Augustus and many

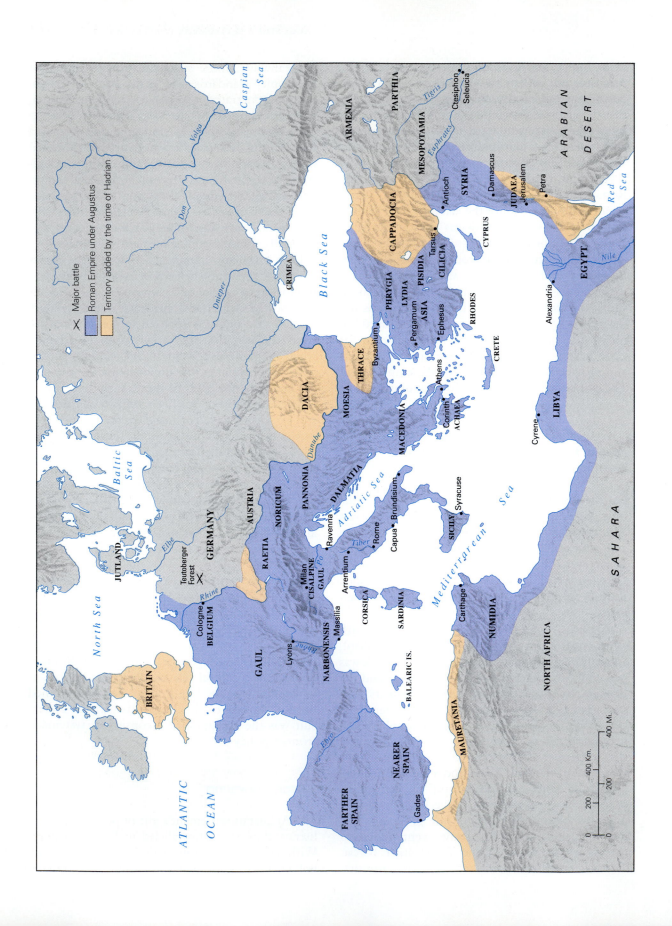

Major battle

Roman Empire under Augustus

Territory added by the time of Hadrian

ATLANTIC OCEAN

North Sea

Baltic Sea

Caspian Sea

Volga

Don

Dnieper

BRITAIN

JUTLAND

GERMANY

Elbe

Cologne

BELGIUM

Teutoberger Forest

Rhine

GAUL

Lyons

Rhône

NARBONENSIS

Massilia

AUSTRIA

RAETIA

NORICUM

PANNONIA

Milan

CISALPINE GAUL

Po

Arrentium

Ravenna

Tiber

Rome

Capua

Brundisium

DALMATIA

Adriatic Sea

Danube

DACIA

MOESIA

THRACE

Byzantium

MACEDONIA

Corinth

ACHAEA

Athens

Black Sea

CRIMEA

ARMENIA

PARTHIA

Tigris

Ctesiphon

Seleucia

MESOPOTAMIA

CAPPADOCIA

Euphrates

Tarsus

CILICIA

PISIDIA

PHRYGIA

LYDIA

ASIA

Pergamum

Ephesus

RHODES

CRETE

CYPRUS

SYRIA

Antioch

Damascus

JUDAEA

Jerusalem

Petra

ARABIAN DESERT

Red Sea

EGYPT

Nile

Alexandria

LIBYA

Cyrene

Mediterranean Sea

SICILY

Syracuse

CORSICA

SARDINIA

BALEARIC IS.

NUMIDIA

Carthage

NORTH AFRICA

MAURETANIA

SAHARA

NEARER SPAIN

FARTHER SPAIN

Gades

Ebro

400 Mi.

400 Km.

200

200

0

0

of his friends actively encouraged poets and writers. Horace, one of Rome's finest poets, offered his own opinion of Augustus and his era:

With Caesar [Augustus] the guardian of the state
Not civil rage nor violence shall drive out peace,
Nor wrath which forges swords
And turns unhappy cities against each other.[4]

These lines are not empty flattery, despite Augustus's support of many contemporary Latin writers. To a generation that had known only vicious civil war, Augustus's settlement was an unbelievable blessing.

The tone and ideal of Roman literature, like that of the Greeks, was humanistic and worldly. Roman poets and prose writers celebrated the dignity of humanity and the range of its accomplishments. They stressed the physical and emotional joys of a comfortable, peaceful life. Their works were highly polished, elegant in style, and intellectual in conception. Roman poets referred to the gods often and treated mythological themes, but always the core of their work was human, not divine.

Virgil (70–19 B.C.), Rome's greatest poet, celebrated the new age in the *Georgics*, a poetic work on agriculture in four books. Virgil delighted in his own farm, and his poems sing of the pleasures of peaceful farm life. The poet also tells how to keep bees, grow grapes and olives, plow, and manage a farm. Throughout the *Georgics* Virgil wrote about things he himself had seen, rather than drawing from the writings of others. Virgil could be vivid and graphic as well as pastoral. Even a small event could be a drama for him. The death of a bull while plowing is hardly epic material; yet Virgil captures the sadness of the event in the image of the farmer unyoking the remaining animal:

Look, the bull, shining under the rough plough,
  falls to the ground
  and vomits from his mouth blood mixed with foam,
  and releases his dying groan.

MAP 6.1 Roman Expansion Under the Empire Following Roman expansion during the Republic, Augustus added vast tracts of Europe to the Roman Empire, which the emperor Hadrian later enlarged by assuming control over parts of central Europe, the Near East, and North Africa.

Sadly moves the ploughman, unharnessing the
  young steer grieving for the death of his brother
  and leaves in the middle of the job
  the plough stuck fast.[5]

Virgil's poetry is robust yet graceful. A sensitive man who delighted in simple things, Virgil left in his *Georgics* a charming picture of life in the Italian countryside during a period of peace.

Virgil's masterpiece is the *Aeneid*, an epic poem that is the Latin equivalent of the Greek *Iliad* and *Odyssey*. In the *Aeneid* Virgil expressed his admiration for Augustus's work by celebrating the shining ideal of a world blessed by the pax Romana. Virgil's account of the founding of Rome and the early years of the city gave final form to the legend of Aeneas, the Trojan hero who escaped to Italy at the fall of Troy. The principal Roman tradition held that Romulus was the founder of Rome, but the legend of Aeneas was known as early as the fifth

Virgil and *The Aeneid* Virgil's great epic poem, *The Aeneid*, became a literary classic immediately on its appearance and has lost none of its power since. The Roman world honored Virgil for his poetic genius not only by treasuring his work but also by portraying him in art. Here two muses, who inspired artists, flank the poet while he writes his epic poem. *(Source: C. M. Dixon)*

century B.C. Virgil linked the legends of Aeneas and Romulus and preserved them both; in so doing, he connected Rome with Greece's heroic past. He also mythologized later aspects of Roman history. Recounting the story of Aeneas and Dido, the queen of Carthage, Virgil made their ill-fated love affair the cause of the Punic wars. But, above all, the *Aeneid* is the expression of Virgil's passionate belief in Rome's greatness. It is a vision of Rome as the protector of the good and noble against the forces of darkness and disruption.

In its own way Livy's history of Rome, entitled simply *Ab Urbe Condita (From the Founding of the City)*, is the prose counterpart of the *Aeneid*. Livy (59 B.C.–A.D. 17) received training in Greek and Latin literature, rhetoric, and philosophy. He even urged the future emperor Claudius to write history. Livy loved and admired the heroes and great deeds

of the republic, but he was also a friend of Augustus and a supporter of the principate. He especially approved of Augustus's efforts to restore republican virtues. Livy's history began with the legend of Aeneas and ended with the reign of Augustus. His theme of the republic's greatness fitted admirably with Augustus's program of restoring the republic. Livy's history was colossal, consisting of 142 books, and only a quarter of it still exists. Livy was a sensitive writer and something of a moralist. Like Thucydides, he felt that history should be applied to the present. His history later became one of Rome's legacies to the modern world. During the Renaissance *Ab Urbe Condita* found a warm admirer in the poet Petrarch and left its mark on Machiavelli, who read it avidly.

The poet Horace (65–8 B.C.) rose from humble beginnings to friendship with Augustus. The son of

Ara Pacis This scene from the Ara Pacis, the Altar of Peace, celebrates Augustus's restoration of peace and the fruits of peace. Here Mother Earth is depicted with her children. The cow and the sheep under the goddess represent the prosperity brought by peace, especially the agricultural prosperity so highly cherished by Virgil. (*Source: Bildarchiv Foto Marburg/Art Resource*)

an ex-slave and tax collector, Horace nonetheless received an excellent education. He loved Greek literature and finished his education in Athens. After Augustus's victory he returned to Rome and became Virgil's friend. Horace happily turned his pen to celebrating Rome's newly won peace and prosperity. One of his finest odes commemorates Augustus's victory over Cleopatra at Actium in 31 B.C. Cleopatra is depicted as a frenzied queen, drunk with desire to destroy Rome. Horace saw in Augustus's victory the triumph of West over East, of simplicity over Oriental excess. One of the truly moving aspects of Horace's poetry, like Virgil's, is his deep and abiding gratitude for the pax Romana.

For Rome, Augustus's age was one of hope and new beginnings. Augustus had put the empire on a new foundation. Constitutional monarchy was firmly established, and government was to all appearances a partnership between princeps and senate. The Augustan settlement was a delicate structure, and parts of it would in time be discarded. Nevertheless, it worked, and by building on it later emperors would carry on Augustus's work.

The solidity of Augustus's work became obvious at his death in A.D. 14. Since the principate was not technically an office, Augustus could not legally hand it to a successor. Augustus had recognized this problem and long before his death had found a way to solve it. He shared his consular and tribunician powers with his adopted son, Tiberius, thus grooming him for the principate. In his will Augustus left most of his vast fortune to Tiberius, and the senate formally requested Tiberius to assume the burdens of the principate. Formalities apart, Augustus had succeeded in creating a dynasty.

THE COMING OF CHRISTIANITY

During the reign of the emperor Tiberius (A.D. 14–37), perhaps in A.D. 29, Pontius Pilate, prefect of Judaea, the Roman province created out of the Jewish kingdom of Judah, condemned Jesus of Nazareth to death. At the time a minor event, this has become one of the best-known moments in history. How did these two men come to their historic meeting? The question is not idle, for Rome was as important as Judaea to Christianity. Jesus was born in a troubled time, when Roman rule aroused

hatred and unrest among the Jews. This climate of hostility affected the lives of all who lived in Judaea, Roman and Jew alike. It formed the backdrop of Jesus' life, and it had a fundamental impact on his ministry. Without an understanding of this age of anxiety in Judaea, Jesus and his followers cannot fully be appreciated.

The entry of Rome into Jewish affairs was anything but peaceful. The civil wars that destroyed the republic wasted the prosperity of Judaea and the entire eastern Mediterranean world. Jewish leaders took sides in the fighting, and Judaea suffered its share of ravages and military confiscations. Peace brought little satisfaction to the Jews. Although Augustus treated Judaea generously, the Romans won no popularity by making Herod king of Judaea (4 B.C.–A.D. 34). King Herod gave Judaea prosperity and security, but the Jews hated his acceptance of Greek culture. He was also a bloodthirsty prince who murdered his own wife and sons. At his death the Jews broke out in revolt. For the next ten years Herod's successor waged almost constant war against the rebels. Added to the horrors of civil war were years of crop failure, which caused famine and plague. Men calling themselves prophets proclaimed the end of the world and the coming of the Messiah, the savior of Israel.

At length the Romans intervened to restore order. Augustus put Judaea under the charge of a prefect answerable directly to the emperor. Religious matters and local affairs became the responsibility of the *Sanhedrin*, the highest Jewish judicial body. Although many prefects tried to perform their duties scrupulously and conscientiously, many others were rapacious and indifferent to Jewish culture. Often acting from fear rather than cruelty, some prefects fiercely stamped out any signs of popular discontent. Pontius Pilate, prefect from A.D. 26 to 36, is typical of such incompetent officials. Although eventually relieved of his duties in disgrace, Pilate brutally put down even innocent demonstrations. Especially hated were the Roman tax collectors, called "publicans," many of whom pitilessly gouged the Jews. *Publicans* and *sinners*—the words became synonymous. Clashes between Roman troops and Jewish guerrillas inflamed the anger of both sides.

In A.D. 40 the emperor Caligula undid part of Augustus's good work by ordering his statue erected in the temple at Jerusalem. The order, though never carried out, further intensified Jewish resentment. Thus the Jews became embittered by Roman rule because of taxes, sometimes unduly harsh enforcement of the law, and misguided religious interference.

Among the Jews two movements spread. First was the rise of the Zealots, extremists who worked and fought to rid Judaea of the Romans. Resolute in their worship of Yahweh, they refused to pay any but the tax levied by the Jewish temple. Their battles with the Roman legionaries were marked by savagery on both sides. As usual, the innocent caught in the middle suffered grievously. As Roman policy grew tougher, even moderate Jews began to hate the conquerors. Judaea came more and more to resemble a tinderbox, ready to burst into flames at a single spark.

The second movement was the growth of militant apocalyptic sentiment—the belief that the coming of the Messiah was near. This belief was an old one among the Jews. But by the first century A.D. it had become more widespread and fervent than ever before. Typical was the Apocalypse of Baruch, which foretold the destruction of the Roman Empire. First would come a period of great tribulation, misery, and injustice. At the worst of the suffering, the Messiah would appear. The Messiah would destroy the Roman legions and all the kingdoms that had ruled Israel. Then the Messiah would inaugurate a period of happiness and plenty for the Jews.

This was no abstract notion among the Jews. As the ravages of war became more widespread and conditions worsened, more and more people prophesied the imminent coming of the Messiah. One such was John the Baptist, "the voice of one crying in the wilderness, Prepare ye the way of the lord."[6] Many Jews did just that. The sect described in the Dead Sea Scrolls readied itself for the end of the world. Its members were probably Essenes, and their social organization closely resembled that of early Christians. Members of this group shared possessions, precisely as John the Baptist urged people to do. Yet this sect, unlike the Christians, also made military preparations for the day of the Messiah.

Jewish religious aspirations were only one part of the story. What can be said of the pagan world of Rome and its empire, into which Christianity was shortly to be born? To answer that question one must first explore the spiritual environment of the pagans, many of whom would soon be caught up in the new Christian religion. The term *pagans* refers to all those who believed in the Greco-Roman gods. Paganism at the time of Jesus' birth can be broadly divided into three spheres: the official state religion of Rome, the traditional Roman cults of hearth and countryside, and the new mystery religions that flowed from the Hellenistic East. The official state religion and its cults honored the traditional deities: Jupiter, Juno, Mars, and such newcomers as Isis (see Chapter 4). This very formal religion was conducted on an official level by socially prominent state priests. It was above all a religion of ritual and grand spectacle, but it provided little emotional or spiritual comfort for the people. The state cults were a bond between the gods and the people, a religious contract to ensure the well-being of Rome. Most Romans felt that the official cults must be maintained, despite their lack of spiritual content, simply for the welfare of the state. After all, observance of the traditional official religion had brought Rome victory, empire, security, and wealth.

For emotional and spiritual satisfaction, many Romans observed the old cults of home and countryside, the same cults that had earlier delighted Cato the Elder (see Chapter 5). These traditional cults brought the Romans back in touch with nature and with something elemental to Roman life. Particularly popular were rustic shrines—often a small building or a sacred tree in an enclosure—to honor the native spirit of the locality. Though familiar and simple, even this traditional religion was not enough for many. They wanted something more personal and immediate. Many common people believed in a supernatural world seen dimly through dreams, magic, miracles, and spells. They wanted some sort of revelation about this supernatural world and security in it after death. Some people turned to astrology in the belief that they could read their destiny in the stars. But that was cold comfort, since they could not change what the stars foretold.

Many people in the Roman Empire found the answer to their need for emotionally satisfying religion and spiritual security in the various Hellenistic mystery cults. Such cults generally provided their adherents with an emotional outlet. For example, the cult of Bacchus was marked by wine-drinking and often by drunken frenzy. The cult of the Great Mother, Cybele, was celebrated with emotional and even overwrought processions, and it offered its worshipers the promise of immortality. The appeal of the mystery religions was not simply that they provided emotional release. They gave their adherents what neither the traditional cults nor philosophy could—above all, security. Yet the mystery religions were by nature exclusive, and none was truly international, open to every human being.

Into this climate of Roman religious yearning, political severity, fanatical Zealotry, and messianic hope came Jesus of Nazareth (ca 5 B.C.–A.D. 29). He was raised in Galilee, stronghold of the Zealots. Yet Jesus himself was a man of peace. Jesus urged his listeners to love God as their father and one another as God's children. The kingdom that he preached was no earthly one, but one of eternal happiness in a life after death. Jesus' teachings are strikingly similar to those of Hillel (30 B.C.–A.D. 9), a rabbi and interpreter of the Scriptures who had also spread the message of devotion to God and love of other people.

Jesus' teachings were Jewish. He declared that he would change not one jot of the Jewish law. His orthodoxy enabled him to preach in the synagogue and the temple. His only deviation from orthodoxy was his insistence that he taught in his own name, not in the name of Yahweh. Was he then the Messiah? A small band of followers thought so, and Jesus claimed that he was. Yet Jesus had his own conception of the Messiah. Unlike the Messiah of the Apocalypse of Baruch, Jesus would not destroy the Roman Empire. He told his disciples flatly that they were to "render unto Caesar the things that are Caesar's." Jesus would establish a spiritual kingdom, not an earthly one. Repeatedly he told his disciples that his kingdom was "not of this world."

Of Jesus' life and teachings the prefect Pontius Pilate knew little and cared even less. All that concerned him was the maintenance of peace and

Pontius Pilate and Jesus This Byzantine mosaic from Ravenna illustrates a dramatic moment in Jesus' trial and crucifixion. Jesus stands accused before Pilate, but Pilate symbolically washes his hands of the whole affair. *(Source: Scala/Art Resource)*

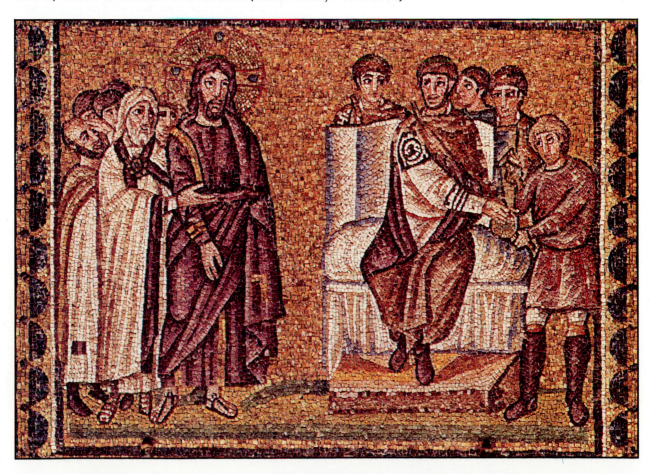

order. The crowds following Jesus at the time of the Passover, a highly emotional time in the Jewish year, alarmed Pilate, who faced a volatile situation. Some Jews believed that Jesus was the long-awaited Messiah. Others were disappointed because he refused to preach rebellion against Rome. Still others who hated and feared Jesus wanted to be rid of him. The last thing Pilate wanted was a riot on his hands. Christian tradition has made much of Pontius Pilate. In the medieval West he was considered a monster. In the Ethiopian church he is considered a saint. Neither monster nor saint, Pilate was simply a hard-bitten Roman official who did his duty, at times harshly. In Judaea his duty was to enforce the law and keep the peace. These were the problems on his mind when Jesus stood before him. Jesus as king of the Jews did not worry him. The popular agitation surrounding Jesus did. To avert riot and bloodshed, Pilate condemned Jesus to death. It is a bitter historical irony that such a gentle man died such a cruel death. After being scourged, he was hung from a cross until he died in the sight of family, friends, enemies, and the merely curious.

Once Pilate's soldiers had carried out the sentence, the entire matter seemed to be closed. Yet on the third day after Jesus' crucifixion, an odd rumor began to circulate in Jerusalem. Some of Jesus' followers were saying he had risen from the dead, while others accused them of having stolen his body. For the earliest Christians and for generations to come, the resurrection of Jesus became a central element of faith—and more than that, a promise: Jesus had triumphed over death, and his resurrection promised all Christians immortality. In Jerusalem, meanwhile, the tumult subsided. Jesus' followers lived quietly and peacefully, unmolested by Roman or Jew. Pilate had no quarrel with them, and Judaism already had many minor sects. Peter (d. A.D. 67?), the first of Jesus' followers, became the head of the sect, which continued to observe Jewish law and religious customs. Peter, a man of traditional Jewish beliefs, felt that Jesus' teachings were meant exclusively for the Jews. Only in their practices of baptism and the Lord's Supper (the Eucharist) did the sect differ from normal Jewish custom. Meanwhile, they awaited the return of Jesus.

Christianity might have remained a purely Jewish sect had it not been for Paul of Tarsus (A.D. 5?–67?). The conversion of Hellenized Jews and of Gentiles (non-Jews) to Christianity caused the sect

grave problems. Were the Gentiles subject to the law of Moses? If not, was Christianity to have two sets of laws? The answer to these questions was Paul's momentous contribution to Christianity. Paul was unlike Jesus or Peter. Born in a thriving, busy city filled with Romans, Greeks, Jews, Syrians, and others, he was at home in the world of Greco-Roman culture. After his conversion to Christianity, he taught that his native Judaism was the preparation for the Messiah and that Jesus by his death and resurrection had fulfilled the prophecy of Judaism and initiated a new age. Paul taught that Jesus was the son of God, the giver of a new law, and preached that Jesus' teachings were to be proclaimed to all, whether Jew or Gentile. Paul thus made a significant break with Judaism, Christianity's parent religion, for Judaism was exclusive and did not usually seek converts.

Paul's influence was far greater than that of any other early Christian. He traveled the length and breadth of the eastern Roman world, spreading his doctrine and preaching of Jesus. To little assemblies of believers in cities as distant as Rome and Corinth, he taught that Jesus had died to save all people. Paul's vision of Christianity won out over Peter's traditionalism. Christianity broke with Judaism and embarked on its own course.

What was Christianity's appeal to the Roman world? What did this obscure sect give people that other religions did not? Christianity possessed many different attractions. One of its appeals was its willingness to embrace both men and women, slaves and nobles. Many of the Eastern mystery religions with which Christianity competed were exclusive in one way or another. Mithraism, a mystery religion descended from Zoroastrianism, spread throughout the entire empire. Mithras the sun-god embodied good and warred against evil. Like Christianity, Mithraism offered elaborate and moving rituals including a form of baptism, a code of moral conduct, and the promise of life after death. Unlike Christianity, however, Mithraism permitted only men to become devotees.

Indeed, Christianity shared many of the features of mystery religions. It possessed a set of beliefs, such as the divinity of Jesus, and a literary history. Paul's epistles, or letters, to various Christian communities were the earliest pieces of literature dealing with Christian beliefs and conduct. Shortly thereafter, some of the disciples wrote *gospels,* or accounts of Jesus' life and teachings. Once people had prepared themselves for conversion by learning of Jesus' message and committing themselves to live by it, they were baptized. Like initiates in mystery religions, they entered the community of believers. The Christian community of believers was strengthened by the sacrament of the Eucharist, the communal celebration of the Lord's Supper. Christianity also had more than a priesthood to officiate at rituals; it developed an ecclesiastical administration that helped to ensure continuity within the new church.

Christianity appealed to common people and to the poor. Its communal celebration of the Lord's Supper gave men and women a sense of belonging. Christianity also offered its adherents the promise of salvation. Christians believed that Jesus on the cross had defeated evil and that he would reward his followers with eternal life after death. Christianity also offered the possibility of forgiveness. Human nature was weak, and even the best Christians would fall into sin. But Jesus loved sinners and forgave those who repented. In its doctrine of salvation and forgiveness alone, Christianity had a powerful ability to give solace and strength to believers.

Christianity was attractive to many because it gave the Roman world a cause. Hellenistic philosophy had attempted to make men and women self-sufficient: people who became indifferent to the outside world could no longer be hurt by it. That goal alone ruled out any cause except the attainment of serenity. The Romans, never innovators in philosophy, merely elaborated this lonely and austere message. Instead of passivity, Christianity stressed the ideal of striving for a goal. Each and every Christian, no matter how poor or humble, supposedly worked to realize the triumph of Christianity on earth. This was God's will, a sacred duty for every Christian. By spreading the word of Christ, Christians played their part in God's plan. No matter how small, the part each Christian played was important. Since this duty was God's will, Christians believed that the goal would be achieved. The Christian was not discouraged by temporary setbacks, believing Christianity to be invincible.

Christianity gave its devotees a sense of community. No Christian was alone. All members of the Christian community strove toward the same goal of fulfilling God's plan. Each individual community was in turn a member of a greater community. And that community, the Church General, was indestructible. After all, Jesus himself had reportedly promised, "Thou art Peter, and upon this rock I will build my church; and the gates of hell shall not prevail against it."[7]

So Christianity's attractions were many, from forgiveness of sin to an exalted purpose for each individual. Its insistence on the individual's importance gave solace and encouragement, especially to the poor and meek. Its claim to divine protection fed hope in the eventual success of the Christian community. Christianity made participation in the universal possible for everyone. The ultimate reward promised by Christianity was eternal bliss after death.

THE JULIO-CLAUDIANS AND THE FLAVIANS (27 B.C.–A.D. 96)

For fifty years after Augustus's death the dynasty that he established—known as the Julio-Claudians because they were all members of the Julian and Claudian clans—provided the emperors of Rome. Some of the Julio-Claudians, such as Tiberius and Claudius, were sound rulers and able administrators. Others, including Caligula and Nero, were weak and frivolous men who exercised their power stupidly and brought misery to the empire. Writers such as the biting and brilliant historian Tacitus (ca A.D. 55–ca 116) and the gossipy Suetonius (ca A.D. 75–150) have left unforgettable—and generally hostile—portraits of these emperors. Yet the venom of Tacitus and Suetonius cannot obscure the fact that Julio-Claudians were responsible for some notable achievements. During their reigns the empire largely prospered.

One of the most momentous achievements of the Julio-Claudians was Claudius's creation of an imperial bureaucracy composed of professional administrators. Even the most energetic emperor could not run the empire alone. The numerous duties and immense responsibilities of the emperor prompted Claudius to delegate power. He began by giving the freedmen of his household official duties, especially in finances. It was a simple, workable system. Claudius knew his ex-slaves well and could discipline them at will. The effect of Claudius's innovations was to enable the emperor to rule the empire more easily and efficiently.

One of the worst defects of Augustus's settlement—the army's ability to interfere in politics—became obvious during the Julio-Claudian period.

Triumph of Titus   After Titus, the son of Vespasian and later himself emperor, conquered Jerusalem, he ordered his soldiers to carry off as spoils of war the sacred objects of the rebellious Jews, most notably in this scene the seven-branched candlestick. *(Source: Art Resource)*

Augustus had created a special standing force, the Praetorian Guard, as an imperial bodyguard. In A.D. 41 one of the praetorians murdered Caligula while others hailed Claudius as the emperor. Under the threat of violence, the senate ratified the praetorians' choice. It was a story repeated frequently. During the first three centuries of the empire, the Praetorian Guard all too often murdered emperors they were supposed to protect and saluted emperors of their own choosing.

In A.D. 68 Nero's inept rule led to military rebellion and his death, thus opening the way to widespread disruption. In A.D. 69, the "Year of the Four Emperors," four men claimed the position of emperor. Roman armies in Gaul, on the Rhine, and in the East marched on Rome to make their commanders emperor. The man who emerged triumphant was Vespasian, commander of the eastern armies, who entered Rome in 70 and restored order. Nonetheless, the Year of the Four Emperors proved the Augustan settlement had failed to end civil war.

Not a brilliant politician, Vespasian did not institute sweeping reforms, as had Augustus, or solve the problem of the army in politics. To prevent usurpers from claiming the throne, Vespasian designated his sons Titus and Domitian as his successors. By establishing the Flavian dynasty (named after his clan), Vespasian turned the principate into an open and admitted monarchy. He also expanded the emperor's power by increasing the size of the budding bureaucracy Claudius had created.

One of Vespasian's first tasks was to suppress rebellions that had erupted at the end of Nero's reign. The most famous had taken place in Judaea, which still seethed long after Jesus' crucifixion. Long-standing popular unrest and atrocities committed by Jews and Romans alike sparked a massive revolt in A.D. 66. Four years later, a Roman army reconquered Judaea and reduced Jerusalem by siege. The Jewish survivors were enslaved, their state destroyed. The mismanagement of Judaea was one of the few—and worst—failures of Roman imperial administration.

The Flavians carried on Augustus's work on the frontiers. Domitian, the last of the Flavians, won additional territory in Germany and consolidated it in two new provinces. He defeated barbarian tribes on the Danube frontier and strengthened that area as well. Even so, Domitian was one of the most hated of Roman emperors because of his cruelty, and he fell victim to an assassin's dagger. Nevertheless, the Flavians had given the Roman world peace and had kept the legions in line. Their work paved the way for the era of the "five good emperors," the golden age of the empire.

THE AGE OF THE "FIVE GOOD EMPERORS" (A.D. 96–180)

In the second century of the Christian era, the Empire of Rome comprehended the fairest part of the earth, and the most civilised portion of mankind. The frontiers of that extensive monarchy were guarded by ancient renown and disciplined valor. The gentle but powerful influence of laws and manners had gradually cemented the union of the provinces. Their peaceful inhabitants enjoyed and abused the advantages of wealth and luxury. The image of a free constitution was preserved with decent reverence: the Roman senate appeared to possess the sovereign authority, and devolved on the emperors all the executive powers of government. During a happy period [A.D. 96–180] of more than fourscore years, the public administration was conducted by the virtue and abilities of Nerva, Trajan, Hadrian, and the two Antonines.[8]

Thus Edward Gibbon (1737–1794) began his monumental *History of the Decline and Fall of the Roman Empire.* Gibbon saw the era of Nerva, Trajan, Hadrian, Antoninus Pius, and Marcus Aurelius —the "five good emperors"—as the happiest in human history, a last burst of summer before an autumn of failure and barbarism. Gibbon recognized a great truth: the age of the Antonines, as the five good emperors are often called, was one of almost unparalleled prosperity for the empire. Wars were generally victorious and confined to the frontiers. Even the serenity of Augustus's day seemed to pale in comparison. These emperors were among the noblest, most dedicated, ablest men in Roman history. Yet fundamental political and military changes had taken place since the time of Augustus's rule.

The Antonine Monarchy

Augustus had claimed that his influence arose from the collection of offices the senate had bestowed on him. However, there was in law no such office as emperor. Augustus was merely the First Citizen. Under the Flavians the principate became a full-blown monarchy, and by the time of the Antonines the principate was an office with definite rights, powers, and prerogatives. In the years between Augustus and the Antonines, the emperor had become an indispensable part of the imperial machinery. In short, without the emperor the empire would quickly fall to pieces. Augustus had been monarch in fact but not in theory; during their reigns, the Antonines were monarchs in both.

The Antonines were not power-hungry autocrats. The concentration of power was the result of empire. The easiest and most efficient way to run the Roman Empire was to invest the emperor with vast powers. Furthermore, Roman emperors on the whole proved to be effective rulers and administrators. As capable and efficient emperors took on new tasks and functions, the emperor's hand was felt in more areas of life and government. Increasingly the emperors became the source of all authority and guidance in the empire. The five good emperors were benevolent and exercised their power intelligently, but they were absolute kings all the same. Lesser men would later throw off the façade of constitutionality and use this same power in a despotic fashion.

Typical of the five good emperors is the career of Hadrian, who became emperor in A.D. 117. He was born in Spain, a fact that illustrates the importance of the provinces in Roman politics. Hadrian received his education at Rome and became an ardent admirer of Greek culture. He caught the attention of his elder cousin Trajan, the future emperor, who started him on a military career. At age nineteen Hadrian served on the Danube frontier, where he learned the details of how the Roman army lived and fought and saw for himself the problems of defending the frontiers. When Trajan became emperor in A.D. 98, Hadrian was given important positions in which he learned how to defend and run the empire. At Trajan's death in 117, Hadrian assumed power.

Roman government had changed since Augustus's day. One of the most significant changes was the enormous growth of the imperial bureaucracy created by Claudius. Hadrian reformed this system by putting the bureaucracy on an organized, official basis. He established imperial administrative departments to handle the work formerly done by imperial freedmen. Hadrian also separated civil service from military service. Men with little talent or taste for the army could instead serve the state as administrators. Hadrian's bureaucracy demanded professionalism from its members. Administrators made a career of the civil service. These innovations made for more efficient running of the empire and increased the authority of the emperor—the ruling power of the bureaucracy.

Changes in the Army

The Roman army had also changed since Augustus's time. The Roman legion had once been a mobile unit, but its duties under the empire no longer called for mobility. The successors of Au-

gustus generally called a halt to further conquests. The army was expected to defend what had already been won. Under the Flavian emperors (A.D. 69–96), the frontiers became firmly fixed. Forts and watch stations guarded the borders. Behind the forts the Romans built a system of roads that allowed the forts to be quickly supplied and reinforced in times of trouble. The army had evolved into a garrison force, with legions guarding specific areas for long periods.

The personnel of the legions was changing, too. Italy could no longer supply all the recruits needed for the army. Increasingly, only the officers came from Italy and from the more romanized provinces. The legionaries were mostly drawn from the less civilized provinces, especially the ones closest to the frontiers. A major trend was already obvious in Hadrian's day: fewer and fewer Roman soldiers were really Roman. In the third century A.D. the barbarization of the army would result in an army indifferent to Rome and its traditions. In the age of

Scene from Trajan's Column   From 101 to 107 Trajan fought the barbarian tribes along the Danube. This scene depicts Roman soldiers unloading supplies at a frontier city. Such walled cities serve as Roman strong points, as well as centers of Roman civilization, with shops, homes, temples, and amphitheaters. *(Source: Alinari/Art Resource)*

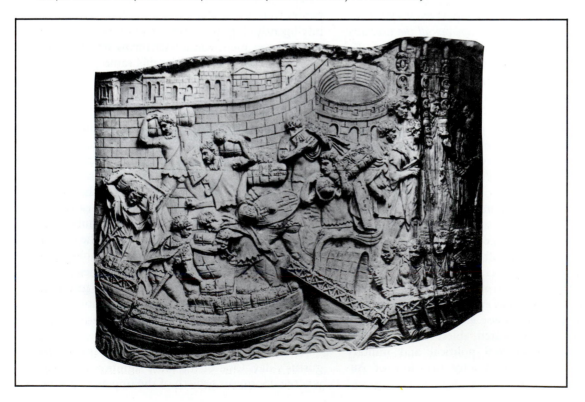

the Antonines, however, the army was still a source of economic stability and a romanizing agent (Map 6.2). Men from the provinces and even barbarians joined the army to learn a trade and to gain Roman citizenship. Even so, the signs were ominous. Veterans from Julius Caesar's campaigns would hardly have recognized Hadrian's troops as Roman legionaries.

LIFE IN THE "GOLDEN AGE"

Many people, both ancient and modern, have considered these years one of the happiest epochs in Western history. But popular accounts have also portrayed Rome as already decadent by the time of the Antonines. If Rome was decadent, who kept the empire running? For that matter, can life in Rome itself be taken as representative of life in other parts of the empire? Rome was unique and must be seen as such. Rome no more resembled a provincial city like Cologne than New York resembles Keokuk, Iowa. Only when the uniqueness of Rome is understood in its own right can one turn to the provinces to obtain a full and reasonable picture of the empire under the Antonines.

Imperial Rome

Rome was truly an extraordinary city, especially by ancient standards. It was also enormous, with a population somewhere between 500,000 and 750,000. Although it could boast of stately palaces, noble buildings, and beautiful residential areas, most people lived in jerrybuilt apartment houses. Fire and crime were perennial problems, even after Augustus created fire and urban police forces. Streets were narrow and drainage inadequate. During the republic, sanitation had been a common problem. Numerous inscriptions record prohibitions against dumping human refuse and even cadavers on the grounds of sanctuaries and cemeteries. Under the empire this situation improved. By comparison with medieval and early modern European cities, Rome was a healthy enough place to live.

Rome was such a huge city that the surrounding countryside could not feed it. Because of the danger of starvation, the emperor, following re-

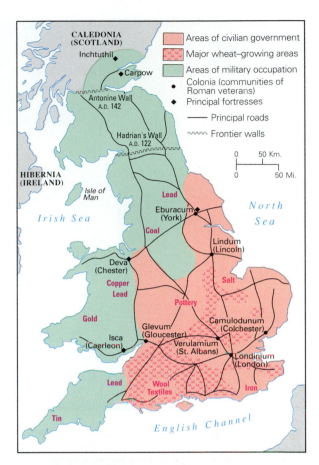

MAP 6.2 Roman Britain   Though the modern state of Great Britain plays a major role in modern international affairs, it was a peripheral part of the Roman Empire, a valuable area but nonetheless definitely on the frontier.

publican practice, provided the citizen population with free grain for bread and, later, oil and wine. By feeding the citizenry the emperor prevented bread riots caused by shortages and high prices. For the rest of the urban population who did not enjoy the rights of citizenship, the emperor provided grain at low prices. This measure was designed to prevent speculators from forcing up grain prices in times of crisis. By maintaining the grain supply the emperor kept the favor of the people and ensured that Rome's poor and idle did not starve.

The emperor also entertained the Roman populace, often at vast expense. The most popular forms of public entertainment were gladiatorial contests and chariot racing. Gladiatorial fighting was originally an Etruscan funerary custom, a blood sacri-

Apartment Houses at Ostia   At heavily populated places such as Rome and Ostia, which was the port of Rome, apartment buildings housed urban dwellers. The brick construction of this building is a good example of solid Roman work. In Rome some apartment buildings were notoriously shoddy and unsafe. *(Source: Art Resource)*

fice for the dead. Even a humane man like Hadrian staged extravagant contests. In A.D. 126 he sponsored six days of such combats, during which 1,835 pairs of gladiators dueled, usually with swords and shields. Many gladiators were criminals, some of whom were sentenced to be slaughtered in the arena. These convicts were given no defensive weapons and stood little real chance of survival. Other criminals were sentenced to fight in the arena as fully armed gladiators. Some gladiators were the slaves of gladiatorial trainers; others were prisoners of war. Still others were free men who volunteered for the arena. Even women at times engaged in gladiatorial combat. What drove these men and women? Some obviously had no other choice. For a criminal condemned to die, the arena was preferable to the imperial mines, where convicts worked digging ore and died under wretched

conditions. At least in the arena the gladiator might fight well enough to win freedom. Others no doubt fought for the love of danger or for fame. Although some Romans protested gladiatorial fighting, most delighted in it—one of their least attractive sides. Not until the fifth century did Christianity put a stop to it.

The Romans were even more addicted to chariot racing than to gladiatorial shows. Under the empire, four permanent teams competed against one another. Each had its own color—red, white, green, or blue. Some Romans claimed that people cared more about their favorite team than about the race itself. Two-horse and four-horse chariots ran a course of seven laps, about five miles. A successful driver could be the hero of the hour. One charioteer, Gaius Appuleius Diocles, raced for twenty-four years. During that time he drove 4,257 starts and won 1,462 of them. His admirers honored him with an inscription that proclaimed him champion of all charioteers.

But people like the charioteer Diocles were no more typical of the common Roman than Babe Ruth is of the average American. Ordinary Romans left their mark in the inscriptions that grace their graves. They were proud of their work and accomplishments, affectionate toward their families and friends, and eager to be remembered after death. Typical Romans did not spend their entire lives in idleness, watching gladiators or chariot races; instead, they had to make a living. They dealt with everyday problems and rejoiced over small pleasures. An impression of them and their cares can be gained from their epitaphs. The funerary inscription of Paprius Vitalis to his wife is particularly engaging: "If there is anything good in the lower regions—I, however, finish a poor life without you—be happy there too, sweetest Thalassia . . . married to me for 40 years."[9]

Even the personal philosophies of typical Romans have come down from antiquity. Marcus Antonius Encolpus erected a funerary inscription to his wife that reads in part:

Do not pass by my epitaph, traveler.
But having stopped, listen and learn, then go your
   way.
There is no boat in Hades, no ferryman Charon,
no caretaker Aiakos, no dog Cerberus.
All we who are dead below
have become bones and ashes, but nothing else.
I have spoken to you honestly, go on, traveler,
lest even while dead I seem loquacious to you.[10]

Others put it more simply: "I was, I am not, I don't care." "To each his own tombstone." These Romans went about their lives as people have always done. Though fond of brutal spectacles, they also had their loves and dreams.

The Provinces

In the provinces and even on the frontiers, the age of the Antonines was one of extensive prosperity, especially in western Europe. The Roman army had beaten back the barbarians and exposed them to the civilizing effects of Roman traders. The resulting peace and security opened Britain, Gaul, Germany, and the lands of the Danube to immigration. Agriculture flourished as large tracts of land came under cultivation. Most of this land was in the hands of free tenant farmers. From the time of Augustus slavery had declined in the empire, as had the growth of latifundia (see page 148). Augustus and his successors encouraged the rise of free farmers. Under the Antonines this trend continued, and the holders of small parcels of land throve as never before. The Antonines provided loans on easy terms to farmers enabling them to rent land previously worked by slaves. It also permitted them to cultivate the new lands that were being opened up. Consequently, the small tenant farmer was becoming the backbone of Roman agriculture.

In continental Europe the army was largely responsible for the new burst of expansion. The areas where legions were stationed readily became romanized. When legionaries retired from the army, they often settled where they had served. Since they had usually learned a trade in the army, they brought essential skills to areas that badly needed trained men. These veterans took their retirement pay and used it to set themselves up in business.

The eastern part of the empire also participated in the boom. The Roman navy had swept the sea of pirates, and Eastern merchants traded throughout the Mediterranean. The flow of goods and produce in the East matched that of the West. Venerable cities like Corinth, Antioch, and Ephesus flourished as rarely before. The cities of the East built extensively, bedecking themselves with new amphitheaters, temples, fountains, and public buildings. For the East the age of the Antonines was the heyday of the city. Life there grew ever richer and more comfortable.

Trade among the provinces increased dramatically. Britain and Belgium became prime grain producers, much of their harvests going to the armies of the Rhine. Britain's famous wool industry probably got its start under the Romans. Italy and southern Gaul produced wine in huge quantities. The wines of Italy went principally to Rome and the Danube, while Gallic wines were shipped to Britain and the Rhineland. Roman colonists had introduced the olive to southern Spain and northern Africa, an experiment so successful that these regions produced most of the oil consumed in the Western empire. In the East, Syrian farmers continued to cultivate the olive, and oil production reached an all-time high. Egypt was the prime grain producer of the East, and tons of Egyptian wheat went to feed the Roman populace. The Roman army in Mesopotamia consumed a high percentage of the raw materials and manufactured products of Syria and Asia Minor. The spread of trade meant the end of isolated and self-contained economies. By the time of the Antonines, the empire had become an economic as well as a political reality (Map 6.3).

One of the most striking features of this period was the growth of industry in the provinces. Cities in Gaul and Germany eclipsed the old Mediterranean manufacturing centers. Italian cities were particularly hard-hit by this development. Cities like Arretium and Capua had dominated the production of glass, pottery, and bronze ware. Yet in the second century A.D., Gaul and Germany took over the pottery market. Lyons in Gaul became the new center of the glassmaking industry. The technique of glass blowing spread to Britain and Germany, and later in the second century Cologne replaced Lyons in glass production. The cities of Gaul were nearly unrivaled in the manufacture of bronze and brass. Gallic craftsmen invented a new technique of tin-plating and decorated their work with Celtic designs. Their wares soon drove Italian products out of the northern European market. For the first time in history, northern Europe was able to rival the Mediterranean as a producer of manufactured goods. Europe had entered fully into the economic and cultural life of the Mediterranean world.

The age of the Antonines was generally one of peace, progress, and prosperity. The work of the Romans in northern and western Europe was a permanent contribution to the history of Western society. The period of the Antonine monarchy was also one of consolidation. Roads and secure sea lanes linked the empire in one vast web. The empire had become a commonwealth of cities, and urban life was its hallmark.

CIVIL WARS AND INVASIONS IN THE THIRD CENTURY

The age of the Antonines gave way to a period of chaos and stress. During the third century A.D. the empire was stunned by civil wars and barbarian invasions. By the time peace was restored, the economy was shattered, cities had shrunk in size, and

agriculture was becoming manorial (see page 181). In the disruption of the third century and the reconstruction of the fourth, the medieval world had its origins.

After the death of Marcus Aurelius, the last of the five good emperors, his son Commodus, a man totally unsuited to govern the empire, came to the throne. His misrule led to his murder and a renewal of civil war. After a brief but intense spasm of fighting, the African general Septimius Severus defeated other rival commanders and established the Severan dynasty (A.D. 193–235). Although Septimius Severus was able to stabilize the empire, his successors proved incapable of disciplining the legions. When the last of the Severi was killed by one of his own soldiers, the empire plunged into still another grim, destructive, and this time prolonged round of civil war.

Over twenty different emperors ascended the throne in the forty-nine years between 235 and 284, and many rebels died in the attempt to seize power. At various times, parts of the empire were lost to rebel generals, one of whom, Postumus, set up his own empire in Gaul for about ten years (A.D. 259–269). Yet other men like the iron-willed Aurelian (A.D. 270–275) dedicated their energies to restoring order. So many military commanders seized rule that the middle of the third century has become known as the age of the "barracks emperors." The Augustan principate had become a military monarchy, and that monarchy was nakedly autocratic.

Barbarians on the Frontiers

The first and most disastrous result of the civil wars was trouble on the frontiers. It was Rome's misfortune that this era of anarchy coincided with immense movements of barbarian peoples. Historians still dispute the precise reason for these migrations, though their immediate cause was pressure from tribes moving westward across Asia. In the sixth

MAP 6.3 The Economic Aspect of the Roman Peace The Roman Empire was not merely a political and military organization but also an intricate economic network through which goods from Armenia and Syria were traded for Western products from as far away as Spain and Britain.

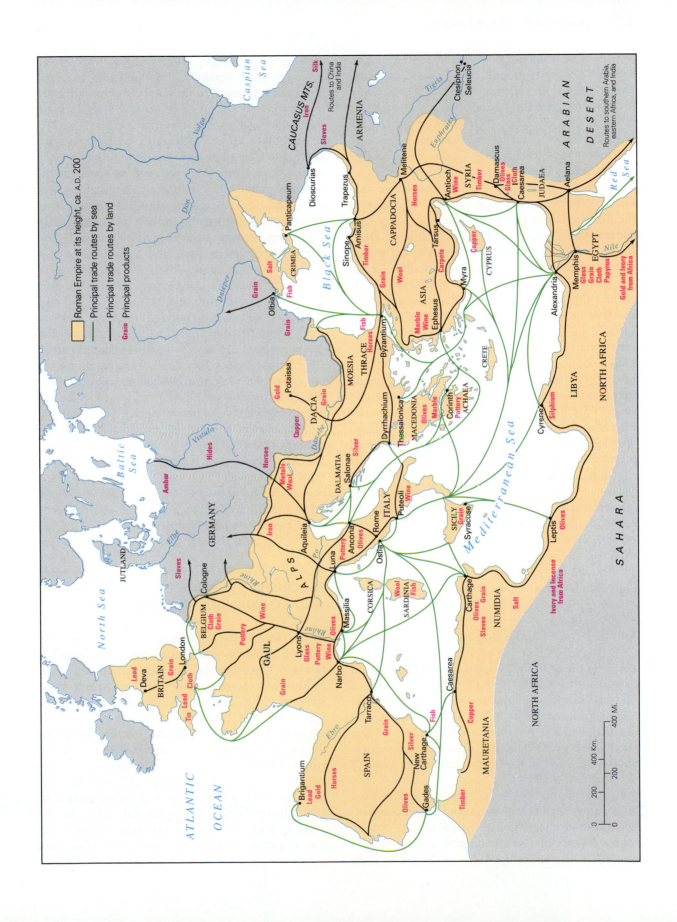

ATLANTIC OCEAN

North Sea

Baltic Sea

Caspian Sea

Black Sea

Mediterranean Sea

Red Sea

Legend

Roman Empire at its height, ca. A.D. 200

Principal trade routes by sea

Principal trade routes by land

Grain Principal products

JUTLAND

BRITAIN — Lead, Deva, Tin, Lead, Cloth, London, Grain

GERMANY — Amber, Hides, Slaves, Cologne

GAUL — BELGIUM Cloth, Grain, Wine, Lyons, Glass, Pottery, Wine, Olives, Narbo, Grain, Massilia, Rhône, Rhine

SPAIN — Brigantium, Lead, Gold, Horses, Tarraco, New Carthage, Silver, Gades, Olives, Ebro

MAURETANIA — Horses, Timber, Copper, Caesarea

NORTH AFRICA — Carthage, Olives, Grain, Slaves, NUMIDIA, Salt, Leptis, Olives, LIBYA, Cyrene, Silphium

ALPS — Aquileia, Iron, Metals, Wool, DALMATIA, Salonae, Silver, Po, Luna, Pottery, Ancona, Olives, ITALY, Rome, Ostia, Puteoli, Wine, CORSICA, SARDINIA, Wool, Fish, SICILY, Syracuse, Grain

DACIA — Gold, Potaissa, Grain, Copper, Danube

MOESIA, THRACE, Byzantium, Horses, Fish, Dyrrhachium, Thessalonica, MACEDONIA, Olives, Marble, CRETE, Corinth, Pottery, ACHAEA, Marble, Wine

Olbia, Grain, Fish, CRIMEA, Salt, Panticapeum, Dioscurias, Slaves, CAUCASUS MTS., Iron, Silk, Routes to China and India, ARMENIA, Trapezus

Dnieper, Don, Volga, Vistula, Elbe

Black Sea — Sinope, Amisus, Timber, ASIA, Grain, Wool, Horses, Marble, Wine, Ephesus, Myra, Carpets, CYPRUS, Copper, Tarsus, CAPPADOCIA, Horses, Meletine, Euphrates, Tigris

Antioch, Wine, SYRIA, Damascus, Olives, Glass, Cloth, Timber, Caesarea, JUDAEA, Aelana, Ctesiphon, Seleucia, Routes to southern Arabia, eastern Africa, and India

EGYPT — Memphis, Glass, Grain, Cloth, Papyrus, Gold and Ivory from Africa, Alexandria, Nile

ARABIAN DESERT

Ivory and Incense from Africa

SAHARA

0 200 400 Km.
0 200 400 Mi.

century A.D., Jordanes, a Christianized Goth, preserved the memory of innumerable wars among the barbarians in his History of the Goths. Goths fought Vandals, Huns fought Goths. Steadily the defeated and displaced tribes moved toward the Roman frontiers. Finally, like "a swarm of bees"—to use Jordanes's image—the Goths, one such people, burst into Europe in A.D. 258.

When the barbarians reached the Rhine and Danube frontiers, they often found huge gaps in the Roman defenses. Typical is the case of Decius, a general who guarded the Danube frontier in Dacia (modern Romania). In A.D. 249 he revolted and invaded Italy in an effort to become emperor. Decius left the frontier deserted, and the Goths easily poured through, looking for new homes. During much of the third century A.D., bands of Goths devastated the Balkans as far south as Greece. They even penetrated Asia Minor. The Alamanni, a German people, swept across the Danube. At one point they entered Italy and reached Milan before they were beaten back. Meanwhile the Franks, still another German folk, hit the Rhine frontier. The Franks then invaded eastern and central Gaul and northeastern Spain. Saxons from Scandinavia sailed into the English Channel in search of loot. In the East the Sassanids, of Persian stock, overran Mesopotamia. If the army had been guarding the borders instead of creating and destroying emperors, none of these invasions would have been possible. The barracks emperors should be credited with one accomplishment, however: they fought barbarians when they were not fighting each other. Only that kept the empire from total ruin.

Turmoil In Farm and Village Life

How did the ordinary people cope with this period of iron and blood? What did it mean to the lives of men and women on farms and in villages? How did local officials continue to serve their emperor and neighbors? Some people became outlaws. Others lived more prosaically. Some voiced their grievances to the emperor, thereby leaving a record of the problems they faced.

In a surprising number of cases, barbarians were less of a problem than lawless soldiers, imperial officials, and local agents. For many ordinary people, official corruption was the tangible and immediate result of the breakdown of central authority. In one instance, some tenant farmers in Lydia (modern Turkey) complained to the emperor about arbitrary arrest and the killing of prisoners. They claimed that police agents had threatened them and prevented them from cultivating the land. Tenant farmers in Phrygia (also in modern Turkey) voiced similar complaints. They suffered extortion at the hands of public officials. Military commanders, soldiers, and imperial agents requisitioned their livestock and compelled the farmers to forced labor. The farmers were becoming impoverished, and many people deserted the land to seek safety elsewhere. The inhabitants of an entire village in Thrace (modern Bulgaria) complained that they were being driven from their homes. From imperial and local officials they suffered insolence and violence. Soldiers demanded to be quartered and given supplies. Many villagers had already abandoned their homes to escape. The remaining villagers warned the emperor that, unless order was restored, they too would flee.

Local officials were sometimes unsympathetic or violent toward farmers and villagers because of their own plight. They were responsible for the collection of imperial revenues. If their area could not meet its tax quota, they paid the deficit from their own pockets. Because the local officials were themselves so hard-pressed, they squeezed whatever they could from the villagers and farmers.

RECONSTRUCTION UNDER DIOCLETIAN AND CONSTANTINE (A.D. 284–337)

At the close of the third century A.D., the emperor Diocletian (r.284–305) put an end to the period of turmoil. Repairing the damage done in the third century was the major work of the emperor Constantine (r.306–337) in the fourth. But the price was high.

Under Diocletian, Augustus's polite fiction of the emperor as first among equals gave way to the emperor as absolute autocrat. The princeps became *dominus*—"lord." The emperor claimed that he was "the elect of God"—that he ruled because of God's favor. Constantine even claimed to be the equal of Jesus' first twelve followers. To underline the emperor's exalted position, Diocletian and

Constantine adopted the gaudy court ceremonies and trappings of the Persian Empire. People entering the emperor's presence prostrated themselves before him and kissed the hem of his robes. Constantine went so far as to import Persian eunuchs to run the palace. The Roman emperor had become an Oriental monarch.

No mere soldier, but rather an adroit administrator, Diocletian gave serious thought to the empire's ailments. He recognized that the empire and its difficulties had become too great for one man to handle. He also realized that during the third century provincial governors had frequently used their positions to foment or participate in rebellions. To solve the first of these problems, Diocletian divided the empire into a western and an eastern half (Map 6.4). Diocletian assumed direct control of the eastern part; he gave the rule of the western part to a colleague, along with the title *augustus,* which had become synonymous with emperor. Diocletian and his fellow augustus further delegated power by appointing two men to assist them. Each man was given the title of *caesar* to indicate his exalted rank. Although this system is known as the *Tetrarchy* because four men ruled the empire, Diocletian was clearly the senior partner and final source of authority.

Each half of the empire was further split into two prefectures, each governed by a prefect responsible to an augustus. Diocletian reduced the power of the old provincial governors by dividing provinces into smaller units. He organized the prefectures into small administrative units called *dioceses,* which were in turn subdivided into small provinces. Provincial governors were also deprived of their military power, leaving them only civil and administrative duties.

Diocletian's political reforms were a momentous step. The Tetrarchy soon failed, but Diocletian's division of the empire into two parts became permanent. Constantine and later emperors tried hard but unsuccessfully to keep the empire together. Throughout the fourth century A.D., the eastern and the western sections drifted apart. In later centuries the western part witnessed the fall of Roman government and the rise of barbarian kingdoms, while the eastern empire evolved into the majestic Byzantine Empire.

The most serious immediate matters confronting Diocletian and Constantine were economic, so-

Diocletian's Tetrarchy The emperor Diocletian's attempt to reform the Roman Empire by dividing rule among four men is represented in this piece of sculpture, which in many features illustrates the transition from ancient to medieval art. Here the four tetrarchs demonstrate their solidarity by clasping one another on the shoulder. Nonetheless each man has his other hand on his sword—a gesture that proved prophetic when Diocletian's reign ended and another struggle for power began. *(Source: Alinari/Art Resource)*

cial, and religious. They needed additional revenues to support the army and the imperial court. Yet the wars and the barbarian invasions had caused widespread destruction and poverty. The fighting had struck a serious blow to Roman agriculture, which the emperors tried to revive. Christianity had become too strong either to ignore or to crush. The responses to these problems by Diocletian, Constantine, and their successors helped create the

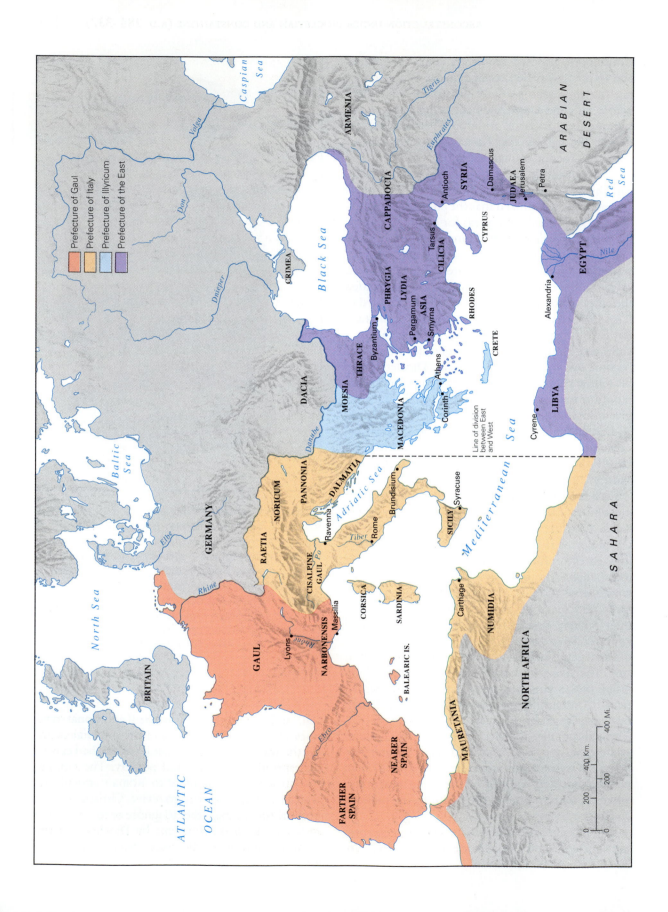

ARABIAN DESERT

Caspian Sea

Volga

Don

Tigris

Euphrates

ARMENIA

CAPPADOCIA

SYRIA

Damascus

Antioch

JUDAEA
Jerusalem
Petra

Red Sea

Tarsus

CILICIA

CYPRUS

EGYPT

Nile

Dnieper

CRIMEA

Black Sea

PHRYGIA

LYDIA

Pergamum
Smyrna

ASIA

RHODES

CRETE

Alexandria

THRACE

Byzantium

Athens

Corinth

Line of division
between East
and West

LIBYA

Cyrene

DACIA

MOESIA

MACEDONIA

Mediterranean Sea

SAHARA

Baltic Sea

Danube

PANNONIA

DALMATIA

Adriatic Sea

Brundisium

Syracuse

GERMANY

Elbe

NORICUM

Ravenna

Rome

Tiber

SICILY

RAETIA

Po

CISALPINE
GAUL

North Sea

Rhine

CORSICA

SARDINIA

Carthage

NUMIDIA

NORTH AFRICA

GAUL

Lyons

Rhône

Massilia

NARBONENSIS

BALEARIC IS.

MAURETANIA

BRITAIN

ATLANTIC OCEAN

NEARER SPAIN

FARTHER SPAIN

Ebro

Prefecture of Gaul
Prefecture of Italy
Prefecture of Illyricum
Prefecture of the East

400 Mi.

400 Km.

200

200

0

0

economic and social patterns that medieval Europe inherited.

Inflation and Taxes

The barracks emperors had dealt with economic hardship by depreciating the currency, cutting the silver content of coins until money was virtually worthless. As a result, the entire monetary system fell into ruin. In Egypt, governors had to order bankers to accept imperial money. The immediate result was crippling inflation throughout the empire.

The empire was less capable of recovery than in earlier times. Wars and invasions had disrupted normal commerce and the means of production. Mines were exhausted in the attempt to supply much-needed ores, especially gold and silver. The turmoil had hit the cities especially hard. Markets were disrupted, and travel became dangerous. Craftsmen, artisans, and traders rapidly left devastated regions. The prosperous industry and commerce of Gaul and the Rhineland declined markedly. Those who owed their prosperity to commerce and the needs of urban life likewise suffered. Cities were no longer places where trade and industry thrived. The devastation of the countryside increased the difficulty of feeding and supplying the cities. The destruction was so extensive that many wondered whether the ravages could be repaired at all.

The response of Diocletian and Constantine to these problems was marked by compulsion, rigidity, and loss of individual freedom. Diocletian's attempt to curb inflation illustrates the methods of absolute monarchy. In a move unprecedented in Roman history, he issued an edict that fixed maximum prices and wages throughout the empire. The measure proved a failure because it was unrealistic as well as unenforceable.

The emperors dealt with the tax system just as strictly and inflexibly. As in the past, local officials bore the responsibility of collecting imperial taxes.

MAP 6.4 The Roman World Divided   Under Diocletian, the Roman Empire was first divided into a western and an eastern half, a development that foreshadowed the medieval division between the Latin West and the Byzantine East.

Constantine made these officials into a hereditary class; son followed father whether he wanted to or not. In this period of severe depression, many localities could not pay their taxes. In such cases these local officials had to make up the difference from their own funds. This system soon wiped out a whole class of moderately wealthy people.

With the monetary system in ruins, most imperial taxes became payable in kind—that is, in goods or produce instead of money. The major drawback of payment in kind is its demands on transportation. Goods have to be moved from where they are grown or manufactured to where they are needed. Accordingly, the emperors locked into their occupations all those involved in the growing, preparation, and transportation of food and essential commodities. A baker or shipper could not go into any other business, and his son took up the trade at his death. The late Roman Empire had a place for everyone, and everyone had a place.

The Decline of Small Farms

The late Roman heritage to the medieval world is most obvious in agriculture. Because of worsening conditions, free tenant farmers were reduced to serfdom. During the third century A.D., many were killed, fled the land to escape the barbarians, or abandoned farms ravaged in the fighting. Consequently, large tracts of land lay deserted. Great landlords with ample resources began at once to reclaim as much of this land as they could. The huge estates that resulted were the forerunners of medieval manors. Like manors, these villas were self-sufficient. Because they often produced more than they consumed, they successfully competed with the declining cities by selling their surplus in the countryside. They became islands of stability in an unsettled world.

While the villas were growing, the small farmers who remained on the land barely held their own. They were too poor and powerless to stand against the tide of chaos. They were exposed to the raids of barbarians or brigands and to the tyranny of imperial officials. For relief they turned to the great landlords. After all, the landowners were men of considerable resources, lords in their own right. They were wealthy and had many people working their land. They were independent and capable of defending themselves. If need be, they could—and at

A Large Roman Villa During the third and fourth centuries, when the Roman Empire was breaking up, large villas such as this one in Carthage became the focus of daily life. The villa was at once a fortress, as the towers at the corner of the building indicate, and the economic and social center of the neighborhood. *(Source: Courtesy, German Archaeological Institute)*

times did—field a small force of their own. Already influential, the landowning class united in protest against the demands of imperial officials.

In return for the protection and security landlords could offer, the small landholders gave over their lands. Free men and their families became clients of the landlords and lost much of their freedom. To guarantee a steady supply of labor, the landlords bound them to the soil. They could no longer decide to move elsewhere. Henceforth they and their families worked their patrons' land, not their own. Free men and women were in effect becoming serfs.

The Legalization of Christianity

In religious affairs Constantine took the decisive step of recognizing Christianity as a legitimate religion. No longer would Christians suffer persecution for their beliefs as they had occasionally experienced earlier. Constantine himself died a Christian in 337. Why had the pagans persecuted Christians in the first place? Polytheism is by nature tolerant of new gods and accommodating in religious matters. Why was Christianity singled out for violence? These questions are still matters of scholarly debate, but some broad answers can be given.

Educated and cultured people like the historian Tacitus opposed Christianity, which struck them as a bizarre new sect.. Tacitus believed that Christians hated the whole human race. As a rule, early Christians, like the Jews, kept to themselves. Romans distrusted and feared their exclusiveness, which seemed unsociable and even subversive. Most pagans genuinely misunderstood Christian practices. They thought that the Lord's Supper, at which Christians said they ate and drank the body and blood of Jesus, was an act of cannibalism. Pagans thought that Christians indulged in immoral and indecent rituals. They considered Christianity one of the worst of the Oriental mystery

ROMAN HISTORY AFTER AUGUSTUS

Period	Important Emperors	Significant Events
Julio-Claudians 27 B.C.–A.D. 68	Augustus 27 B.C.–A.D. 14 Tiberius, 14–37 Caligula, 37–41 Claudius, 41–54 Nero, 54–68	Augustan settlement Beginning of the principate Birth and death of Jesus Expansion into northern and western Europe Creation of the imperial bureaucracy
Year of the Four Emperors 68–69	Nero Galba Otho Vitellius	Civil war Major breakdown of the concept of the principate
Flavians 69–96	Vespasian, 69–79 Titus, 79–81 Domitian, 81–96	Growing trend toward the concept of monarchy Defense and further consolidation of the European frontiers
Antonines 96–192	Nerva, 96–98 Trajan, 98–117 Hadrian, 117–138 Antoninus Pius, 138–161 Marcus Aurelius, 161–180 Commodus, 180–192	The "golden age"—the era of the "five good emperors" Economic prosperity Trade and growth of cities in northern Europe Beginning of barbarian menace on the frontiers
Severi 193–235	Septimius Severus, 193–211 Caracalla, 211–217 Elagabalus, 218–222 Severus Alexander, 222–235	Military monarchy All free men within the empire given Roman citizenship
"Barracks Emperors" 235–284	Twenty-two emperors in forty-nine years	Civil war Breakdown of the Empire Barbarian invasions Severe economic decline
Tetrarchy 284–337	Diocletian, 284–305 Constantine, 306–337	Political recovery Autocracy Legalization of Christianity Transition to the Middle Ages in the West Birth of the Byzantine Empire in the East

cults, for one of the hallmarks of many of those cults was disgusting rituals.

Even these feelings of distrust and revulsion do not entirely account for persecution. The main reason seems to have been sincere religious conviction on the part of the pagans. Time and again, they accused Christians of atheism. Indeed, Christians either denied the existence of pagan gods or called them evil spirits. For this same reason, many Romans hated the Jews. Tacitus no doubt expressed the common view when he said that Jews despised the gods. Christians went even further than Jews—they said that no one should worship pagan gods.

At first some pagans were repelled by the fanaticism of these monotheists. No good could come from scorning the gods. The whole community might end up paying for the wickedness and blasphemy of the Christians. Besides—and this is important—pagans did not demand that Christians *believe* in pagan gods. Greek and Roman religion was never a matter of belief or ethics. It was purely a religion of ritual. One of the clearest statements of pagan theological attitudes comes from the Roman senator Symmachus in the later fourth century A.D.:

We watch the same stars; heaven is the same for us all; the same universe envelops us: what importance is it in what way anyone looks for truth? It is impossible to arrive by one route at such a great secret.[11]

Yet Roman religion was inseparable from the state. An attack on one was an attack on the other. The Romans were being no more fanatical or intolerant than an eighteenth-century English judge who declared the Christian religion part of the law of the land. All the pagans expected was performance of the ritual act, a small token sacrifice. Any Christian who sacrificed went free, no matter what he or she personally believed. The earliest persecutions of the Christians were minor and limited. Even Nero's famous persecution was temporary and limited to Rome. Subsequent persecutions were sporadic and local.

As time went on, pagan hostility decreased. Pagans gradually realized that Christians were not working to overthrow the state and that Jesus was no rival of Caesar. The emperor Trajan forbade his governors to hunt down Christians. Trajan admitted that he thought Christianity an abomination, but he preferred to leave Christians in peace.

The stress of the third century, however, seemed to some emperors the punishment of the gods. What else could account for such anarchy? With the empire threatened on every side, a few emperors thought that one way to appease the gods was by offering them the proper sacrifices. Such sacrifices would be a sign of loyalty to the empire, a show of Roman solidarity. Consequently, a new wave of persecutions began. Yet even they were never very widespread or long-lived; most pagans were not greatly sympathetic to the new round of persecutions. By the late third century, pagans had become used to Christianity. Pagan and Christian alike must have been relieved when Constantine legalized the Christian religion.

In time the Christian triumph would be complete. In 380 the emperor Theodosius made Christianity the official religion of the Roman Empire. At that point Christians began to persecute the pagans for their beliefs. History had come full circle.

The Construction of Constantinople

The triumph of Christianity was not the only event that made Constantine's reign a turning point in Roman history. Constantine took the bold step of building a new capital for the empire. Constantinople, the New Rome, was constructed on the site of Byzantium, an old Greek city on the Bosporus. Throughout the third century, emperors had found Rome and the West hard to defend. The eastern part of the empire was more easily defensible and escaped the worst of the barbarian devastation. It was wealthy and its urban life still vibrant. Moreover, Christianity was more widespread in the East than in the West, and the city of Constantinople was intended to be a Christian center.

THE AWFUL REVOLUTION

Great historical movements will always be the subject of interpretation and speculation. The "fall" of the Roman Empire is a classic example, and it demonstrates excellently how historians try to understand complex historical developments and make

The Arch of Constantine   To celebrate the victory that made him emperor, Constantine built this triumphal arch in Rome. Rather than decorate the arch with the inferior work of his own day, Constantine plundered other Roman monuments, including those of Trajan and Marcus Aurelius. *(Source: C. M. Dixon)*

them understandable to others. Sometimes, as in the case of Rome, the process has a simple beginning. For instance, on the evening of October 15, 1764, Edward Gibbon, a young Englishman, sat in Rome among the ruins of the Capitol listening to the chanting of some monks. As the voices of the Christian present echoed against the stones of the pagan past, Gibbon wondered how the Roman Empire had given way to the medieval world. His curiosity aroused, he dedicated himself to the study of what he considered the greatest problem in history. Twelve years later, in 1776, Gibbon published *The Decline and Fall of the Roman Empire,* one of the monuments of English literature, a brilliant work fashioned with wit, learning, humor, and elegance.

Gibbon's thesis is, as his title indicates, that the Roman Empire, after the first two centuries of existence, declined in strength, vitality, and prosperity, then fell into ruin. His concept of Rome's "decline and fall," a process that he called "the awful revolu-

tion," has dominated historical thought for over two hundred years. Even those who disagree with Gibbon over details have usually accepted his concept of decline and fall, yet one can nonetheless ask whether Gibbon's concept is valid, and whether it is the only way (or even the best way) to explore this historical phenomenon.

There may never be a satisfactory solution to this problem because of its very complexity. Nor is any one answer entirely convincing. Gibbon himself put the blame for the empire's decline largely on the spread of Christianity, which emphasized the virtues of humility, piety, and the belief in an afterlife that was far more important than life here on earth. These qualities, in Gibbon's view, were entirely inadequate for the maintenance of a proud and vigorous empire.

Despite the value of Gibbon's work, Christianity cannot reasonably be made the villain of the piece. True, many very able minds and forceful characters devoted their lives and energies primarily to the Christian church and not to the empire. Yet the numbers involved in these pursuits were small in proportion to the total population. Furthermore, the Byzantine Empire, which evolved from the eastern part of the Roman Empire, demonstrated that Christians could handle the sword as well as the cross.

Ultimately, Gibbon begged his own question, as when he wrote that "instead of inquiring *why* the Roman empire was destroyed, we should rather be surprised that it had subsisted for so long."[12] Yet once Gibbon raised the question of the causes for Rome's fall, other historians were quick to answer it. Some of their answers are nonsensical, others useful; but all demonstrate the very many ways in which people view history and their own relation to it.

To explain the fall of the Roman Empire, some scholars have resorted to pseudoscientific theories. These efforts are in effect an abuse of science. For instance, some writers have looked at historical developments in biological terms. According to them, states and empires develop like living organisms, progressing through periods of birth and growth to maturity and consolidation, followed by decrepitude, decline, and collapse. This argument is simply false analogy, unsupported by any scientific evidence.

Others blame the "collapse" on ridiculous racial theories. They speculate that the Roman people became "mongrelized" when the physically strong, moral, and intelligent Romans intermingled with inferior Asian and African peoples, causing the Romans to lose their physical and moral fiber. This theory, too, can be readily refuted: the eastern, supposedly inferior half of the empire survived a thousand years longer than the "superior" western half. One of the more amusing explanations appeared in the *New England Journal of Medicine* in 1983, when an author speculated that lead poisoning contributed to the fall of the empire. According to this view, the use of lead cooking pots, lead cups, and lead water pipes caused widespread gout and lead poisoning in Roman society. Yet skeletal remains of Romans show no excessive amounts of lead. All of these pseudoscientific explanations suffer from one basic error: they assume that conditions in Rome and Italy were general throughout the Roman Empire. They ignore the simple fact that people lived differently in different parts of the empire, just as Americans in New Mexico live differently from those in Alaska. The government and culture may be essentially the same over a large area, whether in the empire or in the United States, but local circumstances differ widely. Conditions in the city of Rome should not be taken as typical of the empire in general.

Others have offered an economic explanation of the awful revolution—a solution especially popular among Marxist historians. In their view, the Roman economy declined primarily because of its dependence on slave labor. At the same time, Roman expansion in northern Europe led to the growth of new centers of production there. Roman assimilation of barbarian peoples on the European fringe of the empire, combined with the economic development of the area, resulted in economic competition in which Rome's Mediterranean markets declined and economic stagnation set in. This interpretation suffers from two major weaknesses. First, slavery was hardly a significant factor in these events and certainly not the cause of them. In late antiquity slavery was itself in decline and manumission widespread. In fact, these are the very years in which the agricultural slave increasingly gave way to the free tenant farmer, even though the farmer himself was in an economically disadvantaged situation.

The second flaw in the economic view is its overestimation of the competition from northern Europe. It is true that the widespread settlement of retired Roman legionaries on the frontier and the demands of their barbarian customers led to the rise of new economic centers; but this process had existed from the days of Julius Caesar. No one would argue that most of what was produced along the frontier was consumed there. Moreover, this is the very region that was hardest hit by the barbarian invasions and civil wars. Meanwhile, in the core of the Roman Empire, the Mediterranean basin, a sturdy commerce continued over the traditional sea lanes. The later Roman Empire indeed suffered from significant economic problems, but the origins of those difficulties stemmed neither from slavery nor from competition from the European fringe.

Over the years, political explanations for the empire's decline have won the widest acceptance. The Roman imperial government never solved the problem of succession: it never devised a peaceful and regular way to pass on the imperial power when an emperor died. The legions enjoyed too much power, often creating and destroying civil governments at will and in the process gradually destroying the state. The assassinations of emperors and frequent changes of government produced chronic instability, weakening the state's ability to solve its problems.

From the late third century on, successive approaches to Rome's economic difficulties proved disastrous. Emperors depreciated the coinage. The middle classes carried an increasingly heavy tax burden, and the imperial bureaucracy grew bigger, though not more efficient. These factors combined to destroy the ordinary citizen's confidence in the state. Consequently, according to the explanation of political historians, with the economy and society so undermined, the Roman Empire was destroyed by internal difficulties. In this way, most of the economic problems of Rome's decline can be traced to political causes.

Yet there is no real reason even to accept Gibbon's concept of a "fall" or "decline" of the Roman Empire. No one in the late Roman Empire woke up one morning and said, "Oh, I see that the empire has fallen, classical antiquity has ended, and the Middle Ages have begun." Rather, the concept of change and development, instead of decline, has much to recommend it, particularly since so many aspects of the Roman world survived. Both barbarians and popes eagerly embraced Roman political forms and ideas, and a great many aspects of the Roman world survived to influence the medieval and eventually the modern world. Roman law left its traces on the legal and political systems of most European countries. Roman roads, aqueducts, bridges, and buildings remained in use, not as museum pieces but rather as constant practical reminders of the Roman past that became a part of the growing present. The Latin language lay at the root of many of the modern languages of western Europe. It also served as a major cultural link. For almost two thousand years, Latin language and literature remained at the core of Western education. Those who used the old Roman roads or who studied Latin came to some degree under the spell of Rome. Especially in the intellectual realm, Roman attitudes and patterns of thought fertilized the lives and manner of thinking of generation after genera-

tion of Europeans. Slowly, almost imperceptibly, the Roman Empire gave way to the medieval world.

SUMMARY

The Roman emperors expanded the provincial system established during the republic. They gave it more definite organization, both militarily to defend it and bureaucratically to administer it. The result was the pax Romana, a period of peace and prosperity for the empire. Into this climate came Christianity, which was able to spread throughout the Roman world because peace and security made communications within the empire safe and easy. Christianity satisfied people's emotional and spiritual needs in ways that traditional pagan religions did not. Although other mystery religions existed, they were normally exclusive in one way or another. Christianity was open to all, rich and poor, men and women. Paul of Tarsus was the first of many talented Christians to spread the new religion throughout a receptive world. But that world was disrupted in the third century by a combination of barbarian invasions, civil war, and economic decline. The bonds that held the empire together weakened, and only the herculean efforts of the emperors Diocletian and Constantine restored order. Those emperors repulsed the barbarians, defeated rebellious generals, and reformed the economy in a restrictive way. The result was an empire very changed from the time of the Augustan peace, but one that left an enduring legacy for later generations.

NOTES

1. Virgil, *Aeneid* 6.851–853. John Buckler is the translator of all uncited quotations from a foreign language in Chapters 1–6.
2. Augustus, *Res Gestae* 6.34.
3. Ibid., 5.28.
4. Horace, Odes 4.15.
5. Virgil, *Georgics* 3.515–519.
6. Matthew 3:3.
7. Matthew 16:18.

8. Edward Gibbon, *The History of the Decline and Fall of the Roman Empire* (New York: Modern Library, n.d.), 1.1.

9. *Corpus Inscriptionum Latinarum,* vol. 6 (Berlin: G. Reimer, 1882), no. 9792.

10. Ibid., vol. 6, no. 14672.

11. Symmachus, *Relations* 3.10.

12. Gibbon, 2.438.

SUGGESTED READING

Some good general treatments of the empire include B. Levick, *The Government of the Roman Empire: A Source Book* (1984), a convenient collection of sources illustrating the workings of Roman imperial government; P. Garnsey and R. Saller, *The Roman Empire* (1987); and J. Wacher, ed., *The Roman World,* 2 vols. (1987), which attempts a comprehensive survey of the world of the Roman Empire. The role of the emperor is superbly treated by F. Millar, *The Emperor in the Roman World* (1977), and the defense of the empire is studied by E. N. Luttwak, *The Grand Strategy of the Roman Empire* (1976). The army that carried out that strategy is the subject of G. Webster, *The Roman Imperial Army* (1969). Last, a book of far-ranging interest is G. E. M. de St. Croix, *The Class Struggle in the Ancient World* (1981). This book is a Marxist interpretation of Greco-Roman society. Even though de St. Croix has failed to depict that society convincingly in Marxist terms, he offers a number of insights into specific aspects of life, especially during the Roman Empire.

Favorable to Augustus is M. Hammond, *The Augustan Principate* (1933). G. W. Bowersock, *Augustus and the Greek World* (1965), is excellent intellectual history. C. M. Wells, *The German Policy of Augustus* (1972), uses archeological findings to illustrate Roman expansion into northern Europe. H. Schutz, *The Romans in Central Europe* (1985), treats Roman expansion, its problems, and its successes in a vital area of the empire. In *The Augustan Aristocracy* (1985), one of the great Roman historians of this century, R. Syme, studies the new order that Augustus created to help him administer the empire. Rather than study the Augustan poets individually, one can now turn to D. A. West and A. J. Woodman, *Poetry and Politics in the Age of Augustus* (1984). J. B. Campbell, *The Emperor and the Roman Army, 31 B.C.–A.D. 235* (1984), stresses the reliance of the Roman emperor on the army throughout the empire's history. Recent work on the Roman army includes M. Speidel, *Roman Army Studies,* vol. 1 (1984), and L. Keppie, *The Making of the Roman Army from Republic to Empire* (1984). Even though Au-

gustus himself still remains an enigma, F. Millar and E. Segal, eds., *Caesar Augustus: Seven Aspects* (1984), is an interesting volume of essays that attempts, not always successfully, to penetrate the official façade of the emperor. N. Hannestad, *Roman Art and Imperial Policy* (1988), examines the way in which the emperors used art as a means of furthering imperial policy. M. Hammond, *The Antonine Monarchy* (1959), is a classic study of the evolution of the monarchy under the Antonines.

The commercial life of the empire is the subject of an interesting book by K. Greene, *The Archaeology of the Roman Economy* (1986), which offers an intriguing way in which to picture the Roman economy through physical remains. R. Duncan-Jones, *The Economy of the Roman Empire: Quantitative Studies,* 2d ed. (1982), employs new techniques of historical inquiry. The classic treatment, which ranges across the empire, is M. Rostovtzeff, *The Economic and Social History of the Roman Empire* (1957). P. W. de Neeve, *Colonies: Private Farm-Tenancy in Roman Italy* (1983), covers agriculture and the styles of landholding from the republic to the early empire.

Social aspects of the empire are the subject of R. Auguet, *Cruelty and Civilization: The Roman Games* (English translation, 1972); P. Garnsey, *Social Status and Legal Privilege in the Roman Empire* (1970); and A. N. Sherwin-White, *Racial Prejudice in Imperial Rome* (1967). A general treatment is R. MacMullen, *Roman Social Relations, 50 B.C. to A.D. 284* (1981), and a recent contribution is L. A. Thompson, *Romans and Blacks* (1989). N. Kampen, *Image and Status: Roman Working Women in Ostia* (1981), is distinctive for its treatment of ordinary Roman women. An important feature of Roman history is treated by R. P. Saller, *Personal Patronage Under the Early Empire* (1982). J. Humphrey, *Roman Circuses and Chariot Racing* (1985), treats a topic very dear to the hearts of ancient Romans. K. R. Bradley, *Slaves and Masters in the Roman Empire* (1988), discusses social controls in a slaveholding society. Lastly, B. Cunliffe, *Greeks, Romans and Barbarians* (1988), uses archeological and literary evidence to discuss the introduction of Greco-Roman culture into western Europe.

Christianity, paganism, Judaism, and the ways in which they all met have received lively recent attention. K. Wengst, *Pax Romana and the Peace of Jesus Christ* (English translation 1987), is an interesting study of the social atmosphere of the lower classes at the time when Christianity was spreading. More recent is A. Chester, *The Social Context of Early Christianity* (1989). J. Liebeschuetz, *Continuity and Change in Roman Religion* (1979), emphasizes the evolution of Roman religion from the late Republic to the late Empire. M. P. Speidel, *Mithras-Orion, Greek Hero and Roman Army God* (1980), studies the cult of Mithras, a mystery religion that was an early competitor with Christianity. The evolution of Christianity in its Hellenistic background, both pagan and Jewish, can be traced through a series of recent books: R. H. Nash, *Christianity and the Hellenistic World* (1984); T. Barnes, *Early Christianity and the Roman Empire* (1984); S. Benko, *Pagan Rome and Early Christians* (1985); and R. L. Wilken, *The Christians as the Romans Saw Them* (1984). A bit broader than Wilken's book is M. Whittacker, *Jews and Christians: Graeco-Roman Views* (1984). Last, R. Mac-Mullen, *Christianizing the Roman Empire* (1984), treats the growth of the Christian church as seen from a pagan perspective.

Convenient surveys of Roman literature are J. W. Duff's, *Literary History of Rome from the Origins to the Close of the Golden Age* (1953) and *Literary History of Rome in the Silver Age*, 3d ed. (1964).

Ever since Gibbon's *Decline and Fall of the Roman Empire,* one of the masterpieces of English literature, the decline of the empire has been a fertile field of investigation. S. Perowne, *Hadrian* (1987), is a new assessment of the emperor who attempted to limit Roman expansion. Broader are A. M. H. Jones, *The Decline of the Ancient World* (1966); F. W. Walbank, *The Awful Revolution* (1969), and R. MacMullen's two books: *Soldier and Civilian in the Later Roman Empire* (1963) and *Enemies of the Roman Order: Treason, Unrest, and Alienation in the Empire* (1966). S. N. C. Lieu and M. Dodgeon, *Rome's Eastern Frontier, A.D. 226–363* (1988), relies primarily on documents to trace Rome's policy in the East during this difficult period. Two studies analyze the attempts at recovery from the breakdown of the barracks emperors: T. D. Barnes, *The New Empire of Diocletian and Constantine* (1982), which, as its title indicates, concerns itself with the necessary innovations made by the two emperors; and, more narrowly, S. Williams, *Diocletian and the Roman Recovery* (1985). A. Ferrill, *The Fall of the Roman Empire* (1986), with plans and illustrations, offers a military explanation for the "fall" of the Roman Empire. In conclusion, R. MacMullen, *Constantine* (1988), written by a leading scholar in the field, provides a broad and lucid interpretation of Constantine and the significance of his reign.

7

The Making of Europe

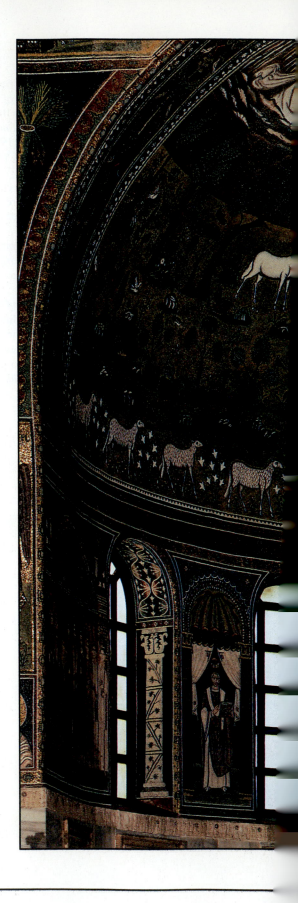

The centuries between approximately 400 and 900 present a paradox. They witnessed the disintegration of the Roman Empire, which had been one of humanity's great political and cultural achievements. On the other hand, these five centuries were a creative and important period, during which Europeans laid the foundations for medieval and modern Europe. It is not too much to say that this period saw the making of Europe.

The basic ingredients that went into the making of a distinctly European civilization were the cultural legacy of Greece and Rome, the customs and traditions of the Germanic peoples, and the Christian faith. The most important of these was Christianity, because it absorbed and assimilated the other two. It reinterpreted the classics in a Christian sense. It instructed the Germanic peoples and gave them new ideals of living and social behavior. Christianity became the cement that held European society together.

During this period the Byzantine Empire, centered at Constantinople, served as a protective buffer between Europe and peoples to the east. The Byzantine Greeks preserved the philosophical and scientific texts of the ancient world, which later formed the basis for study in science and medicine, and produced a great synthesis of Roman law, the Justinian *Code*. In the urbane and sophisticated life led at Constantinople, the Greeks set a standard far above the primitive existence of the West.

In the seventh and eighth centuries, Arabic culture spread around the southern fringes of Europe —to Spain, Sicily, and North Africa, and to Syria, Palestine, and Egypt. The Arabs translated the works of such Greek thinkers as Euclid, Hippocrates, and Galen and made important contributions in mathematics, astronomy, and physics. In Arabic translation, Greek texts trickled to the West, and most later European scientific study rested on the Arabic work.

European civilization resulted from the fusion of the Greco-Roman heritage, Germanic traditions, and the Christian faith.

- How did these components act on one another?
- How did they lead to the making of Europe?
- What influence did the Byzantine and Islamic cultures have on the making of Europe?

This chapter will focus on these questions.

THE GROWTH OF THE CHRISTIAN CHURCH

While many elements of the Roman Empire disintegrated, the Christian church survived and grew. What is the church? Scriptural scholars tell us that the earliest use of the word *church* (in Greek, *ekklesia*) in the New Testament appears in Saint Paul's Letter to the Christians of Thessalonica in northern Greece, written about A.D. 51. By *ekklesia* Paul meant the local community of Christian believers. In Paul's later letters, the term *church* refers to the entire Mediterranean-wide assembly of Jesus' followers. After the legalization of Christianity by the emperor Constantine (see page 182) and the growth of institutional offices and officials, the word *church* was sometimes applied to those officials—much as we use the terms *the college* or *the university* when referring to academic administrators. Then the bishops of Rome—known as "popes" from the Latin word *papa,* meaning "father"—claimed to speak and act as the source of unity for all Christians. The popes claimed to be the successors of Saint Peter and heirs to his authority as chief of the apostles, on the basis of Jesus' words:

You are Peter, and on this rock I will build my church, and the jaws of death shall not prevail against it. I will entrust to you the keys of the kingdom of heaven. Whatever you declare bound on earth shall be bound in heaven; whatever you declare loosed on earth shall be loosed in heaven.[1]

Roman bishops used this text, known as the Petrine Doctrine, to support their assertions of authority over other bishops in the church. Thus the popes maintained that they represented "the church." The word *church,* therefore, has several connotations. Although modern Catholic theology frequently defines the church as "the people of God" and identifies it with local and international Christian communities, in the Middle Ages the institutional and monarchial interpretations tended to be stressed.

Having gained the support of the fourth-century emperors, the church gradually adopted the Roman system of organization. Christianity had a dynamic missionary policy, and the church slowly succeeded in *assimilating*—that is, adapting— pagan peoples, both Germans and Romans, to Christian teaching. Moreover, the church possessed able administrators and leaders and highly literate and creative thinkers. These factors help to explain the survival and growth of the Christian church in the face of repeated Germanic invasions.

The Church and the Roman Emperors

The church benefited considerably from the emperors' support. In return, the emperors expected the support of the Christian church in maintaining order and unity. Constantine had legalized the practice of Christianity within the empire in 312. Although he was not baptized until he was on his deathbed, Constantine encouraged Christianity throughout his reign. He freed the clergy from imperial taxation. At the churchmen's request, he helped settle theological disputes and thus preserve doctrinal unity within the church. Constantine generously endowed the building of Christian churches, and one of his gifts—the Lateran Palace in Rome—remained the official residence of the popes until the fourteenth century. Constantine also declared Sunday a public holiday, a day of rest for the service of God. As the result of its favored position in the empire, Christianity slowly became the leading religion.

In 380 the emperor Theodosius went further than Constantine and made Christianity the official religion of the empire. Theodosius stripped Roman pagan temples of statues, made the practice of the old Roman state religion a treasonable offense, and persecuted Christians who dissented from orthodox doctrine. Most significant, he allowed the church to establish its own courts. Church courts began to develop their own body of law, called "canon law." These courts, not the Roman government, had jurisdiction over the clergy and ecclesiastical disputes. At the death of Theodosius, the Christian church was considerably independent of the Roman state. The foundation for the medieval church's power had been laid.

What was to be the church's relationship to secular powers? How was the Christian to render unto Caesar the things that were Caesar's while returning to God what was due to God? This problem had troubled the earliest disciples of Christ. The toleration of Christianity and the coming to power of Christian emperors in the fourth century did not make it any easier. Striking a balance between responsibility to secular rulers and loyalty to spiritual duties was difficult.

In the fourth century, theological disputes frequently and sharply divided the Christian community. Some disagreements had to do with the nature of Christ. For example, Arianism, which originated with Arius (ca 250–336), a priest of Alexandria, denied that Christ was divine and that he had always existed with God the Father—two propositions of orthodox Christian belief. Arius held that God was by definition uncreated and unchangeable and that he had created Christ as his instrument for the redemption of humankind. Since Christ was created, Arius reasoned, he could not have been coeternal with the Father. Orthodox Christians branded Arianism a *heresy*—the denial of a doctrine of faith. Arianism enjoyed such popularity and provoked such controversy that Constantine, to whom religious disagreement meant civil disorder, interceded. He summoned a council of church leaders to Nicaea in Asia Minor and presided over it personally. The council produced the Nicene Creed, which defined the orthodox position that Christ is "eternally begotten of the Father" and of the same substance as the Father. Arius and those who refused to accept the creed were banished, the first case of civil punishment for heresy. This participation of the emperor in a theological dispute within the church paved the way for later emperors to claim that they could do the same.

So active was the emperor Theodosius's participation in church matters that he eventually came to loggerheads with Bishop Ambrose of Milan (339–397). Theodosius ordered Ambrose to hand over his cathedral church to the emperor. Ambrose's response had important consequences for the future:

At length came the command, "Deliver up the Basilica"; I reply, "It is not lawful for us to deliver it up, nor for your Majesty to receive it. By no law can you violate the house of a private man, and do you think that the house of God may be taken away? It is asserted that all things are lawful to the Emperor, that all things are his. But do not burden your conscience with the thought that you have any right as Emperor over sacred things. Exalt not yourself, but if you would reign the longer, be subject to God. It is written, God's to God and Caesar's to Caesar. The palace is the Emperor's, the Churches are the Bishop's. To you is committed jurisdiction over public, not over sacred buildings."[2]

Ambrose's statement was to serve as the cornerstone of the ecclesiastical theory of state-church

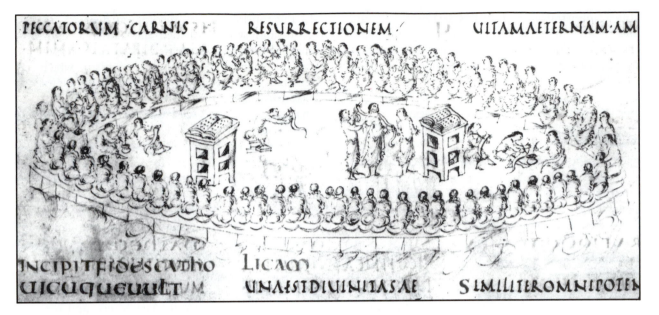

PECCATORVM ·CARNIS · RESVRRECTIONEM · VITAMAETERNAM·AM

INCIPITFIDESCATHO LICAM

QVICVQVEVVLT·um   VNAESTDIVINITASAE   SIMILITEROMNIPOTEN

The Council of Nicaea   (A.D. 325) In this ninth-century pen-and-ink drawing, sixty-six bishops and theologians sit around the presiding bishop while scribes record the proceedings. The Council produced the Nicene Creed, drawn up to defend the orthodox faith against the Arians. *(Source: Bibliotheek der Rijksuniversitet, Utrecht)*

relations throughout the Middle Ages. Ambrose insisted that the church was independent of the state's jurisdiction. He insisted that, in matters relating to the faith or the church, the bishops were to be the judges of emperors, not the other way around. In a Christian society, harmony and peace depended on agreement between the bishop and the secular ruler. But if disagreement developed, the church was ultimately the superior power because the church was responsible for the salvation of all (including the emperor). Theodosius accepted Ambrose's argument and bowed to the church. In later centuries, theologians, canonists, and propagandists repeatedly cited Ambrose's position as the basis of relations between the two powers.

Inspired Leadership

The early Christian church benefited from the brilliant administrative abilities of some church leaders and from identification of the authority and dignity of the bishop of Rome with the grand imperial traditions of the city. Some highly able Roman citizens accepted baptism and applied their intellectual powers and administrative skills to the service of the church rather than the empire. With the empire in decay, educated people joined and worked for the church in the belief that it was the one institution able to provide leadership. Bishop Ambrose, for example, the son of the Roman prefect of Gaul, was a trained lawyer and governor of a province. He is typical of those Roman aristocrats who held high public office, were converted to Christianity, and subsequently became bishops. Such men later provided social continuity from Roman to Germanic rule. As bishop of Milan, Ambrose himself exercised responsibility in the temporal as well as the ecclesiastical affairs of northern Italy.

During the reign of Diocletian (284–305), the Roman Empire had been divided for administrative purposes into geographical units called *dioceses.* Gradually the church made use of this organizational structure. Christian bishops—the leaders of early Christian communities, popularly elected by the Christian people—established their headquarters, or *sees,* in the urban centers of the old Roman dioceses. Their jurisdiction extended throughout all parts of the diocese. The center of the bishop's authority was his cathedral (the word derives from the Latin *cathedra,* meaning "chair"). Thus church leaders capitalized on the Roman imperial method of organization and adapted it to ecclesiastical purposes.

After the removal of the capital and the emperor to Constantinople (page 184), the bishop of Rome exercised vast influence in the West because he had no real competitor there. Bishops of Rome began to identify their religious offices with the imperial traditions of the city. They stressed that Rome had been the capital of a worldwide empire and emphasized the special importance of Rome in the framework of that empire. Successive bishops of Rome reminded Christians in other parts of the world that Rome was the burial place of Saint Peter and Saint Paul. Moreover, according to tradition, Saint Peter, the chief of Christ's first twelve followers, had lived and been executed in Rome. No other city in the world could make such claims. Hence the bishop of Rome was called "Patriarch of the West." In the East the bishops of Antioch, Alexandria, Jerusalem, and Constantinople, because of the special dignity of their sees, also gained the title of *patriarch.* Their jurisdictions extended over lands adjoining their sees; they consecrated bishops, investigated heresy, and heard judicial appeals.

In the fifth century the bishops of Rome began to stress their supremacy over other Christian communities and to urge other churches to appeal to Rome for the resolution of complicated doctrinal issues. Thus Pope Innocent I (401–417) wrote to the bishops of Africa:

We approve your action in following the principle that nothing which was done even in the most remote and distant provinces should be taken as finally settled unless it came to the notice of this See, that any just pronouncement might be confirmed by all the authority of this See, and that the other churches might from thence gather what they should teach.[3]

The prestige of Rome and the church as a whole was also enhanced by the courage and leadership of the Roman bishops. According to tradition, Pope Leo I (440–461) met the advancing army of Attila the Hun in 452 and, through his power of persuasion, saved Rome from destruction. Three years later, Leo persuaded the Vandal leader Gaiseric not to burn the city, though the pope could not prevent a terrible sacking.

By the time Gregory I (590–604) became pope, there was no civic authority left to handle the problems pressing the city. Flood, famine, plague, and invasion by the Lombards made for an almost disastrous situation. Pope Gregory concluded a peace with the Lombards, organized relief services that provided water and food for the citizens, and established hospitals for the sick and dying. The fact that it was Christian leaders, rather than imperial

Pope Gregory I (590–604) and Scribes One of the four "Doctors" (or Learned Fathers) of the Latin Church, Gregory is shown in this tenth-century ivory book cover writing at his desk while the Holy Spirit in the form of a dove whispers in his ear. Below, scribes copy Gregory's works. *(Source: Kunsthistorisches Museum, Vienna)*

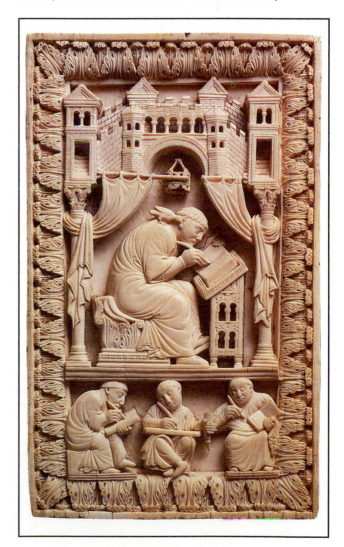

administrators, who responded to the city's dire needs could not help but increase the prestige and influence of the church.

Missionary Activity

The word *catholic* derives from a Greek word meaning "general," "universal," or "worldwide." Christ had said that his teaching was for all peoples, and Christians sought to make their faith catholic—that is, believed everywhere. This could be accomplished only through missionary activity. As Saint Paul had written to the Christian community at Colossae in Asia Minor:

You have stripped off your old behavior with your old self, and you have put on a new self which will progress towards true knowledge the more it is renewed in the image of its creator; and in that image there is no room for distinction between Greek and Jew, between the circumcised or the uncircumcised, or between barbarian or Scythian, slave and free man. There is only Christ; he is everything and he is in everything.[4]

Paul urged Christians to bring the "good news" of Christ to all peoples. The Mediterranean served as the highway over which Christianity spread to the cities of the empire.

During the Roman occupation, Christian communities were scattered throughout Gaul and Britain. The effective beginnings of Christianity in Gaul can be traced to Saint Martin of Tours (ca 316–397), a Roman soldier who, after giving away half his cloak to a naked beggar, had a vision of Christ and was baptized. Martin founded the monastery of Ligugé, the first in Gaul, which became a center for the evangelization of the country districts. In 372 he became bishop of Tours and introduced a rudimentary parish system.

Tradition identifies the conversion of Ireland with Saint Patrick (ca 385–461), one of the most effective missionaries in history. Born in western England to a Christian family of Roman citizenship, Patrick was captured and enslaved by Irish raiders and taken to Ireland, where he worked for six years as a herdsman. He escaped and returned to England, where a vision urged him to Christianize Ireland. In preparation, Patrick studied in Gaul and in 432 was consecrated a bishop. He landed in

Ireland, and at Tara in present-day County Meath —seat of the high kings of Ireland—he made his first converts. With Tara his headquarters, Patrick's missionary activities followed the existing social pattern: he converted the Irish, tribe by tribe, having first baptized the king. In 445, with the approval of Pope Leo I, Patrick established his see in Armagh. The ecclesiastical organization that Patrick set up, however, differed in a fundamental way from church structure on the continent: Armagh was a monastery, and the monastery, rather than the diocese, served as the center of ecclesiastical organization. Local tribes and the monastery were interdependent, with the clan supporting the monastery economically and the monastery providing religious and educational services for the tribe. Patrick also introduced the Roman alphabet and supported the codification of traditional laws. By the time of his death, the majority of the Irish people had received Christian baptism.

A strong missionary fervor characterized Irish Christianity. Perhaps the best representative of Irish-Celtic zeal was Saint Columba (ca 521–597), who established the monastery of Iona on an island in the Inner Hebrides off the west coast of Scotland. Iona served as a base for converting the pagan Picts of Scotland. Columba's proselytizing efforts won him the title "Apostle of Scotland," and his disciples carried the Christian Gospel to the European continent.

The Christianization of the English really began in 597, when Pope Gregory I sent a delegation of monks under the Roman Augustine to Britain to convert the English. Augustine's approach, like Patrick's, was to concentrate on converting the king. When he succeeded in converting Ethelbert, king of Kent, the baptism of Ethelbert's people took place as a matter of course. Augustine established his headquarters, or cathedral seat, at Canterbury, the capital of Kent. Kings who converted, such as Ethelbert and the Frankish chieftain Clovis (see page 211), sometimes had Christian wives. Besides the personal influence a Christian wife exerted on her husband, conversion may have indicated that barbarian kings wanted to enjoy the cultural advantages that Christianity brought, such as literate assistants and an ideological basis for their rule.

In the course of the seventh century, two Christian forces competed for the conversion of the pagan Anglo-Saxons: Roman-oriented missionaries traveling north from Canterbury and Celtic monks from Ireland and northwestern Britain. Monasteries were established at Iona, Lindisfarne, Jarrow, and Whitby (Map 7.1).

The Roman and Celtic traditions differed completely in their forms of church organization, types of monastic life, and methods of arriving at the date of the central feast of the Christian calendar, Easter. At the Synod (ecclesiastical council) of Whitby in 664, the Roman tradition was completely victorious. The conversion of the English and the close attachment of the English church to Rome had far-reaching consequences because Britain later served as a base for the Christianization of the Continent (Map 7.2).

Between the fifth and tenth centuries, the great majority of peoples living on the European continent and the nearby islands accepted the Christian religion—that is, they received baptism, though baptism in itself did not automatically transform people into Christians.

Religion influenced all aspects of tribal life. All members of the tribe participated in religious observances because doing so was a social duty. Religion was not a private or individual matter; the religion of the chieftain or king determined the religion of the people. Thus missionaries concentrated their initial efforts not on the people but on kings or tribal chieftains. According to custom, tribal chiefs negotiated with all foreign powers, including the gods. Because the Christian missionaries represented a "foreign" power (the Christian God), the king dealt with them. If the ruler accepted Christian baptism, his people did so, too. The result was mass baptism.

Once a ruler had marched his people to the waters of baptism, however, the work of Christianization had only begun. Baptism meant either sprinkling the head or immersing the body in water. Conversion meant mental and heartfelt acceptance of the beliefs of Christianity. What does it mean to be a Christian? This question has troubled sincere people from the time of Saint Paul to the present. The problem rests in part in the basic teaching of Jesus in the Gospel:

Then fixing his eyes on his disciples he said: "How happy are you who are poor: yours is the kingdom of God. Happy you who are hungry now: you shall be satisfied. Happy you who weep now: you shall laugh.

MAP 7.1 Anglo-Saxon England   The seven kingdoms of the Heptarchy—Northumbria, Mercia, East Anglia, Essex, Kent, Sussex, and Wessex—dominated but did not subsume Britain. Scotland remained a Pict stronghold while the Celts resisted invasion of their native Wales by Germanic tribes.

"Happy are you when people hate you, drive you out, abuse you, denounce your name as criminal, on account of the Son of Man. Rejoice when that day comes and dance for joy, then your reward will be great in heaven. This was the way their ancestors treated the prophets.

"But alas for you who are rich: you are having your consolation now. Also for you who have your fill now: you shall go hungry. Alas for you who laugh now: you shall mourn and weep.

"But I say this to you who are listening: Love your enemies, do good to those who hate you, bless those who curse you, pray for those who treat you badly. To the man who slaps you on one cheek, present the other cheek too; to the man who takes your cloak from you, do not refuse your tunic. Give to everyone who asks you, and do not ask

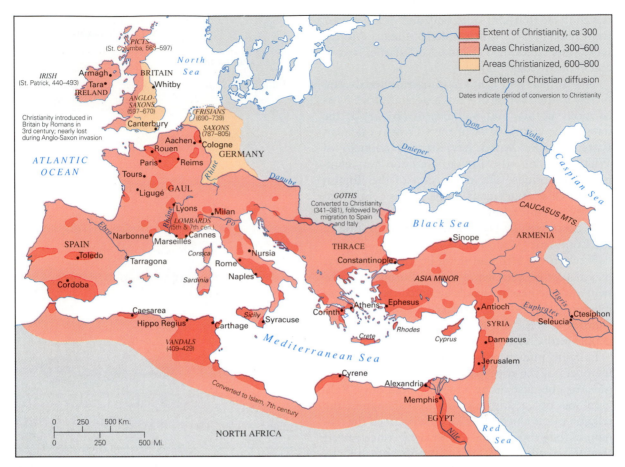

MAP 7.2 The Spread of Christianity   Originating in Judaea, the southern part of modern Israel and Jordan, Christianity spread throughout the Roman world. Roman sea lanes and Roman roads facilitated the expansion.

of your property back from the man who robs you. Treat others as you would like them to treat you."[5]

These ideas are among the most radical and revolutionary the world has heard, and it has proved very difficult to get people to live by them.

The German peoples were warriors who idealized the military virtues of physical strength, ferocity in battle, and loyalty to the leader. Victors in battle enjoyed the spoils of success and plundered the vanquished. The greater the fighter, the more trophies and material goods he collected. Thus the Germans had trouble accepting the Christian precepts of "love your enemies" and "turn the other cheek."

The Germanic tribes found the Christian notions of sin and repentance virtually incomprehensible.

Sin in Christian thought meant disobedience to the will of God as revealed in the Ten Commandments and the teaching of Christ. Good or "moral" behavior to the barbarians meant the observance of tribal customs and practices. Dishonorable behavior caused social ostracism. The inculcation of Christian ideals took a very long time.

Conversion and Assimilation

In Christian theology, conversion involves a turning toward God—that is, a conscious effort to live according to the Gospel message. How did missionaries and priests get masses of pagan and illiterate peoples to understand and live by Christian ideals and teachings? Through preaching, through assimilation, and through the penitential system. Preaching aimed at instruction and edification. Instruction presented the basic teachings of Christianity. Edification was intended to strengthen the newly baptized in their faith through stories about the lives of Christ and the saints. But deeply ingrained pagan customs and practices could not be stamped out by words alone or even by imperial edicts. Christian missionaries often pursued a policy of assimilation, easing the conversion of pagan men and women by stressing similarities between their customs and beliefs and those of Christianity. A letter that Pope Gregory I wrote to Augustine of Canterbury beautifully illustrates this policy. Sent to Augustine in Britain in 601, it expresses the pope's intention that pagan buildings and practices be given a Christian significance:

To our well beloved son Abbot Mellitus: Gregory servant of the servants of God. . . . Therefore, when by God's help you reach our most reverent brother, Bishop Augustine, we wish you to inform him that we have been giving careful thought to the affairs of the English, and have come to the conclusion that the temples of the idols among that people should on no account be destroyed. The idols are to be destroyed, but the temples themselves are to be aspersed with holy water, altars set up in them, and relics deposited there. For if these temples are well-built, they must be purified from the worship of demons and dedicated to the service of the true God. In this way, we hope that the people, seeing that their temples are not destroyed, may abandon their error and, flocking more readily to their accustomed resorts, may come to know and adore the true God. . . . For it is certainly impossible to eradicate all errors from obstinate minds at one stroke,

The Pantheon (Interior)   Originally a temple for the gods, the Pantheon later served as a Christian church. As such, it symbolizes the adaptation of pagan elements to Christian purposes. *(Source: Alinari/Art Resource)*

and whoever wishes to climb to a mountain top climbs gradually step by step, and not in one leap.[6]

How assimilation works is perhaps best appreciated through the example of a festival familiar to all Americans, Saint Valentine's Day. There were two Romans named Valentine. Both were Christian priests, and both were martyred for their beliefs around the middle of February in the third century. Since about 150 B.C. the Romans had celebrated the festival of Lupercalia, at which they asked the gods for fertility for themselves, their fields, and their flocks. This celebration occurred in mid-February, shortly before the Roman New Year and the arrival of spring. Thus the early church "converted" the old festival of Lupercalia into Saint Valentine's Day. (Nothing in the lives of the two Christian martyrs connects them with lovers or the exchange of messages and gifts. That practice began in the later Middle Ages.) The fourteenth of February was still celebrated as a festival, but it had taken on Christian meaning.

Probably more immediate in its impact on the unconverted masses was the penitential system. *Penitentials* were manuals for the examination of conscience. Irish priests wrote the earliest ones, which English missionaries then carried to the Continent. The illiterate penitent knelt beside the priest, who questioned the penitent about sins he or she might have committed. The recommended penance was then imposed. Penance usually meant fasting for three days each week on bread and water, which served as a medicine for the soul. Here is a section of the penitential prepared by Archbishop Theodore of Canterbury (668–690), which circulated widely at the time:

If anyone commits fornication with a virgin he shall do penance for one year. If with a married woman, he shall do penance for four years, two of these entire, and in the other two during the three forty-day periods and three days a week.

A male who commits fornication with a male shall do penance for three years.

If a woman practices vice with a woman, she shall do penance for three years.

Whoever has often committed theft, seven years is his penance, or such a sentence as his priest shall determine, that is, according to what can be arranged with those whom he has wronged. . . .

If a layman slays another with malice aforethought, if he will not lay aside his arms, he shall do penance for seven years; without flesh and wine, three years.

He who defiles his neighbor's wife, deprived of his own wife, shall fast for three years two days a week and in the three forty-day periods.

If [the woman] is a virgin, he shall do penance for one year without meat and wine and mead. . . .

Women who commit abortion before [the fetus] has life, shall do penance for one year or for the three forty-day periods or for forty days, according to the nature of the offense; and if later, that is, more than forty days after conception, they shall do penance as murderesses, that is for three years on Wednesdays and Fridays and in the three forty-day periods. This according to the canons is judged [punishable by] ten years.

If a mother slays her child, if she commits homicide, she shall do penance for fifteen years, and never change except on Sunday.

If a poor woman slays her child, she shall do penance for seven years. In the canon it is said that if it is a case of homicide, she shall do penance for ten years.[7]

As this sample suggests, writers of penitentials were preoccupied with sexual transgressions. Penitentials are much more akin to the Jewish law of the Old Testament than to the spirit of the New Testament. They provide an enormous amount of information about the ascetic ideals of early Christianity and about the crime-ridden realities of Celtic and Germanic societies. Penitentials also reveal the ecclesiastical foundations of some modern attitudes toward sex, birth control, and abortion. Most important, the penitential system contributed to the growth of a different attitude toward religion: formerly public, corporate, and social, religious observances became private, personal, and individual.[8]

CHRISTIAN ATTITUDES TOWARD CLASSICAL CULTURE

Probably the major dilemma the early Christian church faced concerned Greco-Roman culture. The Roman Empire as a social, political, and economic force gradually disintegrated. Its culture, however, survived. In Greek philosophy, art, and architecture, in Roman law, literature, education, and engineering, the legacy of a great civilization continued. The Christian religion had begun and spread within this intellectual and psychological milieu. What was to be the attitude of Christians to the Greco-Roman world of ideas?

Hostility

Christians in the first and second centuries believed that the end of the world was near. Christ had promised to return, and Christians expected to witness that return. Therefore, they considered knowledge useless and learning a waste of time. The important duty of the Christian was to prepare for the Second Coming of the Lord.

Early Christians harbored a strong hatred of pagan Roman culture—in fact, of all Roman civilization. Had not the Romans crucified Christ? Had not the Romans persecuted Christians and subjected them to the most horrible tortures? Did not the Book of Revelation in the New Testament call Rome the great whore of the world, filled with corruption, sin, and every kind of evil? Roman culture was sexual, sensual, and materialistic. The sensual poetry of Ovid, the political poetry of Virgil, even the rhetorical brilliance of Cicero represented a threat, in the eyes of serious Christians, to the spiritual aims and ideals of Christianity. Good Christians who sought the Kingdom of Heaven through the imitation of Christ believed they had to disassociate themselves from the "filth" that Roman culture embodied.

As Saint Paul wrote, "The wisdom of the world is foolishness, we preach Christ crucified." Tertullian (ca 160–220), an influential African Christian writer, condemned all secular literature as foolishness in the eyes of God. He called the Greek philosophers, such as Aristotle, "hucksters of eloquence" and compared them to "animals of self-glorification." "What has Athens to do with Jerusalem," he demanded, "the Academy with the Church? We have no need for curiosity since Jesus Christ, nor for inquiry since the gospel." Tertullian insisted that Christians would find in the Bible all the wisdom they needed.

Compromise and Adjustment

At the same time, Christianity encouraged adjustment to the ideas and institutions of the Roman world. Some biblical texts clearly urged Christians to accept the existing social, economic, and political establishment. Specifically addressing Christians living among non-Christians in the hostile environment of Rome, the author of the First Letter of Saint Peter had written about the obligations of Christians:

Toward Pagans

Always behave honorably among pagans, so that they can see your good works for themselves and, when the day of reckoning comes, give thanks to God for the things which now make them denounce you as criminals.

Toward Civil Authority

For the sake of the Lord, accept the authority of every social institution: the emperor, as the supreme authority, and the governors as commissioned by him to punish criminals and praise good citizenship. God wants you to be good citizens. . . . Have respect for everyone and love for your community; fear God and honour the emperor.[9]

Christians really had little choice. Christianity did not emerge in a social or intellectual vacuum; Jewish and Roman cultures were the only cultures Christians knew. Only men received a formal education, and they went through the traditional curriculum of grammar and rhetoric. They learned to be effective speakers in the forum or the law courts. No other system of education existed. Many early Christians had grown up as pagans, been educated as pagans, and been converted only as adults. Christian attitudes toward women and toward homosexuality illustrate the ways early Christians adopted the views of their contemporary world.

Jesus, whom Christians accept as the Messiah, considered women the equal of men in his plan of salvation. He attributed no disreputable qualities to women, made no comment on the wiles of women, no reference to them as inferior creatures. On the contrary, women were among his earliest and most faithful converts. He discussed his mission with them (John 4:21–25); he accepted the ministrations of a reformed prostitute; and women were the first persons to whom he revealed himself after his resurrection (Matthew 28:9–10). Jewish and Christian writers, however, not Jesus, had the greater influence on the formation of medieval (and modern) attitudes toward women.

Jesus' message emphasized love for God and one's fellow human beings; later writers tended to stress Christianity as a religion of renunciation and asceticism, and they equated sexual activity with women. Their views derive from Platonic-Hellenistic ideas of the contemporary Mediterranean world. The Jewish philosopher Philo of Alexandria, for example, held that since the female represented sense perception and the male the higher, rational soul, the female was inferior to the male. Philo accepted the biblical command to increase and multiply, but argued that the only good of marriage was the production of children for the continuation of the race. Tertullian reminded women that each of them was an Eve, "the first deserter of the divine law; you are the she who persuaded him whom the devil was not valiant enough to attack. You de-

stroyed so easily God's image, man."[10] Female beauty may come from God who created everything, Tertullian wrote, but it should be feared. Women should wear veils or men will be endangered by the sight of them. While early Christian writers repeated such misogynist (hateful of women) statements, perhaps the most revolting image of women comes from St. John Chrysostom (347–407), patriarch of Constantinople, a ruthless critic of contemporary morals. Commenting on female beauty, he wrote that if a man

consider what is stored up inside those beautiful eyes and that straight nose, and the mouth and the cheeks, you will affirm the well-shaped body to be nothing else than a white sepulchre [tomb]; the parts within are full of so much uncleanliness. Moreover, when you see a rag with any of these things on it, such as phlegm or spittle, you cannot bear to touch it, with even the tips of your fingers, nay you cannot even endure looking at it; you are in a flutter of excitement about the storehouses and depositories [women] of these things."[11]

The church fathers acknowledged that God had established marriage for the generation of children, but they believed it was a concession to weak souls who could not bear celibacy. For Saint Augustine, sexual intercourse was the greatest threat to spiritual freedom: "I know nothing which brings the manly mind down from the heights more than a woman's caresses and that joining of bodies without which one cannot have a wife." But since God had clearly sanctioned marriage, Augustine identified original sin with concupiscence (sexual desire). Thus coitus was theoretically good since it was created by God; but in daily life every act of intercourse was evil, and every child was conceived by a sinful act. Celibacy was the highest good; intercourse was little more than animal lust, justified only by procreation in marriage.

Because women were considered incapable of writing on this subject, we have none of their views. The church fathers, by definition, were all males. Since many of them became aware of their physical desires when in the presence of women, misogyny entered Christian thought. Although early Christian writers believed women the spiritual equals of men, Christianity became a male-centered, misogynistic, and sex-negative religion.[12]

Toward homosexuality, according to a controversial study, Christians of the first three or four

The Antioch Chalice This earliest surviving Christian chalice, which dates from the fourth century A.D., combines the typical Roman shape with Christian motifs. The chalice is decorated with figures of Christ and the apostles, leaves, and grapes, which represent the sacrament of the Eucharist. *(Source: The Metropolitan Museum of Art; The Cloisters Collection. Purchase, 1950 (50.4))*

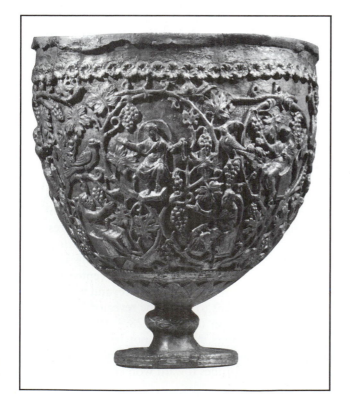

centuries simply imbibed the attitude of the world in which they lived. Many Romans indulged in homosexual activity, and contemporaries did not consider such behavior (or inclinations to it) immoral, bizarre, or harmful. Several emperors were openly homosexual, and homosexuals participated freely in all aspects of Roman life and culture. Early Christians, too, considered homosexuality a conventional expression of physical desire and were no more susceptible to antihomosexual prejudices than pagans were. Some prominent Christians experienced loving same-gender relationships that probably had a sexual element. What eventually led to a change in public and Christian attitudes toward sexual behavior was the shift from the sophisticated urban culture of the Greco-Roman world to the rural culture of medieval Europe.[13]

Even had early Christians wanted to give up Greco-Roman ideas and patterns of thought, they would have had great difficulty doing so. Therefore, they had to adapt their Roman education to their Christian beliefs. Saint Paul himself believed there was a good deal of truth in pagan thought, as long as it was correctly interpreted and understood.

The result was a compromise. Christians gradually came to terms with Greco-Roman culture. Saint Jerome (340–419), a distinguished theologian and linguist, remains famous for his translation of the Old and New Testaments from Hebrew and Greek into vernacular Latin. Called the "Vulgate," his edition of the Bible served as the official translation until the sixteenth century; even today, scholars rely on it. Saint Jerome was also familiar with the writings of such classical authors as Cicero, Virgil, and Terence. He believed that Christians should study the best of ancient thought because it would direct their minds to God. Jerome maintained that the best ancient literature should be interpreted in light of the Christian faith.

Synthesis: Saint Augustine

The finest representative of the blending of classical and Christian ideas, and indeed one of the most brilliant thinkers in the history of the Western world, was Saint Augustine of Hippo (354–430). Aside from the scriptural writers, no one else has had a greater impact on Christian thought in succeeding centuries. Saint Augustine was born into an urban family in what is now Algeria in North Africa. His father was a pagan; his mother, Monica, a devout Christian. Because his family was poor—his father was a minor civil servant—the only avenue to success in a highly competitive world was a classical education.

Augustine's mother believed that a good classical education, though pagan, would make her son a better Christian, so Augustine's father scraped together the money to educate him. The child received his basic education in the local school. By modern and even medieval standards, that education was extremely narrow: textual study of the writings of the poet Virgil, the orator-politician Cicero, the historian Sallust, and the playwright Terence. At that time, learning meant memorization. Education in the late Roman world aimed at appreciation of words, particularly those of renowned and eloquent orators.

At the age of seventeen, Augustine went to nearby Carthage to continue his education. There he took a mistress with whom he lived for fifteen years. At Carthage, Augustine entered a difficult psychological phase and began an intellectual and spiritual pilgrimage that led him through experiments with several philosophies and heretical Christian sects. In 383 he traveled to Rome, where he endured not only illness but also disappointment in his teaching: his students fled when their bills were due.

Finally, in Milan in 387, through the insights he gained from reading Saint Paul's Letter to the Romans, Augustine received Christian baptism. He later became bishop of the seacoast city of Hippo Regius in his native North Africa. He was a renowned preacher to Christians there, a vigorous defender of orthodox Christianity, and the author of over ninety-three books and treatises.

Augustine's autobiography, *The Confessions,* is a literary masterpiece and one of the most influential books in the history of Europe. Written in the form of a prayer, its language is often beautiful:

Great are thou, O Lord, and exceedingly to be praised: great is thy power and of thy wisdom there is no reckoning. And man, indeed, one part of thy creation, has the will to praise thee: yea, man, though he bears his mortality about with him . . . even man, a small portion of thy creation, has the will to praise thee. Thou dost stir him up, that it may delight him to praise thee, for thou hast made us for thyself, and our hearts are restless till they find repose in thee.[14]

Too late have I loved thee, O beauty ever ancient and ever new, too late have I loved thee! And behold! Thou wert within and I without, and it was without that I sought thee. Thou wert with me, and I was not with thee. Those creatures held me far from thee which, were they not in thee, were not at all. Thou didst call, thou didst cry, thou didst break in upon my deafness; thou didst gleam forth, thou didst shine out, thou didst banish my blindness; thou didst send forth thy fragrance, and I drew breath and yearned for thee; I tasted and still hunger and thirst; thou didst touch me, and I was on flame to find thy peace.[15]

The Confessions describes Augustine's moral struggle, the conflict between his spiritual and intellectual aspirations and his sensual and material self. *The Confessions* reveals the change and development of a human mind and personality steeped in the philosophy and culture of the ancient world.

Many Greek and Roman philosophers had taught that knowledge and virtue are the same: a person who really knows what is right will do what is right. Augustine rejected this idea. He believed that a person may know what is right but fail to act righteously because of the innate weakness of the human will. People do not always act on the basis of rational knowledge. Here Augustine made a profound contribution to the understanding of human nature: he demonstrated that a learned person can also be corrupt and evil. *The Confessions,* written in the rhetorical style and language of late Roman antiquity, marks the synthesis of Greco-Roman forms and Christian thought.

Augustine also contributed to the discussion on the nature of the church sparked by the Donatist heretical movement. Promoted by the North African bishop of Carthage, Donatus, Donatism denied the value of sacraments administered by priests or bishops who had denied their faith under persecution or had committed grave sin. For the Donatists, the holiness of the minister was as important as the sacred rites he performed. Donatists viewed themselves as a separate "chosen people" that had preserved its purity and identity in a corrupt world. The true church, therefore, consisted of a small spiritual elite that was an alternative to society. Augustine responded with extensive preaching and the treatise *On Baptism and Against the Donatists* (A.D. 400), written in the best classical Latin. He argued that, through God's action, the rites of the church have an objective and permanent validity,

regardless of the priest's spiritual condition. Being a Christian and a member of the church, Augustine maintained, meant striving for holiness; rather than seeing themselves as apart from society, Christians must live in and transform society. The notion of the church as a special spiritual elite, distinct from and superior to the rest of society, recurred many times in the Middle Ages. Each time it was branded a heresy, and Augustine's arguments were marshaled against it.

When the Visigothic chieftain Alaric conquered Rome in 410, horrified pagans blamed the disaster on the Christians. In response, Augustine wrote *City of God.* This profoundly original work contrasts Christianity with the secular society in which it existed. *City of God* presents a moral interpretation of the Roman government—in fact, of all history. Written in Latin and filled with references to ancient history and mythology, it remained for centuries the standard statement of the Christian philosophy of history.

According to Augustine, history is the account of God acting in time. Human history reveals that there are two kinds of people: those who live according to the flesh in the City of Babylon and those who live according to the spirit in the City of God. The former will endure eternal hellfire, the latter eternal bliss.

Augustine maintained that states came into existence as the result of Adam's fall and people's inclination to sin. The state is a necessary evil, but it can work for the good by providing the peace, justice, and order that Christians need in order to pursue their pilgrimage to the City of God. The particular form of government—whether monarchy, aristocracy, or democracy—is basically irrelevant. Any civil government that fails to provide justice is no more than a band of gangsters.

Although the state results from moral lapse—from sin—neither is the church (the Christian community) entirely free from sin. The church is certainly not equivalent to the City of God. But the church, which is concerned with salvation, is responsible for everyone, including Christian rulers. Churches in the Middle Ages used Augustine's theory to defend their belief in the ultimate superiority of the spiritual power over the temporal. This remained the dominant political theory until the late thirteenth century.

Augustine had no objection to drawing on pagan knowledge to support Christian thought.

Augustine used Roman history as evidence to defend Christian theology. In doing so, he assimilated Roman history, and indeed all of classical culture, into Christian teaching.

MONASTICISM AND THE RULE OF SAINT BENEDICT

Christianity began and spread as a city religion. Since the first century, however, some especially pious Christians had felt that the only alternative to the decadence of urban life was complete separation from the world. All-consuming pursuit of material things, gross sexual promiscuity, and general political corruption disgusted them. They believed that the Christian life as set forth in the Gospel could not be lived in the midst of such immorality. They rejected the values of Roman society and were the first real nonconformists in the church.

The fourth century witnessed a significant change in the relationship of Christianity and the broader society. Until Constantine's legalization of Christianity, Christians were a persecuted minority. The persecutions of Decius in 250 A.D. and Diocletian in 304 were especially severe. Christians greatly revered those men and women who suffered and died for their faith, the *martyrs.* They, like Jesus, made the ultimate sacrifice. The martyrs were the great heroes of the early church. When Christianity was legalized and the persecutions ended, a new problem arose. Where Christians had been a suffering minority, now they came to be identified with the state: non-Christians could not advance in the imperial service. And if Christianity had triumphed, so had "the world," since secular attitudes and values pervaded the church. The church of martyrs no longer existed, and some scholars believe the monasteries provided a way of life for those Christians who wanted to make a total response to Christ's teachings, people who wanted more than a lukewarm Christianity. The monks became the new martyrs. Saint Anthony of Egypt (d. 356), the first monk for whom there is concrete evidence and the father of monasticism, went to Alexandria during the last persecution in the hope of gaining martyrdom. Christians believed that monks, like the martyrs before them, could speak for God and that their prayers had special influence with him.

At first individuals and small groups left the cities and went to live in caves or rude shelters in the desert or mountains. These people were called "hermits," from the Greek word *eremos,* meaning "desert." There is no way of knowing how many hermits there were in the fourth and fifth centuries, partly because their conscious aim was a secret, hidden life known only to God.

Several factors worked against this *eremitical* variety of monasticism in western Europe. First was climate. The cold, snow, ice, and fog that covered much of Europe for many months of the year discouraged isolated living. Dense forests filled with wild animals and wandering barbaric German tribes presented obvious dangers. Furthermore, church leaders did not really approve of eremitical life. Hermits sometimes claimed to have mystical experiences, direct communications with God. No one could verify these experiences. If hermits could communicate directly with the Lord, what need had they for the priest and the institutional church? The church hierarchy, or leaders, encouraged *coenobitic monasticism*—that is, communal living in monasteries. Communal living, moreover, provided an environment for training the aspirant in the virtues of charity, poverty, and freedom from self-deception. The Egyptian ascetic Pachomius (290–346?) organized the first successful coenobitic community at Tabennisi on the Upper Nile. It drew thousands of recruits.

Monasticism had begun in the East. But in the fourth, fifth, and sixth centuries, many experiments in communal monasticism were made in Gaul, Italy, Spain, Anglo-Saxon England, and Ireland. While at Rome Saint Jerome attracted a group of aristocratic women whom he instructed in Scripture and the ideals of ascetic life. After studying both eremitical and coenobitic monasticism in Egypt and Syria, John Cassian established two monasteries near Marseilles in Gaul around 415. One of Cassian's books, *Conferences,* based on conversations he had had with holy men in the East, discussed the dangers of the isolated hermit's life. The abbey or monastery of Lérins on the Mediterranean Sea near Cannes (ca 410) also had significant contacts with monastic centers in the Middle East and North Africa. Lérins encouraged the severely penitential and extremely ascetic behavior common in the East, such as long hours of prayer, fasting, and self-flagellation. It was this tradition of harsh self-mortification that the Roman-British monk Saint Patrick carried from Lérins to Ireland in the fifth century. Church organization in Ireland became closely associated with the monasteries, and Irish monastic life followed the ascetic Eastern form.

Around 540 the Roman senator Cassiodorus retired from public service and established a monastery, the Vivarium, on his estate in Italy. Cassiodorus wanted the Vivarium to become an educational and cultural center and enlisted highly educated and sophisticated men for it. He set the monks to copying both sacred and secular manuscripts, intending this to be their sole occupation. Cassiodorus started the association of monasticism with scholarship and learning. This developed into a great tradition in the medieval and modern worlds. But Cassiodorus's experiment did not become the most influential form of monasticism in European society. The fifth and sixth centuries witnessed the appearance of many other monastic lifestyles.

The Rule of Saint Benedict

In 529 Benedict of Nursia (480–543), who had experimented with both the eremitical and the communal forms of monastic life, wrote a brief set of regulations for the monks who had gathered around him at Monte Cassino between Rome and Naples. Recent research has shown that Benedict's *Rule* derives from a longer, more detailed document known as *The Rule of the Master,* which was actually suitable only for the place for which it was written. Benedict's guide for monastic life proved more adaptable and slowly replaced all others. *The Rule of Saint Benedict* has influenced all forms of organized religious life in the Roman church.

Saint Benedict conceived of his *Rule* as a simple code for ordinary men. It outlined a monastic life of regularity, discipline, and moderation. Each monk had ample food and adequate sleep. Self-destructive acts of mortification were forbidden. In an atmosphere of silence, the monk spent part of the day in formal prayer, which Benedict called the "Work of God." This consisted of chanting psalms and other prayers from the Bible in that part of the monastery church called the "choir." The rest of the day was passed in study and manual labor. After a year of probation, the monk made three vows.

First, the monk vowed stability: he promised to live his entire life in the monastery of his profession. The vow of stability was Saint Benedict's major contribution to Western monasticism; his object was to prevent the wandering so common in his day. Second, the monk vowed conversion of manners—that is, to strive to improve himself and to come closer to God. Third, he promised obedience, the most difficult vow because it meant the complete surrender of his will to the *abbot,* or head of the monastery.

The Rule of Saint Benedict expresses the assimilation of the Roman spirit into Western monasticism. It reveals the logical mind of its creator and the Roman concern for order, organization, and respect for law. Its spirit of moderation and flexibility is reflected in the patience, wisdom, and understanding with which the abbot is to govern and, indeed, with which life is to be led. The *Rule* could be used in vastly different physical and geographical circumstances, in damp and cold Germany as well as in warm and sunny Italy. The *Rule* was quickly adapted for women, and many convents of nuns were established in the early Middle Ages.

Saint Benedict's *Rule* implies that a person who wants to become a monk or nun need have no previous ascetic experience or even a particularly strong bent toward the religious life. Thus it allowed for the admission of newcomers with different backgrounds and personalities. From Chapter 59, "The Offering of Sons by Nobles or by the Poor," and from Benedict's advice to the abbot— "The abbot should avoid all favoritism in the monastery. . . . A man born free is not to be given higher rank than a slave who becomes a monk" (Chapter 2)—we know that men of different social classes belonged to his monastery. This flexibility helps to explain the attractiveness of Benedictine monasticism throughout the centuries. *The Rule of Saint Benedict* is a superior example of the way in which the Greco-Roman heritage and Roman patterns of thought were preserved.

At the same time, the *Rule* no more provides a picture of actual life in a Benedictine abbey of the seventh or eighth (or twentieth) century than the American Constitution of 1789 describes living conditions in the United States today. A code of laws cannot do that. Monasteries were composed of individuals, and human beings defy strict classification according to rules, laws, or statistics. *The Rule of Saint Benedict* had one fundamental purpose.

St. Benedict Holding his *Rule* in his left hand, the seated and cowled Patriarch of Western Monasticism blesses a monk with his right hand. His monastery, Monte Cassino, is in the background. *(Source: Biblioteca Apostolica Vaticana)*

The exercises of the monastic life were designed to draw the individual slowly but steadily away from attachment to the world and love of self and toward the love of God.

The Success of Benedictine Monasticism

Why was the Benedictine form of monasticism so successful? Why did it eventually replace other forms of Western monasticism? The answer lies partly in its spirit of flexibility and moderation and partly in the balanced life it provided. Early Benedictine monks and nuns spent part of the day in prayer, part in study or some other form of intellectual activity, and part in manual labor. The monastic life as conceived by Saint Benedict did not lean too heavily in any one direction; it struck a balance between asceticism and idleness. It thus provided opportunities for persons of entirely different abilities and talents—from mechanics to gardeners to literary scholars. Benedict's *Rule* contrasts sharply with Cassiodorus's narrow concept of the monastery as a place for aristocratic scholars and bibliophiles.

Benedictine monasticism also suited the social circumstances of early medieval society. The German invasions had fragmented European life: the self-sufficient rural estate replaced the city as the basic unit of civilization. A monastery, too, had to be economically self-sufficient. It was supposed to produce from its lands and properties all that was needed for food, clothing, shelter, and liturgical service of the altar. The monastery fitted in—indeed, represented—the trend toward localism.

Benedictine monasticism also succeeded partly because it was so materially successful. In the seventh and eighth centuries, monasteries pushed back forest and wasteland, drained swamps, and experimented with crop rotation. For example, the abbey of Saint Wandrille, founded in 645 near Rouen in northwestern Gaul, sent squads of monks to clear the forests that surrounded it. Within seventy-five years the abbey was immensely wealthy. The abbey of Jumièges, also in the diocese of Rouen, followed much the same pattern. Such Benedictine houses made a significant contribution to the agricultural development of Europe. The communal nature of their organization, whereby property was held in common and profits pooled and reinvested, made this contribution possible.

Finally, monasteries conducted schools for local young people. Some learned about prescriptions and herbal remedies and went on to provide medical treatment for their localities. A few copied manuscripts and wrote books. This training did not go unappreciated in a society desperately in need of it. Local and royal governments drew on the services of the literate men and able administrators the monasteries produced. This was not what Saint Benedict had intended, but the effectiveness of the institution he designed made it perhaps inevitable.

THE MIGRATION OF THE GERMANIC PEOPLES

The migration of peoples from one area to another has been a dominant and continuing feature of European history. Mass movements of Europeans occurred in the fourth through sixth centuries, in the ninth and tenth centuries, and in the twelfth and thirteenth centuries. From the sixteenth century to the present, such movements have been almost continuous, involving not just the European continent but the entire world. The causes of early migrations varied and are not thoroughly understood by scholars. But there is no question that they profoundly affected both the regions to which peoples moved and the ones they left behind.

The *Völkerwanderungen,* or migrations of the Germanic peoples, were important in the decline of the Roman Empire and in the making of European civilization. Many twentieth-century scholars have tried to explain who the Germans were and why they migrated, but historians and sociologists are only beginning to provide satisfactory explanations. The present consensus, based on the study of linguistic and archeological evidence, seems to be that there were not one but many Germanic peo-

ples with very different cultural traditions. Archeological remains—bone fossils, cooking utensils, jewelry, weapons of war, and other artifacts—combined with linguistic data suggest three broad groupings of Germanic peoples. One group lived along the North and Baltic seas in the regions of present-day northern Germany, southern Sweden, and Denmark. A second band inhabited the area between the Elbe and Oder rivers. A third group lived along the Rhine and Weser rivers, closest to the Roman frontier. Although these groupings sometimes showed cultural affiliation, they were very fluid and did not possess political, social, or ethnic solidarity.

Since about 150, Germanic tribes had pressed along the Rhine-Danube frontier of the Roman Empire. Some tribes, such as the Visigoths and Ostrogoths, led a settled existence, engaged in agriculture and trade, and accepted Arian Christianity. Tribes such as the Anglo-Saxons and Huns led a nomadic life unaffected by Roman influences. Scholars do not know exactly when the Mongolian tribe called the Huns began to move westward from China, but about 370 they pressured the Goths along the Rhine-Danube frontier.

Why did the Germans migrate? We do not know. As an authority on the Ostrogoths recently wrote, "Despite a century of keen historical investigation and archaeological excavation, the cause and nature of the *Völkerwanderung* challenge the inquirer as much as ever." Perhaps overpopulation and the resulting food shortages caused migration. Perhaps victorious tribes forced the vanquished to move southward. Probably "the primary stimulus for this gradual migration was the Roman frontier, which increasingly offered service in the army and work for pay around the camps."[16]

Romanization and Barbarization

The Roman Empire, it should be remembered, centered around the Mediterranean. Italy, Spain, and North Africa were the areas most vital to it. Aside from Rome, obviously, Alexandria, Antioch, Ephesus, and later Constantinople represented the great economic, cultural, and population centers. North of Italy, in Gaul, Germany, and Britain, Celtic and Germanic peoples had long predominated. The Roman army had spread a veneer of Roman culture in the territories it controlled, but from the third to the sixth century, as Roman influence declined, native Germanic traditions reasserted themselves.

The Roman army had been the chief means of romanization throughout the empire (see Chapter 6). But from the third century, the army became the chief agent of barbarization. How? In the third and fourth centuries, increasing pressures on the frontiers from the east and north placed greater demands on military manpower, which plague and a declining birthrate had reduced. Therefore, Roman generals recruited barbarians to fill the ranks. They bribed Germanic chiefs with treaties and gold, the masses with grain. By the late third century, a large percentage of military recruits came from the Germanic peoples.

Besides army recruits, several types of barbarian peoples entered the empire and became affiliated with Roman government. The *laeti*, refugees or prisoners of war, were settled with their families in areas of Gaul and Italy under the supervision of Roman prefects and landowners. Generally isolated from the local Roman population, the laeti farmed regions depopulated by plague. The men had to serve in the Roman army. Free barbarian units called *foederati*, stationed near major provincial cities, represented a second type of affiliated barbarian group. Recent research has suggested that rather than giving them land, the Romans assigned the foederati shares of the tax revenues from the region.[17] Living in close proximity to Roman communities, the foederati quickly assimilated into Roman culture. In fact, in the fourth century, some foederati rose to the highest ranks of the army and moved in the most cultured and aristocratic circles. Third, the arrival of the Huns in the West in 376 precipitated the entry of entire peoples, the *gentes*, into the Roman empire. Pressured by defeat in battle, starvation, or the movement of other peoples, tribes such as the Ostrogoths and Visigoths entered in large numbers, perhaps as many as twenty thousand men, women, and children.[18] For example, the Visigoths under the pro-Roman general Fritigern petitioned the emperor Valens to admit them to the empire. Seeing in the hordes of warriors the solution to his manpower problem, Valens agreed. Once the Visigoths were inside the empire, Roman authorities exploited their hunger by forcing them to sell their own people in exchange for dogflesh: "the going rate was one dog for one Goth." The bitterness of those enslaved was aggravated by the arrival of the Ostrogoths. A huge rebellion erupted, and when Valens attempted to put it down, the Goths crushed the Roman army at Adrianople on August 9, 378.[19] This date marks the beginning of massive German invasions into the empire (Map 7.3).

Except for the Lombards, whose conquests of Italy persisted into the mid-eighth century, the movements of Germanic peoples on the Continent ended about 600. Between 450 and 565 the Germans established a number of kingdoms, but none except the Frankish kingdom lasted very long.

Visigothic Eagle   Sixth century. The eagle was a standard symbol of nobility and power among the Germanic peoples. A fine example of Visigothic craftsmanship, this richly jewelled eagle—worn as a cloak clasp or as a brooch—could be afforded only by the wealthiest and most powerful members of the nobility. *(Source: Walters Art Gallery, Baltimore)*

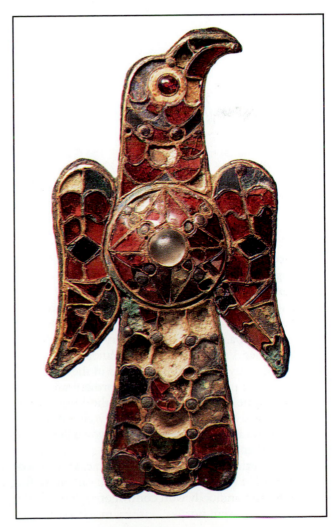

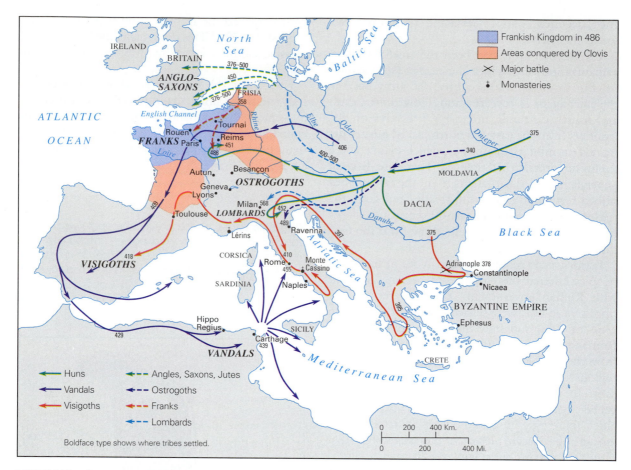

MAP 7.3 The Germanic Migrations   The Germanic tribes infiltrated and settled in all parts of western Europe. The Huns, who were not German ethnically, originated in central Asia. The Huns' victory over the Ostrogoths led the emperor to allow the Visigoths to settle within the empire, a decision that proved disastrous for Rome.

Since the German kingdoms did not have definite geographical boundaries, their locations are approximate. The Visigoths overran much of southwestern Gaul. Establishing their headquarters at Toulouse, they exercised a weak domination over Spain until a great Muslim victory at Guadalete in 711 ended Visigothic rule. The Vandals, whose destructive ways are commemorated in the word *vandal,* settled in North Africa. In northern and western Europe in the sixth century, the Burgundians established rule over lands roughly circumscribed by the old Roman army camps at Lyons, Besançon, Geneva, and Autun.

In northern Italy the Ostrogothic king Theodoric (r. 471–526) established his capital at Ravenna and gradually won control of all Italy, Sicily,

and the territory north and east of the upper Adriatic. Although attached to the customs of his people, Theodoric pursued a policy of assimilation between Germans and Romans. He maintained close relations with the emperor at Constantinople and attracted to his administration able scholars such as Cassiodorus (see page 206) and Boethius (d. ca 524). Boethius's treatise *The Consolation of Philosophy,* a defense of Christianity through the use of Platonic philosophy, was widely read in the Middle Ages. Theodoric's accomplishments were not insignificant, but after his death his administration fell apart.

The most enduring Germanic kingdom was established by the Frankish chieftain Clovis (r. 481–511). Originally only a petty chieftain with headquarters in the region of Tournai in northwestern Gaul (modern Belgium), Clovis began to expand his territories in 486. His defeat of the Gallo-Roman general Syagrius extended his jurisdiction to the Loire River. Clovis's conversion to orthodox Christianity in 496 won him the crucial support of the papacy and the bishops of Gaul. As the defender of Roman Catholicism against heretical German tribes, he went on to conquer the Visigoths, extending his domain as far as the Pyrenees and making Paris his headquarters. Because he was descended from the half-legendary chieftain Merovech, the dynasty Clovis founded has been called "Merovingian." Clovis's sons subjugated the Burgundians in eastern Gaul and the Ostrogothic tribes living north of the Alps.

GERMANIC SOCIETY

Germanic society had originated with Iron Age peoples (800–500 B.C.) in the northern parts of central Europe and the southern regions of Scandinavia. After the Germans replaced the Romans, reestablishing their rule of most of the European continent, German customs and traditions formed the basis of European society for centuries. What patterns of social, political, and economic life characterized the Germans?

Scholars are hampered in answering such questions because the Germans could not write and thus kept no written records before their conversion to Christianity. The earliest information about

Baptism of Clovis (A.D. 496) In this ninth-century ivory carving, St. Remi, bishop of Reims, baptizes the Frankish chieftain by immersing him in a pool of water. Legend holds that on this occasion a dove brought a vial of holy oil from heaven, later used in the coronations of French kings. *(Source: Musée Condé, Chantilly/Laurie Platt Winfrey, Inc.)*

them comes from moralistic accounts by such Romans as the historian Tacitus, who was acquainted only with the tribes living closest to the borders of the empire. Furthermore, Tacitus imposed Greco-Roman categories of tribes and nations on the German peoples he described, ethnographic classifications that have dominated scholarly writing until very recently. Only in the past few decades have anthropologists begun to study early German society on its own terms.

Kinship, Custom, and Class

The Germans had no notion of the state as we in the twentieth century use the term; they thought in social, not political, terms. The basic Germanic social unit was the tribe, or *folk.* Members of the folk believed that they were all descended from a common ancestor. Blood united them. Kinship protected them. Law was custom—unwritten, preserved in the minds of the elders of the tribe, and handed down by word of mouth from generation to generation. Custom regulated everything. Every tribe had its customs, and every member of the tribe knew what they were. Members were subject to their tribe's customary law wherever they went, and friendly tribes respected one another's laws.

In the second and third centuries, Germanic peoples experienced continued stress and pressures from other peoples. A radical restructuring of tribes occurred as tribal groups splintered, some disappeared and new tribes were formed. What bound a tribe, at least temporarily, was a shared peace—peace among those peoples who considered themselves part of a tribe.

Germanic tribes were led by kings or tribal chieftains. The chief was that member of the folk recognized as the strongest and bravest in battle, elected from among the male members of the strongest

Lombard Warrior   This seventh-century warrior rides bareback and without stirrups. *(Source: Historisches Museum, Bern)*

family. He led the tribe in war, settled disputes among its members, conducted negotiations with outside powers, and offered sacrifices to the gods. The period of migrations and conquests of the western Roman Empire witnessed the strengthening of kingship among the Germanic tribes. Tribes that did not migrate did not develop kings.

Closely associated with the king in some southern tribes was the *comitatus,* or "war band." Writing at the end of the first century, Tacitus described the war band as the bravest young men in the tribe. They swore loyalty to the chief, fought with him in battle, and were not supposed to leave the battlefield without him; to do so implied cowardice, disloyalty, and social disgrace. A social egalitarianism existed among members of the war band.

During the *Völkerwanderungen* of the third and fourth centuries, however, and as a result of constant warfare, the war band was transformed into a system of stratified ranks. For example, among the Ostrogoths a warrior-nobility and several other nobilities evolved. Contact with the Romans, who produced such goods as armbands for trade with the barbarians, stimulated demand for armbands. Ostrogothic warriors wanted armbands because of the status and distinctiveness they conferred. Thus armbands, especially the gold ones reserved for the "royal families," promoted the development of hierarchical ranks within war bands. During the Ostrogothic conquest of Italy under Theodoric, warrior-nobles also sought to acquire land, both as a mark of prestige and as a means to power. As land and wealth came into the hands of a small elite class, social inequalities emerged and were gradually strengthened.[20] These inequalities help to explain the origins of the European noble class (see pages 232–233).

Law

As long as custom determined all behavior, the early Germans had no need for written law. Beginning in the late sixth century, however, German tribal chieftains began to collect, write, and publish lists of their customs. Why then? The Christian missionaries who were slowly converting the Germans to Christianity wanted to know the tribal customs, and they encouraged German rulers to set down their customs in written form. Churchmen wanted to read about German ways in order to assimilate the tribes to Christianity. Augustine of Canterbury, for example, persuaded King Ethelbert of Kent to have his folk laws written down: these *Dooms of Ethelbert* date from between 601 and 604, roughly five years after Augustine's arrival in Britain. Moreover, by the sixth century the German kings needed regulations for the Romans under their jurisdiction as well as for their own people.

Today, if a person holds up a bank, American law maintains that the robber attacks both the bank and the state in which it exists—a sophisticated notion involving the abstract idea of the state. In early German law, all crimes were regarded as crimes against a person.

According to the code of the Salian Franks, every person had a particular monetary value to the tribe. This value was called the *wergeld,* which literally means "man-money" or "money to buy off the spear." Men of fighting age had the highest wergeld, then women of child-bearing age, then children, and finally the aged. Everyone's value reflected his or her potential military worthiness. If a person accused of a crime agreed to pay the wergeld and if the victim and his or her family accepted the payment, there was peace (hence the expression "money to buy off the spear"). If the accused refused to pay the wergeld or if the victim's family refused to accept it, a blood feud ensued. Individuals depended on their kin for protection, and kinship served as a force of social control.

Historians and sociologists have difficulty interpreting the early law codes, partly because they are patchwork affairs studded with additions made in later centuries. Yet much historical information can be gleaned from these codes. For example, the Salic Law—the law code of the Salian Franks issued by Clovis—offers a general picture of Germanic life and problems in the early Middle Ages and is typical of the law codes of other tribes, such as the Visigoths, Burgundians, Lombards, and Anglo-Saxons.

The Salic Law lists the money fines to be paid to the victim or the family for such injuries as theft, rape, assault, arson, and murder:

If any person strike another on the head so that the brain appears, and the three bones which lie above the brain shall project, he shall be sentenced to 1200 denars, which make 300 shillings. . . .

If any one have hit a free woman who is pregnant, and she dies, he shall be sentenced to 2800 denars, which make 700 shillings. . . .

If any one have killed a free woman after she has begun bearing children, he shall be sentenced to 2400 denars, which make 600 shillings. . . .

If any one shall have drawn a harrow through another's harvest after it has sprouted, or shall have gone through it with a wagon where there was no road, he shall be sentenced to 120 denars, which make 30 shillings. . . .

If any one shall have killed a free Frank, or a barbarian living under the Salic law, and it have been proved on him, he shall be sentenced to 8000 denars. . . .

But if any one have slain a man who is in the service of the king, he shall be sentenced to 2400 denars, which make 600 shillings.[21]

This is not really a code of law at all, but a list of tariffs or fines for particular offenses. German law aimed at the prevention or reduction of violence. It was not concerned with abstract justice.

At first, Romans had been subject to Roman law and Germans to Germanic custom. As German kings accepted Christianity and as Romans and Germans increasingly intermarried, the distinction between the two laws blurred and, in the course of the seventh and eighth centuries, disappeared. The result would be the new feudal law, to which Romans and Germans were subject alike.

German Life

How did the Germans live? They usually resided in small villages where climate and geography determined the basic patterns of agricultural and pastoral life. In the flat or open coastal regions, German males engaged in animal husbandry, especially cattle raising. They also domesticated pigs, sheep, goats, horses, chickens, and geese. Many tribes lived in small settlements on the edges of clearings where they raised barley, wheat, oats, peas, and beans. They tilled their fields with a simple wooden scratch plow and harvested their grains with a small iron sickle. The kernels of grain were ground with a grindstone, and the resulting flour made into a dough that was baked on clay trays into flat cakes. Much of the grain was fermented into a strong, thick beer. Women performed the heavy work of raising, grinding, and preserving cereals, a mark, some scholars believe, of their low status in a male-dominated society. Women also had responsibility for weaving and spinning the thread that went into the manufacture of clothing and all textiles.

Within the small villages, there were great differences in wealth and status. Free men constituted the largest class. The number of cattle a man possessed indicated his wealth and determined his social status. "Cattle were so much the quintessential indicator of wealth in traditional society that the modern English term 'fee' (meaning cost of goods or services), which developed from the medieval term 'fief,' had its origin in the Germanic term *fihu . . .* , meaning cattle, chattels, and hence, in general, wealth."[22] Free men also shared in tribal warfare. Slaves (prisoners of war) worked as farm laborers, herdsmen, or household servants.

German society was patriarchal: within each household the father had authority over his wives, children, and slaves. The Germans practiced polygamy, and men who could afford them had more than one wife.

Did the Germans produce goods for trade and exchange? Ironworking represented the most advanced craft of the Germanic peoples. Much of northern Europe had iron deposits at or near the earth's surface, and the dense forests provided wood for charcoal. Most villages had an oven and smiths who produced agricultural tools and instruments of war—one-edged swords, arrowheads, and shields. In the first two centuries A.D., the quantity and quality of German goods increased dramatically, and the first steel swords were superior to the weapons of Roman troops. But German goods were produced for war and the subsistence economy, not for trade. Goods were also used for gift-giving, a major social custom. "Gift giving was a means of acquiring prestige and power—the real gain in an exchange accrued not to the receiver but to the giver, who thereby showed his superiority and placed the receiver in his debt."[23] Goods that could not be produced in the village were acquired by raiding and warfare rather than by commercial exchanges. Warfare constituted the main characteristic of Germanic society. Raids between tribes brought the victors booty; the cattle and slaves captured were traded or given as gifts. Warfare determined the economy and the individual's status within the Germanic society.

What was the position of women in Germanic society? Did they hold, as some scholars contend, a higher status than they were to have later in the Middle Ages? The law codes provide the best evidence. The codes show societies that regarded women as family property. The marriageable

Vandal Landowner   The adoption of Roman dress—short tunic, cloak, and sandals—reflects the way the Germanic tribes accepted Roman lifestyles. Likewise both the mosaic art form and the man's stylized appearance show the Germans' assimilation of Roman influences. (Notice that the rider has a saddle but not stirrups.) *(Source: Courtesy of the Trustees of the British Museum)*

daughter went to the highest bidder. A woman of child-bearing years had a very high wergeld. The codes also protected the virtue of women. For example, the Salic Law of the Franks fined a man the large amount of 15 solidi (from *solidus,* a coin originally minted by Constantine and later the basis of much European currency, such as the English shilling) if he pressed the hand of a woman, 35 if he touched her above the elbow. On the other hand, heavy fines did not stop injury, rape, or abduction. Widows were sometimes seized on the battlefields where their dead husbands lay and forced to marry the victors. The sixth-century queen Radegund was forced to marry Chlotar I, the murderer of several

of her relatives. Radegund later escaped her polygamous union and lived out her life in a convent.

A few slaves and peasant women used their beauty to advance their positions. The slave Fredegunda, for whom King Chilperic murdered his Visigothic wife, became a queen and held her position after her husband's death. Another slave, Balthilda, became the wife of Clovis II. During her sons' minority she worked to alleviate the evils of the slave trade.

Some royal women played an important role in the Christianization of the Germanic kingdoms. In the fifth century Clothilde, Clovis's wife, worked to convert her husband. She supported the founding of many monasteries and churches. In sixth-century England, Bertha, wife of Ethelbert of Kent, converted her husband and thus paved the way for the missionary work of Augustine of Canterbury. A few royal women exercised considerable influence and showed they were as capable of bearing responsibilities as men.[24]

Anglo-Saxon England

The island of Britain, conquered by Rome during the reign of Claudius, shared fully in the life of the Roman Empire during the first four centuries of the Christian era. A military aristocracy governed, and the official religion was the cult of the emperor. Towns were planned in the Roman fashion, with temples, public baths, theaters, and amphitheaters. In the countryside, large manors controlled the surrounding lands. Roman merchants brought Eastern luxury goods and Eastern religions—including Christianity—into Britain. The native Britons, a gentle Celtic people, had become thoroughly romanized. Their language was Latin. Their lifestyle was Roman.

But an event in the distant eastern province of Thrace changed all this. In 378 the Visigothic defeat of the emperor Valens at Adrianople (see page 209) forced Rome to retrench. Roman troops were withdrawn from Britain, leaving it unprotected. The savage Picts from Scotland continued to harass the north. Teutonic tribes from modern-day Norway, Sweden, and Denmark—the Angles, Saxons, and Jutes—stepped up their assaults, attacking in a hit-and-run fashion. Their goal was plunder, and at first their invasions led to no permanent settlements. As more Germans arrived, however, they took over the best lands and humbled the Britons. Increasingly, the Britons fled to Wales in the west and across the English Channel to Brittany. The sporadic raids continued for over a century and led to Germanic control of most of Britain. Historians have labeled the period 500 to 1066 "Anglo-Saxon."

The Anglo-Saxon invasion gave rise to a rich body of Celtic mythology, based on the writings of the ninth-century Welsh scholar Nennius; the mythology became known as the Arthurian legends. When Arthur, the illegitimate son of the king of Britain, successfully drew a sword from a stone, Merlin the court magician revealed Arthur's royal parentage. Arthur won recognition as king, and the mysterious Lady of the Lake gave him the invincible sword Excalibur with which he fought many battles against the Saxon invaders. Arthur held his court at Camelot with his knights seated at a Round Table (to avoid quarrels over precedence). Those knights—including Sir Tristan, Sir Lancelot, Sir Galahad, and Sir Percival (Parsifal), who came to represent the ideal of medieval knightly chivalry—played a large role in later medieval and modern literature.

Except for the Jutes, who probably came from Jutland (modern Denmark), the Teutonic tribes came from the least romanized and the least civilized parts of Europe. The Germans destroyed Roman culture in Britain. Tribal custom superseded Roman law.

The beginnings of the Germanic kingdoms in Britain are very obscure, but scholars suspect they came into being in the seventh and eighth centuries. Writing in the eighth century, the scholar Bede described seven kingdoms: the Jutish kingdom of Kent; the Saxon kingdoms of the East Saxons (Essex), South Saxons (Sussex), and West Saxons (Wessex); and the kingdoms of the Angles, Mercians, and Northumbrians (see Map 7.1). The names imply that these peoples thought of themselves in tribal rather than geographical terms. They referred to the kingdom of the West Saxons, for example, rather than simply to Wessex. Because of Bede's categorization, scholars often refer to the Heptarchy, or seven kingdoms, of Anglo-Saxon Britain. The suggestion of total Anglo-Saxon domination, however, is not entirely accurate. Germanic tribes never subdued Scotland, where the Picts remained strong, or Wales, where the Celts and native Britons continued to put up stubborn resistance.

Thus Anglo-Saxon England was divided along racial and political lines. The Teutonic kingdoms in the south, east, and center were opposed by the Britons in the west, who wanted to get rid of the invaders. The Anglo-Saxon kingdoms also fought among themselves, causing boundaries to shift constantly. Finally, in the ninth century, under pressure of the Danish, or Viking, invasions, the Britons and the Germanic peoples were molded together under the leadership of King Alfred of Wessex (r. 871–899).

THE BYZANTINE EAST (ca 400–788)

Constantine (r. 306–337) had tried to maintain the unity of the Roman Empire, but during the fifth and sixth centuries the western and eastern halves drifted apart. Later emperors worked to hold the empire together. Justinian (r. 527–565) waged long and hard-fought wars against the Ostrogoths and temporarily regained Italy and North Africa. But his conquests had disastrous consequences. Justinian's wars exhausted the resources of the Byzantine state, destroyed Italy's economy, and killed a large part of Italy's population. The wars paved the way for the easy conquest of Italy by another Germanic tribe, the Lombards, shortly after Justinian's death. In the late sixth century, the territory of the western Roman Empire came under Germanic sway, while in the East the Byzantine Empire continued the traditions and institutions of the caesars.

Latin Christian culture was only one legacy the Roman Empire bequeathed to the Western world. The Byzantine culture centered at Constantinople —Constantine's "new Rome"—was another. The Byzantine Empire maintained a high standard of living, and for centuries the Greeks were the most civilized people in the Western world. The Byzantine Empire held at bay, or at least hindered, barbarian peoples who could otherwise have wreaked additional devastation on western Europe, retarding its development. Most important, however, is the role of Byzantium as preserver of the wisdom of the ancient world. Throughout the long years when barbarians in western Europe trampled down the old and then painfully built something new, Byzantium protected and then handed on to the West the intellectual heritage of Greco-Roman civilization.

Byzantine East and Germanic West

As imperial authority disintegrated in the West during the fifth century, civic functions were performed first by church leaders and then by German chieftains. Meanwhile, in the East, the Byzantines preserved the forms and traditions of the old Roman Empire and even called themselves Romans. Byzantine emperors traced their lines back past Constantine to Augustus. The senate that sat in Constantinople carried on the traditions and preserved the glory of the old Roman senate. The army that defended the empire was the direct descendant of the old Roman legions. Even the chariot factions of the Roman Empire lived on under the Byzantines, who cheered their favorites as enthusiastically as had the Romans of Hadrian's day.

The position of the church differed considerably in the Byzantine East and the Germanic West. The fourth-century emperors Constantine and Theodosius had wanted the church to act as a unifying force within the empire, but the Germanic invasions made that impossible. The bishops of Rome repeatedly called on the emperors at Constantinople for military support against the invaders, but rarely could the emperors send it. The church in the West steadily grew away from the empire and became involved in the social and political affairs of Italy and the West. Nevertheless, until the eighth century, the popes, who were often selected by the clergy of Rome, continued to send announcements of their elections to the emperors at Constantinople—a sign that the Roman popes long thought of themselves as bishops of the Roman Empire.

The popes were preoccupied with conversion of the Germans, the Christian attitude toward classical culture, and relations with German rulers. Because the Western church concentrated on its missionary function, it took centuries for the clergy to be organized. Most church theology in the West came from the East, and the overwhelming majority of popes were themselves of Eastern origin.

Tensions occasionally developed between church officials and secular authorities in the West. The dispute between Bishop Ambrose of Milan and the emperor Theodosius (see page 193) is a good example. A century later, Pope Gelasius I (492–496) insisted that bishops, not civil authorities, were responsible for the administration of the church. Gelasius maintained that two powers governed the world: the sacred authority of popes and the royal power of kings. Because priests had to answer to God even for the actions of kings, the sacred power was the greater.

Such an assertion was virtually unheard of in the East, where the emperor's jurisdiction over the church was fully acknowledged. The emperor in Constantinople nominated the *patriarch,* as the highest prelate of the Eastern church was called. The emperor looked on religion as a branch of the

Justinian and his Court   The Emperor Justinian (center) with ecclesiastical and court officials personifies the unity of the Byzantine state and the orthodox church in the person of the emperor. Just as the emperor was both king and priest, so all his Greek subjects belonged to the orthodox church. *(Source: Scala/Art Resource)*

state. Religion was such a vital aspect of the social life of the people that the emperor devoted considerable attention to it. He considered it his duty to protect the faith, not only against heathen enemies, but also against heretics within the empire. In case of doctrinal disputes, the emperor, following Constantine's example at Nicaea, summoned councils of bishops and theologians to settle problems.

The steady separation of the Byzantine East and the Germanic West rests partly on the ways Christianity and classical culture were received in the two parts of the Roman Empire. In the West, Christians initially constituted a small, alien minority within the broad Roman culture; they kept apart from the rest of society. Roman society and classical culture were condemned, avoided, and demystified. In Byzantium, by contrast, most Greeks were Christian. *Apologists,* or defenders, of Christianity insisted on harmony between Christianity and clas-

sical culture: they used Greek philosophy to buttress Christian tenets. Politically, as we have seen, emperors beginning with Constantine worked for the unanimity of church and state.

Distinctive attitudes toward the "holy person" illustrate the differences between the two societies. The holy person was a hero whose life and character embodied the spiritual ideals of the group. *Confessors* publicly manifested their faith in Christ. *Martyrs* held to their Christian faith, even suffering death for it and revealing unique courage and fortitude. *Virgins* displayed outstanding qualities of earthly and sexual renunciation. These ideals, Christians believed, existed in the physical body of the holy person. The dead body of the holy person, or *saint* as he or she came to be recognized, became an object of veneration. Saints were *ministers,* who carried people's prayers and petitions to God and interceded with God on behalf of the living. Unlike pagan and Jewish holy persons, the dead saints, because of their intercessory powers, played an extremely important role in Christian worship.

In the Germanic West, the saint had frequently been a socially prominent person, such as a noble or bishop, during his or her lifetime and had exercised real power. The place of the supernatural power associated with the saint was fixed with precision. People knew exactly where a saint's body was buried, because that place was the source of his or her holiness and intercessory influence. Relatively few such sites existed in the Germanic West. In the Byzantine East, on the other hand, Christians accepted many people as bearers or agents of the holy, and the place of spiritual power became very ambiguous. Moreover, the Eastern saint had usually shunned human contact and avoided society and those who exercised power; the Eastern saint had fulfilled no social function in his or her lifetime. Eastern saints drew their spiritual power and influence from outside of society—from a retreat in the desert and from their ability to speak directly to God.

In the East, holiness often touched such socially marginal persons as monks, prostitutes, and soldiers. In the West, holiness was vested in those who had known how to rule, and their posthumous holiness tended to be concentrated in cathedral, monastery, or shrine.[25] Holiness in the West, therefore, could be utilized either for political or economic purposes.

The expansion of the Arabs in the Mediterranean in the seventh and eighth centuries furthered the separation of the churches by dividing the two parts of Christendom. Separation bred isolation. Isolation, combined with prejudice on both sides, bred hostility. Finally, in 1054, a theological disagreement led the bishop of Rome and the patriarch of Constantinople to excommunicate each other. The outcome was a permanent *schism*, or split, between the Roman Catholic and the Greek Orthodox churches.

Despite religious differences, the Byzantine Empire served as a bulwark for the West, protecting it against invasions from the East. The Greeks stopped the Persians in the seventh century. They blunted—though they could not stop—Arab attacks in the seventh and eighth centuries, and they fought courageously against Turkish invaders until the fifteenth century, when they were finally overwhelmed. Byzantine Greeks slowed the impetus of

Slavic incursions in the Balkans and held the Russians at arm's length.

Turning from war to peace, the Byzantines set about civilizing the Slavs, both in the Balkans and in Russia. Byzantine missionaries spread the word of Christ, and one of their triumphs was the conversion of the Russians in the tenth century. The Byzantine missionary Cyril invented a Slavic alphabet using Greek characters, and this script (called the "Cyrillic alphabet") is still in use today. Cyrillic script made possible the birth of Russian literature. Similarly, Byzantine art and architecture became

Woman Carrying Pitcher   This detail from a floor mosaic in the Great Palace at Constantinople shows a buxom peasant woman balancing a huge water ewer on her shoulder. Notice the large earrings. *(Source: Scala/Art Resource)*

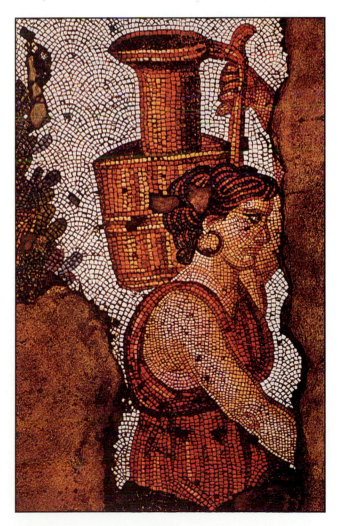

the basis and inspiration of Russian forms. The Byzantines were so successful that the Russians claimed to be the successors of the Byzantine Empire. For a time, Moscow was even known as the "Third Rome" (the second Rome being Constantinople).

The Law Code of Justinian

One of the most splendid achievements of the Byzantine emperors was the preservation of Roman law for the medieval and modern worlds. Roman law had developed from many sources—decisions by judges, edicts of the emperors, legislation passed by the senate, and the opinions of jurists expert in the theory and practice of law. By the fourth century, Roman law had become a huge, bewildering mass. Its sheer bulk made it almost unusable. Some laws had become outdated; some repeated or contradicted others. Faced with this vast, complex, and confusing hodgepodge, the emperor Theodosius decided to clarify and codify the law. He explained the need to do so:

When we consider the enormous multitude of books, the diverse modes of process and the difficulty of legal cases, and further the huge mass of imperial constitutions, which hidden as it were under a rampart of gross mist and darkness precludes men's intellects from gaining a knowledge of them, we feel that we have met a real need of our age, and dispelling the darkness have given light to the laws by a short compendium.[26]

Theodosius's work was only a beginning. He left centuries of Roman law untouched.

A far more sweeping and systematic codification took place under the emperor Justinian. Justinian intended to simplify the law and make it known to everyone. He appointed a committee of eminent jurists to sort through and organize the laws. The result was the *Code,* which distilled the legal genius of the Romans into a coherent whole, eliminated outmoded laws and contradictions, and clarified the law itself. Not content with the *Code,* Justinian set about bringing order to the equally huge body of Roman *jurisprudence,* the science or philosophy of law.

During the second and third centuries, the foremost Roman jurists, at the request of the emperors, had expressed learned opinions on complex legal problems, but often these opinions differed from one another. To harmonize this body of knowledge, Justinian directed his jurists to clear up disputed points and to issue definitive rulings. Accordingly, in 533 his lawyers published the *Digest,* which codified Roman legal thought. Finally, Justinian's lawyers compiled a handbook of civil law, the *Institutes.*

These three works—the *Code, Digest,* and *Institutes*—are the backbone of the *corpus juris civilis,* the "body of civil law," which is the foundation of law for nearly every modern European nation. The work of Justinian and his dedicated band of jurists still affects the modern world nearly fifteen hundred years later.

Byzantine Intellectual Life

Among the Byzantines, education was highly prized, and because of them many masterpieces of ancient Greek literature survived to influence the intellectual life of the modern world. The literature of the Byzantine Empire was predominately Greek, although Latin was long spoken among top politicians, scholars, and lawyers. Indeed, Justinian's *Code* was first written in Latin. Among the large reading public, history was a favorite subject. Generations of Byzantines read the historical works of Herodotus, Thucydides, and others. Some Byzantine historians abbreviated long histories, such as those of Polybius, while others wrote detailed narratives of their own days.

The most remarkable Byzantine historian was Procopius (ca 500–ca 562), who left a rousing account praising Justinian's reconquest of North Africa and Italy. Proof that the wit and venom of ancient writers like Archilochus and Aristophanes lived on in the Byzantine era can be found in Procopius's *Secret History,* a vicious and uproarious attack on Justinian and his wife, the empress Theodora. Though the Byzantines are often depicted as dull and lifeless, such opinions are hard to defend in the face of Procopius's description of Justinian's character:

For he was at once villainous and amenable; as people say colloquially, a moron. He was never truthful with anyone, but always guileful in what he said and did, yet eas-

ily hoodwinked by any who wanted to deceive him. His nature was an unnatural mixture of folly and wickedness.[27]

How much of this is true, how much the hostility of a sanctimonious hypocrite relishing the gossip he spreads, we will never know. Certainly *The Secret History* is robust reading.

Later Byzantine historians chronicled the victories of their emperors and the progress of their barbarian foes. Like Herodotus before them, they were curious about foreigners and left striking descriptions of the Turks, who eventually overwhelmed Byzantium. They sometimes painted unflattering pictures of the uncouth and grasping princes of France and England, whom they encountered on the Crusades.

In mathematics and geometry the Byzantines discovered nothing new. Yet they were exceptionally important as catalysts, for they passed Greco-Roman learning on to the Arabs, who assimilated it and made remarkable advances with it. The Byzantines were equally uncreative in astronomy and natural science, but at least they faithfully learned what the ancients had to teach.

Only when science could be put to military use did the Byzantines make advances. The best-known Byzantine scientific discovery was chemical— "Greek fire," a combustible liquid that was the medieval equivalent of the flame thrower. In mechanics the Byzantines continued the work of Hellenistic and Roman inventors of artillery and siege machinery. Just as Archimedes had devised machines to stop the Romans, so Byzantine scientists improved and modified devices for defending their empire.

The Byzantines devoted a great deal of attention to medicine, and the general level of medical competence was far higher in the Byzantine Empire than it was in the medieval West. The Byzantines assimilated the discoveries of Hellenic and Hellenistic medicine but added very few of their own. The basis of their medical theory was Hippocrates' concept of the four humors (see page 91). Byzantine physicians emphasized the importance of diet and rest and relied heavily on herbal drugs. Perhaps their chief weakness was excessive use of bleeding and burning, which often succeeded only in further weakening an already feeble patient. Hospitals were a prominent feature of Byzantine life, and the army, too, had a medical corps.

THE ARABS AND ISLAM

Around 610, in the important commercial city of Mecca in what is now Saudi Arabia, a merchant called Muhammad began to have religious visions. By the time he died in 632, all Arabia had accepted his creed. A century later, his followers controlled Syria, Palestine, Egypt, North Africa, Spain, and part of France. This Arabic expansion profoundly affected the development of Western civilization. Through centers at Salerno in southern Italy and Toledo in central Spain, Arabic and Greek learning reached the West.

The Arabs

In Muhammad's time, Arabia was inhabited by Semitic tribes, most of them Bedouins. These nomadic peoples grazed goats and sheep on the sparse patches of grass that dotted the vast, semi-arid peninsula. Other Arabs lived in the southern valleys and coastal towns along the Red Sea—in Yemen, Mecca, Medina, and in the northwestern region called "Hejaz." The Hejazi led a more sophisticated life and supported themselves by agriculture and trade. Their caravan routes crisscrossed Arabia and carried goods to Byzantium, Persia, and Syria. The Hejazi had wide commercial dealings but avoided cultural contacts with their Jewish, Christian, and Persian neighbors. The wealth produced by their business transactions led to luxurious and extravagant living in the towns.

Although the nomadic Bedouins condemned the urbanized lifestyle of the Hejazi as immoral and corrupt, Arabs of both types deeply respected one another's local tribal customs. They had no political unity beyond their tribal bonds. Tribal custom regulated their lives. Custom demanded the rigid observance of family obligations and the performance of religious rituals. Custom insisted that an Arab be proud, generous, and swift to take revenge. Custom required courage in public and avoidance of behavior that could bring social disgrace.

Although the various tribes differed markedly, they did have certain religious rules in common. For example, all Arabs kept three months of the year as sacred; during that time, fighting stopped so that everyone could attend holy ceremonies in peace. The city of Mecca was the religious center of the Arab world, and fighting was never tolerated there. All Arabs prayed at the Kaaba, the sanctuary in Mecca. Within the Kaaba was a sacred black stone that Arabs revered because they believed it had fallen from heaven.

What eventually molded the diverse Arab tribes into a powerful political and social unity was the religion founded by Muhammad.

Muhammad and the Faith of Islam

Except for a few vague autobiographical remarks in the Qur'an, the sacred book of Islam, Muhammad (ca 571–632) left no account of his life. Arab tradition accepts as historically true some of the sacred legends that developed about him, but those legends were not written down until about a century after his death. (Similarly, the earliest accounts of the life of Jesus, the Christian Gospels, were not written until forty or fifty years after his death.) Orphaned at the age of six, Muhammad was brought up by his grandfather. As a young man he became a merchant in the caravan trade. Later he entered the service of a wealthy widow, and their subsequent marriage brought him financial independence. The Qur'an reveals him as an extremely devout man, ascetic, self-disciplined, literate but not educated.

Since childhood Muhammad had been subject to strange seizures during which he completely lost consciousness and had visions. After 610 these attacks and the accompanying visions apparently became more frequent. Unsure for a time what he should do, Muhammad discovered his mission after a vision in which the angel Gabriel instructed him to preach. Muhammad described his visions in verse form and used these verses as his *Qur'an*, or "prayer recitation." During Muhammad's lifetime his secretary jotted down these revelations haphazardly. After Muhammad's death, scribes organized the revelations into chapters, and in 651 Muhammad's third successor as religious leader, Othman, arranged to have an official version of them published.

The religion Muhammad founded is called "Islam"; a believer in that faith is called a "Muslim." Muhammad's religion eventually attracted great numbers of people, partly because of the simplicity of its doctrines. The subtle and complex reasoning Christianity had acquired by the seventh century was absent from early Islam. Nor did Islam emphasize study and learning, as did Judaism.

The strictly monotheistic theology outlined in the Qur'an has only a few tenets. Allah, the Muslim God, is all-powerful and all-knowing. Muhammad, Allah's prophet, preached his word and carried his message. Muhammad described himself as the successor both of the Jewish patriarch Abraham and of Christ, and he claimed that his teachings replaced theirs. Muhammad invited and won converts from Judaism and Christianity.

Because Allah is all-powerful, believers must submit themselves to him. (*Islam* literally means "submission to the word of God.") This Islamic belief is closely related to the central feature of Muslim doctrine, the coming Day of Judgment. Muslims need not be concerned about *when* judgment will occur, but they must believe with absolute and total conviction that the Day of Judgment *will* come. Consequently, all of a Muslim's thoughts and actions should be oriented toward the Last Judgment and the rewards of heaven.

In order for a person to merit the rewards of heaven, Muhammad prescribed a strict code of moral behavior. The Muslim must recite a profession of faith in Allah and in Muhammad as God's prophet: "There is no god but Allah and Muhammad is his prophet." The believer must pray five times a day, fast and pray during the sacred month of Ramadan, make a pilgrimage to the holy city of Mecca once during his or her lifetime, and give alms to the poor. The Qur'an forbids alcoholic beverages and gambling. It condemns business *usury* —that is, lending money at interest rates or taking advantage of market demand for products by charging high prices for them. Some foods, such as pork, are forbidden, a dietary regulation adopted from the Mosaic law of the Hebrews.

By earlier Arab standards, the Qur'an sets forth an austere sexual morality. Muslim jurisprudence condemned licentious behavior on the part of men as well as women, which enhanced the status of women in Muslim society. About marriage, illicit intercourse, and inheritance, the Qur'an states:

Islamic Religious Heritage   Reflecting the Judaic and Christian influences on the Islamic faith, this miniature by a Muslim artist illustrates the story from Isaiah 21: 6–9 in which a watchman in the tower reports seeing a man riding on an ass (Jesus) and another riding a camel (Muhammed). *(Source: Edinburgh University Library)*

[Of] . . . women who seem good in your eyes, marry but two, three, or four; and if ye still fear that ye shall not act equitably, then only one. . . .

The whore and the fornicator: whip each of them a hundred times. . . .

The fornicator shall not marry other than a whore; and the whore shall not marry other than a fornicator. . . .

They who defame virtuous women, and fail to bring four witnesses [to swear that they did not], are to be whipped eighty times. . . .

Men who die and leave wives behind shall bequeath to them a year's maintenance.

And your wives shall have a fourth part of what you leave; if you have no issue; but if you have issue, then they shall have an eighth part. . . .

With regard to your children, God commands you to give the male the portion of two females; and if there be more than two females, then they shall have two-thirds of *what their father leaves; but if there be one daughter only, she shall have the half.*

By contrast, Western law has tended to punish prostitutes but not their clients. Westerners tend to think polygamy degrading to women, but in a military society where there were apt to be many widows, polygamy provided women a measure of security. With respect to matters of property, Muslim women were more emancipated than Western women. For example, a Muslim woman retained complete jurisdiction over one-third of her property when she married and could dispose of it in any way she wished. A Western woman had no such power.[28]

The Muslim who faithfully observed the laws of the Qur'an could hope for salvation. According to the Qur'an, salvation is by Allah's grace and choice alone. Technically a Muslim cannot "win" salva-

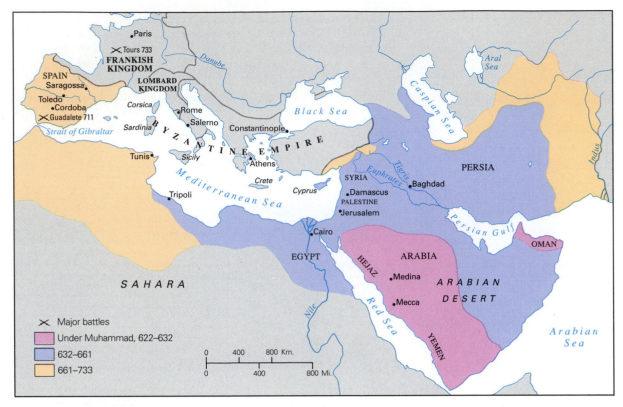

MAP 7.4 The Expansion of Islam to 733   Political weaknesses in the territories they conquered, as well as superior fighting skills, help explain the speed with which the Muslims expanded.

tion as a reward for good behavior. Because Allah is all-knowing and all-powerful, he knows from the moment of a person's conception whether or not that person will be saved. Nevertheless, Muhammad maintained, predestination gave believers the will and courage to try to achieve the impossible. Devout Muslims came to believe that mechanical performance of the faith's basic rules would automatically gain them salvation. Moreover, the believer who suffered and died for his faith in battle was immediately ensured the rewards of the Muslim heaven.

Historians and ecumenically minded theologians have pointed out many similarities among Islam, Christianity, and Judaism. All three religions are monotheistic; all worship the same God. Like Jews, Muslims customarily worshiped together at sundown on Fridays, and no assembly or organized church was essential. Muslims call Jews and Chris-

tians "People of the Book," meaning that all three faiths follow the Hebrew Scriptures.

Islam transcended the public and corporate aspects of tribal religion. Every Muslim hoped that by following the simple requirements of Islam he or she could achieve salvation. For the believer, the petty disputes and conflicts of tribal society paled before the simple teachings of Allah. On this basis, Muhammad united the nomads of the desert and the merchants of the cities. The doctrines of Islam, instead of the ties of local custom, bound all Arabs.

Nevertheless, a schism soon developed within the Islamic faith. In 661 the caliph Ali was assassinated. The title *caliph*, which meant "successor" to the Prophet, combined the ideas of spiritual and political leader of the *umma*, or Muslim community. Ali had claimed the caliphate on the basis of family ties: he was Muhammad's cousin and son-in-law. When Ali was murdered, his followers argued that he had been the Prophet's prescribed successor. These supporters of Ali were called *Shi'ites* or *Shi'a,* Arabic terms meaning "supporters" or "partisans" of Ali. In succeeding generations, Shi'ites emphasized the blood descent from Ali and claimed to have divine knowledge that Muhammad had given to them as his heirs. Other Muslims adhered to the practice and beliefs of the Islamic community, based on the precedents of the Prophet; they were called *Sunnis,* a term derived from the Arabic *Sunna,* the account of Muhammad's sayings and conduct in particular situations. When an issue arose for which the Qur'an offered no solution, Muslim scholars searched for a precedent in the Sunna, which gained an authority comparable to the Qur'an itself. Sunnis identified themselves with religious orthodoxy; they considered the Shi'ites, who claimed special religious knowledge deriving from Ali, heretical. The Shi'ites were always a minority within Islam, but a potentially dangerous one.

Despite this division within Islam, the faith of Allah united the Arabs sufficiently to redirect their warlike energies. Hostilities were launched outward. By the time Muhammad died in 632, he had welded together all the Bedouin tribes. The crescent of Islam, the Muslim symbol, prevailed throughout the Arabian peninsula. During the next century, between 632 and 733, one rich province of the old Roman Empire after another came under Muslim domination—first Syria, then Egypt, and then all of North Africa (Map 7.4). The governmental headquarters of this vast new empire was established at Damascus in Syria by the ruling Umayyad family. A contemporary proverb speaks of the Mediterranean as a Muslim lake. (This is an exaggeration, because Muslim control of the Mediterranean began only during the late ninth and early tenth centuries; and the Byzantines at Constantinople always contested that control.)

In 711 a Muslim force crossed the Strait of Gibraltar and at Guadalete easily defeated the weak Visigothic kingdom in Spain. A few Christian princes supported by the Frankish rulers held out in northern mountain fortresses, but the Muslims controlled most of Spain until the twelfth century. The political history of Spain in the Middle Ages is the history of the *reconquista,* or Christian reconquest of that country.

In 719 the Arabs pushed beyond the Pyrenees

into the kingdom of the Franks. At the Battle of Tours in 733, the Frankish chieftain Charles Martel defeated the Arabs and halted their further expansion. Ultimately Charlemagne (see pages 234–239) expelled them from France.

Muslim expansion was not confined to northern Africa and southern Europe. From the Arabian peninsula, Muslims carried their faith deep into Africa and across Asia all the way to India. In the West, however, Arab political influence was felt

Harvesting Dates This detail from an ivory casket given to a Cordoban prince reflects the importance of fruit cultivation in the Muslim-inspired agricultural expansion in southern Europe in the ninth and tenth centuries. *(Source: Louvre/Cliché des Musées Nationaux, Paris)*

Mosque of Cordoba Ordered by Abd al-Rahman (756–768), founder of the independent Ummayad dynasty in Spain, the mosque at the market city and river port of Cordoba is located on the site of a Roman temple and Visigothic church. The vaulting is supported by twelve aisles of columns rhythmically repeated in every direction. Some architectural historians consider this mosque the most spectacular Islamic building in the world. *(Source: MAS, Barcelona)*

almost exclusively in Spain. A member of the Umayyad dynasty, Abd al-Rahman (r. 756–788), established the Moorish kingdom of Spain with its capital at Cordoba. (The Spanish kingdom and culture were called "Moorish" after the dark-skinned Moors of North Africa, also known as Berber-Arabs, who had conquered the Iberian Peninsula.) Jewish people were generally well treated in Moorish Spain, and Christians were tolerated as long as they paid a small tax.

The Muslims had an enormous impact on agricultural development in Spain. They began the cultivation of rice, sugar cane, oranges, lemons, grapefruit, dates, figs, eggplant, carrots, and, after the eleventh century, cotton. These crops, together with new methods of field irrigation, led to what one scholar has called "a green revolution." Andalusian (southern) Spain developed "a complex and varied agricultural system, whereby a greater variety of soil types were put to efficient use; where fields that had been yielding one crop at most prior to the Islamic invasion were now capable of yielding three or more crops, in rotation; and where agricultural production responded to the demands of an increasingly sophisticated and cosmopolitan urban population by providing the towns with a variety of products unknown in northern Europe."[29]

In the urban areas Muslims made significant advances in thought. Toledo, for example, became an important center of learning, through which Arab intellectual achievements entered and influenced western Europe. Arabic knowledge of science and mathematics, derived from the Chinese, Greeks, and Hindus, was highly sophisticated. The Muslim mathematician al-Khwarizmi (d. 830) wrote the important treatise *Algebra,* the first work in which the word *algebra* is used mathematically. Al-Khwarizmi used Arabic numerals in *Algebra,* and he applied mathematics to problems of physics and astronomy. Scholars at Baghdad translated Euclid's *Elements,* the basic text for plane and solid geometry. Muslims also instructed Westerners in the use of the zero, which permitted the execution of complicated problems of multiplication and long division. Use of the zero represented an enormous advance over clumsy Roman numerals.

Muslim medical knowledge was also far superior to that of Westerners. By the ninth century, Arab physicians had translated most of the treatises of Hippocrates and Galen. Unfortunately, these Greek treatises came to the West as translations from Greek to Arabic to Latin and inevitably lost a great deal in translation. Nevertheless, in the ninth and tenth centuries, Arabic knowledge and experience in anatomy and pharmaceutical prescriptions much enriched Western knowledge. Later, Greek philosophical thought passed to the West by way of Arabic translation.

There is no question that Islam was a significant ingredient in the making of Europe. Muslim expansion meant that Mediterranean civilization would be divided into three spheres of influence: the Byzantine, the Arabic, and the Western. Beginning in the ninth century, Arabic mathematics, medicine, philosophy, and science played a decisive role in the formation of European culture. A few of the words that came into English from Arabic suggest the extent of Arabic influence: *alcohol, admiral, algebra, almanac, candy, cipher, coffee, damask, lemon, orange, sherbet,* and *zero.*

heaven, so there can be only one ruler on earth." By the logic of Islamic law, no political entity outside of Islam could exist permanently. Islam and Christianity each fused the social and political aspects of culture into a self-contained system. In the formation of a distinctively European culture, the Christian faith became the basic cement.

Byzantium played a significant role in the development of both the Latin West and Islam. Byzantium could not confine Islam to Arabia, but it thwarted the Muslim challenge to Christianity by restricting Arab expansion. This Byzantine check permitted a separate medieval Christendom to rise in the West. In the eighth century, spiritual loyalty to Rome enabled the papacy to develop into a supranational authority virtually independent of a secular power. The goals and energy of the bishops of Rome, combined with the military strength of the Carolingian rulers, built a strong Christian faith in the Latin West.[30]

SUMMARY

The civilization that emerged in eighth-century Europe represented a fusion of classical, Christian, and Germanic elements. Latin was the language of educated people, and through the medium of Latin Christian thinkers expressed both their own ideals and religious doctrines and the laws and customs of the Germanic peoples. Christian missionaries preached the Gospel to the Germanic peoples, instructed them in the basic tenets of the Christian faith, and used penitentials to give them a sense of right moral behavior. Monasteries provided a model of Christian living, a pattern of agricultural development, and a place for education and learning. Christianity, because it energetically and creatively fashioned the Germanic and classical legacies, proved the most powerful agent in the making of Europe.

Islam and Byzantium also made contributions. As the ancient world declined, religious faith, rather than imperial rule, became the core of social identity. Each area came to define its world in religious terms. Christians called their world *ecumenical,* meaning universal. Muslims divided the world into two fundamental sections: the House of Islam, which consisted of all those regions where the law of Islam prevailed, and the House of War, which was the rest of the world. "As there is one God in

NOTES

1. Matthew 16:18–19 *(in modern translation).*
2. R. C. Petry, ed., *A History of Christianity: Readings in the History of Early and Medieval Christianity* (Englewood Cliffs, N.J.: Prentice-Hall, 1962), p. 70.
3. H. Bettenson, ed., *Documents of the Christian Church* (Oxford: Oxford University Press, 1947), p. 113.
4. Colossians 3:9–11.
5. Luke 6:20–31.
6. L. Sherley-Price, trans., *Bede: A History of the English Church and People* (Baltimore: Penguin Books, 1962), pp. 86–87.
7. J. T. McNeill and H. Gamer, trans., *Medieval Handbooks of Penance* (New York: Octagon Books, 1965), pp. 184–197.
8. L. White, "The Life of the Silent Majority," in *Life and Thought in the Early Middle Ages,* ed. R. S. Hoyt (Minneapolis: University of Minnesota Press, 1967), p. 100.
9. 1 Peter 2:11–20.
10. V. L. Bullough, *The Subordinate Sex: A History of Attitudes Toward Women* (Urbana: University of Illinois Press, 1973), p. 114.
11. Quoted in ibid., p. 115.
12. Ibid., pp. 118–119.
13. See J. Boswell, *Christianity, Social Tolerance, and Homosexuality: Gay People in Western Europe from the Beginning of the Christian Era to the Fourteenth Century*

(Chicago: University of Chicago Press, 1980), chaps. 3 and 5, esp. pp. 87, 127–131.

14. F. J. Sheed, trans., *The Confessions of St. Augustine* (New York: Sheed & Ward, 1953), bk. 1, pt. 3.

15. Ibid., bk. 10, pt. 27, p. 236.

16. T. Burns, *A History of the Ostrogoths* (Bloomington: Indiana University Press, 1984), pp. 18, 21.

17. See W. Goffart, *Barbarians and Romans: The Techniques of Accommodation* (Princeton, N.J.: Princeton University Press, 1980), chap. 3, and esp. Conclusion, pp. 211–230.

18. See P. J. Geary, *Before France and Germany: The Creation and Transformation of the Merovingian World* (New York: Oxford University Press, 1988), pp. 18–25.

19. Ibid., p. 24.

20. Ibid., pp. 108–112.

21. E. F. Henderson, ed., *Select Historical Documents of the Middle Ages* (London: G. Bell & Sons, 1912), pp. 176–189.

22. Geary, p. 46.

23. Ibid., p. 50.

24. See S. F. Wemple, "Sanctity and Power: The Dual Pursuit of Early Medieval Women," in *Becoming Visible: Women in European History,* 2d ed., ed. R. Bridenthal et al. (Boston: Houghton Mifflin, 1987), pp. 133–136.

25. P. Brown, *Society and the Holy in Late Antiquity* (Berkeley: University of California Press, 1982), pp. 166–195.

26. Quoted in J. B. Bury, *History of the Later Roman Empire,* vol. 1 (New York: Dover, 1958), pp. 233–234.

27. R. Atwater, trans., *Procopius: The Secret History* (Ann Arbor: University of Michigan Press, 1963), bk. 8.

28. J. O'Faolain and L. Martines, eds., *Not in God's Image: Women in History from the Greeks to the Victorians* (New York: Harper & Row, 1973), pp. 108–115.

29. T. F. Glick, *Islamic and Christian Spain in the Early Middle Ages* (Princeton, N.J.: Princeton University Press, 1979), pp. 77–78.

30. See J. Herrin, *The Formation of Christendom* (Princeton, N.J.: Princeton University Press, 1987), pp. 7–8, 477, et passim.

SUGGESTED READING

J. Herrin's *The Formation of Christendom* (1987), which is cited in the Notes, is unquestionably the best recent synthesis of the history of the early Middle Ages; it also contains an excellent discussion of Byzantine, Muslim, and Western art. In addition to the other studies listed in the Notes, students may consult the following works for a more detailed treatment of the early Middle Ages. Both M. Grant, *The Dawn of the Middle Ages* (1981), which emphasizes innovation and development, and P. Brown, *The World of Late Antiquity, A.D. 150–750* (1971), which stresses social and cultural change, are lavishly illustrated and lucidly written introductions to the entire period. Grant has especially valuable material on the Germanic kingdoms, Byzantium, and eastern Europe. J. Pelikan, *The Excellent Empire: The Fall of Rome and the Triumph of the Church* (1987), describes how interpretations of the fall of Rome have influenced our understanding of Western culture.

There is a rich literature on the Christian church and its role in the transition from ancient to medieval civilization. J. Pelikan, *Jesus Through the Centuries: His Place in the History of Culture* (1985), discusses the image of Jesus held by various cultures over the centuries and its function in the development of these cultures. F. Oakley, *The Medieval Experience: Foundations of Western Cultural Singularity* (1974), emphasizes the Christian roots of Western cultural uniqueness. W. Meeks, *The First Urban Christians: The Social World of the Apostle Paul* (1983), provides fascinating material on the early Christians and shows that they came from all social classes. J. Richards, *Consul of God: The Life and Times of Gregory the Great* (1980), is the first significant study in seventy years of this watershed pontificate. History, archeology, and language are critically examined in C. Thomas, *Christianity in Roman Britain to A.D. 500* (1981), a very learned study emphasizing the continuity in Britain's Christian history. P. Brown, *The Cult of the Saints: Its Rise and Function in Latin Christianity* (1982), describes the significance of the saints in popular religion. Students seeking a thorough treatment of Christianity through the sixth century should consult W. H. C. Frend, *The Rise of Christianity* (1984), an almost exhaustive treatment by a leading scholar-theologian. Students seeking to understand early Christian attitudes on sexuality and how they replaced Roman ones should consult the magisterial work of P. Brown, *The Body and Society: Men, Women, and Sexual Renunciation in Early Christianity* (1988), one of the most important studies on Western sexuality published in recent years.

For the synthesis of classical and Christian cultures, see C. N. Cochrane, *Christianity and Classical Culture* (1957), a deeply learned monograph. T. E. Mommsen, "Saint Augustine and the Christian Idea of Progress," *Journal of the History of Ideas* 12 (1951): 346–374, and G. B. Ladner, *The Idea of Reform* (1959), examine ideas of history and progress among the early church fathers. The best biography of Saint Augustine is P. Brown, *Augustine of Hippo* (1967), which treats him as a symbol of change.

For the Germans see, in addition to Burns's work cited in the Notes, J. M. Wallace-Hadrill, *The Barbarian West: The Early Middle Ages A.D. 400–1000* (1962), and A. Lewis, *Emerging Europe, A.D. 400–1000* (1967), both of which describe German customs and society and the Germanic impact on the Roman Empire. A rich but difficult study is H. Wolfram, *History of the Goths,* trans. T. J. Dunlop (1988), which explores German tribal formation and places Gothic history within the context of late Roman society and institutions. F. Lot, *The End of the Ancient World* (1965), emphasizes the economic and social causes of Rome's decline. For Rome itself and the Germans' impact on it, C. Hibbert, *Rome: The Biography of a City* (1985), contains instructive and entertaining material. G. Le Bras, "The Sociology of the Church in the Early Middle Ages," in S. L. Thrupp, ed., *Early Medieval Society* (1967), discusses the Christianization of the barbarians.

The phenomenon of monasticism has attracted interest throughout the centuries. L. Doyle, trans., *St. Benedict's Rule for Monasteries* (1957), presents the monastic guide in an accessible, pocket-size form; a more learned edition is J. McCann, ed. and trans., *The Rule of Saint Benedict* (1952). The best modern edition of the document is T. Fry et al., eds., *RB 1980: The Rule of St. Benedict in Latin and English with Notes* (1981), which contains a history of Western monasticism and a scholarly commentary on the *Rule.* L. Eberle, trans., *The Rule of the Master* (1977), offers the text of and a commentary on Benedict's major source. Especially useful for students is O. Chadwick, *The Making of the Benedictine Ideal* (1981),

a short but profound essay that emphasizes the personality of Saint Benedict in the development of the Benedictine ideal. G. Constable, *Medieval Monasticism: A Select Bibliography* (1976), is a useful research tool. Two beautifully illustrated syntheses by leading authorities are D. Knowles, *Christian Monasticism* (1969), which sketches monastic history through the middle of the twentieth century, and G. Zarnecki, *The Monastic Achievement* (1972), which focuses on the medieval centuries. L. J. Daly, *Benedictine Monasticism* (1965), stresses day-to-day living, while H. W. Workman, *The Evolution of the Monastic Ideal* (1962), shows the impact of the monastic ideal on later religious orders. For women in monastic life, see S. F. Wemple, *Women in Frankish Society: Marriage and the Cloister, 500–900* (1981), an important book with a good bibliography.

For Byzantium and the Arabs, see J. J. Norwich, *Byzantium: The Early Centuries* (1989), an elegantly written sketch; E. Patlagean, "Byzantium in the Tenth and Eleventh Centuries," in *A History of Private Life,* vol. I: *From Pagan Rome to Byzantium* (1987); J. Hussey, *The Byzantine World* (1961); S. Runciman, *Byzantine Civilization* (1956); A. Bridge, *Theodora: Portrait in a Byzantine Landscape* (1984), a romantic and amusing biography of the courtesan who became empress; J. L. Esposito, *Islam: The Straight Path* (1988), an informed and balanced work based on the best modern scholarship; H. A. R. Gibb, *Mohammedianism* (1969); T. Andrae, *Mohammed: The Man and His Faith* (1970); M. Rodinson, *Mohammed* (1974); and W. M. Watt, *Muhammad: Prophet and Statesman* (1961).

8

The Carolingian World: Europe in the Early Middle Ages

The Frankish chieftain Charles Martel defeated Muslim invaders in 733 at the Battle of Tours in central France.[1] At the time, it was only another skirmish in the struggle between Christians and Muslims, but in retrospect it looms as one of the great battles of history: this Frankish victory halted Arab expansion in Europe. A century later, in 843, Charles Martel's three great-great-grandsons, after a bitter war, concluded the Treaty of Verdun, which divided the European continent among themselves.

Between 733 and 843, a distinctly European society emerged. A new kind of social and political organization, later called "feudalism," appeared. And for the first time since the collapse of the Roman Empire, most of western Europe was united under one government. That government reached the peak of its development under Charles Martel's grandson, Charlemagne. Christian missionary activity among the Germanic peoples continued, and strong ties were forged with the Roman papacy. A revival of study and learning, sometimes styled the "Carolingian Renaissance," occurred under Charlemagne.

- How did Charlemagne acquire and govern his vast empire?
- What was the significance of the relations between Carolingian rulers and the church?
- What was the Carolingian Renaissance?
- The culture of the Carolingian Empire has been described as the "first European civilization." What does this mean?
- What was feudalism, and how did it come about?
- What factors contributed to the disintegration of the Carolingian Empire?

These are the questions this chapter will explore.

THE FRANKISH ARISTOCRACY AND THE RISE OF THE CAROLINGIAN DYNASTY

Through a series of remarkable victories over other Germanic tribes, the Franks under Clovis had emerged as the most powerful people in Europe by the early sixth century (see page 211). The Frankish kingdom included most of what is now France and a large section of southwestern Germany. Clovis's baptism into orthodox Christianity won him church support against other Germanic tribes, most of them Arian Christians. By selecting as his "capital" Paris—legendary scene of the martyrdom of Saint Denis, thought to be a disciple of Saint Paul—Clovis identified himself with the cult of Saint Denis and used it to strengthen his rule. Clovis died in 511, and the Merovingian dynasty went on to rule for the next two centuries.

Rule is, of course, too strong a verb. Conquering the vast territories proved easier for the Merovingians than governing them, given their inadequate political institutions. The size of Clovis's kingdom, combined with tribal custom, forced him to divide it among his four sons, because no one king could govern it effectively. Practically, however, Clovis's decision was disastrous, because it led to incessant civil war. The Merovingians bitterly hated each other, and each king fought to deprive his relatives of their portions of the kingdom. Violence and assassination ceased only when one man had killed off all his rivals. Thus in 558 Clovis's youngest son, Lothair, acquired the whole kingdom after he had murdered two nephews and eliminated one rebellious son by burning him and his family alive. After Lothair died, the other sons continued the civil war until one king survived.

In this domestic violence the remarkable Queen Brunhilda (d. 631), wife of King Sigebert of the East Frankish kingdom, played an important role. Her sister Galswintha was murdered by her husband Chilperic, ruler of the West Frankish kingdom, so that he could marry his mistress Fredegunda (see page 215). Brunhilda thereupon instigated war between the two kingdoms. Hatred of Fredegunda led her to continue the war even after the deaths of kings Sigebert and Chilperic. During the reigns of her son and grandson, Brunhilda actually ruled the East Frankish kingdom as well as Burgundy, which was united to the East Frankish kingdom through her designs. Brunhilda displayed great political skills, but her merciless use of violence in pursuit of her goals incurred the bitter enmity of the nobility.

The long period of civil war in the Frankish kingdom may have provided the opportunity for the emergence of a distinct aristocratic class. Recent research in Frankish family history has revealed that a noble ruling class existed before the mid-sixth century. Members of this class belonged to families of

Merovingian Army   This sixth- or seventh-century ivory depicts a nobleman in civilian dress followed by seven warriors. Note that the mounted men do not have stirrups and that they seem to have fought with spears and bows and arrows. The power of the Frankish aristocracy rested on these private armies. *(Source: Rheinisches Landesmuseum, Trier)*

high reputation, who gradually intermarried with members of the old Gallo-Roman senatorial class. They possessed wealth and great villas where they led an aristocratic lifestyle. They exercised rights of lordship over their lands and tenants, dispensing local customary, not royal, law. These families provided almost all the bishops of the church. Because they had a self-conscious awareness of their social, economic, and political distinction from the rest of society, they constituted a noble class.[2]

In the seventh century the central government of the Merovingians could not control these nobles. Primitive and disorganized, the government consisted of a few household officials, the most important of whom was the mayor of the palace. He was in charge of administration and acted as the king's deputy; he also represented the interests of the nobility. Since the Frankish kingdom was divided into East Frankland, West Frankland, and Burgundy, each with its own ruler, and since some territories such as Bavaria were virtually independent, the Merovingian kingdom slowly disintegrated.

Reconstruction of the Frankish kingdom began with the efforts of Pippin of Landen, a member of one aristocratic family. In the early seventh century, he was mayor of the palace in East Frankland. His grandson, Pippin II (d. 714), after a military victory in 687, gained the position of mayor of the palace in both East and West Frankland. It was this Pippin's son Charles Martel who defeated the Muslims at Tours and thus checked Arab expansion into Europe. Charles's wars against the Burgundians and Frisians broke those weakening forces. His victory over the infidels and his successful campaigns within the Frankish kingdom added to his family's prestige a reputation for great military strength. From 714 until his death in 741, Charles Martel thus held the real power in the Frankish kingdom; the Merovingians were kings in name only.

The rise of the Carolingian dynasty—whose name derives from the Latin *Carolus,* for Charles—rested partly on papal support. In the early eighth century, missionaries supported Charles Martel and his son Pippin III as they attempted to bring the various Germanic tribes under their jurisdiction. The most important was the Anglo-Saxon missionary Wynfrith, or Boniface (680–754), as he was later called. Given the semibarbaric peoples with whom he was dealing, Boniface's achievements were remarkable. He helped shape the structure of the German church. He established *The Rule of Saint Benedict* in all the monasteries he founded or reformed. And with the support of Pippin III, he held councils to reform the Frankish church.

Saint Boniface preached throughout Germany against divorce, polygamous unions, and incest. On these matters German custom and ecclesiastical law completely disagreed. The Germans allowed divorce simply by the man's repudiation of his wife; divorce did not require her consent. The Germanic peoples also practiced polygamy and *incest*—sexual relations between brothers and sisters or parents and children—on a wide scale. Church councils and theologians stressed that marriage, validly entered into, could not be ended, and they firmly condemned incest.

Boniface's preaching was not without impact, for in 802 Charles Martel's grandson Charlemagne prohibited incest and decreed that a husband might separate from an adulterous wife. The woman could be punished, and the man could not remarry in her lifetime. Charlemagne also encouraged severe punishment for adulterous men. In so doing, he contributed to the dignity of marriage, the family, and women.

Charles Martel and Pippin III protected Boniface, and he preached Christian obedience to rulers. Because of his staunch adherence to Roman ideas and the Roman pope, the romanization of Europe accompanied its Christianization.

Charles Martel had been king of the Franks in fact but not in title. His son Pippin III (r. 751–768) made himself king in title as well as in fact. In Germanic custom—and custom was law—the kingship had to pass to someone of royal blood. Pippin did not want to murder the ineffectual Merovingian king, but he did want the kingship. Because the missionary activity of Boniface had spread Christian ideas and enhanced papal influence in the Frankish kingdom, Pippin decided to consult the pope. Accordingly, Pippin sent envoys to Rome to ask the pope whether the man with the power was entitled to be king. Pope Zacharias, guided by the Augustinian principle that the real test of kingship is whether it provides for order and justice, responded in 751 that he who has the power should also have the title. This answer constituted recognition of the Carolingians. The Merovingian king was deposed and forced to become a monk.

Just as the emperors Constantine and Theodosius had taken actions in the fourth century that would later be cited as precedents in church-state relations (see pages 193–194), so Pippin III in the mid-eighth century took papal confirmation as official approval of his title. In 751 Pippin III was formally elected king of the Franks by the great lords, or magnates, of the Frankish territory. Two years later, the pope—who needed Pippin's protection from the Lombards—came to Gaul and personally anointed Pippin king at Paris.

Thus an important alliance was struck between the papacy and the Frankish ruler. In 754 Pope Stephen gave Pippin the title of protector of the Roman church. Pippin in turn agreed to restore to the papacy territories in northern Italy recently seized by the Lombards; he promptly marched into Italy and defeated the Lombards. The Carolingian family had received official recognition and anointment from the leading spiritual power in Europe, and the papacy had gained a military protector.

On a second successful campaign in Italy in 756, Pippin made a large donation to the papacy. The gift consisted of estates in central Italy that technically belonged to the Byzantine emperor. Known as the Papal States, they existed on paper, but not in political reality, until the pontificate of Innocent III in the thirteenth century.

Because of his anointment, Pippin's kingship took on a special spiritual and moral character. Before Pippin, only priests and bishops had received anointment. Pippin became the first to be anointed with the sacred oils and acknowledged as *rex et sacerdos* ("king and priest"). Anointment, rather than royal blood, set the Christian king apart. Pippin also cleverly eliminated possible threats to the Frankish throne, and the pope promised him support in the future. When Pippin died, his son Charlemagne succeeded him.

THE EMPIRE OF CHARLEMAGNE

Charles the Great (r. 768–814), generally known as Charlemagne, built on the military and diplomatic foundations of his ancestors. Charles's secretary and biographer, the Saxon Einhard, wrote a lengthy description of this warrior-ruler. It has serious flaws, partly because it is modeled directly on the Roman author Suetonius's *Life of the Emperor Augustus.* Still, it is the earliest medieval biography of a layman, and historians consider it generally accurate:

Charles was large and strong, and of lofty stature, though not disproportionately tall . . . the upper part of his head was round, his eyes very large and animated, nose a little long, hair fair, and face laughing and merry. Thus his appearance was always stately and dignified . . . although his neck was thick and somewhat short, and his belly rather prominent; but the symmetry of the rest of his body concealed these defects. His gait was firm, his whole carriage manly, and his voice clear, but not so strong as his size led one to expect. His health was excellent, except during the four years preceding his death. . . .

Even in those years he consulted rather his own inclinations than the advice of physicians, who were almost hateful to him, because they wanted him to give up roasts, to which he was accustomed, and to eat boiled meat instead. In accordance with the national custom, he took frequent exercise on horseback and in the chase, accomplishments in which scarcely any people in the world can equal the Franks. He enjoyed the exhalations from natural warm springs, and often practiced swimming, in which he was such an adept that none could surpass him; and hence it was that he built his palace at Aix-la-Chapelle [Aachen], and lived there constantly during his latter years until his death. He used not only to invite his sons to his bath, but his nobles and friends, and now and then a troop of his retinue or bodyguard.[3]

Though crude and brutal, Charlemagne was a man of enormous intelligence. He appreciated good literature, such as Saint Augustine's *City of God,* and Einhard considered him an unusually effective speaker. On the other hand, he could not even write his own name.

The security and continuation of his dynasty and the need for diplomatic alliances governed Charlemagne's complicated marriage pattern. The high rate of infant mortality required many sons. Married first to the daughter of Desiderius, king of the Lombards, Charlemagne divorced her on grounds of sterility. His second wife, Hildegard, produced nine children in twelve years. When she died, Charlemagne married Fastrada, daughter of an East Frankish count whose support Charles needed in his campaign against the Saxons. Charlemagne had

a total of four legal wives and six concubines, and even after the age of sixty-five continued to sire children. Though three sons reached adulthood, only one outlived him. Four surviving grandsons, however, ensured perpetuation of the family. The most striking feature of Charlemagne's character

Equestrian Statue of Charlemagne   A medieval king was expected to be fierce (and successful) in battle, to defend the church and the poor, and to give justice to all. This majestic and idealized figure of Charlemagne conveys these qualities. The horse is both the symbol and the means of his constant travels. *(Source: Girandon/Art Resource)*

MAP 8.1 The Carolingian World The extent of Charlemagne's nominal jurisdiction was extraordinary: it was not equalled until the nineteenth century.

Map labels:

SCOTLAND

IRELAND

NORTHUMBRIA
Jarrow
York

NORTH WALES
MERCIA
EAST ANGLIA
ESSEX
KENT
WEST WALES
WESSEX
SUSSEX

DANISH MARCH

SAXONY 804

Utrecht

FLANDERS

AUSTRASIA
Aachen
Fulda
Echternach
Mainz
Rhine

BRITTANY

NEUSTRIA
Rouen
Paris

Tours

ALEMANNIA

BAVARIA 788

Danube

TRIBUTARY

SLAVIC

PEOPLES

AQUITAINE
BURGUNDY
Lyons
Bordeaux
GASCONY

Rhône

VENETIA
Milan
Venice
Pavia

ISTRIA

DALMATIA

LOMBARDY

Roncesvalles

Ebro

SPANISH MARCH 811

UMAYYAD KINGDOM OF SPAIN

Toledo

Cordoba

Barcelona

Marseilles
Lérins

CORSICA

BALEARIC IS.

SARDINIA

PAPAL STATES
Spoleto
Rome
Monte Cassino

DUCHY OF BENEVENTO
Salerno

BYZANTINE EMPIRE

SICILY

Legend:

Monasteries

Frankish Kingdom, 768
Areas conquered by Charlemagne
Tributary peoples
Byzantine Empire

0   150   300 Km.
0   150   300 Mi.

was his phenomenal energy, which helps to explain his great military achievements.[4]

Territorial Expansion

Continuing the expansionist policies of his ancestors, Charlemagne fought more than fifty campaigns and became the greatest warrior of the early Middle Ages. He subdued all of the north of modern France. In the south, the lords of the mountainous ranges of Aquitaine—what is now called "Basque country"—fought off his efforts at total conquest. The Muslims in northeastern Spain were checked by the establishment of strongly fortified areas known as *marches.*

Charlemagne's greatest successes were in today's Germany. There his concerns were basically defensive. In the course of a thirty-year war against the semibarbaric Saxons, he added most of the northwestern German tribes to the Frankish kingdom. Because of their repeated rebellions, Charlemagne ordered, according to Einhard, more than four thousand Saxons slaughtered in one day.

To the south, he also achieved spectacular results. In 773 to 774 the Lombards in northern Italy again threatened the papacy. Charlemagne marched south, overran fortresses at Pavia and Spoleto, and incorporated Lombardy into the Frankish kingdom. To his title as king of the Franks he added king of the Lombards. Charlemagne also ended Bavarian independence and defeated the nomadic Avars, opening the Danubian plain for later settlement. He successfully fought the Byzantine Empire for Venetia (excluding the city of Venice itself), Istria, and Dalmatia and temporarily annexed those areas to his kingdom.

In the west, Charlemagne tried to occupy Basque territory in northwestern Spain. When his long siege of Saragossa proved unsuccessful and the Saxons on his northeastern borders rebelled, Charlemagne decided to withdraw, but the Basques annihilated his rear guard under Count Roland at Roncesvalles (778). This attack represented Charlemagne's only defeat, and he forbade people to talk about it. However, the expedition inspired the great medieval epic *The Song of Roland.* Based on legend and written down about 1100 at the beginning of the European crusading movement, the poem portrays Roland as the ideal chivalric knight and Charlemagne as exercising a sacred kind of kingship. Although many of the epic's details differ from the historical evidence, *The Song of Roland* is important because it reveals the popular image of Charlemagne in later centuries.

By around 805, the Frankish kingdom included all of continental Europe except Spain, Scandinavia, southern Italy, and the Slavic fringes of the East (Map 8.1). Not since the third century A.D. had any ruler controlled so much of the Western world. Not until the reign of Napoleon Bonaparte in the early nineteenth century was the feat to be repeated.

The Government of the Carolingian Empire

Charlemagne ruled a vast rural world dotted with isolated estates and characterized by constant petty violence. His empire was definitely not a state as people today understand that term; it was a collection of primitive peoples and semibarbaric tribes. Apart from a small class of warrior-aristocrats and clergy, almost everyone engaged in agriculture. Trade and commerce played only a small part in the economy. Cities served as the headquarters of bishops and as ecclesiastical centers.

By constant travel, personal appearances, and the sheer force of his personality, Charlemagne sought to awe conquered peoples with his fierce presence and terrible justice. By confiscating the estates of great territorial magnates, he acquired lands and goods with which to gain the support of lesser lords, further expanding the territory under his control.

The political power of the Carolingians rested on the cooperation of the dominant social class, the Frankish aristocracy. By the seventh century, through mutual cooperation and frequent marriage alliances, these families exercised great power that did not derive from the Merovingian kings. The Carolingians themselves had emerged from this aristocracy, and the military and political success that Carolingians such as Pippin II achieved depended on the support of the nobility. The lands and booty with which Charles Martel and Charlemagne rewarded their followers in these noble families enabled the nobles to improve their economic position; but it was only with noble help that the Carolingians were able to wage wars of expansion and suppress rebellions. In short, Carolingian success was a matter of reciprocal help and reward.[5]

Two or three hundred counts from this imperial aristocracy governed at the local level. They had full military and judicial power and held their offices for life but could be removed for misconduct. As a link between local authorities and the central government, Charlemagne appointed officials called *missi dominici,* "agents of the lord king." The empire was divided into visitorial districts. Each year, beginning in 802, two missi, usually a count and a bishop or abbot, visited assigned districts. They held courts and investigated the district's judicial, financial, and clerical activities. They held commissions to regulate crime, moral conduct, the clergy, education, the poor, and many other matters. The missi checked up on the counts and worked to prevent the counts' positions from be-

coming hereditary: strong counts with hereditary estates would have weakened Charlemagne's power. In the "marches" or "marks" (especially barbarous areas) officials called "margraves" had extensive powers to govern their dangerous localities.

A modern state has institutions of government, such as a civil service, courts of law, financial agencies for collecting and apportioning taxes, and police and military powers with which to maintain order internally and defend against foreign attack. These simply did not exist in Charlemagne's empire. Instead, society was held together by dependent relationships cemented by oaths promising faith and loyalty.

Although the empire lacked viable institutions, some Carolingians involved in governing did have vigorous political ideas. The abbots and bishops who served as Charlemagne's advisers worked out what was for their time a sophisticated political ideology. In letters and treatises, they set before their ruler high ideals of behavior and of government. They wrote that a ruler may hold power from God but is responsible to the law. Just as all subjects of the empire were required to obey him, so he, too, was obliged to respect the law. They envisioned a unified Christian society presided over by a king who was responsible for maintaining peace, law, and order and doing justice, without which neither the ruler nor the kingdom had any justification. These views derived largely from Saint Augustine's theories of kingship. Inevitably, they could not be realized in an illiterate, half-Christianized, preindustrial society. But they were the seeds from which medieval and even modern ideas of government were to develop.

A Dual Investiture   As Christ gave authority to St. Peter (Matthew 16:18–20), so Peter invests Pope Leo III (795–816) with the pallium, symbol of archiepiscopal authority, and Charlemagne with the Roman standard, representing civil authority in the West. Leo III commissioned this mosaic to celebrate papal power. *(Source: Scala/Art Resource)*

The Imperial Coronation of Charlemagne (800)

In the autumn of the year 800, Charlemagne paid a momentous visit to Rome. Einhard gave his account of what happened:

His last journey there [to Rome] was due to another factor, namely that the Romans, having inflicted many injuries on Pope Leo—plucking out his eyes and tearing out his tongue, he had been compelled to beg the assistance of the king. Accordingly, coming to Rome in order that he might set in order those things which had exceedingly disturbed the condition of the Church, he remained there the whole winter. It was at the time that he accepted the name of Emperor and Augustus. At first he was so much opposed to this that he insisted that although that day was a great [Christian] feast, he would not have entered the Church if he had known beforehand the pope's intention. But he bore very patiently the jealousy of the Roman Emperors [that is, the Byzantine rulers] who were indignant when he received these titles. He overcame their arrogant haughtiness with magnanimity, a virtue in which he was considerably superior to them, by sending frequent ambassadors to them and in his letters addressing them as brothers.[6]

For centuries scholars have debated the significance of the imperial coronation of Charlemagne. Did Charles plan the ceremony in Saint Peter's on Christmas Day, or did he merely accept the title of emperor? What did he have to gain from it? What meaning did the Frankish chancery (writing office) attach to the imperial title in the eighth century? Did Charlemagne use the imperial title? Did Pope Leo III arrange the coronation in order to identify the Frankish monarchy with the papacy and papal policy?

Though final answers will probably never be found, several things seem certain. First, Charlemagne considered himself a Christian king ruling a Christian people. His motto, *Renovatio romani imperi* ("Revival of the Roman Empire"), "implied a revival of the Western Empire in the image of Augustinian political philosophy."[7] Charles was consciously perpetuating old Roman imperial notions, while at the same time identifying with the new Rome of the Christian church. Charlemagne and his government represented a combination of Frankish practices and Christian ideals, the two basic elements of medieval European society. Second, later German rulers were anxious to gain the imperial title and to associate themselves with the legends of Charlemagne and ancient Rome. They wanted to use the ideology of imperial Rome to strengthen their positions. Finally, ecclesiastical authorities continually cited the event as proof that the dignity of the imperial crown could be granted only by the pope. The imperial coronation of Charlemagne, whether planned by the Carolingian court or by the papacy, was to have a profound effect on the course of German history and on the later history of Europe.

THE CAROLINGIAN INTELLECTUAL REVIVAL

It is ironic that Charlemagne's most enduring legacy was the stimulus he gave to scholarship and learning. Barely literate himself, preoccupied with the control of vast territories, much more a warrior than a thinker, he nevertheless set in motion a cultural revival that had widespread and long-lasting consequences. The revival of learning associated with Charlemagne and his court at Aachen drew its greatest inspiration from seventh- and eighth-century intellectual developments in the Anglo-Saxon kingdom of Northumbria, situated at the northernmost tip of the old Roman world.

Northumbrian Culture

Despite the victory of the Roman forms of Christian liturgy at the Synod of Whitby in 564 (see page 197), Irish-Celtic culture permeated the Roman church in Britain and resulted in a flowering of artistic and scholarly activity. Northumbrian creativity owes a great deal to the intellectual curiosity and collecting zeal of Saint Benet Biscop (ca 628–689). A strong supporter of Benedictine monasticism, Benet Biscop introduced the Roman ceremonial form into new religious houses he founded and encouraged it in older ones. Benet Biscop made five dangerous trips to Italy, raided libraries, and brought back to Northumbria manuscripts, relics, paintings, and other treasures that formed the libraries on which much later study was based.

Northumbrian monasteries produced scores of books: *missals* (used for the celebration of the mass), *psalters* (which contained the 150 psalms and other prayers used by the monks in their devotions), commentaries on the Scriptures, illuminated manuscripts, law codes, and collections of letters and sermons. The finest product of Northumbrian art is probably the Gospel book produced at Lindisfarne around 700. The incredible expense involved in the publication of such a book—for vellum, coloring, and gold leaf—represents in part an aristocratic display of wealth. The script, *uncial*, is a Celtic version of contemporary Greek and Roman handwriting. The illustrations have a strong Eastern quality, combining the abstract style of the Christian Middle East and the narrative approach of classical Roman art. Likewise, the use of

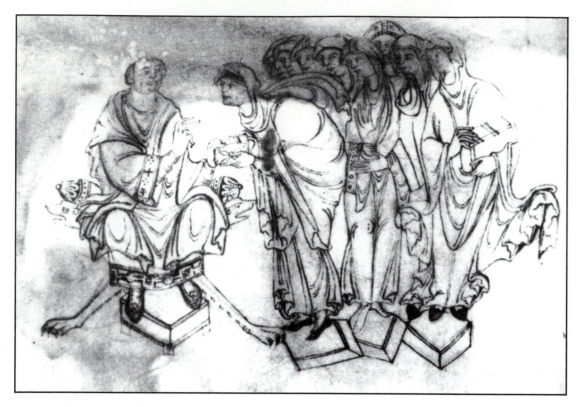

St. Hilda The superior of a mixed monastery of men and women at Whitby in Northumbria, St. Hilda (614–680) here receives a copy of the scholar Aldhelm's treatise *In Praise of Holy Virgins*. The simple drapery of the nuns' clothing with its nervous quality is characteristic of the eleventh-century Anglo-Saxon scriptoria. *(Source: His Grace the Archbishop of Canterbury and the Trustees of Lambeth Palace Library)*

geometrical decorative designs shows the influence of Syrian art. Many scribes, artists, and illuminators must have participated in the book's preparation.

In Anglo-Saxon England, women shared with men in the work of evangelization and in the new Christian learning. Kings and nobles, seeking suitable occupations for daughters who did not or would not marry, founded monasteries for nuns, some of which were *double monasteries*. A double monastery housed both men and women in two adjoining establishments and was governed by one superior, an *abbess*. Double monasteries provided women of the ruling class with something to rule. Nuns and monks worked together. Nuns looked after the children given to the monastery as *oblates* ("offerings"), the elderly who retired at the monastery, and travelers who needed hospitality. Monks provided protection, since in a violent age an isolated house of women invited attack; the monks also did the heavy work on the land. Perhaps the

most famous abbess of the Anglo-Saxon period was Saint Hilda (d. 680). A noblewoman of considerable learning and administrative ability, she ruled the double monastery of Whitby on the Northumbrian coast, advised kings and princes, hosted the famous synod of 664, and encouraged scholars and poets. "She compelled those under her direction to devote time to the study of the Holy Scriptures, and to exercise themselves in works of justice," with the result that five monks from Whitby became bishops. Several generations after Hilda, Saint Boniface (see page 234) wrote many letters to Whitby and other houses of nuns, pleading for copies of books; these attest to the nuns' intellectual reputations.[8]

The finest representative of Northumbrian and indeed all Anglo-Saxon scholarship is the Venerable Bede (ca 673–735). At the age of seven he was given by his parents as an oblate to Benet Biscop's monastery at Wearmouth. Later he was sent to the new monastery at Jarrow five miles away, where, surrounded by the books Benet Biscop had brought from Italy, Bede spent the rest of his life.

The author of learned commentaries on the Scriptures, Bede also devoted himself to other scholarly fields. Modern scholars praise him for his *Ecclesiastical History of the English Nation.* Broader in scope than the title suggests, the work is the chief source of information about early Britain. Bede searched far and wide for his information, discussed the validity of his evidence, compared various sources, and exercised a rare critical judgment. For these reasons, he has been called "the first scientific intellect among the Germanic peoples of Europe."[9]

Bede was probably the greatest master of chronology in the Middle Ages. Bede also popularized the system of dating events from the birth of Christ, rather than from the foundation of the city of Rome, as the Romans had done, or from the regnal years of kings, as the Germans did. Bede introduced the term *anno Domini,* "in the year of the Lord," abbreviated A.D. He fit the entire history of the world into this new dating method. (The reverse dating system of B.C., "before Christ," does not seem to have been widely used before 1700.) Saint Boniface introduced this system of reckoning time throughout the Frankish empire of Charlemagne.

At about the time that monks at Lindisfarne were producing their Gospel book and Bede at Jarrow was writing his *History,* another Northumbrian monk was at work on a nonreligious epic poem that provides considerable information about the society that produced it. The poem *Beowulf* is perhaps the finest expression of eighth-century secular literature. Though the tale is almost childish in its simplicity, scholars have hailed it as a masterpiece of Western heroic literature.

In the epic the great hall of the Danish king Hrothgar has been ravaged by a monster called Grendel. Beowulf, a relative of the Swedish royal house, hears of Grendel's murderous destruction. With a bodyguard of trusted warriors, Beowulf sails to Denmark and destroys Grendel in a brutal battle. Hrothgar and his queen, Wealhtheow, give a great banquet for Beowulf and his followers. Afterward, Grendel's mother enters the hall and carries off one of Hrothgar's closest advisers to avenge her son's death. Beowulf ultimately catches and destroys her. This victory is followed by more feasting, and Beowulf returns home to Sweden laden with rich gifts.

Beowulf later becomes king of a Swedish tribe. When his country is ravaged by a terrible dragon, the aged Beowulf challenges him. In the ensuing battle, Beowulf defeats the dragon but is wounded and dies.[10]

The story resembles ordinary Norse legends but is actually permeated with classical, Germanic, and Christian elements. Though the poem was written in England, all the action takes place in Scandina-

The Venerable Bede This twelfth-century representation of the eighth-century monk cannot pretend to an accurate likeness but shows that later ages respected Bede as a scholar. Note the knife in one hand to sharpen the pen in the other. *(Source: The British Library)*

via. This reflects the "international" quality of the age's culture, or at least the close ties between England and the Continent in the eighth century.

Beowulf's values are military and aristocratic: the central institution in the poem is the *gesith,* the Germanic band of warriors, united to fight with Beowulf. The highest virtue is loyalty to him, and loyalty is maintained by giving gifts. Yet the author was a Christian monk, and the basic theme of the poem is the conflict between good and evil. Beowulf, however, does not exhibit any Christian humility. Never one to hide his light under a bushel, he boasts of his exploits unashamedly. In this he embodies the classical idea of fame: the notion that fame is the greatest achievement because it is all a person leaves behind.

Pagan and Germanic symbols and practices suffuse *Beowulf.* Fighting, feasting, and drinking preoccupy its warrior-heroes. There is no glimpse of those who raised and prepared the food they consume; the author did not think peasants deserved mention. In a famous scene, Hrothgar's beautiful queen, Wealhtheow, enters the great hall, dispensing grace and gifts. The scene suggests that upper-class women served a decorative function in aristocratic society; *Beowulf* also points to their function as peacemakers. But Wealhtheow may have been handing out presents to the warriors because she had custody of and responsibility for her husband's treasure.

In another scene, the body of a dead king, along with considerable treasure, is put on a ship and floated out to sea. That this was a typical method of burial for Scandinavian kings is known from the ship burial uncovered in 1939 at Sutton Hoo in England. Such customs are a far cry from traditional Christian burial. A monk may have composed *Beowulf,* but the persistence of this burial practice indicates that conversion was still imperfect in much of Europe.

Reading *Beowulf,* one enters a world of darkness, cold, gloom, and pessimism, pierced by a weak ray of Christian hope. It is the foremost expression of the psychological complexities and spiritual contradictions of what has been called the heroic age of Scandinavia—the eighth and ninth centuries.

The physical circumstances of life in the seventh and eighth centuries make Northumbrian cultural achievements all the more remarkable. Learning was pursued under terribly primitive conditions. Monasteries such as Jarrow and Lindisfarne stood on the very fringes of the European world. The bar-barian Picts, just an afternoon's walk from Jarrow, were likely to attack at any time.

Food was not the greatest problem. The North Sea and nearby rivers, the Tweed and the Tyne, yielded abundant salmon and other fish, which could be salted or smoked for winter, a nutritious if monotonous diet. Climate was another matter. Winter could be extremely harsh. In 664, for example, deep snow was hardened by frost from early winter until mid-spring. When it melted away, many animals, trees, and plants were found dead. To make matters worse, disease could take terrible tolls. Bede described events in the year 664:

In the same year of our Lord 664 there was an eclipse of the sun on the third day of May at about four o'clock in the afternoon. Also in that year a sudden pestilence first depopulated the southern parts of Britain and then attacked the kingdom of the Northumbrians as well. Raging far and wide for a long time with cruel devastation it struck down a great multitude of men. . . . This same plague oppressed the island of Ireland with equal destruction.[11]

Damp cold with bitter winds blowing across the North Sea must have pierced everything, even stone monasteries. Inside, only one room, the *calefactory* or "warming room," had a fire. Scribes in the *scriptorium,* or "writing room," had to stop frequently to rub circulation back into their numb hands. These monk-artists and monk-writers paid a high physical price for what they gave to posterity.

Had they remained entirely insular, Northumbrian cultural achievements would have been of slight significance. As it happened, an Englishman from Northumbria played a decisive role in the transmission of English learning to the Carolingian Empire and continental Europe.

The Carolingian Renaissance

Charlemagne's empire disintegrated shortly after his death in 814. But the support he gave to education and learning preserved the writings of the ancients and laid the foundations for all subsequent medieval culture. Charlemagne promoted a revival that scholars have named the "Carolingian Renaissance."

At his court at Aachen, Charlemagne assembled learned men from all over Europe. The most important scholar and the leader of the palace school was the Northumbrian Alcuin (ca 735–804). From 781 until his death, Alcuin was the emperor's chief adviser on religious and educational matters. An unusually prolific scholar, Alcuin prepared some of the emperor's official documents and wrote many moral *exempla,* or "models," which set high standards for royal behavior and constitute a treatise on kingship. Alcuin's letters to Charlemagne set forth political theories on the authority, power, and responsibilities of a Christian ruler.

Aside from Alcuin's literary efforts, what did the scholars at Charlemagne's court do? They copied books and manuscripts and built up libraries. They used the beautifully clear handwriting known as "Carolingian minuscule," from which modern Roman type is derived. (This script is called "minuscule" because it has lower-case letters; the Romans had only capitals.) They established schools all across Europe, attaching them to monasteries and cathedrals. They placed great emphasis on the education of priests, trying to make all priests at least able to read, write, and do simple arithmetic. The greatest contribution of the scholars at Aachen was not so much the originality of their ideas as their hard work of salvaging and preserving the thought and writings of the ancients. Thus the Carolingian Renaissance was a rebirth of interest in, study of, and preservation of the ideas and achievements of classical Greece and Rome.

The revival of learning inspired by Charlemagne and directed by Alcuin helped to limit the dangers of illiteracy on the European continent. Although hardly widespread by later standards, basic literacy was established among the clergy and even among some of the nobility. The small group of scholars at Aachen preserved Latin culture from total extinction in the West.

Although the scholars worked with Latin, the common people spoke their local or vernacular languages. The Bretons, for example, retained their local dialect; and the Saxons and Bavarians could not understand each other (see Map 8.1). Communication among the diverse peoples of the Carolingian Empire was possible only through the medium of Latin.

Once basic literacy was established, monastic and other scholars went on to more difficult work. By the middle years of the ninth century, there was a great outpouring of more sophisticated books. Ecclesiastical writers, imbued with the legal ideas of ancient Rome and the theocratic ideals of Saint Augustine, instructed the semibarbaric rulers of the

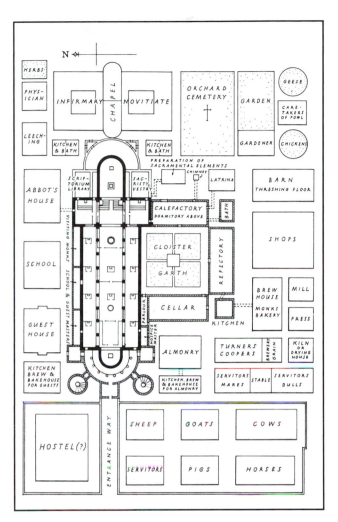

Plan for an Ideal Monastery This is a ninth-century architectural design for a self-supporting monastic community of two hundred and seventy members. The monks' lives mainly focused on the church and the cloister, which appropriately appear in the center of the plan. Note the herb garden close to the physician's quarters. The western entrance for visitors was surrounded by the hostel for poor guests and pens for farm animals—with all the inevitable smells. *(Source: Kenneth John Conant,* Carolingian and Romanesque Architecture, 800–1200. Pelican History of Art, *2nd rev. ed. New York: Pelican, 1978, p. 57)*

West. And it is no accident that medical study in the West began, at Salerno in southern Italy, in the late ninth century, *after* the Carolingian Renaissance.

Alcuin completed the work of his countryman Boniface—the Christianization of northern Europe. Latin Christian attitudes penetrated deeply into the consciousness of European peoples. By the tenth century, the patterns of thought and lifestyles of educated western Europeans were those of Rome and Latin Christianity. Even the violence and destruction of the great invasions of the late ninth and tenth centuries could not destroy the strong foundations laid by Alcuin and his colleagues.

HEALTH AND MEDICAL CARE IN THE EARLY MIDDLE AGES

Scholars' examination of medical treatises, prescription (or herbal) books, manuscript illustrations, and archeological evidence has recently revealed a surprising amount of information about medical treatment in the early Middle Ages. In a society devoted to fighting, warriors and civilians alike stood a strong chance of wounds from sword, spear, battle-ax, or blunt instrument. Trying to eke a living from poor soil with poor tools, perpetually involved in pushing back forest and wasteland, the farmer and his family daily ran the risk of accidents. Poor diet weakened everyone's resistance to disease. People bathed rarely. Low standards of personal hygiene increased the danger of infection. This being the case, what medical attention was available to medieval people?

The Germanic peoples had no rational understanding of the causes and cures of disease. They believed that sickness was due to one of three factors: elf-shot, in which elves hurled darts that produced disease and pain; wormlike creatures in the body; and the number 9. Treatments included charms, amulets, priestly incantations, and potions. Drinks prepared from mistletoe, for example, were thought to serve as an antidote to poison and to make women fertile.

Medical practice consisted primarily of drug and prescription therapy. Through the monks' efforts and recovery of Greek and Arabic manuscripts, a large body of the ancients' prescriptions was preserved and passed on. For almost any ailment, several recipes were likely to exist in the prescription lists. Balsam was recommended for coughs. For asthma, an ointment combining chicken, wormwood, laurel berries, and oil of roses was to be rubbed on the chest. The scores of prescriptions to rid the body of lice, fleas, and other filth reflect

frightful standards of personal hygiene. The large number of prescriptions for eye troubles suggests that they, too, must have been common. This is understandable, given the widespread practice of locating the fireplace in the center of the room. A lot of smoke and soot filtered into the room, rather than going up the chimney. One remedy calls for bathing the eyes in a solution of herbs mixed with honey, balsam, rainwater, salt water, or wine.

Poor diet caused frequent stomach disorders and related ailments such as dysentery, constipation, and diarrhea. The value of dieting and avoiding greasy foods was recognized. For poor circulation, a potion of meadow wort, oak rind, and lustmock was recommended. Pregnant women were advised to abstain from eating the flesh of almost all male animals, because such meat might deform the child. Men with unusually strong sexual appetites were advised to fast and to drink at night the juice of agrimony (an herb of the rose family) boiled in ale. If a man suffered from lack of drive, the same plant boiled in milk gave him "courage."

Physicians were not concerned with the treatment of specific illnesses. They did not examine patients. Physicians or "leeches," as they were known in Anglo-Saxon England, treated only what they could see or deduce from obvious symptoms. Physicians knew little about the pathology of disease or physiological functions. They knew little of internal medicine. They had no accurate standards of weights and measures. Prescriptions called for "a pinch of" or "a handful" or "an eggshell full."

All wounds and open injuries invited infection, and infection invited gangrene. Several remedies were known for wounds. Physicians appreciated the antiseptic properties of honey, and prescriptions recommended that wounds be cleaned with it. When an area or limb had become gangrenous, a good technique of amputation existed. The physician was instructed to cut above the diseased flesh—that is, to cut away some healthy tissue and bone—in order to hasten cure. The juice of white poppy plants—the source of heroin—could be added to wine and drunk as an anesthetic. White poppies, however, grew only in southern Europe and North Africa. If a heavy slug of wine was not enough to dull the patient, he or she had to be held down forcibly while the physician cut. Egg whites, which have a soothing effect, were prescribed for burns.

Teeth survive long periods of burial and give reasonably good information about disease. Evidence from early medieval England shows that the incidence of tooth decay was very low. In the adult population, the rate of cavities was only one-sixth that of today. Cavities below the gum line, however, were very common, because of the prevalence of carbohydrates in the diet. The result was abscesses of the gums. These and other forms of periodontal disease were widespread after the age of thirty.[12]

The spread of Christianity in the Carolingian era had a beneficial effect on medical knowledge and treatment. Several of the church fathers expressed serious interest in medicine. Some of them even knew something about it. The church was deeply concerned about human suffering, whether physical or mental. Christian teaching vigorously supported concern for the poor, sick, downtrodden, and miserable. Churchmen taught that, while all knowledge came from God, he had supplied it so that people could use it for their own benefit.

In the period of the bloodiest violence, the sixth and seventh centuries, medical treatment was provided by monasteries. No other places offered the calm, quiet atmosphere necessary for treatment and recuperation. Monks took care of the sick. They collected and translated the ancient medical treatises. They cultivated herb gardens from which medicines were prepared.

The foundation of a school at Salerno in southern Italy sometime in the ninth century gave a tremendous impetus to medical study by lay people. The school's location attracted Arabic, Greek, and Jewish physicians from all over the Mediterranean region. Students flocked there from northern Europe. The Jewish physician Shabbathai Ben Abraham (931–982) left behind pharmacological notes that were widely studied in later centuries.

By the eleventh century, the medical school at Salerno enjoyed international fame. Its most distinguished professor then was Constantine the African, a native of Carthage who had studied medicine throughout the Middle East. Because of his thorough knowledge of Oriental languages, he served as an important transmitter of Arabic culture to the West. Constantine taught and practiced medicine at Salerno for some years before becoming a monk at Monte Cassino.

Several women physicians also contributed to the celebrity of the school. Trotula, an authority on gynecological problems, wrote a book called *On Female Disorders.* Though not connected with the Salerno medical school, the abbess Hildegard (1098–1179) of Rupertsberg in Hesse, Germany, reputedly treated the emperor Frederick Barbarossa. Hildegard's treatise *Physica* shows a remarkable degree of careful scientific observation.

How available was medical treatment? Most people lived on isolated rural estates and had to take such advice and help as was available locally. Physicians were few in the early Middle Ages. They charged a fee that only the rich could afford. Apparently, most illnesses simply took their course.

The Wound Man This illustration from a fifteenth-century manuscript depicts a "wound man" displaying weapons, sources of injuries, and sores. It may have been used to prompt the aspiring surgeon's memory. *(Source: Courtesy, The Wellcome Institute)*

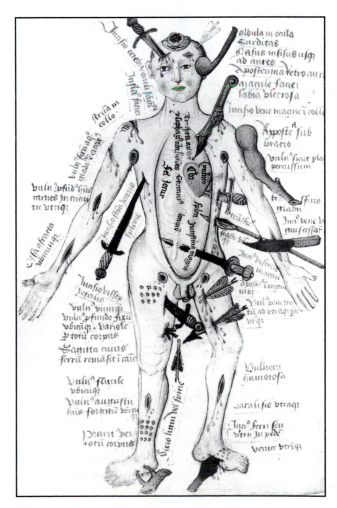

Trotula Famous for her treatise on obstetrics, Trotula was also the most renowned woman teacher at the medical school at Salerno. In this illustration for a twelfth-century manuscript, she holds an orb in her left hand, suggesting that she is ''empress'' of midwives, while instructing with her right hand and pointed finger. *(Source: Courtesy, Wellcome Institute)*

People had to develop a stoical attitude. Death came early. A person of forty was considered old. People's vulnerability to ailments for which there was no probable cure contributed to a fatalistic acceptance of death at an early age. Early medical literature shows that attempts to relieve pain were crude; still, attempts *were* made.

DIVISION AND DISINTEGRATION OF THE CAROLINGIAN EMPIRE (814–987)

Charlemagne left his vast empire to his only surviving son, Louis the Pious (814–840), who had actually been crowned emperor in his father's lifetime. Deeply religious he was, and well educated, but Louis was no soldier. Thus he could not retain the respect and loyalty of the warrior-aristocracy on whom he depended for troops and for administration of his territories. Disintegration began almost at once.

The basic reason for the collapse of the Carolingian Empire is simply that it was too big. Bad roads swarming with thugs and rivers infested with pirates made communication within the empire very difficult. In Charlemagne's lifetime the empire was held together by the sheer force of his personality and driving energy. After his death, it began to fall apart. The empire lacked a bureaucracy like that of the Roman Empire—the administrative machinery necessary for strong and enduring government. It was a collection of tribes held together at the pleasure of warrior-aristocrats, men most interested in strengthening their own local positions and ensuring that they could pass on to their sons the offices and estates they had amassed. Counts, abbots, bishops—both lay and ecclesiastical magnates needed estates to support themselves and reward their followers. In their localities, they simply assumed judicial, military, and financial functions. Why should they obey an unimpressive distant ruler who represented a centralizing power that threatened their local interests? What counted was strength in one's own region and the preservation of family holdings.

The Frankish custom of dividing estates among all male heirs hastened the empire's disintegration. Between 817 and his death in 840, Louis the Pious made several divisions of the empire. Dissatisfied with their portions and anxious to gain the imperial title, Louis's sons—Lothair, Louis the German, and Charles the Bald—fought bitterly among themselves. Finally, in the Treaty of Verdun of 843, the brothers agreed to partition the empire (Map 8.2).

Lothair, the eldest, received the now-empty title of emperor and the "middle kingdom," which included Italy and the territories bordered by the Meuse, Saône, and Rhône rivers in the west and the

Rhine in the east. Almost immediately, this kingdom broke up into many petty principalities extending diagonally across Europe from Flanders to Lombardy. From the tenth century to the twelfth and thirteenth centuries, when French and German monarchs were trying to build strong central governments, this area was constantly contested among them. Even in modern times, the "middle kingdom" of Lothair has been blood-soaked.

The eastern and most Germanic part of the Carolingian Empire passed to Louis the German. The western kingdom went to Charles the Bald; it included the provinces of Aquitaine and Gascony and formed the basis of medieval and modern France. The descendants of Charles the Bald held on in the west until 987, when the leading magnates elected Hugh Capet as king. The heirs of Louis the German ruled the eastern kingdom until 911, but real power was in the hands of local chieftains. Everywhere in the tenth century, fratricidal warfare among the descendants of Charlemagne accelerated the spread of feudalism.

FEUDALISM

The adjective *feudal* is often used disparagingly today to describe something antiquated and barbaric. It is similarly commonplace to think of medieval feudalism as a system that let a small group of lazy military leaders exploit the producing class, the tillers of the soil. This is not a very useful approach. Preindustrial societies from ancient Greece to the American South before the Civil War to some twentieth-century Latin American countries have been characterized by sharp divisions between "exploiters" and "exploited." To call all such societies "feudal" strips the term of significant meaning and distorts our understanding of medieval feudalism. Many twentieth-century scholars have demonstrated that, when feudalism developed, it served the needs of medieval society.

The Two Levels of Feudalism

Webster's *Third New International Dictionary* defines *government* as "the officials collectively comprising the governing body of a political unit and constituting the organization as an active agency." Feudalism, which emerged in western Europe in the

MAP 8.2 Division of the Carolingian Empires, 843
The treaty of Verdun (843), which divided the empire among Charlemagne's grandsons, is frequently taken as the start of the separate development of Germany, France, and Italy. The "Middle Kingdom" of Lothair, however, lacking defensive borders and any political or linguistic unity, quickly broke up into numerous small territories.

ninth century, was a type of government "in which political power was treated as a private possession and was divided among a large number of lords."[13] This kind of government characterized most parts of western Europe from about 900 to 1300. Feudalism actually existed at two social levels: first, at the level of armed retainers who became knights; and second, at the level of royal officials, such as counts, who ruled great feudal principalities. A wide and deep gap in social standing and political function separated these social levels.

In the early eighth century, the Carolingian kings and other powerful men needed bodyguards and retainers, armed men who could fight effectively on horseback. The arrival in western Europe around this time of a Chinese technological invention, the stirrup, revolutionized warfare. The stirrup welded horse and rider into a powerful fighting unit. The stirrup made the rider's seat secure and bolstered human energy with animal power. While an unstirruped horseman could seldom impale an adversary, a rider in stirrups could utilize the galloping animal's force to strike and damage his enemy. Charles Martel recognized the potential of heavily armed and stirruped cavalry, and the invention increased his need for large numbers of retainers. Horses and armor were terribly expensive, and few could afford them. It also took considerable time to train an experienced cavalryman. The value of retainers increased.

Therefore, Charles Martel and other powerful men bound their retainers by oaths of loyalty and ceremonies of homage. Here is an oath of *fealty* (or faithfulness, fidelity) from the ninth century:

Thus shall one take the oath of fidelity:

By the Lord before whom this sanctuary [some religious place] is holy, I will to N. be true and faithful, and love all which he loves and shun all which he shuns, according to the laws of God and the order of the world. Nor will I ever with will or action, through word or deed, do anything which is unpleasing to him, on condition that he will hold to me as I shall deserve it, and that he will perform everything as it was in our agreement when I submitted myself to him and chose his will.[14]

Lords also tried to ensure the support of their retainers with gifts of weapons and jewelry. Some great lords gave their armed cavalrymen estates that produced income to maintain the retainer and his family. These retainers became known as *vassals,* from a Celtic term meaning "servant." Since knights were not involved in any governmental activity, and since only men who exercised political power were considered noble, knights were not

Commendation and Initiation Just as the spiritual power of priests is bequeathed by the laying of the priests' hands on the candidate's head at ordination, so the military virtues of strength and loyalty were conveyed to the warrior by the act of commendation when he placed his clasped hands between the hands of his lord. A kiss, symbolizing peace, often concluded the ceremony. *(Source: Universitätsbibliothek, Heidelberg)*

part of the noble class. Down to the eleventh century, political power was concentrated in the small group of counts.

Counts, descended from the old Frankish aristocracy (see page 232), constituted the second level of feudalism. Under Charles Martel and his heirs, counts monopolized the high offices in the Carolingian Empire. At the local level, they had full judicial, military, and financial power. They held courts that dispensed justice, collected taxes, and waged wars. For most ordinary people, the counts were the government. Charlemagne regularly sent missi to inspect the activities of the counts, but there was slight chance of a corrupt or wicked count being removed from office.

While countships were not hereditary in the eighth century, they tended to remain within the same family. In the eighth and early ninth centuries, regional concentrations of power depended on family connections and political influence at the king's court. The disintegration of the Carolingian Empire, however, served to increase the power of regional authorities. Civil wars weakened the power and prestige of kings, because there was little they could do about domestic violence. Likewise, the great invasions of the ninth century, especially the Viking invasions (see pages 250–253), weakened royal authority. The West Frankish kings could do little to halt the invaders, and the aristocracy had to assume responsibility for defense. Common people turned for protection to the strongest local power, the counts, whom they considered their rightful rulers. Thus, in the ninth and tenth centuries, great aristocratic families increased their authority in the regions of their vested interests. They governed virtually independent territories in which distant and weak kings could not interfere. "Political power had become a private, heritable property for great counts and lords."[15] This is what is meant by feudalism as a form of government.

Because feudal society was a military society, men held the dominant positions in it. A high premium was put on physical strength, fighting skill, and bravery. The legal and social position of women was not as insignificant as might be expected, however. Charters recording gifts to the church indicate that women held land in many areas. Women frequently endowed monasteries, churches, and other religious establishments. The possession of land obviously meant economic power. Moreover, women inherited fiefs, or landed

estates. In southern France and Catalonia in Spain, women inherited feudal property as early as the tenth century. Other kinds of evidence attest to women's status. In parts of northern France, children sometimes identified themselves in legal documents by their mother's name rather than their father's, indicating that the mother's social position in the community was higher than the father's.

In a treatise he wrote in 822 on the organization of the royal household, Archbishop Hincmar of Reims placed the queen directly above the treasurer. She was responsible for giving the knights their annual salaries. She supervised the manorial accounts. Thus, in the management of large households with many knights to oversee and complicated manorial records to supervise, the lady of the manor had highly important responsibilities. With such responsibility went power and influence.[16]

Manorialism

Feudalism concerned the rights, powers, and lifestyle of the military elite; *manorialism* involved the services and obligations of the peasant classes. The economic power of the warring class rested on landed estates, which were worked by peasants. Hence feudalism and manorialism were inextricably linked. Peasants needed protection, and lords demanded something in return for that protection. Free peasants surrendered themselves and their lands to the lord's jurisdiction. The land was given back, but the peasants became tied to the land by various kinds of payments and services. In France, England, Germany, and Italy, local custom determined precisely what those services were, but certain practices became common everywhere. The peasant was obliged to turn over to the lord a percentage of the annual harvest, usually in produce, sometimes in cash. The peasant paid a fee to marry someone from outside the lord's estate. To inherit property the peasant paid a fine, often the best beast the person owned. Above all, the peasant became part of the lord's permanent labor force. With vast stretches of uncultivated virgin land and a tiny labor population, lords encouraged population growth and immigration. The most profitable form of capital was not land but laborers.

In entering into a relationship with a feudal lord, free farmers lost status. Their position became servile, and they became *serfs*. That is, they were bound to the land and could not leave it without the lord's permission. They were also subject to the jurisdiction of the lord's court in any dispute over property and in any case of suspected criminal behavior.

The transition from freedom to serfdom was slow; its speed was closely related to the degree of political order in a given region. Even in the late eighth century, there were still many free peasants. And within the legal category of serfdom there were many economic levels, ranging from the highly prosperous to the desperately poor. Nevertheless, a social and legal revolution was taking place. By the year 800, perhaps 60 percent of the population of western Europe—completely free a century before—had been reduced to serfdom. The ninth-century Viking assaults on Europe created extremely unstable conditions and individual insecurity, leading to additional loss of personal freedom. Chapter 10 will detail the lives of the peasants. As it will show, the later Middle Ages witnessed considerable upward social mobility.

Scandinavian Sword Hilt   (late sixth century) Scandinavian artists attained a high level of achievement in the zoomorphic (or animal) style, though the animals are not recognizable in this fine example of metalwork. The Scandinavians later learned to work in wood and leather from Merovingian, Northumbrian, and Irish artists, but few examples of these techniques survive. *(Source: University Museum of National Antiquities, Oslo)*

GREAT INVASIONS OF THE NINTH CENTURY

After the Treaty of Verdun and the division of Charlemagne's empire among his grandsons, continental Europe presented an easy target for foreign invaders. All three kingdoms were torn by domestic dissension and disorder. No European political power was strong enough to put up effective resistance to external attacks. The frontier and coastal defenses erected by Charlemagne and maintained by Louis the Pious were completely neglected.

From the moors of Scotland to the mountains of Sicily, there arose in the ninth century the Christian prayer, "Save us, O God, from the violence of the Northmen." The Northmen, also known as Normans or Vikings, were Germanic peoples from Norway, Sweden, and Denmark who had remained beyond the sway of the Christianizing and civilizing influences of the Carolingian Empire. Some scholars believe that the name "Viking" derives from the Old Norse word *vik,* meaning "creek." A *Viking,* then, was a pirate who waited in a creek or bay to attack passing vessels.

Charlemagne had established marches, fortresses, and watchtowers along his northern coasts to defend his territory against Viking raids. Their assaults began around 787, and by the mid-tenth century they had brought large chunks of continental Europe and Britain under their sway. In the east they pierced the rivers of Russia as far as the Black Sea (Map 8.3). In the west they sailed as far as Iceland, Greenland, and even the coast of North America, perhaps as far south as Long Island Sound, New York.

The Vikings were superb seamen. Their advanced methods of boatbuilding gave them great speed and maneuverability. Propelled either by oars or by sails, deckless, about 65 feet long, a Viking

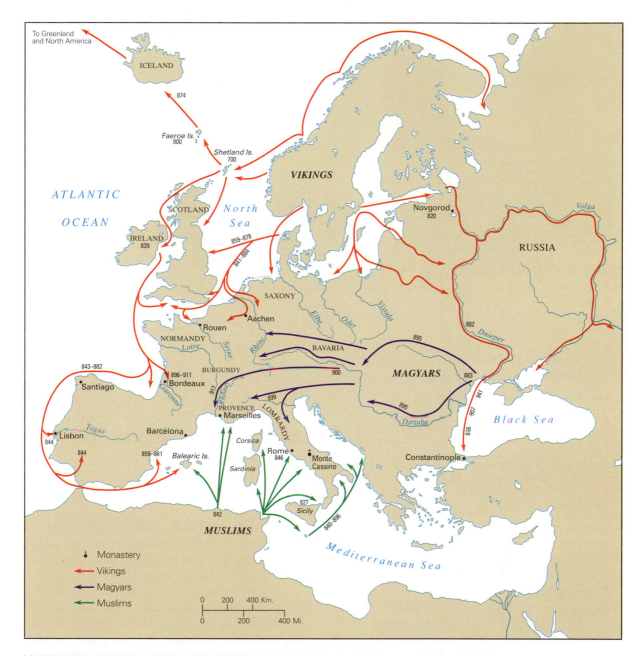

MAP 8.3 The Great Invasions of the Ninth Century   Note the Viking penetration of eastern Europe and their probable expeditions to North America. What impact did their various invasions have on European society?

ship could carry between 40 and 60 men—quite enough to harass an isolated monastery or village. These ships, navigated by thoroughly experienced and utterly fearless sailors, moved through the most complicated rivers, estuaries, and waterways in Europe. The Carolingian Empire, with no navy and no notion of the importance of sea power, was helpless. The Vikings moved swiftly, attacked, and escaped to return again.

Scholars disagree about the reasons for Viking attacks and migrations. Some maintain that overpopulation forced the Vikings to emigrate. Others argue that climatic conditions and crop failures forced migration. Still others insist that the Vikings

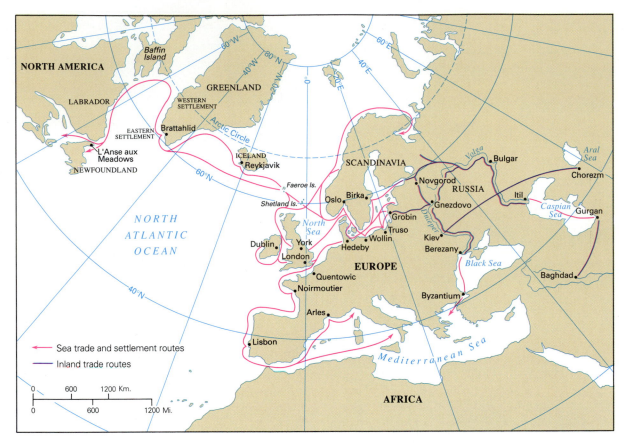

MAP 8.4 Viking Settlement and Trade Routes   Viking trade and settlements extended from Newfoundland and Greenland to deep in Russia.

were looking for trade and new commercial contacts. What better targets for plunder, for example, than the mercantile centers of northern France and Frisia?

Plunder they did. Viking attacks were bitterly savage. At first they attacked and sailed off laden with booty. Later, on returning, they settled down and colonized the areas they had conquered (Map 8.4). Between 876 and 954, Viking control extended from Dublin across the Irish Sea to Britain, across northern Britain between the Dee and the Solway, and then across the North Sea to the Vikings' Scandinavian homelands. These invaders also overran a large part of northwestern France and called the territory "Norsemanland," from which the word *Normandy* derives.

Scarcely had the savagery of the Viking assaults begun to subside when Europe was hit from the east and south. Beginning about 890, Magyar tribes crossed the Danube and pushed steadily westward. (Since people thought of them as return-

ing Huns, the Magyars came to be known as "Hungarians.") They subdued northern Italy, compelled Bavaria and Saxony to pay tribute, and penetrated even into the Rhineland and Burgundy. These roving bandits attacked isolated villages and monasteries, taking prisoners and selling them in the Eastern slave markets. The Magyars were not colonizers; their sole object was booty and plunder.

The Vikings and Magyars depended on fear. In their initial attacks on isolated settlements, many people were put to the sword. The Vikings also seized thousands of captives as slaves from all the countries where their power reached. From the British Isles and territories along the Baltic, the Vikings took *thralls* (slaves) for the markets of Magdeburg on the Elbe River and Regensburg in Bavaria on the Danube, for the fairs of Lyons on the Rhône River, and to supply the huge demand for slaves in the Muslim world. The slave trade represented an important part of Viking commerce. The Icelander Hoskuld Dala-Kolsson of Laxardal paid three marks of silver, three times the price of a common concubine, for a pretty Irish girl; she was one of twelve offered by a Viking trader. No wonder many communities bought peace by paying tribute.

From the south the Muslims also began new encroachments, concentrating on the two southern peninsulas, Italy and Spain. Their goal, too, was plunder. In Italy the monks of Monte Cassino were forced to flee. The Muslims drove northward and sacked Rome in 846. Most of Spain had remained under their domination since the eighth century (see page 225). Expert seamen, they sailed around the Iberian Peninsula, braved the notoriously dangerous shoals and winds of the Atlantic coast, and also attacked the Mediterranean settlements along the coast of Provence. But Muslim attacks on the European continent in the ninth and tenth centuries were less destructive than the Viking and Magyar assaults. Compared to the rich, sophisticated culture of the Arab capitals, northern Europe was primitive, backward, and offered little.

What was the effect of these invasions on the structure of European society? Viking, Magyar, and Muslim attacks accelerated the development of feudalism. Lords capable of rallying fighting men, supporting them, and putting up resistance to the invaders did so. They also assumed political power in their territories. Weak and defenseless people sought the protection of local strongmen. Free peasants sank to the level of serfs. Consequently, European society became further fragmented. Public power became increasingly decentralized.

The ninth-century invaders also left significant traces of their own cultures. As discussed in Chapter 7, the Muslims made an important contribution to European agriculture, primarily through their influence in Spain (see page 225). The Vikings, too, made positive contributions to the areas they settled. They carried everywhere their unrivaled knowledge of shipbuilding and seamanship. The northeastern and central parts of England where the Vikings settled became known as the *Danelaw* because Danish law and customs, not English, prevailed there. Scholars believe that some legal institutions, such as the ancestor of the modern grand jury, originated in the Danelaw. York in northern England, once a Roman army camp and then an Anglo-Saxon town, became a thriving center of Viking trade with Scandinavia. At Dublin on the east coast of Ireland, Viking iron and steel workers and comb makers established a center for

Vikings Invade Britain   In this twelfth-century representation of the Viking invasions, warriors appear to be armed with helmets, spears, and shields. Crossing the rough North Sea and English Channel in open, oar-propelled boats, they had great courage. *(Source: The Pierpont Morgan Library)*

trade with the Hebrides, Iceland, and Norway. The Irish cities of Limerick, Cork, Wexford, and Waterford trace their origins to Viking trading centers.

SUMMARY

Building on the military and diplomatic foundations of his ancestors, Charlemagne waged constant warfare to expand his kingdom. His wars with the Saxons in northwestern Germany and with the

Europe Through the Early Middle Ages

	Government and Law	Economics
300	Constantine removes capital of Roman Empire to Constantinople, ca 315	Growth of serfdom in Roman Empire, ca 200–500
	Huns defeat the Ostrogoths, ca 370	Economic contraction in Roman Empire, 3rd c.
	Bishop Ambrose refuses to yield cathedral church of Milan to Theodosius, thereby asserting church's independence from state, 380	
	Germanic raids of Western Europe, 5th c.	
	Death of Roman emperor Romulus Augustus signals end of empire in the West, 476	
	Clovis issues Salic Law of the Franks, ca 490	
500	Law Code of Justinian, 529	Decline of towns and trade in the West, ca 500–700
	Dooms of Ethelbert, ca 602	
	Spread of Islam across Arabia, southern Europe, Africa, and Asia as far as India, ca 630–733	
700	Charles Martel defeats Muslims at Battle of Tours, 733	Height of Islamic commerce and industry, ca 700–1300
	Pippin III anointed king of the Franks, 754	Agrarian economy predominates in the West, ca 700–1050
	Charlemagne succeeds to the Frankish crown, r. 768–814	
	Charlemagne's territorial gains, 768–805	
800	Imperial coronation of Charlemagne, 800	Height of Byzantine commerce and industry, ca 800–1000
	Treaty of Verdun, 843	
	Viking, Magyar, and Muslim invasions complete disintegration of Carolingian Empire, ca 845–900	

Religion	Culture
Constantine legalizes Christianity, 312	St. Augustine, *The Confessions,* ca 390
Theodosius recognizes Christianity as official imperial religion, 380	Byzantine Greeks preserve Greco-Roman heritage, ca 400–788
Donatist heretical movement reaches its height, ca 400	
Clovis adopts Roman Christianity, 496	
Rule of Saint Benedict, 529	Byzantine church of Santa Sophia, 532–537
Monasteries established throughout Anglo-Saxon England, 7th c.	
Muhammad preaches reform, ca 610	
Publication of Qur'an, 651	
Synod of Whitby, 664	
Missionary work of St. Boniface in Germany, ca 710–750	Lindisfarne Gospel, ca 700
Iconoclasm in Byzantine Empire, 726–843	Bede, *Ecclesiastical History of the English Nation,* ca 700
Pippin III donates Papal States to the papacy, 756	*Beowulf,* ca 700
Foundation of Cluny, 909	Carolingian Renaissance, ca 800–850
Byzantine conversion of Russia, late 10th c.	Byzantines develop Cyrillic script, late 10th c.

Lombards in northern Italy proved successful, and his kingdom ultimately included most of continental Europe. He governed this vast territory through a military elite, the Frankish counts who exercised political, economic, and judicial authority at the local level.

The culture that emerged in Europe between 733 and 843 has justifiably been called the "first" European civilization. That civilization had definite characteristics: it was Christian, feudal, and infused with Latin ideas and models. Almost all people were baptized Christians. Latin was the common language—written as well as spoken—of educated people everywhere. This culture resulted from the mutual cooperation of civil and ecclesiastical authorities. Kings and church leaders supported each others' goals and utilized each others' prestige and power. Kings encouraged preaching and publicized church doctrines, such as the stress on monogamous marriage. In return, church officials urged obedience to royal authority. The support that Charlemagne gave to education and learning, the intellectual movement known as the Carolingian Renaissance, proved his most enduring legacy.

The enormous size of Charlemagne's empire, its lack of viable administrative institutions, the domestic squabbles among his descendants, and the invasions of the Vikings, Magyars, and Muslims—these factors all contributed to the empire's disintegration. As the empire broke down, a new form of decentralized government, later known as feudalism, emerged. In a feudal society public and political power was held by a small group of military leaders. No civil or religious authority could maintain stable government over a very wide area. Local strongmen provided what little security existed. Commerce and long-distance trade were drastically reduced. Because of their agricultural and commercial impact, the Viking and Muslim invaders represent the most dynamic and creative forces of the period.

NOTES

1. For the date of this battle, October 17, 733, see L. White, *Medieval Technology and Social Change* (Oxford: Clarendon Press, 1962), pp. 3 n. 3, 12.
2. See F. Irsigler, "On the Aristocratic Character of Early Frankish Society," in *The Medieval Nobility: Studies on the Ruling Class of France and Germany from the Sixth to the Twelfth Century,* ed. and trans. T. Reuter (New York: North-Holland, 1978), pp. 105–136, esp. p. 123.
3. Einhard, *The Life of Charlemagne,* with a Foreword by S. Painter (Ann Arbor: University of Michigan Press, 1960), pp. 50–51.
4. P. Stafford, *Queens, Concubines, and Dowagers: The King's Wife in the Early Middle Ages* (Athens: University of Georgia Press, 1983), pp. 60–62.
5. See K. F. Werner, "Important Noble Families in the Kingdom of Charlemagne," in Reuter, pp. 174–184.
6. B. D. Hill, ed., *Church and State in the Middle Ages* (New York: John Wiley & Sons, 1970), pp. 46–47.
7. P. Geary, "Carolingians and the Carolingian Empire," in *Dictionary of the Middle Ages,* vol. 3, ed. J. R. Strayer (New York: Charles Scribner's Sons, 1983), p. 110.
8. J. Nicholson, "Feminae Gloriosae: Women in the Age of Bede," in *Medieval Women,* ed. D. Baker (Oxford: Basil Blackwell, 1978), pp. 15–31, esp. p. 19, and C. Fell, *Women in Anglo-Saxon England and the Impact of 1066* (Bloomington: Indiana University Press, 1984), p. 109.
9. R. W. Southern, *Medieval Humanism and Other Studies* (Oxford: Basil Blackwell, 1970), p. 3.
10. D. Wright, trans., *Beowulf* (Baltimore: Penguin Books, 1957), pp. 9–19.
11. L. Sherley-Price, trans., *Bede: A History of the English Church and People* (Baltimore: Penguin Books, 1962), bk. 3, chap. 27, p. 191.
12. See S. Rubin, *Medieval English Medicine* (New York: Barnes & Noble, 1974).
13. J. R. Strayer, "The Two Levels of Feudalism," in *Medieval Statecraft and the Perspectives of History* (Princeton, N.J.: Princeton University Press, 1971), p. 63. This section leans heavily on this seminal study.
14. E. P. Cheney, trans., in *University of Pennsylvania Translations and Reprints,* vol. 4 (Philadelphia: University of Pennsylvania Press, 1898), no. 3, p. 3.
15. Strayer, "The Two Levels," pp. 65–76, esp. p. 71.
16. See D. Herlihy, "Land, Family, and Women in Continental Europe, 701–1200," in *Women in Medieval Society,* ed. S. M. Stuart (Philadelphia: University of Pennsylvania Press, 1976), pp. 13–45.

SUGGESTED READING

A good general introduction to the entire period is "Part III: Formation of Medieval Christendom: Its Rise and Decline," in C. Dawson, *The Formation of Christendom* (1967). The same author's *Religion and the Rise of Western Culture* (1958) emphasizes the religious bases of Western culture. C. H. Talbot, ed., *The Anglo-Saxon Missionaries in Germany* (1954), gives an exciting picture, through biographies and correspondence, of the organization and development of the Christian church in the Carolingian Empire. Chapters 4, 5, and 6 of J. B. Russell, *A History of Medieval Christianity: Prophesy and Order* (1968), describe the mind of the Christian church and how it gradually had an impact on pagan Germanic peoples. The monumental work of F. Kempf et al., *The Church in the Age of Feudalism* (trans. A. Biggs, 1980), Vol. 3 of the History of the Church series, edited by H. Jedin and J. Dolan, contains a thorough treatment of the institutional church in both East and West based on the latest scholarship; this book is primarily for scholars. Significant aspects of spirituality are traced in B. McGinn and J. Meyendorff, eds., *Christian Spirituality: From the Apostolic Fathers to the Twelfth Century* (1985).

Einhard's *Life of Charlemagne,* cited in the Notes, is a good starting point for study of the great chieftain. The best general biography of Charlemagne is D. Bullough, *The Age of Charlemagne* (1965). P. Riche, *Daily Life in the World of Charlemagne* (trans. J. McNamara, 1978), is a richly detailed study of many facets of Carolingian society by a distinguished authority. The same scholar's *Education and Culture in the Barbarian West: From the Sixth Through the Eighth Century* (trans. J. J. Contreni, 1976) provides an excellent, if technical, treatment of Carolingian intellectual activity. Both volumes contain solid bibliographies. For agricultural and economic life, G. Duby, *The Early Growth of the European Economy: Warriors and Peasants from the Seventh to the Twelfth Century* (1978), relates economic behavior to other aspects of human experience in a thoroughly readable style. The importance of technological developments in the Carolingian period is described by L. White, *Medieval Technology and Social Change* (1962), now a classic work. For the meaning of war to the Merovingian and Carolingian kings, see J. M. Wallace-Hadrill, "War and Peace in the Early Middle Ages," in *Early Medieval History* (1975). As the title implies, G. Barraclough, *The Crucible of Europe: The Ninth and Tenth Centuries in European History* (1976), sees those centuries as crucial in the formation of European civilization. E. James, *The Origins of France: From Clovis to the Capetians, 500–1000* (1982), is a solid introductory survey of early French history, with emphasis on family relationships.

In addition to the references to Bede and *Beowulf* in the Notes, D. L. Sayers, trans., *The Song of Roland* (1957), provides an excellent key, in epic form, to the values and lifestyles of the feudal classes. For the eighth-century revival of learning, see W. Levison, *England and the Continent in the Eighth Century* (1946); M. L. W. Laistner, *Thought and Letters in Western Europe, 500–900* (1931); and the beautifully written evocation by P. H. Blair, *Northumbria in the Days of Bede* (1976). E. S. Duckett, *Alcuin, Friend of Charlemagne* (1951), makes light and enjoyable reading. L. Wallach, *Alcuin and Charlemagne,* rev. ed. (1968), is a technical study of Alcuin's treatises, for the advanced student. The best treatment of the theological and political ideas of the period is probably K. F. Morrison, *The Two Kingdoms: Ecclesiology in Carolingian Political Thought* (1964), a difficult book. Wallace-Hadrill's *Early Medieval History* also contains interesting essays on Bede, Boniface, Charlemagne, and England.

Those interested in the role of women and children in early medieval society should see the article by D. Herlihy cited in the Notes and another from the same volume: E. Coleman, "Infanticide in the Early Middle Ages." The best available study of women in this period is S. F. Wemple, *Women in Frankish Society: Marriage and the Cloister, 500 to 900* (1981).

The following studies are also important and useful: J. McNamara, "A Legacy of Miracles: Hagiography and Nunneries in Merovingian Gaul," in J. Kirshner and S. Wemple, eds., *Women of the Medieval World: Essays in Honor of John H. Mundy* (1985); Ann Warren, *Anchorites and Their Patrons in Medieval England* (1985); P. Stafford, *Queens, Concubines, and Dowagers: The King's Wife in the Early Middle Ages* (1983); and the book by C. Fell cited in the Notes.

For health and medical treatment, the curious student should consult W. H. McNeill, *Plagues and Peoples* (1976); A. Castiglioni, *A History of Medicine* (trans. E. B. Krumbhaar, 1941); S. Rubin's book cited in the Notes, esp. pp. 97–149; and the important article by J. M. Riddle, "Theory and Practice in Medieval Medicine," *Viator* 5 (1974): 157–184. Richer than the title might imply, J. C. Russell, *The Control of Late Ancient and Medieval Population* (1985), discusses diet, disease, and demography.

For feudalism and manorialism see, in addition to the references given in the Notes, F. L. Ganshof, *Feudalism* (1961), and J. R. Strayer, "Feudalism in Western Europe," in R. Coulborn, ed., *Feudalism in History* (1956). M. Bloch, *Feudal Society* (trans. L. A. Manyon, 1961), remains important. The more recent treatments of G. Duby, in the book mentioned earlier, and P. Anderson, *Passages from Antiquity to Feudalism* (1978), stress the evolution of social structures and mental attitudes. For the significance of the ceremony of vassalage, see J. Le Goff, "The Symbolic Ritual of Vassalage," in his *Time, Work, and Culture in the Middle Ages* (trans. A. Goldhammer, 1982), a collection of provocative but difficult essays that includes "The Peasants and the Rural World in the Literature of the Early Middle Ages." The best broad treatment of peasant life and conditions is G. Duby, *Rural Economy and Country Life in the Medieval West* (trans. C. Postan, 1968).

J. Brondsted, *The Vikings* (1960), is an excellently illustrated study of many facets of Viking culture. G. Jones, *A History of the Vikings,* rev. ed. (1984), provides a comprehensive survey of the Viking world based on the latest archeological findings and numismatic evidence.

9

Revival, Recovery, and Reform

By the last quarter of the tenth century, after a long and bitter winter of discontent, the first hints of European spring were appearing. The European springtime lasted from the middle of the eleventh century to the end of the thirteenth. This period from about 1050 to 1300 has often been called the "High Middle Ages." The term designates a time of crucial growth and remarkable cultural achievement between two eras of economic, political, and social crisis.

- What were the ingredients of revival, and how did they come about?
- What was the social and political impact of the recovery of Europe?
- How did the reform of the Christian church affect relations between the church and civil authorities?
- What were the Crusades, and how did they manifest the influence of the church and the ideals of medieval society?

These are the questions that will frame discussion in this chapter.

POLITICAL REVIVAL

The eleventh century witnessed the beginnings of political stability in western Europe. Foreign invasions gradually declined, and domestic disorder subsided. This development gave people security in their persons and property. Political order and security provided the foundation for economic recovery and contributed to a slow increase in population.

The Decline of Invasion and Civil Disorder

The most important factor in the revival of Europe after the disasters of the ninth century was the gradual decline in foreign invasions and the reduction of domestic violence. In France, for example, the Norwegian leader Rollo in 911 subdued large parts of what was later called Normandy. The West Frankish ruler Charles the Simple, unable to oust the Vikings, went along with that territorial conquest. He recognized Rollo as duke of Normandy on the condition that Rollo swear allegiance to him and hold the territory as a sort of barrier against future Viking assaults. This agreement, embodied in the Treaty of Saint-Clair-sur-Epte, marks the beginning of the rise of Normandy.

Rollo kept his word. He exerted strong authority over Normandy and in troubled times supported the weak Frankish king. Rollo and his soldiers were baptized as Christians. Although additional Viking settlers arrived, they were easily pacified. The tenth and eleventh centuries saw the steady assimilation of Normans and French. Major attacks on France had ended.

Rollo's descendant, Duke William I (r. 1035–1087), made feudalism work as a system of government. William attached specific quotas of knight service to the lands he distributed, executed vassals who defaulted on their obligations, and forbade the construction of private castles, always the symbol of feudal independence; he also limited private warfare. The duke controlled the currency and supervised the church by participating in the selection of bishops and abbots. By 1066, the year of the Norman invasion of England, the duchy of Normandy was the strongest and most peaceful territory in Europe.

The civil wars and foreign invasions of the ninth and tenth centuries left the territories we now call France divided into provinces and counties where local feudal lords held actual power. Following the death of the last Carolingian ruler in 987, an assembly of nobles met to choose a successor. Accepting the argument of the archbishop of Reims that the French monarchy was elective, the nobles selected Hugh Capet, head of a powerful clan in the West Frankish kingdom. The Capetian kings (so called from the "cope," or cloak, Hugh wore as abbot of Saint-Denis) subsequently saved France from further division. But this was hardly apparent in 987. Compared with the duke of Normandy, the first Capetians were weak; but by hanging on to what they had, they laid the foundations for later political stability.

Recovery followed a different pattern in Anglo-Saxon England. The Vikings had made a concerted effort to conquer and rule the whole island, and probably no part of Europe suffered more. Before the Viking invasions, England had never been united under a single ruler, and in 877 only parts of the kingdom of Wessex survived. The victory of the remarkable Alfred, king of the West Saxons (or

Wessex), over Guthrun the Dane at Edington in 878 inaugurated a great political revival. Alfred and his immediate successors built a system of local defenses and slowly extended royal rule beyond Wessex to other Anglo-Saxon peoples until one law, royal law, replaced local custom. Alfred and his successors also laid the foundations for an efficient system of local government responsible directly to the king. Under the pressure of the Vikings England was gradually united under one ruler.

In 1013 the Danish ruler Swen Forkbeard invaded England: his son Canute completed the subjugation of the island. King of England (1016–1035) and after 1030 king of Norway as well, Canute made England the center of his empire. Canute promoted a policy of assimilation and reconciliation between Anglo-Saxons and Vikings. Slowly the two peoples were molded together. The assimilation of Anglo-Saxon and Viking was personified by King Edward the Confessor (r. 1042–1066), the son of an Anglo-Saxon father and a Norman mother who had taken Canute as her second husband.

In the East, the German king Otto I (r. 936–973) inflicted a crushing defeat on the Hungarians at the banks of the Lech River in 955. This battle halted the Magyars' westward expansion and threat to Germany and made Otto a great hero to the Germans. It also signified the revival of the German monarchy and demonstrated that Otto was a worthy successor to Charlemagne.

When chosen king, Otto had selected Aachen as the site of his coronation to symbolize his intention to continue the tradition of Charlemagne. The basis of his power was to be alliance with and control of the church. Otto asserted the right to control ecclesiastical appointments. Before receiving religious consecration, bishops and abbots had to perform feudal homage for the lands that accompanied the church office. (This practice, later known as "lay investiture," was to create a grave crisis in the eleventh century [see pages 268–270].)

Otto realized that he had to use the financial and military resources of the church to halt feudal anarchy. He used the higher clergy extensively in his administration, and the bulk of his army came from monastic and other church lands. Between 936 and 955 Otto succeeded in breaking the territorial power of the great German dukes.

Some of our knowledge of Otto derives from *The Deeds of Otto*, a history of his reign in heroic verse

written by a nun, Hrotswitha of Gandersheim (ca 935–ca 1003). A learned poet, she also produced six verse plays, and she is considered the first dramatist after the fall of the ancient classical theater. Hrotswitha's literary productions give her an important place in the mainstream of tenth-century civilization.

Otto's coronation by the pope in 962 revived the imperial dignity and laid the foundation for what was later called the Holy Roman Empire. The coronation showed that Otto had the support of the church in Germany and Italy. The uniting of the kingship with the imperial crown advanced German interests. Otto filled a power vacuum in northern Italy and brought peace among the great

Christ Enthroned with Saints and the Emperor Otto I (tenth century) Between 933 and 973, Emperor Otto I founded the church of St. Mauritius in Magdeburg. As a memorial to the event, Otto commissioned the production of this ivory plaque showing Christ accepting a model of the church from the emperor. Ivory was a favorite medium of Ottonian artists, and squat figures in a simple geometrical pattern characterize their work. *(Source: The Metropolitan Museum of Art, Bequest of George Blumenthal, 1941 (41.100.157))*

aristocratic families. The level of order there improved for the first time in over a century. Peace and political stability in turn promoted the revival of northern Italian cities, such as Venice.

By the start of the eleventh century, the Italian maritime cities were seeking a place in the rich Mediterranean trade. Pisa and Genoa fought to break Muslim control of the trade and shipping with the Byzantine Empire and the Far East. Once the Muslim fleets had been destroyed, the Italian cities of Venice, Genoa, and Pisa embarked on the road to prosperity. The eleventh century witnessed their steadily rising strength and wealth. Freedom from invasion and domestic security made economic growth possible all over western Europe. In Spain, the *reconquista*—the Christian reconquest of the land from the Muslims—gained impetus.

Population, Climate, and Mechanization

A steady growth of population also contributed to Europe's general recovery. The decline of foreign invasions and internal civil disorder reduced the number of people killed and maimed. Feudal armies in the eleventh through thirteenth centuries continued their destruction, but they were very small by modern standards and fought few pitched battles. Most medieval conflicts consisted of sieges directed at castles or fortifications. As few as twelve men could defend a castle. With sufficient food and an adequate water supply, they could hold out for a long time. Monastic chroniclers, frequently bored and almost always writing from hearsay evidence, tended to romanticize medieval warfare (as long as it was not in their own neighborhoods). Most conflicts were petty skirmishes with slight loss of life. The survival of more young people—those most often involved in war and usually the most sexually active—meant a population rise.

Nor was there any "natural," or biological, hindrance to population expansion. Between the tenth and fourteenth centuries, Europe was not hit by any major plague or other medical scourge, though leprosy and malaria did strike down some people. Leprosy, caused by a virus, was not very contagious, and it worked slowly. Lepers presented a frightful appearance: the victim's arms and legs rotted away, and gangrenous sores emitted a horrible smell. Physicians had no cure. For these reasons, and because of the command in the thirteenth

chapter of Leviticus that lepers be isolated, medieval lepers were eventually segregated in hospitals called "leprosaria."

Malaria, spread by protozoa-carrying mosquitoes that infested swampy areas, caused problems primarily in Italy. Malaria is characterized by alternate chills and fevers and leaves the afflicted person extremely weak. Peter the Venerable, ninth abbot of Cluny (1122–1156), suffered in his later years from recurring bouts of malaria contracted on a youthful trip to Rome. Still, relatively few people caught malaria or leprosy. Crop failure and the ever-present danger of starvation were much more pressing threats.

The weather cooperated with the revival. Meteorologists believe that a slow but steady retreat of polar ice occurred between the ninth and eleventh centuries. A significant warming trend continued until about 1200. The century between 1080 and 1180 witnessed exceptionally clement weather in England, France, and Germany, with mild winters and dry summers. Good weather helps to explain advances in population growth, land reclamation, and agricultural yield. Increased agricultural output had a profound impact on society: it affected Europeans' health, commerce, industry, and general lifestyle.

The tenth and eleventh centuries also witnessed a remarkable spurt in mechanization, especially in the use of energy. The increase in the number of water mills was spectacular. The Romans had devised a vertical water wheel fitted with blades, "which drove the upper millstone through 90 degree gearing. The gearing permitted a much higher speed of rotation in the stones than in the wheels."[1] An ancient water mill unearthed near Monte Cassino could grind about 1.5 tons of grain in 10 hours, a quantity that would formerly have required the exertions of 40 slaves. The abundance of slave labor in the ancient world had retarded the development of mills, but by the mid-ninth century, on the lands of the abbey of Saint-Germain-des-Prés near Paris, there were 59 water mills. Succeeding generations saw a continued increase. Thus, on the Robec River near Rouen, there were 2 mills in the tenth century, 4 in the eleventh century, 10 in the thirteenth, and 12 in the fourteenth century. *Domesday Book,* William the Conqueror's great survey of English economic resources in the late eleventh century (see page 314), recorded 5,624 water mills. Of the 9,250 manors in England

Arabic Water Mill   Land irrigation, essential to the growth of an agricultural economy, was greatly advanced by Arab inventions such as this *noria*, or water wheel, which harnessed the power of moving water. *(Source: Biblioteca Apostolica Vaticana)*

at that time, 3,463 had at least one mill. One scholar has calculated that on average each mill supplied 50 households. Besides grinding wheat or other grains to produce flour, water mills became essential in fulling, the process of scouring, cleansing, and thickening cloth. Rather than men or women trampling cloth in a trough, wooden hammers were raised and dropped on the cloth by means of a revolving drum connected to the spindle of a water wheel. Water mills revolutionized the means of grinding and fulling by using natural, rather than human, energy.

Successful at adapting waterpower to human needs, medieval engineers soon harnessed windpower. They replaced the wheels driven by water with sails. But while water always flows in the same direction, wind can blow from many directions. Windmill engineers solved this problem very ingeniously by mounting the framed wooden body, which contained the machinery and carried the sails, on a massive upright post free to turn with the wind.[2]

REVIVAL AND REFORM IN THE CHRISTIAN CHURCH

The eleventh century also witnessed the beginnings of a remarkable religious revival. Monasteries, always the leaders in ecclesiastical reform, remodeled themselves under the leadership of the Burgundian abbey of Cluny. Subsequently, new religious orders, such as the Cistercians, were founded and became a broad spiritual movement.

The papacy itself, after a century of corruption and decadence, was cleaned up. The popes worked to clarify church doctrine and codify church law. They and their officials sought to communicate with all the clergy and peoples of Europe through a clearly defined, obedient hierarchy of bishops. The popes wanted the basic loyalty of all members of the clergy. Pope Gregory VII's strong assertion of papal power led to profound changes and serious conflict with secular authorities. The revival of the

Mont St.-Michel   At the summit of a 250-foot cone of rock rising out of the sea and accessible only at low tide, Mont St.-Michel combined fortified castle and monastery. Thirteenth-century monarchs considered it crucial to their power in northwestern France, and it played a decisive role in French defenses against the English during the Hundred Years' War. The abbots so planned the architecture that monastic life went on undisturbed by military activity. *(Source: Giraudon/Art Resource)*

church was manifested in the twelfth and thirteenth centuries by a flowering of popular piety, reflected in the building of magnificent cathedrals.

Monastic Revival

In the early Middle Ages, the best Benedictine monasteries had been citadels of good Christian living and centers of learning. Between the seventh and ninth centuries, religious houses such as Bobbio in northern Italy, Luxeuil in France, and Jarrow in England copied and preserved manuscripts, maintained schools, and set high standards of monastic observance. Charlemagne had encouraged and supported these monastic activities, and the collapse of the Carolingian Empire had disastrous effects.

The Viking, Magyar, and Muslim invaders attacked and ransacked many monasteries across Europe. Some communities fled and dispersed. In the period of political disorder that followed the disintegration of the Carolingian Empire, many religious houses fell under the control and domination of local feudal lords. Powerful laymen appointed themselves or their relatives as abbots, while keeping their wives or mistresses. They took for themselves the lands and goods of monasteries, spending monastic revenues and selling monastic offices. Temporal powers all over Europe dominated the monasteries. The level of spiritual observance and intellectual activity declined.

In 909 William the Pious, duke of Aquitaine, established the abbey of Cluny near Mâcon in Burgundy. This was to be a very important event. In his charter of endowment, Duke William declared that Cluny was to enjoy complete independence from all feudal or secular lordship. The new monastery was to be subordinate only to the authority of Saints Peter and Paul as represented by the pope. The duke then renounced his own possession of and influence over Cluny.

This monastery and its foundation charter came to exert vast religious influence. The first two abbots of Cluny, Berno (910–927) and Odo (927–942), set very high standards of religious behavior. They stressed strict observance of the *Rule of Saint Benedict,* the development of a personal spiritual life by the individual monk, and the importance of the liturgy. Cluny gradually came to stand for clerical celibacy and the suppression of *simony* (the sale of church offices). In the eleventh century, Cluny was fortunate in having a series of highly able abbots who ruled for a long time. These abbots

paid careful attention to sound economic management. In a disorderly world, Cluny gradually came to represent religious and political stability. Therefore, lay persons placed lands under its custody and monastic priories under its jurisdiction for reform. Benefactors wanted to be associated with Cluniac piety. Moreover, properties and monasteries under Cluny's jurisdiction enjoyed special protection, at least theoretically, from violence.[3] In this way hundreds of monasteries, primarily in France and Spain, came under Cluny's authority.

Cluny was not the only center of monastic reform. The abbey of Gorze in Lotharingia (modern Lorraine) exercised a correcting influence on German religious houses. With royal support and through such abbeys as Saint Emmeran at Regensburg, Gorze directed a massive reform of monasteries in central Europe. Recent scholarship has

Consecration of the Church of Cluny   Pope Urban II surrounded by mitred bishops appears on the left, Abbot Hugh of Cluny with cowled monks on the right. A French nobleman who had been a monk of Cluny, Urban coined the term *curia* as the official designation of the central government of the church. *(Source: Bibliothèque Nationale, Paris)*

shown that Gorze and Cluny represented two different monastic traditions. Gorze became a center of literary culture, Cluny of liturgical ceremony. Gorze personified the simple lifestyle, Cluny the elaborate. Gorze accepted lay authority over monasteries, Cluny did not. Gorze served the empire, Cluny the Gregorian reformers (see pages 268–271). In some ways, Gorze stood for the German East, Cluny for the French West.[4]

Deeply impressed lay people showered gifts on monasteries with high reputations. Jewelry, rich vestments, elaborately carved sacred vessels, even lands and properties poured into some houses. But with this wealth came lay influence. As the monasteries became richer, the lifestyle of the monks grew increasingly luxurious. Monastic observance and spiritual fervor declined. Soon fresh demands for reform were heard, and the result was the founding of new religious orders in the late eleventh and

early twelfth centuries. The best representatives of the new reforming spirit were the Cistercians.

In 1098 a group of monks left the rich abbey of Molesmes in Burgundy and founded a new house in the swampy forest of Cîteaux. They had specific goals and high ideals. They planned to avoid all involvement with secular feudal society. They decided to accept only uncultivated lands far from regular habitation. They intended to refuse all gifts of mills, serfs, tithes, ovens—the traditional manorial sources of income. The early Cistercians determined to avoid elaborate liturgy and ceremony and to keep their chant simple. Finally, they refused to allow the presence of high and powerful lay people in their monasteries, because they knew that such influence was usually harmful to careful observance.

The first monks at Cîteaux experienced sickness, a dearth of recruits, and terrible privations. But

Rievaulx Abbey   Taking its name from the nearby Rie River and the valley in which it is situated, both this vast abbey church (completed in 1145) and the accompanying monastic complex were financed by the extremely fine wool produced from the sheep who grazed on these hillsides. The wool clip also supported a monastic community of over 600 in the mid-twelfth century. *(Source: English Heritage. Crown Copyright.)*

their obvious sincerity and high idealism eventually attracted attention. In 1112 a twenty-three-year-old nobleman called Bernard joined the community at Cîteaux, together with thirty of his aristocratic companions. Thereafter, this reforming movement gained impetus. Cîteaux founded 525 new monasteries in the course of the twelfth century, and its influence on European society was profound. Unavoidably, however, Cistercian success brought wealth, and wealth brought power. By the later twelfth century, economic prosperity and political power had begun to compromise the primitive Cistercian ideals.

Reform of the Papacy

Some scholars believe that the monastic revival spreading from Cluny influenced reform of the Roman papacy and eventually of the entire Christian church. Certainly Abbot Odilo of Cluny (994–1048) was a close friend of the German emperor Henry III, who promoted reform throughout the empire. Pope Gregory VII, who carried the ideals of reform to extreme lengths, had spent some time at Cluny. And the man who consolidated the reform movement and strengthened the medieval papal monarchy, Pope Urban II (1088–1099), had been a monk and prior at Cluny. The precise degree of Cluny's impact on the reform movement cannot be measured. But the broad goals of the Cluniac movement and those of the Roman papacy were the same.

The papacy provided little leadership to the Christian peoples of western Europe in the tenth century. Factions in Rome sought to control the papacy for their own material gain. Popes were appointed to advance the political ambitions of their families—the great aristocratic families of the city —and not because of special spiritual qualifications. The office of pope, including its spiritual powers and influence, was frequently bought and sold, though the grave crime of simony had been condemned by Saint Peter. The licentiousness and debauchery of the papal court weakened the pope's religious prestige and moral authority. According to a contemporary chronicler, for example, Pope John XII (955–963), who had secured the papal office at the age of eighteen, wore himself out with sexual excesses before he was twenty-eight.

At the local parish level there were many married priests. Taking Christ as the model for the priestly life, the Roman church had always encouraged clerical celibacy, and it had been an obligation for ordination since the fourth century. But in the tenth and eleventh centuries, probably a majority of European priests were married or living with a woman. Such priests were called "Nicolaites" from a reference in the Book of Revelation to early Christians who advocated a return to pagan sexual practices.

Several factors may account for the uncelibate state of the clergy. The explanation may lie in the basic need for warmth and human companionship. Perhaps village priests could not survive economically on their small incomes and needed the help of a mate. Perhaps the tradition of a married clergy was so deep-rooted by the tenth century that each generation simply followed the example of its predecessor. In any case, the disparity between law and reality shocked the lay community and bred disrespect for the clergy.

Serious efforts at reform began under Pope Leo IX (1049–1054). Not only was Leo related to Emperor Henry III but, as bishop of Toul and a German, he was also an outsider who owed nothing to any Roman faction. Leo traveled widely and held councils at Pavia, Reims, and Mainz that issued decrees against simony, Nicolaism, and violence. Leo's representatives held church councils across Europe, pressing for moral reform. They urged those who could not secure justice at home to appeal to the pope, ultimate source of justice.

By his character and actions, Leo set high moral standards for the West. But the reform of the papacy had legal as well as moral aspects. During Leo's pontificate a new collection of ecclesiastical law was prepared, the *Collection of 74 Titles,* which laid great emphasis on papal authority. In substance the collection stressed the rights, legal position, and supreme spiritual prerogatives of the bishop of Rome as successor of Saint Peter.

Papal reform continued after Leo IX. During the short reign of Nicholas II (1058–1061), a council held in the ancient church of Saint John Lateran in 1059 reached a momentous decision. A new method was devised for electing the pope. Since the eighth century, the priests of the major churches in and around Rome had constituted a special group, called a "college," that advised the pope when he summoned them to meetings. These chief priests were called "cardinals" from the Latin *cardo,* meaning "hinge." The cardinals were the hinges on which the church turned. The Lateran Synod of

1059 decreed that the authority and power to elect the pope rested solely in this college of cardinals. The college retains that power today.

The object of the decree was to reduce royal influence and remove this crucial decision from the secular squabbling of Roman aristocratic factions. When the office of pope was vacant, the cardinals were responsible for governing the church. (In the Middle Ages the college of cardinals numbered around twenty-five or thirty, most of them from Italy. In 1586 the figure was set at seventy. In the 1960s Pope Paul VI virtually doubled that number, appointing men from all parts of the globe to reflect the international character of the church.) By 1073 the progress of reform in the Christian church was well advanced. The election of Cardinal Hildebrand as Pope Gregory VII changed the direction of reform from a moral to a political one.

THE GREGORIAN REVOLUTION

The papal reform movement of the eleventh century is frequently called the Gregorian reform movement, after Pope Gregory VII (1073–1085). The label is not accurate, in that reform began long before Gregory's pontificate and continued after it. Gregory's reign did, however, inaugurate a radical or revolutionary phase that had important political and social consequences.

Pope Gregory VII's Ideas

Cardinal Hildebrand had received a good education at Rome and spent some time at Cluny, where his strict views of clerical life were strengthened. He had served in the papal secretariat under Leo IX and after 1065 was probably the chief influence there. Hildebrand was dogmatic, inflexible, and unalterably convinced of the truth of his own views. He believed that the pope, as the successor of Saint Peter, was the Vicar of God on earth and that papal orders were the orders of God.

Once Hildebrand became pope, the reform of the papacy took on a new dimension. Its goal was not just the moral regeneration of the clergy and centralization of the church under papal authority. Gregory and his assistants began to insist on the "freedom of the church." By this they meant the

freedom of churchmen to obey canon law and freedom from control and interference by lay people.

"Freedom of the church" pointed to the end of *lay investiture*—the selection and appointment of church officials by secular authority. Bishops and abbots were invested with the staff representing pastoral jurisdiction and the ring signifying union with the diocese or monastic community. When laymen gave these symbols, they appeared to be distributing spiritual authority. Ecclesiastical opposition to lay investiture was not new in the eleventh century. It, too, had been part of church theory for centuries. But Gregory's attempt to put theory into practice was a radical departure from tradition. Since feudal monarchs depended on churchmen for the operation of their governments, Gregory's program seemed to spell disaster for stable royal administration. It provoked a terrible crisis.

The Controversy over Lay Investiture

In February 1075 Pope Gregory held a council at Rome. It published decrees not only against Nicolaism and simony but also against lay investiture:

If anyone henceforth shall receive a bishopric or abbey from the hands of a lay person, he shall not be considered as among the number of bishops and abbots. . . . Likewise if any emperor, king . . . or any one at all of the secular powers, shall presume to perform investiture with bishoprics or with any other ecclesiastical dignity . . . he shall feel the divine displeasure as well with regard to his body as to his other belongings.[5]

In short, clerics who accepted investiture from laymen were to be deposed, and laymen who invested clerics were to be *excommunicated* (cut off from the sacraments and all Christian worship).

The church's penalty of excommunication relied for its effectiveness on public opinion. Since most Europeans favored Gregory's moral reforms, he believed that excommunication would compel rulers to abide by his changes. Immediately, however, Henry IV in the empire, William the Conqueror in England, and Philip I in France protested.

The strongest reaction came from Germany. Henry IV had supported the moral aspects of church reform within the empire. In fact, they would not have had much success without him. Most eleventh-century rulers depended on church-

Henry IV and Gregory VII The twelfth-century Cistercian chronicler Otto of Freising depicts Gregory VII expelled from Rome while Henry IV sits beside an anti-pope. Grandson of Henry IV, Otto did not sympathize with Gregory, whom he thought had sown disorder in the church. *(Source: Sächsische Landesbibliothek/Deutsche Fotothek)*

men for their governments; they could not survive without the literacy and administrative knowledge of bishops and abbots. Naturally, then, kings selected and invested most of them. In this respect, as recent research has shown, German kings scarcely varied from other rulers. In two basic ways, however, the relationship of the German kings to the papacy differed from that of other monarchs: the pope crowned the German emperor, and both the empire and the papal states claimed northern Italy.

In addition to the subject of lay investiture, a more fundamental issue was at stake. Gregory's decree raised the question of the proper role of the monarch in a Christian society. Did a king have ultimate jurisdiction over all his subjects, including the clergy? For centuries, tradition had answered this question in favor of the ruler; so it is no wonder that Henry protested the papal assertions about investiture. Indirectly, they undermined imperial power and sought to make papal authority supreme.

An increasingly bitter exchange of letters ensued. Gregory accused Henry of lack of respect for the papacy and insisted that disobedience to the pope was disobedience to God. Henry protested in a now-famous letter beginning, "Henry King not by usurpation, but by the pious ordination of God, to Hildebrand, now not Pope, but false monk."

Within the empire, those who had most to gain from the dispute quickly took advantage of it. In January 1076 the German bishops who had been invested by Henry withdrew their allegiance from the pope. Gregory replied by excommunicating them and suspending Henry from the kingship. The lay nobility delighted in the bind the emperor had been put in: with Henry IV excommunicated and cast outside the Christian fold, they did not have to obey him and could advance their own interests. Gregory hastened to support them. The Christmas season of 1076 witnessed an ironic situation in Germany: the clergy supported the emperor, while the great nobility favored the pope.

Henry outwitted Gregory. Crossing the Alps in January 1077, he approached the pope's residence at Canossa in northern Italy. According to legend, Henry stood for three days in the snow seeking forgiveness. As a priest, Pope Gregory was obliged to grant absolution and to readmit the emperor to the Christian community. Henry's trip to Canossa is often described as the most dramatic incident in the High Middle Ages. Some historians claim that it marked the peak of papal power because the most powerful ruler in Europe, the emperor, had bowed before the pope. Actually, Henry scored a temporary victory. When the sentence of excommunication was lifted, Henry regained the kingship and authority over his rebellious subjects. But in the long run, in Germany and elsewhere, secular rulers were reluctant to pose a serious challenge to the papacy for the next two hundred years.

For Germany the incident at Canossa settled nothing. The controversy over lay investiture and the position of the king in Christian society continued. In 1080 Gregory VII again excommunicated and deposed the emperor; in return, Henry invaded Italy, captured Rome, and controlled the city when Gregory died in 1085. But Henry won no lasting victory. Gregory's successors encouraged Henry's sons to revolt against their father. With lay investiture the ostensible issue, the conflict between the papacy and the successor of Henry IV continued into the twelfth century.

Finally, in 1122, at a conference held at Worms, the issue was settled by compromise. Bishops were to be chosen according to canon law—that is, by the clergy—in the presence of the emperor or his delegate. The emperor surrendered the right of investing bishops with the ring and staff. But since lay rulers were permitted to be present at ecclesiastical elections and to accept or refuse feudal homage from the new prelates, they still possessed an effective veto over ecclesiastical appointments. At the same time, the papacy achieved technical success, because rulers could no longer invest. Papal power was enhanced, and neither side won a clear victory.

William the Conqueror of England and Philip I of France were just as guilty of lay investiture as the German emperor, and both quarreled openly with Gregory. However, Rome's conflict with the western rulers never reached the proportions of the dispute with the German emperor. Gregory VII and his successors had the diplomatic sense to avoid creating three enemies at once.

The long controversy had tremendous social and political consequences in Germany. For half a century, between 1075 and 1125, civil war was chronic in the empire. Preoccupied with Italy and the quarrel with the papacy, emperors could do little about it. The lengthy struggle between papacy and emperor allowed emerging noble dynasties, such as the Zähringer of Swabia, to enhance their

position. As recent research has revealed, by the eleventh century these great German families had achieved a definite sense of themselves as noble.[6] To control their lands, the great lords built castles, symbolizing their increased power and growing independence. (In no European country do more castles survive today.) The castles were both military strongholds and centers of administration for the surrounding territories. The German aristocracy subordinated the knights and reinforced their dependency with strong feudal ties. They reduced free men and serfs to an extremely servile position. Henry IV and Henry V were compelled to surrender rights and privileges to the nobility. When the papal-imperial conflict ended in 1122, the nobility held the balance of power in Germany, and later German kings, such as Frederick Barbarossa (see page 317), would fail in their efforts to strengthen the monarchy against the princely families. For these reasons, particularism, localism, and feudal independence characterized the Holy Roman Empire in the High Middle Ages. The investiture controversy had a catastrophic effect there, severely retarding development of a strong centralized monarchy.

The Papacy in the High Middle Ages

In the late eleventh century and throughout the twelfth, the papacy pressed Gregory's campaign for reform of the church. Pope Urban II laid the real foundations for the papal monarchy by reorganizing the central government of the Roman church, the papal writing office (the chancery), and papal finances. He recognized the college of cardinals as a definite consultative body. These agencies, together with the papal chapel, constituted the papal court, or *curia*—the papacy's administrative bureaucracy and its court of law. The papal curia, although not fully developed until the mid-twelfth century, was the first well-organized institution of monarchial authority in medieval Europe.

The Roman curia had its greatest impact as a court of law. As the highest ecclesiastical tribunal, it formulated canon law for all of Christendom. It was the instrument with which the popes pressed the goals of reform and centralized the church. The curia sent legates to hold councils in various parts of Europe. Councils published decrees and sought to enforce the law. When individuals in any part of

Christian Europe felt they were being denied justice in their local church courts, they could appeal to Rome. Slowly but surely, in the High Middle Ages the papal curia developed into the court of final appeal for all of Christian Europe.

In the course of the twelfth century, appeals to the curia steadily increased. The majority of cases related to disputes over church property or ecclesiastical elections and above all to questions of marriage and annulment. Significantly, most of the popes in the twelfth and thirteenth centuries were themselves canon lawyers. The most famous of them, the man whose pontificate represented the height of medieval papal power, was Innocent III (1198–1216).

Innocent judged a vast number of cases. He compelled King Philip Augustus of France to take back his wife, Ingeborg of Denmark. He arbitrated the rival claims of two disputants to the imperial crown of Germany. He forced King John of England to accept as archbishop of Canterbury a man John did not really want.

By the early thirteenth century, papal efforts at reform begun more than a century before had attained phenomenal success. The popes themselves were men of high principles and strict moral behavior. The frequency of clerical marriage and the level of violence had declined considerably. The practice of simony was much more the exception than the rule.

Yet the seeds of future difficulties were being planted. As the volume of appeals to Rome multiplied, so did the size of the papal bureaucracy. As the number of lawyers increased, so did concern for legal niceties and technicalities, fees, and church offices. As early as the mid-twelfth century, John of Salisbury, an Englishman working in the papal curia, had written that the people condemned the curia for its greed and indifference to human suffering. Nevertheless, the power of the curia continued to grow, as did its bureaucracy.

Thirteenth-century popes devoted their attention to the bureaucracy and their conflicts with the German emperor Frederick II. Some, like Gregory IX (1227–1241), abused their prerogatives to such an extent that their moral impact was seriously weakened. Even worse, Innocent IV (1243–1254) used secular weapons, including military force, to maintain his leadership. These popes badly damaged papal prestige and influence. By the early fourteenth century, the seeds of disorder would grow into a vast and sprawling tree, and once again cries for reform would be heard.

THE CRUSADES

The Crusades of the eleventh and twelfth centuries were the most obvious manifestation of the papal claim to the leadership of Christian society. The enormous popular response to papal calls for crusading reveals the influence of the reformed papacy. The Crusades also reflect the church's new understanding of the noble warrior class. As a distinguished scholar of the Crusades wrote:

At around the turn of the millennium [the year 1000], the attitude of the church toward the military class underwent a significant change. The contrast between militia Christi [war for Christ] and militia saecularis [war for worldly purposes] was overcome and just as rulership earlier had been Christianized . . . , so now was the military profession; it acquired a direct ecclesiastical purpose, for war in the service of the church or for the weak came to be regarded as holy and was declared to be a religious duty not only for the king but also for every individual knight.[7]

Crusades in the late eleventh and early twelfth centuries were holy wars sponsored by the papacy for the recovery of the Holy Land from the Muslim Arabs or the Turks. They grew out of the long conflict between Christians and Muslims in Spain, where by about 1250 Christian kings had regained roughly 90 percent of the peninsula. Throughout this period, Christians alone and in groups left Europe in a steady trickle for the Middle East. Although people of all ages and classes participated in the Crusades, so many knights did so that crusading became a distinctive feature of the upper-class lifestyle. In an aristocratic, military society, men coveted reputations as Crusaders; the Christian knight who had been to the Holy Land enjoyed great prestige. The Crusades manifested the religious and chivalric ideals—as well as the tremendous vitality—of medieval society.

The Roman papacy supported the holy war in Spain and by the late eleventh century had strong reasons for wanting to launch an expedition against Muslim infidels in the Middle East as well. The papacy had been involved in a bitter struggle over investiture with the German emperors. If the

Crusading Scene   Heavily armored Western knights face unencumbered Muslims. Some scholars believe that their dress gave the Muslims a decided advantage in certain battles. *(Source: Bibliothèque Nationale, Paris)*

pope could muster a large army against the enemies of Christianity, his claim to be leader of Christian society in the West would be strengthened. Moreover, in 1054 a serious theological disagreement had split the Greek church of Byzantium and the Roman church of the West. The pope believed that a crusade would lead to strong Roman influence in Greek territories and eventually the reunion of the two churches.

In 1071 at Manzikert in eastern Anatolia, Turkish soldiers in the pay of the Arabs defeated a Greek army and occupied much of Asia Minor. The emperor at Constantinople appealed to the West for support. Shortly afterward, the holy city of Jerusalem, the scene of Christ's preaching and burial, fell to the Turks. Pilgrimages to holy places in the Middle East became very dangerous, and the papacy

was outraged that the holy city was in the hands of infidels.

In 1095 Pope Urban II journeyed to Clermont in France and called for a great Christian holy war against the infidels. He stressed the sufferings and persecution of Christians in Jerusalem. He urged Christian knights who had been fighting one another to direct their energies against the true enemies of God, the Muslims. Urban proclaimed an *indulgence,* or remission of the temporal penalties imposed by the church for sin, to those who would fight for and regain the holy city of Jerusalem. Few speeches in history have had such a dramatic effect as Urban's call at Clermont for the First Crusade.

The response was fantastic. Godfrey of Bouillon, Geoffrey of Lorraine, and many other great lords from northern France immediately had the cross of the Crusader sewn on their tunics. Encouraged by popular preachers like Peter the Hermit and by papal legates in Germany, Italy, and England, thousands of people of all classes joined the crusade. Although most of the Crusaders were French, pilgrims from many regions streamed southward from the Rhineland, through Germany and the Balkans. Of all of the developments of the High Middle Ages, none better reveals Europeans' religious enthusiasm and emotional fervor and the influence of the reformed papacy than the extraordinary outpouring of support for the First Crusade.

Religious convictions inspired many, but mundane motives were also involved. For the curious and the adventurous, the crusade offered foreign travel and excitement. It provided kings, who were trying to establish order and build states, the perfect opportunity to get rid of troublemaking

The Capture of Jerusalem in 1099   As engines hurl stones to breach the walls, Crusaders enter on scaling ladders. Scenes from Christ's passion (above) identify the city as Jerusalem. *(Source: Bibliothèque Nationale, Paris)*

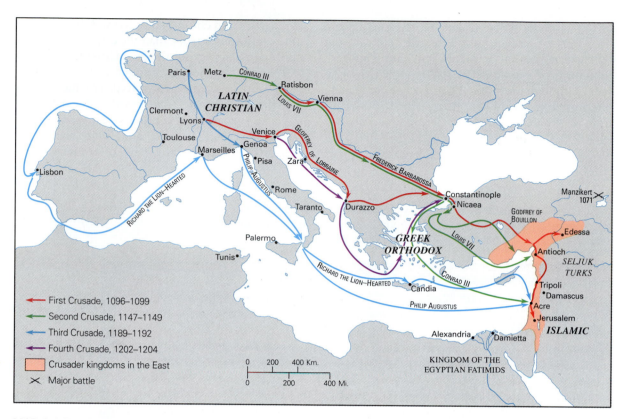

MAP 9.1 The Routes of the Crusades The Crusades led to a major cultural encounter between Muslim and Christian values. What significant intellectual and economic effects resulted?

knights. It gave land-hungry younger sons a chance to acquire fiefs in the Middle East. Even some members of the middle class who stayed at home profited from the crusade. Nobles often had to borrow money from the burghers to pay for their expeditions, and they put up part of their land as security. If a noble did not return home or could not pay the interest on the loan, the middle-class creditor took over the land.

The First Crusade was successful mostly because of the dynamic enthusiasm of the participants. The Crusaders had little more than religious zeal. They knew nothing about the geography or climate of the Middle East. Although there were several counts with military experience among the host, the Crusaders could never agree on a leader, and the entire expedition was marked by disputes among the great lords. Lines of supply were never set up. Starvation and disease wracked the army, and the Turks slaughtered hundreds of noncombat-

ants. Nevertheless, convinced that "God wills it"— the war cry of the Crusaders—the army pressed on and in 1099 captured Jerusalem. Although the Crusaders fought bravely, Arab disunity was a chief reason for their victory. At Jerusalem, Edessa, Tripoli, and Antioch, Crusader kingdoms were founded on the Western feudal model (Map 9.1).

Between 1096 and 1270, the crusading ideal was expressed in eight papally approved expeditions to the East. Despite the success of the First Crusade, none of the later ones accomplished very much. The Third Crusade (1189–1192) was precipitated by the recapture of Jerusalem by the sultan Saladin in 1187. Frederick Barbarossa of the Holy Roman Empire, Richard (Lion-Heart) of England, and Philip Augustus of France participated, and the Third Crusade was better financed than previous ones. But disputes among the leaders and strategic problems prevented any lasting results. In 1208, in one of the most memorable episodes, two expeditions of children set out on a crusade to the Holy Land. One contingent turned back; the other was captured and sold into slavery.

During the Fourth Crusade (1202–1204), careless preparation and inadequate financing had disastrous consequences for Latin-Byzantine relations. When the Crusaders could not pay the Venetians the money promised for transport to the Holy Land, the Venetians forced the Crusaders to divert the expedition to Constantinople. The Venetians wanted to protect their trading interests in the East. Once in Byzantium, the Crusaders sacked the city and established the Latin kingdom of Constantinople. This assault by one Christian people on another—when one of the goals of the crusade was the reunion of the Greek and Latin churches—made the split between the Western and Eastern churches permanent. It also helped to discredit the entire crusading movement. Two later crusades against the Muslims, undertaken by King Louis IX of France, added to his prestige as a pious ruler. Apart from that, the last of the official crusades accomplished nothing at all.

Crusades were also mounted against groups perceived as Christian Europe's social enemies. In 1208 Pope Innocent III proclaimed a crusade against the Albigensians, a heretical sect. The Albigensians, whose name derived from the southern French town of Albi where they were concentrated, rejected orthodox doctrine on the relationship of God and man, the sacraments, and clerical hierarchy. Fearing that religious division would lead to civil disorder, the French monarchy joined the crusade against the Albigensians. Under Count Simon de Montfort, the French inflicted a savage defeat on the Albigensians at Muret in 1213; the county of Toulouse passed to the authority of the French crown. Fearful of encirclement by imperial territories, the popes also promoted crusades against Emperor Frederick II in 1227 and 1239. This use of force against a Christian ruler backfired, damaging papal credibility as the sponsor of peace.

What impact did the Crusades have on women? That is a difficult question. Fewer women than men directly participated, since the Crusades were primarily military expeditions and all societies have perceived war as a masculine enterprise. Given the aristocratic bias of the chroniclers, we have more information about royal and noble ladies who went to the Holy Land than about middle-class and peasant women, though the latter groups contributed

the greater numbers. Eleanor of Aquitaine (1122?–1204) accompanied her husband King Louis VII on the Second Crusade (1147–1149), and the thirteenth-century English chronicler Matthew Paris says that large numbers of women went on the Seventh Crusade (1248–1254) so that they could obtain the crusading indulgence. Women who stayed home assumed their husband's responsibilities in the management of estates, the dispensation of justice to vassals and serfs, and the protection of property from attack. Since Crusaders frequently could finance the expedition only by borrowing, it fell to their wives to repay the loans. These heavy responsibilities brought women a degree of power. The many women who operated inns and shops in the towns through which crusading armies passed profited from the rental of lodgings and the sale of foodstuffs, clothing, arms, and fodder for animals. For prostitutes, also, crusading armies offered business opportunities.

The Crusades introduced some Europeans to Eastern luxury goods, but the Crusades' overall cultural impact on the West remains debatable. By the late eleventh century, strong economic and intellectual ties with the East had already been made. The Crusades testify to the religious enthusiasm of the High Middle Ages. But, as Steven Runciman, a distinguished scholar of the Crusades, concluded in his three-volume history:

The triumphs of the Crusade were the triumphs of faith. But faith without wisdom is a dangerous thing. . . . In the long sequence of interaction and fusion between Orient and Occident out of which our civilization has grown, the Crusades were a tragic and destructive episode. . . . High ideals were besmirched by cruelty and greed, enterprise and endurance by a blind and narrow self-righteousness; and the Holy War itself was nothing more than a long act of intolerance in the name of God, which is the sin against the Holy Ghost.[8]

Along the Syrian and Palestinian coasts, the Crusaders set up a string of feudal states that managed to survive for about two centuries before the Muslims reconquered them. The Crusaders left two more permanent legacies in the Middle East, however, that continue to affect us today. First, the long struggle between Islam and Christendom and the example of persecution set by Christian kings and prelates left an inheritance of deep bitterness; relations between Muslims and their Christian and

Jewish subjects worsened. Second, European merchants, primarily Italians, had established communities in the Crusader states. After those kingdoms collapsed, Muslim rulers still encouraged trade with European businessmen. Commerce with the West benefited both Muslims and Europeans, and it continued to flourish.[9]

SUMMARY

The end of the great invasions signaled the beginning of profound changes in European society—social, political, and ecclesiastical. In the year 1000, having enough to eat was the rare privilege of a few nobles, priests, and monks. By the eleventh century, however, manorial communities were slowly improving their agricultural output through increased mechanization, especially the use of waterpower and windpower; these advances, aided by warmer weather, meant more food and increasing population.

In the eleventh century also, rulers and local authorities gradually imposed some degree of order within their territories. Peace and domestic security, contributed to the rise in population, bringing larger crops for the peasants and improving trading conditions for the townspeople. The church overthrew the domination of lay influences, and the spread of the Cluniac and Cistercian orders marked the ascendancy of monasticism. The Gregorian reform movement with its stress of "the freedom of the church" led to a grave conflict with kings over lay investiture. The papacy achieved a technical success on the religious issue, but in Germany the greatly increased power of the nobility, at the expense of the emperor, represents the significant social consequence. Having put its own house in order, the Roman papacy in the twelfth and thirteenth centuries built the first strong government bureaucracy. In the High Middle Ages, the church exercised general leadership of European society. The Crusades exhibit that leadership.

NOTES

1. J. Gimpel, *The Medieval Machine: The Industrial Revolution of the Middle Ages* (New York: Penguin Books, 1976), p. 7.

2. Ibid., pp. 10–15.

3. See B. Rosenwein, *Rhinoceros Bound: Cluny in the Tenth Century* (Philadelphia: University of Pennsylvania Press, 1982), chap. 2.

4. See K. Hallinger, *Gorze-Kluny: Studien zu den monastichen Lebensformen und Gegensätzen im Hochmittelalter,* Studia Anselmiana xxii-v (Rome: Herder, 1950–1951), esp. p. 40.

5. B. D. Hill, ed., *Church and State in the Middle Ages* (New York: John Wiley & Sons, 1970), p. 68.

6. See J. B. Freed, *The Counts of Falkenstein: Noble Self-consciousness in Twelfth-century Germany,* Transactions of the American Philosophical Society, vol. 74, pt. 6 (Philadelphia, 1984), pp. 9–11.

7. C. Erdmann, *The Origin of the Idea of the Crusade,* trans. M. Baldwin and W. Goffart (Princeton, N.J.: Princeton University Press, 1977), p. 57.

8. S. Runciman, *A History of the Crusades,* vol. 3, *The Kingdom of Acre* (Cambridge: Cambridge University Press, 1955), p. 480.

9. B. Lewis, *The Muslim Discovery of Europe* (New York: W. W. Norton, 1982), pp. 23–25.

SUGGESTED READING

In addition to the references in the Notes, the curious student will find a fuller treatment of many of the topics raised in this chapter in the following works.

Both C. D. Burns, *The First Europe* (1948), and G. Barraclough, *The Crucible of Europe: The Ninth and Tenth Centuries in European History* (1976), survey the entire period and emphasize the transformation from a time of anarchy to one of great creativity; Barraclough also stresses the importance of stable government. His *The Origins of Modern Germany* (1963) is essential for central and eastern Europe. Two studies by G. M. Spiegel—"The Cult of Saint Denis and Capetian Kingship," *Journal of Medieval History* 1 (April 1975): 43–69, and *The Chronicle Tradition of Saint-Denis* (1978)—treat the close relationship between the Capetian dynasty and the royal abbey of Saint-Denis. R. Fletcher, *The Quest for El Cid* (1990), provides an excellent introduction to Spanish social and political conditions through a study of Rodrigo Dias, the eleventh-century soldier of fortune who became the Spanish national hero.

For the Christian church, the papacy, and ecclesiastical developments, G. Barraclough's richly illustrated *The Medieval Papacy* (1968) is a good general survey that emphasizes the development of administrative bureaucracy. The advanced student may tackle W. Ullmann, *A Short History of the Papacy in the Middle Ages* (1972). S. Williams, ed., *The Gregorian Epoch: Reformation, Revolution, Reaction?* (1964), contains significant interpretations of the eleventh-century reform movements. Ullmann's *The Growth of Papal Government in the Middle Ages,* rev. ed. (1970), traces the evolution of papal law and government. G. Tellenbach, *Church, State, and Christian Society at the Time of the Investiture Contest* (1959), emphasizes the revolutionary aspects of the Gregorian reform program. The relationship of the monks to the ecclesiastical crisis of the late eleventh century is discussed by N. F. Cantor, "The Crisis of Western Monasticism," *American Historical Review* 66 (1960), but see also the essential analysis of J. Van Engen, "The 'Crisis of Cenobitism' Reconsidered: Benedictine Monasticism in the Years 1050–1150," *Speculum* 61 (1986): 269–304, as well as H. E. J. Cowdrey, *The Cluniacs and the Gregorian Reform* (1970), an impressive but difficult study. Cowdrey's recent *The Age of Abbot Desiderius: Monte Cassino, the Papacy, and the Normans in the Eleventh and Early Twelfth Centuries* (1983) focuses on Monte Cassino, the oldest black monk monastery. J. B. Russell, *A History of Medieval Christianity* (1968), offers an important and sensitively written survey. The advanced student will benefit considerably from the works by C. Erdmann, J. B. Freed, and B. Rosenwein that are cited in the Notes.

The following studies provide exciting and highly readable general accounts of the Crusades: J. Riley-Smith, *What Were the Crusades?* (1977); R. C. Finucane, *Soldiers of the Faith: Crusaders and Muslims at War* (1983); and R. Payne, *The Dream and the Tomb: A History of the Crusades* (1984). There are excellent articles on many facets of the Crusades, including "The Children's Crusade," "Crusade Propaganda," "Crusader Art and Architecture," and "The Political Crusades"—all written by authorities and based on the latest research—in J. R. Strayer, ed., *The Dictionary of the Middle Ages,* vol. 4 (1984). These articles contain up-to-date bibliographies. C. M. Brand, *Byzantium Confronts the West, 1180–1204* (1968), provides the Greek perspective on the Crusades, while B. Lewis, *The Muslim Discovery of Europe* (1982), gives the Muslim point of view. Serious students will eventually want to consult the multivolume work of K. M. Setton, gen. ed., *A History of the Crusades* (1955–1977).

10

Life in Christian Europe in the High Middle Ages

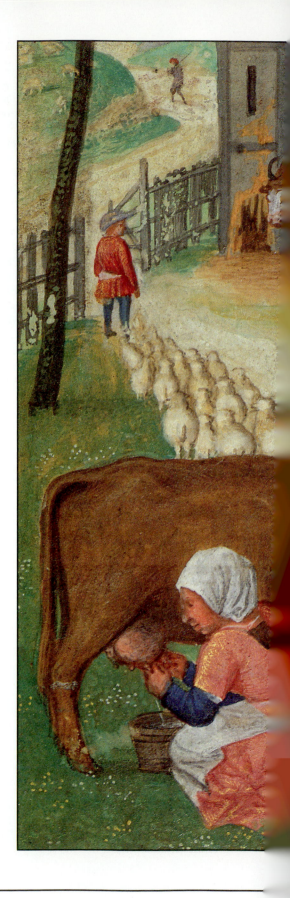

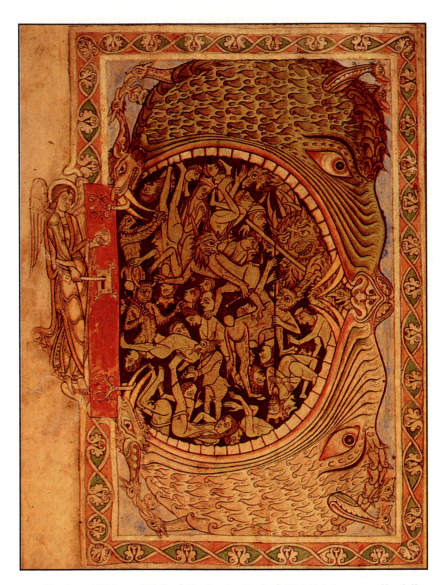

Medieval Vision of Hell   (Winchester Psalter) Frightful demons attack the damned souls—including kings, queens, and monks—in this twelfth-century portrayal of hell. The inscription at the top reads, "Here is hell and the angel closes the gates." *(Source: The British Library)*

fear of nature: storms, thunder, and lightning terrified them. They had a terror of hell, whose geography and awful tortures they knew from sermons. And they certainly saw that the virtuous were not always rewarded but sometimes suffered considerably on earth. These things, which they could not explain, bred a deep pessimism.

No wonder, then, that pilgrimages to shrines of the saints were so popular. They offered hope in a world of gloom. They satisfied a strong emotional

need. They meant change, adventure, excitement. The church granted indulgences to those who visited the shrines of great saints. *Indulgences* were remissions of the penalties that priests imposed on penitents for grave sin. People, however, equated indulgences with salvation itself. They generally believed that the indulgence cut down the amount of time one would spend in hell. Thus indulgences and pilgrimages "promised" salvation. Vast numbers embarked on pilgrimages to the shrines of

Saint James at Santiago de Compostella in Spain, Thomas Becket at Canterbury, Saint-Gilles de Provence, and Saints Peter and Paul at Rome.

THOSE WHO FIGHT

The nobility, though a small fraction of the total population, strongly influenced all aspects of medieval culture—political, economic, religious, educational, and artistic. For that reason, European society in the twelfth and thirteenth centuries may be termed aristocratic. Despite political, scientific, and industrial revolutions, the nobility continued to hold real political and social power in Europe down to the nineteenth century. In order to account for this continuing influence, it is important to understand its development in the High Middle Ages.

During the past twenty years, historians have discovered a great deal about the origins and status of the medieval European nobility. We now know, for example, that ecclesiastical writers in the tenth and eleventh centuries frequently used the term *nobilitas* in reference to the upper classes but did not define it. Clerical writers, however, had no trouble distinguishing who was and was not noble. By the thirteenth century, nobles were broadly described as "those who fight"—those who had the profession of arms. What was a noble? How did the social status and lifestyle of the nobility in the twelfth and thirteenth centuries differ from their tenth-century forms? What political and economic role did the nobility play?

First, in the tenth and eleventh centuries, the social structure in different parts of Europe varied considerably. There were distinct regional customs and social patterns. Broad generalizations about the legal and social status of the nobility, therefore, are dangerous, because they are not universally applicable. For example, in Germany until about 1200, approximately one thousand families, descended from the Carolingian imperial aristocracy and perhaps from the original German tribal nobility, formed the ruling social group. Its members intermarried and held most of the important positions in church and state.[15] Rigid distinctions existed between free and nonfree individuals, preventing the absorption of those of servile birth into the ranks of the nobility. Likewise, in the region

around Paris from the tenth century on, a group of great families held public authority, was self-conscious about its ancestry and honorable status, was bound to the royal house, and was closed to the self-made man. From this aristocracy descended the upper nobility of the High Middle Ages.[16] To the west, however, in the provinces of Anjou and Maine, men of fortune who gained wealth and power became part of the closely related web of noble families by marrying into those families; in these regions, considerable upward mobility existed. Some scholars argue that before the thirteenth century the French nobility was an open caste.[17] Across the English Channel, the English nobility in the High Middle Ages derived from the Norman, Breton, French, and Flemish warriors who helped Duke William of Normandy defeat the Anglo-Saxons at the Battle of Hastings in 1066. In most places, for a son or daughter to be considered a noble, both parents had to be noble. Non-noble women could not usually enter the nobility through marriage, though evidence from Germany shows that some women were ennobled because they had married nobles. There is no evidence of French or English women being raised to the nobility.

Members of the nobility enjoyed a special legal status. A nobleman was free personally and in his possessions. He had immunity from almost all outside authorities. He was limited only by his military obligation to king, duke, or prince. As the result of his liberty, he had certain rights and responsibilities. He raised troops and commanded them in the field. He held courts that dispensed a sort of justice. Sometimes he coined money for use within his territories. He conducted relations with outside powers. He was the political, military, and judicial lord of the people who settled on his lands. He made political decisions affecting them, resolved disputes among them, and protected them in time of attack. The liberty of the noble and the privileges that went with his liberty were inheritable, perpetuated by blood and not by wealth alone.

The nobleman was a professional fighter. His social function, as churchmen described it, was to protect the weak, the poor, and the churches by arms. He possessed a horse and a sword. These, and the leisure time in which to learn how to use them in combat, were the visible signs of his nobility. He was encouraged to display chivalric virtues. Chivalry was a code of conduct originally devised by the clergy to transform the crude and brutal behavior of the knightly class. A knight was supposed to be brave, anxious to win praise, courteous, loyal to his commander, generous, and gracious. The medieval nobility developed independently of knighthood and preceded it; all nobles were knights, but not all knights were noble.[18]

During the eleventh century, the term *chevalier,* meaning "horseman" or "knight," gained wide currency in France. Non-French people gradually adopted it to refer to the nobility, "who sat up high on their war-horses, looking down on the poor masses and terrorizing the monks."[19] In France and England by the twelfth century, the noble frequently used the Latin term *miles,* or "knight." By this time the word connoted moral values, a consciousness of family, and participation in a superior hereditary caste. Those who aspired to the aristocracy desired a castle, the symbol of feudal independence and military lifestyle. Through military

valor, a fortunate marriage, or outstanding service to king or lord, poor knights could and did achieve positions in the upper nobility of France and England. Not so in Germany, where a large class of unfree knights, or *ministerials,* existed. Recruited from the servile dependents of great lords, ministerials fought as warriors or served as stewards who managed nobles' estates or households. In the twelfth century, ministerials sometimes acquired fiefs and wealth. The most important ministerials served the German kings and had significant responsibilities. Legally, however, they remained of servile status: they were not noble.[20] Consequently, in southeastern Germany the term *knight* applied to the servile position of a ministerial.

Infancy and Childhood

Very exciting research has been done on childbirth in the Middle Ages. Most of the information comes from manuscript illuminations, which depict the birth process from the moment of coitus through pregnancy to delivery. An interesting thirteenth-century German miniature from Vienna shows a woman in labor. She is sitting on a chair or stool surrounded by four other women, who are present to help her in the delivery. They could be relatives or neighbors. If they are midwives, the woman in labor is probably noble or rich, since midwives charged a fee. Two midwives seem to be shaking the mother up and down to hasten delivery. One of the women is holding a coriander seed near the mother's vagina. Coriander is an herb of the carrot family, and its seeds were used for cleaning purposes. They were thought to be helpful for expelling gas from the alimentary canal—hence their purported value in speeding up delivery.

The rate of infant mortality (the number of babies who would die before their first birthday) in the High Middle Ages must have been staggering. Such practices as jolting the pregnant woman up and down and inserting a seed into her surely contributed to the death rate of both the newborn and the mother. Natural causes—disease and poor or insufficient food—also resulted in many deaths. Infanticide, however, which was common in the ancient world, seems to have declined in the High Middle Ages. Ecclesiastical pressure worked steadily against it. Infanticide in medieval Europe is another indication of the slow and very imperfect Christianization of European peoples.

Midwives Hastening Delivery Relatives or midwives assist the woman in childbirth by shaking her up and down. Significantly, no physician is present. With such treatment, the death-rate for both mothers and infants was high. *(Source: Österreichische Nationalbibliothek)*

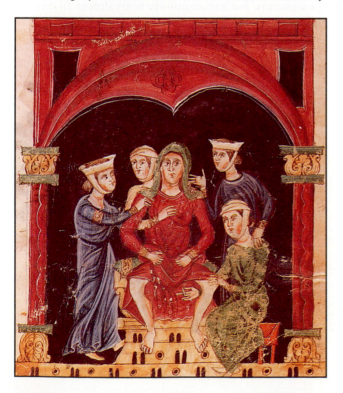

On the other hand, the abandonment of infant children seems to have been the most favored form of family limitation, widely practiced throughout the entire Middle Ages. Abandonment was "the voluntary relinquishing of control over children by their natal parents or guardians, whether by leaving them somewhere, selling them, or legally consigning authority to some other person or institution."[21] Why did parents do this? What became of the children? What was the rate of abandonment? What attitudes did medieval society have toward this practice?

Poverty or local natural disaster led some parents to abandon their children because they could not support them. Before the eleventh century, food was so scarce few parents could feed themselves, let alone children. Thus St. Patrick wrote that, in times of famine, fathers would sell their sons and daughters so that the children could be fed. Parents sometimes gave children away because they were illegitimate or the result of incestuous unions. An eighth-century penitential collection describes the proper treatment for a woman who exposes her unwanted child—that is, leaves it in the open to die —because she has been raped by an enemy or is unable to nourish it. She is not to be blamed, but she should do penance.[22]

Sometimes parents believed that someone of greater means or status might find the child and bring it up in better circumstances than the natal parents could provide. Disappointment in the sex of the child, or its physical weakness or deformity, might also lead parents to abandon it. Finally, some parents were indifferent—they "simply could not be bothered" with the responsibilities of parenthood.[23]

The Christian Middle Ages witnessed a significant development in the disposal of superfluous children: they were given to monasteries as *oblates.* The word *oblate* derives from the Latin *oblatio,* meaning "offering." Boys and girls were given to monasteries or convents as permanent gifts. Saint Benedict (see pages 206–208), in the fifty-ninth chapter of his *Rule,* takes oblation as a normal method for entrance into the monastic life. By the seventh century, church councils and civil codes had defined the practice: "Parents of any social status could donate a child, of either sex, at least up to the age of ten." Contemporaries considered oblation a religious act, since the child was offered to God often in recompense for parental sin. But oblation also served social and economic functions.

Children Given to Creditors Ecclesiastical laws against lending money at interest were widely flouted, and many nobles, having borrowed beyond their ability to repay, fell heavily into debt. As illustrated here, the selling or giving of children to creditors was one solution to indebtedness. *(Source: The Bodleian Library, Oxford)*

The monastery nurtured and educated the child in a familial atmosphere, and it provided career opportunities for the mature monk or nun despite his or her humble origins. Oblation has justifiably been described as "in many ways the most humane form of abandonment ever devised in the West."[24]

The fragmentary medieval evidence prevents the modern student from gaining precise figures on the rate of abandonment. Recent research suggests, however, that abandonment was very common until about the year 1000. The next two hundred years, which saw great agricultural change and relative prosperity, witnessed a low point in abandonment. On the other hand, in the twelfth and thirteenth centuries, the incidence of noble parents giving their younger sons and daughters to religious houses increased dramatically; nobles wanted to preserve the estate intact for the eldest son. Consequently, oblates composed a high percentage of monastic populations. At Winchester in England, for example, 85 percent of the new monks between 1030 and 1070 were oblates. In the early thirteenth

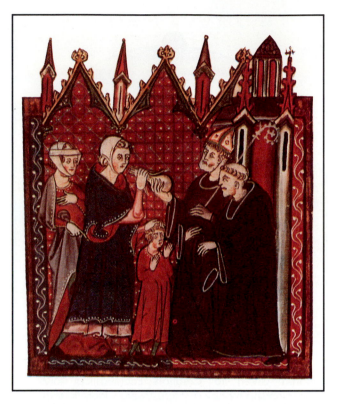

Child Oblate   As St. Benedict allowed (*Rule,* Chap. 59), medieval monasteries frequently received oblates, or children offered by their parents, as permanent members. In this twelfth-century manuscript, a father presents his young son, along with the required dowry, to the abbot (shown with staff). *(Source: Giraudon/Art Resource)*

century, the bishop of Paris observed that children were

. . . cast into the cloister by parents and relatives just as if they were kittens or piglets whom their mothers could not nourish; so that they may die to the world not spiritually but . . . civilly, that is—so that they may be deprived of their hereditary position and that it may devolve on those who remain in the world.

The abandonment of children remained a socially acceptable institution. Ecclesiastical and civil authorities never legislated against it. Moralists reproached parents for abandoning children, because they viewed the child as proof of careless sexuality —not because parents had special obligations to the child. By stressing that all sexual acts have a procreational purpose, and by providing in monastic oblation a humane solution for abandonment,

the Christian church may have actually increased the rate of abandonment.[25]

In addition to abandonment, nobles used other family-planning strategies to preserve family estates, but scholars disagree about the nature of these methods. According to one authority, "The struggle to preserve family holdings intact led them to primogeniture [the exclusive right of the first-born son to inherit] and its corollary, wet nursing, which guaranteed a considerable number of children, males among them."[26] Another student has argued persuasively that nobles deliberately married late or limited the number of their children who could marry by placing them in the church or forbidding them to marry while still laypersons. Nobles may also have practiced birth control. The counts of Falkenstein, who held lordships in Upper Bavaria and Lower Austria, adopted the strategy of late marriages and few children. This custom plus a violent lifestyle ultimately backfired and extinguished the dynasty.[27] Another student, using evidence from tenth-century Saxony, maintains that parents during their lifetimes commonly endowed their sons with estates. This practice allowed sons to marry at a young age and to demonstrate their military prowess.[28] Until we know more about family size and local customs in the High Middle Ages, we cannot generalize about universal practices.

For children of aristocratic birth, the years from infancy to around the age of seven or eight were primarily years of play. Infants had their rattles, as the twelfth-century monk Guibert of Nogent reports, and young children their special toys. Of course, then as now, children would play with anything handy—balls, rings, pretty stones, horns, any small household object. Gerald of Wales, who later became a courtier of King Henry II, describes how as a child he built monasteries and churches in the sand while his brothers were making castles and palaces. Vincent of Beauvais, who composed a great encyclopedia around 1250, recommended that children be bathed twice a day, fed well, and given ample playtime.

Guibert of Nogent speaks in several places in his autobiography of "the tender years of childhood" —the years from six to twelve. Describing the severity of the tutor whom his mother assigned to him, Guibert wrote:

Placed under him, I was taught with such purity and checked with such honesty from the vices which com-

monly spring up in youth that I was kept from ordinary games and never allowed to leave my master's company, or to eat anywhere else than at home, or to accept gifts from anyone without his leave; in everything I had to show self-control in word, look, and deed, so that he seemed to require of me the conduct of a monk rather than a clerk. While others of my age wandered everywhere at will and were unchecked in the indulgence of such inclinations as were natural at their age, I, hedged in with constant restraints and dressed in my clerical garb, would sit and look at the troops of players like a beast awaiting sacrifice. Even on Sundays and saints' days I had to submit to the severity of school exercises.[29]

Guibert's mother had intended him for the church. Other boys and girls had more playtime and freedom.

At about the age of seven, a boy of the noble class who was not intended for the church was placed in the household of one of his father's friends or relatives. There he became a servant to the lord and received his formal training in arms. He was expected to serve the lord at the table, to assist him as a private valet when called on to do so, and, as he gained experience, to care for the lord's horses and equipment. The boy might have a great deal of work to do, depending on the size of the household and the personality of the lord. The work children did, medieval people believed, gave them experience and preparation for later life.

Training was in the arts of war. The boy learned to ride and to manage a horse. He had to acquire skill in wielding a sword, which sometimes weighed as much as 25 pounds. He had to be able to hurl a lance, shoot with a bow and arrow, and care for armor and other equipment. Increasingly, in the eleventh and twelfth centuries, noble youths learned to read and write some Latin. Still, on thousands of charters from that period, nobles signed with a cross (+) or some other mark. Literacy for the nobility became more common in the thirteenth century. Formal training was concluded around the age of twenty-one with the ceremony of knighthood. The custom of knighting, though never universal, seems to have been widespread in France and England but not in Germany. The ceremony of knighthood was one of the most important in a man's life. Once knighted, a young man was supposed to be courteous, generous, and, if possible, handsome and rich. Above all, he was to be loyal to his lord and brave in battle. In a society lacking strong institutions of government, loyalty

was the cement that held aristocratic society together. That is why the greatest crime was called a "felony," which meant treachery to one's lord.

Youth

Knighthood did not necessarily mean adulthood, power, and responsibility. Sons were completely dependent on their fathers for support. Unless a young man's father was dead, he was still considered a youth. He remained a youth until he was in a financial position to marry—that is, until his father died. That might not happen until he was in his late thirties, and marriage at forty was not uncommon. A famous English soldier of fortune, William Marshal, had to wait until he was forty-five to take a wife. One factor—the inheritance of land and the division of properties—determined the lifestyle of the aristocratic nobility. The result was tension, frustration, and sometimes violence.

Once knighted, the young man traveled. His father selected a group of friends to accompany, guide, and protect him. The band's chief pursuit was fighting. They meddled in local conflicts, sometimes departed on crusades, hunted, and did the tournament circuit. The *tournament*, in which a number of men competed from horseback (in contrast to the *joust*, which involved only two competitors), gave the bachelor knight experience in pitched battle. Since the horses and equipment of the vanquished were forfeited to the victors, the knight could also gain a reputation and a profit. Young knights took great delight in spending money on horses, armor, gambling, drinking, and women. Everywhere these bands of youths went they stirred up trouble. It is no wonder that kings supported the Crusades to rid their countries of the violence caused by bands of footloose young knights.

The period of traveling lasted two or three years. Although some young men met violent death and others were maimed or injured, many returned home, still totally dependent on their fathers for support. Serious trouble frequently developed at this stage, for the father was determined to preserve intact the properties of the lordship and to maintain his power and position in the family.

Parents often wanted to settle daughters' futures as soon as possible. Men, even older men, tended to prefer young brides. A woman in her late twenties or thirties would have fewer years of married fertility, limiting the number of children she could produce and thus threatening the family's survival. Therefore, aristocratic girls in the High Middle Ages were married at around the age of sixteen.

The future of many young women was not enviable. For a girl of sixteen, marriage to a man in his thirties was not the most attractive prospect, and marriage to a widower in his forties and fifties was even less so. If there were a large number of marriageable young girls in a particular locality, their "market value" was reduced. In the early Middle Ages, it had been the custom for the groom to present a dowry to the bride and her family, but by the late twelfth century the process was reversed. Thereafter, the size of the marriage portions offered by brides and their families rose higher and higher.

Within noble families and medieval society as a whole, paternal control of the family property and wealth led to serious difficulties. Because marriage was long delayed for men, a considerable age difference existed between husbands and wives and between fathers and sons. Because of this generation gap, as one scholar has written:

The father became an older, distant, but still powerful figure. He could do favors for his sons, but his very presence, once his sons had reached maturity, blocked them in the attainment and enjoyment of property and in the possession of a wife.[30]

Consequently, disputes between the generations were common in the twelfth and thirteenth centuries. Older men held on to property and power. Younger sons wanted a "piece of the action." The conflicts and rebellions in the years 1173 to 1189 involving Henry II of England and his sons Henry, Geoffrey, and John were quite typical.

The relationship between the mother and her sons was also affected. Closer in years to her children than her husband, she was perhaps better able to understand their needs and frustrations. She often served as a mediator between conflicting male generations. One authority on French epic poetry has written, "In extreme need, the heroes betake themselves to their mother, with whom they always find love, counsel and help. She takes them under her protection, even against their father."[31]

A Knightly Tournament or the Battle of the Sexes   The lid of this exquisitely carved French ivory casket shows ladies and gentlemen on a balcony watching a tournament among mounted knights, while men storm the castle of love (left) and a lady and knight tilt with branches of flowers (right). *(Source: Walters Art Gallery, Baltimore)*

When society included so many married young women and unmarried young men, sexual tensions also arose. The young male noble, unable to marry for a long time, could satisfy his lust with peasant girls or prostitutes. But what was a young woman unhappily married to a much older man to do? The literature of courtly love is filled with stories of young bachelors in love with young married women. How hopeless their love was is not known. The cuckolded husband is also a stock figure in such masterpieces as *The Romance of Tristan and Isolde,* Chaucer's *The Merchant's Tale,* and Boccaccio's *Fiammetta's Tale.*

In the High Middle Ages, for economic reasons, a man might remain a bachelor knight—a "youth" —for a very long time. The identification of bachelorhood with youth has survived into modern times, and the social attitude persists that marriage makes a man mature—an adult. Marriage, however, is no guarantee of that.

Power and Responsibility

A male member of the nobility became an adult when he came into the possession of his property. He then acquired vast authority over lands and people. With it went responsibility. In the words of Honorius of Autun:

Soldiers: You are the arm of the Church, because you should defend it against its enemies. Your duty is to aid the oppressed, to restrain yourself from rapine and fornication, to repress those who impugn the Church with evil acts, and to resist those who are rebels against priests. Performing such a service, you will obtain the most splendid of benefices from the greatest of Kings.[32]

Nobles rarely lived up to this ideal, and there are countless examples of nobles attacking the church. In the early thirteenth century, Peter of Dreux, count of Brittany, spent so much of his time attacking the church that he was known as the "Scourge of the Clergy."

The nobles' conception of rewards and gratification did not involve the kind of postponement envisioned by the clergy. They wanted rewards immediately. Since by definition a military class is devoted to war, those rewards came through the pursuit of arms. When nobles were not involved in local squabbles with neighbors—usually disputes over property or over real or imagined slights— they participated in tournaments.

Complete jurisdiction over properties allowed the noble, at long last, to gratify his desire for display and lavish living. Since his status in medieval society depended on the size of his household, he would be anxious to increase the number of his household retainers. The elegance of his clothes, the variety and richness of his table, the number of his horses and followers, the freedom with which he spent money—all were public indications of his social standing. The aristocratic lifestyle was luxurious and extravagant. To maintain it, nobles often had to borrow from financiers or wealthy monasteries.

At the same time, nobles had a great deal of work to do. The responsibilities of a noble in the High Middle Ages depended on the size and extent of his estates, the number of his dependents, and his position in his territory relative to others of his class and to the king. As a vassal he was required to fight for his lord or for the king when called on to do so. By the mid-twelfth century, this service was limited in most parts of western Europe to forty days a year. The noble might have to perform guard duty at his lord's castle for a certain number of days a year. He was obliged to attend his lord's court on important occasions when the lord wanted to put on great displays, such as at Easter, Pentecost, and Christmas. When the lord knighted his eldest son or married off his eldest daughter, he called his vassals to his court. They were expected to attend and to present a contribution known as a "gracious aid."

Throughout the year, a noble had to look after his own estates. He had to appoint prudent and honest overseers and make sure that they paid him the customary revenues and services. Since a great lord's estates were usually widely scattered, he had to travel frequently.

Until the late thirteenth century, when royal authority intervened, a noble in France or England had great power over the knights and peasants on his estates. He maintained order among them and dispensed justice to them. Holding the manorial court, which punished criminal acts and settled disputes, was one of his gravest obligations. The quality of justice varied widely: some lords were vicious tyrants who exploited and persecuted their peasants; others were reasonable and evenhanded. In any case, the quality of life on the manor and its productivity were related in no small way to the temperament and decency of the lord—and his lady.

Women played a large and important role in the functioning of the estate. They were responsible for the practical management of the household's "inner economy"—cooking, brewing, spinning, weaving, caring for yard animals. The lifestyle of the medieval warrior-nobles required constant travel, both for purposes of war and for the supervision of distant properties. When the lord was away for long periods, the women frequently managed the herds, barns, granaries, and outlying fields as well.

Frequent pregnancies and the reluctance to expose women to hostile conditions kept the lady at home and therefore able to assume supervision of the family's fixed properties. When a husband went away on crusade—and this could last anywhere from two to five years, if he returned at all—his wife often became the sole manager of the family properties. When her husband went to the Holy Land between 1060 and 1080, the lady Hersendis was the sole manager of her family's properties in northern France.

Nor were women's activities confined to managing households and estates in their husbands' absence. Medieval warfare was largely a matter of brief skirmishes, and few men were killed in any single encounter. But altogether the number slain ran high, and there were many widows. Aristocratic widows frequently controlled family properties and fortunes and exercised great authority. Although the evidence is scattered and sketchy, there are indications that women performed many of the functions of men. In Spain, France, and Germany they bought, sold, and otherwise transferred property. Gertrude, labeled "Saxony's almighty widow" by the chronicler Ekkehard of Aura, took a leading role in conspiracies against the emperor Henry V. And Eilika Billung, widow of Count Otto of Ballenstedt, built a castle at Burgwerben on the Saale River and, as advocate of the monastery of Goseck, removed one abbot and selected his successor. From her castle at Bernburg, the countess Eilika was also reputed to ravage the countryside.

Throughout the High Middle Ages, fighting remained the dominant feature of the noble lifestyle. The church's preachings and condemnations reduced but did not stop violence. Lateness of inheri-

tance, depriving the nobility of constructive outlets for their energy, together with the military ethos of their culture, encouraged petty warfare and disorder. The nobility thus represented a constant source of trouble for the monarchy. In the thirteenth century, kings drew on the financial support of the middle classes to build the administrative machinery that gradually laid the foundations for strong royal government. The Crusades relieved the rulers of France, England, and the German Empire of some of their most dangerous elements. Complete royal control of the nobility, however, came only in modern times.

THOSE WHO PRAY

Medieval people believed that monks performed an important social service, prayer. In the Middle Ages, prayer was looked on as a vital service, one as crucial as the labor of peasants and the military might of nobles. Just as the knights protected and defended society with the sword and the peasants provided sustenance through their toil, so the monks with their prayers and chants worked to secure God's blessing for society.

Monasticism represented some of the finest aspirations of medieval civilization. The monasteries were devoted to prayer, and their standards of Christian behavior influenced the entire church. The monasteries produced the educated elite that was continually drawn into the administrative service of kings and great lords. Monks kept alive the remains of classical culture and experimented with new styles of architecture and art. They introduced new techniques of estate management and land reclamation. Although relatively few in number in the High Middle Ages, the monks played a significant role in medieval society.

Recruitment

Toward the end of his *Ecclesiastical History of England and Normandy*, when he was well into his sixties, Orderic Vitalis, a monk of the Norman abbey of Saint Evroul, interrupted his narrative to explain movingly how he happened to become a monk:

French Castle Under Siege   Most medieval warfare consisted of small skirmishes and the besieging of castles. If surrounded by a moat and supplied with food and water, a few knights could hold a castle against large armies for a long time. Notice the use of engines to hurl missiles. *(Source: The British Library)*

And so, O glorious God, you didst inspire my father Ode-leric to renounce me utterly and submit me in all things to thy governance. So, weeping, he gave me, a weeping child, into the care of the monk Reginald, and sent me away into exile for love of thee, and never saw me again. And I, a mere boy, did not presume to oppose my father's wishes, but obeyed him in all things, for he promised me for his part that if I became a monk I should taste of the joys of Heaven with the Innocents after my death. . . . And so, a boy of ten, I crossed the English channel and came into Normandy as an exile, unknown to all, knowing no one. Like Joseph in Egypt I heard a language which I could not understand. But thou didst suffer me through thy grace to find nothing but kindness among strangers. I was received as an oblate in the abbey of St. Evroul by the

venerable abbot Mainier in the eleventh year of my life. . . . The name of Vitalis was given me in place of my English name, which sounded harsh to the Normans.[33]

Orderic Vitalis (ca 1075–ca 1140) was one of the leading scholars of his time. As such, he is not a representative figure or even a typical monk. Intellectuals, those who earn their living or spend most of their time working with ideas, are never typical figures of their times. In one respect, however, Orderic was quite representative of the monks of the High Middle Ages: although he had no doubt that God wanted him to be a monk, the decision was actually made by his parents, who gave him to a monastery as a child-oblate. Orderic was the third son of a knight who fought for William the Conqueror at the Battle of Hastings (1066). For his participation in the Norman conquest of England, he was rewarded with lands in western England. Concern for the provision of his two older sons probably led him to give his youngest to the monastery.

Medieval monasteries were religious institutions whose organization and structure fulfilled the social needs of the feudal nobility. The monasteries provided noble children with both an honorable and aristocratic life and opportunities for ecclesiastical careers.[34]

Until well into modern times, and certainly in the Middle Ages, almost everyone believed in the thorough subjection of children to their parents. This belief was the logical consequence of the fact that young noblemen were not expected to work and were therefore totally dependent on their fathers. Some men did become monks as adults, apparently for a wide variety of reasons: belief in a direct call from God, disgust with the materialism and violence of the secular world, the encouragement and inspiration of others, economic failure or lack of opportunity, poverty, sickness, fear of hell. However, most men who became monks, until about the early thirteenth century, seem to have been given as child-oblates by their parents.

In the thirteenth century, the older Benedictine and Cistercian orders had to compete with new orders of friars—the Franciscans and Dominicans. More monks had to be recruited from the middle class, that is, from small landholders or traders in the district near the abbey. As medieval society changed economically, and as European society ever so slowly developed middle-class traits, the monasteries almost inevitably drew their manpower, when they were able, from the middle classes. Until that time, they were preserves of the aristocratic nobility.

The Nuns

Throughout the Middle Ages, social class also defined the kinds of religious life open to women. Kings and nobles usually established convents for their daughters, sisters, aunts, or aging mothers. Entrance was restricted to women of the founder's class. Since a well-born lady could not honorably be apprenticed to a tradesperson, and since her dignity did not permit her to do any kind of manual labor, the sole alternative to life at home was the religious life.

The founder's endowment and support greatly influenced the later social, economic, and political status of the convent. Social and religious bonds between benefactors and communities of nuns frequently continued over many generations. A few convents received large endowments and could accept many women. Amesbury Priory in Wiltshire, England, for example, received a handsome endowment from King Henry II in 1177, and his successors Henry III and Edward I also made lavish gifts. In 1256 Amesbury supported a prioress and 76 nuns, 7 priests, and 16 lay brothers. It owned 200 oxen, 23 horses, 7 cows, 4 calves, 300 pigs, and 4,800 sheep. The convent raised 100 pounds in annual rents and 40 pounds from the wool clip, very large sums at the time. The entrance of such highborn ladies as the dowager queen Eleanor (widow of Henry III), Edward I's daughter Mary, and his niece Isabella of Lancaster stimulated the gift of additional lands and privileges. By 1317 Amesbury had 177 nuns.[35] Most houses of women, however, possessed limited resources and remained small in numbers.

The office of abbess or prioress, the house's superior, customarily went to a nun of considerable social standing. Thus William the Conqueror's daughter Cecelia became abbess of her mother's foundation, Holy Trinity Abbey in Caen, and Henry II's daughter became abbess of Barking. Since an abbess or prioress had responsibility for governing her community and for representing it in any business with the outside world, she was a woman of local power and importance. Sometimes her position brought national prominence. In 1306 Edward I of England summoned several abbesses to Parliament; he wanted their financial support for the expenses connected with knighting his eldest son.

What kind of life did the nuns lead? Religious duties held prime importance. Then there were business responsibilities connected with lands, properties, and rents that preoccupied those women of administrative ability. Sewing, embroidery, and fine needlework were considered the special pursuits of gentlewomen. Nuns in houses with an intellectual tradition copied manuscripts. Although the level of intellectual life in the women's houses varied widely, the careers of two nuns—

Hildegard of Bingen and Isabella of Lancaster—suggest the activities of some nuns in the High Middle Ages.

The tenth child of a lesser noble family, Hildegard (1098–1179) was given when eight years old as an oblate to an abbey in the Rhineland, where she learned Latin and received a good education. Obviously possessed of leadership and administrative talents, Hildegard was sent in 1147 to found the convent of Rupertsberg near Bingen. There she produced a body of writings including the *Scivias (Know the Ways),* a record of her mystical visions that incorporates vast theological learning; the *Physica (On the Physical Elements),* a classification of the natural elements, such as plants, animals, metals, and the movements of the heavenly bodies; a mystery play; and a medical work that led a distinguished twentieth-century historian of science to describe Hildegard as "one of the most original writers of the Latin West in the twelfth century." At the same time, she carried on a vast correspondence with scholars, prelates, and ordinary people and had such a reputation for wisdom that a recent writer has called her "the Dear Abby of the twelfth century to whom everyone came or wrote for advice or comfort." [36] An exceptionally gifted person, Hildegard represents the Benedictine ideal of great learning combined with a devoted monastic life.

As with monks, however, intellectual nuns were not typical of the era. The life of the English nun Isabella of Lancaster better exemplifies the careers of high-born women who became nuns. The niece of King Edward I, she was placed at Amesbury Priory in early childhood, grew up there, made her profession of commitment to the convent life, and became abbess in 1343. Isabella seems to have been a conventional but not devout nun. She traveled widely, spent long periods at the royal court, and with the support of her wealthy relations maintained a residence apart from the priory. She was, however, an able administrator who handled the community finances with prudent skill. Amesbury lacked the intellectual and spiritual standards of Bingen. Isabella's interests were secular and her own literary production was a book of romances.

Prayer and Other Work

In medieval Europe the monasteries of men greatly outnumbered those of women. The pattern of life

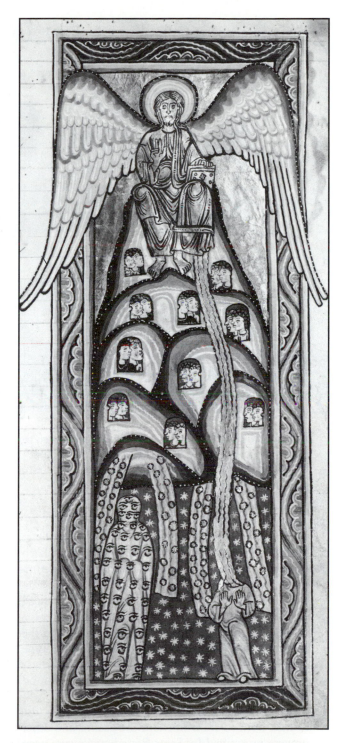

Hildegard of Bingen To describe her gift of visions, Hildegard wrote *Scivias (Know the Ways),* an encyclopedia of Christian salvation. In this first vision, God, enthroned in light at the top of a mountain symbolizing the divine kingdom, embraces all of creation and promises eternal life. *(Source: Rheinisches Bildarchiv)*

Monk Instructing Illuminator   All monks had to learn to read in order to perform the religious services. As illustrated here, a few of the more intellectually and artistically gifted monks were often taught how to copy and to illuminate manuscripts. *(Source: The Pierpont Morgan Library)*

within individual monasteries varied widely from house to house and from region to region. Each monastic community was shaped by the circumstances of its foundation and endowment, by tradition, by the interests of its abbots and members, and by local conditions. It would therefore be a mistake to think that Christian monasticism in the High Middle Ages was everywhere the same. One central activity, however—the work of God—was performed everywhere. Daily life centered around the liturgy.

Seven times a day and once during the night, the monks went to choir to chant the psalms and other prayers prescribed by Saint Benedict. Prayers were offered for peace, rain, good harvests, the civil authorities, the monks' families, and their benefactors. Monastic patrons in turn lavished gifts on the monasteries, which often became very wealthy. Through their prayers the monks performed a valuable service for the rest of society.

Prayer justified the monks' spending a large percentage of their income on splendid objects to enhance the liturgy; monks praised God, they believed, not only in prayer but in everything connected with prayer. They sought to accumulate priestly vestments of the finest silks, velvets, and embroideries, as well as sacred vessels of embossed silver and gold. Thuribles containing sweet-smelling incense brought at great expense from the Orient were used at the altars, following ancient Jewish ritual. The pages of Gospel books were richly decorated with gold leaf, and the books' bindings were ornamented and bejeweled. Every monastery tried to acquire the relics of its patron saint, which necessitated the production of a beautiful reliquary to house the relics. The liturgy, then, inspired a great deal of art, and the monasteries became the crucibles of art in Western Christendom.

The monks fulfilled their social responsibility by praying. It was generally agreed that they could best carry out this duty if they were not distracted by worldly needs. Thus great and lesser lords gave the monasteries lands that would supply the community with necessities. Each manorial unit was responsible for provisioning the abbey for a definite period of time, and the expenses of each manor were supposed to equal its income.

The administration of the abbey's estates and properties consumed considerable time. The operation of a large establishment, such as Cluny in Burgundy or Bury Saint Edmunds in England, which by 1150 had several hundred monks, involved planning, prudence, and wise management. Although the abbot or prior had absolute authority in making assignments, common sense advised that tasks be allotted according to the talents of individual monks.

The usual method of economic organization was the manor. Many monastic manors were small enough and close enough to the abbey to be supervised directly by the abbot. But if a monastery held and farmed vast estates, the properties were divided into administrative units under the supervision of one of the monks of the house. The lands of the German abbey of Saint Emmeran at Regensburg, for example, were divided into thirty-three manorial centers.

Because the *choir monks* were aristocrats, they did not till the land themselves. In each house one monk, the *cellarer* or general financial manager, was responsible for supervising the peasants or lay brothers who did the actual agricultural labor. *Lay brothers* were vowed religious drawn from the servile classes, with simpler religious and intellectual obligations than those of the choir monks. The cellarer had to see to it that the estates of the monastery produced enough income to cover its expenses. Another monk, the *almoner,* was responsible for feeding and caring for the poor of the neighborhood. At the French abbey of Saint-Requier in the eleventh century, 110 persons were fed every day. At Corbie, fifty loaves of bread were distributed daily to the poor.

The *precentor* or *cantor* was responsible for the library and the careful preservation of books. The *sacristan* of the abbey had in his charge all the materials and objects connected with the liturgy—vestments, candles, incense, sacred vessels, altar cloths, and hangings. The *novice master* was responsible for the training of recruits, instructing them in the *Rule,* the chant, the Scriptures, and the history and traditions of the house. For a few of the monks,

work was some form of intellectual activity, such as the copying of books and manuscripts, the preparation of manuals, and the writing of letters.

Although several orders forbade monks to study law and medicine, that rule was often ignored. In the twelfth and thirteenth centuries, many monks gained considerable reputations for their knowledge and experience in the practice of both the canon law of the church and the civil law of their countries. For example, the Norman monk Lanfranc, because of his legal knowledge and administrative ability, became the chief adviser of William the Conqueror.

Although knowledge of medicine was primitive by twentieth-century standards, monastic practitioners were less ignorant than one would suspect. Long before 1066, a rich medical literature had been produced in England. The most important of these treatises was *The Leech Book of Bald (leech* means "medical"). This work exhibits a wide knowledge of herbal prescriptions, ancient authorities, and empirical practice. Bald discusses diseases of the lungs and stomach together with their remedies and demonstrates his acquaintance with surgery. Medical knowledge was sometimes rewarded. King Henry I of England enriched several of his physicians, and Henry II made his medical adviser, the monk Robert de Veneys, abbot of Malmesbury.

The religious houses of medieval Europe usually took full advantage of whatever resources and opportunities their location offered. For example, the raising of horses could produce income in a world that depended on horses for travel and for warfare. Some monasteries, such as the Cistercian abbey of Jervaulx in Yorkshire, became famous for and quite wealthy from their production of prime breeds. In the eleventh and twelfth centuries, a period of considerable monastic expansion, large tracts of swamp, fen, forest, and wasteland were brought under cultivation—principally by the Cistercians. (Map 10.1)

The Cistercians, whose constitution insisted that they accept lands far from human habitation and forbade them to be involved in the traditional feudal-manorial structure, were ideally suited to the agricultural needs and trends of their times. In the Low Countries (present-day Holland, Belgium, and French Flanders) they built dikes to hold back the sea, and the reclaimed land was put to the production of cereals. In the eastern parts of Germany —Silesia, Mecklenburg, and Pomerania—they took the lead in draining swamps and cultivating

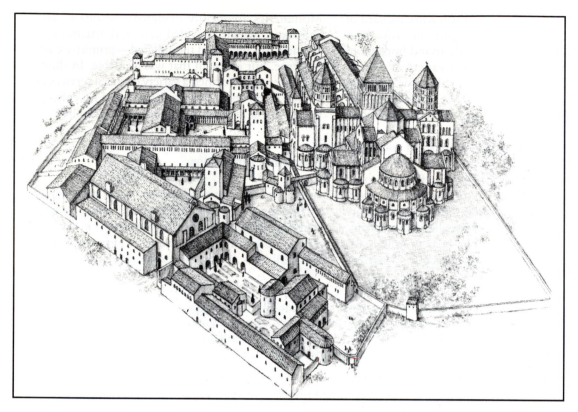

Cluny, ca 1157   Begun in 1085 and supported by the generosity of kings and peasants, the church (right center) and monastery of Cluny was the administrative center of a vast monastic and feudal empire. Note the apse around the east end of the church and the large foreground complex, which served as monastic infirmary and guest hostel. *(Source: The Medieval Academy of America)*

large quantities of rich food. The monks' habits were made of the best cloth available. Cluny's abbots and priors traveled with sizable retinues, as great lords were required to do. The abbots worked to make the liturgy ever more magnificent, and large sums were spent on elaborate vestments and jeweled vessels. Hugh, the sixth abbot (1049–1109), embarked on an extraordinarily expensive building program. He entirely rebuilt the abbey church, and when Pope Urban II consecrated it in 1095, it was the largest church in Christendom. The monks lived like lords, which in a sense they were.

Revenue came from the hundreds of monasteries scattered across France, Italy, Spain, and England that Cluny had reformed in the eleventh century; each year they paid Cluny a cash sum. Novices were expected to make a gift of land or cash when they entered. For reasons of security, knights departing on crusade often placed their estates under Cluny's

authority. Still this income was not enough. The management of Cluny's manors across Europe was entrusted to bailiffs or wardens who were not monks and were given lifetime contracts. Frequently these bailiffs were poor managers and produced no profits. But they could not be removed and replaced. In order to meet expenses, Cluny had to rely on cash reserves. For example, Cluny's estates produced only a small percentage of needed food supplies; the rest had to be paid for from cash reserves.

Cluny had two basic alternatives—improve management to cut costs or borrow money. The abbey could have placed the monastic manors under the jurisdiction of monks, rather than hiring bailiffs who would grow rich as middlemen. It could have awarded annual rather than lifetime contracts, supervised all revenues, and tried to cut costs within the monastery. But Cluny chose the second alternative—borrowing. The abbey spent hoarded reserves of cash and fell into debt.

In contrast to the abbot of Cluny, Suger, the superior of the royal abbey of Saint-Denis near Paris from 1122 to 1151, was a shrewd manager. Though he, too, spared no expense to enhance the beauty of his monastery and church, Suger kept an eye on costs and made sure that his properties were soundly managed. But the management of Saint-Denis was unusual. Far more typical was the economic mismanagement at Cluny. By the later twelfth century, small and great monasteries were facing comparable financial difficulties.

SUMMARY

Generalizations about peasant life in the High Middle Ages must always be qualified according to manorial customs, the weather and geography, and the personalities of local lords. Everywhere, however, the performance of agricultural services and the payment of rents preoccupied peasants. Though peasants led hard lives, the reclamation of waste and forest lands, migration to frontier territory, or flight to a town (see Chap. 11) offered means of social mobility. The Christian faith, though perhaps not understood at an intellectual level, provided a strong emotional and spiritual solace.

By 1100 the knightly class was united in its ability to fight on horseback, its insistence that each member was descended from a valorous ancestor, its privileges, and its position at the top of the social hierarchy. The nobility possessed a strong class consciousness. Aristocratic values and attitudes shaded all aspects of medieval culture. Trained for war, nobles often devoted considerable time to fighting, and intergenerational squabbles were common. Yet a noble might have shouldered heavy judicial, political, and economic responsibilities, depending on the size of his estates.

The monks and nuns exercised a profound influence on matters of the spirit. In their prayers, monks and nuns battled for the Lord, just as the chivalrous knights did on the battlefield. In their chant and rich ceremonial, in their architecture and literary productions, and in the example of many monks' lives, the monasteries inspired Christian peoples to an incalculable degree. As the crucibles of sacred art, the monasteries became the cultural centers of Christian Europe.

NOTES

1. G. Duby, *The Chivalrous Society,* trans. C. Postan (Berkeley: University of California Press, 1977), pp. 90–93.
2. Honorius of Autun, "Elucidarium sive Dialogus de Summa Totius Christianae Theologiae," in *Patrologia Latina,* ed. J. P. Migne (Paris: Garnier Brothers, 1854), vol. 172, col. 1149.
3. E. Power, "Peasant Life and Rural Conditions," in J. R. Tanner et al., *The Cambridge Medieval History,* vol. 7 (Cambridge: Cambridge University Press, 1958), p. 716.
4. Glanvill, "De Legibus Angliae," bk. 5, chap. 5, in *Social Life in Britain from the Conquest to the Reformation,* ed. G. G. Coulton (London: Cambridge University Press, 1956), pp. 338–339.
5. J. B. Freed, *The Friars and German Society in the Thirteenth Century* (Cambridge, Mass.: Medieval Academy of America, 1977), p. 55.
6. See W. C. Jordan, *From Servitude to Freedom: Manumission in the Senonais in the Thirteenth Century* (Philadelphia: University of Pennsylvania Press, 1986), esp. chap. 3, pp. 37–58.
7. See L. White, Jr., *Medieval Technology and Social Change* (Oxford: Clarendon Press, 1962), pp. 59–63.
8. G. Duby, *The Early Growth of the European Economy: Warriors and Peasants from the Seventh to the Twelfth Century* (Ithaca, N.Y.: Cornell University Press, 1978), pp. 213–219.
9. See B. A. Hanawalt, *The Ties That Bound: Peasant Families in Medieval England* (New York: Oxford University Press, 1986), pp. 90–100.
10. Ibid., p. 149.
11. On this quantity and medieval measurements, see D. Knowles, "The Measures of Monastic Beverages," in *The Monastic Order in England* (Cambridge: Cambridge University Press, 1962), p. 717.
12. G. Duby, *Rural Economy and Country Life in the Medieval West,* trans. C. Postan (London: Edward Arnold, 1968), pp. 146–147.
13. S. R. Scargill-Bird, ed., *Custumals of Battle Abbey in the Reigns of Edward I and Edward II* (London: Camden Society, 1887), pp. 213–219.
14. John 19:25–27.
15. J. B. Freed, "The Origins of the European Nobility: The Problem of the Ministerials," *Viator* 7 (1976): 213.
16. Duby, *The Chivalrous Society,* pp. 104–105.
17. See C. Bouchard, "The Origins of the French Nobility," *The American Historical Review* 86 (1981): 501–532.
18. Duby, *The Chivalrous Society,* p. 98.
19. G. Duby, *The Age of the Cathedrals: Art and Society 980–1420,* trans. E. Levieux and B. Thompson (Chi-

cago: University of Chicago Press, 1981), p. 38.

20. Freed, "The Origins of the European Nobility," p. 214.

21. J. Boswell, *The Kindness of Strangers: The Abandonment of Children in Western Europe from Late Antiquity to the Renaissance* (New York: Pantheon Books, 1989), p. 24. This section relies heavily on this important work.

22. Ibid., pp. 214, 223.

23. Ibid., pp. 428–429.

24. Ibid., pp. 238–239.

25. Ibid., pp. 297, 299, and the Conclusion.

26. J. C. Russell, *Late Ancient and Medieval Population Control* (Philadelphia: American Philosophical Society, 1985), p. 180.

27. See J. B. Freed, *The Counts of Falkenstein: Noble Self-Consciousness in Twelfth-Century Germany,* Transactions of the American Philosophical Society, vol. 74, pt. 6 (Philadelphia, 1984), pp. 163–167.

28. R. J. Leyser, *Rule and Conflict in an Early Medieval Society: Ottonian Saxony* (Bloomington: Indiana University Press, 1979), pp. 49, 59.

29. J. F. Benton, ed. and trans., *Self and Society in Medieval France: The Memoirs of Abbot Guibert of Nogent* (New York: Harper & Row, 1970), p. 46.

30. D. Herlihy, "The Generation Gap in Medieval History," *Viator* 5 (1974): 360.

31. Quoted in ibid., p. 361.

32. Honorius of Autun, in *Patrologia Latina,* vol. 172, col. 1148.

33. M. Chibnall, ed. and trans., *The Ecclesiastical History of Orderic Vitalis* (Oxford: Oxford University Press, 1972), 2.xiii.

34. R. W. Southern, *Western Society and the Church in the Middle Ages* (Baltimore: Penguin Books, 1970), pp. 224–230, esp. p. 228.

35. See M. W. Labarge, *A Small Sound of the Trumpet: Women in Medieval Life* (Boston: Beacon Press, 1986), pp. 104–105.

36. J. M. Ferrante, "The Education of Women in the Middle Ages in Theory, Fact, and Fantasy," in *Beyond Their Sex: Learned Women of the European Past,* ed. P. H. Labalme (New York: New York University Press, 1980), pp. 22–24.

SUGGESTED READING

The best short introduction to the material in this chapter is C. Brooke, *The Structure of Medieval Society* (1971), a beautifully illustrated book. The student interested in aspects of medieval slavery, serfdom, or the peasantry should begin with M. Bloch, "How Ancient Slavery Came to an End" and "Personal Liberty and Servitude in the Middle Ages, Particularly in France," in *Slavery and Serfdom in the Middle Ages: Selected Essays* (trans. W. R. Beer, 1975). There is an excellent discussion of these problems in the magisterial work of G. Duby, *Rural Economy and Country Life in the Medieval West* (trans. C. Postan, 1968). G. C. Homans, *English Villagers of the Thirteenth Century* (1975), is a fine combination of sociological and historical scholarship, and the older study of H. S. Bennett, *Life on the English Manor: A Study of Peasant Conditions* (1960), contains much useful information presented in a highly readable fashion. E. L. Ladurie, *Montaillou: Cathars and Catholics in a French Village, 1294–1324* (trans. B. Bray, 1978), is a fascinating glimpse of village life. G. Duby, *The Early Growth of the European Economy,* cited in the Notes, is a superb synthesis by a leading authority. Advanced students should see the same author's *The Three Orders: Feudal Society Imagined* (1980), a brilliant but difficult book.

For the religion of the people, two recent studies are highly recommended: R. and C. Brooke, *Popular Religion in the Middle Ages* (1984), a highly readable synthesis, and B. Ward, *Miracles and the Medieval Mind* (1982), an important and scholarly study. For the development of lay literacy, see M. T. Clanchy, *From Memory to Written Record: England, 1066–1307* (1979).

For the origins and status of the nobility in the High Middle Ages, students are strongly urged to see the recent and important studies by Bouchard, Duby, and Freed cited in the Notes. See, in addition, L. Genicot, "The Nobility in Medieval Francia: Continuity, Break, or Evolution?"; A. Borst, "Knighthood in the High Middle Ages: Ideal and Reality"; and two studies by G. Duby, "The Nobility in Eleventh and Twelfth Century Maconnais" and "Northwestern France: The 'Youth' in Twelfth Century Aristocratic Society." All these articles appear in F. L. Cheyette, ed., *Lordship and Community in Medieval Europe: Selected Readings* (1968). Social mobility among both aristocracy and peasantry are discussed in T. Evergates, *Feudal Society in the Bailliage of Troyes Under the Counts of Champagne, 1152–1284* (1976). K. F. Bosl, "Kingdom and Principality in Twelfth-Century France," and the same author's " 'Noble Unfreedom': The Rise of the Ministerials in Germany," in T. Reuter, ed., *The Medieval Nobility: Studies on the Ruling Classes of France and Germany from the Sixth to the Twelfth Century* (1978), are also fundamental. The older study of M. Bloch, *Feudal Society* (1966), is now somewhat dated. The career of the man described by contemporaries as "the greatest of knights" is celebrated in G. Duby, *William Marshal: The Flowering of Chivalry* (trans. R. Howard, 1985), a remarkable rags-to-riches story.

There is no dearth of good material on the monks in medieval society. The titles listed in the Suggested Reading for Chapter 7 represent a good starting point for study. A. Boyd, *The Monks of Durham* (1975), is an excellently illustrated introductory sketch of many facets of monastic culture in the High Middle Ages. B. D. Hill's articles, "Benedictines" and "Cistercian Order," in J. R. Strayer, ed., *Dictionary of the Middle Ages,* vols. 2 and 3 (1982 and 1983), provide broad surveys of the premier monastic orders and contain useful bibliographies. L. J. Lekai, *The Cistercians: Ideals and Reality* (1977), synthesizes recent research on the white monks and carries their story down to the twentieth century. P. D. Johnson, *Prayer, Patronage, and Power: The Abbey of La Trinité, Vendôme, 1032–1187* (1981), examines one important French monastery in its social environment; this book is a valuable contribution to medieval local history. T. Verdon, ed., *Monasticism and the Arts* (1984), is a rich compilation of papers on various aspects of monastic culture, some of them written by leading scholars. J. Leclercq, *Monks on Marriage: A Twelfth Century View* (1982), studies marital-love literature and gives new insights on medieval attitudes toward sex and marital love. G. Duby, *The Age of the Cathedrals,* cited in the Notes, is especially strong on the monastic origins of medieval art. Both W. Braunfels, *Monasteries of Western Europe: The Architecture of the Orders* (1972), and C. Brooke, *The Monastic World* (1974), have splendid illustrations and good bibliographies. The best study of medieval English Cistercian architecture is P. Fergusson, *Architecture of Solitude: Cistercian Abbeys in Twelfth Century England* (1984).

For women and children, in addition to the titles by Labarge and Boswell cited in the Notes, see E. Power, *Medieval Women* (1976), a nicely illustrated sketch of the several classes of women; D. Herlihy, *Medieval Households* (1985), which treats marriage patterns, family size, sexual relations, and emotional life; A. Macfarlane, *Marriage and Love in England, 1300–1840* (1987); J. McNamara and S. F. Wemple, "Sanctity and Power: The Dual Pursuit of Medieval Women," in R. Bridenthal and C. Koonz, eds., *Becoming Visible: Women in European History* (1987); B. Hanawalt, ed., *Women and Work in Preindustrial Europe* (1986), which describes the activities of women as ale-wives, midwives, businesswomen, nurses, and servants; and Derek Baker, ed., *Medieval Women* (1978), which contains excellent articles on many facets of women's history.

For further treatment of nuns, see, in addition to the titles by Lekai and Brooke above, B. Newman, *Sister of Wisdom: St. Hildegard's Theology of the Feminine* (1987), a learned and lucidly written study; S. Elkins, *Holy Women in Twelfth-Century England* (1985); C. Bynum, *Jesus as Mother: Studies in the Spirituality of the High Middle Ages* (1984), which contains valuable articles on facets of women's religious history and an excellent contrast of the differing spirituality of monks and nuns; and C. Bynum's *Holy Feast and Holy Fast* (1987), which treats the significance of food for nuns and others in medieval society. For health and medical care, B. Rowland, *Medieval Woman's Guide to Health* (1981), makes very interesting reading.

11

The Creativity and Vitality of the High Middle Ages

The High Middle Ages witnessed some of the most remarkable achievements in the entire history of Western society. Europeans displayed tremendous creativity and vitality in many facets of culture. Political rulers tried to establish contact with all their peoples, developed new legal and financial institutions, and slowly consolidated power in the hands of the monarchy. The kings of France and England succeeded in laying the foundations of modern national states. The European economy underwent a remarkable recovery, as evidenced by the growth and development of towns and the revival of long-distance trade. The university, a uniquely Western contribution to civilization and a superb expression of medieval creativity, came into being at the same time. The Gothic cathedral manifested medieval people's deep Christian faith and their appreciation for the worlds of nature, man, and God.

- How did medieval rulers in England, France, and Germany work to solve their problems of government, thereby laying the foundations of the modern state?

- How did medieval towns originate and how do they reveal the beginnings of radical change in medieval society?

- Why did towns become the center of religious heresy, and what was the church's response?

- How did universities evolve, and what needs of medieval society did they serve?

- What does the Gothic cathedral reveal about the ideals, attitudes, and interests of medieval people?

This chapter will focus on these questions.

MEDIEVAL ORIGINS OF THE MODERN STATE

Rome's great legacy to Western civilization had been the concepts of the state and the law; but for almost five hundred years after the disintegration of the Roman Empire in the West, the state as a reality did not exist. Political authority was completely decentralized. Power was spread among many feudal lords, who gave their localities such protection and security as their strength allowed.

The fiefdoms, kingdoms, and territories that covered the continent of Europe did not have the qualities or provide the services of a modern state. They did not have jurisdiction over many people, and their laws affected a relative few. In the mid-eleventh century, there existed many layers of authority —earls, counts, barons, knights—between a king and the ordinary people.

In these circumstances, medieval kings had common goals. The rulers of England, France, and Germany wanted to strengthen and extend royal authority within their territories. They wanted to establish an effective means of communication with all peoples, in order to increase public order. They wanted more revenue and efficient bureaucracies. The solutions they found to these problems laid the foundations for modern national states.

The modern state is an organized territory with definite geographical boundaries that are recognized by other states. It has a body of law and institutions of government. If the state claims to govern according to law, it is guided in its actions by the law. The modern national state counts on the loyalty of its citizens, or at least of a majority of them. In return, it provides order so that citizens can go about their daily work and other activities. It protects its citizens in their persons and property. The state tries to prevent violence and to apprehend and punish those who commit it. It supplies a currency or medium of exchange that permits financial and commercial transactions. The state conducts relations with foreign governments. In order to accomplish even these minimal functions, the state must have officials, bureaucracies, laws, courts of law, soldiers, information, and money. States with these attributes are relatively recent developments.

Unification and Communication

Under the pressure of the Danish (or Viking) invasions of the ninth and tenth centuries, the seven kingdoms of Anglo-Saxon England united under one king (see page 260). At the same time, for reasons historians still cannot fully explain, England was divided into local units called "shires," or counties, each under the jurisdiction of a sheriff appointed by the king. The Danish king Canute (r. 1016–1035) and his successor, Edward the Confessor (r. 1042–1066), exercised broader authority than any contemporary ruler on the Continent. All the English *thegns,* or local chieftains, recognized the central authority of the kingship. The kingdom of England, therefore, had a political head start on the rest of Europe.

When Edward the Confessor died, his cousin Duke William of Normandy—known in English history as William the Conqueror—claimed the English throne and in 1066 defeated the Anglo-Saxon claimant on the battlefield of Hastings. As William subdued the rest of the country, he distributed lands to his Norman followers and assigned specific military quotas to each estate. He also required all feudal lords to swear an oath of allegiance to him as king.

William the Conqueror (r. 1066–1087) preserved the Anglo-Saxon institution of sheriffs representing the king at the local level but replaced Anglo-Saxon sheriffs with Normans. A sheriff had heavy duties. He maintained order in the shire. He caught criminals and punished them in the shire court, over which he presided. He collected taxes

and, when the king ordered him to do so, raised an army of foot soldiers. The sheriff also organized adult males in groups of ten, with each member liable for the good behavior of the others. The Conqueror thus made local people responsible for order in their communities. For all his efforts, the sheriff received no pay. This system, whereby unpaid officials governed the county, served as the basic pattern of English local government for many centuries. It cost the Crown nothing, but it restricted opportunities for public service to the well-to-do.

William also retained another Anglo-Saxon device, the *writ.* This brief administrative order, written in the vernacular (Anglo-Saxon) by a government clerk, was the means by which the central government communicated with people at the local level. Sheriffs were empowered to issue writs relating to matters in their counties.

The Conqueror introduced into England a major innovation, the Norman inquest. At his Christmas court in 1085, William discussed the

The Bayeux Tapestry   Measuring 231 feet by 19½ inches, the Bayeux Tapestry gives a narrative description of the events surrounding the Norman Conquest of England. The tapestry provides an important historical source for the clothing, armor, and lifestyles of the Norman and Anglo-Saxon warrior class. *(Source: Tapisserie de Bayeux et avec autorisation spéciale de la Ville de Bayeux)*

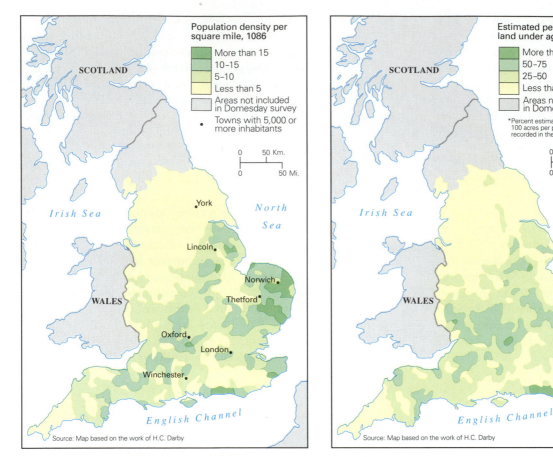

MAP 11.1 Domesday Population and Agriculture, 1086   The incomparably rich evidence of *Domesday Book* enables modern demographers and historians to calculate the English population and land under cultivation in the eleventh century.

state of the kingdom with his vassals and decided to conduct a systematic investigation of the entire country. The survey was to be made by means of *inquests*, or general inquiries, held throughout England. William wanted to determine how much wealth there was in his new kingdom, who held what land, and what lands had been disputed among his vassals since the conquest of 1066. Groups of royal officials or judges were sent to every part of the country. In every village and farm, the priest and six local people were put under oath to answer the questions of the king's commissioners truthfully. In the words of a contemporary chronicler:

He sent his men over all England into every shire and had them find out how many hundred hides there were in the shire [a hide was a measure of land large enough to support one family], or what land and cattle the king himself

had, or what dues he ought to have in twelve months from the shire. Also . . . what or how much everybody had who was occupying land in England, in land or cattle, and how much money it was worth. So very narrowly did he have it investigated, that there was no single hide nor yard of land, nor indeed . . . one ox nor one cow nor one pig was there left out, and not put down in his record: and all these records were brought to him afterwards.[1]

The resulting record, called *Domesday Book* from the Anglo-Saxon word *doom* meaning "judgment," still survives. It is an invaluable source of social and economic information about medieval England (Map 11.1).

The Conqueror's scribes compiled *Domesday Book* in less than a year. *Domesday Book*, a unique document, provided William and his descendants with information vital for the exploitation and government of the country. Knowing the amount of wealth every area possessed, the king could tax accordingly. Knowing the amount of land his vassals had, he could allot knight service fairly. The inclusion of material covering all of England helped English kings to regard their country as one unit.

In 1128 the Conqueror's granddaughter Matilda was married to Geoffrey of Anjou. Their son, who became Henry II of England and inaugurated the Angevin (from Anjou, his father's county) dynasty, inherited the French provinces of Normandy, Anjou, Maine, and Touraine in northwestern France. When Henry married the great heiress Eleanor of Aquitaine in 1152, he claimed lordships over Aquitaine, Poitou, and Gascony in southwestern France. The territory some students call the "Angevin empire" included most of the British Isles and half of France (see Map 11.2). The histories of England and France in the High Middle Ages were thus closely intertwined.

In the early twelfth century, France consisted of a number of virtually independent provinces. Each was governed by its local ruler; each had its own laws and customs; each had its own coinage; each had its own dialect. Unlike the king of England, the king of France had jurisdiction over a very small area. Chroniclers called King Louis VI (r. 1108–1137) roi de Saint-Denis, king of Saint-Denis, because the territory he controlled was limited to Paris and the Saint-Denis area surrounding the city. This region, called the Île-de-France or royal domain, became the nucleus of the French state. The clear goal of the medieval French king was to increase the royal domain and extend his authority (Map 11.2).

The term Saint-Denis had political and religious charisma, which the Crown exploited. Following the precedent of the Frankish chieftain Clovis (see page 232), Louis VI and his Capetian successors strongly supported and identified with the cult of Saint Denis, a deeply revered saint whom the French believed protected the country from danger. Under Saint Denis's banner, the oriflamme, French kings fought their battles and claimed their victories. The oriflamme rested in the abbey of Saint-Denis, which was richly endowed by the Crown and served as the burial place of the French kings. The Capetian kings identified themselves with the cult of Saint Denis in order to tap "national" devotion to him and tie that devotion and loyalty to the monarchy.[2]

The work of unifying France began under Louis VI's grandson Philip II (r. 1180–1223). Rigord,

Philip's biographer, gave him the title "Augustus" (from a Latin word meaning "to increase") because he vastly enlarged the territory of the kingdom of France. By defeating a baronial plot against the Crown, Philip Augustus acquired the northern counties of Artois and Vermandois. When King John of England, who was Philip's vassal for the rich province of Normandy, defaulted on his feudal obligation to come to the French court, Philip declared Normandy forfeit to the French crown. He enforced his declaration militarily, and in 1204 Normandy fell to the French. Within two years Philip also gained the farmlands of Maine, Touraine, and Anjou. By the end of his reign Philip was effectively master of northern France.

In the thirteenth century, Philip Augustus's descendants acquired important holdings in the south. Louis VIII (r. 1223–1226) added the county of Poitou to the kingdom of France by war. Louis IX (r. 1226–1270) gained a vital interest in the Mediterranean province of Provence through his marriage to Margaret of Provence. Louis's son Philip III (r. 1270–1285) secured Languedoc through inheritance. By the end of the thirteenth century, most of the provinces of modern France had been added to the royal domain through diplomacy, marriage, war, and inheritance. The king of France was stronger than any group of nobles who might try to challenge his authority.

Philip Augustus devised a method of governing the provinces and providing for communication between the central government in Paris and local communities. Philip decided that each province would retain its own institutions and laws. But royal agents, called baillis in the north and seneschals in the south, were sent from Paris into the provinces as the king's official representatives with authority to act for him. Often middle-class lawyers, these men possessed full judicial, financial, and military jurisdiction in their districts. The baillis and seneschals were appointed by, paid by, and responsible to the king. Unlike the English sheriffs, they were never natives of the provinces to which they were assigned, and they could not own land there. This policy reflected the fundamental principle of French administration that royal interests superseded local interests.

While English governmental administration was based on the services of unpaid local officials, France was administered by a professional royal bureaucracy. As new territories came under royal control, the bureaucracy expanded. So great was the

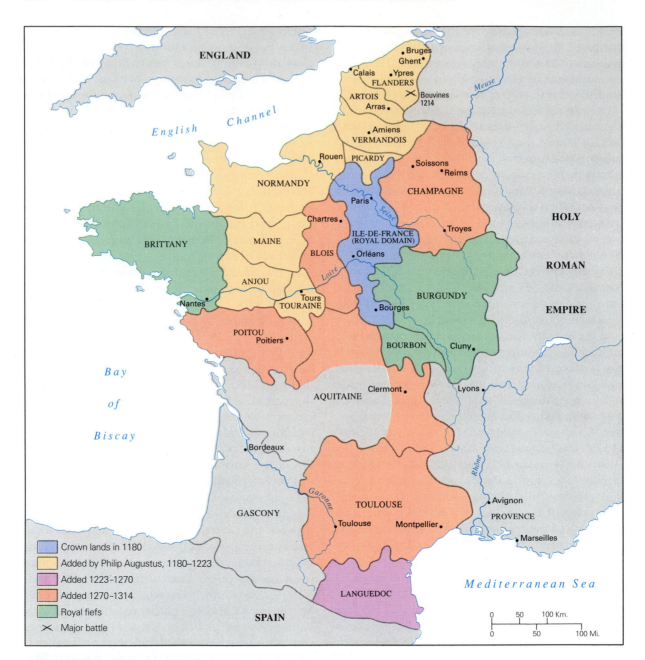

MAP 11.2 The Growth of the Kingdom of France   Some scholars believe that Philip II received the title "Augustus" (from a Latin word meaning "to increase") because he vastly expanded the territories of the kingdom of France.

variety of customs, laws, and provincial institutions that any attempt to impose uniformity would have touched off a rebellion. The French system was characterized by diversity at the local level and centralization at the top. Although it sometimes fell into disrepair, the basic system that Philip Augustus created worked so well that it survived until the Revolution of 1789.

The political problems of Germany differed considerably from those of France and England. The eleventh-century investiture controversy between the German emperor and the Roman papacy had left Germany shattered and divided (see pages 268–270). In the twelfth and thirteenth centuries, Germany was split into hundreds of independent provinces, principalities, bishoprics, duchies, and free cities. Princes, dukes, and local rulers held power over small areas.

There were several barriers to the development of a strong central government. The German rulers lacked a strong royal domain, like that of the French kings, to use as a source of revenue and a base from which to expand royal power. No accepted principle of succession to the throne existed; as a result, the death of the emperor was often followed by disputes, civil war, and anarchy. Moreover, German rulers were continually attracted south by the wealth of the northern Italian cities or by dreams of restoring the imperial glory of Charlemagne. Time after time the German kings got involved in Italian affairs, and in turn the papacy, fearful of a strong German power in northern Italy, interfered in German affairs. German princes took bribes from whichever authority—the emperor or the pope—best supported their own particular ambitions. Consequently, the centralization of authority in Germany, in contrast to that in France and England, occurred very slowly. In medieval Germany, power remained in the hands of numerous princes instead of the king.

Through most of the first half of the twelfth century, civil war wracked Germany as the emperors tried to strengthen their position by playing off baronial factions against one another. When Conrad III died in 1152, the resulting anarchy was so terrible that the *electors*—the seven princes responsible for choosing the emperor—decided that the only alternative to continued chaos was the selection of a strong ruler. They chose Frederick Barbarossa of the house of Hohenstaufen.

Frederick Barbarossa (r. 1152–1190) tried valiantly to unify the empire. Just as the French rulers branched out from their compact domain in the Île-de-France, Frederick tried to use his family duchy of Swabia in southwestern Germany as a power base (Map 11.3). Just as William the Conqueror had done, Frederick required all vassals in Swabia to take an oath of allegiance to him as emperor, no matter who their immediate lord might be. He appointed ministerials to exercise the full imperial authority over administrative districts of Swabia. Ministerials linked the emperor and local communities.

Outside of Swabia, Frederick tried to make feudalism work as a system of government. The princes throughout the empire exercised tremendous power, and Frederick tried to subordinate them to the authority of the royal government. He made alliances with the great lay princes in which they acknowledged that their lands were fiefs of the emperor, and he in turn recognized their military and political jurisdiction over their territories. Frederick also compelled the great churchmen to become his vassals, so that when they died he could control their estates. Frederick solved the problem of chronic violence by making the princes responsible for the establishment of peace within their territories. At a great assembly held at Roncaglia in 1158, private warfare was forbidden in Italy, and severe penalties were laid down for violations of the peace.

Unfortunately, Frederick Barbarossa did not concentrate his efforts and resources in one area. He, too, became embroiled in the affairs of Italy. He, too, wanted to restore the Holy Roman Empire, joining Germany and Italy. In the eleventh and twelfth centuries, the northern Italian cities had grown rich on trade, and Frederick believed that if he could gain the imperial crown, he could cash in on Italian wealth. Frederick saw that, although the Italian cities were populous and militarily strong, they lacked stable governments and were often involved in struggles with one another. The emperor mistakenly believed that moneygrubbing infantrymen could not stand up against his ministerials. He did not realize that the merchant oligarchs who ran the city governments of Milan, the Venetian republic, and Florence considered themselves just as tough as he; they prized their independence and were determined to fight for it. Frederick's desire to control the papacy also attracted him southward. He did not know that the popes feared a strong German state in northern Italy even more than they feared the rich and (the popes suspected) slightly heretical Italian cities.

Between 1154 and 1188, Frederick made six expeditions into Italy. His scorched-earth policy was successful at first, making for significant conquests in the north. The brutality of his methods, however, provoked revolts, and the Italian cities formed an alliance with the papacy. In 1176 Frederick suffered a defeat at Legnano (see Map 11.3). This battle marked the first time a feudal cavalry of armed knights was decisively defeated by bourgeois infantrymen. Frederick was forced to recognize the municipal autonomy of the northern Italian cities. Germany and Italy remained separate countries and followed separate courses of development.

Frederick Barbarossa's Italian ventures contributed nothing to the unification of the German

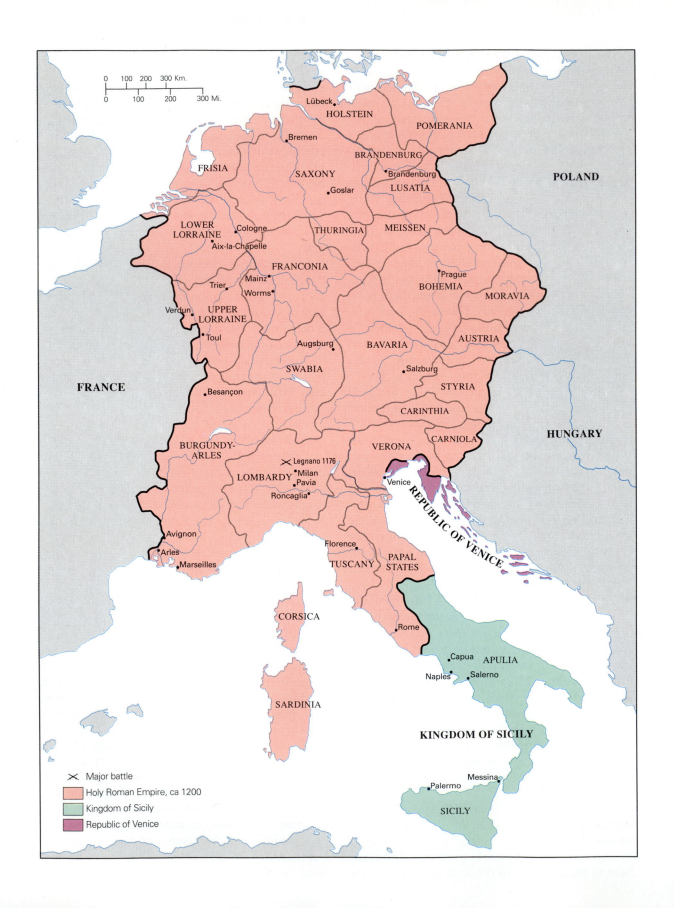

Scale:
0 100 200 300 Km.
0 100 200 300 Mi.

POLAND

FRANCE

HUNGARY

Lübeck
HOLSTEIN
POMERANIA
Bremen
BRANDENBURG
FRISIA
SAXONY
Brandenburg
LUSATIA
Goslar
LOWER
LORRAINE
Cologne
MEISSEN
Aix-la-Chapelle
THURINGIA
FRANCONIA
Trier
Mainz
Prague
Worms
BOHEMIA
MORAVIA
Verdun
UPPER
LORRAINE
Toul
Augsburg
BAVARIA
AUSTRIA
SWABIA
Salzburg
STYRIA
Besançon
CARINTHIA
CARNIOLA
BURGUNDY-
ARLES
Legnano 1176
VERONA
Milan
Venice
LOMBARDY
Pavia
Roncaglia
REPUBLIC OF VENICE
Avignon
Florence
Arles
Marseilles
TUSCANY
PAPAL
STATES
CORSICA
Rome
Capua
APULIA
Naples
Salerno
SARDINIA
KINGDOM OF SICILY
Messina
Palermo
SICILY

✕ Major battle
█ Holy Roman Empire, ca 1200
█ Kingdom of Sicily
█ Republic of Venice

states. Because the empire lacked a stable bureaucratic system of government, his presence was essential for the maintenance of peace. In Frederick's absences, the fires of independence and disorder spread. The princes and magnates consolidated their power, and the unsupervised royal ministerials gained considerable independence. By 1187 Frederick had to accept again the reality of private warfare. The power of the princes cost the growth of a centralized monarchy.

Finance

As medieval rulers expanded territories and extended authority, they required more officials, larger armies, and more money. Officials and armies had to be paid, and kings had to find ways to raise revenue.

In England, William the Conqueror's son Henry I (r. 1100–1135) established a bureau of finance called the "Exchequer" (for the checkered cloth at which his officials collected and audited royal accounts). Henry's income came from a variety of sources: from taxes paid by peasants living on the king's estates; from the *Danegeld,* an old tax originally levied to pay tribute to the Danes; from the *dona,* an annual gift from the church; from money paid to the Crown for settling disputes; and from fines paid by people found guilty of crimes. Henry also received income because of his position as feudal lord. If, for example, one of his vassals died and the son wished to inherit the father's properties, the heir had to pay Henry a tax called *relief.* From the knights Henry took *scutage,* money paid in lieu of the performance of military service. With the scutage collected, Henry could hire mercenary troops. The sheriff in each county was responsible for collecting all these sums and paying them twice a year to the king's Exchequer. Henry, like other medieval kings, made no distinction between his private income and state revenues.

An accurate record of expenditures and income is needed to ensure a state's solvency. Henry assigned a few of the barons and bishops at his court to keep careful records of the moneys paid into and out of the royal treasury. These financial officials, called "barons of the Exchequer," gradually developed a professional organization with its own rules, procedures, and esprit de corps. The Exchequer, which always sat in London, became the first institution of the governmental bureaucracy of England. Because of its work, an almost-complete series of financial records for England dating back to 1130 survives; after 1154 the series is complete.

The development of royal financial agencies in most continental countries lagged behind the English Exchequer. Twelfth-century French rulers derived their income from their royal estates in the Île-de-France. As Philip Augustus and his successors added provinces to the royal domain, the need for money became increasingly acute. Philip made the baillis and seneschals responsible for collecting taxes in their districts. This income came primarily from fines and confiscations imposed by the courts. Three times a year the baillis and seneschals reported to the king's court with the money they had collected.

In the thirteenth century, French rulers found additional sources of revenue. They acquired some income from the church and some from people living in the towns. Townspeople paid *tallage* or the *taille*—a tax arbitrarily laid by the king. In all parts of the country, feudal vassals owed military service to the king when he called for it. Louis IX converted this military obligation into a cash payment, called "host tallage," and thus increased his revenues. Moreover, pervasive anti-Semitism allowed Philip Augustus, Louis VIII, and Louis IX to tax their Jewish subjects mercilessly.

Medieval people believed that a good king lived on the income of his own land and taxed only in time of a grave emergency—that is, a just war. Because the church, and not the state, performed what twentieth-century people call social services, such as education and care of the sick, the aged, and orphaned children, there was no ordinary need for the government to tax. Taxation meant war financing. The French monarchy could not continually justify taxing the people on the grounds of the needs of war. Thus the French kings were slow to develop an efficient bureau of finance. French localism—in contrast to England's early unification—also retarded the growth of a central financial agency. Not until the fourteenth century, as a result of the Hundred Years' War, did a state financial bureau emerge—the Chamber of Accounts.

MAP 11.3 The Holy Roman Empire, ca 1200   Frederick Barbarossa tried to use the feudal bond to tie the different provinces to the imperial monarchy.

In the twelfth century, in finance, law, and bureaucratic development, the papal curia represented the most advanced government. The one secular government other than England that developed a financial bureaucracy was the kingdom of Sicily. Sicily is a good example of how strong government could be built on a feudal base by determined rulers.

Like England, Sicily had come under Norman domination. Between 1061 and 1091, a bold Norman knight, Roger de Hauteville, with a small band of mercenaries had defeated the Muslims and Greeks who controlled the island. Like William the Conqueror in England, Roger introduced Norman feudalism in Sicily and made it work as a system of government. Roger distributed scattered fiefs to his followers, so that no vassal had a centralized power base. He took an inquest of royal properties and rights, and he forbade private warfare. Roger adapted his Norman experience to Arabic and Greek governmental practices. Thus he retained the Muslims' main financial agency, the *diwan,* a sophisticated bureau for record keeping.

His son and heir, Count Roger II (r. 1130–1154), continued the process of state building. He subdued the province of Apulia in southern Italy, united it with his Sicilian lands, and had himself crowned king of Sicily. Roger II organized the economy in the interests of the state; for example, the Crown secured a monopoly on the sale of salt and lumber. With the revenues thus acquired, Roger hired mercenary troops. His judiciary welcomed appeals from local communities. The army, the judiciary, and the *diwan* were staffed by Greeks and Muslims as well as Normans.

Under Frederick II Hohenstaufen (r. 1212–1250), grandson of Roger II, Sicily underwent remarkable development. Frederick, also the grandson and heir of Frederick Barbarossa, was a brilliant legislator and administrator, and he constructed the most advanced bureaucratic state in medieval Europe. The institutions of the kingdom of Sicily

The Chancellery at Palermo   Reflecting the fact that Vandals, Ostrogoths, Greeks, Muslims, and Normans had left their imprint on Sicily, the imperial court bureaucracy kept official records in Greek, Arabic, and Latin, as this manuscript illustration shows. *(Source: Burgerbibliothek Bern)*

were harnessed in the service of the state as represented by the king.

Frederick banned private warfare and placed all castles and towers under royal administration. Frederick also replaced town officials with royal governors. In 1231 he published the *Constitutions of Melfi,* a collection of laws that vastly enhanced royal authority. Both feudal and ecclesiastical courts were subordinated to the king's courts. Each year, royal judges visited all parts of the kingdom, and the supreme court at Capua heard appeals from all lesser courts. Thus churchmen accused of crimes were tried in the royal courts. Royal control of the nobility, of the towns, and of the judicial system added up to great centralization, which required a professional bureaucracy and sound state financing.

In 1224 Frederick founded the University of Naples to train clerks and officials for his bureaucracy. University-educated administrators and lawyers emphasized the stiff principles of Roman law, such as the Justinian maxim that "what pleases the prince has the force of law." Frederick's financial experts regulated agriculture, public works, even business. His customs service carefully supervised all imports and exports, collecting taxes for the Crown on all products. Royal revenues increased tremendously. Moreover, Frederick strictly regulated the currency and forbade the export of gold and silver bullion.

Finally, Frederick secured the tacit consent of his people to regular taxation. This was an incredible achievement when most people believed that taxes should be levied only in time of grave emergency, the just war. Frederick defined emergency broadly. For much of his reign he was involved in a bitter dispute with the papacy. Churchmen hardly considered the emperor's wars with the popes as just, but Frederick's position was so strong that he could ignore criticism and levy taxes.

Frederick's contemporaries called him the "Transformer of the World." He certainly transformed the kingdom of Sicily, creating a state that was in many ways modern. But Frederick was highly ambitious: he wanted to control the entire peninsula of Italy. The popes, fearful of being encircled, waged a long conflict to prevent that. The kingdom of Sicily required constant attention, and Frederick's absences took their toll. Shortly after he died, the unsupervised bureaucracy he had built fell to pieces. The pope, as the feudal overlord of Sicily, called in a French prince to rule.

Frederick showed little interest in Germany. He concentrated his attention on Sicily rather than on the historic Hohenstaufen stronghold in Swabia, and the focus of imperial concerns shifted southward. When he visited the empire, in the expectation of securing German support for his Italian policy, he made sweeping concessions to the princes, bishops, duchies, and free cities. In 1220, for example, he exempted German churchmen from taxation and from the jurisdiction of imperial authorities. In 1231 he gave lay princes the same exemptions and even threw in the right to coin money. Frederick gave away so much that imperial authority was seriously weakened. In the later Middle Ages, lay and ecclesiastical princes held sway in the Holy Roman Empire. The centralizing efforts of Frederick Barbarossa were destroyed by his grandson Frederick II.

Law and Justice

Throughout Europe, the form and application of laws depended on local and provincial custom and practice. In the twelfth and thirteenth centuries, the law was a hodgepodge of Germanic customs, feudal rights, and provincial practices. Kings wanted to blend these elements into a uniform system of rules acceptable and applicable to all their peoples. In France and England, kings successfully contributed to the development of national states through the administration of their laws. Legal developments in continental countries like France were strongly influenced by Roman law, while England slowly built up a unique, unwritten common law.

The French king Louis IX (r. 1226–1270) was famous in his time for his concern for justice. Each French province, even after being made part of the kingdom of France, retained its unique laws and procedures, but Louis IX created a royal judicial system. He established the Parlement of Paris, a kind of supreme court that welcomed appeals from local administrators and from the courts of feudal lords throughout France. By the very act of appealing the decisions of feudal courts to the Parlement of Paris, French people in far-flung provinces were recognizing the superiority of royal justice.

Louis sent royal judges to all parts of the country to check up on the work of the baillis and seneschals and to hear complaints of injustice. He was the first French monarch to publish laws for the entire kingdom. The Parlement of Paris registered (or

Head of French King When the Abbot Suger rebuilt Saint-Denis in the mid-twelfth century, he probably wanted some of the sculpture to reflect the monarchy with which the abbey had long been associated, the Capetian kings, who were the monastery's greatest patrons. This head appeared in the west portal of the church, along with statues of other French kings and queens. *(Source: Walters Art Gallery, Baltimore)*

announced) these laws, which forbade private warfare, judicial duels, gambling, blaspheming, and prostitution. Louis sought to identify justice with the kingship, and gradually royal justice touched all parts of the kingdom.

Under Henry II (r. 1154–1189), England developed and extended a *common law,* a law common to and accepted by the entire country. No other country in medieval Europe did so. Henry I had occasionally sent out *circuit judges* (royal officials who traveled a given circuit or district) to hear civil and criminal cases. Henry II made this way of extending royal justice an annual practice. Every year, royal judges left London and set up court in the

counties. Wherever the king's judges sat, there sat the king's court. Slowly, the king's court gained jurisdiction over all property disputes and criminal actions.

Henry also improved procedure in criminal justice. In 1166 he instructed the sheriffs to summon local juries to conduct inquests and draw up lists of known or suspected criminals. These lists, sworn to by the juries, were to be presented to the royal judges when they arrived in the community. This accusing jury is the ancestor of the modern grand jury.

An accused person formally charged with a crime did *not* undergo trial by jury. He or she was tried by ordeal. The accused was tied hand and foot and dropped in a lake or river. People believed that water was a pure substance and would reject anything foul or unclean. Thus a person who sank was considered innocent, and a person who floated was considered guilty. Trial by ordeal was a ritual that appealed to the supernatural for judgment. God determined innocence or guilt, and thus a priest had to be present to bless the water.

Henry II and others considered this ancient Germanic method irrational and a poor way of determining results, but they knew no alternative. In 1215 the Fourth Lateran Council of the church forbade the presence of priests at trials by ordeal and thus effectively abolished them. Gradually, in the course of the thirteenth century, the king's judges adopted the practice of calling upon twelve people (other than the accusing jury) to consider the question of innocence or guilt. This became the jury of trial, but it was very slowly accepted because medieval people had more confidence in the judgment of God than in that of twelve ordinary people.

One aspect of Henry's judicial reforms encountered stiff resistance from an unexpected source: a friend and former chief adviser whom Henry had made archbishop of Canterbury—Thomas Becket. Henry selected Becket as archbishop in 1162 because he believed he could depend on Becket's support. But when Henry wanted to bring all persons in the kingdom under the jurisdiction of the royal courts, Thomas Becket's opposition led to another dramatic conflict between temporal and spiritual powers.

In the 1160s many literate people accused of crimes claimed "benefit of clergy," even though they were not clerics and often had no intention of being ordained. Benefit of clergy gave the accused the right to be tried in church courts, which meted out mild punishments. A person found guilty in the king's court might suffer mutilation—loss of a hand or foot, castration—or even death. Ecclesiastical punishments tended to be an obligation to say certain prayers or to make a pilgrimage. In 1164 Henry II insisted that everyone, including clerics, be subject to the royal courts. Becket vigorously protested that church law required clerics to be subject to church courts. When he proceeded to excommunicate one of the king's vassals, the issue became more complicated. Because no one was supposed to have any contact with an excommunicated person, it appeared that the church could arbitrarily deprive the king of necessary military forces. The disagreement between Henry II and Becket dragged on for years. The king grew increasingly bitter that his appointment of Becket had proved to be such a mistake. Late in December 1170, in a fit of rage, Henry expressed the wish that Becket be destroyed. Four knights took the king at his word, went to Canterbury, and killed the archbishop in his cathedral as he was leaving evening services.

What Thomas Becket could not achieve in life, he gained in death. The assassination of an archbishop in his own church during the Christmas season turned public opinion in England and throughout western Europe against the king. Within months, miracles were recorded at Becket's tomb, and in a short time Canterbury Cathedral became a major pilgrimage and tourist site. Henry had to back down. He did public penance for the murder and gave up his attempts to bring clerics under the authority of the royal court.

Henry II's sons Richard I, known as Lion-Heart (r. 1189–1199), and John (r. 1199–1216) lacked their father's interest in the work of government. Handsome, athletic, and with an international reputation for military prowess, Richard looked on England as a source of revenue for his military enterprises. Soon after his accession, he departed on crusade to the Holy Land. During his reign he spent only six months in England, and the government was run by ministers trained under Henry II.

Unlike Richard, King John was incompetent as a soldier and unnecessarily suspicious that the barons were plotting against him. His basic problems, however, were financial. King John inherited a heavy debt from his father and brother. The country had paid dearly for Richard's crusading zeal. While returning from the Holy Land, Richard had been captured, and England had paid an enormous

ransom to secure his release. In 1204 John lost the rich province of Normandy to Philip Augustus of France and then spent the rest of his reign trying to get it back. To finance that war, he got in deeper and deeper trouble with his barons. John squeezed as much money as possible from his position as feudal lord. He took scutage, and each time increased the amount due. He forced widows to pay exorbitant fines to avoid unwanted marriages. He sold young girls who were his feudal wards to the highest bidder. These actions antagonized the nobility.

John also alienated the church and the English townspeople. He rejected Pope Innocent III's

The Martyrdom of Thomas Becket Becket's murder evoked many illustrations in the thirteenth century. This illumination faithfully follows the manuscript sources: while one knight held off the archbishop's defenders, the other three attacked. With a powerful stroke, the crown of Becket's head was slashed off and his brains scattered on the cathedral floor. *(Source: Walters Art Gallery, Baltimore)*

nominee to the see of Canterbury. And he infuriated the burghers of the towns by extorting money from them and threatening to revoke their charters of self-government.

All the money John raised did not bring him success. In July 1214, John's coalition of Flemish, German, and English cavalry suffered a severe defeat at the hands of Philip Augustus of France at Bouvines in Flanders. This battle ended English hopes for the recovery of territories from France and also strengthened the barons' opposition to John. On top of his heavy taxation, his ineptitude as a soldier in a society that idealized military glory was the final straw. Rebellion begun by a few hotheaded northern barons eventually grew to involve many of the English nobility, including the archbishop of Canterbury and the earl of Pembroke, the leading ecclesiastical and lay peers. After lengthy negotiations, John met the barons at Runnymede, a meadow along the Thames River. There he was forced to sign the treaty called "Magna Carta," which became the cornerstone of English justice and law.

Magna Carta signifies the principle that the king and the government shall be under the law, that everyone—including the king—must obey the law. It defends the interests of widows, orphans, townspeople, free men, and the church. Some clauses contain the germ of the ideas of due process of law and the right to a fair and speedy trial. Every English king in the Middle Ages reissued Magna Carta as evidence of his promise to observe the law. Because it was reissued frequently and because later generations appealed to Magna Carta as a written statement of English liberties, it acquired an almost sacred importance as a guarantee of law and justice.

In the thirteenth century, the judicial precedents set under Henry II slowly evolved into permanent institutions. The king's judges asserted the royal authority and applied the same principles everywhere in the country. English people found the king's justice more rational and evenhanded than the justice meted out in the baronial courts. Respect for the king's law and courts promoted loyalty to the Crown. By the time of Henry's great-grandson Edward I (r. 1272–1307), one law, the common law, operated all over England.

In the later Middle Ages, the English common law developed features that differed strikingly from the system of Roman law operative in continental Europe. The common law relied on precedents: a decision in an important case served as an authority for deciding similar cases. By contrast, continental judges, trained in Roman law, used the fixed legal maxims of the Justinian *Code* (see page 220) to to decide their cases. Thus the common-law system evolved according to the changing experience of the people, while the Roman-law tradition tended toward an absolutist approach. In countries influenced by the common law, such as Canada and the United States, the court is open to the public; in countries with Roman-law traditions, such as France and the Latin American nations, courts need not be public. Under the common law, people accused in criminal cases have a right to access to the evidence against them; under the other system, they need not. The common law urges judges to be impartial; in the Roman-law system, judges interfere freely in activities in their courtrooms. Finally, whereas torture is foreign to the common-law tradition, it was once widely used in the Roman legal system.

The extension of law and justice led to a phenomenal amount of legal codification all over Europe. The English judge Henry of Bracton (d. 1268) wrote a *Treatise on the Laws and Customs of England;* the French jurist Philippe de Beaumanoir (1250–1296) produced the *Customs of Beaumanoir;* the German scholar Eike von Repgow compiled the *Sachsenspiegel* (ca 1225); and Pope Gregory IX (1227–1241) published a codification of ecclesiastical law, the *Extravagantes.* Legal texts and encyclopedias exalted royal authority, consolidated royal power, and emphasized political and social uniformity. The pressure for social conformity in turn contributed to a rising hostility toward minorities, Jews, and homosexuals.

By the late eleventh century, many towns in western Europe had small Jewish populations. Jews had emigrated in post-Roman times from the large cities of the Mediterranean region to France, the Rhineland, and Britain. During the Carolingian period, Jews had the reputation of being richer and more learned than the semibarbaric peoples among whom they lived. They typically earned their livelihoods in the lesser trades or by lending money at interest, and Jews engaged in trade had to be literate to keep records. The laws of most countries forbade Jews to own land, though they could hold land pledged to them for debts. By the twelfth century, many Jews were usurers: they lent to consumers but primarily to new or growing business enterprises. New towns and underdeveloped areas where cash was scarce welcomed Jewish settlers.

Like other business people, the Jews preferred to live near their work; they also settled close to their synagogue or school. Thus originated the Jews' street or quarter or ghetto. Such neighborhoods gradually became legally defined sections where Jews were required to live.

Jews had been generally tolerated and had become important parts of the urban economies through trade and finance. Some Jews had risen to positions of power and prominence. Through the twelfth century, for example, Jews managed the papal household. The later twelfth and entire thirteenth centuries, however, witnessed increasingly ugly anti-Semitism. Why? Present scholarship does not provide completely satisfactory answers, but we have some clues. Shifting agricultural and economic patterns aggravated social tensions. The indebtedness of peasants and nobles to Jews in an increasingly cash-based economy; the xenophobia that accompanied and followed the Crusades; Christian merchants' and financiers' resentment of Jewish business competition; the spread of vicious accusations of ritual murders or sacrileges against Christian property and persons; royal and papal legislation aimed at social conformity—these factors all contributed to rising anti-Semitism. Thus, from 1180 to 1182, Philip Augustus of France used hostility to Jews as an excuse to imprison them and then to demand heavy ransom for their release. The Fourth Lateran Council of 1215 forbade Jews to hold public office, restricted their financial activities, and required them to wear distinctive clothing. In 1290 Edward I of England capitalized on mercantile and other resentment of Jews to expel them from the country in return for a large parliamentary grant. In 1302 Philip IV of France followed suit by expelling the Jews from his kingdom and confiscating their property. Fear, ignorance, greed, stupidity, and the pressure for social conformity all played a part in anti-Semitism of the High Middle Ages.

Early Christians, as we have seen (pages 202–203), displayed no special prejudice against homosexuals. While some of the church fathers, such as Saint John Chrysostom (347–407), preached against them, a general indifference to homosexual activity prevailed throughout the early Middle Ages. In the early twelfth century, a large homosexual literature circulated. Publicly known homosexuals such as Ralph, archbishop of Tours (1087–1118), and King Richard I of England held high ecclesiastical and political positions.

A Jewish Explusion Subject to ancient and irrational prejudices and lacking legal rights, Jewish people lived and worked in an area, according to the pleasure of kings and lords. The increasing anti-Semitism of the thirteenth century led to their expulsion from many places. Here an entire family with domestic animals is forced to move. Artists commonly used conical caps to identify Jews. (Source: Zentralbibliothek Zürich)

Beginning in the late twelfth century, however, a profound change occurred in public attitudes toward homosexual behavior. Why did this happen, if prejudice against homosexuals cannot be traced to early Christianity? Scholars have only begun to investigate this question, and the root cause of intolerance rarely yields to easy analysis. In the thirteenth century, a fear of foreigners, especially Muslims, became associated with the crusading movement. Heretics were the most despised minority in an age that stressed religious and social uniformity. The notion spread that both Muslims and heretics, the great foreign and domestic menaces to the security of Christian Europe, were inclined to homosexual relations. Finally, the systematization of law and the rising strength of the state made any religious or sexual distinctiveness increasingly unacceptable. Whatever the precise cause, "between 1250 and 1300 homosexual activity passed from being completely legal in most of Europe to incurring the death penalty in all but a few legal compilations."[3] Spain, France, England, Norway, and several Italian city-states adopted laws condemning homosexual acts. Most of these laws remained on statute books until the twentieth century. Anti-Semitism and hostility to homosexuals reflect a dark and evil side to high medieval culture, not the general creativity and vitality of the period.

ECONOMIC REVIVAL

A salient manifestation of Europe's recovery after the tenth-century disorders and of the vitality of the High Middle Ages was the rise of towns and the development of a new business and commercial class. This development was to lay the foundations for Europe's transformation, centuries later, from a rural agricultural society into an industrial urban society—a change with global implications.

Why did these developments occur when they did? What sort of people first populated the towns, and where did they come from? What is known of town life in the High Middle Ages? What relevance did towns have for medieval culture? Part of the answer to at least one of these questions has already been given. Without increased agricultural output, there would not have been an adequate food supply for new town dwellers. Without a rise in population, there would have been no one to people the towns. Without a minimum of peace and political stability, merchants could not have transported and sold goods.

The Rise of Towns

Early medieval society was traditional, agricultural, and rural. The emergence of a new class that was none of these constituted a social revolution. The new class—artisans and merchants—came from the peasantry. They were landless younger sons of large families, driven away by land shortage. Or they were forced by war and famine to seek new possibilities. Or they were unusually enterprising and adventurous, curious and willing to take a chance.

Historians have proposed three basic theories to explain the origins of European towns. Some scholars believe towns began as *boroughs*—that is, as fortifications erected during the ninth-century Viking invasions. According to this view, towns were at first places of defense, into which farmers from the surrounding countryside moved when their area was attacked. Later, merchants were attracted to the fortifications because they had something to sell and wanted to be where customers were. But most residents of early towns made their living by farming outside the town.

Belgian historian Henri Pirenne maintained that towns sprang up when merchants who engaged in long-distance trade gravitated toward attractive or favorable spots, such as a fort. Usually traders settled just outside the walls, in the *faubourgs* or *suburbs*—both of which mean "outside" or "in the shelter of the walls." As their markets prospered and as their number outside the walls grew, the merchants built a new wall around themselves, every century or so. According to Pirenne, a medieval town consisted architecturally of a number of concentric walls, and the chief economic pursuit of its residents was trade and commerce.

A third explanation focuses on the great cathedrals and monasteries, which represented a demand for goods and services. Cathedrals such as Notre Dame in Paris conducted schools, which drew students from far and wide. Consequently, traders and merchants settled near religious establishments to cater to the residents' economic needs. Concentrations of people accumulated, and towns came into being.

All three theories have validity, though none of them explains the origins of *all* medieval towns. Few towns of the tenth and eleventh centuries were "new" in the sense that American towns and cities were new in the seventeenth and eighteenth centuries. They were not carved out of forest and wilderness. Some medieval towns that had become flourishing centers of trade by the mid-twelfth century had originally been Roman army camps. York in northern England, Bordeaux in west central France, and Cologne in west central Germany are good examples of ancient towns that underwent revitalization in the eleventh century. Some Italian seaport cities, such as Venice, Pisa, and Genoa, had been centers of shipping and commerce in earlier times. Muslim attacks and domestic squabbles had cut their populations and drastically reduced the volume of their trade in the early Middle Ages, but trade with Constantinople and the East had never stopped entirely. The restoration of order and political stability promoted rebirth and new development. Pirenne's interpretation accurately describes the Flemish towns of Bruges and Ypres. It does not fit the course of development in the Italian cities or in such centers as London. Moreover, the twelfth century witnessed the foundation of completely new towns, such as Lübeck, Berlin, and Munich.

Whether evolving from a newly fortified place or an old Roman army camp, from a cathedral site or a river junction or a place where several overland routes met, medieval towns had a few common characteristics. Walls enclosed the town. (The terms *burgher* and *bourgeois* derive from the Old English and Old German words *burg, burgh, borg,* and *borough* for "a walled or fortified place." Thus a burgher or bourgeois was originally a person who lived or worked inside the walls.) The town had a marketplace. It often had a mint for the coining of money and a court to settle disputes.

In each town, many people inhabited a small, cramped area. As population increased, towns rebuilt their walls, expanding the living space to accommodate growing numbers. Through an archaeological investigation of the amount of land gradually enclosed by walls, historians have gained a rough estimate of medieval town populations. For example, the walled area of the German city of Cologne equaled 100 hectares in the tenth century (1 hectare = 2.471 acres), about 185 hectares in 1106, about 320 in 1180, and 397 hectares in the

Hammering Cobblestones into place on a roadbed made of loose earth, laborers pave the highways leading from the walled city of Bavay in France. Upkeep of the roads and walls were often a town's greatest expenses. *(Source: Bibliothèque royale Albert 1er, Brussels)*

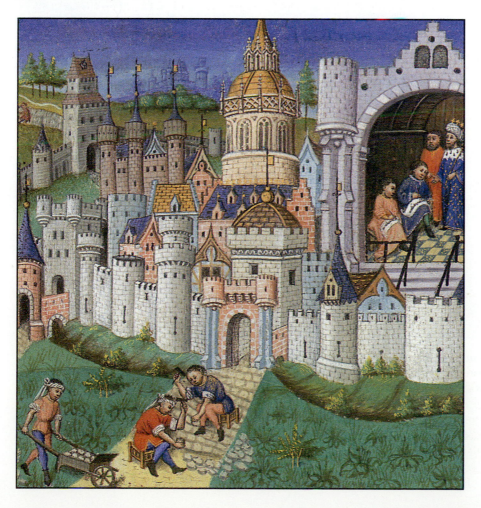

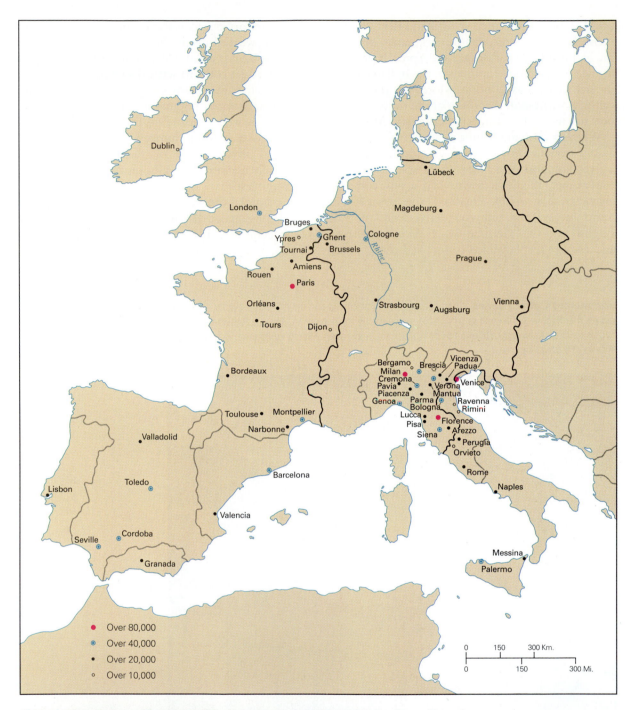

Dublin

Lübeck

London

Magdeburg

Bruges
Ypres Ghent Cologne
Tournai Brussels
Amiens
Rouen
Paris
Orléans
Tours Dijon
Strasbourg Augsburg

Prague

Vienna

Bordeaux

Toulouse Montpellier
Narbonne

Valladolid

Toledo

Lisbon

Valencia

Seville Cordoba
Granada

Bergamo Vicenza
Milan Brescia Padua
Cremona Venice
Pavia Verona
Piacenza Mantua
Genoa Parma Ravenna
Bologna Rimini
Lucca Florence
Pisa Arezzo
Siena Perugia
Orvieto
Rome

Barcelona

Naples

Messina
Palermo

Rhine

- Over 80,000
- Over 40,000
- Over 20,000
- Over 10,000

0   150   300 Km.

0   150   300 Mi.

MAP 11.4 Population of European Urban Areas, ca Late Thirteenth Century   Though there were scores of urban centers in the thirteenth century, the Italian and Flemish towns had the largest concentrations of people. By modern standards, Paris was Europe's only real city.

fourteenth century. In 1180 Cologne's population was at least 32,000; in the mid-fourteenth century, perhaps 40,000.[4] The concentration of the textile industry in the Netherlands brought into being the most populous cluster of cities in western Europe: Ghent with about 56,000 people, Bruges with 27,000, Tournai and Brussels each with perhaps 20,000.[5] Paris, together with Milan, Venice, and Florence, each with about 80,000, led all Europe in population (Map 11.4).

In their backgrounds and abilities, townspeople represented diversity and change. They constituted an entirely new element in medieval society. They fit into none of the traditional categories. Their occupations, their preoccupations, were different from those of the feudal nobility and the laboring peasantry.

The aristocratic nobility glanced down with contempt and derision at the moneygrubbing townspeople but were not above borrowing from them. The rural peasantry peered up with suspicion and fear at the town dwellers. Though some fled to the towns seeking wealth and freedom, what was the point, most farmers wondered, of making money? Only land had real permanence. Nor did the new commercial class make much sense initially to churchmen. The immediate goal of the middle class was obviously not salvation. It was to be a good while before churchmen developed a theological justification for the new class.

Town Liberties

In the words of the Greek poet Alcaeus, "Not houses finely roofed or well built walls, nor canals or dockyards make a city, but men able to use their opportunity."[6] Men and opportunity. That is fundamentally what medieval towns meant—concentrations of people and varieties of chances. No matter where groups of traders congregated, they settled on someone's land and had to secure from king or count, abbot or bishop, permission to live and trade. Aristocratic nobles and churchmen were suspicious of and hostile to the middle class. They soon realized, however, that profits and benefits flowed to them and their territories from the markets set up on their land.

The history of towns in the eleventh through thirteenth centuries consists largely of merchants' efforts to acquire liberties. In the Middle Ages, *liberties* meant special privileges. For the town dweller, liberties included the privilege of living and trading on the lord's land. The most important privilege a medieval townsperson could gain was personal freedom. It gradually developed that an individual who lived in a town for a year and a day, and was accepted by the townspeople, was free of servile obligations and status. More than anything else, perhaps, the liberty of personal freedom that came with residence in a town contributed to the emancipation of the serfs in the High Middle Ages. Liberty meant citizenship, and citizenship in a town implied the right to buy and sell goods there. Unlike foreigners and outsiders of any kind, the full citizen did not have to pay taxes and tolls in the market. Obviously, this increased profits.

In the twelfth and thirteenth centuries, towns fought for, and slowly gained, legal and political rights. Since the tenth century, some English boroughs had held courts with jurisdiction over members of the town in civil and criminal matters. In the twelfth century, such English towns as London and Norwich developed courts that applied a special kind of law, called "law merchant." It dealt with commercial transactions, debt, bankruptcy, proof of sales, and contracts. Law merchant was especially suitable to the needs of the new bourgeoisie. Gradually, towns across Europe acquired the right to hold municipal courts that alone could judge members of the town. In effect, this right gave them judicial independence.[7]

In the acquisition of full rights of self-government, the *merchant guilds* played a large role. Medieval people were long accustomed to communal enterprises. In the late tenth and early eleventh centuries, those who were engaged in foreign trade joined together in merchant guilds; united enterprise provided them greater security and less risk of losses than did individual action. At about the same time, the artisans and craftsmen of particular trades formed their own guilds. These were the butchers, bakers, and candlestick makers. Members of the *craft guilds* determined the quality, quantity, and price of the goods produced and the number of apprentices and journeymen affiliated with the guild. Terrible conflicts were to arise between craft and merchant guilds in the fourteenth century, but that is a later story.

Recent research indicates that, by the fifteenth century, women composed the majority of the adult urban population. Many women were heads of households.[8] They engaged in every kind of urban commercial activity, both as helpmates to their husbands and independently. In many manufacturing trades women predominated, and in some places women were a large percentage of the labor force. In fourteenth-century Frankfurt, for example, about 33 percent of the crafts and trades were entirely female, about 40 percent wholly male, and the remaining crafts roughly divided between the sexes. Craft guilds provided greater opportunity for women than did merchant guilds. In late-twelfth-century Cologne, women and men had equal rights in the turners' guild (the guild for those who made wooden objects on a lathe). Most members of the Paris silk and woolen trades were women, and some achieved the mastership. Widows frequently followed their late husbands' professions, but if they remarried outside the craft, they lost the mastership. Between 1254 and 1271, the chief magistrate of Paris drew up the following regulations for the silk industry:

Any woman who wishes to be a silk spinster [woman who spins] on large spindles in the city of Paris—i.e., reeling, spinning, doubling and re-twisting—may freely do so, provided she observe the following customs and usages of the crafts:

No spinster on large spindles may have more than three apprentices, unless they be her own or her husband's children born in true wedlock; nor may she contract with them for an apprenticeship of less than seven years or for a fee of less than 20 Parisian sols to be paid to her, their mistress. . . . If a working woman comes from outside Paris and wishes to practice the said craft in the city, she must swear before the guardians of the craft that she will practice it well and loyally and conform to its customs and usages. . . . No man of this craft who is without a wife may have more than one apprentice; . . . if, however, both husband and wife practice the craft, they may have two apprentices and as many journeymen as they wish.[9]

Guild records show that women received lower wages than men for the same work, on the grounds that they needed less income.

By the late eleventh century, especially in the towns of the Low Countries and northern Italy, the leaders of the merchant guilds were quite rich and powerful. They constituted an oligarchy in their towns, controlling economic life and bargaining with kings and lords for political independence. Full rights of self-government included the right to hold a town court, the right to select the mayor and other municipal officials, and the right to tax and collect taxes. Kings often levied on their serfs and unfree townspeople the arbitrary tax, tallage. Such a tax (also known as "customs") called attention to the fact that men were not free. Citizens of a town much preferred to levy and collect their own taxes.

A charter that King Henry II of England granted to the merchants of Lincoln around 1157 nicely illustrates the town's rights. The emphasized passages clearly suggest that the merchant guild had been the governing body in the city for almost a century and that anyone who lived in Lincoln for a year and a day was considered free:

Henry, by the grace of God, etc. . . . Know that I have granted to my citizens of Lincoln all their liberties and customs and laws which they had in the time of Edward [King Edward the Confessor] and William and Henry, kings of England. And I have granted them their gild-merchant, comprising men of the city and other merchants of the shire, as well and freely as they had it in the time of our aforesaid predecessors, kings of England. And all the men who live within the four divisions of the city and attend the market, shall stand in relation to gelds [taxes] and customs and the assizes [ordinances or laws] of the city as well as ever they stood in the time of Edward, William and Henry, kings of England. I also confirm to them that if anyone has lived in Lincoln for a year and a day without dispute from any claimant, and has paid the customs, and if the citizens can show by the laws and customs of the city that the claimant has remained in England during that period and has made no claim, then let the defendant remain in peace in my city of Lincoln as my citizen, without [having to defend his] right.[10]

Kings and lords were reluctant to grant towns self-government, fearing loss of authority and revenue if they gave the merchant guilds full independence. But the lords discovered that towns attracted increasing numbers of people to an area—people whom the lords could tax. Moreover, when burghers bargained for a town's political independence, they offered sizable amounts of ready cash. Consequently, feudal lords ultimately agreed to self-government.

Town Life

Protective walls surrounded almost all medieval towns and cities. The valuable goods inside a town were too much of a temptation to marauding bands for the town to be without the security of bricks and mortar. The walls were pierced by gates, and visitors waited at the gates to gain entrance to the town. When the gates were opened early in the morning, guards inspected the quantity and quality of the goods brought in and collected the customary taxes. Part of the taxes went to the king or lord on whose land the town stood, part to the town council for civic purposes. Constant repair of the walls was usually the town's greatest expense.

Peasants coming from the countryside and merchants traveling from afar set up their carts as stalls just inside the gates. The result was that the road nearest the gate was the widest thoroughfare. It was the ideal place for a market, because everyone coming in or going out used it. Most streets in a medieval town were marketplaces as much as passages for transit. Yet they were generally narrow, just wide enough to transport goods.

Medieval cities served, above all else, as markets. In some respects the entire city was a marketplace. The place where a product was made and sold was also typically the merchant's residence. Usually the

Hamburg Cattle Market   In the twelfth and thirteenth centuries, Hamburg, located on the Elbe near the river's mouth on the North Sea, gained great commercial importance, and its alliance (1241) with Lübeck became the basis of the Hanseatic League. Pigs and cattle were among the vast merchandise offered for sale. The market court (background) sold licenses, set prices, and settled disputes. *(Source: Staatsarchiv Hamburg)*

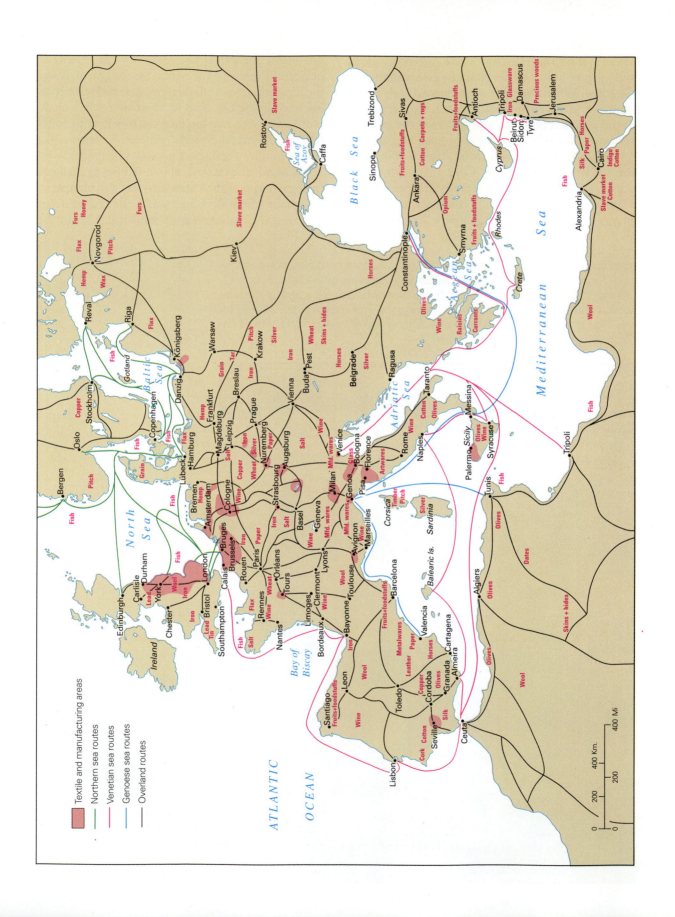

Textile and manufacturing areas

Northern sea routes

Venetian sea routes

Genoese sea routes

Overland routes

ground floor was the scene of production. A window or door opened from the main workroom directly onto the street. The window displayed the finished product, and passersby could look in and see the goods being produced. The merchant's family lived above the business on the second or third floor. As the business and the family expanded, the merchant built additional stories on top of the house.

Because space within the town walls was limited, expansion occurred upward. Second and third stories were built jutting out over the ground floor and thus over the street. Neighbors on the opposite side did the same. Since the streets were narrow to begin with, houses lacked fresh air and light. Initially, houses were made of wood and thatched with straw. Fire represented a constant danger, and because houses were built so close together, fires spread rapidly. Municipal governments consequently urged construction in stone or brick.

Most medieval cities developed haphazardly. There was little town planning. As the population increased, space became more and more limited. Air and water pollution presented serious problems. Many families raised pigs for household consumption in sties next to the house. Horses and oxen, the chief means of transportation and power, dropped tons of dung on the streets every year. It was universal practice in the early towns to dump household waste, both animal and human, into the road in front of one's house. The stench must have been abominable. In 1298 the burgesses of the town of Boutham in Yorkshire, England, received the following order (one long, vivid sentence):

To the bailiffs of the abbot of St. Mary's York, at Boutham. Whereas it is sufficiently evident that the pavement of the said town of Boutham is so very greatly broken up . . . , and in addition the air is so corrupted and infected by the pigsties situated in the king's highways and in the lanes of that town and by the swine feeding and frequently wandering about . . . and by dung and dunghills and many other foul things placed in the streets and lanes, that great repugnance overtakes the king's ministers staying in that town and also others there dwelling

and passing through, the advantage of more wholesome air is impeded, the state of men is grievously injured, and other unbearable inconveniences . . ., to the nuisance of the king's ministers aforesaid and of others there dwelling and passing through, and to the peril of their lives . . . : the king, being unwilling longer to tolerate such great and unbearable defects there, orders the bailiffs to cause the pavement to be suitably repaired within their liberty before All Saints next, and to cause the pigsties, aforesaid streets and lanes to be cleansed from all dung and dunghills, and to cause them to be kept thus cleansed hereafter, and to cause proclamation to be made throughout their bailiwick forbidding any one, under pain of grievous forfeiture, to cause or permit their swine to feed or wander outside his house in the king's streets or the lanes aforesaid.[11]

A great deal of traffic passed through Boutham in 1298 because of the movement of English troops to battlefronts in Scotland. Conditions there were probably not typical. Still, this document suggests that space, air pollution, and sanitation problems bedeviled urban people in medieval times, as they do today.

As the bourgeoisie gained in wealth, they expressed their continuing Christian faith by refurbishing old churches, constructing new ones, and giving stained-glass windows, statues, and carvings. The twelfth-century chronicler William of Newburgh could proudly boast that the city of London had 126 parish churches, in addition to 13 monastic churches and the great cathedral of Saint Paul's.

People wanted to get into medieval cities because they represented a means of economic advancement, social mobility, and improvement in legal status. For the adventurous, the ambitious, and the shrewd, cities offered tremendous opportunities.

MAP 11.5 Trade and Manufacturing in Medieval Europe Note the number of cities and the sources of silver, iron, copper, lead, paper, wool, carpets and rugs, and slaves.

The Revival of Long-Distance Trade

The eleventh century witnessed a remarkable revival of trade, as artisans and craftsmen manufactured goods for local and foreign consumption (Map 11.5). Most trade centered in towns and was controlled by professional traders. Because long-distance trade was risky and required large investments of capital, it could be practiced only by professionals. The transportation of goods involved serious risks. Shipwrecks were common. Pirates infested the sea lanes, and robbers and thieves roamed virtually all of the land routes. Since the risks were so great, merchants preferred to share them. A group of people would thus pool some of their capital to finance an expedition to a distant place. When the ship or caravan returned and the goods brought back were sold, the investors would share the profits. If disaster struck the caravan, an investor's loss was limited to the amount of that individual's investment.

What goods were exchanged? What towns took the lead in medieval "international" trade? In the late eleventh century, the Italian cities, especially Venice, led the West in trade in general and completely dominated the Oriental market. Ships carried salt from the Venetian lagoon, pepper and other spices from North Africa, and silks and purple textiles from the East to northern and western Europe. In the thirteenth century, Venetian caravans brought slaves from the Crimea and Chinese silks from Mongolia to the West. Lombard and Tuscan merchants exchanged those goods at the town markets and regional fairs of France, Flanders, and England. (Fairs were periodic gatherings that attracted buyers, sellers, and goods from all over Europe.) Flanders controlled the cloth industry. The towns of Bruges, Ghent, and Ypres built up a vast industry in the manufacture of cloth. Italian merchants exchanged their products for Flemish tapestries, fine broadcloth, and various other textiles.

Two circumstances help to explain the lead Venice and the Flemish towns gained in long-distance trade. Both enjoyed a high degree of peace and political stability. Geographical factors were equally, if not more, important. Venice was ideally located at the northwestern end of the Adriatic Sea, with easy access to the transalpine land routes as well as the Adriatic and Mediterranean sea lanes. The markets of North Africa, Byzantium, and Russia and the great fairs of Ghent in Flanders and Champagne in France provided commercial opportunities that Venice quickly seized. The geographical situation of Flanders also offered unusual possibilities. Just across the channel from England, Flanders had easy access to English wool. Indeed, Flanders and England developed a very close economic relationship.

Sheep had been raised for their wool in England since Roman times. The rocky soil and damp climate of Yorkshire and Lincolnshire, though poorly suited for agriculture, were excellent for sheep farming. Beginning in the early twelfth century,

but especially after the arrival of Cistercian monks around 1130, the size of the English flocks doubled and then tripled. Scholars have estimated that, by the end of the twelfth century, roughly six million sheep grazed on the English moors and downs. They produced fifty thousand sacks of wool a year.[12] Originally, a "sack" of wool was the burden one packhorse could carry, an amount eventually fixed at 364 pounds; fifty thousand sacks, then, represented huge production.

Wool was the cornerstone of the English medieval economy. Population growth in the twelfth century and the success of the Flemish and Italian textile industries created foreign demand for English wool. The production of English wool stimulated Flemish manufacturing, and the expansion of the Flemish cloth industry in turn spurred the production of English wool. The availability of raw wool also encouraged the development of domestic cloth manufacture within England. The towns of Lincoln, York, Leicester, Northampton, Winchester, and Exeter became important cloth-producing towns. The port cities of London, Hull, Boston, and Bristol thrived on the wool trade. In the thirteenth century, commercial families in these towns grew fabulously rich.

The wool and cloth trades serve as a good barometer of the economic growth and decline of English towns. The supply of wool depended on such natural factors as weather, amount of land devoted to grazing, and prevalence of sheep disease, or *scab*. The price of wool, unlike that of wheat or other foodstuffs, was determined not by supply but by demand. Changes in demand—often the result of political developments over which merchants had no control—could severely damage the wool trade. In the 1320s, for example, violent disorder exploded in the Flemish towns, causing a sharp drop in demand for English wool. When wool exports fell, the economies of London, Hull, and Southampton slumped. Then, during the Hundred Years' War (see pages 362–369), the English crown laid increasingly high export taxes on raw wool, and again the wool trade suffered. On the other hand, the decline of wool exports encouraged the growth of cloth manufacturing in older centers such as Lincoln and in new ones such as Tiverton and Lavenham. In the fourteenth century, these towns experienced some population growth along with considerable prosperity, both of which were directly linked to the cloth industry.

The Commercial Revolution

A steadily expanding volume of international trade from the late eleventh through the thirteenth centuries was a sign of the great economic surge, but it was not the only one. In cities all across Europe, trading and transportation firms opened branch offices. Credit was widely extended, considerably facilitating exchange. Merchants devised the letter of credit, which made unnecessary the slow and dangerous shipment of coin for payment.

A new capitalistic spirit developed. Professional merchants were always on the lookout for new markets and opportunities. They invested surplus capital in new enterprises. They diversified their interests and got involved in a wide variety of operations. The typical prosperous merchant in the later thirteenth century might well be involved in buying and selling, shipping, lending some capital at interest, and other types of banking. Medieval merchants were fiercely competitive.

Some scholars consider capitalism a modern phenomenon, beginning in the fifteenth or sixteenth century. But in their use of capital to make more money, in their speculative pursuits and willingness to gamble, in their competitive spirit, and in the variety of their interests and operations, medieval businessmen displayed the traits of capitalists.

The ventures of the German Hanseatic League illustrate these impulses. The Hanseatic League was a mercantile association of towns. Though scholars trace the league's origin to the foundation of the city of Lübeck in 1159, the mutual protection treaty later signed between Lübeck and Hamburg marks the league's actual expansion. Lübeck and Hamburg wanted mutual security, exclusive trading rights, and, where possible, a monopoly. During the next century, perhaps two hundred cities from Holland to Poland, including Cologne, Brunswick, Dortmund, Danzig, and Riga, joined the league, but Lübeck always remained the dominant member. From the thirteenth to the sixteenth century, the Hanseatic League controlled trade over a Novgorod-Reval-Lübeck-Hamburg-Bruges-London axis, that is, the trade of northern Europe (see Map 11.5). In the fourteenth century, the Hanseatics branched out into southern Germany and Italy by land and into French, Spanish, and Portuguese ports by sea.

Across regular, well-defined trade routes along the Baltic and North seas, the ships of league cities

Hanseatic League Merchants at Hamburg   In the thirteenth century, the merchants of Hamburg and other cities in northern Germany formed an association for the suppression of piracy and the acquisition of commercial privileges in foreign countries. Members of the Hansa traded in furs, fish, wax, and oriental luxury goods. *(Source: Staatsarchiv Hamburg)*

carried furs, wax, copper, fish, grain, timber, and wine. These goods were exchanged for finished products, mainly cloth and salt, from Western cities. At cities such as Bruges and London, Hanseatic merchants secured special trading concessions exempting them from all tolls and allowing them to trade at local fairs. Hanseatic merchants established foreign trading centers, called "factories," the most famous of which was the London Steelyard, a walled community with warehouses, offices, a church, and residential quarters for company representatives.[13]

By the late thirteenth century, Hanseatic merchants had developed an important business technique, the business register. Merchants publicly recorded their debts and contracts and received a league guarantee for them. This device proved a decisive factor in the later development of credit and commerce in northern Europe.[14] These activities required capital, risk-taking, and aggressive pursuit of opportunities—the essential ingredients of capitalism. They also yielded fat profits.

These developments added up to what one modern scholar, who knows the period well, has called "a commercial revolution, . . . probably the greatest turning point in the history of our civilization."[15] This is not a wildly extravagant statement. In the long run, the commercial revolution of the High Middle Ages brought about radical change in European society. One remarkable aspect of this change is that the commercial classes did not constitute a large part of the total population—never more than 10 percent. They exercised an influence far in excess of their numbers.

The commercial revolution created a great deal of new wealth. Wealth meant a higher standard of living. The new availability of something as simple as spices, for example, allowed for variety in food. Dietary habits gradually changed. Tastes became more sophisticated. Contact with Eastern civilizations introduced Europeans to eating utensils such as forks. Table manners improved. Nobles learned to eat with forks and knives, instead of tearing the meat from a roast with their hands. They began to use napkins, instead of wiping their greasy fingers on the dogs lying under the table.

The existence of wealth did not escape the attention of kings and other rulers. Wealth could be taxed, and through taxation kings could create strong and centralized states. In the years to come, alliances with the middle classes were to enable kings to defeat feudal powers and aristocratic interests and to build the states that came to be called "modern."

The commercial revolution also provided the opportunity for thousands of serfs to improve their social position. The slow but steady transformation of European society from almost completely rural and isolated to relatively more sophisticated constituted the greatest effect of the commercial revolution that began in the eleventh century.

Even so, merchants and business people did not run medieval communities, except in central and northern Italy and in the county of Flanders. Most towns remained small. The castle, the manorial village, and the monastery dominated the landscape. The feudal nobility and churchmen determined the preponderant social attitudes, values, and patterns of thought and behavior. The commercial changes of the eleventh through thirteenth centuries did, however, lay the economic foundations for the development of urban life and culture.

MEDIEVAL UNIVERSITIES

Just as the first strong secular states emerged in the thirteenth century, so did the first universities. This was no coincidence. The new bureaucratic states and the church needed educated administrators, and universities were a response to this need. The word *university* derives from the Latin *universitas,* meaning "corporation" or "guild." Medieval universities were educational guilds that produced educated and trained individuals. They were also an expression of the tremendous vitality and creativity of the High Middle Ages. Their organization, methods of instruction, and goals continue to influence institutionalized learning in the Western world.

Origins

In the early Middle Ages, anyone who received education got it from a priest. Priests instructed the clever boys on the manor in the Latin words of the Mass and taught them the rudiments of reading and writing. Few boys acquired elementary literacy, however, and girls did not obtain even that. The peasant who wished to send his son to school had to secure the permission of his lord, because the result of formal schooling tended to be a career in the church or some trade. If a young man were to pursue either, he would have to leave the manor and gain free status. Because the lord stood to lose the services of educated peasants, he limited the number of serfs sent to school.

Few schools were available anyway. Society was organized for war and defense and gave slight support to education. By the late eleventh century, however, social conditions had markedly improved. There was greater political stability, and favorable economic conditions had advanced many people beyond the level of bare subsistence. The curious and able felt the lack of schools and teachers.

Since the time of the Carolingian Empire, monasteries and cathedral schools had offered the only formal instruction available. The monasteries were geared to religious concerns, and the monastic curriculum consisted of studying the Scriptures and the writings of the church fathers. Monasteries wished to maintain an atmosphere of seclusion and silence and were unwilling to accept large numbers of noisy lay students. In contrast, schools attached to cathedrals and run by the bishop and his clergy were frequently situated in bustling cities, and in the eleventh century in Italian cities like Bologna, wealthy businessmen had established municipal schools. Cities inhabited by peoples of many backgrounds and "nationalities" stimulated the growth and exchange of ideas. In the course of the twelfth century, cathedral schools in France and municipal schools in Italy developed into universities (Map 11.6).

The school at Chartres Cathedral in France became famous for its studies of the Latin classics and for the broad literary interests it fostered in its students. The most famous graduate of Chartres was the Englishman John of Salisbury (d. 1180), who wrote *The Statesman's Book,* an important treatise on the corrupting effects of political power. But Chartres, situated in the center of rich farmland, remote from the currents of commercial traffic and intellectual ideas, did not develop into a university. The first European universities appeared in Italy, at Bologna and Salerno.

The growth of the University of Bologna coincided with a revival of interest in Roman law. The study of Roman law as embodied in the Justinian *Code* had never completely died out in the West, but this sudden burst of interest seems to have been inspired by Irnerius (d. 1125), a great teacher at Bologna. His fame attracted students from all over Europe. Irnerius not only explained the Roman law of the Justinian *Code,* he applied it to difficult practical situations. An important school of civil law was founded at Montpellier in France, but Bologna remained the greatest law school throughout the Middle Ages.

At Salerno, interest in medicine had persisted for centuries. Greek and Muslim physicians there had studied the use of herbs as cures and experimented with surgery. The twelfth century ushered in a new interest in Greek medical texts and in the work of Arab and Greek doctors. Students of medicine poured into Salerno and soon attracted royal attention. In 1140, when King Roger II of Sicily took the practice of medicine under royal control, his ordinance stated:

Who, from now on, wishes to practice medicine, has to present himself before our officials and examiners, in order to pass their judgment. Should he be bold enough to disregard this, he will be punished by imprisonment and confiscation of his entire property. In this way we are taking care that our subjects are not endangered by the inexperience of the physicians.[16]

In the first decades of the twelfth century, students converged on Paris. They crowded into the cathedral school of Notre Dame and spilled over into the area later called the "Latin Quarter"— whose name probably reflects the Italian origin of many of the students attracted to Paris by the surge of interest in the classics, logic, and theology. The cathedral school's international reputation had already drawn to Paris scholars from all over Europe, one of the most famous of whom was Peter Abelard.

The son of a minor Breton knight, Peter Abelard (1079–1142) studied in Paris, quickly absorbed a large amount of material, and set himself up as a teacher. Abelard was fascinated by logic, which he believed could be used to solve most problems. He had a brilliant mind and, although orthodox in his philosophical teaching, appeared to challenge ecclesiastical authorities. His book *Sic et Non (Yes and No)* was a list of apparently contradictory propositions drawn from the Bible and the writings of the church fathers. One such proposition, for example, stated that sin is pleasing to God and is not pleasing to God. Abelard used a method of systematic doubting in his writing and teaching. As he put it in the preface of *Sic et Non,* "By doubting we come to questioning, and by questioning we perceive the truth." While other scholars merely asserted theological principles, Abelard discussed and analyzed them. Through reasoning he even tried to describe the attributes of the three persons of the Trinity, the central mystery of the Christian faith. Abelard was severely censured by a church council, but his cleverness, boldness, and imagination made him a highly popular figure among students.

The influx of students eager for learning, together with dedicated and imaginative teachers, created the atmosphere in which universities grew. In northern Europe—at Paris and later at Oxford and Cambridge in England—associations or guilds of professors organized universities. They established the curriculum, set the length of time for study, and determined the form and content of examinations.

SCOTLAND

St. Andrews
Glasgow

North
Sea

DENMARK

Copenhagen

Baltic Sea

IRELAND

Durham
Jarrow
Rivaulx
York

ENGLAND

Petersborough
Cambridge
Bury
St. Edmunds
Oxford
Canterbury
Salisbury
Winchester

ATLANTIC
OCEAN

Ypres
Louvain
Brussels
Amiens
Jumièges
Bec
Laon
Reims
Mont
St. Michel
Notre
Dame
St.-Denis
Paris
Savigny
Chartres
Beauvais
Orléans
Fleury
Tours
Bourges
Cîteaux
Poitiers
Cluny

Cologne
Magdeburg
Berlin
Leipzig
Fulda
HOLY
Mainz
Bamberg
Prague
Heidelberg
ROMAN
Regensburg
Hirsau
Lorch
Vienna
Clairvaux
EMPIRE
Munich
Basel
St.-Gall

FRANCE

Bordeaux
Cahors
Grenoble
Pavia
Padua
Piacenza
Toulouse
Montpellier
Avignon
Bologna
Florence
Vallombrosa
Perugia

Valladolid
Salamanca
Coimbra
SPAIN
Toledo

Corsica

Rome
Monte
Cassino
Naples
Salerno

Sardinia

Seville

Palermo

Sicily

Mediterranean Sea

◆ University
■ Monastery school
🏰 Cathedral school

0   100   200   300 Km.
0   100   200   300 Mi.

Instruction and Curriculum

University faculties grouped themselves according to academic disciplines, called "schools"—law, medicine, arts, and theology. The professors, known as "schoolmen" or "Scholastics," developed a method of thinking, reasoning, and writing in which questions were raised and authorities cited on both sides of the question. The goal of the Scholastic method was to arrive at definitive answers and to provide a rational explanation for what was believed on faith. Schoolmen held that reason and faith constitute two harmonious realms in which the truths of faith and reason complement each other. The Scholastic approach rested on the recovery of classical philosophical texts.

Ancient Greek and Arabic texts had entered Europe in the early twelfth century, primarily through Toledo in Muslim Spain. Thirteenth-century philosophers relied on Latin translations of these texts, especially translations of Aristotle. Aristotle had stressed direct observation of nature, as well as the principles that theory must follow fact and that knowledge of a thing requires an explanation of its causes. The schoolmen reinterpreted Aristotelian texts in a Christian sense.

In exploration of the natural world, Aristotle's axioms were not precisely followed. Medieval scientists argued from authority, such as the Bible, the Justinian *Code,* or an ancient scientific treatise, rather than from direct observation and experimentation, as modern scientists do. Thus the conclusions of medieval scientists were often wrong. Nevertheless, natural science gradually emerged as a discipline distinct from philosophy. Scholastics made important contributions to the advancement of knowledge. They preserved the Greek and Arabic texts that contained the body of ancient scientific knowledge, which would otherwise have been lost. And, in asking questions about nature and the universe, Scholastics laid the foundations for later scientific work.

Many of the problems that Scholastic philosophers raised dealt with theological issues. For exam-

MAP 11.6 Intellectual Centers of Medieval Europe Universities obviously provided more sophisticated instruction than did monastic and cathedral schools. What other factors distinguish the three kinds of intellectual centers?

ple, they addressed the question that interested all Christians, educated and uneducated: how is a person saved? Saint Augustine's thesis—that, as a result of Adam's fall, human beings have a propensity to sin—had become a central feature of medieval church doctrine. The church taught that it possessed the means to forgive the sinful: grace conveyed through the sacraments. However, although grace provided a predisposition to salvation, the Scholastics held that one must also *decide* to use the grace received. In other words, a person must use his or her reason to advance to God.

Thirteenth-century Scholastics devoted an enormous amount of time to collecting and organizing knowledge on all topics. These collections were published as *summa,* or reference books. There were summa on law, philosophy, vegetation, animal life, and theology. Saint Thomas Aquinas (1225–1274), a professor at Paris, produced the most famous collection, the *Summa Theologica,* which deals with a vast number of theological questions.

Aquinas drew an important distinction between faith and reason. He maintained that, although reason can demonstrate many basic Christian principles such as the existence of God, other fundamental teachings such as the Trinity and original sin cannot be proved by logic. That reason cannot establish them does not, however, mean they are contrary to reason. Rather, people understand such doctrines through revelation embodied in Scripture. Scripture cannot contradict reason, nor reason Scripture:

The light of faith that is freely infused into us does not destroy the light of natural knowledge [reason] implanted in us naturally. For although the natural light of the human mind is insufficient to show us these things made manifest by faith, it is nevertheless impossible that these things which the divine principle gives us by faith are contrary to these implanted in us by nature [reason]. Indeed, were that the case, one or the other would have to be false, and, since both are given to us by God, God would have to be the author of untruth, which is impossible. . . . [I]t is impossible that those things which are of philosophy can be contrary to those things which are of faith.[17]

Aquinas also investigated the branch of philosophy called *epistemology,* which is concerned with how a person knows something. Aquinas stated that one knows, first, through sensory perception of the physical world—seeing, hearing, touching, and so on. He maintained that there can be nothing in the mind that is not first in the senses. Second, knowledge comes through reason, the mind exercising its natural abilities. Aquinas stressed the power of human reason to know, even to know God. Proofs of the existence of God exemplify the Scholastic method of knowing.

Aquinas began with the things of the natural world—earth, air, trees, water, birds. Then he inquired about their original source or cause: the mover, creator, planner who started it all. Everything, Aquinas maintained, has an ultimate and essential explanation, a reason for existing. Here he was following Aristotle. Aquinas went further and identified the reason for existing, or first mover, with God. Thomas Aquinas and all medieval intellectuals held that the end of both faith and reason was the knowledge of, and union with, God. His work later became the fundamental text of Roman Catholic doctrine.

At all universities, the standard method of teaching was the *lecture*—that is, a reading. The professor read a passage from the Bible, the Justinian *Code,* or one of Aristotle's treatises. He then explained and interpreted the passage; his interpretation was called a *gloss.* Students wrote down everything. Texts and glosses were sometimes collected and reproduced as textbooks. For example, the Italian Peter Lombard (d. 1160), a professor at Paris, wrote what became the standard textbook in theology, *Sententiae (The Sentences),* a compilation of basic theological principles.

Because books had to be copied by hand, they were extremely expensive, and few students could afford them. Students therefore depended for study on their own or friends' notes accumulated over a period of years. The choice of subjects was narrow. The syllabus at all universities consisted of a core of ancient texts that all students studied and, if they wanted to get ahead, mastered.

There were no examinations at the end of a series of lectures. Examinations were given after three, four, or five years of study, when the student applied for a degree. The professors determined the amount of material students had to know for each degree, and students frequently insisted that the professors specify precisely what that material was. When the candidate for a degree believed himself prepared, he presented himself to a committee of professors for examination.

Examinations were oral and very difficult. If the candidate passed, he was awarded the first, or bachelor's, degree. Further study, about as long, arduous, and expensive as it is today, enabled the graduate to try for the master's and doctor's degrees. All degrees certified competence in a given subject, and degrees were technically licenses to teach. Most students, however, did not become teachers.

GOTHIC ART

Medieval churches stand as the most spectacular manifestations of medieval vitality and creativity. It is difficult for twentieth-century people to appreciate the extraordinary amounts of energy, imagination, and money involved in building them. Between 1180 and 1270 in France alone, eighty cathedrals, about five hundred abbey churches, and tens of thousands of parish churches were constructed. This construction represents a remarkable investment for a country of scarcely eighteen million people. More stone was quarried for churches in medieval France than had been mined in ancient Egypt, where the Great Pyramid alone consumed 40.5 million cubic feet of stone. All these churches displayed a new architectural style. Fifteenth-century critics called the new style "Gothic" because they mistakenly believed the fifth-century Goths had invented it. It actually developed partly in reaction to the earlier "Romanesque" style, which resembled ancient Roman architecture.

Gothic cathedrals were built in towns and reflect both bourgeois wealth and enormous civic pride. The manner in which a society spends its wealth expresses its values. Cathedrals, abbeys, and village churches testify to the deep religious faith and piety of medieval people. If the dominant aspect of medieval culture had not been the Christian faith, the builder's imagination and the merchant's money would have been used in other ways.

From Romanesque Gloom to "Uninterrupted Light"

The relative political stability and increase of ecclesiastical wealth in the eleventh century encouraged the arts of peace. In the ninth and tenth centuries, the Vikings and Magyars had burned hundred of wooden churches. In the eleventh century, the abbots wanted to rebuild in a more permanent fashion, and after the year 1000, church building increased on a wide scale. Because fireproofing was essential, ceilings had to be made of stone. Therefore, builders replaced wooden roofs with arched stone ceilings called "vaults." The stone ceilings were heavy; only thick walls would support them. Because the walls were so thick, the windows were small, allowing little light into the interior of the church. The basic features of such Romanesque architecture are stone vaults in the ceiling, a rounded arch over the nave (the central part of the church), and thick, heavy walls. In northern Europe, twin bell towers often crowned Romanesque churches, giving them a powerful, fortresslike appearance. Built primarily by monasteries, Romanesque churches reflect the quasi-military, aristocratic, and pre-urban society that built them.

The inspiration for the Gothic style originated in the brain of one monk, Suger, abbot of Saint-Denis (1122–1151). When Suger became abbot, he decided to reconstruct the old Carolingian abbey church at Saint-Denis. Work began in 1137. On June 11, 1144, King Louis VII and a large crowd of bishops, dignitaries, and common people witnessed the solemn consecration of the first Gothic church in France.

The basic features of Gothic architecture—the pointed arch, the ribbed vault, and the flying buttress—were not unknown before 1137. What was without precedent was the interior lightness they made possible. Since the ceiling of a Gothic church weighed less than that of a Romanesque church, the walls could be thinner. Stained-glass windows were cut into the stone, flooding the church with light. The bright interior was astounding. Suger, describing his achievement, exulted:

Moreover, it was cunningly provided that . . . the central nave of the old nave should be equalized, by means of geometrical and arithmetical instruments, with the central nave of the new addition; and, likewise, that the dimensions of the old side-aisles should be equalized with the new dimensions of the new side-aisles, except for that elegant and praiseworthy extension, in [the form of] a circular string of chapels, by virtue of which the whole [church] would shine with the wonderful and uninterrupted light of most sacred windows, pervading the interior beauty.[18]

Begun in the Île-de-France, Gothic architecture spread throughout France with the expansion of royal power. French architects were soon invited to design and supervise the construction of churches

Interior of Gothic Cathedral The ribbed vault and pointed arch (and the flying buttress on the exterior) characterize the Gothic style. Stone became the weightless expression of the human spirit, which is raised to the contemplation of the divine through beauty. *(Source: Sonia Halliday)*

in other parts of Europe. For example, William of Sens was commissioned to rebuild Canterbury Cathedral after a disastrous fire in 1174. The distinguished scholar John of Salisbury was then in Canterbury and observed William's work. After John became bishop of Chartres, he wanted William of Sens to assist in the renovation of Chartres Cathedral. Through such contacts the new style traveled rapidly over Europe.

The Creative Outburst

The construction of a Gothic cathedral represented a gigantic investment of time, money, and corporate effort. It was the bishop and the clergy of the cathedral who made the decision to build, but they depended on the support of all the social classes. Bishops raised revenue from contributions by people in their dioceses, and the clergy appealed to the king and the nobility. Since Suger deliberately utilized the Gothic to glorify the French monarchy, the Gothic was called "French royal style" from its inception. Thus the French kings were generous patrons of many cathedrals. Louis IX endowed churches in the Île-de-France—most notably, Sainte-Chapelle, a small chapel to house the crown of thorns. Noble families often gave contributions in order to have their crests in the stained-glass windows. Above all, the church relied on the financial help of those with the greatest amount of ready cash, the commercial classes.

Money was not the only need. A great number of craftsmen had to be assembled: quarrymen, sculptors, stonecutters, masons, mortar makers, carpenters, blacksmiths, glassmakers, roofers. Each master craftsman had apprentices, and unskilled laborers had to be recruited for the heavy work. The construction of a large cathedral was rarely completed in one lifetime; many were never finished at all. Because generation after generation added to the building, many Gothic churches show the architectural influences of two or even three centuries.

Since cathedrals were symbols of bourgeois civic pride, towns competed to build the largest and most splendid church. In northern France in the late twelfth and early thirteenth centuries, cathedrals grew progressively taller. In 1163 the citizens of Paris began Notre Dame Cathedral, intending it to reach the height of 114 feet. When reconstruction on Chartres Cathedral was begun in 1194, it was to be 119 feet. The people of Beauvais exceeded everyone: their church, started in 1247, reached 157 feet. Unfortunately, the weight imposed on the vaults was too great, and the building collapsed in 1284. Medieval people built cathedrals to glorify God—and if mortals were impressed, so much the better.[19]

Cathedrals served secular as well as religious purposes. The sanctuary containing the altar and the bishop's chair belonged to the clergy, but the rest of the church belonged to the people. In addition to marriages, baptisms, and funerals, there were scores of feast days on which the entire town gathered in the cathedral for festivities. Amiens Cathedral could hold the entire town population. Local guilds, which fulfilled the economic, fraternal, and charitable functions of modern labor unions, met in the cathedrals to arrange business deals and plan recreational events and the support of disabled members. Magistrates and municipal officials held political meetings there. Some towns never built town halls, because all civic functions took place in the cathedral. Pilgrims slept there, lovers courted there, traveling actors staged plays there. The cathedral belonged to all.

First and foremost, however, the cathedral was intended to teach the people the doctrines of Christian faith through visual images. Architecture became the servant of theology. The main altar was at the east end, pointing toward Jerusalem, the city of peace. The west front of the cathedral faced the setting sun, and its wall was usually devoted to the scenes of the Last Judgment. The north side, which received the least sunlight, displayed events from the Old Testament. The south side, washed in warm sunshine for much of the day, depicted scenes from the New Testament. This symbolism implied that the Jewish people of the Old Testament lived in darkness and that the Gospel brought by Christ illuminated the world. Every piece of sculpture, furniture, and stained glass had some religious or social significance.

Stained glass beautifully reflects the creative energy of the High Middle Ages. It is both an integral part of Gothic architecture and a distinct form of painting. The glassmaker "painted" the picture with small fragments of glass held together with strips of lead. As Gothic churches became more skeletal and had more windows, stained glass replaced manuscript illumination as the leading kind of painting.

Contributors to the cathedral and workers left their imprints on it. Stonecutters cut their individual marks on each block of stone, partly so that they would be paid. At Chartres the craft and merchant guilds—drapers, furriers, haberdashers, tanners, butchers, bakers, fishmongers, and wine merchants—donated money and are memorialized in stained-glass windows. Thousands of scenes in the cathedral celebrate nature, country life, and the activities of ordinary people. All members of medieval society had a place in the City of God, which the Gothic cathedral represented. No one, from king to peasant, was excluded.

West Front of Notre Dame Cathedral In this powerful vision of the Last Judgment, Christ sits in judgment surrounded by angels, the Virgin, and Saint John. Scenes of paradise fill the arches on Christ's right, scenes of hell on the left. In the lower lintel, the dead arise incorruptible, and in the upper lintel (below Christ's feet), the saved move off to heaven, while devils push the damned to hell. Below, the twelve apostles line the doorway. *(Source: Alinari/Scala/Art Resource)*

Tapestry making also came into its own in the fourteenth century. Heavy woolen tapestries were first made in the monasteries and convents as wall hangings for churches. Because they could be moved and lent an atmosphere of warmth, they subsequently replaced mural paintings. Early tapestries depicted religious scenes, but later hangings produced for the knightly class bore secular designs, especially romantic forests and hunting spectacles.

The drama, derived from the church's liturgy, emerged as a distinct art form during the same period. For centuries, skits based on Christ's Nativity and Resurrection had been performed in monasteries and cathedrals. Beginning in the thirteenth century, plays based on these and other biblical themes and on the lives of the saints were performed in the towns. Guilds financed these "mystery plays," so called because they were based on the mysteries of the Christian faith. Performed first at the cathedral altar, then in the church square, and later in the town marketplace, mystery plays enjoyed great popularity. By combining comical farce based on ordinary life with serious religious scenes, they allowed the common people to understand and identify with religious figures and the mysteries of their faith. While provoking the individual conscience to reform, mystery plays were also an artistic manifestation of local civic pride.

HERESY AND THE FRIARS

As the commercial revolution of the High Middle Ages fostered urban development, the towns experienced an enormous growth of heresy. In fact, in the twelfth and thirteenth centuries, "the most economically advanced and urbanized areas: northern Italy, southern France, Flanders-Brabant, and the lower Rhine Valley" witnessed the strongest heretical movements.[20] Why did heresy flourish in such places? The bishops, usually drawn from the feudal nobility, did not understand urban culture and

Fifteenth-Century Flemish Tapestry   The weavers of Tournai (in present-day Belgium) spent twenty-five years (1450–1475) producing this magnificent tapestry, which is based on the Old Testament story of Jehu, Jezebel, and the sons of Ahab (2 Kings, 9–10). *(Source: Isabella Stewart Gardner Museum, Boston/Art Resource)*

were suspicious of it. Christian theology, formulated for an earlier, rural age, did not address the problems of the more sophisticated mercantile society. The new monastic orders of the twelfth century, deliberately situated in remote, isolated areas, had little relevance to the towns.[21] Finally, townspeople wanted a pious clergy, capable of preaching the Gospel in a manner that satisfied their spiritual needs. They disapproved of clerical ignorance and luxurious living. Critical of the clergy, neglected, and spiritually unfulfilled, townspeople turned to heretical sects.

The term *heresy,* which derives from the Greek *hairesis,* meaning "individual choosing," is older than Christianity. At the end of the fourth century, when Christianity became the official religion of the Roman Empire, religious issues took on a legal dimension. Theologians and kings defined the Roman Empire as a Christian society. Since religion was thought to bind society in a fundamental way, religious unity was essential for social cohesion. A heretic, therefore, threatened not only the religious part of the community, but the community itself. As described in Chapter 7, civil authority could (and did) punish heresy. In the early Middle Ages, the term *heresy* came to be applied to the position of a Christian who chose and stubbornly held to doctrinal error in defiance of church authority.[22]

Ironically, the eleventh-century Gregorian reform movement, which had worked to purify the church of disorder, led to some twelfth- and thirteenth-century heretical movements. Papal efforts to improve the sexual morality of the clergy, for example, had largely succeeded. When Gregory VII forbade married priests to celebrate church ceremonies, he expected public opinion to force priests to put aside their wives and concubines. But Gregory did not foresee the consequences of this order. Laypersons assumed they could remove immoral priests. Critics and heretics could accuse clergymen of immorality and thus weaken their influence. Moreover, by forbidding sinful priests to administer the sacraments, Gregory unwittingly revived the old Donatist heresy, which held that sacraments given by an immoral priest were useless; thus Donatist beliefs spread. The clergy's inability to provide adequate instruction weakened its position.

In northern Italian towns, Arnold of Brescia, a vigorous advocate of strict clerical poverty, denounced clerical wealth. In France, Peter Waldo, a rich merchant of Lyons, gave his money to the poor and preached that only prayers, not sacraments, were needed for salvation. The "Waldensians"—as Peter's followers were called—bitterly attacked the sacraments and church hierarchy, and they carried these ideas across Europe. Another group, known either as the Cathars (from the Greek *katharos,* meaning "pure") or as the Albigensians (from the town of Albi in southern France), rejected not only the hierarchical organization and the sacraments of the church, but the Roman church itself. The Cathars' primary tenet was the dualist belief that God had created spiritual things and the Devil had created material things; thus the soul was good and the body evil. Forces of good and evil battled constantly, and leading a perfect life meant being stripped of all physical and material things. Thus sexual intercourse was evil because it led to the creation of more physical bodies. To free oneself from the power of evil, a person had to lead a life of extreme asceticism, avoiding all material things. Albigensians were divided into the "perfect," who followed the principles of Catharism, and the "believers," who led ordinary lives until their deaths, when they repented and were saved.

The Albigensian heresy won many adherents in southern France. Townspeople admired the virtuous lives of the "perfect," which contrasted very favorably with the luxurious living of the Roman clergy. Women were attracted because the Albigensians treated them as men's equals, and nobles were drawn because they coveted the wealth of the clergy. Faced with widespread defection in southern France, in 1208 Pope Innocent III proclaimed a crusade against the Albigensian heretics. When the papal legate was murdered by a follower of Count Raymond of Toulouse, the greatest lord in southern France and a suspected heretic, the crusade took on a political character; heretical beliefs became fused with feudal rebellion against the French crown. Northern French lords joined the crusade and inflicted severe defeats on the towns of the large southern province of Languedoc. The Albigensian crusade, however, was a political rather than a religious success, and the heresy went underground. In its continuing struggle against heresy, the church gained the support of two remarkable men, Saint Dominic and Saint Francis, and of the orders they founded.

Born in Castile, the province of Spain famous for its zealous Christianity and militant opposition to Islam, Domingo de Gúzman (1170?-1221) received a sound education and was ordained a priest. In 1206 he accompanied his bishop on a mission to preach to the Albigensian heretics in Languedoc. Although the austere simplicity in which they traveled contrasted favorably with the pomp and display of the papal legate in the area, Dominic's efforts had little practical success. Determined to win the heretics back with ardent preaching, Dominic subsequently returned to France with a few followers. In 1216 the group—known as the "Preaching Friars"—won papal recognition as a new religious order. Their name indicates their goal; they were to preach, and in order to preach effectively, they had to study. Dominic sent his recruits to the universities for training in theology.

Francesco di Bernardone (1181–1226), son of a wealthy cloth merchant from the northern Italian town of Assisi, was an extravagant wastrel until he had a sudden conversion. Then he determined to devote himself entirely to living the Gospel. Directed by a vision to rebuild the dilapidated chapel of Saint Damiano in Assisi, Francis sold some of his father's cloth to finance the reconstruction. His enraged father insisted that he return the money and enlisted the support of the bishop. When the bishop told Francis to obey his father, Francis took off all his clothes and returned them to his father. Thereafter he promised to obey only his Father in heaven. Francis was particularly inspired by two biblical texts: "If you seek perfection, go, sell your possessions, and give to the poor. You will have treasure in heaven. Afterward, come back and follow me" (Matthew 19:21); and Jesus' advice to his disciples as they went out to preach, "Take nothing for the journey, neither walking staff nor travelling bag, no bread, no money" (Luke 9:3). Over the centuries, these words had stimulated countless young people. With Francis, however, there was a radical difference: he intended to observe them literally and without compromise. He set out to live and preach the Gospel in absolute poverty.

The simplicity, humility, and joyful devotion with which Francis carried out his mission soon attracted companions. Although he resisted pressure to establish an order, his followers became so numerous that he was obliged to develop some formal structure. In 1221 the papacy approved the "Rule of the Little Brothers of Saint Francis," as the Franciscans were known.

The new Dominican and Franciscan orders differed significantly from older monastic orders such as the Benedictines and the Cistercians. First, the Dominicans and Franciscans were friars, not monks. Their lives and work centered in the cities and university towns, the busy centers of commercial and intellectual life, not the secluded and cloistered world of the monks. Second, the friars stressed apostolic poverty, a life based on the Gospel's teachings, in which they would own no property and depend on Christian people for their material needs. Hence they were called *mendicants,* begging friars. Benedictine and Cistercian abbeys, on the other hand, held land—not infrequently great tracts of land. Finally, the friars drew their members largely from the burgher class, from small property owners and shopkeepers. The monastic orders, by contrast, gathered their members (at least until the thirteenth century) overwhelmingly from the nobility.[23]

The friars represented a response to the spiritual and intellectual needs of the thirteenth century. Exciting new research on the German friars has shown that, while the Franciscans initially accepted uneducated men, the Dominicans always showed a marked preference for university graduates.[24] A more urban and sophisticated society required a highly educated clergy. The Dominicans soon held professorial chairs at leading universities, and they count Thomas Aquinas, probably the greatest medieval philosopher in Europe, as their most famous member. But the Franciscans followed suit at the universities and also produced intellectual leaders. The Franciscans' mission to the towns and the poor, their ideal of poverty, and their compassion for the human condition made them vastly popular. The friars interpreted Christian doctrine for the new urban classes. By living Christianity as well as by preaching it, they won the respect of the medieval bourgeoisie.

Dominic started his order to combat heresy. Francis's followers were motivated by the ideal of absolute poverty. The papacy used the friars to staff a new (1233) ecclesiastical court, the Inquisition. Popes selected the friars to direct the Inquisition because bishops proved unreliable and because special theological training was needed. *Inquisition* means "investigation," and the Franciscans and Dominicans developed expert methods of rooting out unorthodox thought. Modern Americans consider the procedures of the Inquisition exceedingly unjust, and there was substantial criticism of it in the Middle Ages. The accused did not learn the evidence against them or see their accusers; they were subjected to lengthy interrogations often designed to trap them; and torture could be used to extract confessions. Medieval people, however, believed that heretics destroyed the souls of their neighbors. By attacking religion, it was also thought, heretics destroyed the very bonds of society. So successful was the Inquisition that, within a century, heresy had been virtually extinguished.

A CHALLENGE TO RELIGIOUS AUTHORITY

Societies, like individuals, cannot maintain a high level of energy indefinitely. In the later years of the thirteenth century, Europeans seemed to run out of steam. The crusading movement gradually fizzled out. Few new cathedrals were constructed, and if a cathedral had not been completed by 1300, the chances were high that it never would be. The strong rulers of England and France, building on the foundations of their predecessors, increased their authority and gained the loyalty of all their subjects. The vigor of those kings, however, did not pass to their immediate descendants. Meanwhile, the church, which for two centuries had guided Christian society, began to face grave difficulties. A violent dispute between the papacy and the kings of England and France badly damaged the prestige of the pope.

In 1294 King Edward I of England and Philip the Fair of France declared war on each other. To finance this war, both kings laid taxes on the clergy. Kings had been taxing the church for decades. Pope Boniface VIII (1294–1303), arguing from precedent, insisted that kings gain papal consent for taxation of the clergy and forbade churchmen to pay the taxes. But Edward and Philip refused to accept this decree, partly because it hurt royal finances and partly because the papal order threatened royal authority within their countries. Edward immediately denied the clergy the protection of the law, an action that meant its members could be attacked with impunity. Philip halted the shipment of all ecclesiastical revenue to Rome. Boniface had to back down.

Philip the Fair and his ministers continued their attack on all powers in France outside royal authority. Philip arrested a French bishop who was also the papal legate. When Boniface defended the ecclesiastical status and diplomatic immunity of the

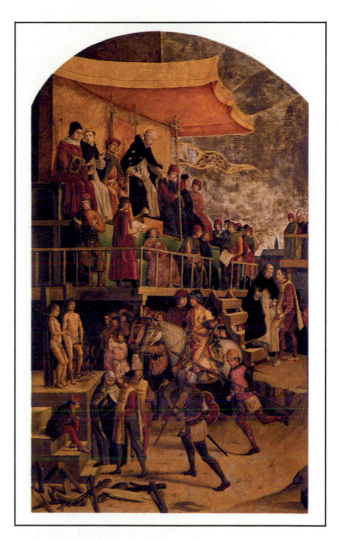

St. Dominic and the Inquisition   The fifteenth-century court painter to the Spanish rulers Ferdinand and Isabella, Pedro Berruguete here portrays an event from the life of St. Dominic: Dominic presides at the trial of Count Raymond of Toulouse who had supported the Albigensian heretics. Raymond, helmeted and on horseback, repented and was pardoned; his companions, who would not repent, were burned. Smoke from the fire has put one of the judges to sleep, and other officials, impervious to the human tragedy, chat among themselves. *(Source: Museo del Prado, Madrid)*

bishop, Philip replied with the trumped-up charge that the pope was a heretic. The papacy and the French monarchy waged a bitter war of propaganda. Finally, in 1302, in a letter entitled *Unam Sanctam* (because its opening sentence spoke of one holy Catholic church), Boniface insisted that all Christians are subject to the pope. Although the letter made no specific reference to Philip, it held that kings should submit to papal authority. Philip's university-trained advisers responded with an argument drawn from Roman law. They maintained that the king of France was completely sovereign in his kingdom and responsible to God alone. French mercenary troops went to Italy and arrested the aged pope at Anagni. Although Boniface was soon freed, he died shortly afterward. The confrontation at Anagni foreshadowed serious difficulties within the Christian church, but religious struggle was only one of the crises that would face Western society in the fourteenth century.

SUMMARY

The High Middle Ages represent one of the most creative periods in the history of Western society. Advances were made in the evolution of strong government and urban life, economic development, architectural design, and education. Through the instruments of justice and finance, the kings of England and France attacked feudal rights and provincial practices, built centralized bureaucracies, and gradually came in contract with all their subjects. In so doing these rulers laid the foundations for modern national states. The German emperors, preoccupied with Italian affairs and with a quest for the imperial crown, allowed feudal and local interests to triumph. Medieval cities—whether beginning around the sites of cathedrals, fortifications, or market towns—recruited people from the countryside and brought into being a new social class, the middle class. Cities provided economic opportunity, which, together with the revival of long-distance trade and a new capitalistic spirit, led to greater wealth, a higher standard of living, and upward social mobility. The soaring Gothic cathedrals that medieval towns erected demonstrate civic pride, deep religious faith, and economic vitality. Universities, institutions of higher learning unique to the West, emerged from cathedral and municipal schools and provided trained officials for the new government bureaucracies. While the Church exercised leadership of Christian society in the High Middle Ages, the clash between the papacy and the kings of France and England at the end of the thirteenth century seriously challenged papal power.

NOTES

1. D. C. Douglas and G. E. Greenaway, eds., *English Historical Documents*, vol. 2 (London: Eyre & Spottiswoode, 1961), p. 853.
2. See G. M. Spiegel, "The Cult of Saint Denis and Capetian Kingship," *Journal of Medieval History* 1 (April 1975): 43–65, esp. 59–64.
3. J. Boswell, *Christianity, Social Tolerance, and Homosexuality: Gay People in Western Europe from the Beginning of the Christian Era to the Fourteenth Century* (Chicago: University of Chicago Press, 1980), pp. 270–293; the quotation is from p. 293. For alternative interpretations, see K. Thomas, "Rescuing Homosexual History," *New York Review of Books*, 4 December 1980, 26ff.; and J. DuQ. Adams, *Speculum* 56 (April 1981): 350ff. For the French monarchy's persecution of the Jews, see J. W. Baldwin, *The Government of Philip Augustus: Foundations of French Royal Power in the Middle Ages* (Berkeley: University of California Press, 1986), pp. 51–52, and W. C. Jordan, *The French Monarchy and the Jews* (Philadelphia: University of Pennsylvania Press, 1989).
4. J. C. Russell, *Medieval Regions and Their Cities* (Bloomington: University of Indiana Press, 1972), p. 91.
5. Ibid., pp. 113–117.
6. Quoted in R. S. Lopez, "Of Towns and Trade," in *Life and Thought in the Early Middle Ages,* ed. R. S. Hoyt (Minneapolis: University of Minnesota Press, 1967), p. 33.
7. H. Pirenne, *Economic and Social History of Medieval Europe* (New York: Harcourt Brace, 1956), p. 53.
8. See D. Herlihy, *Medieval and Renaissance Pistoia: The Social History of an Italian Town, 1200–1430* (New Haven: Yale University Press, 1967), p. 257.
9. Quoted in J. O'Faolain and L. Martines, eds., *Not in God's Image: Women in History from the Greeks to the Victorians* (New York: Harper & Row, 1973), pp. 155–156.
10. Douglas and Greenaway, pp. 969–970.
11. H. Rothwell, ed., *English Historical Documents,* vol. 3 (London: Eyre & Spottiswoode, 1975), p. 854.
12. M. M. Postan, *The Medieval Economy and Society: An Economic History of Britain in the Middle Ages* (Baltimore: Penguin Books, 1975), pp. 213–214.
13. See P. Dollinger, *The German Hansa,* trans. and ed. D. S. Ault and S. H. Steinberg (Stanford, Calif.: Stanford University Press, 1970).
14. C. M. Cipolla, *Before the Industrial Revolution: European Society and Economy, 1000–1700,* 2d ed. (New York: W. W. Norton, 1980), p. 197.
15. R. S. Lopez, "The Trade of Medieval Europe: The South," in *The Cambridge Economic History of Europe,*

vol. 2, ed. M. M. Postan and E. E. Rich (Cambridge: Cambridge University Press, 1952), p. 289.

16. Quoted in H. E. Sigerist, *Civilization and Disease* (Chicago: University of Chicago Press, 1943), p. 102.
17. Quoted in J. H. Mundy, *Europe in the High Middle Ages, 1150–1309* (New York: Basic Books, 1973), pp. 474–475.
18. E. Panofsky, trans. and ed., *Abbot Suger on the Abbey Church of St. Denis and Its Art Treasures* (Princeton, N.J.: Princeton University Press, 1946), p. 101.
19. See J. Gimpel, *The Cathedral Builders* (New York: Grove Press, 1961), pp. 42–49.
20. J. B. Freed, *The Friars and German Society in the Thirteenth Century* (Cambridge, Mass.: Mediaeval Academy of America, 1977), p. 8.
21. Ibid., p. 9.
22. See F. Oakley, *The Western Church in the Later Middle Ages* (Ithaca, N.Y.: Cornell University Press, 1979), p. 175.
23. See Freed, pp. 119–128.
24. Ibid., esp. p. 125.

SUGGESTED READING

The achievements of the High Middle Ages have attracted considerable scholarly attention, and the curious student will have no difficulty finding exciting material on the points raised in this chapter. Three general surveys of the period 1050 to 1300 are especially recommended: J. R. Strayer, *Western Europe in the Middle Ages* (1955), a masterful synthesis; J. W. Baldwin, *The Scholastic Culture of the Middle Ages* (1971), which stresses the intellectual features of medieval civilization; and F. Heer, *The Medieval World* (1963).

R. A. Brown, *The Normans* (1983), revitalizes, on the basis of recent research, the old thesis that the conquerors of England and Sicily were an exceptionally creative force in the eleventh and twelfth centuries. D. Howarth, *1066: The Year of the Conquest* (1981), is a lively and cleverly written account, from Norman, Scandinavian, and English perspectives, of the Norman conquest of England. G. O. Sayles, *The Medieval Foundations of England* (1961), traces political and social conditions to the end of the twelfth century, while H. G. Richardson and G. O. Sayles, *The Governance of Mediaeval England from the Conquest to Magna Carta* (1963), focuses on administrative developments.

Students interested in crime, society, and legal developments will find the following works useful and sound: J. B. Given, *Society and Homicide in Thirteenth-century England* (1977); J. M. Carter, *Rape in Medieval Eng-*

land: An Historical and Sociological Study (1985); R. C. Palmer, *The County Courts of Medieval England, 1150–1350* (1982); and the same scholar's *The Whilton Dispute, 1264–1380: A Social-Legal Study of Dispute Settlement in Medieval England* (1984). Elizabeth M. Hallam, *Domesday Book Through Nine Centuries* (1986), is an excellent recent appreciation of that important document, while J. R. Strayer, *On the Medieval Origins of the Modern State* (1970), is a fine synthesis of political, legal, and administrative developments.

For the Becket controversy, see F. Barlow, *Thomas Becket* (1986), the best recent study; D. Knowles, *Thomas Becket* (1970); and B. Smalley, *The Becket Controversy and the Schools: A Study of Intellectuals in Politics in the Twelfth Century* (1973). J. C. Holt, *Magna Carta* (1969), remains the best modern treatment of the document.

For France, both E. Hallam, *The Capetian Kings of France, 987–1328* (1980), and R. Fawtier, *The Capetian Kings of France* (1962), are readable introductions. Advanced students of medieval French administrative history should see J. Baldwin, *The Government of Philip Augustus: Foundations of French Royal Power in the Middle Ages* (1986); W. C. Jordan, *Louis IX and the Crusade* (1979); and J. R. Strayer, *The Reign of Philip the Fair* (1980). On Germany, G. Barraclough, *The Origins of Modern Germany* (1963), provides an excellent explanation of the problems and peculiarities of the Holy Roman Empire; this is a fine example of the Marxist interpretation of medieval history. M. Pacaut, *Frederick Barbarossa* (trans. A. J. Pomerans, 1980), is perhaps the best one-volume treatment of that important ruler, but P. Munz, *Frederick Barbarossa* (1979), is also important and useful. T. C. Van Cleeve, *The Emperor Frederick II of Hohenstaufen* (1972), gives a thorough modern treatment.

For the economic revival of Europe, see, in addition to the titles by Dollinger, Herlihy, Postan, and Russell given in the Notes, G. J. Hodgett, *A Social and Economic History of Medieval Europe* (1974), a broad survey; C. M. Cipolla, *Before the Industrial Revolution: European Society and Economy, 1000–1700* (1980), which draws on a wealth of recent research to treat demographic shifts, technological change, and business practices; and R. Lopez, *The Commercial Revolution of the Middle Ages* (1976). The effect of climate on population and economic growth is discussed in the remarkable work of E. L. Ladurie, *Times of Feast, Times of Famine: A History of Climate Since the Year 1000* (trans. B. Bray, 1971). A masterful account of agricultural changes and their sociological implications is to be found in G. Duby, *The Early Growth of the European Economy: Warriors and Peasants from the Seventh to the Twelfth Century* (1978).

Students interested in the origins of medieval towns and cities will learn how historians use the evidence of coins, archaeology, tax records, geography, and laws in J. F. Benton, ed., *Town Origins: The Evidence of Medieval*

The High Middle Ages

	Government and Law	Philosophy and Science
1000	Seljuk Turks conquer Muslim Baghdad, 1055 Norman Conquest of England, 1066 Penance of Henry IV at Canossa, 1077	Avicenna, d. 1037 Peter Abelard, 1079–1142
1100	Henry I of England, r. 1100–1135 Louis VI of France, r. 1108–1137 Frederick I of Germany, r. 1152–1190 Henry II of England, r. 1154–1189 Thomas Becket murdered, December 1170 Philip Augustus of France, r. 1180–1223	Origins of universities in the West, ca 1100–1300 Aristotle's works translated into Latin, ca 1140–1260 Windmill invented, ca 1180 Averroës, d. 1198
1200	Spanish victory over Muslims at Las Navas de Tolosa, 1212 Battle of Bouvines, July 1214 Frederick II of Germany and Sicily, r. 1212–1250 Magna Carta, 1215 Louis IX of France, r. 1226–1270 Mongols destroy Baghdad and end the Abbasid caliphate, 1258 Edward I of England, r. 1272–1307 Philip IV (the Fair) of France, r. 1285–1314 War opens between England and France, 1296	Maimonides, d. 1204 Roger Bacon, ca 1214–1294 Thomas Aquinas, 1225–1274 Height of Scholasticism, ca 1250–1277 William of Ockham, ca 1285–1349 Mechanical clock invented, ca 1290
1300	Philip IV orders arrest of Pope Boniface at Anagni, 1303 Hundred Years' War, 1337–1450	Master Eckhart active, ca 1300–1327

Economics	Religion	Arts and Letters
Agrarian economy predominates in the West, ca 700–1050	Byzantine conversion of Russia, ca 988	Romanesque style in architecture and art, ca 1000–1200
Height of Byzantine commerce and industry, ca 800–1000	Beginning of Reform Papacy, 1046	*Song of Roland,* ca 1095
Height of Islamic commerce and industry, ca 900–1300	Schism between Roman and Eastern Orthodox churches, 1054	
Destruction of Byzantine free peasantry, ca 1025–1100	Pope Gregory VII, 1073–1085	
Growth of towns and trade in the West, ca 1050–1300	St. Bernard of Clairvaux, 1090–1153	
Domesday Book, 1086	First Crusade, 1095–1099	
Henry I of England establishes Exchequer, 1130	Height of Cistercian monasticism, ca 1115–1153	*Rubaiyat* of Umar Khayyam, ca 1120
Origin of the Hanseatic League, 1159	Concordat of Worms ends investiture struggle, 1122	Dedication of abbey church at Saint-Denis, June 1144, launches Gothic style
	Hildegard of Bingen (1098–1179) starts to produce theological treatises, ca 1150	
	Crusaders lose Jerusalem, 1187	
	Pope Innocent II, 1198–1216	
	Crusaders take Constantinople (Fourth Crusade), 1204	
	Albigensian Crusade, 1208–1213	
	Founding of Franciscan Order, 1210	
	Fourth Lateran Council, 1215	
	Founding of Dominican Order, 1216	
	Fall of last Christian outposts in Holy Land, 1291	
	Pope Boniface VIII, 1294–1303	
European economic depression, ca 1300–1450	Babylonian Captivity of papacy, 1305–1378	Paintings of Giotto, ca 1305–1337
Black Death begins ca 1347, returns intermittently until eighteenth century		Dante's *Divine Comedy*, ca 1310

England (1968). H. Pirenne, *Early Democracy in the Low Countries* (1932), is an important and standard work. H. Saalman, *Medieval Cities* (1968), gives a fresh description of the layouts of medieval cities, with an emphasis on Germany, and shows how they were places of production and exchange. C. Platt's well-illustrated *The English Medieval Town* (1979) makes excellent use of archaeological data and contains detailed information on the wool and cloth trades. R. Muir, *The English Village* (1980), offers a survey of many aspects of ordinary people's daily lives. For readability, few works surpass J. and F. Gies, *Life in a Medieval City* (1973).

For the new currents of thought in the High Middle Ages, see C. Brooke, *The Twelfth Century Renaissance* (1970), a splendidly illustrated book with copious quotations from the sources; E. Gilson, *Héloise and Abélard* (1960), which treats the medieval origins of modern humanism against the background of Abelard the teacher; D. W. Robertson, Jr., *Abélard and Héloise* (1972), which is highly readable, commonsensical, and probably the best recent study of Abelard and the love affair he supposedly had; C. H. Haskins, *The Renaissance of the Twelfth Century* (1971), a classic; and C. W. Hollister, ed., *The Twelfth Century Renaissance* (1969), a well-constructed anthology with source materials on many aspects of twelfth-century culture. N. Orme, *English Schools in the Middle Ages* (1973), focuses on the significance of schools and literacy in English medieval society, while J. Leclercq, *The Love of Learning and the Desire of God* (1974), discusses monastic literary culture. For the development of literacy among lay people and the formation of a literate mentality, the advanced student should see M. T. Clanchy, *From Memory to Written Record: England, 1066–1307* (1979). Written by outstanding scholars in a variety of fields, R. L. Benson and G. Constable with C. D. Lanham, eds., *Renaissance and Renewal in the Twelfth Century* (1982), contains an invaluable collection of articles.

On the medieval universities, C. H. Haskins, *The Rise of the Universities* (1959), is a good introduction, while H. Rashdall, *The Universities of Europe in the Middle Ages* (1936), is the standard scholarly work. G. Leff, *Paris and Oxford Universities in the Thirteenth and Fourteenth Centuries*

(1968), gives a fascinating sketch and includes a useful bibliography.

N. Pevsner, *An Outline of European Architecture* (1963), provides a good general introduction to Romanesque and Gothic architecture. The following studies are all valuable for the evolution and development of the Gothic style: J. Harvey, *The Gothic World* (1969); the same author's *The Master Builders* (1971); P. Frankl, *The Gothic* (1960); O. von Simson, *The Gothic Cathedral* (1973); and J. Bony, *French Gothic Architecture of the 12th and 13th Centuries* (1983). H. Kraus, *Gold Was the Mortar: The Economics of Cathedral Building* (1979), describes how the cathedrals were financed. D. Grivot and G. Zarnecki, *Gislebertus, Sculptor of Autun* (1961), is the finest appreciation of Romanesque architecture written in English. For the actual work of building, see D. Macaulay, *Cathedral: The Story of Its Construction* (1973), a prize-winning, simply written, and cleverly illustrated re-creation of the problems and duration of cathedral building. J. Gimpel, *The Cathedral Builders* (1961), explores the engineering problems involved in cathedral building and places the subject within its social context. Advanced students will enjoy E. Male, *The Gothic Image: Religious Art in France in the Thirteenth Century* (1958), which contains a wealth of fascinating and useful detail. For the most important cathedrals in France, architecturally and politically, see A. Temko, *Notre Dame of Paris: The Biography of a Cathedral* (1968); G. Henderson, *Chartres* (1968); and A. Katzenellogoben, *The Sculptural Programs of Chartres Cathedral* (1959), by a distinguished art historian. E. Panofsky, *Abbot Suger on the Abbey Church of St.-Denis and Its Art Treasures* (1946), provides a contemporary background account of the first Gothic building, while C. A. Bruzelius, *The Thirteenth-Century Church at St. Denis* (1985), traces later reconstruction. E. G. Holt, ed., *A Documentary History of Art* (1957), contains source materials useful for writing papers. J. Gimpel, *The Medieval Machine: The Industrial Revolution of the Middle Ages* (1977), an extremely useful book, discusses the mechanical and scientific problems involved in early industrialization and shows how construction affected the medieval environment.

12

The Crisis of the Later Middle Ages

During the later Middle Ages, the last book of the New Testament, the Book of Revelation, inspired thousands of sermons and hundreds of religious tracts. The Book of Revelation deals with visions of the end of the world, with disease, war, famine, and death. It is no wonder this part of the Bible was so popular. Between 1300 and 1450, Europeans experienced a frightful series of shocks: economic dislocation, plague, war, social upheaval, and increased crime and violence. Death and preoccupation with death make the fourteenth century one of the most wrenching periods of Western civilization.

The miseries and disasters of the later Middle Ages bring to mind a number of questions.

- What economic difficulties did Europe experience?

- What were the social and psychological effects of repeated attacks of plague and disease?

- Some scholars maintain that war is often the catalyst for political, economic, and social change. Does this theory have validity for the fourteenth century?

- What political and social developments do new national literatures express?

- What provoked the division of the church in the fourteenth century?

- What other ecclesiastical difficulties was the schism a sign of, and what impact did it have on the faith of the common people?

- How can we characterize the dominant features in the lives of ordinary people?

This chapter will focus on these questions.

PRELUDE TO DISASTER

Economic difficulties originating in the later thirteenth century were fully manifest by the start of the fourteenth. In the first decade, the countries of northern Europe experienced a considerable price inflation. The costs of grain, livestock, and dairy products rose sharply. Bad weather made a serious situation worse. An unusual number of storms brought torrential rains, ruining the wheat, oat, and hay crops on which people and animals depended almost everywhere. Since long-distance transportation of food was expensive and difficult, most urban areas depended for bread and meat on areas no more than a day's journey away. Poor harvests—and one in four was likely to be poor—led to scarcity and starvation. Almost all of northern Europe suffered a terrible famine in the years 1315 to 1317.

Hardly had western Europe begun to recover from this disaster when another struck. An epidemic of typhoid fever carried away thousands. In 1316 10 percent of the population of the city of Ypres may have died between May and October alone. Then in 1318 disease hit cattle and sheep, drastically reducing the herds and flocks. Another bad harvest in 1321 brought famine, starvation, and death.

The province of Languedoc in France presents a classic example of agrarian crisis. For over 150 years Languedoc had enjoyed continual land reclamation, steady agricultural expansion, and enormous population growth. Then the fourteenth century opened with four years of bad harvests. Torrential rains in 1310 ruined the harvest and brought on terrible famine. Harvests failed again in 1322 and 1329. In 1332 desperate peasants survived the winter on raw herbs. In the half-century from 1302 to 1348, poor harvests occurred twenty times. The undernourished population was ripe for the Grim Reaper, who appeared in 1348 in the form of the Black Death.

These catastrophes had grave social consequences. Population had steadily increased in the twelfth and thirteenth centuries, and large amounts of land had been put under cultivation. The amount of food yielded, however, did not match the level of population growth. Bad weather had disastrous results. Poor harvests meant that marriages had to be postponed. Later marriages and the deaths caused by famine and disease meant a reduction in population. Meanwhile, the international character of trade and commerce meant that a disaster in one country had serious implications elsewhere. For example, the infection that attacked English sheep in 1318 caused a sharp decline in wool exports in the following years. Without wool, Flemish weavers could not work, and thousands were laid off. Without woolen cloth, the businesses of Flemish, French, and English merchants suf-

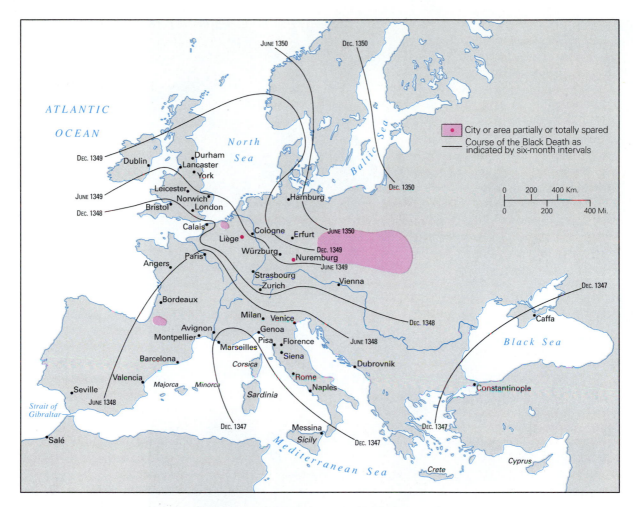

MAP 12.1 The Course of the Black Death in Fourteenth-Century Europe Note the routes that the bubonic plague took across Europe. How do you account for the fact that several regions were spared the "dreadful death"?

fered. Unemployment encouraged many men to turn to crime.

To none of these problems did governments have any solutions. In fact, they even lacked policies. After the death of Edward I in 1307, England was governed by the incompetent and weak Edward II (r. 1307–1327), whose reign was dominated by a series of baronial conflicts. In France the three sons of Philip the Fair, who followed their father to the French throne between 1314 and 1328, took no interest in the increasing economic difficulties. In Germany power drifted into the hands of local rulers. The only actions the governments took tended to be in response to the demands of the upper classes. Economic and social problems were aggravated by the appearance in western Europe of a frightful disease.

THE BLACK DEATH

In 1291 Genoese sailors had opened the Strait of Gibraltar to Italian shipping by defeating the Moroccans. Then, shortly after 1300, important advances were made in the design of Italian merchant ships. A square rig was added to the mainmast, and ships began to carry three masts instead of just one.

The Plague-Stricken   Even as the dead were wrapped in shrouds and collected in carts for mass burial, the disease struck others. The man collapsing has the symptomatic buba on his neck. As Saint Sebastian pleads for mercy (above), a winged devil, bearer of the plague, attacks an angel. *(Source: Walters Art Gallery, Baltimore)*

Additional sails better utilized windpower to propel the ship. The improved design permitted year-round shipping for the first time, and Venetian and Genoese merchant ships could sail the dangerous Atlantic coast even in the winter months. With ships continually at sea, their rats too were constantly on the move, and thus any rat-transmitted disease could spread rapidly.

Scholars dispute the origins of the bubonic plague, often known as the Black Death. Some students hold that it broke out in China or central Asia around 1331, and during the next fifteen years merchants and soldiers carried it over the caravan routes until in 1346 it reached the Crimea in southern Russia. Other scholars believe the plague was endemic in southern Russia. In either case, from the Crimea the plague had easy access to Mediterranean lands and western Europe.

In October 1347, Genoese ships brought the plague to Messina, from where it spread across Sicily. Venice and Genoa were hit in January 1348, and from the port of Pisa the disease spread south to Rome and east to Florence and all Tuscany. By late spring, southern Germany was attacked. Frightened French authorities chased a galley bearing the disease from the port of Marseilles, but not before plague had infected the city, from where it spread to Languedoc and Spain. In June 1348 two ships entered the Bristol Channel and introduced it into England. All Europe felt the scourge of this horrible disease (Map 12.1).

Pathology

Modern understanding of the bubonic plague rests on the research of two bacteriologists, one French and one Japanese, who in 1894 independently identified the bacillus that causes the plague, *Pasteurella pestis* (so labeled after the French scientist's teacher, Louis Pasteur). The bacillus liked to live in the blood stream of an animal or, ideally, in the stomach of a flea. The flea in turn resided in the hair of a rodent, sometimes a squirrel but preferably the hardy, nimble, and vagabond black rat. Why the host black rat moved so much, scientists still do not know, but it often traveled by ship. There the black rat could feast for months on a cargo of grain or live snugly among bales of cloth. Fleas bearing the bacillus also had no trouble nesting in saddlebags.[1] Comfortable, well fed, and

often having greatly multiplied, the black rats ended their ocean voyage and descended on the great cities of Europe.

The plague took two forms—bubonic and pneumonic. In the bubonic form, the rat was the vector, or transmitter, of the disease. In the pneumonic form, the plague was communicated directly from one person to another.

Although by the fourteenth century urban authorities from London to Paris to Rome had begun to try to achieve a primitive level of sanitation, urban conditions remained ideal for the spread of disease. Narrow streets filled with mud, refuse, and human excrement were as much cesspools as thoroughfares. Dead animals and sore-covered beggars greeted the traveler. Houses whose upper stories projected over the lower ones eliminated light and air. And extreme overcrowding was commonplace. When all members of an aristocratic family lived and slept in one room, it should not be surprising that six or eight persons in a middle-class or poor household slept in one bed—if they had one. Closeness, after all, provided warmth. Houses were beginning to be constructed of brick, but many remained of wood, clay, and mud. A determined rat had little trouble entering such a house.

Standards of personal hygiene remained frightfully low. True, most large cities had public bathhouses, but we have no way of knowing how frequently ordinary people used them. People probably bathed rarely. Skin infections, consequently, were common. Lack of personal cleanliness, combined with any number of temporary ailments such as diarrhea and the common cold, weakened the body's resistance to serious disease. Fleas and body lice were universal afflictions: everyone from peasants to archbishops had them. One more bite did not cause much alarm. But if that nibble came from a bacillus-bearing flea, an entire household or area was doomed.

The symptoms of the bubonic plague started with a growth the size of a nut or an apple in the armpit, in the groin, or on the neck. This was the boil, or *buba,* that gave the disease its name and caused agonizing pain. If the buba was lanced and the pus thoroughly drained, the victim had a chance of recovery. The secondary stage was the appearance of black spots or blotches caused by bleeding under the skin. (This syndrome did not give the disease its common name; contemporaries did not call the plague the Black Death. Sometime in the fifteenth century, the Latin phrase *atra mors,* meaning "dreadful death," was translated "black death," and the phrase stuck.) Finally, the victim began to cough violently and spit blood. This stage, indicating the presence of thousands of bacilli in the blood stream, signaled the end, and death followed in two or three days. Rather than evoking compassion for the victim, a French scientist has written, everything about the bubonic plague provoked horror and disgust: "All the matter which exuded from their bodies let off an unbearable stench; sweat, excrement, spittle, breath, so fetid as to be overpowering; urine turbid, thick, black or red."[2]

Medieval people had no rational explanation for the disease nor any effective medical treatment for it. Fourteenth-century medical literature indicates that physicians could sometimes ease the pain, but they had no cure. Most people—lay, scholarly, and medical—believed that the Black Death was caused by some "vicious property in the air" that carried the disease from place to place. When ignorance was joined to fear and ancient bigotry, savage cruelty sometimes resulted. Many people believed that the Jews had poisoned the wells of Christian communities and thereby infected the drinking water. This charge led to the murder of thousands of Jews across Europe. According to one chronicler, sixteen thousand were killed at the imperial city of Strasbourg alone in 1349. Though sixteen thousand is probably a typically medieval numerical exaggeration, the horror of the massacre is not lessened.

The Italian writer Giovanni Boccaccio (1313–1375), describing the course of the disease in Florence in the preface to his book of tales, *The Decameron,* pinpointed the cause of the spread:

Moreover, the virulence of the pest was the greater by reason that intercourse was apt to convey it from the sick to the whole, just as fire devours things dry or greasy when they are brought close to it. Nay, the evil went yet further, for not merely by speech or association with the sick was the malady communicated to the healthy with consequent peril of common death, but any that touched the clothes of the sick or aught else that had been touched or used by them, seemed thereby to contract the disease.[3]

The highly infectious nature of the plague, especially in areas of high population density, was recognized by a few sophisticated Arabs. When the disease struck the town of Salé in Morocco, Ibu Abu Madyan shut in his household with sufficient food and water and allowed no one to enter or leave until the plague had passed. Madyan was entirely successful. The rat that carried the disease-bearing flea avoided travel outside the cities. Thus the countryside was relatively safe. City dwellers who could afford to move fled to the country districts.

The mortality rate cannot be specified, because population figures for the period before the arrival of the plague do not exist for most countries and cities. The largest amount of material survives for England, but it is difficult to use; after enormous scholarly controversy, only educated guesses can be made. Of a total English population of perhaps 4.2 million, probably 1.4 million died of the Black Death in its several visits.[4] Densely populated Italian cities endured incredible losses. Florence lost between half and two-thirds of its 1347 population of 85,000 when the plague visited in 1348. The disease recurred intermittently in the 1360s and 1370s and reappeared many times down to 1700. There have been twentieth-century outbreaks in such places as Hong Kong, Bombay, and Uganda.

Social and Psychological Consequences

Predictably, the poor died more rapidly than the rich, because the rich enjoyed better health to begin with; but the powerful were not unaffected. In England two archbishops of Canterbury fell victim to the plague in 1349, King Edward III's daughter Joan died, and many leading members of the London guilds followed her to the grave.

It is noteworthy that, in an age of mounting criticism of clerical wealth, the behavior of the clergy during the plague was often exemplary. Priests, monks, and nuns cared for the sick and buried the dead. In places like Venice, from where even physicians fled, priests remained to give what ministrations they could. Consequently, their mortality rate was phenomenally high. The German clergy, especially, suffered a severe decline in personnel in the years after 1350. With the ablest killed off, the wealth of the German church fell into the hands of the incompetent and weak. The situation was ripe for reform.

Economic historians and demographers sharply dispute the impact of the plague on the economy in the late fourteenth century. The traditional view that the plague had a disastrous effect has been greatly modified. The clearest evidence comes from

England, where the agrarian economy showed remarkable resilience. While the severity of the disease varied from region to region, it appears that by about 1375 most landlords enjoyed revenues near those of the pre-plague years. By the early fifteenth century seigneurial prosperity reached a medieval peak. Why? The answer appears to lie in the fact that England and many parts of Europe suffered from overpopulation in the early fourteenth century. Population losses caused by the Black Death "led to increased productivity by restoring a more efficient balance between labour, land, and capital."[5] Population decline meant a sharp increase in per capita wealth. Increased demand for labor meant greater mobility among peasant and working classes. Wages rose, providing better distribution of income. The shortage of labor and steady requests for higher wages put landlords on the defensive. They retaliated with such measures as the English Statute of Laborers (1351), which attempted to freeze salaries and wages at pre-1347 levels. The statute could not be enforced and therefore was largely unsuccessful. Some places, such as Florence, experienced economic prosperity as a long-term consequence of the plague.

Even more significant than the social effects were the psychological consequences. The knowledge that the disease meant almost certain death provoked the most profound pessimism. Imagine an entire society in the grip of the belief that it was at the mercy of a frightful affliction about which nothing could be done, a disgusting disease from which family and friends would flee, leaving one to die alone and in agony. It is not surprising that some sought release in orgies and gross sensuality while others turned to the severest forms of asceticism and frenzied religious fervor. Some extremists joined groups of *flagellants*, who collectively whipped and scourged themselves as penance for their and society's sins, in the belief that the Black Death was God's punishment for humanity's wickedness.

Procession of Flagellants Appearing in the Rhine valley and in the Low Countries at the time of the Black Death, groups of flagellants rejected ecclesiastical authority and urged people to re-live the sufferings of Christ's passion by forms of public penance. Flagellants represented a new emotional piety. In this scene they thrash one another. *(Source: Bibliothèque Royale Albert 1er, Brussels)*

The literature and art of the fourteenth century reveal a terribly morbid concern with death. One highly popular artistic motif, the Dance of Death, depicted a dancing skeleton leading away a living person. No wonder survivors experienced a sort of shell shock and a terrible crisis of faith. Lack of confidence in the leaders of society, lack of hope for the future, defeatism, and malaise wreaked enormous anguish and contributed to the decline of the Middle Ages. A long international war added further misery to the frightful disasters of the plague.

THE HUNDRED YEARS' WAR (ca 1337–1453)

In January 1327 Queen Isabella of England, her lover Mortimer, and a group of barons, having deposed and murdered Isabella's incompetent husband, King Edward II, proclaimed his fifteen-year-old son king as Edward III. Isabella and Mortimer, however, held real power until 1330, when Edward seized the reins of government. In 1328 Charles IV of France, the last surviving son of the French king Philip the Fair, died childless. With him ended the Capetian dynasty. An assembly of French barons, meaning to exclude Isabella—who was Charles's sister and the daughter of Philip the Fair—and her son Edward III from the French throne, proclaimed that "no woman nor her son could succeed to the [French] monarchy." The French barons rested their position on the Salic Law, a Germanic law code that forbade females or those descended in the female line to succeed to offices. The barons passed the crown to Philip VI of Valois (r. 1328–1350), a nephew of Philip the Fair. In these actions lie the origins of another phase of the centuries-old struggle between the English and French monarchies, one that was fought intermittently from 1337 to 1453.

Causes

The Hundred Years' War had both distant and immediate causes. In 1259 France and England signed the Treaty of Paris, in which the English king agreed to become—for himself and his successors—vassal of the French crown for the duchy of Aquitaine. The English claimed Aquitaine as an ancient inheritance. French policy, however, was

strongly expansionist, and the French kings resolved to absorb the duchy into the kingdom of France. In 1329 Edward III paid homage to Philip VI for Aquitaine. In 1337 Philip, determined to exercise full jurisdiction there, confiscated the duchy. This action was the immediate cause of the war. Edward III maintained that the only way he could exercise his rightful sovereignty over Aquitaine was by assuming the title of king of France.[6] As the eldest surviving male descendant of Philip the Fair, he believed he could rightfully make this claim. Moreover, the dynastic argument had feudal implications: in order to increase their independent power, French vassals of Philip VI used the excuse that they had to transfer their loyalty to a more legitimate overlord, Edward III. One reason the war lasted so long was that it became a French civil war, with French barons supporting English monarchs in order to thwart the centralizing goals of the French crown.

Economic factors involving the wool trade and the control of Flemish towns had served as justifications for war between France and England for centuries. The causes of the conflicts known as the Hundred Years' War were thus dynastic, feudal, political, and economic. Recent historians have stressed economic factors. The wool trade between England and Flanders served as the cornerstone of both countries' economies; they were closely interdependent. Flanders was a fief of the French crown, and the Flemish aristocracy was highly sympathetic to the monarchy in Paris. But the wealth of Flemish merchants and cloth manufacturers depended on English wool, and Flemish burghers strongly supported the claims of Edward III. The disruption of commerce with England threatened their prosperity.

It is impossible to measure the precise influence of the Flemings on the cause and course of the war. Certainly Edward could not ignore their influence, because it represented money he needed to carry on the war. Although the war's impact on commerce fluctuated, over the long run it badly hurt the wool trade and the cloth industry.

One historian has written in jest that, if Edward III had been locked away in a castle with a pile of toy knights and archers to play with, he would have done far less damage.[7] The same might be said of Philip VI. Both rulers glorified war and saw it as the perfect arena for the realization of their chivalric ideals. Neither king possessed any sort of policy for dealing with his kingdom's social, economic, or political ills.

The Popular Response

The governments of both England and France manipulated public opinion to support the war. Whatever significance modern students ascribe to the economic factor, public opinion in fourteenth-century England held that the war was waged for one reason: to secure for King Edward the French crown he had been denied.[8] Edward III issued letters to the sheriffs describing in graphic terms the evil deeds of the French and listing royal needs. Kings in both countries instructed the clergy to deliver sermons filled with patriotic sentiment. Frequent assemblies of Parliament—which in the fourteenth century were meetings of representatives of the nobility, clergy, counties, and towns, as well as royal officials summoned by the king to provide information or revenue or to do justice—spread royal propaganda for the war. The royal courts sensationalized the wickedness of the other side and stressed the great fortunes to be made from the war. Philip VI sent agents to warn communities about the dangers of invasion and to stress the French crown's revenue needs to meet the attack.

The royal campaign to rally public opinion was highly successful, at least in the early stage of the war. Edward III gained widespread support in the 1340s and 1350s. The English developed a deep hatred of the French and feared that King Philip intended "to have seized and slaughtered the entire realm of England." As England was successful in the field, pride in the country's military proficiency increased.

Most important of all, the Hundred Years' War was popular because it presented unusual opportunities for wealth and advancement. Poor knights and knights that were unemployed were promised regular wages. Criminals who enlisted were granted pardons. The great nobles expected to be rewarded with estates. Royal exhortations to the troops before battles repeatedly stressed that, if victorious, the men might keep whatever they seized. The French chronicler Jean Froissart wrote that, at the time of Edward III's expedition of 1359, men of all ranks flocked to the English king's banner. Some came to acquire honor, but many came in order "to loot and pillage the fair and plenteous land of France."[9]

The Indian Summer of Medieval Chivalry

The period of the Hundred Years' War witnessed the final flowering of the aristocratic code of medieval chivalry. Indeed, the enthusiastic participation of the nobility in both France and England was in response primarily to the opportunity the war provided to display chivalric behavior. What better place to display chivalric qualities than on the field of battle?

War was considered an ennobling experience; there was something elevating, manly, fine, and beautiful about it. When Shakespeare in the sixteenth century wrote of "the pomp and circumstance of glorious war," he was echoing the fourteenth- and fifteenth-century chroniclers who had glorified the trappings of war. Describing the French army before the Battle of Poitiers (1356), a contemporary said:

Then you might see banners and pennons unfurled to the wind, whereon fine gold and azure shone, purple, gules and ermine. Trumpets, horns and clarions—you might hear sounding through the camp; the Dauphin's [title borne by the eldest son of the king of France] great battle made the earth ring.[10]

At Poitiers it was marvelous and terrifying to hear the thundering of the horses' hooves, the cries of the wounded, the sound of the trumpets and clarions, and the shouting of war cries. The tumult was heard at a distance of more than 9 miles. And it was a great grief to behold the flower of all the nobility and chivalry of the world go thus to destruction, death, and martyrdom.

This romantic and "marvelous" view of war holds little appeal for modern men and women, who are more conscious of the slaughter, brutality, dirt, and blood that war inevitably involves. Also, modern thinkers are usually conscious of the broad mass of people, while the chivalric code applied only to the aristocratic military elite. Chivalry had no reference to those outside the knightly class.

The knight was supposed to show courtesy, graciousness, and generosity to his social equals, but certainly not to his social inferiors. When English knights fought French ones, they were social equals fighting according to a mutually accepted code of behavior. The infantry troops were looked on as inferior beings. When a peasant force at Longueil destroyed a contingent of English knights, their comrades mourned them because "it was too much that so many good fighters had been killed by mere peasants."[11]

The Course of the War to 1419

Armies in the field were commanded by rulers themselves; by princes of the blood such as Edward III's son Edward, the Black Prince—so called because of the color of his armor—or by great aristocrats. Knights formed the cavalry; the peasantry served as infantrymen, pikemen, and archers. Edward III set up recruiting boards in the counties to enlist the strongest peasants. Perhaps 10 percent of the adult population of England was involved in the actual fighting or in supplying and supporting the troops. The French contingents were even larger. By medieval standards, the force was astronomically large, especially considering the difficulty of transporting men, weapons, and horses across the English Channel. The costs of these armies stretched French and English resources to the breaking point.

The war was fought almost entirely in France and the Low Countries (Map 12.2). It consisted mainly of a series of random sieges and cavalry raids. In 1335 the French began supporting Scottish incursions into northern England, ravaging the countryside in Aquitaine, and sacking and burning English coastal towns, such as Southampton. Naturally such tactics lent weight to Edward III's propaganda campaign. In fact, royal propaganda on both sides fostered a kind of early nationalism.

During the war's early stages, England was highly successful. At Crécy in northern France in 1346, English longbowmen scored a great victory over French knights and crossbowmen. Although the fire of the longbow was not very accurate, it allowed for rapid reloading, and English archers could send off three arrows to the French crossbowmen's one. The result was a blinding shower of arrows that unhorsed the French knights and caused mass confusion. The firing of cannon—probably the first use of artillery in the West—created further panic. Thereupon the English horsemen charged and butchered the French.

This was not war according to the chivalric rules that Edward III would have preferred. The English victory at Crécy rested on the skill and swiftness of the yeomen archers, who had nothing at all to do with the chivalric ideals for which the war was being fought. Ten years later, Edward the Black Prince, using the same tactics as at Crécy, smashed the French at Poitiers, captured the French king, and held him for ransom. Again, at Agincourt near Arras in 1415, the chivalric English soldier-king Henry V (r. 1413–1422) gained the field over vastly superior numbers. Henry followed up his triumph at Agincourt with the reconquest of Normandy. By 1419 the English had advanced to the walls of Paris (see Map 12.2).

But the French cause was not lost. Though England had scored the initial victories, France won the war.

Joan of Arc and France's Victory

The ultimate French success rests heavily on the actions of an obscure French peasant girl, Joan of Arc, whose vision and work revived French fortunes and led to victory. A great deal of pious and popular legend surrounds Joan the Maid, because of her peculiar appearance on the scene, her astonishing success, her martyrdom, and her canonization by the Catholic church. The historical fact is that she saved the French monarchy, which was the embodiment of France.

Born in 1412 to well-to-do peasants in the village of Domremy in Champagne, Joan of Arc grew up in a religious household. During adolescence she began to hear voices, which she later said belonged to Saint Michael, Saint Catherine, and Saint Margaret. In 1428 these voices spoke to her with great urgency, telling her that the dauphin (the uncrowned King Charles VII) had to be crowned and the English expelled from France. Joan went to the French court, persuaded the king to reject the rumor that he was illegitimate, and secured his support for her relief of the besieged city of Orléans.

MAP 12.2 English Holdings in France During the Hundred Years' War The year 1429 marked the greatest extent of English holdings in France. Why was it unlikely that England could have held these territories permanently?

ENGLAND

Southampton

English Channel

Calais
FLANDERS

NORMANDY
Paris
CHAMPAGNE
Seine

BRITTANY

ANJOU
Loire

BLOIS

BURGUNDY

POITOU

AQUITAINE

Bordeaux
Garonne

GASCONY

TOULOUSE

Rhône

**HOLY
ROMAN
EMPIRE**

0   100 Km.

0   100 Mi.

SPAIN

*Mediterranean
Sea*

**1337
(before the Battle of Crécy)**

Held by the kings
of England

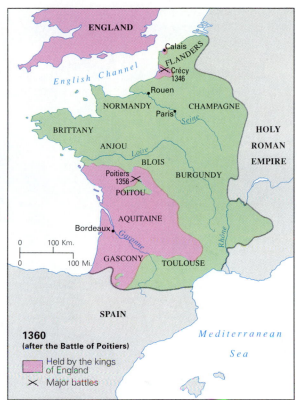

ENGLAND

English Channel

Calais
FLANDERS
Crécy
1346

Rouen

NORMANDY
Paris
CHAMPAGNE
Seine

BRITTANY

ANJOU
Loire

BLOIS

Poitiers
1356
POITOU

BURGUNDY

AQUITAINE

Bordeaux
Garonne

GASCONY
TOULOUSE

Rhône

**HOLY
ROMAN
EMPIRE**

0   100 Km.

0   100 Mi.

SPAIN

*Mediterranean
Sea*

**1360
(after the Battle of Poitiers)**

Held by the kings
of England

✕   Major battles

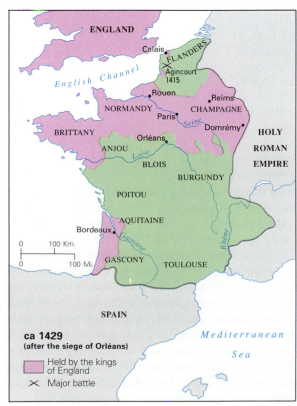

ENGLAND

Calais
FLANDERS
Agincourt
1415

English Channel

Rouen

NORMANDY
Reims
CHAMPAGNE
Paris
Seine
Domrémy

BRITTANY
Orléans
ANJOU
Loire

BLOIS

BURGUNDY

POITOU

AQUITAINE

Bordeaux
Garonne

GASCONY
TOULOUSE

Rhône

**HOLY
ROMAN
EMPIRE**

0   100 Km.

0   100 Mi.

SPAIN

*Mediterranean
Sea*

**ca 1429
(after the siege of Orléans)**

Held by the kings
of England

✕   Major battle

ENGLAND

Calais
FLANDERS

English Channel

NORMANDY
Paris
CHAMPAGNE
Seine

BRITTANY

ANJOU
Loire

BLOIS

BURGUNDY

POITOU

AQUITAINE

Bordeaux
Garonne

GASCONY
TOULOUSE

Rhône

**HOLY
ROMAN
EMPIRE**

0   100 Km.

0   100 Mi.

SPAIN

*Mediterranean
Sea*

**1453
(end of war)**

Held by the kings
of England

The Battle of Crécy, 1346   Pitched battles were unusual in the Hundred Years' War. At Crécy, however, the English (on the right with lions on their royal standard) scored a spectacular victory. The longbow proved a more effective weapon than the French crossbow, and the low-born English archers withstood a charge of the aristocratic French knights. (*Source: Bibliothèque Nationale, Paris*)

The astonishing thing is not that Joan the Maid overcame serious obstacles to see the dauphin, not even that Charles and his advisers listened to her. What is amazing is the swiftness with which they were convinced. French fortunes had been so low for so long that the court believed only a miracle could save the country. Because Joan cut her hair short and dressed like a man, she scandalized the court. But hoping she would provide the necessary miracle, Charles allowed her to accompany the army that was preparing to raise the English siege of Orléans.

In the meantime Joan, herself illiterate, dictated the following letter calling on the English to withdraw:

Jhesus Maria

King of England, and you Duke of Bedford, calling yourself regent of France, you William Pole, Count of Suffolk John Talbot, and you Thomas Lord Scales, calling yourselves Lieutenants of the said Duke of Bedford, do right in the King of Heaven's sight. Surrender to The Maid *sent hither by God the King of Heaven, the keys of all the good towns you have taken and laid waste in France. She comes in God's name to establish the Blood Royal, ready to make peace if you agree to abandon France and repay what you have taken. And you, archers, comrades in arms, gentles and others, who are before the town of Orléans, retire in God's name to your own country. If you do not, expect to hear tidings from* The Maid *who will shortly come upon you to your very great hurt.*[12]

Joan arrived before Orléans on April 28, 1429. Seventeen years old, she knew little of warfare and believed that if she could keep the French troops from swearing and frequenting whorehouses, victory would be theirs. On May 8 the English, weakened by disease and lack of supplies, withdrew from Orléans. Ten days later, Charles VII was crowned king at Reims. These two events marked the turning point in the war.

In 1430 England's allies, the Burgundians, captured Joan and sold her to the English. When the English handed her over to the ecclesiastical authorities for trial, the French court did not intervene. While the English wanted Joan eliminated for obvious political reasons, sorcery (witchcraft) was the ostensible charge at her trial. Witch persecution was increasing in the fifteenth century, and Joan's wearing of men's clothes appeared not only aberrant but indicative of contact with the devil. In 1431 the court condemned her as a heretic—her claim of direct inspiration from God, thereby denying the authority of church officials, constituted heresy—and burned her at the stake in the marketplace at Rouen. A new trial in 1456 rehabilitated her name. In 1920 she was canonized and declared a holy maiden, and today she is revered as the second patron saint of France. The nineteenth-century French historian Jules Michelet extolled Joan of Arc as a symbol of the vitality and strength of the French peasant classes.

The relief of Orléans stimulated French pride and rallied French resources. As the war dragged on, loss of life mounted, and money appeared to be flowing into a bottomless pit, demands for an end increased in England. The clergy and intellectuals pressed for peace. Parliamentary opposition to additional war grants stiffened. Slowly the French reconquered Normandy and, finally, ejected the English from Aquitaine. At the war's end in 1453, only the town of Calais remained in English hands.

Costs and Consequences

For both France and England, the war proved a disaster. In France the English had slaughtered thousands of soldiers and civilians. In the years after the sweep of the Black Death, this additional killing meant a grave loss of population. The English had laid waste to hundreds of thousands of acres of rich farmland, leaving the rural economy of many parts of France a shambles. The war had disrupted trade and the great fairs, resulting in the drastic reduction of French participation in international commerce. Defeat in battle and heavy taxation contributed to widespread dissatisfaction and aggravated peasant grievances.

In England only the southern coastal ports experienced much destruction, and the demographic effects of the Black Death actually worked to restore the land-labor balance (see page 360). The costs of the war, however, were tremendous. England spent over £5 million on the war effort, a huge sum in the fourteenth and fifteenth centuries. Manpower losses had greater social consequences. The knights who ordinarily handled the work of local government as sheriffs, coroners, jurymen, and justices of

Joan of Arc This is how the court scribe who made this sketch in 1429, the year Joan raised the siege of Orleans, imagined her. He had never seen her. *(Source: Archives Nationales, Paris)*

the peace were abroad, and their absence contributed to the breakdown of order at the local level. The English government attempted to finance the war effort by raising taxes on the wool crop. Because of steadily increasing costs, the Flemish and Italian buyers could not afford English wool. Consequently, raw wool exports slumped drastically between 1350 and 1450.

Many men of all social classes had volunteered for service in France in the hope of acquiring booty and becoming rich. The chronicler Walsingham, describing the period of Crécy, tells of the tremendous prosperity and abundance resulting from the spoils of war: "For the woman was of no account who did not possess something from the spoils of . . . cities overseas in clothing, furs, quilts, and utensils . . . tablecloths and jewels, bowls of murra [semiprecious stone] and silver, linen and linen cloths."[13] Walsingham is referring to 1348, in the first generation of war. As time went on, most fortunes seem to have been squandered as fast as they were made.

If English troops returned with cash, they did not invest it in land. In the fifteenth century, returning soldiers were commonly described as beggars and vagabonds, roaming about making mischief. Even the large sums of money received from the ransom of the great—such as the £250,000 paid to Edward III for the freedom of King John of France—and the money paid as indemnities by captured towns and castles did not begin to equal the more than £5 million spent. England suffered a serious net loss.[14]

The long war also had a profound impact on the political and cultural lives of the two countries. Most notably, it stimulated the development of the English Parliament. Between 1250 and 1450, representative assemblies from several classes of society flourished in many European countries. In the English parliaments, French Estates, German diets, and Spanish Cortes, deliberative practices developed that laid the foundations for the representative institutions of modern liberal-democratic nations. While representative assemblies declined in

Soldiers Pillaging a House   In all wars the property and persons of noncombattants have been at the mercy of victorious armies. This scene from the Hundred Years' War shows marauding soldiers ransacking a house for all possible loot. *(Source: The British Library)*

most countries after the fifteenth century, the English Parliament endured. Edward III's constant need for money to pay for the war compelled him to summon not only the great barons and bishops, but knights of the shires and burgesses from the towns as well. Between the outbreak of the war in 1337 and the king's death in 1377, parliamentary assemblies met twenty-seven times. Parliament met in thirty-seven of the fifty years of Edward's reign.[15]

The frequency of the meetings is significant. Representative assemblies were becoming a habit. Knights and burgesses—or the "Commons," as they came to be called—recognized their mutual interests and began to meet apart from the great lords. The Commons gradually realized that they held the country's purse strings, and a parliamentary statute of 1341 required that all nonfeudal levies have parliamentary approval. When Edward III signed the law, he acknowledged that the king of England could not tax without Parliament's consent. Increasingly, during the course of the war, money grants were tied to royal redress of grievances: if the government was to raise money, it had to correct the wrongs its subjects protested.

As the Commons met in a separate chamber—the House of Commons—it also developed its own organization. The "speaker" came to preside over debates in the House of Commons and to represent the Commons before the House of Lords and the king. Clerks kept a record of what transpired during discussions in the Commons.

In England theoretical consent to taxation and legislation was given in one assembly for the entire country. France had no such single assembly; instead, there were many regional or provincial assemblies. Why did a national representative assembly fail to develop in France? The initiative for convening assemblies rested with the king, who needed revenue almost as much as the English ruler. But the French monarchy found the idea of representative assemblies thoroughly distasteful. Large gatherings of the nobility potentially or actually threatened the king's power. The advice of a counselor to King Charles VI (r. 1380–1422), "above all things be sure that no great assemblies of nobles or of *communes* take place in your kingdom," was accepted.[16] Charles VII (r. 1422–1461) even threatened to punish those proposing a national assembly.

The English Parliament was above all else a court of law, a place where justice was done and grievances remedied. No French assembly (except that of Brittany) had such competence. The national assembly in England met frequently. In France general assemblies were so rare that they never got the opportunity to develop precise procedures or to exercise judicial functions.

No one in France wanted a national assembly. Linguistic, geographic, economic, legal, and political differences were very strong. People tended to think of themselves as Breton, Norman, Burgundian, or whatever, rather than French. Through much of the fourteenth and early fifteenth centuries, weak monarchs lacked the power to call a national assembly. Provincial assemblies, highly jealous of their independence, did not want a national assembly. The costs of sending delegates to it would be high, and the result was likely to be increased taxation. Finally, the Hundred Years' War itself hindered the growth of a representative body of government. Possible violence on dangerous roads discouraged people from travel.

In both countries, however, the war did promote the growth of *nationalism*—the feeling of unity and identity that binds together a people who speak the same language, have a common ancestry and customs, and live in the same area. In the fourteenth century, nationalism largely took the form of hostility toward foreigners. Both Philip VI and Edward III drummed up support for the war by portraying the enemy as an alien, evil people. Edward III sought to justify his personal dynastic quarrel by linking it with England's national interests. As the Parliament Roll of 1348 states:

The Knights of the shires and the others of the Commons were told that they should withdraw together and take good counsel as to how, for withstanding the malice of the said enemy *and for the salvation of our said lord the King and his Kingdom of England . . . the King could be aided.*[17]

After victories, each country experienced a surge of pride in its military strength. Just as English patriotism ran strong after Crécy and Poitiers, so French national confidence rose after Orléans. French national feeling demanded the expulsion of the enemy not merely from Normandy and Aquitaine but from French soil. Perhaps no one expressed this national consciousness better than Joan of Arc, when she exulted that the enemy had been "driven out of *France*."

VERNACULAR LITERATURE

Few developments expressed the emergence of national consciousness more vividly than the emergence of national literatures. Across Europe people spoke the language and dialect of their particular locality and class. In England, for example, the common people spoke regional English dialects, while the upper classes conversed in French. Official documents and works of literature were written in Latin or French. Beginning in the fourteenth century, however, national languages—the vernacular—came into widespread use not only in verbal communication but in literature as well. Three masterpieces of European culture, Dante's *Divine Comedy* (1310–1320), Chaucer's *Canterbury Tales* (1387–1400), and Villon's *Grand Testament* (1461), brilliantly manifest this new national pride.

Dante Alighieri (1265–1321) descended from an aristocratic family in Florence, where he held several positions in the city government. Dante called his work a "comedy" because he wrote it in Italian and in a different style from the "tragic" Latin; a later generation added the adjective "divine," referring both to its sacred subject and to Dante's artistry. The *Divine Comedy* is an allegorical trilogy of one hundred cantos (verses) whose three equal parts (1 + 33 + 33 + 33) each describe one of the realms of the next world, Hell, Purgatory, and Paradise. Dante recounts his imaginary journey through these regions toward God. The Roman poet Virgil, representing reason, leads Dante through Hell, where he observes the torments of the damned and denounces the disorders of his own time, especially ecclesiastical ambition and corruption. Passing up into Purgatory, Virgil shows the poet how souls are purified of their disordered inclinations. From Purgatory, Beatrice, a woman Dante once loved and the symbol of divine revelation in the poem, leads him to Paradise. In Paradise, home of the angels and saints, Saint Bernard—representing mystic contemplation—leads Dante to the Virgin Mary. Through her intercession he at last attains a vision of God.

The *Divine Comedy* portrays contemporary and historical figures, comments on secular and ecclesiastical affairs, and draws on Scholastic philosophy. Within the framework of a symbolic pilgrimage to the City of God, the *Divine Comedy* embodies the psychological tensions of the age. A profoundly

Christian poem, it also contains bitter criticism of some church authorities. In its symmetrical structure and use of figures from the ancient world, such as Virgil, the poem perpetuates the classical tradition, but as the first major work of literature in the Italian vernacular, it is distinctly modern.

Geoffrey Chaucer (1340–1400), the son of a London wine merchant, was an official in the administrations of the English kings Edward III and Richard II and wrote poetry as an avocation. Chaucer's *Canterbury Tales* is a collection of stories in lengthy, rhymed narrative. On a pilgrimage to the shrine of Saint Thomas Becket at Canterbury (see page 323), thirty people of various social backgrounds each tell a tale. The Prologue sets the scene and describes the pilgrims, whose characters are further revealed in the story each one tells. For example, the gentle Christian Knight relates a chivalric romance; the gross Miller tells a vulgar story about a deceived husband; the earthy Wife of Bath, who has buried five husbands, sketches a fable about the selection of a spouse; and the elegant Prioress, who violates her vows by wearing jewelry, delivers a homily on the Virgin. In depicting the interests and behavior of all types of people, Chaucer presents a rich panorama of English social life in the fourteenth century. Like the *Divine Comedy, Canterbury Tales* reflects the cultural tensions of the times. Ostensibly Christian, many of the pilgrims are also materialistic, sensual, and worldly, suggesting the ambivalence of the broader society's concern for the next world and frank enjoyment of this one.

Our knowledge of François Villon (1431–1463), probably the greatest poet of late medieval France, derives from Paris police records and his own poetry. Born to desperately poor parents in the year of Joan of Arc's execution, Villon was sent by his guardian to the University of Paris, where he earned the master of arts degree. A rowdy and free-spirited student, he disliked the stuffiness of academic life. In 1455 Villon killed a man in a street brawl; banished from Paris, he joined one of the bands of wandering thieves that harassed the countryside after the Hundred Years' War. For his fellow bandits he composed ballads in thieves' jargon.

Villon's *Lais* (1456), a pun on the word *legs* ("legacy"), is a series of farcical bequests to friends and enemies. "Ballade des Pendus" ("Ballad of the Hanged") was written while contemplating that fate in prison. (His execution was commuted.) Vil-

Dante Alighieri   In this fifteenth-century fresco the poet, crowned with the wreath of poet laureate, holds the book containing the opening lines of his immortal *Commedia*. On the left is Hell and the mountain of purgatory; on the right, the city of Florence. *(Source: Scala/Art Resource)*

lon's greatest and most self-revealing work, the *Grand Testament,* contains another string of bequests, including a legacy to a prostitute, and describes his unshakeable faith in the beauty of life on earth. The *Grand Testament* possesses elements of social rebellion, bawdy humor, and rare emotional depth. While the themes of Dante's and Chaucer's poetry are distinctly medieval, Villon's celebration of the human condition brands him as definitely modern. While he used medieval forms of versification, Villon's language was the despised vernacular of the poor and the criminal.

Perhaps the most versatile and prolific French writer of the later Middle Ages was Christine de Pisan (1363?–1434?). The daughter of a professor of astrology at Bologna whose international reputation won him a post at the French royal court where she received her excellent education, Christine had a broad knowledge of Greek, Latin, French, and Italian literature. The deaths of her father and husband left her with three small children and her mother to support, and she resolved to earn her living with her pen. In addition to poems and books on love, religion, and morality, Christine produced the *Livre de la mutacion de fortune,* a major historical work; a biography of king Charles V; the *Ditié,* celebrating Joan of Arc's victory; and many letters. *The City of Ladies* lists the great women of history and their contributions to society, and *The Book of Three Virtues* provides prudent and practical advice on household management for women of all social classes and at all stages of life. Christine de Pisan's wisdom and wit are illustrated in her autobiographical *Avison-Christine*. She records that a man told her an educated woman is unattractive, since there are so few, to which she responded that an ignorant man was even less attractive, since there are so many.

THE DECLINE OF THE CHURCH'S PRESTIGE

In times of crisis or disaster, people of all faiths have sought the consolation of religion. In the fourteenth century, however, the official Christian church offered very little solace. In fact, the leaders of the church added to the sorrow and misery of the times.

The Babylonian Captivity

From 1309 to 1376, the popes lived in the city of Avignon in southeastern France. In order to control the church and its policies, Philip the Fair of France pressured Pope Clement V to settle in Avignon (see page 347). Clement, critically ill with cancer, lacked the will to resist Philip. This period in church history is often called the Babylonian Captivity (referring to the seventy years the ancient Hebrews were held captive in Mesopotamian Babylon).

The Babylonian Captivity badly damaged papal prestige. The Avignon papacy reformed its financial administration and centralized its government. But the seven popes at Avignon concentrated on bureaucratic matters to the exclusion of spiritual objectives. Though some of the popes led austere lives there, the general atmosphere was one of luxury and extravagance. The leadership of the church was cut off from its historic roots and the source of its ancient authority, the city of Rome. In the absence of the papacy, the Papal States in Italy lacked stability and good government. The economy of Rome had long been based on the presence of the papal court and the rich tourist trade the papacy attracted. The Babylonian Captivity left Rome poverty-stricken. As long as the French crown dominated papal policy, papal influence in England (with which France was intermittently at war) and in Germany declined.

Many devout Christians urged the popes to return to Rome. The Dominican mystic Catherine of Siena, for example, made a special trip to Avignon to plead with the pope to return. In 1377 Pope Gregory XI brought the papal court back to Rome. Unfortunately, he died shortly after the return. At Gregory's death, Roman citizens demanded an Italian pope who would remain in Rome. Determined to influence the papal conclave (the assembly of cardinals who chose the new pope) to elect

an Italian, a Roman mob surrounded Saint Peter's Basilica, blocked the roads leading out of the city, and seized all boats on the Tiber River. Between the time of Gregory's death and the opening of the conclave, great pressure was put on the cardinals to elect an Italian. At the time, none of them protested this pressure.

Sixteen cardinals—eleven Frenchmen, four Italians, and one Spaniard—entered the conclave on April 7, 1378. After two ballots they unanimously chose a distinguished administrator, the archbishop of Bari, Bartolomeo Prignano, who took the name Urban VI. Each of the cardinals swore that Urban had been elected "sincerely, freely, genuinely, and canonically."

Urban VI (1378–1389) had excellent intentions for church reform. He wanted to abolish simony, *pluralism* (holding several church offices at the same time), absenteeism, clerical extravagance, and ostentation. These were the very abuses being increasingly criticized by Christian people across Europe. Unfortunately, Pope Urban went about the work of reform in a tactless, arrogant, and bullheaded manner. The day after his coronation he delivered a blistering attack on cardinals who lived in Rome while drawing their income from benefices elsewhere. His criticism was well founded but ill timed and provoked opposition among the hierarchy before Urban had consolidated his authority.

In the weeks that followed, Urban stepped up attacks on clerical luxury, denouncing individual cardinals by name. He threatened to strike the cardinal archbishop of Amiens. Urban even threatened to excommunicate certain cardinals, and when he was advised that such excommunications would not be lawful unless the guilty had been warned three times, he shouted, "I can do anything, if it be my will and judgment."[18] Urban's quick temper and irrational behavior have led scholars to question his sanity. Whether he was medically insane or just drunk with power is a moot point. In any case, Urban's actions brought on disaster.

In groups of two and three, the cardinals slipped away from Rome and met at Anagni. They declared Urban's election invalid because it had come about under threats from the Roman mob, and they asserted that Urban himself was excommunicated. The cardinals then proceeded to the city of Fondi between Rome and Naples and elected Cardinal Robert of Geneva, the cousin of King Charles V of France, as pope. Cardinal Robert took the name Clement VII. There were thus two popes—Urban at Rome and the antipope Clement VII (1378–1394), who set himself up at Avignon in opposition to the legally elected Urban. So began the Great Schism, which divided Western Christendom until 1417.

The Great Schism

The powers of Europe aligned themselves with Urban or Clement along strictly political lines. France naturally recognized the French antipope, Clement. England, France's historic enemy, recognized Pope Urban. Scotland, whose attacks on England were subsidized by France, followed the French and supported Clement. Aragon, Castile, and Portugal hesitated before deciding for Clement at Avignon. The emperor, who bore ancient hostility to France, recognized Urban VI. At first the Italian city-states recognized Urban; when he alienated them, they opted for Clement.

John of Spoleto, a professor at the law school at Bologna, eloquently summed up intellectual opinion of the schism:

The longer this schism lasts, the more it appears to be costing, and the more harm it does; scandal, massacres, ruination, agitations, troubles and disturbances . . . this dissention is the root of everything: divers tumults, quarrels between kings, seditions, extortions, assassinations, acts of violence, wars, rising tyranny, decreasing freedom, the impunity of villains, grudges, error, disgrace, the madness of steel and of fire given license.[19]

The scandal "rent the seamless garment of Christ," as the church was called, and provoked horror and vigorous cries for reform. The common people, wracked by inflation, wars, and plague, were thoroughly confused about which pope was legitimate. The schism weakened the religious faith of many Christians and gave rise to instability and religious excesses. It brought the church leadership into serious disrepute. At a time when ordinary Christians needed the consolation of religion and confidence in religious leaders, church officials were fighting among themselves for power.

The Conciliar Movement

Calls for church reform were not new. A half-century before the Great Schism, in 1324, Marsiglio of Padua, then rector of the University of Paris, had published *Defensor Pacis (The Defender of the Peace)*. Dealing as it did with the authority of state and church, *Defensor Pacis* proved to be one of the most controversial works written in the Middle Ages.

Marsiglio argued that the state was the great unifying power in society and that the church was subordinate to the state. He put forth the revolutionary ideas that the church had no inherent jurisdiction and should own no property. Authority in the Christian church, according to Marsiglio, should rest in a general council, made up of laymen as well as priests and superior to the pope. These ideas directly contradicted the medieval notion of a society governed by the church and the state, with the church supreme.

Defensor Pacis was condemned by the pope, and Marsiglio was excommunicated. But the idea that a general council representing all of the church had a higher authority than the pope was repeated by John Gerson (1363–1429), a later chancellor of the University of Paris and influential theologian.

Even more earthshaking than the theories of Marsiglio of Padua were the ideas of the English scholar and theologian John Wyclif (1329–1384). Wyclif wrote that papal claims of temporal power had no foundation in the Scriptures, and that the Scriptures alone should be the standard of Christian belief and practice. He urged the abolition of such practices as the veneration of saints, pilgrimages, pluralism, and absenteeism. Sincere Christians, according to Wyclif, should read the Bible for themselves. In response to that idea, the first English translation of the Bible was produced and circulated. Wyclif's views had broad social and economic significance. He urged that the church be stripped of its property. His idea that every Christian free of mortal sin possessed lordship was seized on by peasants in England during a revolt in 1381 and used to justify their goals.

In advancing these views, Wyclif struck at the roots of medieval church structure and religious practices. Consequently, he has been hailed as the precursor of the Reformation of the sixteenth century. Although Wyclif's ideas were vigorously condemned by ecclesiastical authorities, they were widely disseminated by humble clerics and enjoyed great popularity in the early fifteenth century. Wyclif's followers were called "Lollards." The term, which means "mumblers of prayers and psalms," refers to what they criticized. Lollard teaching allowed women to preach and to consecrate the

Eucharist. Women, some well educated, played a significant role in the movement. After Anne, sister of Wenceslaus, king of Germany and Bohemia, married Richard II of England, members of Queen Anne's household carried Lollard principles back to Bohemia, where they were spread by John Hus, rector of the University of Prague.

While John Wyclif's ideas were being spread, two German scholars at the University of Paris, Henry of Langenstein and Conrad of Gelnhausen, produced treatises urging the summoning of a general council. Conrad wrote that the church, as the congregation of all the faithful, was superior to the pope. Although canon law held that only a pope might call a council, a higher law existed: the common good. The common good required the convocation of a council.

In response to continued calls throughout Europe for a council, the two colleges of cardinals—one at Rome, the other at Avignon—summoned a council at Pisa in 1409. A distinguished gathering of prelates and theologians deposed both popes and selected another. Neither the Avignon pope nor the Roman pope would resign, however, and the appalling result was the creation of a threefold schism.

Finally, because of the pressure of the German emperor Sigismund, a great council met at the imperial city of Constance (1414–1418). It had three objectives: to end the schism, to reform the church "in head and members" (from top to bottom), and to wipe out heresy. The council condemned the Lollard ideas of John Hus, and he was burned at the stake. The council eventually deposed both the Roman pope and the successor of the pope chosen at Pisa, and it isolated the Avignon antipope. A conclave elected a new leader, the Roman cardinal Colonna, who took the name Martin V (1417–1431).

Martin proceeded to dissolve the council. Nothing was done about reform. The schism was over, and though councils subsequently met at Basel and at Ferrara-Florence, in 1450 the papacy held a jubilee, celebrating its triumph over the conciliar movement. In the later fifteenth century, the papacy concentrated on Italian problems to the exclusion of universal Christian interests. But the schism and the conciliar movement had exposed the crying need for ecclesiastical reform, thus laying the foundations for the great reform efforts of the sixteenth century.

THE LIFE OF THE PEOPLE

In the fourteenth century, economic and political difficulties, disease, and war profoundly affected the lives of European peoples. Decades of slaughter and destruction, punctuated by the decimating visits of the Black Death, made a grave economic situation virtually disastrous. In many parts of France and the Low Countries, fields lay in ruin or untilled for lack of labor power. In England, as taxes increased, criticisms of government policy and mismanagement multiplied. Crime, always a factor in social history, aggravated economic troubles, and throughout Europe the frustrations of the common people erupted into widespread revolts. But for most people, marriage and the local parish church continued to be the center of their lives.

Marriage

Marriage and the family provided such peace and satisfaction as most people attained. In fact, life for those who were not clerics or nuns meant marriage. Apart from sexual and emotional urgency, the community expected people to marry. For a girl, childhood was a preparation for marriage. In addition to the thousands of chores involved in running a household, girls learned obedience, or at least subordination. Adulthood meant living as a wife or widow. However, sweeping statements about marriage in the Middle Ages have limited validity. Most peasants were illiterate and left slight record of their feelings toward their spouses or about marriage as an institution. The gentry, however, often could write, and the letters exchanged between Margaret and John Paston, upper-middle-class people who lived in Norfolk, England, in the fifteenth century, provide important evidence of the experience of one couple.

John and Margaret Paston were married about 1439, after an arrangement concluded entirely by their parents. John spent most of his time in London fighting through the law courts to increase his family properties and business interests; Margaret remained in Norfolk to supervise the family lands. Her enormous responsibilities involved managing the Paston estates, hiring workers, collecting rents, ordering supplies for the large household, hearing complaints and settling disputes among tenants, and marketing her crops. In these duties she proved herself a remarkably shrewd businessperson. Moreover, when an army of over a thousand men led by the aristocratic thug Lord Moleyns attacked her house, she successfully withstood the siege. When the Black Death entered her area, Margaret moved her family to safety.

Margaret Paston did all this on top of raising eight children (there were probably other children who did not survive childhood). Her husband died before she was forty-three, and she later conducted the negotiations for the children's marriages. Her children's futures, like her estate management, were planned with an eye toward economic and social advancement. When one daughter secretly married the estate bailiff, an alliance considered beneath her, the girl was cut off from the family as if she were dead.[20]

The many letters surviving between Margaret and John reveal slight tenderness toward their children. They seem to have reserved their love for each other, and during many of his frequent absences they wrote to express mutual affection and devotion. How typical the Paston relationship was modern historians cannot say, but the marriage of John and Margaret, although completely arranged by their parents, was based on respect, responsibility, and love.[21]

At what age did people usually marry? The largest amount of evidence on age at first marriage survives from Italy, and a comparable pattern probably existed in northern Europe. For girls, population surveys at Prato place the age at 16.3 years in 1372 and 21.1 in 1470. Chaucer's Wife of Bath says that she married first in her twelfth year. Among the German nobility recent research has indicated that in the Hohenzollern family in the later Middle Ages "five brides were between 12 and 13; five about 14, and five about 15."

Men were older. An Italian chronicler writing about 1354 says that men did not marry before the age of 30. At Prato in 1371, the average age of men at first marriage was 24 years, very young for Italian men, but these data may represent an attempt to regain population losses due to the recent attack of the plague. In England Chaucer's Wife of Bath describes her first three husbands as "goode men, and rich, and old." Among seventeen males in the noble Hohenzollern family, eleven were over 20 years when married, five between 18 and 19, one 16. The general pattern in late medieval Europe was marriage between men in their middle or late twenties and women under twenty.[22]

With marriage for men postponed, was there any socially accepted sexual outlet? Recent research on the southern French province of Languedoc in the fourteenth and fifteenth centuries has revealed the establishment of legal houses of prostitution. Prostitution involves "a socially definable group of women [who] earn their living primarily or exclusively from the commerce of their bodies."[23] Municipal authorities in Toulouse, Montpellier, Albi, and other towns set up houses or red-light districts either outside the city walls or away from respectable neighborhoods. For example, authorities in Montpellier set aside Hot Street for prostitution, required public women to live there, and forbade anyone to molest them. Prostitution thus passed from being a private concern to a social matter requiring public supervision. Publicly owned brothels were more easily policed and supervised than privately run ones. Prostitution was an urban

Prostitute Invites a Traveling Merchant Poverty and male violence drove women into prostitution, which, though denounced by moralists, was accepted as a normal part of the medieval social fabric. In the cities and larger towns where prostitution flourished, public officials passed laws requiring prostitutes to wear a special mark on their clothing, regulated hours of business, forbade women to drag men into their houses, and denied business to women with the "burning sickness," gonorrhea. *(Source: The Bodleian Library, Oxford)*

Domestic Brawl   In all ages the hen-pecked husband has been a popular subject for jests. This elaborate woodcarving from a fifteenth-century English choir stall shows the husband holding distaff and ball of thread, symbolic of wife's work as "spinster," while his wife thrashes him. *(Source: Royal Commission on the Historical Monuments of England)*

phenomenon, because only populous towns had large numbers of unmarried young men, communities of transient merchants, and a culture accustomed to a cash exchange. Although the risk of disease limited the number of years a woman could practice this profession, many women prospered. Some acquired sizable incomes. In 1361 Françoise of Florence, a prostitute working in a brothel in Marseilles, made a will in which she made legacies to various charities and left a large sum as a dowry for a poor girl to marry. Archives in several cities show expensive properties bought by women who named their occupation as prostitution. The towns of Languedoc were not unique. Public authorities in Amiens, Dijon, Paris, Venice, Genoa, London, Florence, Rome, most of the larger German towns, and in the English port of Sandwich set up brothels. Legalized prostitution suggests that public officials believed the prostitute could make a positive contribution to the society; it does not mean the prostitute was respected. Rather, she was scorned and distrusted. Legalized brothels also re-

flect a greater tolerance for male than for female sexuality.[24]

In the later Middle Ages, as earlier—indeed, until the late nineteenth century—economic factors, rather than romantic love or physical attraction, determined whom and when a person married. The young agricultural laborer on the manor had to wait until he had sufficient land. Thus most men had to wait until their fathers died or yielded the holding. The age of marriage was late, and this in turn affected the number of children a couple had. The journeyman craftsman in the urban guild faced the same material difficulties. Prudent young men selected (or their parents selected for them) girls who would bring the most land or money to the union. Once a couple married, the union ended only with the death of one partner.

Deep emotional bonds knit members of medieval families. Most parents delighted in their children, and the church encouraged a cult of paternal care. The church stressed its right to govern and sanctify marriage, and it emphasized monogamy.

Tighter moral and emotional unity within marriages resulted.[25]

Divorce did not exist in the Middle Ages. The church held that a marriage validly entered into could not be dissolved. A valid marriage consisted of the mutual oral consent or promise of two parties. Church theologians of the day urged that marriage be publicized by *banns,* or announcements made in the parish church, and that the couple's union be celebrated and witnessed in a church ceremony and blessed by a priest.

A great number of couples did not observe the church's regulations. Some treated marriage as a private act—they made the promise and spoke the words of marriage to each other without witnesses and then proceeded to enjoy the sexual pleasures of marriage. This practice led to a great number of disputes, because one or the other of the two parties could later deny having made a marriage agreement. The records of the ecclesiastical courts reveal many cases arising from privately made contracts. Evidence survives of marriages contracted in a garden, in a blacksmith's shop, at a tavern, and, predictably, in a bed. The records of church courts that relate to marriage reveal that, rather than suing for divorce, the great majority of petitions asked the court to enforce the marriage contract that one of the parties believed she or he had validly made. Annulments were granted in extraordinary circumstances, such as male impotence, on the grounds that a lawful marriage had never existed.[26]

Life in the Parish

In the later Middle Ages, the land and the parish remained the focus of life for the European peasantry. Work on the land continued to be performed collectively. All men, for example, cooperated in the annual tasks of planting and harvesting. The close association of the cycle of agriculture and the liturgy of the Christian calendar endured. The parish priest blessed the fields before the annual planting, offering prayers on behalf of the people for a good crop. If the harvest was a rich one, the priest led the processions and celebrations of thanksgiving.

How did the common people feel about their work? Since the vast majority were illiterate and inarticulate, it is difficult to say. It is known that the peasants hated the ancient services and obligations on the lords' lands and tried to get them commuted for money rents. When lords attempted to reimpose service duties, the peasants revolted.

In the thirteenth century, the craft guilds provided the small minority of men and women living in towns and cities with the psychological satisfaction of involvement in the manufacture of a superior product. The guild member also had economic security. The craft guilds set high standards for their merchandise. The guilds looked after the sick, the poor, the widowed, and the orphaned. Masters and employees worked side by side.

In the fourteenth century, those ideal conditions began to change. The fundamental objective of the craft guild was to maintain a monopoly on its product, and to do so recruitment and promotion were carefully restricted. Some guilds required a high entrance fee for apprentices; others admitted only relatives of members. Apprenticeship increasingly lasted a long time, seven years. Even after a young man had satisfied all the tests for full membership in the guild and had attained the rank of master, other hurdles had to be passed, such as finding the funds to open his own business or special connections just to get in a guild. Restrictions limited the number of apprentices and journeymen to match the anticipated openings for masters. Women experienced the same exclusion. A careful study of the records of forty-two craft guilds in Cologne, for example, shows that in the fifteenth century all but six became virtual male preserves, either greatly restricting women's participation or allowing so few female members that they cannot be considered mixed guilds.[27] The larger a particular business was, the greater was the likelihood that the master did not know his employees. The separation of master and journeyman and the decreasing number of openings for master craftsmen created serious frustrations. Strikes and riots occurred in the Flemish towns, in France, and in England.

The recreation of all classes reflected the fact that late medieval society was organized for war and that violence was common. The aristocracy engaged in tournaments or jousts; archery and wrestling had great popularity among ordinary people. Everyone enjoyed the cruel sports of bullbaiting and bearbaiting. The hangings and mutilations of criminals were exciting and well-attended events, with all the festivity of a university town before a Saturday football game. Chroniclers exulted in describing executions, murders, and massacres. Here a monk gleefully describes the gory execution of William Wallace in 1305:

Wilielmus Waleis, a robber given to sacrilege, arson and homicide . . . was condemned to most cruel but justly deserved death. He was drawn through the streets of London at the tails of horses, until he reached a gallows of unusual height,. there he was suspended by a halter; but taken down while yet alive, he was mutilated, his bowels torn out and burned in a fire, his head then cut off, his body divided into four, and his quarters transmitted to four principal parts of Scotland.[28]

Violence was as English as roast beef and plum pudding, as French as bread, cheese, and *potage*.

If violent entertainment was not enough to dispel life's cares, alcohol was also available. Beer or ale commonly provided solace to the poor, and the frequency of drunkenness reflects their terrible frustrations.

During the fourteenth and fifteenth centuries, the laity began to exercise increasing control over parish affairs. Churchmen were criticized. The constant quarrels of the mendicant orders (the Franciscans and Dominicans), the mercenary and grasping attitude of the parish clergy, the scandal of the Great Schism and a divided Christendom—all these did much to weaken the spiritual mystique of the clergy in the popular mind. The laity steadily took responsibility for the management of parish lands. Lay people organized associations to vote on and purchase furnishings for the church. And ordinary lay people secured jurisdiction over the structure of the church building, its vestments, books, and furnishings. These new responsibilities of the laity reflect the increased dignity of parishioners in the late Middle Ages.[29]

Fur-Collar Crime

The Hundred Years' War had provided employment and opportunity for thousands of idle and fortune-seeking knights. But during periods of truce and after the war finally ended, many nobles once again had little to do. Inflation also hurt them. Although many were living on fixed incomes, their chivalric code demanded lavish generosity and an aristocratic lifestyle. Many nobles turned to crime as a way of raising money. The fourteenth and fifteenth centuries witnessed a great deal of "fur-collar crime," so called for the miniver fur the nobility alone were allowed to wear on their collars. England provides a good case study of upper-class crime.

Fur-collar crime rarely involved such felonies as homicide, robbery, rape, and arson. Instead, nobles used their superior social status to rob and extort from the weak and then to corrupt the judicial process. Groups of noble brigands roamed the English countryside stealing from both rich and poor. Sir John de Colseby and Sir William Bussy led a gang of thirty-eight knights who stole goods worth £3,000 in various robberies. Operating exactly like modern urban racketeers, knightly gangs demanded that peasants pay "protection money" or else have their hovels burned and their fields destroyed. Members of the household of a certain Lord Robert of Payn beat up a victim and then demanded money for protection from future attack.

Attacks on the rich often took the form of kidnaping and extortion. Individuals were grabbed in their homes, and wealthy travelers were seized on the highways and held for ransom. In northern England a gang of gentry led by Sir Gilbert de Middleton abducted Sir Henry Beaumont; his brother, the bishop-elect of Durham; and two Roman cardinals in England on a peacemaking visit. Only after a ransom was paid were the victims released.[30]

Fur-collar criminals were terrorists, but like some twentieth-century white-collar criminals who commit nonviolent crimes, medieval aristocratic criminals got away with their outrages. When accused of wrongdoing, fur-collar criminals intimidated witnesses. They threatened jurors. They used "pull" or cash to bribe judges. As a fourteenth-century English judge wrote to a young nobleman, "For the love of your father I have hindered charges being brought against you and have prevented execution of indictment actually made."[31]

The ballads of Robin Hood, a collection of folk legends from late medieval England, describe the adventures of the outlaw hero and his band of followers, who lived in Sherwood Forest and attacked and punished those who violated the social system and the law. Most of the villains in these simple tales are fur-collar criminals—grasping landlords, wicked sheriffs such as the famous sheriff of Nottingham, and mercenary churchmen. Robin and his merry men performed a sort of retributive justice. Robin Hood was a popular figure, because he symbolized the deep resentment of aristocratic corruption and abuse; he represented the struggle against tyranny and oppression.

Criminal activity by nobles continued decade after decade because governments were too weak to

The Jacquerie Because social revolt on the part of war-weary, frustrated poor seemed to threaten the natural order of Christian society during the fourteenth and fifteenth centuries, the upper classes everywhere exacted terrible vengeance on peasants and artisans. In this scene some *jacques* are cut down, some beheaded, and others drowned. *(Source: Bibliothèque Nationale, Paris)*

stop it. Then, too, much of the crime was directed against a lord's own serfs, and the line between a noble's legal jurisdiction over his peasants and criminal behavior was a fine one indeed. Persecution by lords, on top of war, disease, and natural disaster, eventually drove long-suffering and oppressed peasants all across Europe to revolt.

Peasant Revolts

Peasant revolts occurred often in the Middle Ages. Early in the thirteenth century, the French preacher Jacques de Vitry asked rhetorically, "How many serfs have killed their lords or burnt their castles?"[32] And in the fourteenth and fifteenth centuries, social and economic conditions caused a great increase in peasant uprisings (Map 12.3).

In 1358, when French taxation for the Hundred Years' War fell heavily on the poor, the frustrations of the French peasantry exploded in a massive uprising called the *Jacquerie*, after a supposedly happy agricultural laborer, Jacques Bonhomme (Good Fellow). Peasants in Picardy and Champagne went on the rampage. Crowds swept through the countryside slashing the throats of nobles, burning their castles, raping their wives and daughters, killing or maiming their horses and cattle. Peasants blamed the nobility for oppressive taxes, for the criminal brigandage of the countryside, for defeat in war, and for the general misery. Artisans, small merchants, and parish priests joined the peasants. Urban and rural groups committed terrible destruction, and for several weeks the nobles were on the defensive. Then the upper class united to repress the revolt with merciless ferocity. Thousands

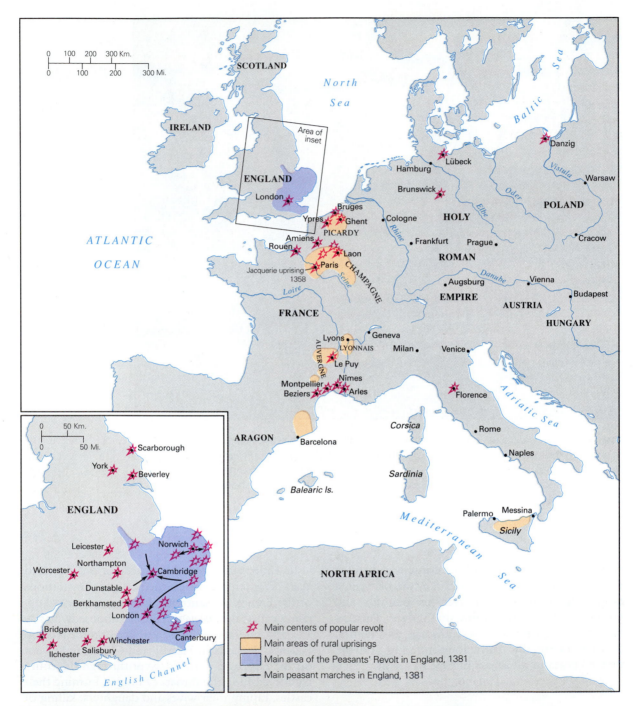

MAP 12.3 Fourteenth-Century Peasant Revolts In the later Middle Ages and early modern times, peasant and urban uprisings were endemic, as common as factory strikes in the industrial world. The threat of insurrection served to check unlimited exploitation.

of the "Jacques," innocent as well as guilty, were cut down.

This forcible suppression of social rebellion, without some effort to alleviate its underlying causes, could only serve as a stopgap measure and drive protest underground. Between 1363 and 1484, serious peasant revolts swept the Auvergne; in 1380 uprisings occurred in the Midi; and in 1420 they erupted in the Lyonnais region of France.

The Peasants' Revolt in England in 1381, involving perhaps a hundred thousand people, was probably the largest single uprising of the entire Middle Ages (see Map 12.3). The causes of the rebellion were complex and varied from place to place. In general, though, the thirteenth century had witnessed the steady commutation of labor services for cash rents, and the Black Death had drastically cut the labor supply. As a result, peasants demanded higher wages and fewer manorial obligations. Thirty years earlier the parliamentary Statute of Laborers of 1351 (see page 361) had declared:

Whereas to curb the malice of servants who after the pestilence were idle and unwilling to serve without securing excessive wages, it was recently ordained ... that such servants, both men and women, shall be bound to serve in return for salaries and wages that were customary ... five or six years earlier.[33]

This statute was an attempt by landlords to freeze wages and social mobility.

The statute could not be enforced. As a matter of fact, the condition of the English peasantry steadily improved in the course of the fourteenth century. Some scholars believe that the peasantry in most places was better off in the period 1350 to 1450 than it had been for centuries before or was to be for four centuries after.

Why then was the outburst in 1381 so serious? It was provoked by a crisis of rising expectations. The relative prosperity of the laboring classes led to demands that the upper classes were unwilling to grant. Unable to climb higher, the peasants found release for their economic frustrations in revolt. But economic grievances combined with other factors. The south of England, where the revolt broke out, had been subjected to frequent and destructive French raids. The English government did little to protect the south, and villages grew increasingly scared and insecure. This fear erupted into revolt. Moreover, decades of aristocratic violence, much

of it perpetrated against the weak peasantry, had bred hostility and bitterness. In France frustration over the lack of permanent victory increased. In England the social and religious agitation of the popular preacher John Ball fanned the embers of discontent. Such sayings as Ball's famous couplet

When Adam delved and Eve span
Who was then the gentleman?

reflect real revolutionary sentiment. Still, the lords of England believed that God had permanently fixed the hierarchical order of society and that nothing people could do would change that order.

The straw that broke the camel's back in England was the reimposition of a head tax on all adult males. Although the tax met widespread opposition in 1380, the royal council ordered the sheriffs to collect it again in 1381 on penalty of a huge fine. Beginning with assaults on the tax collectors, the uprising in England followed much the same course as had the Jacquerie in France. Castles and manors were sacked; manorial records were destroyed. Many nobles, including the archbishop of Canterbury, who had ordered the collection of the tax, were murdered.

Although the center of the revolt lay in the highly populated and economically advanced south and east, sections of the north and the Midlands also witnessed rebellions. Violence took different forms in different places. The townspeople of Cambridge expressed their hostility toward the university by sacking one of the colleges and building a bonfire of academic property. In towns containing skilled Flemish craftsmen, fear of competition led to their being attacked and murdered. Urban discontent merged with rural violence. Apprentices and journeymen, frustrated because the highest positions in the guilds were closed to them, rioted.

The boy-king Richard II (r. 1377–1399) met the leaders of the revolt, agreed to charters ensuring peasants' freedom, tricked them with false promises, and then proceeded to crush the uprising with terrible ferocity. Although the nobility tried to restore ancient duties of serfdom, virtually a century of freedom had elapsed, and the commutation of manorial services continued. Rural serfdom had disappeared in England by 1550.

Conditions in England and France were not unique. In Florence in 1378, the *ciompi,* the poor propertyless workers, revolted. Serious social trouble occurred in Lübeck, Brunswick, and other German cities. In Spain in 1391, aristocratic attempts to impose new forms of serfdom, combined with demands for tax relief, led to massive working-class and peasant uprisings in Seville and Barcelona. These took the form of vicious attacks on Jewish communities. Rebellions and uprisings everywhere reveal deep peasant and working-class frustration and the general socioeconomic crisis of the time.

SUMMARY

Late medieval preachers likened the crises of their times to the Four Horsemen of the Apocalypse in the Book of Revelation, who brought famine, war, disease, and death. The crises of the fourteenth and fifteenth centuries were acids that burned deeply into the fabric of traditional medieval European society. Bad weather brought poor harvests, which contributed to the international economic depression. Disease, over which people also had little control, fostered widespread depression and dissatisfaction. Population losses caused by the Black Death and the Hundred Years' War encouraged the working classes to try to profit from the labor shortage by selling their services higher: they wanted to move up the economic ladder. The ideas of thinkers like John Wyclif, John Hus, and John Ball fanned the flames of social discontent. When peasant frustrations exploded in uprisings, the frightened nobility and upper middle class joined to crush the revolts and condemn heretical preachers as agitators of social rebellion. But the war had heightened social consciousness among the poor.

Albrecht Dürer: The Four Horsemen of the Apocalypse   From right to left, representatives of war, strife, famine, and death gallop across Christian society leaving thousands dead or in misery. The horrors of the age made this subject extremely popular in art, literature, and sermons. *(Source: Courtesy, Museum of Fine Arts, Boston)*

The Hundred Years' War served as a catalyst for the development of representative government in England. The royal policy of financing the war through Parliament-approved taxation gave the middle classes an increased sense of their economic power. They would pay taxes in return for some influence in shaping royal policies.

In France, on the other hand, the war stiffened opposition to national assemblies. The disasters that wracked France decade after decade led the French people to believe that the best solutions to complicated problems lay not in an assembly but in the hands of a strong monarch. France became the model for continental countries in the evolution toward royal absolutism.

The war also stimulated technological experimentation, especially with artillery. Cannon revolutionized warfare, because the stone castle was no longer impregnable against them. Because only central governments, and not private nobles, could afford cannon, they strengthened the military power of national states. After 1325, the cannon, though inaccurate, existed all over Europe.

Religion held society together. European culture was a Christian culture. But the Great Schism weakened the prestige of the church and people's faith in papal authority. The conciliar movement, by denying the church's universal sovereignty, strengthened the claims of secular government to jurisdiction over all their peoples. The later Middle Ages witnessed a steady shift of basic loyalty from the church to the emerging national states.

NOTES

1. W. H. McNeill, *Plagues and Peoples* (New York: Doubleday, 1976), pp. 151–168.
2. Quoted in P. Ziegler, *The Black Death* (Harmondsworth, Eng.: Pelican Books, 1969), p. 20.
3. J. M. Rigg, trans., *The Decameron of Giovanni Boccaccio* (London: J. M. Dent & Sons, 1903), p. 6.
4. Ziegler, pp. 232–239.
5. J. Hatcher, *Plague, Population and the English Economy, 1348–1530* (London: Macmillan Education, 1986), p. 33.
6. See G. P. Cuttino, "Historical Revision: The Causes of the Hundred Years' War," *Speculum* 31 (July 1956): 463–472.
7. N. F. Cantor, *The English: A History of Politics and Society to 1760* (New York: Simon & Schuster, 1967), p. 260.
8. J. Barnie, *War in Medieval English Society: Social Values and the Hundred Years' War* (Ithaca, N.Y.: Cornell University Press, 1974), p. 6.
9. Quoted in Barnie, p. 34.
10. Ibid., p. 73.
11. Ibid., pp. 72–73.
12. W. P. Barrett, trans., *The Trial of Jeanne d'Arc* (London: George Routledge, 1931), pp. 165–166.
13. Quoted in Barnie, pp. 36–37.
14. M. M. Postan, "The Costs of the Hundred Years' War," *Past and Present* 27 (April 1964): 34–53.
15. See G. O. Sayles, *The King's Parliament of England* (New York: W. W. Norton, 1974), app., pp. 137–141.
16. Quoted in P. S. Lewis, "The Failure of the Medieval French Estates," *Past and Present* 23 (November 1962): 6.
17. C. Stephenson and G. F. Marcham, eds., *Sources of English Constitutional History,* rev. ed. (New York: Harper & Row, 1972), p. 217.
18. Quoted in J. H. Smith, *The Great Schism 1378: The Disintegration of the Medieval Papacy* (New York: Weybright & Talley, 1970), p. 141.
19. Ibid., p. 15.
20. A. S. Haskell, "The Paston Women on Marriage in Fifteenth Century England," *Viator* 4 (1973): 459–469.
21. Ibid., p. 471.
22. See D. Herlihy, *Medieval Households* (Cambridge, Mass.: Harvard University Press, 1985), pp. 103–111.
23. L. L. Otis, *Prostitution in Medieval Society: The History of an Urban Institution in Languedoc* (Chicago: University of Chicago Press, 1987), p. 2.
24. Ibid., pp. 25–27, 64–66, 100–106.
25. Ibid., pp. 118–130.
26. See R. H. Helmholz, *Marriage Litigation in Medieval England* (Cambridge: Cambridge University Press, 1974) pp. 28–29, *et passim.*
27. See M. C. Howell, *Women, Production, and Patriarchy in Late Medieval Cities* (Chicago: University of Chicago Press, 1986), pp. 134–135.
28. A. F. Scott, ed., *Everyone a Witness: The Plantagenet Age* (New York: Thomas Y. Crowell, 1976), p. 263.
29. See E. Mason, "The Role of the English Parishioner, 1000–1500," *Journal of Ecclesiastical History* 27 (January 1976): 17–29.
30. B. A. Hanawalt, "Fur Collar Crime: The Pattern of Crime Among the Fourteenth-Century English Nobility," *Journal of Social History* 8 (Spring 1975): 1–14.
31. Ibid., p. 7.
32. Quoted in M. Bloch, *French Rural History,* trans. J. Sondeimer (Berkeley: University of California Press, 1966), p. 169.
33. Stephenson and Marcham, p. 225.

SUGGESTED READING

Students who wish further elaboration of the topics covered in this chapter should consult the following studies, on which the chapter leans extensively. For the Black Death, see R. S. Gottfried, *The Black Death* (1983), a fresh and challenging work, and P. Ziegler, *The Black Death* (1969), a fascinating and highly readable study. For the social implications of disease, see W. H. McNeill, *Plagues and Peoples* (1976); F. F. Cartwright, *Disease and History* (1972); and H. E. Sigerist, *Civilization and Disease* (1970). For the economic effects of the plague, see J. Hatcher, *Plague, Population, and the English Economy, 1348–1550* (1977).

The standard study of the long military conflicts of the fourteenth and fifteenth centuries remains that of E. Perroy, *The Hundred Years' War* (1959). J. Henneman, *Royal Taxation in Fourteenth Century France: The Development of War Financing, 1322–1356* (1971), is an important technical work by a distinguished historian. J. Barnie's *War in Medieval English Society,* cited in the Notes, treats the attitudes of patriots, intellectuals, and the general public. D. Seward, *The Hundred Years' War: The English in France, 1337–1453* (1981), tells an exciting story, and J. Keegan, *The Face of Battle* (1977), chap. 2, "Agincourt," describes what war meant to the ordinary soldier. B. Tuchman, *A Distant Mirror: The Calamitous Fourteenth Century* (1980), gives a vivid picture of many facets of fourteenth-century life, while concentrating on the war. The best treatment of the financial costs of the war is probably M. M. Postan, "The Costs of the Hundred Years' War," mentioned in the Notes. E. Searle and R. Burghart, "The Defense of England and the Peasants' Revolt," *Viator* 3 (1972), is a fascinating study of the peasants' changing social attitudes. For strategy, tactics, armaments, and costumes of war, see H. W. Koch, *Medieval Warfare* (1978), a beautifully illustrated book. R. Barber, *The Knight and Chivalry* (1982), and M. Keen, *Chivalry* (1984), give fresh interpretations of the cultural importance of chivalry.

For political and social conditions in the fourteenth and fifteenth centuries, see the works by Lewis, Sayles, Bloch, Hanawalt, and Helmholz cited in the Notes. The following studies are also useful: P. S. Lewis, *Later Medieval France: The Polity* (1968); L. Romier, *A History of France* (1962); A. R. Meyers, *Parliaments and Estates in Europe to 1789* (1975); R. G. Davies and J. H. Denton, eds., *The English Parliament in the Middle Ages* (1981); I. Kershaw, "The Great Famine and Agrarian Crisis in England, 1315–1322," *Past and Present* 59 (May 1973); K. Thomas, "Work and Leisure in Pre-industrial Society," *Past and Present* 29 (December 1964); R. Hilton, *Bond Men Made Free: Medieval Peasant Movements and the English Rising of 1381* (1973), a comparative study; M.

Keen, *The Outlaws of Medieval Legend* (1961) and "Robin Hood—Peasant or Gentleman?" *Past and Present* 19 (April 1961): 7–18; and P. Wolff, "The 1391 Pogrom in Spain: Social Crisis or Not?" *Past and Present* 50 (February 1971): 4–18. Students are especially encouraged to consult the brilliant achievement of E. L. Ladurie, *The Peasants of Languedoc* (trans. J. Day, 1976). R. H. Hilton, ed., *Peasants, Knights, and Heretics: Studies in Medieval English Social History* (1976), contains a number of valuable articles primarily on the social implications of agricultural change. J. C. Holt, *Robin Hood* (1982), is a soundly researched and highly readable study of the famous outlaw. For the Pastons, see R. Barber, ed., *The Pastons: Letters of a Family in the Wars of the Roses* (1984).

For women's economic status in the late medieval period, see the important study of M. C. Howell, *Women, Production, and Patriarchy in Late Medieval Cities* (1986). B. Hanawalt, *The Ties That Bind: Peasant Families in Medieval England* (1986) gives a living picture of the family lives of ordinary people in rural communities, while D. Nicholas, *The Domestic Life of a Medieval City: Women, Children, and the Family in Fourteenth-Century Ghent* (1985), focuses on an urban society.

The poetry of Dante, Chaucer, and Villon may be read in the following editions: D. Sayers, trans., *Dante: The Divine Comedy,* 3 vols. (1963); N. Coghill, trans., *Chaucer's Canterbury Tales* (1977); P. Dale, trans., *The Poems of Villon* (1973). The social setting of *Canterbury Tales* is brilliantly evoked in D. W. Robertson, Jr., *Chaucer's London* (1968). Students interested in further study of Christine de Pisan should consult A. J. Kennedy, *Christine de Pisan: A Bibliographical Guide* (1984); the best available biography of Pisan is probably C. C. Willard, *Christine de Pisan: Her Life and Works* (1984).

For the religious history of the period, F. Oakley, *The Western Church in the Later Middle Ages* (1979), is an excellent introduction. S. Ozment, *The Age of Reform, 1250–1550* (1980), discusses the Great Schism and the conciliar movement in the intellectual context of the ecclesiopolitical tradition of the Middle Ages. Students seeking a highly detailed and comprehensive work should consult H. Beck et al., *From the High Middle Ages to the Eve of the Reformation,* trans. A. Biggs, vol. 14 in the History of the Church series edited by H. Jedin and J. Dolan (1980). J. Bossy, "The Mass as a Social Institution, 1200–1700," *Past and Present* 100 (August 1983): 29–61, provides a technical study of the central public ritual of the Latin church and its importance to Christian practice, while E. Mason, "The Role of the English Parishioner, 1000–1500," *Journal of Ecclesiastical History* 27 (January 1976): 17–29, describes the influence of lay people on church organization and practice. The older study of J. H. Smith, *The Great Schism 1378,* mentioned in the Notes, is still valuable.

13

European Society in the Age of the Renaissance

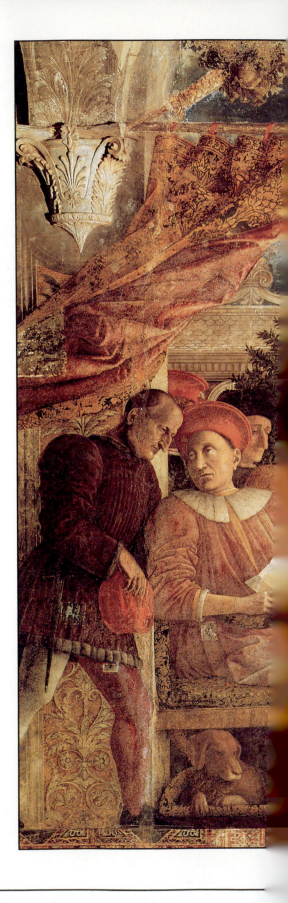

While the Four Horsemen of the Apocalypse carried war, plague, famine, and death across the Continent, a new culture was emerging in southern Europe. The fourteenth century witnessed the beginnings of remarkable changes in many aspects of Italian society. In the fifteenth century, these phenomena spread beyond Italy and gradually influenced society in northern Europe. These cultural changes have been collectively labeled the "Renaissance."

- What does the term *Renaissance* mean?
- How did the Renaissance manifest itself in politics, government, and social organization?
- What were the intellectual and artistic hallmarks of the Renaissance?
- Did the Renaissance involve shifts in religious attitudes?
- What developments occurred in the evolution of the nation-state?

This chapter will concentrate on these questions.

THE EVOLUTION OF THE ITALIAN RENAISSANCE

Economic growth laid the material basis for the Italian Renaissance. The period extending roughly from 1050 to 1300 witnessed phenomenal commercial and financial development, the growing political power of self-governing cities, and great population expansion. Then the period from the late thirteenth to the late sixteenth century was characterized by an incredible efflorescence of artistic energies.[1] Scholars commonly use the term *Renaissance* to describe the cultural achievements of the fourteenth through sixteenth centuries; those achievements rest on the economic and political developments of earlier centuries.

In the great commercial revival of the eleventh century, northern Italian cities led the way. By the middle of the twelfth century, Venice, supported by a huge merchant marine, had grown enormously rich through overseas trade. It profited tremendously from the diversion of the Fourth Crusade to Constantinople (see page 275). Genoa and Milan also enjoyed the benefits of a large volume of trade with the Middle East and northern Europe. These cities fully exploited their geographical positions as natural crossroads for mercantile exchange between the East and West. In the early fourteenth century, furthermore, Genoa and Venice made important strides in shipbuilding that allowed their ships for the first time to sail all year long. Most goods were purchased directly from the producers and sold a good distance away. For example, Italian merchants bought fine English wool directly from the Cistercian abbeys of Yorkshire in northern England. The wool was transported to the bazaars of North Africa either overland or by ship through the Strait of Gibraltar. The risks in such an operation were great, but the profits were enormous. These profits were continually reinvested to earn more.

Scholars tend to agree that the first artistic and literary manifestations of the Italian Renaissance appeared in Florence. Florence possessed enormous wealth despite geographical constraints: it was an inland city without easy access to water transportation. But toward the end of the thirteenth century, Florentine merchants and bankers acquired control of papal banking. From their position as tax collectors for the papacy, Florentine mercantile families began to dominate European banking on both sides of the Alps. These families had offices in Paris, London, Bruges, Barcelona, Marseilles, Tunis and the North African ports, and, of course, Naples and Rome. The profits from loans, investments, and money exchanges that poured back to Florence were pumped into urban industries. Such profits contributed to the city's economic vitality.

The Florentine wool industry, however, was the major factor in the city's financial expansion and population increase. Florence purchased the best-quality wool from England and Spain, developed remarkable techniques for its manufacture into cloth, and employed thousands of workers in the manufacturing process. Florentine weavers produced immense quantities of superb woolen cloth, which brought the highest prices in the fairs, markets, and bazaars of Europe, Asia, and Africa.

By the first quarter of the fourteenth century, the economic foundations of Florence were so strong that even severe crises could not destroy the city. In 1344 King Edward III of England repudiated his huge debts to Florentine bankers and forced some of them into bankruptcy. Florence suffered frightfully from the Black Death, losing at least half of its population. Serious labor unrest, such as the ciompi revolts of 1378 (see page 381), shook the political establishment. Still, the basic Florentine economic structure remained stable. Driving enterprise, technical know-how, and competitive spirit saw Florence through the difficult economic period of the late fourteenth century.

Communes and Republics

The northern Italian cities were *communes,* sworn associations of free men seeking complete political and economic independence from local nobles. The merchant guilds that formed the communes built and maintained the city walls, regulated trade, raised taxes, and kept civil order. In the course of the twelfth century, communes at Milan, Florence, Genoa, Siena, and Pisa fought for and won their independence from surrounding feudal nobles. The nobles, attracted by the opportunities of long-distance and maritime trade, the rising value of urban real estate, the new public offices available in the expanding communes, and the chances for advantageous marriages into rich commercial families, frequently settled within the cities. Marriage vows often sealed business contracts between the rural nobility and the mercantile aristocracy. This merger of the northern Italian feudal nobility and the commercial aristocracy constituted the formation of a new social class, an urban nobility. Within the nobility, groups tied by blood, economic interests, and social connections formed tightly knit alliances to defend and expand their rights.

This new class made citizenship in the communes dependent on a property qualification, years of residence within the city, and social connections. Only a tiny percentage of the male population possessed these qualifications and thus could hold office in the commune's political councils. The *popolo,* a new force, bitterly resented their exclusion from power. The popolo wanted places in the communal government and equality of taxation. Throughout most of the thirteenth century, in city after city, the popolo used armed forces and violence to take over the city governments. Republican governments were established in Bologna, Siena, Parma, Florence, Genoa, and other cities. The victory of the popolo, however, proved temporary. Because they practiced the same sort of political exclusivity as had the noble communes—denying influence to the classes below them, whether the poor, the unskilled, or new immigrants—the popolo never won the support of other groups.

Business Activities in a Florentine Bank   The Florentines early developed new banking devices. One man (left) presents a letter of credit or a bill of exchange, forerunners of the modern check, which allowed credit in distant places. A foreign merchant (right) exchanges one kind of currency for another. The bank profited from the fees it charged for these services. *(Source: Prints Division; New York Public Library; Astor, Lenox and Tilden Foundation)*

Moreover, the popolo could not establish civil order within their cities. Consequently, these movements for republican government failed. By 1300 *signori* (despots, or one-man rulers) or *oligarchies* (the rule of merchant aristocracies) had triumphed everywhere.[2]

For the next two centuries, the Italian city-states were ruled by signori or by constitutional oligarchies. In the signories, despots pretended to observe the law while actually manipulating it to conceal their basic illegality. Oligarchic regimes possessed constitutions, but through a variety of schemes a small, restricted class of wealthy merchants exercised the judicial, executive, and legislative functions of government. Thus in 1422 Venice had a population of 84,000, but 200 men held all power; Florence had about 40,000 people, but 600 men ruled. Oligarchic regimes maintained only a façade of republican government, in which political power theoretically resides in the people and is exercised by their chosen representatives. The Renaissance nostalgia for the Roman form of government, combined with calculating shrewdness, prompted the leaders of Venice, Milan, and Florence to use the old forms.

In the fifteenth century, political power and elite culture centered at the princely courts of despots and oligarchs. "A court was the space and personnel around a prince as he made laws, received ambassadors, made appointments, took his meals, and proceeded through the streets."[3] At his court a prince flaunted his patronage of learning and the arts by munificent gifts to writers, philosophers, and artists. The princely court afforded the despot or oligarch the opportunity to display his wealth. Ceremonies connected with family births, baptisms, marriages, funerals, or triumphant entrances into the city served as occasions for magnificent pageantry and elaborate ritual—all designed to assert the ruler's wealth and power.

The Balance of Power Among the Italian City-States

Renaissance Italians had a passionate attachment to their individual city-states: political loyalty and feeling centered on the local city. This intensity of local feeling perpetuated the dozens of small states and hindered the development of one unified state. Italy, consequently, was completely disunited.

In the fifteenth century, five powers dominated the Italian peninsula: Venice, Milan, Florence, the Papal States, and the kingdom of Naples (Map 13.1). The rulers of the city-states—whether despots in Milan, patrician elitists in Florence, or oligarchs in Venice—governed as monarchs. They crushed urban revolts, levied taxes, killed their enemies, and used massive building programs to employ, and the arts to overawe, the masses.

Venice, with enormous trade and vast colonial empire, ranked as an international power. Though Venice had a sophisticated constitution and was a republic in name, an oligarchy of merchant-aristocrats actually ran the city. Milan was also called a republic, but despots of the Sforza family ruled harshly and dominated the smaller cities of the north. Likewise in Florence the form of government was republican, with authority vested in several councils of state. In reality, between 1434 and 1494, power in Florence was held by the great Medici banking family. Though not public officers, Cosimo (1434–1464) and Lorenzo (1469–1492) ruled from behind the scenes.

Central Italy consisted mainly of the Papal States, which during the Babylonian Captivity had come under the sway of important Roman families.

Pope Alexander VI (1492–1503), aided militarily and politically by his son Cesare Borgia, reasserted papal authority in the papal lands. Cesare Borgia became the hero of Machiavelli's *The Prince* because he began the work of uniting the peninsula by ruthlessly conquering and exacting total obedience from the principalities making up the Papal States.

South of the Papal States was the kingdom of Naples, consisting of virtually all of southern Italy and, at times, Sicily. The kingdom of Naples had long been disputed by the Aragonese and by the French. In 1435 it passed to Aragon.

The major Italian city-states controlled the smaller ones, such as Siena, Mantua, Ferrara, and Modena, and competed furiously among themselves for territory. The large cities used diplomacy, spies, paid informers, and any other means to get information that could be used to advance their ambitions. While the states of northern Europe were moving toward centralization and consolidation, the world of Italian politics resembled a jungle where the powerful dominated the weak.

In one significant respect, however, the Italian city-states anticipated future relations among competing European states after 1500. Whenever one Italian state appeared to gain a predominant position within the peninsula, other states combined to establish a balance of power against the major threat. In 1450, for example, Venice went to war against Milan in protest against Francesco Sforza's acquisition of the title of duke of Milan. Cosimo de' Medici of Florence, a long-time supporter of a Florentine-Venetian alliance, switched his position and aided Milan. Florence and Naples combined with Milan against powerful Venice and the papacy. In the peace treaty signed at Lodi in 1454, Venice received territories in return for recognizing Sforza's right to the duchy. This pattern of shifting alliances continued until 1494. In the formation of these alliances, Renaissance Italians invented the machinery of modern diplomacy; permanent embassies with resident ambassadors in capitals where political relations and commercial ties needed continual monitoring. The resident ambassador is one of the great achievements of the Italian Renaissance.

At the end of the fifteenth century, Venice, Florence, Milan, and the papacy possessed great wealth and represented high cultural achievement. However, their imperialistic ambitions at one another's expense, and their resulting inability to form a common alliance against potential foreign ene-

MAP 13.1 The Italian City-States, ca 1494 In the fifteenth century the Italian city-states represented great wealth and cultural sophistication. The political divisions of the peninsula invited foreign intervention.

mies, made Italy an inviting target for invasion. When Florence and Naples entered into an agreement to acquire Milanese territories, Milan called on France for support.

At Florence the French invasion had been predicted by the Dominican friar Girolamo Savonarola (1452–1498). In a number of fiery sermons between 1491 and 1494, Savonarola attacked what

he considered the paganism and moral vice of the city, the undemocratic government of Lorenzo de' Medici, and the corruption of Pope Alexander VI. For a time Savonarola enjoyed wide popular support among the ordinary people; he became the religious leader of Florence and as such contributed to the fall of the Medici. Eventually, however, people wearied of his moral denunciations, and he was

Palazzo Vecchio, Florence Built during the late thirteenth and early fourteenth centuries as a fortress of defense against both popular uprising and foreign attack, the building housed the *podesta,* the city's highest magistrate, and all the offices of the government. *(Source: Scala/Art Resource)*

Charles's success simply whetted French appetites. In 1508 his son Louis XII formed the League of Cambrai with the pope and the German emperor Maximilian for the purpose of stripping rich Venice of its mainland possessions. Pope Leo X soon found the French a dangerous friend, and in a new alliance called on the Spanish and Germans to expel the French from Italy. This anti-French combination was temporarily successful. In 1519 Charles V succeeded his grandfather Maximilian as Holy Roman emperor. When the French returned to Italy in 1522, there began the series of conflicts called the Habsburg-Valois Wars (named for the German and French dynasties), whose battlefield was often Italy.

In the sixteenth century, the political and social life of Italy was upset by the relentless competition for dominance between France and the empire. The Italian cities suffered severely from the continual warfare, especially in the frightful sack of Rome in 1527 by imperial forces under Charles V. Thus the failure of the city-states to form some federal system, or to consolidate, or at least to establish a common foreign policy, led to the continuation of the centuries-old subjection of the peninsula by outside invaders. Italy was not to achieve unification until 1870.

INTELLECTUAL HALLMARKS OF THE RENAISSANCE

The Renaissance was characterized by self-conscious awareness among fourteenth- and fifteenth-century Italians that they were living in a new era. The realization that something new and unique was happening first came to men of letters in the fourteenth century, especially to the poet and humanist Francesco Petrarch (1304–1374). Petrarch thought that he was living at the start of a new age, a period of light following a long night of Gothic gloom. He believed that the first two centuries of the Roman Empire represented the peak in the development of human civilization. The Germanic invasions had caused a sharp cultural break with the glories of Rome and inaugurated what Petrarch called the "Dark Ages." Medieval people had believed that they were continuing the glories that had been ancient Rome and had recognized no cultural division between the world of the emperors and their own times. But for Petrarch and many of

excommunicated by the pope and executed. Savonarola stands as proof that the common people did not share the worldly outlook of the commercial and intellectual elite. His career also illustrates the internal instability of Italian cities such as Florence, an instability that invited foreign invasion.

The invasion of Italy in 1494 by the French king Charles VIII (r. 1483–1498) inaugurated a new period in Italian and European power politics. Italy became the focus of international ambitions and the battleground of foreign armies. Charles swept down the peninsula with little opposition, and Florence, Rome, and Naples soon bowed before him. When Piero de' Medici, Lorenzo's son, went to the French camp seeking peace, the Florentines exiled the Medicis and restored republican government.

his contemporaries, the thousand-year period between the fourth and the fourteenth centuries constituted a barbarian, or Gothic, or "middle" age. The sculptors, painters, and writers of the Renaissance spoke contemptuously of their medieval predecessors and identified themselves with the thinkers and artists of Greco-Roman civilization. Petrarch believed he was witnessing a new golden age of intellectual achievement—a rebirth or, to use the French word that came into English, a *renaissance*. The division of historical time into periods is often arbitrary and done for the convenience of historians. In terms of the way most people lived and thought, no sharp division exists between the Middle Ages and the Renaissance. Some important poets, writers, and artists, however, believed they were living in a new golden age.

The Renaissance also manifested itself in a new attitude toward men, women, and the world—an attitude that may be described as individualism. A humanism characterized by a deep interest in the Latin classics and the deliberate attempt to revive antique lifestyles emerged, as did a bold new secular spirit.

Individualism

Though the Middle Ages had seen the appearance of remarkable individuals, recognition of such persons was limited. The examples of Saint Augustine in the fifth century and Peter Abelard and Guibert of Nogent in the twelfth—men who perceived themselves as unique and produced autobiographical statements—stand out for that very reason: Christian humility discouraged self-absorption. In the fourteenth and fifteenth centuries, moreover, such characteristically medieval and corporate attachments as the guild and the parish continued to provide strong support for the individual and to exercise great social influence. Yet in the Renaissance intellectuals developed a new sense of historical distance from earlier periods. A large literature specifically concerned with the nature of individuality emerged. This literature represented the flowering of a distinctly Renaissance individualism.

The Renaissance witnessed the emergence of many distinctive personalities who gloried in their uniqueness. Italians of unusual abilities were self-consciously aware of their singularity and unafraid to be unlike their neighbors; they had enormous confidence in their ability to achieve great things.

Leon Battista Alberti (1404–1474), a writer, architect, and mathematician, remarked, "Men can do all things if they will."[4] The Florentine goldsmith and sculptor Benvenuto Cellini (1500–1574) prefaced his *Autobiography* with a sonnet that declares:

My cruel fate hath warr'd with me in vain:
Life, glory, worth, and all unmeasur'd skill,
Beauty and grace, themselves in me fulfill
That many I surpass, and to the best attain.[5]

Cellini, certain of his genius, wrote so that the whole world might appreciate it.

Individualism stressed personality, genius, uniqueness, and the fullest development of capabilities and talents. Artist, athlete, painter, scholar, sculptor, whatever—a person's abilities should be stretched until fully realized. Thirst for fame, a driving ambition, a burning desire for success drove such people to the complete achievement of their potential. The quest for glory was a central component of Renaissance individualism.

The Revival of Antiquity

In the cities of Italy, especially Rome, civic leaders and the wealthy populace showed phenomenal archeological zeal for the recovery of manuscripts, statues, and monuments. Pope Nicholas V (1447–1455), a distinguished scholar, planned the Vatican Library for the nine thousand manuscripts he had collected. Pope Sixtus IV (1471–1484) built that library, which remains one of the richest repositories of ancient and medieval documents.

Patrician Italians consciously copied the lifestyle of the ancients and even searched out pedigrees dating back to ancient Rome. Aeneas Silvius Piccolomini, a native of Siena who became Pope Pius II (1458–1464), once pretentiously declared, "Rome is as much my home as Siena, for my House, the Piccolomini, came in early times from the capital to Siena, as is proved by the constant use of the names Aeneas and Silvius in my family."[6]

The revival of antiquity also took the form of profound interest in and study of the Latin classics. This feature of the Renaissance became known as the "new learning," or simply "humanism," the term of the Florentine rhetorician and historian Leonardo Bruni (1370–1444). The words *humanism* and *humanist* derived ultimately from the Latin *humanitas,* which Cicero used to mean the literary culture needed by anyone who would be considered educated and civilized. Humanists studied the Latin classics to learn what they reveal about human nature. Humanism emphasized human beings, their achievements, interests, and capabilities. Although churchmen supported the new learning, by the later fifteenth century Italian humanism was increasingly a lay phenomenon.

Appreciation for the literary culture of the Romans had never died in the West. Bede and John of Salisbury, for example, had studied and imitated the writings of the ancients. Medieval writers, however, had studied the ancients in order to come to know God. Medieval scholars interpreted the classics in a Christian sense and invested the ancients' poems and histories with Christian meaning.

Renaissance humanists approached the classics differently. Where medieval writers accepted pagan

Brunelleschi: Abraham's Sacrifice of Isaac When the Florentine textile merchants' guild held a competition for designs of the bronze doors of the city Baptistery, Brunelleschi entered this design based on the story in Genesis 22. The Roman altar and the boy removing a thorn from his foot (lower right) show conscious Roman elements in this dramatic, even violent scene. *(Source: Alinari/Art Resource)*

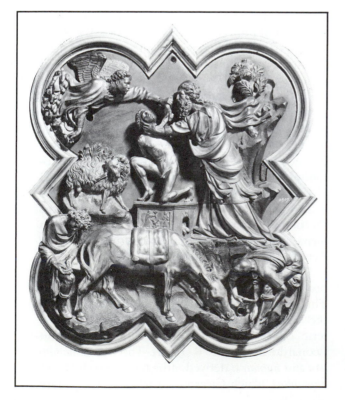

and classical authors uncritically, Renaissance humanists were skeptical of their authority, conscious of the historical distance separating themselves from the ancients, and fully aware that classical writers often disagreed among themselves. Like their medieval predecessors, Renaissance humanists were deeply Christian. They studied the classics to understand human nature, and while they fully grasped the moral thought of pagan antiquity, Renaissance humanists viewed humanity from a strongly Christian perspective: men and women were made in the image and likeness of God. For example, in a remarkable essay, *On the Dignity of Man,* the Florentine writer Pico della Mirandola stressed that man possesses great dignity, because he was made as Adam in the image of God before the Fall and as Christ after the Resurrection. According to Pico, man's place in the universe is somewhere between the beasts and the angels, but because of the divine image planted in him, there are no limits to what he can accomplish. Humanists rejected classical ideas that were opposed to Christianity. Or they sought through reinterpretation an underlying harmony between the pagan and secular and the Christian faith. The fundamental difference between Renaissance humanists and medieval ones is that the former were more self-conscious about what they were doing.[7]

The fourteenth- and fifteenth-century humanists loved the language of the classics and considered it superior to the corrupt Latin of the medieval schoolmen. Renaissance writers were very excited by the purity of ancient Latin. They eventually became concerned more about form than about content, more about the way an idea was expressed than about the significance and validity of the idea. Literary humanists of the fourteenth century wrote each other highly stylized letters imitating ancient authors, and they held witty philosophical dialogues in conscious imitation of the Platonic Academy of the fourth century B.C. Whenever they could, Renaissance humanists heaped scorn on the "barbaric" Latin style of the medievalists. The leading humanists of the early Renaissance were rhetoricians, seeking effective and eloquent communication, both oral and written.

Secular Spirit

Secularism involves a basic concern with the material world instead of eternal and spiritual interests.

A secular way of thinking tends to find the ultimate explanation of everything and the final end of human beings within the limits of what the senses can discover. Medieval business people ruthlessly pursued profits while medieval monks fought fiercely over property. Renaissance people often held strong and deep spiritual interests. Yet in a religious society, such as the medieval, the dominant ideals focused on the otherworldly, on life after death. In a secular society, attention is concentrated on the here and now, often on the acquisition of material things. The fourteenth and fifteenth centuries witnessed the slow but steady growth of secularism in Italy.

The economic changes and rising prosperity of the Italian cities in the thirteenth century worked a fundamental change in social and intellectual attitudes and values. Worries about shifting rates of interest, shipping routes, personnel costs, and employee relations did not leave much time for thoughts about penance and purgatory. The busy bankers and merchants of the Italian cities calculated ways of making and increasing their money. Money allowed greater material pleasures, a more comfortable life, the leisure time to appreciate and patronize the arts. Money could buy many sensual gratifications, and the rich, social-climbing patricians of Venice, Florence, Genoa, and Rome came to see life more as an opportunity to be enjoyed than as a painful pilgrimage to the City of God.

In *On Pleasure,* the humanist Lorenzo Valla (1406–1457) defended the pleasures of the senses as the highest good. Scholars praise Valla as a father of modern historical criticism. His study *On the False Donation of Constantine* (1444) demonstrated by careful textual examination that an anonymous eighth-century document supposedly giving the papacy jurisdiction over vast territories in western Europe was a forgery. Medieval people had accepted the Donation of Constantine as a reality, and the proof that it was an invention weakened the foundations of papal claims to temporal authority. Lorenzo Valla's work exemplifies the application of critical scholarship to old and almost-sacred writings, as well as the new secular spirit of the Renaissance. The tales in the *Decameron* by the Florentine Boccaccio, which describe ambitious merchants, lecherous friars, and cuckolded husbands, portray a frankly acquisitive, sensual, and worldly society. Boccaccio's figures were stock literary characters. Writers, moreover, draw on their imagination as well as social experience, and historians must be

Quentin Metsys: A Banker and His Wife   In this scene from everyday life, the Flemish painter, with quiet sensitivity and remarkable attention to detail, contrasts spiritual and earthly treasures: the clink of coins and the glitter of pearls distracts the wife from her prayerbook. *(Source: Louvre/Cliché des Musées Nationaux, Paris)*

cautious in basing conclusions solely on literature. Still, the *Decameron* contains none of the "contempt of the world" theme so pervasive in medieval literature. Renaissance writers justified the accumulation and enjoyment of wealth with references to ancient authors.

Nor did church leaders do much to combat the new secular spirit. In the fifteenth and early sixteenth centuries, the papal court and the households of the cardinals were just as worldly as those of great urban patricians. Of course, most of the popes and higher church officials had come from the bourgeois aristocracy. Renaissance popes beautified the city of Rome, patronized artists and men of letters, and expended enormous enthusiasm and huge sums of money. A new papal chancellery, begun in 1483 and finished in 1511, stands as one of the architectural masterpieces of the High Renaissance. Pope Julius II (1503–1513) tore down the old Saint Peter's Basilica and began work on the present structure in 1506. Michelangelo's dome for Saint Peter's is still considered his greatest work. Papal interests, far removed from spiritual concerns, fostered rather than discouraged the new worldly attitude.

The broad mass of the people and the intellectuals and leaders of society remained faithful to the Christian church. Few people questioned the basic tenets of the Christian religion. Italian humanists and their aristocratic patrons were antiascetic, anti-Scholastic, and ambivalent, but they were not agnostics or skeptics. The thousands of pious paintings, sculptures, processions, and pilgrimages of the Renaissance period prove that strong religious feeling persisted.

ART AND THE ARTIST

No feature of the Renaissance evokes greater admiration than its artistic masterpieces. The 1400s (*quattrocento*) and 1500s (*cinquecento*) bore witness to a dazzling creativity in painting, architecture, and sculpture. In all the arts, the city of Florence led the way. According to the Renaissance art historian Giorgio Vasari (1511–1574), the painter Perugino once asked why it was in Florence and not elsewhere that men achieved perfection in the arts. The first answer he received was, "There were so many good critics there, for the air of the city makes men quick and perceptive and impatient of mediocrity."[8] But Florence was not the only artistic center. In the period art historians describe as the "High Renaissance" (1500–1527), Rome took the lead. The main characteristics of High Renaissance art—classical balance, harmony, and restraint—are revealed in the masterpieces of Leonardo da Vinci (1452–1519), Raphael (1483–1520), and Michelangelo (1475–1564), all of whom worked in Rome at this time.

Art and Power

In early Renaissance Italy, art manifested corporate power. Powerful urban groups such as guilds or religious confraternities commissioned works of art. The Florentine cloth merchants, for example, delegated Brunelleschi to build the magnificent dome on the cathedral of Florence and selected Ghiberti to design the bronze doors of the baptistry. These works represented the merchants' dominant influence in the community. Corporate patronage is also reflected in the Florentine government's decision to hire Michelangelo to create the sculpture of David, the great Hebrew hero and king. The sub-

ject matter of art through the early fifteenth century, as in the Middle Ages, remained overwhelmingly religious. Religious themes appeared in all media—wood carvings, painted frescoes, stone sculptures, paintings. As in the Middle Ages, art served an educational purpose. A religious picture or statue was intended to spread a particular doctrine, act as a profession of faith, or recall sinners to a moral way of living.

Increasingly in the later fifteenth century, individuals and oligarchs, rather than corporate groups, sponsored works of art. Patrician merchants and bankers, popes and princes supported the arts as a means of glorifying themselves and their families. Vast sums were spent on family chapels, frescoes, religious panels, and tombs. Writing about 1470, the Florentine oligarch Lorenzo de' Medici declared that over the past thirty-five years his family had spent the astronomical sum of 663,755 gold florins for artistic and architectural commissions. Yet "I think it casts a brilliant light on our estate [public reputation] and it seems to me that the monies were well spent and I am very pleased with this." Powerful men wanted to exalt themselves, their families, and their offices. A magnificent style of living, enriched by works of art, served to prove the greatness and the power of the despot or oligarch.[9]

As the fifteenth century advanced, the subject matter of art became steadily more secular. The study of classical texts brought deeper understanding of ancient ideas. Classical themes and motifs, such as the lives and loves of pagan gods and goddesses, figured increasingly in painting and sculpture. Religious topics, such as the Annunciation of the Virgin and the Nativity, remained popular among both patrons and artists, but frequently the patron had himself and his family portrayed. People were conscious of their physical uniqueness and wanted their individuality immortalized. Paintings cost money and thus were also means of displaying wealth.

The style of Renaissance art was decidedly different from that of the Middle Ages. The individual portrait emerged as a distinct artistic genre. In the fifteenth century, members of the newly rich middle class often had themselves painted in a scene of romantic chivalry or in courtly society. Rather than reflecting a spiritual ideal, as medieval painting and sculpture tended to do, Renaissance portraits mirrored reality. The Florentine painter Giotto (1276–1337) led the way in the use of realism; his treatment of the human body and face replaced the formal stiffness and artificiality that had for so long characterized the representation of the human body. The sculptor Donatello (1386–1466) probably exerted the greatest influence of any Florentine artist before Michelangelo. His many statues express an appreciation of the incredible variety of human nature. While medieval artists had depicted the nude human body only in a spiritualized and moralizing context, Donatello revived the classical figure with its balance and self-awareness. The short-lived Florentine Masaccio (1401–1428), sometimes called the father of modern painting, inspired a new style characterized by great realism, narrative power, and remarkably effective use of light and dark. As important as realism was the new "international style," so called because of the wandering careers of influential artists, the close communications and rivalry of princely courts, and the increased trade in works of art. Rich color, decora-

Benozzo Gozzoli: *Journey of the Magi*   Few Renaissance paintings better illustrate art in the service of the princely court, in this case the Medici. Commissioned by Piero de' Medici to adorn his palace chapel, everything in this fresco—the large crowd, the feathers and diamonds adorning many of the personages, the black servant in front— serve to flaunt the power and wealth of the House of Medici. There is nothing especially religious about it; the painting could more appropriately be called "Journey of the Medici." The artist has discreetly placed himself in the crowd, the name Benozzo embroidered on his cap. *(Source: Scala/Art Resource)*

Michelangelo: David In 1501 the new republican government of Florence commissioned the twenty-six-year-old Michelangelo to carve David as a symbol of civic independence and resistance to oligarchial tyranny. Tensed in anticipation of action but certain of victory over his unseen enemy Goliath (1 Samuel 17), this male nude represents the ideal of youthful physical perfection. *(Source: Scala/Art Resource)*

tive detail, curvilinear rhythms, and swaying forms characterized the international style. As the term *international* implies, this style was European, not merely Italian.

Narrative artists depicted the body in a more scientific and natural manner. The female figure is voluptious and sensual. The male body, as in Michelangelo's *David* and *The Last Judgment,* is strong and heroic. Renaissance glorification of the human body reveals the secular spirit of the age. Filippo Brunelleschi (1377–1446) and Piero della Francesca (1420–1492) seem to have pioneered *perspective* in painting, the linear representation of distance and space on a flat surface. *The Last Supper* of Leonardo da Vinci, with its stress on the tension between Christ and the disciples, is an incredibly subtle psychological interpretation.

The Status of the Artist

In the Renaissance the social status of the artist improved. The lower-middle-class medieval master mason had been viewed in the same light as a mechanic. The artist in the Renaissance was considered a free intellectual worker. Artists did not produce unsolicited pictures or statues for the general public; that could mean loss of status. They usually worked on commission from a powerful prince. The artist's reputation depended on the support of powerful patrons, and through them some artists and architects achieved not only economic security but very great wealth. All aspiring artists received a practical (not theoretical) education in a recognized master's workshop. For example, Michelangelo (1475–1564) was apprenticed at age thirteen to the artist Ghirlandaio (1449–1494), although he later denied the fact to make it appear he never had any formal training. The more famous the artist, the more he attracted assistants or apprentices. Lorenzo Ghiberti (1378–1455) had twenty assistants during the period when he was working on the bronze doors of the baptistry in Florence, his most famous achievement.

Ghiberti's salary of two hundred florins a year compared very favorably with that of the head of the city government, who earned five hundred florins. Moreover, at a time when a person could live in a princely fashion on three hundred ducats a year, Leonardo da Vinci was making two thousand annually. Michelangelo was paid three thousand ducats for painting the ceiling of the Sistine

Chapel. When he agreed to work on Saint Peter's Basilica, he refused a salary; he was already a wealthy man.[10]

Renaissance society respected and rewarded the distinguished artist. In 1537 the prolific letter writer, humanist, and satirizer of princes Pietro Aretino (1492–1556) wrote to Michelangelo while he was painting the Sistine Chapel:

To the Divine Michelangelo:

Sir, just as it is disgraceful and sinful to be unmindful of God so it is reprehensible and dishonourable for any man of discerning judgement not to honour you as a brilliant and venerable artist whom the very stars use as a target at which to shoot the rival arrows of their favour. You are so accomplished, therefore, that hidden in your hands lives the idea of a new king of creation. . . . it is surely my duty to honour you with this salutation, since the world has many kings but only one Michelangelo.[11]

When the Holy Roman emperor Charles V (r. 1519–1556) visited the workshop of the great Titian (1477–1576) and stooped to pick up the artist's dropped paintbrush, the emperor was demonstrating that the patron himself was honored in the act of honoring the artist. The social status of the artist of genius was immortally secured.

Renaissance artists were not only aware of their creative power; they boasted about it. Describing his victory over five others, including Brunelleschi, in the competition to design the bronze doors of Florence's baptistry, Ghiberti exulted, "The palm of victory was conceded to me by all the experts and by all my fellow-competitors. By universal consent and without a single exception the glory was conceded to me."[12] Some medieval painters and sculptors had signed their works; Renaissance artists almost universally did so, and many of them incorporated self-portraits, usually as bystanders, in their paintings.

The Renaissance, in fact, witnessed the birth of the concept of the artist as genius. In the Middle Ages, people believed that only God created, albeit through individuals; the medieval conception recognized no particular value in artistic originality. Renaissance artists and humanists came to think that a work of art was the deliberate creation of a unique personality, of an individual who transcended traditions, rules, and theories. A genius had a peculiar gift, which ordinary laws should not inhibit. Cosimo de' Medici described a painter, be-

cause of his genius, as "divine," implying that the artist shared in the powers of God. The word *divine* was widely applied to Michelangelo.

But the student must guard against interpreting Italian Renaissance culture in twentieth-century democratic terms. The culture of the Renaissance was that of a small mercantile elite, a business patriciate with aristocratic pretensions. Renaissance culture did not directly affect the broad middle classes, let alone the vast urban proletariat. A small, highly educated minority of literary humanists and artists created the culture of and for an exclusive elite. They cared little for ordinary people. Renaissance humanists were a smaller and narrower group than the medieval clergy had ever been. High churchmen had commissioned the construction of the Gothic cathedrals, but, once finished, the buildings were for all to enjoy. The modern visitor can still see the deep ruts in the stone floors of Chartres and Canterbury where the poor pilgrims slept at night. Nothing comparable was built in the Renaissance. Insecure, social-climbing merchant princes were hardly egalitarian.[13] The Renaissance continued the gulf between the learned minority and the uneducated multitude that has survived for many centuries.

SOCIAL CHANGE

The Renaissance changed many aspects of Italian, and subsequently European, society. The new developments brought about real breaks with the medieval past. What impact did the Renaissance have on educational theory and practice, on political thought? How did printing, the era's most stunning technological discovery, affect fifteenth- and sixteenth-century society? How did Renaissance culture affect the experience of women? What roles did blacks play in Renaissance society?

Education and Political Thought

One of the central preoccupations of the humanists was education and moral behavior. Humanists poured out treatises, often in the form of letters, on the structure and goals of education and the training of rulers. In one of the earliest systematic programs for the young, Peter Paul Vergerio (1370–1444) wrote Ubertinus, the ruler of Carrara:

For the education of children is a matter of more than private interest; it concerns the State, which indeed regards the right training of the young as, in certain aspects, within its proper sphere. . . . Tutors and comrades alike should be chosen from amongst those likely to bring out the best qualities, to attract by good example, and to repress the first signs of evil. . . . Above all, respect for Divine ordinances is of the deepest importance; it should be inculcated from the earliest years. Reverence towards elders and parents is an obligation closely akin.

We call those studies liberal *which are worthy of a free man; those studies by which we attain and practice virtue and wisdom; that education which calls forth, trains and develops those highest gifts of body and of mind which ennoble men, and which are rightly judged to rank next in dignity to virtue only.*[14.]

Part of Vergerio's treatise specifies subjects for the instruction of young men in public life: history teaches virtue by examples from the past; ethics focuses on virtue itself; and rhetoric or public speaking trains for eloquence.

No book on education had broader influence than Baldassare Castiglione's *The Courtier* (1528). This treatise sought to train, discipline, and fashion the young man into the courtly ideal, the gentleman. According to Castiglione, the educated man of the upper class should have a broad background in many academic subjects, and his spiritual and physical, as well as intellectual, capabilities should be trained. The courtier should have easy familiarity with dance, music, and the arts. Castiglione envisioned a man who could compose a sonnet, wrestle, sing a song and accompany himself on an instrument, ride expertly, solve difficult mathematical problems, and above all speak and write eloquently.

In the sixteenth and seventeenth centuries, *The Courtier* was widely read. It influenced the social mores and patterns of conduct of elite groups in Renaissance and early modern Europe. The courtier became the model of the European gentleman.

No Renaissance book on any topic, however, has been more widely read and studied in all the centuries since its publication than the short political treatise *The Prince*, by Niccolò Machiavelli (1469–1527). Some political scientists maintain that Machiavelli was describing the actual competitive framework of the Italian states with which he was familiar. Other thinkers praise *The Prince* because it revolutionized political theory and destroyed medieval views of the nature of the state. Still other

scholars consider this work a classic because it deals with eternal problems of government and society.

Born to a modestly wealthy Tuscan family, Machiavelli received a good education in the Latin classics. He entered the civil service of the Florentine government and served on thirty diplomatic missions. When the exiled Medicis returned to power in the city in 1512, they expelled Machiavelli from his position as an officer of the city government. In exile he wrote *The Prince*.

The subject of *The Prince* is political power: how the ruler should gain, maintain, and increase it. Machiavelli implicitly addresses the question of the citizen's relationship to the state. As a good humanist, he explores the problems of human nature and concludes that human beings are selfish and out to advance their own interests. This pessimistic view of humanity leads him to maintain that the prince may have to manipulate the people in any way he finds necessary:

For a man who, in all respects, will carry out only his professions of good, will be apt to be ruined amongst so many who are evil. A prince therefore who desires to maintain himself must learn to be not always good, but to be so or not as necessity may require.[15]

The prince should combine the cunning of a fox with the ferocity of a lion to achieve his goals. Asking rhetorically whether it is better for a ruler to be loved or feared, Machiavelli wrote:

This, then, gives rise to the question "whether it be better to be loved than feared, or to be feared than loved." It will naturally be answered that it would be desirable to be both the one and the other; but as it is difficult to be both at the same time, it is much more safe to be feared than to be loved, when you have to choose between the two. For it may be said of men in general that they are ungrateful and fickle, dissemblers, avoiders of danger, and greedy of gain. So long as you shower benefits upon them, they are all yours.[16]

Medieval political theory derived ultimately from Saint Augustine's view that the state arose as a consequence of Adam's fall and people's propensity to sin. The test of good government was whether it provided justice, law, and order. Political theorists and theologians from Alcuin to Marsiglio of Padua had stressed the way government *ought* to be; they set high moral and Christian standards for the ruler's conduct.

The Print Shop Sixteenth-century printing involved a division of labor. Two persons (left) at separate benches set the pieces of type. Another (center, rear) inks the chase (or locked plate containing the set type). Another (right) operates the press, which prints the sheets. The boy removes the printed pages and sets them to dry. Meanwhile, a man carries in fresh paper on his head. *(Source: Bettmann/Hulton)*

Machiavelli maintained that the ruler should be concerned not with the way things ought to be but with the way things actually are. The sole test of a "good" government was whether it was effective, whether the ruler increased his power. Machiavelli did not advocate amoral behavior, but he believed that political action cannot be restricted by moral considerations. While amoral action might be the most effective approach in a given situation, he did not argue for generally amoral behavior rather than moral. In the *Discourses of the Ten Books of Titus Livy,* Machiavelli even showed his strong commitment to republican government. Nevertheless, on the basis of a crude interpretation of *The Prince,* the word *machiavellian* entered the language as a synonym for the politically devious, corrupt, and crafty, indicating actions in which the end justifies the means. The ultimate significance of Machiavelli rests on two ideas: first, that one permanent social order reflecting God's will cannot be established

and, second, that politics has its own laws and ought to be a science.[17]

The Printed Word

Sometime in the thirteenth century, paper money and playing cards from China reached the West. They were *block-printed*—that is, Chinese characters or pictures were carved into a wooden block, inked, and the words or illustrations transferred to paper. Since each word, phrase, or picture was on a separate block, this method of reproduction was extraordinarily expensive and time-consuming.

Around 1455, probably through the combined efforts of three men—Johann Gutenberg, Johann Fust, and Peter Schöffer, all experimenting at Mainz—movable type came into being. The mirror image of each letter (rather than entire words or phrases) was carved in relief on a small block. Individual letters, easily movable, were put together to form words; words separated by blank spaces formed lines of type; and lines of type were brought together to make up a page. Since letters could be arranged into any format, an infinite variety of texts could be printed by reusing and rearranging pieces of type.

By the middle of the fifteenth century, paper was no problem. The knowledge of paper manufacture had originated in China, and the Arabs introduced it to the West in the twelfth century. Europeans quickly learned that durable paper was far less expensive than the vellum (calfskin) and parchment (sheepskin) on which medieval scribes had relied for centuries.

The effects of the invention of movable-type printing were not felt overnight. Nevertheless, within a half-century of the publication of Gutenberg's Bible of 1456, movable type brought about radical changes. Printing transformed both the private and the public lives of Europeans. Governments that "had employed the cumbersome methods of manuscripts to communicate with their subjects switched quickly to print to announce declarations of war, publish battle accounts, promulgate treaties or argue disputed points in pamphlet form. Theirs was an effort 'to win the psychological war.'" Printing made propaganda possible, emphasizing differences between opposing groups, such as Crown and nobility, church and state. These differences laid the basis for the formation of distinct political parties. Printed materials reached an invisible public, allowing silent individuals to join causes and groups of individuals widely separated by geography to form a common identity; this new group consciousness could compete with older, localized loyalties.

Printing also stimulated the literacy of lay people and eventually came to have a deep effect on their private lives. Although most of the earliest books and pamphlets dealt with religious subjects, students, housewives, businessmen, and upper- and middle-class people sought books on all subjects. Printers responded with moralizing, medical, practical, and travel manuals. Pornography as well as piety assumed new forms. Broadsides and flysheets allowed great public festivals, religious ceremonies, and political events to be experienced vicariously by the stay-at-home. Since books and other printed materials were read aloud to illiterate listeners, print bridged the gap between written and oral cultures.[18]

Women in Renaissance Society

During the Renaissance the status of upper-class women declined. If women in the High Middle Ages are compared with those of fifteenth- and sixteenth-century Italy with respect to the kind of work they performed, their access to property and political power, and their role in shaping the outlook of their society, it is clear that ladies in the Renaissance ruling classes generally had less power than comparable ladies in the feudal age.

In the cities of Renaissance Italy, girls received an education similar to boys'. Young ladies learned their letters and studied the classics. Many read Greek as well as Latin, knew the poetry of Ovid and Virgil, and could speak one or two "modern" languages, such as French or Spanish. In this respect, Renaissance humanism represented a real educational advance for women. Some women, though a small minority among humanists, acquired great learning and achieved fame in typically humanist genres—letters, orations, treatises, and poems.

Laura Cereta (1469–1499) illustrates the successes and failures of educated Renaissance women. Educated by her father, who was a member of the governing elite of Brescia in Lombardy, she learned languages, philosophy, theology, and mathematics. She also gained self-confidence and a healthy respect for her own potential. By the age of fifteen, when she married, her literary career was already launched, as her letters to several cardinals attest. For Laura Cereta, however, as for all educated women of the period, the question of marriage forced the issue: she could choose a husband, family, and full participation in social life, or else study and withdrawal from the world. Marriage brought domestic responsibilities and usually prevented women from fulfilling their scholarly potential. Although Laura chose marriage, she was widowed at eighteen, and she spent the remaining twelve years of her life in study. But she had to bear the envy of other women and the hostility of men who felt threatened. In response, Laura condemned "empty women, who strive for no good but exist to adorn themselves . . .'these women of majestic pride, fantastic coiffures, outlandish ornament, and necks bound with gold or pearls [which] bear the glittering symbols of their captivity to men." For Laura Cereta, women's inferiority was derived not from the divine order of things but from women themselves: "For knowledge is not given as a gift, but through study. . . . The free mind, not afraid of labor, presses on to attain the good."[19] Despite Laura's faith in women's potential, men frequently believed that a woman in becoming learned violated nature and thus ceased to be a woman. Brilliant women such as Laura Cereta were severely attacked by men who feared threats to male dominance in the intellectual realm.

Laura Cereta was a prodigy. Ordinary girls of the urban upper middle class, in addition to a classical education, received some training in painting, music, and dance. What were they to do with this training? They were to be gracious, affable, charming—in short, decorative. Renaissance women were better educated than their medieval counterparts. But whereas education trained a young man to rule and to participate in the public affairs of the city, it prepared a woman for the social functions of the home. An educated lady was supposed to know how to attract artists and literati to her husband's court and how to grace her husband's household.

Whatever the practical reality, a striking difference also exists between the medieval literature of courtly love, the etiquette books and romances, and the widely studied Renaissance manual on courtesy and good behavior, Castiglione's *The Courtier*. In the medieval books, manners shaped the man to please the lady; in *The Courtier* the lady was to make herself pleasing to the man. With respect to love and sex, the Renaissance witnessed a downward shift in women's status. In contrast to the medieval tradition of relative sexual equality, Renaissance humanists laid the foundations for the bourgeois double standard. Men, and men alone, operated in the public sphere; women belonged in the home. Castiglione, the foremost spokesman of Renaissance love and manners, completely separated love from sexuality. For women, sex was restricted entirely to marriage. Ladies were bound to chastity, to the roles of wife and mother in a politically arranged marriage. Men, however, could pursue sensual indulgence outside marriage.[20]

Official attitudes toward rape provide another index of the status of women in the Renaissance. A careful study of the legal evidence from Venice in the years 1338 to 1358 is informative. The Venetian shipping and merchant elite held economic and political power and made the laws. Those laws reveal that rape was not considered a particularly serious crime against either the victim or society. Noble youths committed a higher percentage of rapes than their small numbers in Venetian society would imply, despite government-regulated prostitution. The rape of a young girl of marriageable age or a child under twelve was considered a graver crime than the rape of a married woman. Still, the punishment for rape of a noble, marriageable girl was only a fine or about six months' imprisonment. In an age when theft and robbery were punished by mutilation, and forgery and sodomy by burning, this penalty was very mild indeed. When a youth of the upper class was convicted of the rape of a non-noble girl, his punishment was even lighter. By contrast, the sexual assault on a noblewoman by a man of working-class origin, which was extraordinarily rare, resulted in severe penalization because the crime had social and political overtones.

Sofonisba Anguissola: The Artist's Sister Minerva A nobleman's daughter and one of the first Italian women to become a recognized artist, Sofonisba did portraits of her five sisters and of prominent people. The coiffure, elegant gown, necklaces, and rings depict aristocratic dress in the mid-sixteenth century. *(Source: Milwaukee Art Museum, Gift of the Family of Fred Vogel, Jr.)*

In the eleventh century, William the Conqueror had decreed that rapists be castrated, implicitly according women protection and a modicum of respect. But in the early Renaissance, Venetian laws and their enforcement show that the governing oligarchy believed that rape damaged, but only slightly, men's property—women.[21]

Evidence from Florence in the fifteenth century also sheds light on infanticide, which historians are only now beginning to study in the Middle Ages and the Renaissance. Early medieval penitentials and church councils had legislated against abortion and infanticide, though it is known that Pope Innocent III (1198–1216) was moved to establish an orphanage "because so many women were throwing their children into the Tiber."[22] In the fourteenth and early fifteenth centuries, a considerable number of children died in Florence under suspicious circumstances. Some were simply abandoned outdoors. Some were said to have been crushed to death while sleeping in the same bed with their parents. Some died from "crib death" or suffocation. These deaths occurred too frequently to have all been accidental. And far more girls than boys died thus, reflecting societal discrimination against girl children as inferior and less useful than boys. The dire poverty of parents led them to do away with unwanted children.

The gravity of the problem of infanticide, which violated both the canon law of the church and the civil law of the state, forced the Florentine government to build the Foundling Hospital. Supporters of the institution maintained that, without public responsibility, "many children would soon be found dead in the rivers, sewers, and ditches, unbaptized."[23] The large size of the hospital suggests that great numbers of children were abandoned.

Blacks in Renaissance Society

Ever since the time of the Roman republic, a few black people had lived in western Europe. They had come, along with white slaves, as the spoils of war. Even after the collapse of the Roman Empire, Muslim and Christian merchants continued to import them. The evidence of medieval art attests to the presence of Africans in the West and Europeans' awareness of them. In the twelfth and thirteenth centuries, a large cult surrounded Saint Maurice, martyred in the fourth century for refusing to renounce his Christian faith, who was portrayed as a black knight. Saint Maurice received the special veneration of the nobility. The numbers of blacks, though, had always been small.

Beginning in the fifteenth century, however, hordes of black slaves entered Europe. Portuguese explorers imported perhaps a thousand a year and sold them at the markets of Seville, Barcelona, Marseilles, and Genoa. By the mid-sixteenth century, blacks, slave and free, constituted about 10 percent of the populations of the Portuguese cities of Lisbon and Évora; other cities had smaller percentages. In all, blacks made up roughly 3 percent of the Portuguese population. The Venetians specialized in the import of white slaves, but blacks were so greatly in demand at the Renaissance courts of northern Italy that the Venetians defied papal threats of excommunication to secure them. What roles did blacks play in Renaissance society? What image did Europeans have of Africans?

The medieval interest in curiosities, the exotic, and the marvelous continued into the Renaissance. Because of their rarity, black servants were highly prized and much sought after. In the late fifteenth century, Isabella, the wife of Gian Galazzo Sforza, took pride in the fact that she had ten blacks, seven of them females; a black lady's-maid was both a curiosity and a symbol of wealth. In 1491 Isabella of Este, duchess of Mantua, instructed her agent to secure a black girl between four and eight years old, "shapely and as black as possible." The duchess saw the child as a source of entertainment: "we shall make her very happy and shall have great fun with her." She hoped that the little girl would become "the best buffoon in the world."[24] The cruel ancient tradition of a noble household retaining a professional "fool" for the family's amusement persisted through the Renaissance—and even down to the twentieth century.

Adult black slaves filled a variety of positions. Many served as maids, valets, and domestic servants. Italian aristocrats such as the marchesa Elena Grimaldi had their portraits painted with their black page boys to indicate their wealth. The Venetians employed blacks—slave and free—as gondoliers and stevedores on the docks. In Portugal, kings, nobles, laborers, religious institutions such as monasteries and convents, and prostitutes owned slaves. They supplemented the labor force in virtually all occupations—as agricultural laborers, craftsmen, herdsmen, grape pickers, in the manufacture of olive oil, and as seamen on ships going to Lisbon and Africa.[25] Tradition, stretching back at least as far as the thirteenth century, connected blacks with music and dance. In Renaissance Spain and Italy, blacks performed as dancers, as actors and actresses in courtly dramas, and as musicians, sometimes comprising full orchestras.[26] Slavery during the Renaissance foreshadowed the American, especially the later Brazilian, pattern.

Before the sixteenth-century "discoveries" of the non-European world, Europeans had little concrete knowledge of Africans and their cultures. Europeans knew little about them beyond biblical accounts. The European attitude toward Africans was ambivalent. On the one hand, Europeans perceived Africa as a remote place, the home of strange people isolated by heresy and Islam from superior European civilization. Africans' contact even as slaves with Christian Europeans could only "improve" the blacks. Most Europeans' knowledge of the black as a racial type was based entirely on theological speculation. Theologians taught that God was light. Blackness, the opposite of light, therefore represented the hostile forces of the underworld: evil, sin, and the devil. Thus the devil was commonly represented as a black man in medieval and early Renaissance art. Blackness, however, also possessed certain positive qualities. It symbolized the emptiness of worldly goods, the humility of the monastic way of life. Black clothes permitted a conservative and discreet display of wealth. Black vestments and funeral trappings indicated grief, and Christ had said that those who mourn are blessed. Until the exploration and observation of the sixteenth, seventeenth, and nineteenth centuries allowed, ever so slowly, for the development of more scientific knowledge, the Western conception of black people remained bound up with religious notions.[27] In Renaissance society, blacks, like women, were signs of wealth; both were used for display.

Baldung: Adoration of the Magi   Early sixteenth-century German artists produced thousands of adoration scenes depicting a black man as one of the three kings: these paintings were based on direct observation, reflecting the increased presence of blacks in Europe. The elaborate costumes, jewelry, and landscape expressed royal dignity, Christian devotion, and oriental luxury. *(Source: Gemäldegalerie, Staatliche Museen Preussischer Kulturbesitz, Berlin)*

THE RENAISSANCE IN THE NORTH

In the last quarter of the fifteenth century, Italian Renaissance thought and ideals penetrated northern Europe. Students from the Low Countries, France, Germany, and England flocked to Italy, imbibed the "new learning," and carried it back to their countries. Northern humanists interpreted Italian ideas about and attitudes toward classical antiquity, individualism, and humanism in terms of their own traditions. The cultural traditions of northern Europe tended to remain more distinctly Christian, or at least pietistic, than those of Italy. Italian humanists certainly were strongly Christian, as the example of Pico della Mirandola shows. But in Italy secular and pagan themes and Greco-Roman motifs received more humanistic attention. North of the Alps, the Renaissance had a distinctly religious character, and humanists stressed biblical and early Christian themes. What fundamentally distinguished Italian humanists from northern ones is that the latter had a program for broad social reform based on Christian ideals.

Christian humanists were interested in the development of an ethical way of life. To achieve it, they believed that the best elements of classical and Christian cultures should be combined. For example, the classical ideals of calmness, stoical patience, and broad-mindedness should be joined in human conduct with the Christian virtues of love, faith, and hope. Northern humanists also stressed the use of reason, rather than acceptance of dogma, as the foundation for an ethical way of life. Like the Italians, they were impatient with Scholastic philosophy. Christian humanists had a profound faith in the power of human intellect to bring about moral and institutional reform. They believed that, although human nature had been corrupted by sin, it was fundamentally good and capable of improvement through education, which would lead to piety and an ethical way of life.

The work of the French priest Jacques Lefèvre d'Étaples (ca 1455–1536) is one of the early attempts to apply humanistic learning to religious problems. A brilliant thinker and able scholar, he believed that more accurate texts of the Bible would lead people to live better lives. According to Lefèvre, a solid education in the Scriptures would increase piety and raise the level of behavior in Christian society. Lefèvre produced an edition of the Psalms and a commentary on Saint Paul's Epistles. In 1516, when Martin Luther lectured to his students at Wittenberg on Paul's Letter to the Romans, he relied on Lefèvre's texts.

The Englishman Thomas More (1478–1535) towers above other figures in sixteenth-century English social and intellectual history. More's political stance later, at the time of the Reformation (see page 442), a position that in part flowed from his humanist beliefs, cost him his life and has tended to obscure his contribution to Christian humanism.

The early career of Thomas More presents a number of paradoxes that reveal the marvelous complexity of the man. Trained as a lawyer, More lived as a student in the London Charterhouse, a Carthusian monastery. He subsequently married and practiced law, but became deeply interested in the classics; his household served as a model of warm Christian family life and as a mecca for foreign and English humanists. In the career pattern of such Italian humanists as Petrarch, he entered government service under Henry VIII and was sent as ambassador to Flanders. There More found the time to write *Utopia* (1516), which presented a revolutionary view of society.

Utopia, which literally means "nowhere," describes an ideal socialistic community on an island somewhere off the mainland of the New World. All its children receive a good education, primarily in the Greco-Roman classics, and learning does not cease with maturity, for the goal of all education is to develop rational faculties. Adults divide their days equally between manual labor or business pursuits and various intellectual activities.

Because the profits from business and property are held strictly in common, there is absolute social equality. The Utopians use gold and silver both to make chamber pots and to prevent wars by buying off their enemies. By this casual use of precious metals, More meant to suggest that the basic problems in society were caused by greed. Utopian law exalts mercy above justice. Citizens of Utopia lead an ideal, nearly perfect existence because they live by reason; their institutions are perfect. More punned on the word *Utopia,* which he termed "a good place. A good place which is no place."

More's ideas were profoundly original in the sixteenth century. Contrary to the long-prevailing view that vice and violence exist because women and men are basically corrupt, More maintained that acquisitiveness and private property promoted all sorts of vices and civil disorders. Since society protected private property, *society's* flawed institutions were responsible for corruption and war. Today people take this view so much for granted that it is difficult to appreciate how radical it was in the sixteenth century. According to More, the key to improvement and reform of the individual was reform of the social institutions that mold the individual.

Better known by contemporaries than Thomas More was the Dutch humanist Desiderius Erasmus of Rotterdam (1466?–1536). Orphaned as a small boy, Erasmus was forced to enter a monastery. Although he intensely disliked the monastic life, he developed there an excellent knowledge of the Latin language and a deep appreciation for the

Latin classics. During a visit to England in 1499, Erasmus met John Colet, who decisively influenced his life's work: the application of the best humanistic learning to the study and explanation of the Bible. As a mature scholar with an international reputation stretching from Cracow to London, a fame that rested largely on his exceptional knowledge of Greek, Erasmus could boast with truth, "I brought it about that humanism, which among the Italians . . . savored of nothing but pure paganism, began nobly to celebrate Christ."[28]

Erasmus's long list of publications includes *The Adages* (1500), a list of Greek and Latin precepts on ethical behavior; *The Education of a Christian Prince* (1504), which combines idealistic and practical suggestions for the formation of a ruler's character through the careful study of Plutarch, Aristotle, Cicero, and Plato; *The Praise of Folly* (1509), a satire of worldly wisdom and a plea for the simple and spontaneous Christian faith of children; and, most important of all, a critical edition of the Greek New Testament (1516). In the preface to the New Testament, Erasmus explained the purpose of his great work:

Only bring a pious and open heart, imbued above all things with a pure and simple faith. . . . For I utterly dissent from those who are unwilling that the sacred Scriptures should be read by the unlearned translated into their vulgar tongue, as though Christ had taught such subtleties that they can scarcely be understood even by a few theologians. . . . Christ wished his mysteries to be published as openly as possible. I wish that even the weakest woman should read the Gospel—should read the epistles of Paul. And I wish these were translated into all languages, so that they might be read and understood, not only by Scots and Irishmen, but also by Turks and Saracens. . . . Why do we prefer to study the wisdom of Christ in men's writings rather than in the writing of Christ himself?[29]

Two fundamental themes run through all of Erasmus's scholarly work. First, education was the means to reform, the key to moral and intellectual improvement. The core of education ought to be study of the Bible and the classics. Second, the essence of Erasmus's thought is, in his own phrase, "the philosophy of Christ." By this Erasmus meant that Christianity is an inner attitude of the heart or spirit. Christianity is not formalism, special ceremonies, or law; Christianity is Christ—his life and what he said and did, not what theologians have

written. The Sermon on the Mount, for Erasmus, expressed the heart of the Christian message.

While the writings of Colet, Erasmus, and More have strong Christian themes and have drawn the attention primarily of scholars, the stories of the French humanist François Rabelais (1490?–1553) possess a distinctly secular flavor and have attracted broad readership among the literate public. Rabelais's *Gargantua* and *Pantagruel* (serialized between 1532 and 1552) belong among the great comic masterpieces of world literature. These stories' gross and robust humor introduced the adjective *Rabelaisian* into the language.

Gargantua and *Pantagruel* can be read on several levels: as comic romances about the adventures of the giant Gargantua and his son, Pantagruel; as a spoof on contemporary French society; as a program for educational reform; or as illustrations of Rabelais's prodigious learning. The reader enters a world of Renaissance vitality, ribald joviality, and intellectual curiosity. On his travels Gargantua meets various absurd characters, and within their hilarious exchanges there occur serious discussions on religion, politics, philosophy, and education. Rabelais had received an excellent humanistic education in a monastery, and Gargantua discusses the disorders of contemporary religious and secular life. Like More and Erasmus, Rabelais did not denounce institutions directly. Like Erasmus, Rabelais satirized hypocritical monks, pedantic academics, and pompous lawyers. But where Erasmus employed intellectual cleverness and sophisticated wit, Rabelais applied wild and gross humor. Like Thomas More, Rabelais believed that institutions molded individuals and that education was the key to a moral and healthy life. While the middle-class inhabitants of More's Utopia lived lives of restrained moderation, the aristocratic residents of Rabelais's Thélèma lived for the full gratification of their physical instincts and rational curiosity.

Thélèma, the abbey Gargantua establishes, parodies traditional religion and other social institutions. Thélèma, whose motto is "Do as Thou Wilt," admits women *and* men; allows all to eat, drink, sleep, and work when they choose; provides excellent facilities for swimming, tennis, and football; and encourages sexual experimentation and marriage. Rabelais believed profoundly in the basic goodness of human beings and the rightness of instinct.

The most roguishly entertaining Renaissance writer, Rabelais was convinced that "laughter is the

Jan van Eyck: Madonna of Chancellor Rodin The tough and shrewd chancellor who ordered this rich painting visits the Virgin and Christ-Child (though they seem to be visiting him). An angel holds the crown of heaven over the Virgin's head while Jesus, the proclaimed savior of the world, holds it in his left hand and raises his right hand in blessing. Through the colonnade, sculpted with scenes from Genesis, is the city of Bruges. Van Eyck's achievement in portraiture is extraordinary; his treatment of space and figures and his ability to capture the infinitely small and very large prompted the art historian Erwin Panofsky to write that "his eye was at one and the same time a microscope and a telescope." (Source: Louvre/Cliché des Musées Nationaux, Paris)

essence of manhood." A convinced believer in the Roman Catholic faith, he included in Gargantua's education an appreciation for simple and reasonable prayer. Rabelais combined the Renaissance zest for life and enjoyment of pleasure with a classical insistence on the cultivation of the body and the mind.

The distinctly religious orientation of the literary works of the Renaissance in the north also characterized northern art and architecture. Some Flemish painters, notably Jan van Eyck (1366–1441), were the equals of Italian painters. One of the earliest artists successfully to use oil-based paints, van

Eyck, in paintings such as *Ghent Altarpiece* and the portrait of *Giovanni Arnolfini and His Bride,* shows the Flemish love for detail; the effect is great realism and remarkable attention to human personality.

Another Flemish painter, Hieronymous Bosch (ca 1450–1516), frequently used religious themes, but in combination with grotesque fantasies, colorful imagery, and peasant folk legends. Many of Bosch's paintings reflect the confusion and anguish often associated with the end of the Middle Ages. In *Death and the Miser,* Bosch's dramatic treatment of the Dance of Death theme, the miser's gold, increased by usury, is ultimately controlled by diabolical rats and toads, while his guardian angel urges him to choose the crucifix.

A quasi-spiritual aura likewise infuses architectural monuments in the north. The city halls of wealthy Flemish towns such as Bruges, Brussels, Louvain, and Ghent strike the viewer more as shrines to house the bones of saints than as settings for the mundane decisions of politicians and business people. Northern architecture was little influenced by the classical revival so obvious in Renaissance Rome and Florence.

POLITICS AND THE STATE IN THE RENAISSANCE (ca 1450–1521)

The High Middle Ages had witnessed the origins of many of the basic institutions of the modern state. Sheriffs, inquests, juries, circuit judges, professional bureaucracies, and representative assemblies all trace their origins to the twelfth and thirteenth centuries (see page 312). The linchpin for the development of states, however, was strong monarchy, and during the period of the Hundred Years' War, no ruler in western Europe was able to provide effective leadership. The resurgent power of feudal nobilities weakened the centralizing work begun earlier.

Beginning in the fifteenth century, rulers utilized the aggressive methods implied by Renaissance political ideas to rebuild their governments. First in Italy, then in France, England, and Spain, rulers began the work of reducing violence, curbing unruly nobles and troublesome elements, and establishing domestic order. Within the Holy Roman Empire of Germany, the lack of centralization helps to account for the later German distrust of the Roman papacy. Divided into scores of independent principalities, Germany could not deal with the Roman church as an equal.

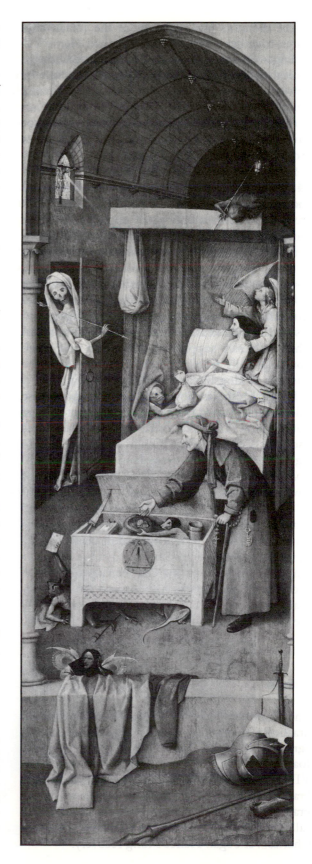

Jerome Bosch: Death and the Miser Netherlandish painters frequently used symbolism, and Bosch (ca 1450–1516) is considered the master artist of symbolism and fantasy. Here rats, which because of their destructiveness symbolize evil, control the miser's gold. Bosch's imagery appealed strongly to twentieth-century surrealist painters. (Source: National Gallery of Art, Washington, D.C., Samuel H. Kress Collection)

NOTES

1. See L. Martines, *Power and Imagination: City-States in Renaissance Italy* (New York: Vintage Books, 1980), esp. pp. 332–333.
2. Ibid., pp. 22–61.
3. Ibid., pp. 221–237, esp. p. 221.
4. Quoted in J. Burckhardt, *The Civilization of the Renaissance in Italy* (London: Phaidon Books, 1951), p. 89.
5. *Memoirs of Benvenuto Cellini; A Florentine Artist; Written by Himself* (London: J. M. Dent & Sons, 1927), p. 2.
6. Quoted in Burckhardt, p. 111.
7. See C. Trinkaus, *In Our Image and Likeness: Humanity and Divinity in Italian Humanist Thought,* vol. 2 (London: Constable, 1970), pp. 505–529.
8. B. Burroughs, ed., *Vasari's Lives of the Artists* (New York: Simon & Schuster, 1946), pp. 164–165.
9. See Martines, chap. 13, esp. pp. 241, 243.
10. See A. Hauser, *The Social History of Art,* vol. 2 (New York: Vintage Books, 1959), chap. 3, esp. pp. 60, 68.
11. G. Bull, trans., *Aretino: Selected Letters* (Baltimore: Penguin Books, 1976), p. 109.
12. Quoted in P. and L. Murray, *A Dictionary of Art and Artists* (Baltimore: Penguin Books, 1963), p. 125.
13. Hauser, pp. 48–49.
14. Quoted in W. H. Woodward, *Vittorino da Feltre and Other Humanist Educators* (Cambridge: Cambridge University Press, 1897), pp. 96–97.
15. C. E. Detmold, trans., *The Historical, Political and Diplomatic Writings of Niccolo Machiavelli* (Boston: J. R. Osgood, 1882), pp. 51–52.
16. Ibid., pp. 54–55.
17. See F. Gilbert, *Machiavelli and Guicciardini: Politics and History in Sixteenth Century Florence* (New York: W. W. Norton, 1984), pp. 197–200.
18. Quoted in E. L. Eisenstein, *The Printing Press as an Agent of Change: Communications and Cultural Transformations in Early Modern Europe,* vol. 1 (New York: Cambridge University Press, 1979), p. 135; for an overall discussion, see pp. 126–159.
19. M. L. King, "Book-lined Cells: Women and Humanism in the Early Italian Renaissance," in *Beyond Their Sex: Learned Women of the European Past,* ed. P. H. Labalme (New York: New York University Press, 1980), pp. 66–81, esp. p. 73.
20. This account rests on J. Kelly-Gadol, "Did Women Have a Renaissance?" in *Becoming Visible: Women in European History,* ed. R. Bridenthal and C. Koontz (Boston: Houghton Mifflin, 1977), pp. 137–161, esp. p. 161.
21. G. Ruggerio, "Sexual Criminality in Early Renaissance Venice, 1338–1358," *Journal of Social History* 8 (Spring 1975): 18–31.
22. Quoted in R. C. Trexler, "Infanticide in Florence: New Sources and First Results," *History of Childhood Quarterly* 1 (Summer 1973): 99.
23. Ibid., p. 100.
24. J. Devisse and M. Mollat, *The Image of the Black in Western Art,* trans. W. G. Ryan, vol. 2 (New York: William Morrow, 1979), pt. 2, pp. 187–188.
25. See A. C. DE. C. M. Saunders, *A Social History of Black Slaves and Freedmen in Portugal, 1441–1555* (New York: Cambridge University Press, 1982), pp. 59, 62–88, 176–179.
26. Ibid., pp. 190–194.
27. Ibid., pp. 255–258.
28. Quoted in E. H. Harbison, *The Christian Scholar and His Calling in the Age of the Reformation* (New York: Charles Scribner's Sons, 1956), p. 109.
29. Quoted in F. Seebohm, *The Oxford Reformers* (London: J. M. Dent & Sons, 1867), p. 256.
30. See J. H. Elliott, *Imperial Spain, 1469–1716* (New York: Mentor Books, 1963), esp. pp. 75, 97–108.

SUGGESTED READING

There are scores of exciting studies available on virtually all aspects of the Renaissance. In addition to the titles given in the Notes, the curious student interested in a broad synthesis should see J. H. Plumb, *The Italian Renaissance* (1965), a superbly written book based on deep knowledge and understanding; this book is probably the best starting point. J. R. Hale, *Renaissance Europe: The Individual and Society, 1480–1520* (1978), is an excellent treatment of individualism by a distinguished authority. J. R. Hale, ed., *A Concise Encyclopaedia of the Italian Renaissance* (1981), is a useful reference tool. F. H. New, *The Renaissance and Reformation: A Short History* (1977), gives a concise balanced account. For Renaissance humanism and education, see P. F. Grendler, *Schooling in Renaissance Italy: Literacy and Learning, 1300–1600* (1989); J. H. Moran, *The Growth of English Schooling, 1340–1548: Learning, Literacy, and Laicization in Pre-Reformation York Diocese* (1985); and J. F. D'Amico, *Renaissance Humanism in Papal Rome: Humanists and Churchmen on the Eve of the Reformation* (1983), which are all highly readable works of outstanding scholarship. The older study of M. P. Gilmore, *The World of Humanism* (1962), has not been superseded on many subjects. For the city where much of it originated, G. A. Brucker, *Renaissance Florence* (1969), gives a good description of Florentine economic, political, social, and cultural history. Learned, provocative, beautifully written, and the work on which this chapter leans heavily, L. Martines, *Power and Imagination: City-States in Renaissance Italy* (1980), is probably the best broad appreciation of the period produced in several decades.

J. R. Hale, *Machiavelli and Renaissance Italy* (1966), is a sound short biography, but advanced students may want to consult the sophisticated intellectual biography of S. de Grazia, *Machiavelli in Hell* (1989), which is based on Machiavelli's literary as well as political writing. F. Gilbert, *Machiavelli and Guicciardini,* mentioned in the Notes, places the two thinkers in their intellectual and social context. C. Singleton, trans., *The Courtier* (1959), presents an excellent picture of Renaissance court life.

The best introduction to the Renaissance in northern Europe and a book that has greatly influenced twentieth-century scholarship is J. Huizinga, *The Waning of the Middle Ages: A Study of the Forms of Life, Thought, and Art in France and the Netherlands in the Dawn of the Renaissance* (1954). This book challenges the whole idea of a Renaissance. L. Febvre, *Life in Renaissance France* (trans. and ed. M. Rothstein, 1977), is a brilliant evocation of French Renaissance civilization by an international authority. The leading northern humanist is sensitively treated in M. M. Phillips, *Erasmus and the Northern Renaissance* (1956), and J. Huizinga, *Erasmus of Rotterdam* (1952). R. Marius, *Thomas More: A Biography* (1984), is an original study of the great English humanist and statesman, but the student may also want to consult E. E. Reynolds, *Thomas More* (1962), and R. W. Chambers, *Thomas More* (1935). J. Leclercq, trans., *The Complete Works of Rabelais* (1963), is easily available.

The following titles should prove useful for various aspects of Renaissance social history: E. L. Eisenstein, *The Printing Press as an Agent of Change: Communications and Cultural Transformations in Early Modern Europe,* 2 vols. (1979), a fundamental work; G. Ruggerio, *Violence in Early Renaissance Venice* (1980), a pioneering study of crime and punishment in a stable society; D. Weinstein and R. M. Bell, *Saints and Society: The Two Worlds of Christendom, 1000–1700* (1982), an essential book for an understanding of the perception of holiness and of the social origins of saints in early modern Europe; J. C. Brown, *Immodest Acts: The Life of a Lesbian Nun in Renaissance Italy* (1985), which is helpful for an understanding of the role and status of women; and I. Maclean, *The Renaissance Notion of Women* (1980). The student who wishes to study blacks in medieval and early modern European society should see the rich and original achievement of J. Devisse and M. Mollat, *The Image of the Black in Western Art,* cited in the Notes.

Renaissance art has understandably inspired vast researches. In addition to Vasari's volume of biographical sketches on the great masters referred to in the Notes, A.

Martindale, *The Rise of the Artist in the Middle Ages and Early Renaissance* (1972), is a splendidly illustrated introduction. B. Berenson, *Italian Painters of the Renaissance* (1957), the work of an American expatriate who was an internationally famous art historian, has become a classic. W. Sypher, *Four Stages of Renaissance Style* (1956), relates drama and poetry to the visual arts of painting and sculpture. One of the finest appreciations of Renaissance art, written by one of the greatest art historians of this century, is E. Panofsky, *Meaning in the Visual Arts* (1955). Both Italian and northern painting are treated in the brilliant study of M. Meiss, *The Painter's Choice: Problems in the Interpretation of Renaissance Art* (1976), a collection of essays dealing with Renaissance style, form, and meaning. The beautifully illustrated work of M. McCarthy, *The Stones of Florence* (1959), celebrates the energy and creativity of the greatest Renaissance city. L. Steinberg, *The Sexuality of Christ in Renaissance Art and in Modern Oblivion* (1983), is a brilliant work that relates Christ's sexuality to incarnational theology. J. M. Saslow, *Ganymede in the Renaissance* (1986), which uses images of Ganymede as a metaphor for emotional and sexual relations between men and youths, provides information on social attitudes toward homosexuality in this period. R. Jones and N. Penny, *Raphael* (1983), celebrates the achievements of that great master.

Students interested in the city of Rome might consult P. Partner, *Renaissance Rome, 1500–1559: A Portrait of a Society* (1979), and the elegantly illustrated study of C. Hibbert, *Rome: The Biography of a City* (1985). Da Vinci's scientific and naturalist ideas and drawings are available in I. A. Richter, ed., *The Notebooks of Leonardo da Vinci* (1985). The magisterial achievement of J. Pope-Hennessy, *Cellini* (1985), is a superb evocation of that artist's life and work.

The following works not only are useful for the political and economic history of the Renaissance but also contain valuable bibliographical information: A. J. Slavin, ed., *The "New Monarchies" and Representative Assemblies* (1965), a collection of interpretations, and R. Lockyer, *Henry VII* (1972), a biography with documents illustrative of the king's reign. For Spain, see M. Defourneaux, *Daily Life in Spain in the Golden Age* (1970); B. Bennasar, *The Spanish Character: Attitudes and Mentalities from the Sixteenth to the Nineteenth Century* (trans. B. Keen, 1979); J. H. Elliott, *Imperial Spain: 1469–1716* (1966); and H. Kamen, *The Spanish Inquisition* (1965). For the Florentine business classes, see I. Origo, *The Merchant of Prato* (1957); G. Brucker, *Two Memoirs of Renaissance Florence: The Diaries of Buonaccorso Pitti and Gregorio Dati* (trans. J. Martines, 1967); and Paul Grendler ed., *An Italian Renaissance Reader* (1987).

14

Reform and Renewal in the Christian Church

The idea of reform is as old as Christianity itself. In his letter to the Christians at Rome, Saint Paul exhorted: "Do not model yourselves on the behavior of the world around you, but let your behavior change, reformed by your new mind. That is the only way to discover the will of God and know what is good, what it is that God wants, what is the perfect thing to do."[1] In the early fifth century, Saint Augustine of Hippo, describing the final stage of world history, wrote, "In the sixth age of the world our reformation becomes manifest, in newness of mind, according to the image of Him who created us." In the middle of the twelfth century, Saint Bernard of Clairvaux complained about the church of his day: "There is as much difference between us and the men of the primitive Church as there is between muck and gold."

The need for reform of the individual Christian and of the institutional church is central to the Christian faith. The Christian humanists of the late fifteenth and early sixteenth centuries—More, Erasmus, Colet, and Lefèvre d'Etaples—urged reform of the church on the pattern of the early church, primarily through educational and social change. Men and women of every period believed the early Christian church represented a golden age, and critics in every period called for reform.

Sixteenth-century cries for reformation, therefore, were hardly new. In fact, many scholars today interpret the sixteenth-century Reformation against the background of reforming trends begun in the fifteenth century.

- What late medieval religious developments paved the way for the adoption and spread of Protestant thought?
- What role did political and social factors play in the several reformations?
- What were the consequences of religious division?
- How were Luther's religious ideas spread?
- Why did the theological ideas of Martin Luther trigger political, social, and economic reactions?
- What appeal had the Reformation for women?
- What response did the Catholic Church make to the movements for reform?

This chapter will explore these questions.

THE CONDITION OF THE CHURCH (ca 1400–1517)

The papal conflict with the German emperor Frederick II in the thirteenth century, followed by the Babylonian Captivity and then the Great Schism, badly damaged the prestige of church leaders. In the fourteenth and fifteenth centuries, leaders of the conciliar movement reflected educated public opinion when they called for the reform of the church "in head and members." The humanists of Italy and the Christian humanists of the north denounced corruption in the church. As Machiavelli put it, "We Italians are irreligious and corrupt above others, because the Church and her representatives set us the worst example."[2] In *The Praise of Folly,* Erasmus condemned the absurd superstitions of the parish clergy and the excessive rituals of the monks. The records of episcopal visitations of parishes, civil court records, and even such literary masterpieces as Chaucer's *Canterbury Tales* and Boccaccio's *Decameron* tend to confirm the sarcasms of the humanists.

Signs of Disorder

The religious life of most people in early sixteenth-century Europe took place at the village or local level. Any assessment of the moral condition of the parish clergy must take into account one fundamental fact: parish priests were peasants, and they were poor. All too frequently, the spiritual quality of their lives was not much better than that of the people to whom they ministered. The clergy identified religion with life; that is, they injected religious symbols and practices into everyday living. Some historians, therefore, have accused the clergy of vulgarizing religion. But if the level of belief and practice was vulgarized, still the lives of rural, isolated, and semipagan people were spiritualized.

In the early sixteenth century, critics of the church concentrated their attacks on three disorders: clerical immorality, clerical ignorance, and clerical pluralism, with the related problem of absenteeism. There was little pressure for doctrinal change; the emphasis was on moral and administrative reform.

Since the fourth century, church law had required that candidates for the priesthood accept absolute celibacy. It had always been difficult to enforce. Many priests, especially those ministering to country people, had concubines, and reports of neglect of the rule of celibacy were common. Immorality, of course, included more than sexual transgressions. Clerical drunkenness, gambling, and indulgence in fancy dress were frequent charges. There is no way of knowing how many priests were guilty of such behavior. But because such conduct was so much at odds with the church's rules and moral standards, it scandalized the educated faithful.

The bishops enforced regulations regarding the education of priests casually. As a result, standards for ordination were shockingly low. When Saint Antonio, archbishop of Florence, conducted a visitation of his metropolitan see in the late fifteenth century, he found churches and service books in a deplorable state and many priests barely able to read and write. The evidence points consistently to the low quality of the Italian clergy. In northern Europe—in England, for example—recent research shows an improvement in clerical educational standards in the early sixteenth century. Nevertheless, parish priests throughout Europe were not as educated as the educated laity. Predictably, Christian humanists, with their concern for learning, condemned the ignorance or low educational level of the clergy. Many priests could barely read and write, and critics laughed at the illiterate priest mumbling Latin words to the Mass that he could not understand.

Absenteeism and pluralism constituted the third major abuse. Many clerics, especially higher ecclesiastics, held several *benefices* (or offices) simultaneously but seldom visited their benefices, let alone performed the spiritual responsibilities those offices entailed. Instead, they collected revenues from all of them and paid a poor priest a fraction of the income to fulfill the spiritual duties of a particular local church.

Many Italian officials in the papal curia held benefices in England, Spain, and Germany. Revenues from those countries paid the Italian priests' salaries, provoking not only charges of absenteeism but nationalistic resentment. King Henry VIII's chancellor Thomas Wolsey was archbishop of York for fifteen years before he set foot in his diocese. The French king Louis XII's famous diplomat Antoine du Prat is perhaps the most notorious example of absenteeism: as archbishop of Sens, the first time he

entered his cathedral was in his own funeral procession. Critics condemned pluralism, absenteeism, and the way money seemed to change hands when a bishop entered into his office.

Although royal governments strengthened their positions and consolidated their territories in the fifteenth and sixteenth centuries, rulers lacked sufficient revenues to pay and reward able civil servants. The Christian church, with its dioceses and abbeys, possessed a large proportion of the wealth of the countries of Europe. What better way to reward government officials, who were usually clerics in any case, than with high church offices? After all, the practice was sanctioned by centuries of tradition. Thus in Spain, France, England, and the Holy Roman Empire—in fact, all over Europe—because church officials served their monarchs, those officials were allowed to govern the church. Churchmen served as royal councilors, diplomats, treasury officials, chancellors, viceroys, and judges. These positions had nothing whatsoever to do with spiritual matters. Bishops worked for their respective states as well as for the church, and they were paid by the church for their services to the state. It is astonishing that so many conscientiously tried to carry out their religious duties on top of their public burdens.

In most countries except England, members of the nobility occupied the highest church positions. The sixteenth century was definitely not a democratic age. The spectacle of proud, aristocratic prelates living in magnificent splendor contrasted very unfavorably with the simple fishermen who were Christ's disciples. Nor did the popes of the period 1450 to 1550 set much of an example. They lived like secular Renaissance princes. Pius II (1458–1464), although deeply learned and a tireless worker, enjoyed a reputation as a clever writer of love stories and Latin poetry. Sixtus IV (1471–1484) beautified the city of Rome, built the famous Sistine Chapel, and generously supported several artists. Innocent VIII (1484–1492) made the papal court a model of luxury and scandal. All three popes used papal power and wealth in order to advance the material interests of their own families.

The court of the Spanish pope Rodrigo Borgia, Alexander VI (1492–1503), who publicly acknowledged his mistress and children, reached new heights of impropriety. Because of the prevalence of intrigue, sexual promiscuity, and supposed poi-

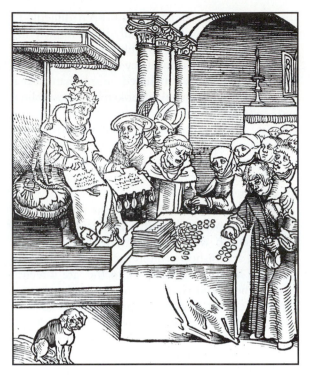

The Church Contrasted   Satirical woodcuts as well as the printed word attacked conditions in the church. Here the attitude of Christ toward money changers is contrasted with the mercenary spirit of the sixteenth-century papacy: Christ drove them from the temple, but the pope kept careful records of revenues owed to the church. *(Source: The Pierpont Morgan Library)*

sonings, the name Borgia became a synonym for moral corruption. Julius II (1503–1513), the nephew of Sixtus IV, donned military armor and personally led papal troops against the French invaders of Italy in 1506. After him, Giovanni de' Medici, the son of Lorenzo de' Medici, carried on as Pope Leo X (1513–1521) the Medicean tradition of being a great patron of the arts.

Signs of Vitality

Calls for reform testify to the spiritual vitality of the church as well as to its problems. In the late fifteenth and early sixteenth centuries, both individuals and groups within the church were working actively for reform. In Spain, for example, Cardinal Francisco Jiménez (1436–1517) visited religious houses, encouraged the monks and friars to keep their rules and constitutions, and set high standards for the training of the diocesan clergy.

In Holland, beginning in the late fourteenth century, a group of pious lay people called the "Brethren of the Common Life" lived in stark simplicity while daily carrying out the Gospel teaching of feeding the hungry, clothing the naked, and visiting the sick. The Brethren also taught in local schools with the goal of preparing devout candidates for the priesthood and the monastic life. Through prayer, meditation, and the careful study of Scripture, the Brethren sought to make religion a personal, inner experience. The spirituality of the Brethren of the Common Life found its finest expression in the classic *The Imitation of Christ* by Thomas à Kempis. Though written in Latin for monks and nuns, *The Imitation* gained wide appeal among lay people. It urges Christians to take Christ as their model and seek perfection in a simple way of life. Like later Protestants, the Brethren stressed the centrality of Scripture in the spiritual life.[3] In the mid-fifteenth century, the movement had founded houses in the Netherlands, in central Germany, and in the Rhineland; it was a true religious revival.

So, too, were the activities of the Oratories of Divine Love in Italy. The oratories were groups of priests living in communities who worked to revive the church through prayer and preaching. They did not withdraw from the world as medieval monks had done but devoted themselves to pastoral and charitable activities such as founding hospitals and orphanages. Oratorians served God in an active ministry.

If external religious observances are a measure of depth of heartfelt conviction, Europeans in the early sixteenth century remained deeply pious and loyal to the Roman Catholic church. Villagers participated in processions honoring the local saints. Middle-class people made pilgrimages to the great shrines, such as Saint Peter's in Rome. The upper classes continued to remember the church in their wills. In England, for example, between 1480 and 1490 almost £30,000, a prodigious sum in those days, was bequeathed to religious foundations. People of all social classes devoted an enormous amount of their time and income to religious causes and foundations.

The papacy also expressed concern for reform. Pope Julius II summoned an ecumenical (universal) council, which met in the church of Saint John Lateran in Rome from 1512 to 1517. Since most of the bishops were Italian and did not represent a broad cross section of international opinion, the term *ecumenical* is not really appropriate. Nevertheless, the bishops and theologians present strove earnestly to reform the church. The council recommended higher standards for education of the clergy and instruction of the common people. The bishops placed the responsibility for eliminating bureaucratic corruption squarely on the papacy and suggested significant doctrinal reforms. But many obstacles stood in the way of ecclesiastical change. Nor did the actions of an obscure German friar immediately force the issue.

MARTIN LUTHER AND THE BIRTH OF PROTESTANTISM

As the result of a personal religious struggle, a German Augustinian friar, Martin Luther (1483–1546), launched the Protestant Reformation of the sixteenth century. Luther was not a typical person of his time; miners' sons who become professors of theology are never typical. But Luther is representative of his time in the sense that he articulated the widespread desire for reform of the Christian church and a deep yearning for salvation. In the sense that concern for salvation was an important motivating force for Luther and other reformers, the sixteenth-century Reformation was in part a continuation of the medieval religious search.

Luther's Early Years

Martin Luther was born at Eisleben in Saxony, the second son of a copper miner and, later, mine owner. At considerable sacrifice, his father sent him to school and then to the University of Erfurt, where Martin earned a master's degree with distinction at the young age of twenty-one. Hans Luther intended his son to proceed to the study of law and a legal career, which for centuries had been the steppingstone to public office and material success. Badly frightened during a thunderstorm, however, Martin Luther vowed to become a friar. Without consulting his father, he entered the monastery of the Augustinian friars at Erfurt in 1505. Luther was ordained a priest in 1507 and after additional study earned the doctorate of theology. From 1512 until his death in 1546, he served as professor of Scripture at the new University of Wittenberg.

Martin Luther was exceedingly scrupulous in his monastic observances and devoted to prayer, penances, and fasting; nevertheless, the young friar's conscience troubled him constantly. The doubts and conflicts felt by any sensitive young person who has just taken a grave step were especially intense in young Luther. He had terrible anxieties about sin and worried continually about his salvation. Luther intensified his monastic observances but still found no peace of mind.

A psychological interpretation of Luther's early life suggests that he underwent a severe inner crisis in the years 1505 to 1515. Luther had disobeyed his father, thus violating one of the Ten Commandments, and serious conflict persisted between them. The religious life seemed to provide no answers to his mental and spiritual difficulties. Three fits that he suffered in the monastic choir during those years may have been outward signs of his struggle.[4] Luther was grappling, as had thousands of medieval people before him, with the problem of salvation and thus the meaning of life. He was also searching for his life's work.

Luther's wise and kindly confessor, Staupitz, directed him to the study of Saint Paul's letters. Gradually, Luther arrived at a new understanding of the Pauline letters and of all Christian doctrine. He came to believe that salvation comes not through external observances and penances but through a simple faith in Christ. Faith is the means by which God sends humanity his grace, and faith is a free gift that cannot be earned. Thus Martin Luther discovered himself, God's work for him, and the centrality of faith in the Christian life.

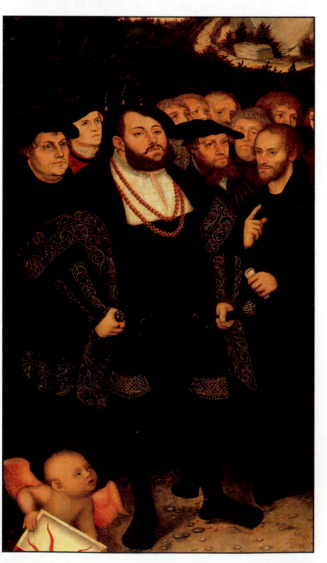

Lucas Cranach the Younger: Luther and the Wittenberg Reformers   The massive figure of John Frederick, Elector of Saxony, who protected and supported Luther, dominates this group portrait. Luther is on the far left, his associate Philip Melancthon in the front row on the right. Luther's face shows a quiet determination. *(Source: The Toledo Museum of Art, Toledo, Ohio; Gift of Edward Drummond Libbey)*

The Ninety-five Theses

An incident illustrative of the condition of the church in the early sixteenth century propelled Martin Luther onto the stage of history and brought about the Reformation in Germany. The University of Wittenberg lay within the ecclesiastical jurisdiction of the archdiocese of Magdeburg. The twenty-seven-year-old archbishop of Magdeburg, Albert, was also administrator of the see of Halberstadt and had been appointed archbishop of Mainz. To hold all three offices simultaneously—blatant pluralism—required papal dispensation. At that moment, Pope Leo X was eager to continue the construction of Saint Peter's Basilica but was hard pressed for funds. Archbishop Albert borrowed money from the Fuggers, a wealthy banking family of Augsburg, to pay for the papal dispensation allowing him to hold the several episcopal benefices. Only a few powerful financiers and churchmen knew the details of the arrangement, but Leo X authorized Archbishop Albert to sell indulgences in Germany to repay the Fuggers.

Wittenberg was in the political jurisdiction of Frederick of Saxony, one of the seven electors of the Holy Roman Empire. When Frederick forbade the sale of indulgences within his duchy, people of Wittenberg, including some of Professor Luther's students, streamed across the border from Saxony into Jütenborg in Thuringia to buy indulgences.

What exactly was an *indulgence*? According to Catholic theology, individuals who sin alienate themselves from God and his love. In order to be reconciled to God, the sinner must confess his or her sins to a priest and do the penance assigned. For example, a person who steals must first return the stolen goods and then perform the penance given by the priest, usually certain prayers or good works. This is known as the temporal (or earthly) penance, since no one knows what penance God will ultimately require.

The doctrine of indulgence rested on three principles. First, God is merciful, but he is also just. Sec-

Hieronymous Bosch: Christ Before Pilate   Pilate (right) grasps the pitcher of water as he prepares to wash his hands. The peasant faces around Christ are vicious, grotesque, even bestial, perhaps signifying humanity's stupidity and blindness. *(Source: Princeton University)*

ond, Christ and the saints, through their infinite virtue, established a "treasury of merits," on which the church, through its special relationship with Christ and the saints, can draw. Third, the church has the authority to grant sinners the spiritual benefits of those merits. Originally an indulgence was a remission of the temporal (priest-imposed) penalties for sin. Beginning in the twelfth century, the papacy and bishops had given Crusaders such indulgences. By the later Middle Ages people widely believed that an indulgence secured total remission of penalties for sin—on earth or in purgatory— and ensured swift entry into heaven.

Archbishop Albert hired the Dominican friar John Tetzel to sell the indulgences. Tetzel mounted an advertising blitz. One of his slogans—"As soon as coin in coffer rings, the soul from purgatory springs"—brought phenomenal success. Men and women could buy indulgences not only for themselves but for deceased parents, relatives, or friends. Tetzel even drew up a chart with specific prices for the forgiveness of particular sins.

Luther was severely troubled that ignorant people believed they had no further need for repentance once they had purchased an indulgence. Thus, according to historical tradition, in the academic fashion of the times, on the eve of All Saints' Day (October 31), 1517, he attached to the door of the church at Wittenberg Castle a list of ninety-five theses (or propositions) on indulgences. By this act

Grünewald: Crucifixion   (ca 1510) The bloodless hands, tortured face, and lacerated body contain an unprecedented depiction of the horrors of physical suffering and reflect the deep emotional piety of northern Europe. Court painter to Albert of Brandenburg, Grünewald later was strongly attracted to Luther's ideas. *(Source: National Gallery of Art, Washington, D.C.; Samuel H. Kress Collection)*

Luther intended only to start a theological discussion of the subject and to defend the theses publicly.

Luther firmly rejected the notion that salvation could be achieved by good works, such as indulgences. Some of his theses challenged the pope's power to grant indulgences, and others criticized papal wealth: "Why does not the Pope, whose riches are at this day more ample than those of the wealthiest of the wealthy, build the one Basilica of St. Peter's with his own money, rather than with that of poor believers . . . ?"[5]

The theses were soon translated from Latin into German, printed, and read throughout the empire. Immediately, broad theological issues were raised. When questioned, Luther rested his fundamental argument on the principle that there was no biblical basis for indulgences. But, replied Luther's opponents, to deny the legality of indulgences was to deny the authority of the pope who had authorized them. The issue was drawn: where did authority lie in the Christian church?

Through 1518 and 1519 Luther studied the history of the papacy. In 1519, in a large public disputation with the Catholic debater John Eck at Leipzig, Luther denied both the authority of the pope and the infallibility of a general council. The Council of Constance, he said, had erred when it condemned John Hus (see page 374).

The papacy responded with a letter condemning some of Luther's propositions, ordering that his books be burned, and giving him two months to recant or be excommunicated. Luther retaliated by publicly burning the letter. By January 3, 1521, when the excommunication was supposed to become final, the controversy involved more than theological issues. The papal legate wrote, "All Germany is in revolution. Nine-tenths shout 'Luther' as their warcry; and the other tenth cares nothing about Luther, and cries 'Death to the court of Rome.' "[6]

In this highly charged atmosphere the twenty-one-year-old emperor Charles V held his first diet (assembly of the Estates of the empire) at Worms and summoned Luther to appear before it. When ordered to recant, Luther replied in language that rang all over Europe:

Unless I am convinced by the evidence of Scripture or by plain reason—for I do not accept the authority of the Pope or the councils alone, since it is established that they have often erred and contradicted themselves—I am bound by the Scriptures I have cited and my conscience is captive to the Word of God. I cannot and will not recant anything, for it is neither safe nor right to go against conscience. God help me. Amen.[7]

Though Luther was declared an outlaw of the empire and denied legal protection, Duke Frederick of Saxony protected him.

Protestant Thought

Between 1520 and 1530, Luther worked out the basic theological tenets that became the articles of faith for his new church and subsequently for all Protestant groups. The word *Protestant* derives from the protest drawn up by a small group of reforming German princes at the Diet of Speyer in 1529. The princes "protested" the decisions of the Catholic majority. At first *Protestant* meant "Lutheran," but with the appearance of many protesting sects, it became a general term applied to all non-Catholic Christians. Lutheran Protestant thought was officially formulated in the Confession of Augsburg in 1530.

Ernst Troeltsch, a German student of the sociology of religion, has defined Protestantism as a "modification of Catholicism, in which the Catholic formulation of questions was retained, while a different answer was given to them." Luther provided new answers to four old, basic theological issues.

First, how is a person to be saved? Traditional Catholic teaching held that salvation was achieved by both faith *and* good works. Luther held that salvation comes by faith alone. Women and men are saved, said Luther, by the arbitrary decision of God, irrespective of good works or the sacraments. God, not people, initiates salvation.

Second, where does religious authority reside? Christian doctrine had long maintained that authority rests both in the Bible and in the traditional teaching of the church. Luther maintained that authority rests in the Word of God as revealed in the Bible alone and as interpreted by an individual's conscience. He urged that each person read and reflect on the Scriptures.

Third, what is the church? Luther re-emphasized the Catholic teaching that the church consists of the entire community of Christian believers. Medieval churchmen, however, had tended to identify the church with the clergy.

Finally, what is the highest form of Christian life? The medieval church had stressed the superiority of the monastic and religious life over the secular. Luther argued that all vocations have equal merit, whether ecclesiastical or secular, and that every person should serve God in his or her individual calling.[8] Protestantism, in sum, represented a reformulation of the Christian heritage.

The Social Impact of Luther's Beliefs

As early as 1521, Luther had a vast following. Every encounter with ecclesiastical or political authorities attracted attention to him. Pulpits and printing presses spread his message all over Germany. By the time of his death, people of all social classes had become Lutheran. What was the immense appeal of Luther's religious ideas?

Recent historical research on the German towns has shown that two significant late medieval developments prepared the way for Luther's ideas. First, since the fifteenth century, city governments had expressed resentment at clerical privileges and immunities. Priests, monks, and nuns paid no taxes and were exempt from civic responsibilities, such as defending the city. Yet religious orders frequently held large amounts of urban property. At Zurich in 1467, for example, religious orders held one-third of the city's taxable property. City governments were determined to integrate the clergy into civic life by reducing their privileges and giving them public responsibilities. Accordingly, the Zurich magistracy subjected the religious to taxes; inspected wills so that legacies to the church and legacies left by churchmen could be controlled; and placed priests and monks under the jurisdiction of the civil courts.

Preacherships also spread Luther's ideas. Critics of the late medieval church, especially informed and intelligent townspeople, condemned the irregularity and poor quality of sermons. As a result, prosperous burghers in many towns established preacherships. Preachers were men of superior education who were required to deliver about a hundred sermons a year, each lasting about forty-five minutes. Endowed preacherships had important consequences after 1517. Luther's ideas attracted many preachers, and in such towns as Stuttgart, Reutlingen, Eisenach, and Jena, preachers became Protestant leaders. Preacherships also encouraged the Protestant form of worship, in which the sermon, not the Eucharist, was the central part of the service.[9]

In the countryside the attraction of the German peasants to Lutheran beliefs was almost predictable. Luther himself came from a peasant background, and he admired the peasants' ceaseless toil. Peasants for their part respected Luther's defiance of church authority. Moreover, they thrilled to the words Luther used in his treatise *On Christian Liberty* (1520): "A Christian man is the most free lord of all and subject to none." Taken by themselves, these words easily contributed to social unrest. Fifteenth-century Germany had witnessed several peasant revolts. In the early sixteenth century, the economic condition of the peasantry varied from place to place but was generally worse than it had been in the fifteenth century and deteriorating. Crop failures in 1523 and 1524 aggravated an explosive situation. In 1525 representatives of the Swabian peasants met at the city of Memmingen and drew up the Twelve Articles, which expressed their grievances. The Twelve Articles condemn lay and ecclesiastical lords and summarize the agrarian crisis of the early sixteenth century. The articles complain that nobles had seized village common lands, which traditionally had been used by all; that they had imposed new rents on manorial properties and new services on the peasants working those properties; and that they had forced the poor to pay unjust death duties in the form of the peasants' best horses or cows. Wealthy, socially mobile peasants especially resented these burdens, which they emphasized as new.[10] The peasants believed their demands conformed to Scripture and cited Luther as a theologian who could prove that they did.

Luther wanted to prevent rebellion. Initially he sided with the peasants, and in his tract *An Admonition to Peace* he blasted the lords:

We have no one on earth to thank for this mischievous rebellion, except you lords and princes, especially you blind bishops and mad priests and monks. . . . In your government you do nothing but flay and rob your subjects in order that you may lead a life of splendor and pride, until the poor common folk can bear it no longer.[11]

But nothing justified the use of armed force, he warned: "The fact that rulers are unjust and wicked does not excuse tumult and rebellion; to punish wickedness does not belong to everybody, but to the worldly rulers who bear the sword." As for biblical support for the peasants' demands, he main-

The Folly of Indulgences   In this woodcut the Church's sale of indulgences is viciously satirized. With one claw in the holy water symbolizing the rite of purification (Psalm 50), and the other claw resting on the coins paid for indulgences, the Church in the form of a rapacious eagle with its right hand stretched out for offerings, writes out an indulgence with excrement—which represents its worth. Fools, in a false security, sit in the animal's gaping mouth, representing hell, to which a devil delivers the pope in a three-tiered crown and holding the keys to heaven originally given to St. Peter. *(Source: Kunstsammlungen der Veste Coburg)*

tained that Scripture had nothing to do with earthly justice or material . . . or material gain.[12]

Massive revolts first broke out near the Swiss frontier and then swept through Swabia, Thuringia, the Rhineland, and Saxony. The crowds' slogans came directly from Luther's writings. "God's righteousness" and the "Word of God" were in-voked in the effort to secure social and economic justice. The peasants who expected Luther's support were soon disillusioned. He had written of the "freedom" of the Christian, but he had meant the freedom to obey the Word of God, for in sin men and women lose their freedom and break their relationship with God. Freedom for Luther meant independence from the authority of the Roman church; it did *not* mean opposition to legally established secular powers. Firmly convinced that rebellion hastened the end of civilized society, he wrote a tract *Against the Murderous, Thieving Hordes of the Peasants:* "Let everyone who can smite, slay, and stab [the peasants], secretly and openly, remembering that nothing can be more poisonous, hurtful or devilish than a rebel."[13] The nobility ferociously crushed the revolt. Historians estimate that over 75,000 peasants were killed in 1525.

Luther took literally these words of Saint Paul's Letter to the Romans: "Let every soul be subject to the higher powers. For there is no power but of God: the powers that be are established by God.

Whosoever resists the power, resists the ordinance of God: and they that resist shall receive to themselves damnation."[14] As it developed, Lutheran theology exalted the state, subordinated the church to the state, and everywhere championed "the powers that be." The consequences for German society were profound and have redounded into the twentieth century. The revolt of 1525 strengthened the authority of lay rulers. Peasant economic conditions, however, moderately improved. For example, in many parts of Germany, enclosed fields, meadows, and forests were returned to common use.

Scholars in many disciplines have attributed Luther's fame and success to the invention of the

Battle of Gaisbeuren during the Peasants' War, 1525   When peasants' economic and social grievances merged with religious discontent, Luther wrote that the peasants misunderstood the Gospel and could not use it to change the social order. Because his appeal did not persuade the peasants to stop the violence, Luther called on the princes to exercise their right to the sword to end the disorder. A couple of peasants have guns, but most seem armed only with staves. *(Source: Siegfried Lauterwasser)*

printing press, which rapidly reproduced and made known his ideas. Equally important was Luther's incredible skill with language. Some thinkers have lavished praise on the Wittenberg reformer; others have bitterly condemned him. But, in the words of psychologist Erik Erikson:

The one matter on which professor and priest, psychiatrist and sociologist, agree is Luther's immense gift for language: his receptivity for the written word; his memory for the significant phrase; and his range of verbal expression (lyrical, biblical, satirical, and vulgar) which in English is paralleled only by Shakespeare.[15]

Language proved to be the weapon with which this peasant's son changed the world.

Educated people and humanists, like the peasants, were much attracted by Luther's words. He advocated a simpler, personal religion based on faith, a return to the spirit of the early church, the centrality of the Scriptures in the liturgy and in Christian life, abolition of elaborate ceremonial—precisely the reforms the northern humanists had been calling for. Ulrich Zwingli (1484–1531), for example, a humanist of Zurich, was strongly influenced by Luther's bold stand; it stimulated Zwingli's reforms in that Swiss city. The nobleman Ulrich von Hutten (1488–1523), who had published several humanistic tracts, in 1519 dedicated his life to the advancement of Luther's Reformation. And the Frenchman John Calvin (1509–1564), often called the organizer of Protestantism, owed a great deal to Luther's thought.

The publication of Luther's German translation of the New Testament in 1523 democratized religion. His insistence that everyone should read and reflect on the Scriptures attracted the literate and thoughtful middle classes partly because Luther appealed to their intelligence. Moreover, the business classes, preoccupied with making money, envied the church's wealth, disapproved of the luxurious lifestyle of some churchmen, and resented tithes and ecclesiastical taxation. Luther's doctrines of salvation by faith and the priesthood of all believers not only raised the religious status of the commercial classes but protected their pocketbooks as well.

Hymns, psalms, and Luther's two catechisms (1529), compendiums of basic religious knowledge, also show the power of language in spreading the ideals of the Reformation. The reformers knew "that rhyme, meter, and melodies could forcefully impress minds and affect sensibilities." Such hymns as the famous "A Mighty Fortress Is Our God" expressed deep human feelings, were easily remembered, and imprinted on the mind central points of doctrine. Luther's *Larger Catechism* contained brief sermons on the main articles of faith, while the *Shorter Catechism* gave concise explanations of doctrine in question-and-answer form. Both catechisms stressed the importance of the Ten Commandments, the Lord's Prayer, the Apostle's Creed, and the sacraments for the believing Christian. Although originally intended for the instruction of pastors, these catechisms became powerful techniques for the indoctrination of men and women of all ages, especially the young.[16]

What appeal did Luther's message have for women? Luther's argument that all vocations have equal merit in the sight of God gave dignity to those who performed ordinary, routine, domestic tasks. The abolition of monasticism in Protestant territories led to the exaltation of the home, which Luther and other reformers stressed as the special domain of the wife. The Christian home, in contrast to the place of business, became the place for the exercise of the gentler virtues—love, tenderness, reconciliation, the carrying of one another's burdens. The Protestant abolition of private confession to a priest freed women from embarrassing explorations of their sexual lives and activities. Protestants established schools where girls, as well as boys, became literate in the catechism and the Bible. Finally, the reformers stressed marriage as the cure for clerical concupiscence. Protestantism thus proved attractive to the many women who had been priests' concubines and mistresses: now they became legal and honorable wives.[17]

For his time, Luther held enlightened views on matters of sexuality and marriage. He wrote to a young man, "Dear lad, be not ashamed that you desire a girl, nor you my maid, the boy. Just let it lead you into matrimony and not into promiscuity, and it is no more cause for shame than eating and drinking."[18] Luther was confident that God took delight in the sexual act and denied that original sin affected the goodness of creation. He believed, however, that marriage was a woman's career. A student recorded Luther as saying, early in his public ministry, "Let them bear children until they are dead of it; that is what they are for." A happy marriage to the ex-nun Katharine von Bora mellowed him, and another student later quoted him as saying, "Next to God's Word there is no more precious treasure than holy matrimony. God's highest gift on earth is a pious, cheerful, God-fearing, home-keeping wife, with whom you may live peacefully, to whom you may entrust your goods, and body and life."[19] Though Luther deeply loved his "dear Katie," he believed that women's concerns revolved exclusively around the children, the kitchen, and the church. A happy woman was a patient wife, an efficient manager, and a good mother. Kate was an excellent financial manager (which Luther—much inclined to give money and goods away—was not). Himself a stern if often indulgent father, Luther held that the father should rule his household while the wife controlled its economy. With many relatives and constant visitors, Luther's was a large and happy household, a model for Protestants if an abomination for Catholics. The wives of other reformers, though they exercised no leadership role in the reform, shared their husbands' work and concerns.

GERMANY AND THE PROTESTANT REFORMATION

The history of the Holy Roman Empire in the later Middle Ages is a story of dissension, disintegration, and debility. Unlike Spain, France, and England, the empire lacked a strong central power. The Golden Bull of 1356 legalized what had long existed—government by an aristocratic federation. Each of seven electors—the archbishops of Mainz, Trier, and Cologne, the margrave of Brandenburg, the duke of Saxony, the count palatine of the Rhine, and the king of Bohemia—gained virtual sovereignty in his own territory. The agreement ended disputed elections in the empire; it also reduced the central authority of the emperor. Germany was characterized by weak borders, localism, and chronic disorder. The nobility strengthened their territories, while imperial power declined.

Against this background of decentralization and strong local power, Martin Luther had launched a movement to reform the church. Two years after Luther posted the Ninety-five Theses, the electors chose as emperor a nineteen-year-old Habsburg prince who ruled as Charles V. Luther's interests and motives were primarily religious, but many people responded to his teachings for political, so-

cial, or economic reasons. How did the goals and interests of the emperor influence the course of the Reformation in Germany? What impact did the upheaval in the Christian church have on the political condition in Germany?

The Rise of the Habsburg Dynasty

The marriage in 1477 of Maximilian I of the house of Habsburg and Mary of Burgundy was a decisive event in early modern European history. Through this union with the rich and powerful duchy of Burgundy, the Austrian house of Habsburg, already the strongest ruling family in the empire, became an international power.

In the fifteenth and sixteenth centuries, as in the Middle Ages, relations among states continued to be greatly affected by the connections of royal families. Marriage often determined the diplomatic status of states. The Habsburg-Burgundian marriage angered the French, who considered Burgundy part of French territory. Louis XI of France repeatedly ravaged parts of the Burgundian Netherlands until he was able to force Maximilian to accept French terms: the Treaty of Arras (1482) emphatically declared Burgundy a part of the kingdom of France. The Habsburgs, however, never really renounced their claim to Burgundy, and intermittent warfare over it continued between France and Maximilian. Within the empire, German principalities that resented Austria's pre-eminence began to see that they shared interests with France. The marriage of Maximilian and Mary inaugurated centuries of conflict between the Austrian house of Habsburg and the kings of France. And Germany was to be the chief arena of the struggle.

"Other nations wage war; you, Austria, marry." Historians dispute the origins of the adage, but no one questions its accuracy. The heir of Mary and Maximilian, Philip of Burgundy, married Joanna of Castile, daughter of Ferdinand and Isabella of Spain. Philip and Joanna's son Charles V (1500–1558) fell heir to a vast conglomeration of territories. Through a series of accidents and unexpected deaths, Charles inherited Spain from his mother, together with her possessions in the New World and the Spanish dominions in Italy, Sicily, Sardinia, and Naples. From his father he inherited the Habsburg lands in Austria, southern Germany,

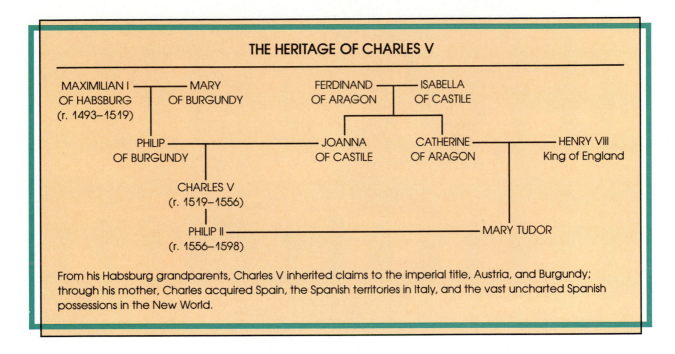

THE HERITAGE OF CHARLES V

MAXIMILIAN I OF HABSBURG (r. 1493–1519) ——— MARY OF BURGUNDY

FERDINAND OF ARAGON ——— ISABELLA OF CASTILE

PHILIP OF BURGUNDY ——— JOANNA OF CASTILE

CATHERINE OF ARAGON ——— HENRY VIII King of England

CHARLES V (r. 1519–1556)

PHILIP II (r. 1556–1598) ——— MARY TUDOR

From his Habsburg grandparents, Charles V inherited claims to the imperial title, Austria, and Burgundy; through his mother, Charles acquired Spain, the Spanish territories in Italy, and the vast uncharted Spanish possessions in the New World.

the Low Countries, and Franche-Comté in east central France.

Charles's inheritance was an incredibly diverse collection of states and peoples, each governed in a different manner and held together only by the person of the emperor (Map 14.1). Charles's Italian adviser, the grand chancellor Gattinara, told the young ruler: "God has set you on the path toward world monarchy." Charles not only believed this; he was convinced that it was his duty to maintain the political and religious unity of Western Christendom. In this respect Charles V was the last medieval emperor.

Charles needed and in 1519 secured the imperial title. Forward-thinking Germans proposed governmental reforms. They urged placing the administration in the hands of an imperial council whose president, the emperor's appointee, would have ultimate executive power. Reforms of the imperial finances, the army, and the judiciary were also recommended. Such ideas did not interest the young emperor at all. When he finally arrived in Germany from Spain and opened his first diet at Worms in January 1521, he naively announced that "the empire from of old has had not many masters, but one, and it is our intention to be that one." Charles went on to say that he was to be treated as of greater account than his predecessors because he

was more powerful than they had been. In view of the long history of aristocratic power, Charles's notions were pure fantasy.

Charles continued the Burgundian policy of his grandfather Maximilian. That is, German revenues and German troops were subordinated to the needs of other parts of the empire, first Burgundy and then Spain. Habsburg international interests came before the need for reform in Germany.

The Political Impact of Luther's Beliefs

In the sixteenth century, the practice of religion remained a public matter. Everyone participated in the religious life of the community, just as almost everyone shared in the local agricultural work. Whatever spiritual convictions individuals held in the privacy of their consciences, the emperor, king, prince, magistrate, or other civil authority determined the official form of religious practice within his jurisdiction. Almost everyone believed that the presence of a faith different from that of the majority represented a political threat to the security of the state. Only a tiny minority, and certainly none of the princes, believed in religious liberty.

Against this background, the religious storm launched by Martin Luther swept across Germany.

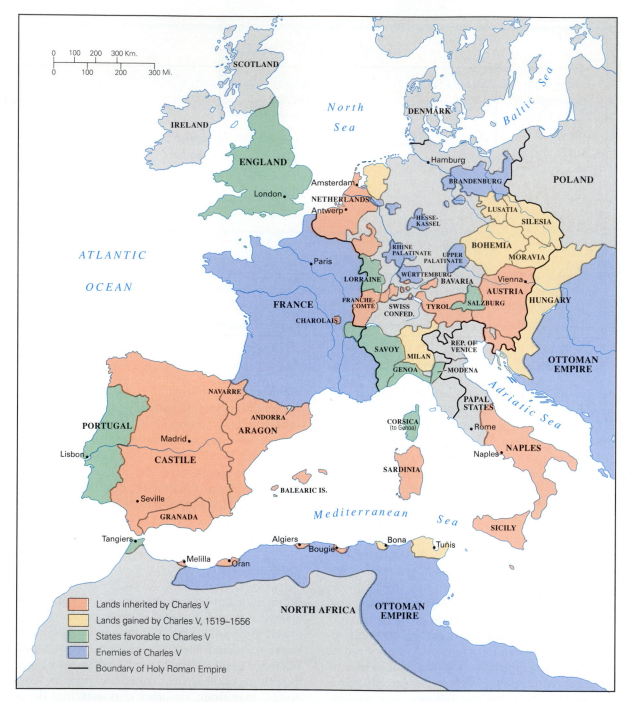

MAP 14.1 The European Empire of Charles V Charles V exercised theoretical jurisdiction over more territory than anyone since Charlemagne. This map does not show
his Latin American and Asian possessions.

Legend:
- Lands inherited by Charles V
- Lands gained by Charles V, 1519–1556
- States favorable to Charles V
- Enemies of Charles V
- Boundary of Holy Roman Empire

Titian: The Emperor Charles V   (1548) Court painter to Charles V, Titian portrayed him shortly after the emperor's defeat of the league of German Protestant princes at the battle of Mühlberg near Leipzig. In this idealization, one of the earliest equestrian portraits, Charles appears as heroic victor, chivalric knight, and defender of the church. *(Source: Museo del Prado, Madrid)*

Several elements in his religious reformation stirred patriotic feelings. Anti-Roman sentiment ran high. Humanists lent eloquent intellectual support. And Luther's translation of the New Testament into German evoked national pride.

For decades devout lay people and churchmen had called on the German princes to reform the church. In 1520 Luther took up the cry in his *Appeal to the Christian Nobility of the German Nation*. Unless the princes destroyed papal power in Germany, Luther argued, reform was impossible. He urged the princes to confiscate ecclesiastical wealth and to abolish indulgences, dispensations, pardons, and clerical celibacy. He told them that it was their public duty to bring about the moral reform of the church. Luther based his argument in part on the papacy's financial exploitation of Germany:

How comes it that we Germans must put up with such robbery and such extortion of our property at the hands of the pope? If the Kingdom of France has prevented it, why do we Germans let them make such fools and apes of us? It would all be more bearable if in this way they only stole our property; but they lay waste the churches and rob Christ's sheep of their pious shepherds, and destroy the worship and the Word of God. As it is they do nothing for the good of Christendom; they only wrangle about the incomes of bishoprics and prelacies, and that any robber could do.[20]

These words fell on welcome ears and itchy fingers. Luther's appeal to German patriotism gained him strong support, and national feeling influenced many princes otherwise confused by or indifferent to the complexities of the religious issues.

The church in Germany possessed great wealth. And, unlike other countries, Germany had no strong central government to check the flow of gold to Rome. Rejection of Roman Catholicism and adoption of Protestantism would mean the legal confiscation of lush farmlands, rich monasteries, and wealthy shrines. Some German princes, such as the prince-archbishop of Cologne, Hermann von Wied, were sincerely attracted to Lutheranism, but many civil authorities realized that they had a great deal to gain by embracing the new faith. A steady stream of duchies, margraviates, free cities, and bishoprics secularized church property, accepted Lutheran theological doctrines, and adopted simpler services conducted in German. The decision reached at Worms in 1521 to condemn Luther and his teaching was not enforced because the German princes did not want to enforce it.

Charles V was a vigorous defender of Catholicism, and contemporary social and political theory denied the possibility of two religions coexisting peacefully in one territory. Thus many princes used the religious issue to extend their financial and political independence. When doctrinal differences became linked to political ambitions and financial receipts, the results proved unfortunate for the improvement of German government. The Protestant movement ultimately proved a political disaster for Germany.

Charles V must share blame with the German princes for the disintegration of imperial authority in the empire. He neither understood nor took an interest in the constitutional problems of Germany, and he lacked the material resources to oppose Protestantism effectively there. Throughout his reign he was preoccupied with his Flemish, Spanish, Italian, and American territories. Moreover, the Turkish threat prevented him from acting effectively against the Protestants; Charles's brother Ferdinand needed Protestant support against the Turks who besieged Vienna in 1529.

Five times between 1521 and 1555, Charles V went to war with the Valois kings of France. The issue each time was the Habsburg lands acquired by the marriage of Maximilian and Mary of Burgundy. Much of the fighting occurred in Germany. The cornerstone of French foreign policy in the sixteenth and seventeenth centuries was the desire to keep the German states divided. Thus Europe witnessed the paradox of the Catholic king of France supporting the Lutheran princes in their challenge to his fellow Catholic, Charles V. French foreign policy contributed to the continuing division of Germany. The long dynastic struggle commonly called the Habsburg-Valois Wars advanced the cause of Protestantism and promoted the political fragmentation of the German empire.

Finally, in 1555, Charles agreed to the Peace of Augsburg, which, in accepting the status quo, officially recognized Lutheranism. Each prince was permitted to determine the religion of his territory. Most of northern and central Germany became Lutheran, while the south remained Roman Catholic. There was no freedom of religion, however. Princes or town councils established state churches to which all subjects of the area had to belong. Dissidents, whether Lutheran or Catholic, had to convert or leave. The political difficulties Germany inherited from the Middle Ages had been compounded by the religious crisis of the sixteenth century.

THE GROWTH OF THE PROTESTANT REFORMATION

By 1555 much of northern Europe had broken with the Roman Catholic church. All of Scandinavia, England (except under Mary Tudor), Scotland, and such self-governing cities as Geneva and Zurich in Switzerland and Strasbourg in Germany had rejected the religious authority of Rome and adopted new faiths. Because a common religious faith had been the one element uniting all of Europe for almost a thousand years, the fragmentation of belief led to profound changes in European life and society. The most significant new form of Protestantism was Calvinism, of which the Peace of Augsburg had made no mention at all.

Calvinism

In 1509, while Luther was studying for the doctorate at Wittenberg, John Calvin (1509–1564) was born in Noyon in northwestern France. Luther inadvertently launched the Protestant Reformation. Calvin, however, had the greater impact on future generations. His theological writings profoundly influenced the social thought and attitudes of Europeans and English-speaking peoples all over the world, especially in Canada and the United States. Although he had originally intended to have an ecclesiastical career, Calvin studied law, which had a decisive impact on his mind and later thought. In 1533 he experienced a religious crisis, as a result of which he converted to Protestantism.

Convinced that God selects certain people to do his work, Calvin believed that God had specifically called him to reform the church. Accordingly, he accepted an invitation to assist in the reformation of the city of Geneva. There, beginning in 1541, Calvin worked assiduously to establish a Christian society ruled by God through civil magistrates and reformed ministers. Geneva, "a city that was a Church," became the model of a Christian community for sixteenth-century Protestant reformers.

To understand Calvin's Geneva, it is necessary to understand Calvin's ideas. These he embodied in *The Institutes of the Christian Religion,* first published in 1536 and definitively issued in 1559. The cornerstone of Calvin's theology was his belief in the absolute sovereignty and omnipotence of God and the total weakness of humanity. Before the infinite power of God, he asserted, men and women are as insignificant as grains of sand.

Calvin did not ascribe free will to human beings, because that would detract from the sovereignty of God. Men and women cannot actively work to achieve salvation; rather, God in his infinite wisdom decided at the beginning of time who would be saved and who damned. This viewpoint constitutes the theological principle called *predestination:*

John Calvin   The lean, ascetic face with the strong jaw reflects the iron will and determination of the organizer of Protestantism. The fur collar represents his training in law. *(Source: Bibliothèque Nationale/Snark/Art Resource)*

Predestination we call the eternal decree of God, by which he has determined in himself, what he would have become of every individual of mankind. For they are not all created with a similar destiny; but eternal life is foreordained for some, and eternal damnation for others. . . . In conformity, therefore, to the clear doctrine of the Scripture, we assert, that by an eternal and immutable counsel, God has once for all determined, both whom he would admit to salvation, and whom he would condemn to destruction. We affirm that this counsel, as far as concerns the elect, is founded on his gratuitous mercy, totally irrespective of human merit; but that to those whom he devotes to condemnation, the gate of life is closed by a just and irreprehensible, but incomprehensible, judgment. How exceedingly presumptuous it is only to inquire into the causes of the Divine will; which is in fact, and is justly entitled to be, the cause of everything that exists. . . . For *the will of God is the highest justice; so that what he wills must be considered just, for this very reason, because he wills it.*[21]

Though the doctrine of predestination dates back to Saint Augustine and Saint Paul, many people have found it a pessimistic view of the nature of God, who, they feel, revealed himself in the Old and New Testaments as merciful as well as just. Calvin maintained that while individuals cannot know whether they will be saved—and the probability is that they will be damned—good works are a "sign" of election. In any case, people should concentrate on worshiping God and doing his work and not waste time worrying about salvation. Though the doctrine of predestination may strike *us* as pessimistic, it inspired an enormous amount of energy in the sixteenth and later centuries.

Calvin aroused Genevans to a high standard of morality. He had two remarkable assets: complete mastery of Scripture and exceptional fluency in French. Through his sermons and a program of religious education, God's laws and man's were enforced in Geneva. Calvin's powerful sermons delivered the Word of God and thereby monopolized the strongest contemporary means of communication, preaching. Through his *Genevan Catechism,* published in 1541, children and adults memorized set questions and answers and acquired a summary of their faith and a guide for daily living. Calvin's sermons and his *Catechism* gave a whole generation of Genevans thorough instruction in the reformed religion.[22]

In the reformation of the city, the Genevan Consistory also exercised a powerful role. This body consisted of twelve laymen, plus the Company of Pastors of which Calvin was the permanent moderator (presider). The duties of the Consistory were "to keep watch over every man's life [and] to admonish amiably those whom they see leading a disorderly life." While Calvin emphasized that the Consistory's activities should be thorough and "its eyes may be everywhere," corrections were only "medicine to turn sinners to the Lord."[23] Thus austere living, public fasting, and evening curfew became the order of the day. Fashionable clothes, dancing, card playing, and heavy drinking were absolutely prohibited. The Consistory investigated the private morals of citizens but was unwilling to punish the town prostitutes as severely as Calvin would have preferred. Calvin exercised some political influence through the Consistory, but the civil magistrates in Geneva maintained control.

Calvin reserved his harshest condemnation for religious dissenters, declaring them "dogs and swine":

God makes plain that the false prophet is to be stoned without mercy. We are to crush beneath our heel all affections of nature when His honor is concerned. The father should not spare his child, nor brother his brother, nor husband his own wife or the friend who is dearer to him than life. No human relationship is more than animal unless it be grounded in God.[24]

Calvin translated his words into action. In the 1550s the Spanish humanist Michael Servetus had gained international notoriety for his publications denying the Christian dogma of the Trinity, which holds that God is three divine persons, Father, Son, and Holy Spirit. Servetus had been arrested by the Inquisition but escaped to Geneva, where he hoped for support. He was promptly rearrested. At his trial he not only held to his belief that there is no scriptural basis for the Trinity but rejected child baptism and insisted that a person under twenty cannot commit a mortal sin. The city fathers considered this last idea dangerous to public morality, "especially in these days when the young are so corrupted." Though Servetus begged that he be punished by banishment, Calvin and the town council maintained that the denial of child baptism and the Trinity amounted to a threat to all society. Whispering "Jesus, Son of the eternal God, have pity on me," Servetus was burned at the stake.

To many sixteenth-century Europeans, Calvin's Geneva seemed "the most perfect school of Christ since the days of the Apostles." Religious refugees from France, England, Spain, Scotland, and Italy visited the city. Subsequently, the Reformed church of Calvin served as the model for the Presbyterian church in Scotland, the Huguenot church in France, and the Puritan churches in England and New England. For women, the Calvinist provision for congregational participation and vernacular liturgy helped to satisfy their desire for belonging to and participating in a meaningful church organization.

Calvinism became the compelling force in international Protestantism. The Calvinist ethic of the "calling" dignified all work with a religious aspect. Hard work, well done, was pleasing to God. This doctrine encouraged an aggressive, vigorous activism. In the *Institutes* Calvin provided a systematic theology for Protestantism. The Reformed church of Calvin had a strong and well-organized machinery of government. These factors, together with the social and economic applications of Calvin's theology, made Calvinism the most dynamic force in sixteenth- and seventeenth-century Protestantism.

The Anabaptists

The name *Anabaptist* derives from a Greek word meaning "to baptize again." The Anabaptists, sometimes described as the "left wing of the Reformation," believed that only adults could make a free choice about religious faith, baptism, and entry into the Christian community. Thus they considered the practice of baptizing infants and children preposterous and claimed there was no scriptural basis for it. They wanted to rebaptize believers who had been baptized as children. Anabaptists took the Gospel and, at first, Luther's teachings absolutely literally and favored a return to the kind of church that had existed among the earliest Christians—a voluntary association of believers who had experienced an inner light.

Anabaptists maintained that only a few people would receive the inner light. This position meant that the Christian community and the Christian state were not identical. In other words, Anabaptists believed in the separation of church and state

and in religious tolerance. They almost never tried to force their values on others. In an age that believed in the necessity of state-established churches, Anabaptist views on religious liberty were thought to undermine that concept.

Each Anabaptist community or church was entirely independent; it selected its own ministers and ran its own affairs. In 1534 the community at Münster in Germany, for example, established a legal code that decreed the death penalty for insubordinate wives. Moreover, the Münster community also practiced polygamy and forced all women under a certain age to marry or face expulsion or execution.

Anabaptists admitted women to the ministry. They shared goods as the early Christians had done, refused all public offices, and would not serve in

Calvinist Worship   A converted house in Lyons, France, serves as a church for the simple Calvinist service. Although Calvin's followers believed in equality and elected officials administered the church, here men and women are segregated, and some people sit on hard benches while others sit in upholstered pews. Beside the pulpit an hourglass hangs to time the preacher's sermon. (Could the dog sit still for that long?) *(Source: Bibliothèque publique et universitaire, Geneva)*

the armed forces. In fact, they laid great stress on pacifism. A favorite Anabaptist scriptural quotation was "By their fruits you shall know them," suggesting that if Christianity was a religion of peace, the Christian should not fight. Good deeds were the sign of Christian faith, and to be a Christian meant to imitate the meekness and mercy of Christ. With such beliefs Anabaptists were inevitably a minority. Anabaptism later attracted the poor, the unemployed, the uneducated. Geographically, Anabaptists drew their members from depressed urban areas—from among the followers of Zwingli in Zurich and from Basel, Augsburg, and Nuremberg.

Ideas such as absolute pacifism and the distinction between the Christian community and the state brought down on these unfortunate people fanatical hatred and bitter persecution. Zwingli, Luther, Calvin, and Catholics all saw—quite correctly—the separation of church and state as leading ultimately to the complete secularization of society. The powerful rulers of Swiss and German society immediately saw the connection between religious heresy and economic dislocation. Civil authorities feared that the combination of religious differences and economic grievances would lead to civil disturbances. In Saxony, in Strasbourg, and in the Swiss cities, Anabaptists were either banished or cruelly executed by burning, beating, or drowning. Their community spirit and the edifying example of their lives, however, contributed to the survival of Anabaptist ideas.

Later, the Quakers with their gentle pacifism; the Baptists with their emphasis on an inner spiritual light; the Congregationalists with their democratic church organization; and, in 1787, the authors of the United States Constitution with their concern for the separation of church and state—all these trace their origins in part to the Anabaptists of the sixteenth century.

The English Reformation

As on the Continent, the Reformation in England had social and economic causes as well as religious ones. As elsewhere, too, Christian humanists had for decades been calling for the purification of the church. When the political matter of the divorce of King Henry VIII (r. 1509–1547) became en-

meshed with other issues, a complete break with Rome resulted.

Demands for ecclesiastical reform dated back at least to the fourteenth century. The Lollards (see page 374) had been driven underground in the fifteenth century but survived in parts of southern England and the Midlands. Working-class people, especially cloth workers, were attracted to their ideas. The Lollards stressed the individual's reading and interpretation of the Bible, which they considered the only standard of Christian faith and holiness. Consequently, they put no stock in the value of the sacraments and were vigorously anticlerical. Lollards opposed ecclesiastical wealth, the veneration of the saints, prayers for the dead, and all war. Although they had no notion of justification by faith, like Luther they insisted on the individual soul's direct responsibility to God.

The work of the English humanist William Tyndale (ca 1494–1536) stimulated cries for reform. Tyndale visited Luther at Wittenberg in 1524, and a year later at Antwerp he began printing an English translation of the New Testament. From Antwerp, merchants carried the New Testament into England, where it was distributed by Lollards. Fortified with copies of Tyndale's English Bible and some of Luther's ideas, the Lollards represented the ideal of "a personal, scriptural, non-sacramental, and lay-dominated religion."[25] In this manner, doctrines that would later be called Protestant flourished underground in England before any official or state-approved changes.

In the early sixteenth century, the ignorance of much of the parish clergy, and the sexual misbehavior of some, compared unfavorably with the education and piety of lay people. Even more than the ignorance of the lower clergy, the wealth of the English church fostered resentment and anticlericalism. The church controlled perhaps 20 percent of the land and also received an annual tithe of the produce of lay people's estates. The church even charged a mortuary fee, a tax to bury the dead, which people resented. Mortuary fees led to frequent lawsuits.

The career of Thomas Wolsey (1474?–1530) provides an extreme example of pluralism in the English church in the early sixteenth century. The son of a butcher, Wolsey became a priest and in 1507 secured an appointment as chaplain to Henry VII. In 1509 Henry VIII made Wolsey a privy councillor, where his remarkable ability and energy won him rapid advancement. In 1515 he became a cardinal and lord chancellor, and in 1518 papal legate. As papal legate he ruled the English church, with final authority in all matters relating to marriage, wills, the clergy, and ecclesiastical appointments. Wolsey had more power than any previous royal minister, and he used that power to amass a large number of church offices, including the rich bishoprics of Winchester and Lincoln and the abbacy of Saint Albans. He displayed the vast wealth these positions brought him with ostentation and arrogance, which in turn fanned the flames of anticlericalism. The divorce of Henry VIII ignited all these glowing coals.

Having fallen in love with a woman named Anne Boleyn, Henry wanted his marriage to Catherine of Aragon annulled. Legal, diplomatic, and theological problems stood in his way, however. When Henry married Catherine he had secured a dispensation from Pope Julius II to eliminate all doubts and legal technicalities about Catherine's previous union with Henry's late brother, Arthur. For eighteen years Catherine and Henry lived together in what contemporaries thought a happy marriage. Catherine produced six children, although only the princess Mary survived childhood.

Around 1527 Henry began to insist, on the basis of a passage in the Old Testament Book of Leviticus, that God was denying him a male heir to punish him for marrying his brother's widow.[26] Henry claimed that he wanted to spare England the dangers of a disputed succession. The anarchy and disorders of the Wars of the Roses would be repeated if a woman, the princess Mary, inherited the throne.

Henry went about the business of ensuring a peaceful succession in an extraordinary manner. He petitioned Pope Clement VII for an annulment of his marriage to Catherine. Henry wanted the pope to declare that a legal marriage with Catherine had never existed, in which case Princess Mary was illegitimate and thus ineligible to succeed to the throne. The pope was an indecisive man whose attention at the time was focused on the Lutheran revolt in Germany and the Habsburg-Valois struggle for control of Italy. But there is a stronger reason why Clement could not grant Henry's petition. Henry argued that Pope Julius's dispensation had contradicted the law of God—that a man may not marry his brother's widow. The English king's request reached Rome at the very time that Luther was widely publishing tracts condemning the papacy as the core of wickedness. Had Clement granted Henry's annulment and thereby admitted that his recent predecessor, Julius II, had erred, Clement would have given support to the Lutheran assertion that popes substitute their own evil judgments for the law of God. This Clement could not do, so he delayed acting on Henry's request.[27] The capture and sack of Rome in 1527 by the emperor Charles V, Queen Catherine's nephew, thoroughly tied the pope's hands.

Accordingly, Henry determined to get his divorce in England. The convenient death of the archbishop of Canterbury allowed Henry to appoint a new archbishop, Thomas Cranmer (1489–1556). Cranmer heard the case in his archiepiscopal court, granted the annulment, and thereby paved the way for Henry's marriage to Anne Boleyn. English public opinion was against this marriage and strongly favored Queen Catherine as a woman much wronged. The marriage between Henry and Anne was publicly announced on May 28, 1533. In September the princess Elizabeth was born.

Since Rome had refused to support Henry's matrimonial plans, he decided to remove the English church from papal jurisdiction. Henry used Parliament to legalize the Reformation in England. The Act in Restraint of Appeals (1533) declared the king to be the supreme sovereign in England and forbade all judicial appeals to the papacy, thus establishing the Crown as the highest legal authority in the land. The Act for the Submission of the Clergy (1534) required churchmen to submit to the king and forbade the publication of all ecclesiastical laws without royal permission. The Supremacy Act of 1534 declared the king the supreme head of the Church of England. Both the Act in Restraint of Appeals and the Supremacy Act led to heated debate in the House of Commons. An authority on the Reformation Parliament has written that probably only a small number of those who voted the Restraint of Appeals actually knew they were voting for a permanent break with Rome.[28] Some opposed the king. John Fisher, the bishop of Rochester, a distinguished scholar and humanist who had preached the oration at the funeral of Henry VII, lashed the clergy with scorn for their

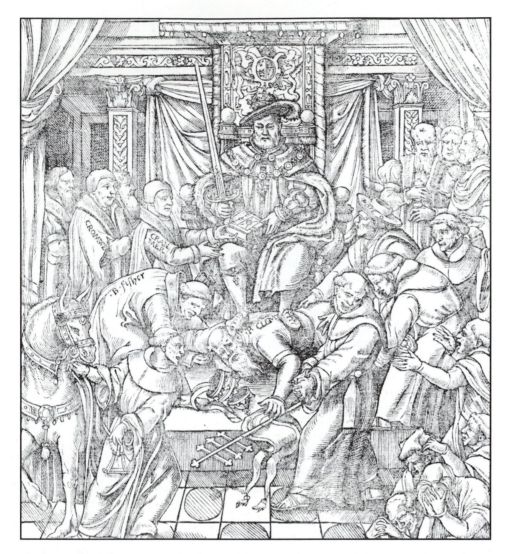

Henry VIII's "Victory"   This cartoon shows Henry VIII, assisted by Cromwell and Cranmer, triumphing over Pope Clement VII. Though completely removed from the historical facts, such illustrations were effectively used to promote antipapal feeling in late sixteenth-century England. *(Source: Fotomas Index)*

cowardice. Another humanist, Thomas More, resigned the chancellorship: he could not take the oath required by the Supremacy Act because it rejected papal authority and made the king head of the English church. Fisher, More, and other dissenters were beheaded.

When Anne Boleyn failed to produce a male child, Henry VIII charged her with adulterous incest and in 1536 had her beheaded. Parliament promptly proclaimed the princess Elizabeth illegitimate and, with the royal succession thoroughly

confused, left the throne to whomever Henry chose. His third wife, Jane Seymour, gave Henry the desired son, Edward, but died in childbirth. Henry went on to three more wives. Before he passed to his reward in 1547, he got Parliament to reverse the decision of 1536, relegitimating Mary and Elizabeth and fixing the succession first in his son and then in his daughters.

Between 1535 and 1539, under the influence of his chief minister, Thomas Cromwell, Henry decided to dissolve the English monasteries because he wanted their wealth. The king ended nine hundred years of English monastic life, dispersed the monks and nuns, and confiscated their lands. Hundreds of properties were later sold to the middle and upper classes and the proceeds spent on war. The dissolution of the monasteries did not achieve a more equitable distribution of land and wealth. Rather, the "bare ruined choirs where late the sweet birds sang"—as Shakespeare described the desolate religious houses—testified to the loss of a valuable aesthetic and cultural force in English life. The redistribution of land, however, greatly strengthened the upper classes and tied them to the Tudor dynasty.

Did the religious changes have broad popular support? Recent scholarly research has emphasized that the English Reformation came from above. The surviving evidence does not allow us to gauge the degree of opposition to (or support for) Henry's break with Rome. Certainly, many lay people wrote to the king, begging him to spare the monasteries. "Most laypeople acquiesced in the Reformation because they hardly knew what was going on, were understandably reluctant to jeopardise life or limb, a career or the family's good name."[29] But all did not quietly acquiesce. In 1536 popular opposition in the north to the religious changes led to the Pilgrimage of Grace, a massive multi-class rebellion that proved the largest in English history. In 1546 serious rebellions in East Anglia and in the west, despite possessing economic and Protestant components, reflected considerable public opposition to the state-ordered religious changes.[30]

Henry's motives combined personal, political, social, and economic elements. Theologically he retained such traditional Catholic practices and doctrines as auricular confession, clerical celibacy, and *transubstantiation* (the doctrine of the real presence of Christ in the bread and wine of the Eucharist, these elements retaining only the appearance and taste of bread and wine). Meanwhile, Protestant literature circulated, and Henry approved the selection of men with known Protestant sympathies as tutors for his son.

The nationalization of the church and the dissolution of the monasteries led to important changes in governmental administration. Vast tracts of land came temporarily under the Crown's jurisdiction, and new bureaucratic machinery had to be developed to manage those properties. Thomas Cromwell reformed and centralized the king's household, the council, the secretariats, and the Exchequer. New departments of state were set up. Surplus funds from all departments went into a liquid fund to be applied to areas where there were deficits. This balancing resulted in greater efficiency and economy. In Henry VIII's reign can be seen the growth of the modern centralized bureaucratic state.

For several decades after Henry's death in 1547, the English church shifted left and right. In the short reign of Henry's sickly son Edward VI (1547–1553), strongly Protestant ideas exerted a significant influence on the religious life of the country. Archbishop Thomas Cranmer simplified

Holbein: Sir Thomas More   This powerful portrait (1527), revealing More's strong character and humane sensitivity, shows Holbein's complete mastery of detail—down to the stubble on More's chin. The chain was an emblem of More's service to Henry VIII. *(Source: The Frick Collection, New York)*

the liturgy, invited Protestant theologians to England, and prepared the first *Book of Common Prayer* (1549). In stately and dignified English, the *Book of Common Prayer* included, together with the Psalter, the order for all services of the Church of England.

The equally brief reign of Mary Tudor (1553–1558) witnessed a sharp move back to Catholicism. The devoutly Catholic daughter of Catherine of Aragon, Mary rescinded the Reformation legislation of her father's reign and fully restored Roman Catholicism. Mary's marriage to her cousin Philip of Spain, son of the emperor Charles V, proved highly unpopular in England, and her persecution and execution of several hundred Protestants further alienated her subjects. During her reign, many Protestants fled to the Continent. Mary's death raised to the throne her sister Elizabeth (r. 1558–1603) and inaugurated the beginnings of religious stability.

At the beginning of her reign, Elizabeth's position was insecure. Although the populace cheered her accession, many questioned her legitimacy. On the one hand, Catholics wanted a Roman Catholic ruler. On the other hand, a vocal number of returned English exiles wanted all Catholic elements in the Church of England destroyed. The latter, because they wanted to "purify" the church, were called "Puritans."

Elizabeth had been raised a Protestant, but if she had genuine religious convictions she kept them to herself. Probably one of the shrewdest politicians in English history, Elizabeth chose a middle course between Catholic and Puritan extremes. She insisted on dignity in church services and political order in the land. She did not care what people believed as long as they kept quiet about it. Avoiding precise doctrinal definitions, Elizabeth had herself styled "Supreme Governor of the Church of England, Etc.," and left it to her subjects to decide what the "Etc." meant.

The parliamentary legislation of the early years of Elizabeth's reign—laws sometimes labeled the "Elizabethan Settlement"—required outward conformity to the Church of England and uniformity in all ceremonies. Everyone had to attend Church of England services; those who refused were fined. In 1563 a convocation of bishops approved the Thirty-nine Articles, a summary in thirty-nine short statements of the basic tenets of the Church of England. During Elizabeth's reign, the Anglican church (from the Latin *Ecclesia Anglicana*), as the Church of England was called, moved in a moder-

ately Protestant direction. Services were conducted in English, monasteries were not re-established, and the clergy were allowed to marry. But the bishops remained as church officials, and apart from language, the services were quite traditional.

The Establishment of the Church of Scotland

Reform of the church in Scotland did not follow the English model. In the early sixteenth century, the church in Scotland presented an extreme case of clerical abuse and corruption, and Lutheranism initially attracted sympathetic support. In Scotland as elsewhere, political authority was the decisive influence in reform. The monarchy was very weak, and factions of virtually independent nobles competed for power. King James V and his daughter Mary, Queen of Scots (r. 1560–1567), staunch Catholics and close allies of Catholic France, opposed reform. The Scottish nobles supported it. One man, John Knox (1505?–1572), dominated the movement for reform in Scotland.

In 1559 Knox, a dour, narrow-minded, and fearless man with a reputation as a passionate preacher, set to work reforming the church. He had studied and worked with Calvin in Geneva and was determined to structure the Scottish church after the model of Calvin's Geneva. In 1560 Knox persuaded the Scottish parliament, which was dominated by reform-minded barons, to enact legislation ending papal authority. The Mass was abolished and attendance at it forbidden under penalty of death. Knox then established the Presbyterian Church of Scotland, so named because *presbyters,* or ministers—not bishops—governed it. The Church of Scotland was strictly Calvinist in doctrine, adopted a simple and dignified service of worship, and laid great emphasis on preaching. Knox's *Book of Common Order* (1564) became the liturgical directory for the church. The Presbyterian Church of Scotland was a national, or state, church, and many of its members maintained close relations with English Puritans.

Protestantism in Ireland

To the ancient Irish hatred of English political and commercial exploitation, the Reformation added the bitter antagonism of religion. Henry VIII wanted to "reduce that realm to the knowledge of

God and obedience to us." English rulers in the sixteenth century regarded the Irish as barbarians, and a policy of complete extermination was rejected only because "to enterprise [attempt] the whole extirpation and total destruction of all the Irishmen in the land would be a marvelous sumptious charge and great difficulty."[31] In other words, it would have cost too much.

In 1536, on orders from London, the Irish parliament, which represented only the English landlords and the people of the Pale (the area around Dublin), approved the English laws severing the church from Rome and making the English king sovereign over ecclesiastical organization and practice. The Church of Ireland was established on the English pattern, and the (English) ruling class adopted the new reformed faith. Most of the Irish, probably for political reasons, defiantly remained Roman Catholic. Monasteries were secularized. Catholic property was confiscated and sold and the profits shipped to England. With the Roman church driven underground, the Catholic clergy acted as national as well as religious leaders.

Lutheranism in Sweden, Norway, and Denmark

In Sweden, Norway, and Denmark, the monarchy took the initiative in the religious Reformation. The resulting institutions were Lutheran state churches. Since the late fourteenth century, the Danish kings had ruled Sweden and Norway as well as Denmark. In 1520 the Swedish nobleman Gustavus Vasa led a successful revolt against Denmark, and Sweden became independent. As king, Gustavus Vasa seized church lands and required the bishops' loyalty to the Swedish crown. The Wittenberg-educated Swedish reformer Olaus Petri (1493–1552) translated the New Testament into Swedish and, with the full support of Gustavus Vasa, organized the church along strict Lutheran lines. This consolidation of the Swedish monarchy in the sixteenth century was to profoundly affect the development of Germany in the seventeenth century.

Christian III, king of Denmark (r. 1503–1559) and of Norway (r. 1534–1559), secularized church property and set up a Lutheran church. Norway, which was governed by Denmark until 1814, adopted Lutheranism as its state religion under Danish influence.

THE CATHOLIC AND THE COUNTER-REFORMATIONS

Between 1517 and 1547, the reformed versions of Christianity known as Protestantism made remarkable advances. All of England, Scandinavia, much of Scotland and Germany, and sizable parts of France and Switzerland adopted the creeds of Luther, Calvin, and other reformers. Still, the Roman Catholic church made a significant comeback. After about 1540, no new large areas of Europe, except for the Netherlands, accepted Protestant beliefs (Map 14.2).

Historians distinguish between two types of reform within the Catholic church in the sixteenth and seventeenth centuries. The Catholic Reformation began before 1517 and sought renewal basically through the stimulation of a new spiritual fervor. The Counter-Reformation started in the 1540s as a reaction to the rise and spread of Protestantism. The Counter-Reformation involved Catholic efforts to convince or coerce dissidents or heretics to return to the church lest they corrupt the entire community of Catholic believers. Fear of the "infection" of all Christian society by the religious dissident was a standard sixteenth-century attitude. If the heretic could not be persuaded to reconvert, counter-reformers believed it necessary to call on temporal authorities to defend Christian society by expelling or eliminating the dissident. The Catholic Reformation and the Counter-Reformation were not mutually exclusive; in fact, after about 1540 they progressed simultaneously.

The Slowness of Institutional Reform

The Renaissance princes who sat on the throne of Saint Peter were not blind to the evils that existed. Modest reform efforts had begun with the Lateran Council called in 1512 by Pope Julius II. The Dutch pope Adrian VI (1522–1523) instructed his legate in Germany to

say that we frankly confess that God permits this [Lutheran] persecution of his church on account of the sins of men, especially those of the priests and prelates. . . . We know that in this Holy See now for some years there have been many abominations, abuses in spiritual things, excesses in things commanded, in short that all has become perverted. . . . We have all turned aside in our ways, nor

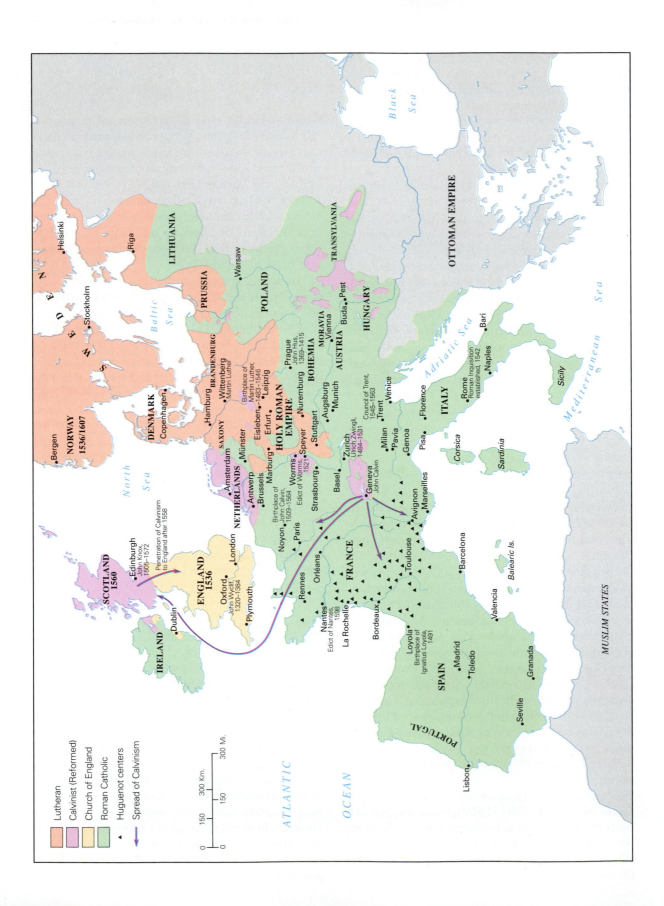

Black Sea

OTTOMAN EMPIRE

LITHUANIA

Helsinki
Riga

Baltic Sea

PRUSSIA

Warsaw

POLAND

TRANSYLVANIA

Stockholm

S W E D E N

HUNGARY

Pest

Buda

MORAVIA

Vienna

AUSTRIA

Adriatic Sea

Bari

BRANDENBURG

NORWAY
1536/1607

Bergen

DENMARK

Copenhagen

Hamburg

Wittenberg
Martin Luther

Birthplace of
Martin Luther,
1483–1546

Leipzig

SAXONY

Eisleben

Erfurt

Prague
John Hus,
1369–1415

BOHEMIA

Nuremberg

Augsburg

Munich

Council of Trent,
1545–1563

Venice

ITALY

Florence

Rome
Roman Inquisition
established, 1542

Naples

Sicily

Mediterranean Sea

North Sea

HOLY ROMAN
EMPIRE

Münster

Amsterdam

NETHERLANDS

Antwerp

Brussels

Marburg

Stuttgart

Speyer

Worms

Edict of Worms,
1521

Zurich
Ulrich Zwingli,
1484–1531

Milan

Pavia

Genoa

Pisa

Corsica

Sardinia

Birthplace of
John Calvin,
1509–1564

Noyon

Paris

Basel

Strasbourg

Geneva
John Calvin

Marseilles

Avignon

SCOTLAND
1560

Edinburgh
John Knox,
1505–1572

Penetration of Calvinism
to England after 1558

ENGLAND
1536

London

Oxford
John Wyclif,
1320–1384

Plymouth

Dublin

IRELAND

Rennes

Orléans

FRANCE

Toulouse

Nantes
Edict of Nantes,
1598

La Rochelle

Bordeaux

Barcelona

Valencia

Balearic Is.

Loyola
Birthplace of
Ignatius Loyola,
1491

Madrid

Toledo

SPAIN

Seville

Granada

PORTUGAL

Lisbon

ATLANTIC

OCEAN

MUSLIM STATES

Lutheran
Calvinist (Reformed)
Church of England
Roman Catholic
Huguenot centers
Spread of Calvinism

300 Mi.

300 Km.

150

150

0

0

was there, for a long time, any who did right—no, not one.[32]

Adrian VI tried desperately to reform the church and to check the spread of Protestantism. His reign lasted only thirteen months, however, and the austerity of his life and his Dutch nationality provoked the hostility of pleasure-loving Italian curial bureaucrats.

Overall, why did the popes, spiritual leaders of the Western church, move so slowly? The answers lie in the personalities of the popes themselves, their preoccupation with political affairs in Italy, and the awesome difficulty of reforming so complicated a bureaucracy as the Roman curia.

Clement VII, a true Medici, was far more interested in elegant tapestries and Michelangelo's painting of the Last Judgment than in theological disputes in barbaric Germany. Indecisive and vacillating, Pope Clement must bear much of the responsibility for the great spread of Protestantism. While Emperor Charles V and the French king Francis I competed for the domination of divided Italy, the papacy worried about the security of the Papal States. Clement tried to follow a middle course, backing first the emperor and then the French ruler. At the Battle of Pavia in 1525, Francis I suffered a severe defeat and was captured. In a reshuffling of diplomatic alliances, the pope switched from Charles and the Spaniards to Francis I. The emperor was victorious once again, however, and in 1527 his Spanish and German mercenaries sacked and looted Rome and captured the pope. Obviously, papal concern about Italian affairs and the Papal States diverted attention from reform.

The idea of reform was closely linked to the idea of a general council representing the entire church. A strong contingent of countries beyond the Alps —Spain, Germany, and France—wanted to reform the vast bureaucracy of Latin officials, reducing offices, men, and revenues. Popes from Julius II to Clement VII, remembering fifteenth-century conciliar attempts to limit papal authority, resisted calls for a council. The papal bureaucrats who were

Raphael: Pope Leo X and His Cousins   In this dynastic portrait of the Medici family, so suggested by the Medici ball on the back of the chair, the pope sits clothed in velvet and damask, while his cousins Cardinals Guilio de' Medici (later Pope Clement VII) and Luigi de Rossi stand. A fine humanist and musician, Cardinal Guilio was one of the most handsome men ever elected pope. The book on the table is opened to the beginning of St. John's Gospel, indicating Leo's namesake, Giovanni or John; weak eyesight forced him to use an eyeglass to read. *(Source: Alinari/Art Resource)*

the popes' intimates warned the popes against a council, fearing loss of power, revenue, and prestige. Five centuries before, Saint Bernard of Clairvaux had anticipated the situation: "The most grievous danger of any Pope lies in the fact that, encompassed as he is by flatterers, he never hears the truth about his own person and ends by not wishing to hear it."

The Council of Trent

In the papal conclave that followed the death of Clement VII, Cardinal Alexander Farnese promised two German cardinals that if he were elected

MAP 14.2 The Protestant and the Catholic Reformations   The reformations shattered the religious unity of Western Christendom. What common cultural traits predominated in regions where a particular branch of the Christian faith was maintained or took root?

pope he would summon a council. He won the election and ruled as Pope Paul III (1534–1549). This Roman aristocrat, humanist, and astrologer, who immediately made his teenage grandsons cardinals, seemed an unlikely person to undertake serious reform. Yet Paul III appointed as cardinals several learned and reform-minded men, such as Gian Pietro Caraffa (later Pope Paul IV); established the Inquisition in the Papal States; and—true to his word—called a council, which finally met at Trent, an imperial city close to Italy.

The Council of Trent met intermittently from 1545 to 1563. It was called not only to reform the church but to secure reconciliation with the Protestants. Lutherans and Calvinists were invited to participate, but their insistence that the Scriptures be the sole basis for discussion made reconciliation impossible. International politics repeatedly cast a shadow over the theological debates. Charles V opposed discussions on any matter that might further alienate his Lutheran subjects, fearing the loss of additional imperial territory to Lutheran princes.

The Council of Trent   This seventeenth-century engraving depicts one of the early and sparsely attended sessions of the Council of Trent. The tridentine sessions of 1562–1563 drew many more bishops and laymen, but there were never many representatives from northern Europe. *(Source: Photo Vatican Museums)*

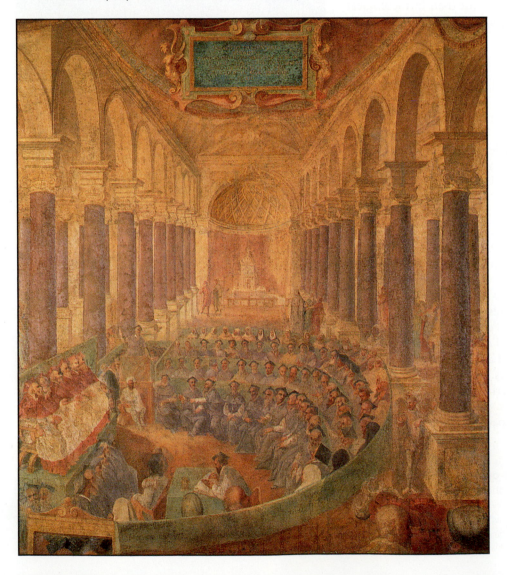

Meanwhile, the French kings worked against the reconciliation of Roman Catholicism and Lutheranism. As long as religious issues divided the German states, the empire would be weakened, and a weak and divided empire meant a stronger France. Portugal, Poland, Hungary, and Ireland sent representatives, but very few German bishops attended.

Another problem was the persistence of the conciliar theory of church government. Some bishops wanted a concrete statement asserting the supremacy of a church council over the papacy. The adoption of the conciliar principle could have led to a divided church. The bishops had a provincial and national outlook; only the papacy possessed an international religious perspective. The centralizing tenet was established that all acts of the council required papal approval.

In spite of the obstacles, the achievements of the Council of Trent are impressive. It dealt with both doctrinal and disciplinary matters. The council gave equal validity to the Scriptures and to tradition as sources of religious truth and authority. It reaffirmed the seven sacraments and the traditional Catholic teaching on transubstantiation. Thus Lutheran and Calvinist positions were rejected.

The council tackled the problems arising from ancient abuses by strengthening ecclesiastical discipline. Tridentine (from *Tridentum,* the Latin word for Trent) decrees required bishops to reside in their own dioceses, suppressed pluralism and simony, and forbade the sale of indulgences. Clerics who kept concubines were to give them up. The jurisdiction of bishops over all the clergy of their dioceses was made almost absolute, and bishops were ordered to visit every religious house within the diocese at least once every two years. In a highly original canon, the council required every diocese to establish a seminary for the education and training of the clergy; the council even prescribed the curriculum and insisted that preference for admission be given to sons of the poor. Finally, great emphasis was laid on preaching and instructing the laity, especially the uneducated.

The Council of Trent did not meet everyone's expectations. Reconciliation with Protestantism was not achieved, nor was reform brought about immediately. Nevertheless, the Tridentine decrees laid a solid basis for the spiritual renewal of the church and for the enforcement of correction. For four centuries, the doctrinal and disciplinary legislation of Trent served as the basis for Roman Catholic faith, organization, and practice.

New Religious Orders

The establishment of new religious orders within the church reveals a central feature of the Catholic Reformation. These new orders developed in response to one crying need: to raise the moral and intellectual level of the clergy and people. Education was a major goal of them all.

The Ursuline order of nuns, founded by Angela Merici (1474–1540), attained enormous prestige for the education of women. The daughter of a country gentleman, Angela Merici worked for many years among the poor, sick, and uneducated around her native Brescia in northern Italy. In 1535 she established the Ursuline order to combat heresy through Christian education. The first women's religious order concentrating exclusively on teaching young girls, the Ursulines sought to re-Christianize society by training future wives and mothers. Approved as a religious community by Paul III in 1544, the Ursulines rapidly grew and spread to France and the New World. Their schools in North America, stretching from Quebec to New Orleans, provided superior education for young women and inculcated the spiritual ideals of the Catholic Reformation.

The Society of Jesus, founded by Ignatius Loyola (1491–1556), a former Spanish soldier, played a powerful international role in resisting the spread of Protestantism, converting Asians and Latin American Indians to Catholicism, and spreading Christian education all over Europe. While recuperating from a severe battle wound in his legs, Loyola studied a life of Christ and other religious books and decided to give up his military career and become a soldier of Christ. During a year spent in seclusion, prayer, and personal mortification, he gained the religious insights that went into his great classic, *Spiritual Exercises.* This work, intended for study during a four-week period of retreat, directed the individual imagination and will to the reform of life and a new spiritual piety.

Loyola was apparently a man of considerable personal magnetism. After study at the universities in Salamanca and Paris, he gathered a group of six companions and in 1540 secured papal approval of the new Society of Jesus, whose members were called "Jesuits." Their goals were the reform of the church primarily through education, preaching the Gospel to pagan peoples, and fighting Protestantism. Within a short time, the Jesuits had attracted many recruits.

Pope Paul III's Confirmation of the Jesuit Constitutions   On the right Ignatius Loyola receives the constitutions of the Society of Jesus by direct illumination from God. At left the pope approves them. When the constitutions were read to him, Paul III supposedly murmured, "There is the finger of God." *(Source: Historical Picture Service, Chicago)*

The Society of Jesus was a highly centralized, tightly knit organization. Candidates underwent a two-year novitiate, in contrast to the usual one-year probation. Although new members took the traditional vows of poverty, chastity, and obedience, the emphasis was on obedience. Carefully selected members made a fourth vow of obedience to the pope and the governing members of the society. As faith was the cornerstone of Luther's life, so obedience became the bedrock of the Jesuit tradition.

The Jesuits had a modern, quasi-military quality; they achieved phenomenal success for the papacy and the reformed Catholic church. Jesuit schools adopted humanist curricula and methods, and while they first concentrated on the children of the poor, they were soon educating the sons of the nobility. As confessors and spiritual directors to kings, Jesuits exerted great political influence. Operating on the principle that the end sometimes justifies the means, they were not above spying. Indifferent to physical comfort and personal safety, they carried Christianity to India and Japan before 1550, to Brazil, North America, and the Congo in the seventeenth century. Within Europe, the Jesuits brought southern Germany and much of eastern Europe back to Catholicism.

The Sacred Congregation of the Holy Office

In 1542 Pope Paul III established the Sacred Congregation of the Holy Office with jurisdiction over the Roman Inquisition, a powerful instrument of the Counter-Reformation. The Inquisition was a committee of six cardinals with judicial authority over all Catholics and the power to arrest, imprison, and execute. Under the fanatical Cardinal Caraffa, it vigorously attacked heresy.

The Roman Inquisition operated under the principles of Roman law. It accepted hearsay evidence, was not obliged to inform the accused of charges against them, and sometimes applied torture. Echoing one of Calvin's remarks about heresy, Cardinal Caraffa wrote, "No man is to lower himself by showing toleration towards any sort of heretic, least of all a Calvinist."[33] The Holy Office published the *Index of Prohibited Books,* a catalogue of forbidden reading.

Within the Papal States, the Inquisition effectively destroyed heresy (and some heretics). Outside the papal territories, however, its influence was slight. Governments had their own judicial systems for the suppression of treasonable activities, as religious heresy was then considered. The republic of Venice is a good case in point.

In the sixteenth century, Venice was one of the great publishing centers of Europe. The Inquisition and the Index could have badly damaged the Venetian book trade, but authorities there cooperated with the Holy Office only when heresy became a great threat to the security of the republic. The Index had no influence on scholarly research in nonreligious areas, such as law, classical literature, and mathematics. As a result of the Inquisition, Venetians and Italians were *not* cut off from the main currents of European learning.[34]

SUMMARY

Demands for the reform of the Christian church go back very far in European history. In the fifteenth and early sixteenth centuries, movements such as the Brethren of the Common Life, Lollardy, the Oratories of Divine Love, and the efforts of the Roman papacy itself paved the way for institutional reform. Martin Luther's strictly religious call for reform, rapidly spread by preaching, hymns, and the printing press, soon became enmeshed in social, economic, and political issues. The German peasants interpreted Luther's ideas in an economic sense: Christian liberty for them meant the end of harsh manorial burdens. Princes used the cloak of the new religious ideas both to acquire the material wealth of the Church and to thwart the centralizing goals of the emperor. In England the political issue of the royal succession triggered that country's break with Rome, and in Switzerland and France the political and social ethos of Calvinism attracted many people. The Protestant doctrine that all callings have equal merit in God's sight and its stress on the home as the special domain of women drew women to Protestantism. The reformulation of Roman Catholic doctrine at the Council of Trent; the new religious orders such as the Jesuits and the Ursulines; and the Roman Inquisition all represent the Catholic response to the demands for reform.

The age of the Reformation presents very real paradoxes. The break with Rome and the rise of Lutheran, Anglican, Calvinist, and other faiths destroyed the unity of Europe as an organic Christian society. Saint Paul's exhortation, "There should be no schism in the body [of the church]. . . . You are all one in Christ,"[35] was widely ignored. On the other hand, religious belief remained tremendously strong. In fact, the strength of religious convictions caused political fragmentation. In the later sixteenth century and through most of the seventeenth, religion and religious issues continued to play a major role in the lives of individuals and in the policies and actions of governments. Religion, whether Protestant or Catholic, decisively influenced the growth of national states.

Scholars have maintained that the sixteenth century witnessed the beginnings of the modern world. They are both right and wrong. Although most of the church reformers rejected the idea of religious toleration, they helped pave the way for it. They also paved the way for the eighteenth-century revolt from the Christian God, one of the strongest supports of life in Western culture. In this respect, the Reformation marked the beginning of the modern world, with its secularism and rootlessness. At the same time, it can equally be argued that the sixteenth century represented the culmination of the Middle Ages. Martin Luther's anxieties about salvation show him to be very much a medieval man. His concerns had deeply troubled serious individuals since the time of Saint Augustine. In modern times, such concerns have tended to take different forms.

NOTES

1. Romans 12:2–3.
2. Quoted in J. Burckhardt, *The Civilization of the Renaissance in Italy* (London: Phaidon Books, 1951), p. 262.

The Later Middle Ages, Renaissance, and Protestant

	Government and Law	Philosophy and Science
1300	Hundred Years' War, 1337–1453 Political chaos in Germany, ca 1350–1450	Master Eckhart, active ca 1300–1327
1400	Appearance of Joan of Arc, 1429–1431 Medici domination of Florence begins, 1434 Princes in Germany consolidate power, ca 1450–1500 Capture of Constantinople by Ottoman Turks, 1453 Wars of the Roses in England, 1453–1471 Unification of Spain under Ferdinand and Isabella, 1492 French invade Italy, 1494	Printing with movable type, ca 1450
1500	Troops of Holy Roman Emperor Charles V (r. 1519–1546) sack Rome, 1527 Revolt of the Netherlands, 1566–1609 St. Bartholemew's Day Massacre, 1572 Defeat of Spanish Armada, 1588 Edict of Nantes, 1598	Erasmus, *The Praise of Folly,* 1509 Machiavelli, *The Prince,* 1513 Thomas More, *Utopia,* 1516 Castiglione, *The Courtier,* 1528 Copernicus, *On the Revolutions,* 1543 Francis Bacon, *The Advancement of Learning,* 1605

and Catholic Reformations, 1300–1600

Economics	Religion	Arts and Letters
European economic depression, ca 1300–1450	Babylonian captivity of papacy, 1309–1372	Dante, *The Devine Comedy,* 1300–1321
Black Death, begins 1347; recurs intermittently until 18th c.	John Wyclif, ca 1330–1384	Petrarch, 1304–1374
Height of Hanseatic League, ca 1350–1450	Great Schism of papacy, 1377–1417	Boccaccio, *The Decameron,* ca 1350
The Jacquerie in France, 1358		Jan van Eyck, 1366–1441
Laborers' revolt in Florence, 1378		Brunelleschi, 1377–1446
Peasants' Revolt in England, 1381		Chaucer, *Canterbury Tales,* ca 1385–1400
Columbus reaches the Americas, 1492	Council of Constance, 1414–1418	Masaccio, 1401–1428
Portugal gains control of East Indian spice trade, 1498–1511	Pragmatic Sanction of Bourges, 1438	Botticelli, 1444–1510
	Expulsion of Jews from Spain, 1492	Leonardo da Vinci, 1452–1519
		Albrecht Dürer, 1471–1528
		Michelangelo, 1475–1564
		Raphael, 1483–1520
		Rabelais, ca 1490–1553
Balboa discovers the Pacific, 1513	Lateran Council undertakes reform of clerical abuses, 1512–1517	Cervantes, 1547–1616
Magellan's crew circumnavigates the earth, 1519–1522	Concordat of Bologna, 1516	Shakespeare, 1564–1616
Spain gains control of Central and South America, ca 1520–1550	Martin Luther proclaims the Ninety-Five Theses, 1517	Rubens, 1577–1640
Peasants' Revolt in Germany, 1524	Henry VIII of England breaks with Rome, 1529–1534	
	Anabaptists take over Münster, 1534	
	Loyola founds the Society of Jesus, 1540	
	Calvin establishes a theocracy in Geneva, 1541	
	Council of Trent, 1545–1563	
	Peace of Augsburg, 1555	

3. See R. R. Post, *The Modern Devotion: Confrontation with Reformation and Humanism* (Leiden: E. J. Brill, 1968), esp. pp. 237–238, 255, 323–348.

4. E. Erikson, *Young Man Luther: A Study in Psychoanalysis and History* (New York: W. W. Norton, 1962).

5. Quoted in T. C. Mendenhall et al., eds., *Ideas and Institutions in European History: 800–1715* (New York: Henry Holt, 1948), p. 220.

6. Quoted in O. Chadwick, *The Reformation* (Baltimore: Penguin Books, 1976), p. 55.

7. Quoted in E. H. Harbison, *The Age of Reformation* (Ithaca, N.Y.: Cornell University Press, 1963), p. 52.

8. This passage is based heavily on Harbison, pp. 52–55.

9. See S. E. Ozment, *The Reformation in the Cities: The Appeal of Protestantism to Sixteenth-Century Germany and Switzerland* (New Haven: Yale University Press, 1975), pp. 32–45.

10. See S. E. Ozment, *The Age of Reform, 1250–1550: An Intellectual and Religious History of Late Medieval and Reformation Europe* (New Haven: Yale University Press, 1980), pp. 273–279.

11. Quoted in ibid., p. 280.

12. Ibid., p. 281.

13. Ibid., p. 284.

14. Romans 13:1–2.

15. Erikson, p. 47.

16. G. Strauss, *Luther's House of Learning: Indoctrination of the Young in the German Reformation* (Baltimore: Johns Hopkins University Press, 1978), esp. pp. 159–162, 231–233.

17. See R. H. Bainton, *Women of the Reformation in Germany and Italy* (Minneapolis: Augsburg, 1971), pp. 9–10; and Ozment, *The Reformation in the Cities,* pp. 53–54, 171–172.

18. Quoted in H. G. Haile, *Luther: An Experiment in Biography* (Garden City, N.Y.: Doubleday, 1980), p. 272.

19. Quoted in J. Atkinson, *Martin Luther and the Birth of Protestantism* (Baltimore: Penguin Books, 1968), pp. 247–248.

20. *Martin Luther: Three Treatises* (Philadelphia: Muhlenberg Press, 1947), pp. 28–31.

21. J. Allen, trans., *John Calvin: The Institutes of the Christian Religion* (Philadelphia: Westminster Press, 1930), bk. 3, chap. 21, paras. 5, 7.

22. E. W. Monter, *Calvin's Geneva* (New York: John Wiley & Sons, 1967), pp. 98–108.

23. Ibid., p. 137.

24. Quoted in Bainton, pp. 69–70.

25. A. G. Dickens, *The English Reformation* (New York: Schocken Books, 1964), p. 36.

26. Leviticus 18:16, 20, 21.

27. See R. Marius, *Thomas More: A Biography* (New York: Alfred A. Knopf, 1984), pp. 215–216.

28. See S. E. Lehmberg, *The Reformation Parliament 1529–1536* (Cambridge: Cambridge University Press, 1970), pp. 174–176, 204–205.

29. J. J. Scarisbrick, *The Reformation and the English People* (Oxford: Basil Blackwell, 1984), pp. 81–84, esp. p. 81.

30. Ibid.

31. Quoted in P. Smith, *The Age of the Reformation,* rev. ed. (New York: Henry Holt, 1951), p. 346.

32. Ibid., p. 84.

33. Quoted in Chadwick, p. 270.

34. See P. Grendler, *The Roman Inquisition and the Venetian Press, 1540–1605* (Princeton, N.J.: Princeton University Press, 1977).

35. 1 Corinthians 1:25, 27.

SUGGESTED READING

There are many easily accessible and lucidly written general studies of the reformations of the sixteenth century. P. Chaunu, ed., *The Reformation* (1989), is a lavishly illustrated anthology of articles by an international team of scholars, a fine appreciation of both theological and historical developments, with an up-to-date bibliography. H. Hillerbrand, *Men and Ideas in the Sixteenth Century* (1969), and the books by Chadwick and Harbison listed in the Notes are all good general introductions. P. Smith, *The Age of the Reformation,* rev. ed. (1951), is an older, broad, and often anecdotal treatment. L. W. Spitz, *The Protestant Reformation, 1517–1559* (1985), provides a sound and comprehensive survey that incorporates the latest scholarly research. For the current trend in scholarship, interpreting the Reformation against the background of fifteenth-century reforming developments, see the excellent study of J. F. D'Amico, *Renaissance Humanism in Papal Rome: Humanists and Churchmen on the Eve of the Reformation* (1983), and J. H. Overfield, *Humanism and Scholasticism in Late Medieval Germany* (1984), which portrays the intellectual life of the German universities, the milieu from which the Protestant Reformation emerged. Older studies include H. A. Oberman, *The Harvest of Medieval Theology: Gabriel Biel and Late Medieval Nominalism* (1963); R. R. Post, *The Modern Devotion* (1968); G. Strauss, ed., *Manifestations of Discontent in Germany on the Eve of the Reformation* (1971), a useful and exciting collection of documents; and S. Ozment, *The Age of Reform, 1250–1550: An Intellectual and Religious History of Late Medieval and Reformation Europe* (1980), which combines intellectual and social history. For the condition of the church in the late fifteenth and early sixteenth centuries, see D. Hay, *The Church in Italy in the Fifteenth Century* (1977), and P. Heath, *The English Parish Clergy on the Eve of the Reformation* (1969); J.

Moran, *The Growth of English Schooling, 1340–1548* (1985) also contains useful material.

For the central figure of the early Reformation, Martin Luther, students should see the works by Atkinson, Erikson, and Haile mentioned in the Notes, as well as H. Boehmer, *Martin Luther: Road to Reformation* (1960), a well-balanced work treating Luther's formative years. Students may expect thorough and sound treatments of Luther's theology in the following distinguished works: H. Bornkamm, *Luther in Mid-Career, 1521–1530* (1983); A. E. McGrath, *Luther's Theology of the Cross: Martin Luther on Justification* (1985); M. Brecht, *Martin Luther: His Road to Reformation* (trans. J. L. Schaaf, 1985), which includes an exploration of Luther's background and youth; and J. Pelikan, *Reformation of Church and Dogma, 1300–1700* (1986).

The best study of John Calvin is W. J. Bouwsma, *John Calvin: A Sixteenth-Century Portrait* (1988), an authoritative study that situates Calvin within Renaissance culture. See also F. Wendel, *Calvin: The Origins and Development of His Thought* (trans. P. Mairet, 1963). J. T. McNeill, *History and Character of Calvinism* (1954), presents useful information, while W. E. Monter, *Calvin's Geneva* (1967), is an excellent account of the effect of Calvin's reforms on the social life of that Swiss city. R. T. Kendall, *Calvinism and English Calvinism to 1649* (1981), presents English conditions, while R. M. Mitchell, *Calvin and the Puritan's View of the Protestant Ethic* (1979), interprets the socioeconomic implications of Calvin's thought. Students interested in the left wing of the Reformation should see the profound though difficult work of G. H. Williams, *The Radical Reformers* (1962).

For various aspects of the social history of the period, see in addition to the titles by Bainton and Ozment cited in the Notes, S. Ozment, *Magdalena and Balthasar* (1987), which reveals many features of social life through the letters of a Nuremburg couple; L. P. Buck and J. W. Zophy, eds., *The Social History of the Reformation* (1972), and K. von Greyerz, ed., *Religion and Society in Early Modern Europe, 1500–1800* (1984), both of which contain interesting essays on religion, society, and popular culture. Two books listed in the Notes make important contributions to social history: S. Ozment, *The Reformation in the Cities,* and G. Strauss, *Luther's House of Learning,* which describes how plain people were imbued with Reformation ideals and patterns of behavior. R. L. De Molen, *Leaders of the Reformation* (1984), contains provocative portraits of several figures including Zwingli, Loyola, Cromwell, and Calvin. For women's studies in the German context, see M. Wiesner, *Women in the Sixteenth Century: A Bibliography* (1983), a useful reference tool; and S. M. Wyntjes, "Women in the Refor-

mation Era," in R. Bridenthal and C. Koonz, eds., *Becoming Visible: Women in European History* (1977), an interesting general survey. The best recent treatment of marriage and the family is S. Ozment, *When Fathers Ruled: Family Life in Reformation Europe* (1983). Ozment's edition of *Reformation Europe: A Guide to Research* (1982) contains not only helpful references but valuable articles on such topics as "The German Peasants," "The Anabaptists," and "The Confessional Age: The Late Reformation in Germany." For Servetus, see R. H. Bainton, *Hunted Heretic: The Life and Death of Michael Servetus* (1953), which remains valuable.

For England, in addition to the fundamental work by Dickens cited in the Notes, K. Thomas, *Religion and the Decline of Magic* (1971), provides a useful treatment of pre-Reformation popular religion, as does J. J. Scarisbrick, *The Reformation and the English People,* also mentioned in the Notes, and S. T. Bindoff, *Tudor England* (1959), a good short synthesis. The marital trials of Henry VIII are treated in both the sympathetic study of G. Mattingly, *Catherine of Aragon* (1949), and H. A. Kelly, *The Matrimonial Trials of Henry VIII* (1975). A persuasive treatment of Henry VIII's possible syphilis and its effects on his children is given in F. S. Cartwright, *Disease and History* (1972). The legal implications of Henry VIII's divorces have been thoroughly analyzed in J. J. Scarisbrick, *Henry VIII* (1968), an almost definitive biography. On the dissolution of the English monasteries, see D. Knowles, *The Religious Orders in England,* vol. 3 (1959), one of the finest examples of historical prose in English written in the twentieth century. Knowles's *Bare Ruined Choirs* (1976) is an attractively illustrated abridgment of *Religious Orders.* G. R. Elton, *The Tudor Revolution in Government* (1959), discusses the modernization of English government under Thomas Cromwell, while the same author's *Reform and Reformation: England, 1509–1558* (1977) combines political and social history in a broad study. Many aspects of English social history are discussed in J. Youings, *Sixteenth Century England* (1984), a beautifully written work, which is highly recommended. The biography of Thomas More by R. Marius, listed in the Notes, provides a thorough and perceptive study of the great humanist, lord chancellor, and saint.

P. Janelle, *The Catholic Reformation* (1951), is a comprehensive treatment of the Catholic Reformation from a Catholic point of view, and A. G. Dickens, *The Counter Reformation* (1969), gives the Protestant standpoint in a beautifully illustrated book. The definitive study of the Council of Trent was written by H. Jedin, *A History of the Council of Trent,* 3 vols. (1957–1961). For the Jesuits, see M. Foss, *The Founding of the Jesuits, 1540* (1969), and W. B. Bangert, *A History of the Society of Jesus* (1972).

15

The Age of European Expansion and Religious Wars

etween 1560 and 1648 two developments dramatically altered the world in which Europeans lived: overseas expansion and the reformations of the Christian churches. Overseas expansion broadened Europeans' geographical horizons and brought them into confrontation with ancient civilizations in Africa, Asia, and the Americas. These confrontations led first to conquest, then to exploitation, and finally to profound social changes in both Europe and the conquered territories. Likewise, the Renaissance and the reformations drastically changed intellectual, political, religious, and social life in Europe. War and religious issues dominated politics. Though religion was commonly used to rationalize international conflict, wars were fought for power and territorial expansion.

Meanwhile, Europeans carried their political, religious, and social attitudes to their territories.

- Why, in the sixteenth and seventeenth centuries, did a relatively small group living on the edge of the Eurasian land mass gain control of the major sea lanes of the world and establish political and economic hegemony on distant continents?
- What effect did overseas expansion have on Europe and on conquered societies?
- What were the causes and consequences of the religious wars in France, the Netherlands, and Germany?
- How did the religious crises of this period affect the status of women?
- How and why did slave labor become the dominant form of labor organization in the New World?
- What religious and intellectual developments led to the growth of skepticism?
- What literary masterpieces of the English-speaking world did this period produce?

This chapter will address these questions.

DISCOVERY, RECONNAISSANCE, AND EXPANSION

Historians have variously called the period from 1450 to 1650 the "Age of Discovery," "Age of Reconnaissance," and "Age of Expansion." All three labels are appropriate. The "Age of Discovery" refers to the era's phenomenal advances in geographical knowledge and technology, often achieved through trial and error. In 1350 it took as long to sail from the eastern end of the Mediterranean to the western end as it had taken a thousand years earlier. Even in the fifteenth century, Europeans knew little more about the earth's surface than the Romans had. By 1650, however, Europeans had made an extensive reconnaissance—or preliminary exploration—and had sketched fairly accurately the physical outline of the whole earth. Much of the geographical information they had gathered was tentative and not fully understood—hence the appropriateness of the term the "Age of Reconnaissance."

The designation of the era as the "Age of Expansion" refers to the migration of Europeans to other parts of the world. This colonization resulted in political control of much of South and North America; coastal regions of Africa, India, China, and Japan; and many Pacific islands. Political hegemony was accompanied by economic exploitation, religious domination, and the introduction of European patterns of social and intellectual life. The sixteenth-century expansion of European society launched a new age in world history.

Overseas Exploration and Conquest

The outward expansion of Europe began with the Viking voyages across the Atlantic in the ninth and tenth centuries. Under Eric the Red and Leif Ericson, the Vikings discovered Greenland and the eastern coast of North America. The Vikings made permanent settlements in, and a legal imprint on, Iceland, Ireland, England, Normandy, and Sicily (see pages 250–253). The Crusades of the eleventh through thirteenth centuries were another phase in Europe's attempt to explore and exploit peoples on the periphery of the Continent. But weak support from the West, the lack of a strong territorial base, and sheer misrule combined to make the medieval Crusader kingdoms short-lived. In the mid-fifteenth century, Europe seemed ill prepared for further international ventures. By 1450 a grave new threat had appeared in the East—the Ottoman Turks.

Combining excellent military strategy with efficient administration of their conquered territories, the Turks had subdued most of Asia Minor and begun to settle on the western side of the Bosporus.

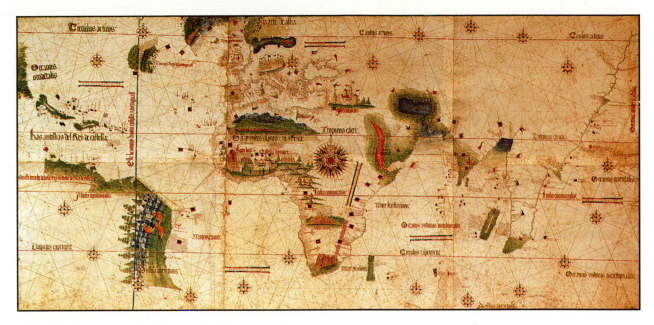

The Cantino Map (1502), named for the agent secretly commissioned to design it in Lisbon for the Duke of Ferrara, an avid Italian map collector, reveals such a good knowledge of the African continent, of the islands of the West Indies, and of the shoreline of present-day Venezuela, Guiana, and Brazil in South America that modern scholars suspect there may have been clandestine voyages to the Americas shortly after Columbus's. *(Source: Biblioteca Estense Universitaria, Modena)*

The Ottoman Turks under Sultan Mohammed II (r. 1451–1481) captured Constantinople in 1453, pressed northwest into the Balkans, and by the early sixteenth century controlled the eastern Mediterranean. The Turkish menace badly frightened Europeans. In France in the fifteenth and sixteenth centuries, twice as many books were printed about the Turkish threat as about the American discoveries. Yet the fifteenth and sixteenth centuries witnessed a fantastic continuation, on a global scale, of European expansion.

Political centralization in Spain, France, and England helps to explain those countries' outward push. In the fifteenth century, Isabella and Ferdinand had consolidated their several kingdoms to achieve a more united Spain. The Catholic rulers revamped the Spanish bureaucracy and humbled dissident elements, notably the Muslims and the Jews. The Spanish monarchy was stronger than ever before and in a position to support foreign ventures; it could bear the costs and dangers of exploration. But Portugal, situated on the extreme southwestern edge of the European continent, got the start on the rest of Europe. Still insignificant as a European land power despite its recently secured frontiers, Portugal sought greatness in the unknown world overseas.

Portugal's taking of Ceuta, an Arab city in northern Morocco, in 1415 marked the beginning of European exploration and control of overseas territory. The objectives of Portuguese policy included the historic Iberian crusade to Christianize Muslims and the search for gold, for an overseas route to the spice markets of India, and for the mythical Christian ruler of Ethiopia, Prester John.

In the early phases of Portuguese exploration, Prince Henry (1394–1460), called "the Navigator" because of the annual expeditions he sent down the western coast of Africa, played the leading role. In the fifteenth century, most of the gold that reached Europe came from the Sudan in West Africa and from Ashanti blacks living near the area of present-day Ghana. Muslim caravans brought the gold from the African cities of Niani and Timbuktu and carried it north across the Sahara to Mediterranean ports. Then the Portuguese muscled in on this commerce in gold. Prince Henry's carefully planned expeditions succeeded in reaching

Guinea, and under King John II (r. 1481–1495) the Portuguese established trading posts and forts on the Guinea coast and penetrated into the continent all the way to Timbuktu (see Map 15.1). Portuguese ships transported gold to Lisbon, and by 1500 Portugal controlled the flow of gold to Europe. The golden century of Portuguese prosperity had begun.

Still the Portuguese pushed farther south down the west coast of Africa. In 1487 Bartholomew Diaz rounded the Cape of Good Hope at the

Columbus Lands on San Salvador The printed page and illustrations such as this German woodcut spread reports of Columbus's voyage all over Europe. According to Columbus, a group of naked Indians greeted the Spaniards' arrival. Pictures of the Indians as "primitive" and "uncivilized" instilled prejudices that centuries have not erased. *(Source: New York Public Library)*

southern tip, but storms and a threatened mutiny forced him to turn back. On a second expedition (1497–1499), the Portuguese mariner Vasco da Gama reached India and returned to Lisbon loaded with samples of Indian wares. King Manuel (r. 1495–1521) promptly dispatched thirteen ships under the command of Pedro Alvares Cabral, assisted by Diaz, to set up trading posts in India. On April 22, 1500, the coast of Brazil in South America was sighted and claimed for the crown of Portugal. Cabral then proceeded south and east around the Cape of Good Hope and reached India. Half the fleet was lost on the return voyage, but the six spice-laden vessels that dropped anchor in Lisbon harbor in July 1501 more than paid for the entire expedition. Thereafter, convoys were sent out every March. Lisbon became the entrance port for Asian goods into Europe—but this was not accomplished without a fight.

For centuries the Muslims had controlled the rich spice trade of the Indian Ocean, and they did not surrender it willingly. Portuguese commercial activities were accompanied by the destruction or seizure of strategic Muslim coastal forts, which later served Portugal as both trading posts and military bases. Alfonso de Albuquerque, whom the Portuguese crown appointed as governor of India (1509–1515), decided that these bases and not inland territories should control the Indian Ocean. Accordingly, his cannon blasted open the ports of Calicut, Ormuz, Goa, and Malacca, the vital centers of Arab domination of south Asian trade. This bombardment laid the foundation for Portuguese imperialism in the sixteenth and seventeenth centuries: a strange way to bring Christianity to "those who were in darkness." As one scholar wrote about the opening of China to the West, "while Buddha came to China on white elephants, Christ was borne on cannon balls."[1]

In March 1493, between the voyages of Diaz and da Gama, Spanish ships entered Lisbon harbor bearing a triumphant Italian explorer in the service of the Spanish monarchy. Christopher Columbus (1451–1506), a Genoese mariner, had secured Spanish support for an expedition to the East. He sailed from Palos, Spain, to the Canary Islands and crossed the Atlantic to the Bahamas, landing in October 1492 on an island that he named "San Salvador" and believed to be the coast of India.

Columbus explained his motives in *Book of the First Navigation and Discovery of the Indies:*

And Your Highnesses, as Catholic Christians and Princes devoted to the Holy Christian Faith and the propagators thereof, and enemies of the sect of Mahomet and of all idolatries and heresies, resolved to send me Christopher Columbus to the said regions of India, to see the said princes and peoples and lands and [to observe] the disposition of them and of all, and the manner in which may be undertaken their conversion to our Holy Faith, and ordained that I should not go by land (the usual way) to the Orient, but by the route of the Occident, by which no one to this day knows for sure that anyone has gone.[2]

Like most people of his day, Christopher Columbus was deeply religious. The crew of his flagship, *Santa Maria,* recited vespers every night and sang a hymn to the Virgin before going to bed. Nevertheless, the Spanish fleet, sailing westward to find the East, sought wealth as well as souls to convert.

Between 1492 and 1502, Columbus made four voyages to America, discovering all the major islands of the Caribbean—Haiti (which he called "Dominica" and the Spanish named "Hispaniola"), San Salvador, Puerto Rico, Jamaica, Cuba, Trinidad—and Honduras in Central America. Columbus believed until he died that the islands he found were off the coast of India. In fact, he had opened up for the rulers of Spain a whole new world. The Caribbean islands—the West Indies—represented to Spanish missionary zeal millions of Indian natives for conversion to Christianity. Hispaniola, Cuba, and Puerto Rico also offered gold.

Forced labor, disease, and starvation in the Spaniards' gold mines rapidly killed off the Indians of Hispaniola. When Columbus arrived in 1492, the population had been approximately 100,000; in 1570, 300 people survived. Indian slaves from the Bahamas and black Africans from Guinea were then imported to do the mining.

The search for precious metals determined the direction of Spanish exploration and expansion into South America. When it became apparent that placer mining (in which ore is separated from soil by panning) in the Caribbean islands was slow and the rewards slim, new routes to the East and new sources of gold and silver were sought.

In 1519 the Spanish ruler Charles V commissioned Ferdinand Magellan (1480–1521) to find a direct route to the Moluccan Islands off the southeast coast of Asia. Magellan sailed southwest across the Atlantic to Brazil and proceeded south around Cape Horn into the Pacific Ocean (Map 15.1). He crossed the Pacific, sailing west, to the Malay Archipelago, which he called the "Western Isles." (Some of these islands were conquered in the 1560s and named the "Philippines" for Philip II of Spain.)

Though Magellan was killed, the expedition continued, returning to Spain in 1522 from the east by way of the Indian Ocean, the Cape of Good Hope, and the Atlantic. Terrible storms, mutiny, starvation, and disease haunted this voyage. Nevertheless, it verified the theory that the earth was round and brought information about the vastness of the Pacific. Magellan also proved that the earth was much larger than Columbus had estimated.

In the West Indies, the slow recovery of gold, the shortage of a healthy labor force, and sheer restlessness speeded up Spain's search for wealth. In 1519, the year Magellan departed on his worldwide expedition, a brash and determined Spanish adventurer, Hernando Cortez (1485–1547), crossed from Hispaniola to mainland Mexico with six hundred men, seventeen horses, and ten cannon. Within three years, Cortez had conquered the fabulously rich Aztec Empire, taken captive the Aztec emperor Montezuma, and founded Mexico City as the capital of New Spain. The subjugation of northern Mexico took longer, but between 1531 and 1550 the Spanish gained control of Zacatecas and Guanajuato, where rich silver veins were soon tapped.

Another Spanish conquistador, Francisco Pizarro (1470–1541), repeated Cortez's feat in Peru. Between 1531 and 1536, with even fewer resources, Pizarro crushed the Inca Empire in western South America and established the Spanish viceroyalty of Peru with its center at Lima. In 1545 the Spanish opened at Potosí in the Peruvian highlands what became the richest silver mines in the New World.

Between 1525 and 1575, the riches of the Americas poured into the Spanish port of Seville and the Portuguese capital of Lisbon. For all their new wealth, however, Lisbon and Seville did not become important trading centers. It was the Flemish city of Antwerp, controlled by the Spanish Habsburgs, that developed into the great entrepôt for overseas bullion and Portuguese spices and served as the commercial and financial capital of the entire European world.

Since the time of the great medieval fairs, cities of the Low Countries (so called because much of the land lies below sea level) had been important

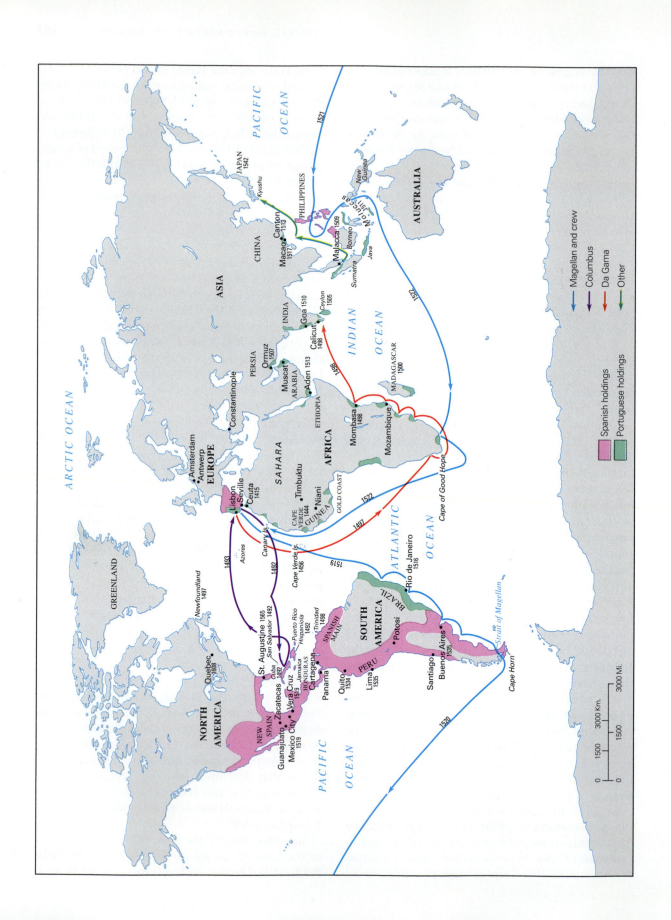

PACIFIC OCEAN

1521

ARCTIC OCEAN

ASIA

JAPAN
1542

Kyushu

Canton
1513

CHINA

Macao
1517

PHILIPPINES

New Guinea

MOLUCCAS

1521

INDIA

Goa 1510

Calicut
1498

Ceylon
1505

INDIAN OCEAN

PERSIA

Ormuz
1507

Muscat

ARABIA

Aden 1513

ETHIOPIA

Constantinople

Sumatra

Borneo

Java

Malacca 1509

MADAGASCAR
1500

1502

Amsterdam
Antwerp

EUROPE

SAHARA

AFRICA

Mombasa
1498

Mozambique

Lisbon
Seville

Ceuta
1415

Timbuktu

Niani

CAPE VERDE

GUINEA

GOLD COAST

Cape of Good Hope

1522

1497

1493

Azores

Canary Is.

1492

Cape Verde Is.
1456

1519

ATLANTIC OCEAN

GREENLAND

Newfoundland
1497

St. Augustine 1565

Cuba
San Salvador 1492

Puerto Rico
Hispaniola
1492

Jamaica

Trinidad
1498

Honduras

Cartagena

Panama

Quito
1534

Lima
1535

PERU

SPANISH MAIN

SOUTH AMERICA

BRAZIL

Rio de Janeiro
1516

Potosi

Santiago

Buenos Aires
1535

Strait of Magellan

Cape Horn

1520

NORTH AMERICA

Quebec
1608

NEW SPAIN

Zacatecas

Guanajuato

Mexico City
1519

Vera Cruz

AUSTRALIA

PACIFIC OCEAN

Magellan and crew
Columbus
Da Gama
Other

Spanish holdings
Portuguese holdings

3000 Mi.
3000 Km.
1500
1500
0
0

sites for the exchange of products from the Baltic and Italy. Antwerp, ideally situated on the Scheldt River at the intersection of many trading routes, steadily expanded as the chief intermediary for international commerce and finance. English woolens; Baltic wheat, fur, and timber; Portuguese spices; German iron and copper; Spanish fruit; French wines and dyestuffs; Italian silks, marbles, and mirrors; together with vast amounts of cash—all were exchanged at Antwerp. The city's harbor could dock 2,500 vessels at once, and 5,000 merchants from many nations gathered daily in the *bourse* (or exchange). Spanish silver was drained to the Netherlands to pay for food and luxury goods. Even so, the desire for economic independence from Spain was to play a major role in the Netherlands' revolt in the late sixteenth century.

By the end of the sixteenth century, Amsterdam had overtaken Antwerp as the financial capital of Europe. The Dutch had also embarked on foreign exploration and conquest. The Dutch East India Company, founded in 1602, became the major organ of Dutch imperialism and within a few decades expelled the Portuguese from Ceylon and other East Indian islands. By 1650 the Dutch West India Company had successfully intruded on the Spanish possessions in America, in the process gaining control of much of the African and American trade.

English and French explorations lacked the immediate, sensational results of the Spanish and Portuguese. In 1497 John Cabot, a Genoese merchant living in London, sailed for Brazil but discovered Newfoundland. The next year he returned and explored the New England coast and perhaps as far south as Delaware. Since these expeditions found no spices or gold, King Henry VII lost interest in exploration. Between 1534 and 1541, the Frenchman Jacques Cartier made several voyages and explored the Saint Lawrence region of Canada, but the first permanent French settlement, at Quebec, was not founded until 1608.

MAP 15.1 Overseas Exploration and Conquest. Fifteenth and Sixteenth Centuries The voyages of discovery marked another phase in the centuries-old migrations of European peoples. Consider the major contemporary significance of each of the three voyages depicted on the map.

The Explorers' Motives

The expansion of Europe was not motivated by demographic pressures. The Black Death had caused serious population losses from which Europe had not recovered in 1500. Few Europeans emigrated to North or South America in the sixteenth century. Half of those who did sail to begin a new life in America died en route; half of those who reached the New World eventually returned to their homeland. Why, then, did explorers brave the Atlantic and Pacific oceans, risking their lives to discover new continents and spread European culture?

The reasons are varied and complex. People of the sixteenth century were still basically medieval in the sense that their attitudes and values were shaped by religion and expressed in religious terms. In the late fifteenth century, crusading fervor remained a basic part of the Portuguese and Spanish national ideal. The desire to Christianize Muslims and pagan peoples played a central role in European expansion. Queen Isabella of Spain, for example, showed a fanatical zeal for converting the Muslims to Christianity, and she concentrated her efforts on the Arabs in Granada. After the abortive crusading attempts of the thirteenth century, Isabella and other rulers realized full well that they lacked the material resources to mount the full-scale assault on Islam necessary for victory. Crusading impulses thus shifted from the Muslims to the pagan peoples of Africa and the Americas.

Moreover, after the reconquista, enterprising young men of the Spanish upper classes found economic and political opportunities severely limited. As a recent study of the Castilian city of Ciudad Real shows, the ancient aristocracy controlled the best agricultural land and monopolized urban administrative posts. Great merchants and a few nobles (surprisingly, since Spanish law forbade noble participation in commercial ventures) dominated the textile and leather-glove manufacturing industries. Consequently, many ambitious men emigrated to the Americas to seek their fortunes.[3]

Government sponsorship and encouragement of exploration also help to account for the results of the various voyages. Mariners and explorers could not afford, as private individuals, the massive sums needed to explore mysterious oceans and to control remote continents. The strong financial support of Prince Henry the Navigator led to Portugal's phenomenal success in the spice trade. Even

Market at Cartagena   Founded in 1533 as a port on the Caribbean Sea, Cartagena (modern Colombia) became the storage depot for precious metals waiting shipment to Spain. In this fanciful woodcut, male Indians wearing tunics composed of overlapping feathers and nude females sell golden necklaces, fish, fruit, and grain. *(Source: Rare Book Division, New York Public Library; Astor, Lenox and Tilden Foundations)*

the grudging and modest assistance of Isabella and Ferdinand eventually brought untold riches—and complicated problems—to Spain. The Dutch in the seventeenth century, through such government-sponsored trading companies as the Dutch East India Company, reaped enormous wealth, and although the Netherlands was a small country in size, it dominated the European economy in 1650. In England, by contrast, Henry VII's lack of interest in exploration delayed English expansion for a century.

Scholars have frequently described the European discoveries as a manifestation of Renaissance curiosity about the physical universe, the desire to know more about the geography and peoples of the world. There is truth to this explanation. Cosmography, natural history, and geography aroused enormous interest among educated people in the fifteenth and sixteenth centuries. Just as science fiction and speculation about life on other planets excite readers today, quasi-scientific literature about Africa, Asia, and the Americas captured the imaginations of literate Europeans. Oviedo's *General History of the Indies* (1547), a detailed eyewitness account of plants, animals, and peoples, was widely read.

Spices were another important incentive to voyages of discovery. Introduced into western Europe by the Crusaders in the twelfth century, nutmeg, mace, ginger, cinnamon, and pepper added flavor and variety to the monotonous diet of Europeans. Spices were also used in the preparation of medicinal drugs and incense for religious ceremonies. In the late thirteenth century, the Venetian Marco Polo (1254?–1324?), the greatest of medieval travelers, had visited the court of the Chinese emperor. The widely publicized account of his travels in the *Book of Various Experiences* stimulated the trade in spices between Asia and Italy. The Venetians came to hold a monopoly of the trade in western Europe.

Spices were grown in India and China, shipped across the Indian Ocean to ports on the Persian Gulf, and then transported by Arabs across the Arabian Desert to Mediterranean ports. But the rise of the Ming Dynasty in China in the late fourteenth century resulted in the expulsion of foreigners. And the steady penetration of the Ottoman Turks into the eastern Mediterranean and of hostile Muslims across North Africa forced Europeans to seek a new route to the Asian spice markets.

The basic reason for European exploration and expansion, however, was the quest for material profit. Mariners and explorers frankly admitted this. As Bartholomew Diaz put it, his motives were "to serve God and His Majesty, to give light to those who were in darkness and to grow rich as all men desire to do." When Vasco da Gama reached the port of Calicut, India, in 1498, a native asked what the Portuguese wanted. Da Gama replied, "Christians and spices."[4] The bluntest of the Spanish conquistadors, Hernando Cortez, announced as he prepared to conquer Mexico, "I have come to win gold, not to plow the fields like a peasant."[5]

Spanish and Portuguese explorers carried the fervent Catholicism and missionary zeal of the Iberian Peninsula to the New World, and once in America they urged home governments to send clerics. At bottom, however, wealth was the driving motivation. A sixteenth-century diplomat, Ogier Gheselin de Busbecq, summed up this paradoxical attitude well: in expeditions to the Indies and the Antipodes, he said, "religion supplies the pretext and gold the motive."[6]

Technological Stimuli to Exploration

Technological developments were the key to Europe's remarkable outreach. By 1350 *cannon*—iron or bronze guns that fired iron or stone balls—had been fully developed in western Europe. These pieces of artillery emitted frightening noises and great flashes of fire and could batter down fortresses and even city walls. Sultan Mohammed II's siege of Constantinople in 1453 provides a classic illustration of the effectiveness of cannon fire.

Constantinople had very strong walled fortifications. The sultan secured the services of a Western technician who built fifty-six small cannon and a gigantic gun that could hurl stone balls weighing about eight hundred pounds. The gun could be moved only by several hundred oxen and loaded and fired only by about a hundred men working together. Reloading took two hours. This awkward but powerful weapon breached the walls of Constantinople before it cracked on the second day of the bombardment. Lesser cannon finished the job.

Early cannon posed serious technical difficulties. Iron cannon were cheaper than bronze to construct, but they were difficult to cast effectively and were liable to crack and injure the artillerymen. Bronze guns, made of copper and tin, were less subject than iron to corrosion, but they were very expensive. All cannon were extraordinarily difficult to move, required considerable time for reloading, and were highly inaccurate. They thus proved inefficient for land warfare. However, they could be used at sea.

The mounting of cannon on ships and improved techniques of shipbuilding gave impetus to European expansion. Since ancient times, most seagoing vessels had been narrow, open boats called *galleys,* propelled largely by manpower. Slaves or convicts who had been sentenced to the galleys manned the oars of the ships that sailed the Mediterranean, and both cargo ships and warships carried soldiers for defense. Though well suited to the placid and thoroughly explored waters of the Mediterranean, galleys could not withstand the rough winds and uncharted shoals of the Atlantic. The need for sturdier craft, as well as population losses caused by the Black Death, forced the development of a new style of ship that would not require soldiers for defense or much manpower to sail.

In the course of the fifteenth century, the Portuguese developed the *caravel,* a small, light, three-masted sailing ship. Though somewhat slower than the galley, the caravel held more cargo and was highly maneuverable. When fitted with cannon, it could dominate larger vessels, such as the round ships commonly used as merchantmen. The substitution of windpower for manpower, and artillery fire for soldiers, signaled a great technological advance and gave Europeans navigational and fighting ascendancy over the rest of the world.[7]

Other fifteenth-century developments in navigation helped make possible the conquest of the Atlantic. The magnetic compass enabled sailors to determine their direction and position at sea. The *astrolabe,* an instrument developed by Muslim navigators in the twelfth century and used to determine the altitude of the sun and other celestial bodies, permitted mariners to plot their *latitude,* or position north or south of the equator. Steadily improved maps and sea charts provided information about distance, sea depths, and general geography.

The Economic Effects of Spain's Discoveries in the New World

The sixteenth century has often been called the "Golden Century" of Spain. The influence of Spanish armies, Spanish Catholicism, and Spanish wealth was felt all over Europe. This greatness rested largely on the influx of precious metals from the New World.

The mines at Zacatecas and Guanajuato in Mexico and Potosí in Peru poured out huge quantities of precious metals. To protect this treasure from French and English pirates, armed convoys transported it each year to Spain. Between 1503 and 1650, 16 million kilograms of silver and 185,000 kilograms of gold entered the port of Seville. Scholars have long debated the impact of all this bullion on the economies of Spain and Europe as a whole. Spanish predominance, however, proved temporary.

In the sixteenth century, Spain experienced a steady population increase, creating a sharp rise in the demand for food and goods. Spanish colonies in the Americas also represented a demand for products. Since Spain expelled some of its best farmers and business people, the Jews in 1492 and the Muslims in the sixteenth and seventeenth centuries, the Spanish economy suffered and could not meet the new demands. Prices rose. Because the costs of manufacturing cloth and other goods increased, Spanish products could not compete in the international market with cheaper products made elsewhere. The textile industry was badly hurt. Prices spiraled upward, faster than the government could levy taxes to dampen the economy. (Higher taxes would have cut the public's buying power; with fewer goods sold, prices would have come down.)

Did the flood of American silver bullion *cause* the inflation? Prices rose most steeply before 1565, but bullion imports reached their peak between 1580 and 1620. Thus there is no direct correlation between silver imports and the inflation rate. Did the substantial population growth accelerate the inflation rate? Perhaps, since when the population pressure declined after 1600, prices gradually stabilized. One fact is certain: the price revolution severely strained governmental budgets. Several times between 1557 and 1647, Philip II and his successors were forced to repudiate the state debt, which in turn undermined confidence in the government. By the seventeenth century, the economy was a shambles.

As Philip II paid his armies and foreign debts with silver bullion, the Spanish inflation was transmitted to the rest of Europe. Between 1560 and 1600, much of Europe experienced large price increases. Prices doubled and in some cases quadrupled, and wages did not keep pace with prices. Spain suffered most severely, but all European countries were affected. People who lived on fixed incomes, such as the continental nobles, were badly hurt because their money bought less. Those who owed fixed sums of money, such as the middle class, prospered: in a time of rising prices, debts had less value each year. Food costs rose most sharply, and the poor fared worst of all.

Colonial Administration

Columbus, Cortez, and Pizarro claimed the lands they had "discovered" for the crown of Spain.

How were they to be governed? According to the Spanish theory of absolutism, the Crown was entitled to exercise full authority over all imperial lands. In the sixteenth century the Crown divided its New World territories into four viceroyalties or administrative divisions: New Spain, which consisted of Mexico, Central America, and present-day California, Arizona, New Mexico, and Texas, with the capital at Mexico City; Peru, originally all the lands in continental South America, later reduced to the territory of modern Peru, Chile, Bolivia, and Ecuador, with the viceregal seat at Lima; New Granada, including present-day Venezuela, Colombia, Panama, and after 1739 Ecuador, with Bogotá as its administrative center; and La Plata, consisting of Argentina, Uruguay, and Paraguay, with Buenos Aires as the capital. Within each territory, the viceroy or imperial governor exercised broad military and civil authority as the direct representative of the sovereign in Madrid. The viceroy presided over the *audiencia,* a board of twelve to fifteen judges, which served as his advisory council and the highest judicial body. The enlightened Spanish king Charles III (1716–1788) introduced the system of *intendants.* These royal officials possessed broad military, administrative, and financial authority within their intendancy and were responsible, not to the viceroy, but to the monarchy in Madrid.

From the early sixteenth century to the beginning of the nineteenth, the Spanish monarchy acted on the mercantilist principle that the colonies existed for the financial benefit of the mother country. The mining of gold and silver was always the most important industry in the colonies. The Crown claimed the *quinto,* one-fifth of all precious metals mined in South America. Gold and silver yielded the Spanish monarchy 25 percent of its total income. In return, it shipped manufactured goods to America and discouraged the development of native industries.

The Portuguese governed their colony of Brazil in a similar manner. After the union of the crowns of Portugal and Spain in 1580, Spanish administrative forms were introduced. Local officials called *corregidores* held judicial and military powers. Mercantilist policies placed severe restrictions on Brazilian industries that might compete with those of Portugal. In the seventeenth century the use of black slave labor made possible the cultivation of coffee and cotton, and in the eighteenth century Brazil led the world in the production of sugar. The unique feature of colonial Brazil's culture and society was its thoroughgoing intermixture of Indians, whites, and blacks.

POLITICS, RELIGION, AND WAR

In 1559 France and Spain signed the Treaty of Cateau-Cambrésis, which ended the long conflict known as the Habsburg-Valois Wars. This event marks a watershed in early modern European history. Spain was the victor. France, exhausted by the struggle, had to acknowledge Spanish dominance in Italy, where much of the war had been fought. Spanish governors ruled in Sicily, Naples, and Milan, and Spanish influence was strong in the Papal States and Tuscany.

Emperor Charles V had divided his attention between the Holy Roman Empire and Spain. Under his son Philip II (r. 1556–1598), however, the center of the Habsburg empire and the political center of gravity for all of Europe shifted westward to Spain. Before 1559, Spain and France had fought bitterly for control of Italy; after 1559, the two Catholic powers aimed their guns at Protestantism. The Treaty of Cateau-Cambrésis ended an era of strictly dynastic wars and initiated a period of conflicts in which politics and religion played the dominant roles.

Because a variety of issues were stewing, it is not easy to generalize about the wars of the late sixteenth century. Some were continuations of struggles between the centralizing goals of monarchies and the feudal reactions of nobilities. Some were crusading battles between Catholics and Protestants. Some were struggles for national independence or for international expansion.

These wars differed considerably from earlier wars. Sixteenth- and seventeenth-century armies were bigger than medieval ones; some forces numbered as many as fifty thousand men. Because large armies were expensive, governments had to reorganize their administrations to finance them. The use of gunpowder altered both the nature of war and popular attitudes toward it. Guns and cannon killed and wounded from a distance, indiscriminately. Writers scorned gunpowder as a coward's weapon that allowed a common soldier to kill a gentleman. The Italian poet Ariosto lamented:

Through thee is martial glory lost, through
Thee the trade of arms becomes a worthless art:
And at such ebb are worth and chivalry that
The base often plays the better part.[8]

Gunpowder weakened the notion, common during the Hundred Years' War, that warfare was an ennobling experience. Governments had to utilize propaganda, pulpits, and the printing press to arouse public opinion to support war.[9]

Late sixteenth-century conflicts fundamentally tested the medieval ideal of a unified Christian society governed by one political ruler, the emperor, to whom all rulers were theoretically subordinate, and one church, to which all people belonged. The Protestant Reformation had killed this ideal, but few people recognized it as dead. Catholics continued to believe that Calvinists and Lutherans could be reconverted; Protestants persisted in thinking that the Roman church should be destroyed. Most people believed that a state could survive only if its members shared the same faith. Catholics and Protestants alike feared people of the other faith living in their midst. The settlement finally achieved in 1648, known as the Peace of Westphalia, signaled the end of the medieval ideal.

The Origins of Difficulties in France (1515–1559)

In the first half of the sixteenth century, France continued the recovery begun under Louis XI (see page 410). The population losses caused by the plague and the disorders accompanying the Hundred Years' War had created such a labor shortage that serfdom virtually disappeared. Cash rents replaced feudal rents and servile obligations. This development clearly benefited the peasantry. Meanwhile, the declining buying power of money hurt the nobility. Increasing French population in the late fifteenth and sixteenth centuries brought new lands under cultivation, but the division of property among sons meant that most peasant holdings were very small. Domestic and foreign trade picked up; mercantile centers such as Rouen and Lyons expanded; and in 1517 a new port city was founded at Le Havre.

The charming and cultivated Francis I (r. 1515–1547) and his athletic, emotional son Henry II (r. 1547–1559) governed through a small, efficient council. Great nobles held titular authority in the provinces as governors, but Paris-appointed baillis and seneschals continued to exercise actual fiscal and judicial responsibility (see page 315). In 1539 Francis issued an ordinance that placed the whole of France under the jurisdiction of the royal law courts and made French the language of those courts. This act had a powerful centralizing impact. The taille, a tax on land, provided what strength the monarchy had and supported a strong standing army. Unfortunately, the tax base was too narrow for France's extravagant promotion of the arts and ambitious foreign policy.

Deliberately imitating the Italian Renaissance princes, the Valois monarchs lavished money on a magnificent court, a vast building program, and Italian artists. Francis I commissioned the Paris architect Pierre Lescot to rebuild the palace of the Louvre. Francis secured the services of Michelangelo's star pupil, Il Rosso, who decorated the wing of the Fontainebleau château, subsequently called the Gallery Francis I, with rich scenes of classical and mythological literature. After acquiring Leonardo da Vinci's Mona Lisa, Francis brought Leonardo himself to France, where he soon died. Henry II built a castle at Dreux for his mistress, Diana de Poitiers, and a palace in Paris, the Tuileries, for his wife, Catherine de' Medici. Art historians credit Francis I and Henry II with importing Italian Renaissance art and architecture to France. Whatever praise these monarchs deserve for their cultural achievement, they spent far more than they could afford.

The Habsburg-Valois Wars, waged intermittently through the first half of the sixteenth century, also cost more than the government could afford. Financing the war posed problems. In addition to the time-honored practices of increasing taxes and heavy borrowing, Francis I tried two new devices to raise revenue: the sale of public offices and a treaty with the papacy. The former proved to be only a temporary source of money. The offices sold tended to become hereditary within a family, and once a man bought an office he and his heirs were tax-exempt. The sale of public offices thus created a tax-exempt class called the "nobility of the robe," which held positions beyond the jurisdiction of the Crown.

Rossi and Primaticcio: The Gallery of Francis I Flat paintings alternating with rich sculpture provide a rhythm that directs the eye down the long gallery at Fontainebleau, constructed between 1530 and 1540. Francis I sought to re-create in France the elegant Renaissance lifestyle found in Italy. *(Source: Art Resource)*

The treaty with the papacy was the Concordat of Bologna (see page 411), in which Francis agreed to recognize the supremacy of the papacy over a universal council. In return, the French crown gained the right to appoint all French bishops and abbots. This understanding gave the monarchy a rich supplement of money and offices and a power over the church that lasted until the Revolution of 1789. The Concordat of Bologna helps to explain why France did not later become Protestant: in effect, it established Catholicism as the state religion. Because they possessed control over appointments and had a vested financial interest in Catholicism, French rulers had no need to revolt from Rome.

However, the Concordat of Bologna perpetuated disorders within the French church. Ecclesiastical offices were used primarily to pay and reward civil servants. Churchmen in France, as elsewhere, were promoted to the hierarchy not for any special spiritual qualifications but because of their services to the state. Such bishops were unlikely to work to elevate the intellectual and moral standards of the parish clergy. Few of the many priests in France devoted scrupulous attention to the needs of their parishioners. The teachings of Luther and Calvin, as the presses disseminated them, found a receptive audience.

Luther's tracts first appeared in France in 1518, and his ideas attracted some attention. After the publication of Calvin's *Institutes* in 1536, sizable numbers of French people were attracted to the "reformed religion," as Calvinism was called. Because Calvin wrote in French rather than Latin, his ideas gained wide circulation. Initially, Calvinism

Triple Profile Portrait   This portrait from the late sixteenth century exemplifies the very high finish and mannered sophistication of the School of Fontainebleau. These courtiers served Henry III, one of the weak sons of Henry II (*Source: Milwaukee Art Museum, Gift of Women's Exchange*)

drew converts from among reform-minded members of the Catholic clergy, the industrious middle classes, and artisan groups. Most Calvinists lived in major cities, such as Paris, Lyons, Meaux, and Grenoble.

In spite of condemnation by the universities, government bans, and massive burnings at the stake, the numbers of Protestants grew steadily. When Henry II died in 1559, there were 40 well-organized Protestant churches and 2,150 mission stations in France. Perhaps one-tenth of the population had become Calvinist.

Religious Riots and Civil War in France (1559–1589)

For thirty years, from 1559 to 1589, violence and civil war divided and shattered France. The feebleness of the monarchy was the seed from which the weeds of civil violence germinated. The three weak sons of Henry II who occupied the throne could not provide the necessary leadership. Francis II (r.

1559–1560) died after seventeen months. Charles IX (r. 1560–1574) succeeded at the age of ten and was thoroughly dominated by his opportunistic mother, Catherine de' Medici, who would support any party or position to maintain her influence. The intelligent and cultivated Henry III (r. 1574–1589) divided his attention between debaucheries with his male lovers and frantic acts of repentance.

The French nobility took advantage of this monarchial weakness. In the second half of the sixteenth century, between two-fifths and one-half of the nobility at one time or another became Calvinist. Just as German princes in the Holy Roman Empire had adopted Lutheranism as a means of opposition to the emperor Charles V, so French nobles frequently adopted the "reformed religion" as a religious cloak for their independence. No one believed that peoples of different faiths could coexist peacefully within the same territory. The Reformation thus led to a resurgence of feudal disorder. Armed clashes between Catholic royalist lords and Calvinist antimonarchial lords occurred in many parts of France.

Among the upper classes the Catholic-Calvinist conflict was the surface issue, but the fundamental object of the struggle was power. At lower social levels, however, religious concerns were paramount. Working-class crowds composed of skilled craftsmen and the poor wreaked terrible violence on people and property. Both Calvinists and Catholics believed that the others' books, services, and ministers polluted the community. Preachers incited violence, and ceremonies like baptisms, marriages, and funerals triggered it. Protestant pastors encouraged their followers to destroy statues and liturgical objects in Catholic churches. Catholic priests urged their flocks to shed the blood of the Calvinist heretics.

In 1561 in the Paris church of Saint-Médard, a Protestant crowd cornered a baker guarding a box containing the consecrated Eucharistic bread. Taunting "Does your God of paste protect you now from the pains of death?" the mob proceeded to kill the poor man.[10] Calvinists believed that the Catholic emphasis on symbols in their ritual desecrated what was truly sacred and promoted the worship of images. In scores of attacks on Catholic churches, religious statues were knocked down, stained-glass windows smashed, and sacred vestments, vessels, and Eucharistic elements defiled. In 1561 a Catholic crowd charged a group of just-

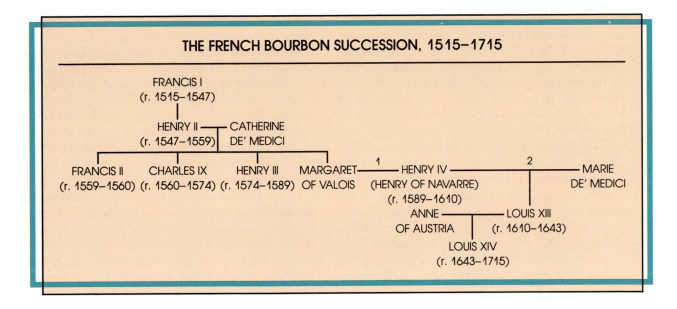

THE FRENCH BOURBON SUCCESSION, 1515–1715

FRANCIS I
(r. 1515–1547)

HENRY II —— CATHERINE
(r. 1547–1559)   DE' MEDICI

FRANCIS II   CHARLES IX   HENRY III   MARGARET —— 1 —— HENRY IV —— 2 —— MARIE
(r. 1559–1560)   (r. 1560–1574)   (r. 1574–1589)   OF VALOIS   (HENRY OF NAVARRE)   DE' MEDICI
(r. 1589–1610)

ANNE —————— LOUIS XIII
OF AUSTRIA   (r. 1610–1643)

LOUIS XIV
(r. 1643–1715)

released Protestant prisoners, killed them, and burned their bodies in the street. Hundreds of Huguenots, as French Calvinists were called, were tortured, had their tongues cut out or throats slit, were maimed or murdered.

In the fourteenth and fifteenth centuries, crowd action—attacks on great nobles and rich prelates—had expressed economic grievances. In contrast, religious rioters of the sixteenth century believed that they could assume the power of public magistrates and rid the community of corruption. Municipal officials criticized the crowds' actions, but the participation of pastors and priests in these riots lent them some legitimacy.[11]

A savage Catholic attack on Calvinists in Paris on August 24, 1572 (Saint Bartholomew's Day), followed the usual pattern. The occasion was a religious ceremony, the marriage of the king's sister Margaret of Valois to the Protestant Henry of Navarre, which was intended to help reconcile Catholics and Huguenots. Among the many Calvinists present for the wedding festivities was the admiral Gaspard de Coligny, head of one of the great noble families of France and leader of the Huguenot party. Coligny had recently replaced Catherine de' Medici in influence over the young king Charles IX. When, the night before the wedding, the leader of the Catholic aristocracy, Henry of Guise, had Coligny attacked, rioting and slaughter followed. The Huguenot gentry in Paris were massacred, and

religious violence spread to the provinces. Between August 25 and October 3, perhaps twelve thousand Huguenots perished at Meaux, Lyons, Orléans, and Paris. The contradictory orders of the unstable Charles IX worsened the situation.

The Saint Bartholomew's Day massacre led to fighting that launched the War of the Three Henrys, a civil conflict among factions led by the Catholic Henry of Guise, the Protestant Henry of Navarre, and King Henry III, who succeeded the tubercular Charles IX. Though he remained Catholic, King Henry realized that the Catholic Guise group represented his greatest danger. The Guises wanted, through an alliance of Catholic nobles called the "Holy League," not only to destroy Calvinism but to replace Henry III with a member of the Guise family. France suffered fifteen more years of religious rioting and domestic anarchy. Agriculture in many areas was destroyed; commercial life declined severely; starvation and death haunted the land.

What ultimately saved France was a small group of Catholic moderates called *politiques* who believed that only the restoration of strong monarchy could reverse the trend toward collapse. No religious creed was worth the incessant disorder and destruction. Therefore, the politiques favored accepting the Huguenots as an officially recognized and organized pressure group. (But religious toleration, the full acceptance of peoples of different religious persuasions within a pluralistic society—with the minorities having the same civil liberties as the majority, developed only in the eighteenth century.) The death of Catherine de' Medici, followed by the assassinations of Henry of Guise and King Henry III, paved the way for the accession of Henry of Navarre, a politique who became Henry IV (r. 1589–1610).

This glamorous prince, "who knew how to fight, to make love, and to drink," as a contemporary remarked, wanted above all a strong and united France. He knew, too, that the majority of the French were Roman Catholics. Declaring "Paris is worth a Mass," Henry knelt before the archbishop of Bourges and was received into the Roman Catholic church. Henry's willingness to sacrifice religious principles to political necessity saved France. The Edict of Nantes, which Henry published in 1598, granted to Huguenots liberty of conscience and liberty of public worship in two hundred fortified towns, such as La Rochelle. The reign of Henry IV and the Edict of Nantes prepared the way for French absolutism in the seventeenth century by helping to restore internal peace in France.

The Netherlands Under Charles V

In the last quarter of the sixteenth century, the political stability of England, the international prestige of Spain, and the moral influence of the Roman papacy all became mixed up with the religious crisis in the Low Countries. The Netherlands was the pivot around which European money, diplomacy, and war revolved. What began as a movement for the reformation of the church developed into a struggle for Dutch independence.

The emperor Charles V (r. 1519–1556) had inherited the seventeen provinces that compose present-day Belgium and Holland (see page 432). Ideally situated for commerce between the Rhine and Scheldt rivers, the great towns of Bruges, Ghent, Brussels, Arras, and Amsterdam made their living by trade and industry. The French-speaking southern towns produced fine linens and woolens, while the wealth of the Dutch-speaking northern cities rested on fishing, shipping, and international banking. The city of Antwerp was the largest port and the greatest money market in Europe. In the cities of the Low Countries, trade and commerce had produced a vibrant cosmopolitan atmosphere, personified by the urbane Erasmus of Rotterdam.

Each of the seventeen provinces of the Netherlands possessed historical liberties: each was self-governing and enjoyed the right to make its own laws and collect its own taxes. Only the recognition of a common ruler in the person of the emperor Charles V united the provinces. Delegates from the various provinces met together in the Estates General, but important decisions had to be referred back to each province for approval. In the middle of the sixteenth century, the provinces of the Netherlands had a limited sense of federation.

In the Low Countries, as elsewhere, corruption in the Roman church and the critical spirit of the Renaissance provoked pressure for reform. Lutheran tracts and Dutch translations of the Bible flooded the seventeen provinces in the 1520s and 1530s, attracting many people to Protestantism. Charles V's government responded with condemnation and mild repression. This policy was not particularly effective, however, because ideas circulated freely in the cosmopolitan atmosphere of the commercial centers. But Charles's Flemish loyalty checked the spread of Lutheranism. Charles had been born in Ghent and raised in the Netherlands; he was Flemish in language and culture. He identified with the Flemish and they with him.

In 1556, however, Charles V abdicated, dividing his territories between his brother Ferdinand, who received Austria and the Holy Roman Empire, and his son Philip, who inherited Spain, the Low Countries, Milan and the kingdom of Sicily, and the Spanish possessions in America. Charles delivered his abdication speech before the Estates General at Brussels. The emperor was then fifty-five years old, white-haired, and so crippled in the legs that he had to lean for support on the young Prince William of Orange. According to one contemporary account of the emperor's appearance:

His under lip, a Burgundian inheritance, as faithfully transmitted as the duchy and county, was heavy and hanging, the lower jaw protruding so far beyond the upper that it was impossible for him to bring together the few fragments of teeth which still remained, or to speak a whole sentence in an intelligible voice.[12]

Charles spoke in Flemish. His small, shy, and sepulchral son Philip responded in Spanish; he could speak neither French nor Flemish. The Netherlanders had always felt Charles one of themselves. They were never to forget that Philip was a Spaniard.

The Revolt of the Netherlands (1566–1587)

By the 1560s, there was a strong, militant minority of Calvinists in most of the cities of the Netherlands. The seventeen provinces possessed a large middle-class population, and the reformed religion, as a contemporary remarked, had a powerful appeal "to those who had grown rich by trade and were therefore ready for revolution."[13] Calvinism appealed to the middle classes because of its intellectual seriousness, moral gravity, and emphasis on any form of labor well done. It took deep root among the merchants and financiers in Amsterdam and the northern provinces. Working-class people were also converted, partly because their employers would hire only fellow Calvinists. Well organized and with the backing of rich merchants, Calvinists quickly gained a wide following. Lutherans taught respect for the powers that be. Calvinist reformed religion, however, tended in the 1570s to encourage opposition to "illegal" civil authorities.

In 1559 Philip II appointed his half-sister Margaret as regent of the Netherlands (1559–1567). A proud, energetic, and strong-willed woman, who once had Ignatius Loyola as her confessor, Margaret pushed Philip's orders to wipe out Protestantism. She introduced the Inquisition. Her more immediate problem, however, was revenue to finance the government of the provinces. Charles V had steadily increased taxes in the Low Countries. When Margaret appealed to the Estates General, they claimed that the Low Countries were more heavily taxed than Spain. Nevertheless, Margaret raised taxes and succeeded in uniting the opposition to the government's fiscal policy with the opposition to official repression of Calvinism.

In August of 1566, a year of very high grain prices, fanatical Calvinists, primarily of the poorest

To Purify the Church   The destruction of pictures and statues representing biblical events, Christian doctrine, or sacred figures was a central feature of the Protestant Reformation. Here Dutch Protestant soldiers destroy what they consider idols in the belief that they are purifying the church. *(Source: Fotomas Index)*

classes, embarked on a rampage of frightful destruction. As in France, Calvinist destruction in the Low Countries was incited by popular preaching, and attacks were aimed at religious images as symbols of false doctrines, not at people. The cathedral of Notre Dame at Antwerp was the first target. Begun in 1124 and finished only in 1518, this church stood as a monument to the commercial prosperity of Flanders, the piety of the business classes, and the artistic genius of centuries. On six successive summer evenings, crowds swept through the nave. While the town harlots held tapers to the greatest concentration of artworks in northern Europe, people armed with axes and sledgehammers smashed altars, paintings, books, tombs, ecclesiastical vestments, missals, manuscripts, ornaments, stained-glass windows, and sculptures. Before the havoc was over, thirty more churches had been sacked and irreplaceable libraries burned. From Antwerp the destruction spread to Brussels and Ghent and north to the provinces of Holland and Zeeland.

From Madrid, Philip II sent twenty thousand Spanish troops under the duke of Alva to pacify the Low Countries. Alva interpreted "pacification" to mean the ruthless extermination of religious and political dissidents. On top of the Inquisition he opened his own tribunal, soon called the "Council of Blood." On March 3, 1568, fifteen hundred men were executed. Even Margaret was sickened and resigned her regency. Alva resolved the financial crisis by levying a 10 percent sales tax on every transaction, which in a commercial society caused widespread hardship and confusion.

For ten years, between 1568 and 1578, civil war raged in the Netherlands between Catholics and Protestants and between the seventeen provinces and Spain. A series of Spanish generals could not halt the fighting. In 1576 the seventeen provinces united under the leadership of Prince William of Orange, called "the Silent" because of his remarkable discretion. In 1578 Philip II sent his nephew Alexander Farnese, duke of Parma and the great-grandson of the Alexander Farnese who was Pope Paul III (see page 448), to crush the revolt once and for all. A general with a superb sense of timing, an excellent knowledge of the geography of the Low Countries, and a perfect plan, Farnese arrived with an army of German mercenaries. Avoiding pitched battles, he fought by patient sieges. One by one the cities of the south fell—Maastricht, Tournai,

Bruges, Ghent, and finally the financial capital of northern Europe, Antwerp. Calvinism was forbidden in these territories, and Protestants were compelled to convert or leave. The collapse of Antwerp marked the farthest extent of Spanish jurisdiction and ultimately the religious division of the Netherlands.

The ten southern provinces, the Spanish Netherlands (the future Belgium), remained under the control of the Spanish Habsburgs. The seven northern provinces, led by Holland, formed the Union of Utrecht and in 1581 declared their independence from Spain. Thus was born the United Provinces of the Netherlands (Map 15.2).

Geography and sociopolitical structure differentiated the two countries. The northern provinces were ribboned with sluices and canals and therefore were highly defensible. Several times the Dutch had broken the dikes and flooded the countryside to halt the advancing Farnese. In the southern provinces the Ardennes Mountains interrupt the otherwise flat terrain. In the north the commercial aristocracy possessed the predominant power; in the south the landed nobility had the greater influence. The north was Protestant; the south remained Catholic.

Philip II and Alexander Farnese did not accept this geographical division, and the struggle continued after 1581. The United Provinces repeatedly begged the Protestant Queen Elizabeth of England for assistance.

The crown on the head of Elizabeth I (see page 444) did not rest easily. She had steered a moderately Protestant course between the Puritans, who sought the total elimination of Roman Catholic elements in the English church, and the Roman Catholics, who wanted full restoration of the old religion. Elizabeth survived a massive uprising by the Catholic north in 1569 to 1570. She survived two serious plots against her life. In the 1570s the presence in England of Mary, Queen of Scots, a Roman Catholic and the legal heir to the English throne, produced a very embarrassing situation. Mary was the rallying point of all opposition to Elizabeth, yet the English sovereign hesitated to set the terrible example of regicide by ordering Mary executed.

Elizabeth faced a grave dilemma. If she responded favorably to Dutch pleas for military support against the Spanish, she would antagonize Philip II. The Spanish king had the steady flow of silver from the Americas at his disposal, and Elizabeth, lacking such treasure, wanted to avoid war. But if she did not help the Protestant Netherlands and they were crushed by Farnese, the likelihood was that the Spanish would invade England.

Three developments forced Elizabeth's hand. First, the wars in the Low Countries—the chief market for English woolens—badly hurt the English economy. When wool was not exported, the Crown lost valuable customs revenues. Second, the murder of William the Silent in July 1584 eliminated not only a great Protestant leader but the chief military check on the Farnese advance. Third, the collapse of Antwerp appeared to signal a Catholic sweep through the Netherlands. The next step, the English feared, would be a Spanish invasion of their island. For these reasons, Elizabeth pumped £250,000 and two thousand troops into the Protestant cause in the Low Countries between 1585 and 1587. Increasingly fearful of the plots of Mary, Queen of Scots, Elizabeth finally signed her death warrant. Mary was beheaded on February 18, 1587. Sometime between March 24 and 30, the news of Mary's death reached Philip II.

Philip II and the Spanish Armada

Philip pondered the Dutch and English developments at the Escorial northwest of Madrid. Begun in 1563 and completed under the king's personal supervision in 1584, the monastery of Saint Lawrence of the Escorial served as a residence for Jeromite monks, a tomb for the king's Habsburg ancestors, and a royal palace for Philip and his family. The vast buildings resemble a gridiron, the instrument on which Saint Lawrence (d. 258) had supposedly been roasted alive. The royal apartments were in the center of the Italian Renaissance building complex. King Philip's tiny bedchamber possessed a concealed sliding window that opened directly onto the high altar of the monastery church so he could watch the services and pray along with the monks. In this somber atmosphere, surrounded by a community of monks and close to the bones of his ancestors, the Catholic ruler of Spain and much of the globe passed his days.

Philip of Spain considered himself the international defender of Catholicism and the heir to the medieval imperial power. Hoping to keep England within the Catholic church when his wife Mary

MAP 15.2 The Netherlands, 1578–1609 Though small in geographical size, the Netherlands held a strategic position in the religious struggles of the sixteenth century. Why?

Tudor died, Philip had asked Elizabeth to marry him; she had emphatically refused. Several popes had urged him to move against England. When Pope Sixtus V (1585–1590) heard of the death of the Queen of Scots, he promised to pay Philip one million gold ducats the moment Spanish troops landed in England. Alexander Farnese had repeatedly warned that, to subdue the Dutch, he would have to conquer England and cut off the source of Dutch support. Philip also worried that the vast amounts of South American silver he was pouring into the conquest of the Netherlands seemed to be going down a bottomless pit. Two plans for an expedition were considered. Philip's naval adviser recommended that a fleet of 150 ships sail from Lisbon, attack the English navy in the Channel, and invade England. Another proposal had been to assemble a collection of barges and troops in Flanders to stage a cross-Channel assault. With the expected support of English Catholics, Spain would achieve a great victory. Farnese opposed this plan as militarily unsound.

Philip compromised. He prepared a vast fleet to sail from Lisbon to Flanders, fight off Elizabeth's navy *if* it attacked, rendezvous with Farnese, and escort his barges across the English Channel. The expedition's purpose was to transport the Flemish army.

On May 9, 1588, *la felicissima armada*—"the most fortunate fleet," as it was ironically called in official documents—sailed from Lisbon harbor. The Spanish fleet of 130 vessels carried 123,790 cannonballs and perhaps 30,000 men, every one of whom had confessed his sins and received the Eucharist. An English fleet of about 150 ships met the Spanish in the Channel. The English fleet was composed of smaller, faster, more maneuverable ships, many of which had greater firing power than the Spanish. A combination of storms and squalls, spoiled food and rank water, inadequate Spanish ammunition, and, to a lesser extent, English fire ships that caused the Spanish to scatter, gave England the victory. Many Spanish ships went down on the journey home around Ireland; perhaps 65 managed to reach home ports.

The battle in the Channel has frequently been described as one of the decisive battles in the history of the world. In fact, it had mixed consequences. Spain soon rebuilt its navy, and after 1588 the quality of the Spanish fleet improved. The destruction of the Armada did not halt the flow of silver from the New World. More silver reached Spain between 1588 and 1603 than in any other fifteen-year period. The war between England and Spain dragged on for years.

The defeat of the Spanish Armada was decisive, however, in the sense that it prevented Philip II from reimposing unity on western Europe by force. He did not conquer England, and Elizabeth con-

Defeat of the Spanish Armada   The crescent-shaped Spanish formation was designed to force the English to fight at close quarters—by ramming and boarding. When the English sent burning ships against the Spaniards, the crescent broke up, the English pounced on individual ships, and an Atlantic gale swept the Spaniards into the North Sea, finishing the work of destruction. *(Source: National Maritime Museum, London)*

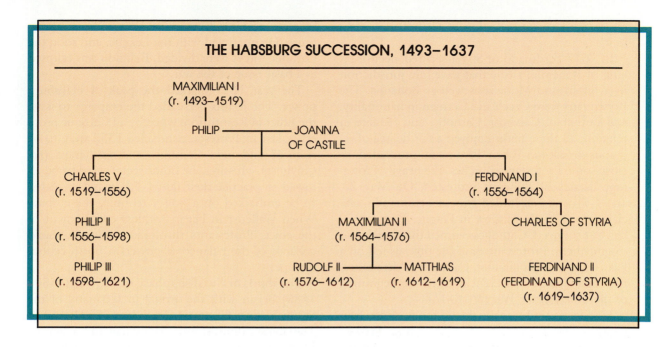

THE HABSBURG SUCCESSION, 1493–1637

MAXIMILIAN I
(r. 1493–1519)

PHILIP —— JOANNA OF CASTILE

CHARLES V
(r. 1519–1556)

FERDINAND I
(r. 1556–1564)

PHILIP II
(r. 1556–1598)

MAXIMILIAN II
(r. 1564–1576)

CHARLES OF STYRIA

PHILIP III
(r. 1598–1621)

RUDOLF II —— MATTHIAS
(r. 1576–1612)   (r. 1612–1619)

FERDINAND II
(FERDINAND OF STYRIA)
(r. 1619–1637)

tinued her financial and military support of the Dutch. In the Netherlands neither side gained significant territory. The borders of 1581 tended to become permanent. In 1609 Philip III of Spain (r. 1598–1621) agreed to a truce, in effect recognizing the independence of the United Provinces. In seventeenth-century Spain memory of the defeat of the Armada contributed to a spirit of defeatism. In England the victory contributed to a David and Goliath legend that enhanced English national sentiment.

The Thirty Years' War (1618–1648)

While Philip II dreamed of building a second armada and Henry IV began the reconstruction of France, the political-religious situation in central Europe deteriorated. An uneasy truce had prevailed in the Holy Roman Empire since the Peace of Augsburg of 1555 (see page 437). The Augsburg settlement, in recognizing the independent power of the German princes, further undermined any authority of the central government. The Habsburg ruler in Vienna enjoyed the title of emperor but had no imperial power.

According to the Augsburg settlement, the faith of the prince determined the religion of his subjects. Later in the century, though, Catholics grew

alarmed because Lutherans, in violation of the Peace of Augsburg, were steadily acquiring German bishoprics. The spread of Calvinism further confused the issue. The Augsburg settlement had pertained only to Lutheranism and Catholicism, but Calvinists ignored it and converted several princes. Lutherans feared that the Augsburg principles would be totally undermined by Catholic and Calvinist gains. Also, the militantly active Jesuits had reconverted several Lutheran princes to Catholicism. In an increasingly tense situation, Lutheran princes formed the Protestant Union (1608) and Catholics retaliated with the Catholic League (1609). Each alliance was determined that the other should make no religious (that is, territorial) advance. The empire was composed of two armed camps.

Dynastic interests were also involved in the German situation. When Charles V abdicated in 1556, he had divided his possessions between his son Philip II and his brother Ferdinand I. This partition began the Austrian and Spanish branches of the Habsburg family. Ferdinand inherited the imperial title and the Habsburg lands in central Europe, including Austria. Ferdinand's grandson Matthias had no direct heirs and promoted the candidacy of his fiercely Catholic cousin, Ferdinand of Styria. The Spanish Habsburgs strongly supported the goals of their Austrian relatives: the unity of the empire and the preservation of Catholicism within it.

In 1617 Ferdinand of Styria secured election as king of Bohemia, a title that gave him jurisdiction over Silesia and Moravia as well as Bohemia. The Bohemians were Czech and German in nationality, and Lutheran, Calvinist, Catholic, and Hussite in religion; all these faiths enjoyed a fair degree of religious freedom. When Ferdinand proceeded to close some Protestant churches, the heavily Protestant Estates of Bohemia protested. On May 23, 1618, Protestants hurled two of Ferdinand's officials from a castle window in Prague. They fell 70 feet but survived: Catholics claimed that angels had caught them; Protestants said the officials fell on a heap of soft horse manure. Called the "defenestration of Prague," this event marked the beginning of the Thirty Years' War (1618–1648).

Historians traditionally divide the war into four phases. The first, or Bohemian, phase (1618–1625) was characterized by civil war in Bohemia between the Catholic League, led by Ferdinand, and the Protestant Union, headed by Prince Frederick of the Palatinate. The Bohemians fought for religious liberty and independence from Habsburg rule. In 1618 the Bohemian Estates deposed Ferdinand and gave the crown of Bohemia to Frederick, thus uniting the interests of German Protestants with those of the international enemies of the Habsburgs. Frederick wore his crown only a few months. In 1620 he was totally defeated by Catholic forces at the Battle of the White Mountain. Ferdinand, who had recently been elected Holy Roman emperor as Ferdinand II, followed up his victories by wiping out Protestantism in Bohemia through forcible conversions and the activities of militant Jesuit missionaries. Within ten years, Bohemia was completely Catholic.

The second, or Danish, phase of the war (1625–1629)—so called because of the participation of King Christian IV of Denmark (r. 1588–1648), the ineffective leader of the Protestant cause—witnessed additional Catholic victories. The Catholic imperial army led by Albert of Wallenstein scored smashing victories. It swept through Silesia, north through Schleswig and Jutland to the Baltic, and east into Pomerania. Wallenstein had made himself indispensable to the emperor Ferdinand, but he was an unscrupulous opportunist who used his vast riches to build an army loyal only to himself. The general seemed interested more in carving out an

empire for himself than in aiding the Catholic cause. He quarreled with the League, and soon the Catholic forces were divided. Religion was eclipsed as a basic issue of the war.

The year 1629 marked the peak of Habsburg power. The Jesuits persuaded the emperor to issue the Edict of Restitution, whereby all Catholic properties lost to Protestantism since 1552 were to be restored and only Catholics and Lutherans (*not* Calvinists, Hussites, or other sects) were to be allowed to practice their faiths. Ferdinand appeared to be embarked on a policy to unify the empire. When Wallenstein began ruthless enforcement of the edict, Protestants throughout Europe feared collapse of the balance of power in north central Europe.

The third, or Swedish, phase of the war (1630–1635) began with the arrival in Germany of the Swedish king Gustavus Adolphus (1594–1632). The ablest administrator of his day and a devout Lutheran, Gustavus Adolphus intervened to support the oppressed Protestants within the empire and to assist his relatives, the exiled dukes of Mecklenburg. Cardinal Richelieu, the chief minister of King Louis XIII of France (r. 1610–1643), subsidized the Swedes, hoping to weaken Habsburg power in Europe. In 1631, with a small but well-disciplined army equipped with superior muskets and warm uniforms, Gustavus Adolphus won a brilliant victory at Breitenfeld. Again in 1632 he was victorious at Lützen, though he was fatally wounded in the battle.

The participation of the Swedes in the Thirty Years' War proved decisive for the future of Protestantism and later German history. When Gustavus Adolphus landed on German soil, he had already brought Denmark, Poland, Finland, and the smaller Baltic states under Swedish influence. The Swedish victories ended the Habsburg ambition of uniting all the German states under imperial authority.

The death of Gustavus Adolphus, followed by the defeat of the Swedes at the Battle of Nördlingen in 1634, prompted the French to enter the war on the side of the Protestants. Thus began the French, or international, phase of the Thirty Years' War (1635–1648). For almost a century, French foreign policy had been based on opposition to the Habsburgs, because a weak empire divided into scores of independent principalities enhanced France's international stature. In 1622, when the Dutch had re-

Jan Asselyn: Charge by the Swedish Cavalry   A Dutch landscape painter, Asselyn did this dramatic scene of the Protestant king Gustavus Adolphus leading cavalry regiments against the imperial forces under General Wallenstein at the Battle of Lützen near Leipzig in 1632. Gustavus Adolphus defeated Wallenstein but was killed in the battle. *(Source: Herzog Anton Ulrich-Museums Braunschweig; Photo B. P. Keiser)*

sumed the war against Spain, the French had supported Holland. Now, in 1635, Cardinal Richelieu declared war on Spain and again sent financial and military assistance to the Swedes and the German Protestant princes. The war dragged on. French, Dutch, and Swedes, supported by Scots, Finns, and German mercenaries, burned, looted, and destroyed German agriculture and commerce. The Thirty Years' War lasted so long because neither side had the resources to win a quick, decisive victory. Finally, in October 1648, peace was achieved.

The treaties signed at Münster and Osnabrück, commonly called the "Peace of Westphalia," mark a turning point in European political, religious, and social history. The treaties recognized the sovereign, independent authority of the German princes. Each ruler could govern his particular territory and make war and peace as well. With power in the hands of more than three hundred princes, with no central government, courts, or means of controlling unruly rulers, the Holy Roman Empire as a real state was effectively destroyed (Map 15.3).

The independence of the United Provinces of the Netherlands was acknowledged. The international stature of France and Sweden was also greatly improved. The political divisions within the empire, the weak German frontiers, and the acquisition of the province of Alsace increased France's size and

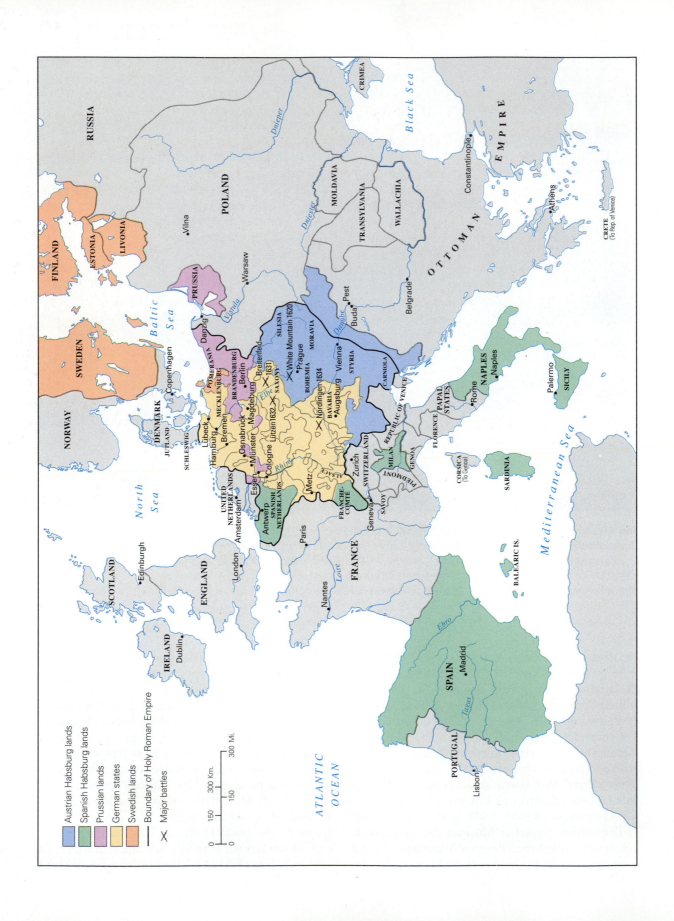

RUSSIA

POLAND

FINLAND

ESTONIA

LIVONIA

SWEDEN

NORWAY

Vilna

Warsaw

PRUSSIA

Danzig

Copenhagen

DENMARK

JUTLAND

SCHLESWIG

POMERANIA

MECKLENBURG

BRANDENBURG

Berlin

Lübeck

Hamburg

Bremen

Magdeburg

Breitenfeld

Lützen 1632

Saxony 1631

White Mountain 1620

SILESIA

Prague

BOHEMIA

MORAVIA

Vienna

Pest

Buda

Belgrade

MOLDAVIA

TRANSYLVANIA

WALLACHIA

CRIMEA

Black Sea

OTTOMAN EMPIRE

Constantinople

Athens

CRETE
(To Rep. of Venice)

Baltic Sea

North Sea

Osnabruck

Münster

Cologne

Essen

Nördlingen 1634

BAVARIA

Augsburg

STYRIA

CARNIOLA

REPUBLIC OF VENICE

Rhine

Elbe

Dnieper

Dniester

Danube

Vistula

UNITED NETHERLANDS

Amsterdam

Antwerp

SPANISH NETHERLANDS

Metz

FRANCHE-COMTÉ

Geneva

Zurich

SWITZERLAND

ALSACE

MILAN

SAVOY

PIEDMONT

GENOA

FLORENCE

PAPAL STATES

Rome

NAPLES

Naples

Palermo

SICILY

CORSICA
(To Genoa)

SARDINIA

BALEARIC IS.

Mediterranean Sea

Paris

FRANCE

Loire

Nantes

SCOTLAND

Edinburgh

ENGLAND

London

IRELAND

Dublin

ATLANTIC OCEAN

SPAIN

Madrid

Ebro

Tagus

PORTUGAL

Lisbon

Austrian Habsburg lands
Spanish Habsburg lands
Prussian lands
German states
Swedish lands
Boundary of Holy Roman Empire
Major battles

300 Mi.
150
0

300 Km.
150
0

Soldiers Pillage a Farmhouse   Billeting troops on civilian populations caused untold hardships. In this late seventeeth-century Dutch illustration, brawling soldiers take over a peasant's home, eat his food, steal his possessions, and insult his family. Peasant retaliation sometimes proved swift and bloody. *(Source: Rijksmuseum, Amsterdam)*

prestige. The treaties allowed France to intervene at will in German affairs. Sweden received a large cash indemnity and jurisdiction over German territories along the Baltic Sea. The powerful Swedish presence in northeastern Germany subsequently posed a major threat to the future kingdom of Brandenburg-Prussia. The treaties also denied the papacy the right to participate in German religious affairs —a restriction symbolizing the reduced role of the church in European politics.

In religion, the Westphalian treaties stipulated that the Augsburg agreement of 1555 should stand

MAP 15.3 Europe in 1648   Which country emerged from the Thirty Years' War as the strongest European power? What dynastic house was that country's major rival in the early modern period?

permanently. The sole modification was that Calvinism, along with Catholicism and Lutheranism, would become a legally permissible creed. In practice, the north German states remained Protestant, the south German states Catholic. The war settled little.

Germany After the Thirty Years' War

The Thirty Years' War was a disaster for the German economy and society, probably the most destructive event in German history before the twentieth century. Population losses were frightful. Perhaps one-third of the urban residents and two-fifths of the inhabitants of rural areas died. Entire areas of Germany were depopulated, partly by military actions, partly by disease—typhus, dysentery, bubonic plague, and syphilis accompanied the movements of armies—and partly by the thousands of refugees who fled to safer areas.

In the late sixteenth and early seventeenth centuries, all Europe experienced an economic crisis primarily caused by the influx of silver from South America. Because the Thirty Years' War was fought on German soil, these economic difficulties were badly aggravated in the empire. Scholars still cannot estimate the value of losses in agricultural land and livestock, in trade and commerce. The trade of southern cities like Augsburg, already hard hit by the shift in transportation routes from the Mediterranean to the Atlantic, was virtually destroyed by the fighting in the south. Meanwhile, towns like Lübeck, Hamburg, and Bremen in the north and Essen in the Ruhr area actually prospered because of the many refugees they attracted. The destruction of land and foodstuffs, compounded by the flood of Spanish silver, brought on a severe price rise. During and after the war, inflation was worse in Germany than anywhere else in Europe.

Agricultural areas suffered catastrophically. The population decline caused a rise in the value of labor, and owners of great estates had to pay more for agricultural workers. Farmers who needed only small amounts of capital to restore their lands started over again. Many small farmers, however, lacked the revenue to rework their holdings and had to become day laborers. Nobles and landlords bought up many small holdings and acquired great estates. In some parts of Germany, especially east of the Elbe River in areas like Mecklenburg and Pomerania, peasants' loss of land led to the rise of a new serfdom.[14] Thus the Thirty Years' War contributed to the legal and economic decline of the largest segment of German society.

CHANGING ATTITUDES

The age of religious wars revealed extreme and violent contrasts. It was a deeply religious period in which men fought passionately for their beliefs; 70 percent of the books printed dealt with religious subjects. Yet the times saw the beginnings of religious skepticism. Europeans explored new continents, partly with the missionary aim of Christianizing the peoples they encountered. Yet the Spanish, Portuguese, Dutch, and English proceeded to dominate and enslave the Indians and blacks they encountered. While Europeans indulged in gross sensuality, the social status of women declined. The exploration of new continents reflects deep curiosity and broad intelligence, yet Europeans believed in witches and burned thousands at the stake. Sexism, racism, and skepticism had all originated in ancient times. But late in the sixteenth century they began to take on their familiar modern forms.

The Status of Women

Do new ideas about women appear in this period? Theological and popular literature on marriage in Reformation Europe helps to answer this question. These manuals emphasize the qualities expected of each partner. A husband was obliged to provide for the material welfare of his wife and children. He should protect his family while remaining steady and self-controlled. Especially was a husband and father to rule his household, firmly but justly. But he was not to behave like a tyrant, a guideline counselors repeated frequently. A wife should be mature, a good household manager, and subservient and faithful to her spouse. The husband also owed fidelity, and both Protestant and Catholic moralists rejected the double standard of sexual morality as a threat to family unity. Counselors believed that marriage should be based on mutual respect and trust. While they discouraged impersonal unions arranged by parents, they did not think romantic attachments—based on physical attraction and emotional love—a sound basis for an enduring relationship.

Moralists held that the household was a woman's first priority. She might assist in her own or her husband's business and do charitable work. Involvement in social or public activities, however, was inappropriate because it distracted the wife from her primary responsibility, her household. If women suffered under their husbands' yoke, writers explained that submission was their punishment inherited from Eve, penance for man's fall, like the pain of childbearing. Moreover, they said, a woman's lot was no worse than a man's: he must earn the family's bread by the sweat of his brow.[15]

Catholics viewed marriage as a sacramental union, which, validly entered into, could not be dissolved. Protestants stressed the contractual form of marriage, whereby each partner promised the other support, companionship, and the sharing of mutual goods. Protestants recognized a mutual right to divorce and remarriage for various reasons, including adultery and irreparable breakdown.[16] Society in the early modern period was patriarchal. While women neither lost their identity nor lacked meaningful work, the all-pervasive assumption was that men ruled. Leading students of the Lutherans, Catholics, French Calvinists, and English Puritans tend to concur that there was no amelioration in women's definitely subordinate status.

There are some remarkable success stories, however. Elizabeth Hardwick, the orphaned daughter of an obscure English country squire, made four careful marriages, each of which brought her more property and carried her higher up the social ladder. She managed her estates, amounting to more than 100,000 acres, with a degree of business sense rare in any age. The two great mansions she built, Chatsworth and Hardwick, stand today as monuments to her acumen. Having established several aristocratic dynasties, she died in 1608, past her eightieth year, one of the richest people in England.[17]

Artists' drawings of plump, voluptuous women and massive, muscular men reveal the contemporary standards of physical beauty. It was a sensual age that gloried in the delights of the flesh. Some people, such as the humanist poet Aretino, found sexual satisfaction with both sexes. Reformers and public officials simultaneously condemned and condoned sexual "sins." The oldest profession had many practitioners, and when in 1566 Pope Pius IV expelled all the prostitutes from Rome, so many people left and the city suffered such a loss of revenue that in less than a month the pope was forced to rescind the order. Scholars debated Saint Augustine's notion that whores serve a useful social function by preventing worse sins. Prostitution was common because desperate poverty forced women and young men into it. Since the later Middle Ages, licensed houses of prostitution had been common in urban centers (see page 375). The general public took the matter for granted. Consequently, civil authorities in both Catholic and Protestant countries licensed houses of public prostitution. These establishments were intended for the convenience of single men, and some Protestant cities, such as Geneva and Zurich, installed officials in the brothels with the express purpose of preventing married men from patronizing them.

Moralists naturally railed against prostitution. For example, Melchior Ambach, the Lutheran editor of many tracts against adultery and whoring, wrote in 1543 that if "houses of women" for single and married men were allowed, why not provide a "house of boys" for womenfolk who lacked a husband to service them? "Would whoring be any worse for the poor, needy female sex?"[18] Ambach, of course, was not being serious: by treating infidelity from the perspective of female rather than male customers, he was still insisting that prostitution destroyed the family and society.

Single women of the middle and working classes in the sixteenth and seventeenth centuries worked in many occupations and professions—as butchers, shopkeepers, nurses, goldsmiths, and midwives and in the weaving and printing industries. Women who were married normally assisted in their husbands' businesses. What became of the thousands of women who left convents and nunneries during the Reformation? This question concerns primarily women of the upper classes, who formed the dominant social group in the religious houses of late medieval Europe.

Luther and the Protestant reformers believed that celibacy had no scriptural basis, that young girls were forced by their parents into convents and once there were bullied by men into staying. Therefore, reformers favored the suppression of women's religious houses and encouraged ex-nuns to marry. Marriage, the reformers maintained, not only gave women emotional and sexual satisfaction, it freed them from clerical domination, cultural deprivation, and sexual repression.[19] It would appear, consequently, that these women passed from clerical domination to subservience to husbands.

If some nuns in the Middle Ages lacked a genuine religious vocation and if some religious houses witnessed financial mismanagement and moral laxness, convents nevertheless provided women of the upper classes with scope for their literary, artistic, medical, or administrative talents if they could not or would not marry. With the closing of convents, marriage became virtually the only occupation for upper-class Protestant women. This helps explain why Anglicans, Calvinists, and Lutherans established communities of religious women, such as the Lutheran one at Kaiserwerth in the Rhineland, in the eighteenth and nineteenth centuries.[20]

The Great European Witch Hunt

The great European witch scare reveals something about contemporary attitudes toward women. The period of the religious wars witnessed a startling increase in the phenomenon of witch-hunting, whose prior history was long but sporadic. "A witch," according to Chief Justice Coke of England, "was a person who hath conference with the Devil to consult with him or to do some act." This definition by the highest legal authority in England demon-

Witches Worshiping the Devil In medieval Christian art, a goat symbolizes the damned at the Last Judgment, following Christ's statement that the Son of Man would separate believers from nonbelievers, as a shepherd separates the sheep from the goats (Matthew 25: 31–32). In this manuscript illustration, a witch arrives at a sabbat and prepares to venerate the devil in the shape of a goat by kissing its anus. *(Source: Bodleian Library, Oxford)*

strates that educated people, as well as the ignorant, believed in witches. Witches were thought to be individuals who could mysteriously injure other people or animals—by causing a person to become blind or impotent, for instance, or by preventing a cow from giving milk. Belief in witches dates back to the dawn of time. For centuries, tales had circulated about old women who made nocturnal travels on greased broomsticks to *sabbats,* or assemblies of witches, where they participated in sexual orgies and feasted on the flesh of infants. In the popular imagination witches had definite characteristics. The vast majority were married women or widows between fifty and seventy years old, crippled or bent with age, with pockmarked skin. They often practiced midwifery or folk medicine, and most had sharp tongues and were quick to scold.

In the sixteenth century, religious reformers' extreme notions of the devil's powers and the insecurity created by the religious wars contributed to the growth of belief in witches. The idea developed that witches made pacts with the devil in return for the power to work mischief on their enemies. Since pacts with the devil meant the renunciation of God, witchcraft was considered heresy, and all religions persecuted it.

Fear of witches took a terrible toll of innocent lives in parts of Europe. In southwestern Germany, 3,229 witches were executed between 1561 and 1670, most by burning. The communities of the Swiss Confederation tried 8,888 persons between 1470 and 1700 and executed 5,417 of them as witches. In all the centuries before 1500, witches in England had been suspected of causing perhaps "three deaths, a broken leg, several destructive storms and some bewitched genitals." Yet between 1559 and 1736, witches were thought to have caused thousands of deaths, and in that period almost 1,000 witches were executed in England.[21]

Historians and anthropologists have offered a variety of explanations for the great European witch hunt. Some scholars maintain that charges of witchcraft were a means of accounting for inexplicable misfortunes. Just as the English in the fifteenth century had blamed their military failures in France on Joan of Arc's sorcery, so in the seventeenth century the English Royal College of Physicians attributed undiagnosable illnesses to witchcraft. Some scholars hold that in small communities, which typically insisted on strict social conformity, charges of witchcraft were a means of attacking and eliminating the nonconformist; witches, in other words, served the collective need for scapegoats. The evidence of witches' trials, some writers suggest, shows that women were not accused because they harmed or threatened their neighbors; rather, their communities believed such women worshiped the devil, engaged in wild sexual activities with him, and ate infants. Other scholars argue the exact opposite: that people were tried and executed as witches because their neighbors feared their evil powers. Finally, there is the theory that the unbridled sexuality attributed to witches was a psychological projection on the part of their accusers, resulting from Christianity's repression of sexuality.

Though these different hypotheses exist, scholars still cannot fully understand the phenomenon. The exact reasons for the persecution of women as witches probably varied from place to place. Nevertheless, given the broad strand of misogyny (hatred of women) in Western religion, the ancient belief in the susceptibility of women (so-called weaker vessels) to the devil's allurements, and the pervasive seventeenth-century belief about women's multiple and demanding orgasms and thus their sexual insatiability, it is not difficult to understand why women were accused of all sorts of mischief and witchcraft. Charges of witchcraft provided a legal basis for the execution of tens of thousands of women. As the most important capital crime for women in early modern times, witchcraft has considerable significance for the history and status of women.[22]

European Slavery and the Origins of American Racism

Almost all peoples in the world have engaged in the enslavement of other human beings at some time in their histories. Since ancient times, victors in battle have enslaved conquered peoples. In the later Middle Ages slavery was deeply entrenched in southern Italy, Sicily, Crete, and Mediterranean Spain. The bubonic plague, famines, and other epidemics created a severe shortage of agricultural and domestic workers throughout Europe, encouraging Italian merchants to buy slaves from the Balkans, Thrace, southern Russia, and central Anatolia for sale in the West. In 1364 the Florentine government allowed the unlimited importation of slaves, so long as they were not Roman Catholics. Between 1414 and 1423, at least ten thousand slaves were sold in Venice alone. The slave trade represents one aspect of Italian business enterprise during the Renaissance: where profits were lucrative, papal threats of excommunication completely failed to stop Genoese slave traders. The Genoese set up colonial stations in the Crimea and along the Black Sea, and according to an international authority on slavery, these outposts were "virtual laboratories" for the development of slave plantation agriculture in the New World.[23] This form of slavery had nothing to do with race; almost all slaves were white. How, then, did black African slavery enter the European picture and take root in the New World?

In 1453 the Ottoman capture of Constantinople halted the flow of white slaves from the Black Sea region and the Balkans. Mediterranean Europe, cut off from its traditional source of slaves, had no alternative source for slave labor but sub-Saharan Africa. The centuries-old trans-Saharan trade was greatly stimulated by finding a ready market in the vineyards and sugar plantations of Sicily and Majorca. By the later fifteenth century, the Mediterranean had developed an "American" form of slavery before the discovery of America.

Meanwhile, the Genoese and other Italians had colonized the Canary Islands in the western Atlantic. Prince Henry the Navigator's sailors (see pages 459–460) discovered the Madeira Islands and made settlements there. In this stage of European expansion, "the history of slavery became inextricably tied up with the history of sugar." Though it was an expensive luxury that only the affluent could afford, population increases and monetary expansion in the fifteenth century led to an increasing demand for sugar. Resourceful Italians provided the capital, cane, and technology for sugar cultivation on plantations in southern Portugal, Madeira, and the Canary Islands. Meanwhile, in the port of Lisbon alone between 1490 and 1520, 302,000 black slaves arrived (Map 15.4). From Lisbon, where African slaves performed most of the manual labor and constituted 10 percent of the city's population, slaves were transported to the sugar plantations of Madeira, the Azores, the Cape Verde Islands, and then Brazil. Sugar and the small Atlantic islands gave New World slavery its distinctive shape. Columbus himself, who spent a decade in Madeira, took sugar plants on his voyages to "the Indies."[24]

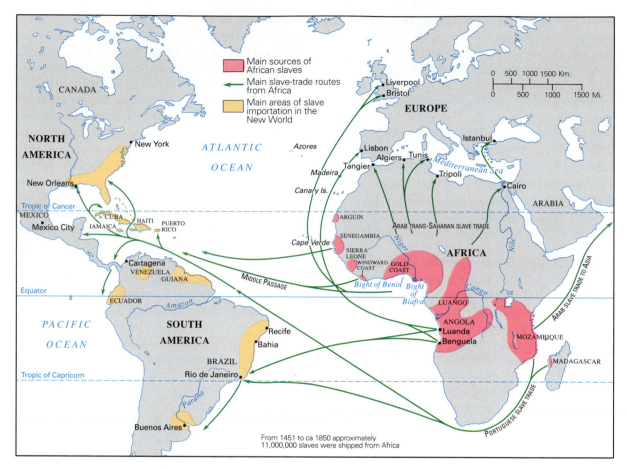

MAP 15.4 The African Slave Trade Decades before the discovery of America, Greek, Russian, Bulgarian, Armenian, and then black slaves worked the plantation economies of southern Italy, Sicily, Portugal, and Mediterranean Spain—thereby serving as models for the American form of slavery.

As already discussed, European expansion across the Atlantic led to the economic exploitation of the Americas. In the New World the major problem settlers faced was a shortage of labor. As early as 1495, the Spanish solved the problem by enslaving the native Indians. In the next two centuries, the Portuguese, Dutch, and English followed suit.

Unaccustomed to any form of forced labor, certainly not to panning gold for more than twelve hours a day in the broiling sun, the Indians died "like fish in a bucket," as one Spanish settler reported.[25] In 1515 a Spanish missionary, Bartolomé de Las Casas (1474–1566), who had seen the evils of Indian slavery, urged the future emperor Charles V to end Indian slavery in his American dominions. Las Casas recommended the importation of

blacks from Africa, both because church law did not strictly forbid black slavery and because he thought blacks could better survive under South American conditions. Charles agreed, and in 1518 the African slave trade began. (When the blacks arrived, Las Casas immediately regretted his suggestion.) Columbus's introduction of sugar plants, moreover, stimulated the need for black slaves; and the experience and model of plantation slavery in Portugal and the Atlantic islands encouraged the establishment of a similar agricultural pattern in the New World.

Several European nations participated in the African slave trade. Portugal brought the first slaves to Brazil; by 1600, 4,000 were being imported annually. After its founding in 1621, the Dutch

West India Company, with the full support of the government of the United Provinces, transported thousands of Africans to Brazil and the Caribbean. Only in the late seventeenth century, with the chartering of the Royal African Company, did the English get involved. Thereafter, large numbers of African blacks poured into the West Indies and North America. In 1790 there were 757,181 blacks in a total U.S. population of 3,929,625. When the first census was taken in Brazil in 1798, blacks numbered about 2 million in a total population of 3.25 million.

Settlers brought to the Americas the racial attitudes they had absorbed in Europe. Settlers' beliefs and attitudes toward blacks derived from two basic sources: Christian theological speculation (see page 405) and Muslim ideas. In the sixteenth and seventeenth centuries, the English, for example, were extremely curious about Africans' lives and customs, and slavers' accounts were extraordinarily popular. Travel literature depicted Africans as savages because of their eating habits, morals, clothing, and social customs; as barbarians because of their language and methods of war; and as heathens because they were not Christian. English people saw similarities between apes and Africans; thus the terms *bestial* and *beastly* were frequently applied to Africans. Africans were believed to possess a potent sexuality. One seventeenth-century observer considered Africans "very lustful and impudent, . . . (for a Negroes hiding his members, their extraordinary greatness) is a token of their lust." African women were considered sexually aggressive with a "temper hot and lascivious."[26]

"At the time when Columbus sailed to the New World, Islam was the largest world religion, and the only world religion that showed itself capable of expanding rapidly in areas as far apart and as different from each other as Senegal [in northwest Africa], Bosnia [in the Balkans], Java, and the Philippines." Medieval Arabic literature emphasized blacks' physical repulsiveness, mental inferiority, and primitivism. In contrast to civilized peoples from the Mediterranean to China, Muslim writers claimed, sub-Saharan blacks were the only peoples who had produced no sciences or stable states. The fourteenth-century Arab historian ibn-Khaldun wrote that "the only people who accept slavery are the Negroes, owing to their low degree of humanity and their proximity to the animal stage."

Though black kings, Khaldun alleged, sold their subjects without even a pretext of crime or war, the victims bore no resentment because they gave no thought to the future and had "by nature few cares and worries; dancing and rhythm are for them inborn."[27] It is easy to see how such absurd images developed into the classic stereotypes used to justify black slavery in South and North America in

African Slave and Indian Woman A black slave approaches an Indian prostitute. Unable to explain what he wants, he points with his finger; she eagerly grasps for the coin. The Spanish caption above moralizes on the black man using stolen money—yet the Spaniards ruthlessly expropriated all South American mineral wealth. *(Source: New York Public Library)*

the seventeenth, eighteenth, and nineteenth centuries. Medieval Christians and Muslims had similar notions of blacks as inferior and primitive people ideally suited to enslavement. Perhaps centuries of commercial contacts between Muslim and Mediterranean peoples had familiarized the latter with Muslim racial attitudes. In any case, these were the racial beliefs that the Portuguese, Spanish, Dutch, and English brought to the New World.

LITERATURE AND ART

The age of religious wars and overseas expansion also experienced an extraordinary degree of intellectual and artistic ferment. This effervescence can be seen in the development of the essay as a distinct literary genre, in other prose, poetry, and drama, in art, and in music.

The Essay: Michel de Montaigne

Decades of religious fanaticism, bringing famine, civil anarchy, and death, led both Catholics and Protestants to doubt that any one faith contained absolute truth. The late sixteenth and seventeenth centuries witnessed the beginning of modern skepticism. *Skepticism* is a school of thought founded on doubt that total certainty or definitive knowledge is ever attainable. The skeptic is cautious and critical and suspends judgment. Perhaps the finest representative of early modern skepticism is the Frenchman Michel de Montaigne (1533–1592).

Montaigne came from a bourgeois family that had made a fortune selling salted herring and in 1477 had purchased the title and property of Montaigne in Gascony. Montaigne received a classical education before studying law and securing a judicial appointment in 1554. Though a member of the nobility, in embarking on a judicial career he identified with the new nobility of the robe. He condemned the ancient nobility of the sword for being more concerned with war and sports than with the cultivation of the mind.

At the age of thirty-eight, Montaigne resigned his judicial post, retired to his estate, and devoted the rest of his life to study, contemplation, and the effort to understand himself. Like the Greeks, he believed that the object of life was to "know thyself," for self-knowledge teaches men and women how to live in accordance with nature and God. Montaigne developed a new literary genre, the essay—from the French *essayer,* meaning "to test or try"—to express his thoughts and ideas.

Montaigne's *Essays* provide insight into the mind of a remarkably humane, tolerant, and civilized man. He was a humanist; he loved the Greek and Roman writers and was always eager to learn from them. In his essay "On Solitude," he quoted the Roman poet Horace:

Reason and sense remove anxiety,
Not villas that look out upon the sea

Some said to Socrates that a certain man had grown no better by his travels. "I should think not," he said; "he took himself along with him. . . ."
We should have wife, children, goods, and above all health, if we can; but we must not bind ourselves to them so strongly that our happiness depends on them. We must reserve a back shop all our own, entirely free, in which to establish our real liberty and our principal retreat and solitude.[28]

From the ancient authors, especially the Roman Stoic Seneca, Montaigne acquired a sense of calm, inner peace, and patience. The ancient authors also inculcated in him a tolerance and broad-mindedness. Montaigne had grown up during the French civil wars, perhaps the worst kind of war. Religious ideology had set family against family, even brother against brother. He wrote:

In this controversy . . . France is at present agitated by civil wars, the best and soundest side is undoubtedly that which maintains both the old religion and the old government of the country. However, among the good men who follow that side . . . we see many whom passion drives outside the bounds of reason, and makes them sometimes adopt unjust, violent, and even reckless courses.[29]

Though he remained a Catholic, Montaigne possessed a detachment, an independence, an openness of mind, and a willingness to look at all sides of a question. As he wrote, "I listen with attention to the judgment of all men; but so far as I can remember, I have followed none but my own.

Though I set little value upon my own opinion, I set no more on the opinions of others."

In a violent and cruel age, Montaigne was a gentle and sensitive man. In his famous essay "On Cruelty," he stated:

Among other vices I cruelly hate cruelty, both by nature and by judgment, as the extreme of all vices. . . .

I live in a time when we abound in incredible examples of this vice, through the license of our civil wars; and we see in the ancient histories nothing more extreme than what we experience of this every day. But that has not reconciled me to it at all.[30]

In the book-lined tower where Montaigne passed his days, he became a deeply learned man. Yet he was not ignorant of the world of affairs, and he criticized scholars and bookworms who ignored the life around them. Montaigne's essay "On Cannibals" reflects the impact of overseas discoveries on Europeans' consciousness. His tolerant mind rejected the notion that one culture is superior to another:

I long had a man in my house that lived ten or twelve years in the New World, discovered in these latter days, and in that part of it where Villegaignon landed [Brazil]. . . .

I find that there is nothing barbarous and savage in [that] nation, by anything that I can gather, excepting, that every one gives the title of barbarism to everything that is not in use in his own country. As, indeed, we have no other level of truth and reason, than the example and idea of the opinions and customs of the place wherein we live.[31]

In his belief in the nobility of human beings in the state of nature, uncorrupted by organized society, and in his cosmopolitan attitude toward different civilizations, Montaigne anticipated many eighteenth-century thinkers.

The thought of Michel de Montaigne marks a sharp break with the past. Faith and religious certainty had characterized the intellectual attitudes of Western society for a millennium. Montaigne's rejection of any kind of dogmatism, his secularism, and his skepticism thus represent a basic change. In his own time and throughout the seventeenth century, few would have agreed with him. The publication of his ideas, however, anticipated a basic shift in attitudes. Montaigne inaugurated an era of doubt. "Wonder," he said, "is the foundation of all philosophy, research is the means of all learning, and ignorance is the end."[32]

Elizabethan and Jacobean Literature

In addition to the essay as a literary genre, the period fostered remarkable creativity in other branches of literature. England, especially in the latter part of Elizabeth's reign and in the first years of her successor James I (r. 1603–1625), fostered remarkable creativity. The terms *Elizabethan* and *Jacobean* (referring to the reign of James) are used to designate the English music, poetry, prose, and drama of this period. The poetry of Sir Philip Sidney (1554–1586), such as *Astrophel and Stella*, strongly influenced later poetic writing. *The Faerie Queene* of Edmund Spenser (1552–1599) endures as one of the greatest moral epics in any language. The rare poetic beauty of the plays of Christopher Marlowe (1564–1593), such as *Tamburlaine* and *The Jew of Malta*, paved the way for the work of Shakespeare. Above all, the immortal dramas of Shakespeare and the stately prose of the Authorized or King James Bible mark the Elizabethan and Jacobean periods as the golden age of English literature.

William Shakespeare (1564–1616), the son of a successful glove manufacturer who rose to the highest municipal office in the Warwickshire town of Stratford-on-Avon, chose a career on the London stage. By 1592 he had gained recognition as an actor and playwright. Between 1599 and 1603, Shakespeare performed in the Lord Chamberlain's Company and became co-owner of the Globe Theatre, which after 1603 presented his plays.

Shakespeare's genius lies in the originality of his characterizations, the diversity of his plots, his understanding of human psychology, and his unexcelled gift for language. Shakespeare was a Renaissance man in his deep appreciation for classical culture, individualism, and humanism. Such plays as *Julius Caesar, Pericles,* and *Antony and Cleopatra* deal with classical subjects and figures. Several of his comedies have Italian Renaissance settings. The nine history plays, including *Richard II, Richard III,* and *Henry IV,* enjoyed the greatest popularity among Shakespeare's contemporaries.

A Royal Hunt In the sixteenth and seventeenth centuries, hunting remained an aristo-cratic pasttime. Here a courtier, having slain a deer, presents the dagger to Queen Elizabeth I. *(Source: By permission of the Folger Shakespeare Library)*

Written during the decade after the defeat of the Spanish Armada, the history plays express English national consciousness. Lines such as these from *Richard II* reflect this sense of national greatness with unparalleled eloquence:

This royal Throne of Kings, this sceptre'd Isle,
This earth of Majesty, this seat of Mars,
This other Eden, demi-paradise,
This fortress built by Nature for herself,
Against infection and the hand of war:

This happy breed of men, this little world,
This precious stone, set in the silver sea,
Which serves it in the office of a wall,
Or as a moat defensive to a house,
Against the envy of less happier Lands,
This blessed plot, this earth, this Realm, this England.

Shakespeare's later plays, above all the tragedies *Hamlet, Othello,* and *Macbeth,* explore an enormous range of human problems and are open to an almost infinite variety of interpretations. *Othello,* which the nineteenth-century historian Thomas Macaulay called "perhaps the greatest work in the world," portrays an honorable man destroyed by a flaw in his own character and the satanic evil of his supposed friend Iago. *Macbeth's* central theme is exorbitant ambition. Shakespeare analyzes the psychology of sin in the figures of Macbeth and Lady Macbeth, whose mutual love under the pressure of ambition leads to their destruction. The central figure in *Hamlet,* a play suffused with individuality, wrestles with moral problems connected with revenge and with man's relationship to life and death. The soliloquy in which Hamlet debates suicide is perhaps the most widely quoted passage in English literature:

To be, or not to be: that is the question:
Whether 'tis nobler in the mind to suffer
The slings and arrows of outrageous fortune,
Or to take arms against a sea of troubles,
And by opposing end them? . .

Hamlet's sad cry, "There is nothing either good or bad but thinking makes it so," expresses the anguish and uncertainty of modern man. *Hamlet* has always enjoyed great popularity, because in his many-faceted personality people have seen an aspect of themselves.

Shakespeare's dynamic language bespeaks his extreme sensitivity to the sounds and meanings of words. Perhaps no phrase better summarizes the reason for his immortality than this line, slightly modified, from *Antony and Cleopatra:* "Age cannot wither [him], nor custom stale/ [his] infinite variety."

The other great masterpiece of the Jacobean period was the *Authorized Bible.* At a theological conference in 1604, a group of Puritans urged James I to support a new translation of the Bible. The king in turn assigned the task to a committee of scholars, who published their efforts in 1611. Based on the best scriptural research of the time and divided into chapters and verses, the Authorized Version is actually a revision of earlier Bibles more than an original work. Yet it provides a superb expression of the mature English vernacular in the early seventeenth century. Thus Psalm 37:

Fret not thy selfe because of evill doers, neither bee thou
envious against the workers of iniquitie.

For they shall soone be cut downe like the grasse; and
wither as the greene herbe.
Trust in the Lord, and do good, so shalt thou dwell in
the land, and verely thou shalt be fed.
Delight thy selfe also in the Lord; and he shall give thee
the desires of thine heart.
Commit thy way unto the Lord: trust also in him, and
he shall bring it to passe.
And he shall bring forth thy righteousness as the light,
and thy judgement as the noone day.

The Authorized Version, so called because it was produced under royal sponsorship—it had no official ecclesiastical endorsement—represented the Anglican and Puritan desire to encourage lay people to read the Scriptures. It quickly achieved great popularity and displaced all earlier versions. British settlers carried this Bible to the North American colonies, where it became known as the *King James Bible.* For centuries the King James Bible has had a profound influence on the language and lives of English-speaking peoples.

Baroque Art and Music

Throughout European history, the cultural tastes of one age have often seemed quite unsatisfactory to the next. So it was with the baroque. The term *baroque* itself may have come from the Portuguese word for an "odd-shaped, imperfect pearl" and was commonly used by late-eighteenth-century art critics as an expression of scorn for what they considered an overblown, unbalanced style. The hostility of these critics, who also scorned the Gothic style of medieval cathedrals in favor of a classicism inspired by antiquity and the Renaissance, has long since passed. Specialists agree that the triumphs of the baroque marked one of the high points in the history of Western culture.

The early development of the baroque is complex, but most scholars stress the influence of Rome and the revitalized Catholic church of the later sixteenth century. The papacy and the Jesuits encouraged the growth of an intensely emotional, exuberant art. These patrons wanted artists to go beyond the Renaissance focus on pleasing a small, wealthy cultural elite. They wanted artists to appeal to the senses and thereby touch the souls and kindle the faith of ordinary churchgoers, while

proclaiming the power and confidence of the re-formed Catholic church. In addition to this underlying religious emotionalism, the baroque drew its sense of drama, motion, and ceaseless striving from the Catholic Reformation. The interior of the famous Jesuit Church of Jesus in Rome—the Gesù—combined all these characteristics in its lavish, shimmering, wildly active decorations and frescoes.

Taking definite shape in Italy after 1600, the baroque style in the visual arts developed with exceptional vigor in Catholic countries—in Spain and Latin America, Austria, southern Germany, and Poland. Yet baroque art was more than just "Catholic art" in the seventeenth century and the first half of the eighteenth. True, neither Protestant England nor the Netherlands ever came fully under the spell of the baroque, but neither did Catholic France. And Protestants accounted for some of the finest examples of baroque style, especially in music. The baroque style spread partly because its tension and bombast spoke to an agitated age, which was experiencing great violence and controversy in politics and religion.

In painting, the baroque reached maturity early with Peter Paul Rubens (1577–1640), the most outstanding and representative of baroque painters. Studying in his native Flanders and in Italy, where he was influenced by masters of the High Renaissance such as Michelangelo, Rubens developed his own rich, sensuous, colorful style, which was characterized by animated figures, melodramatic contrasts, and monumental size. Although Rubens excelled in glorifying monarchs such as Queen Mother Marie de' Medici of France, he was also a devout Catholic. Nearly half of his pictures treat Christian subjects. Yet one of Rubens's trademarks was fleshy, sensual nudes, who populate his canvases as Roman goddesses, water nymphs, and remarkably voluptuous saints and angels.

Veronese: Mars and Venus United by Love (ca 1580) Taking a theme from classical mythology, the Venetian painter Veronese celebrates in clothing, architecture, and landscape the luxurious wealth of the aristocracy. The lush and curvaceous Venus and the muscular and powerfully built Mars suggest the anticipated pleasures of sexual activity and the frank sensuality of the age. (Source: The Metropolitan Museum of Art, New York, John Stewart Kennedy Fund, 1910)

Velázquez: Juan de Pareja This portrait (1650) of the Spanish painter Velázquez's one-time assistant, a black man of obvious intellectual and sensual power and himself a renowned religious painter, suggests the integration of some blacks in seventeenth-century society. The elegant lace collar attests to his middle-class status. (Source: The Metropolitan Museum of Art)

Rubens was enormously successful. To meet the demand for his work, he established a large studio and hired many assistants to execute his rough sketches and gigantic murals. Sometimes the master artist added only the finishing touches. Rubens's wealth and position—on occasion he was given special diplomatic assignments by the Habsburgs—attest that distinguished artists continued to enjoy the high social status they had won in the Renaissance.

In music, the baroque style reached its culmination almost a century later in the dynamic, soaring lines of the endlessly inventive Johann Sebastian Bach (1685–1750), one of the greatest composers the Western world has ever produced. Organist and choirmaster of several Lutheran churches across Germany, Bach was equally at home writing secular concertos and sublime religious cantatas. Bach's organ music, the greatest ever written, combined the baroque spirit of invention, tension, and emotion in an unforgettable striving toward the infinite. Unlike Rubens, Bach was not fully appreciated in his lifetime, but since the early nineteenth century his reputation has grown steadily.

SUMMARY

In the sixteenth and seventeenth centuries, Europeans for the first time gained access to large parts of the globe. European peoples had the intellectual curiosity, driving ambition, and scientific technology to attempt feats that were as difficult and expensive then as going to the moon is today. Exploration and exploitation contributed to a more sophisticated standard of living, in the form of spices and Asian luxury goods, and to a terrible international inflation resulting from the influx of South American silver and gold. Governments, the upper classes, and the peasantry were badly hurt by the inflation. Meanwhile, the middle class of bankers, shippers, financiers, and manufacturers prospered for much of the seventeenth century.

European expansion and colonization took place against a background of religious conflict and rising national consciousness. The seventeenth century was by no means a secular period. Though the medieval religious framework had broken down, people still thought largely in religious terms. Europeans explained what they did politically and economically in terms of religious doctrine. Religious ideology served as a justification for a variety of goals, such as the French nobles' opposition to the Crown and the Dutch struggle for political and economic independence from Spain. In Germany, religious hatreds and foreign ambitions led to the Thirty Years' War. After 1648 the divisions between Protestant and Catholic tended to become permanent. Religious skepticism and racial attitudes were harbingers of developments to come.

NOTES

1. Quoted in C. M. Cipolla, *Guns, Sails, and Empires: Technological Innovation and the Early Phases of European Expansion, 1400–1700* (New York: Minerva Press, 1965), pp. 115–116.
2. Quoted in S. E. Morison, *Admiral of the Ocean Sea: A Life of Christopher Columbus* (Boston: Little, Brown, 1946), p. 154.
3. See C. R. Phillips, *Ciudad Real, 1500–1750: Growth, Crisis, and Readjustment in the Spanish Economy* (Cambridge, Mass.: Harvard University Press, 1979), pp. 103–104, 115.
4. Quoted in Cipolla, p. 132.
5. Quoted in F. H. Littell, *The Macmillan Atlas History of Christianity* (New York: Macmillan, 1976), p. 75.
6. Quoted in Cipolla, p. 133.
7. J. H. Parry, *The Age of Reconnaissance* (New York: Mentor Books, 1963), chaps. 3 and 5.
8. Quoted in J. Hale, "War and Public Opinion in the Fifteenth and Sixteenth Centuries," *Past and Present* 22 (July 1962): 29.
9. See ibid., pp. 18–32.
10. Quoted in N. Z. Davis, "The Rites of Violence: Religious Riot in Sixteenth Century France," *Past and Present* 59 (May 1973): 59.
11. See ibid., pp. 51–91.
12. Quoted in J. L. Motley, *The Rise of the Dutch Republic* (Philadelphia: David McKay, 1898), 1.109.
13. Quoted in P. Smith, *The Age of the Reformation* (New York: Henry Holt, 1951), p. 248.
14. H. Kamen, "The Economic and Social Consequences of the Thirty Years' War," *Past and Present* 39 (April 1968): 44–61.
15. This passage is based heavily on S. Ozment, *When Fathers Ruled: Family Life in Reformation Europe* (Cambridge, Mass.: Harvard University Press, 1983), pp. 50–99.
16. Ibid., pp. 85–92.
17. See D. Durant, *Bess of Hardwick: Portrait of an Elizabethan Dynast* (London: Weidenfeld & Nicolson, 1977).
18. Quoted in Ozment, p. 56.
19. Ozment, pp. 9–14.
20. See F. Biot, *The Rise of Protestant Monasticism* (Baltimore: Helicon Press, 1968), pp. 74–78.
21. N. Cohn, *Europe's Inner Demons: An Enquiry Inspired by the Great Witch-Hunt* (New York: Basic Books, 1975), pp. 253–254; K. Thomas, *Religion and the Decline of Magic* (New York: Charles Scribner's Sons, 1971), pp. 450-455.
22. See E. W. Monter, "The Pedestal and the Stake: Courtly Love and Witchcraft," in *Becoming Visible: Women in European History*, ed. R. Bridenthal and C. Koonz (Boston: Houghton Mifflin, 1977), pp. 132–135; and A. Fraser, *The Weaker Vessel* (New York: Random House, 1985), pp. 100–103.
23. C. Verlinden, *The Beginnings of Modern Colonization*, trans. Y. Freccero (Ithaca, N. Y.: Cornell University Press, 1970), pp. 5–6, 80–97.
24. This section leans heavily on D. B. Davis, *Slavery and Human Progress* (New York: Oxford University Press, 1984), pp. 54–62.
25. Quoted in D. P. Mannix with M. Cowley, *Black Car-*

goes: A History of the Atlantic Slave Trade, (New York: Viking Press, 1968), p. 5.

26. Ibid., p. 19.
27. Davis, pp. 43–44.
28. D. M. Frame, trans., *The Complete Works of Montaigne* (Stanford, Calif.: Stanford University Press, 1958), pp. 175–176.
29. Ibid., p. 177.
30. Ibid., p. 306.
31. C. Cotton, trans., *The Essays of Michel de Montaigne* (New York: A. L. Burt, 1893), pp. 207, 210.
32. Ibid., p. 523.

SUGGESTED READING

Perhaps the best starting point for the study of European society in the age of exploration is a work cited in the Notes: J. H. Parry, *The Age of Reconnaissance,* which treats the causes and consequences of the voyages of discovery. Parry's splendidly illustrated *The Discovery of South America* (1979) examines Europeans' reactions to the maritime discoveries and treats the entire concept of new *discoveries.* The urbane studies of C. M. Cipolla present fascinating material on technological and sociological developments written in a lucid style: *Guns, Sails, and Empires,* mentioned in the Notes; *Clocks and Culture, 1300–1700* (1967); *Cristofano and the Plague: A Study in the History of Public Health in the Age of Galileo* (1973); and *Public Health and the Medical Profession in the Renaissance* (1976). S. E. Morison's *Admiral of the Ocean Sea,* cited in the Notes, is the standard biography of Columbus. The advanced student should consult F. Braudel, *Civilization and Capitalism, Fifteenth–Eighteenth Century,* trans. Sian Reynolds: vol. 1, *The Structures of Everyday Life* (1981); vol. 2, *The Wheels of Commerce* (1982); and vol. 3, *The Perspective of the World* (1984). These three fat volumes combine vast erudition, a global perspective, and remarkable illustrations.

For the religious wars, in addition to the references in the Suggested Reading for Chapter 14 and the Notes to this chapter, see J. H. M. Salmon, *Society in Crisis: France in the Sixteenth Century* (1975), which traces the fate of French institutions during the civil wars. N. Sutherland, *Catherine de' Medici and the Ancien Regime* (1966), provides a sympathetic account of that queen's policies and problems in governing France. A. N. Galpern, *The Religions of the People in Sixteenth-Century Champagne* (1976), is a useful case study in religious anthropology, and W. A. Christian, Jr., *Local Religion in Sixteenth-Century Spain* (1981), traces the attitudes and practices of ordinary people.

A cleverly illustrated introduction to the Low Countries is K. H. D. Kaley, *The Dutch in the Seventeenth Century* (1972). The old study of J. L. Motley, cited in the Notes, still provides a good comprehensive treatment and makes fascinating reading. For Spanish military operations in the Low Countries, see G. Parker, *The Army of Flanders and the Spanish Road, 1567–1659: The Logistics of Spanish Victory and Defeat in the Low Countries' Wars* (1972). The same author's *Spain and the Netherlands, 1559–1659: Ten Studies* (1979) contains useful essays, of which students may especially want to consult "Why Did the Dutch Revolt Last So Long?" For the later phases of the Dutch-Spanish conflict, see J. I. Israel, *The Dutch Republic and the Hispanic World, 1606–1661* (1982), which treats the struggle in global perspective.

Of the many biographies of Elizabeth of England, see L. B. Smith, *Elizabeth Tudor: Portrait of a Queen* (1980), and C. Haight, *Elizabeth I* (1988). W. T. MacCaffrey, *Queen Elizabeth and the Making of Policy, 1572–1588* (1981), examines the problems posed by the Reformation and how Elizabeth solved them. J. E. Neale, *Queen Elizabeth I* (1957), remains valuable, and L. B. Smith, *The Elizabethan Epic* (1966), is a splendid evocation of the age of Shakespeare with Elizabeth at the center. The best recent biography is C. Erickson, *The First Elizabeth* (1983), a fine, psychologically resonant portrait.

Nineteenth- and early twentieth-century historians described the defeat of the Spanish Armada as a great victory for Protestantism, democracy, and capitalism, which those scholars tended to link together. Recent historians have treated the event in terms of its contemporary significance. For a sympathetic but judicious portrait of the man who launched the Armada, see G. Parker, *Philip II* (1978). D. Howarth, *The Voyage of the Armada* (1982), discusses the expedition largely in terms of the individuals involved, while G. Mattingly, *The Armada* (1959), gives the diplomatic and political background; both Howarth and Mattingly tell very exciting tales. M. Lewis, *The Spanish Armada* (1972), also tells a good story, but strictly from the English perspective. The best recent account of the Armada is G. Parker and C. Martin, *The Spanish Armada* (1988). Significant aspects of Portuguese culture are treated in A. Hower and R. Preto-Rodas, eds., *Empire in Transition: The Portuguese World in the Time of Camões* (1985).

C. V. Wedgwood, *The Thirty Years' War* (1961), must be qualified in light of recent research on the social and economic effects of the war. G. Parker, *The Thirty Years' War* (1984), is an important but densely written work. A variety of opinions on the causes and results of the war are given in T. K. Rabb's anthology, *The Thirty Years' War* (1981). Several articles in the scholarly journal *Past and Present* provide some of the latest important findings. Two of these articles, by H. Kamen and J. Hale, respectively, are mentioned in the Notes; the others are J. V. Polisensky, "The Thirty Years' War and the Crises and Revolutions of Sixteenth Century Europe," 39 (1968), and M. Roberts, "Queen Christina and the General Crisis of the Seventeenth Century," 22 (1962), which treats the overall significance of Swedish participation.

As background to the intellectual changes instigated by the Reformation, D. C. Wilcox, *In Search of God and Self: Renaissance and Reformation Thought* (1975), contains a perceptive analysis, and T. Ashton, ed., *Crisis in Europe, 1560–1660* (1967), is fundamental. On witches and witchcraft see, in addition to the titles by N. Cohn and K. Thomas in the Notes, J. B. Russell, *Witchcraft in the Middle Ages* (1976) and *Lucifer: The Devil in the Middle Ages* (1984); R. Kieckhefer, *European Witch Trials: Their Foundations in Popular and Learned Culture, 1300–1500* (1976), which places the subject within the social context; H. C. E. Midelfort, *Witch Hunting in Southwestern Germany: The Social and Intellectual Foundations* (1972), a sensitive and informed work; E. W. Monter, *Witchcraft in France and Switzerland* (1976), which discusses the subject with wit and wisdom; C. Ginzburg, *The Night Battle: Witchcraft and Agrarian Cults in the Sixteenth and Seventeenth Centuries* (1983), for small Italian communities; J. C. Baroja, *The World of Witches* (1964), for Spain; and the recent study of G. R. Quaife, *Godly Zeal and Furious Rage: The Witch in Early Modern Europe* (1987), an excellent and lucidly written synthesis.

For women, marriage, and the family, see L. Stone, *The Family, Sex, and Marriage in England, 1500–1800* (1977), a controversial work; D. Underdown, "The Taming of the Scold," and S. Amussen, "Gender, Family, and the Social Order," in A. Fletcher and J. Stevenson, eds., *Order and Disorder in Early Modern England* (1985); A. Macfarlane, *Marriage and Love in England: Modes of Reproduction, 1300–1848* (1986); C. R. Boxer, *Women in Iberian Expansion Overseas, 1415–1815* (1975), an invaluable study of women's role in overseas emigration; S. M. Wyntjes, "Women in the Reformation Era," in R. Bridenthal and C. Koonz, eds., *Becoming Visible: Women in European History* (1977), a quick survey of conditions in different countries; A. Clark, *The Working Life of Women in the Seventeenth Century* (1968); K. M. Wilson,

ed., *Women Writers of the Renaissance and Reformation* (1987); M. J. M. Ezell, *The Patriarch's Wife: Literary Evidence and the History of the Family* (1987); L. Pollock, *A Lasting Relationship: Parents and Children over Three Centuries* (1987); and L. Schwoerer, *Lady Russel: One of the Best Women* (1988). S. Ozment's *When Fathers Ruled,* a work listed in the Notes, is a seminal study concentrating on Germany and Switzerland.

As background to slavery and racism in North and South America, students should see J. L. Watson, ed., *Asian and African Systems of Slavery* (1980), a valuable collection of essays, as well as two works mentioned in the Notes: Davis's, *Slavery and Human Progress,* which shows how slavery was viewed as a progressive force in the expansion of the Western world; and Mannix and Cowley's *Black Cargoes,* a hideously fascinating account of the slave trade. For North American conditions, interested students should consult W. D. Jordan, *The White Man's Burden: Historical Origins of Racism in the United States* (1974). The excellent essays in G. M. Frederickson, *The Arrogance of Race: Historical Perspectives on Slavery, Racism, and Social Inequality* (1988), stress the social and economic circumstances associated with the rise of plantation slavery. For Caribbean and South American developments, see F. P. Bowser, *The African Slave in Colonial Peru* (1974); J. S. Handler and F. W. Lange, *Plantation Slavery in Barbados: An Archeological and Historical Investigation* (1978); and R. E. Conrad, *Children of God's Fire: A Documentary History of Black Slavery in Brazil* (1983).

The leading authority on Montaigne is D. M. Frame. See his *Montaigne's Discovery of Man* (1955) and his translation *The Complete Works of Montaigne* (1958). For baroque art, see V. L. Tapié, *The Age of Grandeur: Baroque Art and Architecture* (1961), a standard work, and J. Montagu, *Roman Baroque Sculpture: The Industry of Art* (1985), an original and entertaining recent study.

16

Absolutism and Constitutionalism in Western Europe (ca 1589–1715)

expenses against that revenue. One of the first French officials to appreciate the significance of overseas trade, Sully subsidized the Company for Trade with the Indies. He started a countrywide highway system and even dreamed of an international organization for the maintenance of peace.

In twelve short years, Henry IV and Sully restored public order in France and laid the foundations for economic prosperity. By the standards of the time, Henry IV's government was progressive and promising. His murder in 1610 by a crazed fanatic led to a severe crisis.

After the death of Henry IV, the queen-regent Marie de' Medici led the government for the child-king Louis XIII (r. 1610–1643), but in fact feudal nobles and princes of the blood dominated the political scene. In 1624 Marie de' Medici secured the appointment of Armand Jean du Plessis—Cardinal Richelieu (1585–1642)—to the council of ministers. It was a remarkable appointment. The next year Richelieu became president of the council, and after 1628 he was first minister of the French crown. Richelieu used his strong influence over King Louis XIII to exalt the French monarchy as the embodiment of the French state. One of the greatest servants of the French state, Richelieu set in place the cornerstone of French absolutism, and his work served as the basis for France's cultural domination of Europe in the later seventeenth century.

Richelieu's policy was the total subordination of all groups and institutions to the French monarchy. The French nobility, with its selfish and independent interests, had long constituted the foremost threat to the centralizing goals of the Crown and to a strong national state. Therefore, Richelieu tried to break the power of the nobility. He leveled castles, long the symbol of feudal independence. He crushed aristocratic conspiracies with quick executions. For example, when the duke of Montmorency, the first peer of France and the godson of Henry IV, became involved in a revolt in 1632, he was summarily put to death.

The constructive genius of Cardinal Richelieu is best reflected in the administrative system he established. He extended the use of the royal commissioners called intendants. France was divided into thirty-two *généralités* ("districts"), in each of which a royal intendant had extensive responsibility for justice, police, and finances. The intendants were authorized "to decide, order and execute all that they see good to do." Usually members of the upper middle class or minor nobility, the intendants were appointed directly by the monarch, to whom they were solely responsible. They could not be natives of the districts where they held authority; thus they had no vested interest in their localities. The intendants recruited men for the army, supervised the collection of taxes, presided over the administration of local law, checked up on the local nobility, and regulated economic activities—commerce, trade, the guilds, marketplaces—in their districts. They were to use their power for two related purposes: to enforce royal orders in the généralités of their jurisdiction and to weaken the power and influence of the regional nobility. The system of government by intendants derived from Philip Augustus's baillis and seneschals, and ultimately from Charlemagne's missi dominici. As the intendants' power grew during Richelieu's administration, so did the power of the centralized state.

The cardinal perceived that Protestantism often served as a cloak for the political intrigues of ambitious lords. When the Huguenots revolted in 1625, under the duke of Rohan, Richelieu personally supervised the siege of their walled city, La Rochelle, and forced it to surrender. Thereafter, fortified cities were abolished. Huguenots were allowed to practice their faith, but they no longer possessed armed strongholds or the means to be an independent party in the state. Another aristocratic prop was knocked down.

French foreign policy under Richelieu was aimed at the destruction of the fence of Habsburg territories that surrounded France. Consequently, Richelieu supported the Habsburgs' enemies. In 1631 he signed a treaty with the Lutheran king Gustavus Adolphus, promising French support against the Catholic Habsburgs in what has been called the Swedish phase of the Thirty Years' War (see page 478). French influence became an important factor in the political future of the German Empire. Richelieu acquired for France extensive rights in Alsace in the east and Arras in the north.

Richelieu's efforts at centralization extended even to literature. In 1635 he gave official recognition to a group of philologists who were interested in grammar and rhetoric. Thus was born the French Academy. With Richelieu's encouragement, the Academy began the preparation of a dictionary to standardize the French language; it was completed in 1694. The French Academy survives as a prestigious society and its membership now includes people outside the field of literature.

All of these new policies, especially war, cost money. In his *Political Testament* Richelieu wrote, "I have always said that finances are the sinews of the state." He fully realized that revenues determine a government's ability to inaugurate and enforce policies and programs. A state secures its revenues through taxation. But the political and economic structure of France greatly limited the government's ability to tax. Seventeenth-century France remained "a collection of local economies and local societies dominated by local elites." The rights of some assemblies in some provinces, such as Brittany, to vote their own taxes; the hereditary exemption from taxation of many wealthy members of the nobility and the middle class; and the royal pension system drastically limited the government's power to tax.

Richelieu—and later Louis XIV—temporarily solved their financial problems by securing the cooperation of local elites. The central government shared the proceeds of tax revenue with local powers. It never gained all the income it needed. Because the French monarchy could not tax at will, it never completely controlled the financial system. In practice, therefore, French absolutism was strictly limited.[2]

In building the French state, Richelieu believed he had to resort to drastic measures against persons and groups within France and to conduct a tough anti-Habsburg foreign policy. He knew also that his approach sometimes seemed to contradict traditional Christian teaching. As a priest and bishop, how did he justify his policies? He developed his own *raison d'état* ("reason of state"): "What is done for the state is done for God, who is the basis and foundation of it." Richelieu had no doubt that "the French state was a Christian state . . . governed by a Christian monarch with the valuable aid of an enlightened Cardinal Minister." "Where the interests of the state are concerned," the cardinal himself wrote, God absolves actions which, if privately committed, would be a crime."[3]

Richelieu persuaded Louis XIII to appoint his protégé Jules Mazarin (1602–1661) as his successor. An Italian diplomat of great charm, Mazarin had served on the council of state under Richelieu, acquiring considerable political experience. He became a cardinal in 1641 and a French citizen in 1643. When Louis XIII followed Richelieu to the grave in 1643 and a regency headed by Queen Anne of Austria governed for the child-king Louis XIV, Mazarin became the dominant power in the

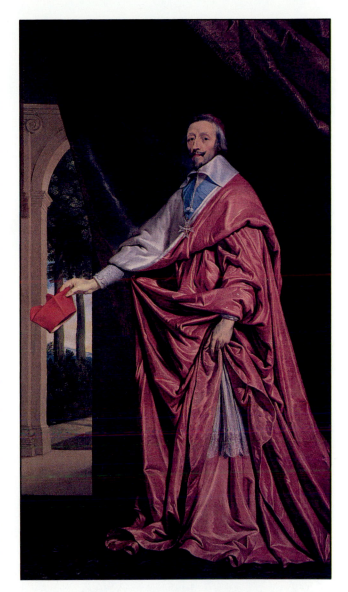

Philippe de Champaigne: Cardinal Richelieu This portrait, with its penetrating eyes, expression of haughty and imperturable cynicism, and dramatic sweep of red robes, suggests the authority, grandeur, and power that Richelieu wished to convey as first minister of France. *(Source: Reproduced by courtesy of the Trustees, The National Gallery, London)*

government. He continued the centralizing policies of Richelieu, but his attempts to increase royal revenues led to the civil wars known as the "Fronde."

The word *fronde* means "slingshot" or "catapult," and a *frondeur* was originally a street urchin who threw mud at the passing carriages of the rich.

The term came to be used for anyone who opposed the policies of the government. The policies of Richelieu and Mazarin had vastly increased the political power of the monarchy. By 1660 the state bureaucracy included about sixty thousand officeholders who represented a great expansion of the royal presence, a broad means of extracting the wealth of the working people. Naturally, these officeholders and state bureaucrats were the bitter tar-

Coysevox: Louis XIV (1687–1689) The French court envisioned a new classical age with the Sun King as emperor and his court a new Rome. This statue depicts Louis in a classical pose, clothed (except for the wig) as for a Roman military triumph. *(Source: Caisse Nationale des Monuments Historiques et des Sites, Paris. Copyright 1990 ARS N.Y./SPADEM)*

gets of the exploited peasants and artisans. On the other hand, these officials, who considered their positions the path to economic and social advancement, felt they were manipulated by the Crown and their interests ignored.[4] When in 1648 Mazarin proposed new methods of raising state income, bitter civil war ensued between the monarchy on the one side and the frondeurs (the nobility and middle class) on the other. Riots and public turmoil wracked Paris and the nation. Violence continued intermittently for the next twelve years.

The conflicts of the Fronde had three significant results for the future. It became apparent that the government would have to compromise with the bureaucrats and social elites who controlled local institutions and constituted the state bureaucracy. These groups were already largely exempt from taxation, and Louis XIV confirmed their privileged social status. Second, the French economy was badly disrupted and would take years to rebuild. Finally, the Fronde had a traumatic effect on the young Louis XIV. The king and his mother were frequently threatened and sometimes treated as prisoners by aristocratic factions. On one occasion a mob broke into the royal bedchamber to make sure the king was actually there; it succeeded in giving him a bad fright. Louis never forgot such humiliations. The period of the Fronde formed the cornerstone of his political education and of his conviction that the sole alternative to anarchy was absolute monarchy. The personal rule of Louis XIV represented the culmination of the process of centralization, but it also witnessed the institutionalization of procedures that would ultimately undermine the absolute monarchy.

The Absolute Monarchy of Louis XIV

According to the court theologian Bossuet, the clergy at the coronation of Louis XIV in Reims Cathedral asked God to cause the splendors of the French court to fill all who beheld it with awe. God subsequently granted that prayer. In the reign of Louis XIV (1643–1715), the longest in European history, the French monarchy reached the peak of absolutist development. In the magnificence of his court, in his absolute power, in the brilliance of the culture over which he presided and which permeated all of Europe, and in his remarkably long life, the "Sun King" dominated his age. No wonder scholars have characterized the second half of the seventeenth century as the "Grand Century," the "Age of Magnificence," and, echoing the eighteenth-century philosopher Voltaire, the "Age of Louis XIV."

Who was this phenomenon, of whom it was said that when Louis sneezed, all Europe caught cold? Born in 1638, king at the age of five, he entered into personal, or independent, rule in 1661. One of the first tales recorded about him gained wide circulation during his lifetime. Taken as a small child to his father's deathbed, he identified himself as *Louis Quatorze* ("Louis the fourteenth"). Since neither Louis nor his father referred to himself with numerals, the story is probably untrue. But it reveals the incredible sense of self that contemporaries, both French and foreign, believed that Louis possessed throughout his life.

In old age, Louis claimed that he had grown up learning very little, but recent historians think he was being modest. True, he knew little Latin and only the rudiments of arithmetic and thus by Renaissance standards was not well educated. On the other hand, he learned to speak Italian and Spanish fluently; he spoke and wrote elegant French; he knew some French history and more European geography than the ambassadors accredited to his court. He imbibed the devout Catholicism of his mother, Anne of Austria, and throughout his long life scrupulously performed his religious duties. Religion, Anne, and Mazarin all taught Louis that God had established kings as his rulers on earth. The royal coronation consecrated him to God's service, and he was certain—to use Shakespeare's phrase—that there was a divinity that doth hedge a king. Though kings were a race apart, they could not do as they pleased: they must obey God's laws and rule for the good of the people.

Louis's education was more practical than formal. Under Mazarin's instruction, he studied state papers as they arrived, and he attended council meetings and sessions at which French ambassadors were dispatched abroad and foreign ambassadors received. He learned by direct experience and gained professional training in the work of government. Above all, the misery he suffered during the Fronde gave Louis an eternal distrust of the nobility and a profound sense of his own isolation. Accordingly, silence, caution, and secrecy became political tools for the achievement of his goals. His characteristic answer to requests of all kinds became the enigmatic "Je verrai" ("I shall see").

Louis grew up with an absolute sense of his royal dignity. Contemporaries considered him tall and distinguished in appearance but inclined to heaviness because of the gargantuan meals in which he indulged. A highly sensual man easily aroused by an attractive female face and figure, Louis nonetheless ruled without the political influence of either his wife, Queen Maria Theresa, whom he married as the result of a diplomatic agreement with Spain, or his mistresses. One contemporary described him this way: "He has an elevated, distinguished, proud, intrepid, agreeable air . . . a face that is at the same time sweet and majestic. . . . His manner is cold; he speaks little except to people with whom he is familiar . . . [and then] he speaks well and effectively, and says what is apropos. . . . [H]e has natural goodness, is charitable, liberal, and properly acts out the role of king."[5] Louis XIV was a consummate actor, and his "terrifying majesty" awed all who saw him. He worked extremely hard and succeeded in being "every moment and every inch a king." Because he so relished the role of monarch, historians have had difficulty distinguishing the man from the monarch.

Historians have often said that Louis XIV introduced significant governmental innovations, the greatest of which was "the complete domestication of the nobility." By this phrase scholars meant that he exercised complete control over the powerful social class that historically had opposed the centralizing goals of the French monarchy. Recent research has demonstrated that notions of "domestication" represent a gross exaggeration. What Louis XIV actually achieved was the cooperation or collaboration of the nobility. Throughout France the nobility agreed to participate in projects that both exalted the monarchy and reinforced the aristocrats' ancient prestige. Thus the relationship between the Crown and the nobility constituted collaboration, rather than absolute control.

In the province of Languedoc, for example, Louis and his agents persuaded the notables to support the construction of the Canal des Deux Mers, a waterway linking the Mediterranean Sea and the Atlantic Ocean. Royal encouragement for the manufacture of luxury draperies in Languedocian towns likewise tied provincial business people to national goals, although French cloths subsequently proved unable to compete with cheaper Dutch ones. Above all, in the campaign for the repression of the Huguenots, the interests of the monarchy and nobility coincided. Aristocrats repeatedly petitioned Louis XIV to close Protestant churches and schools and to expel Huguenot ministers. In 1685 the king ultimately agreed. In each instance, through mutual collaboration, the nobility and the king achieved goals that neither could have won without the other. For his part, Louis won increased military taxation from the Estates of Languedoc. In return, Louis graciously granted the nobility and dignitaries privileged social status and increased access to his person, which meant access to the enormous patronage the king had to dispense. French government rested on the social and political structure of seventeenth-century France, a structure in which the nobility historically exercised great influence. In this respect, therefore, French absolutism was not so much modern as the last phase of a historical feudal society.[6]

Louis XIV installed his royal court at Versailles, a small town 10 miles from Paris. He required all the great nobility of France, at the peril of social, political, and sometimes economic disaster, to come live at Versailles for at least part of the year. Today Versailles stands as the best surviving museum of a vanished society on earth. In the seventeenth century, it became a model of rational order, the center of France and thus the center of Western civilization, the perfect symbol of the king's power.

Louis XIII began Versailles as a hunting lodge, a retreat from a queen he did not like. His son's architects, Le Nôtre and Le Vau, turned what the duke of Saint-Simon called "the most dismal and thankless of sights" into a veritable paradise. Wings were added to the original building to make the palace U-shaped. Everywhere at Versailles the viewer had a sense of grandeur, vastness, and elegance. Enormous state rooms became display galleries for inlaid tables, Italian marble statuary, Gobelin tapestries woven at the state factory in Paris, silver ewers, and beautiful (if uncomfortable) furniture. If genius means attention to detail, Louis XIV and his designers had it: the decor was perfected down to the last doorknob and keyhole. In the gigantic Hall of Mirrors, later to reflect so much of German as well as French history, hundreds of candles illuminated the domed ceiling, where allegorical paintings celebrated the king's victories.

The art and architecture of Versailles served as fundamental tools of state policy under Louis XIV. Architecture was another device the king used to overawe his subjects and foreign visitors. Versailles was seen as a reflection of French genius. Thus the Russian tsar Peter the Great imitated Versailles in the construction of his palace, Peterhof, as did the Prussian emperor Frederick the Great in his palace at Potsdam outside Berlin.

As in architecture, so too in language. Beginning in the reign of Louis XIV, French became the language of polite society and the vehicle of diplomatic exchange. French also gradually replaced Latin as the language of international scholarship and learning. The wish of other kings to ape the courtly style of Louis XIV and the imitation of French intellectuals and artists spread the language all over Europe. The royal courts of Sweden, Russia, Poland, and Germany all spoke French. In the eighteenth century, the great Russian aristocrats were more fluent in French than in Russian. In England the first Hanoverian king, George I, spoke fluent French and only halting English. France inspired a cosmopolitan European culture in the late seventeenth century, and that culture was inspired by the king. That is why the French today revere Louis XIV as one of their greatest national heroes: because of the culture that he inspired and symbolized.

Against this background of magnificent splendor, as Saint-Simon describes him, Louis XIV

. . . reduced everyone to subjection, and brought to his court those very persons he cared least about. Whoever was old enough to serve did not dare demur. It was still another device to ruin the nobles by accustoming them to equality and forcing them to mingle with everyone indiscriminately. . . .

Upon rising, at bedtime, during meals, in his apartments, in the gardens of Versailles, everywhere the courtiers had a right to follow, he would glance right and left to see who was there; he saw and noted everyone; he missed no one, even those who were hoping they would not be seen. . . .

Louis XIV took great pains to inform himself on what was happening everywhere, in public places, private homes, and even on the international scene. . . . Spies and informers of all kinds were numberless. . . .

But the King's most vicious method of securing information was opening letters.[7]

Though this passage was written by one of Louis's severest critics, all agree that the king used court ceremonial to undermine the power of the great nobility. By excluding the highest nobles from his councils, he weakened their ancient right to advise the king and to participate in government; they became mere instruments of royal policy. Operas, fetes, balls, gossip, and trivia occupied the nobles' time and attention. Through painstaking attention to detail and precisely calculated showmanship, Louis XIV reduced the major threat to his power. He separated power from status and grandeur: he secured the nobles' cooperation, and the nobility enjoyed the status and grandeur in which they lived.

Louis dominated the court, and in his scheme of things, the court was more significant than the government. In government Louis utilized several councils of state, which he personally attended, and the intendants, who acted for the councils throughout France. A stream of questions and instructions flowed between local districts and Versailles, and under Louis XIV a uniform and centralized administration was imposed on the country. In 1685 France was the strongest and most highly centralized state in Europe.

Councilors of state came from the recently ennobled or the upper middle class. Royal service provided a means of social mobility. These professional bureaucrats served the state in the person of the king, but they did not share power with him. Louis stated that he chose bourgeois officials because he wanted "people to know by the rank of the men who served him that he had no intention of sharing power with them."[8] If great ones were the king's advisers, they would seem to share the royal authority; professional administrators from the middle class would not.

Throughout his long reign and despite increasing financial problems, he never called a meeting of the Estates General. The nobility, therefore, had no means of united expression or action. Nor did Louis have a first minister; he kept himself free from worry about the inordinate power of a Richelieu. Louis's use of spying and terror—a secret police force, a system of informers, and the practice of opening private letters—foreshadowed some of the devices of the modern state. French government remained highly structured, bureaucratic, centered at Versailles, and responsible to Louis XIV.

Financial and Economic Management Under Louis XIV: Colbert

Finance was the grave weakness of Louis XIV's absolutism. An expanding professional bureaucracy, the court of Versailles, and extensive military reforms (discussed later in this chapter) cost a great amount of money. The French method of collecting taxes consistently failed to produce enough revenue. Tax farmers, agents who purchased from the Crown the right to collect taxes in a particular district, pocketed the difference between what they raked in and what they handed over to the state. Consequently, the tax farmers profited, while the government got far less than the people paid. In addition, by an old agreement between the Crown and the nobility, the king could freely tax the common people, provided he did not tax the nobles. The nobility thereby relinquished a role in government: since they did not pay taxes, they could not legitimately claim a say in how taxes were spent. Louis, however, lost enormous potential revenue. The middle classes, moreover, secured many tax exemptions. With the rich and prosperous classes exempt, the tax burden fell heavily on those least able to pay, the poor peasants.

Hall of Mirrors, Versailles The grandeur and elegance of the Sun King's reign are reflected in the Hall of Mirrors, where the king's victories were celebrated in paintings on the domed ceiling. Hundreds of candles lit up the dome. *(Source: Michael Holford)*

The Spider and the Fly   In reference to the insect symbolism (upper left), the caption on the lower left side of this illustration states, "The noble is the spider, the peasant the fly." The other caption (upper right) notes, "The more people have, the more they want. The poor man brings everything—wheat, fruit, money, vegetables. The greedy lord sitting there ready to take everything will not even give him the favor of a glance." This satirical print summarizes peasant grievances. *(Source: New York Public Library)*

The king named Jean-Baptiste Colbert (1619–1683), the son of a wealthy merchant-financier of Reims, as controller-general of finances. Colbert came to manage the entire royal administration and proved himself a financial genius. Colbert's central principle was that the wealth and the economy of France should serve the state. He did not invent the system called "mercantilism," but he rigorously applied it to France.

Mercantilism is a collection of governmental policies for the regulation of economic activities, especially commercial activities, by and for the state. In seventeenth- and eighteenth-century economic theory, a nation's international power was thought to be based on its wealth, specifically its gold supply. To accumulate gold, a country should always

sell more goods abroad than it bought. Colbert believed that a successful economic policy meant more than a favorable balance of trade, however. He insisted that the French sell abroad and buy *nothing* back. France should be self-sufficient, able to produce within its borders everything the subjects of the French king needed. Consequently, the outflow of gold would be halted, debtor states would pay in bullion, and, with the wealth of the nation increased, its power and prestige would be enhanced.

Colbert attempted to accomplish self-sufficiency through state support for both old industries and newly created ones. He subsidized the established cloth industries at Abbeville, Saint-Quentin, and Carcassonne. He granted special royal privileges to the rug and tapestry industries at Paris, Gobelin, and Beauvais. New factories at Saint-Antoine in Paris manufactured mirrors to replace Venetian imports. Looms at Chantilly and Alençon competed with English lacemaking, and foundries at Saint-Étienne made steel and firearms that reduced Swedish imports. To ensure a high-quality finished product, Colbert set up a system of state inspection and regulation. To ensure order within every industry, he compelled all craftsmen to organize into guilds, and within every guild he gave the masters absolute power over their workers. Colbert encouraged skilled foreign craftsmen and manufacturers to immigrate to France, and he gave them special privileges. To improve communications, he built roads and canals, the most famous linking the Mediterranean and the Bay of Biscay. To protect French goods, he abolished many domestic tariffs and enacted high foreign tariffs, which prevented foreign products from competing with French ones.

Colbert's most important work was the creation of a powerful merchant marine to transport French goods. He gave bonuses to French shipowners and shipbuilders and established a method of maritime conscription, arsenals, and academies for the training of sailors. In 1661 France possessed 18 unseaworthy vessels; by 1681 it had 276 frigates, galleys, and ships of the line. Colbert tried to organize and regulate the entire French economy for the glory of the French state as embodied in the king.

Colbert hoped to make Canada—rich in untapped minerals and some of the best agricultural land in the world—part of a vast French empire. He gathered four thousand peasants from western

France and shipped them to Canada, where they peopled the province of Quebec. (In 1608, one year after the English arrived at Jamestown, Virginia, Sully had established the city of Quebec, which became the capital of French Canada.) Subsequently, the Jesuit Marquette and the merchant Joliet sailed down the Mississippi River and took possession of the land on both sides, as far south as present-day Arkansas. In 1684 the French explorer La Salle continued down the Mississippi to its mouth and claimed vast territories and the rich delta for Louis XIV. The area was called, naturally, "Louisiana."

How successful were Colbert's policies? His achievement in the development of manufacturing was prodigious. The textile industry, especially in woolens, expanded enormously, and "France . . . had become in 1683 the leading nation of the world in industrial productivity."[9] The commercial classes prospered, and between 1660 and 1700 their position steadily improved. The national economy, however, rested on agriculture. Although French peasants did not become serfs, as did the peasants of eastern Europe, they were mercilessly taxed. After 1685 other hardships afflicted them: poor harvests, continuing deflation of the currency, and fluctuation in the price of grain. Many peasants emigrated. With the decline in population and thus in the number of taxable people (the poorest), the state's resources fell. A totally inadequate tax base and heavy expenditure for war in the later years of the reign made Colbert's goals unattainable.

The Revocation of the Edict of Nantes

We now see with the proper gratitude what we owe to God . . . for the best and largest part of our subjects of the so-called reformed religion have embraced Catholicism, and now that, to the extent that the execution of the Edict of Nantes remains useless, we have judged that we can do nothing better to wipe out the memory of the troubles, of the confusion, of the evils that the progress of this false religion has caused our kingdom . . . than to revoke entirely the said Edict.[10]

Thus, in 1685, Louis XIV revoked the Edict of Nantes, by which his grandfather Henry IV had granted liberty of conscience to French Huguenots. The new law ordered the destruction of churches, the closing of schools, the Catholic baptism of Huguenots, and the exile of Huguenot pastors who refused to renounce their faith. Why? There had been so many mass conversions during previous years (many of them forced) that Madame de Maintenon, Louis's second wife, could say that "nearly all the Huguenots were converted." Some Huguenots had emigrated. Richelieu had already deprived French Calvinists of political rights. Why, then, did Louis, by revoking the edict, persecute some of his most loyal and industrially skilled subjects, force others to flee abroad, and provoke the outrage of Protestant Europe?

Recent scholarship has convincingly shown that Louis XIV was basically tolerant. He insisted on religious unity not for religious but for political reasons. His goal was "one king, one law, one faith." He hated division within the realm and insisted that religious unity was essential to his royal dignity and to the security of the state. The seventeenth century, moreover, was not a tolerant one. While France in the early years of Louis's reign permitted religious liberty, it was not a popular policy. In fact, as mentioned earlier, aristocrats had petitioned Louis to crack down on Protestants. But the revocation was solely the king's decision, and it won him enormous praise. "If the flood of congratulation means anything, it . . . was probably the one act of his reign that, at the time, was popular with the majority of his subjects."[11]

While contemporaries applauded Louis XIV, scholars in the eighteenth century and later damned him for the adverse impact that revocation had on the economy and foreign affairs. Tens of thousands of Huguenot craftsmen, soldiers, and business people emigrated, depriving France of their skills and tax revenues and carrying their bitterness to Holland, England, and Prussia. Modern scholarship has greatly modified this picture. While Huguenot settlers in northern Europe aggravated Protestant hatred for Louis, the revocation of the Edict of Nantes had only minor and scattered effects on French economic development.[12]

French Classicism

Scholars characterize the art and literature of the age of Louis XIV as "French classicism." By this they mean that the artists and writers of the late seventeenth century deliberately imitated the subject matter and style of classical antiquity; that their work resembled that of Renaissance Italy; and that French art possessed the classical qualities of discipline, balance, and restraint. Classicism was the official style of Louis's court. In painting, however, French classicism had already reached its peak before 1661, the beginning of the king's personal government.

Nicholas Poussin (1594–1665) is generally considered the finest example of French classicist painting. Poussin spent all but eighteen months of his creative life in Rome because he found the atmosphere in Paris uncongenial. Deeply attached to classical antiquity, he believed that the highest aim of painting was to represent noble actions in a logical and orderly, but not realistic, way. His masterpiece, *The Rape of the Sabine Women,* exhibits these qualities. Its subject is an incident in Roman history; the figures of people and horses are ideal representations, and the emotions expressed are studied, not spontaneous. Even the buildings are exact architectural models of ancient Roman structures.

Poussin, whose paintings still had individualistic features, did his work before 1661. After Louis's accession to power, the principles of absolutism molded the ideals of French classicism. Individualism was not allowed, and artists' efforts were directed to the glorification of the state as personified

Poussin: The Rape of the Sabine Women (ca 1636) Considered the greatest French painter of the seventeenth century, Poussin in this dramatic work shows his complete devotion to the ideals of classicism. The heroic figures are superb physical specimens, but hardly life-like. *(Source: The Metropolitan Museum of Art, New York, Harris Brisbane Dick Fund, 1946 (46.160)).*

by the king. Precise rules governed all aspects of culture, with the goal of formal and restrained perfection.

Contemporaries said that Louis XIV never ceased playing the role of grand monarch on the stage of his court. If the king never fully relaxed from the pressures and intrigues of government, he did enjoy music and theater and used them as a backdrop for court ceremonial. Louis favored Jean-Baptiste Lully (1632–1687), whose orchestral works combine lively animation with the restrained austerity typical of French classicism. Lully also composed court ballets, and his operatic productions achieved a powerful influence throughout Europe. Louis supported François Couperin (1668–1733), whose harpsichord and organ works possess the regal grandeur the king loved, and Marc-Antoine Charpentier (1634–1704), whose solemn religious music entertained him at meals. Charpentier received a pension for the *Te Deums,* hymns of thanksgiving, he composed to celebrate French military victories.

Louis XIV loved the stage, and in the plays of Molière and Racine his court witnessed the finest achievements in the history of the French theater. When Jean-Baptiste Poquelin (1622–1673), the son of a prosperous tapestry maker, refused to join his father's business and entered the theater, he took the stage name "Molière." As playwright, stage manager, director, and actor, Molière produced comedies that exposed the hypocrisies and follies of society through brilliant caricature. *Tartuffe* satirized the religious hypocrite, *Le Bourgeois Gentilhomme* attacked the social parvenu, and *Les Femmes Savantes (The Learned Women)* mocked the fashionable pseudo-intellectuals of the day. In structure Molière's plays followed classical models, but they were based on careful social observation. Molière made the bourgeoisie the butt of his ridicule; he stopped short of criticizing the nobility, thus reflecting the policy of his royal patron.

While Molière dissected social mores, his contemporary Jean Racine (1639–1699) analyzed the power of love. Racine based his tragic dramas on Greek and Roman legends, and his persistent theme is the conflict of good and evil. Several plays —*Andromaque, Bérénice, Iphigénie,* and *Phèdre*— bear the names of women and deal with the power of passion in women. Louis preferred *Mithridate* and *Britannicus* because of the "grandeur" of their themes. For simplicity of language, symmetrical structure, and calm restraint, the plays of Racine represent the finest examples of French classicism. His tragedies and Molière's comedies are still produced today.

Louis XIV's Wars

Just as the architecture and court life at Versailles served to reflect the king's glory, and as the economy of the state under Colbert was managed to advance the king's prestige, so did Louis XIV use war to exalt himself above the other rulers and nations of Europe. He visualized himself as a great military hero. "The character of a conqueror," he remarked, "is regarded as the noblest and highest of titles." Military glory was his aim. In 1666 Louis appointed François le Tellier (later marquis of Louvois) as secretary of war. Louvois created a professional army, which was modern in the sense that the French state, rather than private nobles, employed the soldiers. The king himself took personal command of the army and directly supervised all aspects and details of military affairs.

A commissariat was established to feed the troops, in place of their ancient practice of living off the countryside. An ambulance corps was designed to look after the wounded. Uniforms and weapons were standardized. Finally, a rational system of recruitment, training, discipline, and promotion was imposed. With this new military machine, for the first time in Europe's history one national state, France, was able to dominate the politics of Europe.

Louis continued on a broader scale the expansionist policy begun by Cardinal Richelieu. In 1667, using a dynastic excuse, he invaded Flanders, part of the Spanish Netherlands, and Franche-Comté in the east. In consequence he acquired twelve towns, including the important commercial centers of Lille and Tournai (Map 16.1). Five years later, Louis personally led an army of over a hundred thousand men into Holland, and the Dutch ultimately saved themselves only by opening the dikes and flooding the countryside. This war, which lasted six years and eventually involved the Holy Roman Empire and Spain, was concluded by the Treaty of Nijmegen (1678). Louis gained additional Flemish towns and all of Franche-Comté.

Encouraged by his successes, by the weakness of the German Empire, and by divisions among the

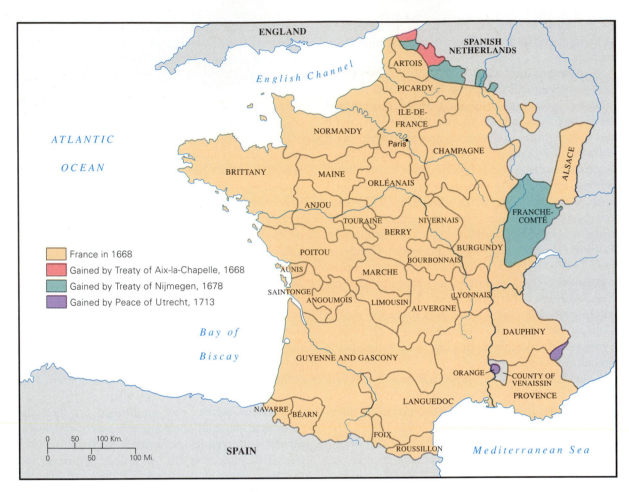

MAP 16.1 The Acquisitions of Louis XIV, 1668–1713 The desire for glory and the weakness of his German neighbors encouraged Louis' expansionist policy. But he paid a high price for his acquisitions.

other European powers, Louis continued his aggression. In 1681 he seized the city of Strasbourg and three years later sent his armies into the province of Lorraine. At that moment the king seemed invincible. In fact, Louis had reached the limit of his expansion at Nijmegen. The wars of the 1680s and 1690s brought him no additional territories. In 1689 the Dutch prince William of Orange, a bitter foe of Louis XIV, became king of England. William joined the League of Augsburg—which included the Habsburg emperor, the kings of Spain and Sweden, and the electors of Bavaria, Saxony, and the Palatinate—adding British resources and men to the alliance. Neither the French nor the league won any decisive victories. France lacked the means to win; it was financially exhausted.

Louis was attempting to support an army of 200,000 men, in several different theaters of war, against the great nations of Europe, the powerful Bank of Amsterdam, and (after 1694) the Bank of England. This task far exceeded French resources. Le Peletier, Colbert's successor as minister of finance, resorted to devaluation of the currency and to the old device of creating and selling offices, tax exemptions, and titles of nobility. These measures failed to produce adequate revenue. So the weight of taxation fell on the already overburdened peasants. They expressed their frustrations in widespread revolts that hit all parts of France in the last decades of the century.

A series of bad harvests between 1688 and 1694 brought catastrophe. Cold, wet summers reduced the harvests by an estimated one-third to two-thirds. The price of wheat skyrocketed. The result was widespread starvation, and in many provinces the death rate rose to several times the normal figure. Parish registers reveal that France buried at least a tenth of its population in those years. Rising grain prices, new taxes for war on top of old ones, a slump in manufacturing and thus in exports, and the constant nuisance of pillaging troops—all these meant great suffering for the French people. France wanted peace at any price. Louis XIV granted a respite for five years, while he prepared for the conflict later known as the War of the Spanish Succession.

This struggle (1701–1713), provoked by the territorial disputes of the past century, also involved the dynastic question of the succession to the Spanish throne. It was an open secret in Europe that the king of Spain, Charles II (r. 1665–1700), was mentally defective and sexually impotent. In 1698 the European powers, including France, agreed by treaty to partition, or divide, the vast Spanish possessions between the king of France and the Holy Roman Emperor, who were Charles II's brothers-in-law. When Charles died in 1700, however, his will left the Spanish crown and the worldwide Spanish Empire to Philip of Anjou, Louis XIV's grandson. While the will specifically rejected union of the French and Spanish crowns, Louis was obviously the power in France, not his seventeen-year-old grandson. Louis reneged on the treaty and accepted the will.

The Dutch and the English would not accept French acquisition of the Spanish Netherlands and of the rich trade with the Spanish colonies. The union of the Spanish and French crowns, moreover, would have totally upset the European balance of power. The Versailles declaration that "the Pyrenees no longer exist" provoked the long-anticipated crisis.

In 1701 the English, Dutch, Austrians, and Prussians formed the Grand Alliance against Louis XIV. They claimed that they were fighting to prevent France from becoming too strong in Europe, but during the previous half-century, overseas maritime rivalry among France, Holland, and England had created serious international tension. The secondary motive of the allied powers was to check France's expanding commercial power in North America, Asia, and Africa. In the ensuing series of conflicts, two great soldiers dominated the alliance against France: Eugene, prince of Savoy, representing the Holy Roman Empire, and the Englishman John Churchill, subsequently duke of Marlborough. Eugene and Churchill inflicted a severe defeat on Louis in 1704 at Blenheim in Bavaria. Marlborough followed with another victory at Ramillies near Namur in Brabant.

The war was finally concluded at Utrecht in 1713, where the principle of partition was applied. Louis's grandson Philip remained the first Bourbon king of Spain on the understanding that the French and Spanish crowns would never be united. France surrendered Newfoundland, Nova Scotia, and the Hudson Bay territory to England, which also acquired Gibraltar, Minorca, and control of the African slave trade from Spain. The Dutch gained little because Austria received the former Spanish Netherlands (Map 16.2)

The Peace of Utrecht had important international consequences. It represented the balance-of-power principle in operation, setting limits on the extent to which any one power, in this case France, could expand. The treaty completed the decline of Spain as a great power. It vastly expanded the British Empire. Finally, Utrecht gave European powers experience in international cooperation, thus preparing them for the alliances against France at the end of the century.

The Peace of Utrecht marked the end of French expansionist policy. In Louis's thirty-five-year quest for military glory, his main territorial acquisition was Strasbourg. Even revisionist historians, who portray the aging monarch as responsible in negotiation and moderate in his demands, acknowledge "that the widespread misery in France during the period was in part due to royal policies, especially the incessant wars."[13] To raise revenue for the wars, forty thousand additional offices had been sold, thus increasing the number of families exempt from future taxation. In 1714 France hovered on the brink of financial bankruptcy. Louis had exhausted the country without much compensation. It is no wonder that when he died on September I, 1715, Saint-Simon wrote, "Those . . . wearied by the heavy and oppressive rule of the King and his ministers, felt a delighted freedom. . . . Paris . . . found relief in the hope of liberation. . . . The provinces . . . quivered with delight . . . [and] the people, ruined, abused, despairing, now thanked God for a deliverance which answered their most ardent desires."[14]

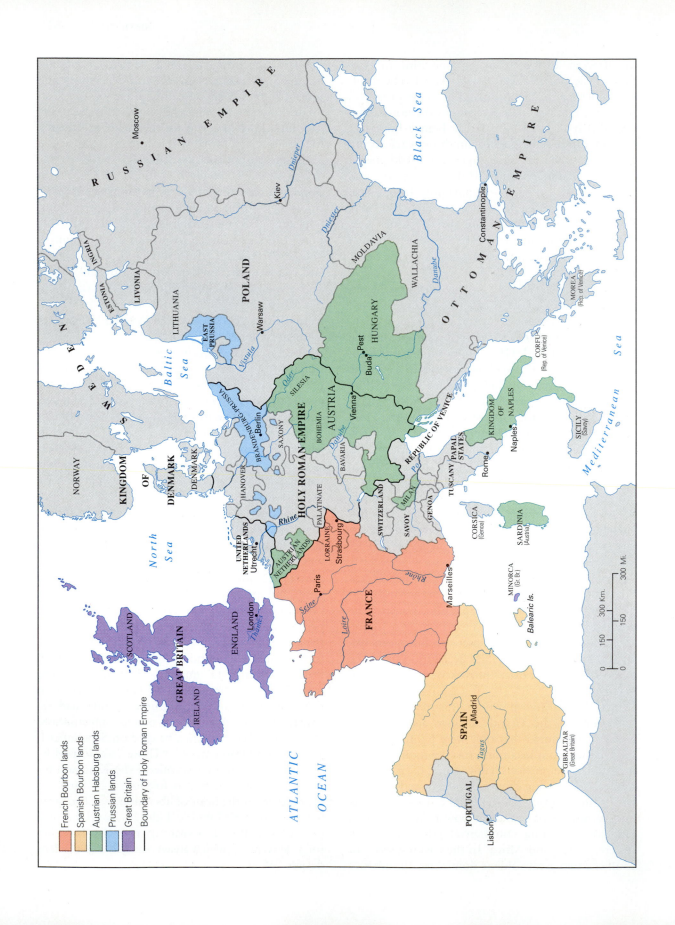

RUSSIAN EMPIRE

• Moscow

Dnieper

Dniester

• Kiev

Black Sea

OTTOMAN EMPIRE

Constantinople •

MOREA
(Rep. of Venice)

Mediterranean Sea

CORFU
(Rep. of Venice)

SICILY
(Savoy)

POLAND

MOLDAVIA

WALLACHIA

Danube

Warsaw •

LITHUANIA

LIVONIA

ESTONIA

Baltic Sea

EAST PRUSSIA

Vistula

Oder

SILESIA

BRANDENBURG-PRUSSIA

Berlin •

SAXONY

BOHEMIA

HUNGARY

Pest •

Buda •

AUSTRIA

Vienna •

BAVARIA

Danube

HOLY ROMAN EMPIRE

KINGDOM OF NAPLES

Naples •

SARDINIA
(Austria)

REPUBLIC OF VENICE

Po

PAPAL STATES

Rome •

TUSCANY

GENOA

MILAN

SAVOY

SWITZERLAND

PALATINATE

HANOVER

Elbe

Rhine

NORWAY

KINGDOM OF DENMARK

DENMARK

S W E D E N

North Sea

UNITED NETHERLANDS

Utrecht •

AUSTRIAN NETHERLANDS

LORRAINE

Strasbourg •

Paris •

Seine

Loire

Rhône

FRANCE

Marseilles •

CORSICA
(Genoa)

MINORCA
(Gr. Br.)

Balearic Is.

SCOTLAND

GREAT BRITAIN

ENGLAND

London •

Thames

IRELAND

ATLANTIC OCEAN

SPAIN

Madrid •

Tagus

GIBRALTAR
(Great Britain)

PORTUGAL

Lisbon •

French Bourbon lands

Spanish Bourbon lands

Austrian Habsburg lands

Prussian lands

Great Britain

Boundary of Holy Roman Empire

300 Mi.

300 Km.

150

150

0

0

The Decline of Absolutist Spain in the Seventeenth Century

Spanish absolutism and greatness had preceded that of the French. In the sixteenth century, Spain (or, more precisely, the kingdom of Castile) had developed the standard features of absolute monarchy: a permanent bureaucracy staffed by professionals employed in the various councils of state, a standing army, and national taxes, the *servicios,* which fell most heavily on the poor.

France depended on financial and administrative unification within its borders; Spain had developed an international absolutism on the basis of silver bullion from Peru. Spanish gold and silver, armies, and glory had dominated the Continent for most of the sixteenth century, but by the 1590s the seeds of disaster were sprouting. While France in the seventeenth century represented the classic model of the modern absolute state, Spain was experiencing steady decline. The lack of a strong middle class, largely the result of the expulsion of the Jews and Moors (see page 414), the agricultural crisis and population decline, the failure to invest in productive enterprises, the intellectual isolation and psychological malaise—all combined to reduce Spain, by 1715, to a second-rate power.

The fabulous and seemingly inexhaustible flow of silver from Mexico and Peru had led Philip II (see page 475) to assume the role of defender of Roman Catholicism in Europe. In order to humble the Dutch and to regain control of all the Low Countries, Philip believed that England, the Netherlands' greatest supporter, had to be crushed. He poured millions of Spanish ducats and all of Spanish hopes into the vast fleet that sailed in 1588.

MAP 16.2 Europe in 1715 The series of treaties commonly called the Peace of Utrecht (April 1713–November 1715) ended the War of the Spanish Succession and redrew the map of Europe. A French Bourbon king succeeded to the Spanish throne on the understanding that the French not attempt to unite the French and Spanish crowns. France surrendered to Austria the Spanish Netherlands (later Belgium), then in French hands; and France recognized the Hohenzollern rulers of Prussia. Spain ceded Gibraltar to Great Britain, for which it has been a strategic naval station ever since. Spain also granted to Britain the *asiento,* the contract for supplying African slaves to America.

When the "Invincible Armada" went down, a century of Spanish pride and power went with it. After 1590 a spirit of defeatism and disillusionment crippled almost all efforts at reform.

Philip II's Catholic crusade had been financed by the revenues of the Spanish-Atlantic economy. These included, in addition to silver and gold bullion, the sale of cloth, grain, oil, and wine to the colonies. In the early seventeenth century, the Dutch and English began to trade with the Spanish colonies, cutting into the revenues that had gone to Spain. Mexico and Peru themselves developed local industries, further lessening their need to buy from Spain. Between 1610 and 1650, Spanish trade with the colonies fell 60 percent.

At the same time, the native Indians and African slaves, who worked the South American silver mines under conditions that would have shamed the ancient Egyptian pharaohs, suffered frightful epidemics of disease. Moreover, the lodes started to run dry. Consequently, the quantity of metal produced for Spain steadily declined. Nevertheless, in Madrid royal expenditures constantly exceeded income. The remedies applied in the face of a mountainous state debt and declining revenues were devaluation of the coinage and declarations of bankruptcy. In 1596, 1607, 1627, 1647, and 1680, Spanish kings found no solution to the problem of an empty treasury other than to cancel the national debt. Given the frequency of cancellation, public confidence in the state naturally deteriorated.

Spain, in contrast to the other countries of western Europe, had only a tiny middle class. Disdain for money, in a century of increasing commercialism and bourgeois attitudes, reveals a significant facet of the Spanish national character. Public opinion, taking its cue from the aristocracy, condemned moneymaking as vulgar and undignified. Those with influence or connections sought titles of nobility and social prestige. Thousands entered economically unproductive professions or became priests, monks, and nuns: there were said to be nine thousand monasteries in the province of Castile alone. The flood of gold and silver had produced severe inflation, pushing the costs of production in the textile industry higher and higher, to the point that Castilian cloth could not compete in colonial and international markets. Many businessmen found so many obstacles in the way of profitable enterprise that they simply gave up.[15]

Spanish aristocrats, attempting to maintain an extravagant lifestyle they could no longer afford, increased the rents on their estates. High rents and heavy taxes in turn drove the peasants from the land. Agricultural production suffered, and the peasants departed for the large cities, where they swelled the ranks of unemployed beggars.

Their most Catholic majesties, the kings of Spain, had no solutions to these dire problems. If one can discern personality from pictures, the portraits of Philip III (r. 1598–1622), Philip IV (r. 1622–1665), and Charles II hanging in the Prado, the Spanish national museum in Madrid, reflect the increasing weakness of the dynasty. Their faces—the small, beady eyes, the long noses, the jutting Habsburg jaws, the pathetically stupid expressions—tell a story of excessive inbreeding and decaying monarchy. The Spanish kings all lacked force of character. Philip III, a pallid, melancholy, and deeply pious man "whose only virtue appeared to reside in a total absence of vice," handed the government over to the lazy duke of Lerma, who used it to advance his personal and familial wealth. Philip IV left the management of his several kingdoms to Count Olivares.

Olivares was an able administrator. He did not lack energy and ideas; he devised new sources of revenue. But he clung to the grandiose belief that the solution to Spain's difficulties rested in a return to the imperial tradition. Unfortunately, the imperial tradition demanded the revival of war with the Dutch, at the expiration of a twelve-year truce in 1622, and a long war with France over Mantua (1628–1659). Spain thus became embroiled in the Thirty Years' War. These conflicts, on top of an empty treasury, brought disaster.

In 1640 Spain faced serious revolts in Catalonia and Portugal; in 1643 the French inflicted a crushing defeat on a Spanish army in Belgium. By the Treaty of the Pyrenees of 1659, which ended the French-Spanish wars, Spain was compelled to surrender extensive territories to France. This treaty marked the end of Spain as a great power.

Seventeenth-century Spain was the victim of its past. It could not forget the grandeur of the sixteenth century and look to the future. The bureaucratic councils of state continued to function as symbols of the absolute Spanish monarchy. But because those councils were staffed by aristocrats, it was the aristocracy that held the real power. Spanish absolutism had been built largely on slave-pro-

duced gold and silver. When the supply of bullion decreased, the power and standing of the Spanish state declined.

The most cherished Spanish ideals were military glory and strong Roman Catholic faith. In the seventeenth century, Spain lacked the finances and the manpower to fight the expensive wars in which it foolishly got involved. Spain also ignored the new mercantile ideas and scientific methods, because they came from heretical nations, Holland and England. The incredible wealth of South America destroyed what remained of the Spanish middle class and created contempt for business and manual labor.

The decadence of the Habsburg dynasty and the lack of effective royal councilors also contributed to Spanish failure. Spanish leaders seemed to lack the will to reform. Pessimism and fatalism permeated national life. In the reign of Philip IV, a royal council was appointed to plan the construction of a canal linking the Tagus and Manzanares rivers in Spain. After interminable debate, the committee decided that "if God had intended the rivers to be navigable, He would have made them so."

In the brilliant novel *Don Quixote*, the Spanish writer Miguel de Cervantes (1547–1616) produced one of the great masterpieces of world literature. *Don Quixote*—on which the modern play *Man of La Mancha* is based—delineates the whole fabric of sixteenth-century Spanish society. The main character, Don Quixote, lives in a world of dreams, traveling about the countryside seeking military glory. From the title of the book, the English language has borrowed the word *quixotic*. Meaning "idealistic but impractical," the term characterizes seventeenth-century Spain. As a leading scholar has written, "The Spaniard convinced himself that reality was what he felt, believed, imagined. He filled the world with heroic reverberations. Don Quixote was born and grew."[16]

CONSTITUTIONALISM

The seventeenth century, which witnessed the development of absolute monarchy, also saw the appearance of the constitutional state. While France and later Prussia, Russia, and Austria (see Chapter 17) solved the question of sovereignty with the absolutist state, England and Holland evolved to-

Diego Velázquez: The Spinners (1599–1600) Spain's master of realism captures women workers in a tapestry workshop and three ladies inspecting a tapestry in the background. Or so people long believed. Modern critics see a mythological weaving competition between the low-born Arachne on the right and the goddess of arts and crafts on the left. (The gutsy Arachne lost and was turned into a spider.) Art historians also have their debates and conflicting interpretations. *(Source: Museo del Prado, Madrid)*

ward the constitutional state. What is constitutionalism? Is it identical to democracy?

Constitutionalism is the limitation of government by law. Constitutionalism also implies a balance between the authority and power of the government on the one hand and the rights and liberties of the subjects on the other. The balance is often very delicate.

A nation's constitution may be written or unwritten. It may be embodied in one basic document, occasionally revised by amendment or judi-cial decision, like the Constitution of the United States. Or a constitution may be partly written and partly unwritten and include parliamentary statutes, judicial decisions, and a body of traditional procedures and practices, like the English and Canadian constitutions. Whether written or unwritten, a constitution gets its binding force from the government's acknowledgment that it must respect that constitution—that is, that the state must govern according to the laws. Likewise, in a constitutional state, the people look on the law and the constitution as the protectors of their rights, liberties, and property.

Modern constitutional governments may take either a republican or a monarchial form. In a constitutional republic, the sovereign power resides in the electorate and is exercised by the electorate's representatives. In a constitutional monarchy, a king or queen serves as the head of state and possesses some residual political authority, but again the ultimate or sovereign power rests in the electorate.

A constitutional government is not, however, quite the same as a democratic government. In a complete democracy, *all* the people have the right to participate either directly, or indirectly through their elected representatives, in the government of the state. Democratic government, therefore, is intimately tied up with the *franchise* (the vote). Most men could not vote until the late nineteenth century. Even then, women—probably the majority in Western societies—lacked the franchise; they gained the right to vote only in the twentieth century. Consequently, although constitutionalism developed in the seventeenth century, full democracy was achieved only in very recent times.

The Decline of Royal Absolutism in England (1603–1649)

In 1588 Queen Elizabeth I of England exercised very great personal power; by 1689 the English monarchy was severely circumscribed. Change in England was anything but orderly. Seventeenth-century England displayed little political stability. It executed one king, experienced a bloody civil war, experimented with military dictatorship, then restored the son of the murdered king, and finally, after a bloodless revolution, established constitutional monarchy. Political stability came only in the 1690s. How do we account for the fact that, after such a violent and tumultuous century, England laid the foundations for constitutional monarchy? What combination of political, socioeconomic, and religious factors brought on a civil war in 1642 to 1649 and then the constitutional settlement of 1688 to 1689?

The extraordinary success of Elizabeth I had rested on her political shrewdness and flexibility, her careful management of finances, her wise selection of ministers, her clever manipulation of Parliament, and her sense of royal dignity and devotion to hard work. The aging queen had always refused to discuss the succession. After her Scottish cousin James Stuart succeeded her as James I (r. 1603–1625), Elizabeth's strengths seemed even greater than they actually had been.

King James was well educated, learned, and, with thirty-five years' experience as king of Scotland, politically shrewd. But he was not as interested in displaying the majesty and mystique of monarchy as Elizabeth had been. He also lacked the common touch. Urged to wave at the crowds who waited to greet their new ruler, James complained that he was tired and threatened to drop his breeches "so they can cheer at my arse." The new king failed to live up to the role expected of him in England. Moreover, James's Scottish accent, in a society already hostile to the Scots and where proper spoken English was becoming a matter of concern, proved another disadvantage.[17]

James was devoted to the theory of the divine right of kings. He expressed his ideas about divine right in his essay "The Trew Law of Free Monarchy." According to James I, a monarch has a divine (or God-given) right to his authority and is responsible only to God. Rebellion is the worst of political crimes. If a king orders something evil, the subject should respond with passive disobedience but should be prepared to accept any penalty for noncompliance.

Unfortunately, he lectured the House of Commons: "There are no privileges and immunities which can stand against a divinely appointed King." This notion, implying total royal jurisdiction over the liberties, persons, and properties of English men and women, formed the basis of the Stuart concept of absolutism. Such a view ran directly counter to the long-standing English idea that a person's property could not be taken away without due process of law. James's expression of such views before the English House of Commons constituted a grave political mistake.

The House of Commons guarded the state's pocketbook, and James and later Stuart kings badly needed to open that pocketbook. Elizabeth had bequeathed to James a sizable royal debt. Through prudent management the debt could have been gradually reduced, but James I looked on all revenues as a happy windfall to be squandered on a lavish court and favorite courtiers. In reality, the extravagance displayed in James's court, as well as the public flaunting of his male lovers, weakened respect for the monarchy.

Elizabeth had also left to her Stuart successors a House of Commons that appreciated its own financial strength and intended to use that strength to acquire a greater say in the government of the state. The knights and burgesses who sat at Westminster in the late sixteenth and early seventeenth centuries wanted to discuss royal expenditures, religious reform, and foreign affairs. In short, the Commons wanted what amounted to sovereignty.

Profound social changes had occurred since the sixteenth century. The English House of Commons during the reigns of James I and his son Charles I (r. 1625–1649) was very different from the assembly Henry VIII had manipulated into passing his Reformation legislation. A social revolution had brought about the change. The dissolution of the monasteries and the sale of monastic land had enriched many people. Agricultural techniques like the draining of wasteland and the application of fertilizers improved the land and its yield. In the seventeenth century old manorial common land was enclosed and turned into sheep runs; breeding was carefully supervised, and the size of the flocks increased. In these activities, as well as in renting and leasing parcels of land, precise accounts were kept.

Many people invested in commercial ventures at home, such as the expanding cloth industry, and through partnerships and joint stock companies engaged in foreign enterprises. Many also made prudent marriages. All these developments led to a great deal of social mobility. Both in commerce and in argiculture, the English in the late sixteenth and early seventeenth centuries were capitalists, investing their profits to make more money. Though the international inflation of the period hit everywhere, in England commercial and agricultural income rose faster than prices. Wealthy country gentry, rich city merchants, and financiers invested abroad.

The typical pattern was for the commercially successful to set themselves up as country gentry, thus creating an elite group that possessed a far greater proportion of land and of the national wealth in 1640 than had been the case in 1540. Small wonder that in 1640 someone could declare in the House of Commons, probably accurately, "We could buy the House of Lords three times over." Increased wealth had also produced a better-educated and more articulate House of Commons. Many members had acquired at least a smattering of legal knowledge, and they used that knowledge to search for medieval precedents from which to argue against the king. The class that dominated the Commons wanted political power corresponding to its economic strength.

In England, unlike France, there was no social stigma attached to paying taxes. Members of the House of Commons were willing to tax themselves provided they had some say in the expenditure of those taxes and in the formulation of state policies. The Stuart kings, however, considered such ambitions intolerable presumption and a threat to their divine-right prerogative. Consequently, at every Parliament between 1603 and 1640, bitter squabbles erupted between the Crown and the wealthy, articulate, and legal-minded Commons. Charles I's attempt to govern without Parliament (1629–1640), and to finance his government by arbitrary nonparliamentary levies, brought the country to a crisis.

An issue graver than royal extravagance and Parliament's desire to make law also disturbed the English and embittered relations between the king and the House of Commons. That problem was religion. In the early seventeenth century, increasing numbers of English people felt dissatisfied with the Church of England established by Henry VIII and reformed by Elizabeth. Many Puritans (see page 444) believed that Reformation had not gone far enough. They wanted to "purify" the Anglican church of Roman Catholic elements—elaborate vestments and ceremonial, the position of the altar in the church, even the giving and wearing of wedding rings.

It is very difficult to establish what proportion of the English population was Puritan. According to the present scholarly consensus, the dominant religious groups in the early seventeenth century were Calvinist; their more zealous members were Puritans. It also seems clear that many English men and women were attracted by the socioeconomic implications of John Calvin's theology. Calvinism emphasized hard work, sobriety, thrift, competition, and postponement of pleasure, and it tended to link sin and poverty with weakness and moral corruption. These attitudes fit in precisely with the economic approaches and practices of many (successful) business people and farmers. These values have frequently been called the "Protestant ethic," "middle-class ethic," or "capitalist ethic." While it is hazardous to identify capitalism and progress with Protestantism—there were many successful Catholic capitalists—the "Protestant virtues" represented the prevailing values of members of the House of Commons.

James I and Charles I both gave the impression of being highly sympathetic to Roman Catholicism. Charles supported the policies of William Laud (1573–1645), archbishop of Canterbury, who tried to impose elaborate ritual and rich ceremonial on all churches. Laud insisted on complete uniformity of church services and enforced that uniformity through an ecclesiastical court called the "Court of High Commission." People believed the country was being led back to Roman Catholicism. In 1637 Laud attempted to impose two new elements on the church organization in Scotland: a new prayer book, modeled on the Anglican *Book of Common Prayer*, and bishoprics, which the Presbyterian Scots firmly rejected. The Scots therefore revolted. In order to finance an army to put down the Scots, King Charles was compelled to summon Parliament in November 1640.

For eleven years Charles I had ruled without Parliament, financing his government through extraordinary stopgap levies, considered illegal by most English people. For example, the king revived a medieval law requiring coastal districts to help pay the cost of ships for defense, but levied the tax, called "ship money," on inland as well as coastal countries. When the issue was tested in the courts, the judges, having been suborned, decided in the king's favor.

Most members of Parliament believed that such taxation without consent amounted to arbitrary and absolute despotism. Consequently, they were not willing to trust the king with an army. Accordingly, this Parliament, commonly called the "Long Parliament" because it sat from 1640 to 1660, proceeded to enact legislation that limited the power of the monarch and made arbitrary government impossible.

In 1641 the Commons passed the Triennial Act, which compelled the king to summon Parliament every three years. The Commons impeached Archbishop Laud and abolished the Court of High Commission. It went further and threatened to abolish the institution of episcopacy. King Charles, fearful of a Scottish invasion—the original reason for summoning Parliament—accepted these measures. Understanding and peace were not achieved, however, partly because radical members of the Commons pushed increasingly revolutionary propositions, partly because Charles maneuvered to rescind those he had already approved. An uprising in Ireland precipitated civil war.

Ever since Henry II had conquered Ireland in 1171, English governors had mercilessly ruled the land, and English landlords had ruthlessly exploited the Irish people. The English Reformation had made a bad situation worse: because the Irish remained Catholic, religious differences became united with economic and political oppression. Without an army, Charles I could neither come to terms with the Scots nor put down the Irish rebellion, and the Long Parliament remained unwilling to place an army under a king it did not trust. Charles thus instigated military action against parliamentary forces. He recruited an army drawn from the nobility and their cavalry staff, the rural gentry, and mercenaries. The parliamentary army was composed of the militia of the city of London, country squires with business connections, and men with a firm belief in the spiritual duty of serving.

The English civil war (1642–1649) tested whether sovereignty in England was to reside in the king or in Parliament. The civil war did not resolve that problem, although it ended in 1649 with the execution of King Charles on the charge of high treason—a severe blow to the theory of divine-right monarchy. The period between 1649 and 1660, called the "Interregnum" because it separated two monarchial periods, witnessed England's solitary experience of military dictatorship.

Puritanical Absolutism in England: Cromwell and the Protectorate

The problem of sovereignty was vigorously debated in the middle years of the seventeenth century. In *Leviathan,* the English philosopher and political theorist Thomas Hobbes (1588–1679) maintained that sovereignty is ultimately derived from the people, who transfer it to the monarchy by implicit contract. The power of the ruler is absolute, but kings do not hold their power by divine right. This view pleased no one in the seventeenth century.

When Charles I was beheaded on January 30, 1649, the kingship was abolished. A *commonwealth*, or republican form of government, was proclaimed. Theoretically, legislative power rested in the surviving members of Parliament and executive power in a council of state. In fact, the army that had defeated the royal forces controlled the government, and Oliver Cromwell controlled the army. Though called the "Protectorate," the rule of Cromwell (1653–1658) constituted military dictatorship.

Oliver Cromwell (1599–1658) came from the country gentry, the class that dominated the House of Commons in the early seventeenth century. He himself had sat in the Long Parliament. Cromwell rose in the parliamentary army and achieved nationwide fame by infusing the army with his Puritan convictions and molding it into the highly effective military machine, called the "New Model Army," that defeated the royalist forces.

The army had prepared a constitution, the Instrument of Government (1653), that invested executive power in a lord protector (Cromwell) and a council of state. The instrument provided for triennial parliaments and gave Parliament the sole power to raise taxes. But after repeated disputes, Cromwell tore the document up. He continued the standing army and proclaimed quasi-martial law. He divided England into twelve military districts, each governed by a major general. The major generals acted through the justices of the peace, though they sometimes overrode them. On the issue of religion, Cromwell favored broad toleration, and the Instrument of Government gave all Christians, except Roman Catholics, the right to practice their faith. Toleration meant state protection of many different Protestant sects, however, and most English people had no enthusiasm for such a notion; the idea was far ahead of its time. As for Irish Catholicism, Cromwell identified it with sedition. In 1649 he crushed rebellion in Ireland with merciless savagery, leaving a legacy of Irish hatred for England that has not yet subsided. The state rigorously censored the press, forbade sports, and kept the theaters closed in England.

Cromwell's regulation of the nation's economy had features typical of seventeenth-century absolutism. The lord protector's policies were mercantilist, similar to those Colbert established in France. Cromwell enforced a navigation act requiring that English goods be transported on English ships.

The navigation act was a great boost to the development of an English merchant marine and brought about a short but successful war with the commercially threatened Dutch. Cromwell also welcomed the immigration of Jews, because of their skills, and they began to return to England after four centuries of absence.

Absolute government collapsed when Cromwell died in 1658. Fed up with military rule, the English

Periodical Sheet on the Civil War Single sheets or broadsides spread the positions of the opposing sides to the nonliterate public. *Mercurius Rusticus,* intended for country people, conveyed the royalist argument. *(Source: The British Library)*

Cromwell Dismisses the Rump Parliament In 1648 the army disposed of its enemies in Parliament; those who remained were known as the Rump Parliament. After the execution of Charles I and the establishment of the Commonwealth, legislative power in England theoretically rested in Parliament. But in 1653, concluding that he could not work with this body, Cromwell turned out the Rump. In this satirical Dutch print, Cromwell ordered members to go home. The sign on the wall reads, "This house is to let." *(Source: The British Library/Pat Hodgson Library)*

longed for a return to civilian government, restoration of the common law, and social stability. Moreover, the strain of creating a community of puritanical saints proved too psychologically exhausting. Government by military dictatorship was an unfortunate experiment that the English never forgot or repeated. By 1660 they were ready to restore the monarchy.

The Restoration of the English Monarchy

The Restoration of 1660 re-established the monarchy in the person of Charles II (r. 1660–1685), eldest son of Charles I. At the same time both houses of Parliament were restored, together with the established Anglican church, the courts of law, and the system of local government through justices of the peace. The Restoration failed to resolve two serious problems. What was to be the attitude of the state toward Puritans, Catholics, and dissenters from the established church? And what was to be the constitutional position of the king—that is, what was to be the relationship between the king and Parliament?

About the first of these issues, Charles II, a relaxed, easygoing, and sensual man, was basically indifferent. He was not interested in doctrinal issues. The new members of Parliament were, and they proceeded to enact a body of laws that sought to compel religious uniformity. Those who refused to receive the sacrament of the Church of England could not vote, hold public office, preach, teach, attend the universities, or even assemble for meetings, according to the Test Act of 1673. These restrictions could not be enforced. When the Quaker William Penn held a meeting of his Friends and was arrested, the jury refused to convict him.

In politics, Charles II was determined "not to set out in his travels again," which meant that he intended to get along with Parliament. Charles II's solution to the problem of the relationship between the king and the House of Commons had profound importance for later constitutional development. Generally good rapport existed between the king and the strongly royalist Parliament that had restored him. This rapport was due largely to the king's appointment of a council of five men who served both as his major advisers and as members of Parliament, thus acting as liaison agents between the executive and the legislature. This body —known as the "Cabal" from the names of its five members (Clifford, Arlington, Buckingham, Ashley-Cooper, and Lauderdale)—was an ancestor of the later cabinet system (see page 524). It gradually came to be accepted that the Cabal was answerable in Parliament for the decisions of the king. This development gave rise to the concept of ministerial responsibility: royal ministers must answer to the Commons.

Harmony between the Crown and Parliament rested on the understanding that Charles would summon frequent parliaments and that Parliament would vote him sufficient revenues. However, although Parliament believed Charles had a virtual divine right to govern, it did not grant him an adequate income. Accordingly, in 1670 Charles entered into a secret agreement with Louis XIV. The French king would give Charles £200,000 annually, and in return Charles would relax the laws against Catholics, gradually re-Catholicize England, support French policy against the Dutch, and convert to Catholicism himself.

When the details of this secret treaty leaked out, a great wave of anti-Catholic fear swept England. This fear was compounded by a crucial fact: although Charles had produced several bastards, he had no legitimate children. It therefore appeared that his brother and heir, James, duke of York, who had publicly acknowledged his Catholicism, would inaugurate a Catholic dynasty. The combination of hatred for the French absolutism embodied in Louis XIV, hostility to Roman Catholicism, and fear of a permanent Catholic dynasty produced virtual hysteria. The Commons passed an exclusion bill denying the succession to a Roman Catholic, but Charles quickly dissolved Parliament and the bill never became law.

James II (r. 1685–1688) did succeed his brother. Almost at once the worst English anti-Catholic fears, already aroused by Louis XIV's revocation of the Edict of Nantes, were realized. In direct violation of the Test Act, James appointed Roman Catholics to positions in the army, the universities, and local government. When these actions were tested in the courts, the judges, whom James had appointed, decided for the king. The king was suspending the law at will and appeared to be reviving the absolutism of his father and grandfather. He went further. Attempting to broaden his base of support with Protestant dissenters and nonconformists, James issued a declaration of indulgence granting religious freedom to all.

Two events gave the signals for revolution. First, seven bishops of the Church of England petitioned the king that they not be forced to read the declaration of indulgence because of their belief that it was an illegal act. They were imprisoned in the Tower of London but subsequently acquitted amid great public enthusiasm. Second, in June 1688 James's second wife produced a male heir. A Catholic dynasty seemed assured. The fear of a Roman Catholic monarchy, supported by France and ruling outside the law, prompted a group of eminent persons to offer the English throne to James's Protestant daughter, Mary, and her Dutch husband, Prince William of Orange. In December 1688 James II, his queen, and their infant son fled to France and became pensioners of Louis XIV. Early in 1689, William and Mary were crowned king and queen of England.

The Triumph of England's Parliament: Constitutional Monarchy and Cabinet Government

The English call the events of 1688 to 1689 the "Glorious Revolution." The revolution was indeed glorious in the sense that it replaced one king with another with a minimum of bloodshed. It also represented the destruction, once and for all, of the idea of divine-right monarchy. William and Mary accepted the English throne from Parliament and in so doing explicitly recognized the supremacy of Parliament. The revolution of 1688 established the principle that sovereignty, the ultimate power in the state, was divided between king and Parliament and that the king ruled with the consent of the governed.

The men who brought about the revolution quickly framed their intentions in the Bill of Rights, the cornerstone of the modern British constitution. The basic principles of the Bill of Rights were formulated in direct response to Stuart absolutism. Law was to be made in Parliament; once made, it could not be suspended by the Crown. Parliament had to be called at least every three years. Both elections to and debate in Parliament were to be free, in the sense that the Crown was not to interfere in them (this aspect of the bill was widely disregarded in the eighteenth century). Judges would hold their offices "during good behavior," a provision that assured the independence of the judiciary. No longer could the Crown get the judicial decisions it wanted by threats of removal. There was to be no standing army in peacetime—a limitation designed to prevent the repetition of either Stuart or Cromwellian military government. The Bill of Rights granted "that the subjects which are Protestants may have arms for their defense suitable to their conditions and as allowed by law,"[18] meaning that Catholics could not possess firearms because the Protestant majority feared them. Additional legislation granted freedom of worship to Protestant dissenters and nonconformists and required that the English monarch always be Protestant.

The Glorious Revolution found its best defense in the political philosopher John Locke's *Second Treatise* of *Civil Government* (1690). Locke (1632–1704) maintained that people set up civil governments in order to protect life, liberty, and property. A government that oversteps its proper function—protecting the natural rights of life, liberty, and property—becomes a tyranny. (By "natural" rights, Locke meant rights basic to all men because all have the ability to reason.) Under a tyrannical government, the people have the natural right to rebellion. Rebellion can be avoided if the government carefully respects the rights of citizens and if the people zealously defend their liberty. Recognizing the close relationship between economic and political freedom, Locke linked economic liberty and private property with political freedom. Locke

served as the great spokesman for the liberal English revolution of 1688 to 1689 and for representative government. His idea, inherited from ancient Greece and Rome (see Chapter 4), that there are natural or universal rights, equally valid for all peoples and societies, played a powerful role in eighteenth-century Enlightenment thought. His ideas on liberty and tyranny were especially popular in colonial America.

The events of 1688 to 1689 did not constitute a *democratic* revolution. The revolution placed sovereignty in Parliament, and Parliament represented the upper classes. The great majority of English people acquired no say in their government. The English revolution established a constitutional monarchy; it also inaugurated an age of aristocratic government, which lasted at least until 1832 and in many ways until 1914.

In the course of the eighteenth century, the cabinet system of government evolved. The term *cabinet* derives from the small private room in which English rulers consulted their chief ministers. In a cabinet system, the leading ministers, who must have seats in and the support of a majority of the House of Commons, formulate common policy and conduct the business of the country. During the administration of one royal minister, Sir Robert Walpole, who led the cabinet from 1721 to 1742, the idea developed that the cabinet was responsible to the House of Commons. The Hanoverian king George I (r. 1714–1727) normally presided at cabinet meetings throughout his reign, but his son and heir George II (r. 1727–1760) discontinued the practice. The influence of the Crown in decision making accordingly declined. Walpole enjoyed the favor of the monarchy and of the House of Commons and came to be called the king's first, or "prime," minister. In the English cabinet system, both legislative and executive power are held by the leading ministers, who form the government.

The Dutch Republic in the Seventeenth Century

In the late sixteenth century, the seven northern provinces of the Netherlands, of which Holland and Zeeland were the most prosperous, had succeeded in throwing off Spanish domination. This success was based on their geographical lines of defense, the wealth of their cities, the military strategy of William the Silent, the preoccupation of Philip II of Spain with so many additional concerns, and the northern provinces' vigorous Calvinism. In 1581 the seven provinces of the Union of Utrecht had formed the United Provinces (see page 474). Philip II continued to try to crush the Dutch, but in 1609 his son Philip III agreed to a truce that implicitly recognized the independence of the United Provinces. At the time neither side expected the peace to be permanent. The Peace of Westphalia in 1648, however, confirmed the Dutch republic's independence.

The seventeenth century witnessed an unparalleled flowering of Dutch scientific, artistic, and literary achievement. In this period, often called the "golden age of the Netherlands," Dutch ideas and

Vermeer: A Woman Weighing Gold (ca 1657) Vermeer painted pictures of middle-class women involved in ordinary activities in the quiet interiors of their homes. Unrivaled among Dutch masters for his superb control of light, in this painting Vermeer illuminates the pregnant woman weighing gold on her scales, as Christ in the painting on the wall weighs the saved and the damned. *(Source: National Gallery of Art, Washington; Widener Collection)*

attitudes played a profound role in shaping a new and modern world-view. At the same time, the Republic of the United Provinces of the Netherlands represents another model of the development of the modern constitutional state.

Within each province an oligarchy of wealthy merchants called "regents" handled domestic affairs in the local Estates. The provincial Estates held virtually all the power. A federal assembly, or States General, handled matters of foreign affairs, such as war. But the States General did not possess sovereign authority, since all issues had to be referred back to the local Estates for approval. The States General appointed a representative, the *stadholder,* in each province. As the highest executive there, the stadholder carried out ceremonial functions and was responsible for defense and good order. The sons of William the Silent, Maurice and William Louis, held the office of stadholder in all seven provinces. As members of the House of Orange, they were closely identified with Dutch patriotism. The regents in each province jealously guarded local independence and resisted efforts at centralization. Nevertheless, Holland, which had the largest navy and the most wealth, dominated the republic and the States General. Significantly, the Estates assembled at Holland's capital, The Hague.

The government of the United Provinces fits none of the standard categories of seventeenth-century political organization. The Dutch were not monarchial, but fiercely republican. The government was controlled by wealthy merchants and financiers. Though rich, their values were not aristocratic but strongly middle class, emphasizing thrift, hard work, and simplicity in living. The Dutch republic was not a strong federation but a confederation—that is, a weak union of strong provinces. The provinces were a temptation to powerful neighbors, yet the Dutch resisted the long Spanish effort at reconquest and withstood both French and English attacks in the second half of the century. Louis XIV's hatred of the Dutch was proverbial. They represented all that he despised—middle-class values, religious toleration, and political independence.

The political success of the Dutch rested on the phenomenal commercial prosperity of the Netherlands. The moral and ethical bases of that commercial wealth were thrift, frugality, and religious toleration. John Calvin had written, "From where do the merchant's profits come except from his own diligence and industry." This attitude undoubtedly encouraged a sturdy people who had waged a centuries-old struggle against the sea.

Alone of all European peoples in the seventeenth century, the Dutch practiced religious toleration. Peoples of all faiths were welcome within their borders. Although there is scattered evidence of anti-Semitism, Jews enjoyed a level of acceptance and absorption in Dutch business and general culture unique in early modern Europe. It is a testimony to the urbanity of Dutch society that in a century when patriotism was closely identified with religious uniformity, the Calvinist province of Holland allowed its highest official, Jan van Oldenbarneveldt, to continue to practice his Roman Catholic faith. As long as business people conducted their religion in private, the government did not interfere with them.

Toleration also paid off: it attracted a great deal of foreign capital and investment. Deposits at the Bank of Amsterdam were guaranteed by the city council, and in the middle years of the century the bank became Europe's best source of cheap credit and commercial intelligence and the main clearinghouse for bills of exchange. People of all races and creeds traded in Amsterdam, at whose docks on the Amstel River five thousand ships were berthed. Joost van den Vondel, the poet of Dutch imperialism, exulted:

God, God, the Lord of Amstel cried, hold every
    conscience free;
And Liberty ride, on Holland's tide, with billowing sails
    to sea,
And run our Amstel out and in; let freedom gird the
    bold,
And merchant in his counting house stand elbow deep in
    gold.[19]

The fishing industry was the cornerstone of the Dutch economy. For half the year, from June to December, fishing fleets combed the dangerous English coast and the North Sea, raking in tiny herring. Profits from herring stimulated shipbuilding, and even before 1600 the Dutch were offering the lowest shipping rates in Europe. The merchant marine was the largest in Europe. In 1650 contemporaries estimated that the Dutch had sixteen thousand merchant ships, half the European total. All the wood for these ships had to be imported: the Dutch bought whole forests from Norway. They also bought entire vineyards from French growers before the grapes were harvested. They controlled the Baltic grain trade, buying entire wheat and rye crops in Poland, east Prussia, and Swedish Pomerania. Because they dealt in bulk, nobody could undersell the Dutch. Foreign merchants coming to Amsterdam could buy anything from precision lenses for the newly invented microscope to muskets for an army of five thousand. Although Dutch cities became famous for their exports—diamonds and linens from Haarlem, pottery from Delft—Dutch wealth depended less on exports than on transport.

In 1602 a group of the regents of Holland formed the Dutch East India Company, a joint stock company. The investors each received a percentage of the profits proportional to the amount of money they had put in. Within half a century, the Dutch East India Company had cut heavily into Portuguese trading in East Asia. The Dutch seized the Cape of Good Hope, Ceylon, and Malacca and established trading posts in each place. In the 1630s the Dutch East India Company was paying its investors about a 35 percent annual return on their investments. The Dutch West India

Job Berckheyde: The Amsterdam Stock Exchange Small shareholders (through brokers) as well as rich capitalists could buy and sell and, by various combinations, speculate without having any money at all in the Amsterdam stock market. Shares in the Dutch East India Company were major objects of speculation. The volume, fluidity, and publicity of the Exchange were its new and distinctly modern features. *(Source: Museum Boymans-van Beuningen, Rotterdam)*

Company, founded in 1621, traded extensively with Latin America and Africa (Map 16.3).

Trade and commerce brought the Dutch prodigious wealth. In the seventeenth century, the Dutch enjoyed the highest standard of living in Europe, perhaps in the world. Amsterdam and Rotterdam built massive granaries where the surplus of one year could be stored against possible shortages the next. Thus, excepting the 1650s when bad harvests reduced supplies, food prices fluctuated very little. By the standards of Cologne, Paris, or London, salaries were high for all workers—except women. All classes of society, including unskilled laborers, ate well. The low price of bread meant that, compared to other places in Europe, a higher percentage of the worker's income could be spent on fish, cheese, butter, vegetables, even meat. A

scholar recently described the Netherlands as "an island of plenty in a sea of want." Consequently, the Netherlands experienced very few of the food riots that characterized the rest of Europe.[20]

Although the initial purpose of the Dutch East and West India Companies was commercial—the import of spices and silks to Europe—the Dutch found themselves involved in the imperialist exploitation of parts of East Asia and Latin America, with great success. In 1652 the Dutch founded Cape Town on the southern tip of Africa as a fueling station for ships planning to cross the Pacific. But war with France and England in the 1670s hurt the United Provinces. The long War of the Spanish Succession, in which the Dutch supported England against France, was a costly drain on Dutch manpower and financial resources. The peace signed in

MAP 16.3 Seventeenth-century Dutch Commerce Dutch wealth rested on commerce, and commerce depended on the huge Dutch merchant marine, manned by perhaps 48,000 sailors. The fleet carried goods from all parts of the globe to the port of Amsterdam.

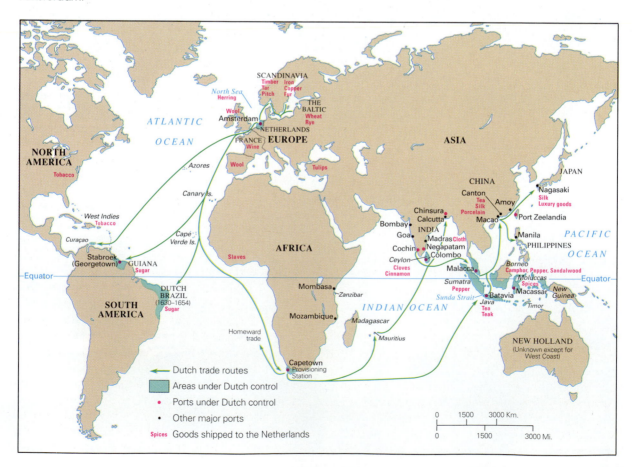

Pieter Claesz: Still Life The term "still life" became popular after 1650 as a reference to paintings of inanimate objects—flowers, fruit, all kinds of food, tableware, musical instruments—and the term was usually applied to Dutch paintings. As this scene suggests, the enormously successful Dutch commercial society took great pleasure in sensuous materialism. Yet the tortoise, a symbol of long life, and the watch, a reminder of the passage of time, imply that all is vanity. *(Source: Louvre/Cliché des Musées Nationaux, Paris)*

1715 to end the war marked the beginning of Dutch economic decline.

SUMMARY

According to Thomas Hobbes, the central drive in every human is "a perpetual and restless desire of Power, after Power, that ceaseth only in Death." The seventeenth century solved the problem of sovereign power in two fundamental ways: absolutism and constitutionalism. The France of Louis XIV witnessed the emergence of the fully absolutist state. The king commanded all the powers of the state: judicial, military, political, and, to a great extent, ecclesiastical. France developed a centralized bureaucracy, a professional army, a state-directed economy, all of which Louis personally supervised. For the first time in history, all the institutions and powers of the national state were effectively controlled by a single person. The king saw himself as the representative of God on earth, and it has been said that "to the seventeenth century imagination God was a sort of image of Louis XIV."[21]

As Louis XIV personifies absolutism, so Stuart England exemplifies the evolution of the first modern constitutional state. The conflicts between Parliament and the first two Stuart rulers, James I and Charles I, tested where sovereign power would rest in the state. The resulting civil war did not solve the problem. The Instrument of Government, the document produced in 1653 by the victorious parliamentary army, provided for a balance of governmental authority and recognition of popular rights; as such, the Instrument has been called the first modern constitution. Unfortunately, it lacked public support. James II's absolutist tendencies brought on the Glorious Revolution of 1688 to 1689, and the people who made that revolution settled three basic issues. Sovereign power was divided between king and Parliament, with Parliament enjoying the greater share. Government was to be based on the rule of law. And the liberties of English people were made explicit in written form, in the Bill of Rights. The framers of the English constitution left to later generations the task of making constitutional government work.

The models of governmental power established by seventeenth-century England and France strongly influenced other states then and ever since. As the American novelist William Faulkner wrote, "The past isn't dead; it's not even past."

NOTES

1. G. Parker and L. M. Smith, "Introduction," and N. Steensgaard, "The Seventeenth Century Crisis," in *The General Crisis of the Seventeenth Century,* ed. G. Parker and L. M. Smith (London: Routledge & Kegan Paul, 1985), pp. 1–53, esp. p. 12.
2. J. B. Collins, *Fiscal Limits of Absolutism: Direct Taxation in Early Seventeenth Century France* (Berkeley: University of California Press, 1988), pp. 1, 3–4, 215–222.
3. Cited in J. H. Elliot, *Richelieu and Olivares* (Cambridge: Cambridge University Press, 1984), p. 135; and in W. F. Church, *Richelieu and Reason of State* (Princeton, N.J.: Princeton University Press, 1972), p. 507.
4. D. Parker, *The Making of French Absolutism* (New York: St. Martin's Press, 1983), pp. 146–148.
5. Quoted in J. Wolf, *Louis XIV* (New York: W. W. Norton, 1968), p. 115.
6. See W. Beik, *Absolutism and Society in Seventeenth Century France: State Power and Provincial Aristocracy in Languedoc* (Cambridge: Cambridge University Press, 1985), pp. 279–302.
7. S. de Gramont, ed., *The Age of Magnificence: Memoirs of the Court of Louis XIV by the Duc de Saint Simon* (New York: Capricorn Books, 1964), pp. 141–145.
8. Quoted in Wolf, p. 146.
9. Quoted in A. Trout, *Jean-Baptiste Colbert* (Boston: Twayne, 1978), p. 128.
10. Quoted in Wolf, p. 394.
11. Ibid.
12. See W. C. Scoville, *The Persecution of the Huguenots and French Economic Development: 1680–1720* (Berkeley: University of California Press, 1960).
13. W. F. Church, *Louis XIV in Historical Thought: From Voltaire to the Annales School* (New York: W. W. Norton, 1976), p. 92.
14. Gramont, p. 183.
15. J. H. Elliott, *Imperial Spain, 1469–1716* (New York: Mentor Books, 1963), pp. 306–308.
16. B. Bennassar, *The Spanish Character: Attitudes and Mentalities from the Sixteenth to the Nineteenth Century* trans. B. Keen (Berkeley: University of California Press, 1979), p. 125.
17. For a revisionist interpretation, see J. Wormald, "James VI and I: Two Kings or One?" *History* 62 (June 1983): 187–209.
18. C. Stephenson and G. F. Marcham, *Sources of English Constitutional History* (New York: Harper & Row, 1937), p. 601.
19. Quoted in D. Maland, *Europe in the Seventeenth Century* (New York: Macmillan, 1967), pp. 198–199.
20. S. Schama, *The Embarrassment of Riches: An Interpretation of Dutch Culture in the Golden Age* (New York: Alfred A. Knopf, 1987), pp. 165–170.
21. Quoted in C. J. Friedrich and C. Blitzer, *The Age of Power* (Ithaca, N.Y.: Cornell University Press, 1957), p. 112.

SUGGESTED READING

Students who wish to explore the problems presented in this chapter in greater depth will easily find a rich and exciting literature, with many titles available in paperback editions. The following surveys all provide good background material. G. Parker, *Europe in Crisis, 1598–1618* (1980), provides a sound introduction to the social, economic, and religious tensions of the period. R. S. Dunn, *The Age of Religious Wars, 1559–1715,* 2d ed. (1979), examines the period from the perspective of the confessional strife between Protestants and Catholics, but there is also stimulating material on absolutism and constitutionalism. T. Aston, ed., *Crisis in Europe, 1560–1660* (1967), contains essays by leading historians. P. Anderson, *Lineages of the Absolutist State* (1974), is a Marxist interpretation of absolutism in western and eastern Europe. M. Beloff, *The Age of Absolutism* (1967), concentrates on the social forces that underlay administrative change. H. Rosenberg, "Absolute Monarchy and Its Legacy," in N. F. Cantor and S. Werthman, eds., *Early Modern Europe, 1450–1650* (1967), is a seminal study. The classic treatment of constitutionalism remains that of C. H. McIlwain, *Constitutionalism: Ancient and Modern* (1940), written by a great scholar during the rise of German fascism. S. B. Crimes, *English Constitutional History* (1967), is an excellent survey with useful chapters on the sixteenth and seventeenth centuries.

Louis XIV and his age have predictably attracted the attention of many scholars. J. Wolf's *Louis XIV,* cited in the Notes, remains the best available biography. Two works of W. H. Lewis, *The Splendid Century* (1957) and *The Sunset of the Splendid Century* (1963), make delightful light reading, especially for the beginning student. The advanced student will want to consult the excellent historiographical analysis by W. F. Church mentioned in the Notes, *Louis XIV in Historical Thought.* Perhaps the best works of the Annales school on the period are P.

Goubert, *Louis XIV and Twenty Million Frenchmen* (1972), and his heavily detailed *The Ancien Régime: French Society, 1600–1750,* 2 vols. (1969–1973), which contains invaluable material on the lives and work of ordinary people. For the French economy and financial conditions, the old study of C. W. Cole, *Colbert and a Century of French Mercantilism,* 2 vols. (1939), is still valuable but should be supplemented by R. Bonney, *The King's Debts: Finance and Politics in France, 1589–1661* (1981), and by the works of Trout and Scoville listed in the Notes. Scoville's book is a significant contribution to revisionist history. For Louis XIV's foreign policy and wars, see R. Hatton, "Louis XIV: Recent Gains in Historical Knowledge," *Journal of Modern History* 45 (1973), and her edited work *Louis XIV and Europe* (1976), an important collection of essays. Hatton's *Europe in the Age of Louis XIV* (1979) is a splendidly illustrated survey of many aspects of seventeenth-century European culture. O. Ranum, *Paris in the Age of Absolutism* (1968), describes the geographical, political, economic, and architectural significance of the cultural capital of Europe, while V. L. Tapie, *The Age of Grandeur: Baroque Art and Architecture* (1960), also emphasizes the relationship between art and politics with excellent illustrations.

For Spain and Portugal, in addition to the works in the Notes, see M. Defourneaux, *Daily Life in Spain in the Golden Age* (1976), highly useful for an understanding of ordinary people and of Spanish society; and C. R. Phillips, *Ciudad Real, 1500–1750: Growth, Crisis, and Readjustment in the Spanish Economy* (1979), a significant case study.

The following works all offer solid material on English political and social issues of the seventeenth century: M. Ashley, *England in the Seventeenth Century,* rev. ed. (1980), and *The House of Stuart: Its Rise and Fall* (1980); C. Hill, *A Century of Revolution* (1961); J. P. Kenyon, *Stuart England* (1978); and K. Wrightson, *English Society, 1580–1680* (1982). Perhaps the most comprehensive treatments of Parliament are C. Russell's *Crisis of Parliaments, 1509–1660* (1971) and *Parliaments and English Politics, 1621–1629* (1979). On the background of the English civil war, L. Stone, *The Crisis of the Aristocracy* (1965) and *The Causes of the English Revolution* (1972), are standard works, while both B. Manning, *The English People and the English Revolution* (1976), and D. Underdown, *Revel, Riot, and Rebellion* (1985), discuss the extent of popular involvement; Underdown's is the more sophisticated treatment. For English intellectual currents, see J. O. Appleby, *Economic Thought and Ideology in Seventeenth Century England* (1978); and C. Hill, *Intellectual Origins of the English Revolution* (1966) and *Society and Puritanism in Pre-revolutionary England* (1964).

For the several shades of Protestant sentiment in the early seventeenth century, see P. Collinson, *The Religion of Protestants* (1982). C. M. Hibbard, *Charles I and the Popish Plot* (1983), treats Roman Catholic influence; like Collinson's work, it is an excellent, fundamental reference for religious issues, though the older work of W. Haller, *The Rise of Puritanism* (1957), is still valuable. For women, see R. Thompson, *Women in Stuart England and America* (1974), and A. Fraser, *The Weaker Vessel* (1985). For Cromwell and the Interregnum, C. Firth, *Oliver Cromwell and the Rule of the Puritans in England* (1956); C. Hill, *God's Englishman* (1972); and A. Fraser, *Cromwell, the Lord Protector* (1973), are all valuable. J. Morrill, *The Revolt of the Provinces,* 2d ed. (1980), is the best study of religious neutralism, while C. Hill, *The World Turned Upside Down* (1972), discusses radical thought during the period.

For the Restoration and the Glorious Revolution, see R. Hutton, *Charles II: King of England, Scotland and Ireland* (1989), and A. Fraser, *Royal Charles: Charles II and the Restoration* (1979), two highly readable biographies; R. Ollard, *The Image of the King: Charles I and Charles II* (1980), which examines the nature of monarchy; J. Miller, *James II: A Study in Kingship* (1977); J. Childs, *The Army, James II, and the Glorious Revolution* (1980); J. R. Jones, *The Revolution of 1688 in England* (1972); and L. G. Schwoerer, *The Declaration of Rights, 1689* (1981), a fine assessment of that fundamental document. The ideas of John Locke are analyzed by J. P. Kenyon, *Revolution Principles: The Politics of Party, 1689–1720* (1977). R. Hutton, *The Restoration, 1658–1667* (1985), is a thorough if somewhat difficult narrative.

On Holland, K. H. D. Haley, *The Dutch Republic in the Seventeenth Century* (1972), is a splendidly illustrated appreciation of Dutch commercial and artistic achievements, while J. L. Price, *Culture and Society in the Dutch Republic During the Seventeenth Century* (1974), is a sound scholarly work. R. Boxer, *The Dutch Seaborne Empire* (1980), and the appropriate chapters of D. Maland's *Europe in the Seventeenth Century,* cited in the Notes, are useful for Dutch overseas expansion and the reasons for Dutch prosperity. The following works focus on the economic and cultural life of the leading Dutch city: V. Barbour, *Capitalism in Amsterdam in the Seventeenth Century* (1950), and D. Regin, *Traders, Artists, Burghers: A Cultural History of Amsterdam in the Seventeenth Century* (1977). J. M. Montias, *Artists and Artisans in Delft: A Socioeconomic Study of the Seventeenth Century* (1982), examines another major city. The leading statesmen of the period may be studied in these biographies: H. H. Rowen, *John de Witt, Grand Pensionary of Holland, 1625–1672* (1978); S. B. Baxter, *William the III and the Defense of European Liberty, 1650–1702* (1966); and J. den Tex, *Oldenbarnevelt,* 2 vols. (1973).

Many facets of the lives of ordinary French, Spanish, English, and Dutch people are discussed by P. Burke, *Popular Culture in Early Modern Europe* (1978), an important and provocative study.

17

Absolutism in Eastern Europe to 1740

The seventeenth century witnessed a struggle between constitutionalism and absolutism in eastern Europe. With the notable exception of the kingdom of Poland, monarchial absolutism was everywhere triumphant in eastern Europe; constitutionalism was decisively defeated. Absolute monarchies emerged in Austria, Prussia, and Russia. This was a development of great significance: these three monarchies exercised enormous influence until 1918, and they created a strong authoritarian tradition that is still dominant in eastern Europe.

Although the monarchs of eastern Europe were greatly impressed by Louis XIV and his model of royal absolutism, their states differed in several important ways from that of their French counterpart. Louis XIV built French absolutism on the heritage of a well-developed medieval monarchy and a strong royal bureaucracy. And when Louis XIV came to the throne, the powers of the nobility were already somewhat limited, the French middle class was relatively strong, and the peasants were generally free from serfdom. Eastern absolutism rested on a very different social reality: a powerful nobility, a weak middle class, and an oppressed peasantry composed of serfs.

These differences in social conditions raise three major questions.

- Why did the basic structure of society in eastern Europe move away from that of western Europe in the early modern period?

- How and why, in their different social environments, did the rulers of Austria, Prussia, and Russia manage to build powerful absolute monarchies, which proved more durable than that of Louis XIV?

- Finally, how did the absolute monarchs' interaction with artists and architects contribute to the splendid achievements of baroque culture?

These are the questions that this chapter will explore.

LORDS AND PEASANTS IN EASTERN EUROPE

When absolute monarchy took shape in eastern Europe in the seventeenth century, it built on social and economic foundations laid between roughly 1400 and 1650. In those years, the princes and the landed nobility of eastern Europe rolled back the gains made by the peasantry during the High Middle Ages and reimposed a harsh serfdom on the rural masses. The nobility also reduced the importance of the towns and the middle classes. This process differed profoundly from developments in western Europe at the same time. In the west, peasants won greater freedom, and the urban capitalistic middle class continued its rise. Thus the east that emerged contrasted sharply with the west —another aspect of the shattered unity of medieval Latin Christendom.

The Medieval Background

Between roughly 1400 and 1650, nobles and rulers re-established serfdom in the eastern lands of Bohemia, Silesia, Hungary, eastern Germany, Poland, Lithuania, and Russia. The east—the land east of the Elbe River in Germany, which historians often call "East Elbia"—gained a certain social and economic unity in the process. But eastern peasants lost their rights and freedoms. They became bound first to the land they worked and then, by degrading obligations, to the lords they served.

This development was a tragic reversal of trends in the High Middle Ages. The period from roughly 1050 to 1300 had been a time of general economic expansion characterized by the growth of trade, towns, and population. Expansion also meant clearing the forests and colonizing the frontier beyond the Elbe River. Anxious to attract German settlers to their sparsely populated lands, the rulers and nobles of eastern Europe had offered potential newcomers economic and legal incentives. Large numbers of incoming settlers obtained land on excellent terms and gained much greater personal freedom. These benefits were also gradually extended to the local Slavic populations, even those of central Russia. Thus by 1300 there had occurred a very general improvement in peasant conditions in eastern Europe. Serfdom all but disappeared. Peasants bargained freely with their landlords and moved about as they pleased. Opportunities and improvements east of the Elbe had a positive impact on western Europe, where the weight of serfdom was also reduced between 1100 and 1300.

After about 1300, however, as Europe's population and economy both declined grievously, mainly because of the Black Death, the east and the west went in different directions. In both east and west there occurred a many-sided landlord reaction, as lords sought to solve their tough economic problems by more heavily exploiting the peasantry. Yet this reaction generally failed in the west. In many western areas by 1500, almost all of the peasants were completely free, and in the rest of western Europe serf obligations had declined greatly. East of the Elbe, however, the landlords won. By 1500 eastern peasants were well on their way to becoming serfs again.

Throughout eastern Europe, as in western Europe, the drop in population and prices in the fourteenth and fifteenth centuries caused severe labor shortages and hard times for the nobles. Yet rather than offer better economic and legal terms to keep old peasants and attract new ones, eastern landlords used political and police power to turn the tables on peasants. They did this in two ways.

First, the lords made their kings and princes issue laws that restricted or eliminated the peasants' precious, time-honored right of free movement. Thus a peasant could no longer leave to take advantage of better opportunities elsewhere without the lord's permission, and the lord had no reason to make such concessions. In Prussian territories by 1500, the law required that runaway peasants be hunted down and returned to their lords; a runaway servant was to be nailed to a post by one ear and given a knife to cut himself loose. Until the middle of the fifteenth century, medieval Russian peasants had been free to move wherever they wished and seek the best landlord. Thereafter this freedom was gradually curtailed, so that by 1497 a Russian peasant had the right to move only during a two-week period after the fall harvest. Eastern peasants were losing their status as free and independent men and women.

Second, lords steadily took more and more of their peasants' land and imposed heavier and heavier labor obligations. Instead of being independent farmers paying reasonable, freely negotiated rents, peasants tended to become forced laborers on the lords' estates. By the early 1500s, lords in many territories could command their peasants to work for them without pay as many as six days a week. A German writer of the mid-sixteenth century described peasants in eastern Prussia who "do not possess the heritage of their holdings and have to serve their master whenever he wants them."[1]

The gradual erosion of the peasantry's economic position was bound up with manipulation of the legal system. The local lord was also the local prosecutor, judge, and jailer. As a matter of course, he ruled in his own favor in disputes with his peasants. There were no independent royal officials to provide justice or uphold the common law.

The Consolidation of Serfdom

Between 1500 and 1650, the social, legal, and economic conditions of peasants in eastern Europe continued to decline. Free peasants lost their freedom and became serfs. In Poland, for example, nobles gained complete control over their peasants in 1574, after which they could legally inflict the death penalty on their serfs whenever they wished. In Prussia a long series of oppressive measures reached their culmination in 1653. Not only were all the old privileges of the lords reaffirmed, but peasants were assumed to be in "hereditary subjugation" to their lords unless they could prove the contrary in the lords' courts, which was practically impossible. Prussian peasants were serfs tied to their lords as well as to the land.

In Russia the right of peasants to move from a given estate was "temporarily" suspended in the 1590s and permanently abolished in 1603. In 1649 a new law code completed the process. At the insistence of the lower nobility, the Russian tsar lifted the nine-year time limit on the recovery of runaways. Henceforth runaway peasants were to be returned to their lords whenever they were caught, as long as they lived. The last small hope of escaping serfdom was gone. Control of serfs was strictly the lords' own business, for the new law code set no limits on the lords' authority over their peasants. Although the political development of the various eastern states differed, the legal re-establishment of permanent hereditary serfdom was the common fate of peasants in the east by the middle of the seventeenth century.

The consolidation of serfdom between 1500 and 1650 was accompanied by the growth of estate agriculture, particularly in Poland and eastern Germany. In the sixteenth century, European economic expansion and population growth resumed after the great declines of the late Middle Ages. Prices for agricultural commodities also rose sharply as gold and silver flowed in from the New World. Thus Polish and German lords had powerful economic incentives to increase the production of their estates. And they did.

Punishing Serfs   This seventeenth-century illustration from Olearius's famous *Travels to Moscovy* suggests what eastern serfdom really meant. The scene is set in eastern Poland. There, according to Olearius, a common command of the lord was, "Beat him till the skin falls from the flesh." *(Source: University of Illinois, Champaign)*

Lords seized more and more peasant land for their own estates and then demanded and received ever more unpaid serf labor on those enlarged estates. Even when the estates were inefficient and technically backward, as they generally were, the great Polish nobles and middle-rank German lords squeezed sizable, cheap, and thus very profitable surpluses out of their impoverished peasants. These surpluses in wheat and timber were easily sold to big foreign merchants, who exported them to the growing cities of the west. The poor east helped feed the much wealthier west.

The re-emergence of serfdom in eastern Europe in the early modern period was clearly a momentous human development, and historians have advanced a variety of explanations for it. As always, some scholars have stressed the economic interpretation. Agricultural depression and population de-

cline in the fourteenth and fifteenth centuries led to a severe labor shortage, they have argued, and thus eastern landlords naturally tied their precious peasants to the land. With the return of prosperity and the development of export markets in the sixteenth century, the landlords finished the job, grabbing the peasants' land and making them work as unpaid serfs on the enlarged estates. This argument by itself is not very convincing, for almost identical economic developments "caused" the opposite result in the west. Indeed, some historians have maintained that labor shortage and subsequent expansion were key factors in the virtual disappearance of western serfdom.

It seems fairly clear, therefore, that political rather than economic factors were crucial in the simultaneous rise of serfdom in the east and decline of serfdom in the west. Specifically, eastern lords enjoyed much greater political power than their western counterparts. In the late Middle Ages, when much of eastern Europe experienced innumerable wars and general political chaos, the noble landlord class greatly increased its political power at the expense of the ruling monarchs. There were, for example, many disputed royal successions, so that weak kings were forced to grant political favors to win the support of the nobility. Thus while strong "new monarchs" were rising in Spain, France, and England and providing effective central government, kings were generally losing power in the east. Such weak kings could not resist the demands of the lords regarding their peasants.

Moreover, most eastern monarchs did not want to resist even if they could. The typical king was only first among equals in the noble class. He, too, thought mainly in private rather than public terms. He, too, wanted to squeeze as much as he could out of his peasants and enlarge his estates. The western concept and reality of sovereignty, as embodied in a king who protected the interests of all his people, was not well developed in eastern Europe before 1650.

The political power of the peasants was also weaker in eastern Europe and declined steadily after about 1400. Although there were occasional bloody peasant uprisings against the oppression of the landlords, they never succeeded. Nor did eastern peasants effectively resist day-by-day infringements on their liberties by their landlords. Part of the reason was that the lords, rather than the kings, ran the courts—one of the important concessions nobles extorted from weak monarchs. It has also been suggested that peasant solidarity was weaker in the east, possibly reflecting the lack of long-established village communities on the eastern frontier.

Finally, with the approval of weak kings, the landlords systematically undermined the medieval privileges of the towns and the power of the urban classes. Instead of selling their products to local merchants in the towns, as required in the Middle Ages, the landlords sold directly to big foreign capitalists. For example, Dutch ships sailed up the rivers of Poland and eastern Germany to the loading docks of the great estates, completely short-circuiting the local towns. Moreover, "town air" no longer "made people free," for the eastern towns lost their medieval right of refuge and were compelled to return runaways to their lords. The population of the towns and the importance of the urban middle classes declined greatly. This development both reflected and promoted the supremacy of noble landlords in most of eastern Europe in the sixteenth century.

THE RISE OF AUSTRIA AND PRUSSIA

Despite the strength of the nobility and the weakness of many monarchs before 1600, strong kings did begin to emerge in many lands in the course of the seventeenth century. War and the threat of war aided rulers greatly in their attempts to build absolute monarchies. There was an endless struggle for power, as eastern rulers not only fought each other but also battled with hordes of Asiatic invaders. In this atmosphere of continuous wartime emergency, monarchs reduced the political power of the landlord nobility. Cautiously leaving the nobles the unchallenged masters of their peasants, the absolutist monarchs of eastern Europe gradually gained and monopolized political power in three key areas. They imposed and collected permanent taxes without consent. They maintained permanent standing armies, which policed their subjects in addition to fighting abroad. And they conducted relations with other states as they pleased.

As with all general historical developments, there were important variations on the absolutist theme in eastern Europe. The royal absolutism created in Prussia was stronger and more effective than that established in Austria. This advantage gave Prussia a thin edge over Austria in the struggle for power in east-central Europe in the eighteenth century. That edge had enormous long-term political significance, for it was a rising Prussia that unified the German people in the nineteenth century and imposed on them a fateful Prussian stamp.

Austria and the Ottoman Turks

Like all the other peoples and rulers of central Europe, the Habsburgs of Austria emerged from the Thirty Years' War (see pages 477–481) impoverished and exhausted. The effort to root out Protestantism in the German lands had failed utterly, and the authority of the Holy Roman Empire and its Habsburg emperors had declined almost to the vanishing point. Yet defeat in central Europe also opened new vistas. The Habsburg monarchs were forced to turn inward and eastward in the attempt to fuse their diverse holdings into a strong unified state.

An important step in this direction had actually been taken in Bohemia during the Thirty Years' War. Protestantism had been strong among the Czechs, a Slavic people concentrated in Bohemia. In 1618 the Czech nobles who controlled the Bohemian Estates—the semiparliamentary body of Bohemia—had risen up against their Habsburg king. Not only was this revolt crushed, but the old Czech nobility was wiped out as well. Those Czech nobles who did not die in 1620 at the Battle of the White Mountain (see page 478), a momentous turning point in Czech history, had their estates confiscated. The Habsburg king, Ferdinand II (r. 1619–1637), then redistributed the Czech lands to a motley band of aristocratic soldiers of fortune, who had nothing in common with the Czech-speaking peasants.

In fact, after 1650, 80 to 90 percent of the Bohemian nobility was of recent foreign origin and owed everything to the Habsburgs. With the help of this new nobility, the Habsburgs established strong direct rule over reconquered Bohemia. The condition of the enserfed peasantry worsened: three days per week of unpaid labor—the *robot*—became the norm, and a quarter of the serfs worked for their lords every day but Sundays and religious holidays. Serfs also paid the taxes, which further strengthened the alliance between the Habsburg monarch and the Bohemian nobility. Protestantism was also stamped out, in the course of which a growing unity of religion was brought about. The reorganization of Bohemia was a giant step toward absolutism.

After the Thirty Years' War, Ferdinand III centralized the government in the hereditary German-speaking provinces, most notably Austria, Styria, and the Tyrol, which formed the second part of the Habsburg holdings. For the first time, Ferdinand III's reign saw the creation of a permanent standing army, which stood ready to put down any internal opposition. The Habsburg monarchy was then ready to turn toward the vast plains of Hungary, which it claimed as the third and largest part of its dominion, in opposition to the Ottoman Turks.

The Ottomans had come out of Anatolia, in present-day Turkey, to create one of history's greatest military empires. At their peak in the middle of the sixteenth century under Suleiman the Magnificent (r. 1520–1566), they ruled the most powerful empire in the world. Their possessions stretched from western Persia across North Africa and up into the heart of central Europe (Map 17.1). Apostles of Islam, the Ottoman Turks were old and determined foes of the Catholic Habsburgs. Their armies had almost captured Vienna in 1529, and for more than 150 years thereafter the Ottomans ruled all of the Balkan territories, almost all of Hungary, and part of southern Russia.

The Ottoman Empire was originally built on a fascinating and very non-European conception of state and society. There was an almost complete absence of private landed property. All the agricultural land of the empire was the personal hereditary property of the sultan, who exploited the land as he saw fit according to Ottoman political theory. There was, therefore, no security of landholding and no hereditary nobility. Everyone was dependent on the sultan and virtually his slave.

Indeed, the top ranks of the bureaucracy were staffed by the sultan's slave corps. Every year the sultan levied a "tax" of one to three thousand male children on the conquered Christian populations in the Balkans. These and other slaves were raised in Turkey as Muslims and trained to fight and to administer. The most talented slaves rose to the top of the bureaucracy; the less fortunate formed the brave and skillful core of the sultan's army, the so-called janissary corps.

As long as the Ottoman Empire expanded, the system worked well. As the sultan won more territory, he could impose his slave tax on larger populations. Moreover, he could amply reward loyal and effective servants by letting them draw a carefully defined income from conquered Christian peasants on a strictly temporary basis. For a long time, Christian peasants in eastern Europe were economically exploited less by the Muslim Turks than by Christian nobles, and they were not forced to convert to Islam. After about 1570, however, the powerful, centralized Ottoman system slowly began to disintegrate as the Turks' western advance was stopped. Temporary Muslim landholders became hard-to-control permanent oppressors. Weak sultans left the glory of the battlefield for the delights of the harem, and the army lost its dedication and failed to keep up with European military advances.

Yet in the late seventeenth century, under vigorous reforming leadership, the Ottoman Empire succeeded in marshaling its forces for one last mighty blow at Christian Europe. After wresting

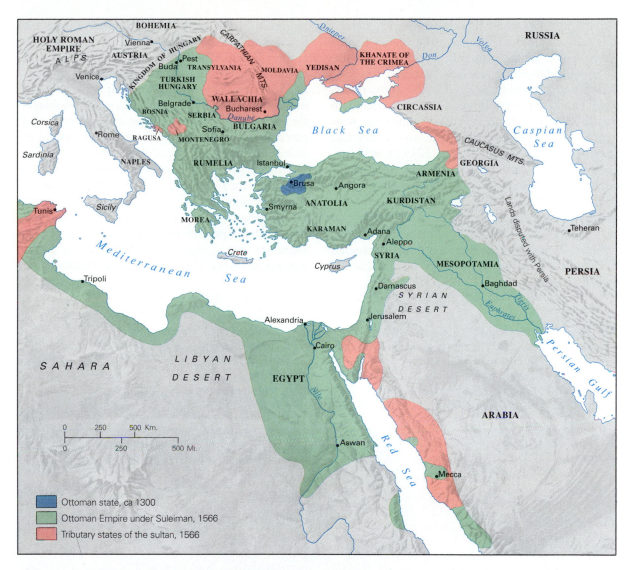

MAP 17.1 The Ottoman Empire at Its Height, 1566 The Ottomans, like their great rivals the Habsburgs, rose to rule a far-flung dynastic empire encompassing many different peoples and ethnic groups. The army and the bureaucracy served to unite the disparate territories into a single state.

territory from Poland, fighting a long inconclusive war with Russia, and establishing an alliance with Louis XIV of France, the Turks turned again on Austria. A huge Turkish army surrounded Vienna and laid siege to it in 1683. But after holding out against great odds for two months, the city was relieved at the last minute by a mixed force of Habsburg, Saxon, Bavarian, and Polish troops, and the Ottomans were forced to retreat. Soon the retreat became a rout. As their Russian and Venetian allies attacked on other fronts, the Habsburgs conquered

all of Hungary and Transylvania (part of present-day Romania) by 1699 (Map 17.2).

The Turkish wars and this great expansion strengthened the Habsburg army and promoted some sense of unity in the Habsburg lands. The Habsburgs moved to centralize their power and make it as absolute as possible. These efforts to create a fully developed, highly centralized, absolutist state were only partly successful.

The Habsburg state was composed of three separate and distinct territories—the old "hereditary provinces" of Austria, the kingdom of Bohemia, and the kingdom of Hungary. These three parts were tied together primarily by their common ruler, the Habsburg monarch. Each part had its own laws and political life, for the three noble-dominated Estates continued to exist, though with reduced powers. The Habsburgs themselves were well aware of the fragility of the union they had forged. In 1713 Charles VI (r. 1711–1740) proclaimed the so-called Pragmatic Sanction, which stated that the Habsburg possessions were never to be divided and were always to be passed intact to a single heir, who might be female since Charles had no sons. Charles spent much of his reign trying to get this principle accepted by the various branches of the Habsburg family, by the three different Es-

tates of the realm, and by the states of Europe. His fears turned out to be well founded.

The Hungarian nobility, despite its reduced strength, effectively thwarted the full development of Habsburg absolutism. Time and again throughout the seventeenth century, Hungarian nobles—the most numerous in Europe, making up 5 to 7 percent of the Hungarian population—rose in revolt against the attempts of Vienna to impose absolute rule. They never triumphed decisively, but neither were they ever crushed and replaced, as the Czech nobility had been in 1620.

Hungarians resisted because many of them were Protestants, especially in the area long ruled by the more tolerant Turks, and they hated the heavy-handed attempts of the conquering Habsburgs to

The Siege of Vienna, 1683   Seeking to tunnel under the city walls and blow them up with mines, a huge Turkish army besieged the Habsburg capital and penetrated the outer fortifications on September 2, 1683. As the Turks launched the final assault on the city ten days later, a relief army led by John Sobieski, the King of Poland (shown in foreground), arrived and delivered a successful surprise attack. This painting shows the battle at its height. *(Source: Heeresgeschichtliches Museum, Vienna)*

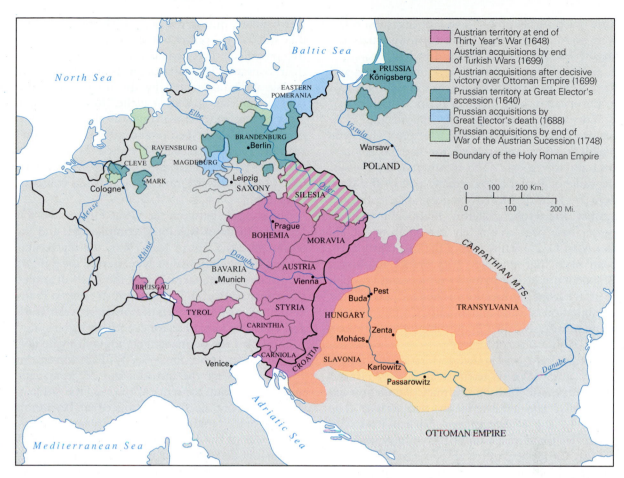

MAP 17.2 The Growth of Austria and Brandenburg-Prussia to 1748 Austria expanded to the southwest into Hungary and Transylvania at the expense of the Ottoman Empire. It was unable to hold the rich German province of Silesia, however, which was conquered by Brandenburg-Prussia.

re-Catholicize everyone. Moreover, the lords of Hungary often found a powerful military ally in Turkey. Finally, the Hungarian nobility, and even part of the Hungarian peasantry, had become attached to a national ideal long before most of the other peoples of eastern Europe. They were determined to maintain as much independence and local control as possible. Thus when the Habsburgs were bogged down in the War of the Spanish Succession (see page 513), the Hungarians rose in one last patriotic rebellion under Prince Francis Rákóczy in 1703. Rákóczy and his forces were eventually defeated, but this time the Habsburgs had to accept a definitive compromise. Charles VI restored many of the traditional privileges of the Hungarian aristocracy in return for Hungarian ac-

ceptance of hereditary Habsburg rule. Thus Hungary, unlike Austria or Bohemia, never came close to being fully integrated into a centralized, absolute Habsburg state.

Prussia in the Seventeenth Century

After 1400 the status of east German peasants declined steadily; their serfdom was formally spelled out in the early seventeenth century. While the local princes lost political power and influence, a revitalized landed nobility became the undisputed ruling class. The Hohenzollern family, which ruled through its senior and junior branches as the electors of Brandenburg and the dukes of Prussia, had little real princely power. The Hohenzollern rulers were nothing more than the first among equals, the largest landowners in a landlord society.

Nothing suggested that the Hohenzollerns and their territories would ever play an important role in European or even German affairs. The elector of Brandenburg's right to help choose the Holy Roman emperor with six other electors was of little practical value, and the elector had no military strength whatsoever. The territory of his cousin, the duke of Prussia, was actually part of the kingdom of Poland. Moreover, geography conspired against the Hohenzollerns. Brandenburg, their power base, was completely cut off from the sea (see Map 17.2). A tiny part of the vast north European plain that stretches from France to Russia, Brandenburg lacked natural frontiers and lay open to attack from all directions. The land was poor, a combination of sand and swamp. Contemporaries contemptuously called Brandenburg the "sand-box of the Holy Roman Empire."[2]

Brandenburg was a helpless spectator in the Thirty Years' War, its territory alternately ravaged by Swedish and Habsburg armies. Population fell drastically, and many villages disappeared. The power of the Hohenzollerns reached its lowest point. Yet the devastation of the country prepared the way for Hohenzollern absolutism, because foreign armies dramatically weakened the political power of the Estates—the representative assemblies of the realm. This weakening of the Estates helped the very talented young elector Frederick William (r. 1640–1688), later known as the "Great Elector," to ride roughshod over traditional parliamentary liberties and to take a giant step toward royal absolutism. This constitutional struggle, often unjustly neglected by historians, was the most crucial in Prussian history for hundreds of years, until that of the 1860s.

When he came to power in 1640, the twenty-year-old Great Elector was determined to unify his three quite separate provinces and to add to them by diplomacy and war. These provinces were Brandenburg itself, the area around Berlin; Prussia, inherited in 1618 when the junior branch of the Hohenzollern family died out; and completely separate, scattered holdings along the Rhine in western Germany, inherited in 1614 (see Map 17.2). Each of the three provinces was inhabited by Germans; but each had its own Estates, whose power had increased until about 1600 as the power of the rulers declined. Although the Estates had not

met regularly during the chaotic Thirty Years' War, they still had the power of the purse in their respective provinces. Taxes could not be levied without their consent. The Estates of Brandenburg and Prussia were dominated by the nobility and the landowning classes, known as the "Junkers." But it must be remembered that this was also true of the English Parliament before and after the civil war. Had the Estates successfully resisted the absolutist demands of the Great Elector, they, too, might have evolved toward more broadly based constitutionalism.

The struggle between the Great Elector and the provincial Estates was long, complicated, and intense. After the Thirty Years' War, the representatives of the nobility zealously reasserted the right of the Estates to vote taxes, a right the Swedish armies of occupation had simply ignored. Yet first in Brandenburg in 1653 and then in Prussia between 1661 and 1663, the Great Elector eventually had his way.

To pay for the permanent standing army he first established in 1660, Frederick William forced the Estates to accept the introduction of permanent taxation without consent. Moreover, the soldiers doubled as tax collectors and policemen, becoming the core of the rapidly expanding state bureaucracy. The power of the Estates declined rapidly thereafter, for the Great Elector had both financial independence and superior force. He turned the screws of taxation: the state's total revenue tripled during his reign. The size of the army leaped about tenfold. In 1688 a population of one million was supporting a peacetime standing army of thirty thousand. Many of the soldiers were French Huguenot immigrants, whom the Great Elector welcomed as the talented, hard-working citizens they were.

In accounting for the Great Elector's fateful triumph, two factors appear central. As in the formation of every absolutist state, war was a decisive factor. The ongoing struggle between Sweden and Poland for control of the Baltic after 1648 and the wars of Louis XIV in western Europe created an atmosphere of permanent crisis. The wild Tartars of southern Russia swept through Prussia in the winter of 1656 to 1657, killing and carrying off as slaves more than fifty thousand people, according to an old estimate. This invasion softened up the Estates and strengthened the urgency of the elector's demands for more money for more soldiers. It was no accident that, except for commercially minded Holland, constitutionalism won out only in England, the only major country to escape devastating foreign invasions in the seventeenth century.

Second, the nobility had long dominated the government through the Estates, but only for its own narrow self-interest. When the crunch came, the Prussian nobles proved unwilling to join the representatives of the towns in a consistent common front against royal pretensions. The nobility was all too concerned with its own rights and privileges, especially its freedom from taxation and its unlimited control over the peasants. When, therefore, the Great Elector reconfirmed these privileges in 1653 and after, even while reducing the political power of the Estates, the nobility growled but did not bite. It accepted a compromise whereby the bulk of the new taxes fell on towns, and royal au-

thority stopped at the landlords' gates. The elector could and did use naked force to break the liberties of the towns. The main leader of the urban opposition in the key city of Königsberg, for example, was simply arrested and imprisoned for life without trial.

The Consolidation of Prussian Absolutism

By the time of his death in 1688, the Great Elector had created a single state out of scattered principalities. But his new creation was still small and fragile. All the leading states of Europe had many more people—France with twenty million was fully twenty times as populous—and strong monarchy

Molding the Prussian Spirit   Discipline was strict and punishment brutal in the Prussian army. This scene, from an eighteenth-century book used to teach school children, shows one soldier being flogged while another is being beaten with canes as he walks between rows of troops. The officer on horseback proudly commands. *(Source: University of Illinois, Champaign)*

A Prussian Giant Grenadier Frederick William I wanted tall, handsome soldiers. He dressed them in tight bright uniforms to distinguish them from the peasant population from which most soldiers came. He also ordered several portraits of his favorites from his court painter, J. C. Merk. Grenadiers wore the distinctive mitre cap instead of an ordinary hat so that they could hurl their heavy hand grenades unimpeded by a broad brim. *(Source: Copyright reserved to Her Majesty Queen Elizabeth II)*

was still a novelty. Moreover, the Great Elector's successor, Elector Frederick III, "the Ostentatious" (r. 1688–1713), was weak of body and mind.

Like so many of the small princes of Germany and Italy at the time, Frederick III imitated Louis XIV in every possible way. He built his own very expensive version of Versailles. He surrounded himself with cultivated artists and musicians and basked in the praise of toadies and sycophants. His only real political accomplishment was to gain the title of king from the Holy Roman emperor, a Habsburg, in return for military aid in the War of the Spanish Succession, and in 1701 he was crowned King Frederick I.

This tendency toward luxury-loving, happy, and harmless petty tyranny was completely reversed by Frederick William I, "the Soldiers' King" (r. 1713–1740). A crude, dangerous psychoneurotic, Frederick William I was nevertheless the most talented reformer ever produced by the Hohenzollern family. It was he who truly established Prussian absolutism and gave it its unique character. It was he who created the the best army in Europe, for its size, and who infused military values into a whole society. In the words of a leading historian of Prussia:

For a whole generation, the Hohenzollern subjects were victimized by a royal bully, imbued with an obsessive bent for military organization and military scales of value. This left a deep mark upon the institutions of Prussiandom and upon the molding of the "Prussian spirit."[3]

Frederick William's attachment to the army and military life was intensely emotional. He had, for example, a bizarre, almost pathological love for tall soldiers, whom he credited with superior strength and endurance. Austere and always faithful to his wife, he confided to the French ambassador: "The most beautiful girl or woman in the world would be a matter of indifference to me, but tall soldiers —they are my weakness." Like some fanatical modern-day basketball coach in search of a championship team, he sent his agents throughout both Prussia and all of Europe, tricking, buying, and kidnaping top recruits. Neighboring princes sent him their giants as gifts to win his gratitude. Prussian mothers told their sons: "Stop growing or the recruiting agents will get you."[4]

Profoundly military in temperament, Frederick William always wore an army uniform, and he lived the highly disciplined life of the professional soldier. He began his work by five or six in the morning; at ten he almost always went to the parade ground to drill or inspect his troops. A man of violent temper, Frederick William personally punished the most minor infractions on the spot: a missing button off a soldier's coat quickly provoked a savage beating with his heavy walking stick.

Frederick William's love of the army was also based on a hardheaded conception of the struggle for power and a dog-eat-dog view of international politics. Even before ascending the throne, he bitterly criticized his father's ministers: "They say that they will obtain land and power for the king with the pen; but I say it can be done only with the sword." Years later he summed up his life's philosophy in his instructions to his son: "A formidable army and a war chest large enough to make this army mobile in times of need can create great respect for you in the world, so that you can speak a word like the other powers."[5] This unshakable belief that the welfare of king and state depended on the army above all else reinforced Frederick William's passion for playing soldier.

The cult of military power provided the rationale for a great expansion of royal absolutism. As the ruthless king himself put it: "I must be served with life and limb, with house and wealth, with honour and conscience, everything must be committed except eternal salvation—that belongs to God, but all else is mine."[6] To make good these extraordinary demands, Frederick William created a strong centralized bureaucracy. More commoners probably rose to top positions in the civil government than at any other time in Prussia's history. The last traces of the parliamentary Estates and local self-government vanished.

The king's grab for power brought him into considerable conflict with the noble landowners, the Junkers. In his early years, he even threatened to destroy them; yet, in the end, the Prussian nobility was not destroyed but enlisted—into the army. Responding to a combination of threats and opportunities, the Junkers became the officer caste. By 1739 all but 5 of 245 officers with the rank of major or above were aristocrats, and most of them were native Prussians. A new compromise had been worked out, whereby the proud nobility imperiously commanded the peasantry in the army as well as on its estates.

Coarse and crude, penny-pinching and hardworking, Frederick William achieved results.

Above all, he built a first-rate army on the basis of third-rate resources. The standing army increased from 38,000 to 83,000 during his reign. Prussia, twelfth in Europe in population, had the fourth largest army by 1740. Only the much more populous states of France, Russia, and Austria had larger forces, and even France's army was only twice as large as Prussia's. Moreover, soldier for soldier, the Prussian army became the best in Europe, astonishing foreign observers with its precision, skill, and discipline. For the next two hundred years, Prussia and then Prussianized Germany would almost always win the crucial military battles.

Frederick William and his ministers also built an exceptionally honest and conscientious bureaucracy, which not only administered the country but tried with some success to develop it economically. Finally, like the miser he was, living very frugally off the income of his own landholdings, the king loved his "blue boys" so much that he hated to "spend" them. This most militaristic of kings was, paradoxically, almost always at peace.

Nevertheless, the Prussian people paid a heavy and lasting price for the obsessions of the royal drillmaster. Civil society became rigid and highly disciplined. Prussia became the "Sparta of the North"; unquestioning obedience was the highest virtue. As a Prussian minister later summed up, "To keep quiet is the first civic duty."[7] Thus the policies of Frederick William I combined with harsh peasant bondage and Junker tyranny to lay the foundations for probably the most militaristic country of modern times.

THE DEVELOPMENT OF RUSSIA

One of the favorite parlor games of nineteenth-century Russian (and non-Russian) intellectuals was debating whether Russia was a Western and European or a non-Western Asiatic society. This question was particularly fascinating because it was unanswerable. To this day Russia differs fundamentally from the West in some basic ways, though Russian history has paralleled that of the West in other ways. A good case can be made for either position: thus the hypnotic attraction of Russian history.

The differences between Russia and the West were particularly striking before 1700, when

NORWAY

SWEDEN

FINLAND

Barents Sea

Arkhangelsk

L. Onega

L. Ladoga

Stockholm

Helsinki

St. Petersburg

ESTONIA

Novgorod

NOVGOROD

Pskov

Riga

LATVIA

Tver

Volga

RUSSIANS

Nizhni Novgorod

Vladimir

×Kazan

LITHUANIA

Danzig

Königsberg

Vilna

GREAT

Moscow

Smolensk

Minsk

Ryazan

URAL MTS.

SIBERIA

Ob

Kama

Samara

COSSACKS

Ural

Uralsk

KIRGHIZ

POLAND

Warsaw

Brest

Pinsk

Chernigov

Kiev

UKRAINIANS

×Poltava

COSSACKS

Saratov

Volga

Don

Dnieper

Baltic Sea

HUNGARY

CARPATHIAN MTS.

BESSARABIA

WALLACHIA

Belgrade

Tsaritsyn

(New) Saray

Saray

Astrakhan×

Rostov

CRIMEA

Black Sea

Constantinople

OTTOMAN EMPIRE

Ankara

Athens

Tiflis

GEORGIA

ARMENIA

Aral Sea

Caspian Sea

	Principality of Moscow, ca 1300
	Acquisitions by Ivan III's accession (1462)
	Acquisitions under Ivan III (1462–1505)
	Acquisitions by death of Ivan the Terrible (1584)
	Acquisitions by Peter the Great's accession (1689)
	Acquisitions under Peter the Great (1689–1725)
×	Major battles

0   200   400 Km.

0   200   400 Mi.

Russia's overall development began to draw progressively closer to that of its Western neighbors. These early differences and Russia's long isolation from Europe explain why little has so far been said here about Russia. Yet it is impossible to understand how Russia has increasingly influenced and been influenced by western European civilization since roughly the late seventeenth century without looking at the course of early Russian history. Such a brief survey will also help explain how, when absolute monarchy finally and decisively triumphed under the rough guidance of Peter the Great in the early eighteenth century, it was a quite different type of absolute monarchy from that of France or even Prussia.

The Vikings and the Kievan Principality

In antiquity the Slavs lived as a single people in central Europe. With the start of the mass migrations of the late Roman Empire, the Slavs moved in different directions and split into three groups. Between the fifth and ninth centuries, the eastern Slavs, from whom the Ukrainians, the Russians, and the White Russians descend, moved into the vast and practically uninhabited area of present-day European Russia and the Ukraine (Map 17.3).

This enormous area consisted of an immense virgin forest to the north, where most of the eastern Slavs settled, and an endless prairie grassland to the south. Probably organized as tribal communities, the eastern Slavs, like many North American pioneers much later, lived off the great abundance of wild game and a crude "slash and burn" agriculture. After clearing a piece of the forest to build log cabins, they burned the stumps and brush. The ashes left a rich deposit of potash and lime, and the land gave several good crops before it was exhausted. The people then moved on to another untouched area and repeated the process.

In the ninth century, the Vikings, those fearless warriors from Scandinavia, appeared in the lands of the eastern Slavs. Called "Varangians" in the old

MAP 17.3 The Expansion of Russia to 1725 After the disintegration of the Kievan state and the Mongol conquest, the princes of Moscow and their descendants gradually extended their rule over an enormous territory.

Russian chronicles, the Vikings were interested primarily in international trade, and the opportunities were good, since the Muslim conquests of the eighth century had greatly reduced Christian trade in the Mediterranean. Moving up and down the rivers, the Vikings soon linked Scandinavia and northern Europe to the Black Sea and to the Byzantine Empire with its capital at Constantinople. They built a few strategic forts along the rivers, from which they raided the neighboring Slavic tribes and collected tribute. Slaves were the most important article of tribute, and *Slav* even became the word for "slave" in several European languages.

In order to increase and protect their international commerce, the Vikings declared themselves the rulers of the eastern Slavs. According to tradition, the semilegendary chieftain Ruirik founded the princely dynasty about 860. In any event, the Varangian ruler Oleg (r. 878–912) established his residence at Kiev. He and his successors ruled over a loosely united confederation of Slavic territories—the Kievan state—until 1054. The Viking prince and his clansmen quickly became assimilated into the Slavic population, taking local wives and emerging as the noble class.

Assimilation and loss of Scandinavian ethnic identity was speeded up by the conversion of the Vikings and local Slavs to Eastern Orthodox Christianity by missionaries from the Byzantine Empire. The written language of these missionaries, an early form of Slavic now known as Old Church Slavonic, was subsequently used in all religious and nonreligious documents in the Kievan principality. Thus the rapidly Slavified Vikings left two important legacies for the future. They created a loose unification of Slavic territories under a single ruling prince and a single ruling dynasty. And they imposed a basic religious unity by accepting Orthodox Christianity, as opposed to Roman Catholicism, for themselves and the eastern Slavs.

Even at its height under Great Prince Iaroslav the Wise (r. 1019–1054), the unity of the Kievan principality was extremely tenuous. Trade, rather than government, was the main concern of the rulers. Moreover, the Slavified Vikings failed to find a way of peacefully transferring power from one generation to the next. In medieval western Europe this fundamental problem of government was increasingly resolved by resort to the principle of primogeniture: the king's eldest son received the crown as his rightful inheritance when his father died. Civil war was thus averted; order was preserved. In early Kiev, however, there were apparently no fixed rules, and much strife accompanied each succession.

Possibly to avoid such chaos, before his death in 1054 Great Prince Iaroslav divided the Kievan principality among his five sons, who in turn divided their properties when they died. Between 1054 and 1237, Kiev disintegrated into more and more competing units, each ruled by a prince claiming to be a descendant of Ruirik. Even when only one prince was claiming to be the great prince, the whole situation was very unsettled.

The princes divided their land like private property because they thought of it as private property. A given prince owned a certain number of farms or landed estates and had them worked directly by his people, mainly slaves, called *kholops* in Russian. Outside of these estates, which constituted the princely domain, the prince exercised only very limited authority in his principality. Excluding the clergy, two kinds of people lived there: the noble *boyars* and the commoner peasants.

The boyars were the descendants of the original Viking warriors, and they also held their lands as free and clear private property. Although the boyars normally fought in princely armies, the customary law declared that they could serve any prince they wished. The ordinary peasants were also truly free. The peasants could move at will wherever opportunities were greatest. In the touching phrase of the times, theirs was "a clean road, without boundaries."[8] In short, fragmented princely power, private property, and personal freedom all went together.

The Mongol Yoke and the Rise of Moscow

The eastern Slavs, like the Germans and the Italians, might have emerged from the Middle Ages weak and politically divided, had it not been for a development of extraordinary importance—the Mongol conquest of the Kievan state. Wild nomadic tribes from present-day Mongolia, the Mongols were temporarily unified in the thirteenth century by Jenghiz Khan (1162–1227), one of history's greatest conquerors. In five years his armies subdued all of China. His successors then wheeled westward, smashing everything in their path and reaching the plains of Hungary victorious before they pulled back in 1242. The Mongol army—the Golden Horde—was savage in the extreme, often

slaughtering the entire populations of cities before burning them to the ground. En route to Mongolia in 1245, Archbishop John of Plano Carpini, the famous papal ambassador to Mongolia, passed through Kiev, which the Mongols had sacked in 1242, and wrote an unforgettable eyewitness account:

The Mongols went against Russia and enacted a great massacre in the Russian land. They destroyed towns and fortresses and killed people. They besieged Kiev which had been the capital of Russia, and after a long siege they took it and killed the inhabitants of the city. For this reason, when we passed through that land, we found lying in the field countless heads and bones of dead people; for this city had been extremely large and very populous, whereas now it has been reduced to nothing: barely two hundred houses stand there, and those people are held in the harshest slavery.[9]

Having devastated and conquered, the Mongols ruled the eastern Slavs for more than two hundred years. They built their capital of Saray on the lower Volga (see Map 17.3). They forced all the bickering Slavic princes to submit to their rule and to give them tribute and slaves. If the conquered peoples rebelled, the Mongols were quick to punish with death and destruction. Thus the Mongols unified the eastern Slavs, for the Mongol khan was acknowledged by all as the supreme ruler.

The Mongol unification completely changed the internal political situation. Although the Mongols conquered, they were quite willing to use local princes as their obedient servants and tax collectors. Therefore, they did not abolish the title of great prince, bestowing it instead on the prince who served them best and paid them most handsomely.

Beginning with Alexander Nevsky in 1252, the previously insignificant princes of Moscow became particularly adept at serving the Mongols. They loyally put down popular uprisings and collected the khan's harsh taxes. By way of reward, the princes of Moscow emerged as hereditary great princes. Eventually the Muscovite princes were able to destroy their princely rivals and even to replace the khan as supreme ruler. In this complex process, two princes of Moscow after Alexander Nevsky— Ivan I and Ivan III—were especially noteworthy.

Ivan I (r. 1328–1341) was popularly known as Ivan the Moneybag. A bit like Frederick William of Prussia, he was extremely stingy and built up a large personal fortune. This enabled him to buy more property and to increase his influence by loaning money to less frugal princes to pay their Mongol taxes. Ivan's most serious rival was the prince of Tver, whom the Mongols at one point appointed as great prince.

In 1327 the population of Tver revolted against Mongol oppression, and the prince of Tver joined his people. Ivan immediately went to the Mongol capital of Saray, where he was appointed commander of a large Russian-Mongol army, which then laid waste to Tver and its lands. For this proof of devotion, the Mongols made Ivan the general tax collector for all the Slavic lands they had subjugated and named him great prince. Ivan also convinced the metropolitan of Kiev, the leading churchman of all eastern Slavs, to settle in Moscow; Ivan I thus gained greater prestige. The church gained a powerful advocate before the khan.

In the next hundred-odd years, in the course of innumerable wars and intrigues, the great princes of Moscow significantly increased their holdings. Then, in the reign of Ivan III (r. 1462–1505), the long process was largely completed. After purchasing Rostov, Ivan conquered and annexed other principalities, of which Novgorod with its lands extending as far as the Baltic Sea was most crucial (see Map 17.3). Thus, more than four hundred years after Iaroslav the Wise had divided the embryonic Kievan state, the princes of Moscow defeated all the rival branches of the house of Ruirik to win complete princely authority.

Another dimension to princely power developed. Not only was the prince of Moscow the *unique* ruler, he was the *absolute* ruler, the autocrat, the *tsar*—the Slavic contraction for "caesar," with all its connotations. This imperious conception of absolute power is expressed in a famous letter from the aging Ivan III to the Holy Roman Emperor Frederick III (r. 1440–1493). Frederick had offered Ivan the title of king in conjunction with the marriage of his daughter to Ivan's nephew. Ivan proudly refused:

We by the grace of God have been sovereigns over our domains from the beginning, from our first forebears, and our right we hold from God, as did our forebears. . . . As in the past we have never needed appointment from anyone, so now do we not desire it.[10]

The Muscovite idea of absolute authority was powerfully reinforced by two developments. First,

about 1480 Ivan III stopped acknowledging the khan as his supreme ruler. There is good evidence to suggest that Ivan and his successors saw themselves as khans. Certainly they assimilated the Mongol concept of kingship as the exercise of unrestrained and unpredictable power.

Second, after the fall of Constantinople to the Turks in 1453, the tsars saw themselves as the heirs of both the caesars and Orthodox Christianity, the one true faith. All the other kings of Europe were heretics: only the tsars were rightful and holy rulers. This idea was promoted by Orthodox churchmen, who spoke of "holy Russia" as the "Third Rome." As the monk Pilotheus stated: "Two Romes have fallen, but the third stands, and a fourth there will not be."[11] Ivan's marriage to the daughter of the last Byzantine emperor further enhanced the aura of an imperial inheritance for Moscow. Worthy successor to the mighty khan and the true Christian emperor, the Muscovite tsar was a king above all others.

Tsar and People to 1689

By 1505 the great prince of Moscow, the tsar, had emerged as the single hereditary ruler of "all the Russias"—all the lands of the eastern Slavs—and he was claiming unrestricted power as his God-given right. In effect, the tsar was demanding the same kind of total authority over all his subjects that the princely descendants of Ruirik had long exercised over their slaves on their own landed estates. This was an extremely radical demand.

As peasants had begun losing their freedom of movement in the fifteenth century, so had the noble boyars begun to lose power and influence. Ivan III pioneered in this regard, as in so many others. When Ivan conquered the principality of Novgorod in the 1480s, he confiscated fully 80 percent of the land, executing the previous owners or resettling them nearer Moscow. He then kept more than half of the confiscated land for himself and distributed the remainder to members of a newly emerging service nobility. The boyars had previously held their land as hereditary private property and been free to serve the prince of their choosing. The new service nobility held the tsar's land on the explicit condition that they serve in the tsar's army. Moreover, Ivan III began to require boyars outside of Novgorod to serve him if they wished to retain their lands. Since there were no

St. Basil's Cathedral in Moscow, with its sloping roofs and colorful onion-shaped domes, is a striking example of powerful Byzantine influences on Russian culture. According to tradition, an enchanted Ivan the Terrible blinded the cathedral's architects to ensure that they would never duplicate their fantastic achievement, which still dazzles the beholder in today's Red Square. *(Source: George Holton/Photo Researchers)*

competing princes left to turn to, the boyars had to yield.

The rise of the new service nobility accelerated under Ivan IV (r. 1533–1584), the famous Ivan the Terrible. Having ascended the throne at age three, Ivan suffered insults and neglect at the hands of the haughty boyars after his mother mysteriously died, possibly poisoned, when he was just eight. At age sixteen he suddenly pushed aside his hated boyar advisers. In an awe-inspiring ceremony, complete with gold coins pouring down on his head, he majestically crowned himself and officially took the august title of tsar for the first time.

Selecting the beautiful and kind Anastasia of the popular Romanov family for his wife and queen, the young tsar soon declared war on the remnants of Mongol power. He defeated the faltering khanates of Kazan and Astrakhan between 1552 and 1556, adding vast new territories to Russia. In the course of these wars, Ivan virtually abolished the old distinction between hereditary boyar private property and land granted temporarily for service. All nobles, old and new, had to serve the tsar in order to hold any land.

The process of transforming the entire nobility into a service nobility was completed in the second part of Ivan the Terrible's reign. In 1557 Ivan turned westward, and for the next twenty-five years Muscovy waged an exhausting, unsuccessful war primarily with the large Polish-Lithuanian state, which controlled not only Poland but much of the Ukraine in the sixteenth century. Quarreling with the boyars over the war and blaming them for the sudden death of his beloved Anastasia in 1560, the increasingly cruel and demented Ivan turned to strike down all who stood in his way.

Above all, he struck down the ancient Muscovite boyars with a reign of terror. Leading boyars, their relatives, and even their peasants and servants were executed en masse by a special corps of unquestioning servants. Dressed in black and riding black horses, they were forerunners of the modern dictator's secret police. Large estates were confiscated, broken up, and reapportioned to the lower service nobility. The great boyar families were severely reduced. The newer, poorer, more nearly equal service nobility, still less than half a percent of the total population, was totally dependent on the autocrat.

Ivan also took giant strides toward making all commoners servants of the tsar. His endless wars and demonic purges left much of central Russia depopulated. It grew increasingly difficult for the lower service nobility to squeeze a living for themselves out of the peasants left on their landholdings. As the service nobles demanded more from the remaining peasants, more and more peasants fled toward the wild, recently conquered territories to the east and south. There they formed free groups and outlaw armies known as "Cossacks." The Cossacks maintained a precarious independence beyond the reach of the oppressive landholders and the tsar's hated officials. The solution to this problem was to complete the tying of the peasants to the land, making them serfs perpetually bound to serve the noble landholders, who were bound in turn to serve the tsar.

In the time of Ivan the Terrible, urban traders and artisans were also bound to their towns and jobs, so that the tsar could tax them more heavily. Ivan assumed that the tsar owned Russia's trade and industry, just as he owned all the land. In the course of the sixteenth and seventeenth centuries, the tsars therefore took over the mines and industries and monopolized the country's important commercial activities. The urban classes had no security in their work or property, and even the wealthiest merchants were basically dependent agents of the tsar. If a new commercial activity became profitable, it was often taken over by the tsar and made a royal monopoly. This royal monopolization was in sharp contrast to developments in western Europe, where the capitalist middle classes were gaining strength and security in their private property. The tsar's service obligations checked the growth of the Russian middle classes, just as they led to decline of the boyars, rise of the lower nobility, and the final enserfment of the peasants.

Ivan the Terrible's system of autocracy and compulsory service struck foreign observers forcibly. Sigismund Herberstein, a German traveler to Russia, wrote in 1571: "All the people consider themselves to be *kholops*, that is slaves of their Prince." At the same time, Jean Bodin, the French thinker who did so much to develop the modern concept of sovereignty, concluded that Russia's political system was fundamentally different from those of all other European monarchies and comparable only to that of the Turkish empire. In both Turkey and Russia, as in other parts of Asia and Africa, "the prince is become lord of the goods and persons of his subjects . . . governing them as a master of a family does his slaves."[12] The Mongol inheritance weighed heavily on Russia.

Ivan the Terrible Ivan IV, the first to take the title Tsar of Russia, executed many Muscovite boyars and their peasants and servants. His ownership of all the land, trade, and industry restricted economic development. *(Source: National Museum, Copenhagen, Denmark)*

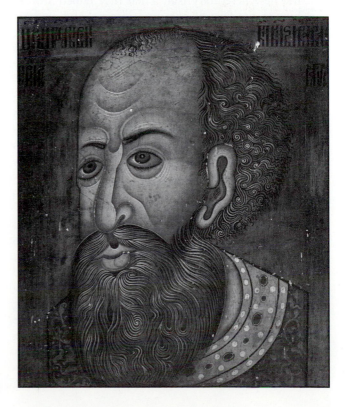

slaves."[12] The Mongol inheritance weighed heavily on Russia.

As has so often occurred in Russia, the death of an iron-fisted tyrant—in this case, Ivan the Terrible in 1584—ushered in an era of confusion and violent struggles for power. Events were particularly chaotic after Ivan's son Theodore died in 1598 without an heir. The years 1598 to 1613 are aptly called the "Time of Troubles."

The close relatives of the deceased tsar intrigued against and murdered each other, alternately fighting and welcoming the invading Swedes and Poles, who even occupied Moscow. Most serious for the cause of autocracy, there was a great social upheaval as Cossack bands marched northward, rallying peasants and slaughtering nobles and officials. The mass of Cossacks and peasants called for the "true tsar," who would restore their freedom of movement and allow them to farm for whomever they pleased, who would reduce their heavy taxes and lighten the yoke imposed by the landlords.

This social explosion from below, which combined with a belated surge of patriotic opposition to Polish invaders, brought the nobles, big and small, to their senses. In 1613 they elected Ivan's sixteen-year-old grandnephew, Michael Romanov, the new hereditary tsar. Then they rallied around him in the face of common internal and external threats. Michael's election was a real restoration, and his reign saw the gradual re-establishment of tsarist autocracy. Michael was understandably more kindly disposed toward the supportive nobility than toward the sullen peasants. Thus, while peasants were completely enserfed in 1649, Ivan's heavy military obligations on the nobility were relaxed considerably. In the long reign of Michael's successor, the pious Alexis (r. 1645–1676), this asymmetry of obligations was accentuated. The nobility gained more exemptions from military service, while the peasants were further ground down.

The result was a second round of mass upheaval and protest. In the later seventeenth century, the unity of the Russian Orthodox church was torn apart by a great split. The surface question was the religious reforms introduced in 1652 by the patriarch Nikon, a dogmatic purist who wished to bring "corrupted" Russian practices of worship into line with the Greek Orthodox model. The self-serving church hierarchy quickly went along, but the intensely religious common people resisted. They saw Nikon as the anti-Christ, who was stripping

them of the only thing they had—the true religion of "holy Russia."

Great numbers left the church and formed illegal communities of "Old Believers," who were hunted down and persecuted. As many as twenty thousand people burned themselves alive, singing the "hallelujah" in their chants three times rather than twice as Nikon had demanded and crossing themselves in the old style, with two rather than three fingers, as they went down in flames. After the great split, the Russian masses were alienated from the established church, which became totally dependent on the state for its authority.

Again the Cossacks revolted against the state, which was doggedly trying to catch up with them on the frontiers and reduce them to serfdom. Under Stenka Razin they moved up the Volga River in 1670 and 1671, attracting a great undisciplined army of peasants, murdering landlords and high church officials, and proclaiming freedom from oppression. This rebellion to overthrow the established order was finally defeated by the government. In response, the thoroughly scared upper classes tightened the screws of serfdom even further. Holding down the peasants, and thereby maintaining the tsar, became almost the principal obligation of the nobility until 1689.

The Reforms of Peter the Great

It is now possible to understand the reforms of Peter the Great (r. 1682–1725) and his kind of monarchial absolutism. Contrary to some historians' assertions, Peter was interested primarily in military power and not in some grandiose westernization plan. A giant for his time, at six feet seven inches, and possessing enormous energy and will power, Peter was determined to redress the defeats the tsar's armies had occasionally suffered in their wars with Poland and Sweden since the time of Ivan the Terrible.

To be sure, these western foes had never seriously threatened the existence of the tsar's vast kingdom, except perhaps when they had added to the confusion of civil war and domestic social upheaval in the Time of Troubles. Russia had even gained a large mass of the Ukraine from the kingdom of Poland in 1667 (see Map 17.3). And tsarist forces had completed the conquest of the primitive tribes of all Siberia in the seventeenth century. Muscovy, which had been as large as all the rest of Europe combined in 1600, was three times as large as the rest of Europe in 1682 and by far the largest kingdom on earth. But territorial expansion was the soul of tsardom. Therefore, it was natural that the seventeen-year-old Peter would seek further gains when he overturned the regency in 1689 and assumed personal rule. The thirty-six years of that rule knew only one year of peace.

When Peter took control in 1689, the heart of his army still consisted of cavalry made up of boyars and service nobility. Foot soldiers played a secondary role, and the whole army served on a part-time basis. The Russian army was lagging behind the professional standing armies being formed in Europe in the seventeenth century. The core of such armies was a highly disciplined infantry—an infantry that fired and refired rifles as it fearlessly advanced, until it charged with bayonets fixed. Such a large, permanent army was enormously expensive and could be created only at the cost of great sacrifice. Given the desire to conquer more territory, Peter's military problem was serious.

Peter's solution was, in essence, to tighten up Muscovy's old service system and really make it work. He put the nobility back in harness with a vengeance. Every nobleman, great or small, was once again required to serve in the army or in the civil administration—for life. Since a more modern army and government required skilled technicians and experts, Peter created schools and even universities. One of his most hated reforms required five years of compulsory education away from home for every young nobleman. Peter established an interlocking military-civilian bureaucracy with fourteen ranks, and he decreed that all must start at the bottom and work toward the top. Some people of non-noble origins rose to high positions in the embryonic meritocracy. Peter searched out talented foreigners—twice in his reign he went abroad to study and observe—and placed them in his service. These measures combined to make the army and government more powerful and efficient.

Peter also greatly increased the service requirements of the commoners. He established a regular standing army of more than 200,000 soldiers, made up mainly of peasants commanded by officers from the nobility. In addition, special forces of Cossacks and foreigners numbered more than 100,000. The departure of a drafted peasant boy was celebrated by his family and village almost like

"The Bronze Horseman" This equestrian masterpiece of Peter the Great, finished for Catherine the Great in 1783, dominates the center of St. Petersburg (modern Leningrad). The French sculptor Falconnet has captured the tsar's enormous energy, power, and determination. *(Source: Courtesy of The Conway Library, Courtauld Institute of Art)*

a funeral, as indeed it was, since the recruit was drafted for life. The peasantry also served with its taxes, which increased threefold during Peter's reign, as people—"souls"—replaced land as the primary unit of taxation. Serfs were also arbitrarily assigned to work in the growing number of factories and mines. Most of these industrial enterprises were directly or indirectly owned by the state, and they were worked almost exclusively for the military. In general, Russian serfdom became more oppressive under the reforming tsar.

The constant warfare of Peter's reign consumed 80 to 85 percent of all revenues but brought only modest territorial expansion. Yet the Great Northern War with Sweden, which lasted from 1700 to 1721, was crowned in the end by Russian victory. After initial losses, Peter's new war machine crushed the smaller army of Sweden's Charles XII in the Ukraine at Poltava in 1709, one of the most significant battles in Russian history. Sweden never really regained the offensive, and Russia eventually annexed Estonia and much of present-day Latvia (see Map 17.3), lands that had never before been under Russian rule. Russia became the dominant power on the Baltic Sea and very much a European Great Power. If victory or defeat is the ultimate historical criterion, Peter's reforms were a success.

There were other important consequences of Peter's reign. Because of his feverish desire to use modern technology to strengthen the army, many Westerners and Western ideas flowed into Russia for the first time. A new class of educated Russians began to emerge. At the same time, vast numbers of Russians, especially among the poor and weak, hated Peter's massive changes. The split between the enserfed peasantry and the educated nobility thus widened, even though all were caught up in the endless demands of the sovereign.

A new idea of state interest, distinct from the tsar's personal interests, began to take hold. Peter himself fostered this conception of the public interest by claiming time and again to be serving the common good. For the first time, a Russian tsar attached explanations to his decrees in an attempt to gain the confidence and enthusiastic support of the populace. Yet, as before, the tsar alone decided what the common good was. Here was a source of future tension between tsar and people.

In sum, Peter built on the service obligations of old Muscovy. His monarchial absolutism was truly the culmination of the long development of a unique Russian civilization. Yet the creation of a more modern army and state introduced much that was new and Western to that civilization. This development paved the way for Russia to move much closer to the European mainstream in its thought and institutions during the Enlightenment, especially under that famous administrative and sexual lioness, Catherine the Great.

ABSOLUTISM AND THE BAROQUE

The rise of royal absolutism in eastern Europe had many consequences. Nobles served their powerful rulers in new ways, while the great inferiority of the urban middle classes and the peasants was reconfirmed. Armies became larger and more professional, while taxes rose and authoritarian traditions were strengthened. Nor was this all. Royal absolu-

tism also interacted with baroque culture and art, baroque music and literature. Inspired in part by Louis XIV of France, the great and not-so-great rulers called on the artistic talent of the age to glorify their power and magnificence. This exaltation of despotic rule was particularly striking in the lavish masterpieces of architecture.

Palaces and Power

As soaring Gothic cathedrals expressed the idealized spirit of the High Middle Ages, so dramatic baroque palaces symbolized the age of absolutist power. By 1700 palace building had become a veritable obsession for the rulers of central and eastern Europe. Their baroque palaces were clearly intended to overawe the people with the monarch's strength. The great palaces were also visual declarations of equality with Louis XIV and were therefore modeled after Versailles to a greater or lesser extent. One such palace was Schönbrunn, an enormous Viennese Versailles, begun in 1695 by Emperor Leopold to celebrate Austrian military victories and Habsburg might. Charles XI of Sweden, having reduced the power of the aristocracy, ordered the construction in 1693 of his Royal Palace, which dominates the center of Stockholm to this day. Frederick I of Prussia began his imposing new royal residence in Berlin in 1701, the same year he attained the title of king.

Petty princes also contributed mightily to the palace-building mania. Frederick the Great of Prussia noted that every descendant of a princely family "imagines himself to be something like Louis XIV. He builds his Versailles, has his mistresses, and maintains his army."[13] The not-very-important elector-archbishop of Mainz, the ruling prince of that city, confessed apologetically that "building is a craze which costs much, but every fool likes his own hat."[14] The archbishop of Mainz's own "hat" was an architectural gem, like that of another churchly ruler, the prince-bishop of Würzburg.

In central and eastern Europe, the favorite noble servants of royalty became extremely rich and powerful, and they, too, built grandiose palaces in the capital cities. These palaces were in part an extension of the monarch, for they surpassed the buildings of less favored nobles and showed all the high road to fame and fortune. Take, for example, the palaces of Prince Eugene of Savoy. A French nobleman by birth and education, Prince Eugene entered the service of Emperor Leopold I with the relief of the besieged Vienna in 1683, and he became Austria's most famous military hero. It was he who reorganized the Austrian army, smashed the Turks, fought Louis XIV to a standstill, and generally guided the triumph of absolutism in Austria. Rewarded with great wealth by his grateful royal employer, Eugene called on the leading architects of the day, J. B. Fischer von Erlach and Johann Lukas von Hildebrandt, to consecrate his glory in stone and fresco. Fischer built Eugene's Winter (or Town) Palace in Vienna, and he and Hildebrandt collaborated on the prince's Summer Palace on the city's outskirts.

The Summer Palace was actually two enormous buildings, the Lower Belvedere and the Upper Belvedere, completed in 1713 and 1722 respectively and joined by one of the most exquisite gardens in Europe. The Upper Belvedere, Hildebrandt's

Würzburg, the Prince-Bishop's Palace   The baroque style brought architects, painters, and sculptors together in harmonious, even playful partnership. This magnificent monumental staircase, designed by Johann Balthasar Neumann in 1735, merges into the vibrant ceiling frescos by Giovanni Battista Tiepolo. A man is stepping out of the picture, and a painted dog resembles a marble statue. *(Source: Erich Lessing Culture and Fine Arts Archive)*

masterpiece, stood gracefully, even playfully, behind a great sheet of water. One entered through magnificent iron gates into a hall where sculptured giants crouched as pillars; then one moved on to a great staircase of dazzling whiteness and ornamentation. Even today, the emotional impact of this building is great: here art and beauty create a sense of immense power and wealth.

Palaces like the Upper Belvedere were magnificent examples of the baroque style. They expressed the baroque delight in bold, sweeping statements, which were intended to provide a dramatic emotional experience. To create this experience, baroque masters dissolved the traditional artistic frontiers: the architect permitted the painter and the artisan to cover the undulating surfaces with wildly colorful paintings, graceful sculptures, and fanciful carvings. Space was used in a highly original way, to blend everything together in a total environment. These techniques shone in all their glory in the churches of southern Germany and in the colossal halls of palaces like that of Ludwig II of Bavaria. Artistic achievement and political statement reinforced each other.

Royal Cities

Absolute monarchs and baroque architects were not content with fashioning ostentatious palaces. They remodeled existing capital cities, or even built new ones, to reflect royal magnificence and the centralization of political power. Karlsruhe, founded in 1715 as the capital city of a small German principality, is one extreme example. There, broad, straight avenues radiated out from the palace, so that all roads—like all power—were focused on the ruler. More typically, the monarch's architects added new urban areas alongside the old city; these areas then became the real heart of the expanding capital.

The distinctive features of these new additions were their broad avenues, their imposing government buildings, and their rigorous mathematical layout. Along these major thoroughfares the nobles built elaborate baroque townhouses; stables and servants' quarters were built on the alleys behind. Wide avenues also facilitated the rapid movement of soldiers through the city to quell any disturbance (the king's planners had the needs of the military constantly in mind). Under the arcades along the avenues appeared smart and very expensive shops, the first department stores, with plate-glass windows and fancy displays.

The new avenues brought reckless speed to the European city. Whereas everyone had walked through the narrow, twisting streets of the medieval town, the high and mighty raced down the broad boulevards in their elegant carriages. A social gap opened between the wealthy riders and the gaping, dodging pedestrians. "Mind the carriages!" wrote one eighteenth-century observer in Paris:

Here comes the black-coated physician in his chariot, the dancing master in his coach, the fencing master in his surrey—and the Prince behind six horses at the gallop as if he were in the open country. . . . The threatening wheels of the overbearing rich drive as rapidly as ever over stones stained with the blood of their unhappy victims.[15]

Speeding carriages on broad avenues, an endless parade of power and position: here was the symbol and substance of the baroque city.

The Growth of St. Petersburg

No city illustrated better than St. Petersburg the close ties among politics, architecture, and urban development in this period. In 1700, when the Great Northern War between Russia and Sweden began, the city did not exist. There was only a small Swedish fortress on one of the water-logged islands at the mouth of the Neva River, where it flows into the Baltic Sea. In 1702 Peter the Great's armies seized this desolate outpost. Within a year the reforming tsar had decided to build a new city there and to make it, rather than ancient Moscow, his capital.

Since the first step was to secure the Baltic coast, military construction was the main concern for the next eight years. A mighty fortress was built on Peter Island, and a port and shipyards were built across the river on the mainland, as a Russian navy came into being. The land was swampy and uninhabited, the climate damp and unpleasant. But Peter cared not at all: for him, the inhospitable northern marshland was a future metropolis, gloriously bearing his name.

After the decisive Russian victory at Poltava in 1709 greatly reduced the threat of Swedish armies, Peter moved into high gear. In one imperious decree after another, he ordered his people to build a city that would equal any in the world. Such a city

St. Petersburg, ca 1760   Rastrelli's remodeled Winter Palace, which housed the royal family until the Russian Revolution of 1917, stands on the left along the Neva River. The Navy Office with its famous golden spire and other government office buildings are nearby and across the river. Russia became a naval power and St. Petersburg a great port. *(Source: Michael Holford)*

had to be Western and baroque, just as Peter's army had to be Western and permanent. From such a new city, his "window on Europe," Peter also believed it would be easier to reform the country militarily and administratively.

These general political goals matched Peter's architectural ideas, which had been influenced by his travels in western Europe. First, Peter wanted a comfortable, "modern" city. Modernity meant broad, straight, stone-paved avenues, houses built in a uniform line and not haphazardly set back from the street, large parks, canals for drainage, stone bridges, and street lighting. Second, all building had to conform strictly to detailed architectural regulations set down by the government. Finally, each social group—the nobility, the merchants, the artisans, and so on—was to live in a certain section of town. In short, the city and its population were to conform to a carefully defined urban plan of the baroque type.

Peter used the traditional but reinforced methods of Russian autocracy to build his modern capital. The creation of St. Petersburg was just one of the heavy obligations he dictatorially imposed on all social groups in Russia. The peasants bore the heaviest burdens. Just as the government drafted peasants for the army, it also drafted twenty-five to forty thousand men each summer to labor in St. Petersburg for three months, without pay. Every ten to fifteen peasant households had to furnish one such worker each summer and then pay a special tax in order to feed that worker in St. Petersburg.

Peasants hated this forced labor in the capital, and each year one-fourth to one-third of those sent risked brutal punishment and ran away. Many peasant construction workers died each summer from hunger, sickness, and accidents. Many also died because peasant villages tended to elect old men or young boys to labor in St. Petersburg, since strong

From Reformation to Revolution in Europe, 1600–1800

	Government and Law	Philosophy and Science
1600	Edict of Nantes, 1598	Francis Bacon, 1561–1626
	Thirty Years' War, 1618–1648	Galileo, 1564–1642
	Richelieu dominates French government, 1624–1643	Johannes Kepler, 1571–1630
		Thomas Hobbes, 1588–1679
	Frederick William, Elector of Brandenburg, r. 1640–1688	René Descartes, 1596–1650
	English Civil War, 1642–1649	John Locke, 1632–1704
	Louis XIV, r. 1643–1715	Isaac Newton, 1642–1727
	Peace of Westphalia, 1648	
	The Fronde in France, 1648–1660	
1650	Protectorate in England, 1653–1658	Newton, *Principia Mathematica,* 1687
	Leopold I, Habsburg emperor, r. 1658–1705	Montesquieu, 1689–1755
	Treaty of the Pyrenees, 1659	Locke, *Second Treatise on Civil Government,* 1690
	Restoration of English monarchy, 1660	Voltaire, 1694–1778
	Siege of Vienna, 1683	
	Revocation of Edict of Nantes, 1685	
	Glorious Revolution in England, 1688–1689	
	Peter the Great of Russia, r. 1689–1725	
1700	War of the Spanish Succession, 1701–1713	David Hume, 1711–1776
	Peace of Utrecht, 1713	Diderot, 1713–1784
	Frederick William I of Prussia, r. 1713–1740	Condorcet, 1743–1794
	Louis XV of France, r. 1715–1774	
	Frederick the Great of Prussia, r. 1740–1786	
	Maria Theresa of Austria, r. 1740–1780	
1750	Seven Years' War, 1756–1763	Publication of the *Encyclopedia,* edited by Diderot and d'Alembert, 1751–1765
	Catherine the Great of Russia, r. 1762–1796	Rousseau, *The Social Contract,* 1762
	Partition of Poland, 1772–1795	Adam Smith, *The Wealth of Nations,* 1776
	Louis XVI of France, r. 1774–1792	
	American Revolution, 1776–1783	
	Beginning of the French Revolution, 1789	Jenner's smallpox vaccine, 1796

Economics	Religion	Arts and Letters
"Time of Troubles" in Russia, 1598–1613	Huguenot revolt in France, 1625	Baroque movement in the arts, ca 1550–1725
Chartering of English East India Company, 1600		Rubens, 1577–1640
English Poor Law, 1601		Molière, 1622–1673
Chartering of Dutch East India Company, 1602		
France establishes first Canadian settlement, at Quebec, 1608		
Height of mercantilism in Europe, ca 1650–1750	Patriarch Nikon's reforms split Russian Orthodox church, 1652	Construction of baroque palaces and remodeling of capital cities throughout central and eastern Europe, ca 1650–1725
Principle of peasants' "hereditary subjugation" to their lords affirmed in Prussia, 1653	Test Act excludes Roman Catholics from public office in England, 1673	J. S. Bach, 1685–1750
Colbert's economic reforms in France, ca 1663–1683	Revocation of Edict of Nantes, 1685	Fontenelle, *Conversations on the Plurality of Worlds,* 1686
Cossack revolt in Russia, 1670–1671	James II attempts to restore Roman Catholicism as state religion, 1685–1688	The Enlightment, ca 1690–1790
		Voltaire, 1694–1778
	Bayle, *Historical and Critical Dictionary,* 1697	
Newcomen develops steam engine, 1705	John Wesley, 1703–1791	Foundation of St. Petersburg, 1701
Last appearance of bubonic plague in western Europe, ca 1720		
Enclosure movement in England, ca 1730–1830		
Start of general European population increase, ca 1750		W. A. Mozart, 1756–1791
James Hargreaves invents spinning jenny, ca 1765		Romantic movement in the arts, ca 1790–1850
Richard Arkwright invents water frame, ca 1765		Wordsworth, 1770–1850
James Watt's steam engine promotes industrial breakthrough, 1780s		

and able-bodied men were desperately needed on the farm in the busy summer months. Thus beautiful St. Petersburg was built on the shoveling, carting, and paving of a mass of conscripted serfs.

Peter also drafted more privileged groups to his city, but on a permanent basis. Nobles were summarily ordered to build costly stone houses and palaces in St. Petersburg and to live in them most of the year. The more serfs a noble possessed, the bigger his dwelling had to be. Merchants and artisans were also commanded to settle and build in St. Petersburg. These nobles and merchants were then required to pay for the city's avenues, parks, canals, embankments, pilings, and bridges, all of which were very costly in terms of both money and lives because they were built on a swamp. The building of St. Petersburg was, in truth, an enormous direct tax levied on the wealthy, who in turn forced the peasantry to do most of the work. The only immediate beneficiaries were the foreign architects and urban planners. No wonder so many Russians hated Peter's new city.

Yet the tsar had his way. By the time of his death in 1725, there were at least six thousand houses and numerous impressive government buildings in St. Petersburg. Under the remarkable women who ruled Russia throughout most of the eighteenth century, St. Petersburg blossomed fully as a majestic and well-organized city, at least in its wealthy showpiece sections. Peter's youngest daughter, the quick-witted, sensual beauty, Elizabeth (r. 1741–1762), named as her chief architect Bartolomeo Rastrelli, who had come to Russia from Italy as a boy of fifteen in 1715. Combining Italian and Russian traditions into a unique, wildly colorful St. Petersburg style, Rastrelli built many palaces for the nobility and all the larger government buildings erected during Elizabeth's reign. He also rebuilt the Winter Palace as an enormous, aqua-colored royal residence, now the Hermitage Museum. There Elizabeth established a flashy, luxury-loving, and slightly crude court, which Catherine the Great in turn made truly imperial. All the while St. Petersburg grew rapidly, and its almost 300,000 inhabitants in 1782 made it one of the world's largest cities. Peter and his successors had created out of nothing a magnificent and harmonious royal city, which unmistakably proclaimed the power of Russia's rulers and the creative potential of the absolutist state.

SUMMARY

From about 1400 to 1650, social and economic developments in eastern Europe increasingly diverged from those in western Europe. In the east, peasants and townspeople lost precious freedoms, while the nobility increased its power and prestige. It was within this framework of resurgent serfdom and entrenched nobility that Austrian and Prussian monarchs fashioned absolutist states in the seventeenth and early eighteenth centuries. These monarchs won absolutist control over standing armies, permanent taxes, and legislative bodies. But they did not question the underlying social and economic relationships. Indeed, they enhanced the privileges of the nobility, which furnished the leading servitors for enlarged armies and growing state bureaucracies.

In Russia, the social and economic trends were similar, but the timing of political absolutism was different. Mongol conquest and rule was a crucial experience, and a harsh, indigenous tsarist autocracy was firmly in place by the reign of Ivan the Terrible in the sixteenth century. More than a century later, Peter the Great succeeded in tightening up Russia's traditional absolutism and modernizing it by reforming the army, the bureaucracy, and the defense industry. In Russia and throughout eastern Europe, war and the needs of the state in time of war weighed heavily in the triumph of absolutism.

Triumphant absolutism interacted spectacularly with the arts. Baroque art, which had grown out of the Catholic Reformation's desire to move the faithful and exalt the true faith, admirably suited the secular aspirations of eastern European rulers. They built grandiose baroque palaces, monumental public squares, and even whole cities to glorify their power and majesty. Thus baroque art attained magnificent heights in eastern Europe, symbolizing the ideal and harmonizing with the reality of imperious royal absolutism.

NOTES

1. Quoted in F. L. Carsten, *The Origins of Prussia* (Oxford: Clarendon Press, 1954), p. 152.
2. Ibid., p. 175.

3. H. Rosenberg, *Bureaucracy, Aristocracy, and Autocracy: The Prussian Experience, 1660–1815* (Boston: Beacon Press, 1966), p. 38.

4. Quoted in R. Ergang, *The Potsdam Fuhrer: Frederick William I, Father of Prussian Militarism* (New York: Octagon Books, 1972), pp. 85, 87.

5. Ibid., pp. 6–7, 43.

6. Quoted in R. A. Dorwart, *The Administrative Reforms of Frederick William I of Prussia* (Cambridge, Mass.: Harvard University Press, 1953), p. 226.

7. Quoted in Rosenberg, p. 40.

8. Quoted in R. Pipes, *Russia Under the Old Regime* (New York: Charles Scribner's Sons, 1974), p. 48.

9. Quoted in N. V. Riasanovsky, *A History of Russia* (New York: Oxford University Press, 1963), p. 79.

10. Quoted in I. Grey, *Ivan III and the Unification of Russia* (New York: Collier Books, 1967), p. 39.

11. Quoted in Grey, p. 42.

12. Both quoted in Pipes, pp. 65, 85.

13. Quoted in Ergang, p. 13.

14. Quoted in J. Summerson, in *The Eighteenth Century: Europe in the Age of Enlightenment,* ed. A. Cobban (New York: McGraw-Hill, 1969), p. 80.

15. Quoted in L. Mumford, *The Culture of Cities* (New York: Harcourt Brace Jovanovich, 1938), p. 97.

SUGGESTED READING

All of the books cited in the Notes are highly recommended. Carsten's *The Origin of Prussia* is the best study on early Prussian history, and Rosenberg's *Bureaucracy, Aristocracy, and Autocracy* is a masterful analysis of the social context of Prussian absolutism. In addition to Ergang's *The Potsdam Fuhrer,* an exciting and critical biography of ramrod Frederick William I, there is G. Ritter, *Frederick the Great* (1968), a more sympathetic study of the talented son by one of Germany's leading conservative historians. G. Craig, *The Politics of the Prussian Army, 1640–1945* (1964), expertly traces the great influence of the military on the Prussian state over three hundred years. R. J. Evans, *The Making of the Habsburg Empire, 1550–1770* (1979), and R. A. Kann, *A History of the Habsburg Empire, 1526–1918* (1974), analyze the development of absolutism in Austria, as does A. Wandruszka, *The House of Habsburg* (1964). J. Stoye, *The Siege of Vienna* (1964), is a fascinating account of the last great Ottoman offensive, which is also treated in the interesting

study by P. Coles, *The Ottoman Impact on Europe, 1350–1699* (1968). The Austro-Ottoman conflict is also a theme of L. S. Stavrianos, *The Balkans Since 1453* (1958), and D. McKay's fine biography, *Prince Eugene of Savoy* (1978). A good general account is provided in D. McKay and H. Scott, *The Rise of the Great Powers, 1648–1815* (1983), and R. Vierhaus, *Germany in the Age of Absolutism* (1988), offers a good survey of the different German states.

On eastern European peasants and serfdom, D. Chirot, ed., *The Origins of Backwardness in Eastern Europe: Economics and Politics from the Middle Ages Until the Twentieth Century* (1989), is a wide-ranging introduction, which may be compared with J. Blum, "The Rise of Serfdom in Eastern Europe," *American Historical Review* 62 (July 1957): 807–836. E. Levin, *Sex and Society in the World of the Orthodox Slavs, 900–1700* (1989), carries family history to eastern Europe, while R. Mousnier, *Peasant Uprisings in Seventeenth-Century France, Russia, and China* (1970), is a fine comparative study. J. Blum, *Lord and Peasant in Russia from the Ninth to the Nineteenth Century* (1961), provides a good look at conditions in rural Russia, and P. Avrich, *Russian Rebels, 1600–1800* (1972), treats some of the violent peasant upheavals those conditions produced. R. Hellie, *Enserfment and Military Change in Muscovy* (1971), is outstanding, as is A. Yanov's provocative *Origins of Autocracy: Ivan the Terrible in Russian History* (1981). In addition to the fine surveys by Pipes and Riasanovsky cited in the Notes, J. Billington, *The Icon and the Axe* (1970), is a stimulating history of early Russian intellectual and cultural developments, such as the great split in the church. M. Raeff, *Origins of the Russian Intelligentsia* (1966), skillfully probes the mind of the Russian nobility in the eighteenth century. B. H. Sumner, *Peter the Great and the Emergence of Russia* (1962), is a fine brief introduction, which may be compared with the brilliant biography by Russia's greatest prerevolutionary historian, V. Klyuchevsky, *Peter the Great* (English trans., 1958), and with N. Riasanovsky, *The Image of Peter the Great in Russian History and Thought* (1985). G. Vernadsky and R. Fisher, eds., *A Source Book of Russian History from Early Times to 1917,* 3 vols. (1972), is an invaluable, highly recommended collection of documents and contemporary writings.

Three good books on art and architecture are E. Hempel, *Baroque Art and Architecture in Central Europe* (1965); G. Hamilton, *The Art and Architecture of Russia* (1954); and N. Pevsner, *An Outline of European Architecture,* 6th ed. (1960).

18

Toward a New World-view

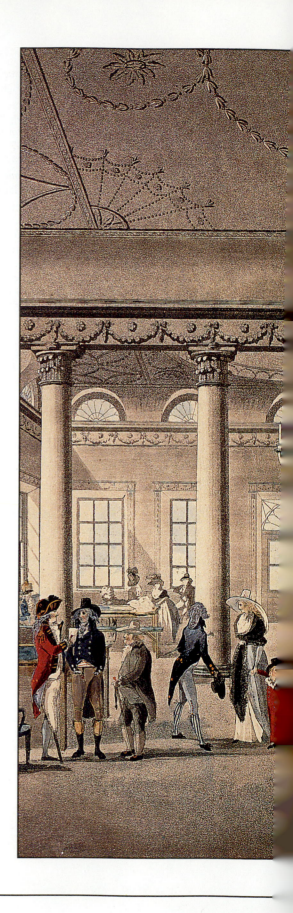

*M*ost people are not philosophers, but nevertheless they have a basic outlook on life, a more or less coherent world-view. At the risk of oversimplification, one may say that the world-view of medieval and early modern Europe was primarily religious and theological. Not only did Christian or Jewish teachings form the core of people's spiritual and philosophical beliefs, but religious teachings also permeated all the rest of human thought and activity. Political theory relied on the divine right of kings, for example, and activities ranging from marriage and divorce to eating habits and hours of business were regulated by churches and religious doctrines.

In the course of the eighteenth century, this religious and theological world-view of the educated classes of western Europe underwent a fundamental transformation. Many educated people came to see the world primarily in secular and scientific terms. And while few abandoned religious beliefs altogether, many became openly hostile toward established Christianity. The role of churches and religious thinking in earthly affairs and in the pursuit of knowledge was substantially reduced. Among many in the upper and middle classes, a new critical, scientific, and very "modern" world-view took shape.

- Why did this momentous change occur?
- How did this new outlook on life affect society and politics?

This chapter will focus on these questions.

THE SCIENTIFIC REVOLUTION

The foremost cause of the change in world-view was the scientific revolution. Modern science— precise knowledge of the physical world based on the union of experimental observations with sophisticated mathematics—crystallized in the seventeenth century. Whereas science had been secondary and subordinate in medieval intellectual life, it became independent and even primary for many educated people in the eighteenth century.

The emergence of modern science was a development of tremendous long-term significance. A noted historian has even said that the scientific revolution of the late sixteenth and seventeenth centuries "outshines everything since the rise of Christianity and reduces the Renaissance and Reformation to the rank of mere episodes, mere internal displacements, within the system of medieval Christendom." The scientific revolution was "the real origin both of the modern world and the modern mentality."[1] This statement is an exaggeration, but not much of one. Of all the great civilizations, only that of the West developed modern science. It was with the scientific revolution that Western society began to acquire its most distinctive traits.

Though historians agree that the scientific revolution was enormously important, they approach it in quite different ways. Some scholars believe that the history of scientific achievement in this period had its own basic "internal" logic and that "nonscientific" factors had quite limited significance. These scholars write brilliant, often highly technical, intellectual studies, but they neglect the broader historical context. Other historians stress "external" economic, social, and religious factors, brushing over the scientific developments themselves. Historians of science now realize that these two approaches need to be brought together, but they are only beginning to do so. It is best, therefore, to examine the milestones on the fateful march toward modern science first and then to search for nonscientific influences along the route.

Scientific Thought in 1500

Since developments in astronomy and physics were at the heart of the scientific revolution, one must begin with the traditional European conception of the universe and movement in it. In the early 1500s, traditional European ideas about the universe were still based primarily on the ideas of Aristotle, the great Greek philosopher of the fourth century B.C. These ideas had gradually been recovered during the Middle Ages and then brought into harmony with Christian doctrines by medieval theologians. According to this revised Aristotelian view, a motionless earth was fixed at the center of the universe. Around it moved ten separate, transparent, crystal spheres. In the first eight spheres were embedded, in turn, the moon, the sun, the five known planets, and the fixed stars. Then followed two spheres added during the Middle Ages to account for slight changes in the positions of the stars over the centuries. Beyond the tenth sphere was heaven, with the throne of God and the souls of the saved. Angels kept the spheres moving in perfect circles.

Aristotle's views, suitably revised by medieval philosophers, also dominated thinking about physics and motion on earth. Aristotle had distinguished sharply between the world of the celestial spheres and that of the earth—the sublunar world. The spheres consisted of a perfect, incorruptible "quintessence," or fifth essence. The sublunar world, however, was made up of four imperfect, changeable elements. The "light" elements—air and fire—naturally moved upward, while the "heavy" elements—water and earth—naturally moved downward. The natural directions of motion did not always prevail, however, for elements were often mixed together and could be affected by an outside force such as a human being. Aristotle and his followers also believed that a uniform force moved an object at a constant speed and that the object would stop as soon as that force was removed.

Aristotle's ideas about astronomy and physics were accepted with minor revisions for two thousand years, and with good reason. First, they offered an understandable, common-sense explanation for what the eye actually saw. Second, Aristotle's science, as interpreted by Christian theologians, fit neatly with Christian doctrines. It established a home for God and a place for Christian souls. It put human beings at the center of the universe and made them the critical link in a "great chain of being" that stretched from the throne of God to the most lowly insect on earth. Thus science was primarily a branch of theology, and it reinforced religious thought. At the same time, medieval "scientists" were already providing closely reasoned explanations of the universe, explanations they felt were worthy of God's perfect creation.

The Copernican Hypothesis

The desire to explain and thereby glorify God's handiwork led to the first great departure from the medieval system. This departure was the work of the Polish clergyman and astronomer Nicolaus Copernicus (1473–1543). As a young man, Copernicus studied church law and astronomy in various

Ptolemy's System This 1543 drawing shows how the changing configurations of the planets moving around the earth form the twelve different constellations, or "signs," of the zodiac. The learned astronomer on the right is using his knowledge to predict the future for the king on the left. *(Source: Mary Evans Picture Library/ Photo Researchers)*

European universities. He saw how professional astronomers were still dependent for their most accurate calculations on the work of Ptolemy, the last great ancient astronomer, who had lived in Alexandria in the second century A.D. Ptolemy's achievement had been to work out complicated rules to explain the minor irregularities in the movement of the planets. These rules enabled stargazers and astrologers to track the planets with greater precision. Many people then (and now) believed that the changing relationships between planets and stars influenced and even determined the future.

The young Copernicus was uninterested in astrology and felt that Ptolemy's cumbersome and occasionally inaccurate rules detracted from the majesty of a perfect Creator. He preferred an old Greek idea being discussed in Renaissance Italy: that the sun rather than the earth was at the center of the universe. Finishing his university studies and returning to a church position in east Prussia, Copernicus worked on his hypothesis from 1506 to 1530. Never questioning the Aristotelian belief in crystal spheres or the idea that circular motion was most perfect and divine, Copernicus theorized that the stars and planets, including the earth, revolve around a fixed sun. Yet Copernicus was a cautious man. Fearing the ridicule of other astronomers, he did not publish his *Oh the Revolutions of the Heavenly Spheres* until 1543, the year of his death.

Copernicus's theory had enormous scientific and religious implications, many of which the conservative Copernicus did not anticipate. First, it put the stars at rest, their apparent nightly movement simply a result of the earth's rotation. Thus it destroyed the main reason for believing in crystal spheres capable of moving the stars around the earth. Second, Copernicus's theory suggested a universe of staggering size. If in the course of a year the earth moved around the sun and yet the stars appeared to remain in the same place, then the universe was unthinkably large or even infinite. Finally, by characterizing the earth as just another planet, Copernicus destroyed the basic idea of Aristotelian physics—that the earthly world was quite different from the heavenly one. Where, then, was the realm of perfection? Where was heaven and the throne of God?

The Copernican theory quickly brought sharp attacks from religious leaders, especially Protestants. Hearing of Copernicus's work even before it was published, Martin Luther spoke of him as the "new astrologer who wants to prove that the earth moves and goes round. . . . The fool wants to turn the whole art of astronomy upside down." Luther noted that "as the Holy Scripture tells us, so did Joshua bid the sun stand still and not the earth." Calvin also condemned Copernicus, citing as evidence the first verse of Psalm 93: "The world also is established that it cannot be moved." "Who," asked Calvin, "will venture to place the authority of Copernicus above that of the Holy Spirit?"[2] Catholic reaction was milder at first. The Catholic church had never been hypnotized by literal interpretations of the Bible, and not until 1616 did it officially declare the Copernican theory false.

This slow reaction also reflected the slow progress of Copernicus's theory for many years. Other events were almost as influential in creating doubts about traditional astronomical ideas. In 1572 a new star appeared and shone very brightly for almost two years. The new star, which was actually a distant exploding star, made an enormous impression on people. It seemed to contradict the idea that the heavenly spheres were unchanging and therefore perfect. In 1577 a new comet suddenly moved through the sky, cutting a straight path across the supposedly impenetrable crystal spheres. It was time, as a typical scientific writer put it, for "the radical renovation of astronomy."[3]

From Tycho Brahe to Galileo

One astronomer who agreed was Tycho Brahe (1546–1601). Born into a leading Danish noble family and earmarked for a career in government, Brahe was at an early age tremendously impressed by a partial eclipse of the sun. It seemed to him "something divine that men could know the motions of the stars so accurately that they were able a long time beforehand to predict their places and relative positions."[4] Completing his studies abroad and returning to Denmark, Brahe established himself as Europe's leading astronomer with his detailed observations of the new star of 1572. Aided by generous grants from the king of Denmark, which made him one of the richest men in the country, Brahe built the most sophisticated observatory of his day. For twenty years he meticulously observed the stars and planets with the naked eye. An imposing man who had lost a piece of his nose in a duel and replaced it with a special bridge of gold and silver alloy, a noble who exploited his peasants arrogantly and approached the heavens humbly, Brahe's great contribution was his mass of data. His limited understanding of mathematics prevented him, however, from making much sense out of his data. Part Ptolemaic, part Copernican, he believed that all the planets revolved around the sun and that the entire group of sun and planets revolved in turn around the earth-moon system.

It was left to Brahe's brilliant young assistant, Johannes Kepler (1571–1630), to go much further. Kepler was a medieval figure in many ways. Coming from a minor German noble family and trained for the Lutheran ministry, he long believed that the universe was built on mystical mathematical relationships and a musical harmony of the heavenly bodies. Working and reworking Brahe's mountain of observations in a staggering sustained effort after the Dane's death, this brilliant mathematician eventually went beyond mystical intuitions.

Kepler formulated three famous laws of planetary motion. First, building on Copernican theory, he demonstrated in 1609 that the orbits of the planets around the sun are elliptical rather than circular. Second, he demonstrated that the planets do not move at a uniform speed in their orbits. Third, in 1619 he showed that the time a planet takes to make its complete orbit is precisely related to its distance from the sun. Kepler's contribution was monumental. Whereas Copernicus had speculated, Kepler proved mathematically the precise relations of a sun-centered (solar) system. His work demolished the old system of Aristotle and Ptolemy, and in his third law he came close to formulating the idea of universal gravitation.

While Kepler was unraveling planetary motion, a young Florentine named Galileo Galilei (1564–1642) was challenging all the old ideas about motion. Like so many early scientists, Galileo was a poor nobleman first marked for a religious career. However, he soon became fascinated by mathematics. A brilliant student, Galileo became a professor of mathematics in 1589 at age twenty-five. He proceeded to examine motion and mechanics in a new way. Indeed, his great achievement was the elaboration and consolidation of the modern experimental method. Rather than speculate about what might or should happen, Galileo conducted controlled experiments to find out what actually *did* happen.

In his famous acceleration experiment, he showed that a uniform force—in this case, gravity —produced a uniform acceleration. Here is how Galileo described his pathbreaking method and conclusion in his *Two New Sciences:*

A piece of wooden moulding . . . was taken; on its edge was cut a channel a little more than one finger in breadth. Having made this groove very straight, smooth and polished, and having lined it with parchment, also as smooth and polished as possible, we rolled along it a hard, smooth and very round bronze ball. . . . Noting . . . the time required to make the descent . . . we now rolled the ball only one-quarter the length of the channel; and hav-

ing measured the time of its descent, we found it precisely one-half of the former. . . . In such experiments [over many distances], repeated a full hundred times, we always found that the spaces traversed were to each other as the squares of the times, and that this was true for all inclinations of the plane.[5]

With this and other experiments, Galileo also formulated the law of inertia. That is, rather than rest being the natural state of objects, an object continues in motion forever unless stopped by some external force. Aristotelian physics was in a shambles.

In the tradition of Brahe, Galileo also applied the experimental method to astronomy. His astronomical discoveries had a great impact on scientific development. On hearing of the invention of the telescope in Holland, Galileo made one for himself and trained it on the heavens. He quickly discovered the first four moons of Jupiter, which clearly suggested that Jupiter could not possibly be embedded in any impenetrable crystal sphere. This discovery provided new evidence for the Copernican theory, in which Galileo already believed.

Galileo then pointed his telescope at the moon. He wrote in 1610 in *Siderus Nuncius:*

I feel sure that the moon is not perfectly smooth, free from inequalities, and exactly spherical, as a large school of philosophers considers with regard to the moon and the other heavenly bodies. On the contrary, it is full of inequalities, uneven, full of hollows and protuberances, just like the surface of the earth itself, which is varied. . . . The next object which I have observed is the essence or substance of the Milky Way. By the aid of a telescope anyone may behold this in a manner which so distinctly appeals to the senses that all the disputes which have tormented philosophers through so many ages are exploded by the irrefutable evidence of our eyes, and we are freed from wordy disputes upon the subject. For the galaxy is nothing else but a mass of innumerable stars planted together in clusters. Upon whatever part of it you direct the telescope straightway a vast crowd of stars presents itself to view; many of them are tolerably large and extremely bright, but the number of small ones is quite beyond determination.[6]

Reading these famous lines, one feels that a crucial corner in Western civilization is being turned. The traditional religious and theological worldview, which rested on determining and accepting

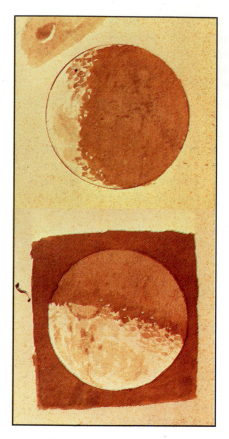

Galileo's Paintings of the Moon   When Galileo published the results of his telescopic observations of the moon, he added these paintings to illustrate the marvels he had seen. Galileo made two telescopes, which are shown here. The larger one magnifies 14 times, the smaller 20 times. *(Source: Biblioteca Nazionale Centrale, Florence; Museum of Science, Florence/Scala/Art Resource)*

the proper established authority, is beginning to give way in certain fields to a critical, scientific method. This new method of learning and investigating was the greatest accomplishment of the entire scientific revolution, for it has proved capable of great extension. A historian investigating documents of the past, for example, is not much different from a Galileo studying stars and rolling balls.

Galileo was employed in Florence by the Medici grand dukes of Tuscany, and his work eventually aroused the ire of some theologians. The issue was presented in 1624 to Pope Urban VII, who permitted Galileo to write about different possible systems of the world, as long as he did not presume to judge which one actually existed. After the publication in Italian of his widely read *Dialogue on the Two Chief Systems of the World* in 1632, which too openly lampooned the traditional views of Aristotle and Ptolemy and defended those of Copernicus, Galileo was tried for heresy by the papal Inquisition. Imprisoned and threatened with torture, the aging Galileo recanted, "renouncing and cursing" his Copernican errors. Of minor importance in the development of science, Galileo's trial later became for some writers the perfect symbol of the inevitable conflict between religious belief and scientific knowledge.

Newton's Synthesis

The accomplishments of Kepler, Galileo, and other scientists had taken effect by about 1640. The old astronomy and physics were in ruins, and several fundamental breakthroughs had been made. The new findings had not, however, been fused together in a new synthesis, a single explanatory system that would comprehend motion both on earth and in the skies. That synthesis, which prevailed until the twentieth century, was the work of Isaac Newton (1642–1727).

Newton was born into lower English gentry and attended Cambridge University. A great genius who spectacularly united the experimental and theoretical-mathematical sides of modern science, Newton was also fascinated by alchemy. He sought the elixir of life and a way to change base metals into gold and silver. Not without reason did the twentieth-century economist John Maynard Keynes call Newton the "last of the magicians." Newton was intensely religious. He had a highly suspicious nature, lacked all interest in women and sex, and in 1693 suffered a nervous breakdown from which he later recovered. He was far from being the perfect rationalist so endlessly eulogized by writers in the eighteenth and nineteenth centuries.

Of his intellectual genius and incredible powers of concentration there can be no doubt, however. Arriving at some of his most basic ideas about physics in 1666 at age twenty-four, but unable to prove these theories mathematically, he attained a professorship and studied optics for many years. In 1684 Newton returned to physics for eighteen extraordinarily intensive months. For weeks on end he seldom left his room except to read his lectures. His meals were sent up, but he usually forgot to eat them, his mind fastened like a vise on the laws of the universe. He opened the third book of his immortal *Mathematical Principles of Natural Philosophy*, published in Latin in 1687 and generally known as the *Principia,* with these lines:

In the preceding books I have laid down the principles of philosophy [that is, science]. . . . These principles are the laws of certain motions, and powers or forces, which chiefly have respect to philosophy. . . . It remains that from the same principles I now demonstrate the frame of the System of the World.

Newton made good his grandiose claim. His towering accomplishment was to integrate in a single explanatory system the astronomy of Copernicus, as corrected by Kepler's laws, with the physics of Galileo and his predecessors. Newton did this by means of a set of mathematical laws that explain motion and mechanics. These laws of dynamics are complex, and it took scientists and engineers two hundred years to work out all their implications. Nevertheless, the key feature of the Newtonian synthesis was the law of universal gravitation. According to this law, every body in the universe attracts every other body in the universe in a precise mathematical relationship, whereby the force of attraction is proportional to the quantity of matter of the objects and inversely proportional to the square of the distance between them. The whole universe—from Kepler's elliptical orbits to Galileo's rolling balls—was unified in one majestic system.

Causes of the Scientific Revolution

With a charming combination of modesty and self-congratulation, Newton once wrote: "If I have seen further [than others], it is by standing on the

Isaac Newton This portrait suggests the depth and complexity of the great genius. Is the powerful mind behind those piercing eyes thinking of science or of religion, or perhaps of both? *(Source: Scala/Art Resource)*

shoulders of Giants."[7] Surely the path from Copernicus to Newton confirms the "internal" view of the scientific revolution as a product of towering individual genius. The problems of science were inherently exciting, and solution of those problems was its own reward for inquisitive, high-powered minds. Yet there were certainly broader causes as well.

The long-term contribution of medieval intellectual life and medieval universities to the scientific revolution was much more considerable than historians unsympathetic to the Middle Ages once believed. By the thirteenth century, permanent universities with professors and large student bodies had been established in western Europe. The universities were supported by society because they trained the lawyers, doctors, and church leaders society required. By 1300 philosophy had taken its place alongside law, medicine, and theology. Medieval philosophers developed a limited but real independence from theologians and a sense of free inquiry. They nobly pursued a body of knowledge and tried to arrange it meaningfully by means of abstract theories.

Within this framework, science was able to emerge as a minor but distinct branch of philosophy. In the fourteenth and fifteenth centuries, first in Italy and then elsewhere in Europe, leading universities established new professorships of mathematics, astronomy, and physics (natural philosophy) within their faculties of philosophy. The prestige of the new fields was still low among both professors and students. Nevertheless, this pattern of academic science, which grew out of the medieval commitment to philosophy and did not change substantially until the late eighteenth century, undoubtedly promoted scientific development. Rational, critical thinking was applied to scientific problems by a permanent community of scholars. And an outlet existed for the talents of a Galileo or a Newton: all the great pathfinders either studied or taught at universities.

The Renaissance also stimulated scientific progress. One of the great deficiencies of medieval science was its rather rudimentary mathematics. The recovery of the finest works of Greek mathematics—a by-product of Renaissance humanism's ceaseless search for the knowledge of antiquity—greatly improved European mathematics well into the early seventeenth century. The recovery of more texts also showed that classical mathematicians had their differences, and Europeans were forced to try to resolve these ancient controversies by means of their own efforts. Finally, the Renaissance pattern of patronage, especially in Italy, was often scientific as well as artistic and humanistic. Various rulers and wealthy business people supported scientific investigations, just as the Medicis of Florence supported those of Galileo.

The navigational problems of long sea voyages in the age of overseas expansion were a third factor in the scientific revolution. Ship captains on distant shores needed to be able to chart their positions as accurately as possible, so that reliable maps could be drawn and the risks of international trade reduced. As early as 1484, the king of Portugal appointed a commission of mathematicians to perfect tables to help seamen find their latitude. This resulted in the first European navigation manual.

The problem of fixing longitude was much more difficult. In England, the government and the great capitalistic trading companies turned to science and scientific education in an attempt to solve this pressing practical problem. When the famous Elizabethan financier Sir Thomas Gresham left a large amount of money to establish Gresham College in London, he stipulated that three of the college's seven professors had to concern themselves exclusively with scientific subjects. The professor of astronomy was directed to teach courses on the science of navigation. A seventeenth-century popular ballad took note of the new college's calling:

This college will the whole world measure
Which most impossible conclude,
And navigation make a pleasure
By finding out the longitude.[8]

At Gresham College scientists had, for the first time in history, an important, honored role in society. They enjoyed close ties with the top officials of the Royal Navy and with the leading merchants and shipbuilders. Gresham College became the main center of scientific activity in England in the first half of the seventeenth century. The close tie between practical men and scientists also led to the establishment in 1662 of the Royal Society of London, which published scientific papers and sponsored scientific meetings.

Navigational problems were also critical in the development of many new scientific instruments, such as the telescope, the barometer, the thermom-

State Support   Governments supported scientific research because they thought it might be useful. Here Louis XIV visits the French Royal Academy of Sciences in 1671 and examines a plan for better military fortifications. The great interest in astronomy, anatomy, and geography is evident. *(Source: Bibliothèque Nationale, Paris)*

eter, the pendulum clock, the microscope, and the air pump. Better instruments, which permitted more accurate observations, often led to important new knowledge. Galileo with his telescope was by no means unique.

Better instruments were part of a fourth factor in the scientific revolution, the development of better ways of obtaining knowledge about the world. Two important thinkers, Francis Bacon (1561–1626) and René Descartes (1596–1650), represented key aspects of this improvement in scientific methodology.

The English politician and writer Francis Bacon was the greatest early propagandist for the new experimental method, as Galileo was its greatest early practitioner. Rejecting the Aristotelian and medieval method of using speculative reasoning to build general theories, Bacon argued that new knowledge had to be pursued through empirical, experimental research. That is, the researcher who wants to learn more about leaves or rocks should not speculate about the subject but rather collect a multitude of specimens and then compare and analyze them. Thus freed from sterile medieval speculation, the facts will speak for themselves, and important general principles will then emerge. Knowledge will increase. Bacon's contribution was to formalize the empirical method, which had already been used by Brahe and Galileo, into the general theory of inductive reasoning known as *empiricism.*

Bacon claimed that the empirical method would result not only in more knowledge, but in highly practical, useful knowledge. According to Bacon, scientific discoveries like those so avidly sought at Gresham College would bring about much greater control over the physical environment and make people rich and nations powerful. Thus Bacon helped provide a radically new and effective justification for private and public support of scientific inquiry.

The French philosopher René Descartes was a true genius who made his first great discovery in

René Descartes dismissed the scientific theories of Aristotle and his medieval disciples as outdated dogma. A brilliant philosopher and mathematician, he formulated rules for abstract, deductive reasoning and the search for comprehensive scientific laws. *(Source: Royal Museum of Fine Arts, Copenhagen)*

mathematics. As a twenty-three-year-old soldier serving in the Thirty Years' War, he experienced on a single night in 1619 a life-changing intellectual vision. Descartes saw that there was a perfect correspondence between geometry and algebra and that geometrical, spatial figures could be expressed as algebraic equations and vice versa. A great step forward in the history of mathematics, Descartes' discovery of analytic geometry provided scientists with an important new tool. Descartes also made contributions to the science of optics, but his greatest achievement was to develop his initial vision into a whole philosophy of knowledge and science.

Like Bacon, Descartes scorned traditional science and had great faith in the powers of the human mind. Yet Descartes was much more sys-

tematic and mathematical than Bacon. He decided it was necessary to doubt everything that could reasonably be doubted and then, as in geometry, to use deductive reasoning from self-evident principles to ascertain scientific laws. Descartes' reasoning ultimately reduced all substances to "matter" and "mind"—that is, to the physical and the spiritual. His view of the world as consisting of two fundamental entities is known as *Cartesian dualism.* Descartes was a profoundly original and extremely influential thinker.

It is important to realize that the modern scientific method, which began to crystallize in the late seventeenth century, has combined Bacon's inductive experimentalism and Descartes' deductive, mathematical rationalism. Neither of these extreme approaches was sufficient by itself. Bacon's inability to appreciate the importance of mathematics and his obsession with practical results clearly showed the limitations of antitheoretical empiricism. Likewise, some of Descartes' positions—he believed, for example, that it was possible to deduce the whole science of medicine from first principles—aptly demonstrated the inadequacy of rigid, dogmatic rationalism. Significantly, Bacon faulted Galileo for his use of abstract formulas, while Descartes criticized the great Italian for being too experimental and insufficiently theoretical. Thus the modern scientific method has typically combined Bacon and Descartes. It has joined precise observations and experimentalism with the search for general laws that may be expressed in rigorously logical, mathematical language.

Finally, there is the question of science and religion. Just as some historians have argued that Protestantism led to the rise of capitalism, others have concluded that Protestantism was a fundamental factor in the rise of modern science. Protestantism, particularly in its Calvinist varieties, supposedly made scientific inquiry a question of individual conscience and not of religious doctrine. The Catholic church, on the other hand, supposedly suppressed scientific theories that conflicted with its teachings and thus discouraged scientific progress.

The truth of the matter is more complicated. *All* religious authorities—Catholic, Protestant, and Jewish—opposed the Copernican system to a greater or lesser extent until about 1630, by which time the scientific revolution was definitely in progress. The Catholic church was initially less hostile than Protestant and Jewish religious leaders.

This early Catholic toleration and the scientific interests of Renaissance Italy help account for the undeniable fact that Italian scientists played a crucial role in scientific progress right up to the trial of Galileo in 1633. Thereafter, the Counter-Reformation church became more hostile to science, a change that helps account for the decline of science in Italy (but not in Catholic France) after 1640. At the same time, some Protestant countries became quite "pro-science," especially if the country lacked a strong religious authority capable of imposing religious orthodoxy on scientific questions.

This was the case with England after 1630. English religious conflicts became so intense that it was impossible for the authorities to impose religious unity on anything, including science. It is significant that the forerunners of the Royal Society agreed to discuss only "neutral" scientific questions, so as not to come to blows over closely related religious and political disputes. The work of Bacon's many followers during Cromwell's commonwealth helped solidify the neutrality and independence of science. Bacon advocated the experimental approach precisely because it was open-minded and independent of any preconceived religious or philosophical ideas. Neutral and useful, science became an accepted part of life and developed rapidly in England after about 1640.

Some Consequences of the Scientific Revolution

The ˌrise of modern science had many consequences, some of which are still unfolding. First, it went hand in hand with the rise of a new and expanding social group—the scientific community. Members of this community were linked together by learned societies, common interests, and shared values. Expansion of knowledge was the primary goal of this community, and scientists' material and psychological rewards depended on their success in this endeavor. Thus science became quite competitive, and even more scientific advance was inevitable.

Second, the scientific revolution introduced not only new knowledge about nature but also a new and revolutionary way of obtaining such knowledge—the modern scientific method. In addition to being both theoretical and experimental, this method was highly critical, and it differed profoundly from the old way of getting knowledge about nature. It refused to base its conclusions on tradition and established sources, on ancient authorities and sacred texts.

The scientific revolution had few consequences for economic life and the living standards of the masses until the late eighteenth century at the very earliest. True, improvements in the techniques of navigation facilitated overseas trade and helped enrich leading merchants. But science had relatively few practical economic applications, and the hopes of the early Baconians were frustrated. The close link between theoretical, or pure, science and applied technology, which we take for granted today, simply did not exist before the nineteenth century. Thus the scientific revolution of the seventeenth century was first and foremost an intellectual revolution. It is not surprising that for more than a hundred years its greatest impact was on how people thought and believed.

THE ENLIGHTENMENT

The scientific revolution was the single most important factor in the creation of the new world-view of the eighteenth-century Enlightenment. This world-view, which has played a large role in shaping the modern mind, was based on a rich mix of ideas, sometimes conflicting, for intellectuals delight in playing with ideas just as athletes delight in playing games. Despite this diversity, three central concepts stand out.

The most important and original idea of the Enlightenment was that the methods of natural science could and should be used to examine and understand all aspects of life. This was what intellectuals meant by *reason*, a favorite word of Enlightenment thinkers. Nothing was to be accepted on faith. Everything was to be submitted to the rational, critical, scientific way of thinking. This approach brought the Enlightenment into a head-on conflict with the established churches, which rested their beliefs on the special authority of the Bible and Christian theology. A second important Enlightenment concept was that the scientific method was capable of discovering the laws of human society as well as those of nature. Thus was social science born. Its birth led to the third key idea, that of progress. Armed with the proper method of discovering the laws of human existence, Enlightenment thinkers believed it was at least possible to create better societies and better people. Their belief was strengthened by some genuine improvements in economic and social life during the eighteenth century (see Chapters 19 and 20).

The Enlightenment was therefore profoundly secular. It revived and expanded the Renaissance concentration on worldly explanations. In the course of the eighteenth century, the Enlightenment had a profound impact on the thought and culture of the urban middle and upper classes. It did not have much appeal for the poor and the peasants.

The Emergence of the Enlightenment

The Enlightenment did not reach its maturity until about 1750. Yet it was the generation that came of age between the publication of Newton's masterpiece in 1687 and the death of Louis XIV in 1715 that tied the crucial knot between the scientific revolution and a new outlook on life.

Talented writers of that generation popularized hard-to-understand scientific achievements for the educated elite. The most famous and influential popularizer was a versatile French man of letters, Bernard de Fontenelle (1657–1757). Fontenelle practically invented the technique of making highly complicated scientific findings understandable to a broad nonscientific audience. He set out to make science witty and entertaining, as easy to read as a novel. This was a tall order, but Fontenelle largely succeeded.

His most famous work, *Conversations on the Plurality of Worlds* of 1686, begins with two elegant figures walking in the gathering shadows of a large park. One is a woman, a sophisticated aristocrat, and the other is her friend, perhaps even her lover. They gaze at the stars, and their talk turns to a passionate discussion of . . . astronomy! He confides that "each star may well be a different world." She is intrigued by his novel idea: "Teach me about these stars of yours." And he does, gently but persistently stressing how error is giving way to truth. At one point he explains:

There came on the scene . . . one Copernicus, who made short work of all those various circles, all those solid skies, which the ancients had pictured to themselves. The

former he abolished; the latter he broke in pieces. Fired with the noble zeal of a true astronomer, he took the earth and spun it very far away from the center of the universe, where it had been installed, and in that center he put the sun, which had a far better title to the honor.[9]

Rather than tremble in despair in the face of these revelations, Fontenelle's lady rejoices in the advance of knowledge. Fontenelle thus went beyond entertainment to instruction, suggesting that the human mind was capable of making great progress.

This idea of progress was essentially a new idea of the later seventeenth century. Medieval and Reformation thinkers had been concerned primarily with sin and salvation. The humanists of the Renaissance had emphasized worldly matters, but they had been backward-looking. They had believed it might be possible to equal the magnificent accomplishments of the ancients, but they did not ask for more. Fontenelle and like-minded writers had come to believe that, at least in science and mathematics, their era had gone far *beyond* antiquity. Progress, at least intellectual progress, was clearly possible. During the eighteenth century, this idea would sink deeply into the consciousness of the European elite.

Fontenelle and other literary figures of his generation were also instrumental in bringing science into conflict with religion. Contrary to what is often assumed, many seventeenth-century scientists, both Catholic and Protestant, believed that their work exalted God. They did not draw antireligious implications from their scientific findings. The greatest scientist of them all, Isaac Newton, was a devout if unorthodox Christian who saw all of his studies as directed toward explaining God's message. Newton devoted far more of his time to angels and biblical prophecies than to universal gravitation, and he was convinced that all of his inquiries were equally scientific.

Fontenelle, on the other hand, was skeptical about absolute truth and cynical about the claims of organized religion. Since such unorthodox views could not be stated openly in Louis XIV's France, Fontenelle made his point through subtle editorializing about science. His depiction of the cautious Copernicus as a self-conscious revolutionary was typical. In his *Eulogies of Scientists*, Fontenelle exploited with endless variations the basic theme of rational, progressive scientists versus prejudiced, reactionary priests. Time and time again, Fontenelle's fledgling scientists attended church and studied theology; then, at some crucial moment, each was converted from the obscurity of religion to the clarity of science.

The progressive and antireligious implications that writers like Fontenelle drew from the scientific revolution reflected a very real crisis in European thought at the end of the seventeenth century. This crisis had its roots in several intellectual uncertainties and dissatisfactions, of which the demolition of Aristotelian-medieval science was only one.

A second uncertainty involved the whole question of religious truth. The destructive wars of religion had been fought, in part, because religious freedom was an intolerable idea in the early seventeenth century. Both Catholics and Protestants had believed that religious truth was absolute and therefore worth fighting and dying for. It was also generally believed that a strong state required unity in religious faith. Yet the disastrous results of the many attempts to impose such religious unity, such as Louis XIV's expulsion of the French Huguenots in 1685, led some people to ask if ideological conformity in religious matters was really necessary. Others skeptically asked if religious truth could ever be known with absolute certainty and concluded that it could not.

The most famous of these skeptics was Pierre Bayle (1647–1706), a French Huguenot who took refuge in Holland. A teacher by profession and a crusading journalist by inclination, Bayle critically examined the religious beliefs and persecutions of the past in his *Historical and Critical Dictionary,* published in 1697. Demonstrating that human beliefs had been extremely varied and very often mistaken, Bayle concluded that nothing can ever be known beyond all doubt. In religion as in philosophy, humanity's best hope was open-minded toleration. Bayle's skeptical views were very influential. Many eighteenth-century writers mined his inexhaustible vein of critical skepticism for ammunition in their attacks on superstition and theology. Bayle's four-volume *Dictionary* was found in more private libraries of eighteenth-century France than any other book.

The rapidly growing travel literature on non-European lands and cultures was a third cause of uncertainty. In the wake of the great discoveries, Europeans were learning that the peoples of China, India, Africa, and the Americas all had their own very different beliefs and customs. Europeans

shaved their faces and let their hair grow. The Turks shaved their heads and let their beards grow. In Europe a man bowed before a woman to show respect. In Siam a man turned his back on a woman when he met her, because it was disrespectful to look directly at her. Countless similar examples discussed in the travel accounts helped change the perspective of educated Europeans. They began to look at truth and morality in relative rather than absolute terms. Anything was possible, and who could say what was right or wrong? As one Frenchman wrote: "There is nothing that opinion, prejudice, custom, hope, and a sense of honor cannot do." Another wrote disapprovingly of religious skeptics who were corrupted "by extensive travel

Popularizing Science The frontispiece illustration of Fontenelle's *Conversations on the Plurality of Worlds* invites the reader to share the pleasures of astronomy with an elegant lady and an entertaining teacher. *(Source: University of Illinois, Champaign)*

and lose whatever shreds of religion that remained with them. Every day they see a new religion, new customs, new rites."[10]

A fourth cause and manifestation of European intellectual turmoil was John Locke's epoch-making *Essay Concerning Human Understanding*. Published in 1690—the same year Locke published his famous *Second Treatise of Civil Government* (see page 524)—Locke's essay brilliantly set forth a new theory about how human beings learn and form their ideas. In doing so, he rejected the prevailing view of Descartes, who had held that all people are born with certain basic ideas and ways of thinking. Locke insisted that all ideas are derived from experience. The human mind is like a blank tablet (*tabula rasa*) at birth, a tablet on which environment writes the individual's understanding and beliefs. Human development is therefore determined by education and social institutions, for good or for evil. Locke's *Essay Concerning Human Understanding* passed through many editions and translations. It was, along with Newton's *Principia,* one of the dominant intellectual inspirations of the Enlightenment.

The Philosophes and Their Ideas

By the death of Louis XIV in 1715, many of the ideas that would soon coalesce into the new world-view had been assembled. Yet Christian Europe was still strongly attached to its traditional beliefs, as witnessed by the powerful revival of religious orthodoxy in the first half of the eighteenth century. By the outbreak of the American Revolution in 1775, however, a large portion of western Europe's educated elite had embraced many of the new ideas. This acceptance was the work of one of history's most influential groups of intellectuals, the *philosophes*. It was the philosophes who proudly and effectively proclaimed that they, at long last, were bringing the light of knowledge to their ignorant fellow creatures in a great Age of Enlightenment.

Philosophe is the French word for "philosopher," and it was in France that the Enlightenment reached its highest development. The French philosophes were indeed philosophers. They asked fundamental philosophical questions about the meaning of life, about God, human nature, good and evil, and cause and effect. But, in the tradition of Bayle and Fontenelle, they were not content with abstract arguments or ivory-tower speculations among a tiny minority of scholars and professors. They wanted to influence and convince a broad audience.

The philosophes were intensely committed to reforming society and humanity, yet they were not free to write as they wished, since it was illegal in France to criticize openly either church or state. Their most radical works had to circulate in France in manuscript form, very much as critical works are passed from hand to hand in unpublished form in dictatorships today. Knowing that direct attacks would probably be banned or burned, the philosophes wrote novels and plays, histories and philosophies, dictionaries and encyclopedias, all filled with satire and double meanings to spread the message.

One of the greatest philosophes, the baron de Montesquieu (1689–1755), brilliantly pioneered this approach in *The Persian Letters,* an extremely influential social satire published in 1721. Montesquieu's work consisted of amusing letters supposedly written by Persian travelers, who see European customs in unique ways and thereby cleverly criticize existing practices and beliefs.

Having gained fame using wit as a weapon against cruelty and superstition, Montesquieu settled down on his family estate to study history and politics. His interest was partly personal for, like many members of the high French nobility, he was dismayed that royal absolutism had triumphed in France under Louis XIV. But Montesquieu was also inspired by the example of the physical sciences, and he set out to apply the critical method to the problem of government in *The Spirit of Laws* (1748). The result was a complex comparative study of republics, monarchies, and despotisms—a great pioneering inquiry in the emerging social sciences.

Showing that forms of government were related to history, geography, and customs, Montesquieu focused on the conditions that would promote liberty and prevent tyranny. He argued that despotism could be avoided if political power were divided and shared by a diversity of classes and orders holding unequal rights and privileges. A strong, independent upper class was especially important, according to Montesquieu, because in order to prevent the abuse of power, "it is necessary that by the arrangement of things, power checks power." Admiring greatly the English balance of power among the king, the houses of Parliament, and the independent courts, Montesquieu believed that in France the thirteen high courts—the *parlements*—were front-line defenders of liberty against royal despotism. Apprehensive about the uneducated poor, Montesquieu was clearly no democrat, but his theory of separation of powers had a great impact on France's wealthy, well-educated elite. The constitutions of the young United States in 1789 and of France in 1791 were based in large part on this theory.

The most famous and in many ways most representative philosophe was François Marie Arouet, who was known by the pen name of Voltaire (1694–1778). In his long career, this son of a comfortable middle-class family wrote over seventy witty volumes, hobnobbed with kings and queens, and died a millionaire because of shrewd business speculations. His early career, however, was turbulent. In 1717 Voltaire was imprisoned for eleven months in the Bastille in Paris for insulting the regent of France. In 1726 a barb from his sharp tongue led a great French nobleman to have him beaten and arrested. This experience made a deep impression on Voltaire. All his life he struggled against legal injustice and class inequalities before the law.

Released from prison after promising to leave the country, Voltaire lived in England for three years. Sharing Montesquieu's enthusiasm for English institutions, Voltaire then wrote various works praising England and popularizing English scientific progress. Newton, he wrote, was history's greatest man, for he had used his genius for the benefit of humanity. "It is," wrote Voltaire, "the man who sways our minds by the prevalence of reason and the native force of truth, not they who reduce mankind to a state of slavery by force and downright violence . . . that claims our reverence and admiration."[11] In the true style of the Enlightenment, Voltaire mixed the glorification of science and reason with an appeal for better people and institutions.

Yet, like almost all of the philosophes, Voltaire was a reformer and not a revolutionary in social and political matters. Returning to France, he was eventually appointed royal historian in 1743, and his *Age of Louis XIV* portrayed Louis as the dignified leader of his age. Voltaire also began a long correspondence with Frederick the Great, and he accepted Frederick's invitation to come brighten up the Prussian court in Berlin. The two men later quarreled, but Voltaire always admired Frederick as a free thinker and an enlightened monarch.

Unlike Montesquieu, Voltaire pessimistically concluded that the best one could hope for in the way of government was a good monarch, since human beings "are very rarely worthy to govern themselves." Nor did he believe in social equality in human affairs. The idea of making servants equal to their masters was "absurd and impossible." The only realizable equality, Voltaire thought, was that "by which the citizen only depends on the laws which protect the freedom of the feeble against the ambitions of the strong."[12]

Voltaire's philosophical and religious positions were much more radical. In the tradition of Bayle, his voluminous writings challenged—often indirectly—the Catholic church and Christian theology at almost every point. Though he was considered by many devout Christians to be a shallow blasphemer, Voltaire's religious views were influential and quite typical of the mature Enlightenment. The essay on religion from his widely read *Philosophical Dictionary* sums up many of his criticisms and beliefs:

I meditated last night; I was absorbed in the contemplation of nature; I admired the immensity, the course, the harmony of these infinite globes which the vulgar do not know how to admire.

I admired still more the intelligence which directs these vast forces. I said to myself: "One must be blind not to be dazzled by this spectacle; one must be stupid not to recognize its author; one must be mad not to worship the Supreme Being."

I was deep in these ideas when one of those genii who fill the intermundane spaces came down to me . . . and transported me into a desert all covered with piles of bones. . . . He began with the first pile. "These," he said, "are the twenty-three thousand Jews who danced before a calf, with the twenty-four thousand who were killed while lying with Midianitish women. The number of those massacred for such errors and offences amounts to nearly three hundred thousand.

"In the other piles are the bones of the Christians slaughtered by each other because of metaphysical disputes. . . ."

"What!" I cried, "brothers have treated their brothers like this, and I have the misfortune to be of this brotherhood! . . . Why assemble here all these abominable monuments to barbarism and fanaticism?"

Voltaire leans forward at left to exchange ideas with Frederick the Great across the table, as Prussian officials look on. As this painting suggests, Voltaire's radicalism was mainly intellectual and philosophical, not social or political. *(Source: Bildarchiv Preussischer Kulturbesitz)*

"To instruct you. . . . Follow me now." . . .

I saw a man with a gentle, simple face, who seemed to me to be about thirty-five years old. From afar he looked with compassion upon those piles of whitened bones, through which I had been led to reach the sage's dwelling place. I was astonished to find his feet swollen and bleeding, his hands likewise, his side pierced, and his ribs laid bare by the cut of the lash. "Good God!" I said to him, "is it possible for a just man, a sage, to be in this state? . . . Was it . . . by priests and judges that you were so cruelly assassinated?"

With great courtesy he answered, "Yes."

"And who were these monsters?"

"They were hypocrites."

"Ah! that says everything; I understand by that one word that they would have condemned you to the cruelest punishment. Had you then proved to them, as Socrates

did, that the Moon was not a goddess, and that Mercury was not a god?"

"No, it was not a question of planets. My countrymen did not even know what a planet was; they were all arrant ignoramuses. Their superstitions were quite different from those of the Greeks."

"Then you wanted to teach them a new religion?"

"Not at all; I told them simply: 'Love God with all your heart and your neighbor as yourself, for that is the whole of mankind's duty.' Judge yourself if this precept is not as old as the universe; judge yourself if I brought them a new religion." . . .

"Did you not say once that you were come not to bring peace, but a sword?"

"It was a scribe's error; I told them that I brought peace and not a sword. I never wrote anything; what I said can have been changed without evil intention."

"You did not then contribute in any way by your teaching, either badly reported or badly interpreted, to those frightful piles of bones which I saw on my way to consult with you?"

"I have only looked with horror upon those who have made themselves guilty of all these murders."

. . . [Finally] I asked him to tell me in what true religion consisted.

"Have I not already told you? Love God and your neighbor as yourself." . . .

"Well, if that is so, I take you for my only master."[13]

This passage requires careful study, for it suggests several Enlightenment themes of religion and philosophy. As the opening paragraphs show, Voltaire clearly believed in a God. But the God of Voltaire and most philosophes was a distant, deistic God, a great Clockmaker who built an orderly universe and then stepped aside and let it run. The passage also reflects the philosophes' hatred of all forms of religious intolerance. They believed that people had to be wary of dogmatic certainty and religious disputes, which often led to fanaticism and savage, inhuman action. Simple piety and human kindness—the love of God and the golden rule—were religion enough, even Christianity enough, as Voltaire's interpretation of Christ suggests.

The ultimate strength of the philosophes lay in their numbers, dedication, and organization. The philosophes felt keenly that they were engaged in a common undertaking that transcended individuals. Their greatest and most representative intellectual achievement was, quite fittingly, a group effort—the seventeen-volume *Encyclopedia: The Rational Dictionary of the Sciences, the Arts, and the Crafts,* edited by Denis Diderot (1713–1784) and Jean le Rond d'Alembert (1717–1783). Diderot and d'Alembert made a curious pair. Diderot began his career as a hack writer, first attracting attention with a skeptical tract on religion that was quickly

Canal with Locks   The articles on science and the industrial arts in the *Encyclopedia* carried lavish explanatory illustrations. This typical engraving from the section on water and its uses shows advances in canal building and reflects the encyclopedists' faith in technical progress. *(Source: University of Illinois, Champaign)*

One of the most famous salons was that of Madame Geoffrin, the unofficial godmother of the *Encyclopedia*. Having lost her parents at an early age, the future Madame Geoffrin was married at fifteen by her well-meaning grandmother to a rich and boring businessman of forty-eight. It was the classic marriage of convenience—the poor young girl and the rich old man—and neither side ever pretended that love was a consideration. After dutifully raising her children, Madame Geoffrin sought to break out of her gilded cage as she entered middle age. The very proper businessman's wife became friendly with a neighbor, the marquise de Tencin, an aristocratic beauty who had settled down to run a salon that counted Fontenelle and the philosopher Montesquieu among its regular guests.

When the marquise died in 1749, Madame Geoffrin tactfully transferred these luminaries to her spacious mansion for regular dinners. At first Madame Geoffrin's husband loudly protested the arrival of this horde of "parasites." But his wife's will was much stronger than his, and he soon opened his purse and even appeared at the twice-weekly dinners. "Who was that old man at the end of the table who never said anything?" an innocent newcomer asked one evening. "That," replied Madame Geoffrin without the slightest emotion, "was my husband. He's dead."[16]

When Monsieur Geoffrin's death became official, Madame Geoffrin put the large fortune and spacious mansion she inherited to good use. She welcomed the encyclopedists, and her generous financial aid helped to save their enterprise from collapse, especially after the first eight volumes were burned by the authorities in 1759. She also corresponded with the king of Sweden and Catherine the Great of Russia. Madame Geoffrin was, however, her own woman. She remained a practicing

Madame Geoffrin's Salon   In this stylized group portrait a famous actor reads to a gathering of leading philosophes and aristocrats in 1755. Third from the right presiding over her gathering is Madame Geoffrin, next to the sleepy ninety-eight-year-old Bernard de Fontenelle. *(Source: Giraudon/Art Resource)*

Christian and would not tolerate attacks on the church in her house. The plain and long-neglected Madame Geoffrin managed to become the most renowned hostess of the eighteenth century.

There were many other hostesses, but Madame Geoffrin's greatest rival, Madame du Deffand, was one of the most interesting. While Madame Geoffrin was middle-class, pious, and chaste, Madame du Deffand was a skeptic from the nobility who lived fast and easy, at least in her early years. Another difference was that women—mostly highly intelligent, worldly members of the nobility—were fully the equal of men in Madame du Deffand's intellectual salon. Forever pursuing fulfillment in love and life, Madame du Deffand was an accomplished and liberated woman. An exceptionally fine letter writer, she carried on a vast correspondence and counted Voltaire as her most enduring friend.

The salons seem to have functioned as informal schools, where established hostesses bonded with younger women and passed their skills to them. Madame du Deffand's closest female friend was Julie de Lespinasse, a beautiful, talented young woman whom she befriended and made her protégée. The never-acknowledged illegitimate daughter of noble parents, Julie de Lespinasse had a hard youth, but she flowered in Madame du Deffand's drawing room—so much so that she was eventually dismissed by her jealous patroness.

Once again Julie de Lespinasse triumphed. Her friends gave her money so that she could form her own salon. Her highly informal gatherings—she was not rich enough to supply more than tea and cake—attracted the keenest minds in France and Europe. As one philosophe wrote:

She could unite the different types, even the most antagonistic, sustaining the conversation by a well-aimed phrase, animating and guiding it at will. . . . Politics, religion, philosophy, news: nothing was excluded. Her circle met daily from five to nine. There one found men of all ranks in the State, the Church, and the Court, soldiers and foreigners, and the leading writers of the day.[17]

Thus in France the ideas of the Enlightenment thrived in a social setting that graciously united members of the intellectual, economic, and social elites. Never before and never again would social and intellectual life be so closely and so pleasantly joined. In such an atmosphere, the philosophes, the French nobility, and the upper middle class intermingled and increasingly influenced one another. Critical thinking became fashionable and flourished alongside hopes for human progress through greater knowledge.

THE DEVELOPMENT OF ABSOLUTISM

How did the Enlightenment influence political developments? To this important question there is no easy answer. On the one hand, the philosophes were primarily interested in converting people to critical scientific thinking and were not particularly concerned with politics. On the other hand, such thinking naturally led to political criticism and interest in political reform. Educated people, who belonged mainly to the nobility and middle class, came to regard political change as both possible and desirable. A further problem is that Enlightenment thinkers had different views on politics. Some, led by the nobleman Montesquieu, argued for curbs on monarchial power in order to promote liberty, and some French judges applied such theories in practical questions.

Until the American Revolution, however, most Enlightenment thinkers believed that political change could best come from above—from the ruler—rather than from below, especially in central and eastern Europe. There were several reasons for this essentially moderate belief. First, royal absolutism was a fact of life, and the kings and queens of Europe's leading states clearly had no intention of giving up their great powers. Therefore, the philosophes realistically concluded that a benevolent absolutism offered the best opportunities for improving society. Critical thinking was turning the art of good government into an exact science. It was necessary only to educate and "enlighten" the monarch, who could then make good laws and promote human happiness. Second, philosophes turned toward rulers because rulers seemed to be listening, treating them with respect, and seeking their advice. Finally, although the philosophes did not dwell on this fact, they distrusted the masses. Known simply as "the people" in the eighteenth century, the peasant masses and the urban poor were, according to the philosophes, still enchained by religious superstitions and violent passions. No doubt the people were maturing, but they were still children in need of firm parental guidance.

Encouraged and instructed by the philosophes, several absolutist rulers of the later eighteenth century tried to govern in an "enlightened" manner. Yet, because European monarchs had long been locked in an intense international competition, a more enlightened state often meant in practice a more effective state, a state capable of expanding its territory and defeating its enemies. Moreover, reforms from above had to be grafted onto previous historical developments and existing social structures. Little wonder, then, that the actual programs and accomplishments of these rulers varied greatly. Let us therefore examine the evolution of monarchial absolutism at close range before trying to form any overall judgment regarding the meaning of what historians have often called the "enlightened absolutism" of the later eighteenth century.

The "Greats": Frederick of Prussia and Catherine of Russia

Just as the French culture and absolutism of Louis XIV provided models for European rulers in the late seventeenth century, the Enlightenment teachings of the French philosophes inspired European monarchs in the second half of the eighteenth century. French was the international language of the educated classes, and the education of future kings and queens across Europe lay in the hands of French tutors espousing Enlightenment ideas. France's cultural leadership was reinforced by the fact that it was still the wealthiest and most populous country in Europe. Thus absolutist monarchs in several west German and Italian states, as well as in Spain and Portugal, proclaimed themselves more enlightened. By far the most influential of the new-style monarchs were Frederick II of Prussia and Catherine II of Russia, both styled "the Great."

Frederick the Great Frederick II (r. 1740–1786), commonly known as Frederick the Great, built masterfully on the work of his father, Frederick William I (see pages 543–545). This was somewhat surprising for, like many children with tyrannical parents, he rebelled against his family's wishes in his early years. Rejecting the crude life of the barracks, Frederick embraced culture and literature, even writing poetry and fine prose in French, a language his father detested. He threw off his father's dour Calvinism and dabbled with atheism. After

trying unsuccessfully to run away at age eighteen in 1730, he was virtually imprisoned and even compelled to watch his companion in flight beheaded at his father's command. Yet, like many other rebellious youths, Frederick eventually reached a reconciliation with his father, and by the time he came to the throne ten years later, Frederick was determined to use the splendid army that his father had left him.

When, therefore, the emperor of Austria, Charles VI, also died in 1740 and his young and beautiful daughter, Maria Theresa, became ruler of the Habsburg dominions, Frederick suddenly and without warning invaded her rich, all-German province of Silesia. This action defied solemn Prussian promises to respect the Pragmatic Sanction, which guaranteed Maria Theresa's succession—but no matter. For Frederick, it was the opportunity of a lifetime to expand the size and power of Prussia. Although Maria Theresa succeeded in dramatically rallying the normally quarrelsome Hungarian nobility, her multinational army was no match for Prussian precision. In 1742, as other greedy powers were falling on her lands in the general European War of the Austrian Succession (1740–1748), she was forced to cede all of Silesia to Prussia (see Map 17.2). In one stroke, Prussia doubled its population to six million people. Now Prussia unquestionably towered above all the other German states and stood as a European Great Power.

Though successful in 1742, Frederick had to spend much of his reign fighting against great odds to save Prussia from total destruction. Maria Theresa was determined to regain Silesia, and when the ongoing competition between Britain and France for colonial empire brought renewed conflict in 1756, her able chief minister fashioned an aggressive alliance with France and Russia. During the Seven Years' War (1756–1763), the aim of the alliance was to conquer Prussia and divide up its territory, just as Frederick II and other monarchs had so recently sought to partition the Austrian Empire. Frederick led his army brilliantly, striking repeatedly at vastly superior forces invading from all sides. At times he believed all was lost, but he fought on with stoic courage. In the end, he was miraculously saved: Peter III came to the Russian throne in 1762 and called off the attack against Frederick, whom he greatly admired.

In the early years of his reign, Frederick II had kept his enthusiasm for Enlightenment culture strictly separated from a brutal concept of international politics. He wrote:

Of all States, from the smallest to the biggest, one can safely say that the fundamental rule of government is the principle of extending their territories. . . . The passions of rulers have no other curb but the limits of their power. Those are the fixed laws of European politics to which every politician submits.[18]

But the terrible struggle of the Seven Years' War tempered Frederick and brought him to consider how more humane policies for his subjects might also strengthen the state.

Thus Frederick went beyond a superficial commitment to Enlightenment culture for himself and his circle. He tolerantly allowed his subjects to believe as they wished in religious and philosophical matters. He promoted the advancement of knowledge, improving his country's schools and universities. Moreover, Frederick tried to improve the lives of his subjects more directly. As he wrote his friend Voltaire, "I must enlighten my people, cultivate their manners and morals, and make them as happy as human beings can be, or as happy as the means at my disposal permit." The legal system and the bureaucracy were Frederick's primary tools. Prussia's laws were simplified, torture of prisoners was abolished, and judges decided cases quickly and impartially. Prussian officials became famous for their hard work and honesty. After the Seven Years' War ended in 1763, Frederick's government also energetically promoted the reconstruction of agriculture and industry in his war-torn country. In all this Frederick set a good example. He worked hard and lived modestly, claiming that he was "only the first servant of the state." Thus Frederick justified monarchy in terms of practical results and said nothing of the divine right of kings.

Frederick's dedication to high-minded principles went only so far, however. He never tried to change Prussia's existing social structure. True, he condemned serfdom in the abstract, but he accepted it in practice and did not even free the serfs on his own estates. He accepted and extended the privileges of the nobility, which he saw as his primary ally in the defense and extension of his realm. It became practically impossible for a middle-class person to gain a top position in the government. The Junker nobility remained the backbone of the army and the entire Prussian state.

Catherine the Great Catherine the Great of Russia (r. 1762–1796) was one of the most remarkable rulers who ever lived, and the philosophes adored her. Catherine was a German princess from Anhalt-Zerbst, a totally insignificant principality sandwiched between Prussia and Saxony. Her father commanded a regiment of the Prussian army, but her mother was related to the Romanovs of Russia, and that proved to be her chance.

Peter the Great had abolished the hereditary succession of tsars so that he could name his successor and thus preserve his policies. This move opened a period of palace intrigue and a rapid turnover of rulers until Peter's youngest daughter Elizabeth came to the Russian throne in 1741. A crude, shrewd woman noted for her hard drinking and hard loving—one of her official lovers was an illiterate shepherd boy—Elizabeth named her nephew Peter heir to the throne and chose Catherine to be his wife in 1744. It was a mismatch from the beginning. The fifteen-year-old Catherine was intelligent and attractive; her husband was stupid and ugly, his face badly scarred by smallpox. Ignored by her childish husband, Catherine carefully studied Russian, endlessly read writers like Bayle and Voltaire, and made friends at court. Soon she knew what she wanted. "I did not care about Peter," she wrote in her *Memoirs,* "but I did care about the crown."[19]

As the old empress Elizabeth approached death, Catherine plotted against her unpopular husband. A dynamic, sensuous woman, Catherine used her sexuality to good political advantage. She selected as her new lover a tall, dashing young officer named Gregory Orlov, who with his four officer brothers commanded considerable support among the soldiers stationed in St. Petersburg. When Peter came to the throne in 1762, his decision to withdraw Russian troops from the coalition against Prussia alienated the army. Nor did Peter III's attempt to gain support from the Russian nobility by freeing it from compulsory state service succeed. At the end of six months, Catherine and the military conspirators deposed Peter III in a palace revolution. Then the Orlov brothers murdered him. The German princess became empress of Russia.

Catherine had drunk deeply at the Enlightenment well. Never questioning the common assumption that absolute monarchy was the best form of government, she set out to rule in an enlightened manner. One of her most enduring goals was to bring the sophisticated culture of western

Catherine as Equestrian   Catherine took advantage of her intelligence and good looks to maneuver her husband Peter III off the throne and get herself crowned as Russia's new monarch. Strongly influenced by the Enlightenment, she cultivated the French philosophes and instituted moderate domestic reforms only to reverse them in the aftermath of Pugachev's rebellion. *(Source: Sovfoto)*

Europe to backward Russia. To do so, she imported Western architects, sculptors, musicians, and intellectuals. She bought masterpieces of Western art in wholesale lots and patronized the philosophes. An enthusiastic letter writer, she corresponded extensively with Voltaire and praised him as the "champion of the human race." When the French government banned the *Encyclopedia,* she offered to publish it in St. Petersburg. She discussed reform with Diderot in St. Petersburg; and when Diderot needed money, she purchased his library for a small fortune but allowed him to keep it during his lifetime. With these and countless similar actions, Catherine skillfully won a good press for herself and for her country in the West. Moreover, this intellectual ruler, who wrote plays and loved good talk, set the tone for the entire Russian nobility. Peter the Great westernized Russian armies, but it was Catherine who westernized the thinking of the Russian nobility.

Catherine's second goal was domestic reform, and she began her reign with sincere and ambitious projects. Better laws were a major concern. In 1767 she drew up enlightened instructions for the special legislative commission she appointed to prepare a new law code. No new unified code was ever produced, but Catherine did restrict the practice of torture and allowed limited religious toleration. She also tried to improve education and strengthen local government. The philosophes applauded these measures and hoped more would follow.

Such was not the case. In 1773 a simple Cossack soldier named Emelian Pugachev sparked a gigantic uprising of serfs, very much as Stenka Razin had done a century earlier (see page 552). Proclaiming himself the true tsar, Pugachev issued "decrees" abolishing serfdom, taxes, and army service. Thousands joined his cause, slaughtering landlords and officials over a vast area of southwestern Russia. Pugachev's untrained hordes eventually proved no match for Catherine's noble-led regular army. Betrayed by his own company, Pugachev was captured and savagely executed.

Pugachev's rebellion was a decisive turning point in Catherine's domestic policy. On coming to the throne she had condemned serfdom in theory, but she was smart enough to realize that any changes would have to be very gradual or else she would quickly follow her departed husband. Pugachev's rebellion put an end to any illusions she might have had about reforming serfdom. The peasants were clearly dangerous, and her empire rested on the support of the nobility. After 1775 Catherine gave the nobles absolute control of their serfs. She extended serfdom into new areas, such as the Ukraine. In 1785 she formalized the nobility's privileged position, freeing them forever from taxes and state service. She also confiscated the lands of the Russian Orthodox church and gave them to favorite officials. Under Catherine, the Russian nobility attained its most exalted position, and serfdom entered its most oppressive phase.

Catherine's third goal was territorial expansion, and in this respect she was extremely successful. Her armies subjugated the last descendants of the Mongols, the Crimean Tartars, and began the conquest of the Caucasus.

Her greatest coup by far was the partitioning of Poland. Poland showed the dangers of failing to build a strong absolutist state. For decades all important decisions had required the unanimous agreement of all the Polish nobles, which meant that nothing could ever be done. When between 1768 and 1772 Catherine's armies scored unprecedented victories against the Turks and thereby threatened to disturb the balance of power between Russia and Austria in eastern Europe, Frederick of Prussia obligingly came forward with a deal. He proposed that Turkey be let off easily, and that Prussia, Austria, and Russia each compensate itself by taking a gigantic slice of Polish territory. Catherine jumped at the chance. The first partition of Poland took place in 1772. Two more partitions, in 1793 and 1795, gave all three powers more Polish territory, and the kingdom of Poland simply vanished from the map (Map 18.1).

Expansion helped Catherine keep the nobility happy, for it provided her with vast new lands to give to her faithful servants. Expansion also helped Catherine reward her lovers, of whom twenty-one have been definitely identified. On all these royal favorites she lavished large estates with many serfs,

as if to make sure there were no hard feelings when her interest cooled. Until the end this remarkable woman—who always believed that, in spite of her domestic setbacks, she was slowly civilizing Russia—kept her zest for life. Fascinated by a new twenty-two-year-old flame when she was a roly-poly grandmother in her sixties, she happily reported her good fortune to a favorite former lover: "I have come back to life like a frozen fly; I am gay and well."[20]

Absolutism in France and Austria

The Enlightenment's influence on political developments in France and Austria was complex. In France, the monarchy maintained its absolutist claims, and some philosophes like Voltaire believed that the king was still the best source of needed reform. At the same time, discontented nobles and learned judges drew on thinkers such as Montesquieu for liberal arguments, and they sought with some success to limit the king's power. In Austria, two talented rulers did manage to introduce major reforms, although traditional power politics were more important than Enlightenment teachings.

Louis XV of France In building French absolutism, Louis XIV had successfully drawn on the middle class to curb the political power of the nobility. As long as the Grand Monarch lived, the nobility could only grumble and, like the duke of Saint-Simon in his *Memoirs,* scornfully lament the rise of "the vile bourgeoisie." But when Louis XIV finally died in 1715, to be succeeded by his five-year-old great-grandson, Louis XV (r. 1715–1774), the Sun King's elaborate system of absolutist rule was challenged in a general reaction. Favored by the duke of Orléans, who governed as regent until 1723, the nobility made a strong comeback.

Most important, the duke restored to the high court of Paris—the Parlement—the right to "register" and thereby approve the king's decrees. This was a fateful step. The judges of the Parlement of Paris had originally come from the middle class, and their high position reflected the way that Louis XIV (and earlier French monarchs) had chosen to use that class to build the royal bureaucracy so necessary for an absolutist state. By the eighteenth century, however, these middle-class judges had risen to become hereditary nobles. Moreover, although Louis XIV had curbed the political power of the nobility, he had never challenged its enormous social prestige. Thus high position in the government continued to bestow the noble status that middle-class officials wanted, either immediately or after three generations of continuous service. The judges of Paris, like many high-ranking officials, actually owned their government jobs and freely passed them on as private property from father to son. By supporting the claim of this well-entrenched and increasingly aristocratic group to register the king's laws, the duke of Orléans sanctioned a counterweight to absolute power.

These implications became clear when the heavy expenses of the War of the Austrian Succession plunged France into financial crisis. In 1748 Louis XV appointed a finance minister who decreed a 5 percent income tax on every individual, regardless of social status. Exemption from most taxation had long been a hallowed privilege of the nobility, and other important groups—the clergy, the large towns, and some wealthy bourgeoisie—had also gained special tax advantages over time. The result

was a vigorous protest from many sides, and the Parlement of Paris refused to ratify the tax law. The monarchy retreated; the new tax was dropped.

Following the disastrously expensive Seven Years' War, the conflict re-emerged. The government tried to maintain emergency taxes after the war ended. The Parlement of Paris protested and even challenged the basis of royal authority, claiming that the king's power must necessarily be limited to protect liberty. Once again the government caved in and withdrew the wartime taxes in 1764. Emboldened by its striking victory and widespread support from France's educated elite, the judicial opposition in Paris and the provinces pressed its demands. In a barrage of pamphlets and legal briefs, it asserted that the king could not levy taxes without the consent of the Parlement of Paris acting as the representative of the entire nation.

Indolent and sensual by nature, more interested in his many mistresses than in affairs of state, Louis XV finally roused himself for a determined defense of his absolutist inheritance. "The magistrates," he

MAP 18.1 The Partition of Poland and Russia's Expansion, 1772–1795 Though all three of the great eastern absolutist states profited from the division of large but weak Poland, Catherine's Russia gained the most.

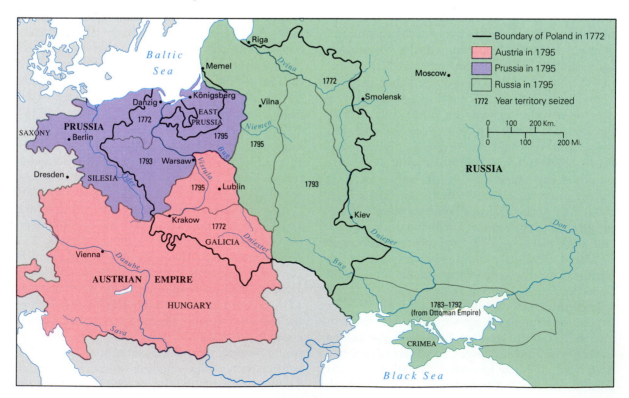

angrily told the Parlement of Paris in a famous face-to-face confrontation, "are my officers. . . . In my person only does the sovereign power rest."[21] In 1768 Louis appointed a tough career official named René de Maupeou as chancellor and ordered him to crush the judicial opposition.

Maupeou abolished the Parlement of Paris and exiled its members to isolated backwaters in the provinces. He created a new and docile parlement of royal officials, and he began once again to tax the privileged groups. A few philosophes like Voltaire applauded these measures: the sovereign was using his power to introduce badly needed reforms that had been blocked by a self-serving aristocratic elite. Most philosophes and educated public opinion as a whole sided with the old parlements, however, and there was widespread dissatisfaction with royal despotism. Yet the monarchy's power was still great enough for Maupeou simply to ride over the opposition, and Louis XV would probably have prevailed—if he had lived to a very ripe old age.

But Louis XV died in 1774. The new king, Louis XVI (r. 1774–1792), was a shy twenty-year-old with good intentions. Taking the throne, he is reported to have said: "What I should like most is to be loved."[22] The eager-to-please monarch decided to yield in the face of such strong criticism from so much of France's elite. He dismissed Maupeou and repudiated the strong-willed minister's work. The old Parlement of Paris was reinstated, as enlightened public opinion cheered and people hoped for moves toward representative government. Such moves were not forthcoming. Instead, a weakened but unrepentant monarchy faced a judicial opposition that claimed to speak for the entire French nation. Increasingly locked in stalemate, the country was drifting toward renewed financial crisis and political upheaval.

The Austrian Habsburgs   Joseph II (r. 1780–1790) was a fascinating individual. For an earlier generation of historians he was the "revolutionary emperor," a tragic hero whose lofty reforms were undone by the landowning nobility he dared to challenge. More recent scholarship has revised this romantic interpretation and stressed how Joseph II continued the state-building work of his mother, the empress Maria Theresa, a remarkable but old-fashioned absolutist.

Maria Theresa's long reign (1740–1780) began with her neighbors, led by Frederick II of Prussia, invading her lands and trying to dismember them

(see page 584). Emerging from the long War of the Austrian Succession in 1748 with only the serious loss of Silesia, Maria Theresa and her closest ministers were determined to introduce reforms that would make the state stronger and more efficient. Three aspects were most important in these reforms. First, Maria Theresa introduced measures to bring relations between church and state under government control. Like some medieval rulers, the most devout and very Catholic Maria Theresa aimed at limiting the papacy's political influence in her realm. Second, a whole series of administrative reforms strengthened the central bureaucracy, smoothed out some provincial differences, and revamped the tax system, taxing even the lands of nobles without special exemptions. Finally, the government sought to improve the lot of the agricultural population, cautiously reducing the power of lords over both their hereditary serfs and their partially free peasant tenants.

Coregent with his mother from 1765 onward and a strong supporter of change, Joseph II moved forward rapidly when he came to the throne in 1780. He controlled the established Catholic church even more closely, in an attempt to ensure that it produced better citizens. He granted religious toleration and civic rights to Protestants and Jews—a radical innovation that impressed his contemporaries. In even more spectacular peasant reforms, Joseph abolished serfdom in 1781, and in 1789 he decreed that all peasant labor obligations be converted into cash payments. This ill-conceived measure was violently rejected not only by the nobility but by the peasants it was intended to help, since their primitive barter economy was woefully lacking in money. When a disillusioned Joseph died prematurely at forty-nine, the entire Habsburg empire was in turmoil. His brother Leopold (r. 1790–1792) was forced to cancel Joseph's radical edicts in order to re-establish order. Peasants lost most of their recent gains, and once again they were required to do forced labor for their lords, as in the 1770s under Maria Theresa.

An Overall Evaluation

Having examined the evolution of monarchial absolutism in four leading states, we can begin to look for meaningful generalizations and to evaluate the overall influence of Enlightenment thought on politics. That thought, it will be remembered,

Maria Theresa   and her husband pose with eleven of their sixteen children at Schön-brunn palace. Joseph, the heir to the throne, stands at the center of the star pattern. Wealthy women often had very large families, in part because they seldom nursed their babies as poor women usually did. *(Source: Kunsthistorisches Museum, Vienna)*

was clustered in two distinct schools: the liberal critique of unregulated monarchy promoted by Montesquieu and the defenders of royal absolutism led by Voltaire.

It is clear that France diverged from its eastern neighbors in its political development in the eighteenth century. Although neither the French monarchy nor the eastern rulers abandoned the absolutist claims and institutions they had inherited, the monarch's capacity to govern in a truly absolutist manner declined substantially in France, and this was not the case in eastern Europe. The immediate cause of this divergence was the political resurgence of the French nobility after 1715 and the growth of judicial opposition, led by the Parlement

of Paris. More fundamentally, however, the judicial and aristocratic opposition in France achieved its still rather modest successes because it received major support from educated public opinion, which increasingly made the liberal critique of unregulated royal authority its own. In France, then, the proponents of absolute monarchy were increasingly on the defensive, as was the French monarchy itself.

The situation in eastern Europe was different. The liberal critique of absolute monarchy remained an intellectual curiosity, and proponents of reform from above held sway. Moreover, despite their differences, the leading eastern European monarchs of the later eighteenth century all claimed that they were acting on the principles of the Enlightenment. The philosophes generally agreed with this assessment and cheered them on. Beginning in the mid-nineteenth century, historians developed the idea of a common "enlightened despotism" or "enlightened absolutism," and they canonized Frederick, Catherine, and Joseph as its most outstanding examples. More recent research has raised doubts about this old interpretation and has led to a fundamental re-evaluation.

First, there is general agreement that these absolutists, especially Catherine and Frederick, did encourage and spread the cultural values of the Enlightenment. Perhaps this was their greatest achievement. Skeptical in religion and intensely secular in basic orientation, they unabashedly accepted the here and now and sought their happiness in the enjoyment of it. At the same time, they were proud of their intellectual accomplishments and good taste, and they supported knowledge, education, and the arts. No wonder the philosophes felt the monarchs were kindred spirits.

Historians also agree that the absolutists believed in change from above and tried to enact needed reforms. Yet the results of these efforts brought only very modest improvements, and the life of the peasantry remained very hard in the eighteenth century. Thus some historians have concluded that these monarchs were not really sincere in their reform efforts. Others disagree, arguing that powerful nobilities blocked the absolutists' genuine commitment to reform. (The old interpretation of Joseph II as the tragic "revolutionary emperor" forms part of this argument.)

The emerging answer to this confusion is that the later eastern absolutists were indeed committed to reform, but that humanitarian objectives were of quite secondary importance. Above all, the absolutists wanted reforms that would strengthen the state and allow them to compete militarily with their neighbors. Modern scholarship has stressed, therefore, how Catherine, Frederick, and Joseph were in many ways simply continuing the state building of their predecessors, reorganizing their armies and expanding their bureaucracies to raise more taxes and troops. The reason for this continuation was simple. The international political struggle was brutal, and the stakes were high. First Austria under Maria Theresa, and then Prussia under Frederick the Great, had to engage in bitter fighting to escape dismemberment, while decentralized Poland was coldly divided and eventually liquidated.

Yet, in their drive for more state power, the later absolutists were also innovators, and the idea of an era of enlightened absolutism retains a certain validity. Sharing the Enlightenment faith in critical thinking and believing that knowledge meant power, these absolutists really were more enlightened because they put their state-building reforms in a new, broader perspective. Above all, they considered how more humane laws and practices could help their populations become more productive and satisfied, and thus able to contribute more substantially to the welfare of the state. It was from this perspective that they introduced many of their most progressive reforms, tolerating religious minorities, simplifying legal codes, and promoting practical education.

The primacy of state as opposed to individual interests—a concept foreign to North Americans long accustomed to easy dominion over a vast continent—also helps to explain some puzzling variations in social policies. For example, Catherine the Great took measures that worsened the peasants' condition because she looked increasingly to the nobility as her natural ally and sought to strengthen it. Frederick the Great basically favored the status quo, limiting only the counterproductive excesses of his trusted nobility against its peasants. On the other hand, Joseph II believed that greater freedom for peasants was the means to strengthen his realm, and he acted accordingly. Each enlightened absolutist sought greater state power, but each believed a different policy would attain it.

In conclusion, the eastern European absolutists of the later eighteenth century combined old-fashioned state building with the culture and critical thinking of the Enlightenment. In doing so, they succeeded in expanding the role of the state in the life of society. Unlike the successors of Louis XIV, they perfected bureaucratic machines that were to prove surprisingly adaptive and capable of enduring into the twentieth century.

SUMMARY

This chapter has focused on the complex development of a new world-view in Western civilization. This new view of the world was essentially critical and secular, drawing its inspiration from the scientific revolution and crystallizing in the Enlightenment.

The decisive breakthroughs in astronomy and physics in the seventeenth century, which demolished the imposing medieval synthesis of Aristotelian philosophy and Christian theology, had only limited practical consequences despite the expectations of scientific enthusiasts like Bacon. Yet the impact of new scientific knowledge on intellectual life became great. Interpreting scientific findings and Newtonian laws in an antitraditional, antireligious manner, the French philosophes of the Enlightenment extolled the superiority of rational, critical thinking. This new method, they believed, promised not just increased knowledge but even the discovery of the fundamental laws of human society. Although they reached different conclusions when they turned to social and political realities, the philosophes nevertheless succeeded in spreading their radically new world-view. That was a momentous accomplishment.

NOTES

1. H. Butterfield, *The Origins of Modern Science* (New York: Macmillan, 1951), p. viii.
2. Quoted in A. G. R. Smith, *Science and Society in the Sixteenth and Seventeenth Centuries* (New York: Harcourt Brace Jovanovich, 1972), p. 97.
3. Quoted in Butterfield, p. 47.
4. Quoted in Smith, p. 100.
5. Ibid., pp. 115–116.
6. Ibid., p. 120.
7. A. R. Hall, *From Galileo to Newton, 1630–1720* (New York: Harper & Row, 1963), p. 290.
8. Quoted in R. K. Merton, *Science, Technology and Society in Seventeenth-century England*, rev. ed. (New York: Harper & Row, 1970), p. 164.
9. Quoted in P. Hazard, *The European Mind, 1680–1715* (Cleveland: Meridian Books, 1963), pp. 304–305.
10. Ibid., pp. 11–12.
11. Quoted in L. M. Marsak, ed., *The Enlightenment* (New York: John Wiley & Sons, 1972), p. 56.
12. Quoted in G. L. Mosse et al., eds., *Europe in Review* (Chicago: Rand McNally, 1964), p. 156.
13. F. M. Arouet de Voltaire, *Oeuvres completes,* vol. 8 (Paris: Firmin-Didot, 1875), pp. 188–190.
14. Quoted in P. Gay, "The Unity of the Enlightenment," *History* 3 (1960): 25.
15. See E. Fox-Genovese, "Women in the Enlightenment," in *Becoming Visible: Women in European History,* 2d ed., ed. R. Bridenthal, C. Koonz, and S.

Stuard (Boston: Houghton Mifflin, 1987), esp. pp. 252–259 and 263–265.
16. Quoted in G. P. Gooch, *Catherine the Great and Other Studies* (Hamden, Conn.: Archon Books, 1966), p. 112.
17. Ibid., p. 149.
18. Quoted in L. Krieger, *Kings and Philosophers, 1689–1789* (New York: W. W. Norton, 1970), p. 257.
19. Ibid., p. 15.
20. Ibid., p. 53.
21. Quoted in R. R. Palmer, *The Age of Democratic Revolution,* vol. 1 (Princeton, N.J.: Princeton University Press, 1959), pp. 95–96.
22. Quoted in G. Wright, *France in Modern Times* (Chicago: Rand McNally, 1960), p. 42.

SUGGESTED READING

The first three authors cited in the Notes—H. Butterfield, A. G. R. Smith, and A. R. Hall—have written excellent general interpretations of the scientific revolution. These may be compared with an outstanding recent work by M. Jacob, *The Cultural Meaning of the Scientific Revolution* (1988), which has a useful bibliography. The older study of England by R. Merton, mentioned in the Notes, also analyzes ties between science and the larger community. A. Debus, *Man and Nature in the Renaissance* (1978), is good on the Copernican revolution, while M. Boas, *The Scientific Renaissance, 1450–1630* (1966), is especially insightful about the influence of magic on science and about Galileo's trial. T. Kuhn, *The Structure of Scientific Revolutions* (1962), is a challenging, much-discussed attempt to understand major breakthroughs in scientific thought over time. E. Andrade, *Sir Isaac Newton* (1958), is a good short biography, which may be compared with F. Manuel, *The Religion of Isaac Newton* (1974).

The work of P. Hazard listed in the Notes is a classic study of the formative years of Enlightenment thought, and his *European Thought in the Eighteenth Century* (1954) is also recommended. A famous, controversial interpretation of the Enlightenment is that of C. Becker, *The Heavenly City of the Eighteenth Century Philosophes* (1932), which maintains that the world-view of medieval Christianity continued to influence the philosophes greatly. Becker's ideas are discussed interestingly in R. O. Rockwood, ed., *Carl Becker's Heavenly City Revisited* (1958). P. Gay has written several major studies on the Enlightenment: *Voltaire's Politics* (1959) and *The Party of Humanity* (1971) are two of the best. I. Wade, *The Structure and Form of the French Enlightenment* (1977), is a major synthesis. F. Baumer's *Religion and the Rise of Skepticism*

(1969), H. Payne's *The Philosophes and the People* (1976), and H. Chisick, *The Limits of Reform in the Enlightenment: Attitudes Toward the Education of the Lower Classes in Eighteenth-Century France* (1981), are interesting studies of important aspects of Enlightenment thought. On women, see the stimulating study by E. Fox-Genovese cited in the Notes, as well as S. Spencer, ed., *French Women and the Age of Enlightenment* (1984), and K. Rogers's *Feminism in Eighteenth-Century England* (1982). Above all, one should read some of the philosophes and let them speak for themselves. Two good anthologies are C. Brinton, ed., *The Portable Age of Reason* (1956), and F. Manuel, ed., *The Enlightenment* (1951). Voltaire's most famous and very amusing novel *Candide* is highly recommended, as are S. Gendzier, ed., *Denis Diderot: The Encyclopedia: Selections* (1967), and A. Wilson's biography, *Diderot* (1972).

In addition to the works mentioned in the Suggested Reading for Chapters 16 and 17, the monarchies of Europe are carefully analyzed in C. Tilly, ed., *The Formation of National States in Western Europe* (1975), and in J. Gagliardo, *Enlightened Despotism* (1967), both of which have useful bibliographies. M. Anderson, *Historians and Eighteenth-Century Europe* (1979), is a valuable introduction to modern scholarship. Other recommended studies on the struggle for power and reform in different countries are: F. Ford, *Robe and Sword* (1953), which discusses the resurgence of the French nobility after the death of Louis XIV; R. Herr, *The Eighteenth-Century Revolution in Spain* (1958), on the impact of Enlightenment thought in Spain; and P. Bernard, *Joseph II* (1968). There are several fine works on Russia. J. Alexander, *Catherine the Great: Life and Legend* (1989), is the best biography of the famous ruler. I. de Madariaga's masterful *Russia in the Age of Catherine the Great* (1981) and D. Ransel's solid *Politics of Catherinean Russia* (1975) are recommended. The ambitious reader should also look at A. N. Radishchev, *A Journey from St. Petersburg to Moscow* (English trans., 1958), a famous 1790 attack on Russian serfdom and an appeal to Catherine the Great to free the serfs, for which Radishchev was exiled to Siberia.

The culture of the time may be approached through A. Cobban, ed., *The Eighteenth Century* (1969), a richly illustrated work with excellent essays, and C. B. Behrens, *The Ancien Régime* (1967). C. Rosen, *The Classical Style: Haydn, Mozart, Beethoven* (1972), brilliantly synthesizes music and society, as did Mozart himself in his great opera *The Marriage of Figaro*, where the count is the buffoon and his servant the hero.

19

The Expansion of Europe in the Eighteenth Century

The world of absolutism and aristocracy, a combination of raw power and elegant refinement, was a world apart from that of ordinary men and women. For the overwhelming majority of the population in the eighteenth century, life remained a struggle with poverty and uncertainty, with the landlord and the tax collector. In 1700 peasants on the land and artisans in their shops lived little better than had their ancestors in the Middle Ages. Only in science and thought, and there only among a few intellectual leaders, had Western society succeeded in going beyond the great achievements of the High Middle Ages, achievements that in turn owed so much to Greece and Rome.

Everyday life was a struggle because European societies, despite their best efforts, still could not produce very much by modern standards. Ordinary people might work like their beasts in the fields, and they often did, but there was seldom enough good food, warm clothing, and decent housing. Life went on; history went on. The wars of religion ravaged Germany in the seventeenth century; Russia rose to become a Great Power; the kingdom of Poland simply disappeared; monarchs and nobles continuously jockeyed for power and wealth. In 1700 or even 1750, the idea of progress—of substantial improvement in the lives of great numbers of people—was still only the dream of a small elite in fashionable salons.

Yet the economic basis of European life was beginning to change. In the course of the eighteenth century, the European economy emerged from the long crisis of the seventeenth century, responded to challenges, and began to expand once again. Some areas were more fortunate than others. The rising Atlantic powers—Holland, France, and above all England—and their colonies led the way. Agriculture and industry, trade and population, began a surge comparable to that of the eleventh- and twelfth-century springtime of European civilization. But this time, development was not cut short. This time, the response to new challenges led toward one of the most influential developments in human history, the Industrial Revolution, considered in Chapter 22.

- What were the causes of this renewed surge?
- Why were the fundamental economic underpinnings of European society beginning to change at this time, and what were the dimensions of these changes?
- How did these changes affect people and their work?

These are the questions this chapter will address.

AGRICULTURE AND THE LAND

At the end of the seventeenth century, the economy of Europe was agrarian, as it had been for several hundred years. With the possible exception of Holland, at least 80 percent of the people of all western European countries drew their livelihoods from agriculture. In eastern Europe the percentage was considerably higher.

Men and women lavished their attention on the land, plowing fields and sowing seed, reaping harvests and storing grain. The land repaid these efforts, year after year yielding up the food and most of the raw materials for industry that made life possible. Yet the land was stingy. Even in a rich agricultural region like the Po Valley in northern Italy, every bushel of wheat sown yielded on average only 5 or 6 bushels of grain at harvest during the seventeenth century. The average French yield in the same period was somewhat less. Such yields were barely more than those attained in fertile, well-watered areas in the thirteenth century or in ancient Greece. By modern standards, output was distressingly low. (For each bushel of wheat seed sown today on fertile land with good rainfall, an American or French farmer can expect roughly 40 bushels of produce.) In 1700 European agriculture was much more ancient and medieval than it was modern.

If the land was stingy, it was also capricious. In most regions of Europe in the sixteenth and seventeenth centuries, harvests were poor, or even failed completely, every eight or nine years. The vast majority of the population who lived off the land might survive a single bad harvest by eating less and drawing on their reserves of grain. But when the land's caprices combined with persistent bad weather—too much rain rotting the seed or drought withering the young stalks—the result was catastrophic. Meager grain reserves were soon exhausted, and the price of grain soared. Provisions from other areas with better harvests were hard to obtain.

In such crisis years, which periodically stalked Europe in the seventeenth and even into the eighteenth century, a terrible tightening knot in the belly forced people to use substitutes—the "famine foods" of a desperate population. People gathered chestnuts and stripped bark in the forests; they cut dandelions and grass; and they ate these substitutes to escape starvation. In one community in Norway in the early 1700s, people were forced to wash dung from the straw in old manure piles in order to bake a pathetic substitute for bread. Even cannibalism occurred in the seventeenth century.

Such unbalanced and inadequate food in famine years made people weak and extremely susceptible to illness and epidemics. Eating material unfit for human consumption, such as bark or grass,

Farming the Land   Agricultural methods in Europe changed very slowly from the Middle Ages to the early eighteenth century. This realistic picture from Diderot's *Encyclopedia* has striking similarities with agricultural scenes found in medieval manuscripts. *(Source: University of Illinois, Champaign)*

resulted in dysentery and intestinal ailments of many kinds. Influenza and smallpox preyed with particular savagery on populations weakened by famine. In famine years, the number of deaths soared far above normal. A third of a village's population might disappear in a year or two. The 1690s were as dismal as many of the worst periods of earlier times. One county in Finland, probably typical of the entire country, lost fully 28 percent of its inhabitants in 1696 and 1697. Certain well-studied villages in the Beauvais region of northern France suffered a similar fate. In preindustrial Europe, the harvest was the real king, and the king was seldom generous and often cruel.

To understand why Europeans produced barely enough food in good years and occasionally agonized through years of famine throughout the later seventeenth century, one must follow the plowman, his wife, and his children into the fields to observe their battle for food and life. There the ingenious pattern of farming that Europe had developed in the Middle Ages, a pattern that allowed fairly large numbers of people to survive but could never produce material abundance, was still dominant.

The Open-Field System

The greatest accomplishment of medieval agriculture was the open-field system of village agriculture developed by European peasants (see Chapter 10). That system divided the land to be cultivated by the peasants of a given village into several large fields, which were in turn cut up into long, narrow strips. The fields were open, and the strips were not enclosed into small plots by fences or hedges. An individual peasant family—if it were fortunate—held a number of strips scattered throughout the various large fields. The land of those who owned but did not till, primarily the nobility, the clergy, and wealthy townspeople, was also in scattered strips. The peasants farmed each large field as a community, with each family following the same pattern of plowing, sowing, and harvesting in accordance with tradition and the village leaders.

The ever-present problem was exhaustion of soil. If the community planted wheat year after year in a field, the nitrogen in the soil was soon depleted and crop failure was certain. Since the supply of manure for fertilizer was limited, the only way for the land to recover its life-giving fertility was for a field to lie fallow for a period of time. In the early Middle Ages, a year of fallow was alternated with a year of cropping, so that half the land stood idle in a given year. With time, three-year rotations were introduced, especially on more fertile lands. This system permitted a year of wheat or rye to be followed by a year of oats or beans, and only then by a year of fallow. Even so, only awareness of the tragic consequences of continuous cropping forced undernourished populations to let a third (or half) of their crop land lie idle, especially when the fallow had to be plowed two or three times a year to keep down the weeds.

Traditional village rights reinforced the traditional pattern of farming. In addition to rotating the field crops in a uniform way, villages maintained open meadows for hay and natural pasture. These lands were "common" lands, set aside primarily for the draft horses and oxen so necessary in the fields, but open to the cows and pigs of the village community as well. After the harvest, the men and women of the village also pastured their animals on the wheat or rye stubble. In many places such pasturing followed a brief period, also established by tradition, for the gleaning of grain. Poor women would go through the fields picking up the few single grains that had fallen to the ground in the course of the harvest. The subject of a great nineteenth-century painting, *The Gleaners* by Jean François Millet, this backbreaking work by hard-working but impoverished women meant quite literally the slender margin of survival for some people in the winter months.

In the age of absolutism and nobility, state and landlord continued to levy heavy taxes and high rents as a matter of course. In so doing they stripped the peasants of much of their meager earnings. The level of exploitation varied. Conditions for the rural population were very different in different areas.

Generally speaking, the peasants of eastern Europe were worst off. As we have seen in Chapter 17, they were still serfs, bound to their lords in hereditary service. Though serfdom in eastern Europe in the eighteenth century had much in common with medieval serfdom in central and western Europe, it was, if anything, harsher and more oppressive. In much of eastern Europe there were few limitations on the amount of forced labor the lord could require, and five or six days of unpaid work per week on the lord's land was not uncommon. Well into

Millet: The Gleaners   Poor French peasant women search for grains and stalks the harvesters (in the background) have missed. The open-field system seen here could still be found in parts of Europe in 1857, when this picture was painted. Millet is known for his great paintings expressing social themes. *(Source: Louvre/Cliché des Musées Nationaux, Paris)*

the nineteenth century, individual Russian serfs and serf families were regularly sold with and without land. Serfdom was often very close to slavery. The only compensating factor in much of eastern Europe was that, as with slavery, differences in well-being among serfs were slight. In Russia, for example, the land available to the serfs for their own crops was divided among them almost equally.

Social conditions were better in western Europe. Peasants were generally free from serfdom. In France, western Germany, and the Low Countries, they owned land and could pass it on to their chil-

dren. Yet life in the village was unquestionably hard, and poverty was the great reality for most people. For the Beauvais region of France at the beginning of the eighteenth century, it has been carefully estimated that in good years and bad only a tenth of the peasants could live satisfactorily off the fruits of their landholdings. Owning considerably less than half of the land, the peasants of the Beauvais region had to pay heavy royal taxes, the church's tithe, and dues to the lord, as well as set aside seed for the next season. Left with only half of their crop for their own use, these peasants had to toil and till for others and seek work for wages in a variety of jobs. It was a constant scramble for a meager living. And this was in a rich agricultural region in a country where peasants were comparatively well off. The privileges of Europe's ruling elites weighed heavily on the people of the land.

Agricultural Revolution

One possible way for European peasants to improve their difficult position was to take land from those who owned but did not labor. Yet the social and political conditions that enabled the ruling elites to squeeze the peasants were ancient and deep-rooted, and powerful forces stood ready to crush any protest. Only with the coming of the French Revolution were European peasants, mainly in France, able to improve their position by means of radical mass action.

Technological progress offered another possibility. The great need was for new farming methods that would enable Europeans to produce more and eat more. The uncultivated fields were the heart of the matter. If peasants (and their noble landlords) could replace the idle fallow with crops, they could increase the land under cultivation by 50 percent. So remarkable were the possibilities and the results that historians have often spoken of the progressive

Enclosing the Fields   This aerial photograph captures key aspects of the agricultural revolution. Though the long ridges and furrows of the old open-field system still stretch across the whole picture, hedge rows now cut through the long strips to divide the land into several enclosed fields. *(Source: © British Crown copyright/MOD reproduced with the permission of the Controller of Her Britannic Majesty's Stationery Office)*

elimination of the fallow, which occurred slowly throughout Europe from the mid-seventeenth century on, as an agricultural revolution.

This agricultural revolution, which took longer than historians used to believe, was a great milestone in human development. The famous French scholar Marc Bloch, who gave his life in the resistance to the Nazis in World War Two, summed it up well: "The history of the conquest of the fallow by new crops, a fresh triumph of man over the earth that is just as moving as the great land clearing of the Middle Ages, [is] one of the noblest stories that can be told."[1]

Because grain crops exhaust the soil and make fallowing necessary, the secret to eliminating the fallow lies in alternating grain with certain nitrogen-storing crops. Such crops not only rejuvenate the soil even better than fallowing, but give more produce as well. The most important of these land-reviving crops are peas and beans, root crops such as turnips and potatoes, and clovers and grasses. In the eighteenth century, peas and beans were old standbys; turnips, potatoes, and clover were newcomers to the fields. As time went on, the number of crops that were systematically rotated grew, and farmers developed increasingly sophisticated patterns of rotation to suit different kinds of soils. For example, farmers in French Flanders near Lille in the late eighteenth century used a ten-year rotation, alternating a number of grain, root, and hay crops in a given field on a ten-year schedule. Continuous experimentation led to more scientific farming.

Improvements in farming had multiple effects. The new crops made ideal feed for animals. Because peasants and larger farmers had more fodder —hay and root crops—for the winter months, they could build up their small herds of cattle and sheep. More animals meant more meat and better diets for the people. More animals also meant more manure for fertilizer, and therefore more grain for bread and porridge. The vicious cycle in which few animals meant inadequate manure, which meant little grain and less fodder, which led to fewer animals, and so on, could be broken. The cycle became positive: more animals meant more manure, which meant more grain and more fodder, which meant more animals, which meant better diets.

Advocates of the new rotations, who included an emerging group of experimental scientists, some government officials, and a few big landowners, believed that new methods were scarcely possible

Surveyors Measuring Enclosing open farmland met with much resistance, especially from poorer peasants and some nobility. It was more successful in England as illustrated in this scene from a nineteenth-century map of Bedfordshire. *(Source: Courtesy, Bedfordshire County Council)*

within the traditional framework of open fields and common rights. A farmer who wanted to experiment with new methods would have to get all the landholders in a village to agree to the plan, and advocates of improvement maintained that this would be difficult if not impossible, given peasant caution and the force of tradition. Therefore, they argued that innovating agriculturalists needed to enclose and consolidate their scattered holdings into compact, fenced-in fields, in order to farm more effectively. In doing so, the innovators also needed to enclose their individual shares of the natural pasture, the common. According to this view, a revolution in village life and organization was the necessary price of technical progress.

That price seemed too high to many rural people. Above all, the village poor believed that they were being asked to pay an unfair and disproportionate share of the bill. With land distributed very unequally all across Europe by 1700, large groups of village poor held small, inadequate holdings, or very little land at all. Common rights were precious to these poor peasants. The rights to glean and to graze a cow on the common, to gather firewood in the lord's forest and pick berries in the marsh, were vital because they helped poor peasants retain a modicum of independence and status and avoid falling into the growing group of landless, "proletarian" wage workers. Thus, when the small landholders and the village poor could effectively oppose the enclosure of the open fields and the common pasture, they did so. Moreover, in many countries they usually found allies among the larger, predominately noble landowners, who were also wary of enclosure because it required large investments and posed risks for them as well. Only powerful social and political pressures could overcome the combined opposition.

The old system of unenclosed open fields and the new system of continuous rotation coexisted in Europe for a very long time. In large parts of central Russia, for example, the old system did not disappear until after the Bolshevik Revolution in 1917. It could also be found in much of France and Germany in the early years of the nineteenth century, because peasants there had successfully opposed efforts to introduce the new techniques in the late eighteenth century. Indeed, until the end of the eighteenth century, the promise of the new system was extensively realized only in the Low Countries and in England.

The Leadership of the Low Countries and England

The new methods of the agricultural revolution originated in the Low Countries. The vibrant, dynamic middle-class society of seventeenth-century republican Holland was the most advanced in Europe in many areas of human endeavor. In shipbuilding and navigation, in commerce and banking, in drainage and agriculture, the people of the Low Countries, especially the Dutch, provided models the jealous English and French sought to copy or to cripple.

By the middle of the seventeenth century, intensive farming was well established throughout much of the Low Countries. Enclosed fields, continuous rotation, heavy manuring, and a wide variety of crops—all these innovations were present. Agriculture was highly specialized and commercialized. The same skills that grew turnips produced flax to be spun into linen for clothes and tulip bulbs to lighten the heart with their beauty. The fat cattle of Holland, so beloved by Dutch painters, gave the most milk in Europe. Dutch cheeses were already world-renowned.

The reasons for early Dutch leadership in farming were basically twofold. In the first place, since the end of the Middle Ages the Low Countries had been one of the most densely populated areas in Europe. Thus, in order to feed themselves and provide employment, the Dutch were forced at an early date to seek maximum yields from their land and to increase the cultivated area through the steady draining of marshes and swamps. Even so, they had to import wheat from Poland and eastern Germany.

The pressure of population was connected with the second cause, the growth of towns and cities in the Low Countries. Stimulated by commerce and overseas trade, Amsterdam grew from 30,000 inhabitants to 200,000 in its golden seventeenth century. The growth of urban population provided Dutch peasants with good markets for all they could produce and allowed each region to specialize in what it did best. Thus the Dutch could develop their potential, and the Low Countries became "the Mecca of foreign agricultural experts who came . . . to see Flemish agriculture with their own eyes, to write about it and to propagate its methods in their home lands."[2]

The English were the best students. Indeed, they were such good students it is often forgotten that they had teachers at all. Drainage and water control was one subject in which they received instruction. Large parts of seventeenth-century Holland had once been sea and sea marsh, and the efforts of centuries had made the Dutch the world's leaders in the skills of drainage. In the first half of the seventeenth century, Dutch experts made a great contribution to draining the extensive marshes, or fens, of wet and rainy England.

The most famous of these Dutch engineers, Cornelius Vermuyden, directed one large drainage project in Yorkshire and another in Cambridgeshire. The project in Yorkshire was supported by Charles I and financed by a group of Dutch capitalists, who were to receive one-third of all land reclaimed in return for their investment. Despite local opposition, Vermuyden drained the land by means of a large canal—his so-called Dutch river—and settlers cultivated the new fields in the Dutch fashion. In the Cambridge fens, Vermuyden and his Dutch workers eventually reclaimed 40,000 acres, which were then farmed intensively in the Dutch manner. Although all these efforts were disrupted in the turbulent 1640s by the English civil war, Ver-

Dutch Villagers turned perishable milk into valuable cheeses that could be conveniently shipped to many markets. In this workshop scene a girl carries buckets of milk to women who are pressing curds together to form a solid. The finished cheeses—big red rounds of Gouda—stand on shelves to the right. *(Source: Courtesy, Dutch Dairy Bureau)*

muyden and his countrymen largely succeeded. Swampy wilderness was converted into thousands of acres of some of the best land in England. On such new land, where traditions and common rights were not firmly established yet, farmers introduced new crops and new rotations fairly easily.

Dutch experience was also important to Viscount Charles Townsend (1674–1738), one of the pioneers of English agricultural improvement. This lord from the upper reaches of the English aristocracy learned about turnips and clover while serving as English ambassador to Holland. In the 1710s, he was using these crops in the sandy soil of his large estates in Norfolk in eastern England, already one of the most innovative agricultural areas in the country. When Lord Charles retired from politics in 1730 and returned to Norfolk, it was said that he spoke of turnips, turnips, and nothing but turnips.

This led some wit to nickname his lordship "Turnip" Townsend. But Townsend had the last laugh. Draining extensively, manuring heavily, and sowing crops in regular rotation without fallowing, the farmers who leased Townsend's lands produced larger crops. They and he earned higher incomes. Those who had scoffed reconsidered. By 1740 agricultural improvement in various forms had become something of a craze among the English aristocracy.

Jethro Tull (1674–1741), part crank and part genius, was another important English innovator. A true son of the early Enlightenment, Tull constantly tested accepted ideas about farming in an effort to develop better methods through empirical research. He was especially enthusiastic about using horses for plowing, in preference to slower-moving oxen. He also advocated sowing seed with drilling equipment, rather than scattering it by

Selective Breeding meant bigger livestock and more meat on English tables. This gigantic champion, one of the new improved shorthorn breed, was known as the Newbus Ox. Such great fat beasts were pictured in the press and praised by poets. *(Source: Institute of Agricultural History and Museum of English Rural Life, University of Reading)*

hand. Drilling distributed seed evenly and at the proper depth. There were also improvements in livestock, inspired in part by the earlier successes of English country gentlemen in breeding ever-faster horses for the races and fox hunts that were their passions. Selective breeding of ordinary livestock was a marked improvement over the old pattern, which has been graphically described as little more than "the haphazard union of nobody's son with everybody's daughter."

By the mid-eighteenth century, English agriculture was in the process of a radical transformation. The eventual result was that by 1870 English farmers produced 300 percent more food than they had produced in 1700, although the number of people working the land had increased by only 14 percent. This great surge of agricultural production provided food for England's rapidly growing urban population. It was a tremendous achievement.

The Cost of Enclosure

What was the cost of technical progress in England, and to what extent did its payment result in social injustice? Scholars agree that the impetus for enclosing the fields came mainly from the powerful ruling class, the English aristocracy. Owning large estates, the aristocracy benefited directly from higher yields that could support higher rents, and it was able and ready to make expensive investments in the new technology. Beyond these certainties, there are important differences of interpretation among historians.

Many historians stress the initiative and enterprise of the big English landowners, which they contrast with the inertia and conservatism of continental landowners, big and small. They also assert that the open fields were enclosed fairly, with both large and small owners receiving their fair share after the strips were surveyed and consolidated.

Other historians argue that fairness was more apparent than real. The large landowners controlled Parliament, which made the laws. They had Parliament pass hundreds of "enclosure acts," each of which authorized the fencing of open fields in a given village and the division of the common in proportion to one's property in the open fields. The heavy legal and surveying costs of enclosure were also divided among the landowners. This meant that many peasants who had small holdings had to sell out to pay their share of the expenses. Similarly, the landless cottagers lost their age-old access to the common pasture without any compensation whatsoever. This dealt landless families a serious blow, because it deprived women of the means to raise animals for market and earn vital income. In the spirited words of one critical historian, "Enclosure (when all the sophistications are allowed for) was a plain enough case of class robbery, played according to the fair rules of property and law laid down by a Parliament of property-owners and lawyers."[3]

In assessing these conflicting interpretations, one needs to put eighteenth-century developments in a longer historical perspective. In the first place, as much as half of English farmland was already enclosed by 1750. A great wave of enclosure of English open fields into sheep pastures had already occurred in the sixteenth and early seventeenth centuries, a wave that had already dispossessed many English peasants in order to produce wool for the growing textile industry. In the later seventeenth and early eighteenth centuries, many open fields were enclosed fairly harmoniously by mutual agreement among all classes of landowners in English villages. Thus parliamentary enclosure, the great bulk of which occurred after 1760 and particularly during the Napoleonic wars early in the nineteenth century, only completed a process that was in full swing. Nor did an army of landless cottagers and farm laborers appear only in the last years of the eighteenth century. Much earlier, and certainly

by 1700 because of the early enclosures for sheep runs, there were perhaps two landless agricultural workers in England for every independent farmer. In 1830, after the enclosures were complete, the proportion of landless laborers on the land was not substantially greater.

Indeed, by 1700 a highly distinctive pattern of landownership and production existed in England. At one extreme were a few large landowners, at the other a large mass of landless cottagers, who labored mainly for wages and who could graze only a pig or a cow on the village common. In between stood two other groups: small, independent peasants farmers who owned their own land, and substantial tenant farmers who rented land from the big landowners, hired wage laborers, and sold their output on a cash market. Yet the small, independent English peasant farmers had been declining in number since the sixteenth-century enclosures (and even before), and they continued to do so in the eighteenth century. They could not compete with the rising group of profit-minded, market-oriented tenant farmers.

These tenant farmers, many of whom had formerly been independent owners, were the key to mastering the new methods of farming. Well financed by the large landowners, the tenant farmers fenced fields, built drains, and improved the soil with fertilizers. Such improvements actually increased employment opportunities for wage workers in some areas. So did new methods of farming, for land was farmed more intensively without the fallow, and new crops like turnips required more care and effort. Thus enclosure did not force people off the land and into the towns by eliminating jobs, as has sometimes been claimed.

At the same time, by eliminating common rights and greatly reducing the access of poor men and women to the land, the eighteenth-century enclosure movement marked the completion of two major historical developments in England—the rise of market-oriented estate agriculture and the emergence of a landless rural proletariat. By 1815 a tiny minority of wealthy English (and Scottish) landowners held most of the land and pursued profits aggressively, leasing their holdings through agents at competitive prices to middle-sized farmers. These farmers produced mainly for cash markets and relied on landless laborers for their workforce. These landless laborers may have lived as well in 1800 as in 1700 in strictly economic terms. But they had lost that bit of independence and self-respect that common rights had provided. They had become completely dependent on cash wages earned in agriculture or in rural industry for their survival. In no other European country had this "proletarianization"—this transformation of large numbers of small peasant farmers into landless rural wage earners—gone so far as it had in England by the late eighteenth century. And, as in the earlier English enclosure movement, the village poor found the cost of economic change and technical progress heavy and unjust.

THE BEGINNING OF THE POPULATION EXPLOSION

Another factor that affected the existing order of life and forced economic changes in the eighteenth century was the remarkable growth of European population, the beginning of the "population explosion." This population explosion continued in Europe until the twentieth century, by which time it was affecting non-Western areas of the globe. What caused the growth of population, and what did the challenge of more mouths to feed and more hands to employ do to the European economy?

FIGURE 19.1 The Growth of Population in England, 1000–1800 England is a good example of both the uneven increase of European population before 1700 and the third great surge of growth, which began in the eighteenth century. *(Source: E. A. Wrigley,* Population and History. *New York: McGraw-Hill, 1969)*

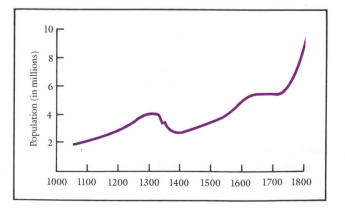

Limitations on Population Growth

Many commonly held ideas about population in the past are wrong. One such mistaken idea is that people always married young and had large families. A related error is the belief that past societies were so ignorant that they could do nothing to control their numbers and that population was always growing too fast. On the contrary, until 1700 the total population of Europe grew slowly much of the time, and it followed an irregular cyclical pattern (Figure 19.1).

The cyclical pattern of European population growth had a great influence on many aspects of social and economic life over time, although striking local and regional differences often make generalization difficult. As we have seen, the terrible ravages of the Black Death caused a sharp drop in population and prices after 1350 and also created a labor shortage throughout Europe (see page 534). Lords in eastern Europe responded to this labor shortage by reversing the trend toward personal freedom and gradually reinstituting serfdom. This landlord reaction failed in western Europe, however, where serf obligations had declined or even disappeared by 1500. Moreover, the era of labor shortages and low food prices after the Black Death resulted in an increased standard of living for peasants and artisans. Indeed, some economic historians calculate that, for those common people in western Europe who managed to steer clear of warfare and of power struggles within the ruling class, the later Middle Ages was an era of exceptional well-being.

But peasant and artisan well-being was eroded in the course of the sixteenth century. The second great surge of population growth indicated by Figure 19.1 outstripped the growth of agricultural production after about 1500. There was less food per person, and food prices rose more rapidly than wages, a development intensified by the inflow of precious metals from the Americas and a general if uneven European price revolution. The result was a substantial decline in living standards for the great majority of people throughout Europe. This decline aggravated especially the plight of both the urban and the rural poor. By 1600 the pressure of population on resources was severe in much of Europe, and widespread poverty was an undeniable reality.

For this reason, population growth slowed and stopped in seventeenth-century Europe. Births and deaths, fertility and mortality, were in a crude but effective balance. The birthrate—annual births as a proportion of the population—was fairly high, but far lower than it would have been if all women between ages fifteen and forty-five had been having as many children as biologically possible. The death rate in normal years was also high, though somewhat lower than the birthrate. As a result, the population grew modestly in normal years at a rate of perhaps 0.5 to 1 percent, or enough to double the population in 70 to 140 years. This is, of course, a generalization encompassing many different patterns. In areas like Russia and colonial New England, where there was a great deal of frontier to be settled, the annual rate of increase might well have exceeded 1 percent. In a country like France, where the land had long been densely settled, the rate of increase might have been less than 0.5 percent.

Although population growth of even 1 percent per year is fairly modest by the standards of many African and Latin American countries today—some of which are growing at about 3 percent annually—it will produce a very large increase over a long period. An annual increase of even 1 percent will result in sixteen times as many people in three hundred years. Such gigantic increases simply did not occur in agrarian Europe before the eighteenth century. In certain abnormal years and tragic periods—the Black Death was only the most extreme and extensive example—many more people died than were born. Total population fell sharply, even catastrophically. A number of years of modest growth would then be necessary to make up for those who had died in an abnormal year. Such savage increases in deaths occurred periodically in the seventeenth century on a local and regional scale, and these demographic crises combined with birthrates far below the biological potential to check the growth of population until after 1700.

The grim reapers of demographic crisis were famine, epidemic disease, and war. Famine, the inevitable result of poor farming methods and periodic crop failures, was particularly murderous because it was accompanied by disease. With a brutal one-two punch, famine stunned and weakened a population, and disease finished it off. Disease could also ravage independently, even in years of adequate harvests. Bubonic plague returned again and again in Europe for more than three hundred years after its ravages in the fourteenth century. Epidemics of dysentery and smallpox also operated independently of famine.

War was another scourge. The indirect effects were more harmful than the organized killing. War spread disease. Soldiers and camp followers passed venereal disease through the countryside to scar and kill. Armies requisitioned scarce food supplies for their own use and disrupted the agricultural cycle. The Thirty Years' War (see pages 477–481) witnessed all possible combinations of distress. In the German states, the number of inhabitants declined by more than *two-thirds* in some large areas and by at least one-third almost everywhere else. The Thirty Years' War reduced the total German population by no less than 40 percent. But numbers inadequately convey the dimensions of such human tragedy. One needs the vision of the artist. The great sixteenth-century artist Albrecht Dürer captured the horror of demographic crisis in his chilling woodcut *The Four Horsemen of the Apocalypse* (see page 382). Death, accompanied by his trusty companions War, Famine, and Conflict, takes his merciless ride of destruction. The narrow victory of life over death that prevails in normal times is being undone.

The New Pattern of the Eighteenth Century

In the eighteenth century, the population of Europe began to grow markedly. This increase in numbers occurred in all areas of Europe—western and eastern, northern and southern, dynamic and stagnant. Growth was especially dramatic after about 1750, as Figure 19.2 shows.

Although it is certain that Europe's population grew greatly, it is less clear why. Painstaking and innovative research in population history has shown that, because population grew everywhere, it is best to look first for general factors, rather than focus on those limited to individual countries or to certain levels of social and economic development. What, then, caused fewer people to die or, possibly, more babies to be born? In some kinds of families in some areas, women may have had more babies than before (see page 631). Yet the basic cause was a decline in mortality—fewer deaths.

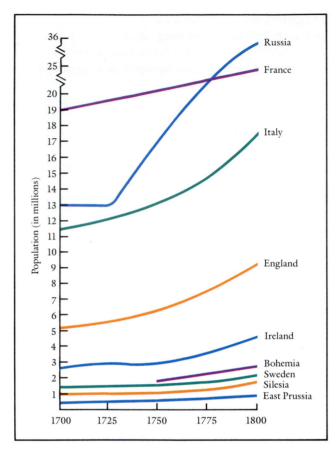

FIGURE 19.2 The Increase of Population in Europe in the Eighteenth Century   France's large population continued to support French political and intellectual leadership. Russia emerged as Europe's most populous state because natural increase was complemented by growth from territorial expansion.

The bubonic plague mysteriously disappeared. Following the Black Death in the fourteenth century, plagues had remained a part of the European experience, striking again and again with savage force, particularly in towns. As a German writer of the early sixteenth century noted, "It is remarkable and astonishing that the plague should never wholly cease, but it should appear every year here and there, making its way from one place to another. Having subsided at one time, it returns within a few years by a circuitous route."[4]

As late as 1720, a ship from Syria and the Levant, where plague was ever-present, brought the monstrous disease to Marseilles. In a few weeks, forty thousand of the city's ninety thousand inhabitants died. The epidemic swept southern France, killing one-third, one-half, even three-fourths of those in the larger towns. Once again an awful fear swept across Europe. But the epidemic passed, and that was the last time plague fell on western and central Europe. The final disappearance of plague was due in part to stricter measures of quarantine in Mediterranean ports and along the Austrian border with Turkey. Human carriers of plague were carefully isolated. Chance and plain good luck were more important, however.

It is now understood that bubonic plague is, above all, a disease of rats. More precisely, it is the black rat that spreads major epidemics, for the black rat's flea is the principal carrier of the plague bacillus. After 1600, for reasons unknown, a new rat of Asiatic origin—the brown, or wander, rat—began to drive out and eventually eliminate its black competitor. In the words of a noted authority, "This revolution in the animal kingdom must have gone far to break the lethal link between rat and man."[5] Although the brown rat also contracts the plague, another kind of flea is its main parasite. That flea carries the plague poorly and, for good measure, has little taste for human blood.

Advances in medical knowledge did not contribute much to reducing the death rate in the eighteenth century. The most important advance in preventive medicine in this period was inoculation against smallpox. This great improvement was long confined mainly to England and probably did little to reduce deaths throughout Europe until the latter part of the century. However, improvements in the water supply and sewerage promoted somewhat better public health and helped reduce such diseases as typhoid and typhus in some urban areas of western Europe. It has also been argued recently that eighteenth-century improvements in water supply and in the drainage of swamps and marshes reduced Europe's large and dangerous insect population. Filthy flies and mosquitoes played a major role in spreading serious epidemics and also in transmitting common diseases, especially those striking children and young adults. Thus early public health measures were probably more important than historians have previously believed, and they helped the decline in mortality that began with the disappearance of plague to continue into the early nineteenth century.

Human beings also became more successful in their efforts to safeguard the supply of food and protect against famine. The eighteenth century was a time of considerable canal and road building in western Europe. These advances in transportation, which were among the more positive aspects of strong absolutist states, lessened the impact of local crop failure and famine. Emergency supplies could be brought in. The age-old spectacle of localized starvation became less frequent. Wars became more gentlemanly and less destructive than in the seventeenth century and spread fewer epidemics. New foods, particularly the potato, were introduced. Potatoes served as an important alternative source of vitamins A and C for the poor, especially when the grain crops were skimpy or failed. In short, population grew in the eighteenth century primarily because years of abnormal death rates were less catastrophic. Famines, epidemics, and wars continued to occur, but their severity moderated.

The growth of population in the eighteenth century cannot be interpreted as a sign of human progress, however. As we have seen, serious population pressure on resources existed by 1600 and continued throughout the seventeenth century. Thus renewed population growth in the eighteenth century maintained or even increased the imbalance between the number of people and the economic opportunities available to them. There was only so much land available, and tradition slowed the adoption of better farming methods. Therefore, agriculture could not provide enough work for the rapidly growing labor force, and poor people in the countryside had to look for new ways to make a living.

THE GROWTH OF COTTAGE INDUSTRY

The growth of population increased the number of rural workers with little or no land, and this in turn contributed to the development of industry in rural areas. The poor in the countryside needed increasingly to supplement their earnings from agriculture with other types of work, and capitalists from the city were eager to employ them, often at lower wages than urban workers usually commanded. Manufacturing with hand tools in peasant cottages and worksheds grew markedly in the eighteenth century. Rural industry became a crucial feature of the European economy.

To be sure, peasant communities had always made some clothing, processed some food, and

constructed some housing for their own use. But in the High Middle Ages, peasants did not produce manufactured goods on a large scale for sale in a market. Industry in the Middle Ages was dominated and organized by urban craft guilds and urban merchants, who jealously regulated handicraft production and sought to maintain it as an urban monopoly. By the eighteenth century, however, the pressures of rural poverty and the need to employ landless proletarians were overwhelming the efforts of urban artisans to maintain their traditional control over industrial production. A new system was expanding lustily.

Doctor in Protective Clothing   Most doctors believed, incorrectly, that poisonous smells carried the plague. This doctor has placed strong-smelling salts in his "beak" to protect himself against deadly plague vapors. *(Source: Germanisches Nationalmuseum, Nuremberg)*

The new system has had many names. It has often been called "cottage industry" or "domestic industry," to distinguish it from the factory industry that came later. In recent years, some scholars have preferred to speak of "protoindustrialization," by which they usually mean a stage of rural industrial development with wage workers and hand tools that necessarily preceded the emergence of large-scale factory industry. The focus on protoindustrialization has been quite valuable, because it has sparked renewed interest in Europe's early industrial development and shown again that the mechanized factories grew out of a vibrant industrial tradition. However, the evolving concept of protoindustrialization also has different versions, some of which are rigid and unduly deterministic. Thus the phrase *putting-out system,* widely used by contemporaries to describe the key features of eighteenth-century rural industry, still seems a more approriate term for the new form of industrial production.

The Putting-out System

The two main participants in the putting-out system were the merchant-capitalist and the rural worker. The merchant loaned or "put out" raw materials to several cottage workers, who processed the raw materials in their own homes and returned the finished product to the merchant. For example, a merchant would provide raw wool, and the workers would spin and weave the wool into cloth. The merchant then paid the outworkers for their work by the piece and proceeded to sell the finished product. There were endless variations on this basic relationship. Sometimes rural workers would buy their own materials and work as independent producers before they sold to the merchant. Sometimes several workers toiled together to perform a complicated process in a workshop. The relative importance of earnings from the land and from industry varied greatly for handicraft workers, although industrial wages usually became more im-

Linen Industry in Ireland Many steps went into making textiles. Here the women are beating away the coarse woody part of the flax plant so that the man can draw the soft part through a series of combs. The fine flax fibers will then be spun into thread and woven into cloth by this family enterprise. *(Source: The Mansell Collection)*

Rural Industry in Action   This French engraving suggests just how many things could be made in the countryside with simple hand tools. These men are making inexpensive but long-lasting wooden shoes, which were widely worn by the poor. *(Source: University of Illinois, Champaign)*

portant for a given family with time. In all cases, however, the putting-out system was a kind of capitalism. Merchants needed large amounts of capital, which they held in the form of goods being worked up and sold in distant markets. They sought to make profits and increase the capital in their businesses.

The putting-out system grew because it had competitive advantages. Underemployed labor was abundant, and poor peasants and landless laborers would work for low wages. Since production in the countryside was unregulated, workers and merchants could change procedures and experiment as they saw fit. Because they did not need to meet rigid guild standards, which maintained quality but discouraged the development of new methods, cottage industry became capable of producing many kinds of goods. Textiles, all manner of knives, forks, and housewares, buttons and gloves, clocks and musical instruments could be produced quite satisfactorily in the countryside. Luxury goods for the rich, such as exquisite tapestries and fine porce-

lain, demanded special training, close supervision, and centralized workshops. Yet such goods were as exceptional as those who used them. The skills of rural industry were sufficient for everyday articles.

Rural manufacturing did not spread across Europe at an even rate. It appeared first in England and developed most successfully there, particularly for the spinning and weaving of woolen cloth. By 1500 half of England's textiles were being produced in the countryside. By 1700 English industry was generally more rural than urban and heavily reliant on the putting-out system. Continental countries developed rural industry more slowly.

In France at the time of Louis XIV, Colbert had revived the urban guilds and used them as a means to control the cities and collect taxes (see page 508). But the pressure of rural poverty proved too great. In 1762 the special privileges of urban manufacturing were abolished in France, and the already-developing rural industries were given free rein from then on. The royal government in France had come to believe that the best way to help the

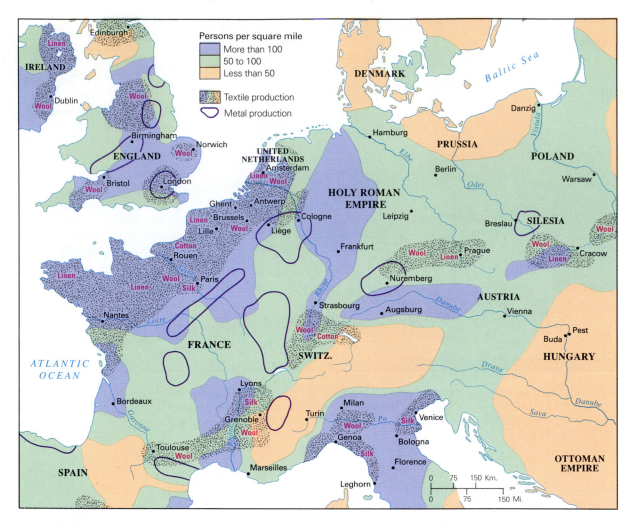

MAP 19.1 Industry and Population in Eighteenth-Century Europe   The growth of cottage manufacturing in rural areas helped country people to increase their income and contributed to increases in the population. This putting-out system began in England, and most of the work was in the textile industry.

poor in the countryside was to encourage the growth of cottage manufacturing. Thus in France, as in Germany and other areas, the later part of the eighteenth century witnessed a remarkable expansion of rural industry in certain densely populated regions (Map 19.1). The pattern established in England was spreading to the Continent.

The Textile Industry

Throughout most of history, until at least the nineteenth century, the industry that has employed the most people has been textiles. The making of linen, woolen, and eventually cotton cloth was the typical activity of cottage workers engaged in the putting-out system. A look inside the cottage of the English rural textile worker illustrates a way of life as well as an economic system.

The rural worker lived in a small cottage, with tiny windows and little space. Indeed, the worker's cottage was often a single room that served as workshop, kitchen, and bedroom. There were only a few pieces of furniture, of which the weaver's loom was by far the largest and most important. That loom had changed somewhat in the early eighteenth century, when John Kay's invention of the flying shuttle enabled the weaver to throw the shuttle back and forth between the threads with one hand. Aside from that improvement, however, the loom was as it had been for much of history. In the cottage there were also spinning wheels, tubs for dyeing cloth and washing raw wool, and carding pieces to comb and prepare the raw material.

These different pieces of equipment were necessary because cottage industry was first and foremost a family enterprise. All the members of the family helped in the work, so that "every person from seven to eighty (who retained their sight and who could move their hands) could earn their bread," as one eighteenth-century English observer put it.[6] While the women and children prepared the raw material and spun the thread, the man of the house wove the cloth. There was work for everyone, even the youngest. After the dirt was beaten out of the raw cotton, it had to be thoroughly cleaned with strong soap in a tub, where tiny feet took the place of the agitator in a washing machine. George Crompton, the son of Samuel Crompton, who in 1784 invented the mule for cotton spinning, recalled that "soon after I was able to walk I was employed in the cotton manufacture.... My mother tucked up my petticoats about my waist, and put me into the tub to tread upon the cotton at the bottom."[7] Slightly older children and aged relatives carded and combed the cotton or wool, so

The Weaver's Repose   This painting by Decker Cornelis Gerritz (1594–1637) captures the pleasure of release from long hours of toil in cottage industry. The loom realistically dominates the cramped living space and the family's modest possessions. *(Source: Musées Royaux des Beaux-Arts, Brussels. Copyright A.C.I.)*

that the woman and the older daughter she had taught could spin it into thread. Each member had a task. The very young and very old worked in the family unit as a matter of course.

There was always a serious imbalance in this family enterprise: the work of four or five spinners was needed to keep one weaver steadily employed. Therefore, the wife and the husband had constantly to try to find more thread and more spinners. Widows and unmarried women—those "spinsters" who spun for their living—were recruited by the wife. Or perhaps the weaver's son went off on horseback to seek thread. The need for more thread might even lead the weaver and his wife to become small capitalist employers. At the end of the week, when they received the raw wool or cotton from the merchant-manufacturer, they would put out some of this raw material to other cottages. The following week they would return to pick up the thread and pay for the spinning—spinning that would help keep the weaver busy for a week until the merchant came for the finished cloth.

Relations between workers and employers were often marked by sharp conflict. An English popular song written about 1700, called "The Clothier's Delight, or the Rich Men's Joy and the Poor Men's Sorrow," has the merchant boasting of his countless tricks used to "beat down wages":

We heapeth up riches and treasure great store
Which we get by griping and grinding the poor.
* And this is a way for to fill up our purse*
* Although we do get it with many a curse.*[8]

There were constant disputes over weights of materials and the quality of the cloth. Merchants accused workers of stealing raw materials, and weavers complained that merchants delivered underweight bales. Suspicions abounded.

There was another problem, at least from the merchant-capitalist's point of view. Rural labor was cheap, scattered, and poorly organized. For these reasons it was hard to control. Cottage workers tended to work in spurts. After they got paid on Saturday afternoon, the men in particular tended to drink and relax for two or three days. Indeed, Monday was called "holy Monday" because inactivity was so religiously observed. By the end of the week the weaver was probably working feverishly to make his quota. But if he did not succeed, there was little the merchant could do. When times were

good and the merchant could easily sell everything produced, the weaver and his family did fairly well and were particularly inclined to loaf, to the dismay of the capitalist. Thus the putting-out system in the textile industry had definite shortcomings from the employer's point of view. There was an imbalance between spinning and weaving. Labor relations were often poor, and the merchant was unable to control the quality of the cloth or the schedule of the workers. Ambitious merchant-capitalists therefore intensified their search for ways to produce more efficiently and to squeeze still more work out of "undisciplined" cottage workers.

BUILDING THE ATLANTIC ECONOMY

In addition to agricultural improvement, population pressure, and expanding cottage industry, the expansion of Europe in the eighteenth century was characterized by the growth of world trade. Spain and Portugal revitalized their empires and began drawing more wealth from renewed development. Yet, once again, the countries of northwestern Europe—the Netherlands, France, and above all Great Britain—benefited most. Great Britain (formed in 1707 by the union of England and Scotland in a single kingdom) gradually became the leading maritime power. In the eighteenth century, British ships and merchants succeeded in dominating long-distance trade, particularly the fast-growing intercontinental trade across the Atlantic Ocean. The British played the critical role in building a fairly unified Atlantic economy, which offered remarkable opportunities for them and their colonists.

Mercantilism and Colonial Wars

Britain's commercial leadership in the eighteenth century had its origins in the mercantilism of the seventeenth century (see page 508). European mercantilism was a system of economic regulations aimed at increasing the power of the state. As practiced by a leading advocate like Colbert under Louis XIV, mercantilism aimed particularly at creating a favorable balance of foreign trade in order to increase a country's stock of gold. A country's gold holdings served as an all-important treas-

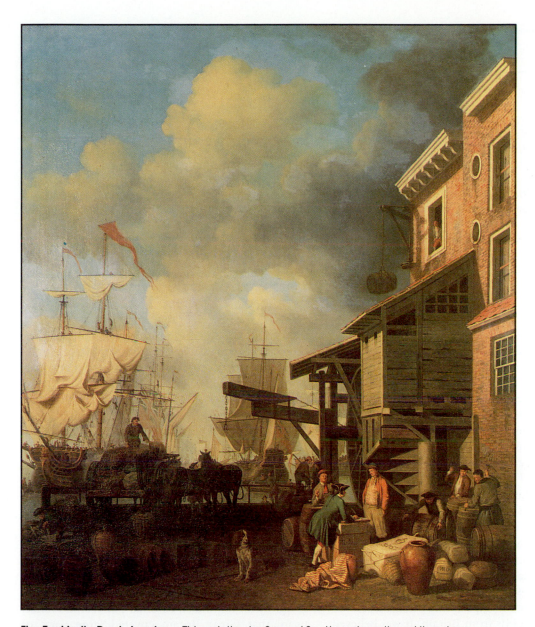

The East India Dock, London   This painting by Samuel Scott captures the spirit and excitement of British maritime expansion. Great sailing ships line the quay, bringing profit and romance from far-off India. London grew in population from 350,000 in 1650 to 900,000 in 1800, when it was twice as big as Paris, its nearest rival. *(Source: Courtesy of Board of Trustees of the Victoria & Albert Museum)*

ure chest, to be opened periodically to pay for war in a violent age.

Early English mercantilists shared these views. What distinguished English mercantilism was the unusual idea that governmental economic regulations could and should serve the private interest of individuals and groups as well as the public needs of the state. As Josiah Child, a very wealthy brewer and director of the East India Company, put it, in the ideal economy "Profit and Power ought jointly to be considered."[9] In France and other continental countries, by contrast, seventeenth-century mercantilists generally put the needs of the state far above those of business people and workers. And

COLONIAL COMPETITION AND WAR, 1651–1763

1651–1663	British Navigation Acts create the mercantile system, which is not seriously modified until 1786
1652–1674	Three Anglo-Dutch wars damage Dutch shipping and commerce
1664	New Amsterdam is seized and renamed New York
1701–1714	War of the Spanish Succession
1713	Peace of Utrecht: Britain wins parts of Canada from France and control of the western African slave trade from Spain
1740–1748	War of the Austrian Succession, resulting in no change in territorial holdings in North America
1756–1763	Seven Years' War (known in North America as the French and Indian War), a decisive victory for Britain
1763	Treaty of Paris: Britain receives all French territory on the North American mainland and achieves dominance in India

they seldom saw a possible union of public and private interests for a common good.

The result of the English desire to increase both military power and private wealth was the mercantile system of the Navigation Acts. Oliver Cromwell established the first of these laws in 1651, and the restored monarchy of Charles II extended them further in 1660 and 1663; these Navigation Acts of the seventeenth century were not seriously modified until 1786. The acts required that most goods imported from Europe into England and Scotland be carried on British-owned ships with British crews or on ships of the country producing the article. Moreover, these laws gave British merchants and shipowners a virtual monopoly on trade with the colonies. The colonists were required to ship their products—sugar, tobacco, and cotton—on British (or American) ships and to buy almost all of their European goods from Britain. It was believed that these economic regulations would provide British merchants and workers with profits and employment, and colonial plantation owners and farmers with a guaranteed market for their products. And the the emerging British empire would develop a shipping industry with a large number of tough, experienced deep-water seamen, who could be drafted when necessary into the Royal Navy to protect the island nation and its colonial possessions.

The Navigation Acts were a form of economic warfare. Their initial target was the Dutch, who were far ahead of the English in shipping and for-

eign trade in the mid-seventeenth century. The Navigation Acts, in conjunction with three Anglo-Dutch wars between 1652 and 1674, did seriously damage Dutch shipping and commerce. The thriving Dutch colony of New Amsterdam was seized in 1664 and renamed "New York." By the later seventeenth century, when the Dutch and the English became allies to stop the expansion of France's Louis XIV, the Netherlands was falling behind England in shipping, trade, and colonies.

As the Netherlands followed Spain into relative decline, France stood clearly as England's most serious rival in the competition for overseas empire. Rich in natural resources and endowed with a population three or four times that of England, continental Europe's leading military power was already building a powerful fleet and a worldwide system of rigidly monopolized colonial trade. And France, aware that Great Britain coveted large parts of Spain's American empire, was determined to revitalize its Spanish ally. Thus, from 1701 to 1763, Britain and France were locked in a series of wars to decide, in part, which nation would become the leading maritime power and claim a lion's share of the profits of Europe's overseas expansion (Map 19.2).

MAP 19.2 The Economy of the Atlantic Basin in 1701 The growth of trade encouraged both economic development and military conflict in the Atlantic Basin.

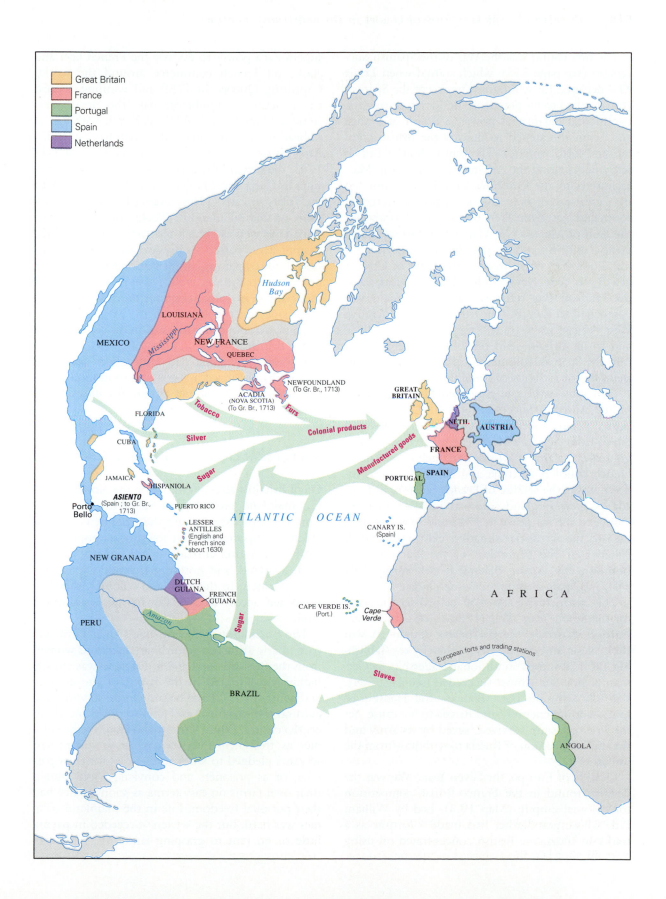

Great Britain
France
Portugal
Spain
Netherlands

Hudson
Bay

LOUISIANA

MEXICO

NEW FRANCE

QUEBEC

Mississippi

NEWFOUNDLAND
(To Gr. Br., 1713)

ACADIA
(NOVA SCOTIA)
(To Gr. Br., 1713)

FLORIDA

Tobacco

Furs

GREAT
BRITAIN

NETH.

AUSTRIA

Silver

Colonial products

Manufactured goods

FRANCE

CUBA

Sugar

JAMAICA

HISPANIOLA

PORTUGAL

SPAIN

ASIENTO
(Spain ; to Gr. Br.,
1713)

Porto
Bello

PUERTO RICO

LESSER
ANTILLES
(English and
French since
about 1630)

ATLANTIC   OCEAN

CANARY IS.
(Spain)

NEW GRANADA

AFRICA

DUTCH
GUIANA

FRENCH
GUIANA

PERU

Amazon

Sugar

CAPE VERDE IS.
(Port.)

Cape
Verde

European forts and trading stations

Slaves

BRAZIL

ANGOLA

The first round was the War of the Spanish Succession (see page 513), which started when Louis XIV declared his willingness to accept the Spanish crown willed to his grandson. Besides upsetting the continental balance of power, a union of France and Spain threatened to destroy the British colonies in North America. The thin ribbon of British settlements along the Atlantic seaboard from Massachusetts to the Carolinas would be surrounded by a great arc of Franco-Spanish power stretching south and west from French Canada to Florida and the Gulf of Mexico (see Map 19.2). Defeated by a great coalition of states after twelve years of fighting, Louis XIV was forced in the Peace of Utrecht (1713) to cede Newfoundland, Nova Scotia, and the Hudson Bay territory to Britain. Spain was compelled to give Britain control of the lucrative West African slave trade—the so-called *asiento*— and to let Britain send one ship of merchandise into the Spanish colonies annually, through Porto Bello on the Isthmus of Panama.

France was still a mighty competitor. The War of the Austrian Succession (1740–1748), which started when Frederick the Great of Prussia seized Silesia from Austria's Maria Theresa (see page 584), gradually became a world war, including Anglo-French conflicts in India and North America. Indeed, it was the seizure of French territory in Canada by New England colonists in 1745 that led France to sue for peace in 1748 and to accept a return to the territorial situation existing in North America at the beginning of the war. France's Bourbon ally, Spain, defended itself surprisingly well, and Spain's empire remained intact.

This inconclusive stand-off helped set the stage for the Seven Years' War (1756–1763). In central Europe, Austria's Maria Theresa sought to win back Silesia and crush Prussia, thereby re-establishing the Habsburgs' traditional leadership in German affairs. She almost succeeded (see page 584), skillfully winning both France—the Habsburgs' long-standing enemy—and Russia to her cause. Yet the Prussian state survived, saved by its army and the sudden decision of Russia to withdraw from the war in 1762.

Outside of Europe, the Seven Years' War was the decisive round in the Franco-British competition for colonial empire (Map 19.3). Led by William Pitt, whose grandfather had made a fortune as a trader in India, the British concentrated on using superior sea power to destroy the French fleet and choke off French commerce around the world. Capturing Quebec in 1759 and winning a great naval victory at Quiberon Bay, the British also strangled France's valuable sugar trade with its Caribbean islands and smashed French forts in India. After Spain entered the war on France's side in 1761, the surging British temporarily occupied Havana in Cuba and Manila in the Philippines. With the Treaty of Paris (1763), France lost all its possessions on the mainland of North America. French Canada as well as French territory east of the Mississippi River passed to Britain, and France ceded Louisiana to Spain as compensation for Spain's loss of Florida to Britain. France also gave up most of its holdings in India, opening the way to British dominance on the subcontinent. By 1763 British naval power, built in large part on the rapid growth of the British shipping industry after the passage of the Navigation Acts, had triumphed decisively. Britain had realized its goal of monopolizing a vast trading and colonial empire for its exclusive benefit.

Land and Wealth in North America

Of all Britain's colonies, those on the North American mainland proved most valuable in the long run. The settlements along the Atlantic coast provided an important outlet for surplus population, so that migration abroad limited poverty in England, Scotland, and northern Ireland. The settlers also benefited. In the mainland colonies, they had privileged access to virtually free and unlimited land.

The possibility of having one's own farm was particularly attractive to ordinary men and women from the British Isles. Land in England was already highly concentrated in the hands of the nobility and gentry in 1700 and became more so with agricultural improvement and enclosures in the eighteenth century. White settlers who came to the colonies as free men and women, or as indentured servants pledged to work seven years for their passage, or as prisoners and convicts, could obtain their own farms on easy terms as soon as they had their personal freedom. Life in the mainland colonies was hard, but the settlers succeeded in paying little or no rent to grasping landlords, and taxes

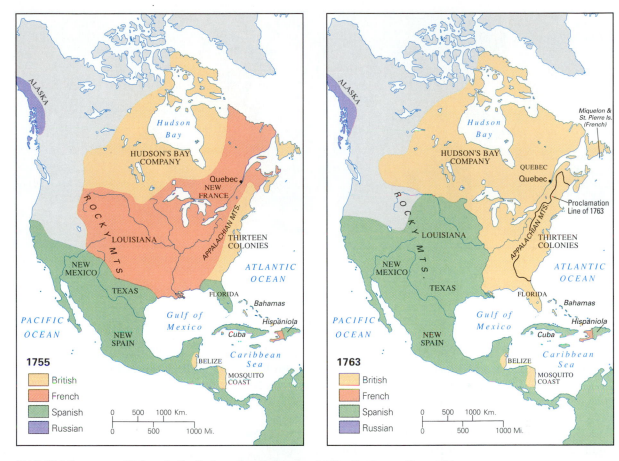

MAP 19.3 European Claims in North America Before and After the Seven Years' War (1756–1763)   France lost its vast claims in North America, though the British government then prohibited colonists from settling west of a line drawn in 1763. The British wanted to avoid costly wars with Indians living in the newly conquered territory.

were very low. Unlike the great majority of European peasants, who had to accept high rents and taxes as part of the order of things, American farmers could keep most of what they managed to produce.

The availability of land made labor expensive in the colonies. This basic fact, rather than any repressive aspects of the Navigation Acts, limited the growth of industry in the colonies. The advantage for colonists was in farming, and farm they did.

Cheap land and scarce labor were also critical factors in the growth of slavery in the southern colonies. By 1700 British indentured servants were carefully avoiding the Virginia lowlands, where black slavery was spreading, and by 1730 the large

plantations there had gone over completely to black slaves. Slave labor permitted an astonishing tenfold increase in tobacco production between 1700 and 1774 and created a wealthy aristocratic planter class in Maryland and Virginia.

In the course of the eighteenth century, the farmers of New England and the middle colonies began to produce more food than they needed. They exported ever more foodstuffs, primarily to the West Indies. There the owners of the sugar plantations came to depend on the mainland colonies for grain and dried fish to feed their slaves. The plantation owners, whether they grew tobacco in Virginia and Maryland or sugar in the West Indies, had the exclusive privilege of supplying the British

Tobacco   was a key commodity in the Atlantic trade. This engraving from 1775 shows a merchant and his slaves preparing a cargo for sail. *(Source: The British Library)*

Isles with their products. Englishmen could not buy cheaper sugar from Brazil, nor were they allowed to grow tobacco in the home islands. Thus the colonists, too, had their place in the protective mercantile system of the Navigation Acts. The American shipping industry grew rapidly in the eighteenth century, for example, because colonial shippers enjoyed the same advantages as their fellow citizens in Britain.

The abundance of almost-free land resulted in a rapid increase in the colonial population in the eighteenth century. In a mere three-quarters of a century after 1700, the white population of the mainland colonies multiplied a staggering ten times, as immigrants arrived and colonial couples raised large families. In 1774, 2.2 million whites and 330,000 blacks inhabited what would soon become the independent United States.

Rapid population growth did not reduce the settlers to poverty. On the contrary, agricultural development resulted in fairly high standards of living, in eighteenth-century terms, for mainland colonists. There was also an unusual degree of economic equality by European standards. Few people were extremely rich, and few were extremely poor. Remarkably, on the eve of the American Revolution, white men or women in the mainland British colonies probably had the highest average income and standard of living in the world.[10] Thus it is clear just how much the colonists benefited from hard work and the mercantile system created by the Navigation Acts.

The Growth of Foreign Trade

England also profited greatly from the mercantile system. Above all, the rapidly growing and increasingly wealthy agricultural populations of the mainland colonies provided an expanding market for English manufactured goods. This situation was extremely fortunate, for England in the eighteenth century was gradually losing, or only slowly expanding, its sales to many of its traditional European markets. However, rising demand for manufactured goods in North America, as well as in the West Indies, Africa, and Latin America, allowed English cottage industry to continue to grow and diversify. Merchant-capitalists and manufacturers found new and exciting opportunities for profit and wealth.

Since the late Middle Ages, England had relied very heavily on the sale of woolen cloth in foreign markets. Indeed, as late as 1700, woolen cloth was the only important manufactured good exported from England, and fully 90 percent of it was sold to Europeans. In the course of the eighteenth century, the states of continental Europe were trying to develop their own cottage textile industries in an effort to deal with rural poverty and overpopulation. Like England earlier, these states adopted protectionist, mercantilist policies. They tried by means of tariffs and other measures to exclude competing goods from abroad, whether English woolens or the cheap but beautiful cotton calicos the English East India Company brought from India and sold in Europe.

France had already closed its markets to the English in the seventeenth century. In the eighteenth century, German states purchased much less woolen cloth from England and encouraged cottage production of coarse, cheap linens, which became a feared competitor in all of central and southern Europe. By 1773 England was selling only about two-thirds as much woolen cloth to northern and western Europe as it had in 1700. The decline of many markets on the Continent meant that the English economy badly needed new markets and new products in order to develop and prosper.

Protected colonial markets came to the rescue, more than offsetting stagnating trade with Europe. The markets of the Atlantic economy led the way, as may be seen in Figure 19.3. English exports of manufactured goods to continental Europe increased very modestly, from roughly £2.9 million in 1700 to only £3.3 million in 1773. Meanwhile, sales of manufactured products to the Atlantic economy—primarily the mainland colonies of North America and the West Indian sugar islands, with an important assist from West Africa and Latin America—soared from £500,000 to £4.0 million. Sales to other "colonies"—Ireland and India—also rose substantially in the eighteenth century.

English exports became much more balanced and diversified. To America and Africa went large quantities of metal items—axes to frontier settlers, firearms, chains for slaveowners. There were also clocks and coaches, buttons and saddles, china and furniture, musical instruments and scientific equipment, and a host of other things. By 1750 half the nails made in England were going to the colonies. Foreign trade became the bread and butter of some industries.

Thus the mercantile system formed in the seventeenth century to attack the Dutch and to win power and profit for England continued to shape

trade in the eighteenth century. The English concentrated in their hands much of the demand for manufactured goods from the growing Atlantic economy. The pressure of demand from three continents on the cottage industry of one medium-sized country heightened the efforts of English merchant-capitalists to find new and improved ways to produce more goods. By the 1770s England stood on the threshold of epoch-making industrial changes which will be described later in Chapter 22.

Revival in Colonial Latin America

When the last Spanish Habsburg, the feeble-minded Charles II, died in 1700 (see page 513), Spain's vast empire lay ready for dismemberment. Yet, in one of those striking reversals with which history is replete, Spain revived. The empire held together and even prospered, while a European-oriented landowning aristocracy enhanced its position in colonial society.

FIGURE 19.3 Exports of English Manufactured Goods, 1700–1774   While trade between England and Europe stagnated after 1700, English exports to Africa and the Americas boomed and greatly stimulated English economic development. *(Source: R. Davis, English Foreign Trade, 1700–1774, Economic History Review, 2d series, 15 (1962); 302–303)*

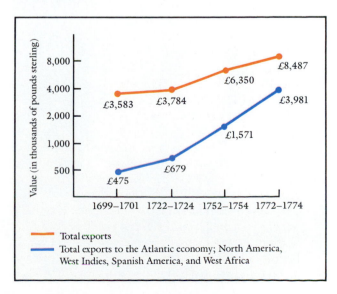

Spain recovered in part because of better leadership. Louis XIV's grandson, who took the throne as Philip V (r. 1700–1746), brought new men and fresh ideas with him from France and rallied the Spanish people to his Bourbon dynasty in the long War of the Spanish Succession. When peace was restored, a series of reforming ministers reasserted royal authority, overhauling state finances and strengthening defense.

Revitalization in Madrid had positive results in the colonies. The colonies succeeded in defending themselves from numerous British attacks and even increased in size. Spain received Louisiana from France in 1763, and missionaries and ranchers extended Spanish influence all the way to northern California.

Political success was matched by economic improvement. After declining markedly in the seventeenth century, silver mining recovered in Mexico and Peru. Output quadrupled between 1700 and 1800, when Spanish America accounted for half of world silver production. Silver mining also encouraged food production for large mining camps and gave the *Creoles*—people of Spanish blood born in America—the means to purchase more and more European luxuries and manufactured goods. A class of wealthy merchants arose to handle this flourishing trade, which often relied on smuggled goods from Great Britain. As in British North America, industry remained weak, although workshops employing forced Indian labor were occupied with fashioning Mexican and Peruvian wool into coarse fabrics for purchase by the Latin American masses. Spain's colonies were an important element of the Atlantic economy.

Economic development strengthened the Creole elite, which came to rival the top government officials dispatched from Spain. Creole estate owners controlled much of the land, the main source of wealth. Small independent farmers were rare. The estate owners strove to become a genuine European aristocracy, and they believed that work in the fields was the proper occupation of an impoverished peasantry. The defenseless Indians suited their needs. As the Indian population recovered in numbers, slavery and periodic forced labor gave way to widespread debt peonage from 1600 on. Under this system, a planter or rancher would keep the estate's Christianized, increasingly Hispanicized Indians in perpetual debt bondage by periodically advancing food, shelter, and a little money. In this way, debt peonage was a form of agricultural serfdom.

There were also Creoles of modest means, especially in the cities. The large middle group in Spanish colonies consisted of racially mixed *mestizos,* the offspring of Spanish men and Indian women. The most talented mestizos realistically aspired to join the Creoles, for enough wealth and power could make one white. This ambition siphoned off the most energetic mestizos and lessened the buildup of any lower-class discontent. Thus, by the end of the colonial era, roughly 20 percent of the population was classified as white and about 30 percent as

Charles Willson Peale: General John Cadwalader, His First Wife Elizabeth Lloyd, and Their Daughter Anne With their rich imported satins and elegant household furnishings, represented by the elaborately carved table on the left, this colonial American family proclaims its prosperity, refinement, and high social standing. American demand for foreign goods was voracious. *(Source: Philadelphia Museum of Art; The Cadwalader Collection)*

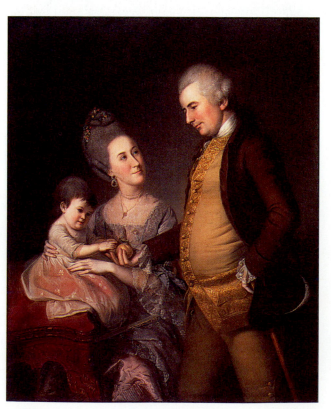

Porto Bello Located on the isthmus of Panama, little Porto Bello was a major port in Spanish America. When ships arrived for 40-day trade fairs, it bustled with the energy of merchants, slaves, and soldiers. *(Source: The Pierpont Morgan Library)*

mestizo. Pure-blooded Indians accounted for most of the remainder, for only on the sugar plantations of Cuba and Puerto Rico did black slavery ever take firm root in Spanish America.

The situation was quite the opposite in Portuguese Brazil. As in the West Indies, enormous numbers of blacks were brought in chains to work the sugar plantations. About half the population of Brazil was of African origin in the early nineteenth century. Even more than in the Spanish territories, the people of Brazil intermingled sexually and culturally. In contrast to North America, where racial lines were hard and fast, at least in theory, colonial Brazil made a virtue of miscegenation, and the population grew to include every color in the racial rainbow.

SUMMARY

While some European intellectual elites were developing a new view of the world in the eighteenth century, Europe as a whole was experiencing a gradual but far-reaching expansion. As agriculture showed signs of modest improvement across the Continent, first the Low Countries and then England launched changes that gradually revolutionized agriculture. Plague disappeared, and the populations of all countries grew significantly, encouraging the growth of wage labor, cottage industry, and merchant capitalism.

Europeans also continued their overseas expansion, fighting for empire and profit and, in particular, consolidating their hold on the Americas. A revived Spain and its Latin American colonies participated fully in this expansion. As in agriculture and cottage industry, however, England and its empire proved most successful. The English concentrated much of the growing Atlantic trade in their hands, a development that challenged and enriched English industry and intensified the search for new methods of production. Thus, by the 1770s, England was approaching an economic breakthrough fully as significant as the great political upheaval destined to develop shortly in neighboring France.

NOTES

1. M. Bloch, *Les caractères originaux de l'histoire rurale française,* vol. 1 (Paris: Librarie Armand Colin, 1960), pp. 244–245.
2. B. H. Slicher van Bath, *The Agrarian History of Western Europe, A.D. 500–1850* (New York: St. Martin's Press, 1963), p. 240.
3. E. P. Thompson, *The Making of the English Working Class* (New York: Vintage Books, 1966), p. 218.
4. Quoted in E. E. Rich and C. H. Wilson, eds., *The Cambridge Economic History of Europe,* vol. 4 (Cambridge: Cambridge University Press, 1967), p. 74.
5. Ibid., p. 85.
6. Quoted in I. Pinchbeck, *Women Workers and the Industrial Revolution, 1750–1850* (New York: F. S. Crofts, 1930), p. 113.
7. Quoted in S. Chapman, *The Lancashire Cotton Industry* (Manchester, Eng.: Manchester University Press, 1903), p. 13.
8. Quoted in P. Mantoux, *The Industrial Revolution in the Eighteenth Century* (New York: Harper & Row, 1961), p. 75.
9. Quoted in C. Wilson, *England's Apprenticeship, 1603–1763* (London: Longmans, Green, 1965), p. 169.
10. G. Taylor, "America's Growth Before 1840," *Journal of Economic History* 24 (December 1970): pp. 427–444.

SUGGESTED READING

The works by B. H. Slicher van Bath and M. Bloch listed in the Notes are wide-ranging general introductions to the gradual transformation of European agriculture. Bloch's classic has been translated as *French Rural History* (1966). J. Blum, *The End of the Old Order in Rural Europe* (1978), is an impressive comparative study. J. de Vries, *The Dutch Rural Economy in the Golden Age, 1500–1700* (1974), skillfully examines the causes of early Dutch leadership in farming, while A. Kussmaul, *A General View of the Rural Economy of England, 1538–1840* (1989), charts the path of agricultural progress in England. Two recommended and complementary studies on landowning nobilities are R. Forster, *The Nobility of Toulouse in the Eighteenth Century* (1960), and G. E. Mingay, *English Landed Society in the Eighteenth Century* (1963). A. Goodwin, ed., *The European Nobility in the Eighteenth Century* (1967), is an exciting group of essays on aristocrats in different countries. R. and E. Forster, eds., *European Society in the Eighteenth Century* (1969), assembles a rich collection of contemporary writing on a variety of economic and social topics. E. Le Roy Ladurie, *The Peasants of Languedoc* (1976), a brilliant and challenging study of rural life in southern France for several centuries, complements J. Goody et al., eds., *Family and Inheritance: Rural Society in Western Europe, 1200–1800* (1976). Life in small-town France comes alive in P. Higonnet, *Pont-de-Montvert: Social Structure and Politics in a French Village, 1700–1914* (1971), while O. Hufton deals vividly and sympathetically with rural migration, work, women, and much more in *The Poor in Eighteenth-Century France* (1974).

An ambitious reexamination with extensive bibliographical references by M. Gutman, *Toward the Modern Economy: Early Modern Industry in Europe, 1500–1800* (1988), highlights the creativity of rural industry, as do J. Goodman and K. Honeyman in *Gainful Pursuits: The Making of Industrial Europe, 1600–1914* (1988). The classic study by P. Mantoux, cited in the Notes, and D. Landes, *The Unbound Prometheus* (1969), lay more stress on the growing limitations of cottage production. G. Gullickson, *Spinners and Weavers of Auffay: Rural Industry and the Sexual Division of Labor in a French Village, 1750–1850* (1986), and M. Sonenscher, *The Hatters of Eighteenth-Century France* (1987), are valuable studies.

Two excellent multivolume series, *The Cambridge Economic History of Europe,* mentioned in the Notes, and C. Cipolla, ed., *The Fontana Economic History of Europe,* cover the sweep of economic developments from the Middle Ages to the present and have extensive bibliographies. So does R. Cameron, *A Concise Economic History of the World* (1989), which deals mainly with Europe. F. Braudel, *Civilization and Capitalism, Fifteenth–Eighteenth Century* (1981–1984), is a monumental and highly recommended three-volume synthesis. In the area of trade and colonial competition, V. Barbour, *Capitalism in Amsterdam* (1963), and C. R. Boxer, *The Dutch Seaborne Empire* (1970), are very interesting on Holland. J. Brewer, *The Sinews of Power: War, Money, and the English State, 1688–1783* (1989), looks at English victories, while G. Parker,

The Military Revolution: Military Technology in the Rise of the West (1988), a masterful, beautifully illustrated work, explores the roots of European power and conquest. W. Dorn, *The Competition for Empire, 1740–1763* (1963), D. K. Fieldhouse, *The Colonial Empires* (1971), and R. Davies, *The Rise of Atlantic Economies* (1973), are all valuable works on the struggle for empire. R. Pares, *Yankees and Creoles* (1956), is a short, lively work on trade between the mainland colonies and the West Indies, and M. Rediker, *Between the Devil and the Deep Blue Sea: Merchant Seamen, Pirates, and the Anglo-American Maritime World, 1700–1750* (1987), captures the spirit of ships and sailors. E. Williams, *Capitalism and Slavery* (1966), provocatively argues that slavery provided the wealth necessary for England's industrial development. Another exciting work is J. Nef, *War and Human Progress* (1968), which examines the impact of war on economic and industrial development in European history between about 1500 and 1800.

Three very fine books on the growth of population are M. Flinn's concise *The European Demographic System, 1500–1800* (1981); E. A. Wrigley's demanding *Population and History* (1969); and T. McKeown's scholarly *The Modern Rise of Population* (1977). J. Komlos, *Nutrition and Economic Development in the Eighteenth-Century Habsburg Monarchy* (1989), and W. McNeill, *Plagues and Peoples* (1976), are both noteworthy. For England, C. Wilson's volume mentioned in the Notes is highly recommended, as is P. Langford, *A Polite and Commercial People: England, 1727–1783* (1989). Further works on England can be found in the Suggested Reading for Chapter 22. The greatest novel of eighteenth-century English society is Henry Fielding's unforgettable *Tom Jones,* although Jane Austen's novels about country society, *Emma* and *Pride and Prejudice,* are not far behind.

20

The Life of the People

The discussion of agriculture and industry in the last chapter showed the ordinary man and woman at work, straining to make ends meet and earn a living. Yet work is only part of human experience. What about the rest?

- What changes occurred in marriage and the family by the end of the eighteenth century?
- What was life like for children?
- What did people eat, and how did diet and medical care affect people's health?
- What were the patterns of popular religion in the era of the Enlightenment?

These questions help us better understand how the peasant masses and urban poor really lived in western Europe before the age of revolution at the end of the eighteenth century. They are the focus of this chapter.

MARRIAGE AND THE FAMILY

The basic unit of social organization is the family. It is within the structure of the family that human beings love, mate, and reproduce themselves. It is primarily the family that teaches the child, imparting values and customs that condition an individual's behavior for a lifetime. The family is also an institution woven into the web of history. It evolves and changes, assuming different forms in different times and places.

Extended and Nuclear Families

In many traditional Asian and African societies, the typical family has often been an extended family. A newly married couple, instead of establishing their own home, will go to live with either the bride's or the groom's family. The couple raise their children while living under the same roof with their own brothers and sisters, who may also be married. The family is a big, three- or four-generation clan, headed by a patriarch or perhaps a matriarch, and encompassing everyone from the youngest infant to the oldest grandparent.

Extended families, it is often said, provide security for adults and children in traditional agrarian peasant economies. Everyone has a place within the extended family, from cradle to grave. Sociologists frequently assume that the extended family gives way to the conjugal, or nuclear, family with the advent of industrialization and urbanization. In a society characterized by nuclear families, couples establish their own households and their own family identities when they marry. They live with the children they raise, apart from their parents. Something like this is indeed happening in much of Asia and Africa today. And since Europe was once agrarian and preindustrial, it has often been believed that the extended family must also have prevailed in Europe before being destroyed by the Industrial Revolution.

In recent years innovative historians have developed new ways to test such old ideas. Above all, historians have analyzed the entries in previously neglected parish registers, in which local priests and pastors recorded the births, deaths, and marriages of the people in their church parishes. As a result, knowledge about the details of family life for the mass of people before the nineteenth century has greatly increased. Many simplistic old beliefs have been disproved by one of the most exciting advances in historical scholarship in the last generation. Yet it is important to realize that only a tiny percentage of all European villages have been studied, while perplexing local and regional variations have also been discovered. Thus many questions remain, and there is still much research to be done.

Despite these qualifications, it seems clear that the extended, three-generation family was a great rarity in western and central Europe by 1700. Indeed, the extended family may never have been common in Europe, although it is hard to know about the Middle Ages because fewer records survive. When young European couples married, they normally established their own households and lived apart from their parents. When a three-generation household came into existence, it was usually a parent who moved in with a married child, rather than a newly married couple moving in with either set of parents. The married couple, and the children that were sure to follow, were on their own from the beginning.

Perhaps because European couples set up separate households when they married, people did not marry young in the seventeenth and early eighteenth centuries. Indeed, the average person, who was neither rich nor aristocratic, married surprisingly late, many years after reaching adulthood and many more after beginning to work. In one well-studied, apparently typical English village, both men and women married for the first time at an average age of twenty-seven or older in the seventeenth and eighteenth centuries. A similar pattern existed in early-eighteenth-century France. Moreover, a substantial portion of men and women never married at all.

Between two-fifths and three-fifths of European women capable of bearing children—that is, women between fifteen and forty-four—were unmarried at any given time. The contrast with traditional non-Western societies is once again striking. In those societies, the pattern has very often been almost universal and very early marriage. The union of a teenage bride and teenage groom has been the general rule.

The custom of late marriage combined with a nuclear-family household was a distinctive characteristic of European society. The consequences have been tremendous, though still only partially explored. It seems likely that the agressive dynamism and creativity that have characterized European society were due in large part to the pattern of marriage and family. This pattern fostered and required self-reliance and independence. In preindustrial western Europe in the sixteenth through eighteenth centuries, marriage normally joined a mature man and a mature woman—two adults who had already experienced a great deal of life and could transmit self-reliance and real skills to the next generation.

Why was marriage delayed? The main reason was that couples normally could not marry until they could support themselves economically. The land was still the main source of income. The peasant son often needed to wait until his father's death to inherit the family farm and marry his sweetheart. Similarly, the peasant daughter and her family needed to accumulate a small dowry to help her fiancé buy land or build a house.

There were also laws and regulations to temper impetuous love and physical attraction. In some areas, couples needed the legal permission or tacit approval of the local lord or landowner in order to marry. In Austria and Germany, there were legal re-strictions on marriage, and well into the nineteenth century poor couples had particular difficulty securing the approval of local officials. These officials believed that freedom to marry for the lower classes would mean more landless paupers, more abandoned children, and more money for welfare. Thus prudence, custom, and law combined to postpone the march to the altar. This pattern helped society maintain some kind of balance between the number of people and the available economic resources.

Work away from Home

Many young people worked within their families until they could start their own households. Boys plowed and wove; girls spun and tended the cows. Many others left home temporarily to work elsewhere. In the towns, a lad might be apprenticed to a craftsman for seven or fourteen years to learn a trade. During that time he would not be permitted to marry. In most trades he earned little and worked hard, but if he were lucky he might eventually be admitted to a guild and establish his economic independence. More often, the young man would drift from one tough job to another: hired hand for a small farmer, wage laborer on a new road, carrier of water in a nearby town. He was always subject to economic fluctuations, and unemployment was a constant threat.

Girls also temporarily left their families to work, at an early age and in large numbers. The range of opportunities open to them was more limited, however. Service in another family's household was by far the most common job. Even middle-class families often sent their daughters into service and hired others as servants in return. Thus a few years away from home as a servant were often a normal part of growing up. If all went well, the girl (or boy) would work hard and save some money for parents and marriage. At the least, there would be one less mouth to feed at home.

The legions of young servant girls worked hard but had little real independence. Sometimes the employer paid the girl's wages directly to her parents. Constantly under the eye of her mistress, the servant girl found her tasks were many—cleaning, shopping, cooking, caring for the baby. Often the work was endless, for there were no laws to limit

Chardin: The Kitchen Maid Lost in thought as she pauses in her work, perhaps this young servant is thinking about her village and loved ones there. Chardin was one of eighteenth-century France's greatest painters, and his scenes from everyday life provide valuable evidence for the historian. *(Source: National Gallery of Art, Washington, D.C. Samuel H. Kress Collection)*

exploitation. Few girls were so brutalized that they snapped under the strain of such treatment like Varka—the Russian servant girl in Chekhov's chilling story "Sleepy"—who, driven beyond exhaustion, finally quieted her mistress's screaming child by strangling it in its cradle. But court records are full of complaints by servant girls of physical mis-

treatment by their mistresses. There were many others like the fifteen-year-old English girl in the early eighteenth century who told the judge that her mistress had not only called her "very opprobrious names, as Bitch, Whore and the like," but also "beat her without provocation and beyond measure."[1]

There was also the pressure of seducers and sexual attack. In theory, domestic service offered protection and security for a young girl leaving home. The girl had food, lodging, and a new family. She did not drift in a strange and often dangerous environment. But, in practice, she was often the easy prey of a lecherous master, or his sons, or his friends. Indeed, "the evidence suggests that in all European countries, from Britain to Russia, the upper classes felt perfectly free to exploit sexually girls who were at their mercy."[2] If the girl became pregnant, she was quickly fired and thrown out in disgrace to make her own way. Prostitution and petty thievery were often the harsh consequences of unwanted pregnancy. "What are we?" exclaimed a bitter Parisian prostitute. "Most of us are unfortunate women, without origins, without education, servants and maids for the most part."[3]

Premarital Sex and Birth-control Practices

Did the plight of some ex-servant girls mean that late marriage in preindustrial Europe went hand in hand with premarital sex and many illegitimate children? For most of western and central Europe, until at least 1750, the answer seems to be no. English parish registers, in which the clergy recorded the births and deaths of the population, seldom list more than one bastard out of every twenty children baptized. Some French parishes in the seventeenth century had extraordinarily low rates of illegitimacy, with less than 1 percent of the babies born out of wedlock. Illegitimate babies were apparently a rarity, at least as far as the official church records are concerned.

At the same time, premarital sex was clearly commonplace. In one well-studied English village, one-third of all first children were conceived before the couple was married, and many were born within three months of the marriage ceremony. In the mid-eighteenth century, one-fifth of the French women in the village of Auffay, in Normandy, were pregnant when they got married, although only 2 percent of all babies in the village were born to unwed mothers. No doubt many of these French and English couples were already betrothed, or at least "going steady," before they entered into an intimate relationship, and pregnancy simply set the marriage date once and for all. But the very low rates of illegitimate birth also reflect the powerful social controls of the traditional village, particularly the open-field village with its pattern of cooperation and common action. Irate parents and village elders, indignant priests and authoritative landlords, all combined to pressure any young people who wavered about marriage in the face of unexpected pregnancy. These controls meant that premarital sex was not entered into lightly. In the countryside it was generally limited to those contemplating marriage.

Once a woman was married, she generally had several children. This does not mean that birth control within marriage was unknown in western and central Europe before the nineteenth century. But it was primitive and quite undependable. The most common method was *coitus interruptus*—withdrawal by the male before ejaculation. The French, who were apparently early leaders in contraception, were using this method extensively to limit family size by the end of the eighteenth century. Withdrawal as a method of birth control was in keeping with the European pattern of nuclear family, in which the father bore the direct responsibility of supporting his children. Withdrawal—a male technique—was one way to meet that responsibility.

Mechanical and other means of contraception were not unknown in the eighteenth century, but they appear to have been used mainly by certain sectors of the urban population. The "fast set" of London used the "sheath" regularly, although primarily to protect against venereal disease, not pregnancy. Prostitutes used various contraceptive techniques to prevent pregnancy, and such information was probably available to anyone who really sought it. The second part of an indictment for adultery against a late-sixteenth-century English vicar charged that the wayward minister was "also an instructor of young folks [in] how to commit the sin of adultery or fornication and not to beget or bring forth children."[4]

New Patterns of Marriage and Illegitimacy

In the second half of the eighteenth century, the pattern of late marriage and few illegitimate children began to break down. It is hard to say why. Certainly, changes in the economy had a gradual but profound impact. The growth of cottage industry created new opportunities for earning a living, opportunities not tied to the land. Cottage industry tended to develop in areas where the land was poor in quality and divided into small, inadequate holdings. As cottage industry took hold in such areas, young people attained greater independence and did not have to wait to inherit a farm in order to get married. A scrap of ground for a garden and a cottage for the loom and spinning wheel could be quite enough for a modest living. A contemporary observer of an area of rapidly growing cottage industry in Switzerland at the end of the eighteenth century described these changes: "The increased and sure income offered by the combination of cottage manufacture with farming hastened and multiplied marriages and encouraged the division of landholdings, while enhancing their value; it also promoted the expansion and embellishment of houses and villages."[5] The pattern of cottage industry stimulating a lower age of marriage and thus more rapid population growth was also widely observed in England.

Cottage workers married not only earlier but for different reasons. Nothing could be so businesslike, so calculating, as a peasant marriage that was often dictated by the needs of the couple's families. After 1750, however, courtship became more extensive and freer as cottage industry grew. It was easier to yield to the attraction of the opposite sex and fall in love. Members of the older generation were often shocked by the lack of responsibility they saw in the early marriages of the poor, the union of "people with only two spinning wheels and not even a bed." But the laws and regulations they imposed, especially in Germany, were often disregarded. Unions based on love rather than on economic considerations were increasingly the pattern for cottage workers. Factory workers, numbers of whom first began to appear in England after about 1780, followed the path blazed by cottage workers.

Changes in the timing and motivation of marriage went hand in hand with a rapid increase in illegitimate births between about 1750 and 1850. Some historians even speak of an "illegitimacy explosion." In Frankfurt, Germany, for example, only about 2 percent of all births were illegitimate in the early 1700s. This figure rose to 5 percent in about 1760, to about 10 percent in 1800, and peaked at about 25 percent around 1850. In Bordeaux, France, illegitimate births rose steadily until by 1840 one out of every three babies was born out of wedlock. Small towns and villages less frequently experienced such startlingly high illegitimacy rates, but increases from a range of 1 to 3 percent initially to 10 to 20 percent between 1750 and 1850 were commonplace. A profound sexual and cultural transformation was taking place. Fewer girls were abstaining from premarital intercourse, and, more important, fewer boys were marrying the girls they got pregnant.

It is hard to know exactly why this change occurred and what it meant. The old idea of a safe, late, economically secure marriage did not reflect economic and social realities. The growing freedom of thought in the turbulent years beginning with the French Revolution in 1789 influenced sexual and marital behavior in both towns and villages. And illegitimate births, particularly in Germany, were also the result of open rebellion against class laws limiting the right of the poor to marry. Unable to show a solid financial position and thereby obtain a marriage license, couples asserted their independence and lived together anyway. Children were the natural and desired result of "true love" and greater freedom. Eventually, when the stuffy, old-fashioned propertied classes gave in and repealed their laws against "imprudent marriage," poor couples once again went to the altar, often accompanied by their children, and the number of illegitimate children declined.

More fundamentally, the need of a growing population to seek work outside farming and the village made young people more mobile. Mobility in turn encouraged new sexual and marital relationships, which were less subject to parental pressure and village tradition. As in the case of young servant girls who became pregnant and were then forced to fend for themselves, some of these relationships promoted loose living or prostitution. This resulted in more illegitimate births and strengthened an urban subculture of habitual illegitimacy.

Early Sexual Emancipation?

It has been suggested that the increase in illegitimate births represented a stage in the emancipation of women. According to this view, new economic opportunities outside the home, in the city and later in the factory, revolutionized women's attitudes about themselves. Young working women became individualistic and rebelled against old restrictions like late marriage. They sought fulfillment in the pleasure of sexuality. Since there was little birth control, freer sex for single women meant more illegitimate babies.

No doubt single working women in towns and cities were of necessity more independent and self-reliant. Yet, until at least the late nineteenth century, it seems unlikely that such young women were motivated primarily by visions of emancipation and sexual liberation. Most women were servants or textile workers. These jobs paid poorly, and the possibility of a truly independent, "liberated" life was correspondingly limited. Most women in the city probably looked to marriage and family life as an escape from hard, poorly paid work

and as the foundation of a satisfying life. Moreover, illegitimacy increased in rural areas as well as in urban ones, so an interpretation based on changed attitudes in towns and cities does not account for the entire phenomenon.

Promises of marriage from men of the working girl's own class led naturally enough to sex, which was widely viewed as part of serious courtship. In one medium-sized French city in 1787 to 1788, the great majority of unwed mothers stated that sexual intimacy had followed promises of marriage. Their sisters in rural Normandy reported again and again that they had been "seduced in anticipation of marriage."[6] Many soldiers, day laborers, and male servants were no doubt sincere in their proposals. But their lives were insecure, and many hesitated to

Peasants Begging   In seventeenth-century France, many heavily taxed peasants found it very difficult to afford enough to eat. Although charity was becoming more fashionable, many peasant families were reduced to begging. *(Source: The Metropolitan Museum of Art)*

take on the heavy economic burdens of wife and child. Nor were their backbones any longer stiffened by the traditional pressures of the village.

Thus it became increasingly difficult for a woman to convert pregnancy into marriage, and in a growing number of cases the intended marriage did not take place. The romantic yet practical dreams and aspirations of many young working women and men in towns and villages were frustrated by low wages, inequality, and changing economic and social conditions. Old patterns of marriage and family were breaking down among the common people. Only in the late nineteenth century would more stable patterns reappear.

INFANTS AND CHILDREN

In the traditional framework of agrarian Europe, women married late but then began bearing children rapidly. If a woman married before she was thirty, and if both she and her husband lived to forty-five, the chances were roughly one in two that she would give birth to six or more children. The newborn child entered a dangerous world. Infant mortality was high. One in five was sure to die, and one in three was quite likely to, in the poorer areas. Newborn children were very likely to catch infectious diseases of the stomach and chest, which were not understood. Thus little could be done for an ailing child, even in rich families. Childhood itself was dangerous because of adult indifference, neglect, and even brutality. Parents in early modern Europe could count themselves fortunate if half their children lived to adulthood.

Child Care and Nursing

Women of the lower classes generally breast-fed their infants, and for much longer periods than is customary today. Breast-feeding decreases the likelihood of pregnancy for the average woman by delaying the resumption of ovulation. Although women may have been only vaguely aware of the link between nursing and not getting pregnant, they were spacing their children—from two to three years apart—and limiting their fertility by nursing their babies. If a newborn baby died, nurs-

ing stopped and a new life could be created. Nursing also saved lives: the breast-fed infant was more likely to survive on its mother's milk than on any artificial foods. In many areas of Russia, where common practice was to give a new child a sweetened (and germ-laden) rag to suck on for its subsistence, half the babies did not survive the first year.

In contrast to the laboring poor, the women of the aristocracy and upper middle class seldom nursed their own children. The upper-class woman felt that breast-feeding was crude, common, and well beneath her dignity. Instead, she hired a wet nurse to suckle her child. The urban mother of more modest means—the wife of a shopkeeper or artisan—also commonly used a wet nurse, sending her baby to some poor woman in the country as soon as possible.

Wet-nursing was a very widespread and flourishing business in the eighteenth century, a dismal business within the framework of the putting-out system. The traffic was in babies rather than in wool and cloth, and two or three years often passed before the wet-nurse worker finished her task. The great French historian Jules Michelet described with compassion the plight of the wet nurse, who was still going to the homes of the rich in early-nineteenth-century France:

People do not know how much these poor women are exploited and abused, first by the vehicles which transport them (often barely out of their confinement), and afterward by the employment offices which place them. Taken as nurses on the spot, they must send their own child away, and consequently it often dies. They have no contact with the family that hires them, and they may be dismissed at the first caprice of the mother or doctor. If the change of air and place should dry up their milk, they are discharged without any compensation. If they stay here [in the city] they pick up the habits of the easy life, and they suffer enormously when they are forced to return to their life of [rural] poverty. A good number become servants in order to stay in the town. They never rejoin their husbands, and the family is broken.[7]

Other observers noted the flaws of wet-nursing. It was a common belief that a nurse passed her bad traits to the baby with her milk. When a child turned out poorly, it was assumed that "the nurse changed it." Many observers charged that nurses were often negligent and greedy. They claimed that there were large numbers of "killing nurses" with whom no child ever survived. The nurse let the child die quickly, so that she could take another child and another fee. No matter how the adults fared in the wet-nurse business, the child was a certain loser.

Foundlings and Infanticide

In the ancient world and in Asian societies, it was not uncommon to allow or force newborn babies, particularly girl babies, to die when there were too many mouths to feed. To its great and eternal credit, the early medieval church, strongly influenced by Jewish law, denounced infanticide as a pagan practice and insisted that every human life was sacred. The willful destruction of newborn children became a crime punishable by death. And yet, as the reference to "killing nurses" suggests, direct and indirect methods of eliminating unwanted babies did not disappear. There were, for example, many cases of "overlaying"—parents rolling over and suffocating the child placed between them in their bed. Such parents claimed they were drunk and had acted unintentionally. In Austria in 1784, suspicious authorities made it illegal for parents to take children under five into bed with them. Severe poverty on the one hand and increasing illegitimacy on the other conspired to force the very poor to thin their own ranks.

The young girl—very likely a servant—who could not provide for her child had few choices. If she would not stoop to abortion or the services of a killing nurse, she could bundle up her baby and leave it on the doorstep of a church. In the late seventeenth century, Saint Vincent de Paul was so distressed by the number of babies brought to the steps of Notre Dame in Paris that he established a home for foundlings. Others followed his example. In England the government acted on a petition calling for a foundling hospital "to prevent the frequent murders of poor, miserable infants at birth" and "to suppress the inhuman custom of exposing newborn children to perish in the streets."

In much of Europe in the eighteenth century, foundling homes became a favorite charity of the rich and powerful. Great sums were spent on them. The foundling home in St. Petersburg, perhaps the most elaborate and lavish of its kind, occupied the

Abandoned Children   At this Italian foundlings' home a frightened, secretive mother could discreetly deposit her baby. *(Source: The Bettmann Archive)*

former palaces of two members of the high nobility. In the early nineteenth century it had 25,000 children in its care and was receiving 5,000 new babies a year. At their best, the foundling homes of the eighteenth century were a good example of Christian charity and social concern in an age of great poverty and inequality.

Yet the foundling home was no panacea. By the 1770s one-third of all babies born in Paris were immediately abandoned to the foundling home by their mothers. Fully a third of all those foundlings were abandoned by married couples, a powerful commentary on the standard of living among the

The Five Senses Published in 1774, J. B. Basedow's *Elementary Reader* helped spread new attitudes toward child development and education. Drawing heavily on the theories of Locke and Rousseau, the German educator advocated nature study and contact with everyday life. In this illustration for Basedow's reader, gentle teachers allow uncorrupted children to learn about the five senses through direct experience. *(Source: Caroline Buckler)*

with the establishment of Christian schools, which taught the catechism and prayers as well as reading and writing. The Church of England and the dissenting congregations established "charity schools" to instruct the children of the poor. As early as 1717, Prussia made attendance at elementary schools compulsory. Inspired by the old Protestant idea that every believer should be able to read and study the Bible in the quest for personal salvation, and by the new idea of a population capable of effectively serving the state, Prussia led the way in the development of universal education. Religious mo-

tives were also extremely important elsewhere. From the middle of the seventeenth century, Presbyterian Scotland was convinced that the path to salvation lay in careful study of the Scriptures, and this belief led to an effective network of parish schools for rich and poor alike. The Enlightenment commitment to greater knowledge through critical thinking reinforced interest in education in the eighteenth century.

The result of these efforts was a remarkable growth of basic literacy between 1600 and 1800, especially after 1700. Whereas in 1600 only one male in six was barely literate in France and Scotland, and one in four in England, by 1800 almost 90 percent of the Scottish male population was literate. At the same time, two out of three males were literate in France; and in advanced areas such as Normandy, literacy approached 90 percent (Map 20.1). More than half of English males were literate by 1800. In all three countries the bulk of the jump occurred in the eighteenth century. Women were also increasingly literate, although they probably lagged behind men somewhat in most countries. Some elementary education was becoming a reality for European peoples, and schools were of growing significance in everyday life.

THE EUROPEAN'S FOOD

Plague and starvation, which recurred often in the seventeenth century, gradually disappeared in the eighteenth century. This phenomenon probably accounts in large part for the rapid growth in the total number of Europeans and for their longer lives. The increase in the average life span, allowing for regional variations, was substantial. In 1700 the average European could expect at birth to live only twenty-five years. A century later, a newborn European could expect to live fully ten years longer, to age thirty-five. The doubling of the adult life span meant that there was more time to produce and create, and more reason for parents to stress learning and preparation for adulthood.

People also lived longer because ordinary years were progressively less deadly. People ate better and somewhat more wisely. Doctors and hospitals probably saved a few more lives than they had in the past. How and why did health and life expectancy improve, and how much did they improve? And what were the differences between rich and poor? To answer these questions, it is necessary first to follow the eighteenth-century family to the table and then to see what contribution doctors made.

Diets and Nutrition

Although the accomplishments of doctors and hospitals are constantly in the limelight today, the greater, if less spectacular, part of medicine is preventive medicine. The great breakthrough of the second half of the nineteenth century was the development of public health techniques—proper sanitation and mass vaccinations—to prevent outbreaks of communicable diseases. Even before the nineteenth century, when medical knowledge was slight and doctors were of limited value, prevention was the key to longer life. Warm, dry housing, good clothing, and plentiful food make for healthier populations, much more capable of battling disease. Clothing and housing for the masses probably improved only modestly in the eighteenth century, but the new agricultural methods and increased agricultural output had a beneficial effect. The average European ate more and better food and was healthier as a result in 1800 than in 1700. This pattern is apparent if we look at the fare of the laboring poor.

At the beginning of the eighteenth century, ordinary men and women depended on grain as fully as they had in the past. Bread was quite literally the staff of life. Peasants in the Beauvais region of France ate two pounds of bread a day, washing it down with water, green wine, beer, or a little skimmed milk. Their dark bread was made from a

MAP 20.1 Literacy in France on the Eve of the French Revolution Literacy rates varied widely between and within states in eighteenth-century Europe. Northern France was clearly ahead of southern France.

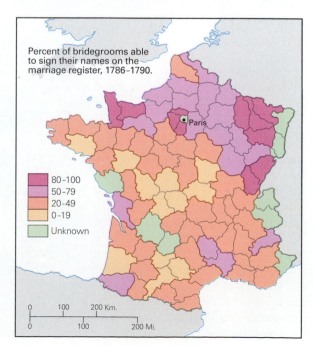

Percent of bridegrooms able to sign their names on the marriage register, 1786–1790.

- 80–100
- 50–79
- 20–49
- 0–19
- Unknown

Paris

0   100   200 Km.
0   100   200 Mi.

mixture of rough-ground wheat and rye—the standard flour of the poor. The poor also ate grains in soup and gruel. In rocky northern Scotland, for example, people depended on oatmeal, which they often ate half-cooked so it would swell in their stomachs and make them feel full. No wonder, then, that the supply of grain and the price of bread were critical questions for most people.

The poor, rural and urban, also ate a fair quantity of vegetables. Indeed, vegetables were considered "poor people's food." Peas and beans were probably the most common; grown as field crops in much of Europe since the Middle Ages, they were eaten fresh in late spring and summer. Dried, they became the basic ingredients in the soups and stews of the long winter months. In most regions, other vegetables appeared in season on the tables of the poor, primarily cabbages, carrots, and wild greens. Fruit was uncommon and limited to the summer months.

The European poor loved meat and eggs, but even in England—the wealthiest country in Europe in 1700—they seldom ate their fill. Indeed, the poor ate less meat in 1700 than in 1500, because their general standard of living had declined as the population surged in the sixteenth century (see page 606). Now meat was just too expensive. When the poor did eat meat—on a religious holiday or at a wedding or other special occasion—it was most likely lamb or mutton. Sheep could survive on rocky soils and did not compete directly with humans for the slender resources of grain.

Le Nain: Peasant Family A little wine and a great deal of dark bread: the traditional food of the poor French peasantry accentuates the poetic dignity of this masterpiece, painted about 1640 by Louis Le Nain. *(Source: Louvre/Cliché des Musées Nationaux, Paris)*

Milk was rarely drunk. It was widely believed that milk caused sore eyes, headaches, and a variety of ills, except among the very young and very old. Milk was used primarily to make cheese and butter, which the poor liked but could afford only occasionally. Medical and popular opinion considered whey, the watery liquid left after milk was churned, "an excellent temperate drink."

The diet of the rich—aristocrats, officials, and the comfortable bourgeoisie—was traditionally quite different from that of the poor. The men and women of the upper classes were rapacious carnivores, and a person's standard of living and economic well-being were often judged by the amount of meat eaten. A truly elegant dinner among the great and powerful consisted of one rich meat after another: a chicken pie, a leg of lamb, a grilled steak, for example. Three separate meat courses might be followed by three fish courses, laced with piquant sauces and complemented with sweets, cheeses, and nuts of all kinds. Fruits and vegetables were not often found on the tables of the rich. The long-standing dominance of meat and fish in the diet of the upper classes continued throughout the eighteenth century. There was extravagant living, and undoubtedly great overeating and gluttony, not only among the aristocracy but also among the prosperous professional classes.

There was also an enormous amount of over-drinking among the rich. The English squire, for example, who loved to ride with his hounds, loved drink with a similar passion. He became famous as the "four-bottle man." With his dinner he drank red wine from France or white wine from the Rhineland, and with his dessert he took sweet but strong port or Madeira from Portugal. Sometimes he ended the evening under the table in a drunken stupor, but very often he did not. The wine and the meat were consumed together in long hours of sustained excess, permitting the gentleman and his guests to drink enormous quantities.

The diet of small traders, master craftsmen, minor bureaucrats—the people of the towns and cities—was probably less monotonous than that of the peasantry. The markets, stocked by market gardens in the outskirts, provided a substantial variety of meats, vegetables, and fruits, although bread and beans still formed the bulk of the poor family's diet.

There were also regional dietary differences in 1700. Generally speaking, northern, Atlantic Europe ate better than southern, Mediterranean Europe. The poor of England probably ate best of all. Contemporaries on both sides of the Channel often contrasted the Englishman's consumption of meat with the French peasant's greater dependence on bread and vegetables. The Dutch were also considerably better fed than the average European, in large part because of their advanced agriculture and diversified gardens.

The Impact of Diet on Health

How were the poor and the rich served by their quite different diets? Good nutrition depends on a balanced supply of food as well as on an adequate number of calories. Modern research has shown that the chief determinant of nutritional balance is the relationship between carbohydrates (sugar and starch) and proteins. A diet consisting primarily of carbohydrates is seriously incomplete.

At first glance, the diet of the laboring poor, relying as it did on carbohydrates, seems very unsatisfactory. Even when a peasant got his daily two or three pounds of bread, his supply of protein and essential vitamins would appear too low. A closer look reveals a somewhat brighter picture. Most bread was "brown" or "black," made from wheat or rye. The flour of the eighteenth century was a whole-meal flour, produced by stone grinding. It contained most of the bran—the ground-up husk —and the all-important wheat germ. The bran and germ contain higher proportions of some minerals, vitamins, and good-quality proteins than does the rest of the grain. Only when they are removed does bread become a foodstuff providing relatively more starch and less of the essential nutrients.

In addition, the field peas and beans eaten by poor people since Carolingian days contained protein that complemented the proteins in whole-meal bread. The proteins in whey, cheese, and eggs, which the poor ate at least occasionally, also supplemented the bread and vegetables. Indeed, a leading authority concludes that if a pint of milk and some cheese and whey were eaten each day, the balance of the poor people's diet "was excellent, far better indeed than in many of our modern diets."[11]

The basic bread-and-vegetables diet of the poor *in normal times* was adequate. It protected effectively against most of the disorders associated with a deficiency of the vitamin B complex, for example.

The lack of sugar meant that teeth were not so plagued by cavities. Constipation was almost unknown to peasants and laborers living on coarse cereal breads, which provided the roughage modern diets lack. The common diet of the poor also generally warded off anemia, although anemia among infants was not uncommon.

The key dietary problem was probably getting enough green vegetables (or milk), particularly in the late winter and early spring, to ensure adequate supplies of vitamins A and C. A severe deficiency of vitamin C produces scurvy, a disease that leads to rotting gums, swelling of the limbs, and great weakness. Before the season's first vegetables, many people had used up their bodily reserves of vitamin C and were suffering from mild cases of scurvy. Sailors on long voyages suffered most. By the end of the sixteenth century, the exceptional antiscurvy properties of lemons and limes led to the practice of supplying some crews with a daily ration of lemon juice, which had highly beneficial effects. "Scurvy grass"—a kind of watercress—also guarded against scurvy, and this disease was increasingly controlled on even the longest voyages.

The practice of gorging on meat, sweets, and spirits caused the rich their own nutritional problems. They, too, were very often deficient in vitamins A and C because of their great disdain for fresh vegetables. Gout was a common affliction of the overfed and underexercised rich. No wonder they were often caricatured as dragging their flabby limbs and bulging bellies to the table, to stuff their swollen cheeks and poison their livers. People of moderate means, who could afford some meat and dairy products with fair regularity but who had not abandoned the bread and vegetables of the poor, were probably best off from a nutritional standpoint.

New Foods and New Knowledge

In nutrition and food consumption, Europe in the early eighteenth century had not gone beyond its medieval accomplishments. This situation began to change markedly as the century progressed. Although the introduction of new methods of farming was confined largely to the Low Countries and England, a new food—the potato—came to the aid of the poor everywhere.

Introduced into Europe from the Americas, along with corn, squash, tomatoes, chocolate, and many other useful plants, the humble potato is actually an excellent food. It contains a good supply of carbohydrates and calories and is rich in vitamins A and C, especially if it is not overcooked and the skin is eaten. The lack of vitamins from green vegetables was one of the biggest deficiencies in the poor person's winter and early spring diet. But the potato, which gave a much higher caloric yield than grain for a given piece of land, provided the needed vitamins and helped prevent scurvy. Doctors, increasingly aware of the dietary benefits of potatoes, prescribed them for the general public and in institutions such as schools and prisons.

For some poor people, especially desperately poor peasants who needed to get every possible calorie from a tiny plot of land, the potato replaced grain as the primary food in the eighteenth century. This happened first in Ireland, where rebellion in the seventeenth century had led to English repression and the perfection of a system of exploitation worthy of the most savage Eastern tyrant. The foreign (and Protestant) English landlords took the best land, forcing large numbers of poor (and Catholic) peasants to live off tiny scraps of rented ground. By 1700 the poor in Ireland lived almost exclusively on the bountiful fruits of the potato plot. This dependence placed the Irish in a precarious position, and when the potato crop failed in 1845 and 1846, there was widespread famine and starvation.

Elsewhere in Europe, potatoes took hold more slowly, because many people did not like to eat them. Therefore, potatoes were first fed to pigs and livestock, and there was even debate over whether they were fit for humans. In Germany the severe famines caused by the Seven Years' War (1756–1763) settled the matter: potatoes were edible and not just "famine food." By the end of the century, the potato was an important dietary supplement in much of Europe.

There was also a general growth of market gardening, and a greater variety of vegetables appeared in towns and cities. Potatoes, cabbages, peas, beans, radishes, spinach, asparagus, lettuce, parsnips, carrots, and other vegetables were sold in central markets and streets. In the course of the eighteenth century, the large towns and cities of maritime Europe began to receive semitropical fruits, such as oranges, lemons, and limes, from Portugal and the West Indies, although they were not cheap.

The growing variety of food was matched by some improvement in knowledge about diet and nutrition. For the poor, such improvement was limited primarily to the insight that the potato and other root crops improved health in the winter and helped to prevent scurvy. The rich began to be aware of the harmful effects of their meat-laden, wine-drowned meals.

The waning influence of Galen's medical teachings was another aspect of progress. Galen's Roman synthesis of ancient medical doctrines held that the four basic elements—air, fire, water, and earth—combine to produce in each person a complexion and a corresponding temperament. Foods were grouped into four categories appropriate for each complexion. Galen's notions dominated the dietary thinking of the seventeenth-century medical profession; for instance, "Galen said that the flesh of a hare preventeth fatness, causeth sleep and cleanseth the blood."

The growth of scientific experimentation in the seventeenth century led to a generally beneficial questioning of the old views. Haphazardly, by trial and error, and influenced by advances in chemistry, saner ideas developed. Not all changes in the eighteenth century were for the better, however. Bread began to change, most noticeably in England. Rising incomes and new tastes led to a shift from whole-meal black or brown bread to white bread made from finely ground and sifted flour. On the Continent, such white bread was generally limited to the well-to-do. To the extent that the preferred wheaten flour was stone-ground and sifted for coarse particles only, white bread remained satisfactory. But the desire for "bread as white as snow" was already leading to a decline in nutritional value.

The coarser bran, which is necessary for roughage, and at least some of the germ, which darkened the bread but contained many of the grain's nutrients, were already being sifted out to some extent. Bakers in English cities added the chemical alum to their white loaves to make them smoother, whiter, and larger. In the nineteenth century, "improvements" in milling were to lead to the removal of almost all the bran and germ from the flour, leaving it perfectly white and greatly reduced in nutritional value. The only saving grace in this sad deterioration was that people began to eat less bread and therefore to depend on it less.

Another sign of nutritional decline was the growing consumption of sweets in general and sugar in particular. Initially a luxury, sugar dropped rapidly in price, as slave-based production increased in the Americas, and the sweetener was much more widely used in the eighteenth century. This development probably led to an increase in cavities and to other ailments as well. Overconsumption of refined sugar can produce, paradoxically, low blood sugar (hypoglycemia) and, for some individuals at least, a variety of physical and mental ailments. Of course the greater or lesser poverty of the laboring poor saved most of them from the problems of the rich and well-to-do.

MEDICAL SCIENCE AND THE SICK

Advances in medical science played a very small part in improving the health and lengthening the lives of people in the eighteenth century. Such seventeenth-century advances as William Harvey's discovery of the circulation of blood were not soon translated into better treatment. The sick had to await the medical revolution of the later nineteenth century for much help from doctors.

Yet developments in medicine reflected the general thrust of the Enlightenment. The prevailing focus on discovering the laws of nature and on human problems, rather than on God and the heavens, gave rise to a great deal of research and experimentation. The century saw a remarkable rise in the number of doctors, and a high value was placed on their services. Thus, when the great breakthroughs in knowledge came in the nineteenth century, they could be rapidly diffused and applied. Eighteenth-century medicine, in short, gave promise of a better human existence, but most of the realization lay far in the future.

The Medical Professionals

Care of the sick was the domain of several competing groups: faith healers, apothecaries, surgeons, and physicians. Since the great majority of common ailments have a tendency to cure themselves, each group could point to successes and win adherents. When the doctor's treatment made the patient worse, as it often did, the original medical problem could always be blamed.

Faith healers, who had been among the most important kinds of physicians in medieval Europe, remained active. They and their patients believed that demons and evil spirits caused disease by lodging in people and that the proper treatment was to exorcise or drive out the offending devil. This demonic view of disease was strongest in the countryside, as was faith in the healing power of religious relics, prayer, and the laying on of hands. Faith healing was particularly effective in the treatment of mental disorders like hysteria and depression, where the link between attitude and illness is most direct.

Apothecaries, or pharmacists, sold a vast number of herbs, drugs, and patent medicines for every conceivable "temperament and distemper." Early pharmacists were seldom regulated, and they frequently diagnosed as freely as the doctors whose prescriptions they filled. Their prescriptions were incredibly complex—a hundred or more drugs might be included in a single prescription—and often very expensive. Some of the drugs undoubtedly worked. For example, strong laxatives were given to the rich for their constipated bowels. Indeed, the medical profession continued to believe that regular "purging" of the bowels was essential for good health and the treatment of illness. Much purging was harmful, however, and only bloodletting for the treatment of disease was more effective in speeding patients to their graves.

Drugs were prescribed and concocted in a helter-skelter way. With so many different drugs being combined, it was impossible to isolate cause and effect. Nor was there any standardization. A complicated prescription filled by ten different pharmacists would result in ten different preparations with different medical properties.

Surgeons competed vigorously with barbers and "bone benders," the forerunners of chiropractors. The eighteenth-century surgeon (and patient) labored in the face of incredible difficulties. Almost all operations were performed without any painkiller, for anesthesia was believed too dangerous. The terrible screams of people whose limbs were being sawed off echoed through hospitals and across battlefields. Such operations were common, because a surgeon faced with an extensive wound sought to obtain a plain surface that could be cau-

terized with fire. Thus, if a person broke an arm or a leg and the bone stuck out, off came the limb. Many patients died from the agony and shock of such operations.

Surgery was also performed in the midst of filth and dirt. There simply was no knowledge of bacteriology and the nature of infection. The simplest wound treated by a surgeon festered, often fatally. In fact, surgeons encouraged wounds to fester in the belief—a remnant of Galen's theory—that the pus was beneficially removing the base portions of the body.

Physicians, the fourth major group, were trained like surgeons. They were apprenticed in their teens to a practicing physician for several years of on-the-job training. This training was then rounded out with hospital work or some university courses. To their credit, physicians in the eighteenth century were increasingly willing to experiment with new methods, but the hand of Galen lay heavily on them. Bloodletting was still considered a medical cure-all. It was the way "bad blood," the cause of illness, was removed and the balance of humors necessary for good health restored. According to a physician practicing medicine in Philadelphia in 1799, bleeding was proper at the onset of all inflammatory fevers, in all inflammations, and for "asthma, sciatic pains, coughs, head-aches, rheumatisms, the apoplexy, epilepsy, and bloody fluxes."[12] It was also necessary after all falls, blows, and bruises.

Physicians, like apothecaries, laid great stress on purging. They also generally believed that disease was caused by bad odors, and for this reason they carried canes whose heads contained ammonia salts. As they made their rounds in the filthy, stinking hospitals, physicians held their canes to their noses to protect themselves from illness.

While ordinary physicians were bleeding, apothecaries purging, surgeons sawing, and faith healers praying, the leading medical thinkers were attempting to pull together and assimilate all the information and misinformation they had been accumulating. The attempt was ambitious: to systematize medicine around simple, basic principles, as Newton had done in physics. But the schools of thought resulting from such speculation and theorizing did little to improve medical care. Proponents of *animism* explained life and disease in terms of *anima*, the "sensitive soul," which they believed was present throughout the body and prevented its decay and self-destruction. Another school, *vitalism,* stressed "the vital principle," which inhabited all parts of the body. Vitalists tried to classify diseases systematically.

More interesting was the *homeopathic* system of Samuel Hahnemann of Leipzig. Hahnemann believed that very small doses of drugs that produce certain symptoms in a healthy person will cure a sick person with those symptoms. This theory was probably preferable to most eighteenth-century treatments, in that it was a harmless alternative to the extravagant and often fatal practices of bleeding, purging, drug taking, and induced vomiting. The patient gained confidence, and the body had at least a fighting chance of recovering.

Hospitals and Mental Illness

Hospitals were terrible throughout most of the eighteenth century. There was no isolation of patients. Operations were performed in the patient's bed. The nurses were old, ignorant, greedy, and often drunk women. Fresh air was considered harmful, and infections of every kind were rampant. Diderot's article in the *Encyclopedia* on the Hôtel-Dieu in Paris, the "richest and most terrifying of all French hospitals," vividly describes normal conditions of the 1770s:

Imagine a long series of communicating wards filled with sufferers of every kind of disease who are sometimes packed three, four, five or even six into a bed, the living alongside the dead and dying, the air polluted by this mass of unhealthy bodies, passing pestilential germs of their afflictions from one to the other, and the spectacle of suffering and agony on every hand. That is the Hôtel-Dieu.

The result is that many of these poor wretches come out with diseases they did not have when they went in, and often pass them on to the people they go back to live with. Others are half-cured and spend the rest of their days in an invalidism as hard to bear as the illness itself; and the rest perish, except for the fortunate few whose strong constitutions enable them to survive.[13]

No wonder the poor of Paris hated hospitals and often saw confinement there as a plot to kill paupers.

In the last years of the century, the humanitarian concern already reflected in Diderot's description

Knives for Bloodletting   In the eighteenth century doctors continued to use these highly esteemed instruments for almost every illness, with disastrous results. *(Source: Courtesy, World Heritage Museum. Photo: Caroline Buckler)*

of the Hôtel-Dieu led to a movement for hospital reform throughout western Europe. Efforts were made to improve ventilation and eliminate filth, on the grounds that bad air caused disease. The theory was wrong, but the results were beneficial, since the spread of infection was somewhat reduced.

Mental hospitals, too, were incredibly savage institutions. The customary treatment for mental illness was bleeding and cold water, administered more to maintain discipline than to effect a cure. Violent persons were chained to the wall and forgotten. A breakthrough of sorts occurred in the 1790s, when William Tuke founded the first humane sanatorium in England. In Paris an innovative warden, Philippe Pinel, took the chains off the mentally disturbed in 1793 and tried to treat them as patients rather than as prisoners.

In the eighteenth century, there were all sorts of wildly erroneous ideas about mental illness. One

Hospital Life   Patients crowded into hospitals like this one in Hamburg in 1746 had little chance of recovery. A priest by the window administers last rites, while in the center a surgeon coolly saws off the leg of a man who has received no anesthesia. *(Source: Germanisches Nationalmuseum, Nuremberg)*

was that moonlight caused madness, a belief reflected in the word *lunatic*—someone harmed by lunar light. Another mid-eighteenth-century theory, which lasted until at least 1914, was that masturbation caused madness, not to mention acne, epilepsy, and premature ejaculation. Thus parents, religious institutions, and schools waged relentless war on masturbation by males, although they were curiously uninterested in female masturbation. In the nineteenth century, this misguided idea was to reach its greatest height, resulting in increasingly drastic medical treatment. Doctors ordered their "patients" to wear mittens, fitted them with wooden braces between the knees, or simply tied them up in strait jackets.

Medical Experiments and Research

In the second half of the eighteenth century, medicine in general turned in a more practical and ex-perimental direction. Some of the experimentation was creative quackery involving the recently discovered phenomenon of electricity. One magnificent quack, James Graham of London, opened a great hall filled with the walking sticks, crutches, eyeglasses, and ear trumpets of supposedly cured patients, which he kept as symbols of his victory over disease. Great glass globes and the rich perfumes of burning incense awaited all who entered. Graham's principal treatment involved his Celestial Bed, which was lavishly decorated with magnets and electrical devices. Graham claimed that by sleeping in it youths would keep their good looks, their elders would be rejuvenated, and couples would have beautiful, healthy children. The fee for a single night in the Medico-Magnetico-Musico-Electrical Bed was £100—a great sum of money.

The rich could buy expensive treatments, but the prevalence of quacks and the general lack of knowledge meant they often got little for their money. Because so many treatments were harmful, the poor were probably much less deprived by their almost total lack of access to medical care than one might think.

Renewed experimentation and the intensified search for solutions to human problems also led to some real, if still modest, advances in medicine after 1750. The eighteenth century's greatest medical triumph was the conquest of smallpox.

With the progressive decline of bubonic plague, smallpox became the most terrible of the infectious diseases. In the words of the historian Thomas Macaulay, "smallpox was always present, filling the churchyard with corpses, tormenting with constant fears all whom it had not stricken." In the seventeenth century, one in every four deaths in the British Isles was due to smallpox, and it is estimated that sixty million Europeans died of it in the eighteenth century. Fully 80 percent of the population was stricken at some point in life, and 25 percent of the total population was left permanently scarred. If ever a human problem cried out for solution, it was smallpox.

The first step in the conquest of this killer came in the early eighteenth century. An English aristocrat whose great beauty had been marred by the pox, Lady Mary Wortley Montagu, learned about the practice of inoculation in the Ottoman Empire while her husband was serving as British ambassador there. She had her own son successfully inoculated in Constantinople and was instrumental in spreading the practice in England after her return in 1722.

Inoculation against smallpox had long been practiced in the Middle East. The skin was deliberately broken, and a small amount of matter taken from the pustule of a smallpox victim was applied. The person thus contracted a mild case of smallpox that gave lasting protection against further attack.

The Fight Against Smallpox   This Russian illustration dramatically urges parents to inoculate their children against smallpox. The good father's healthy youngsters flee from their ugly and infected playmates, who hold their callous father responsible for their shameful fate. *(Source: Yale Medical Library)*

Inoculation was risky, however, and about one person in fifty died from it. In addition, people who had been inoculated were just as infectious as those who had caught the disease by chance. Inoculated people thus spread the disease, and the practice of inoculation against smallpox was widely condemned in the 1730s.

Success in overcoming this problem in British colonies led the British College of Physicians in 1754 to strongly advocate inoculation. Moreover, a successful search for cheaper methods led to something approaching mass inoculation in England in the 1760s. One specialist treated seventeen thousand patients and only five died. Both the danger and the cost had been reduced, and deadly smallpox struck all classes less frequently. On the Continent, the well-to-do were also inoculated, beginning with royal families like those of Maria Theresa and Catherine the Great. The practice then spread to the middle classes. By the later years of the century, smallpox inoculation played some part in the decline of the death rate and the increase in population.

The final breakthrough against smallpox came at the end of the century. Edward Jenner (1749–1823), a talented country doctor, noted that in the English countryside there was a long-standing belief that dairy maids who had contracted cowpox did not get smallpox. Cowpox produces sores on the cow's udder and on the hands of the milker. The sores resemble those of smallpox, but the disease is mild and not contagious.

For eighteen years Jenner practiced a kind of Baconian science, carefully collecting data on protection against smallpox by cowpox. Finally, in 1796 he performed his first vaccination on a young boy, using matter taken from a milkmaid with cowpox. Two months later he inoculated the boy with smallpox pus, but the disease did not take. In the next two years, twenty-three successful vaccinations were performed, and in 1798 Jenner published his findings. There was some skepticism and hostility, but after Austrian medical authorities replicated Jenner's results, the new method of treatment spread rapidly. Smallpox soon declined to the point of disappearance in Europe and then throughout the world. Jenner eventually received prizes of totaling £30,000 from the British government for his great discovery, a fitting recompense for a man who gave an enormous gift to humanity and helped lay the foundation for the science of immunology in the nineteenth century.

RELIGION AND CHRISTIAN CHURCHES

Though the critical spirit of the Enlightenment spread among the educated elite in the eighteenth century, the great mass of ordinary men and women remained firmly committed to the Christian religion, especially in rural areas. Religion offered answers to life's mysteries and gave comfort and courage in the face of sorrow and fear. Religion also remained strong because it was usually embedded in local traditions and everyday social experience.

Yet the popular religion of village Europe was everywhere enmeshed in a larger world of church hierarchies and state power. These powerful outside forces sought to regulate religious life at the local level. These efforts created tensions that helped set the scene for a vigorous religious revival in Germany and England.

The Institutional Church

As in the Middle Ages, the local parish church remained the basic religious unit all across Europe. Still largely coinciding with the agricultural village, the parish fulfilled many needs. The parish church was the focal point of religious devotion, which went far beyond sermons and Holy Communion. The parish church organized colorful processions and pilgrimages to local shrines. Even in Protestant countries, where such activities were severely restricted, congregations gossiped and swapped stories after services, and neighbors came together in church for baptisms, marriages, funerals, and special events. Thus the parish church was woven into the very fabric of community life.

Moreover, the local church had important administrative tasks. Priests and parsons were truly the bookkeepers of agrarian Europe, and it is because parish registers were so complete that historians have learned so much about population and family life. Parishes also normally distributed charity to the destitute, looked after orphans, and provided whatever primary education was available.

The many tasks of the local church were usually the responsibility of a resident priest or pastor, a full-time professional working with assistants and lay volunteers. Moreover, all clerics—whether Catholic, Protestant, or Orthodox—shared the fate of middlemen in a complicated institutional system. Charged most often with ministering to poor peasants, the priest or parson was the last link in a powerful church-state hierarchy that was everywhere determined to control religion down to the grassroots. However, the regulatory framework of belief, which went back at least to the fourth century, when Christianity became the official religion of the Roman Empire, had undergone important changes since 1500.

The Protestant Reformation had begun as a culmination of medieval religiosity and a desire to purify Christian belief. Martin Luther, the greatest of the reformers (see Chapter 14), preached that all men and women were saved from their sins and God's damnation only by personal faith in Jesus Christ. The individual could reach God directly, without need of priestly intermediaries. This was the revolutionary meaning of Luther's "priesthood of all believers," which broke forever the monopoly of the priestly class over medieval Europe's most priceless treasure—eternal salvation.

As the Reformation gathered force, with peasant upheaval and doctrinal competition, Luther turned more conservative. The monkish professor called on willing German princes to put themselves at the head of official churches in their territories. Other monarchs in northern Europe followed suit. Protestant authorities, with generous assistance from state-certified theologians like Luther, then proceeded to regulate their "territorial churches" strictly, selecting personnel and imposing detailed rules. They joined with Catholics to crush the Anabaptists (see Chapter 14), who, with their belief in freedom of conscience and separation of church and state, had become the real revolutionaries. Thus the Reformation, initially so radical in its rejection of Rome and its stress on individual religious experience, eventually resulted in a bureaucratization of the church and local religious life in Protestant Europe.

The Reformation era also increased the practical power of Catholic rulers over "their" churches, but it was only in the eighteenth century that some Catholic monarchs began to impose striking reforms. These reforms, which had their counterparts in Orthodox Russia, had a very "Protestant" aspect. They increased state control over the Catholic church, making it less subject to papal influence.

Spain provides a graphic illustration of changing church-state relations in Catholic lands. A deeply Catholic country with devout rulers, Spain nevertheless took firm control of ecclesiastical appointments. Papal proclamations could not even be read in Spanish churches without prior approval from the government. Spain also asserted state control over the Spanish Inquisition (see Chapter 13), which had been ruthlessly pursuing heresy as an independent agency under Rome's direction for two hundred years. In sum, Spain went far toward creating a "national" Catholic church, as France had done earlier.

A more striking indication of state power and papal weakness was the fate of the Society of Jesus. As the most successful of the Catholic Reformation's new religious orders (see Chapter 14), the well-educated Jesuits were extraordinary teachers, missionaries, and agents of the papacy. In many Catholic countries, the Jesuits exercised tremendous political influence, since individual members held high government positions and Jesuit colleges formed the minds of Europe's Catholic nobility. Yet, by playing politics so effectively, the Jesuits eventually raised a broad coalition of enemies that destroyed their order. Especially bitter controversies over the Jesuits rocked the entire Catholic hierarchy in France. Following the earlier example of Portugal, the French king ordered the Jesuits out of France in 1763 and confiscated their property. France and Spain then pressured Rome to dissolve the Jesuits completely. In 1773 a reluctant pope caved in, although the order was revived after the French Revolution.

Some Catholic rulers also turned their reforming efforts on monasteries and convents, believing that the large monastic clergy should make a more practical contribution to social and religious life. Austria, a leader in controlling the church (see page 584), showed how far the process could go. Whereas Maria Theresa sharply restricted entry into "unproductive" orders, Joseph II recalled the radical initiatives of the Protestant Reformation. In his Edict on Idle Institutions, Joseph abolished contemplative orders, henceforth permitting only orders that were engaged in teaching, nursing, or other practical work. The number of monks plunged from 65,000 to 27,000. The state also expropriated the dissolved monasteries and used their great wealth for charitable purposes and higher salaries for ordinary priests.

Catholic Piety

Catholic territorial churches also sought to purify religious practice somewhat. As might be expected, Joseph II went the furthest. Above all, he and his agents sought to root out what they considered to be idolatry and superstition. Yet pious peasants saw only an incomprehensible attack on the true faith and drew back in anger. Joseph's sledgehammer approach and the resulting reaction dramatized an underlying tension between Christian reform and popular piety after the Reformation.

Protestant reformers had taken very seriously the commandment that "Thou shalt not make any graven image" (Exodus 20:4), and their radical reforms had reordered church interiors. Relics and crucifixes had been permanently removed from crypt and altar, while stained-glass windows had been smashed and walls and murals covered with whitewash. Processions and pilgrimages, saints and shrines—all such nonessentials had been rigorously suppressed in the attempt to recapture the vital core of the Christian religion. Such revolutionary changes had often troubled ordinary churchgoers, but by the late seventeenth century,

Planting Crosses After their small wooden crosses were blessed at church as part of the Rogation Days' ceremonies in early May, French peasants traditionally placed them in their fields and pastures to protect the seed and help the crops grow. This illustration shows the custom being performed in the French Alps in the mid-nineteenth century, when it was still widely practiced. *(Source: Library of Congress)*

"Clipping the Church"   The ancient English ceremony of dancing around the church once each year on the night before Lent undoubtedly had pre-Christian origins, for its purpose was to create a magical protective chain against evil spirits and the devil. The Protestant reformers did their best to stamp them out, but such "pagan practices" sometimes lingered on. *(Source: Somerset Archaeological and Natural History Society)*

these reforms had been thoroughly routinized by official Protestant churches.

The situation was quite different in Catholic Europe around 1700. First of all, the visual contrast was striking; baroque art (see Chapter 15) had lavished rich and emotionally exhilarating figures and images on Catholic churches, just as Protestants had removed theirs. From almost every indication, people in Catholic Europe remained intensely religious. More than 95 percent of the population probably attended church for Easter Communion, the climax of the Catholic church year.

The tremendous popular strength of religion in Catholic countries reflected the fact that religious practice went far beyond Sunday churchgoing and was an important part of community life. Thus, although Catholics reluctantly confessed their sins to the priest, they enthusiastically joined together in public processions to celebrate the passage of the liturgical year. In addition to the great processional days—such as Palm Sunday, the joyful re-enactment of Jesus' triumphal entry into Jerusalem, or Rogations, with its chanted supplications and penances three days before the bodily ascent of Jesus into heaven on Ascension Day—each parish had its own local processions. Led by its priest, a congregation might march around the village, or across the countryside to a local shrine or chapel. There were endless variations. In the southern French Alps, the people looked forward especially to "high-mountain" processions in late spring. Parishes came together from miles around on some high mountain. There the assembled priests asked God to bless the people with healthy flocks and pure waters, and then all joined together in an enormous picnic. Before each procession, the priest explained its religious significance to kindle group piety. But processions were also folklore and tradition, an escape from work and a form of recreation. A holiday atmosphere sometimes reigned on longer processions, with drinking and dancing and couples disappearing into the woods.

Devout Catholics held many religious beliefs that were marginal to the Christian faith, often of obscure or even pagan origin. On the feast of Saint Anthony, priests were expected to bless salt and bread for farm animals to protect them from disease. One saint's relics could help cure a child of fear, and there were healing springs for many ailments. The ordinary person combined a strong Christian faith with a wealth of time-honored superstitions.

Parish priests and Catholic hierarchies were frequently troubled by the limitations of their parishioners' Christian understanding. One parish priest in France, who kept an invaluable daily diary, lamented that his parishioners were "more superstitious than devout . . . and sometimes appear as baptized idolaters."[14]

Many parish priests in France, often acting on instructions from their bishops, made an effort to purify popular religious culture. For example, one priest tried to abolish pilgrimages to a local sacred spring of Our Lady, reputed to revive dead babies

long enough for a proper baptism. French priests denounced particularly the "various remnants of paganism" found in popular bonfire ceremonies during Lent, in which young men, "yelling and screaming like madmen," tried to jump over the bonfires in order to help the crops grow and protect themselves from illness. One priest saw rational Christians turning back into pagan animals —"the triumph of Hell and the shame of Christianity."[15]

Yet, whereas Protestant reformers had already used the power of the territorial state to crush such practices, Catholic church leaders generally proceeded cautiously in the eighteenth century. They knew that old beliefs—such as the belief common throughout Europe that the priest's energetic ringing of church bells and his recitation of ritual prayers would protect the village from hail and thunderstorms—were an integral part of the people's religion. Thus Catholic priests and hierarchies generally preferred a compromise between theological purity and the people's piety, realizing perhaps that the line between divine truth and mere superstition is not easily drawn.

Protestant Revival

By the late seventeenth century, official Protestant churches had completed their vast reforms and had generally settled into a smug complacency. In the Reformation heartland, one concerned German minister wrote that the Lutheran church "had become paralyzed in forms of dead doctrinal conformity" and badly needed a return to its original inspiration.[16] This voice was one of many that would prepare and then guide a powerful Protestant revival, a revival largely successful because it answered the intense but increasingly unsatisfied needs of common people.

The Protestant revival began in Germany. It was known as "Pietism," and three aspects helped explain its powerful appeal. First, Pietism called for warm emotional religion that everyone could experience. Enthusiasm—in prayer, in worship, in preaching, in life itself—was the key concept. "Just as a drunkard becomes full of wine, so must the congregation become filled with spirit," declared one exuberant writer. Another said simply, "The heart must burn."[17]

Second, Pietism reasserted the earlier radical stress on the "priesthood of all believers," thereby reducing the large gulf between the official clergy and the Lutheran laity. Bible reading and study were enthusiastically extended to all classes, and this provided a powerful spur for popular education as well as individual religious development. Finally, Pietists believed in the practical power of Christian rebirth in everyday affairs. Reborn Christians were expected to lead good, moral lives and come from all walks of life.

Pietism had a major impact on John Wesley (1703–1791), who served as the catalyst for popular religious revival in England. Wesley came from a long line of ministers, and when he went to Oxford University to prepare for the clergy, he mapped a fanatically earnest "scheme of religion." Like some students during final-exam period, he organized every waking moment. After becoming a teaching fellow at Oxford, he organized a Holy Club for similarly minded students, who were soon known contemptuously as "Methodists" because they were so methodical in their devotion. Yet, like the young Luther, Wesley remained intensely troubled about his own salvation, even after his ordination as an Anglican priest in 1728.

Wesley's anxieties related to grave problems of the faith in England. The Church of England was shamelessly used by the government to provide favorites with high-paying jobs and sinecures. Building of churches practically stopped while the population grew, and in many parishes there was a grave shortage of pews. Services and sermons had settled into an uninspiring routine. That the properly purified religion had been separated from local customs and social life was symbolized by church doors that were customarily locked on weekdays. Moreover, the skepticism of the Enlightenment was making inroads among the educated classes, and deism was becoming popular. Some bishops and church leaders acted as if they believed that doctrines like the Virgin Birth or the Ascension were little more than particularly elegant superstitions.

Living in an atmosphere of religious decline and uncertainty, Wesley became profoundly troubled by his lack of faith in his own salvation. Yet spiritual counseling from a sympathetic Pietist minister from Germany prepared Wesley for a mystical, emotional "conversion" in 1738. He described this critical turning point in his *Journal:*

In the evening I went to a [Christian] society in Aldersgate Street where one was reading Luther's preface to the Epistle to the Romans. *About a quarter before nine, while he was describing the change which God works in the heart through faith in Christ, I felt my heart strangely warmed. I felt I did trust in Christ, Christ alone for salvation; and an assurance was given me that he had taken away* my *sins, even* mine, *and saved* me *from the law of sin and death.*[18]

Wesley's emotional experience resolved his intellectual doubts. Moreover, he was convinced that any person, no matter how poor or simple, might have a similar heartfelt conversion and gain the same blessed assurance.

Wesley took the good news to the people. Since existing churches were often overcrowded and the

John Wesley preached that all who truly believe in Christ may gain eternal salvation. Shown here preaching from his father's tomb, Wesley waited until the 1780s to organize the Methodists into a separate denomination. *(Source: E. T. Archive)*

Pluralism reflected corruption in the Church of England. With the help of powerful friends, the "pluralist" parson satirized in this eighteenth-century cartoon has received appointments to four different parishes. Employing poor assistants to do the preaching, he collects a handsome unearned income. *(Source: Bettmann/Hulton)*

church-state establishment was hostile, Wesley preached in open fields. People came in large numbers. Of critical importance was Wesley's rejection of Calvinist predestination—the doctrine of salvation granted only to a select few (see Chapter 14). Expanding on earlier Dutch theologians' views, he preached that *all* men and women who earnestly sought salvation might be saved. It was a message of hope and joy, of free will and universal salvation.

Traveling some 225,000 miles by horseback and preaching more than 40,000 sermons in fifty years, Wesley's ministry won converts, formed Methodist cells, and eventually resulted in a new denomination. Evangelicals in the Church of England and the old dissenting groups also followed Wesley's

example, giving impetus to an even broader awakening among the lower classes. That result showed that in England, as throughout Europe despite different churches and different practices, religion remained a vital force in the lives of the people.

SUMMARY

In recent years, imaginative research has greatly increased the specialist's understanding of ordinary life and social patterns in the past. The human experience, as recounted by historians, has become richer and more meaningful, and many mistaken ideas have fallen. This has been particularly true of eighteenth-century, agrarian Europe. The intimacies of family life, the contours of women's history and of childhood, and vital problems of medicine and religion are emerging from obscurity. Nor is this all. A deeper, truer understanding of the life of common people can shed light on the great economic and political developments of long-standing concern, to be seen in the next chapter.

NOTES

1. Quoted in J. M. Beattie, "The Criminality of Women in Eighteenth-century England," *Journal of Social History* 8 (Summer 1975): 86.
2. W. L. Langer, "Infanticide: A Historical Survey," *History of Childhood Quarterly* 1 (Winter 1974): 357.
3. Quoted in R. Cobb, *The Police and the People: French Popular Protest, 1789–1820* (Oxford: Clarendon Press, 1970), p. 238.
4. Quoted in E. A. Wrigley, *Population and History* (New York: McGraw-Hill, 1969), p. 127.
5. Quoted in D. S. Landes, ed., *The Rise of Capitalism* (New York: Macmillan, 1966), pp. 56–57.
6. G. Gullickson, *Spinners and Weavers of Auffay: Rural Industry and the Sexual Division of Labor in a French Village, 1750–1850* (Cambridge: Cambridge University Press, 1986), p. 186. Also see L. A. Tilly, J. W. Scott, and M. Cohen, "Women's Work and European Fertility Patterns," *Journal of Interdisciplinary History* 6 (Winter 1976): 447–476.
7. J. Michelet, *The People*, trans. with an introduction by J. P. McKay (Urbana: University of Illinois Press, 1973; original publication, 1846), pp. 38–39.
8. J. Brownlow, *The History and Design of the Foundling Hospital* (London, 1868), p. 7.
9. Quoted in B. W. Lorence, "Parents and Children in Eighteenth-century Europe," *History of Childhood Quarterly* 2 (Summer 1974): 1–2.
10. Ibid., pp. 13, 16.
11. J. C. Drummond and A. Wilbraham, *The Englishman's Food: A History of Five Centuries of English Diet* 2d ed. (London: Jonathan Cape, 1958), p. 75.
12. Quoted in L. S. King, *The Medical World of the Eighteenth Century* (Chicago: University of Chicago Press, 1958), p. 320.
13. Quoted in R. Sand, *The Advance to Social Medicine* (London: Staples Press, 1952), pp. 86–87.
14. Quoted in I. Woloch, *Eighteenth-century Europe: Tradition and Progress, 1715–1789* (New York: W. W. Norton, 1982), p. 292.
15. Quoted in T. Tackett, *Priest and Parish in Eighteenth-century France* (Princeton, N.J.: Princeton University Press, 1977), p. 214.
16. Quoted in K. Pinson, *Pietism as a Factor in the Rise of German Nationalism* (New York: Columbia University Press, 1934), p. 13.
17. Ibid., pp. 43–44.
18. Quoted in S. Andrews, *Methodism and Society* (London: Longmans, Green, 1970), p. 327.

SUGGESTED READING

Though long ignored in many general histories of the Western world, social topics of the kind considered in this chapter have come into their own in recent years. The articles cited in the Notes are typical of the exciting work being done, and the reader is strongly advised to take time to look through recent volumes of some leading journals: *Journal of Social History, Past and Present,* and *Journal of Interdisciplinary History.* In addition, the number of book-length studies has expanded rapidly and continues to do so. Several of these studies are mentioned in the Notes, and the books by Wrigley, Drummond and Wilbraham, and Tackett are especially useful.

Among general introductions to the history of the family, women, and children, J. Casey, *The History of the Family* (1989), is recommended. P. Laslett, *The World We Have Lost* (1965), is an exciting, pioneering investigation of England before the Industrial Revolution, though some of his conclusions have been weakened by further research. L. Stone, *The Family, Sex and Marriage in England, 1500–1800* (1977), is a provocative general interpretation, and L. Tilly and J. Scott, *Women, Work and Family* (1978), is excellent. Two valuable works on women, both with good bibliographies, are M. Boxer and J. Quataert, eds., *Connecting Spheres: Women in the Western World, 1500 to the Present* (1987), and R. Bridenthal, C. Koonz, and S. Stuard, eds., *Becoming Visible: Women in European History,* 2d ed. (1987). P. Aries, *Centuries of Childhood: A Social History of Family Life* (1962), is another stimulating study. E. Shorter, *The Making of the Modern Family* (1975), is a lively controversial interpretation, which should be compared with the excellent study by M. Segalen, *Love and Power in the Peasant Family: Rural France in the Nineteenth Century* (1983). T. Rabb and R. I. Rothberg, eds., *The Family in History* (1973), is a good collection of articles dealing with both Europe and the United States. A. MacFarlane, *The Family Life of Ralph Josselin* (1970), is a brilliant re-creation of the intimate family circle of a seventeenth-century English clergyman who kept a detailed diary; MacFarlane's *Origins of English Individualism: The Family, Property and Social Transi-*

tion (1978) is a major work. I. Pinchbeck and M. Hewitt, *Children in English Society* (1973), is a good introduction. Various aspects of sexual relationships are treated imaginatively by M. Foucault, *The History of Sexuality* (1981), and R. Wheaton and T. Hareven, eds., *Family and Sexuality in French History* (1980).

J. Burnett, *A History of the Cost of Living* (1969), has a great deal of interesting information about what people spent their money on in the past. J. Knyveton, *Diary of a Surgeon in the Year 1751–1752* (1937), gives a contemporary's unforgettable picture of both eighteenth-century medicine and social customs, as do D. and R. Porter, *Patient's Progress: Doctors and Doctoring in Eighteenth-Century England* (1989), and M. Romsey, *Professional and Popular Medicine in France, 1770–1830: The Social World of Medical Practice* (1988). Good introductions to the evolution of medical practices are B. Ingles, *History of Medicine* (1965); O. Bettmann, *A Pictorial History of Medicine* (1956); and H. Haggard's old but interesting *Devils, Drugs, and Doctors* (1929). W. Boyd, *History of Western Education* (1966), is a standard survey, while R. Houston, *Literacy in Early Modern Europe: Culture and Education, 1500–1800* (1988), is brief and engaging. M. D. George, *London Life in the Eighteenth Century* (1965), is a delightfully written book, while D. Roche, *The People of Paris* (1987), presents an unforgettable portrait of the Paris poor in the eighteenth century. G. Rude, *The Crowd in History, 1730–1848* (1964), is an innovative effort to see politics and popular protest from below. An important series edited by R. Forster and O. Ranuum considers neglected social questions such as diet, abandoned children, and deviants, as does P. Burke's excellent study, *Popular Culture in Early Modern Europe* (1978). J. Gillis, *For Better, for Worse: Marriage in Britain Since 1500* (1985), admirably covers the subject.

Good works on religious life include J. Delumeau, *Catholicism Between Luther and Voltaire: A New View of the Counter-Reformation* (1977); B. Semmel, *The Methodist Revolution* (1973); and J. Bettey, *Church and Community: The Parish Church in English Life* (1979).

21

The Revolution in Politics, 1775–1815

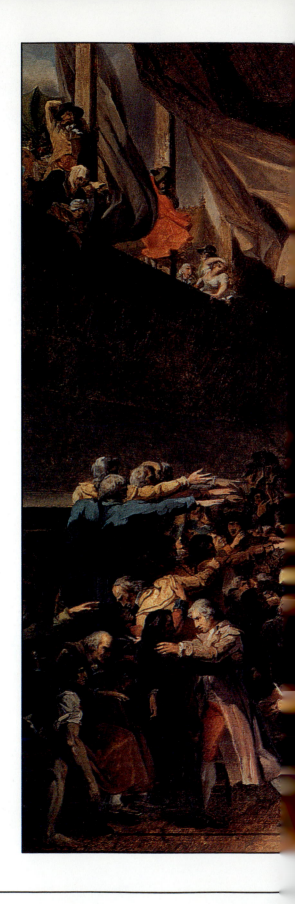

The last years of the eighteenth century were a time of great upheaval. A series of revolutions and revolutionary wars challenged the old order of kings and aristocrats. The ideas of freedom and equality, ideas that have not stopped shaping the world since that era, flourished and spread. The revolution began in North America in 1775. Then in 1789 France, the most influential country in Europe, became the leading revolutionary nation. It established first a constitutional monarchy, then a radical republic, and finally a new empire under Napoleon. The armies of France also joined forces with patriots and radicals abroad in an effort to establish new governments based on new principles throughout much of Europe. The world of modern domestic and international politics was born.

- What caused this era of revolution?
- What were the ideas and objectives of the men and women who rose up violently to undo the established system?
- What were the gains and losses for privileged groups and for ordinary people in a generation of war and upheaval?

These are the questions underlying this chapter's examination of the French and American revolutions.

LIBERTY AND EQUALITY

Two ideas fueled the revolutionary period in both America and Europe: liberty and equality. What did eighteenth-century politicians and other people mean by liberty and equality, and why were those ideas so radical and revolutionary in their day?

The call for liberty was first of all a call for individual human rights. Even the most enlightened monarchs customarily claimed that it was their duty to regulate what people wrote and believed. Liberals of the revolutionary era protested such controls from on high. They demanded freedom to worship according to the dictates of their consciences instead of according to the politics of their prince. They demanded the end of censorship and the right to express their beliefs freely in print and at public meetings. They demanded freedom from arbitrary laws and from judges who simply obeyed orders from the government.

These demands for basic personal freedoms, which were incorporated into the American Bill of Rights and other liberal constitutions, were very far-reaching. Indeed, eighteenth-century revolutionaries demanded more freedom than most governments today believe it is desirable to grant. The Declaration of the Rights of Man, issued at the beginning of the French Revolution, proclaimed, "Liberty consists in being able to do anything that does not harm another person." A citizen's rights had, therefore, "no limits except those which assure to the other members of society the enjoyment of these same rights." Liberals called for the freedom of the individual to develop and to create to the fullest possible extent. In the context of the aristocratic and monarchial forms of government that then dominated Europe, this was a truly radical idea.

The call for liberty was also a call for a new kind of government. The revolutionary liberals believed that the people were sovereign—that is, that the people alone had the authority to make laws limiting the individual's freedom of action. In practice, this system of government meant choosing legislators who represented the people and who were accountable to them. Moreover, liberals of the revolutionary era believed that every people—that is, every ethnic group—had this right of self-determination and, thus, the right to form a free nation.

By equality, eighteenth-century liberals meant that all citizens were to have identical rights and civil liberties. Above all, the nobility had no right to special privileges based on the accident of birth.

Liberals did not define equality as meaning that everyone should be equal economically. Quite the contrary. As Thomas Jefferson wrote in an early draft of the American Declaration of Independence, before changing "property" to the more noble-sounding "happiness," everyone was equal in "the pursuit of property." Jefferson and other liberals certainly did not expect equal success in that pursuit. Great differences in wealth and income between rich and poor were perfectly acceptable to liberals. The essential point was that everyone should legally have an equal chance. French liberals and revolutionaries said they wanted "careers opened to talent." They wanted employment in government, in business, and in the professions to be based on ability, not on family background or legal status.

Equality of opportunity was a very revolutionary idea in eighteenth-century Europe. Legal inequality between classes and groups was the rule, not the exception. Society was still legally divided into groups with special privileges, such as the nobility and the clergy, and groups with special burdens, like the peasantry. In many countries, various middle-class groups—professionals, business people, townspeople, and craftsmen—enjoyed privileges that allowed them to monopolize all sorts of economic activity. It was this kind of economic inequality, an inequality based on artificial legal distinctions, against which liberals protested.

The Roots of Liberalism

The ideas of liberty and equality—the central ideas of classical liberalism—have deep roots in Western history. The ancient Greeks and the Judeo-Christian tradition had affirmed for hundreds of years the sanctity and value of the individual human being. The Judeo-Christian tradition, reinforced by the Reformation, had long stressed personal responsibility on the part of both common folk and exalted rulers, thereby promoting the self-discipline without which liberty becomes anarchy. The hounded and persecuted Protestant radicals of the later sixteenth century had died for the revolutionary idea that individuals were entitled to their own religious beliefs.

Although the liberal creed had roots deep in the Western tradition, classical liberalism first crystallized at the end of the seventeenth century and during the Enlightenment of the eighteenth century. Liberal ideas reflected the Enlightenment's stress on human dignity and human happiness on earth. Liberals shared the Enlightenment's general faith in science, rationality, and progress: the adoption of liberal principles meant better government and a better society for all. Almost all the writers of the Enlightenment were passionately committed to greater personal liberty. They preached religious toleration, freedom of press and speech, and fair and equal treatment before the law.

Certain English and French thinkers were mainly responsible for joining the Enlightenment's concern for personal freedom and legal equality to a theoretical justification of liberal self-government.

The two most important were John Locke and the baron de Montesquieu, considered earlier. Locke (see page 524) maintained that England's long political tradition rested on "the rights of Englishmen" and on representative government through Parliament. Locke admired especially the great Whig nobles who had made the bloodless revolution of 1688 to 1689, and he argued that if a government oversteps its proper function of protecting the natural rights of life, liberty, and private property, it becomes a tyranny. Montesquieu (see page 576) was also inspired by English constitutional history. He, too, believed that powerful "intermediary groups"—such as the judicial nobility of which he was a proud member—offered the best defense of liberty against despotism.

The Marquis de Lafayette was the most famous great noble to embrace the liberal revolution. Shown here directing a battle in the American Revolution, he returned to champion liberty and equality in France. For admirers he was the "hero of two worlds." *(Source: Jean-Loup Charmet)*

The Attraction of Liberalism

The belief that representative institutions could defend their liberty and interests appealed powerfully to ambitious and educated bourgeois. Yet it is important to realize that liberal ideas about individual rights and political freedom also appealed to much of the aristocracy, at least in western Europe and as formulated by Montesquieu. Representative government did not mean democracy, which liberal thinkers tended to equate with mob rule. Rather, they envisioned voting for representatives as being restricted to those who owned property, those with "a stake in society." England had shown the way. After 1688 it had combined a parliamentary system and considerable individual liberty with a restricted franchise and unquestionable aristocratic pre-eminence. In the course of the eighteenth century, many leading French nobles, led by a judicial nobility inspired by Montesquieu, were increasingly eager to follow the English example.

Eighteenth-century liberalism, then, appealed not only to the middle class, but also to some aristocrats. It found broad support among the educated elite and the substantial classes in western Europe. What it lacked from the beginning was strong mass support. For comfortable liberals, the really important questions were theoretical and political. They had no need to worry about their stomachs and the price of bread. For the much more numerous laboring poor, the great questions were immediate and economic. Getting enough to eat was the crucial challenge. These differences in outlook and well-being were to lead to many misunderstandings and disappointments for both groups in the revolutionary era.

THE AMERICAN REVOLUTION, 1775–1789

The era of liberal revolution began in the New World. The thirteen mainland colonies of British North America revolted against their home country and then succeeded in establishing a new unified government.

Americans have long debated the meaning of their revolution. Some have even questioned whether or not it was a real revolution, as opposed to a war for independence. According to some scholars, the Revolution was conservative and defensive in that its demands were for the traditional liberties of English citizens; Americans were united against the British, but otherwise they were a satisfied people, not torn by internal conflict. Other scholars have argued that, on the contrary, the American Revolution was quite radical. It split families between patriots and Loyalists and divided the country. It achieved goals that were fully as advanced as those obtained by the French in their great revolution a few years later.

How does one reconcile these positions? Both contain large elements of truth. The American revolutionaries did believe they were demanding only the traditional rights of English men and women. But those traditional rights were liberal rights, and in the American context they had very strong democratic and popular overtones. Thus the American Revolution was fought in the name of established ideals that were still quite radical in the context of the times. And in founding a government firmly based on liberal principles, the Americans set an example that had a forceful impact on Europe and speeded up political development there.

The Origins of the Revolution

The American Revolution had its immediate origins in a squabble over increased taxes. The British government had fought and decisively won the Seven Years' War (see page 618) on the strength of its professional army and navy. The American colonists had furnished little real aid. The high cost of the war to the British, however, had led to a doubling of the British national debt. Anticipating further expense defending its recently conquered western lands from Indian uprisings like that of Pontiac, the British government in London set about reorganizing the empire with a series of bold, largely unprecedented measures. Breaking with tradition, the British decided to maintain a large army in North America after peace was restored in 1763. Moreover, they sought to exercise strict control over their newly conquered western lands and to tax the colonies directly. In 1765 the government pushed through Parliament the Stamp Act, which levied taxes on a long list of commercial and legal documents, diplomas, pamphlets, newspapers, almanacs, dice, and playing cards. A stamp glued to each article indicated the tax had been paid.

The effort to increase taxes as part of tightening up the empire seemed perfectly reasonable to the British. Heavier stamp taxes had been collected in

The Boston Tea Party   This contemporary illustration shows men disguised as Indians dumping East India Company tea into Boston's harbor. The enthusiastic crowd cheering from the wharf indicates widespread popular support. *(Source: Library of Congress)*

Great Britain for two generations, and Americans were being asked only to pay a share of their own defense costs. Moreover, Americans had been paying only very low local taxes. The Stamp Act would have doubled taxes to about 2 shillings per person per year. No other people in the European or colonial world (except the Poles) paid so little. The British, meanwhile, paid the highest taxes in the Western world in about 1765—26 shillings per person. It is not surprising that taxes per person in the newly independent American nation were much higher in 1785 than in 1765, when the British no longer subsidized American defense. The colonists protested the Stamp Act vigorously and violently, however, and after rioting and boycotts against British goods, Parliament reluctantly repealed the new tax.

As the fury of the Stamp Act controversy revealed, much more was involved than taxes. The key question was political. To what extent could the home government refashion the empire and reassert its power while limiting the authority of colonial legislatures and their elected representatives? Accordingly, who should represent the colonies, and who had the right to make laws for Americans? While a troubled majority of Americans searched hard for a compromise, some radicals began to proclaim that "taxation without representation is tyranny." The British government replied that Americans were represented in Parliament, albeit indirectly (like most English people themselves), and that the absolute supremacy of Parliament throughout the empire could not be questioned. Many Americans felt otherwise. As John Adams put it, "A Parliament of Great Britain can have no more rights to tax the colonies than a Parliament of Paris." Thus imperial reorganization and parliamentary supremacy came to appear as grave threats to Americans' existing liberties and time-honored institutions.

Americans had long exercised a great deal of independence and gone their own way. In British North America, unlike England and Europe, no powerful established church existed, and personal freedom in questions of religion was taken for granted. The colonial assemblies made the important laws, which were seldom overturned by the home government. The right to vote was much more widespread than in England. In many parts of colonial Massachusetts, for example, as many as 95 percent of the adult males could vote.

Moreover, greater political equality was matched by greater social and economic equality. Neither a hereditary nobility nor a hereditary serf population existed, although the slavery of the Americas consigned blacks to a legally oppressed caste. Independent farmers were the largest group in the country and set much of its tone. In short, the colonial experience had slowly formed a people who felt themselves separate and distinct from the home country. The controversies over taxation intensified those feelings of distinctiveness and separation and brought them to the fore.

In 1773 the dispute over taxes and representation flared up again. The British government had permitted the financially hard-pressed East India Company to ship its tea from China directly to its

agents in the colonies, rather than through London middlemen who sold to independent merchants in the colonies. Thus the company secured a vital monopoly on the tea trade, and colonial merchants were suddenly excluded from a highly profitable business. The colonists were quick to protest.

In Boston, men disguised as Indians had a rowdy "tea party" and threw the company's tea into the harbor. This led to extreme measures. The so-called Coercive Acts closed the port of Boston, curtailed local elections and town meetings, and greatly expanded the royal governor's power. County conventions in Massachusetts protested vehemently and urged that the acts be "rejected as the attempts of a wicked administration to enslave America." Other colonial assemblies joined in the denunciations. In September 1774, the First Continental Congress met in Philadelphia, where the more radical members argued successfully against conces-

The Signing of the Declaration, July 4, 1776   John Trumbull's famous painting shows the dignity and determination of America's revolutionary leaders. An extraordinarily talented group, they succeeded in rallying popular support without losing power to more radical forces in the process. *(Source: Yale University Art Gallery)*

sions to the Crown. Compromise was also rejected by the British Parliament, and in April 1775 fighting began at Lexington and Concord.

Independence

The fighting spread, and the colonists moved slowly but inevitably toward open rebellion and a declaration of independence. The uncompromising attitude of the British government and its use of German mercenaries went a long way toward dissolving long-standing loyalties to the home country and rivalries among the separate colonies. *Common Sense* (1775), a brilliant attack by the recently arrived English radical Thomas Paine (1737–1809), also mobilized public opinion in favor of independence. A runaway best seller with sales of 120,000 copies in a few months, Paine's tract ridiculed the idea of a small island ruling a great continent. In his call for freedom and republican government, Paine expressed Americans' growing sense of separateness and moral superiority.

On July 4, 1776, the Second Continental Congress adopted the Declaration of Independence. Written by Thomas Jefferson, the Declaration of Independence boldly listed the tyrannical acts committed by George III (r. 1760–1820) and confidently proclaimed the natural rights of humankind and the sovereignty of the American states. Sometimes called the world's greatest political editorial, the Declaration of Independence in effect universalized the traditional rights of English people and made them the rights of all humanity. It stated that "all men are created equal . . . they are endowed by their Creator with certain unalienable rights . . . among these are life, liberty, and the pursuit of happiness." No other American political document has ever caused such excitement, both at home and abroad.

Many American families remained loyal to Britain; many others divided bitterly. After the Declaration of Independence, the conflict often took the form of a civil war pitting patriot against Loyalist. The Loyalists tended to be wealthy and politically moderate. Many patriots, too, were wealthy—individuals such as John Hancock and George Washington—but willingly allied themselves with farmers and artisans in a broad coalition. This coalition harassed the Loyalists and confiscated their property to help pay for the American war effort. The broad social base of the revolutionaries tended to make the liberal revolution democratic. State governments extended the right to vote to many more people in the course of the war and re-established themselves as republics.

On the international scene, the French sympathized with the rebels from the beginning. They wanted revenge for the humiliating defeats of the Seven Years' War. Officially neutral until 1778, they supplied the great bulk of guns and gunpowder used by the American revolutionaries, very much as neutral great powers supply weapons for "wars of national liberation" in our day. By 1777 French volunteers were arriving in Virginia, and a dashing young nobleman, the marquis de Lafayette (1757–1834), quickly became one of Washington's most trusted generals. In 1778 the French government offered a formal alliance to the American ambassador in Paris, Benjamin Franklin, and in 1779 and 1780 the Spanish and Dutch declared war on Britain. Catherine the Great of Russia helped organize a League of Armed Neutrality in order to protect neutral shipping rights, which Britain refused to recognize.

Thus by 1780 Great Britain was engaged in an imperial war against most of Europe as well as the thirteen colonies. In these circumstances, and in the face of severe reverses in India, the West Indies, and at Yorktown in Virginia, a new British government decided to cut its losses. American negotiators in Paris were receptive. They feared that France wanted a treaty that would bottle up the new United States east of the Alleghenies and give British holdings west of the Alleghenies to France's ally, Spain. Thus the American negotiators ditched the French and accepted the extraordinarily favorable terms Britain offered.

By the Treaty of Paris of 1783, Britain recognized the independence of the thirteen colonies and ceded all its territory between the Appalachians and the Mississippi River to the Americans. Out of the bitter rivalries of the Old World, the Americans snatched dominion over half a continent.

Framing the Constitution

The liberal program of the American Revolution was consolidated by the federal Constitution, the Bill of Rights, and the creation of a national republic. Assembling in Philadelphia in the summer of 1787, the delegates to the Constitutional Convention were determined to end the period of economic depression, social uncertainty, and very weak central government that had followed independence. The delegates decided, therefore, to grant the federal, or central, government important powers: regulation of domestic and foreign trade, the right to levy taxes, and the means to enforce its laws.

Strong rule was placed squarely in the context of representative self-government. Senators and congressmen would be the lawmaking delegates of the voters, and the president of the republic would be an elected official. The central government was to operate in Montesquieu's framework of checks and balances. The executive, legislative, and judicial branches would systematically balance each other. The power of the federal government would in turn be checked by the powers of the individual states.

When the results of the secret deliberations of the Constitutional Convention were presented to the states for ratification, a great public debate began. The opponents of the proposed constitution—the Anti-Federalists—charged that the framers of the new document had taken too much power from the individual states and made the federal government too strong. Moreover, many Anti-Federalists feared for the personal liberties and individual freedoms for which they had just fought. In order to overcome these objections, the Federalists solemnly promised to spell out these basic freedoms as soon as the new constitution was adopted. The result was the first ten amendments to the Constitution, which the first Congress passed shortly after it met in New York in March 1789. These amendments formed an effective bill of rights to safeguard the individual. Most of them—trial by jury, due process of law, right to assemble, freedom from unreasonable search—had their origins in English law and the English Bill of Rights of 1689. Others—the freedoms of speech, the press, and religion—reflected natural-law theory and the American experience.

The American Constitution and the Bill of Rights exemplified the great strengths and the limits of what came to be called "classical liberalism." Liberty meant individual freedoms and political safeguards. Liberty also meant representative government but did not necessarily mean democracy with its principle of one person, one vote.

Equality—slaves excepted—meant equality before the law, not equality of political participation or economic well-being. Indeed, economic inequal-ity was resolutely defended by the elite who framed the Constitution. The right to own property was guaranteed by the Fifth Amendment, and if the government took private property, the owner was to receive "just compensation." The radicalism of liberal revolution in America was primarily legal and political, not economic or social.

The Revolution's Impact on Europe

Hundreds of books, pamphlets, and articles analyzed and romanticized the American upheaval. Thoughtful Europeans noted, first of all, its enormous long-term implications for international politics. A secret report by the Venetian ambassador to Paris in 1783 stated what many felt: "If only the union of the Provinces is preserved, it is reasonable to expect that, with the favorable effects of time, and of European arts and sciences, it will become the most formidable power in the world."[1] More generally, American independence fired the imaginations of those few aristocrats who were uneasy with their privileges and of those commoners who yearned for greater equality. Many Europeans believed that the world was advancing now and that America was leading the way. As one French writer put it in 1789: "This vast continent which the seas surround will soon change Europe and the universe."

Europeans who dreamed of a new era were fascinated by the political lessons of the American Revolution. The Americans had begun with a revolutionary defense against tyrannical oppression, and they had been victorious. They had then shown how rational beings could assemble together to exercise sovereignty and write a permanent constitution—a new social contract. All this gave greater reality to the concepts of individual liberty and representative government. It reinforced one of the primary ideas of the Enlightenment, the idea that a better world was possible.

THE FRENCH REVOLUTION, 1789–1791

No country felt the consequences of the American Revolution more directly than France. Hundreds of French officers served in America and were inspired by the experience. The most famous of these, the young and impressionable marquis de Lafayette, left home as a great aristocrat determined only to fight France's traditional foe, England. He returned with a love of liberty and firm republican convictions. French intellectuals and publicists engaged in passionate analysis of the federal Constitution, as well as the constitutions of the various states of the new United States. The American Revolution undeniably hastened upheaval in France.

Yet the French Revolution did not mirror the American example. It was more violent and more complex, more influential and more controversial, more loved and more hated. For Europeans and most of the rest of the world, it was the great revolution of the eighteenth century, *the* revolution that opened the modern era in politics.

The Breakdown of the Old Order

Like the American Revolution, the French Revolution had its immediate origins in the financial difficulties of the government. As we noted in Chapter 18, the efforts of Louis XV's ministers to raise taxes had been thwarted by the Parlement of Paris, strengthened in its opposition by widespread popular support (see pages 588–589). When renewed efforts to reform the tax system met a similar fate in 1776, the government was forced to finance all of its enormous expenditures during the American war with borrowed money. The national debt and the annual budget deficit soared. By the 1780s fully half of France's annual budget went for ever-increasing interest payments on the ever-increasing debt. Another quarter went to maintain the military, while 6 percent was absorbed by the costly and extravagant king and his court at Versailles. Less than one-fifth of the entire national budget was available for the productive functions of the state, such as transportation and general administration. It was an impossible financial situation.

One way out would have been for the government to declare partial bankruptcy, forcing its creditors to accept greatly reduced payments on the debt. The powerful Spanish monarchy had regularly repudiated large portions of its debt in earlier times, and France had done likewise, after an attempt to establish a French national bank ended in financial disaster in 1720. Yet by the 1780s the French debt was held by an army of aristocratic and bourgeois creditors, and the French monarchy, though absolute in theory, had become far too weak for such a drastic and unpopular action.

France and America Made in France about 1784, this figurine commemorates the vital support that France gave to the colonists in the American Revolution. Arrayed in Roman armor, a majestic Louis XVI hands documents entitled "American independence" and "freedom of the seas" to Benjamin Franklin. Franklin was lionized as a sage and a liberator while American ambassador to France. *(Source: The Providence Athenaeum, Providence, Rhode Island)*

Nor could the king and his ministers, unlike modern governments, print money and create inflation to cover their deficits. Unlike England and Holland, which had far larger national debts relative to their populations, France had no central bank, no paper currency, and no means of creating credit. French money was good gold coin. Therefore, when a depressed economy and a lack of public confidence made it increasingly difficult for the government to obtain new gold loans in 1786, it had no alternative but to try to increase taxes. And since France's tax system was unfair and out of date, increased revenues were possible only through fundamental reforms. Such reforms, which would affect all groups in France's complex and fragmented society, opened a Pandora's box of social and political demands.

Legal Orders and Social Realities

As in the Middle Ages, France's 25 million inhabitants were still legally divided into three orders or "estates"—the clergy, the nobility, and everyone else. As the nation's first estate, the clergy numbered about 100,000 and had important privileges. It owned about 10 percent of the land and paid only a "voluntary gift" to the government every five years. Moreover, the church levied a tax (the tithe) on landowners, which averaged somewhat less than 10 percent. Much of the church's income was actually drained away from local parishes by political appointees and worldly aristocrats at the top of the church hierarchy, to the intense dissatisfaction of the poor parish priests.

The second legally defined estate consisted of some 400,000 noblemen and noblewomen—the descendants of "those who fought" in the Middle Ages. The nobles owned outright about 25 percent of the land in France, and they, too, were taxed very lightly. Moreover, nobles continued to enjoy certain manorial rights, or privileges of lordship, that dated back to medieval times and allowed them to tax the peasantry for their own profit. This was done by means of exclusive rights to hunt and fish, village monopolies on baking bread and pressing grapes for wine, fees for justice, and a host of other "useful privileges." In addition, nobles had "honorific privileges," such as the right to precedence on public occasions and the right to wear a sword. These rights conspicuously proclaimed the nobility's legal superiority and exalted social position.

Everyone else was a commoner, a member of the third estate. A few commoners were rich merchants or highly successful doctors and lawyers. Many more were urban artisans and unskilled day laborers. The vast majority of the third estate consisted of the peasants and agricultural workers in the countryside. Thus the third estate was a conglomeration of vastly different social groups, united only by their shared legal status as distinct from the privileged nobility and clergy.

In discussing the long-term origins of the French Revolution, historians have long focused on growing tensions between the nobility and the comfortable members of the third estate, usually known as the bourgeoisie, or middle class. A dominant historical interpretation has held sway for at least two generations. According to this interpretation, the bourgeoisie was basically united by economic position and class interest. Aided by the general economic expansion discussed in Chapter 19, the middle class grew rapidly in the eighteenth century, tripling to about 2.3 million persons, or about 8 percent of France's population. Increasing in size, wealth, culture, and self-confidence, this rising bourgeoisie became progressively exasperated by archaic "feudal" laws restraining the economy and by the growing pretensions of a reactionary nobility, which was closing ranks against middle-class needs and aspirations. As a result, the French bourgeoisie eventually rose up to lead the entire third estate in a great social revolution, a revolution that destroyed feudal privileges and established a capitalist order based on individualism and a market economy.

In recent years, a flood of new research has challenged these accepted views, and once again the French Revolution is a subject of heated scholarly debate. Above all, revisionist historians have questioned the existence of a growing social conflict between a progressive capitalistic bourgeoisie and a reactionary feudal nobility in eighteenth-century France. Instead, these historians see both bourgeoisie and nobility as highly fragmented, riddled with internal rivalries. The great nobility, for example, was profoundly separated from the lesser nobility by differences in wealth, education, and worldview. Differences within the bourgeoisie—between wealthy financiers and local lawyers, for example—were no less profound. Rather than standing as unified blocs against each other, nobility and bourgeoisie formed two parallel social ladders, increasingly linked together at the top by wealth, marriage, and Enlightenment culture.

Revisionist historians stress three developments in particular. First, the nobility remained a fluid and relatively open order. Throughout the eighteenth century, substantial numbers of successful commoners continued to seek and obtain noble status through government service and purchase of expensive positions conferring nobility. Thus the nobility of the robe continued to attract the wealthiest members of the middle class and to permit social mobility. Second, key sections of the nobility were no less liberal than the middle class, which, until revolution actually began, generally supported the judicial opposition led by the Parlement of Paris. Finally, the nobility and the bourgeoisie were not really at odds in the economic sphere. Both looked to investment in land and government service as their preferred activities, and the ideal of the merchant-capitalist was to gain enough wealth to retire from trade, purchase estates, and live nobly as a large landowner. At the same time, wealthy nobles often acted as aggressive capitalists, investing especially in mining, metallurgy, and foreign trade.

The revisionists have clearly shaken the belief that the bourgeoisie and the nobility were inevitably locked in growing conflict before the Revolution. But in stressing the similarities between the two groups, especially at the top, revisionists have also reinforced the view, long maintained by historians, that the Old Regime had ceased to correspond with social reality by the 1780s. Legally, society was still based on rigid orders inherited from the Middle Ages. In reality, France had already moved far toward being a society based on wealth and economic achievement, where an emerging elite that included both aristocratic and bourgeois notables was frustrated by a bureaucratic monarchy that had long claimed the right to absolute power.

The Formation of the National Assembly

The Revolution was under way by 1787, though no one could have realized what was to follow. Spurred by a depressed economy and falling tax receipts, Louis XVI's minister of finance revived old proposals to impose a general tax on all landed property, as well as provincial assemblies to help administer the tax, and he convinced the king to call an Assembly of Notables to gain support for the idea. The assembled notables, who were mainly important noblemen and high-ranking clergy, were not in favor of it. In return for their support, they demanded that control over all government spending be given to the provincial assemblies, which they expected to control. When the government refused, the notables responded that such sweeping tax changes required the approval of the Estates General, the representative body of all three estates, which had not met since 1614.

Facing imminent bankruptcy, the king tried to reassert his authority. He dismissed the notables and established new taxes by decree. In stirring language, the Parlement of Paris promptly declared the royal initiative null and void. The Parlement went so far as to specify some of the "fundamental laws" against which no king could transgress, such as national consent to taxation and freedom from arbitrary arrest and imprisonment. When the king tried to exile the judges, a tremendous wave of pro-

test swept the country. Frightened investors also refused to advance more loans to the state. Finally, in July 1788, a beaten Louis XVI called for a spring session of the Estates General. Absolute monarchy was collapsing.

What would replace it? Throughout the unprecedented election campaign of 1788 and 1789, that question excited France. All across the country, clergy, nobles, and commoners came together in their respective orders to draft petitions for change and to elect their respective delegates to the Estates General. The local assemblies of the clergy showed considerable dissatisfaction with the church hierarchy, and two-thirds of the delegates were chosen from the poorer parish priests, who were commoners by birth. The nobles, already badly split by wealth and education, remained politically divided. A conservative majority was drawn from the poorer and more numerous provincial nobility, but fully a third of the nobility's representatives were liberals committed to major changes.

As for the third estate, there was great popular participation in the elections. Almost all male commoners twenty-five years or older had the right to vote. However, voting required two stages, which meant that most of the representatives finally selected by the third estate were well-educated, prosperous members of the middle class. Most of them were not businessmen, but lawyers and government officials. Social status and prestige were matters of particular concern to this economic elite. There were no delegates from the great mass of laboring poor, which included the peasants and also the artisans.

The petitions for change from the three estates showed a surprising degree of agreement on most issues, as recent research has clearly revealed. There was general agreement that royal absolutism should give way to constitutional monarchy, in which laws and taxes would require the consent of an Estates General meeting regularly. All agreed that, in the future, individual liberties must be guaranteed by law and that the position of the parish clergy had to be improved. It was generally acknowledged that economic development required reforms, such as the abolition of internal trade barriers. The striking similarities in the grievance petitions of the clergy, nobility, and third estate reflected the broad commitment of France's elite to liberalism.

Yet an increasingly bitter quarrel undermined this consensus during the intense campaign: *how*

Fan: Opening of the Legislature   In 1789 the first meeting of the Estates General since 1614 was recorded not only in the annals of French history but in the most ordinary objects, including this painted fan. *(Source: Musée Carnavalet/Bulloz)*

would the Estates General vote, and precisely *who* would lead in the political reorganization that was generally desired? The Estates General of 1614 had sat as three separate houses. Any action had required the agreement of at least two branches, a requirement that had guaranteed control by the privileged orders—the nobility and the clergy. Immediately after its victory over the king, the aristocratic Parlement of Paris, mainly out of respect for tradition but partly to enhance the nobility's political position, ruled that the Estates General should once again sit separately. The ruling was quickly denounced by certain middle-class intellectuals and some liberal nobles. They demanded instead a single assembly dominated by representatives of the third estate, to ensure fundamental reforms. Reflecting a growing hostility toward aristocratic aspirations, the abbé Sieyès argued in 1789, in his famous pamphlet *What Is the Third Estate?*, that the nobility was a tiny, overprivileged minority and that the neglected third estate constituted the true strength of the French nation. When the government agreed that the third estate should have as many delegates as the clergy and the nobility combined, but then rendered its act meaningless by upholding voting by separate order, middle-

class leaders saw fresh evidence of an aristocratic conspiracy.

In May 1789 the twelve hundred delegates of the three estates paraded in medieval pageantry through the streets of Versailles to an opening session resplendent with feudal magnificence. The estates were almost immediately deadlocked. Delegates of the third estate refused to transact any business until the king ordered the clergy and nobility to sit with them in a single body. Finally, after a six-week war of nerves, a few parish priests began to go over to the third estate, which on June 17 voted to call itself the "National Assembly." On June 20, excluded from their hall because of "repairs," the delegates of the third estate moved to a large indoor tennis court. There they swore the famous Oath of the Tennis Court, pledging never to disband until they had written a new constitution.

The king's actions were then somewhat contradictory. On June 23 he made a conciliatory speech to a joint session, urging reforms, and then ordered the three estates to meet together. At the same time, he apparently followed the advice of relatives and court nobles, who urged him to dissolve the Estates General by force. The king called an army of eighteen thousand troops toward Versailles, and on July 11 he dismissed his finance minister and his other more liberal ministers. Faced with growing opposition since 1787, Louis XVI had resigned himself to bankruptcy. Now he sought to reassert his divine and historic right to rule. The middle-class delegates had done their best, but they were resigned to being disbanded at bayonet point. One third-estate delegate reassured a worried colleague: "You won't hang—you'll only have to go back home."[2]

The Revolt of the Poor and the Oppressed

While the third estate pressed for symbolic equality with the nobility and clergy in a single legislative body at Versailles, economic hardship gripped the masses of France in a tightening vise. Grain was the basis of the diet of ordinary people, and in 1788 the harvest had been extremely poor. The price of bread, which had been rising gradually since 1785, began to soar. By July 1789 the price of bread in the provinces climbed as high as eight sous per pound. In Paris, where bread was subsidized by the government in an attempt to prevent popular unrest, the price rose to four sous. The poor could scarcely afford to pay two sous per pound, for even at that price a laborer with a wife and three children had to spend half of his wages to buy the family's bread.

Harvest failure and high bread prices unleashed a classic economic depression of the preindustrial age. With food so expensive and with so much uncertainty, the demand for manufactured goods collapsed. Thousands of artisans and small traders were thrown out of work. By the end of 1789, almost half of the French people would be in need of relief. One person in eight was a pauper, living in extreme want. In Paris the situation was desperate in July 1789: perhaps 150,000 of the city's 600,000 people were without work.

Against this background of dire poverty and excited by the political crisis, the people of Paris entered decisively onto the revolutionary stage. They believed in a general, though ill-defined, way that the economic distress had human causes. They believed that they should have steady work and enough bread to survive. Specifically, they feared that the dismissal of the king's moderate finance minister would throw them at the mercy of aristocratic landowners and grain speculators. Stories

like that quoting the wealthy financier Joseph François Foulon as saying that the poor "should eat grass, like my horses," and rumors that the king's troops would sack the city began to fill the air. Angry crowds formed, and passionate voices urged action. On July 13 the people began to seize arms for the defense of the city, and on July 14 several hundred of the most determined people marched to the Bastille to search for gunpowder.

A medieval fortress with walls 10 feet thick and eight great towers each a hundred feet high, the Bastille had long been used as a prison. It was guarded by eighty retired soldiers and thirty Swiss guards. The governor of the fortress-prison refused to hand over the powder, panicked, and ordered his men to fire, killing ninety-eight people attempting to enter. Cannon were brought to batter the main gate, and fighting continued until the governor of the prison surrendered. While he was being taken under guard to city hall, a band of men broke through and hacked him to death. His head and that of the mayor of Paris, who had been slow to give the crowd arms, were stuck on pikes and paraded through the streets. The next day, a committee of citizens appointed the marquis de Lafayette commander of the city's armed forces. Paris was lost to the king, who was forced to recall the finance minister and to disperse his troops. The uprising had saved the National Assembly.

As the delegates resumed their long-winded and inconclusive debates at Versailles, the people in the countryside sent them a radical and unmistakable message. All across France, peasants began to rise in spontaneous, violent, and effective insurrection against their lords, ransacking manor houses and burning feudal documents that recorded the peasants' obligations. Neither middle-class landowners, who often owned manors and village monopolies, nor the larger, more prosperous farmers were spared. In some areas, the nobles and bourgeoisie combined forces and organized patrols to protect their property. Yet the peasant insurrection went on. Recent enclosures were undone, old common lands were reoccupied, and the forests were seized. Taxes went unpaid. Fear of vagabonds and outlaws —the so-called Great Fear—seized the countryside and fanned the flames of rebellion. The long-suffering peasants were doing their best to free themselves from aristocratic privilege and exploitation.

Faced with chaos, yet afraid to call on the king to restore order, some liberal nobles and middle-class delegates at Versailles responded to peasant demands with a surprise maneuver on the night of August 4, 1789. The duke of Aiguillon, one of France's greatest noble landowners, declared that

in several provinces the whole people forms a kind of league for the destruction of the manor houses, the ravaging of the lands, and especially for the seizure of the archives where the title deeds to feudal properties are kept. It seeks to throw off at last a yoke that has for many centuries weighted it down.[3]

He urged equality in taxation and the elimination of feudal dues. In the end, all the old exactions were abolished, generally without compensation: serfdom where it still existed, exclusive hunting rights for nobles, fees for justice, village monopolies, the right to make peasants work on the roads,

and a host of other dues. Though a clarifying law passed a week later was less generous, the peasants ignored the "fine print." They never paid feudal dues again. Thus the French peasantry, which already owned about 30 percent of all the land, quickly achieved a great and unprecedented victory. Henceforth, the French peasants would seek mainly to consolidate their triumph. As the Great Fear subsided, they became a force for order and stability.

A Limited Monarchy

The National Assembly moved forward. On August 27, 1789, it issued the Declaration of the Rights of Man. This great liberal document had a

Storming the Bastille   This representation by an untrained contemporary artist shows civilians and members of the Paris militia—the "conquerors of the Bastille"—on the attack. This successful action had enormous practical and symbolic significance, and July 14 has long been France's most important national holiday. *(Source: Musée Carnavalet/Photo Hubert Josse)*

"To Versailles"   This print is one of many commemorating the women's march on Versailles. Notice on the left that the fashionable lady from the well-to-do is a most reluctant revolutionary. *(Source: Photo Flammarion)*

very American flavor, and Lafayette even discussed his draft in detail with the American ambassador in Paris, Thomas Jefferson, the author of the American Declaration of Independence. According to the French declaration, "men are born and remain free and equal in rights." Mankind's natural rights are "liberty, property, security, and resistance to oppression." Also, "every man is presumed innocent until he is proven guilty." As for law, "it is an expression of the general will; all citizens have the right to concur personally or through their representatives in its formation. . . . Free expression of thoughts and opinions is one of the most precious rights of mankind: every citizen may therefore speak, write, and publish freely." In short, this clarion call of the liberal revolutionary ideal guaranteed equality before the law, representative government for a sovereign people, and individual freedom. This revolutionary credo, only two pages long, was propagandized throughout France and Europe and around the world.

Moving beyond general principles to draft a constitution proved difficult. The questions of how much power the king should retain and whether he could permanently veto legislation led to another deadlock. Once again the decisive answer came from the poor, in this instance the poor women of Paris.

To understand what happened, one must remember that the work and wages of women and children were essential in the family economy of the laboring poor. In Paris great numbers of women worked, particularly within the putting-out system in the garment industry—making lace, fancy dresses, embroidery, ribbons, bonnets, corsets, and so on. Many of these goods were beautiful luxury items, destined for an aristocratic and international clientele.[4] Immediately after the fall of the Bastille, many of France's great court nobles began to leave Versailles for foreign lands, so that a plummeting demand for luxuries intensified the general economic crisis. International markets also declined, and the church was no longer able to give its traditional grants of food and money to the poor. Unemployment and hunger increased further, and the result was another popular explosion.

On October 5 some seven thousand desperate women marched the 12 miles from Paris to Versailles to demand action. A middle-class deputy looking out from the Assembly saw "multitudes arriving from Paris including fishwives and bullies from the market, and these people wanted nothing but bread." This great crowd invaded the Assembly, "armed with scythes, sticks and pikes." One coarse, tough old woman directing a large group of younger women defiantly shouted into the debate: "Who's that talking down there? Make the chatterbox shut up. That's not the point: the point is that we want bread."[5] Hers was the genuine voice of the people, essential to any understanding of the French Revolution.

The women invaded the royal apartments, slaughtered some of the royal bodyguards, and furiously searched for the despised queen, Marie Antoinette. "We are going to cut off her head, tear out her heart, fry her liver, and that won't be the end of it," they shouted, surging through the palace in a frenzy. It seems likely that only the intervention of Lafayette and the National Guard saved the royal family. But the only way to calm the disorder was for the king to go and live in Paris, as the crowd demanded.

The next day, the king, the queen, and their son left for Paris in the midst of a strange procession. The heads of two aristocrats, stuck on pikes, led the way. They were followed by the remaining members of the royal bodyguard, unarmed and surrounded and mocked by fierce men holding sabers and pikes. A mixed and victorious multitude surrounded the king's carriage, hurling crude insults at the queen. There was drinking and eating among the women. "We are bringing the baker, the baker's wife, and the baker's boy," they joyfully sang. The National Assembly followed the king to Paris. Reflecting the more radical environment, it adopted a constitution that gave the virtually imprisoned "baker" only a temporary veto in the lawmaking process. And, for a time, he and the government made sure that the masses of Paris did not lack bread.

The next two years, until September 1791, saw the consolidation of the liberal Revolution. Under middle-class leadership, the National Assembly abolished the French nobility as a legal order and pushed forward with the creation of a constitutional monarchy, which Louis XVI reluctantly agreed to accept in July 1790. In the final constitution, the king remained the head of state, but all lawmaking power was placed in the hands of the National Assembly, elected by the economic upper half of French males. Eighty-three departments of approximately equal size replaced the complicated old patchwork of provinces with their many historic differences. The jumble of weights and measures that varied from province to province was reformed, leading to the introduction of the simple, rational metric system in 1793. The National Assembly promoted economic freedom. Monopolies, guilds, and workers' combinations were prohibited, and barriers to trade within France were abolished in the name of economic liberty. Thus the National Assembly applied the critical spirit of the Enlightenment to reform France's laws and institutions completely.

The Assembly also threatened nobles who had emigrated from France with the loss of their lands. It nationalized the property of the church and abolished the monasteries as useless relics of a distant past. The government used all former church property as collateral to guarantee a new paper currency, the *assignats,* and then sold these properties in an attempt to put the state's finances on a solid footing. Although the church's land was sold in large blocks, a procedure that favored nimble speculators and the rich, peasants eventually purchased much of it as it was subdivided. These purchases strengthened their attachment to the revolutionary state.

The most unfortunate aspect of the reorganization of France was that it brought the new government into conflict with the Catholic church. Many middle-class delegates to the National Assembly, imbued with the rationalism and skepticism of the eighteenth-century philosophes, harbored a deep distrust of popular piety and "superstitious religion." They were interested in the church only to the extent that they could seize its land and use the church to strengthen the new state. Thus they established a national church, with priests chosen by voters. In the face of resistance, the National Assembly required the clergy to take a loyalty oath to the new government. The clergy became just so many more employees of the state. The pope formally condemned this attempt to subjugate the church. Against such a backdrop, it is not surprising that only half the priests of France took the oath of allegiance. The result was a deep division within both the country and the clergy itself on the religious question, and confusion and hostility among French Catholics were pervasive. The attempted reorganization of the Catholic church was the revolutionary government's first important failure.

WORLD WAR AND REPUBLICAN FRANCE, 1791–1799

When Louis XVI accepted the final version of the completed constitution in September 1791, a young and still obscure provincial lawyer and member of the National Assembly named Maximilien Robespierre (1758–1794) evaluated the work of two years and concluded, "The Revolution is over." Robespierre was both right and wrong. He was right in the sense that the most constructive and lasting reforms were in place. Nothing substantial in the way of liberty and equality would be gained in the next generation, though much would be lost. He was wrong in the sense that a much more radical stage lay ahead. New heroes and new ideologies were to emerge in revolutionary wars and international conflict.

Foreign Reactions and the Beginning of War

The outbreak and progress of revolution in France produced great excitement and a sharp division of opinion in Europe and the United States. Liberals and radicals saw a mighty triumph of liberty over despotism. In Great Britain, especially, they hoped that the French example would lead to a fundamental reordering of the political system. That system, which had been consolidated in the revolution of 1688 to 1689 (see Chapter 16), placed Parliament in the hands of the aristocracy and a few wealthy merchants; the great majority of people had very little say in the government. After the French Revolution began, conservative leaders like Edmund Burke (1729–1797) were deeply troubled by the aroused spirit of reform. In 1790 Burke published *Reflections on the Revolution in France,* one of the great intellectual defenses of European conservatism. He defended inherited privileges in general and those of the English monarchy and aristocracy in particular. He glorified the unrepresentative Parliament and predicted that thoroughgoing reform like that occurring in France would lead only to chaos and tyranny. Burke's work sparked vigorous debate.

One passionate rebuttal came from a young writer in London, Mary Wollstonecraft (1759–1797). Born into the middle class, Wollstonecraft was schooled in adversity by a mean-spirited father

Mary Wollstonecraft Painted by an unknown artist when Mary Wollstonecraft was thirty-two and writing her revolutionary *Vindication of the Rights of Woman,* this portrait highlights the remarkable strength of character that energized Wollstonecraft's brilliant intellect. *(Source: The Board of Trustees of the National Museums and Galleries on Merseyside, Walker Art Gallery)*

who beat his wife and squandered his inherited fortune. Determined to be independent in a society that generally expected women of her class to become homebodies and obedient wives, she struggled for years to earn her living as a governess and teacher—practically the only acceptable careers for single, educated women—before attaining success as a translator and author. Interested in politics and believing that "A desperate disease requires a powerful remedy" in Great Britain as well as France, Wollstonecraft was incensed by Burke's book. She immediately wrote a blistering, widely read attack, *A Vindication of the Rights of Man* (1790).

Then, fired up on controversy and commitment, she made a daring intellectual leap. She developed for the first time the logical implications of natural-law philosophy in her masterpiece, *A Vindication of the Rights of Woman* (1792). To fulfill the liberating promise of the French Revolution and to eliminate the economic and sexual inequality she had felt so keenly, she demanded that

the Rights of Women be respected . . . [and] JUSTICE for one-half of the human race. . . . It is time to effect a revolution in female manners, time to restore to them their lost dignity, and make them, as part of the human species, labor, by reforming themselves, to reform the world.

Setting high standards for women—"I wish to persuade women to endeavor to acquire strength, both of mind and body"—Wollstonecraft broke with those who had a low opinion of women's intellectual potential. She advocated rigorous co-education, which would make women better wives and mothers, good citizens, and even economically independent. "Women might certainly study the art of healing, and be physicians, as well as nurses." Women could manage businesses and enter politics. Men themselves would benefit from women's rights, for Wollstonecraft believed that "the two sexes mutually corrupt and improve each other."[6] Marking the birth of the modern women's movement for equal rights, Wollstonecraft's strikingly original analysis testified to the power of the Revolution to excite and inspire outside of France.

The kings and nobles of continental Europe, who had at first welcomed the revolution in France as weakening a competing power, began to feel no less threatened than Burke and his supporters. At their courts they listened to the diatribes of great court nobles who had fled France and were urging intervention in France's affairs. When Louis XVI and Marie Antoinette were arrested and returned to Paris after trying unsuccessfully to slip out of France in June 1791, the monarchs of Austria and Prussia issued the Declaration of Pillnitz. This carefully worded statement declared their willingness to intervene in France, but only with the unanimous agreement of all the Great Powers, which they did not expect to receive. Austria and Prussia expected their threat to have a sobering effect on revolutionary France without causing war.

The crowned heads of Europe misjudged the revolutionary spirit in France. When the National Assembly disbanded, it sought popular support by decreeing that none of its members would be eligible for election to the new Legislative Assembly. This meant that, when the new representative body was duly elected and convened in October 1791, it had

a different character. The great majority were still prosperous, well educated, and middle class, but they were younger and less cautious than their predecessors. Loosely allied as "Jacobins," so named after their political club, the new representatives to the Assembly were passionately committed to liberal revolution.

The Jacobins increasingly lumped "useless aristocrats" and "despotic monarchs" together, and they easily whipped themselves into a patriotic fury with bombastic oratory. So the courts of Europe were attempting to incite a war of kings against France; well then, "we will incite a war of people against kings. . . . Ten million Frenchmen, kindled by the fire of liberty, armed with the sword, with reason, with eloquence would be able to change the face of the world and make the tyrants tremble on their thrones."[7] Only Robespierre and a very few others argued that people do not welcome liberation at the point of a gun. Such warnings were brushed aside. France would "rise to the full height of her mission," as one deputy urged. In April 1792 France declared war on Francis II, archduke of Austria and king of Hungary and Bohemia.

France's crusade against tyranny went poorly at first. Prussia joined Austria in the Austrian Netherlands (present-day Belgium), and French forces broke and fled at their first encounter with armies of this First Coalition. The road to Paris lay open, and it is possible that only conflict between the eastern monarchs over the division of Poland saved France from defeat.

Military reversals and Austro-Prussian threats caused a wave of patriotic fervor to sweep France. The Legislative Assembly declared the country in danger. Volunteer armies from the provinces streamed through Paris, fraternizing with the people and singing patriotic songs like the stirring *Marseillaise,* later the French national anthem.

In this supercharged wartime atmosphere, rumors of treason by the king and queen spread in Paris. Once again, as in the storming of the Bastille, the common people of Paris acted decisively. On August 10, 1792, a revolutionary crowd attacked the royal palace at the Tuileries, capturing it after heavy fighting with the Swiss guards. The king and his family fled for their lives to the nearby Legislative Assembly, which suspended the king from all his functions, imprisoned him, and called for a new National Convention to be elected by universal male suffrage. Monarchy in France was on its deathbed, mortally wounded by war and revolt.

The Second Revolution

The fall of the monarchy marked a rapid radicalization of the Revolution, a phase that historians often call the "second revolution." Louis's imprisonment was followed by the September Massacres, which sullied the Revolution in the eyes of most of its remaining foreign supporters. Wild stories seized the city that imprisoned counter-revolutionary aristocrats and priests were plotting with the allied invaders. As a result, angry crowds invaded the prisons of Paris and summarily slaughtered half the men and women they found. In late September 1792, the new, popularly elected National Convention proclaimed France a republic. The republic adopted a new revolutionary calendar, and citizens were expected to address each other with the friendly "thou" of the people, rather than with the formal "you" of the rich and powerful.

All of the members of the National Convention were Jacobins and republicans, and the great majority continued to come from the well-educated middle class. But the convention was increasingly divided into two well-defined, bitterly competitive groups—the Girondists, named after a department in southwestern France, and the Mountain, led by Robespierre and another young lawyer, Georges Jacques Danton. The Mountain was so called because its members sat on the uppermost left-hand benches of the assembly hall. Many indecisive Convention members seated in the "Plain" below floated back and forth between the rival factions.

This division was clearly apparent after the National Convention overwhelmingly convicted Louis XVI of treason. By a single vote, 361 of the 720 members of the Convention then unconditionally sentenced him to death in January 1793. Louis died with tranquil dignity on the newly invented guillotine. One of his last statements was, "I am innocent and shall die without fear. I would that my death might bring happiness to the French, and ward off the dangers which I foresee."[8]

Both the Girondists and the Mountain were determined to continue the "war against tyranny." The Prussians had been stopped at the indecisive Battle of Valmy on September 20, 1792, one day before the republic was proclaimed. Republican armies then successfully invaded Savoy and captured Nice. A second army corps invaded the German Rhineland and took the city of Frankfurt. To the north, the revolutionary armies won their first major battle at Jemappes and occupied the entire Austrian Netherlands by November 1792. Everywhere they went, French armies of occupation chased the princes, "abolished feudalism," and found support among some peasants and middle-class people.

But the French armies also lived off the land, requisitioning food and supplies and plundering local treasures. The liberators looked increasingly like foreign invaders. International tensions mounted. In February 1793 the National Convention, at war with Austria and Prussia, declared war on Britain, Holland, and Spain as well. Republican France was now at war with almost all of Europe, a great war that would last almost without interruption until 1815.

As the forces of the First Coalition drove the French from the Austrian Netherlands, peasants in western France revolted against being drafted into the army. They were supported and encouraged in their resistance by devout Catholics, royalists, and foreign agents.

In Paris the quarrelsome National Convention found itself locked in a life-and-death political struggle between the Girondists and the Mountain. The two groups were in general agreement on questions of policy. Sincere republicans, they hated privilege and wanted to temper economic liberalism with social concern. Yet personal hatreds ran deep. The Girondists feared a bloody dictatorship by the Mountain, and the Mountain was no less convinced that the more moderate Girondists would turn to conservatives and even royalists in order to retain power. With the middle-class delegates so bitterly divided, the laboring poor of Paris emerged as the decisive political factor.

The great mass of the Parisian laboring poor always constituted—along with the peasantry in the summer of 1789—the elemental force that drove the Revolution forward. It was the artisans, shopkeepers, and day laborers who had stormed the Bastille, marched on Versailles, driven the king from the Tuileries, and carried out the September Massacres. The petty traders and laboring poor were often known as the *sans-culottes*, "without breeches," because they wore trousers instead of the knee breeches of the aristocracy and the solid middle class. The immediate interests of the sans-culottes were mainly economic, and in the spring of 1793 the economic situation was as bad as the military situation. Rapid inflation, unemployment, and food shortages were again weighing heavily on the poor.

Moreover, by the spring of 1793, the sans-culottes were keenly interested in politics. Encouraged by the so-called angry men, such as the passionate young ex-priest and journalist Jacques Roux, the sans-culottes were demanding radical political action to guarantee them their daily bread. At first the Mountain joined the Girondists in violently rejecting these demands. But in the face of military defeat, peasant revolt, and hatred of the Girondists, the Mountain and especially Robespierre became more sympathetic. The Mountain joined with sans-culottes activists in the city government to engineer a popular uprising, which forced the Convention to arrest thirty-one Girondist deputies for treason on June 2. All power passed to the Mountain.

Robespierre and others from the Mountain joined the recently formed Committee of Public Safety, to which the Convention had given dictatorial power to deal with the national emergency. These developments in Paris triggered revolt in leading provincial cities, such as Lyons and Marseilles, where moderates denounced Paris and demanded a decentralized government. The peasant revolt spread, and the republic's armies were driven back on all fronts. By July 1793 only the areas around Paris and on the eastern frontier were firmly controlled by the central government. Defeat appeared imminent.

Total War and the Terror

A year later, in July 1794, the Austrian Netherlands and the Rhineland were once again in the hands of conquering French armies, and the First Coalition was falling apart. This remarkable change of fortune was due to the revolutionary government's success in harnessing, for perhaps the first time in history, the explosive forces of a planned economy, revolutionary terror, and modern nationalism in a total war effort.

Robespierre and the Committee of Public Safety advanced with implacable resolution on several fronts in 1793 and 1794. In an effort to save revolutionary France, they collaborated with the fiercely patriotic and democratic sans-culottes. They established, as best they could, a planned economy with egalitarian social overtones. Rather than let supply and demand determine prices, the government decreed the maximum allowable prices, fixed in paper assignats, for a host of key products. Though the

state was too weak to enforce all its price regulations, it did fix the price of bread in Paris at levels the poor could afford. Rationing and ration cards were introduced to make sure that the limited supplies of bread were shared fairly. Quality was also controlled. Bakers were permitted to make only the "bread of equality"—a brown bread made of a mixture of all available flours. White bread and pastries were outlawed as frivolous luxuries. The poor of Paris may not have eaten well, but at least they ate.

They also worked, mainly to produce arms and munitions for the war effort. Craftsmen and small manufacturers were told what to produce and when to deliver. The government nationalized many small workshops and requisitioned raw materials and grain from the peasants. Sometimes planning and control did not go beyond orders to meet the latest emergency: "Ten thousand soldiers lack shoes. You will take the shoes of all the aristocrats in Strasbourg and deliver them ready for transport to headquarters at 10 A.M. tomorrow." Failures to control and coordinate were failures of means and not of desire: seldom if ever before had a government attempted to manage an economy so thoroughly. The second revolution and the ascendancy of the sans-culottes had produced an embryonic emergency socialism, which was to have great influence on the subsequent development of socialist ideology.

While radical economic measures supplied the poor with bread and the armies with weapons, a Reign of Terror (1793–1794) was solidifying the home front. Special revolutionary courts, responsible only to Robespierre's Committee of Public Safety, tried rebels and "enemies of the nation" for political crimes. Drawing on popular, sans-culottes support centered in the local Jacobin clubs, these local courts ignored normal legal procedures and judged severely. Some 40,000 French men and women were executed or died in prison. Another 300,000 suspects crowded the prisons and often brushed close to death in a revolutionary court.

Robespierre's Reign of Terror was one of the most controversial phases of the French Revolution. Most historians now believe that the Reign of Terror was not directed against any single class. Rather, it was a political weapon directed impartially against all who might oppose the revolutionary government. For many Europeans of the time, however, the Reign of Terror represented a terrifying perversion of the generous ideals that existed in

1789. It strengthened the belief that France had foolishly replaced a weak king with a bloody dictatorship.

The third and perhaps most decisive element in the French republic's victory over the First Coalition was its ability to continue drawing on the explosive power of patriotic dedication to a national state and a national mission. This is the essence of modern nationalism. With a common language and a common tradition, newly reinforced by the ideas of popular sovereignty and democracy, the French people were stirred by a common loyalty. The shared danger of foreign foes and internal rebels unified all classes in a heroic defense of the nation.

In such circumstances, war was no longer the gentlemanly game of the eighteenth century, but a life-and-death struggle between good and evil. Everyone had to participate in the national effort. According to a famous decree of August 23, 1793,

The young men shall go to battle and the married men shall forge arms. The women shall make tents and clothes, and shall serve in the hospitals; children shall tear rags into lint. The old men will be guided to the public places of the cities to kindle the courage of the young warriors and to preach the unity of the Republic and the hatred of kings.

Like the wars of religion, war in 1793 was a crusade; this war, though, was fought for a secular rather than a religious ideology.

Because all unmarried young men were subject to the draft, the French armed forces swelled to one million men in fourteen armies. A force of this size was unprecedented in the history of European warfare. The soldiers were led by young, impetuous generals, who had often risen rapidly from the ranks and personified the opportunities the Revolution seemed to offer gifted sons of the people. These generals used mass attacks at bayonet point

The Reign of Terror   A man, woman, and child accused of political crimes are brought before a special revolutionary committee for trial. The Terror's iron dictatorship crushed individual rights as well as treason and opposition. *(Source: Photo Flammarion)*

THE FRENCH REVOLUTION

May 5, 1789	Estates General convene at Versailles
June 17, 1789	Third Estate declares itself the National Assembly
June 20, 1789	Oath of the Tennis Court
July 14, 1789	Storming of the Bastille
July–August 1789	The Great Fear in the countryside
August 4, 1789	National Assembly abolishes feudal privileges
August 27, 1789	National Assembly issues Declaration of the Rights of Man
October 5, 1789	Parisian women march on Versailles and force royal family to return to Paris
November 1789	National Assembly confiscates church lands
July 1790	Civil Constitution of the Clergy establishes a national church
	Louis XVI reluctantly agrees to accept a constitutional monarchy
June 1791	Arrest of the royal family while attempting to flee France
August 1791	Declaration of Pillnitz by Austria and Prussia
April 1792	France declares war on Austria
August 1792	Parisian mob attacks palace and takes Louis XVI prisoner
September 1792	September Massacres
	National Convention declares France a republic and abolishes monarchy
January 1793	Execution of Louis XVI
February 1793	France declares war on Britain, Holland, and Spain
	Revolts in provincial cities
March 1793	Bitter struggle in the National Convention between Girondists and the Mountain
April–June 1793	Robespierre and the Mountain organize the Committee of Public Safety and arrest Girondist leaders
September 1793	Price controls to aid the sans-culottes and mobilize war effort
1793–1794	Reign of Terror in Paris and the provinces
Spring 1794	French armies victorious on all fronts
July 1794	Execution of Robespierre
	Thermidorean Reaction begins
1795–1799	The Directory
1795	End of economic controls and suppression of the sans-culottes
1797	Napoleon defeats Austrian armies in Italy and returns triumphant to Paris
1798	Austria, Great Britain, and Russia form the Second Coalition against France
1799	Napoleon overthrows the Directory and seizes power

by their highly motivated forces to overwhelm the enemy. By the spring of 1794, French armies were victorious on all fronts. The republic was saved.

The Thermidorian Reaction and the Directory, 1794–1799

The success of the French armies led Robespierre and the Committee of Public Safety to relax the emergency economic controls, but they extended the political Reign of Terror. Their lofty goal was increasingly an ideal democratic republic, where justice would reign and there would be neither rich

nor poor. Their lowly means were unrestrained despotism and the guillotine, which struck down any who might seriously question the new order. In March 1794, to the horror of many sans-culottes, Robespierre's Terror wiped out many of the "angry men," led by the radical social democrat Jacques Hébert. Two weeks later, several of Robespierre's long-standing collaborators, led by the famous orator Danton, marched up the steps to the guillotine. Knowing that they might be next, a strange assortment of radicals and moderates in the Convention organized a conspiracy. They howled down Robespierre when he tried to speak to the National Convention on 9 Thermidor (July 27, 1794). On the following day, it was Robespierre's turn to be shaved by the revolutionary razor.

As Robespierre's closest supporters followed their leader, France unexpectedly experienced a thorough reaction to the despotism of the Reign of Terror. In a general way, this "Thermidorian reaction" recalled the early days of the Revolution. The respectable middle-class lawyers and professionals who had led the liberal revolution of 1789 reasserted their authority, drawing support from their own class, the provincial cities, and the better-off peasants. The National Convention abolished many economic controls, printed more paper currency, and let prices rise sharply. It severely restricted the local political organizations where the sans-culottes had their strength. And all the while, the wealthy bankers and newly rich speculators celebrated the sudden end of the Terror with an orgy of self-indulgence and ostentatious luxury.

The collapse of economic controls, coupled with runaway inflation, hit the working poor very hard. The gaudy extravagance of the rich wounded their pride. The sans-culottes accepted private property, but they believed passionately in small business and the right of all to earn a decent living. Increasingly disorganized after Robespierre purged their radical leaders, the common people of Paris finally revolted against the emerging new order in early 1795. The Convention quickly used the army to suppress these insurrections. For the first time since the fall of the Bastille, bread riots and uprisings by Parisians living on the edge of starvation were effectively put down by a government that made no concessions to the poor.

In the face of all these catastrophes, the revolutionary fervor of the laboring poor finally subsided. As far as politics was concerned, their interest and influence would remain very limited until 1830. There arose, especially from the women, a great cry for peace and a turning toward religion. As the government looked the other way, the women brought back the Catholic church and the worship of God. In one French town, women fought with each other over which of their children should be baptized first. After six tumultuous years, the women of the poor concluded that the Revolution was a failure.

As for the middle-class members of the National Convention, they wrote yet another constitution, which they believed would guarantee their economic position and political supremacy. The mass of the population could vote only for electors, who would be men of means. Electors then elected the members of a reorganized Legislative Assembly, as well as key officials throughout France. The Assembly also chose the five-man executive—the Directory.

The Directory continued to support French military expansion abroad. War was no longer so much a crusade as a means to meet the ever-present, ever-unsolved economic problem. Large, victorious French armies reduced unemployment at home, and they were able to live off the territories they conquered and plundered.

The unprincipled action of the Directory reinforced widespread disgust with war and starvation. This general dissatisfaction revealed itself clearly in the national elections of 1797, which returned a large number of conservative and even monarchist deputies who favored peace at almost any price. Fearing for their skins, the members of the Directory used the army to nullify the elections and began to govern dictatorially. Two years later, Napoleon Bonaparte ended the Directory in a coup d'état and substituted a strong dictatorship for a weak one. Truly, the Revolution was over.

THE NAPOLEONIC ERA, 1799–1815

For almost fifteen years, from 1799 to 1814, France was in the hands of a keen-minded military dictator of exceptional ability. One of history's most fascinating leaders, Napoleon Bonaparte realized the need to put an end to civil strife in France, in order to create unity and consolidate his rule. And he did. But Napoleon saw himself as a man of destiny, and the glory of war and the dream of universal empire proved irresistible. For years he spiraled from victory to victory; but in the end he was destroyed by a mighty coalition united in fear of his restless ambition.

Napoleon's Rule of France

In 1799, when he seized power, young General Napoleon Bonaparte was a national hero. Born in Corsica into an impoverished noble family in 1769, Napoleon left home to become a lieutenant in the French artillery in 1785. After a brief and unsuccessful adventure fighting for Corsican independence in 1789, he returned to France as a

French patriot and a dedicated revolutionary. Rising rapidly in the new army, Napoleon was placed in command of French forces in Italy and won brilliant victories there in 1796 and 1797. His next campaign, in Egypt, was a failure, but Napoleon made his way back to France before the fiasco was generally known. His reputation remained intact.

Napoleon soon learned that some prominent members of the Legislative Assembly were plotting against the Directory. The dissatisfaction of these plotters stemmed not so much from the fact that the Directory was a dictatorship as from the fact that it was a weak dictatorship. Ten years of upheaval and uncertainty had made firm rule much more appealing than liberty and popular politics to these disillusioned revolutionaries. The abbé Sieyès personified this evolution in thinking. In 1789 he had written in his famous pamphlet, *What Is the Third Estate?*, that the nobility was grossly overprivi-

David: Napoleon Crossing the Alps Bold and commanding, with flowing cape and surging stallion, the daring young Napoleon Bonaparte leads his army across the Alps from Italy to battle the Austrians in 1797. This painting by the great Jacques-Louis David (1748–1825) is a stirring glorification of Napoleon, a brilliant exercise in mythmaking. *(Source: Louvre/Cliché des Musées Nationaux, Paris)*

leged and that the entire people should rule the French nation. Now Sieyès's motto was "confidence from below, authority from above."

Like the other members of his group, Sieyès wanted a strong military ruler. The flamboyant thirty-year-old Napoleon was ideal. Thus the conspirators and Napoleon organized a takeover. On November 9, 1799, they ousted the Directors, and the following day soldiers disbanded the Assembly at bayonet point. Napoleon was named first consul of the republic, and a new constitution consolidating his position was overwhelmingly approved in a plebiscite in December 1799. Republican appearances were maintained, but Napoleon was already the real ruler of France.

The essence of Napoleon's domestic policy was to use his great and highly personal powers to maintain order and put an end to civil strife. He did so by working out unwritten agreements with powerful groups in France, whereby these groups received favors in return for loyal service. Napoleon's bargain with the solid middle class was codified in the famous Civil Code of 1804, which reasserted two of the fundamental principles of the liberal and essentially moderate revolution of 1789: equality of all citizens before the law and absolute security of wealth and private property. Napoleon and the leading bankers of Paris established a privately owned Bank of France, which loyally served the interests of both the state and the financial oligarchy. Napoleon's defense of the economic status quo also appealed to the peasants, who had bought some of the lands confiscated from the church and nobility. Thus Napoleon reconfirmed the gains of the peasantry and reassured the middle class, which had already lost a large number of its revolutionary illusions in the face of social upheaval.

At the same time, Napoleon accepted and strengthened the position of the French bureaucracy. Building on the solid foundations that revolutionary governments had inherited from the Old Regime, he perfected a thoroughly centralized state. A network of prefects, subprefects, and centrally appointed mayors depended on Napoleon and served him well. Nor were members of the old nobility slighted. In 1800 and again in 1802, Napoleon granted amnesty to a hundred thousand émigrés on the condition that they return to France and take a loyalty oath. Members of this returning elite soon ably occupied many high posts in the expanding centralized state. Only a thousand diehard monarchists were exempted and remained abroad. Napoleon also created a new imperial nobility in order to reward his most talented generals and officials.

Napoleon's great skill in gaining support from important and potentially hostile groups is illustrated by his treatment of the Catholic church in France. In 1800 the French clergy was still divided into two groups: those who had taken an oath of allegiance to the revolutionary government and those in exile or hiding who had refused to do so. Personally uninterested in religion, Napoleon wanted to heal the religious division so that a united Catholic church in France could serve as a bulwark of order and social peace. After long and arduous negotiations, Napoleon and Pope Pius VII (1800–1823) signed the Concordat of 1801. The pope gained for French Catholics the precious right to practice their religion freely, but Napoleon gained the most politically. His government now nominated bishops, paid the clergy, and exerted great influence over the church in France.

The domestic reforms of Napoleon's early years were his greatest achievement. Much of his legal and administrative reorganization has survived in France to this day. More generally, Napoleon's domestic initiatives gave the great majority of French people a welcome sense of order and stability. And when Napoleon added the glory of military victory, he rekindled a spirit of national unity that would elude France throughout most of the nineteenth century.

Order and unity had their price: Napoleon's authoritarian rule. Women, who had participated actively in revolutionary politics, had no political rights under the Napoleonic Code. Under the law, women were dependents, of either their fathers or their husbands, and they could not make contracts or even have bank accounts in their own names. Free speech and freedom of the press—fundamental rights of the liberal revolution, enshrined in the Declaration of the Rights of Man—were continually violated. Napoleon constantly reduced the number of newspapers in Paris. By 1811 only four were left, and they were little more than organs of government propaganda. The occasional elections were a farce. Later laws prescribed harsh penalties for political offenses.

These changes in the law were part of the creation of a police state in France. Since Napoleon was usually busy making war, this task was largely left to Joseph Fouché, an unscrupulous opportun-

ist who had earned a reputation for brutality during the Reign of Terror. As minister of police, Fouché organized a ruthlessly efficient spy system, which kept thousands of citizens under continuous police surveillance. People suspected of subversive activities were arbitrarily detained, placed under house arrest, or even consigned to insane asylums. After 1810 political suspects were held in state prisons, as they had been during the Terror. There were about 2,500 such political prisoners in 1814.

Napoleon's Wars and Foreign Policy

Napoleon was above all a military man, and a great one. After coming to power in 1799, he sent peace feelers to Austria and Great Britain, the two remaining members of the Second Coalition, which had been formed against France in 1798. When these overtures were rejected, French armies led by Napoleon decisively defeated the Austrians. In the Treaty of Lunéville (1801) Austria accepted the loss of its Italian possessions, and German territory on the west bank of the Rhine was incorporated into France. Once more, as in 1797, the British were alone, and war-weary, like the French.

Still seeking to consolidate his regime domestically, Napoleon concluded the Treaty of Amiens with Great Britain in 1802. Britain agreed to return Trinidad and the Caribbean islands, which it had seized from France in 1793. The treaty said very little about Europe, though. France remained in control of Holland, the Austrian Netherlands, the west bank of the Rhine, and most of the Italian peninsula. Napoleon was free to reshape the German states as he wished. To the dismay of British business people, the Treaty of Amiens did not provide for expansion of the commerce between Britain and the Continent. It was clearly a diplomatic triumph for Napoleon, and peace with honor and profit increased his popularity at home.

In 1802 Napoleon was secure but unsatisfied. Ever a romantic gambler as well as a brilliant administrator, he could not contain his power drive. Aggressively redrawing the map of Germany so as to weaken Austria and attract the secondary states of southwestern Germany toward France, Napoleon was also mainly responsible for renewed war with Great Britain. Regarding war with Britain as inevitable, he threatened British interests in the eastern Mediterranean and tried to restrict British trade with all of Europe. Britain had technically

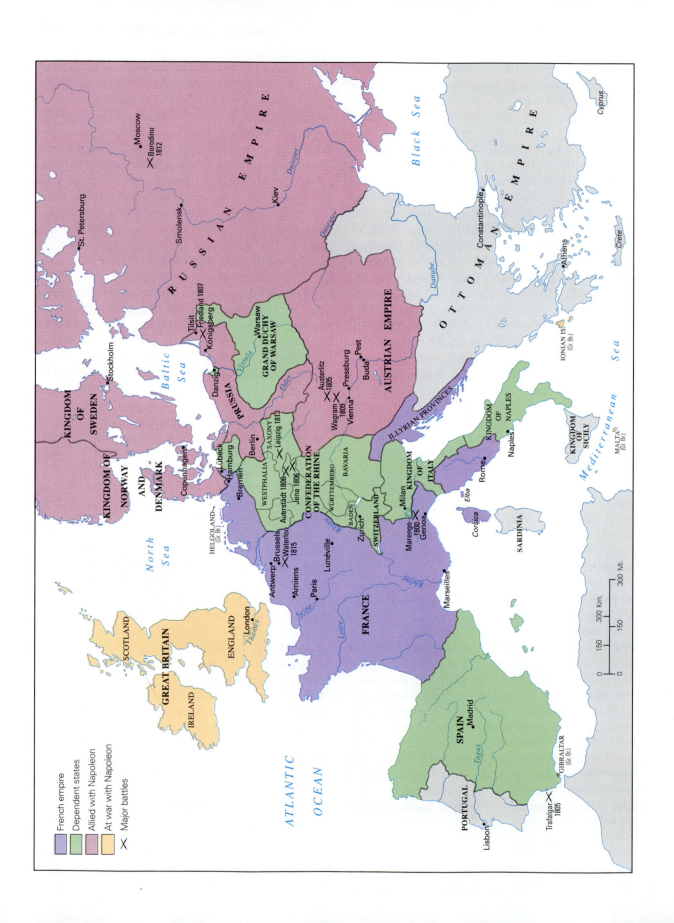

RUSSIAN EMPIRE

Moscow
×Borodino
1812

St. Petersburg

Smolensk

Kiev

Dnieper

Black Sea

OTTOMAN EMPIRE

Constantinople

Athens

Crete

Cyprus

KINGDOM OF SWEDEN

Stockholm

Tilsit
×Friedland 1807
Königsberg

Danzig

GRAND DUCHY OF WARSAW

Warsaw

Vistula

Oder

AUSTRIAN EMPIRE

Austerlitz
1805×

Pressburg

Pest
Buda

Vienna
×Wagram
1809

Danube

PRUSSIA

Baltic Sea

KINGDOM OF NORWAY AND DENMARK

Copenhagen

Lübeck
Hamburg
Bremen

Berlin

SAXONY
×Leipzig 1813

WESTPHALIA
×Auerstädt 1806
×Jena 1806

CONFEDERATION OF THE RHINE

WÜRTTEMBERG

BAVARIA

BADEN

SWITZERLAND
Zurich

Rhine

KINGDOM OF ITALY

Milan

×Marengo
1800
Genoa

ILLYRIAN PROVINCES

KINGDOM OF NAPLES

Rome
Elba

Naples

KINGDOM OF SICILY

IONIAN IS.
(Gr. Br.)

MALTA
(Gr. Br.)

Mediterranean Sea

NORTH SEA

HELGOLAND
(Gr. Br.)

Brussels
×Waterloo
1815

Antwerp
Amiens
Paris
Lunéville

Seine

Loire

Rhône

Marseilles

FRANCE

Corsica

SARDINIA

ATLANTIC OCEAN

SCOTLAND

GREAT BRITAIN

London
Thames

ENGLAND

IRELAND

SPAIN

Madrid

Tagus

GIBRALTAR
(Gr. Br.)

PORTUGAL

Lisbon

×Trafalgar
1805

300 Mi.
300 Km.
150
150
0
0

French empire
Dependent states
Allied with Napoleon
At war with Napoleon
× Major battles

violated the Treaty of Amiens by failing to evacuate the island of Malta, but it was Napoleon's decision to renew war in May 1803. He concentrated his armies in the French ports on the Channel in the fall of 1803 and began making preparations to invade England. Yet Great Britain remained dominant on the seas. When Napoleon tried to bring his Mediterranean fleet around Gibraltar to northern France, a combined French and Spanish fleet was, after a series of mishaps, virtually annihilated by Lord Nelson at the Battle of Trafalgar on October 21, 1805. Invasion of England was henceforth impossible. Renewed fighting had its advantages, however, for the first consul used the wartime atmosphere to have himself proclaimed emperor in late 1804.

Austria, Russia, and Sweden joined with Britain to form the Third Coalition against France shortly before the Battle of Trafalgar. Actions like Napoleon's assumption of the Italian crown had convinced both Alexander I of Russia and Francis II of Austria that Napoleon was a threat to their interests and to the European balance of power. Yet the Austrians and the Russians were no match for Napoleon, who scored a brilliant victory over them at the Battle of Austerlitz in December 1805. Alexander I decided to pull back, and Austria accepted large territorial losses in return for peace as the Third Coalition collapsed.

Victorious at Austerlitz, Napoleon proceeded to reorganize the German states to his liking. In 1806 he abolished many of the tiny German states, as well as the ancient Holy Roman Empire, whose emperor had traditionally been the ruler of Austria. Napoleon established by decree a German Confederation of the Rhine, a union of fifteen German states minus Austria, Prussia, and Saxony. Naming himself "protector" of the confederation, Napoleon firmly controlled western Germany.

Napoleon's intervention in German affairs alarmed the Prussians, who had been at peace with France for more than a decade. Expecting help from his ally Russia, Frederick William III of Prussia mobilized his armies. Napoleon attacked and won two more brilliant victories in October 1806 at Jena and Auerstädt, where the Prussians were outnumbered two to one. The war with Prussia

and Russia continued into the following spring, and after Napoleon's larger armies won another victory, Alexander I of Russia wanted peace.

For several days in June 1807, the young tsar and the French emperor negotiated face to face on a raft anchored in the middle of the Niemen River. All the while, the helpless Frederick William rode back and forth on the shore, anxiously awaiting the results. As the German poet Heinrich Heine said later, Napoleon had but to whistle and Prussia would have ceased to exist. In the subsequent treaties of Tilsit, Prussia lost half of its population, while Russia accepted Napoleon's reorganization of western and central Europe. Alexander also promised to enforce Napoleon's recently decreed economic blockade against British goods and to declare war on Britain if Napoleon could not make peace on favorable terms with his island enemy.

After the victory of Austerlitz and even more after the treaties of Tilsit, Napoleon saw himself as the emperor of Europe and not just of France. The so-called Grand Empire he built had three parts. The core was an ever-expanding France, which by 1810 included Belgium, Holland, parts of northern Italy, and much German territory on the east bank of the Rhine. Beyond French borders Napoleon established a number of dependent satellite kingdoms, on the thrones of which he placed (and replaced) the members of his large family. Third, there were the independent but allied states of Austria, Prussia, and Russia. Both satellites and allies were expected after 1806 to support Napoleon's continental system and cease trade with Britain.

The impact of the Grand Empire on the peoples of Europe was considerable. In the areas incorporated into France and in the satellites (Map 21.1), Napoleon introduced many French laws, abolishing feudal dues and serfdom where French revolutionary armies had not already done so. Some of the peasants and middle class benefited from these reforms. Yet while he extended progressive measures to his cosmopolitan empire, Napoleon had to put the prosperity and special interests of France first in order to safeguard his power base. Levying heavy taxes in money and men for his armies, Napoleon came to be regarded more as a conquering tyrant than as an enlightened liberator.

The first great revolt occurred in Spain. In 1808 a coalition of Catholics, monarchists, and patriots rebelled against Napoleon's attempts to make Spain a French satellite with a Bonaparte as its king.

Map 21.1 Napoleonic Europe in 1810

French armies occupied Madrid, but the foes of Napoleon fled to the hills and waged uncompromising guerrilla warfare. Spain was a clear warning. Resistance to French imperialism was growing.

Yet Napoleon pushed on, determined to hold his complex and far-flung empire together. In 1810, when the Grand Empire was at its height, Britain still remained at war with France, helping the guerrillas in Spain and Portugal. The continental system, organized to exclude British goods from the Continent and force that "nation of shopkeepers" to its knees, was a failure. Instead, it was France that suffered from Britain's counter-blockade, which created hard times for French artisans and the middle class. Perhaps looking for a scapegoat, Napoleon turned on Alexander I of Russia, who

had been fully supporting Napoleon's war of prohibitions against British goods.

Napoleon's invasion of Russia began in June 1812 with a force that eventually numbered 600,000, probably the largest force yet assembled in a single army. Only one-third of this force was French, however; nationals of all the satellites and allies were drafted into the operation. Originally planning to winter in the Russian city of Smolensk if Alexander did not sue for peace, Napoleon reached Smolensk and recklessly pressed on. The great battle of Borodino that followed was a draw, and the Russians retreated in good order. Alexander ordered the evacuation of Moscow, which then burned, and refused to negotiate. Finally, after five weeks in the burned-out city, Napoleon or-

Goya: The Third of May, 1808   This great painting screams in outrage at the horrors of war, which Goya witnessed in Spain. Spanish rebels, focused around the Christ-like figure at the center, are gunned down by anonymous French soldiers, grim forerunners of modern death squads and their atrocities. *(Source: Museo del Prado, Madrid)*

THE NAPOLEONIC ERA

November 1799	Napoleon overthrows the Directory
December 1799	French voters overwhelmingly approve Napoleon's new constitution
1800	Napoleon founds the Bank of France
1801	France defeats Austria and acquires Italian and German territories in the Treaty of Lunéville
	Napoleon signs a concordat with the pope
1802	Treaty of Amiens with Britain
December 1804	Napoleon crowns himself emperor
October 1805	Battle of Trafalgar: Britain defeats the French and Spanish fleets
December 1805	Battle of Austerlitz: Napoleon defeats Austria and Prussia
1807	Treaties of Tilsit: Napoleon redraws the map of Europe
1810	Height of the Grand Empire
June 1812	Napoleon invades Russia with 600,000 men
Winter 1812	Disastrous retreat from Russia
March 1814	Russia, Prussia, Austria, and Britain form the Quadruple Alliance to defeat France
April 1814	Napoleon abdicates and is exiled to Elba
February–June 1815	Napoleon escapes from Elba and rules France until suffering defeat at Battle of Waterloo

dered a retreat. That retreat was one of the great military disasters in history. The Russian army and the Russian winter cut Napoleon's army to pieces. Only 30,000 men returned to their homelands.

Leaving his troops to their fate, Napoleon raced to Paris to raise yet another army. Possibly he might still have saved his throne if he had been willing to accept a France reduced to its historical size—the proposal offered by Austria's foreign minister Metternich. But Napoleon refused. Austria and Prussia deserted Napoleon and joined Russia and Great Britain in the Fourth Coalition. All across Europe, patriots called for a "war of liberation" against Napoleon's oppression, and the well-disciplined regular armies of Napoleon's enemies closed in for the kill. This time the coalition held together, cemented by the Treaty of Chaumont, which created a Quadruple Alliance to last for twenty years. Less than a month later, on April 4, 1814, a defeated, abandoned Napoleon abdicated his throne. After this unconditional abdication, the victorious allies granted Napoleon the island of Elba off the coast of Italy as his own tiny state. Napoleon was even allowed to keep his imperial title, and France was required to pay him a large yearly income of 2 million francs.

The allies also agreed to the restoration of the Bourbon dynasty, in part because demonstrations led by a few dedicated French monarchists indicated some support among the French people for that course of action. The new monarch, Louis XVIII (r. 1814–1824), tried to consolidate that support by issuing the Constitutional Charter, which accepted many of France's revolutionary changes and guaranteed civil liberties. Indeed, the Charter gave France a constitutional monarchy roughly similar to that established in 1791, although far fewer people had the right to vote for representatives to the resurrected Chamber of Deputies. Moreover, after Louis XVIII stated firmly that his government would not pay any war reparations, France was treated leniently by the allies, who agreed to meet in Vienna to work out a general peace settlement.

Yet Louis XVIII—old, ugly, and crippled by gout—totally lacked the glory and magic of Napoleon. Hearing of political unrest in France and diplomatic tensions in Vienna, Napoleon staged a daring escape from Elba in February 1815. Landing in France, he issued appeals for support and marched on Paris with a small band of followers. French officers and soldiers who had fought so long for their emperor responded to the call. Louis XVIII fled, and once more Napoleon took command. But Napoleon's gamble was a desperate long shot, for the allies were united against him. At the end of a frantic period known as the Hundred Days, they crushed his forces at Waterloo on June 18, 1815, and imprisoned him on the rocky island of St. Helena, far off the western coast of Africa. Old Louis XVIII returned again—this time "in the baggage of the allies," as his detractors scornfully put it—and recommended his reign. The allies now dealt more harshly with the apparently incorrigible French (see Chapter 22). And Napoleon, doomed to suffer crude insults at the hands of sadistic English jailers on distant St. Helena, could take revenge only by writing his memoirs, skillfully nurturing the myth that he had been Europe's revolutionary liberator, a romantic hero whose lofty work had been undone by oppressive reactionaries. An era had ended.

SUMMARY

The revolution that began in America and spread to France was a liberal revolution. Inspired by English history and some of the teachings of the Enlightenment, revolutionaries on both sides of the Atlantic sought to establish civil liberties and equality before the law within the framework of representative government. Success in America was subsequently matched by success in France. There, liberal nobles and an increasingly class-conscious middle class overwhelmed declining monarchial absolutism and feudal privilege, thanks to the common people—the sans-culottes and the peasants. The government and society established by the Declaration of the Rights of Man and the French constitution of 1791 were remarkably similar to those created in America by the federal Constitution and the Bill of Rights. Thus the new political system, based on electoral competition and civil equality, came into approximate harmony with France's evolving social structure, which had become increasingly based on wealth and achievement rather than on tradition and legal privileges.

Yet the Revolution in France did not end with the liberal victory of 1789 to 1791. As Robespierre led the determined country in a total war effort against foreign foes, French revolutionaries became more democratic, radical, and violent. Their effort succeeded, but at the price of dictatorship—first by Robespierre himself and then by the Directory and Napoleon. Some historians blame the excesses of the French revolutionaries for the emergence of dictatorship, while others hold the conservative monarchs of Europe responsible. In any case, historians have often concluded that the French Revolution ended in failure.

This conclusion is highly debatable, though. After the fall of Robespierre, the solid middle class, with its liberal philosophy and Enlightenment world-view, reasserted itself. Under the Directory, it salvaged a good portion of the social and political gains that it and the peasantry had made between 1789 and 1791. In so doing, the middle-class leaders repudiated the radical social and economic measures associated with Robespierre, but they never re-established the old pattern of separate legal orders and absolute monarchy. Napoleon built on the policies of the Directory. With considerable success he sought to add the support of the old nobility and the church to that of the middle class and the peasantry. And though Napoleon sharply curtailed thought and speech, he effectively promoted the reconciliation of old and new, of centralized government and careers open to talent, of noble and bourgeois in a restructured property-owning elite. Little wonder, then, that Louis XVIII had no choice but to accept a French society solidly based on wealth and achievement. In granting representative government and civil liberties to facilitate his restoration to the throne in 1814, Louis XVIII submitted to the rest of the liberal triumph of 1789 to 1791. The core of the French Revolution had survived a generation of war and dictatorship. Old Europe would never be the same.

NOTES

1. Quoted in R. R. Palmer, *The Age of the Democratic Revolution,* vol. 1 (Princeton, N.J.: Princeton University Press, 1959), p. 239.
2. G. Lefebvre, *The Coming of the French Revolution* (New York: Vintage Books, 1947), p. 81.
3. P. H. Beik, ed., *The French Revolution* (New York: Walker, 1970), p. 89.
4. O. Hufton, "Women in Revolution," *Past and Present* 53 (November 1971): 91–95.
5. G. Pernoud and S. Flaisser, eds., *The French Revolution* (Greenwich, Conn.: Fawcett, 1960), p. 61.

6. Quotations from Wollstonecraft are drawn from E. W. Sunstein, *A Different Face: The Life of Mary Wollstonecraft* (New York: Harper & Row, 1975), pp. 208, 211; and H. R. James, *Mary Wollstonecraft: A Sketch* (London: Oxford University Press, 1932), pp. 60, 62, 69.

7. L. Gershoy, *The Era of the French Revolution, 1789–1799* (New York: Van Norstrand, 1957), p. 150.

8. Pernoud and Flaisser, pp. 193–194.

SUGGESTED READING

For fascinating eyewitness reports on the French Revolution, see the edited works by Beik and Pernoud and Flaisser mentioned in the Notes. In addition, A. Young's *Travels in France During the Years 1787, 1788 and 1789* (1969) offers an engrossing contemporary description of France and Paris on the eve of revolution. Edmund Burke, *Reflections on the Revolution in France,* first published in 1790, is the classic conservative indictment. The intense passions the French Revolution has generated may be seen in the nineteenth-century French historians, notably the enthusiastic Jules Michelet, *History of the French Revolution;* the hostile Hippolyte Taine; and the judicious Alexis de Tocqueville, whose masterpiece, *The Old Regime and the French Revolution,* was first published in 1856. Important general studies on the entire period include the work of R. R. Palmer, cited in the Notes, which paints a comparative international picture; E. J. Hobsbawm, *The Age of Revolution, 1789–1848* (1962); C. Breunig, *The Age of Revolution and Reaction, 1789–1850* (1970); O. Connelly, *French Revolution—Napoleonic Era* (1979); and L. Dehio, *The Precarious Balance: Four Centuries of the European Power Struggle* (1962).

Recent decades have seen a wealth of new scholarship and interpretation, culminating in a profusion of works published to coincide with the French Revolution's bicentenary of 1989. A. Cobban, *The Social Interpretation of the French Revolution* (1964), and F. Furet, *Interpreting the French Revolution* (1981), are major reassessments of long-dominant ideas, which are admirably presented in N. Hampson, *A Social History of the French Revolution* (1963), and in the volume by Lefebvre listed in the Notes. R. Chartier, *The Cultural Origins of the French Revolution* (1989), and W. Doyle, *Origins of the French Revolution* (1981), are excellent on long-term developments. Among recent studies, which generally are often quite critical of revolutionary developments, several are noteworthy: J. Bosher, *The French Revolution* (1988); S.

Schama, *Citizens: A Chronicle of the French Revolution* (1989); W. Doyle, *The Oxford History of the French Revolution* (1989); and D. Sutherland, *France, 1789–1815: Revolution and Counterrevolution* (1986).

Two valuable anthologies concisely presenting a range of interpretations are F. Kafker and J. Laux, eds., *The French Revolutions: Conflicting Interpretations,* 4th ed. (1989), and G. Best, ed., *The Permanent Revolution: The French Revolution and Its Legacy, 1789–1989* (1988). G. Rude makes the men and women of the great days of upheaval come alive in his *The Crowd in the French Revolution* (1959), while R. R. Palmer studies sympathetically the leaders of the Terror in *Twelve Who Ruled* (1941). Four other particularly interesting, detailed works are D. Jordan, *The Revolutionary Career of Maximilien Robespierre* (1985); J. P. Bertaud, *The Army of the French Revolution: From Citizen-Soldier to Instrument of Power* (1988); C. L. R. James, *The Black Jacobins* (1938, 1980), on black slave revolt in Haiti; and J. C. Herold, *Mistress to an Age* (1955), on the remarkable Madame de Staël. Other significant studies on aspects of revolutionary France include P. Jones's pathbreaking *The Peasantry in the French Revolution* (1988); D. Jordan's vivid *The King's Trial: Louis XVI vs. the French Revolution* (1979); W. Sewell, Jr.'s imaginative *Work and Revolution in France: The Language of Labor from the Old Regime to 1848* (1980); and L. Hunt's innovative *Politics, Culture, and Class in the French Revolution* (1984). Mary Wollstonecraft's dramatic life is the subject of several good biographies, including those by Sunstein and James cited in the Notes.

Two important works placing political developments in a comparative perspective are P. Higonnet, *Sister Republics: The Origins of French and American Republicanism* (1988), and E. Morgan, *Inventing the People: The Rise of Popular Sovereignty in England and America* (1988). B. Bailyn, *The Ideological Origins of the American Revolution* (1967), is also noteworthy.

The best synthesis on Napoleonic France is L. Bergeron, *France Under Napoleon* (1981). P. Geyl, *Napoleon, For and Against* (1949), is a delightful discussion of changing historical interpretations of Napoleon, which may be compared with a more recent treatment by R. Jones, *Napoleon: Man and Myth* (1977). Good biographies are J. M. Thompson, *Napoleon Bonaparte: His Rise and Fall* (1952); F. H. M. Markham, *Napoleon* (1964); and V. Cronin, *Napoleon Bonaparte* (1972). Wonderful novels inspired by this period include Raphael Sabatini's *Scaramouche,* a swashbuckler of revolutionary intrigue with accurate historical details; Charles Dickens's classic *Tale of Two Cities;* and Leo Tolstoy's monumental saga of Napoleon's invasion of Russia (and much more), *War and Peace.*

22

The Revolution in
Energy and Industry

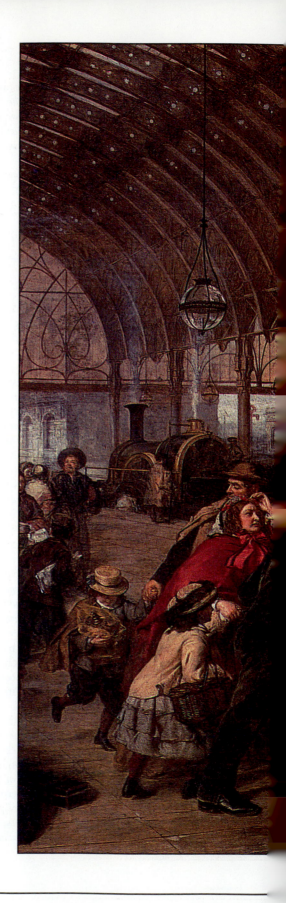

While the revolution in France was opening a new political era, another revolution was beginning to transform economic and social life. This was the Industrial Revolution, which began in England around the 1780s and started to influence continental Europe after 1815. Because the Industrial Revolution was less dramatic than the French Revolution, some historians see industrial development as basically moderate and evolutionary. In the long perspective, however, it was rapid and brought about radical changes. Perhaps only the development of agriculture during Neolithic times had a similar impact and significance.

The Industrial Revolution profoundly modified much of human experience. It changed patterns of work, transformed the social class structure, and eventually even altered the international balance of political power. The Industrial Revolution also helped ordinary people gain a higher standard of living, as the widespread poverty of the preindustrial world was gradually reduced.

Unfortunately, the improvement in the European standard of living was quite limited until about 1850, for at least two reasons. First, even in England only a few key industries experienced a technological revolution. Many more industries continued to use old methods, especially on the Continent, and this held down the increase in total production. Second, the increase in total population, which began in the eighteenth century (see pages 607–609), continued all across Europe as the era of the Industrial Revolution unfolded. As a result, the rapid growth in population threatened—quite literally—to eat up the growth in production and to leave individuals poorer than ever. Thus rapid population growth formed a somber background for European industrialization and made the wrenching transformation more difficult.

- What, then, was the Industrial Revolution?
- What were its origins, and how did it develop?
- How did the changes it brought affect people and society in an era of continued rapid population growth?

These are the questions this chapter will seek to answer. Chapter 24 will examine in detail the emergence of accompanying changes in urban civilization.

THE INDUSTRIAL REVOLUTION IN ENGLAND

The Industrial Revolution began in England. It was something new in history, and it was quite unplanned. With no models to copy and no idea of what to expect, England had to pioneer not only in industrial technology but also in social relations and urban living. Between 1793 and 1815, these formidable tasks were complicated by almost constant war with France. As the trailblazer in economic development, as France was in political change, England must command special attention.

Eighteenth-Century Origins

Although many aspects of the English Industrial Revolution are still matters for scholarly debate, it is generally agreed that the industrial changes that did occur grew out of a long process of development. First of all, the expanding Atlantic economy of the eighteenth century served mercantilist England remarkably well. The colonial empire that England aggressively built, augmented by a strong position in Latin America and in the African slave trade, provided a growing market for English manufactured goods. So did England itself. In an age when it was much cheaper to ship goods by water than by land, no part of England was more than 20 miles from navigable water. Beginning in the 1770s, a canal-building boom greatly enhanced this natural advantage (Map 22.1). Nor were there any tariffs within the country to hinder trade, as there were in France before 1789 and in politically fragmented Germany.

Agriculture played a central role in bringing about the Industrial Revolution in England. English farmers were second only to the Dutch in productivity in 1700, and they were continuously adopting new methods of farming as the century went on. The result, especially before 1760, was a period of bountiful crops and low food prices. The ordinary English family did not have to spend almost everything it earned just to buy bread. It could spend more on other items, on manufactured goods—leather shoes or a razor for the man, a bonnet or a shawl for the woman, toy soldiers for the son, and a doll for the daughter. Thus demand for goods within the country complemented the demand from the colonies.

England had other assets that helped give rise to the industrial leadership. Unlike eighteenth-century France, England had an effective central bank and well-developed credit markets. The monarchy and the aristocratic oligarchy, which had jointly ruled the country since 1688, provided stable and predictable government. At the same time, the government let the domestic economy operate fairly freely and with few controls, encouraging personal initiative, technical change, and a free market. Finally, England had long had a large class of hired agricultural laborers, rural proletarians whose numbers were further increased by the enclosure movement of the late eighteenth century. These rural wage earners were relatively mobile—compared to village-bound peasants in France and western Germany, for example—and along with cottage workers they formed a potential industrial labor force for capitalist entrepreneurs.

All these factors combined to initiate the Industrial Revolution, a term first coined by awed contemporaries in the 1830s to describe the burst of major inventions and technical changes they had witnessed in certain industries. This technical revolution went hand in hand with an impressive quickening in the annual rate of industrial growth in England. Thus industry grew at only 0.7 percent between 1700 and 1760—before the Industrial Revolution—but it grew at the much higher rate of 3 percent between 1801 and 1831, when industrial transformation was in full swing.[1] The decisive quickening of growth probably came in the 1780s, after the American war for independence and just before the French Revolution.

Therefore, the great economic and political revolutions that shaped the modern world occurred almost simultaneously, though they began in different countries. The Industrial Revolution was, however, a longer process than the political upheavals. It was not complete in England until 1850, and it had no real impact on continental countries until after 1815.

The First Factories

The pressure to produce more goods for a growing market was directly related to the first decisive breakthrough of the Industrial Revolution—the creation of the world's first large factories in the English cotton textile industry. Technological in-

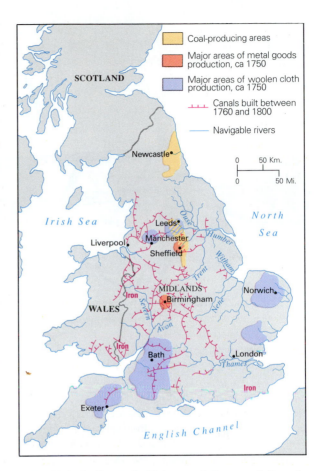

MAP 22.1 Cottage Industry and Transportation in Eighteenth-Century England England had an unusually good system of navigable waterways even before river-linking canals made it better.

novations in the manufacture of cotton cloth led to a new system of production and social relationships. Since no other industry experienced such a rapid or complete transformation before 1830, these trailblazing developments deserve special consideration.

Although the putting-out system of merchant capitalism (see pages 610–612) was expanding all across Europe in the eighteenth century, this pattern of rural industry was most fully developed in England. Thus it was in England, under the pressure of growing demand, that the system's limitations first began to outweigh its advantages. This was especially true in the textile industry after about 1760.

The constant shortage of thread in the textile industry focused attention on ways of improving

Hargreave's Spinning Jenny   The loose cotton strands on the slanted bobbins passed up to the sliding carriage and then on to the spindles in back for fine spinning. By 1783 one woman could spin by hand a hundred threads at a time on an improved model. *(Source: University of Illinois, Champaign)*

spinning. Many a tinkering worker knew that a better spinning wheel promised rich rewards. Spinning of the traditional raw materials—wool and flax—proved hard to change, but cotton was different. Cotton textiles had first been imported into England from India by the East India Company, and by 1760 there was a tiny domestic industry in northern England. After many experiments over a generation, a gifted carpenter and jack-of-all-trades, James Hargreaves, invented his cotton-spinning jenny about 1765. At almost the same moment a barber-turned-manufacturer named Richard Arkwright invented (or possibly pirated) another kind of spinning machine, the water frame. These breakthroughs produced an explosion in the infant cotton textile industry in the 1780s, when it was increasing the value of its output at an unprecedented rate of about 13 percent each year. By 1790 the new machines produced ten times as much cotton yarn as had been made in 1770.

Hargreaves's jenny was simple and inexpensive. It was also hand operated. In early models, from six to twenty-four spindles were mounted on a sliding carriage, and each spindle spun a fine, slender thread. The woman moved the carriage back and forth with one hand and turned a wheel to supply power with the other. Now it was the weaver who could not keep up with his vastly more efficient wife.

Arkwright's water frame employed a different principle. It quickly acquired a capacity of several hundred spindles and demanded much more power—water-power. The water frame thus required large specialized mills, factories that employed as many as a thousand workers from the very beginning. The water frame could spin only coarse, strong thread, which was then put out for respinning on hand-powered cottage jennies. Around 1790 an alternative technique invented by Samuel Crompton also began to require more power than the human arm could supply. After that time, all cotton spinning was gradually concentrated in factories.

The first consequences of these revolutionary developments were more beneficial than is generally believed. Cotton goods became much cheaper, and they were bought and treasured by all classes. In the past, only the wealthy could afford the comfort and cleanliness of underwear, which was called "body linen" because it was made from expensive linen cloth. Now millions of poor people, who had earlier worn nothing underneath their coarse, filthy outer garments, could afford to wear cotton slips and underpants, as well as cotton dresses and shirts.

Families using cotton in cottage industry were freed from their constant search for adequate yarn from scattered, part-time spinners, since all the thread needed could be spun in the cottage on the jenny or obtained from a nearby factory. The wages of weavers, now hard pressed to keep up with the spinners, rose markedly until about 1792. Weavers were among the best-paid workers in England. They were known to walk proudly through the streets with £5 notes stuck in their hatbands, and they dressed like the middle class.

One result of this unprecedented prosperity was that large numbers of agricultural laborers became handloom weavers. The growth of handloom cotton weaving was an outstanding example of how breakthroughs in factory production normally stimulated complementary increases in handicraft output. It was also an example of how further mechanization threatened certain groups of handicraft workers, for mechanics and capitalists soon sought to invent a power loom to save on labor costs. This Edmund Cartwright achieved in 1785. But the power looms of the factories worked poorly at first, and handloom weavers continued to receive good wages until at least 1800.

Working conditions in the early factories were less satisfactory than those of cottage weavers and spinners. But until the late 1780s, most English factories were in rural areas, where they had access to waterpower. These factories employed a relatively small percentage of all cotton textile workers. People were reluctant to work in them, partly because they resembled the poorhouses where destitute inmates had to labor for very little pay. Therefore, factory owners turned to young children as a source of labor. More precisely, they turned to children who had been abandoned by their parents and put in the care of local parishes. The parish officers often "apprenticed" such unfortunate orphans to factory owners. The parish thus saved money, and the factory owners gained workers over whom they exercised almost the authority of slaveowners.

Apprenticed as young as five or six years of age, the boy and girl workers were forced by law to labor for their "master" for as many as fourteen years. Housed, fed, and locked up nightly in factory dormitories, the young workers received little or no pay for their toil. Hours were appalling—commonly thirteen or fourteen hours a day, six days a week. Harsh physical punishment maintained brutal discipline. To be sure, poor children typically worked long hours from an early age in the eighteenth century, and frequently outside the home for a brutal master. But the wholesale coercion of orphans as factory apprentices constituted exploitation on a truly unprecedented scale. This exploitation ultimately piqued the conscience of reformers and reinforced humanitarian attitudes toward children and their labor in the early nineteenth century.

The creation of the world's first modern factories in the English cotton textile industry in the 1770s and 1780s, which grew out of the putting-out system of cottage production, was a major historical development. Both symbolically and in substance, the big new cotton mills marked the beginning of the Industrial Revolution in England. By 1831 the largely mechanized cotton textile industry towered above all others, accounting for fully 22 percent of the country's entire industrial production.

The Problem of Energy

The growth of the cotton textile industry might have been stunted or cut short, however, if water from rivers and streams had remained the primary source of power for the new factories. But this did not occur. Instead, an epoch-making solution was found to the age-old problem of energy and power. It was this solution to the energy problem—a problem that has reappeared in recent times—that permitted continued rapid development in cotton textiles, the gradual generalization of the factory system, and the triumph of the Industrial Revolution in England and Scotland.

Human beings, like all living organisms, require energy. Adult men and women need 2,000 to

4,000 calories (units of energy) daily, simply to fuel their bodies, work, and survive. Energy comes from a variety of sources; energy also takes different forms, and one form may be converted into another. Plants have been converting solar energy into caloric matter for eons. And human beings have used their toolmaking abilities to construct machines that convert one form of energy into another for their own benefit.

Prehistoric people relied on plants and plant-eating animals as their sources of energy. With the development of agriculture, early civilizations were able to increase the number of useful plants and thus the supply of energy. Some plants could be fed to domesticated animals, like the horse. Stronger than human beings, these animals converted the energy in the plants into work.

In the medieval period, people began to develop water mills to grind their grain and windmills to pump water and drain swamps. More efficient use of water and wind in the sixteenth and seventeenth centuries enabled human beings to accomplish more; intercontinental sailing ships are a prime example. Nevertheless, even into the eighteenth century, society continued to rely for energy mainly on plants, and human beings and animals continued to perform most work. This dependence meant that Western civilization remained poor in energy and power.

Lack of power lay at the heart of the poverty that afflicted the large majority of people. The man behind the plow and the woman at the spinning wheel could employ only horsepower and human muscle in their labor. No matter how hard they worked, they could not produce very much. What people needed were new sources of energy and more power at their disposal. Then they would be able to work more efficiently, produce more, and live better.

Where was more energy to be found? Almost all energy came directly or indirectly from plants and therefore from the land: grain for people, hay for animals, and wood for heat. The land was also the principal source of raw materials needed for industrial production: wool and flax for clothing; leather for shoes; wood for housing, tools, and ironmaking. And though swamps could be drained and marshes reclaimed from the sea, it was difficult to expand greatly the amount of land available. True, its yield could be increased, as by the elimination of fallow; nonetheless, there were definite limits to such improvements.

The shortage of energy was becoming particularly severe in England by the eighteenth century. Because of the growth of population, most of the great forests of medieval England had long ago been replaced by fields of grain and hay. Wood was in ever shorter supply; yet it remained tremendously important. It was the primary source of heat for all homes and industries. It was also the key to transportation, since ships and wagons were made of wood. Moreover, wood was, along with iron ore, the basic raw material of the iron industry. Processed wood (charcoal) was the fuel mixed with iron ore in the blast furnace to produce pig iron. The iron industry's appetite for wood was enormous, and even very modest and constant levels of iron production had gone far toward laying bare the forests of England, as well as parts of continental Europe. By 1740 the English iron industry was stagnating. Vast forests enabled Russia in the eighteenth century to become the world's leading producer of iron, much of which was exported to England. But Russia's potential for growth was limited, too, and in a few decades Russia would reach the barrier of inadequate energy that was already holding England back.

The Steam Engine Breakthrough

As this early energy crisis grew worse, England looked toward its abundant and widely scattered reserves of coal as an alternative to its vanishing wood. Coal was first used in England in the late Middle Ages as a source of heat. By 1640 most homes in London were heated with it, and it also provided heat for making beer, glass, soap, and other products. Coal was not used, however, to produce mechanical energy or to power machinery. It was there that coal's potential was enormous, as a simple example shows.

One pound of good bituminous coal contains about 3,500 calories of heat energy. A miner who eats 3,500 calories of food can dig out 500 pounds of coal a day, using hand tools. Even an extremely inefficient converter, which transforms only 1 percent of the heat energy in coal into mechanical energy, will produce 27 horsepower-hours of work from the 500 pounds of coal the miner cut out of the earth. The miner, by contrast, produces only about 1 horsepower-hour in the course of a day. Much more energy is consumed by the converter, but much more work can be done.

Making Charcoal After wood was carefully cut and stacked, iron masters slowly burned it to produce charcoal. Before the Industrial Revolution, a country's iron industry depended greatly on the size of its forests. *(Source: University of Illinois, Champaign)*

Early steam engines were just such inefficient converters. As more coal was produced, mines were dug deeper and deeper and were constantly filling with water. Mechanical pumps, usually powered by animals walking in circles at the surface, had to be installed. At one mine, fully five hundred horses were used in pumping. Such power was expensive and bothersome. In an attempt to overcome these disadvantages, Thomas Savery in 1698 and Thomas Newcomen in 1705 invented the first primitive steam engines.

Both engines were extremely inefficient. Both burned coal to produce steam, which was then injected into a cylinder or reservoir. In Newcomen's engine, the steam in the cylinder was cooled, creating a partial vacuum in the cylinder. This vacuum allowed the pressure of the earth's atmosphere to push the piston in the cylinder down and operate a pump. By the early 1770s, many of the Savery engines and hundreds of the Newcomen engines were operating successfully, though inefficiently, in English and Scottish mines.

In the early 1760s, a gifted young Scot named James Watt (1736–1819) was drawn to a critical study of the steam engine. Watt was employed at the time by the University of Glasgow as a skilled craftsman making scientific instruments. The Scottish universities were pioneers in practical technical education, and in 1763 Watt was called on to repair a Newcomen engine being used in a physics course. After a series of observations, Watt saw why the Newcomen engine wasted so much energy: the cylinder was being heated and cooled for every single stroke of the piston. To remedy this problem, Watt added a separate condenser, where the steam could be condensed without cooling the cylinder.

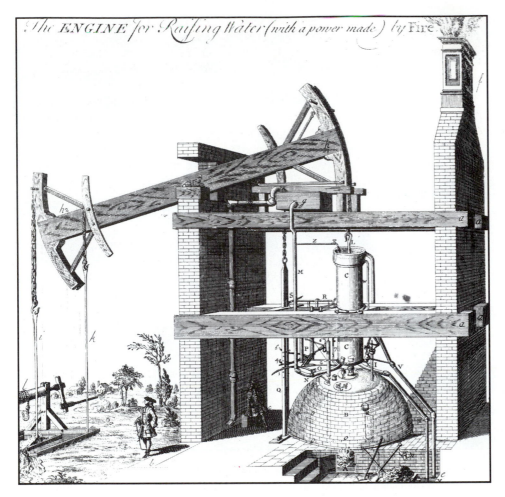

The ENGINE *for Raifing Water (with a power made) by* Fire

The Newcomen Engine   The huge steam-filled cylinder (C) was cooled by injecting water from the tank above (G) through a pipe (M). Atmospheric pressure then pushed down the piston, raised the beam, and pumped water from the mine. *(Source: Reproduced by permission of the Trustees of the Science Museum, London)*

This splendid invention greatly increased the efficiency of the steam engine.

To invent something in a laboratory is one thing; to make it a practical success is quite another. Watt needed skilled workers, precision parts, and capital, and the relatively advanced nature of the English economy proved essential. A partnership with a wealthy, progressive toymaker provided risk capital and a manufacturing plant. In the craft tradition of locksmiths, tinsmiths, and millwrights, Watt found skilled mechanics who could install, regulate, and repair his sophisticated engines. From ingenious manufacturers like the cannonmaker John Wilkinson, who learned to bore cylinders with a fair degree of accuracy, Watt was gradually able to purchase precision parts. This support allowed him to

create an effective vacuum and regulate a complex engine. In more than twenty years of constant effort, Watt made many further improvements. By the late 1780s, the steam engine was a practical and commercial success in England.

The steam engine of Watt and his followers was the Industrial Revolution's most fundamental advance in technology. For the first time in history, humanity had, at least for a few generations, almost unlimited power at its disposal. For the first time, inventors and engineers could devise and implement all kinds of power equipment to aid people in their work. For the first time, abundance was at least a possibility for ordinary men and women.

The steam engine was quickly put to use in several industries in England. It made possible the production of ever more coal to feed steam engines elsewhere. The steam-power plant began to replace waterpower in the cotton-spinning mills during the 1780s, contributing greatly to that industry's phenomenal rise. Steam also took the place of waterpower in flour mills, in the malt mills used in breweries, in the flint mills supplying the china industry, and in the mills exported by England to the West Indies to crush sugar cane.

Steam power promoted important breakthroughs in other industries. The English iron industry was radically transformed. The use of powerful, steam-driven bellows in blast furnaces helped ironmakers switch over rapidly from limited charcoal to unlimited coke (which is made from coal) in the smelting of pig iron after 1770. In the 1780s Henry Cort developed the puddling furnace, which allowed pig iron to be refined in turn with coke. Strong, skilled ironworkers—the puddlers—"cooked" molten pig iron in a great vat, raking off globs of refined iron for further processing. Cort also developed heavy-duty, steam-powered rolling mills, which were capable of spewing out finished iron in every shape and form.

The economic consequence of these technical innovations was a great boom in the English iron industry. In 1740 annual British iron production was only 17,000 tons. With the spread of coke smelting and the first impact of Cort's inventions, production reached 68,000 tons in 1788, 125,000 tons in 1796, and 260,000 tons in 1806. In 1844 Britain produced 3 million tons of iron. This was truly amazing expansion. Once scarce and expensive, iron became the cheap, basic building block of the economy.

The Coming of the Railroads

Sailing ships had improved noticeably since the Age of Discovery, and the second half of the eighteenth century saw extensive construction of hard and relatively smooth roads, particularly in France before the Revolution. Yet it was passenger traffic that benefited most from this construction. Overland shipment of freight, relying solely on horsepower, was still quite limited and frightfully expensive; shippers used rivers and canals for heavy freight whenever possible. It was logical, therefore, that inventors would try to use steam power.

As early as 1800, an American ran a "steamer on wheels" through city streets. Other experiments followed. In the 1820s, English engineers created steam cars capable of carrying fourteen passengers at 10 miles an hour—as fast as the mail coach. But the noisy, heavy steam automobiles frightened passing horses and damaged themselves as well as the roads with their vibrations. For the rest of the century, horses continued to reign on highways and city streets.

The coal industry had long been using plank roads and rails to move coal wagons within mines and at the surface. Rails reduced friction and allowed a horse or a human being to pull a heavier load. Thus, once a rail capable of supporting a heavy locomotive was developed in 1816, all sorts of experiments with steam engines on rails went forward. In 1825, after ten years of work, George Stephenson built an effective locomotive. In 1830 his *Rocket* sped down the track of the just-completed Liverpool and Manchester Railway at 16 miles per hour. This was the world's first important railroad, fittingly steaming in the heart of industrial England.

The line from Liverpool to Manchester was a financial as well as a technical success, and many private companies were quickly organized to build more rail lines. These companies had to get permission for their projects from Parliament and pay for the rights of way they needed; otherwise, their freedom was great. Within twenty years, they had completed the main trunk lines of Great Britain. Other countries were quick to follow.

The significance of the railroad was tremendous. The railroad dramatically reduced the cost and uncertainty of shipping freight overland. This advance had many economic consequences. Previously, markets had tended to be small and local; as the barrier of high transportation costs was lowered, they became larger and even nationwide. Larger markets encouraged larger factories with more sophisticated machinery in a growing number of industries. Such factories could make goods more cheaply and gradually subjected most cottage workers and many urban artisans to severe competitive pressures.

In all countries, the construction of railroads contributed to the growth of a class of urban workers. Cottage workers, farm laborers, and small peasants did not generally leave their jobs and homes to go directly to work in factories. However, the building of railroads created a strong demand for labor, especially unskilled labor, throughout a country. Hard work on construction gangs was done in the open air with animals and hand tools. Many landless farm laborers and poor peasants, long accustomed to leaving their villages for temporary employment, went to build railroads. By the time the work was finished, life back home in the village often seemed dull and unappealing, and many men drifted to towns in search of work—with the railroad companies, in construction, in factories. By the time they sent for their wives and sweethearts to join them, they had become urban workers.

The railroad changed the outlook and values of the entire society. The last and culminating invention of the Industrial Revolution, the railroad dramatically revealed the power and increased the speed of the new age. Racing down a track at 16 miles per hour or, by 1850, at a phenomenal 50 miles per hour was a new and awesome experience.

As a noted French economist put it after a ride on the Liverpool and Manchester in 1833, "There are certain impressions that one cannot put into words!"

Some great painters, notably J. M. W. Turner (1775–1851) and Claude Monet (1840–1926), succeeded in expressing this sense of power and awe. So did the massive new train stations, the cathedrals of the industrial age. Leading railway engineers like Isambard Kingdom Brunel and Thomas Brassey, whose tunnels pierced mountains and whose bridges spanned valleys, became public idols —the astronauts of their day. Everyday speech absorbed the images of railroading. After you got up a "full head of steam," you "highballed" along. And if you didn't "go off the track," you might "toot your own whistle." The railroad fired the imagination.

The Liverpool and Manchester Railway   This hand-colored engraving celebrates the opening of the world's first major railroad on September 15, 1830. Railroad construction reshaped the built environment and proclaimed the coming of a new age. (Source: Mr. and Mrs. M. G. Powell)

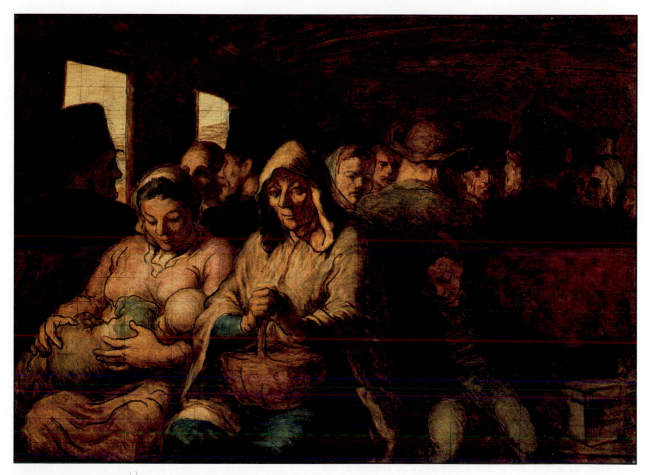

The Third-Class Carriage   The French artist Honoré Daumier was fascinated by the railroad and its human significance. This great painting focuses on the peasant grand-mother, absorbed in memories. The nursing mother represents love and creativity; the sleeping boy, innocence. *(Source: The Metropolitan Museum of Art. Bequest of Mrs. H. O. Havemeyer, 1929. The H. O. Havemeyer Collection (29. 100. 129))*

Industry and Population

In 1851 London was the site of a famous industrial fair. This Great Exposition was held in the newly built Crystal Palace, an architectural masterpiece made entirely of glass and iron, both of which were now cheap and abundant. For the millions who visited, one fact stood out. The little island of Britain —England, Wales, and Scotland—was the "work-shop of the world." It alone produced two-thirds of the world's coal and more than half of its iron and cotton cloth. More generally, it has been carefully estimated that, in 1860, Britain produced a truly remarkable 20 percent of the entire world's output of industrial goods, whereas it had pro-duced only about 2 percent of the world total

in 1750.[2] Experiencing revolutionary industrial change, Britain became the first industrial nation (Map 22.2).

As the British economy significantly increased its production of manufactured goods, the gross na-tional product (GNP) rose roughly fourfold at con-stant prices between 1780 and 1851. In other words, the British people increased their wealth and their national income dramatically. At the same time, the population of Great Britain boomed, growing from about 9 million in 1780 to almost 21 million in 1851. Thus growing numbers con-sumed much of the increase in total production. According to one recent study, average consump-tion per person increased by only 75 percent be-tween 1780 and 1851, as the growth in the total

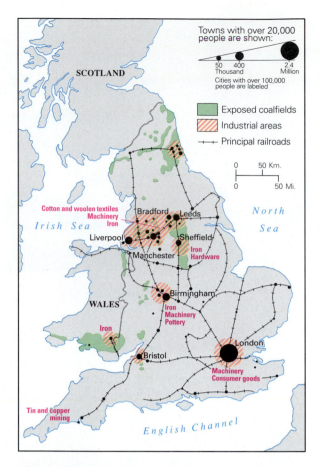

MAP 22.2 The Industrial Revolution in England, ca 1850 Industry concentrated in the rapidly growing cities of the north and the midlands, where rich coal and iron deposits were in close proximity.

population ate up a large part of the fourfold increase in gross national product in those years.[3]

Although the question is still debated, many economic historians now believe that rapid population growth in Great Britain was not harmful because it facilitated industrial expansion. More people meant a more mobile labor force, with a wealth of young workers in need of employment and ready to go where the jobs were. Contemporaries were much less optimistic. In his famous and influential *Essay on the Principle of Population* (1798), Thomas Malthus (1766–1834) argued that population would always tend to grow faster than the food supply. In Malthus's opinion, the only hope of warding off such "positive checks" to population growth as war, famine, and disease was "prudential restraint." That is, young men and women had to limit the growth of population by the old tried-and-

true means of marrying late in life. But Malthus was not optimistic about this possibility. The powerful attraction of the sexes would cause most people to marry early and have many children.

The wealthy English stockbroker and leading economist David Ricardo (1772–1823) coldly spelled out the pessimistic implications of Malthus's thought. Ricardo's depressing "iron law of wages" posited that, because of the pressure of population growth, wages would always sink to the subsistence level. That is, wages would be just high enough to keep the workers from starving. With Malthus and Ricardo setting the tone, there is little wonder that economics was soon dubbed "the dismal science."

Malthus, Ricardo, and their many followers were proved wrong—in the long run. However, as the great economist Keynes quipped in the Great Depression of the 1930s, "we are all dead in the long run." Those who lived through the Industrial Revolution could not see the long run in advance. As modern quantitative studies show, until the 1820s, or even the 1840s, contemporary observers might reasonably conclude that the economy and the total population were racing neck and neck, with the outcome very much in doubt. The closeness of the race added to the difficulties inherent in the unprecedented journey toward industrial civilization.

There was another problem as well. Perhaps workers, farmers, and ordinary people did not get their rightful share of the new wealth. Perhaps only the rich got richer, while the poor got poorer or made no progress. We will turn to this great issue after looking at the process of industrialization in continental countries in the nineteenth century.

INDUSTRIALIZATION IN CONTINENTAL EUROPE

The new technologies developed in the British Industrial Revolution were adopted rather slowly by businesses in continental Europe. Yet, by the end of the nineteenth century, several European countries, as well as the United States, had also industrialized their economies to a considerable but variable degree. This meant that the process of Western industrialization proceeded gradually, with uneven jerks and national (and regional) variations.

Scholars are still struggling to explain these variations, especially since good answers may offer valu-

The Crystal Palace   The Great Exhibition of 1851 attracted more than six million visitors, many of whom journeyed to London on the newly built railroads. Companies and countries displayed their products and juries awarded prizes in the strikingly modern Crystal Palace. *(Source: The Bridgeman Art Library)*

able lessons in our own time for poor countries seeking to improve their material condition through industrialization and economic development. The latest findings on the Western experience are encouraging. They suggest that there were alternative paths to the industrial world in the nineteenth century and that, today as then, there is no need to follow a rigid, predetermined British model.

National Variations

European industrialization, like most economic developments, requires some statistical analysis as part of the effort to understand it. Comparative data on industrial production in different countries over time help to give us an overview of what happened. One set of data, the work of a Swiss scholar, compares the level of industrialization on a per capita basis in several countries from 1750 to 1913. These data are far from perfect because there are gaps in the underlying records. But they reflect basic trends and are presented in Table 22.1 for closer study.

As the heading of Table 22.1 makes clear, this is a per capita comparison of levels of industrialization —a comparison of how much industrial product was available, on average, to each person in a given country in a given year. Therefore, all the numbers in Table 22.1 are expressed in terms of a single index number of 100, which equals the per capita level of industrial goods in Great Britain (and Ireland) in 1900. Every number is thus a percentage

	1750	1800	1830	1860	1880	1900	1913
Great Britain	10	16	25	64	87	100	115
Belgium	9	10	14	28	43	56	88
United States	4	9	14	21	38	69	126
France	9	9	12	20	28	39	59
Germany	8	8	9	15	25	52	85
Austria-Hungary	7	7	8	11	15	23	32
Italy	8	8	8	10	12	17	26
Russia	6	6	7	8	10	15	20

Note: All entries are based on an index value of 100, equal to the per capita level of industrialization in Great Britain in 1900.

Source: P. Bairoch, "International Industrialization Levels from 1750 to 1980," *Journal of European Economic History* 11 (Spring 1982): 294. Data for Great Britain are actually for the United Kingdom, thereby including Ireland with England, Wales, and Scotland.

TABLE 22.1 Per Capita Levels of Industrialization, 1750–1913

of the 1900 level in Great Britain and is directly comparable. The countries are listed in roughly the order that they began to use large-scale, power-driven technology.

What does this overview of European industrialization tell us? First, and very significantly, one sees that in 1750 all countries were fairly close together and that Britain was only slightly ahead of its archenemy, France. Second, Britain then opened up a noticeable lead over all continental countries by 1800, and that gap progressively widened as the British Industrial Revolution accelerated to 1830 and reached full maturity by 1860. The British level of per capita industrialization was twice the French level in 1830, for example, and more than three times the French level in 1860. All other large countries (except the United States) had fallen even further behind Britain than France had at both dates. Sophisticated quantitative history confirms the primacy and relative rapidity of Britain's Industrial Revolution.

Third, variations in the timing and in the extent of industrialization in the continental powers and the United States are also apparent. Belgium, independent in 1831 and rich in iron and coal, led in adopting Britain's new technology. France developed factory production more gradually, and most historians now detect no burst in French mechanization and no acceleration in the growth of overall

industrial output that may accurately be called revolutionary. They stress instead France's relatively good pattern of early industrial growth, which has been unjustly tarnished by the spectacular rise of Germany and the United States after 1860. By 1913 Germany was rapidly closing in on Britain, while the United States had already passed the first industrial nation in per capita production.

Finally, all European states (as well as the United States, Canada, and Japan) managed to raise per capita industrial levels in the nineteenth century. These continent-wide increases stood in stark contrast to the large and tragic decreases that occurred at the same time in most non-Western countries, and most notably in China and India. European countries industrialized to a greater or lesser extent even as most of the non-Western world *de*industrialized. Thus differential rates of wealth- and power-creating industrial development, which heightened disparities within Europe, also greatly magnified existing inequalities between Europe and the rest of the world. We shall return to this momentous change in Chapter 26.

The Challenge of Industrialization

The different patterns of industrial development suggest that the process of industrialization was far from automatic. Indeed, building modern industry was an awesome challenge. To be sure, the eighteenth century was throughout Europe an era of agricultural improvement, population increase, expanding foreign trade, and growing cottage industry. England led in these developments, but other countries participated in the general trend. Thus, when the pace of English industry began to accelerate in the 1780s, continental businesses began to adopt the new methods as they proved their profitability. English industry enjoyed clear superiority, but at first the Continent was not very far behind.

By 1815, however, the situation was quite different. In spite of wartime difficulties, English industry maintained the momentum of the 1780s and continued to grow and improve between 1789 and 1815. On the Continent, the unending political and economic upheavals that began with the French Revolution had another effect. They disrupted trade, created runaway inflation, and fostered social anxiety. War severed normal communications between England and the Continent, severely handicapping continental efforts to use new British machinery and technology. Moreover, the years from 1789 to 1815 were, even for the privileged French economy, a time of "national catastrophe"—in the graphic words of a leading French scholar.[4] Thus, whatever the French Revolution and the Napoleonic era meant politically, economically and industrially they meant that France and the rest of Europe were further behind Britain in 1815 than in 1789.

This widening gap made it more difficult if not impossible for other countries to follow the British pattern in energy and industry after 1815. Above all, in the newly mechanized industries British goods were being produced very economically, and these goods had come to dominate world markets completely while the continental states were absorbed in war between 1792 and 1815. Continental firms had little hope of competing with mass-produced British goods in foreign markets for a long time. In addition, British technology had become so advanced and complicated that very few engineers or skilled technicians outside England understood it. Moreover, the technology of steam power had grown much more expensive. It involved large investments in the iron and coal industries and, after 1830, required the existence of railroads, which were very costly. Continental business people had great difficulty finding the large

sums of money the new methods demanded, and there was a shortage of laborers accustomed to working in factories. Landowners and government officials were often so suspicious of the new form of industry and the changes it brought that they did little at first to encourage it. All these disadvantages slowed the spread of modern industry (Map 22.3).

After 1815, however, when continental countries began to face up to the British challenge, they had at least three important advantages. First, most continental countries had a rich tradition of putting-out enterprise, merchant-capitalists, and skilled urban artisans. Such a tradition gave continental firms the ability to adapt and survive in the face of new market conditions. Second, continental capitalists did not need to develop, ever so slowly and expensively, their own advanced technology. Instead, they could simply "borrow" the new methods developed in Great Britain, as well as engineers and some of the financial resources they lacked. European countries like France and Russia also had a third asset that many non-Western areas lacked in the nineteenth century. They had strong independent governments, which did not fall under foreign political control. These governments could fashion economic policies to serve their own interests, as they proceeded to do. They would eventually use the power of the state to promote the growth of industry and catch up with Britain.

Agents of Industrialization

The British realized the great value of their technical discoveries and tried to keep their secrets to themselves. Until 1825 it was illegal for artisans and skilled mechanics to leave Britain; until 1843 the export of textile machinery and other equipment was forbidden. Many talented, ambitious workers, however, slipped out of the country illegally and introduced the new methods abroad.

One such man was William Cockerill, a Lancashire carpenter. He and his sons began building cotton-spinning equipment in French-occupied Belgium in 1799. In 1817 the most famous son, John Cockerill, purchased the old summer palace of the deposed bishops of Liège in southern Belgium. Cockerill converted the palace into a large industrial enterprise, which produced machinery, steam engines, and then railway locomotives. He also established modern ironworks and coal mines.

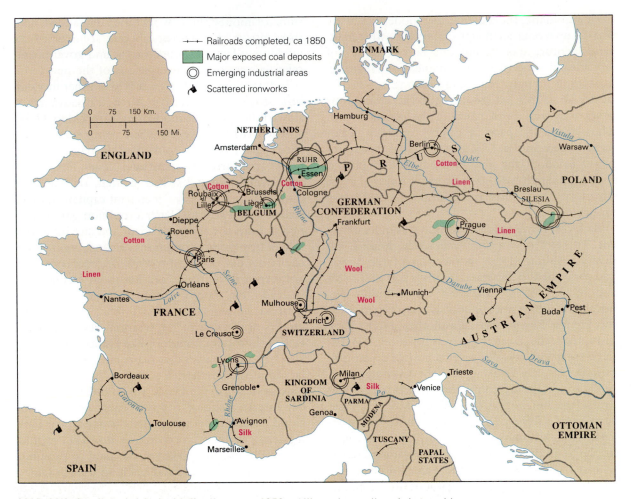

MAP 22.3 Continental Industrialization, ca 1850   Although continental countries were beginning to make progress by 1850, they still lagged far behind England. For example, continental railroad building was still in an early stage, whereas the English rail system was essentially complete.

Cockerill's plants in the Liège area became an industrial nerve center, continually gathering new information and transmitting it across Europe. Many skilled British workers came, illegally, to work for Cockerill, and some went on to found their own companies throughout Europe. Newcomers brought the latest plans and secrets, so that Cockerill could boast that, ten days after an industrial advance occurred in Britain, he knew all about it in Belgium. Thus, British technicians and skilled workers were a powerful force in the spread of early industrialization.

Another agent of industrialization was Fritz Harkort, a pioneer in the German machinery industry. Serving in England as a Prussian army officer during the Napoleonic wars, Harkort was impressed and enchanted with what he saw. He concluded that Germany had to match all these English achievements as quickly as possible. Setting up shop in an abandoned castle in the still-tranquil Ruhr Valley, Harkort felt an almost religious calling to build steam engines and become the "Watt of Germany."

Harkort's basic idea was simple, but it was enormously difficult to carry out. Lacking skilled laborers to do the job, Harkort turned to England for experienced, though expensive, mechanics. He could not be choosy, and he longed for the day when he could afford to replace the haughty foreigners with his fellow Germans. Getting materials also posed a great problem. He had to import the thick iron boilers that he needed from England at great cost. Moreover, German roads were so bad that steam engines had to be built at the works, completely dismantled and shipped piece by piece to the buyer, and then reassembled by Harkort's technicians. In spite of all these problems, Harkort built and sold engines, winning fame and praise. His ambitious efforts over sixteen years also resulted in large financial losses for himself and his partners, and in 1832 he was forced out of his company by his financial backers, who cut back operations to reduce losses. His career illustrates both the great efforts of a few important business leaders to duplicate the British achievement and the difficulty of the task.

Entrepreneurs like Harkort were obviously exceptional. Most continental businesses adopted factory technology slowly, and handicraft methods lived on. Indeed, as recent research on France has shown, continental industrialization usually brought substantial but uneven expansion of handicraft industry in both rural and urban areas for a time. Artisan production of luxury items grew in France, as the rising income of the international middle class created foreign demand for silk scarfs, embroidered needlework, perfumes, and fine wines.

Support from the government often helped business people in continental countries to overcome some of their difficulties. Tariff protection was one such support. For example, after Napoleon's wars ended in 1815, France was suddenly flooded with cheaper and better English goods. The French government responded by laying high tariffs on many English imports, in order to protect the French economy. After 1815 continental governments bore the cost of building roads and canals to improve transportation, and they also bore to a significant extent the cost of building railroads.

The career of the German journalist and thinker Friedrich List (1789–1846) reflects government's greater role in industrialization on the Continent than in England. List considered the growth of modern industry of the utmost importance because manufacturing was a primary means of increasing

A Silesian Ironworks, 1841   This plant is using the new British method of smelting iron with coke. Silesia and the Ruhr region emerged as the main centers of German heavy industry in the nineteenth century, but that development was only beginning when this picture was painted. *(Source: Deutsches Museum Munich)*

people's well-being and relieving their poverty. Moreover, List was a dedicated nationalist. He wrote that the "wider the gap between the backward and advanced nations becomes, the more dangerous it is to remain behind." For an agricultural nation was not only poor but weak, increasingly unable to defend itself and maintain its political independence. To promote industry was to defend the nation.

The practical policy List focused on in articles and in his *National System of Political Economy* (1841) was the tariff. He supported the formation of a customs union, or *Zollverein,* among the separate German states. Such a tariff union came into being in 1834. It allowed goods to move between the German member states without tariffs, and a single uniform tariff was erected against all other nations. List wanted a high protective tariff, which would encourage infant industries, allowing them to develop and eventually to hold their own against their more advanced British counterparts. List denounced the English doctrine of free trade as little more than England's attempt "to make the rest of the world, like the Hindus, its serfs in all industrial and commercial relations." By the 1840s List's ideas were increasingly popular in Germany and elsewhere.

Banks, like governments, also played a larger and more creative role on the Continent than in England. Previously, almost all banks in Europe had been private, organized as secretive partnerships. Such banks were content to deal with a few rich clients and a few big merchants. They avoided industry. In the 1830s two important Belgian banks pioneered in a new direction. They operated as big corporations with many stockholders, large and small. Thus their financial resources were large. The banks were able to use that money to develop industrial companies. They became, in short, industrial banks.

Similar banks became important in France and Germany in the 1850s. They established and developed many railroads and many companies working in heavy industry. The most famous such bank was the Crédit Mobilier of Paris, founded by Isaac and Émile Pereire, two young Jewish journalists from Bordeaux. The Crédit Mobilier advertised extensively. It used the savings of thousands of small investors, as well as the resources of big ones. The activities of the bank were far-reaching; it built railroads all over France and Europe. As Émile Pereire had said in 1835, "It is not enough to outline

gigantic programs on paper. I must write my ideas on the earth."

Industrial banks like the Crédit Mobilier mobilized the savings of thousands of small investors and invested those savings in industry and transportation, particularly in the 1850s. In doing so, the directors of these banks helped their countries find the capital needed for industrialization. They also often made themselves very wealthy.

CAPITAL AND LABOR

Industrial development brought new social relations and intensified problems between capital and labor. A new group of factory owners and industrial capitalists arose. These men strengthened the wealth and size of the middle class, which had previously been made up mainly of merchants and professional people. The nineteenth century became the golden age of the middle class. Modern industry also created a much larger group, the factory workers. For the first time, large numbers of men and women came together under one roof to work with complicated machinery for major capitalists and large companies. What was the nature of relations between these two new groups—capital and labor? Did the new industrial middle class ruthlessly exploit the workers, as Karl Marx and others have charged?

The New Class of Factory Owners

Early industrialists operated in a highly competitive economic system. As the careers of Watt and Harkort illustrate, there were countless production problems, and success and large profits were by no means certain. Manufacturers, therefore, waged a constant battle to cut their production costs and stay afloat. Much of the profit had to go back into the business for new and better machinery. "Dragged on by the frenzy of this terrible life," according to one of the dismayed critics, the struggling manufacturer had "no time for niceties. He must conquer or die, make a fortune or drown himself."[5]

The early industrialists came from a variety of backgrounds. Many, like Harkort, were from well-established merchant families, who provided capital and contacts. Others, like Watt and Cockerill, were of modest means, especially in the early days. Artisans and skilled workers of exceptional ability had unparalleled opportunities. The ethnic and religious groups that had been discriminated against in the traditional occupations controlled by the landed aristocracy jumped at the new chances. Quakers and Scots were tremendously important in England; Protestants and Jews dominated banking in Catholic France. Many of the industrialists were newly rich, and, not surprisingly, they were very proud and self-satisfied.

As factories grew larger, opportunities declined, at least in well-developed industries. It became considerably harder for a gifted but poor young mechanic to end up as a wealthy manufacturer. Formal education became more important as a means of advancement, and formal education at the advanced level was expensive. In England by 1830 and in France and Germany by 1860, leading industrialists were more likely to have inherited their well-established enterprises, and they were financially much more secure than their fathers and grandfathers. They were also aware of a greater gap between themselves and their workers.

The New Factory Workers

The social consequences of the Industrial Revolution have long been hotly debated. The condition of English workers during the transformation has always generated the most controversy among historians, because England was the first country to industrialize and because the social consequences seem harshest there. Before 1850, other countries had not proceeded very far with industrialization, and almost everyone agrees that the economic conditions of European workers improved after 1850. The countries that followed England were able to benefit from English experience in social as well as technical matters. Thus the experience of English workers to about 1850 deserves special attention. (Industrial growth also promoted rapid urbanization with its own awesome problems, as will be shown in Chapter 24.)

From the beginning, the Industrial Revolution in England had its critics. Among the first were the romantic poets. William Blake (1757–1827) called the early factories "satanic mills" and protested against the hard life of the London poor. William Wordsworth (1770–1850) lamented the destruction of the rural way of life and the pollution of the

land and water. Some handicraft workers—notably the Luddites, who attacked whole factories in northern England in 1812 and after—smashed the new machines, which they believed were putting them out of work. Doctors and reformers wrote eloquently of problems in the factories and new towns, while Malthus and Ricardo (see page 702) concluded that workers would earn only enough to stay alive.

This pessimistic view was accepted and reinforced by Friedrich Engels (1820–1895), the future revolutionary and colleague of Karl Marx. After studying conditions in northern England, this young middle-class German published in 1844 *The Condition of the Working Class in England,* a blistering indictment of the middle classes. "At the bar of world opinion," he wrote, "I charge the English middle classes with mass murder, wholesale robbery, and all the other crimes in the calendar."[6] The new poverty of industrial workers was worse than the old poverty of cottage workers and agricultural laborers, according to Engels. The culprit was industrial capitalism, with its relentless competition and constant technical change. Engels's charge of middle-class exploitation and increasing worker poverty was embellished by Marx and later socialists. It was extremely influential.

Meanwhile, other observers believed that conditions were improving for the working class. Andrew Ure wrote in 1835 in his study of the cotton industry that conditions in most factories were not harsh and were even quite good. Edwin Chadwick, a great and conscientious government official, well acquainted with the problems of the working class, concluded that the "whole mass of the laboring community" was increasingly able "to buy more of the necessities and minor luxuries of life."[7] Nevertheless, if all the contemporary assessments were counted up, those who thought conditions were getting worse for working people would probably be the majority.

In an attempt to go beyond the contradictory judgments of contemporaries, some historians have looked at different kinds of sources. Statistical evidence is one such source. If working people suffered a great economic decline, as Engels and later socialists asserted, then they must have bought less and less food, clothing, and other necessities as time went on. The purchasing power of the working person's wages must have declined drastically.

Scholarly statistical studies, which continue to multiply rapidly in an age of easy calculations with computer technology, have weakened the idea that the condition of the working class got much worse with industrialization. On the other hand, the most recent studies also confirm the view that the early years of the Industrial Revolution were hard ones for English and Scottish workers. There was little or no increase in the purchasing power of the average British worker from about 1780 to about 1820. The years from 1792 to 1815, a period of almost constant warfare with France, were particularly difficult. Food prices rose faster than wages, and the living conditions of the laboring poor declined. Only after 1820, and especially after 1840, did real wages rise substantially, so that the average worker earned and consumed roughly 50 percent more in real terms in 1850 than in 1770.[8] In short, there was considerable economic improvement for workers throughout Great Britain by 1850, but that improvement was hard-won and slow in coming.

This important conclusion must be qualified, though. Increased purchasing power meant more goods, but it did not necessarily mean greater happiness. More goods may have provided meager compensation for work that was more dangerous and monotonous, for example. Also, statistical studies do not say anything about how the level of unemployment may have risen, for the simple reason that there are no good unemployment statistics from this period. Furthermore, the hours in the average workweek increased; to an unknown extent, workers earned more simply because they worked more. Finally, the wartime decline was of great importance. The war years were formative years for the new factory labor force. They were also some of the hardest yet experienced. They colored the early experience of modern industrial life in somber tones.

Another way to consider workers' standard of living is to look at the goods that they purchased. Again the evidence is somewhat contradictory. Speaking generally, workers ate somewhat more food of higher nutritional quality as the Industrial Revolution progressed, except during wartime. Diets became more varied; people ate more potatoes, dairy products, fruits, and vegetables. Clothing improved, but housing for working people probably deteriorated somewhat. In short, per capita use of specific goods supports the position that the standard of living of the working classes rose, at least moderately, after the long wars with France.

Conditions of Work

What about working conditions? Did workers eventually earn more only at the cost of working longer and harder? Were workers exploited harshly by the new factory owners?

The first factories were cotton mills, which began functioning along rivers and streams in the 1770s. Cottage workers, accustomed to the putting-out system, were reluctant to work in factories even when they received relatively good wages, because factory work was different from what they were used to and unappealing. In the factory, workers had to keep up with the machine and follow its tempo. They had to show up every day and work long, monotonous hours. Factory workers had to adjust their daily lives to the shrill call of the factory whistle.

Cottage workers were not used to that kind of life and discipline. All members of the family worked hard and long, but in spurts, setting their own pace. They could interrupt their work when they wanted to. Women and children could break up their long hours of spinning with other tasks. On Saturday afternoon the head of the family delivered the week's work to the merchant-manufacturer and got paid. Saturday night was a time of relaxation and drinking, especially for the men. Recovering from his hangover on Tuesday, the weaver bent to his task on Wednesday and then worked frantically to meet his deadline on Saturday. Like some students today, he might "pull an all-nighter" on Thursday or Friday in order to get his work in.

Also, early factories resembled English poorhouses, where totally destitute people went to live on welfare. Some poorhouses were industrial prisons, where the inmates had to work in order to receive their food and lodging. The similarity between large brick factories and large stone poorhouses increased the cottage workers' fear of factories and their hatred of factory discipline.

It was cottage workers' reluctance to work in factories that prompted the early cotton mill owners to turn to abandoned and pauper children for their labor. As we have seen (page 695), they contracted with local officials to employ large numbers of these children, who had no say in the matter. Pauper children were often badly treated and terribly overworked in the mills, as they were when they were apprenticed as chimney sweeps, market girls, shoemakers, and so forth. In the eighteenth cen-

Cotton Mill Workers Family members often worked side by side in industry. Here women and children are combing raw cotton and drawing it into loose strands called rovings, which will then be spun into fine thread. *(Source: The Mansell Collection)*

tury, semiforced child labor seemed necessary and was socially accepted. From our modern point of view, it was cruel exploitation and a blot on the record of the new industrial system.

By 1790 the early pattern was rapidly changing. The use of pauper apprentices was in decline, and in 1802 it was forbidden by Parliament. Many more factories were being built, mainly in urban areas, where they could use steam rather than waterpower and attract a work force more easily than in the countryside. The need for workers was great. Indeed, people came from near and far to work in the cities, both as factory workers and as laborers, builders, and domestic servants. Yet, as they took these new jobs, working people did not simply give in to a system of labor that had formerly repelled them. Rather, they helped modify the system by carrying over old, familiar working traditions.

For one thing, they often came to the mills and the mines as family units. This was how they had worked on farms and in the putting-out system.

The mill or mine owner bargained with the head of the family and paid him or her for the work of the whole family. In the cotton mills, children worked for their mothers or fathers, collecting wastes and "piecing" broken threads together. In the mines, children sorted coal and worked the ventilation equipment. Their mothers hauled coal in the narrow tunnels below the surface, while their fathers hewed with pick and shovel at the face of the seam.

The preservation of the family as an economic unit in the factories from the 1790s on made the new surroundings more tolerable, both in Great Britain and in other countries during the early stages of industrialization. Parents disciplined their children, making firm measures socially acceptable, and directed their upbringing. The presence of the whole family meant that children and adults worked the same long hours (twelve-hour shifts were normal in cotton mills in 1800). In the early years, some very young children were employed solely to keep the family together. Jedediah Strutt, for example, believed children should be at least ten years old to work in his mills, but he reluctantly employed seven-year-olds to satisfy their parents. Adult workers were not particularly interested in limiting the minimum working age or hours of their children, as long as they worked side by side. Only when technical changes threatened to place control and discipline in the hands of impersonal managers and foremen did they protest against inhuman conditions in the name of their children.

Some enlightened employers and social reformers in Parliament definitely felt otherwise. They argued that more humane standards were necessary, and they used widely circulated parliamentary reports to influence public opinion. For example, Robert Owen (1771–1858), a very successful manufacturer in Scotland, testified in 1816 before an investigating committee on the basis of his experience. He stated that "very strong facts" demonstrated that employing children under ten years of age as factory workers was "injurious to the children, and not beneficial to the proprietors." The parliamentary committee asked him to explain, and the testimony proceeded as follows:

"Seventeen years ago, a number of individuals, with myself, purchased the New Lanark establishment from the late Mr Dale, of Glasgow. At that period I find that there were 500 children, who had been taken from poor-houses, chiefly in Edinburgh. . . . The hours of work at that time were thirteen, inclusive of meal times, and an hour and a half was allowed for meals. I very soon discovered that although those children were very well fed, well clothed, well lodged, and very great care taken of them when out of the mills, their growth and their minds were materially injured by being employed at those ages within the cotton mills for eleven and a half hours per day. . . . Their limbs were generally deformed, their growth was stunted, and although one of the best school-masters upon the old plan was engaged to instruct those children every night, in general they made but a very slow progress, even in learning the common alphabet. . . ."

"Do you think the age of ten the best period for the admission of children into full and constant employment for ten or eleven hours per day, within woollen, cotton, and other mills or manufactories?"

"I do not."

"What other period would you recommend for their full admission to full work?"

"Twelve years."[9]

Owen's testimony rang true because he had already raised the age of employment in his mills and was promoting education for young children. Workers also provided graphic testimony at such hearings, as the reformers pressed Parliament to pass corrective laws. They scored some important successes.

Their first major accomplishment was the Factory Act of 1833. It limited the factory workday for children between nine and thirteen to eight hours

Girl Dragging Coal Tubs   Published by reformers in Parliament in 1842, this picture shocked public opinion and contributed to the Mines Act of 1842. *(Source: The British Library)*

and that of adolescents between fourteen and eighteen to twelve hours, although the act made no effort to regulate hours of work for children at home or in small businesses. The law also prohibited the factory employment of children under nine; they were to be enrolled in the elementary schools factory owners were required to establish. The employment of children declined rapidly. Thus the Factory Act broke the pattern of whole families working together in the factory because efficiency required standardized shifts for all workers.

Ties of blood and kinship were important in other ways in Great Britain in the formative years between about 1790 and 1840. Many manufacturers and builders hired workers not directly but through subcontractors. They paid the subcontractors on the basis of what the subcontractors and their crews produced—for smelting so many tons of pig iron or moving so much dirt or gravel for a canal or roadbed. Subcontractors in turn hired and fired their own workers, many of whom were friends and relations. The subcontractor might be as harsh as the greediest capitalist, but the relationship between subcontractor and work crew was close and personal. This kind of personal relationship had traditionally existed in cottage industry and in urban crafts, and it was more acceptable to many workers than impersonal factory discipline. This system also provided people an easy way to find a job. Even today, a friend or relative who is a supervisor is frequently worth a hundred formal application forms.

Ties of kinship were particularly important for newcomers, who often traveled considerable distances to find work. Many urban workers in Great Britain were from Ireland. Forced out of rural Ireland by population growth and deteriorating economic conditions from 1817 on, Irish in search of jobs could not be choosy; they took what they could get. As early as 1824, most of the workers in the Glasgow cotton mills were Irish; in 1851 one-sixth of the population of Liverpool was Irish. Even when Irish workers were not related directly by blood, they were held together by ethnic and religious ties. Like other immigrant groups elsewhere, they worked together, formed their own neighborhoods, and not only survived but thrived.

It is important to remember that many kinds of employment changed slowly during and after the Industrial Revolution in Great Britain. Within industry itself, the pattern of small-scale production with artisan skills lived on in many trades, even as

some others were revolutionized. For example, as in the case of cotton and coal, the British iron industry was completely dominated by large-scale capitalist firms by 1850. One iron magnate in Wales employed six thousand workers in his plant, and many large ironworks had over a thousand people on their payroll. Yet the firms that fashioned iron into small metal goods, such as tools, tableware, and toys, employed on average fewer than ten workers, who used time-honored handicraft skills. Only gradually after 1850 did some owners find ways to reorganize such handicraft industries with new machines and new patterns of work. The survival of small workshops and artisan crafts gave many workers an alternative to factory employment.

Old, familiar jobs outside industry provided other alternatives for individual workers. In 1850 more British people still worked on farms than in any other occupation. The second largest occupation was domestic service, which counted more than a million household servants, 90 percent of whom were women. Thus many traditional jobs lived on, and this also helped ease the transition to industrial civilization.

In Great Britain and in other countries later on, workers gradually built a labor movement to improve working conditions and to serve their needs. In 1799, partly in panicked reaction to the French Revolution, Parliament had passed the Combination Acts outlawing unions and strikes. These acts were widely disregarded by workers. Societies of skilled factory workers organized unions, as printers, papermakers, carpenters, and other such craftsmen had long since done. The unions sought to control the number of skilled workers, limit apprenticeship to members' own children, and bargain with owners over wages. They were not afraid to strike; there was, for example, a general strike of adult cotton spinners in Manchester in 1810. In the face of widespread union activity, Parliament repealed the Combination Acts in 1824, and unions were tolerated though not fully accepted after 1825.

The next stage in the development of the British trade-union movement was the attempt to create a single large national union. This effort was led not so much by working people as by social reformers like Robert Owen. Owen, the self-made cotton manufacturer quoted earlier, had pioneered in industrial relations by combining firm discipline with concern for the health, safety, and hours of his

"Be United and Industrious" This handsome membership certificate of the "new model" Amalgamated Society of Engineers exalts the nobility of skilled labor and the labor movement. Union members are shown rejecting the call of Mars, the God of War, and accepting well-deserved honors from the Goddess of Peace. Other figures represent the strength of union solidarity, famous English inventors, and the trades of the members. *(Source: E. T. Archive)*

workers. After 1815 he experimented with cooperative and socialist communities, including one at New Harmony, Indiana. Then, in 1834, Owen organized one of the largest and most visionary of the early national unions, the Grand National Consolidated Trades Union. When this and other grandiose schemes collapsed, the British labor movement moved once again after 1851 in the direction of craft unions. The most famous of these "new model unions" was the Amalgamated Society of Engineers. These unions won real benefits for members by fairly conservative means and thus became an accepted part of the industrial scene.

British workers also engaged in direct political activity in defense of their own interests. After the collapse of Owen's national trade union, a great deal of the energy of working people went into the Chartist movement, whose goal was political democracy. The key Chartist demand—that all men be given the right to vote—became the great hope of millions of aroused people. Workers were also active in campaigns to limit the workday in the factories to ten hours and to permit duty-free importation of wheat into Great Britain to secure cheap bread. Thus working people played an active role in shaping the new industrial system. Clearly, they were neither helpless victims nor passive beneficiaries.

The Sexual Division of Labor

The era of the Industrial Revolution witnessed major changes in the sexual division of labor. In preindustrial Europe most people generally worked in family units. By tradition, certain jobs were defined by sex—women and girls for milking and spinning, men and boys for plowing and weaving. But many tasks might go to either sex, because particular circumstances dictated a family's response in its battle for economic survival. This pattern of family employment carried over into early factories and subcontracting, but it collapsed as child labor was restricted and new attitudes emerged. A different sexual division of labor gradually arose to take its place. The man emerged as the family's primary wage earner, while the woman found only limited job opportunities. Generally denied good jobs at good wages in the growing urban economy, women were expected to concentrate on unpaid housework, child care, and craft work at home.

This new pattern of "separate spheres" had several aspects. First, all studies agree that married women were much less likely to work full-time for wages outside the house after the first child arrived, although they often earned small amounts doing putting-out handicrafts at home and taking in boarders. Second, when married women did work for wages outside the house, they usually came from the poorest, most desperate families, where the husbands were poorly paid, sick, unemployed, or missing. Third, these poor married (or widowed) women were joined by legions of young unmarried women, who worked full-time but only in certain jobs. Fourth, all women were generally confined to low-paying, dead-end jobs. Virtually no occupation open to women paid a living wage—a wage sufficient for a person to live independently. Men predominated in the better-paying, more promising employments. Evolving gradually as family labor declined, but largely in place in the urban sector of the British economy by 1850, the new sexual division of labor constituted a major development in the history of women and of the family.

If the reorganization of paid work along gender lines is widely recognized, there is as yet no agreement on its causes. One school of scholars sees little connection with industrialization and finds the answer in the deeply ingrained sexist attitudes of a "patriarchal tradition," which predated the economic transformation. These scholars stress the role of male-dominated craft unions in denying women access to good jobs and in reducing them to unpaid maids dependent on their husbands. Other scholars, believing that the gender roles of women and men can vary enormously with time and culture, look more to a combination of economic and biological factors in order to explain why the mass of women were either unwilling or unable to halt the emergence of a sex-segregated division of labor.

Three ideas stand out in this more recent interpretation. First, the new and unfamiliar discipline of the clock and the machine was especially hard on married women. Above all, relentless factory discipline conflicted with child care in a way that labor on the farm or in the cottage had not. A woman operating ear-splitting spinning machinery could mind a child of seven or eight working beside her (until such work was outlawed), but she could no longer pace herself through pregnancy, even though overwork during pregnancy heightened the already high risks of childbirth. Nor could a woman breast-feed her baby on the job, although breast-feeding saved lives. Thus a working-class woman had strong incentives to concentrate on child care within her home, if her family could afford it.

Second, running a household in conditions of primitive urban poverty was an extremely demanding job in its own right. There were no supermarkets or discount department stores, no running water or public transportation. Everything had to be done on foot. As in the poor sections of many inner cities today, shopping and feeding the family constituted a never-ending challenge. The woman marched from one tiny shop to another, dragging her tired children (for who was to watch them?) and struggling valiantly with heavy sacks, tricky shopkeepers, and walk-up apartments. Yet another brutal job outside the house—a "second shift"—had limited appeal for the average married woman. Thus women might well accept the emerging division of labor as the best available strategy for family survival in the industrializing society.[10]

Third, why were the women who did work for wages outside the home segregated and confined to certain "women's jobs"? No doubt the desire of males to monopolize the best opportunities and hold women down provides part of the answer. Yet, as Jane Humphries has argued, sex-segregated employment also formed a collective response to the new industrial system. Previously, at least in theory, young people worked under a watchful parental eye. The growth of factories and mines brought unheard-of opportunities for girls and boys to mix on the job, free of familial supervision. Continuing to mix after work, they were "more likely to form liaisons, initiate courtships, and respond to advances."[11] Such intimacy also led to more unplanned pregnancies and fueled the illegitimacy explosion that had begun in the late eighteenth century and that gathered force until at least 1850 (see pages 631–632). Thus segregation of jobs by gender was partly an effort by older people to help control the sexuality of working-class youth.

Investigations into the British coal industry before 1842 provide a graphic example of this concern. The middle-class men leading the inquiry often failed to appreciate the physical effort of the girls and women who dragged with belt and chain the unwheeled carts of coal along narrow underground passages. But they professed horror at the sight of girls and women working without shirts, which was a common practice because of the heat, and they quickly assumed the prevalence of licentious sex with the male miners, who also wore very little clothing. In fact, most girls and married women worked for related males in a family unit that provided considerable protection and restraint. Yet many witnesses from the working class believed that "blackguardism and debauchery" were common and that "They are best out of the pits, the lasses." Some miners stressed particularly the sexual danger of letting girls work past puberty. As one explained,

"I consider it a scandal for girls to work in the pits. Till they are 12 or 14 they may work very well but after that

it's an abomination. . . . The work of the pit does not hurt them, it is the effect on their morals that I complain of, and after 14 they should not be allowed to go. . . . [A]fter that age it is dreadful for them."[12]

The Mines Act of 1842 prohibited underground work for all women, as well as for boys under ten.

Some women who had to support themselves protested against being excluded from coal mining, which paid higher wages than most other jobs open to women. But provided they were part of families that could manage economically, the girls and the women who had worked underground were generally pleased with the law. In explaining her satisfaction in 1844, one mother of four provided a real insight into why many women accepted the emerging sexual division of labor:

While working in the pit I was worth to my [miner] husband seven shillings a week, out of which we had to pay 2½ shillings to a woman for looking after the younger children. I used to take them to her house at 4 o'clock in the morning, out of their own beds, to put them into hers. Then there was one shilling a week for washing; besides, there was mending to pay for, and other things. The house was not guided. The other children broke things; they did not go to school when they were sent; they would be playing about, and get ill-used by other children, and their clothes torn. Then when I came home in the evening, everything was to do after the day's labor, and I was so tired I had no heart for it; no fire lit, nothing cooked, no water fetched, the house dirty, and nothing comfortable for my husband. It is all far better now, and I wouldn't go down again.[13]

Industrial Revolution in England greatly increased output in certain radically altered industries, stimulated the large handicraft and commercial sectors, and speeded up overall economic growth. Rugged Scotland industrialized at least as fast as England, and Great Britain became the first industrial nation. By 1850 the level of British per capita industrial production surpassed continental levels by a growing margin, and Britain savored a near monopoly in world markets for mass-produced goods. Thus continental countries inevitably took rather different paths to the urban industrial society. They relied more on handicraft production in both towns and villages, and only in the 1840s did railroad construction begin to create a strong demand for iron, coal, and railway equipment that speeded up the process of industrialization.

The rise of modern industry had a profound impact on people and their lives. In the early stages Britain again led the way, experiencing in a striking manner the long-term social changes accompanying the economic transformation. Factory discipline and Britain's stern capitalist economy weighed heavily on working people, who, however, actively fashioned their destinies, refusing to be passive victims. Improvements in the standard of living came slowly, although they were substantial by 1850. The era of industrialization fostered new attitudes toward child labor, encouraged protective factory legislation, and called forth an assertive labor movement. It also promoted a more rigid division of roles and responsibilities within the family that was detrimental to women, another gradual but profound change of revolutionary proportions.

SUMMARY

Western society's industrial breakthrough grew out of a long process of economic and social change, in which the rise of capitalism, overseas expansion, and the growth of rural industry stood out as critical preparatory developments. Eventually taking the lead in all of these developments, and also profiting from stable government, abundant natural resources, and a flexible labor force, England experienced between roughly the 1780s and the 1850s an epoch-making transformation, one that is still aptly termed the Industrial Revolution.

Building on technical breakthroughs, power-driven equipment, and large-scale enterprise, the

NOTES

1. N. F. R. Crafts, *British Economic Growth During the Industrial Revolution* (Oxford: Oxford University Press, 1985), p. 32. These estimates are for Great Britain as a whole.
2. P. Bairoch, "International Industrialization Levels from 1750 to 1980," *Journal of European Economic History* 11 (Spring 1982): 269–333.
3. Crafts, pp. 45, 95–102.
4. M. Lévy-Leboyer, *Les banques européennes et l'industrialisation dans la première moitié du XIXe siècle* (Paris: Presses Universitaires de France, 1964), p. 29.
5. J. Michelet, *The People,* trans. with an introduction by J. P. McKay (Urbana: University of Illinois Press, 1973; original publication, 1846), p. 64.

6. F. Engels, *The Condition of the Working Class in England,* trans. and ed. W. O. Henderson and W. H. Chaloner (Stanford, Calif.: Stanford University Press, 1968), p. xxiii.
7. Quoted in W. A. Hayek, ed., *Capitalism and the Historians* (Chicago: University of Chicago Press, 1954), p. 126.
8. Crafts, p. 95.
9. Quoted in E. R. Pike, *"Hard Times": Human Documents of the Industrial Revolution* (New York: Praeger, 1966), p. 109.
10. See, especially, J. Brenner and M. Rama, "Rethinking Women's Oppression," *New Left Review* 144 (March–April 1984): 33–71, and sources cited there.
11. J. Humphries, " '. . . The Most Free from Objection . . .' The Sexual Division of Labor and Women's Work in Nineteenth-Century England," *Journal of Economic History* 47 (December 1987): 948.
12. Ibid., p. 941; Pike, p. 266.
13. Quoted in Pike, p. 208.

SUGGESTED READING

There is a vast and exciting literature on the Industrial Revolution. R. Cameron, *A Concise Economic History of the World* (1989), provides an introduction to the issues and has a carefully annotated bibliography. J. Goodman and K. Honeyman, *Gainful Pursuits: The Making of Industrial Europe, 1600–1914* (1988); D. S. Landes, *The Unbound Prometheus: Technological Change and Industrial Development in Western Europe from 1750 to the Present* (1969); and S. Pollard, *Peaceful Conquest: The Industrialization of Europe* (1981), are excellent general treatments of European industrial growth. These studies also suggest the range of issues and interpretations. M. Berg, *The Age of Manufactures: Industry, Innovation and Work in Britain, 1700–1820* (1985); P. Mathias, *The First Industrial Nation: An Economic History of Britain, 1700–1914* (1969); P. Mantoux, *The Industrial Revolution in the Eighteenth Century* (1961), admirably discuss the various aspects of the English breakthrough and offer good bibliographies, as does the work by Crafts mentioned in the Notes. W. Rostow, *The Stages of Economic Growth: A Non-Communist Manifesto* (1960), is a popular, provocative study.

H. Kirsch, *From Domestic Manufacturing to Industrial Revolution: The Case of the Rhineland Textile Districts* (1989), and M. Neufield, *The Skilled Metalworkers of Nuremberg: Craft and Class in the Industrial Revolution* (1985), examine the persistence and gradual transformation of handicraft techniques. R. Cameron brilliantly traces the spread of railroads and industry across Europe in *France and the Economic Development of Europe, 1800–1914* (1961). The works of A. S. Milward and S. B. Saul, *The Economic Development of Continental Europe, 1780–1870* (1973) and *The Development of the Economies of Continental Europe, 1850–1914* (1977), may be compared with J. Clapham's old-fashioned classic, *Economic Development of France and Germany* (1963). C. Kindleberger, *Economic Growth in France and Britain, 1851–1950* (1964), is a stimulating study, especially for those with some background in economics. Other important works in recent years on industrial developments are C. Tilly and E. Shorter, *Strikes in France, 1830–1848* (1974); D. Ringrose, *Transportation and Economic Stagnation in Spain, 1750–1850* (1970); L. Schofer, *The Formation of a Modern Labor Force* (1975), which focuses on the Silesian part of Germany; and W. Blackwell, *The Industrialization of Russia,* 2d ed. (1982). L. Moch, *Paths to the City: Regional Migration in Nineteenth-century France* (1983), and W. Schivelbusch, *Disenchanted Night: The Industrialization of Light in the Nineteenth Century* (1983), imaginatively analyze quite different aspects of industrialization's many consequences.

The debate between "optimists" and "pessimists" about the consequences of industrialization in England goes on. P. Taylor, ed., *The Industrial Revolution: Triumph or Disaster?* (1970), is a useful introduction to different viewpoints, while Hayek's collection of essays, cited in the Notes, stresses positive aspects. It is also fascinating to compare Friedrich Engels's classic condemnation, *The Condition of the Working Class in England,* with Andrew Ure's optimistic defense, *The Philosophy of Manufactures,* first published in 1835 and reprinted recently. E. P. Thompson continues and enriches the Engels tradition in *The Making of the English Working Class* (1963), an exciting book rich in detail and early working-class lore. E. R. Pike's documentary collection, *"Hard Times,"* cited in the Notes, provides fascinating insights into the lives of working people. An unorthodox but moving account of a doomed group is D. Bythell, *The Handloom Weavers* (1969). F. Klingender, *Art and the Industrial Revolution,* rev. ed. (1968), is justly famous, and M. Ignatieff, *A Just Measure of Pain* (1980), is an engrossing study of prisons during English industrialization. D. S. Landes, *Revolution in Time: Clocks and the Making of the Modern World* (1983), is a brilliant integration of industrial and cultural history.

Among general studies, G. S. R. Kitson Clark, *The Making of Victorian England* (1967), is particularly imaginative. A. Briggs, *Victorian People* (1955), provides an engrossing series of brief biographies. H. Ausubel discusses a major reformer in *John Bright* (1966), and B. Harrison skillfully illuminates the problem of heavy drinking in *Drink and the Victorians* (1971). The most famous contemporary novel dealing with the new industrial society is Charles Dickens's *Hard Times,* an entertaining but exaggerated story. *Mary Barton* and *North and South* by Elizabeth Gaskell are more realistic portrayals, and both are highly recommended.

23

Ideologies and Upheavals, 1815–1850

The momentous economic and political transformation of modern times began in the late eighteenth century with the Industrial Revolution in England and then the French Revolution. Until about 1815, these economic and political revolutions were separate, involving different countries and activities and proceeding at very different paces. The Industrial Revolution created the factory system and new groups of capitalists and industrial workers in northern England, but almost continuous warfare with France checked its spread to continental Europe. Meanwhile, England's ruling aristocracy suppressed all forms of political radicalism at home and joined with crowned heads abroad to oppose and eventually defeat revolutionary and Napoleonic France. The economic and political revolutions worked at cross-purposes and even neutralized each other.

After peace returned in 1815, the situation changed. Economic and political changes tended to fuse, reinforcing each other and bringing about what the historian Eric Hobsbawm has incisively called the "dual revolution." For instance, the growth of the industrial middle class encouraged the drive for representative government, while the demands of the French sans-culottes in 1793 and 1794 inspired many socialist thinkers. Gathering strength and threatening almost every aspect of the existing political and social framework, the dual revolution rushed on to alter completely first Europe and then the world. Much of world history in the last two centuries can be seen as the progressive unfolding of the dual revolution.

Yet three qualifications must be kept firmly in mind. In Europe in the nineteenth century, as in Asia and Africa in more recent times, the dual revolution was not some inexorable mechanical monster grinding peoples and cultures into a homogenized mass. The economic and political transformation it wrought was built on complicated histories, strong traditions, and highly diverse cultures. Radical change was eventually a constant, but the particular results varied enormously.

Nor should the strength of the old forces be underestimated. In central and eastern Europe especially, the traditional elites—the monarchs, noble landowners, and bureaucrats—long proved capable of defending their privileges and even of redirecting the dual revolution to serve their interests.

Finally, the dual revolution posed a tremendous intellectual challenge. The meanings of the economic, political, and social changes that were occurring, as well as the ways they could be shaped by human action, were anything but clear. These questions fascinated observers and stimulated new ideas and ideologies.

- What ideas did thinkers develop to describe and shape the transformation going on before their eyes?
- How did the artists and writers of the Romantic movement also reflect and influence changes in this era?
- How did the political revolution, derailed in France and resisted by European monarchs, eventually break out again after 1815?
- Why did the revolutionary surge triumph briefly in 1848, then fail almost completely?

These are the questions this chapter will explore.

THE PEACE SETTLEMENT

The eventual triumph of revolutionary economic and political forces was by no means certain in 1814. Quite the contrary. The conservative, aristocratic monarchies with their preindustrial armies and economies (Great Britain excepted) appeared firmly in control once again. France had been decisively defeated by the off-again, on-again alliance of Russia, Prussia, Austria, and Great Britain. That alliance had been strengthened and reaffirmed in March 1814, when the allies pledged not only to defeat France but to hold it in line for twenty years thereafter. The Quadruple Alliance had then forced Napoleon to abdicate in April 1814 and restored the Bourbon dynasty to the French throne (see page 687). But there were many other international questions outstanding, and the allies agreed to meet in Vienna to fashion a general peace settlement. Interrupted by Napoleon's desperate gamble during the Hundred Days, the allies concluded their negotiations at the Congress of Vienna after Napoleon's defeat at Waterloo.

Most people felt profound longing for peace. The great challenge for political leaders in 1814 was to construct a peace settlement that would last and not sow the seeds of another war. Their efforts were largely successful and contributed to a century

The Great Powers negotiated the main questions of the peace settlement in intimate sessions at the Congress of Vienna. This painting shows the Duke of Wellington, standing at the far left; seated at far left is the Prussian Prince of Hardinberg. Wellington had just led the allied forces to victory against Napoleon at Waterloo. *(Source: Windsor Castle, Royal Library© 1990. Her Majesty Queen Elizabeth II)*

unmarred by destructive, generalized war (Map 23.1).

The Congress of Vienna

The allied powers were concerned first and foremost with the defeated enemy, France. Agreeing to the restoration of the Bourbon dynasty, the allies signed the first Peace of Paris with Louis XVIII on May 30, 1814.

The allies were quite lenient toward France. France was given the boundaries it possessed in 1792, which were larger than those of 1789. France lost only the territories it had conquered in Italy, Germany, and the Low Countries, in addition to a few colonial possessions. Although there was some

sentiment for levying a fine on France to pay for the war, the allies did not press the matter when Louis XVIII stated firmly that his government would not pay any reparations. France was even allowed to keep the art treasures Napoleon's agents had looted from the museums of Europe. Thus the victorious powers did not punish harshly, and they did not foment a spirit of injustice and revenge in the defeated country.

When the four allies met together at the Congress of Vienna, assisted in a minor way by a host of delegates from the smaller European states, they also agreed to raise a number of formidable barriers against renewed French aggression. The Low Countries—Belgium and Holland—were united under an enlarged Dutch monarchy capable of opposing France more effectively. Moreover, Prussia

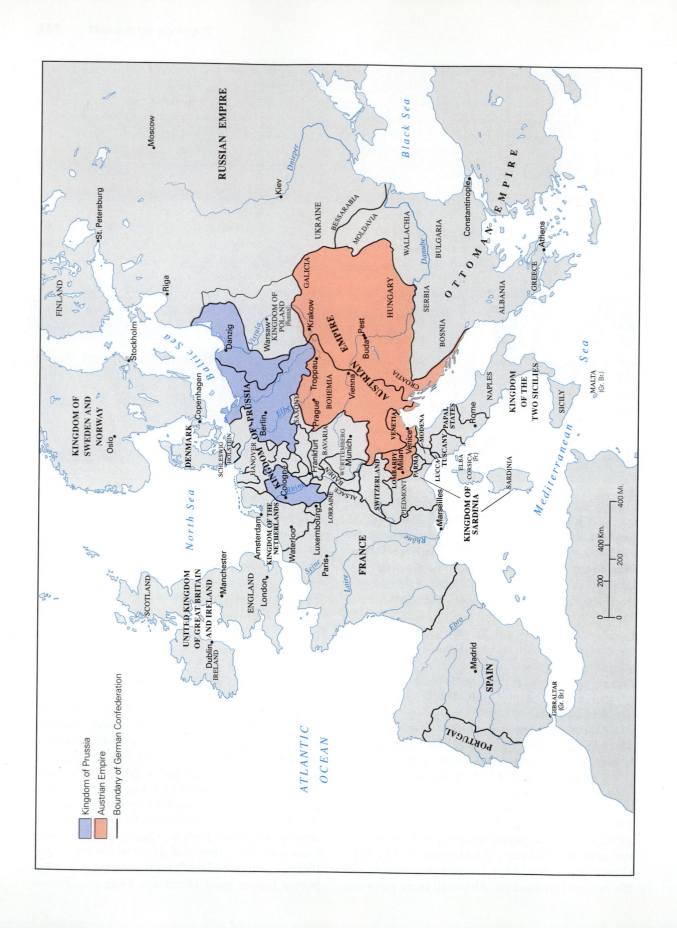

RUSSIAN EMPIRE

Moscow

FINLAND

St. Petersburg

Riga

KINGDOM OF SWEDEN AND NORWAY

Stockholm

Oslo

Copenhagen

DENMARK

Baltic Sea

Danzig

Vistula

Warsaw

KINGDOM OF POLAND (Russia)

UKRAINE

Kiev

Dnieper

Black Sea

Constantinople

GALICIA

BESSARABIA

MOLDAVIA

WALLACHIA

BULGARIA

SERBIA

BOSNIA

Krakow

HUNGARY

AUSTRIAN EMPIRE

Buda

Pest

ALBANIA

GREECE

Athens

O T T O M A N   E M P I R E

SCHLESWIG
HOLSTEIN

HANOVER

KINGDOM OF PRUSSIA

Berlin

Elbe

SAXONY

Prague

BOHEMIA

Troppau

Vienna

CROATIA

VENETIA

Venice

Milan

LOMBARDY

PARMA

MODENA

PAPAL STATES

Rome

NAPLES

KINGDOM OF THE TWO SICILIES

SICILY

MALTA (Gr. Br.)

Mediterranean Sea

Frankfurt

BAVARIA

Munich

WÜRTTEMBERG

BADEN

SWITZERLAND

PIEDMONT

LUCCA

TUSCANY

ELBA

CORSICA (Fr.)

SARDINIA

KINGDOM OF SARDINIA

Cologne

Rhine

KINGDOM OF THE NETHERLANDS

Amsterdam

Waterloo

Luxembourg

ALSACE

LORRAINE

FRANCE

Paris

Seine

Loire

Marseilles

Rhône

North Sea

UNITED KINGDOM OF GREAT BRITAIN AND IRELAND

SCOTLAND

Manchester

ENGLAND

London

Dublin

IRELAND

ATLANTIC OCEAN

Ebro

Madrid

SPAIN

GIBRALTAR (Gr. Br.)

PORTUGAL

400 Mi.

400 Km.

200

200

0

0

Kingdom of Prussia

Austrian Empire

Boundary of German Confederation

received considerably more territory on France's eastern border, so as to stand as the "sentinel on the Rhine" against France. In these ways the Quadruple Alliance combined leniency toward France with strong defensive measures. They held out a carrot with one hand and picked up a bigger stick with the other.

In their moderation toward France the allies were motivated by self-interest and traditional ideas about the balance of power. To Metternich and Castlereagh, the foreign ministers of Austria and Great Britain, as well as their French counterpart Talleyrand, the balance of power meant an international equilibrium of political and military forces, which would preserve the freedom and independence of each of the Great Powers. Such a balance would discourage aggression by any combination of states or, worse, the domination of Europe by any single state. As they saw it, the task of the powers was thus twofold. They had to make sure that France would not dominate Europe again, and they also had to arrange international relations so that none of the victors would be tempted to strive for domination in its turn. Such a balance involved many considerations and all of Europe.

The balance of power was the mechanism used by the Great Powers—Austria, Britain, Prussia, Russia, and France—to settle their own dangerous disputes at the Congress of Vienna. There was general agreement among the victors that each of them should receive compensation in the form of territory for their successful struggle against the French. Great Britain had already won colonies and strategic outposts during the long wars, and these it retained. Metternich's Austria gave up territories in Belgium and southern Germany but expanded greatly elsewhere, taking the rich provinces of Venetia and Lombardy in northern Italy as well as its former Polish possessions and new lands on the eastern coast of the Adriatic (see Map 23.1). There was also agreement that Prussia and Russia should be compensated. But where, and to what extent? That was the ticklish question that almost led to renewed war in January 1815.

The vaguely progressive, impetuous Alexander I of Russia had already taken Finland and Bessarabia

on his northern and southern borders. Yet he burned with ambition to restore the ancient kingdom of Poland, on which he expected to bestow the benefits of his rule. The Prussians were willing to go along and give up their Polish territories, provided they could swallow up the large and wealthy kingdom of Saxony, their German neighbor to the south.

These demands were too much for Castlereagh and Metternich, who feared an unbalancing of forces in central Europe. In an astonishing about-face, they turned for diplomatic support to the wily Talleyrand and the defeated France he represented. On January 3, 1815, Great Britain, Austria, and France signed a secret alliance directed against Russia and Prussia. As Castlereagh concluded somberly, it appeared that the "peace we have so dearly purchased will be of short duration."[1]

The outcome, however, was compromise rather than war. When rumors of the alliance were intentionally leaked, the threat of war caused the rulers of Russia and Prussia to moderate their demands. They accepted Metternich's proposal: Russia established a small Polish kingdom, and Prussia received two-fifths rather than all of Saxony (see Map 23.1). This compromise was very much within the framework of balance-of-power ideology and eighteenth-century diplomacy: Great Powers became greater, but not too much greater. In addition, France had been able to intervene and tip the scales in favor of the side seeking to prevent undue expansion of Russia and Prussia. In so doing, France regained its Great Power status and was no longer isolated, as Talleyrand gleefully reported to Louis XVIII.

Unfortunately for France, as the final touches were being put on the peace settlement at Vienna, Napoleon suddenly reappeared on the scene. Escaping from his "comic kingdom" on the island of Elba in February 1815 and rallying his supporters for one last campaign during the Hundred Days, Napoleon was defeated at Waterloo and exiled to St. Helena. Yet the resulting peace—the second Peace of Paris—was still relatively moderate toward France. Fat old Louis XVIII was restored to his throne for a second time. France lost some territory, had to pay an indemnity of 700 million francs, and had to support a large army of occupation for five years.

The rest of the settlement already concluded at the Congress of Vienna was left intact. The members of the Quadruple Alliance did, however, agree

MAP 23.1 Europe in 1815 Europe's leaders re-established a balance of political power after the defeat of Napoleon.

to meet periodically to discuss their common interests and to consider appropriate measures for the maintenance of peace in Europe. This agreement marked the beginning of the European "congress system," which lasted long into the nineteenth century and settled international crises through diplomatic conferences.

Intervention and Repression

There was also a domestic political side to the re-establishment of peace. Within their own countries, the leaders of the victorious states were much less flexible. In 1815, under Metternich's leadership, Austria, Prussia, and Russia embarked on a crusade against the ideas and politics of the dual revolution. The crusade lasted until 1848.

The first step was the Holy Alliance, formed by Austria, Prussia, and Russia in September 1815. First proposed by Russia's Alexander I, the alliance proclaimed the intention of the three eastern monarchs to rule exclusively on the basis of Christian principles and to work together to maintain peace and justice on all occasions. Castlereagh refused to sign, characterizing the vague statement of principle as "a piece of sublime mysticism and nonsense." Yet it soon became a symbol of the repression of liberal and revolutionary movements all over Europe.

In 1820 revolutionaries succeeded in forcing the monarchs of Spain and the southern Italian kingdom of the Two Sicilies to grant liberal constitutions against their wills. Metternich was horrified: revolution was rising once again. Calling a conference at Troppau in Austria, under the provisions of the Quadruple Alliance, he and Alexander I proclaimed the principle of active intervention to maintain all autocratic regimes whenever they were threatened. Austrian forces then marched into Naples and restored Ferdinand I to the throne of the Two Sicilies. The French armies of Louis XVIII likewise restored the Spanish regime—after the Congress of Troppau had rejected Alexander's offer to send his Cossacks across Europe to teach the Spanish an unforgettable lesson.

Great Britain remained aloof, arguing that intervention in the domestic politics of foreign states was not an object of British diplomacy. In particular, Great Britain opposed any attempts by the restored Spanish monarchy to reconquer its former Latin American possessions, which had gained

their independence during and after the Napoleonic wars. Encouraged by the British position, the young United States proclaimed its celebrated Monroe Doctrine in 1823. This bold document declared that European powers were to keep their hands off the New World and in no way attempt to re-establish their political system there. In the United States, constitutional liberalism, an ongoing challenge to the conservatism of continental Europe, retained its cutting edge.

In the years following the crushing of liberal revolution in southern Italy in 1821 and in Spain in 1823, Metternich continued to battle against liberal political change. Sometimes he could do little, as in the case of the new Latin American republics. Nor could he undo the dynastic changes of 1830 and 1831 in France and Belgium. Nonetheless, until 1848 Metternich's system proved quite effective in central Europe, where his power was the greatest.

Metternich's policies dominated not only Austria and the Italian peninsula but the entire German Confederation, which the peace settlement of Vienna had called into being. The confederation was composed of thirty-eight independent German states, including Prussia and Austria. (Neither Prussia's eastern territories nor the Hungarian half of the Austrian Empire was included in the confederation.) These states met in complicated assemblies dominated by Austria, with Prussia a willing junior partner in the planning and execution of repressive measures.

It was through the German Confederation that Metternich had the infamous Carlsbad Decrees issued in 1819. The decrees required the thirty-eight German member states to root out subversive ideas in their universities and newspapers. The decrees also established a permanent committee with spies and informers to investigate and punish any liberal or radical organizations. Metternich's ruthless imposition of repressive internal policies on the governments of central Europe contrasted with the intelligent moderation he had displayed in the general peace settlement of 1815.

Metternich and Conservatism

Metternich's determined defense of the status quo made him a villain in the eyes of most progressive, optimistic historians of the nineteenth century. Yet rather than denounce the man, it is more useful to try to understand him and the general conservatism he represented.

Born into the middle ranks of the landed nobility of the Rhineland, Prince Klemens von Metternich (1773–1859) was an internationally oriented aristocrat. In 1795 his splendid marriage to Eleonora von Kaunitz, granddaughter of a famous Austrian statesman and heiress to vast estates, opened the door to the highest court circles and a brilliant diplomatic career. Austrian ambassador to Napoleon's court in 1806 and Austrian foreign minister from 1809 to 1848, the cosmopolitan Metternich always remained loyal to his class and jealously defended its rights and privileges to the day he died. Like most other conservatives of his time, he did so with a clear conscience. The nobility was one of Europe's most ancient institutions, and conservatives regarded tradition as the basic source of human institutions. In their view, the proper state and society remained that of pre-1789 Europe, which rested on a judicious blend of monarchy, bureaucracy, and aristocracy.

Metternich's commitment to conservatism was coupled with a passionate hatred of liberalism. He firmly believed that liberalism, as embodied in revolutionary America and France, had been responsible for a generation of war with untold bloodshed and suffering. Liberal demands for representative government and civil liberties had unfortunately captured the imaginations of some middle-class lawyers, business people, and intellectuals. Metternich thought that these groups had been and still were engaged in a vast conspiracy to impose their beliefs on society and destroy the existing order. Like many other conservatives then and since, Metternich blamed liberal revolutionaries for stirring up the lower classes, whom he believed to be indifferent or hostile to liberal ideas, desiring nothing more than peace and quiet.

The threat of liberalism appeared doubly dangerous to Metternich because it generally went with national aspirations. Liberals, especially liberals in central Europe, believed that each people, each national group, had a right to establish its own independent government and seek to fulfill its own destiny. The idea of national self-determination was repellent to Metternich. It not only threatened the existence of the aristocracy, it also threatened to destroy the Austrian Empire and revolutionize central Europe.

The vast Austrian Empire of the Habsburgs was a great dynastic state. Formed over centuries by war, marriage, and luck, it was made up of many peoples speaking many languages (Map 23.2). The Germans, long the dominant element, had supported and profited by the long-term territorial expansion of Austria; yet they accounted for only a quarter of the population. The Magyars (Hungarians), a substantially smaller group, dominated the kingdom of Hungary—which was part of the Austrian Empire—though they did not account for a majority of the population even there.

The Czechs, the third major group, were concentrated in Bohemia and Moravia. There were also large numbers of Italians, Poles, and Ukrainians, as well as smaller groups of Slovenes, Croats, Serbs, Ruthenians, and Rumanians. The various Slavic peoples, together with the Italians and the Rumanians, represented a widely scattered and completely divided majority in an empire dominated by

Metternich This portrait by Sir Thomas Lawrence reveals much of Metternich the man. Handsome, refined, and intelligent, Metternich was a great aristocrat passionately devoted to the defense of his class and its interests. *(Source: Copyright reserved to Her Majesty Queen Elizabeth II)*

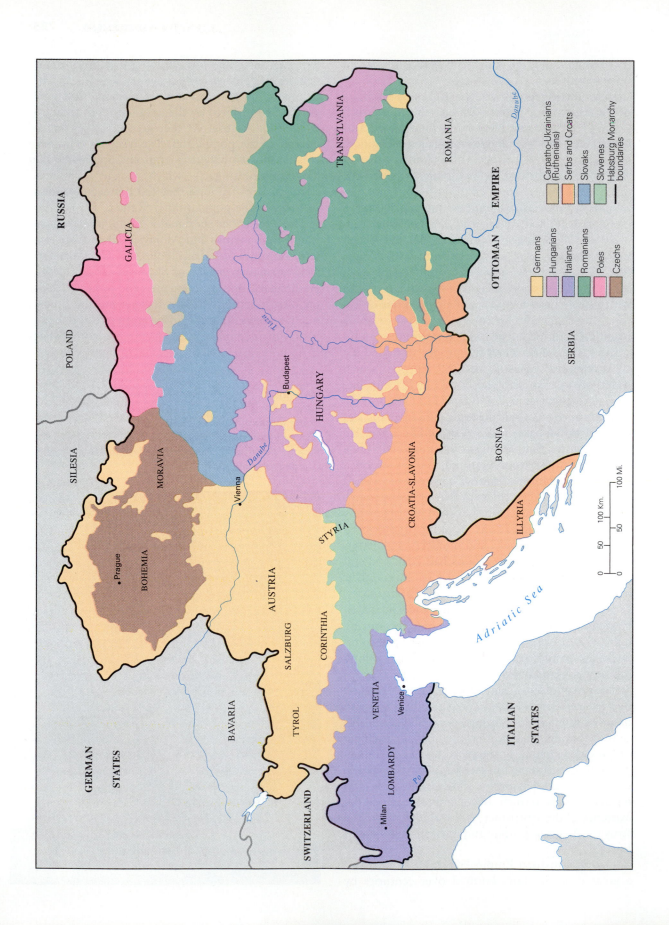

RUSSIA

GALICIA

POLAND

SILESIA

MORAVIA

Prague • BOHEMIA

GERMAN

STATES

BAVARIA

TYROL

SWITZERLAND

SALZBURG

AUSTRIA

Vienna •

CORINTHIA

STYRIA

HUNGARY

Budapest •

Danube

Tisza

TRANSYLVANIA

ROMANIA

OTTOMAN EMPIRE

SERBIA

BOSNIA

CROATIA-SLAVONIA

ILLYRIA

VENETIA

Venice •

LOMBARDY

Milan •

Po

ITALIAN STATES

Adriatic Sea

	Germans		Carpatho-Ukrainians (Ruthenians)
	Hungarians		Serbs and Croats
	Italians		Slovaks
	Romanians		Slovenes
	Poles		Habsburg Monarchy boundaries
	Czechs		

Scale: 0 50 100 Km. / 0 50 100 Mi.

Germans and Hungarians. Different ethnic groups often lived in the same provinces and even the same villages. Thus the different parts and provinces of the empire differed in languages, customs, and institutions. They were held together primarily by their ties to the Habsburg emperor.

The multinational state Metternich served was both strong and weak. It was strong because of its large population and vast territories; it was weak because of its many and potentially dissatisfied nationalities. In these circumstances, Metternich virtually had to oppose liberalism and nationalism, for Austria was simply unable to accommodate those ideologies of the dual revolution. Other conservatives supported Austria because they could imagine no better fate for the jumble of small nationalities wedged precariously between masses of Germans and hordes of Russians in east central Europe. Castlereagh even went so far as to say that Austria was the "great hinge upon which the fate of Europe must ultimately depend." Metternich's repressive conservatism may not hold appeal for many people today, but it had understandable roots in the dilemma of a multinational state in an age of rising nationalism.

RADICAL IDEAS AND EARLY SOCIALISM

The years following the peace settlement of 1815 were years of profound intellectual activity. Intellectuals and social observers were seeking to understand the revolutionary changes that had occurred and were still taking place. These efforts led to ideas that still motivate the world.

Almost all of these basic ideas were radical. In one way or another they opposed the old, deeply felt conservatism that Metternich exemplified so well. The revived conservatism, with its stress on tradition, a hereditary monarchy, a strong and privileged landowning aristocracy, and an official church, was rejected by radicals. Instead, radicals developed and refined alternative visions—alterna-

MAP 23.2 Peoples of the Habsburg Monarchy, 1815 The old dynastic state was a patchwork of nationalities. Note the widely scattered pockets of Germans and Hungarians.

tive ideologies—and tried to convince society to act on them. With time, they were very successful.

Liberalism

The principal ideas of liberalism—liberty and equality—were by no means defeated in 1815. First realized successfully in the American Revolution and then achieved in part in the French Revolution, this political and social philosophy continued to pose a radical challenge to revived conservatism. Liberalism demanded representative government as opposed to autocratic monarchy, equality before the law as opposed to legally separate classes. The idea of liberty also continued to mean specific individual freedoms: freedom of the press, freedom of speech, freedom of assembly, and freedom from arbitrary arrest. In Europe, only France with Louis XVIII's Constitutional Charter and Great Britain with its Parliament and historic rights of English men and women had realized much of the liberal program in 1815. Even in those countries, liberalism had not fully succeeded; and elsewhere, liberal demands were still a call for revolutionary change.

Although liberalism still had its cutting edge, it was not as sharp a tool as it had been. This was true because liberalism in the early nineteenth century resolutely opposed government intervention in social and economic affairs, even if the need for action seemed great to social critics and reformers. This form of liberalism is often called "classical" liberalism in the United States, in order to distinguish it sharply from modern American liberalism, which usually favors more government programs to meet social needs and to regulate the economy. Classical liberalism's decline in radicalism was especially evident in its economic principles, which called for unrestricted private enterprise and no government interference in the economy. This philosophy was popularly known as the doctrine of *laissez faire*.

The idea of a free economy had first been persuasively formulated by a Scottish professor of philosophy, Adam Smith (1723–1790). Smith, whose *Inquiry into the Nature and Causes of the Wealth of Nations* (1776) founded modern economics, was highly critical of eighteenth-century mercantilism. Mercantilism, he said, meant stifling government regulations as well as unjust privileges for private monopolies and government favorites. Far preferable was free competition, which would give all citizens a fair and equal opportunity to do what they did best. Smith argued effectively that freely competitive private enterprise would result in greater income for everyone, not just the rich.

Unlike some of his contemporaries, Smith applauded the modest rise in real wages of British workers in the eighteenth century and went so far as to say, "No society can surely be flourishing and happy, of which the far greater part of the members are poor and miserable." Smith also believed that greater competition meant higher wages for workers, since manufacturers and "masters are always and everywhere in a sort of tacit, but constant and uniform, combination, not to raise the wages of laborers above their actual rate." In short, Adam Smith was a spokesman for general economic development, not narrow business interests.

In the early nineteenth century, the British economy was progressively liberalized, as old restrictions on trade and industry were relaxed or eliminated. This liberalization promoted continued economic growth in the Industrial Revolution. At the same time, however, economic liberalism and laissez-faire economic thought were tending to become a doctrine serving business interests. Businessmen used the doctrine to defend their right to do exactly as they wished in their factories. Labor unions were outlawed because they supposedly restricted free competition and the individual's "right to work."

The teachings of Thomas Malthus (1766–1834) and David Ricardo (1772–1823) helped especially to make economic liberalism an ideology of business interests in many people's minds. As we have seen (page 702), Malthus argued that population would always tend to grow faster than the supply of food. This led Ricardo to formulate his "iron law of wages," which said that, because of the pressure of population growth, wages would be just high enough to keep the workers from starving. Malthus and Ricardo thought of themselves as objective social scientists. Yet their teachings were often used by industrial and middle-class interests in England, the Continent, and the United States to justify opposing any kind of government action to protect or improve the lot of workers: if workers were poor, it was their own fault, the result of their breeding like rabbits.

In the early nineteenth century, liberal political ideals also became more closely associated with narrow class interests. Early-nineteenth-century liberals favored representative government, but they generally wanted property qualifications attached to the right to vote. In practice, this meant limiting the vote to well-to-do aristocratic landowners, substantial businessmen, and successful members of the professions. Workers and peasants as well as the lower middle class of shopkeepers, clerks, and artisans did not own the necessary property and thus could not vote.

As liberalism became increasingly middle-class after 1815, some intellectuals and foes of conservatism felt that it did not go nearly far enough. Inspired by memories of the French Revolution and the contemporary example of exuberant Jacksonian democracy in the young American republic, they called for universal voting rights, at least for males. Giving all men the vote, they felt, would allow the masses to join in government and would lead to democracy.

Many people who believed in democracy also believed in the republican form of government. They detested the power of the monarchy, the privileges of the aristocracy, and the great wealth of the upper middle class. These democrats and republicans were more radical than the liberals. Taking for granted much of the liberal program, they sought to go beyond it. Democrats and republicans were also more willing than most liberals to endorse violent upheaval to achieve goals. All of this meant that liberals and radical, democratic republicans could join forces against conservatives only up to a point.

Nationalism

Nationalism was a second radical idea in the years after 1815, an idea destined to have an enormous influence in the modern world. In a summation of this complex ideology, three points stand out. First, nationalism has normally evolved from a real or imagined *cultural* unity, manifesting itself especially in a common language, history, and territory. Second, nationalists have usually sought to turn this cultural unity into *political* reality, so that the territory of each people coincides with its state boundaries. It was this goal that made nationalism so potentially explosive in central and eastern Europe after 1815, when there were either too few states (Austria, Russia, and the Ottoman Empire) or too many (the Italian peninsula and the German Confederation) and when different peoples overlapped and intermingled. Third, modern nationalism had its immediate origins in the French Revolution and the Napoleonic wars. Nationalism was effectively harnessed by the French republic during the Reign of Terror to help repel foreign foes, and all across Europe patriots tried to kindle nationalist flames in the war against Napoleon. Thus by 1815 there were already hints of nationalism's remarkable ability to spread and develop.

Between 1815 and 1850, most people who believed in nationalism also believed in either liberalism or radical, democratic republicanism. In more recent times, however, many governments have been very nationalistic without favoring liberty and democracy. Why, then, was love of liberty almost synonymous with love of nation in the early nineteenth century?

A common faith in the creativity and nobility of the people was perhaps the single most important reason for linking these two concepts. Liberals and especially democrats saw the people as the ultimate source of all government. The people (or some of them) elected their officials and governed themselves within a framework of personal liberty. Yet such self-government would be possible only if the people were united by common traditions and common loyalties. In practice, common loyalties rested above all on a common language. Thus liberals and nationalists agreed that a shared language forged the basic unity of a people, a unity that transcended local or provincial interests and even class differences.

Early nationalists usually believed that every nation, like every citizen, had the right to exist in freedom and to develop its character and spirit. They were confident that the independence and freedom of other nations, as in the case of other citizens within a nation, would not lessen the freedom of their own country. Rather, the symphony of nations would promote the harmony and ultimate unity of all peoples. As the French historian Jules Michelet put it in *The People* in 1846, each citizen "learns to recognize his country . . . as a note in the grand concert; through it he himself participates and loves the world." Similarly, the Italian patriot

Giuseppe Mazzini believed that "in laboring according to the true principles of our country we are laboring for Humanity." Thus the liberty of the individual and the love of a free nation overlapped greatly in the early nineteenth century.

Nationalism also had a negative side to it. Even as they talked of serving the cause of humanity, early nationalists stressed the differences among peoples. The German pastor and philosopher Johann Herder (1744–1803) had argued that every people has its own particular spirit and genius, which it expresses through its culture and language. Yet Herder (and others after him) could not define the uniqueness of the French, German, and Slavic peoples without comparing and contrasting one people with another. Thus, even early nationalism developed a strong sense of "we" and "they."

"They" were often the enemy. The leader of the Czech cultural revival, the passionate democrat and nationalist historian Francis Palacký, is a good example of this tendency. In his histories he lauded the achievements of the Czech people, which he characterized as a long struggle against brutal German domination. To this "we–they" outlook, it was all too easy for nationalists to add two other highly volatile ingredients: a sense of national mission and a sense of national superiority. As Mazzini characteristically wrote, "Peoples never stop before they have achieved the ultimate aim of their existence, before having fulfilled their mission." Even Michelet, so alive to the aspirations of other peoples, could not help speaking in 1846 of the "superiority of France"; the principles espoused in the French Revolution had made France the "salvation of mankind."

German and Spanish nationalists had a very different opinion of France. To them the French often seemed as oppressive as the Germans seemed to the Czechs, as hateful as the Russians seemed to the Poles. The despised enemy's mission might seem as oppressive as the American national mission seemed to the Mexicans after the U.S. annexation of Texas. In 1845 the American journalist and strident nationalist John Louis O'Sullivan wrote that taking land from an "imbecile and distracted Mexico" was a laudable step in the "fulfillment of our manifest destiny to overspread the continent allotted by Providence for the free development of our yearly multiplying millions."[2]

Early nationalism was thus ambiguous. Its main thrust was liberal and democratic. But below the surface lurked ideas of national superiority and national mission, which could lead to aggressive crusades and counter-crusades, as had happened in the French Revolution and in the "wars of liberation" against Napoleon.

French Utopian Socialism

To understand the rise of socialism, one must begin with France. Despite the fact that France lagged far behind Great Britain in developing modern industry, almost all the early socialists were French. Although they differed on many specific points, these French thinkers were acutely aware that the political revolution in France and the rise of modern industry in England had begun a transformation of society. Yet they were disturbed by what they saw. Liberal practices in politics and economics appeared to be fomenting selfish individualism and splitting the community into isolated fragments. There was, they believed, an urgent need for a further reorganization of society to establish cooperation and a new sense of community. Starting from this shared outlook, individual French thinkers went in many different directions. They searched the past, analyzed existing conditions, and fashioned luxurious utopias. Yet certain ideas tied their critiques and visions together.

Early French socialists believed in economic planning. Inspired by the emergency measures of 1793 and 1794 in France, they argued that the government should rationally organize the economy and not depend on destructive competition to do the job. Early socialists also shared an intense desire to help the poor and to protect them from the rich. With passionate moral fervor, they preached that the rich and the poor should be more nearly equal economically. Finally, socialists believed that most private property should be abolished and replaced by state or community ownership. Planning, greater economic equality, and state ownership of property: these were the key ideas of early French socialism and of all socialism since.

One of the most influential early socialist thinkers was a nobleman, Count Henri de Saint-Simon (1760–1825). A curious combination of radical thinker and successful land speculator, Saint-Simon optimistically proclaimed the tremen-

dous possibilities of industrial development: "The age of gold is before us!" The key to progress was proper social organization. Such an arrangement of society required the "parasites"—the court, the aristocracy, lawyers, churchmen—to give way, once and for all, to the "doers"—the leading scientists, engineers, and industrialists. The doers would carefully plan the economy and guide it forward by undertaking vast public works projects and establishing investment banks. Saint-Simon also stressed in highly moralistic terms that every social institution ought to have as its main goal improved conditions for the poor. Saint-Simon's stress on industry and science inspired middle-class industrialists and bankers, like the Pereire brothers, founders of the Crédit Mobilier (see page 708).

After 1830 the socialist critique of capitalism became sharper. Charles Fourier (1772–1837), a lonely, saintly man with a tenuous hold on reality, described a socialist utopia in lavish mathematical detail. Hating the urban wage system, Fourier envisaged self-sufficient communities of 1,620 people living communally on 5,000 acres devoted to a combination of agriculture and industry. Although Fourier waited in vain each day at noon in his apartment for a wealthy philanthropist to endow his visionary schemes, he was very influential. Several utopian communities were founded along the lines he prescribed, mainly in the United States.

Fourier was also an early proponent of the total emancipation of women. Extremely critical of middle-class family life, Fourier believed that most marriages were only another kind of prostitution. According to Fourier, young single women were shamelessly "sold" to their future husbands for dowries and other financial considerations. Therefore, Fourier called for the abolition of marriage, free unions based only on love, and complete sexual freedom. Many middle-class men and women found these ideas, which were shared and even practiced by some followers of Saint Simon, shocking and immoral. The socialist program for the liberation of women as well as workers appeared to them as doubly dangerous and revolutionary.

Louis Blanc (1811–1882), a sharp-eyed, intelligent journalist, was much more practical. In his *Organization of Work* (1839), he urged workers to agitate for universal voting rights and to take control of the state peacefully. Blanc believed that the full power of the state should be directed at setting up government-backed workshops and factories to

Fourier's Utopia   The vision of a harmonious planned community freed from capitalism and selfish individualism radiates from this 1847 illustration of Fourier's principles. *(Source: Mary Evans Picture Library/Photo Researchers)*

guarantee full employment. The right to work had to become as sacred as any other right. Finally, there was Pierre Joseph Proudhon (1809–1865), a self-educated printer, who wrote a pamphlet in 1840 entitled *What Is Property?* His answer was that it was nothing but theft. Property was profit that was stolen from the worker, who was the source of all wealth. Unlike most socialists, Proudhon feared the power of the state and was often considered an anarchist.

Thus a variety of French thinkers blazed the way with utopian socialism in the 1830s and 1840s. Their ideas were very influential, particularly in Paris, where poverty-stricken workers with a revolutionary tradition were attentive students. Yet the economic arguments of the French utopians were weak, and their specific programs usually seemed too fanciful to be taken seriously. To Karl Marx was left the task of establishing firm foundations for modern socialism.

The Birth of Marxian Socialism

In 1848 the thirty-year-old Karl Marx (1818–1883) and the twenty-eight-year-old Friedrich Engels (1820–1895) published the *Communist Manifesto,* the bible of socialism. The son of a Jewish lawyer who had converted to Christianity, the atheistic young Marx had studied philosophy at the University of Berlin before turning to journalism and economics. He read widely in French socialist thought and was influenced by it. He shared Fourier's view of middle-class marriage as legalized prostitution, and he too looked forward to the emancipation of women and the abolition of the family. But by the time he was twenty-five, he was developing his own socialist ideas.

Early French socialists often appealed to the middle class and the state to help the poor. Marx ridiculed such appeals as naive. He argued that the interests of the middle class and those of the

The Marx Family   In 1849 the exiled Marx settled in London. There he wrote *Capital*, the weighty exposition of his socialist theories, and worked to organize the working class. With his coauthor and financial supporter Friedrich Engels (right), Marx is shown here with his daughters, ironically a picture of middle-class respectability. *(Source: Culver Pictures)*

industrial working class are inevitably opposed to each other. Indeed, according to the *Manifesto*, the "history of all previously existing society is the history of class struggles." In Marx's view, one class had always exploited the other, and with the advent of modern industry, society was split more clearly than ever before: between the middle class—the bourgeoisie—and the modern working class—the proletariat. Moreover, the bourgeoisie had reduced everything to a matter of money and "naked self-interest." "In a word, for exploitation, veiled by religious and political illusions, the bourgeoisie had substituted naked, shameless, direct brutal exploitation."

Just as the bourgeoisie had triumphed over the feudal aristocracy, Marx predicted, the proletariat was destined to conquer the bourgeoisie in a violent revolution. While a tiny minority owned the means of production and grew richer, the ever-poorer proletariat was constantly growing in size and in class consciousness. In this process, the proletariat was aided, according to Marx, by a portion of the bourgeoisie who had gone over to the proletariat and who (like Marx and Engels) "had raised themselves to the level of comprehending theoretically the historical moment." And the critical moment was very near. "Let the ruling classes tremble at a Communist revolution. The proletarians have nothing to lose but their chains. They have a world to win. WORKING MEN OF ALL COUNTRIES, UNITE!" So ends the *Communist Manifesto*.

In brief outline, Marx's ideas may seem to differ only slightly from the wild and improbable ideas of the utopians of his day. Yet whatever one may think of the validity of Marx's analysis, he must be taken seriously. He united sociology, economics, and all human history in a vast and imposing edifice. He synthesized in his socialism not only French utopian schemes but English classical economics and German philosophy—the major intellectual currents of his day. Moreover, after the young Marx fled to England as a penniless political refugee following the revolutions of 1848, he continued to show a rare flair for combining complex theorization with both lively popular writing and practical organizational ability. This combination of theoretical and practical skills contributed greatly to the subsequent diffusion of Marx's socialist synthesis after 1860, as will be shown in Chapter 25 (see page 817).

Marx's debt to England was great. He was the last of the classical economists. Following David Ricardo, who had taught that labor was the source of all value, Marx went on to argue that profits were really wages stolen from the workers. Moreover, Marx incorporated Engels's charges of terrible oppression of the new class of factory workers in England; thus his doctrines seemed to be based on hard facts.

Marx's theory of historical evolution was built on the philosophy of the German Georg Hegel (1770–1831). Hegel believed that history is "ideas in motion": each age is characterized by a dominant set of ideas, which produces opposing ideas and eventually a new synthesis. The idea of being had been dominant initially, for example, and it had produced its antithesis, the idea of nonbeing. This idea in turn had resulted in the synthesis of becoming. Thus history has pattern and purpose.

Marx retained Hegel's view of history as a dialectic process of change but made economic relationships between classes the driving force. This dialectic explained the decline of agrarian feudalism and the rise of industrial capitalism. And Marx stressed again and again that the "bourgeoisie, historically, has played a most revolutionary part. . . . During its rule of scarcely one hundred years the bourgeoisie has created more massive and more colossal productive forces than have all preceding generations together." Here was a convincing explanation for people trying to make sense of the dual revolution. Marx's next idea, that it was now the bourgeoisie's turn to give way to the socialism of revolutionary workers, appeared to many the irrefutable capstone of a brilliant interpretation of humanity's long development. Thus Marx pulled together powerful ideas and insights to create one of the great secular religions out of the intellectual ferment of the early nineteenth century.

THE ROMANTIC MOVEMENT

Radical concepts of politics and society were accompanied by comparable changes in literature and other arts during the dual revolution. The early nineteenth century marked the acme of the romantic movement, which profoundly influenced the arts and enriched European culture immeasurably.

The romantic movement was in part a revolt against classicism and the Enlightenment. Classicism was essentially a set of artistic rules and standards that went hand in glove with the Enlightenment's belief in rationality, order, and restraint. The classicists believed that the ancient Greeks and Romans had discovered eternally valid aesthetic rules and that playwrights and painters should continue to follow them. Classicists could enforce these rules in the eighteenth century because they dominated the courts and academies for which artists worked.

Forerunners of the romantic movement appeared from about 1750 on. Of these, Rousseau (see page 581)—the passionate advocate of feeling, freedom, and natural goodness—was the most influential. Romanticism then crystallized fully in the 1790s, primarily in England and Germany. The French Revolution kindled the belief that radical reconstruction was also possible in cultural and artistic life (even though many early English and German romantics became disillusioned with events in France and turned from liberalism to conservatism in politics). Romanticism gained strength until the 1840s.

Romanticism

Romanticism was characterized by a belief in emotional exuberance, unrestrained imagination, and spontaneity in both art and personal life. In Germany early romantics of the 1770s and 1780s called themselves the "Storm and Stress" (*Sturm und Drang*) group, and many romantic artists of the early nineteenth century lived lives of tremendous emotional intensity. Suicide, duels to the death, madness, and strange illnesses were not uncommon among leading romantics. Romantic artists typically led bohemian lives, wearing their hair long and uncombed in preference to powdered wigs and living in cold garrets rather than frequenting stiff drawing rooms. They rejected materialism and sought to escape to lofty spiritual heights through their art. Great individualists, the romantics believed the full development of one's unique human potential to be the supreme purpose in life. The romantics were driven by a sense of an unlimited universe and by a yearning for the unattained, the unknown, the unknowable.

Nowhere was the break with classicism more apparent than in romanticism's general conception of nature. Classicism was not particularly interested in nature. In the words of the eighteenth-century English author Samuel Johnson, "A blade of grass is always a blade of grass; men and women are my subjects of inquiry." Nature was portrayed by classicists as beautiful and chaste, like an eighteenth-century formal garden. The romantics, on the other hand, were enchanted by nature. Sometimes they found it awesome and tempestuous, as in Théodore Géricault's painting *The Raft of the Medusa,* which shows the survivors of a shipwreck adrift in a turbulent sea. Others saw nature as a source of spiritual inspiration. As the great English landscape artist John Constable declared, "Nature is Spirit visible."

Most romantics saw the growth of modern industry as an ugly, brutal attack on their beloved nature and on the human personality. They sought escape—in the unspoiled Lake District of northern England, in exotic North Africa, in an idealized Middle Ages. Yet some romantics found a vast, awesome, terribly moving power in the new industrial landscape. In ironworks and cotton mills they saw the flames of hell and the evil genius of Satan himself. One of John Martin's last and greatest paintings, *The Great Day of His Wrath* (1850), vividly depicts the Last Judgment foretold in Revelation 6, when the "sun became black as sackcloth of hair, and the moon became as blood; and the stars of heaven fell unto the earth." Martin's romantic masterpiece was inspired directly by a journey through the "Black country" of the industrial Midlands in the dead of night. According to Martin's son:

The glow of the furnaces, the red blaze of light, together with the liquid fire, seemed to him truly sublime and awful. He could not imagine anything more terrible even in the regions of everlasting punishment. All he had done or attempted in ideal painting fell far short, very far short, of the fearful sublimity.[3]

Fascinated by color and diversity, the romantic imagination turned toward the study and writing of history with a passion. For romantics, history was not a minor branch of philosophy from which philosophers picked suitable examples to illustrate their teachings. History was beautiful, exciting, and important in its own right. It was the art of change over time—the key to a universe that was now perceived to be organic and dynamic. It was no longer perceived to be mechanical and static as it had to

Constable: The Hay Wain   Constable's love of a spiritualized and poetic nature radiates from this masterpiece of romantic art. Exhibited in Paris in 1824, *The Hay Wain* created a sensation and made a profound impression on the young Delacroix. *(Source: Courtesy of the Trustees, The National Gallery, London)*

the philosophes of the eighteenth-century Enlightenment.

Historical studies supported the development of national aspirations and encouraged entire peoples to seek in the past their special destinies. This trend was especially strong in Germany and eastern Europe. As the famous English historian Lord Acton put it, the growth of historical thinking associated with the romantic movement was a most fateful step in the story of European thought.

Literature

Britain was the first country where romanticism flowered fully in poetry and prose, and the British romantic writers were among the most prominent in Europe. Wordsworth, Coleridge, and Scott were all active by 1800, to be followed shortly by Byron, Shelley, and Keats. All were poets: romanticism found its distinctive voice in poetry, as the Enlightenment had in prose.

A towering leader of English romanticism, William Wordsworth (1770–1850) traveled in France after his graduation from Cambridge. There he fell passionately in love with a French woman, who bore him a daughter. He was deeply influenced by the philosophy of Rousseau and the spirit of the early French Revolution. Back in England, prevented by war and the Terror from returning to France, Wordsworth settled in the countryside with his sister Dorothy and Samuel Taylor Coleridge (1772–1834).

In 1798 the two poets published their *Lyrical Ballads,* one of the most influential literary works in the history of the English language. In defiance of classical rules, Wordsworth and Coleridge abandoned flowery poetic conventions for the language of ordinary speech, simultaneously endowing simple subjects with the loftiest majesty. This twofold rejection of classical practice was at first ignored and then harshly criticized, but by 1830 Wordsworth had triumphed.

One of the best examples of Wordsworth's romantic credo and genius is "Daffodils":

I wandered lonely as a cloud
That floats on high o'er vales and hills,
When all at once I saw a crowd,
A host, of golden daffodils;
Beside the lake, beneath the trees,
Fluttering and dancing in the breeze.

Continuous as the stars that shine
And twinkle on the Milky Way,
They stretched in never-ending line
Along the margin of a bay:
Ten thousand saw I at a glance,
Tossing their heads in sprightly dance.

The waves beside them danced, but they
Out-did the sparkling waves in glee:
A poet could not but be gay,
In such a jocund company:
I gazed—and gazed—but little thought
What wealth the show to me had brought:

For oft, when on my couch I lie
In vacant or in pensive mood,
They flash upon that inward eye
Which is the bliss of solitude;
And then my heart with pleasure fills,
And dances with the daffodils.

Here indeed are simplicity and love of nature in commonplace forms. Here, too, is Wordsworth's romantic conviction that nature has the power to elevate and instruct, especially when interpreted by a high-minded poetic genius. Wordsworth's conception of poetry as the "spontaneous overflow of powerful feeling recollected in tranquility" is well illustrated by the last stanza.

Born in Edinburgh, Walter Scott (1771–1832) personified the romantic movement's fascination with history. Raised on his grandfather's farm, Scott fell under the spell of the old ballads and tales of the Scottish border. He was also deeply influenced by German romanticism, particularly by the immortal poet and dramatist Johann Wolfgang von Goethe (1749–1832). Scott translated Goethe's famous *Gotz von Berlichingen,* a play about a sixteenth-century knight who revolted against centralized authority and championed individual freedom—at least in Goethe's romantic drama. A natural storyteller, Scott then composed long narrative poems and a series of historical novels. Scott excelled in faithfully recreating the spirit of bygone ages and great historical events, especially those of Scotland.

At first, the strength of classicism in France inhibited the growth of romanticism there. Then, between 1820 and 1850, the romantic impulse broke through in the poetry and prose of Lamartine, Alfred de Vigny, Victor Hugo, Alexander Dumas, and George Sand. Of these, Victor Hugo (1802–1885) was the greatest in both poetry and prose.

Son of a Napoleonic general, Hugo achieved an amazing range of rhythm, language, and image in his lyric poetry. His powerful novels exemplified the romantic fascination with fantastic characters, strange settings, and human emotions. The hero of Hugo's famous *Hunchback of Notre Dame* (1831) is the great cathedral's deformed bellringer, a "human gargoyle" overlooking the teeming life of fifteenth-century Paris. A great admirer of Shakespeare, whom classical critics had derided as undisciplined and excessive, Hugo also championed romanticism in drama. His play *Hernani* (1830) consciously broke all the old rules, as Hugo renounced his early conservatism and equated freedom in literature with liberty in politics and society. Hugo's political evolution was thus exactly the opposite of Wordsworth's, in whom youthful radicalism gave way to middle-aged caution. As the contrast between the two artists suggests, romanticism was a cultural movement compatible with many political beliefs.

Amandine Aurore Lucie Dupin (1804–1876), a strong-willed and gifted woman generally known by her pen name, George Sand, defied the narrow conventions of her time in an unending search for self-fulfillment. After eight years of unhappy marriage in the provinces, she abandoned her dullard of a husband and took her two children to Paris to pursue a career as a writer. There Sand soon achieved fame and wealth, eventually writing over eighty novels on a variety of romantic and social themes. All were shot through with a typically romantic love of nature and moral idealism. George Sand's striking individualism went far beyond her flamboyant preference for men's clothing and cigars and her notorious affairs with the poet Alfred de Musset and the composer Frédéric Chopin, among others. Her semi-autobiographical novel *Lélia* was shockingly modern, delving deeply into her tortuous quest for sexual and personal freedom.

In central and eastern Europe, literary romanticism and early nationalism often reinforced each other. Seeking a unique greatness in every people, well-educated romantics plumbed their own histories and cultures. Like modern anthropologists, they turned their attention to peasant life and transcribed the folk songs, tales, and proverbs that the cosmopolitan Enlightenment had disdained. The brothers Jacob and Wilhelm Grimm were particularly successful at rescuing German fairy tales from oblivion. In the Slavic lands, romantics played a decisive role in converting spoken peasant languages into modern written languages. The greatest of all Russian poets, Alexander Pushkin (1799–1837), rejecting eighteenth-century attempts to force Russian poetry into a classical strait jacket, used his lyric genius to mold the modern literary language.

Art and Music

The greatest and most moving romantic painter in France was Eugène Delacroix (1798–1863), probably the illegitimate son of the French foreign minister Talleyrand. Delacroix was a master of dramatic, colorful scenes that stir the emotions. He was fascinated with remote and exotic subjects, whether lion hunts in Morocco or the languishing, sensuous women of a sultan's harem. Yet he was also a passionate spokesman for freedom. His masterpiece, *Liberty Leading the People,* celebrated the nobility of popular revolution in general and revolution in France in particular.

In England the most notable romantic painters were J. M. W. Turner (1775–1851) and John Constable (1776–1837). Both were fascinated by nature, but their interpretations of it contrasted sharply, aptly symbolizing the tremendous emotional range of the romantic movement. Turner depicted nature's power and terror; wild storms and sinking ships were favorite subjects. Constable painted gentle Wordsworthian landscapes in which human beings were at one with their environment, the comforting countryside of unspoiled rural England.

It was in music that romanticism realized most fully and permanently its goals of free expression and emotional intensity. Whereas the composers of the eighteenth century had remained true to well-defined structures, like the classical symphony, the great romantics used a great range of forms to create a thousand musical landscapes and evoke a host of powerful emotions. Romantic composers also transformed the small classical orchestra, tripling its size by adding wind instruments, percussion, and more brass and strings. The crashing chords evoking the surge of the masses in Chopin's "Revolutionary" etude, the bottomless despair of the funeral march in Beethoven's Third Symphony, the solemn majesty of a great religious event in Schumann's Rhenish Symphony—such were the modern orchestra's musical paintings that plumbed the depths of human feeling.

This range and intensity gave music and musicians much greater prestige than in the past. Music no longer simply complemented a church service or helped a nobleman digest his dinner. Music became a sublime end in itself. It became for many the greatest of the arts, precisely because it achieved the most ecstatic effect and most perfectly realized the endless yearning of the soul. It was worthy of great concert halls and the most dedicated sacrifice. The unbelievable one-in-a-million performer—the great virtuoso who could transport the listener to ecstasy and hysteria—became a cultural hero. The composer Franz Liszt (1811–1886) vowed to do for the piano what Paganini had done for the violin, and he was lionized as the greatest pianist of his age. People swooned for Liszt as they scream for rock stars today.

Though romanticism dominated music until late in the nineteenth century, no composer ever surpassed its first great master, Ludwig van Beethoven (1770–1827). Extending and breaking open classical forms, Beethoven used contrasting themes and tones to produce dramatic conflict and inspiring resolutions. As the contemporary German novelist Ernst Hoffmann (1776–1822) wrote, "Beethoven's music sets in motion the lever of fear, of awe,

Heroes of Romanticism   Observed by a portrait of Byron and bust of Beethoven, Liszt plays for friends. From left to right sit Alexander Dumas, George Sand (characteristically wearing men's garb), and Marie d'Agoult, Liszt's mistress. Standing are Victor Hugo, Paganini, and Rossini. (*Source: Bildarchiv Preussischer Kulturbesitz*)

of horror, of suffering, and awakens just that infinite longing which is the essence of Romanticism." Beethoven's range was tremendous; his output included symphonies, chamber music, sonatas for violin and piano, masses, an opera, and a great many songs.

At the peak of his fame, in constant demand as a composer and recognized as the leading concert pianist of his day, Beethoven began to lose his hearing. He considered suicide but eventually overcame despair: "I will take fate by the throat; it will not bend me completely to its will."[4] Beethoven continued to pour out immortal music. Among other achievements, he fully exploited for the first time the richness and beauty of the piano. Beethoven never heard much of his later work, including the unforgettable choral finale to the Ninth Symphony, for his last years were silent, spent in total deafness.

REFORMS AND REVOLUTIONS

While the romantic movement was developing, liberal, national, and socialist forces battered against the conservatism of 1815. In some countries, change occurred gradually and peacefully. Elsewhere, pressure built up like steam in a pressure cooker without a safety valve and eventually caused an explosion in 1848. Three important countries —Greece, Great Britain, and France—experienced variations on this basic theme.

National Liberation in Greece

National, liberal revolution, frustrated in Italy and Spain by conservative statesmen, succeeded first after 1815 in Greece. Since the fifteenth century, the Greeks had been living under the domination of the Ottoman Turks. In spite of centuries of foreign rule, the Greeks had survived as a people, united by their language and the Greek Orthodox religion. It was perfectly natural that the general growth of national aspirations and a desire for independence would inspire some Greeks in the early nineteenth century. This rising national movement led to the formation of secret societies and then to revolt in 1821, led by Alexander Ypsilanti, a Greek patriot and a general in the Russian army.

The Great Powers, particularly Metternich, were opposed to all revolution, even revolution against the Islamic Turks. They refused to back Ypsilanti and supported the Ottoman Empire. Yet for many Europeans the Greek cause became a holy one. Educated Americans and Europeans were in love with the culture of classical Greece; Russians were stirred by the piety of their Orthodox brethren. Writers and artists, moved by the romantic impulse, responded enthusiastically to the Greek struggle. The flamboyant, radical poet Lord Byron went to Greece and died there in the struggle "that Greece might still be free." Turkish atrocities toward the rebels fanned the fires of European outrage and Greek determination. One of Delacroix's romantic masterpieces memorialized the massacre at Chios, where the Turks slaughtered nearly 100,000 Greeks.

The Greeks, though often quarreling among themselves, battled on against the Turks and hoped for the eventual support of European governments. In 1827 Great Britain, France, and Russia responded to popular demands at home and directed Turkey to accept an armistice. When the Turks refused, the navies of these three powers trapped the Turkish fleet at Navarino and destroyed it. Russia then declared another of its periodic wars of expansion against the Turks. This led to the establishment of a Russian protectorate over much of present-day Rumania, which had also been under Turkish rule. Great Britain, France, and Russia finally declared Greece independent in 1830 and installed a German prince as king of the new country in 1832. In the end the Greeks had won: a small nation had gained its independence in a heroic war against a foreign empire.

Liberal Reform in Great Britain

Eighteenth-century British society had been both flexible and remarkably stable. It was dominated by the landowning aristocracy, but that class was neither closed nor rigidly defined. Successful business and professional people could buy land and become gentlefolk, while the common people had more than the usual opportunities of the preindustrial world. Basic civil rights for all were balanced by a tradition of deference to one's social superiors. Parliament was manipulated by the king and was thoroughly undemocratic. Only about 6 percent of

Delacroix: Massacre at Chios   The Greek struggle for freedom and independence won the enthusiastic support of liberals, nationalists, and romantics. The Ottoman Turks were seen as cruel oppressors holding back the course of history, as in this powerful masterpiece by Delacroix. *(Source: Louvre/Cliché des Musées Nationaux, Paris)*

the population could vote for representatives to Parliament, and by the 1780s there was growing interest in some kind of political reform.

But the French Revolution threw the aristocracy into a panic for a generation, making it extremely hostile to any attempts to change the status quo. The Tory party, completely controlled by the landed aristocracy, was particularly fearful of radical movements at home and abroad. Castlereagh

initially worked closely with Metternich to restrain France and restore a conservative balance in central Europe. This same intense conservatism motivated the Tory government at home. After 1815 the aristocracy defended its ruling position by repressing every kind of popular protest.

The first step in this direction began with revision of the Corn Laws in 1815. Corn Laws to regulate the foreign grain trade had long existed, but

THE PRELUDE TO 1848

March 1814	Russia, Prussia, Austria, and Britain form the Quadruple Alliance to defeat France
April 1814	Napoleon abdicates
May–June 1814	Restoration of the Bourbon monarchy; Louis XVIII issues Constitutional Charter providing for civil liberties and representative government
	First Peace of Paris: allies combine leniency with defensive posture toward France
October 1814– June 1815	Congress of Vienna peace settlement: establishes balance-of-power principle and creates the German Confederation
February 1815	Napoleon escapes from Elba and marches on Paris
June 1815	Battle of Waterloo
September 1815	Austria, Prussia, and Russia form the Holy Alliance to repress liberal and revolutionary movements
November 1815	Second Peace of Paris and renewal of Quadruple Alliance: punishes France and establishes the European "congress system"
1819	Carlsbad Decrees: Metternich imposes harsh measures throughout the German Confederation
1820	Revolution in Spain and the Kingdom of the Two Sicilies
	Congress of Troppau: Metternich and Alexander I of Russia proclaim principle of intervention to maintain autocratic regimes
1821	Austria crushes liberal revolution in Naples and restores the Sicilian autocracy
	Greek revolt against the Ottoman Turks
1823	French armies restore the Spanish regime
	United States proclaims the Monroe Doctrine
1824	Reactionary Charles X succeeds Louis XVIII in France
1830	Charles X repudiates the Constitutional Charter; insurrection and collapse of government; Louis Philippe succeeds to the throne and maintains a narrowly liberal regime until 1848
	Greece wins independence from the Ottoman Empire
1832	Reform Bill expands British electorate and encourages the middle class
1839	Louis Blanc, *Organization of Work*
1840	Pierre Joseph Proudhon, *What Is Property?*
1846	Jules Michelet, *The People*
1848	Karl Marx and Friedrich Engels, *The Communist Manifesto*

they were not needed during a generation of war with France because the British had been unable to import cheap grain from eastern Europe. As shortages occurred and agricultural prices skyrocketed, a great deal of marginal land had been brought under cultivation. This development had been a bonanza for the landed aristocracy, whose fat rent rolls became even fatter. Peace meant that grain could be imported again and that the price of wheat and bread would go down. To almost everyone except the aristocracy, lower prices seemed highly desirable. The aristocracy, however, rammed far-reaching changes in the Corn Laws through Par-

liament. The new law prohibited the importation of foreign grain unless the price at home rose above 80 shillings per quarter-ton—a level reached only in time of harvest disaster before 1790. Seldom has a class legislated more selfishly for its own narrow economic advantage.

The change in the Corn Laws, coming at a time of widespread unemployment and postwar adjustment, led to protests and demonstrations by urban laborers. They were supported by radical intellectuals, who campaigned for a reformed House of Commons that would serve the nation and not just the aristocracy. In 1817 the Tory government responded by temporarily suspending the traditional rights of peaceable assembly and habeas corpus. Two years later, Parliament passed the infamous Six Acts, which among other things controlled a heavily taxed press and practically eliminated all mass meetings. These acts followed an enormous but orderly protest, at Saint Peter's Fields in Manchester, that had been savagely broken up by armed cavalry. Nicknamed the "Battle of Peterloo," in scornful reference to the British victory at Waterloo, this incident expressed the government's determination to repress and stand fast.

Ongoing industrial development was not only creating urban and social problems but also strengthening the upper middle classes. The new manufacturing and commercial groups insisted on a place for their new wealth alongside the landed wealth of the aristocracy in the framework of political power and social prestige. They called for certain kinds of liberal reform: reform of town government, organization of a new police force, and more rights for Catholics and dissenters. In the 1820s a less frightened Tory government moved in the direction of better urban administration, greater economic liberalism, and civil equality for Catholics. The prohibition on imports of foreign grain was replaced by a heavy tariff. These actions encouraged the middle classes to press on for reform of Parliament, so they could have a larger say in government and perhaps repeal the revised Corn Law, that symbol of aristocratic domination.

The Whig party, though led like the Tories by great aristocrats, had by tradition been more responsive to commercial and manufacturing interests. In 1830 a Whig ministry introduced "an act to amend the representation of the people of England and Wales." Defeated, then passed by the House of Commons, this reform bill was rejected by the House of Lords. But when in 1832 the Whigs got the king to promise to create enough new peers to pass the law, the House of Lords reluctantly gave in rather than see its snug little club ruined by upstart manufacturers and plutocrats. A mighty surge of popular protest had helped the king and lords make up their minds.

The Reform Bill of 1832 had profound significance. The House of Commons had emerged as the all-important legislative body. In the future, an obstructionist House of Lords could always be brought into line by the threat of creating new peers. The new industrial areas of the country gained representation in the Commons, and many old "rotten boroughs"—electoral districts with very few voters that the landed aristocracy had bought and sold—were eliminated.

The redistribution of seats reflected the shift in population to the northern manufacturing counties and the gradual emergence of an urban society. As a result of the Reform Bill of 1832, the number of voters increased about 50 percent. Comfortable middle-class groups in the urban population, as well as some substantial farmers who leased their land, received the vote. Thus the pressures building in Great Britain were successfully—though only temporarily—released. A major reform had been achieved peacefully, without revolution or civil war. More radical reforms within the system appeared difficult but not impossible.

The principal radical program was embodied in the "People's Charter" of 1838 and the Chartist movement (see page 714). Partly inspired by the economic distress of the working class, the Chartists' core demand was universal male (not female) suffrage. They saw complete political democracy and rule by the common people as the means to a good and just society. Hundreds of thousands of people signed gigantic petitions calling on Parliament to grant all men the right to vote, first and most seriously in 1839, again in 1842, and yet again in 1848. Parliament rejected all three petitions. In the short run, the working poor failed with their Chartist demands, but they learned a valuable lesson in mass politics.

While calling for universal male suffrage, many working-class people joined with middle-class manufacturers in the Anti–Corn Law League, founded in Manchester in 1839. Mass participation made possible a popular crusade against the tariff on imported grain and against the landed aristocracy. People were fired up by dramatic popular orators such as John Bright and Richard Cobden. These fighting liberals argued that lower food prices and more jobs in industry depended on repeal of the Corn Laws. Much of the working class agreed. The climax of the movement came in 1845. In that year Ireland's potato crop failed, and rapidly rising food prices marked the beginning of the Irish famine. Famine prices for food and even famine itself also seemed likely in England. To avert the impending catastrophe, the Tory prime minister Robert Peel joined with the Whigs and a minority of his own party to repeal the Corn Laws in 1846. England escaped famine. Thereafter, free trade became al-most sacred doctrine in Great Britain.

The following year, the Tories passed a bill de-signed to help the working classes, but in a differ-ent way. This was the Ten Hours Act of 1847, which limited the workday for women and young people in factories to ten hours. Tory aristocrats continued to champion legislation regulating fac-tory conditions. They were competing vigorously with the middle class for the support of the work-ing class. This healthy competition between a still-vigorous aristocracy and a strong middle class was a crucial factor in Great Britain's peaceful evolu-tion. The working classes could make temporary al-liances with either competitor to better their own conditions.

The people of Ireland did not benefit from this political competition. Long ruled as a conquered people, the great mass of the population (outside the northern counties of Ulster, which were partly Presbyterian) were Irish Catholic peasants, who rented their land from a tiny minority of Church of England Protestants, many of whom lived in Eng-land (see Chapter 20). Ruthlessly exploited and growing rapidly in numbers, Irish peasants had come to depend on the potato crop, the size of which varied substantially from year to year. Potato failures cannot be detected in time to plant other crops, nor can potatoes be stored for more than a year. Moreover, Ireland's precarious potato econ-omy was a subsistence economy, which therefore lacked a well-developed network of roads and trade capable of distributing other foods in time of disas-ter. When the crop failed in 1845, the Irish were very vulnerable.

In 1846, 1848, and 1851, the potato crop failed again in Ireland and throughout much of Europe. The general result was high food prices, widespread

Evictions of Irish Peasants   who could not pay their rent continued for decades after the famine. Surrounded by a few meager possessions, this family has been turned out of its cottage in the 1880s. The door is nailed shut to prevent their return. *(Source: Lawrence Collection, National Library of Ireland, Dublin)*

Delacroix: Liberty Leading the People This great romantic painting glorifies the July Revolution in Paris in 1830. Raising high the revolutionary tricolor, Liberty unites the worker, bourgeois, and street child in a righteous crusade against privilege and oppression. *(Source: Louvre/Cliché des Musées Nationaux, Paris)*

suffering, and, frequently, social upheaval. In Ireland, the result was unmitigated disaster—the Great Famine. Blight attacked the young plants, and the tubers rotted. Widespread starvation and mass fever epidemics followed. Total losses of population were staggering. Fully 1 million emigrants fled the famine between 1845 and 1851, going primarily to the United States and Great Britain, and at least 1.5 million people died or went unborn because of the disaster. The British government's efforts at famine relief were too little and too late. At the same time, the government energetically supported the heartless demands of landowners with armed force. Tenants who could not pay their rents

were evicted and their homes broken up or burned. Famine or no, Ireland remained a conquered province, a poor agricultural land that had gained little from the liberal reforms and the industrial developments that were transforming Great Britain.

The Revolution of 1830 in France

Louis XVIII's Constitutional Charter of 1814—theoretically a gift from the king but actually a response to political pressures—was basically a liberal constitution (see page 687). The economic gains of the middle class and the prosperous peasantry were fully protected; great intellectual and artistic freedom was permitted; and a real parliament with upper and lower houses was created. Immediately after Napoleon's abortive Hundred Days, the moderate, worldly-wise king refused to bow to the wishes of diehard aristocrats like his brother Charles, who wished to sweep away all the revolutionary changes and return to a bygone age of royal absolutism and aristocratic pretension. Instead, Louis appointed as his ministers moderate royalists, who sought and obtained the support of a majority of the representatives elected to the lower Chamber of Deputies between 1816 and Louis's death in 1824.

Louis XVIII's charter was anything but democratic. Only about 100,000 of the wealthiest people out of a total population of 30 million had the right to vote for the deputies who, with the king and his ministers, made the laws of the nation. Nonetheless, the "notable people" who did vote came from very different backgrounds. There were wealthy businessmen, war profiteers, successful professionals, ex-revolutionaries, large landowners from the middle class, Bourbons, and Bonapartists.

The old aristocracy with its pre-1789 mentality was a minority within the voting population. It was this situation that Louis's successor, Charles X (r. 1824–1830), could not abide. Crowned in a lavish, utterly medieval, five-hour ceremony in the cathedral of Reims in 1824, Charles was a true reactionary. He wanted to re-establish the old order in France. Increasingly blocked by the opposition of the deputies, Charles finally repudiated the Constitutional Charter in an attempted coup in July 1830. He issued decrees stripping much of the wealthy middle class of its voting rights, and he censored the press. The reaction was an immediate insurrection. In "three glorious days" the government collapsed. Paris boiled with revolutionary excitement, and Charles fled. Then the upper middle class, which had fomented the revolt, skillfully seated Charles's cousin, Louis Philippe, duke of Orléans, on the vacant throne.

Louis Philippe (r. 1830–1848) accepted the Constitutional Charter of 1814, adopted the red, white, and blue flag of the French Revolution, and admitted that he was merely the "king of the French people." In spite of such symbolic actions, the situation in France remained fundamentally unchanged. Casimir Périer, a wealthy banker and Louis Philippe's new chief minister, bluntly told a deputy who complained when the vote was extended only from 100,000 to 170,000 citizens, "The trouble with this country is that there are too many people like you who imagine that there has been a revolution in France."[5] The wealthy "notable" elite actually tightened its control as the old aristocracy retreated to the provinces to sulk harmlessly. For the upper middle class there had been a change in dynasty, in order to protect the status quo and the narrowly liberal institutions of 1815. Republicans, democrats, social reformers, and the poor of Paris were bitterly disappointed. They had made a revolution, but it seemed for naught.

THE REVOLUTIONS OF 1848

In 1848 revolutionary political and social ideologies combined with economic crisis and the romantic impulse to produce a vast upheaval. Only the most advanced and the most backward major countries—reforming Great Britain and immobile Russia—escaped untouched. Governments toppled; monarchs and ministers bowed or fled. National independence, liberal-democratic constitutions, and social reform: the lofty aspirations of a generation seemed at hand. Yet, in the end, the revolutions failed. Why was this so?

A Democratic Republic in France

The late 1840s in Europe were hard economically and tense politically. The potato famine in Ireland in 1845 and in 1846 had echoes on the Continent. Bad harvests jacked up food prices and caused misery and unemployment in the cities. "Prerevolutionary" outbreaks occurred all across Europe: an abortive Polish revolution in the northern part of Austria in 1846, a civil war between radicals and conservatives in Switzerland in 1847, and an armed uprising in Naples, Italy, in January 1848. Revolution was almost universally expected, but it took revolution in Paris—once again—to turn expectations into realities.

From its beginning in 1830, Louis Philippe's "bourgeois monarchy" was characterized by stubborn inaction. There was a glaring lack of social legislation, and politics was dominated by corruption and selfish special interests. The king's chief minister in the 1840s, François Guizot, was complacency personified. Guizot was especially satisfied with the electoral system. Only the rich could vote for deputies, and many of the deputies were docile government bureaucrats. It was the government's stubborn refusal to consider electoral reform that touched off popular revolt in Paris. Barricades went up on the night of February 22, 1848, and by February 24 Louis Philippe had abdicated in favor of his grandson. But the common people in arms would tolerate no more monarchy. This refusal led to the proclamation of a provisional republic, headed by a ten-man executive committee and certified by cries of approval from the revolutionary crowd.

In the flush of victory, there was much about which Parisian revolutionaries could agree. A generation of historians and journalists had praised the First French Republic, and their work had borne fruit: the revolutionaries were firmly committed to a republic as opposed to any form of constitutional monarchy, and they immediately set about drafting a constitution for France's Second Republic. Moreover, they wanted a truly popular and democratic republic, so that the healthy, life-giving forces of the common people—the peasants and the workers—could reform society with wise legislation. In practice, building such a republic meant giving the right to vote to every adult male, and this was quickly done. Revolutionary compassion and sympathy for freedom were expressed in the freeing of all slaves in French colonies, abolition of the death penalty, and the establishment of a ten-hour workday for Paris.

Yet there were profound differences within the revolutionary coalition in Paris. On the one hand, there were the moderate, liberal republicans of the middle class. They viewed universal manhood suffrage as the ultimate concession to be made to popular forces and strongly opposed any further radical social measures. On the other hand were the radical republicans. Influenced by the critique of capitalism and unbridled individualism elaborated by a generation of utopian socialists, and appalled by the poverty and misery of the urban poor, the radical republicans were committed to socialism. To be sure, socialism came in many utopian shapes and sizes for the Parisian working poor and their leaders, but that did not make their commitment to it any less real. Finally, wedged in between these groups were individuals like the poet Lamartine and the democrat Ledru-Rollin, who were neither doctrinaire socialists nor stand-pat liberals and who sought to escape an impending tragedy.

Daumier: The Legislative Belly   Protected by freedom of the press after 1830, French radicals bitterly attacked the do-nothing government of Louis Philippe. Here Daumier savagely ridicules the corruption of the Chamber of Deputies. *(Source: ©1990 The Art Institute of Chicago. All Rights Reserved.)*

Worsening depression and rising unemployment brought these conflicting goals to the fore. Louis Blanc (see page 730), who along with a worker named Albert represented the republican socialists in the provisional government, pressed for recognition of a socialist right to work. Blanc asserted that permanent government-sponsored cooperative workshops should be established for workers. Such workshops would be an alternative to capitalist employment and a decisive step toward a new social order.

The moderate republicans wanted no such thing. They were willing to provide only temporary relief. The resulting compromise set up national workshops—soon to become a vast program of pick-and-shovel public works—and established a special commission under Louis Blanc to "study the question." This satisfied no one. As bad as the national workshops were, though, they were better than nothing. An army of desperate poor from the French provinces and even from foreign countries streamed into Paris to sign up. The number enrolled in the workshops soared from 10,000 in March to 120,000 by June, and another 80,000 were trying unsuccessfully to join.

While the workshops in Paris grew, the French masses went to the polls in late April. Voting in most cases for the first time, the people elected to the new Constituent Assembly about five hundred moderate republicans, three hundred monarchists, and one hundred radicals who professed various brands of socialism. One of the moderate republicans was the author of *Democracy in America,* Alexis de Tocqueville (1805–1859), who had predicted the overthrow of Louis Philippe's government. To this brilliant observer, socialism was the most characteristic aspect of the revolution in Paris.

This socialist revolution was evoking a violent reaction not only among the frightened middle and upper classes but also among the bulk of the population—the peasants. The French peasants owned land, and according to Tocqueville, "private property had become with all those who owned it a sort of bond of fraternity."[6] The countryside, Tocqueville wrote, had been seized with a universal hatred of radical Paris. Returning from Normandy to take his seat in the new Constituent Assembly, Tocqueville saw that a majority of the members were firmly committed to the republic and strongly opposed to the socialists, and he shared their sentiments.

The clash of ideologies—of liberal capitalism and socialism—became a clash of classes and arms after the elections. The new government's executive committee dropped Louis Blanc and thereafter included no representative of the Parisian working class. Fearing that their socialist hopes were about to be dashed, the workers invaded the Constituent Assembly on May 15 and tried to proclaim a new revolutionary state. But the government was ready and used the middle-class National Guard to squelch this uprising. As the workshops continued to fill and grow more radical, the fearful but powerful propertied classes in the Assembly took the offensive. On June 22 the government dissolved the national workshops in Paris, giving the workers the choice of joining the army or going to workshops in the provinces.

The result was a spontaneous and violent uprising. Frustrated in their attempts to create a socialist society, masses of desperate people were now losing even their life-sustaining relief. As a voice from the crowd cried out when the famous astronomer François Arago counseled patience, "Ah, Monsieur Arago, you have never been hungry!"[7] Barricades sprang up in the narrow streets of Paris, and a terrible class war began. Working people fought with the courage of utter desperation, but the government had the army and the support of peasant France. After three terrible "June Days" and the death or injury of more than ten thousand people, the republican army under General Louis Cavaignac stood triumphant in a sea of working-class blood and hatred.

The revolution in France thus ended in spectacular failure. The February coalition of the middle and working classes had in four short months become locked in mortal combat. In place of a generous democratic republic, the Constituent Assembly completed a constitution featuring a strong executive. This allowed Louis Napoleon, nephew of Napoleon Bonaparte, to win a landslide victory in the election of December 1848. The appeal of his great name, as well as the desire of the propertied classes for order at any cost, had produced a semi-authoritarian regime.

The Austrian Empire in 1848

Throughout central Europe, news of the upheaval in France evoked feverish excitement and eventu-

THE REVOLUTIONS OF 1848

February	Revolt in Paris against Louis Philippe's "bourgeois monarchy"; Louis Philippe abdicates; proclamation of a provisional republic
February–June	Establishment and rapid growth of government-sponsored workshops in France
March 3	Hungarians under Kossuth demand autonomy from Austrian Empire
March 13	Uprising of students and workers in Vienna; Metternich flees to London
March 19–21	Frederick William IV of Prussia is forced to salute the bodies of slain revolutionaries in Berlin and agrees to a liberal constitution and merger into a new German state
March 20	Ferdinand I of Austria abolishes serfdom and promises reforms
March 26	Workers in Berlin issue a series of socialist demands
April 22	French voters favor moderate republicans over radicals 5 : 1
May 15	Parisian socialist workers invade the Constitutional Assembly and unsuccessfully proclaim a new revolutionary state
May 18	Frankfurt Assembly begins writing a new German constitution
June 17	Austrian army crushes working-class revolt in Prague
June 22–26	French government abolishes the national workshops, provoking an uprising June Days: republican army defeats rebellious Parisian working class
October	Austrian army besieges and retakes Vienna from students and working-class radicals
December	Conservatives force Ferdinand I of Austria to abdicate in favor or young Francis Joseph
	Frederick William IV disbands Prussian Constituent Assembly and grants Prussia a conservative constitution
	Louis Napoleon wins a landslide victory in French presidential elections
March 1849	Frankfurt Assembly elects Frederick William IV of Prussia emperor of the new German state; Frederick William refuses and reasserts royal authority in Prussia
June –August 1849	Habsburg and Russian forces defeat the Hungarian independence movement

ally revolution. Liberals demanded written constitutions, representative government, and greater civil liberties. When governments hesitated, popular revolts followed. Urban workers and students served as the shock troops, but they were allied with middle-class liberals and peasants. In the face of this united front, monarchs collapsed and granted almost everything. The popular revolutionary coalition, having secured great and easy victories, then broke down as it had in France. The traditional forces—the monarchy, the aristocracy, and the regular army—recovered their nerve, reasserted their authority, and took back many though not all of the concessions. Reaction was everywhere victorious.

The revolution in the Austrian Empire began in Hungary. Nationalism had been growing among Hungarians since about 1790, and in 1848, under the leadership of Louis Kossuth, the Hungarians demanded national autonomy, full civil liberties, and universal suffrage. When the monarchy in Vienna hesitated, Viennese students and workers took to the streets on March 13 and added their own demands. Peasant disorders broke out in parts of the empire. The Habsburg emperor Ferdinand I (r. 1835–1848) capitulated and promised reforms and a liberal constitution. Metternich fled in disguise toward London. The old order seemed to be collapsing with unbelievable rapidity.

The coalition of revolutionaries was not completely stable, though. The Austrian Empire was overwhelmingly agricultural, and serfdom still existed. On March 20, as part of its capitulation before upheaval, the monarchy abolished serfdom with its degrading forced labor and feudal services. Peasants throughout the empire felt they had won a

Defending the Barricades in Prague   Tearing up the cobblestones and barricading
the streets, men and women fought with fierce determination in the revolutions of 1848.
(Source: Sphinx Publishers)

victory reminiscent of that in France in 1789.
Newly free, men and women of the land lost interest in the political and social questions agitating
the cities. The government had in the peasants a
potential ally of great importance, especially since,
in central Europe as in France, the army was largely
composed of peasants.

   The coalition of March was also weakened—and
ultimately destroyed—by conflicting national aspirations. In March the Hungarian revolutionary
leaders pushed through an extremely liberal, almost democratic, constitution granting widespread voting rights and civil liberties and ending
feudal obligations. So far, well and good. Yet the
Hungarian revolutionaries were also nationalists
with a mission. They wanted the ancient Crown of
Saint Stephen, with its mosaic of provinces and na-

tionalities, transformed into a unified, centralized
Hungarian nation. To the minority groups that
formed half the population of the kingdom of
Hungary—the Croats, the Serbs, and the Rumanians—such unification was completely unacceptable. Each felt entitled to political autonomy and
cultural independence. The Habsburg monarchy in
Vienna exploited the fears of the minority groups,
and they were soon locked in armed combat with
the new Hungarian government.

   In a somewhat different way, Czech nationalists
based in Bohemia and the city of Prague, led by the
Czech historian Palacký, came into conflict with
German nationalists. Like the minorities in Hungary, the Czechs saw their struggle for autonomy as
a struggle against a dominant group, the Germans.
Thus the national aspirations of different peoples

in the Austrian Empire came into sharp conflict, and the monarchy was able to play off one group against the other.

Nor was this all. The urban working classes of poor artisans and day laborers were not as radical in the Austrian Empire as they were in France, but then neither were the middle class and lower middle class. Throughout Austria and the German states, where Metternich's brand of absolutism had so recently ruled supreme, the middle class wanted liberal reform, complete with constitutional monarchy, limited voting rights, and modest social measures. They wanted a central European equivalent of the English Reform Bill of 1832 and the Corn Law repeal of 1846. When the urban poor rose in arms—as they did in the Austrian cities of Vienna, Prague, and Milan and throughout the German Confederation as well, presenting their own demands for socialist workshops and universal voting rights for men—the prosperous middle classes recoiled in alarm. As in Paris, the union of the urban poor and the middle class was soon a mere memory, and a bad memory at that.

Finally, the conservative aristocratic forces gathered around Emperor Ferdinand I regained their nerve and reasserted their great strength. The archduchess Sophia, a conservative but intelligent and courageous Bavarian princess married to the emperor's brother, provided a rallying point. Deeply ashamed of the emperor's collapse before a "mess of students,"[8] she insisted that Ferdinand, who had no heir, abdicate in favor of her eighteen-year-old son, Francis Joseph. Powerful nobles who held high positions in the government, the army, and the church agreed completely. They organized around Sophia in a secret conspiracy to reverse and crush the revolution.

Their first breakthrough came when one of the most dedicated members of the group, Prince Alfred Windischgrätz, bombarded Prague and savagely crushed a working-class revolt there on June 17. Other Austrian officials and nobles began to lead the minority nationalities of Hungary against the revolutionary government proclaimed by the Hungarian patriots. In late July 1848 another Austrian army reconquered Austria's possessions in northern Italy, where Italian patriots had seized power in March. Thus revolution failed as miserably in Italy as everywhere else. At the end of October, the well-equipped, predominantly peasant troops of the regular Austrian army attacked the student and working-class radicals in Vienna and retook the city at the cost of more than four thousand casualties. Thus the determination of the Austrian aristocracy and the loyalty of its army were the final ingredients in the triumph of reaction and the defeat of revolution.

Sophia's son Francis Joseph (r. 1848–1916) was crowned emperor of Austria immediately after his eighteenth birthday in December 1848. Only in Hungary were the Austrian forces at first unsuccessful in establishing control on the new emperor's behalf. Yet another determined conservative, Nicholas I of Russia (r. 1825–1855), obligingly lent his iron hand. On June 6, 1849, 130,000 Russian troops poured into Hungary. After bitter fighting—in which the Hungarian army supported the revolutionary Hungarian government—they subdued the country. For a number of years the Habsburgs ruled Hungary as a conquered territory.

Prussia and the Frankfurt Assembly

The rest of the states in the German Confederation generally recapitulated the ebb and flow of developments in France and Austria. The key difference was the additional goal of unifying the thirty-eight states of the German Confederation, with the possible exception of Austria, into a single sovereign nation. Therefore, events in Germany were extraordinarily complex, since they were occurring not only in the individual principalities but at the all-German level as well.

After Austria, Prussia was the largest and most influential German kingdom. Prior to 1848, the goal of middle-class Prussian liberals had been to transform absolutist Prussia into a liberal constitutional monarchy. Such a monarchy would then take the lead in merging itself and all the other German states into a liberal, unified nation. The agitation following the fall of Louis Philippe encouraged Prussian liberals to press their demands. When these were not granted, the artisans and factory workers in Berlin exploded, joining temporarily with the middle-class liberals in the struggle against the monarchy. The autocratic yet paternalistic Frederick William IV (r. 1840–1861), already displaying the instability that later became insanity, vacillated. Humiliated by the revolutionary crowd, which forced him to salute from his balcony the blood-spattered corpses of workers who had fallen in an uprising on March 18, the nearly hysterical king finally caved in. On March 21 he promised to grant Prussia a liberal constitution and to merge it into a new national German state that was to be created. He appointed two wealthy businessmen from the Rhineland—perfect representatives of moderate liberalism—to form a new government.

The situation might have stabilized at this point if the workers had not wanted much more and the Prussian aristocracy much less. On March 26 the workers issued a series of radical and vaguely socialist demands that troubled their middle-class allies: universal voting rights, a ministry of labor, a minimum wage, and a ten-hour day. At the same time, a wild-tempered Prussian landowner and aristocrat,

Revolutionary Justice in Vienna   As part of the conservative resurgence, in October 1848 the Austrian minister of war ordered up reinforcements for an army marching on Hungary. In a last defiant gesture the outraged revolutionaries in Vienna seized the minister and lynched him from a lamppost for treason. The army then reconquered the city in a week of bitter fighting. *(Source: Mary Evans Picture Library/Photo Researchers)*

Otto von Bismarck, joined the conservative clique gathered around the king to urge counter-revolution. While these tensions in Prussia were growing, an elected assembly met in Berlin to write a constitution for the Prussian state.

To add to the complexity of the situation, a self-appointed committee of liberals from various German states successfully called for the formation of a national constituent assembly to begin writing a federal constitution for a unified German state. That body met for the first time on May 18 in Saint Paul's Church in Frankfurt. The Frankfurt National Assembly was a most curious revolutionary body. It was really a serious middle-class body whose 820 members included some 200 lawyers; 100 professors; many doctors, judges, and officials; and 140 businessmen for good measure.

Convened to write a constitution, the learned body was soon absorbed in a battle with Denmark over the provinces of Schleswig and Holstein. Jurisdiction over them was a hopelessly complicated issue from a legal point of view. Britain's foreign minister Lord Palmerston once said that only three people had ever understood the Schleswig-Holstein question, and of those one had died, another had gone mad, and he himself had forgotten the answer. The provinces were inhabited primarily by Germans but were ruled by the king of Denmark, although Holstein was a member of the German Confederation. When Frederick VII, the new nationalistic king of Denmark, tried to integrate both provinces into the rest of his state, the Germans there revolted.

Hypnotized by this conflict, the National Assembly at Frankfurt debated ponderously and finally called on the Prussian army to oppose Denmark in the name of the German nation. Prussia responded and began war with Denmark. As the Schleswig-Holstein issue demonstrated, the national ideal was a crucial factor motivating the German middle classes in 1848.

Almost obsessed with the fate of Germans under Danish rule, many members of the National Assembly also wanted to bring the German-speaking provinces of Austria into the new German state. Yet resurgent Austria resolutely opposed any division of its territory. Once this Austrian action made a "big German state" impossible, the National Assembly completed its drafting of a liberal constitution. Finally, in March 1849, the Assembly elected King Frederick William of Prussia emperor of the new German national state (minus Austria and Schleswig-Holstein).

By early 1849, however, reaction had been successful almost everywhere. Frederick William reasserted his royal authority, disbanded the Prussian Constituent Assembly, and granted his subjects a limited, essentially conservative, constitution. Reasserting that he ruled by divine right, Frederick William contemptuously refused to accept the "crown from the gutter." The reluctant revolutionaries in Frankfurt had waited too long and acted too timidly.

When Frederick William, who really wanted to be emperor but only on his own authoritarian terms, tried to get the small monarchs of Germany to elect him emperor, Austria balked. Supported by Russia, Austria forced Prussia to renounce all its schemes of unification in late 1850. The German Confederation was re-established. After two turbulent years, the political map of the German states remained unchanged. Attempts to unite the Germans—first in a liberal national state and then in a conservative Prussian empire—had failed completely.

SUMMARY

In 1814 the victorious allied powers sought to restore peace and stability in Europe. Dealing moderately with France and wisely settling their own differences, the allies laid the foundations for beneficial international cooperation throughout much of the nineteenth century. Led by Metternich, the conservative powers also sought to prevent the spread of subversive ideas and radical changes in domestic politics. Yet European thought has seldom been more powerfully creative than after 1815, and ideologies of liberalism, nationalism, and socialism all developed to challenge the existing order. The Romantic movement, breaking decisively with the dictates of classicism, reinforced the spirit of change and revolutionary anticipation.

All of these forces culminated in the liberal and nationalistic revolutions of 1848. Political, economic, and social pressures that had been building since 1815 exploded dramatically, but the upheavals of 1848 were abortive and very few revolutionary goals were realized. The moderate, nationalistic middle classes were unable to consolidate their initial victories in France or elsewhere in Europe. Instead, they drew back when artisans, factory workers, and radical socialists rose up to present their own much more revolutionary demands. This retreat facilitated the efforts of dedicated aristocrats in central Europe and made possible the crushing of Parisian workers by a coalition of solid bourgeoisie and landowning peasantry in France. A host of fears, a sea of blood, and a torrent of disillusion had drowned the lofty ideals and utopian visions of a generation. The age of romantic revolution was over.

NOTES

1. Quoted in A. J. May, *The Age of Metternich, 1814–1848* rev. ed. (New York: Holt, Rinehart & Winston, 1963), p. 11.
2. Quoted in H. Kohn, *Nationalism* (New York: Van Nostrand, 1955), pp. 141–142.
3. Quoted in F. D. Klingender, *Art and the Industrial Revolution* (St. Albans, Eng.: Paladin, 1972), p. 117.
4. Quoted in F. B. Artz, *From the Renaissance to Romanticism: Trends in Style in Art, Literature, and Music, 1300–1830* (Chicago: University of Chicago Press, 1962), pp. 276, 278.
5. Quoted in G. Wright, *France in Modern Times* (Chicago: Rand McNally, 1960), p. 145.
6. A. de Tocqueville, *Recollections* (New York: Columbia University Press, 1949), p. 94.
7. M. Agulhon, *1848* (Paris: Éditions du Seuil, 1973), pp. 68–69.
8. Quoted in W. L. Langer, *Political and Social Upheaval, 1832–1852* (New York: Harper & Row, 1969), p. 361.

SUGGESTED READING

All of the works cited in the Notes are highly recommended. May's is a good brief survey, while Kohn has written perceptively on nationalism in many books. Wright's *France in Modern Times* is a lively introduction to French history with stimulating biographical discussions; Langer's is a balanced synthesis with an excellent bibliography. Among general studies, C. Moraze, *The Triumph of the Middle Classes* (1968), a wide-ranging procapitalist interpretation, may be compared with E. J. Hobsbawm's flexible Marxism in *The Age of Revolution,*

1789–1848 (1962). For English history, A. Briggs's socially oriented *The Making of Modern England, 1784–1867* (1967) and D. Thomson's *England in the Nineteenth Century, 1815–1914* (1951) are excellent. Restoration France is sympathetically portrayed by G. de Bertier de Sauvigny in *The Bourbon Restoration* (1967), while R. Price, *A Social History of Nineteenth-Century France* (1987), is a fine synthesis incorporating recent research. T. Hamerow studies the social implications of the dual revolution in Germany in *Restoration, Revolution, Reaction 1815–1871* (1966), which may be compared with H. Treitschke's bombastic, pro-Prussian *History of Germany in the Nineteenth Century* (1915–1919), a classic of nationalistic history, and L. Snyder, *Roots of German Nationalism* (1978). H. James, *A German Identity, 1770–1990* (1989), and J. Sheehan, *Germany, 1770–1866* (1989), are stimulating general histories that skillfully incorporate recent research. E. Kedourie, *Nationalism* (1960), is a stimulating critique of the new faith. H. Kissinger, *A World Restored* (1957), offers not only a provocative interpretation of the Congress of Vienna but also insights into the mind of Richard Nixon's famous secretary of state. Compare that volume with H. Nicolson's entertaining *The Congress of Vienna* (1946). On 1848, L. B. Namier's highly critical *1848: The Revolution of the Intellectuals* (1964) and P. Robertson's *Revolutions of 1848: A Social History* (1960) are outstanding. I. Deak, *The Lawful Revolution: Louis Kossuth and the Hungarians, 1848–49* (1979), is a noteworthy study of an interesting figure.

On early socialism and Marxism, there are A. Lindemann's stimulating survey, *A History of European Socialism* (1983), and W. Sewell, Jr.'s *Work and Revolution in France: The Language of Labor from the Old Regime to 1848* (1980), as well as G. Lichtheim's high-powered *Marxism* (1961) and his *Short History of Socialism* (1970). Fourier is treated sympathetically in J. Beecher, *Charles Fourier* (1986). J. Schumpeter, *Capitalism, Socialism and Democracy* (1947), is magnificent but difficult, a real mind-stretcher. Also highly recommended is B. Taylor, *Eve and the New Jerusalem: Socialism and Feminism in the Nineteenth Century* (1983), which explores fascinating English attempts to emancipate workers and women at the same time. On liberalism, there are R. Heilbroner's entertaining *The Worldly Philosophers* (1967) and G. de Ruggiero's classic *History of European Liberalism* (1959). J. Barzun, *Classic, Ro-*

mantic and Modern (1961), skillfully discusses the emergence of romanticism. R. Stromberg, *An Intellectual History of Modern Europe,* 3d ed. (1981), and F. Baumer, *Modern European Thought: Continuity and Change in Ideas, 1600–1950* (1970), are valuable surveys. The important place of religion in nineteenth-century thought is considered from different perspectives in H. McLeod, *Religion and the People of Western Europe* (1981), and O. Chadwick, *The Secularization of the European Mind in the Nineteenth Century* (1976). Two good church histories with useful bibliographies are J. Altholz, *The Churches in the Nineteenth Century* (1967), and A. Vidler, *The Church in an Age of Revolution: 1789 to the Present Day* (1961).

The thoughtful reader is strongly advised to delve into the incredibly rich writing of contemporaries. J. Bowditch and C. Ramsland, eds., *Voices of the Industrial Revolution* (1961), is an excellent starting point, with well-chosen selections from leading economic thinkers and early socialists. H. Hugo, ed., *The Romantic Reader,* is another fine anthology. Mary Shelley's *Frankenstein,* a great romantic novel, draws an almost lovable picture of the famous monster and is highly recommended. Jules Michelet's compassionate masterpiece *The People,* a famous historian's anguished examination of French social divisions on the eve of 1848, draws one into the heart of the period and is highly recommended. Alexis de Tocqueville covers some of the same ground less romantically in his *Recollections,* which may be compared with Karl Marx's white-hot "instant history," *Class Struggles in France, 1848–1850* (1850). Great novels that accurately portray aspects of the times are Victor Hugo, *Les Misérables,* an exciting story of crime and passion among France's poor; Honoré de Balzac, *La Cousine Bette* and *Le Père Goriot;* and Thomas Mann, *Buddenbrooks,* a wonderful historical novel that traces the rise and fall of a prosperous German family over three generations during the nineteenth century.

24

Life in Urban Society

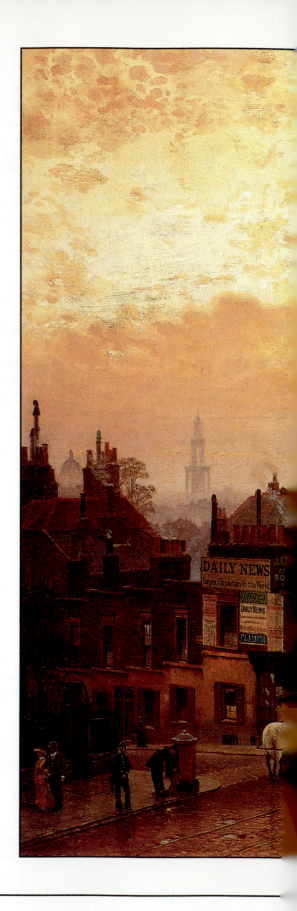

The era of intellectual and political upheaval that culminated in the revolutions of 1848 was also an era of rapid urbanization. After 1848, Western political development veered off in a novel and uncharted direction, but the growth of towns and cities rushed forward with undiminished force. Thus Western society was urban and industrial in 1900, as surely as it had been rural and agrarian in 1800. The urbanization of society was both a result of the Industrial Revolution and a reflection of its enormous long-term impact.

- What was life like in the cities, and how did it change?
- What did the emergence of urban industrial society mean for rich and poor and those in between?
- How did families cope with the challenges and respond to the opportunities of the developing urban civilization?
- Finally, what changes in science and thought inspired and gave expression to this new civilization?

These are the questions this chapter will investigate.

TAMING THE CITY

The growth of industry posed enormous challenges for all elements of Western society, from young factory workers confronting relentless discipline to aristocratic elites maneuvering to retain political power. As we saw in Chapter 22, the early consequences of economic transformation were mixed and far-reaching, and by no means wholly negative. By 1850 at the latest, working conditions were improving and real wages were definitely rising for the mass of the population, and they continued to do so until 1914. Thus, given the poverty and uncertainty of preindustrial life, some historians maintain that the history of industrialization in the nineteenth century is probably better written in terms of increasing opportunities than of greater hardships.

Critics of this relatively optimistic view of industrialization claim that it neglects the quality of life in urban areas. They stress that the new industrial towns and cities were awful places, where people, especially poor people, suffered from bad housing, lack of sanitation, and a sense of hopelessness. They ask if these drawbacks did not more than cancel out higher wages and greater opportunity. An examination of urban development provides some answers to this complex question.

Industry and the Growth of Cities

Since the Middle Ages, European cities had been centers of government, culture, and large-scale commerce. They had also been congested, dirty, and unhealthy. People were packed together almost as tightly as possible within the city limits. The typical city was a "walking city": for all but the wealthiest classes, walking was the only available form of transportation.

Infectious disease spread with deadly speed in cities, and people were always more likely to die in the city than in the countryside. In the larger towns, more people died each year than were born, on the average, and urban populations were able to maintain their numbers only because newcomers were continuously arriving from rural areas. Little could be done to improve these conditions. Given the pervasive poverty, absence of urban transportation, and lack of medical knowledge, the deadly and overcrowded conditions could only be accepted fatalistically. They were the urban equivalents of bad weather and poor crops, the price of urban excitement and opportunity.

Clearly, deplorable urban conditions did not originate with the Industrial Revolution. What the Industrial Revolution did was to reveal those conditions more nakedly than ever before. The steam engine freed industrialists from dependence on the energy of fast-flowing streams and rivers, so that by 1800 there was every incentive to build new factories in urban areas. Cities had better shipping facilities than the countryside and thus better supplies of coal and raw materials. There were also many hands wanting work in the cities, for cities drew people like a magnet. And it was a great advantage for a manufacturer to have other factories nearby to supply the business's needs and buy its products. Therefore, as industry grew, there was also a rapid expansion of already overcrowded and unhealthy cities.

The challenge of the urban environment was felt first and most acutely in Great Britain. The number

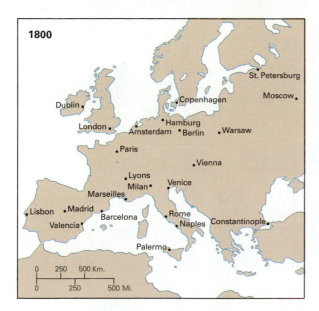

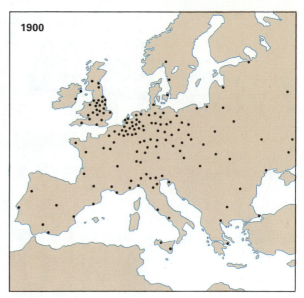

MAP 24.1 European Cities of 100,000 or More, 1800 and 1900   There were more large cities in Great Britain in 1900 than in all Europe in 1800.

of people living in cities of 20,000 or more in England and Wales jumped from 1.5 million in 1801 to 6.3 million in 1851 and reached 15.6 million by 1891. Such cities accounted for 17 percent of the total English population in 1801, 35 percent as early as 1851, and fully 54 percent in 1891. Other countries duplicated the English pattern as they industrialized. An American observer was hardly exaggerating when he wrote in 1899 that "the most remarkable social phenomenon of the present century is the concentration of population in cities" (Map 24.1).[1]

In the 1820s and 1830s, people in Britain and France began to worry about the condition of their cities. In those years, the populations of a number of British cities were increasing by 40 to 70 percent each decade. With urban areas expanding at such previously undreamed-of rates, people's fatalistic acceptance of overcrowded, unsanitary urban living conditions began to give way to active concern. Something had to be done.

On one point everyone could agree: except on the outskirts, each town and city was using every scrap of land to the fullest extent. Parks and open areas were almost nonexistent. A British parliamentary committee reported in 1833 that "with a rapidly increasing population, lodged for the most part in narrow courts and confined streets, the means of occasional exercise and recreation in fresh air are every day lessened, as inclosures [of vacant areas] take place and buildings spread themselves on every side."[2] Buildings were erected on the smallest possible lots, in order to pack the maximum number of people into a given space. Narrow houses were built wall to wall, in long rows. These row houses had neither front nor back yards, and only a narrow alley in back separated one row from the next. Or buildings were built around tiny courtyards completely enclosed on all four sides. Many people lived in cellars and attics. These tiny rooms were often overcrowded. "Six, eight, and even ten occupying one room is anything but uncommon," wrote a doctor from Aberdeen in Scotland for a government investigation in 1842.

These highly concentrated urban populations lived in extremely unsanitary and unhealthy conditions. Open drains and sewers flowed alongside or down the middle of unpaved streets. Because of poor construction and an absence of running water, the sewers often filled with garbage and excrement. Toilet facilities were primitive in the extreme. In parts of Manchester, as many as two hundred people shared a single outhouse. Such privies filled up rapidly, and since they were infrequently emptied, sewage often overflowed and seeped into cellar dwellings.

The extent to which filth lay underfoot and the smell of excrement filled the air is hard to believe;

A COURT FOR KING CHOLERA.

Filth and Disease This 1852 drawing from *Punch* tells volumes about the unhealthy living conditions of the urban poor. In the foreground children play with a dead rat and a woman scavenges a dungheap. Cheap rooming houses provide shelter for the frightfully overcrowded population. *(Source: The British Library)*

yet it was abundantly documented between 1830 and 1850. One London construction engineer found, for example, that the cellars of two large houses on a major road were "full of night-soil [human excrement], to the depth of three feet, which had been permitted for years to accumulate from the overflow of the cesspools." Moreover, some courtyards in poorer neighborhoods became dunghills, collecting excrement that was sometimes sold as fertilizer. By the 1840s there was among the better-off classes a growing, shocking "realization that, to put it as mildly as possible, millions of English men, women, and children were living in shit."[3]

Who or what was responsible for these awful conditions? The crucial factors were the tremendous pressure of more people and the *total* absence of public transportation. People simply had to jam themselves together if they were to be able to walk to shops and factories. Another factor was that government in Great Britain, both local and national, was slow to provide sanitary facilities and establish adequate building codes. This slow pace was probably attributable more to a need to explore and identify what precisely should be done than to rigid middle-class opposition to government action. Certainly Great Britain had no monopoly on overcrowded and unhealthy urban conditions; many continental cities were every bit as bad.

Most responsible of all was the sad legacy of rural housing conditions in preindustrial society, combined with appalling ignorance. As the author of a recent study concludes, there "were rural slums of a horror not surpassed by the rookeries of London. . . . The evidence shows that the decent cottage was the exception, the hovel the rule."[4]

Thus housing was far down on the newcomer's list of priorities, and it is not surprising that many people carried the filth of the mud floor and the dung of the barnyard with them to the city.

Indeed, ordinary people generally took dirt and filth for granted, and some even prized it. One English miner told an investigator, "I do not think it usual for the lasses [in the coal mines] to wash their bodies; my sisters never wash themselves." As for the men, "their legs and bodies are as black as your hat." When poor people were admitted to English workhouses, they often resisted the required bath. One man protested that it was "equal to robbing him of a great coat which he had had for some years."[5]

The Public Health Movement

Although cleanliness was not next to godliness in most people's eyes, it was becoming so for some reformers. The most famous of these was Edwin Chadwick, one of the commissioners charged with the administration of relief to paupers under the revised Poor Law of 1834. Chadwick was a good Benthamite—that is, a follower of the radical philosopher Jeremy Bentham (1748–1832). Bentham had taught that public problems ought to be dealt with on a rational, scientific basis and according to the "greatest good for the greatest number." Applying these principles, Chadwick soon saw that much more than economics was involved in the problems of poverty and the welfare budget. Indeed, he soon became convinced that disease and death actually caused poverty, simply because a sick worker was an unemployed worker and orphaned children were poor children. Most important, Chadwick believed that disease could be prevented by quite literally cleaning up the urban environment. That was his "sanitary idea."

Building on a growing number of medical and sociological studies, Chadwick collected detailed reports from local Poor Law officials on the "sanitary conditions of the laboring population." After three years of investigation, these reports and Chadwick's hard-hitting commentary were published in 1842 to wide publicity. This mass of evidence proved that disease was related to filthy environmental conditions, which were in turn caused largely by lack of drainage, sewers, and garbage collection. Putrefying, smelly excrement was no longer simply disgusting. For reformers like Chad-

wick, it was a threat to the entire community. It polluted the atmosphere and caused disease.

The key to the energetic action Chadwick proposed was an adequate supply of clean piped water. Such water was essential for personal hygiene, public bathhouses, street cleaning, firefighting, and industry. Chadwick correctly believed that the stinking excrement of communal outhouses could be dependably carried off by water through sewers at less than one-twentieth the cost of removing it by hand. The cheap iron pipes and tile drains of the industrial age would provide running water and sewerage for all sections of town, not just the wealthy ones. In 1848, with the cause strengthened by the cholera epidemic of 1846, Chadwick's report became the basis of Great Britain's first public health law, which created a national health board and gave

Sewer Scavenger Growing cities had many rubbish collectors, who sifted through garbage for things to sell and "recycle." Some worked in the sewers, like this London scavenger. Sewer scavengers occasionally found valuable items, but their occupation was unhealthy and extremely dangerous. (Source: Museum of London)

cities broad authority to build modern sanitary systems.

The public health movement won dedicated supporters in the United States, France, and Germany from the 1840s on. As in Great Britain, governments accepted at least limited responsibility for the health of all citizens. Moreover, they adopted increasingly concrete programs of action, programs that broke decisively with the age-old fatalism of urban populations in the face of shockingly high mortality. Thus, despite many people's skepticism about sanitation, European cities were making real progress toward adequate water supplies and sewage systems by the 1860s and 1870s. And city dwellers were beginning to reap the reward of better health.

The Bacterial Revolution

Effective control of communicable disease required a great leap forward in medical knowledge and biological theory as well as clean water supply and good sewers. Reformers like Chadwick were seriously handicapped by the prevailing *miasmatic theory* of disease—the belief that people contract disease when they breathe the bad odors of decay and putrefying excrement; in short, the theory that smells cause disease. The miasmatic theory was a reasonable deduction from empirical observations: cleaning up filth did produce laudable results. Yet the theory was very incomplete.

Keen observation by doctors and public health officials in the 1840s and 1850s pinpointed the role of bad drinking water in the transmission of disease and suggested that contagion was *spread through* filth and not caused by it. Moreover, some particularly horrid stenches, such as that of the sewage-glutted Thames River at London in 1858, did not lead to widely feared epidemics, and this fact also weakened the miasmatic idea.

The breakthrough was the development of the *germ theory* of disease by Louis Pasteur (1822–1895), a French chemist who began studying fermentation in 1854. For ages people had used fermentation to make bread and wine, beer and cheese, but without really understanding what was going on. And from time to time, beer and wine would mysteriously spoil for no apparent reason. Responding to the calls of big brewers for help, Pasteur used his microscope to develop a simple test brewers could use to monitor the fermentation

process and avoid spoilage. Continuing his investigations, Pasteur found that fermentation depended on the growth of living organisms, and that the activity of these organisms could be suppressed by heating the beverage—by *pasteurizing it.* The breathtaking implication was that specific diseases were caused by specific living organisms—germs—and that those organisms could be controlled in people as well as in beer, wine, and milk.

By 1870 the work of Pasteur and others had demonstrated the general connection between germs and disease. When, in the middle of the 1870s, the German country doctor Robert Koch and his coworkers developed pure cultures of harmful bacteria and described their life cycles, the dam broke. Over the next twenty years, researchers—mainly Germans—identified the organisms responsible for disease after disease, often identifying several in a single year. These discoveries led to the development of a number of effective vaccines and the emergence of modern immunology.

Acceptance of the germ theory brought about dramatic improvements in the deadly environment of hospitals and surgery. The English surgeon Joseph Lister (1827–1912) had noticed that patients with simple fractures were much less likely to die than those with compound fractures, in which the skin was broken and internal tissues were exposed to the air. In 1865, when Pasteur showed that the air was full of bacteria, Lister immediately grasped the connection between aerial bacteria and the problem of wound infection. He reasoned that a chemical disinfectant applied to a wound dressing would "destroy the life of the floating particles." Lister's "antiseptic principle" worked wonders. In the 1880s, German surgeons developed the more sophisticated practice of sterilizing not only the wound but everything—hands, instruments, clothing—that entered the operating room.

The achievements of the bacterial revolution coupled with the ever-more-sophisticated public health movement saved millions of lives, particularly after about 1890. Mortality rates began to decline dramatically in European countries (Figure 24.1), as the awful death sentences of the past—diphtheria, typhoid and typhus, cholera, yellow fever—became vanishing diseases. City dwellers benefited especially from these developments. By 1910 the death rates for people of all ages in urban areas were generally no greater than in rural areas, and sometimes they were less. Particularly striking was the decline in infant mortality in the cities after 1890. By 1910, in many countries, an urban mother was less likely than a rural mother to see her child die before its first birthday. A great silent revolution had occurred: the terrible ferocity of death from disease-carrying bacteria in the cities had almost been tamed.

Urban Planning and Public Transportation

Public health was only part of the urban challenge. Overcrowding, bad housing, and lack of transportation could not be solved by sewers and better medicine; yet in these areas, too, important transformations significantly improved the quality of urban life after midcentury.

More effective urban planning was one of the keys to improvement. Urban planning was in decline by the early nineteenth century, but after 1850 its practice was revived and extended. France took the lead during the rule of Napoleon III (1848–1870), who sought to stand above class conflict and promote the welfare of all his subjects through government action. He believed that rebuilding much of Paris would provide employment, improve living conditions, and testify to the power and glory of his empire. In the baron Georges Haussmann, an aggressive, impatient Alsatian whom he placed in charge of Paris, Napoleon III found an authoritarian planner capable of bulldozing both buildings and opposition. In twenty years Paris was quite literally transformed (Map 24.2).

The Paris of 1850 was a labyrinth of narrow, dark streets, the results of desperate overcrowding. In a central city not twice the size of New York's Central Park lived more than one-third of the city's one million inhabitants. Terrible slum conditions and extremely high death rates were facts of life. There were few open spaces and only two public parks for the entire metropolis. Public transportation played a very small role in this enormous walking city.

Haussmann and his fellow planners proceeded on many interrelated fronts. With a bold energy that often shocked their contemporaries, they razed old buildings in order to cut broad, straight, tree-lined boulevards through the center of the city as well as in new quarters on the outskirts. These boulevards, designed in part to prevent the easy construction and defense of barricades by revolutionary crowds, permitted traffic to flow freely. Their

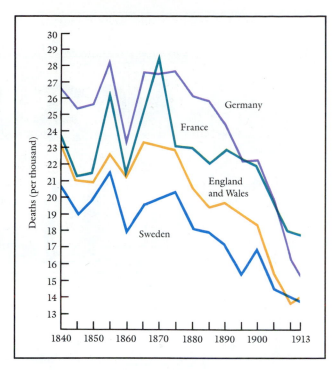

FIGURE 24.1 The Decline of Death Rates in England and Wales, Germany, France, and Sweden, 1840–1913 A rising standard of living, improvements in public health, and better medical knowledge all contributed to the dramatic decline of death rates in the nineteenth century.

creation also demolished some of the worst slums. New streets stimulated the construction of better housing, especially for the middle classes. Small neighborhood parks and open spaces were created throughout the city, and two very large parks suitable for all kinds of holiday activities were developed on either side of the city. The city also improved its sewers, and a system of aqueducts more than doubled the city's supply of good fresh water.

Haussmann and Napoleon III tried to make Paris a more beautiful city, and to a large extent they succeeded. The broad, straight boulevards, such as those radiating out like the spokes of a wheel from the Arch of Triumph and those centering on the new Opera House, afforded impressive vistas. If for most people Paris remains one of the world's most beautiful and enchanting cities, it is in part because of the transformations of Napoleon III's Second Empire.

Rebuilding Paris provided a new model for urban planning and stimulated modern urbanism

Apartment Living in Paris This drawing shows how different social classes lived close together in European cities about 1850. Passing the middle-class family on the first (American second) floor, the economic condition of the tenants declined until one reached abject poverty in the garret. *(Source: Bibliothèque Nationale, Paris)*

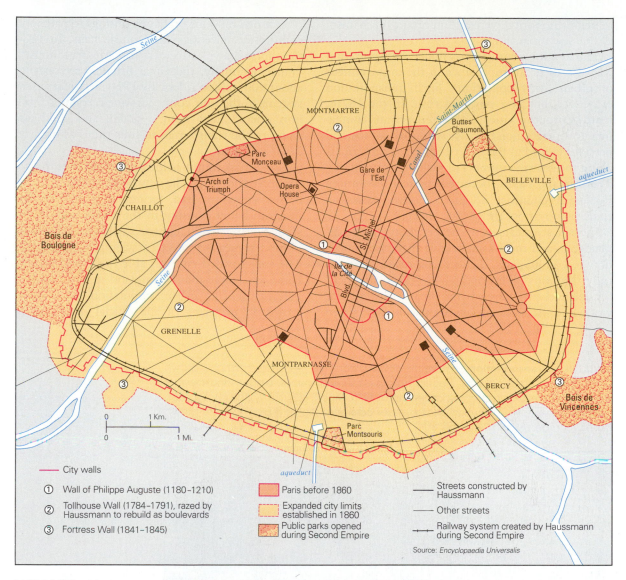

MAP 24.2 The Modernization of Paris, ca 1850–1870   Broad boulevards, large parks, and grandiose train stations transformed Paris. The cutting of the new north-south axis —known as the Boulevard Saint-Michel—was one of Haussmann's most controversial projects. It razed much of Paris's medieval core and filled the Île de la Cité with massive government buildings.

throughout Europe, particularly after 1870. In city after city, public authorities mounted a coordinated attack on many of the interrelated problems of the urban environment. As in Paris, improvements in public health through better water supply and waste disposal often went hand in hand with new boulevard construction. Cities like Vienna and Cologne followed the Parisian example of tearing down old walled fortifications and replacing them

with broad, circular boulevards on which office buildings, town halls, theaters, opera houses, and museums were erected. These ring roads and the new boulevards that radiated out from them toward the outskirts eased movement and encouraged urban expansion (see Map 24.2). *Zoning expropriation laws,* which allowed a majority of the owners of land in a given quarter of the city to impose major street or sanitation improvements on a reluctant minority, were an important mechanism of the new urbanism.

The development of mass public transportation was also of great importance in the improvement of urban living conditions. Such transportation came late, but in a powerful rush. In the 1870s, many European cities authorized private companies to operate horse-drawn streetcars, which had been developed in the United States, to carry riders along the growing number of major thoroughfares. Then, in the 1890s, occurred the real revolution: European countries adopted another American transit innovation, the electric streetcar.

Electric streetcars were cheaper, faster, more dependable, and more comfortable than their horse-drawn counterparts. Service improved dramatically. Millions of Europeans—workers, shoppers, schoolchildren—hopped on board during the workweek. And on weekends and holidays, street-

cars carried millions on happy outings to parks and countryside, racetracks and music halls. In 1886 the horse-drawn streetcars of Austria-Hungary, France, Germany, and Great Britain were carrying about 900 million riders. By 1910 electric streetcar systems in the four countries were carrying 6.7 billion riders.[6] Each man, woman, and child was using public transportation four times as often in 1910 as in 1886.

Good mass transit helped greatly in the struggle for decent housing. The new boulevards and horse-drawn streetcars had facilitated a middle-class move to better housing in the 1860s and 1870s; similarly, after 1890, electric streetcars gave people of modest means access to new, improved housing. The still-crowded city was able to expand and become less congested. In England in 1901, only 9 percent of the urban population was "overcrowded" in terms of the official definition of

Mass Public Transportation   Before the 1890s, urban Europeans relied on horse-drawn streetcars for transportation. Electric trolleys—faster, cheaper, bigger, and cleaner than their horse-drawn counterparts—improved service dramatically. This photograph of Berlin dates from 1901 when electric street cars were rapidly replacing horse-drawn buses. *(Source: Ullstein Bilderdienst)*

more than two persons per room. On the Continent, many city governments in the early twentieth century were building electric streetcar systems that provided transportation to new public and private housing developments in outlying areas of the city for the working classes. Poor, overcrowded housing, long one of the blackest blots on the urban landscape, was in retreat—another example of the gradual taming of the urban environment.

RICH AND POOR AND IN BETWEEN

General improvements in health and in the urban environment had beneficial consequences for all kinds of people. Yet differences in living conditions between social classes remained gigantic.

Social Structure

How much had the almost-completed journey to an urban, industrialized world changed the social framework of rich and poor? The first great change was a substantial and undeniable increase in the standard of living for the average person. The real wages of British workers, for example, which had already risen by 1850, almost doubled between 1850 and 1906. Similar unmistakable increases occurred in continental countries as industrial development quickened after 1850. Ordinary people took a major step forward in the centuries-old battle against poverty, reinforcing efforts to improve many aspects of human existence.

There is another side to the income coin, however, and it must be stressed as well. Greater economic rewards for the average person did *not* eliminate poverty, nor did they make the wealth and income of the rich and the poor significantly more equal. In almost every advanced country around 1900, the richest 5 percent of all households in the population received one-third of all national income. The richest one-fifth of households received anywhere from 50 to 60 percent of all national income, while the entire bottom four-fifths received only 40 to 50 percent. Moreover, the bottom 30 percent of households received 10 percent or less of all income. These enormous differences are illustrated in Figure 24.2.

The middle classes, smaller than they are today, accounted for less than 20 percent of the popula-

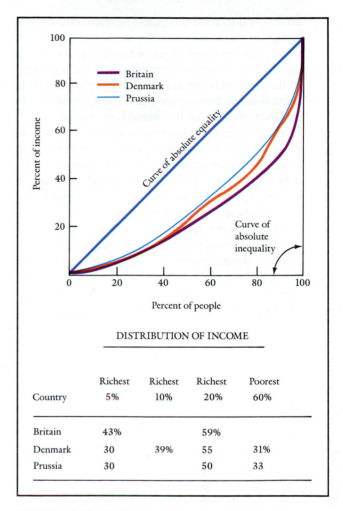

FIGURE 24.2 The Distribution of Income in Britain, Denmark, and Prussia in 1913   The so-called Lorenz curve is useful for showing the degree of economic inequality in a given society. The closer the actual distribution of income lies to the (theoretical) curve of absolute equality, where each 20 percent of the population receives 20 percent of all income, the more incomes are nearly equal. European society was very far from any such equality before World War One. Notice that incomes in Prussia were somewhat more equal than those in Britain. *(Source: S. Kuznets,* Modern Economic Growth, *Yale University Press, New Haven, 1966, pp. 208–209)*

DISTRIBUTION OF INCOME

Country	Richest 5%	Richest 10%	Richest 20%	Poorest 60%
Britain	43%		59%	
Denmark	30	39%	55	31%
Prussia	30		50	33

tion; thus the statistics show that the upper and middle classes alone received more than one-half of all income. The poorest four-fifths—the working classes, including peasants and agricultural laborers—received less altogether than the two richest classes. And since many wives and teenagers in poor families worked for wages, these figures actually understate the enduring gap between rich and poor. Moreover, income taxes on the wealthy were light or nonexistent. Thus the gap between rich and poor remained enormous at the beginning of the twentieth century. It was probably almost as great as it had been in the age of agriculture and aristocracy, before the Industrial Revolution.

The great gap between rich and poor endured, in part, because industrial and urban development made society more diverse and less unified. By no means did society split into two sharply defined opposing classes, as Marx had predicted. Instead, economic specialization enabled society to produce more effectively and in the process created more new social groups than it destroyed. There developed an almost unlimited range of jobs, skills, and earnings; one group or subclass shaded off into another in a complex, confusing hierarchy. Thus the tiny elite of the very rich and the sizable mass of the dreadfully poor were separated from each other by many subclasses, each filled with individuals struggling to rise or at least to hold their own in the social order. In this atmosphere of competition and hierarchy, neither the middle classes nor the working classes acted as a unified force. The age-old pattern of great economic inequality remained firmly intact.

The Middle Classes

By the beginning of the twentieth century, the diversity and range within the urban middle class were striking. Indeed, it is more meaningful to think of a confederation of middle classes, loosely united by occupations requiring mental rather than physical skill. At the top stood the upper middle class, composed mainly of the most successful business families from banking, industry, and large-scale commerce. These families were the prime beneficiaries of modern industry and scientific progress. As people in the upper middle class gained in income and progressively lost all traces of radicalism after the trauma of 1848, they were almost irresistibly drawn toward the aristocratic lifestyle.

As the aristocracy had long divided the year between palatial country estates and lavish townhouses during "the season," so the upper middle class purchased country places or built beach houses for weekend and summer use. (Little wonder that a favorite scenario in late-nineteenth-century middle-class novels was a mother and children summering gloriously in the country home, with only sporadic weekend intrusions by a distant, shadowy father.) The number of servants was an important indicator of wealth and standing for the middle class, as it had always been for the aristocracy. Private coaches and carriages, ever an expensive item in the city, were also signs of rising social status. More generally, the rich businessman and certainly his son devoted less time to business and more to "culture" and easy living than was the case in less wealthy or well-established commercial families.

The topmost reaches of the upper middle class tended to shade off into the old aristocracy to form a new upper class. This was the 5 percent of the population that, as we have seen, received roughly one-third of the national income in European countries before 1914. Much of the aristocracy welcomed this development. Having experienced a sharp decline in its relative income in the course of industrialization, the landed aristocracy had met big business coming up the staircase and was often delighted to trade titles, country homes, and snobbish elegance for good hard cash. Some of the best bargains were made through marriages to American heiresses. Correspondingly, wealthy aristocrats tended increasingly to exploit their agricultural and mineral resources as if they were business people. Bismarck was not the only proud nobleman to make a fortune distilling brandy on his estates.

Below the wealthy upper middle class were much larger, much less wealthy, and increasingly diversified middle-class groups. Here one found the moderately successful industrialists and merchants, as well as professionals in law and medicine. This was the middle middle class, solid and quite comfortable but lacking great wealth. Below them were independent shopkeepers, small traders, and tiny manufacturers—the lower middle class. Both of these traditional elements of the middle class expanded modestly in size with economic development.

Meanwhile, the traditional middle class was gaining two particularly important additions. The expansion of industry and technology created a growing demand for experts with specialized knowledge. The most valuable of the specialties became solid middle-class professions. Engineering, for example, emerged from the world of skilled labor as a full-fledged profession of great importance, considerable prestige, and many branches.

Architects, chemists, accountants, and surveyors— to name only a few—first achieved professional standing in this period. They established criteria for advanced training and certification and banded together in organizations to promote and defend their interests.

Management of large public and private institutions also emerged as a kind of profession, as governments provided more services and as very large corporations like railroads came into being. Government officials and many private executives were not capitalists in the sense that they owned business enterprises. But public and private managers did have specialized knowledge and the capacity to earn a good living. And they shared most of the values of the business-owning entrepreneurs and the older professionals.

Industrialization also expanded and diversified the lower middle class. The number of independent, property-owning shopkeepers and small business people grew and so did the number of white-collar employees—a mixed group of traveling salesmen, bookkeepers, store managers, and clerks who staffed the offices and branch stores of large corporations. White-collar employees were propertyless and often earned no more than the better-paid skilled or semiskilled workers did. Yet white-collar workers were fiercely committed to the middle class and to the ideal of moving up in society. In the Balkans, for example, clerks let their fingernails grow very long to distinguish themselves from people who worked with their hands. The tie, the suit, and soft clean hands were no-less-subtle marks of class distinction than wages.

Relatively well educated but without complex technical skills, many white-collar groups aimed at achieving professional standing and the accompanying middle-class status. Elementary school teachers largely succeeded in this effort. From being miserably paid part-time workers in the early nineteenth century, teachers rode the wave of mass education to respectable middle-class status and income. Nurses also rose from the lower ranks of unskilled labor to precarious middle-class standing. Dentistry was taken out of the hands of the working-class barbers and placed in the hands of highly trained (and middle-class) professionals.

In spite of their growing occupational diversity and conflicting interests, the middle classes were loosely united by a certain style of life. Food was the largest item in the household budget, for middle-class people liked to eat very well. In France and Italy, the middle classes' love of good eating meant that, even in large cities, activity ground almost to a halt between half past twelve and half past two on weekdays, as husbands and schoolchildren returned home for the midday meal. Around eight in the evening, the serious business of eating was taken up once again.

The English were equally attached to substantial meals, which they ate three times a day if income allowed. The typical English breakfast of bacon and eggs, toast and marmalade, and stewed fruits—not to mention sardines, kidneys, or fresh fish—always astonished French and German travelers, though large-breakfast enthusiasts like the Dutch and Scandinavians were less awed. The European middle classes consumed meat in abundance, and a well-off family might spend 10 percent of its substantial earnings on meat alone. In the 1890s, even a very prosperous English family—with an income of, say, $10,000 a year while the average working-class family earned perhaps $400 a year—spent fully a quarter of its income on food and drink.

Spending on food was also great because the dinner party was this class's favored social occasion. A wealthy family might give a lavish party for eight to twelve almost every week, while more modest households would settle for once a month. Throughout middle-class Europe, such dinners were served in the "French manner" (which the French had borrowed from the Russian aristocracy): eight or nine separate courses, from appetizers at the beginning to coffee and liqueurs at the end. In summer, a picnic was in order. But what a picnic! For a party of ten, one English cookbook suggested 5 pounds of cold salmon, a quarter of lamb, 8 pounds of pickled brisket, a beef tongue, a chicken pie, salads, cakes, and 6 pounds of strawberries. An ordinary family meal normally consisted of only four courses—soup, fish, meat, and dessert.

The middle-class wife could cope with this endless procession of meals, courses, and dishes because she had both servants and money at her disposal. The middle classes were solid members of what some contemporary observers called the "servant-keeping classes." Indeed, the employment of at least one enormously helpful full-time maid to cook and clean was the best single sign that a family had crossed the vague line separating the working classes from the middle classes. The greater its income, the greater the number of servants a family employed. The all-purpose servant gave way to a

"A Corner of the Table"   With photographic precision this 1904 oil painting by the French academic artist Paul-Émile Chabas (1867–1937) skillfully idealizes the elegance and intimacy of a sumptuous dinner party. *(Source: Bibliothèque des Arts Decoratifs/Jean-Loup Charmet)*

cook and a maid, then to a cook, a maid, and a boy, and so on. A prosperous English family, far up the line with $10,000 a year, in 1900 spent fully one-fourth of its income on a hierarchy of ten servants: a manservant, a cook, a kitchen maid, two house-maids, a serving maid, a governess, a gardener, a coachman, and a stable boy. Domestic servants were the second largest item in the budget of the middle classes. Food and servants together absorbed about one-half of income at all levels of the middle classes.

Well fed and well served, the middle classes were also well housed by 1900. Many quite prosperous families rented rather than owned their homes. Apartment living, complete with tiny rooms for servants under the eaves of the top floor, was commonplace (outside Great Britain), and wealthy investors and speculative builders found good prof-

its in middle-class housing. By 1900 the middle classes were also quite clothes-conscious. The factory, the sewing machine, and the department store had all helped to reduce the cost and expand the variety of clothing. Middle-class women were particularly attentive to the fickle dictates of fashion.

Education was another growing expense, as middle-class parents tried to provide their children with ever-more-crucial advanced education. The keystones of culture and leisure were books, music, and travel. The long realistic novel, the heroics of Wagner and Verdi, the diligent striving of the dutiful daughter on a piano, and the packaged tour to a foreign country were all sources of middle-class pleasure.

Finally, the middle classes were loosely united by a shared code of expected behavior and morality. This code was strict and demanding. It laid great stress on hard work, self-discipline, and personal achievement. Men and women who fell into crime or poverty were generally assumed to be responsible for their own circumstances. Traditional Christian morality was reaffirmed by this code and preached tirelessly by middle-class people who took pride in their own good conduct and regular church attendance. Drinking and gambling were denounced as vices; sexual purity and fidelity were celebrated as virtues. In short, the middle-class person was supposed to know right from wrong and was expected to act accordingly.

The Working Classes

About four out of five people belonged to the working classes at the turn of the century. Many members of the working classes—that is, people whose livelihoods depended on physical labor and who did not employ domestic servants—were still small landowning peasants and hired farm hands. This was especially true in eastern Europe. In western and central Europe, however, the typical worker had left the land. In Great Britain, less than 8 percent of the people worked in agriculture, while in rapidly industrializing Germany only one person in four was employed in agriculture and forestry. Even in less industrialized France, less than half the people depended on the land in 1900.

The urban working classes were even less unified and homogeneous than the middle classes. In the first place, economic development and increased specialization expanded the traditional range of working-class skills, earnings, and experiences. Meanwhile, the old sharp distinction between highly skilled artisans and unskilled manual workers was gradually breaking down. To be sure, highly skilled printers and masons, as well as unskilled dock workers and common laborers, continued to exist. But between these extremes there were ever-more semiskilled groups, many of which were composed of factory workers and machine tenders (Figure 24.3).

In the second place, skilled, semiskilled, and unskilled workers had widely divergent lifestyles and cultural values, and their differences contributed to a keen sense of social status and hierarchy within the working classes. The result was great variety and limited class unity.

Highly skilled workers, who comprised about 15 percent of the working classes, were a real "labor aristocracy." By 1900 they were earning about £2 a week in Great Britain, or roughly $10 a week and $500 per year. This was only about two-thirds the income of the bottom ranks of the servant-keeping classes. But it was fully twice as much as the earnings of unskilled workers, who averaged about $5 per week, and substantially more than the earnings of semiskilled workers, who averaged perhaps $7 per week. Other European countries had a similar range of earnings.

The most "aristocratic" of the highly skilled workers were construction bosses and factory foremen, men who had risen from the ranks and were fiercely proud of their achievement. The labor aristocracy also included members of the traditional highly skilled handicraft trades that had not been mechanized or placed in factories. These included makers of scientific and musical instruments, cabinetmakers, potters, jewelers, bookbinders, engravers, and printers. This group as a whole was under constant long-term pressure. Irregularly but inexorably, factory methods were being extended to more crafts, and many skilled artisans were being replaced by lower-paid semiskilled factory workers. Traditional woodcarvers and watchmakers virtually disappeared, for example, as the making of furniture and timepieces was put into the factory.

At the same time, a contrary movement was occurring. The labor aristocracy was consistently being enlarged by the growing need for highly skilled workers, such as shipbuilders, machine-tool makers, railway locomotive engineers, fine cotton textile spinners, and some metalworkers. Thus the labor elite was in a state of flux as individuals and whole crafts moved in and out of it.

FIGURE 24.3 The Urban Social Hierarchy

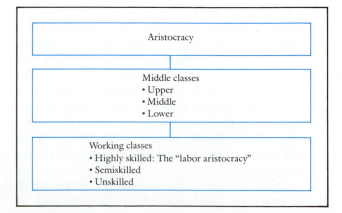

To maintain its precarious standing, the upper working class adopted distinctive values and strait-laced, almost puritanical, behavior. Like the middle classes, the labor aristocracy was strongly committed to the family and to economic improvement. Families in the upper working class saved money regularly, worried about their children's education, and valued good housing. Despite these similarities, which superficial observers were quick to exaggerate, skilled workers viewed themselves not as aspirants to the middle class but as the pacesetters and natural leaders of all the working classes. Well aware of the degradation not so far below them, they practiced self-discipline and stern morality.

The upper working class in general frowned on heavy drinking and sexual permissiveness. The organized temperance movement was strong in the countries of northern Europe, such as Great Britain, where a generation advocated tea as the "cup that cheers but does not inebriate." As one German labor aristocrat somberly warned, "the path to the brothel leads through the tavern" and from there quite possibly to drastic decline or total ruin for person and family.[7]

Men and women of the labor aristocracy were quick to find fault with those below them who failed to meet their standards. In 1868 William Lovett, an English labor aristocrat if ever there was one, denounced "this ignorant recklessness and improvidence that produce the swarms of half-starved, neglected, and ignorant children we see in all directions; who mostly grow up to become the burdens and often the pests of society, which the industrious and frugal have to support."[8] Finally, many members of the labor aristocracy had definite political and philosophical beliefs, whether Christian or socialist or both. Such beliefs further strengthened the firm moral code of the upper working class.

Below the labor aristocracy stood semiskilled and unskilled urban workers. The enormous complexity of this sector of the world of labor is not easily summarized. Workers in the established crafts—carpenters, bricklayers, pipefitters—stood near the top of the semiskilled hierarchy, often flirting with (or having backslid from) the labor elite. A large number of the semiskilled were factory workers, who earned highly variable but relatively good wages and whose relative importance in the labor force was increasing.

Below the semiskilled workers was a larger group of unskilled, who included day laborers such as longshoremen, wagon-driving teamsters, teenagers, and every kind of "helper." Many of these people had real skills and performed valuable services, but they were unorganized and divided, united only by the common fate of meager earnings. The same lack of unity characterized street vendors and market people—self-employed workers who competed savagely with each other and with the established shopkeepers of the lower middle class.

One of the largest components of the unskilled group was domestic servants, whose numbers grew steadily in the nineteenth century. In advanced Great Britain, for example, one out of every seven employed persons was a domestic servant in 1911. The great majority were women; indeed, one out of every three girls in Britain between the ages of fifteen and twenty was a domestic servant. Throughout Europe and America, a great many female domestics in the cities were recent migrants from rural areas. As in earlier times, domestic service was still hard work at low pay with limited personal independence. For the full-time general maid in a lower-middle-class family, there was an unending routine of babysitting, shopping, cooking, and cleaning. In the great households, the girl was at the bottom of a rigid hierarchy; status-conscious butlers and housekeepers were determined to stand almost as far above her as the wealthy master and mistress.

Nonetheless, domestic service had real attractions for "rough country girls" with strong hands and few specialized skills. Marriage prospects were better, or at least more varied, in the city. And though wages were low, they were higher and more regular than in hard agricultural work. Finally, as one London observer noted, young girls and other migrants were drawn to the city by "the contagion of numbers, the sense of something going on, the theaters and the music halls, the brightly lighted streets and busy crowds—all, in short, that makes the difference between the Mile End fair on a Saturday night, and a dark and muddy country lane, with no glimmer of gas and with nothing to do."[9]

Many young domestics from the countryside made a successful transition to working-class wife and mother. Yet, with an unskilled or unemployed husband and a growing family, such a woman often had to join the broad ranks of working women in the "sweated industries." These industries resembled the old putting-out and cottage industries of the eighteenth and early nineteenth cen-

Sweated Industry About 1900   This moving photograph shows an English family making cheap toys at home for low wages. Women and children were the backbone of sweated industry, and this husband may be filling in while unemployed. *(Source: University of Reading, Institute of Agricultural History and Museum of English Rural Life)*

turies. The women normally worked at home, though sometimes together in some loft or garret, for tiny merchant-manufacturers. Paid by the piece and not by the hour, these women (and their young daughters), for whom organization was impossible, earned pitiful wages and lacked any job security.

Some women did hand-decorating of every conceivable kind of object; the majority, however, made clothing, especially after the advent of the sewing machine. Foot-powered sewing machines allowed the poorest wife or widow in the foulest dwelling to rival and eventually supplant the most highly skilled male tailor. By 1900 only a few such tailors lingered on in high-priced "tailor-made" shops. An army of poor women accounted for the bulk of the inexpensive "ready-made" clothes displayed on department store racks and in tiny shops. All of these considerations graphically illustrate the rise and fall of groups and individuals within the working classes.

The urban working classes sought fun and recreation, and they found it. Across the face of Europe, drinking was unquestionably the favorite leisure-time activity of working people. For many middle-class moralists, as well as moralizing historians since, love of drink has been a curse of the modern age—a sign of social dislocation and popular suffering. Certainly, drinking was deadly serious business. One English slum dweller recalled that "drunkenness was by far the commonest cause of dispute and misery in working class homes. On account of it one saw many a decent family drift down through poverty into total want."[10]

Generally, however, heavy "problem" drinking declined by the late nineteenth century, as it became less and less socially acceptable. This decline reflected in part the moral leadership of the upper working class. At the same time, drinking became more public and social, especially as on-the-job drinking, an ancient custom of field laborers and urban artisans, declined. Cafés and pubs became increasingly bright, friendly places. Working-class political activities, both moderate and radical, were also concentrated in taverns and pubs. Moreover, social drinking by married couples and sweethearts became an accepted and widespread practice for the

Renoir: Le Moulin de la Galette à Montmartre   In this 1876 masterpiece the impressionist painter Auguste Renoir (1841–1919) has transformed a popular outdoor dance hall of the Parisian masses into an enchanted fairyland. Renoir was a joyous artist, and his work optimistically affirmed the beauty and value of modern life. *(Source: Musée d'Orsay/Cliché des Musées Nationaux, Paris)*

first time. This greater participation by women undoubtedly helped to civilize the world of drink and hard liquor.

The two other leisure-time passions of the working classes were sports and music halls. By the late nineteenth century there had been a great decline in "cruel sports," such as bullbaiting and cockfighting, throughout Europe. Their place was filled by modern spectator sports, of which racing and soccer were the most popular. There was a great deal of gambling on sports events, and for many a working person the desire to decipher the racing forms was a powerful incentive toward literacy. Music halls and vaudeville theaters, the working-class counterparts of middle-class opera and classical theater, were enormously popular throughout Europe. In the words of one English printer, "It is to the music halls that the vast body of working people look for recreation and entertainment."[11] In 1900 there were more than fifty in London alone. Music hall audiences were thoroughly mixed, which may account for the fact that drunkenness, sexual intercourse and pregnancy before marriage, marital difficulties, and problems with mothers-in-law were favorite themes of broad jokes and bittersweet songs.

In more serious moments, religion and the Christian churches continued to provide working people with solace and meaning. The eighteenth-century vitality of popular religion in Catholic countries and the Protestant rejuvenation exemplified by German Pietism and English Methodism (see pages 652–654) carried over into the nineteenth century. Indeed, many historians see the early early nineteenth century as an age of religious revival. Yet historians also recognize that, by the last two or three decades of the nineteenth century, a considerable decline in both church attendance and church donations was occurring in most European countries. And it seems clear that this decline was greater for the urban working classes than for their rural counterparts or for the middle classes.

What did the decline in working-class church attendance really mean? Some have argued that it accurately reflected a general decline in faith and religious belief. Others disagree, noting correctly that most working-class families still baptized their children and considered themselves Christians. Although more research is necessary, it appears that the urban working classes in Europe did become more secular and less religious in the late nineteenth and early twentieth centuries. They rarely repudiated the Christian religion, but it tended to play a diminishing role in their daily lives.

Part of the reason was that the construction of churches failed to keep up with the rapid growth of urban population, especially in new working-class neighborhoods. Thus the vibrant, materialistic urban environment undermined popular religious impulses, which were poorly served in the cities. Equally important, however, was the fact that throughout the nineteenth century both Catholic and Protestant churches were normally seen as they saw themselves—as conservative institutions defending social order and custom. Therefore, as the European working classes became more politically conscious, they tended to see the established (or quasi-established) "territorial church" as defending what they wished to change and allied with their political opponents. Especially the men of the urban working classes developed vaguely anti-church attitudes, even though they remained neutral or positive toward religion. They tended to regard regular church attendance as "not our kind of thing"—not part of urban working-class culture.

The pattern was different in the United States. There, most churches also preached social conservatism in the nineteenth century. But because church and state had always been separated and because there was always a host of competing denominations and even different religions, working people identified churches much less with the political and social status quo. Instead, individual churches in the United States were often closely identified with an ethnic group rather than with a social class; and churches thrived, in part, as a means of asserting ethnic identity.

THE FAMILY

Urban life wrought many fundamental changes in the family. Although much is still unknown, it seems clear that by the late nineteenth century the family had stabilized considerably after the disruption of the late eighteenth and early nineteenth centuries. The home became more important for both men and women. The role of women and attitudes toward children underwent substantial change, and adolescence emerged as a distinct stage of life. These are but a few of the transformations that affected all social classes in varying degrees.

Premarital Sex and Marriage

By 1850 the preindustrial pattern of lengthy courtship and mercenary marriage was pretty well dead among the working classes. In its place, the ideal of romantic love had triumphed. As one French observer in a small seaport remarked about 1850, "The young men are constantly letting partners with handsome dowries go begging. When they marry, it's ordinarily for inclination and not for advantage."[12]

Couples were ever more likely to come from different, even distant, towns and to be more nearly the same age, further indicating that romantic sentiment was replacing tradition and financial considerations. The calculating practice whereby wealthy old craftsmen took pretty young brides, who as comfortable middle-aged widows later married poor apprentices, was increasingly heard of only in old tales and folk songs.

Economic considerations in marriage long remained much more important to the middle classes than to the working classes. In France, dowries and elaborate legal marriage contracts were standard practice among the middle classes, and marriage was for many families life's most crucial financial transaction. A popular author advised young Frenchmen that "marriage is in general a means of increasing one's credit and one's fortune and of insuring one's success in the world."[13] This preoccupation with money led many middle-class men, in France and elsewhere, to marry late, after they were established economically, and to choose women considerably younger and less sexually experienced than themselves. These differences between husband and wife became a source of tension in many middle-class marriages.

A young woman of the middle class found her romantic life carefully supervised by her well-meaning mother, who schemed for a proper marriage and guarded her daughter's virginity like the family's credit. After marriage, middle-class morality sternly demanded fidelity.

Middle-class boys were watched, too, but not as vigilantly. By the time they reached late adolescence, they had usually attained considerable sexual experience with maids or prostitutes. With marriage a distant, uncertain possibility, it was all too easy for the young man of the middle classes to turn to the urban underworld of whoredom and sexual exploitation to satisfy his desires.

In the early nineteenth century, sexual experimentation before marriage had also triumphed, as had illegitimacy. There was an "illegitimacy explosion" between 1750 and 1850 (see page 632). By the 1840s, as many as one birth in three was occurring outside of wedlock in many large cities. Although poverty and economic uncertainty undoubtedly prevented many lovers from marrying, there were also many among the poor and propertyless who saw little wrong with having illegitimate offspring. One young Bavarian woman answered happily when asked why she kept having illegitimate children: "It's O.K. to make babies. . . . The king has o.k.'d it!"[14] Thus the pattern of romantic ideals, premarital sexual activity, and widespread illegitimacy was firmly established by midcentury among the urban working classes.

It is hard to know how European couples managed sex, pregnancy, and marriage after 1850, because such questions were considered improper both in polite conversation and in public opinion polls. Yet there are many telltale clues. In the second half of the century the rising rate of illegitimacy was reversed: more babies were born to married mothers. Some observers have argued that this shift reflected the growth of puritanism and a lessening of sexual permissiveness among the unmarried. This explanation, however, is unconvincing.

The percentage of brides who were pregnant continued to be high and showed little or no tendency to decline. In many parts of urban Europe around 1900, as many as one woman in three was going to the altar an expectant mother. Moreover, unmarried people almost certainly used the cheap condoms and diaphragms the industrial age had made available to prevent pregnancy, at least in predominately Protestant countries.

Unmarried young people were probably engaging in just as much sexual activity as their parents and grandparents who had created the illegitimacy explosion of 1750 to 1850. But toward the end of the nineteenth century, pregnancy usually meant marriage and the establishment of a two-parent household. This important development reflected the growing respectability of the working classes, as well as their gradual economic improvement. Skipping out was less acceptable, and marriage was less of an economic disaster. Thus the urban working-class couple became more stable, and their stability strengthened the family as an institution.

Prostitution

In Paris alone, 155,000 women were registered as prostitutes between 1871 and 1903, and 750,000 others were suspected of prostitution in the same years. Men of all classes visited prostitutes, but the middle and upper classes supplied much of the motivating cash. Thus, though many middle-class men abided by the publicly professed code of stern puritanical morality, others indulged their appetites for prostitutes and sexual promiscuity.

My Secret Life, the anonymous eleven-volume autobiography of an English sexual adventurer from the servant-keeping classes, provides a remarkable picture of such a man. Beginning at an early age with a maid, the author becomes progressively obsessed with sex and devotes his life to living his sexual fantasies. In almost every one of his innumerable encounters all across Europe, this man of wealth simply buys his pleasure. Usually meetings are arranged in a businesslike manner: regular and part-time prostitutes quote their prices; working-class girls are corrupted by hot meals and baths.

At one point, he offers a young girl a sixpence for a kiss and gets it. Learning that the pretty, unskilled working girl earns nine pence a day, he offers her the equivalent of a week's salary for a few moments of fondling. When she finally agrees, he savagely exults that "*her* want was my opportunity."[15] Later he offers more money for more gratification, and when she refuses, he tries unsuccessfully to rape her in a hackney cab. On another occasion he takes a farm worker by force: "Her tears ran down. If I had not committed a rape, it looked uncommonly like one." He then forces his victim to take money to prevent a threatened lawsuit, while the foreman advises the girl to keep quiet and realize that "you be in luck if he likes you."

Obviously atypical in its excesses, the encyclopedic thoroughness of *My Secret Life* does reveal the dark side of sex and class in urban society. Thinking of their wives largely in terms of money and social position, the men of the comfortable classes often purchased sex and even affection from poor girls both before and after marriage. Moreover, the great continuing differences between rich and poor made for every kind of debauchery and sexual exploitation, including the brisk trade in poor virgins that the author of *My Secret Life* particularly relished. Brutal sexist behavior was part of life—a part the sternly moral women (and men) of the upper working class detested and tried to shield their daughters from. For many poor young women, prostitution, like domestic service, was a stage of life. Having passed through it for two or three years in their early twenties, they went on in their mid-twenties to marry (or live with) men of their own class and establish homes and families.

Kinship Ties

Within working-class homes, ties to relatives after marriage—kinship ties—were in general much stronger than superficial social observers have recognized. Most newlyweds tried to live near their parents, though not in the same house. Indeed, for many married couples in the cities, ties to mothers and fathers, uncles and aunts, became more important, and ties to nonrelated acquaintances became weaker.

Toulouse-Lautrec: à La Mie   Nobleman by birth and cripple by accident, Henri de Toulouse-Lautrec (1864–1901) was irresistibly drawn to the night life of Paris and its sexual underworld. This portrait of an aging prostitute and her reptilian companion is a powerful study in degradation. *(Source: S. A. Denio Collection and General Income. Courtesy, Museum of Fine Arts, Boston)*

People turned to their families for help in coping with sickness, unemployment, death, and old age. Although governments were generally providing more welfare services by 1900, the average couple and their children inevitably faced crises. Funerals, for example, were an economic catastrophe, requiring a sudden large outlay for special clothes, carriages, and burial services. Unexpected death or desertion could leave the bereaved or abandoned, especially widows and orphans, in need of financial aid or perhaps a foster home. Relatives responded to such cries, knowing full well that their time of need and repayment would undoubtedly come.

Relatives were also valuable at less tragic moments. If a couple was very poor, an aged relation often moved in to cook and mind the children so the wife could earn badly needed income outside the home. Sunday dinners were often shared, as were outgrown clothing and useful information. Often the members of a large family group all lived in the same neighborhood.

Women and Family Life

Industrialization and the growth of modern cities brought great changes to the lives of European women. These changes were particularly consequential for married women, and most women did marry in the nineteenth century.

The work of most wives became quite distinct and separate from that of their husbands. Husbands became wage earners in factories and offices, while wives tended to stay home and manage the household and care for the children. The preindustrial pattern among both peasants and cottage workers, in which husbands and wives worked together and divided up household duties and child rearing, declined. Only in a few occupations, such as retail trade, did married couples live where they worked and struggle together to make their mom-and-pop operations a success. Factory employment for married women also declined as the early practice of hiring entire families in the factory disappeared.

As economic conditions improved late in the nineteenth century, married women tended to work outside the home only in poor families. One old English worker recalled that "the boy wanted to get into a position that would enable him to keep a wife and family, as it was considered a thoroughly unsatisfactory state of affairs if the wife had

to work to help maintain the home."[16] The ideal was a strict division of labor by sex: the wife as mother and homemaker, the husband as wage earner.

This rigid division of labor meant that married women faced great injustice if they tried to move into the man's world, the world of employment outside the home. Husbands were unsympathetic or hostile. Well-paying jobs were off limits to women, and a woman's wage was almost always less than a man's, even for the same work.

Moreover, married women were subordinated to their husbands by law and lacked many basic legal rights. In England, the situation was summed up in a famous line from the jurist William Blackstone: "In law husband and wife are one person, and the husband is that person." Thus a wife in England had no legal identity, and hence no right to own property in her own name. Even the wages she might earn belonged to her husband. In France, the Napoleonic Code also enshrined the principle of female subordination and gave the wife few legal rights regarding property, divorce, and custody of the children. Legal inferiority for women permeated Western society.

With middle-class women suffering, sometimes severely, from a lack of legal rights and with all women facing discrimination in education and employment, there is little wonder that some women rebelled and began the long-continuing fight for equality of the sexes and the rights of women. Their struggle proceeded on two main fronts. First, following in the steps of women like Mary Wollstonecraft (see page 675), organizations founded by middle-class feminists campaigned for equal legal rights for women as well as access to higher education and professional employment. These organizations scored some significant victories, like the law giving English married women full property rights in 1882. In the years before 1914, middle-class feminists increasingly shifted their attention to securing the right to vote for women.

Women inspired by utopian and especially Marxian socialism blazed a second path. Often scorning the programs of middle-class feminists, socialist women leaders argued that the liberation of (working-class) women would come only with the liberation of the entire working class through revolution. In the meantime, they championed the cause of working women and won some practical improvements, especially in Germany, where the socialist movement was most effectively organized. In a

Women Workers Founded in 1869, the German Social Democratic party became the strongest socialist party in Europe. Women were active in the socialist movement, as this engraving from 1890 of a meeting of workers in Berlin illustrates. *(Source: Bildarchiv Preussischer Kulturbesitz)*

general way, these different approaches to women's issues reflected the diversity of classes in the urban society.

If the ideology and practice of rigidly separate roles undoubtedly narrowed women's horizons and caused some women to rebel, there was a brighter side to the same coin. As home and children became the typical wife's main concerns, her control and influence there apparently became increasingly strong throughout Europe. Among the English working classes, it was the wife who generally determined how the family's money was spent. In many families the husband gave all his earnings to his wife to manage, whatever the law might read. She returned to him only a small allowance for carfare, beer, tobacco, and union dues. All the major domestic decisions, from the children's schooling and religious instruction to the selection of new furniture or a new apartment, were hers. In France women had even greater power in their assigned domain. One English feminist noted in 1908 that "though legally women occupy a much inferior status than men [in France], in practice they constitute the superior sex. They are the power behind the throne." Another Englishwoman believed that

"in most French households, women reign with unchallenged sway."[17]

Women ruled at home partly because running the urban household was a complicated, demanding, and valuable task. Twice-a-day food shopping, penny-pinching, economizing, and the growing crusade against dirt—not to mention child rearing—were a full-time occupation. Nor were there any laborsaving appliances to help. Working yet another job for wages outside the home had limited appeal for most married women, unless such earnings were essential for family survival.

The wife also guided the home because a good deal of her effort was directed toward pampering her husband as he expected. In countless humble households, she saw that he had meat while she ate bread, that he relaxed by the fire while she did the dishes.

The woman's guidance of the household went hand in hand with the increased emotional importance of home and family. The home she ran was idealized as a warm shelter in a hard and impersonal urban world. By the 1820s one observer of the comfortable middle classes in Marseilles had noted, for example, that "the family father, obliged to occupy himself with difficult business problems during the day, can relax only when he goes home. . . . Family evenings together are for him a time of the purest and most complete happiness."[18]

In time the central place of the family spread down the social scale. For a child of the English slums in the early 1900s,

home, however, poor, was the focus of all love and interests, a sure fortress against a hostile world. Songs about its beauties were ever on people's lips. "Home, sweet home," first heard in the 1870s, had become "almost a second national anthem." Few walls in lower-working-class houses lacked "mottoes"—colored strips of paper, about nine inches wide and eighteen inches in length, attesting to domestic joys: EAST, WEST, HOME'S BEST; BLESS OUR HOME; GOD IS MASTER OF THIS HOUSE; HOME IS THE NEST WHERE ALL IS BEST.[19]

By 1900 home and family were what life was all about for millions of people of all classes.

Women also developed stronger emotional ties to their husbands. Even in the comfortable classes, marriages were increasingly founded on sentiment

and sexual attraction rather than on money and calculation. Affection and eroticism became more central to the couple after marriage. Gustave Droz, whose best seller *Mr., Mrs., and Baby* went through 121 editions between 1866 and 1884, saw love within marriage as the key to human happiness. He condemned men who made marriage sound dull and practical, men who were exhausted by prostitutes and rheumatism and who wanted their young wives to be little angels. He urged women to follow their hearts and marry a man more nearly their own age:

A husband who is stately and a little bald is all right, but a young husband who loves you and who drinks out of your glass without ceremony, is better. Let him, if he ruffles your dress a little and places a kiss on your neck as he passes. Let him, if he undresses you after the ball, laughing like a fool. You have fine spiritual qualities, it is true, but your little body is not bad either and when one loves, one loves completely. Behind these follies lies happiness.[20]

Many French marriage manuals of the late 1800s stressed that women had legitimate sexual needs, such as the "right to orgasm." Perhaps the French

A Working-Class Home, 1875   Emotional ties within ordinary families grew stronger in the nineteenth century. *(Source: Illustrated London News, LXVI, 1875. Photo courtesy of Boston Public Library)*

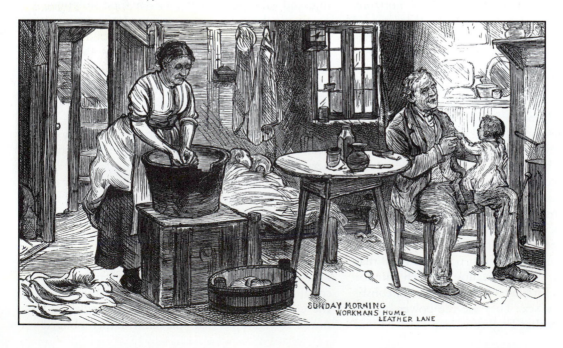

were a bit more enlightened in these matters than other nationalities. But the rise of public socializing by couples in cafés and music halls, as well as franker affection within the family, suggest a more erotic, pleasurable intimate life for women throughout Western society. This, too, helped make the woman's role as mother and homemaker acceptable and even satisfying.

Child Rearing

One of the most striking signs of deepening emotional ties within the family was the mother's love and concern for her tiny infants. This was a sharp break with the past. It may seem scarcely believable today that the typical mother in preindustrial Western society was very often indifferent toward her baby. This indifference—unwillingness to make real sacrifices for the welfare of the infant—was giving way among the comfortable classes by the later part of the eighteenth century, but the ordinary mother adopted new attitudes only as the nineteenth century progressed. The baby became more important, and women became better mothers.

Mothers increasingly breast-fed their infants, for example, rather than paying wet nurses to do so. Breast-feeding involved sacrifice—a temporary loss of freedom, if nothing else. Yet in an age when there was no good alternative to mother's milk, it saved lives. The surge of maternal feeling also gave rise to a wave of specialized books on child rearing and infant hygiene, such as Droz's phenomenally successful book. Droz urged fathers to get into the act and pitied those "who do not know how to roll around on the carpet, play at being a horse and a great wolf, and undress their baby."[21] Another sign, from France, of increased affection is that fewer illegitimate babies were abandoned as foundlings, especially after about 1850. Moreover, the practice of swaddling disappeared completely. Instead, ordinary mothers allowed their babies freedom of movement and delighted in their spontaneity.

The loving care lavished on infants was matched by greater concern for older children and adolescents. They, too, were wrapped in the strong emotional ties of a more intimate and protective family. For one thing, European women began to limit the number of children they bore, in order to care adequately for those they had. It was evident by the end of the century that the birthrate was declining

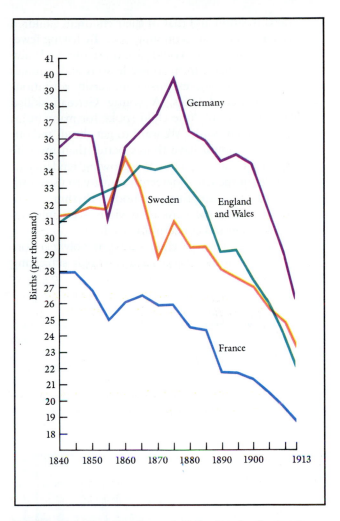

FIGURE 24.4 The Decline of Birthrates in England and Wales, France, Germany, Sweden, 1840–1913 Women had fewer babies for a variety of reasons, including the fact that their children were increasingly less likely to die before reaching adulthood. Compare with Figure 24.2 on page 765.

across Europe, as Figure 24.4 shows, and it continued to do so until after World War Two. The Englishwoman who married in the 1860s, for example, had an average of about six children; her daughter marrying in the 1890s had only four; and her granddaughter marrying in the 1920s had only two or possibly three.

The most important reason for this revolutionary reduction in family size, in which the comfortable and well-educated classes took the lead, was parents' desire to improve their economic and social position and that of their children. Children were no longer an economic asset. By having fewer youngsters, parents could give those they had valuable advantages, from music lessons and summer vacations to long, expensive university educations and suitable dowries. A young German skilled worker with only one child spoke for many in his class when he said, "We want to get ahead, and our daughter should have things better than my wife and sisters did."[22] Thus the growing tendency of couples in the late nineteenth century to use a variety of contraceptive methods—rhythm, withdrawal, and mechanical devices—certainly reflected increased concern for children.

Indeed, many parents were probably *too* concerned about their children, unwittingly subjecting

The Drawing Room   The middle-class ideal of raising cultured, educated, and properly protected young women is captured in this illustration. A serious mother lovingly teachers her youngest child while the older daughters practice their genteel skills. A drawing room was a kind of nineteenth-century family room, mercifully spared the tyranny of television. *(Source: Bettmann/Hulton)*

them to an emotional pressure cooker of almost unbearable intensity. The result was that many children and especially adolescents came to feel trapped and in desperate need of greater independence.

Biological and medical theories led parents to believe in the possibility that their own emotional characteristics were passed on to their offspring and that they were thus directly responsible for any abnormality in a child. The moment the child was conceived was thought to be of enormous importance. "Never run the risk of conception when you are sick or over-tired or unhappy," wrote one influential American woman. "For the bodily condition of the child, its vigor and magnetic qualities, are much affected by conditions ruling this great moment."[23] So might the youthful "sexual excess" of the father curse future generations. Although this was true in the case of syphilis, which could be transmitted to unborn children, the rigid determinism of such views left little scope for the child's individual development.

Another area of excessive parental concern was the sexual behavior of the child. Masturbation was viewed with horror, for it represented an act of independence and even defiance. Diet, clothing, games, and sleeping were carefully regulated. Girls were discouraged from riding horses and bicycling because rhythmic friction simulated masturbation. Boys were dressed in trousers with shallow and widely separated pockets. Between 1850 and 1880, there were surgical operations for children who persisted in masturbating. Thereafter until about 1905, various restraining apparatuses were more often used.

These and less blatant attempts to repress the child's sexuality were a source of unhealthy tension, often made worse by the rigid division of sexual roles within the family. It was widely believed that mother and child love each other easily, but that relations between father and child are necessarily difficult and often tragic. The father was a stranger; his world of business was far removed from the maternal world of spontaneous affection. Moreover, the father was demanding, often expecting the child to succeed where he himself had failed and making his love conditional on achievement. Little wonder that the imaginative literature of the late nineteenth century came to deal with the emotional and destructive elements of father-son relationships. In the Russian Feodor Dostoevsky's great novel *The Brothers Karamazov* (1880–1881), for example, four sons work knowingly or unknowingly to destroy their father. Later, at the murder trial, one of the brothers claims to speak for all mankind and screams out: "Who doesn't wish his father dead?"

Sigmund Freud (1856–1939), the Viennese founder of psychoanalysis, formulated the most striking analysis of the explosive dynamics of the family, particularly the middle-class family in the late nineteenth century. A physician by training, Freud began his career treating mentally ill patients. He noted that the hysteria of his patients appeared to originate in bitter early childhood experiences, wherein the child had been obliged to repress strong feelings. When these painful experiences were recalled and reproduced under hypnosis or through the patient's free association of ideas, the patient could be brought to understand his or her unhappiness and eventually to deal with it.

One of Freud's most influential ideas concerned the Oedipal tensions resulting from the son's instinctive competition with the father for the mother's love and affection. More generally, Freud postulated that much of human behavior is motivated by unconscious emotional needs, whose nature and origins are kept from conscious awareness by various mental devices he called "defense mechanisms." Freud concluded that much unconscious psychological energy is sexual energy, which is repressed and precariously controlled by rational thinking and moral rules. If Freud exaggerated the sexual and familial roots of adult behavior, that exaggeration was itself a reflection of the tremendous emotional intensity of family life in the late nineteenth century.

The working classes probably had more avenues of escape from such tensions than did the middle classes. Unlike their middle-class counterparts, who remained economically dependent on their families until a long education was finished or a proper marriage secured, working-class boys and girls went to work when they reached adolescence. Earning wages on their own, they could bargain with their parents for greater independence within the household by the time they were sixteen or seventeen. If they were unsuccessful, they could and did leave home, to live cheaply as paying lodgers in other working-class homes. Thus the young person from the working classes broke away from the family more easily when emotional ties became oppressive. In the twentieth century, middle-class youth would follow this lead.

SCIENCE AND THOUGHT

Major changes in Western thought accompanied the emergence of urban society. Two aspects of these complex intellectual developments stand out as especially significant. Scientific knowledge expanded rapidly and came to influence the Western world-view even more profoundly than it had since the Scientific Revolution and the early Enlightenment. And, between about the 1840s and the 1890s, European literature underwent a shift from soaring romanticism to tough-minded realism.

The Triumph of Science

As the pace of scientific advance quickened and as theoretical advances resulted in great practical benefits, science exercised growing influence on human thought. The intellectual achievements of the Scientific Revolution had resulted in few such benefits, and theoretical knowledge had also played a relatively small role in the Industrial Revolution in England. But breakthroughs in industrial technology enormously stimulated basic scientific inquiry, as researchers sought to explain theoretically how such things as steam engines and blast furnaces actually worked. The result was an explosive growth of fundamental scientific discoveries from the 1830s onward. And in contrast to earlier periods, these theoretical discoveries were increasingly transformed into material improvements for the general population.

A perfect example of the translation of better scientific knowledge into practical human benefits was the work of Pasteur and his followers in biology and the medical sciences. Another was the development of the branch of physics known as *thermodynamics.* Building on Newton's laws of mechanics and on studies of steam engines, thermodynamics investigated the relationship between heat and mechanical energy. By midcentury, physicists had formulated the fundamental laws of thermodynamics, which were then applied to mechanical engineering, chemical processes, and many other fields. The *law of conservation of energy* held that different forms of energy—such as heat, electricity, and magnetism—could be converted but neither created nor destroyed. Nineteenth-century thermodynamics demonstrated that the physical world is governed by firm, unchanging laws.

Chemistry and electricity were two other fields characterized by extremely rapid progress. Chemists devised ways of measuring the atomic weight of different elements, and in 1869 the Russian chemist Dmitri Mendeleev (1834–1907) codified the rules of chemistry in the periodic law and the periodic table. Chemistry was subdivided into many specialized branches, such as *organic chemistry*—the study of the compounds of carbon. Applying theoretical insights gleaned from this new field, researchers in large German chemical companies discovered ways of transforming the dirty, useless coal tar that accumulated in coke ovens into beautiful, expensive synthetic dyes for the world of fashion. The basic discoveries of Michael Faraday (1791–1867) on electromagnetism in the 1830s and 1840s resulted in the first dynamo (generator) and opened the way for the subsequent development of electric motors, electric lights, and electric streetcars.

The triumph of science and technology had at least three significant consequences. First, though ordinary citizens continued to lack detailed scientific knowledge, everyday experience and innumerable popularizers impressed the importance of science on the popular mind.

As science became more prominent in popular thinking, the philosophical implications of science formulated in the Enlightenment spread to broad sections of the population. Natural processes appeared to be determined by rigid laws, leaving little room for either divine intervention or human will. Yet scientific and technical advances had also fed the Enlightenment's optimistic faith in human progress, which now appeared endless and automatic to many middle-class minds.

Finally, the methods of science acquired unrivaled prestige after 1850. For many, the union of careful experiment and abstract theory was the only reliable route to truth and objective reality. The "unscientific" intuitions of poets and the revelations of saints seemed hopelessly inferior.

Social Science and Evolution

From the 1830s onward, many thinkers tried to apply the objective methods of science to the study of society. In some ways these efforts simply perpetuated the critical thinking of the philosophes. Yet there were important differences. The new "social scientists" had access to the massive sets of numerical data that governments had begun to collect, on everything from children to crime, from population to prostitution. In response, they developed new statistical methods to analyze these facts "scientifically" and supposedly to test their theories. And the systems of the leading nineteenth-century social scientists were more unified, all-encompassing, and dogmatic than those of the philosophes. Marx was a prime example (see pages 731–733).

Another extremely influential system builder was the French philosopher Auguste Comte (1798–1857). Initially a disciple of the utopian socialist Saint-Simon (see page 730), Comte wrote a six-volume *System of Positive Philosophy* (1830–1842), which was largely overlooked during the romantic era. But when the political failures of 1848 completed the swing to realism, Comte's philosophy came into its own. Its influence has remained great to this day.

Comte postulated that all intellectual activity progresses through predictable stages:

The great fundamental law. . . is this:—that each of our leading conceptions—each branch of our knowledge—passes successively through three different theoretical conditions: the Theological, or fictitious; the Metaphysical, or abstract; and the Scientific, or positive. . . . The first is the necessary point of departure of human understanding, and the third is the fixed and definitive state. The second is merely a transition.[24]

By way of example, Comte noted that the prevailing explanation of cosmic patterns had shifted, as knowledge of astronomy developed, from the will of God (the theological) to the will of an orderly Nature (the metaphysical) to the rule of unchanging laws (the scientific). Later, this same intellectual progression took place in increasingly complex fields—physics, chemistry, and finally the study of society. By applying the scientific or *positivist* method, Comte believed, his new discipline of sociology would soon discover the eternal laws of human relations. This colossal achievement would in turn enable expert social scientists to impose a disciplined harmony and well-being on less enlightened citizens. Dismissing the "fictions" of traditional religions, Comte became the chief priest of the religion of science and rule by experts.

Comte's stages of knowledge exemplify the nineteenth-century fascination with the idea of evolution and dynamic development. Thinkers in many fields, like the romantic historians and "scientific" Marxists, shared and applied this basic concept. In geology, Charles Lyell (1797–1875) effectively discredited the long-standing view that the earth's surface had been formed by short-lived cataclysms, such as biblical floods and earthquakes. Instead, according to Lyell's principle of uniformitarianism, the same geological processes that are at work today slowly formed the earth's surface over an immensely long time. The evolutionary view of biological development, first proposed by the Greek Anaximander in the sixth century B.C., re-emerged in a more modern form in the work of Jean Baptiste Lamarck (1744–1829). Lamarck asserted that all forms of life had arisen through a long process of continuous adjustment to the environment.

Lamarck's work was flawed—he believed that characteristics parents acquired in the course of their lives could be inherited by their children—and was not accepted, but it helped prepare the way for Charles Darwin (1809–1882), the most influential of all nineteenth-century evolutionary thinkers. As the official naturalist on a five-year scientific cruise to Latin America and the South Pacific beginning in 1831, Darwin carefully collected specimens of the different animal species he encountered on the voyage. Back in England, convinced by fossil evidence and by his friend Lyell that the earth and life on it were immensely ancient, Darwin came to doubt the general belief in a special divine creation of each species of animals. Instead, he concluded, all life had gradually evolved from a common ancestral origin in an unending "struggle for survival." After long hesitation, Darwin published his research, which immediately attracted wide attention.

Darwin's great originality lay in suggesting precisely *how* biological evolution might have occurred. His theory is summarized in his title, *On the Origin of Species by the Means of Natural Selection* (1859). Decisively influenced by Malthus's gloomy theory that populations naturally grow faster than their food supplies, Darwin argued that chance differences among the members of a given species help some to survive while others die. Thus the variations that prove useful in the struggle for survival are selected naturally and gradually spread to the entire species through reproduction. Darwin did not explain why such variations occurred in the first place, and not until the early twentieth century did the study of genetics and the concept of mutation provide some answers.

As the capstone of already-widespread evolutionary thinking, Darwin's theory had a powerful and many-sided influence on European thought and the European middle classes. Darwin was hailed as the great scientist par excellence, the "Newton of biology," who had revealed once again the powers of objective science. Darwin's findings also reinforced the teachings of secularists like Comte and Marx, who scornfully dismissed religious belief in favor of agnostic or atheistic materialism. In the great cities especially, religion was on the defensive. Finally, many writers applied the theory of biological evolution to human affairs. Herbert Spencer (1820–1903), an English disciple of Auguste Comte, saw the human race as driven forward to

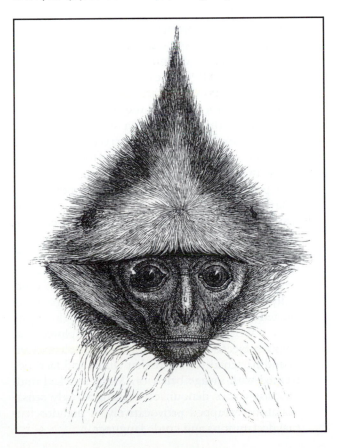

Attracting Females was an integral part of the struggle for survival, according to Darwin. He theorized that those males who were most attractive to females would have the most offspring, like this type of monkey that had developed ornamental hair with devastating sex appeal. Darwin used this illustration in *The Descent of Man* (1871). *(Source: Library of Congress)*

ever-greater specialization and progress by the brutal economic struggle that efficiently determined the "survival of the fittest." The poor were the ill-fated weak, the prosperous the chosen strong. Understandably, Spencer and other Social Darwinists were especially popular with the upper middle class.

Realism in Literature

In 1868 Émile Zola (1840–1902), the giant of the realist movement in literature, defended his violently criticized first novel against charges of pornography and corruption of morals. Such accusations were meaningless, Zola claimed: he was only a purely objective scientist using "the modern method, the universal instrument of inquiry of which this age makes such ardent use to open up the future."

I chose characters completely dominated by their nerves and their blood, deprived of free-will, pushed to each action of their lives by the fatality of their flesh. . . . I have simply done on living bodies the work of analysis which surgeons perform on corpses.[25]

Zola's literary manifesto articulated the key themes of realism, which had emerged in the 1840s and continued to dominate Western culture and style until the 1890s. Realist writers believed that literature should depict life exactly as it was. Forsaking poetry for prose and the personal, emotional viewpoint of the romantics for strict, scientific objectivity, the realists simply observed and recorded —content to let the facts speak for themselves.

The major realist writers focused their extraordinary powers of observation on contemporary everyday life. Emphatically rejecting the romantic search for the exotic and the sublime, they energetically pursued the typical and the commonplace. Beginning with a dissection of the middle classes, from which most of them sprang, many realists eventually focused on the working classes, especially the urban working classes, who had been neglected in imaginative literature before this time. They put a microscope to many unexplored and taboo subjects—sex, strikes, violence, alcoholism—and hastened to report that slums and factories teemed with savage behavior. Many shocked middle-class critics denounced realism as ugly sensationalism, wrapped provocatively in pseudoscientific declarations and crude language.

The realists' claims of objectivity did not prevent the elaboration of a definite world-view. Unlike the romantics, who had gloried in individual freedom and an unlimited universe, realists such as Zola were strict determinists. Human beings, like atoms, were components of the physical world, and all human actions were caused by unalterable natural laws. Heredity and environment determined human behavior; good and evil were merely social conventions.

The realist movement began in France, where romanticism had never been completely dominant, and three of its greatest practitioners—Balzac, Flaubert, and Zola—were French. Honoré de Balzac (1799–1850) spent thirty years writing a vastly ambitious panorama of postrevolutionary French life. Known collectively as *The Human Comedy,* this series of nearly one hundred books vividly portrays more than two thousand characters from virtually all sectors of French society. Balzac pictures urban society as grasping, amoral, and brutal, characterized by a Darwinian struggle for wealth and power. In *Le Père Goriot* (1835), the hero, a poor student from the provinces, eventually surrenders his idealistic integrity to feverish ambition and society's all-pervasive greed.

Madame Bovary (1857), the masterpiece of Gustave Flaubert (1821–1880), is far narrower in scope than Balzac's work but unparalleled in its depth and accuracy of psychological insight. Unsuccessfully prosecuted as an outrage against public morality and religion, Flaubert's carefully crafted novel tells the ordinary, even banal, story of a frustrated middle-class housewife who has an adulterous love affair and is betrayed by her lover. Without moralizing, Flaubert portrays the provincial middle class as petty, smug, and hypocritical.

Zola was most famous for his seamy, animalistic view of working-class life. But he also wrote gripping, carefully researched stories featuring the stock exchange, the big department store, and the army, as well as urban slums and bloody coal strikes. Like many later realists, Zola sympathized with socialism, a sympathy evident in his overpowering *Germinal* (1885).

Realism quickly spread beyond France. In England, Mary Ann Evans (1819–1880), who wrote under the pen name George Eliot, brilliantly achieved a more deeply felt, less sensational kind of realism. "It is the habit of my imagination," George Eliot wrote, "to strive after as full a vision of the medium in which a character moves as one of the character itself." Her great novel *Middlemarch: A Study of Provincial Life* examines masterfully the ways in which people are shaped by their social medium as well as their own inner strivings, conflicts, and moral choices. Thomas Hardy (1840–1928) was more in the Zola tradition. His novels, such as *Tess of the D'Urbervilles* and *Return of the Native,* depicted men and women frustrated and crushed by fate and bad luck.

The greatest Russian realist, Count Leo Tolstoy (1828–1910), combined realism in description and character development with an atypical moralizing, which came to dominate his later work. Tolstoy's greatest work was *War and Peace,* a monumental novel set against the historical background of Napoleon's invasion of Russia in 1812. Tolstoy probes deeply into the lives of a multitude of unforgettable characters, such as the ill-fated Prince Andrei; the shy, fumbling Pierre; and the enchanting, level-headed Natasha. Tolstoy goes to great pains to develop his fatalistic theory of history, which regards free will as an illusion and the achievements of even the greatest leaders as only the channeling of historical necessity. Yet Tolstoy's central message is one that most of the people discussed in this chapter would readily accept: human love, trust, and everyday family ties are life's enduring values.

Thoroughgoing realism (or "naturalism," as it was often called) arrived late in the United States, most arrestingly in the work of Theodore Dreiser (1871–1945). Dreiser's first novel, *Sister Carrie* (1900), the story of an ordinary farm girl who does well going wrong in Chicago, so outraged conventional morality that the publisher withdrew the book. The United States subsequently became a bastion of literary realism in the twentieth century after the movement had faded away in Europe.

Degas: Women Ironing   Realism replaced romanticism as the dominant trend in the visual arts for a long generation after 1850. This French work by Edgar Degas (1834–1917) accurately captures the hard work and fatigue of unskilled labor. *(Source: Musée d'Orsay/Cliché des Musées Nationaux, Paris)*

SUMMARY

The Industrial Revolution had a decisive influence on the urban environment. The populations of towns and cities grew rapidly because it was economically advantageous to locate factories and offices in urban areas. This rapid growth worsened long-standing overcrowding and unhealthy living conditions and posed a frightening challenge for society. Eventually government leaders, city planners, reformers, scientists, and ordinary citizens responded. They took effective action in public health and provided themselves with other badly needed urban services. Gradually they tamed the ferocious savagery of the traditional city.

As urban civilization came to prevail, there were major changes in family life. Especially among the lower classes, family life became more stable, more loving, and less mercenary. These improvements had a price, though. Sex roles for men and women became sharply defined and rigidly separate. Women especially tended to be locked into a subordinate and stereotypical role. Nonetheless, on balance, the quality of family life improved for all family members. Better, more stable family relations reinforced the benefits for the masses of higher real wages, increased social security, political participation, and education.

While the quality of urban and family life improved, the class structure became more complex and diversified than before. Urban society featured many distinct social groups, which existed in a state of constant flux and competition. The gap between rich and poor remained enormous and really quite traditional in mature urban society, although there were countless gradations between the extremes. Large numbers of poor women in particular continued to labor as workers in sweated industries, as domestic servants, and as prostitutes in order to satisfy the demands of their masters in the servant-keeping classes. Urban society in the late nineteenth century represented a great step forward for humanity, but it remained very unequal.

Inequality was a favorite theme of realist novelists like Balzac and Zola. More generally, literary realism reflected Western society's growing faith in science, progress, and evolutionary thinking. The emergence of urban, industrial civilization accelerated the secularization of the Western world-view.

NOTES

1. A. Weber, *The Growth of Cities in the Nineteenth Century* (New York: Columbia University Press, 1899), p. 1.
2. Quoted in W. Ashworth, *The Genesis of Modern British Town Planning* (London: Routledge & Kegan Paul, 1954), p. 17.
3. S. Marcus, "Reading the Illegible," in *The Victorian City: Images and Realities,* ed. H. J. Dyos and Michael Wolff, vol. 1 (London: Routledge & Kegan Paul, 1973), p. 266.
4. E. Gauldie, *Cruel Habitations: A History of Working-Class Housing, 1780–1918* (London: George Allen & Unwin, 1974), p. 21.
5. Quoted in E. Chadwick, *Report on the Sanitary Condition of the Labouring Population of Great Britain,* ed. M. W. Flinn (Edinburgh: University of Edinburgh Press, 1965; original publication, 1842), pp. 315–316.
6. J. P. McKay, *Tramways and Trolleys: The Rise of Urban Mass Transport in Europe* (Princeton, N.J.: Princeton University Press, 1976), p. 81.
7. Quoted in R. P. Neuman, "The Sexual Question and Social Democracy in Imperial Germany," *Journal of Social History* 7 (Winter 1974): 276.
8. Quoted in B. Harrison, "Underneath the Victorians," *Victorian Studies* 10 (March 1967): 260.
9. Quoted in J. A. Banks, "The Contagion of Numbers," in Dyos and Wolff, vol. 1, p. 112.
10. Quoted in R. Roberts, *The Classic Slum: Salford Life in the First Quarter of the Century* (Manchester, Eng.: University of Manchester Press, 1971), p. 95.
11. Quoted in B. Harrison, "Pubs," in Dyos and Wolff, vol. 1, p. 175.
12. Quoted in E. Shorter, *The Making of the Modern Family* (New York: Basic Books, 1975), p. 150.
13. Quoted in T. Zeldin, *France, 1848–1945* (Oxford, Eng.: Clarendon Press, 1973), vol. 1, p. 288.
14. Quoted in J. M. Phayer, "Lower-Class Morality: The Case of Bavaria," *Journal of Social History* 8 (Fall 1974): 89.
15. Quoted in S. Marcus, *The Other Victorians: A Study of Sexuality and Pornography in Mid-Nineteenth-Century England* (New York: Basic Books, 1966), p. 142.
16. Quoted in G. S. Jones, "Working-Class Culture and Working-Class Politics in London, 1870–1900: Notes on the Remaking of a Working Class," *Journal of Social History* 7 (Summer 1974): 486.
17. Quoted in Zeldin, vol. 1, p. 346.
18. Quoted in Shorter, pp. 230–231.
19. Roberts, p. 35.
20. Quoted in Zeldin, vol. 1, p. 295.
21. Ibid., vol. 1, p. 328.
22. Quoted in Neuman, p. 281.
23. Quoted by S. Kern, "Explosive Intimacy: Psychodynamics of the Victorian Family," *History of Childhood Quarterly* 1 (Winter 1974): 439.
24. A. Comte, *The Positive Philosophy of Auguste Comte,* trans. H. Martineau, vol. 1 (London: J. Chapman, 1853), pp. 1–2.
25. Quoted in G. J. Becker, ed., *Documents of Modern Literary Realism* (Princeton, N.J.: Princeton University Press, 1963), p. 159.

SUGGESTED READING

All of the books and articles cited in the Notes are highly recommended; each in its own way is an important contribution to social history and the study of life in the urban society. Note that the *Journal of Social History,* which has a strong European orientation, is excellent both for its articles and for its reviews of new books. The book mentioned by T. Zeldin, *France, 1848–1945,* 2 vols. (1973, 1977), is a pioneering social history that opens many doors, as is the ambitious synthesis by T. Hamerow, *The Birth of a New Europe: State and Society in the Nineteenth Century* (1983).

On the European city, D. Harvey, *Consciousness and the Urban Experience* (1985), is provocative, and D. Pickney, *Napoleon III and the Rebuilding of Paris* (1972), is fascinating, as are G. Masur, *Imperial Berlin* (1970), and M. Hamm, ed., *The City in Russian History* (1976). So also are N. Evenson's beautifully illustrated *Paris: A Century of Change, 1878–1978* (1979); and D. Grew's authoritative *Town in the Ruhr: A Social History of Bochum, 1860–1914* (1979). J. Siegel, *Bohemian Paris: Culture, Politics, and the Boundaries of Bourgeois Life, 1830–1930* (1986), and J. Merriman, ed., *French Cities in the Nineteenth Century: Class, Power, and Urbanization* (1982), are important works on France. D. Olsen's scholarly *Growth of Victorian*

London (1978) complements H. Mayhew's wonderful contemporary study, *London Labour and the Labouring Poor* (1861), reprinted recently. M. Crichton's realistic historical novel on organized crime, *The Great Train Robbery* (1976), is excellent. J. J. Tobias, *Urban Crime in Victorian England* (1972), is a lively, scholarly approach to declining criminal activity in the nineteenth century, with a wealth of detail. J. P. Goubert, *The Conquest of Water: The Advent of Health in the Industrial Age* (1989), and G. Rosen, *History of Public Health* (1958), are excellent introductions to sanitary and medical developments. For society as a whole, J. Burnett, *History of the Cost of Living* (1969), cleverly shows how different classes spent their money, and B. Tuchman, *The Proud Tower* (1966), draws an unforgettable portrait of people and classes before 1914. J. Laver's handsomely illustrated *Manners and Morals in the Age of Optimism, 1848–1914* (1966) investigates the urban underworld and relations between the sexes. Sexual attitudes are also examined by E. Trudgill, *Madonnas and Magdalenas: The Origin and Development of Victorian Sexual Attitudes* (1976), and J. Phayer, *Sexual Liberation and Religion in Nineteenth Century Europe* (1977). G. Alter, *Family and Female Life Course: The Women of Verviers, Belgium, 1849–1880* (1988), and A. McLaren, *Sexuality and Social Order: Birth Control in Nineteenth-Century France* (1982), explore attitudes toward family planning.

Women are coming into their own in historical studies. In addition to the general works by Shorter, Wrigley, Stone, and Tilly and Scott cited in Chapter 20, there are a growing number of eye-opening specialized investigations. These include L. Davidoff, *The Best Circles* (1973), and P. Jalland, *Women, Marriage and Politics, 1860–1914* (1986), on upper-class society types; O. Banks, *Feminism and Family Planning in Victorian England* (1964); and P. Branca, *Women in Europe Since 1750* (1978). M. J. Peterson, *Love and Work in the Lives of Victorian Gentlewomen* (1989), and L. Holcombe, *Victorian Ladies at Work* (1973), examine middle-class women at work. M. Vicinus, ed., *Suffer and Be Still* (1972) and *A Widening Sphere* (1981), are far-ranging collections of essays on women's history, as is R. Bridenthal, C. Koonz, and S. Stuard, eds., *Becoming Visible: Women in European History,* 2d ed.

(1987). Feminism is treated perceptively in R. Evans, *The Feminists: Women's Emancipation in Europe, America, and Australia* (1979); K. Blair, *The Clubwoman as Feminist: True Womanhood Redefined, 1868–1914* (1980); and C. Moses, *French Feminism in the Nineteenth Century* (1984). J. Gillis, *Youth and History* (1974), is a good introduction. D. Ransel, ed., *The Family in Imperial Russia* (1978), is an important work on the subject, as is J. Donzelot, *The Policing of Families* (1979), which stresses the loss of family control of all aspects of life to government agencies.

Among studies of special groups, J. Scott, *The Glass-Workers of Carmaux* (1974), is outstanding on skilled French craftsmen, and D. Lockwood, *The Blackcoated Worker* (1958), carefully examines class consciousness in the English lower middle class. J. R. Wegs, *Growing Up Working Class: Continuity and Change Among Viennese Youth, 1890–1938* (1989), is recommended. Two fine studies on universities and their professors are S. Rothblatt, *Revolution of the Dons: Cambridge and Society in Victorian England* (1968), and F. Ringer, *The Decline of the German Mandarins* (1969). Servants and their employers receive excellent treatment in T. McBride, *The Domestic Revolution: The Modernization of Household Service in England and France, 1820–1920* (1976), and B. Smith, *Ladies of the Leisure Class: The Bourgeoises of Northern France in the Nineteenth Century* (1981), which may be compared with the innovative study by M. Miller, *The Bon Marché: Bourgeois Culture and the Department Store, 1869–1920* (1981).

On Darwin, M. Ruse, *The Darwinian Revolution* (1979), is a good starting point, as are P. Bowler, *Evolution: The History of an Idea*, rev. ed. (1989), and G. Himmelfarb, *Darwin and the Darwinian Revolution* (1968). O. Chadwick, *The Secularization of the European Mind in the Nineteenth Century* (1976), analyzes the impact of science (and other factors) on religious belief. The masterpieces of the great realist social novelists remain one of the best and most memorable introductions to nineteenth-century culture and thought. In addition to the novels discussed in this chapter, and those cited in the Suggested Reading for Chapters 22 and 23, I. Turgenev's *Fathers and Sons* and Zola's *The Dram-Shop (L'Assommoir)* are especially recommended.

25

The Age of Nationalism, 1850–1914

The revolutions of 1848 closed one era and opened another. Urban industrial society began to take strong hold on the Continent and in the young United States, as it already had in Great Britain. Internationally, the repressive peace and diplomatic stability of Metternich's time were replaced by a period of war and rapid change. In thought and culture, exuberant romanticism gave way to hard-headed realism. In the Atlantic economy, the hard years of the 1840s were followed by good times and prosperity throughout most of the 1850s and 1860s. Perhaps most important of all, Western society progressively found, for better or worse, a new and effective organizing principle, capable of coping with the many-sided challenge of the dual revolution and the emerging urban civilization. That principle was nationalism—dedication to and identification with the nation-state.

The triumph of nationalism is a development of enormous historical significance. It was by no means completely predictable. After all, nationalism had been a powerful force since at least 1789. Yet it had repeatedly failed to realize its goals, most spectacularly so in 1848.

- Why, then, did nationalism become in one way or another an almost universal faith in Europe and in the United States between 1850 and 1914?

- More specifically, how did nationalism evolve so that it appealed not only to predominately middle-class liberals but to the broad masses of society as well?

These are the weighty questions this chapter will seek to answer.

NAPOLEON III IN FRANCE

Early nationalism was at least liberal and idealistic and often democratic and radical as well. The ideas of nationhood and popular sovereignty posed an awesome revolutionary threat to conservatives like Metternich. Yet, from the vantage point of the twentieth century, it is clear that nationalism wears many masks: it may be democratic and radical, as it was for Mazzini and Michelet; but it can also flourish in dictatorial states, which may be conservative,

fascist, or communist. Napoleon I's France had already combined national devotion with authoritarian rule. Significantly, it was Napoleon's nephew, Louis Napoleon, who revived and extended this merger. It was he who showed how governments could reconcile popular and conservative forces in an authoritarian nationalism. In doing so, he provided a model for political leaders elsewhere.

The Second Republic and Louis Napoleon

The overwhelming victory of Louis Napoleon Bonaparte in the French presidential election of December 1848 has long puzzled historians. The nephew of Napoleon I, Louis Napoleon had lived most of his life outside of France and played no part in French politics before 1848. Why did universal manhood suffrage give such an unproven nobody 5.5 million votes, while the runner-up, General Cavaignac of June Days fame (see page 746), polled only 1.5 million and the other three candidates (including the poet Lamartine) received insignificant support?

The usual explanation is that, though Louis Napoleon had only his great name in common with his uncle, that was enough. According to some historians, the Napoleonic legend—a monument to the power of romanticism between 1820 and 1848 —had transformed a dictator into a demigod in the minds of the unsophisticated French masses. Another explanation, popularized by Karl Marx, has stressed the fears of middle-class and peasant property owners in the face of the socialist challenge of urban workers. These classes wanted protection. They wanted a tough cop with a big stick on the beat. They found him in Louis Napoleon, who had indeed served briefly as a special constable in London at the height of the Chartist agitation.

These explanations are not wrong, but there was more to Louis Napoleon's popularity than stupidity and fear. In late 1848 Louis Napoleon had a positive "program" for France, which was to guide him throughout most of his long reign. This program had been elaborated earlier in two pamphlets, *Napoleonic Ideas* and *The Elimination of Poverty,* which Louis Napoleon had written while imprisoned for a farcical attempt to overthrow Louis Philippe's government. The pamphlets had been widely circulated prior to the presidential election.

Louis Napoleon believed that the government should represent the people and that it should also try hard to help them economically. How was this to be done? Parliaments and political parties were not the answer, according to Louis Napoleon. Politicians represented special-interest groups, particularly middle-class ones. When they ran a parliamentary government, they stirred up class hatred because they were not interested in helping the poor. This had occurred under Louis Philippe, and it was occurring again under the Second Republic. The answer was a strong, even authoritarian, national leader, like the first Napoleon, who would serve all the people, rich and poor. This leader would be linked to the people by direct democracy and universal male suffrage. Sovereignty would flow from the entire population to the leader and would not be diluted or corrupted by politicians and legislative bodies.

These political ideas went hand in hand with Louis Napoleon's vision of national unity and social progress. Rather than doing nothing or providing only temporary relief for the awful poverty of the poor, the state and its leader had a sacred duty to provide jobs and stimulate the economy. All classes would benefit by such action.

Louis Napoleon's political and social ideas were at least vaguely understood by large numbers of French peasants and workers in December 1848. To many common people he appeared to be both a strong man *and* a forward-looking champion of their interests, and that is why they voted for him.

Elected to a four-year term, President Louis Napoleon had to share power with a conservative National Assembly. With some misgivings he signed a bill to increase greatly the role of the Catholic church in primary and secondary education. In France, as elsewhere in Europe after 1848, the anxious well-to-do saw religion as a bulwark against radicalism. As one leader of the church in France put it, "There is only one recipe for making those who own nothing believe in property-rights: that is to make them believe in God, who dictated the Ten Commandments and who promises eternal punishment to those who steal."[1] Very reluctantly, Louis Napoleon also signed another conservative law depriving many poor people of the right to vote. He took these conservative measures for two main reasons: he wanted the Assembly to vote funds to pay his personal debts, and he wanted it to change the constitution so he could run for a second term.

The Assembly did neither. Thus in 1851 Louis Napoleon began to organize a conspiracy with key army officers. On December 2, 1851, he illegally dismissed the Assembly and seized power in a *coup d'état.* There was some armed resistance in Paris and other cities, but the actions of the Assembly had left the Second Republic with few defenders. Restoring universal male suffrage, Louis Napoleon called on the French people, as his uncle had done, to legalize his actions. They did: 92 percent voted to make him a strong president for ten years. A year later, 97 percent agreed in a national plebiscite to make him hereditary emperor. For the third time, and by the greatest margin yet, the authoritarian Louis Napoleon was overwhelmingly elected to lead the French nation.

Napoleon III's Second Empire

Louis Napoleon—now Emperor Napoleon III—experienced both success and failure between 1852 and 1870. His greatest success was with the economy, particularly in the 1850s. His government encouraged the new investment banks and massive railroad construction that were at the heart of the Industrial Revolution on the Continent. General economic expansion was also fostered by the government's ambitious program of public works, which included the rebuilding of Paris to improve the urban environment. The profits of business people soared with prosperity, and the working classes did not fare poorly either. Their wages more than kept up with inflation, and jobs were much easier to find.

Louis Napoleon always hoped that economic progress would reduce social and political tensions. This hope was at least partially realized. Until the mid-1860s, there was little active opposition and even considerable support for his government from France's most dissatisfied group, the urban workers. Napoleon III's regulation of pawnshops and his support of credit unions and better housing for the working class were evidence of positive concern in the 1850s. In the 1860s he granted workers the right to form unions and the right to strike—important economic rights denied by earlier governments.

At first, political power remained in the hands of the emperor. He alone chose his ministers, and they had great freedom of action. At the same time, Napoleon III restricted but did not abolish the Assembly. Members were elected by universal male suffrage every six years, and Louis Napoleon and his government took the parliamentary elections

Rebuilding Paris Expensive and time consuming, boulevard construction in Paris brought massive demolition, considerable slum clearance, and protests of ruin to the old city. In addition to expecting economic benefits, Napoleon III rightly believed that broad boulevards would be harder for revolutionaries to barricade than narrow twisting streets. *(Source: The Mansell Collection)*

very seriously. They tried to entice notable people, even those who had opposed the regime, to stand as government candidates in order to expand the base of support. Moreover, the government used its officials and appointed mayors to spread the word that the election of the government's candidates—and the defeat of the opposition—was the key to roads, schools, tax rebates, and a thousand other local concerns.

In 1857 and again in 1863, Louis Napoleon's system worked brilliantly and produced overwhelming electoral victories. Yet in the course of the 1860s Napoleon III's electoral system gradually disintegrated, for several reasons. France's problems in Italy and the rising power of Prussia led to increasing criticism at home from his Catholic and nationalist supporters. With increasing effectiveness, the middle-class liberals who had

always detested his dictatorship continued to denounce his rule as a disgrace to France's republican tradition.

Napoleon was always sensitive to the public mood. Public opinion, he once said, always wins the last victory. Thus in the 1860s he progressively liberalized his empire. He gave the Assembly greater powers and the opposition candidates greater freedom, which they used to good advantage. In 1869 the opposition, consisting of republicans, monarchists, and liberals, polled almost 45 percent of the vote.

The following year, a sick and weary Louis Napoleon once again granted France a new constitution, which combined a basically parliamentary regime with a hereditary emperor as chief of state. In a final great plebiscite on the eve of a disastrous war with Prussia, 7.5 million Frenchmen voted in favor of the new constitution, and only 1.5 million opposed it. Napoleon III's attempt to reconcile a strong national state with universal manhood suffrage was still evolving, in a democratic direction.

NATION BUILDING IN ITALY AND GERMANY

Louis Napoleon's triumph in 1848 and his authoritarian rule in the 1850s provided the old ruling classes of Europe with a new model in politics. To what extent was it possible that the expanding urban middle classes and even the growing working classes might, like people in rural areas, rally to a strong and essentially conservative national state? This was one of the great political questions in the 1850s and 1860s. In central Europe, a resounding and definitive answer came with the national unification of Italy and Germany.

Italy to 1850

Italy had never been a united nation prior to 1860. Part of Rome's great empire in ancient times, the Italian peninsula was divided in the Middle Ages into competing city-states, which led the commercial and cultural revival of the West with amazing creativity. A battleground for great powers after 1494, Italy had been reorganized in 1815 at the Congress of Vienna. The rich northern provinces of Lombardy and Venetia were taken by Metternich's Austria. Sardinia and Piedmont were under the rule of an Italian monarch, and Tuscany with its famous capital of Florence shared north central Italy with several smaller states. Central Italy and Rome were ruled by the papacy, which had always considered an independent political existence necessary to fulfill its spiritual mission. Naples and Sicily were ruled, as they had been for almost a hundred years, by a branch of the Bourbons. Metternich was not wrong in dismissing Italy as "a geographical expression" (Map 25.1).

Between 1815 and 1848, the goal of a unified Italian nation captured the imaginations of increasing numbers of Italians. There were three basic approaches. The first was the radical program of the idealistic patriot Mazzini, who preached a centralized democratic republic based on universal suffrage and the will of the people. The second was that of Gioberti, a Catholic priest, who called for a federation of existing states under the presidency of a progressive pope. Finally, there were those who looked for leadership toward the autocratic kingdom of Sardinia-Piedmont, much as many Germans looked toward Prussia.

The third alternative was strengthened by the failures of 1848, when Austria smashed and discredited Mazzini's republicanism. Almost by accident, Sardinia's monarch Victor Emmanuel retained the liberal constitution granted under duress in March 1848. This constitution provided for a fair degree of civil liberties and real parliamentary government, complete with elections and parliamentary control of taxes. To the Italian middle classes, Sardinia appeared to be a liberal, progressive state, ideally suited to achieve the goal of national unification. By contrast, Mazzini's brand of democratic republicanism seemed quixotic and too radical. As for the papacy, the initial cautious support by Pius IX (1846–1878) for unification had given way to fear and hostility after he was temporarily driven from Rome during the upheavals of 1848. For a long generation, the papacy would stand resolutely opposed not only to national unification but to most modern trends. In 1864, in the *Syllabus of Errors,* Pius IX strongly denounced rationalism, socialism, separation of church and state, and religious liberty, denying that "the Roman pontiff can and ought to reconcile and align himself with progress, liberalism, and modern civilization."

Cavour and Garibaldi

Sardinia had the good fortune of being led by a brilliant statesman, Count Camillo Benso di Cavour, the dominant figure in the Sardinian government from 1850 until his death in 1861. Cavour's development was an early sign of the coming tacit alliance between the aristocracy and the solid middle class throughout much of Europe. Beginning as a successful manager of his father's large landed estates in Piedmont, Cavour was also an economic liberal. He turned toward industry and made a substantial fortune in sugar mills, steamships, banks, and railroads. Economically secure, he then entered the world of politics and became chief minister in the liberalized Sardinian monarchy. Cavour's national goals were limited and realistic. Until 1859 he sought unity only for the states of northern and perhaps central Italy in a greatly expanded

MAP 25.1 The Unification of Italy, 1859–1870   The leadership of Sardinia-Piedmont and nationalist fervor were decisive factors in the unification of Italy.

kingdom of Sardinia. It was not one of his goals to incorporate the Papal States or the kingdom of the Two Sicilies, with their very different cultures and governments, into an Italy of all the Italians. Cavour was a moderate nationalist.

In the 1850s Cavour worked to consolidate Sardinia as a liberal state capable of leading northern Italy. His program of highways and railroads, of civil liberties and opposition to clerical privilege, increased support for Sardinia throughout northern Italy. Yet Cavour realized that Sardinia could not drive Austria out of Lombardy and Venetia and unify northern Italy under Victor Emmanuel without the help of a powerful ally. He sought that ally in the person of Napoleon III, who sincerely believed in the general principle of nationality, as well as modest expansion for France.

In a complicated series of diplomatic maneuvers, Cavour worked for a secret diplomatic alliance with Napoleon III against Austria. Finally, in July 1858, he succeeded and goaded Austria into attacking Sardinia. Napoleon III came to Sardinia's defense. Then, after the victory of the combined Franco-Sardinian forces, Napoleon III did a complete about-face. Nauseated by the gore of war and criticized by French Catholics for supporting the pope's declared enemy, Napoleon III abandoned Cavour. He made a compromise peace with the Austrians at Villafranca in July 1859. Sardinia would receive only Lombardy, the area around Milan. The rest of the map of Italy would remain essentially unchanged. Cavour resigned in a rage.

Yet Cavour's plans were salvaged by popular revolts and Italian nationalism. While the war against Austria had raged in the north, dedicated nationalists in central Italy had risen and driven out their rulers. Nationalist fervor seized the urban masses. Large crowds demonstrated, chanting, "Italy and Victor Emmanuel!" and singing passionately, "Foreigners, get out of Italy!" Buoyed up by this enthusiasm, the leaders of the nationalist movement in central Italy ignored the compromise peace of Villafranca and called for fusion with Sardinia. This was not at all what France and the other Great Powers wanted, but the nationalists held firm and eventually had their way. Cavour returned to power in early 1860, and the people of central Italy voted overwhelmingly to join a greatly enlarged kingdom of Sardinia. Cavour had achieved his original goal of a north Italian state (see Map 25.1).

For superpatriots like Giuseppe Garibaldi (1807–1882), the job of unification was still only half done. The son of a poor sailor, Garibaldi personified the romantic, revolutionary nationalism of

Garibaldi and His Red Shirts   Four days after landing in western Sicily, Garibaldi's forces won the Battle of Calatafimi, pictured here with the flamboyant patriot exhorting his troops at the center. Within two weeks Garibaldi took Palermo and established a provisional government in Sicily. *(Source: Museo del Risorgimento, Milan. Photo: Glancarlo Costa)*

Mazzini and 1848. As a lad of seventeen, he had traveled to Rome and been converted to the "New Italy, the Italy of all the Italians." As he later wrote in his *Autobiography,* "The Rome that I beheld with the eyes of youthful imagination was the Rome of the future—the dominant thought of my whole life." Sentenced to death in 1834 for his part in an uprising in Genoa, Garibaldi escaped to South America. For twelve years he led a guerrilla band in Uruguay's struggle for independence. "Shipwrecked, ambushed, shot through the neck," he found in a tough young woman, Anna da Silva, a mate and companion in arms. Their first children nearly starved in the jungle while Garibaldi, clad in his long red shirt, fashioned a legend not unlike that of the Cuban Ché Guevara in recent times. He returned to Italy to fight in 1848 and led a corps of volunteers against Austria in 1859. By the spring of 1860, Garibaldi had emerged as a powerful independent force in Italian politics.

Partly to use him and partly to get rid of him, Cavour secretly supported Garibaldi's bold plan to "liberate" Sicily. Landing in Sicily in May 1860, Garibaldi's guerrilla band of a thousand "Red Shirts" captured the imagination of the Sicilian peasantry. Outwitting the twenty-thousand-man royal army, the guerrilla leader took Palermo. Then he and his men crossed to the mainland, marched triumphantly toward Naples, and prepared to attack Rome and the pope. But the wily Cavour quickly sent Sardinian forces to occupy most of the Papal States (but not Rome) and to intercept Garibaldi.

Cavour realized that an attack on Rome would bring about war with France, and he also feared Garibaldi's popular appeal. Therefore, he immediately organized a plebiscite in the conquered territories. Despite the urging of some of his more radical supporters, the patriotic Garibaldi did not oppose Cavour, and the people of the south voted to join Sardinia. When Garibaldi and Victor Emmanuel rode through Naples to cheering crowds, they symbolically sealed the union of north and south, of monarch and people.

Cavour had succeeded. He had controlled Garibaldi and had turned popular nationalism in a conservative direction. The new kingdom of Italy, which did not include Venice until 1866 or Rome until 1870, was neither radical nor democratic. Italy was a parliamentary monarchy under Victor Emmanuel, but in accordance with the Sardinian constitution only a small minority of Italians had the right to vote. There was a definite division between the propertied classes and the common people. There was also a great social and cultural gap between the progressive, industrializing north and the stagnant, agrarian south. This gap would increase, since peasant industries in the south would not be able to survive. Italy was united politically. Other divisions remained.

Germany Before Bismarck

In the aftermath of 1848, while Louis Napoleon consolidated his rule and Cavour schemed, the German states were locked in a political stalemate. With Russian diplomatic support, Austria had blocked the halfhearted attempt of Frederick William IV of Prussia (r. 1840–1861) to unify Germany "from above." This action contributed to a growing tension between Austria and Prussia, as each power sought to block the other within the reorganized German Confederation (see pages 724–751). Stalemate also prevailed in the domestic politics of the individual states, as Austria, Prussia, and the smaller German kingdoms entered a period of reaction and immobility.

At the same time, powerful economic forces were undermining the political status quo. As we have seen, modern industry grew rapidly in Europe throughout the 1850s. Nowhere was this growth more rapid than within the German customs union (*Zollverein*). Developing gradually under Prussian leadership after 1818 and founded officially in 1834 to stimulate trade and increase the revenues of member states, the customs union had not included Austria. After 1848 it became a crucial factor in the Austro-Prussian rivalry.

Tariff duties were substantially reduced so that Austria's highly protected industry could not bear to join. In retaliation, Austria tried to destroy the Zollverein by inducing the south German states to leave it, but without success. Indeed, by the end of 1853 all the German states except Austria had joined the customs union. A new Germany excluding Austria was becoming an economic reality, and the middle class and business groups were finding solid economic reasons to bolster their idealistic support of national unification. Thus economic developments helped Prussia greatly in its struggle against Austria's supremacy in German affairs.

The national uprising in Italy in 1859 made a profound impression in the German states. In Prussia, great political change and war—perhaps with Austria, perhaps with France—seemed quite possible. Along with his top military advisers, the tough-minded William I of Prussia (r. 1861–1888), who had replaced the unstable Frederick William IV as regent in 1858 and become king himself in 1861, was convinced of the need for major army reforms. William I wanted to double the size of the highly disciplined regular army. He also wanted to reduce the importance of the reserve militia, a semipopular force created during the Napoleonic wars. Of course, reform of the army meant a bigger defense budget and higher taxes.

Prussia had emerged from 1848 with a parliament of sorts, and by 1859 the Prussian parliament was in the hands of the liberal middle class. The middle class, like the landed aristocracy, was overrepresented by the Prussian electoral system, and it wanted society to be less, not more, militaristic. Above all, middle-class representatives wanted to establish once and for all that the parliament, not the king, had the ultimate political power. They also wanted to ensure that the army was responsible to the people and not a "state within a state." These demands were popular. The parliament rejected the military budget in 1862, and the liberals triumphed so completely in new elections that the conservatives "could ride to the parliament building in a single coach." King William considered abdicating in favor of his more liberal son. In the end, he called on Count Otto von Bismarck to head a new ministry and defy the parliament. It was a momentous choice.

Otto von Bismarck A fierce political fighter with a commanding personality and a brilliant mind, Bismarck was devoted to Prussia and its king and aristocracy. Uniforms were worn by civilian officials as well as by soldiers in Prussia. (Source: Brown Brothers)

Bismarck Takes Command

The most important figure in German history between Luther and Hitler, Otto von Bismarck (1815–1898) has been the object of enormous interest and debate. A great hero to some, a great villain to others, Bismarck was above all a master of politics. Born into the Prussian landowning aristocracy, the young Bismarck was a wild and tempestuous student, given to duels and drinking. Proud of his Junker heritage—"my fathers have been born and have lived and died in the same rooms for centuries"—and always devoted to his Prussian sovereign, Bismarck had a strong personality and an unbounded desire for power.

Bismarck entered the civil service, which was the only socially acceptable career except the army for a Prussian aristocrat. But he soon found bureaucratic life unbearable and fled to his ancestral estate. "My pride," he admitted, "bids me command rather than obey."[2] Yet in his drive for power, power for himself and for Prussia, Bismarck was extraordinarily flexible and pragmatic. "One must always have two irons in the fire," he once said. He kept his options open, pursuing one policy and then another as he moved with skill and cunning toward his goal.

Bismarck first honed his political skills as a diplomat. Acquiring a reputation as an ultraconservative in the Prussian assembly in 1848, he fought against Austria as the Prussian ambassador to the German Confederation from 1851 to 1859. Transferred next to St. Petersburg and then to Paris, Bismarck worked toward a basic goal that was well known by 1862—to build up Prussia's strength and consolidate Prussia's precarious Great Power status.

To achieve this goal, Bismarck was convinced that Prussia had to control completely the northern, predominately Protestant part of the German Confederation. He saw three possible paths open before him. He might work with Austria to divide up the smaller German states lying between them. Or he might combine with foreign powers—France and Italy, or even Russia—against Austria. Or he might ally with the forces of German nationalism to defeat and expel Austria from German affairs. Each possibility was explored in many complicated diplomatic maneuvers, but in the end the last path was the one Bismarck took.

That Bismarck would join with the forces of German nationalism to increase Prussia's power seemed unlikely when he took office as chief minister in 1862. Bismarck's appointment made a strong but unfavorable impression. His speeches were a sensation and a scandal. Declaring that the government would rule without parliamentary consent, Bismarck lashed out at the middle-class opposition: "The great questions of the day will not be decided by speeches and resolutions—that was the blunder of 1848 and 1849—but by blood and iron." In 1863 he told the Prussian parliament, "If a compromise cannot be arrived at and a conflict arises, then the conflict becomes a question of power. Whoever has the power then acts according to his opinion." Denounced for this view that "might makes right," Bismarck had the bureaucracy go right on collecting taxes, even though the parliament refused to approve the budget. Bismarck reorganized the army. And for four years, from 1862 to 1866, the voters of Prussia continued to express their opposition by sending large liberal majorities to the parliament.

The Austro-Prussian War of 1866

Opposition at home spurred the search for success abroad. The ever-knotty question of Schleswig-Holstein provided a welcome opportunity. When the Danish king tried again, as in 1848, to bring the provinces into a centralized Danish state against the will of the German Confederation, Prussia joined Austria in a short and successful war against Denmark in 1864. Then Bismarck maneuvered Austria into a tricky position. Prussia and Austria agreed to joint administration of the conquered provinces, thereby giving Bismarck a weapon he could use either to force Austria into peacefully accepting Prussian domination in northern Germany or to start a war against Austria.

Bismarck knew that a war with Austria would have to be a localized war. He had to be certain that Prussian expansion did not provoke a mighty armed coalition, such as the coalition that had almost crushed Frederick the Great in the eighteenth century. Russia, the great bear to the east, was no problem. Bismarck had already gained Alexander II's gratitude by supporting Russia's repression of a Polish uprising in 1863. Napoleon III—the "sphinx without a riddle," according to Bismarck—was another matter. But Bismarck charmed him into neutrality with vague promises of more territory along the Rhine. Thus, when Austria proved unwilling to give up its historic role in German affairs, Bismarck was in a position to engage in a war of his own making.

The Austro-Prussian War of 1866 lasted only seven weeks. Utilizing railroads to mass troops and the new breechloading needle gun for maximum firepower, the reorganized Prussian army overran northern Germany and defeated Austria decisively at the Battle of Sadowa in Bohemia. Anticipating Prussia's future needs, Bismarck offered Austria realistic, even generous, peace terms. Austria paid no reparations and lost no territory to Prussia, although Venice was ceded to Italy. But the German Confederation was dissolved, and Austria agreed to withdraw from German affairs. The states north of the Main River were grouped in a new North German Confederation led by an expanded Prussia. The mainly Catholic states of the south were permitted to remain independent, while forming military alliances with Prussia. Bismarck's fundamental goal of Prussian expansion was being realized (Map 25.2).

The Taming of the Parliament

Bismarck had long been convinced that the old order he so ardently defended should make peace—on its own terms—with the liberal middle class and the nationalist movement. Inspired somewhat by Louis Napoleon, he realized that nationalism was not necessarily hostile to conservative, authoritarian government. Moreover, Bismarck believed that, because of the events of 1848, the German

Scale:
0 50 100 Km.
0 50 100 Mi.

DENMARK

SWEDEN

North Sea

Baltic Sea

SCHLESWIG

Kiel

HOLSTEIN

Lübeck

Hamburg

Bremen

MECKLENBURG

POMERANIA

WEST PRUSSIA

EAST PRUSSIA

Königsberg

Danzig

Neman

OLDENBURG

HANOVER

Hanover

BRANDENBURG

Berlin

P   R   U   S   S   I   A

POSEN

Vistula

Warta

RUSSIAN   EMPIRE

Warsaw

Amsterdam

NETHERLANDS

WESTPHALIA

Essen

P   R   U

Leipzig

Weimar

Dresden

SAXONY

SILESIA

POLAND

Oder

Antwerp

BELGIUM

Cologne

Bonn

RHINE PROVINCE

Ruhr

Elbe

Moselle

Frankfurt

Sadowa 1866 ✕

Prague

Kraków

Sedan 1870

Luxembourg

Main

BOHEMIA

Olmütz

MORAVIA

Verdun

LORRAINE

Rhine

Neckar

Karlsruhe

Stuttgart

WÜRTTEMBERG

BAVARIA

Nuremberg

Vltava

Morava

A U S T R I A N   E M P I R E

Nancy

Strasbourg

ALSACE

BADEN

Munich

Inn

Danube

Vienna

Pest

Buda

FRANCE

SWITZERLAND

Innsbruck

ITALY

▨ Prussia before 1866

▨ Conquered by Prussia in Austro-Prussian War, 1866

▨ Austrian territories excluded from German Confederation, 1867

▨ Joined with Prussia to form German Confederation, 1867

▨ South German states joining with Prussia to form German Empire, 1871

▨ Won by Prussia in Franco-Prussian War, 1871

✕ Major battles

— German Confederation boundary, 1815–1866

— Bismarck's German Empire, 1871

MAP 25.2 The Unification of Germany, 1866–1871   This map deserves careful study. Note how Prussian expansion, Austrian expulsion from the old German Confederation, and the creation of a new German Empire went hand in hand. Austria lost no territory but Prussia's neighbors in the north suffered grievously or simply disappeared.

middle class could be led to prefer the reality of national unity to a long, uncertain battle for truly liberal institutions. During the constitutional struggle over army reform and parliamentary authority, he had delayed but not abandoned this goal. Thus, during the attack on Austria in 1866, he increasingly identified Prussia's fate with the "national development of Germany."

In the aftermath of victory, Bismarck fashioned a federal constitution for the new North German Confederation. Each state retained its own local government, but the king of Prussia was to be president of the confederation and the chancellor—

"His First Thought" This 1896 cartoon provides a brilliant commentary on German middle-class attitudes. Suddenly crippled, the man's first thought is "Disaster! Now I can no longer be an army reserve officer." Being a part-time junior officer, below the dominant aristocratic career officers, became a great middle-class status symbol. *(Source: Caroline Buckler)*

Bismarck—was to be responsible only to the president. The federal government—William I and Bismarck—controlled the army and foreign affairs. There was also a legislature, consisting of two houses that shared equally in the making of laws. Delegates to the upper house were appointed by the different states, but members of the lower house were elected by universal, equal manhood suffrage. With this radical innovation, Bismarck opened the door to popular participation and went over the head of the middle class directly to the people. All the while, however, ultimate power rested as securely as ever in the hands of Prussia and its king and army.

Events within Prussia itself were even more significant than those at the federal level. In the flush of victory, the ultraconservatives expected Bismarck to suspend the Prussian constitution or perhaps abolish the Prussian parliament altogether. Yet he did nothing of the sort. Instead, he held out an olive branch to the parliamentary opposition. Marshaling all his diplomatic skill, Bismarck asked the parliament to pass a special indemnity bill to approve after the fact all of the government's spending between 1862 and 1866. Most of the liberals snatched at the chance to cooperate. For four long years, they had opposed and criticized Bismarck's "illegal" measures. And what had happened? Bismarck, the king, and the army had persevered, and in the end these conservative forces had succeeded beyond the wildest dreams of the liberal middle class. In 1866 German unity was in sight, and the people were going to be allowed to participate actively in the new state. Many liberals repented their "sins" and were overjoyed that Bismarck would forgive them.

None repented more ardently or more typically than Hermann Baumgarten, a mild-mannered, thoroughly decent history professor and member of the liberal opposition. In his essay "A Self Criticism of German Liberalism," he confessed in 1866:

We thought by agitation we could transform Germany. But . . . almost all the elements of our political system have been shown erroneous by the facts themselves. . . . Yet we have experienced a miracle almost without parallel. The victory of our principles would have brought us misery, whereas the defeat of our principles has brought boundless salvation.[3]

The constitutional struggle was over. The German middle class was bowing respectfully before Bismarck and the monarchial authority and aristocratic superiority he represented. The middle class did not stand upright again in the years before 1914.

The Franco-Prussian War of 1870–1871

The rest of the story of German unification is anticlimactic. In 1867 Bismarck brought the four south German states into the customs union and established a customs parliament. But the south Germans were reluctant to go further because of their different religious and political traditions. Bismarck realized that a patriotic war with France would drive the south German states into his arms. The French obligingly played their part. The apparent issue—whether a distant relative of Prussia's William I (and France's Napoleon III) might become king of Spain—was only a diplomatic pretext. By 1870 the French leaders of the Second Empire, alarmed by their powerful new neighbor on the Rhine, had decided on a war to teach Prussia a lesson.

As soon as war against France began in 1870, Bismarck had the wholehearted support of the south German states. With other governments standing still—Bismarck's generosity to Austria in 1866 was paying big dividends—German forces under Prussian leadership decisively defeated Louis Napoleon's armies at Sedan on September 1, 1870. Three days later, French patriots in Paris proclaimed yet another French republic and vowed to continue fighting. But after five months, in January 1871, a starving Paris surrendered, and France went on to accept Bismarck's harsh peace terms. By this time, the south German states had agreed to join a new German Empire. The victorious William I was proclaimed emperor of Germany in the Hall of Mirrors in the palace of Versailles. Europe had a nineteenth-century German "sun king." As in the 1866 constitution, the king of Prussia and his ministers had ultimate power in the new empire, and the lower house of the legislature was elected popularly by universal male suffrage.

The Franco-Prussian War of 1870 to 1871, which Europeans generally saw as a test of nations in a pitiless Darwinian struggle for existence, released an enormous surge of patriotic feeling in Germany. Bismarck's genius, the invincible Prussian army, the solidarity of king and people in a unified nation—these and similar themes were trumpeted endlessly during and after the war. The weakest of the Great Powers in 1862—after Austria, Britain, France, and Russia—Prussia fortified by the other Germans states had become the most powerful state in Europe in less than a decade. Most Germans were enormously proud, enormously relieved. And they were somewhat drunk with success, blissfully imagining themselves the fittest and best of the European species. Semi-authoritarian nationalism had triumphed. Only a few critics remained dedicated to the liberal ideal of truly responsible parliamentary government.

NATION BUILDING IN THE UNITED STATES

Closely linked to general European developments in the nineteenth century, the United States experienced the full drama of midcentury nation building and felt the power of nationalism to refashion politics and remake states. Yet in the United States competing national aspirations served first to divide rather than unite. Only after a bitter civil war was nationalism successfully harnessed to the building of a transcontinental giant.

Slavery and Territorial Expansion

Formed in the process of revolt against Great Britain, the young "United" States was divided by slavery from its birth. Then, as the new federal Constitution was being written, the Northwest Ordinance of 1787 effectively extended the seaboard patterns of free and slave labor into the vast area west of the Appalachian Mountains and east of the Mississippi, with the Ohio River serving as the fatal dividing line. The purchase of the entire Louisiana Territory from France in 1803 opened another enormous area for settlement, as the native American Indians continued to be pushed to the fringes or decimated. Thus the stage was set for growing regional tensions as American economic development carried the free and the slaveholding states in very different directions.

In the North, white settlers broke the soil north of the Ohio and extended the pattern of family farm agriculture. Ingenious Yankees began building English-model factories, drawing first on New England farm girls housed in company dormitories and then on families of Irish immigrants. By 1850

Slavery and Cotton   The intense activity and the systematic exploitation of slave labor on large cotton plantations come alive in this contemporary painting. Slaves of both sexes and of all ages pick the cotton and transport it to smoke-belching worksheds, shown in the background, for later processing in cotton gins. *(Source: Courtesy Jay P. Altmayer)*

an industrializing, urbanizing North was also building an efficient system of canals and railroads and attracting most of the rising tide of European immigrants.

In the South, by contrast, industry and cities did not develop, and newcomers avoided the region. And while fully three-quarters of all Southern white families were small farmers and owned no slaves in 1850, plantation owners holding twenty or more slaves and producing a market crop dominated the economy and the society, as they had since colonial times. Turning increasingly from tobacco, sugar cane, and rice, the rich, profit-minded slaveowners used gangs of black slaves to claim a vast new kingdom, a kingdom where cotton was the king. Expanding into fertile virgin lands and relying after 1793 on Eli Whitney's newly invented cotton engine (or "gin," for short), which separated the sticky green seeds from the fluffy fiber and did the work of fifty workers, the cotton kingdom eventually stretched across most of the Deep South, from the Carolinas westward to Arkansas and eastern

Texas. By 1850, it produced 5 million bales a year (as opposed to only 4,000 bales in 1791) and profitably satisfied an apparently insatiable demand from cotton mills in Great Britain, other European countries, and New England.

The rise of the slave-based cotton empire had momentous consequences for the republic. First, it revitalized slave-based agriculture and created great wealth, and not just for rich Southern slaveholders. Cotton accounted for two-thirds of the value of all American exports by the 1850s, and many economic historians believe it provided the critical "leading sector" that ignited rapid economic growth in the United States. Second, the large profits flowing from cotton production led influential Southerners to defend slavery and even argue that it benefited slaves as well as masters (and, indirectly, poor whites). In defending their "peculiar institution," Southern whites developed a strong cultural identity and saw themselves as a close-knit "we" distinct from a Northern "they." Third, prodded by bitter battles over the protective tariff and by passionate antislavery crusaders, Northern whites also came to see their free-labor system as being no less economically and morally superior. Thus regional antagonisms intensified.

These antagonisms came to a climax after 1848, when a recently defeated Mexico ceded to the United States half a million square miles of territory stretching from west Texas to the Pacific Ocean. Whether and to what extent Congress should permit slavery in this conquered area became the all-absorbing and highly divisive political

issue. Attitudes hardened on both sides, and outbreaks of violence multiplied, involving even the U.S. Congress. In one famous incident in 1856, a hotheaded representative from South Carolina used his heavy cane to beat an abolitionist senator from Massachusetts almost to death as he sat at his desk on the Senate floor. By 1860 many Northerners warned ominously of a "Slave Power" plot to destroy freedom everywhere, and Southerners denounced the power of "lord King Numbers" to strangle and ruin the South (Map 25.3). In

MAP 25.3 Slavery in the United States, 1860 This map illustrates the nation on the eve of the Civil War. Although many issues contributed to the developing opposition between North and South, slavery was the fundamental, enduring force that underlay all others. Lincoln's prediction, "I believe this government cannot endure permanently half slave and half free," tragically proved correct.

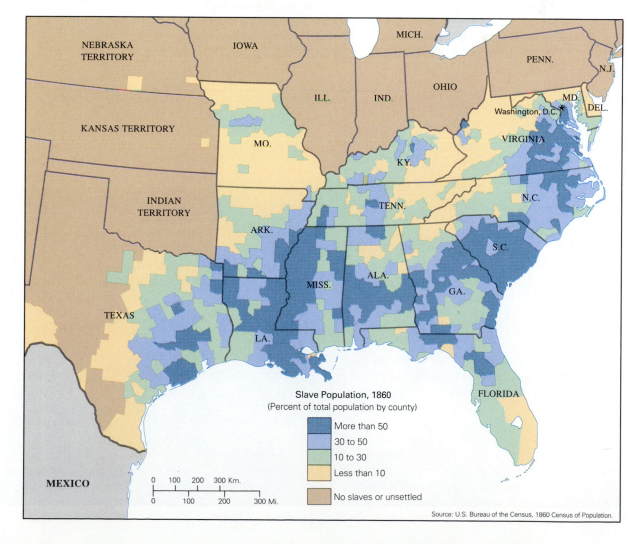

Abraham Lincoln's famous words, the United States was a "house divided" by contradictory economic systems and conflicting values.

Civil War and Reunification

Lincoln's election as president in 1860 gave Southern "fire-eaters" the chance they had been waiting for. Having agitated for years for the end of the Union, they now trumpeted the fact that Lincoln had not even campaigned in the South as an insult and called for secession and Southern independ-

ence. Southern moderates countered that secession would lead to war and then to emancipation, possibly through bloody slave revolts. Alexander H. Stephens, future vice-president of the Southern Confederacy, declared prophetically, "I consider slavery much more secure in the Union than out of it."[4] But radicals in South Carolina quickly voted to leave the Union, and the rest of the Deep South followed suit. Confederate troops then fired on an indefensible federal fort in the heart of South Carolina's Charleston harbor, in a successful effort to provoke Northern retaliation and thus cause the cautious but proud Upper South—Virginia, Ten-

The Battle of Gettysburg, July 1–3, 1863 marked the high point of the Confederate advance and was the greatest battle of the war. This painting commemorates the climax on the third day, when Confederate General Robert E. Lee commanded Pickett's division to charge the Union center. Coming toward the viewer in the face of terrible fire, the brave Southerners have reached the first Union line. But General Hancock, shown with arm extended in the left foreground, is ordering the Northern counterattack that will decimate Pickett's troops and force the Confederates back into Virginia. *(Source: Photograph by Al Freni© 1985 Time-Life Books, Inc. Courtesy, The Seventh Regiment Fund, Inc.)*

nessee, and North Carolina—to join the gamble for an independent Southern nation.

The long Civil War (1861–1865) was the bloodiest conflict in all of American history, but in the end the South was decisively defeated and the Union was preserved. To historians explaining this outcome, it is clear that the vastly superior population, industry, and transportation of the North placed the South at a great, probably fatal disadvantage. Yet less obvious factors tied to morale and national purpose were also extremely important. The enormous gap between the slaveowning elite and the poor whites made it impossible for the South to build effectively on the patriotism of 1861. As the war ground on, many ordinary whites felt that the burden of war was falling mainly on their shoulders, because big planters resisted taxation and used loopholes to avoid the draft. Desertions from Southern armies mounted rapidly from the summer of 1863, as soldiers became disillusioned and responded to moving calls for help at home. "Before God, Edward, unless you come home we must die," wrote one of many desperate wives with sick and hungry children.[5]

Slavery itself weakened the South's war effort. Although blacks were used on the home front in countless ways, owners generally tried to keep their valuable property on their plantations, in order to prevent runaways and possible slave rebellion. Nor would planters accept the idea of a black Southern soldier or of freedom for blacks as a last-ditch means of fully mobilizing the South.

In the North, by contrast, most people prospered during the war years. Enthusiasm remained high, and certain dominant characteristics of American life and national culture took shape. Powerful business corporations emerged, steadfastly supported by the Republican party during and after the war. The vision of an ethnically diverse but still unified nation gained strength, for on the battlefield immigrants and native-born were all "damn Yankees" in Southern eyes. The Homestead Act of 1862, which gave western land to those who would settle it, and the Emancipation Proclamation of 1863, which freed the slaves in rebellious states, reinforced tremendously the concept of free labor taking its chances in a market economy. Finally, the success of Lincoln and the North in holding the Union together seemed to confirm that the "manifest destiny" of the United States was indeed to straddle a continent as a great (and presumably virtuous)

world power. Thus a new American nationalism grew out of the war to prevent the realization of Southern nationhood.

Northern victory also led to a "national" policy of sorts toward American blacks, although the path was complicated and often contradictory. With Northern armies occupying large parts of the Southern states until 1877, Congress guaranteed the legal freedom of blacks during the Reconstruction era and thwarted devious efforts of former masters to virtually re-enslave the freed black population. But Northern efforts to "reconstruct" the South did not include land reform. Freed blacks were generally forced to continue laboring for whites, but now as tenants under unfavorable sharecropping conditions. Blacks also faced very pervasive discrimination. Thus, as a result of war and reunification, the life of blacks in the Southern states moved much closer to that of the small number of blacks in the North, who had long been free but unequal citizens.

THE MODERNIZATION OF RUSSIA

In Russia, unlike Italy and Germany, there was no need to build a single state out of a jumble of principalities. The Russian Empire was already an enormous multinational state, a state that contained all the ethnic Russians and many other nationalities as well. As in the United States at midcentury, the long-term challenge facing the government was to hold the existing state together, either by means of political compromise or by military force. Thus Russia's rulers saw nationalism as a subversive ideology in the early nineteenth century, and they tried with some success to limit its development among their non-Russian subjects.

Yet old autocratic Russia found itself in serious trouble after 1853. It became clear to Russia's leaders that the country had to embrace the process of *modernization*. A vague and often overworked term, modernization is a great umbrella under which some writers place most of the major developments of the last two hundred or even five hundred years. Yet defined narrowly—as changes that enable a country to compete effectively with the leading countries at a given time—modernization can be a useful concept. It fits Russia after the Crimean War particularly well.

The "Great Reforms"

In the 1850s Russia was a poor agrarian society. Industry was little developed, and almost 90 percent of the population lived on the land. Agricultural techniques were backward: the ancient open-field system reigned supreme. Serfdom was still the basic social institution. Bound to the lord on a hereditary basis, the peasant serf was little more than a slave. Individual serfs and serf families were regularly sold, with and without land, in the early nineteenth century. Serfs were obliged to furnish labor services or money payments as the lord saw fit. Moreover, the lord could choose freely among the serfs for army recruits, who had to serve for twenty-five years, and he could punish a serf with deportation to Siberia whenever he wished. Sexual exploitation of female serfs by their lords was common.

Serfdom had become the great moral and political issue for the government by the 1840s, but it might still have lasted many more years had it not been for the Crimean War of 1853 to 1856. The war began as a dispute with France over who should protect certain Christian shrines in the Ottoman Empire. Because the fighting was concentrated in the Crimean peninsula on the Black Sea, Russia's transportation network of rivers and wagons failed to supply the distant Russian armies adequately. France and Great Britain, aided by Sardinia and the Ottoman Empire, inflicted a humiliating defeat on Russia.

The military defeat marked a turning point in Russian history. The Russian state had been built on the military, and Russia had not lost a major war for a century and a half. This defeat demonstrated that Russia had fallen behind the rapidly industrializing nations of western Europe in many areas. At the very least, Russia needed railroads, better armaments, and reorganization of the army if it was to maintain its international position. Moreover, the disastrous war had caused hardship and raised the specter of massive peasant rebellion. Reform of serfdom was imperative. And, as the new tsar, Alexander II (r. 1855–1881), told the serf owners, it would be better if reform came from above. Military disaster thus forced Alexander II and his ministers along the path of rapid social change and general modernization.

The first and greatest of the reforms was the freeing of the serfs in 1861. Human bondage was abolished forever, and the emancipated peasants received, on the average, about half of the land. Yet they had to pay fairly high prices for their land, and because the land was owned collectively, each peasant village was jointly responsible for the payments of all the families in the village. The government hoped that collective responsibility would strengthen the peasant village as a social unit and prevent the development of a class of landless peasants. In practice, collective ownership and responsibility made it very difficult for individual peasants to improve agricultural methods or leave their villages. Thus the effects of the reform were limited, for it did not encourage peasants to change their old habits and attitudes.

Most of the later reforms were also halfway measures. In 1864 the government established a new institution of local government, the *zemstvo*. Members of this local assembly were elected by a three-class system of towns, peasant villages, and noble landowners. A zemstvo executive council dealt with local problems. The establishment of the zemstvos marked a significant step toward popular participation, and Russian liberals hoped it would lead to a national parliament. They were soon disappointed. The local zemstvo remained subordinate to the traditional bureaucracy and the local nobility, who were heavily favored by the property-based voting system. More successful was reform of the legal system, which established independent courts and equality before the law. Education was also liberalized somewhat, and censorship was relaxed but not removed.

The Industrialization of Russia

Until the twentieth century, Russia's greatest strides toward modernization were economic rather than political. Industry and transport, both so vital to the military, were transformed in two industrial surges. The first of these came after 1860. The government encouraged and subsidized private railway companies, and construction boomed. In 1860 the empire had only about 1,250 miles of railroads; by 1880 it had about 15,500 miles. The railroads enabled agricultural Russia to export grain and thus earn money for further industrialization. Domestic manufacturing was stimulated, and by the end of the 1870s Russia had a well-developed railway-equipment industry. Industrial suburbs grew up around Moscow and St. Petersburg, and a class of modern factory workers began to take shape.

Novgorod Merchants Drinking Tea   This late nineteenth-century photograph suggests how Russian businessmen were slow to abandon traditional dress and attitudes. Stern authoritarians and staunchly devoted to church and tsar, they were often suspicious of foreigners as well as the lawyers and journalists who claimed to speak for the nation's middle class. *(Source: Bettmann/Hulton)*

Industrial development strengthened Russia's military forces and gave rise to territorial expansion to the south and east. Imperial expansion greatly excited many ardent Russian nationalists and superpatriots, who became some of the government's most enthusiastic supporters. Industrial development also contributed mightily to the spread of Marxian thought and the transformation of the Russian revolutionary movement after 1890.

In 1881 Alexander II was assassinated by a small group of terrorists. The era of reform came to an abrupt end, for the new tsar, Alexander III (r. 1881–1894), was a determined reactionary. Russia, and indeed all of Europe, experienced hard times economically in the 1880s. Political modernization remained frozen until 1905, but economic modernization sped forward in the massive industrial surge of the 1890s. As it had after the Crimean

War, nationalism played a decisive role. The key leader was Sergei Witte, the tough, competent minister of finance from 1892 to 1903. Early in his career, Witte found in the writings of Friedrich List (see page 707) an analysis and a program for action. List had stressed the peril for Germany of remaining behind England in the 1830s and 1840s. Witte saw the same threat of industrial backwardness threatening Russia's power and greatness.

Witte moved forward on several fronts. A railroad manager by training, he believed that railroads were "a very powerful weapon . . . for the direction of the economic development of the country."[6] Therefore, the government built railroads rapidly, doubling the network to 35,000 miles by the end of the century. The gigantic trans-Siberian line connecting Moscow with Vladivostok on the Pacific Ocean 5,000 miles away was Witte's

Building the Trans-Siberian Railroad   Constructed largely in the 1890s as part of Witte's industrialization drive, the world's longest railroad facilitated Russian penetration of northern China and Korea. That penetration then led to war with Japan. *(Source: Bettmann/Hulton)*

pride, and it was largely completed during his term of office. Following List's advice, Witte established high protective tariffs to build Russian industry, and he put the country on the gold standard of the "civilized world" in order to strengthen Russian finances.

Witte's greatest innovation, however, was to use the West to catch up with the West. He aggressively encouraged foreigners to use their abundant capital and advanced technology to build great factories in backward Russia. As he told the tsar, "The inflow of foreign capital is . . . the only way by which our industry will be able to supply our country quickly with abundant and cheap products."[7] This policy was brilliantly successful, especially in southern Russia. There, in the eastern Ukraine, foreign capitalists and their engineers built an enormous and very modern steel and coal industry almost from scratch in little more than a decade. By 1900 only the United States, Germany, and Great Britain were producing more steel than Russia. The Russian petroleum industry had even pulled up alongside that of the United States and was producing and refining half the world's output of oil.

Witte knew how to keep foreigners in line. Once a leading foreign businessman came to him and an-

grily demanded that the Russian government fulfill a contract it had signed and pay certain debts immediately. Witte asked to see the contract. He read it and then carefully tore it to pieces and threw it in the wastepaper basket without a word of explanation. It was just such a fiercely independent Russia that was catching up with the advanced nations of the West.

The Revolution of 1905

Catching up partly meant vigorous territorial expansion, for this was the age of Western imperialism. By 1903 Russia had established a sphere of influence in Chinese Manchuria and was casting greedy eyes on northern Korea. When the protests of equally imperialistic Japan were ignored, the Japanese launched a surprise attack in February 1904. To the world's amazement, Russia suffered repeated losses and was forced in August 1905 to accept a humiliating defeat.

As is often the case, military disaster abroad brought political upheaval at home. The business and professional classes had long wanted to match economic with political modernization. Their minimal goal was to turn the last of Europe's absolutist monarchies into a liberal, representative regime. Factory workers, strategically concentrated in the large cities, had all the grievances of early industrialization and were organized in a radical labor movement. Peasants had gained little from the era of reforms and were suffering from poverty and overpopulation. Finally, nationalist sentiment was emerging among the empire's minorities. The politically and culturally dominant ethnic Russians were only about 45 percent of the population, and by 1900 some intellectuals among the subject nationalities were calling for self-rule and autonomy. Separatist nationalism was strongest among the Poles and Ukrainians. With the army pinned down in Manchuria, all these currents of discontent converged in the revolution of 1905.

The beginning of the revolution pointed up the incompetence of the government. On a Sunday in January 1905, a massive crowd of workers and their families converged peacefully on the Winter Palace in St. Petersburg to present a petition to the tsar. The workers were led by a trade-unionist priest named Father Gapon, who had been secretly supported by the police as a preferable alternative to more radical unions. Carrying icons and respectfully singing "God Save the Tsar," the workers did not know Nicholas II had fled the city. Suddenly troops opened fire, killing and wounding hundreds. The "Bloody Sunday" massacre turned ordinary workers against the tsar and produced a wave of general indignation.

Outlawed political parties came out into the open, and by the summer of 1905 strikes, peasant uprisings, revolts among minority nationalities, and troop mutinies were sweeping the country. The revolutionary surge culminated in October 1905 in a great paralyzing general strike, which forced the government to capitulate. The tsar issued the October Manifesto, which granted full civil rights and promised a popularly elected Duma (parliament) with real legislative power. The manifesto split the opposition. It satisfied most moderate and liberal demands, but the Social Democrats rejected it and led a bloody workers' uprising in Moscow in December 1905. Frightened middle-class moderates helped the government repress the uprising and survive as a constitutional monarchy.

On the eve of the opening of the first Duma in May 1906, the government issued the new constitution, the Fundamental Laws. The tsar retained great powers. The Duma, elected indirectly by universal male suffrage, and a largely appointive upper house could debate and pass laws, but the tsar had an absolute veto. As in Bismarck's Germany, the emperor appointed his ministers, who did not need to command a majority in the Duma.

The disappointed, predominately middle-class liberals, the largest group in the newly elected Duma, saw the Fundamental Laws as a great step backward. Efforts to cooperate with the tsar's ministers soon broke down. The government then dismissed the Duma, only to find that a more hostile and radical opposition was elected in 1907. After three months of deadlock, the second Duma was also dismissed. Thereupon the tsar and his reactionary advisers unilaterally rewrote the electoral law so as to increase greatly the weight of the propertied classes at the expense of workers, peasants, and national minorities.

The new law had the intended effect. With landowners assured half the seats in the Duma, the government finally secured a loyal majority in 1907 and again in 1912. Thus armed, the tough, energetic chief minister, Peter Stolypin, pushed through important agrarian reforms designed to break down collective village ownership of land and to encourage the more enterprising peasants—the so-called wager on the strong. On the eve of the First World War, Russia was partially modernized, a conservative constitutional monarchy with a peasant-based but industrializing economy.

THE RESPONSIVE NATIONAL STATE, 1871–1914

For central and western Europe, the unification of Italy and Germany by "blood and iron" marked the end of a dramatic period of nation building. After 1871 the heartland of Europe was organized in strong national states. Only on the borders of Europe—in Ireland and Russia, in Austria-Hungary and the Balkans—did subject peoples still strive for political unity and independence. Despite national differences, European domestic politics after 1871 had a common framework, the firmly established national state. The common themes within that framework were the emergence of mass politics and growing mass loyalty toward the national state.

For good reason, ordinary people—the masses of an industrializing, urbanizing society—felt increasing loyalty to their governments. More and more people could vote. By 1914 universal manhood suffrage was the rule rather than the exception. This development had as much psychological as political significance. Ordinary men were no longer denied the right to vote because they lacked wealth or education. They counted; they could influence the government to some extent. They were becoming "part of the system."

Women also began to demand the right to vote. The women's suffrage movement achieved its first success in the western United States, and by 1913 women could vote in twelve states. Europe, too, moved slowly in this direction. In 1914 Norway gave the vote to most women. Elsewhere, women like the English Emmeline Pankhurst were very militant in their demands. They heckled politicians and held public demonstrations. These efforts generally failed before 1914, but they prepared the way for the triumph of the women's suffrage movement immediately after World War One.

As the right to vote spread, politicians and parties in national parliaments represented the people more responsively. Most countries soon had many political parties. The multiparty system meant that parliamentary majorities were built on shifting coalitions, which were unstable but did give parties leverage. Parties could obtain benefits for their supporters. Governments increasingly passed laws to alleviate general problems and to help specific groups. Governments seemed to care, and they seemed more worthy of support.

The German Empire

Politics in Germany after 1871 reflected many of these developments. The new German Empire was a federal union of Prussia and twenty-four smaller states. Much of the everyday business of government was conducted by the separate states, but there was a strong national government with a chancellor—until 1890, Bismarck—and a popularly elected parliament, called the *Reichstag.* Although Bismarck refused to be bound by a parliamentary majority, he tried nonetheless to maintain such a majority. This situation gave the political parties opportunities. Until 1878 Bismarck relied mainly on the National Liberals, who had rallied to him after 1866. They supported legislation useful for further economic and legal unification of the country.

Less wisely, they backed Bismarck's attack on the Catholic church, the so-called *Kulturkampf,* or "struggle for civilization." Like Bismarck, the middle-class National Liberals were particularly alarmed by Pius IX's declaration of papal infallibility in 1870. That dogma seemed to ask German Catholics to put loyalty to their church above loyalty to their nation. Only in Protestant Prussia did the Kulturkampf have even limited success. Catholics throughout the country generally voted for the Catholic Center party, which blocked passage of national laws hostile to the church. Finally, in 1878, Bismarck abandoned his attack. Indeed, he and the Catholic Center party entered into an uneasy but mutually advantageous alliance. The reasons were largely economic.

After a worldwide financial bust in 1873, European agriculture was in an increasingly difficult position. Wheat prices plummeted as cheap grain poured in from the United States, Canada, and Russia. New lands were opening up in North America and Russia, and the combination of railroads and technical improvements in shipping cut freight rates for grain drastically. European peasants with their smaller, less efficient farms could not compete in cereal production, especially in western and southern Germany. The peasantry there was largely Catholic, and the Catholic Center party was thus converted to the cause of higher tariffs to protect the economic interests of its supporters.

The same competitive pressures caused the Protestant Junkers, who owned large estates in eastern Germany, to embrace the cause of higher tariffs. They were joined by some of the iron and steel magnates of the Prussian Rhineland and Westphalia, who had previously favored free trade. With three such influential groups lobbying energetically, Bismarck was happy to go along with a new protective tariff in 1879. In doing so, he won new supporters in the parliament—the Center party of the Catholics and the Conservative party of the Prussian landowners—and he held on to most of the National Liberals.

Bismarck had been looking for a way to increase taxes and raise more money for the government. The solution was higher tariffs. Many other governments acted similarly. The 1880s and 1890s saw a widespread return to protectionism. France, in particular, established very high tariffs to protect agriculture and industry, peasants and manufacturers. Thus the German government and other

Bismarck and William II   Shown here visiting Bismarck's country estate in 1888, shortly after he became emperor of Germany (and king of Prussia), the young and impetuous William II soon quarrelled with his chief minister. Determined to rule, not merely to reign, his dismissal of Bismarck in 1890 was a fatal decision. *(Source: Bildarchiv Preussicher Kulturbesitz)*

governments responded to a major economic problem and simultaneously won greater loyalty.

At the same time, Bismarck tried to stop the growth of German socialism because he genuinely feared its revolutionary language and allegiance to a movement transcending the nation-state. In 1878, after two attempts on the life of William I by radicals (though not socialists), Bismarck succeeded in ramming through the Reichstag a law repressing socialists. Socialist meetings and publications were strictly controlled. The Social Democratic party was outlawed and driven underground. However, German socialists displayed a discipline and organization worthy of the Prussian army itself. Bismarck had to try another tack.

Thus Bismarck's state pioneered with social measures designed to win the support of working-class people. In 1883 he pushed through the parliament the first of several modern social security laws to help wage earners. The laws of 1883 and 1884 established national sickness and accident insur-

ance; the law of 1889 established old-age pensions and retirement benefits. Henceforth sick, injured, and retired workers could look forward to regular weekly benefits from the state. This national social security system, paid for through compulsory contributions by wage earners and employers as well as grants from the state, was the first of its kind anywhere. It was to be fifty years before similar measures would be taken in the United States. Bismarck's social security system did not wean workers from socialism, but it did protect them from some of the uncertainties of the complex urban industrial world. This enormously significant development was a product of political competition and governmental efforts to win popular support.

Increasingly, the great issues in German domestic politics were socialism and the Marxian Social Democratic party. In 1890 the new emperor, the young, idealistic, and unstable William II (r. 1888–1918), opposed Bismarck's attempt to renew the law outlawing the Social Democratic party. Eager to rule in his own right, as well as to earn the support of the workers, William II forced Bismarck to resign. After the "dropping of the pilot," German foreign policy changed profoundly and mostly for the worse, but the government did pass new laws to aid workers and to legalize socialist political activity.

Yet William II was no more successful than Bismarck in getting workers to renounce socialism. Indeed, socialist ideas spread rapidly, and more and more Social Democrats were elected to the parliament in the 1890s. After opposing a colonial war in German Southwest Africa in 1906 and thus suffering important losses in the general elections of 1907, the German Social Democratic party broadened its base in the years before World War One. In the elections of 1912, the party scored a great victory, becoming the largest single party in the Reichstag. The "revolutionary" socialists were, however, becoming less and less revolutionary in Germany. In the years before World War One, the strength of socialist opposition to greater military spending and imperialist expansion declined greatly. German socialists marched under the national banner.

Republican France

In 1871 France seemed hopelessly divided once again. The patriotic republicans who proclaimed the Third Republic in Paris after the military disaster at Sedan refused to admit defeat. They defended Paris with great heroism for weeks, living off rats and zoo animals, until they were quite literally starved into submission by German armies in January 1871. When national elections then sent a large majority of conservatives and monarchists to the National Assembly, the traumatized Parisians exploded and proclaimed the Paris Commune in March 1871. Vaguely radical, the leaders of the Commune wanted to govern Paris without interference by the conservative French countryside. The National Assembly, led by the aging politician Adolphe Thiers, would hear none of it. The Assembly ordered the French army into Paris and brutally crushed the Commune. Twenty thousand people died in the fighting. As in June 1848, it was Paris against the provinces, French against French.

Out of this tragedy France slowly formed a new national unity, achieving considerable stability before 1914. How is one to account for this? Luck played a part. Until 1875 the monarchists in the "republican" National Assembly had a majority but could not agree who should be king. The compromise Bourbon candidate refused to rule except under the white flag of his ancestors—a completely unacceptable condition. In the meantime, Thiers's slaying of the radical Commune and his other firm measures showed the fearful provinces and the middle class that the Third Republic might be moderate and socially conservative. France therefore retained the republic, though reluctantly. As President Thiers cautiously said, it was "the government which divides us least."

Another stabilizing factor was the skill and determination of the moderate republican leaders in the early years. The most famous of these was Léon Gambetta, the son of an Italian grocer, a warm, easygoing, unsuccessful lawyer turned professional politician. A master of emerging mass politics, Gambetta combined eloquence with the personal touch as he preached a republic of truly equal opportunity. Gambetta was also instrumental in establishing absolute parliamentary supremacy between 1877 and 1879, when the deputies challenged Marshall MacMahon and forced the somewhat autocratic president to resign. By 1879 the great majority of members of both the upper and the lower houses of the parliament were republicans. Although these republicans were split among many parliamentary groups and later among several parties—a situation that led to constant coalition politics and the rapid turnover of ministers—the Third Republic had firm foundations after almost a decade.

The moderate republicans sought to preserve their creation by winning the hearts and minds of the next generation. Trade unions were fully legalized, and France acquired a colonial empire. More important, under the leadership of Jules Ferry, the moderate republicans of small towns and villages passed a series of laws between 1879 and 1886 establishing free compulsory elementary education for both girls and boys. At the same time, they greatly expanded the state system of public tax-supported schools. Thus France shared fully in the general expansion of public education, which served as a critical nation-building tool throughout the Western world in the late nineteenth century.

In France most elementary and much secondary education had traditionally been in the parochial schools of the Catholic church, which had long been hostile to republics and to much of secular life. Free compulsory elementary education in France became secular republican education. The pledge of allegiance and the national anthem replaced the catechism and the "Ave Maria." Militant young elementary teachers carried the ideology of patriotic republicanism into every corner of France. In their classes, they sought to win the loyalty of the young citizens to the republic, so that France would never again vote en masse for dictators like the two Napoleons.

Although these reforms disturbed French Catholics, many of them rallied to the republic in the 1890s. The limited acceptance of the modern world by the more liberal Pope Leo XIII (1878–1903) eased tensions between church and state. Unfortunately, the Dreyfus affair changed all that.

Alfred Dreyfus, a Jewish captain in the French army, was falsely accused and convicted of treason. His family never doubted his innocence and fought unceasingly to reopen the case, enlisting the support of prominent republicans and intellectuals such as the novelist Émile Zola. In 1898 and 1899, the case split France apart. On one side was the army, which had manufactured evidence against Dreyfus, joined by anti-Semites and most of the Catholic establishment. On the other side stood the civil libertarians and most of the more radical republicans.

This battle, which eventually led to Dreyfus's being declared innocent, revived republican feeling against the church. Between 1901 and 1905, the government severed all ties between the state and the Catholic church, after centuries of close relations. The salaries of priests and bishops were no longer paid by the government, and all churches were given to local committees of lay Catholics. Catholic schools were put completely on their own financially, and in a short time they lost a third of their students. The state school system's power of indoctrination was greatly strengthened. In France,

Captain Alfred Dreyfus Leaving an 1899 reconsideration of his original court martial, Dreyfus receives an insulting "guard of dishonor" from soldiers whose backs are turned. Top army leaders were determined to brand Dreyfus as a traitor. *(Source: Bibliothèque Nationale, Paris)*

only the growing socialist movement, with its very different and thoroughly secular ideology, stood in opposition to patriotic, republican nationalism.

Great Britain and Ireland

Britain in the late nineteenth century has often been seen as a shining example of peaceful and successful political evolution. Germany was stuck with a manipulated parliament that gave an irresponsible emperor too much power; France had a quarrelsome parliament that gave its presidents too little power. Great Britain, in contrast, seemed to enjoy an effective two-party parliament that skillfully guided the country from classical liberalism to full-fledged democracy with hardly a misstep.

This view of Great Britain is not so much wrong as incomplete. After the right to vote was granted to males of the solid middle class in 1832, opinion leaders and politicians wrestled with the uncertainties of a further extension of the franchise. In his famous essay *On Liberty,* published in 1859, the philosopher John Stuart Mill (1806–1873), the leading heir to the Benthamite tradition (see page 759), probed the problem of how to protect the rights of individuals and minorities in the emerging age of mass electoral participation. Mill pleaded eloquently for the practical and moral value inherent in safeguarding individual differences and unpopular opinions. In 1867 Benjamin Disraeli and the Conservatives extended the vote to all middle-class males and the best-paid workers. The son of a Jewish stockbroker, himself a novelist and urban dandy, the ever-fascinating Disraeli (1804–1881) was willing to risk this "leap in the dark" in order to gain new supporters. The Conservative party, he believed, needed to broaden its traditional base of aristocratic and landed support if it was to survive. After 1867 English political parties and electoral campaigns became more modern, and the "lower orders" appeared to vote as responsibly as their "betters." Hence the Third Reform Bill of 1884 gave the vote to almost every adult male.

While the House of Commons was drifting toward democracy, the House of Lords was content to slumber nobly. Between 1901 and 1910, however, that bastion of aristocratic conservatism tried to reassert itself. Acting as supreme court of the land, it ruled against labor unions in two important decisions. And after the Liberal party came to power in 1906, the Lords vetoed several measures passed by the Commons, including the so-called People's Budget. The Lords finally capitulated, as they had done in 1832, when the king threatened to create enough new peers to pass the bill.

Aristocratic conservatism yielded to popular democracy, once and for all. The result was that extensive social welfare measures, slow to come to Great Britain, were passed in a spectacular rush between 1906 and 1914. During those years, the Liberal party, inspired by the fiery Welshman David Lloyd George (1863–1945), substantially raised taxes on the rich as part of the People's Budget. This income helped the government pay for national health insurance, unemployment benefits, old-age pensions, and a host of other social measures. The state was integrating the urban masses socially as well as politically.

This record of accomplishment was only part of the story, though. On the eve of World War One, the ever-emotional, ever-unanswered question of Ireland brought Great Britain to the brink of civil war. In the 1840s, Ireland had been decimated by famine, which fueled an Irish revolutionary movement. Thereafter, the English slowly granted concessions, such as the abolition of the privileges of the Anglican church and rights for Irish peasants. The Liberal prime minister William Gladstone (1809–1898), who had proclaimed twenty years earlier that "my mission is to pacify Ireland," introduced bills to give Ireland self-government in 1886 and in 1893. They failed to pass. After two decades of relative quiet, Irish nationalists in the British Parliament saw their chance. They supported the Liberals in their battle for the People's Budget and received a home-rule bill for Ireland in return.

Thus Ireland, the emerald isle, achieved self-government—but not quite, for Ireland is composed of two peoples. As much as the Irish Catholic majority in the southern counties wanted home rule, precisely that much did the Irish Protestants of the northern counties of Ulster come to oppose it. Motivated by the accumulated fears and hostilities of generations, the Protestants of Ulster refused to submerge themselves in a Catholic Ireland, just as Irish Catholics had refused to submit to a Protestant Britain.

The Ulsterites vowed to resist home rule in northern Ireland. By December 1913 they had raised 100,000 armed volunteers, and they were supported by much of English public opinion.

Thus in 1914 the Liberals in the House of Lords introduced a compromise home-rule law that did not apply to the northern counties. This bill, which openly betrayed promises made to Irish nationalists, was rejected and in September the original home-rule plan was passed but simultaneously suspended for the duration of the hostilities. The momentous Irish question had been overtaken by earth-shattering world war in August 1914.

Irish developments illustrated once again the power of national feeling and national movements in the nineteenth century. Moreover, they were proof that governments could not elicit greater loyalty unless they could capture and control that elemental current of national feeling. Though Great Britain had much going for it—power, Parliament, prosperity—none of these availed in the face of the conflicting nationalisms espoused by Catholics and Protestants in northern Ireland. Similarly, progressive Sweden was powerless to stop the growth of the Norwegian national movement, which culminated in Norway's breaking away from Sweden and becoming a fully independent nation in 1905. In this light, one can also see how hopeless was the case of the Ottoman Empire in Europe in the later nineteenth century. It was only a matter of time before the Serbs, Bulgarians, and Romanians would break away, and they did.

The Austro-Hungarian Empire

The dilemma of conflicting nationalisms in Ireland also helps one appreciate how desperate the situation in the Austro-Hungarian Empire had become by the early twentieth century. In 1849 Magyar nationalism had driven Hungarian patriots to declare an independent Hungarian republic, which was savagely crushed by Russian and Austrian armies (see pages 746–749). Throughout the 1850s, Hungary was ruled as a conquered territory, and Emperor Francis Joseph and his bureaucracy tried hard to centralize the state and Germanize the language and culture of the different nationalities.

Then, in the wake of defeat by Prussia in 1866, a weakened Austria was forced to strike a compromise and establish the so-called dual monarchy. The empire was divided in two, and the nationalistic Magyars gained virtual independence for Hungary. Henceforth each half of the empire agreed to deal with its own "barbarians"—its own minorities

"No Home Rule"   Posters like this one helped to foment pro-British, anti-Catholic sentiment in the northern Irish counties of Ulster before the First World War. The rifle raised defiantly and the accompanying rhyme are a thinly veiled threat of armed rebellion and civil war. *(Source: Reproduced with kind permission of the Trustees of the Ulster Museum)*

—as it saw fit. The two states were joined only by a shared monarch and common ministries for finance, defense, and foreign affairs. After 1867 the disintegrating force of competing nationalisms continued unabated, for both Austria and Hungary had several "Irelands" within their borders.

In Austria, ethnic Germans were only one-third of the population, and by the late 1890s many Germans saw their traditional dominance threatened by Czechs, Poles, and other Slavs. A particularly emotional and divisive issue in the Austrian parliament was the language used in government and elementary education at the local level. From 1900 to 1914, the parliament was so divided that ministries generally could not obtain a majority and ruled instead by decree. Efforts by both conservatives and socialists to defuse national antagonisms by stressing economic issues cutting across ethnic lines—endeavors that led to the introduction of universal male suffrage in 1907—proved largely unsuccessful.

One aspect of such national antagonisms was anti-Semitism, which was particularly virulent in Austria. The Jewish populations of Austrian cities grew very rapidly after Jews obtained full legal equality in 1867, and by 1900 Jews constituted 10 percent of the population of Vienna. Many Jewish business people were quite successful in banking and retail trade, while Jewish artists, intellectuals, and scientists, like the world-famous Sigmund Freud, played a major role in making Vienna a leading center of European culture and modern thought. When extremists charged the Jews with controlling the economy and corrupting German culture with alien ideas and ultramodern art, anxious Germans of all classes tended to listen. The popular mayor of Vienna from 1897 to 1910, Dr. Karl Lueger, combined anti-Semitic rhetoric with calls for "Christian socialism" and municipal ownership of basic services. Lueger appealed especially to the German lower middle class—and to an unsuccessful young artist named Adolf Hitler.

In Hungary, the Magyar nobility in 1867 restored the constitution of 1848 and used it to dominate both the Magyar peasantry and the minority populations until 1914. Only the wealthiest one-fourth of adult males had the right to vote, making

The Language Ordinances of 1897,   which were intended to satisfy the Czechs by establishing equality between German and the local language in non-German districts of Austria, produced a powerful backlash among Germans. This wood engraving shows troops dispersing German protesters of the new law before the parliament building. *(Source: Österreichische Nationalbibliothek)*

the parliament the creature of the Magyar elite. Laws promoting use of the Magyar (Hungarian) language in schools and government were rammed through and bitterly resented, especially by the Croatians and Rumanians. While Magyar extremists campaigned loudly for total separation from Austria, the radical leaders of the subject nationalities dreamed in turn of independence from Hungary. Unlike most major countries, which harnessed nationalism to strengthen the state after 1871, the Austro-Hungarian Empire was progressively weakened and destroyed by it.

MARXISM AND THE SOCIALIST MOVEMENT

Nationalism served, for better or worse, as a new unifying principle. But what about socialism? Did the rapid growth of socialist parties, which were generally Marxian parties, dedicated to an international proletarian revolution, mean that national states had failed to gain the support of workers? Certainly, many prosperous and conservative citizens were greatly troubled by the socialist movement. And many historians have portrayed the years before 1914 as a time of increasing conflict between revolutionary socialism on the one hand and a nationalist alliance between conservative aristocracy and the prosperous middle class on the other. This question requires close examination.

The Socialist International

The growth of socialist parties after 1871 was phenomenal. Neither Bismarck's antisocialist laws nor his extensive social security system checked the growth of the German Social Democratic party, which espoused the Marxian ideology. By 1912 it had attracted millions of followers and was the largest party in the parliament. Socialist parties also grew in other countries, though nowhere else with quite such success. In 1883 Russian exiles in Switzerland founded a Russian Social Democratic party, which grew rapidly in the 1890s and thereafter, despite internal disputes. In France, various socialist parties re-emerged in the 1880s after the carnage of the Commune. Most of them were finally unified in a single, increasingly powerful Marxian party, called the French Section of the Workers International, in 1905. Belgium and Austria-Hungary also had strong socialist parties of the Marxian persuasion.

As the name of the French party suggests, Marxian socialist parties were eventually linked together in an international organization. As early as 1848, Marx had laid out his intellectual system in the *Communist Manifesto* (see pages 731–733). He had declared that "the working men have no country," and he had urged proletarians of all nations to unite against their governments. Joining the flood of radicals and republicans who fled continental Europe for England and America after the revolutions of 1848, Marx settled in London. Poor and depressed, he lived on his meager earnings as a journalist and on the gifts of his friend Engels. Marx never stopped thinking of revolution. Digging deeply into economics and history, he concluded that revolution follows economic crisis and tried to prove it in *Critique of Political Economy* (1859) and his greatest theoretical work, *Capital* (1867).

The bookish Marx also excelled as a practical organizer. In 1864 he played an important role in founding the First International of socialists—the International Working Men's Association. In the following years, he battled successfully to control the organization and used its annual meetings as a means of spreading his realistic, "scientific" doctrines of inevitable socialist revolution. Then Marx enthusiastically embraced the passionate, vaguely radical patriotism of the Paris Commune and its terrible conflict with the French National Assembly as a giant step toward socialist revolution. This impetuous action frightened many of his early supporters, especially the more moderate British labor leaders. The First International collapsed.

Yet international proletarian solidarity remained an important objective for Marxists. In 1889, as the individual parties in different countries grew stronger, socialist leaders came together to form the Second International, which lasted until 1914. Although the International was only a federation of various national socialist parties, it had great psychological impact. Every three years, delegates from the different parties met to interpret Marxian doctrines and plan coordinated action. May 1—May Day—was declared an annual international one-day strike, a day of marches and demonstrations. A permanent executive for the International was established. Many feared and many others rejoiced in the growing power of socialism and the Second International.

Socialist Clubs   helped spread Marxian doctrines among the working classes. There workers (and intellectuals) from different backgrounds debated the fine points and developed a sense of solidarity. *(Source: Bildarchiv Preussischer Kulturbesitz)*

Unions and Revisionism

Was socialism really radical and revolutionary in these years? On the whole, it was not. Indeed, as socialist parties grew and attracted large numbers of members, they looked more and more toward gradual change and steady improvement for the working class, less and less toward revolution. The mainstream of European socialism became militantly moderate; that is, socialists increasingly combined radical rhetoric with sober action.

Workers themselves were progressively less inclined to follow radical programs. There were several reasons for this. As workers gained the right to vote and to participate politically in the nation-state, their attention focused more on elections than on revolutions. And as workers won real, tangible benefits, this furthered the process. Workers were not immune to patriotic education and indoc-

trination during military service, however ardently socialist intellectuals might wish the contrary. Nor were workers a unified social group.

Perhaps most important of all, workers' standard of living rose substantially after 1850 as the promise of the Industrial Revolution was at least partially realized. In Great Britain, for example, workers could buy almost twice as much with their wages in 1906 as in 1850, and most of the increase came after 1870. Workers experienced similar increases in most continental countries after 1850, though much less strikingly in late-developing Russia. Improvement in the standard of living was much more than merely a matter of higher wages. The quality of life improved dramatically in urban areas. For all these reasons, workers tended more and more to become militantly moderate: they demanded gains, but they were less likely to take to the barricades in pursuit of them.

The growth of labor unions reinforced this trend toward moderation. In the early stages of industrialization, modern unions were generally prohibited by law. A famous law of the French Revolution had declared all guilds and unions illegal in the name of "liberty" in 1791. In Great Britain, attempts by workers to unite were considered criminal conspiracies after 1799. Other countries had similar laws, and these obviously hampered union development. In France, for example, about two hundred workers were imprisoned each year between 1825 and 1847 for taking part in illegal combinations. Unions were considered subversive bodies, only to be hounded and crushed.

From this sad position workers struggled to escape. Great Britain led the way in 1824 and 1825, when unions won the right to exist but (generally) not the right to strike. After the collapse of Robert Owen's attempt to form one big union in the 1830s (see page 713), new and more practical kinds of unions appeared. Limited primarily to highly skilled workers such as machinists and carpenters, the "new model unions" avoided both radical politics and costly strikes. Instead, their sober, respectable leaders concentrated on winning better wages and hours for their members through collective bargaining and compromise. This approach helped pave the way to full acceptance in Britain in the 1870s, when unions won the right to strike without being held legally liable for the financial damage inflicted on employers. After 1890 unions for unskilled workers developed, and between 1901 and 1906 the legal position of British unions was further strengthened.

Germany was the most industrialized, socialized, and unionized continental country by 1914. German unions were not granted important rights until 1869, and until the antisocialist law was repealed in 1890, they were frequently harassed by the government as socialist fronts. Nor were socialist leaders particularly interested in union activity, believing as they did in the iron law of low wages and the need for political revolution. The result was that, as late as 1895, there were only about 270,000 union members in a male industrial workforce of nearly 8 million. Then, with German industrialization still storming ahead and almost all legal harassment eliminated, union membership skyrocketed to roughly 3 million in 1912.

This great expansion both reflected and influenced the changing character of German unions. Increasingly, unions in Germany focused on bread-and-butter issues—wages, hours, working conditions—rather than on instilling pure socialist doctrine. Genuine collective bargaining, long opposed by socialist intellectuals as a "sellout," was officially recognized as desirable by the German Trade Union Congress in 1899. When employers proved unwilling to bargain, a series of strikes forced them to change their minds.

Between 1906 and 1913, successful collective bargaining was gaining a prominent place in German industrial relations. In 1913 alone, over 10,000 collective bargaining agreements affecting 1.25 million workers were signed. Further gradual improvement, not revolution, was becoming the primary objective of the German trade-union movement.

The German trade unions and their leaders were —in fact, if not in name—thoroughgoing revisionists. *Revisionism*—that most awful of sins in the eyes of militant Marxists in the twentieth century—was an effort by various socialists to update Marxian doctrines to reflect the realities of the time. Thus the socialist Edward Bernstein argued in 1899 in his *Evolutionary Socialism* that Marx's predictions of ever-greater poverty for workers and ever-greater concentration of wealth in ever-fewer hands had been proved false. Therefore, Bernstein suggested, socialists should reform their doctrines and tactics. They should combine with other progressive forces to win gradual evolutionary gains for workers through legislation, unions, and further economic development. These views were formally denounced as heresy by the German Social Democratic party and later by the entire Second International. Nevertheless, the revisionist, gradualist approach continued to gain the tacit acceptance of many German socialists, particularly in the trade unions.

Moderation found followers elsewhere. In France, the great humanist and socialist leader Jean Jaurès formally repudiated revisionist doctrines in order to establish a unified socialist party, but he remained at heart a gradualist. Questions of revolutionary versus gradualist policies split Russian Marxists.

Socialist parties before 1914 had clear-cut national characteristics. Russians and socialists in the Austro-Hungarian Empire tended to be the most radical. The German party talked revolution and practiced reformism, greatly influenced by its enormous trade-union movement. The French party talked revolution and tried to practice it, unrestrained by a trade-union movement that was both very weak and very radical. In England, the socialist but non-Marxian Labour party, reflecting the well-established union movement, was formally committed to gradual reform. In Spain and Italy, Marxian socialism was very weak. There anarchism, seeking to smash the state rather than the bourgeoisie, dominated radical thought and action.

In short, socialist policies and doctrines varied from country to country. Socialism itself was to a large extent "nationalized" behind the imposing façade of international unity. This helps explain why, when war came in 1914, socialist leaders almost without exception supported their governments.

SUMMARY

From the mid-nineteenth century on, Western society became nationalistic as well as urban and industrial. Nation-states and strong-minded national leaders gradually enlisted widespread support and gave men and women a sense of belonging. Even socialism became increasingly national in orientation, gathering strength as a champion of working-class interests in domestic politics. Yet, while nationalism served to unite peoples, it also drove them apart. Though most obvious in the United States before the Civil War and in Austria-Hungary and Ireland, this was in a real sense true for all of Western civilization. The universal national faith, which reduced social tensions within states, promoted a bitter, almost Darwinian competition between states and thus ominously threatened the progress and unity it had helped to build.

NOTES

1. Quoted in G. Wright, *France in Modern Times* (Chicago: Rand McNally, 1960), p. 179.
2. Quoted in O. Pflanze, *Bismarck and the Development of Germany: The Period of Unification, 1815–1871* (Princeton, N.J.: Princeton University Press, 1963), p. 60.
3. Quoted in H. Kohn, *The Mind of Germany: The Education of a Nation* (New York: Charles Scribner's Sons & Macmillan, 1960), pp. 156–161.
4. Quoted in R. Sewell, *A House Divided: Sectionalism and Civil War, 1848–1865* (Baltimore: Johns Hopkins University Press, 1988), p. 79.
5. Ibid., p. 124.
6. Quoted in T. von Laue, *Sergei Witte and the Industrialization of Russia* (New York: Columbia University Press, 1963), p. 78.
7. Quoted in J. P. McKay, *Pioneers for Profit: Foreign Entrepreneurship and Russian Industrialization, 1885–1913* (Chicago: University of Chicago Press, 1970), p. 11.

SUGGESTED READING

In addition to the general works mentioned in the Suggested Reading for Chapter 23, which treat the entire nineteenth century, G. Craig, *Germany, 1866–1945* (1980), and B. Moore, *Social Origins of Dictatorship and Democracy* (1966), are outstanding. R. Anderson, *France, 1870–1914* (1977), provides a good introduction and has a useful bibliography.

Among specialized works of high quality, D. Harvey, *Napoleon III and His Comic Empire* (1988), and R. Williams, *Gaslight and Shadows* (1957), brings the world of Napoleon III vibrantly alive, while Karl Marx's *The Eighteenth Brumaire of Louis Napoleon* is a famous denunciation of the *coup d'état*. E. Weber, *France, Fin de Siècle* (1986) and the engaging collective biography by R. Shattuck, *The Banquet Years* (1968), capture the spirit of Paris at the end of the century. E. Weber, *Peasants into Frenchmen* (1976), stresses the role of education and modern communications in the transformation of rural France after 1870. E. Thomas, *The Women Incendiaries* (1966), examines radical women in the Paris Commune. G. Chapman, *The Dreyfus Case: A Reassessment* (1955), and D. Johnson, *France and the Dreyfus Affair* (1967), are careful examinations of the famous case. In *Jean Barois,* Nobel Prize winner R. M. Du Gard accurately recreates in novel form the Dreyfus affair, and Émile Zola's novel *The Debacle* treats the Franco-Prussian War realistically.

D. M. Smith has written widely on Italy, and his *Garibaldi* (1956) and *Italy: A Modern History,* rev. ed. (1969) are recommended. P. Schroeder, *Austria, Great Britain and the Crimean War* (1972), is an outstanding and highly original diplomatic study. In addition to the important studies on Bismarck and Germany by Pflanze and Kohn cited in the Notes, see E. Eyck, *Bismarck and the German Empire* (1964). F. Stern, *Gold and Iron* (1977), is a fascinating examination of relations between Bismarck and his financial adviser, the Jewish banker Bleichröder. L. Cecil, *Wilhelm II: Prince and Emperor, 1859–1900* (1989), probes the character and politics of Germany's ruler. G.

Iggers, *The German Conception of History* (1968); K. D. Barkin, *The Controversy over German Industrialization, 1890–1902* (1970); and E. Spencer, *Management and Labor in Imperial Germany: Ruhr Industrialists as Employers* (1984), are valuable in-depth investigations. H. Glasser, ed., *The German Mind in the Nineteenth Century* (1981), is an outstanding anthology, as are R. E. Joeres and M. Maynes, eds., *German Women in the Eighteenth and Nineteenth Centuries* (1986), and P. Mendes-Flohr, ed., *The Jew in the Modern World: A Documentary History* (1980). C. Schorske, *Fin de Siècle Vienna: Politics and Culture* (1980), and P. Gay, *Freud, Jews, and Other Germans* (1978), are brilliant on aspects of modern culture. A. Sked, *The Decline and Fall of the Habsburg Empire, 1815–1918* (1989), and R. Kann, *The Multinational Empire*, 2 vols. (1950, 1964), probe the intricacies of the nationality problem in Austria-Hungary, while S. Stavrianos has written extensively on southeastern Europe, including *The Balkans, 1815–1914* (1963). In addition to the excellent introduction to the United States in the era of regional conflict by Sewell, which is cited in the Notes and which has an annotated bibliography, Southern nationalism has been interpreted from different perspectives by P. Escott, *After Secession: Jefferson Davis and the Failure of Confederate Nationalism* (1974), and D. Faust, *The Creation of Confederate Nationalism* (1988). E. Foner, *A Short History of Reconstruction* (1989), is highly recommended.

In addition to the studies on Russian industrial development by von Laue and McKay cited in the Notes, P. Gatrell, *The Tsarist Economy, 1850–1917* (1986), and A. Rieber, *Merchants and Entrepreneurs in Imperial Russia* (1982), are recommended. Among fine studies on Russian development, H. Rogger, *Russia in the Age of Modernization and Revolution, 1881–1917* (1983), which has an excellent bibliography; T. Emmons, *The Russian Landed Gentry and the Peasant Emancipation of 1861* (1968); and H. Troyat, *Daily Life in Russia Under the Last Tsar* (1962), are especially recommended. T. Friedgut, *Iuzovka and Revolution: Life and Work in Russia's Donbass, 1869–1924* (1989); R. Zelnik, *Labor and Society in Tsarist Russia, 1855–1870* (1971); and R. Johnson, *Peasant and Proletarian: The Working Class of Moscow at the End of the Nineteenth Century* (1979), skillfully treat different aspects of working-class life and politics. W. E. Mosse, *Alexander II and the Modernization of Russia* (1958), provides a good discussion of midcentury reforms, while C. Black, ed., *The Transformation of Russian Society* (1960), offers a collection of essays on Russian modernization. I. Turgenev's great novel *Fathers and Sons* probes the age-old conflict of generations as well as nineteenth-century Russian revolutionary thought.

G. Dangerfield, *The Strange Death of Liberal England* (1961), brilliantly examines social tensions in Ireland as well as Englishwomen's struggle for the vote before 1914. W. Arnstein convincingly shows how the Victorian aristocracy survived and even flourished in nineteenth-century Britain in F. Jaher, ed., *The Rich, the Well-Born, and the Powerful* (1973), an interesting collection of essays on social elites in history. The theme of aristocratic strength and survival is expanded in A. Mayer's provocative *Persistence of the Old Regime: Europe to the Great War* (1981).

On late-nineteenth-century socialism, C. Schorske, *German Social Democracy, 1905–1917* (1955), is a modern classic. V. Lidtke, *The Outlawed Party* (1966), and J. Quataert, *Reluctant Feminists in German Social Democracy, 1885–1917* (1979), are also recommended for the study of the German socialists. H. Goldberg, *The Life of Jean Jaurès* (1962), is a sympathetic account of the great French socialist leader. P. Stearns, who has written several books on European labor history, considers radical labor leaders in *Revolutionary Syndicalism and French Labor* (1971). D. Geary, ed., *Labour and Socialist Movements in Europe Before 1914* (1989), contains excellent studies on developments in different countries and has up-to-date bibliographies.

26

The West and the World

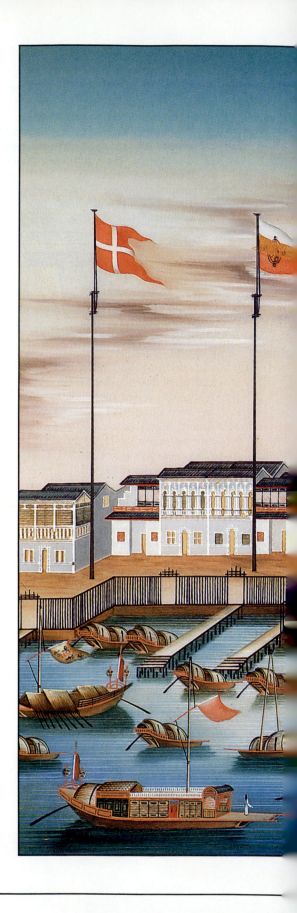

While industrialization and nationalism were transforming urban life and Western society, Western society itself was reshaping the world. At the peak of its power and pride, the West entered the third and most dynamic phase of the aggressive expansion that began with the Crusades and continued with the great discoveries and the rise of seaborne colonial empires. An ever-growing stream of products, people, and ideas flowed out of Europe in the nineteenth century. Hardly any corner of the globe was left untouched. The most spectacular manifestations of Western expansion came in the late nineteenth century, when the leading European nations established or enlarged their far-flung political empires. The political annexation of territory in the 1880s—the "new imperialism," as it is often called by historians—was the capstone of a profound underlying economic and technological process.

- How and why did this many-sided, epoch-making expansion occur in the nineteenth century?
- What were some of its consequences for the West and the rest of the world?

These are the questions this chapter will examine.

INDUSTRIALIZATION AND THE WORLD ECONOMY

The Industrial Revolution created, first in Great Britain and then in continental Europe and North America, a growing and tremendously dynamic economic system. In the course of the nineteenth century, that system was extended across the face of the earth. Some of this extension into non-Western areas was peaceful and beneficial for all concerned, for the West had many products and techniques the rest of the world desired. If peaceful methods failed, however, Europeans did not stand on ceremony. They used their superior military power to force non-Western nations to open their doors to Western economic interests. In general, Westerners fashioned the global economic system so that the largest share of the ever increasing gains from trade, technology, and migration flowed to the West and its propertied classes.

The Rise of Global Inequality

The Industrial Revolution in Europe marked a momentous turning point in human history. Indeed, it is only by placing Europe's economic breakthrough in a global perspective that one can truly appreciate its revolutionary implications and consequences.

From such a global perspective, the ultimate significance of the Industrial Revolution was that it allowed those regions of the world that industrialized in the nineteenth century to increase their wealth and power enormously in comparison to those that did not. As a result, a gap between the industrializing regions—mainly Europe and North America—and the nonindustrializing ones—mainly Africa, Asia, and Latin America—opened up and grew steadily throughout the nineteenth century. Moreover, this pattern of uneven global development became institutionalized, or built into the structure of the world economy. Thus we evolved a "lopsided world," a world of rich lands and poor.

Historians have long been aware of this gap, but it is only recently that historical economists have begun to chart its long-term evolution with some precision. Their findings are extremely revealing, although one must understand that they contain a margin of error and other limitations as well. The findings of one such study are summarized in Figure 26.1. This figure compares the long-term evolution of average income per person in today's "developed" (or industrialized) regions—defined as western and eastern Europe, North America, and Japan—with that found in the "Third World"—a term that is now widely used by international organizations and by scholars to group Africa, Asia, and Latin America into a single unit. To get these individual income figures, researchers estimate a country's gross national product (GNP) at different points in time, convert those estimates to some common currency, and divide by the total population.

Figure 26.1 highlights three main points. First, in 1750 the average standard of living was no higher in Europe as a whole than in the rest of the world. In 1750 Europe was still a poor agricultural society. Moreover, the average per-person income in the wealthiest European country (Great Britain) was less than twice that in the poorest non-Western land. By 1970, however, the average person in the wealthiest countries had an income fully twenty-five times as great as that received by the average person in the poorest countries of Africa and Asia.

Second, it was industrialization that opened the gaps in average wealth and well-being among countries and regions. One sees that Great Britain had jumped well above the European average by 1830, when the first industrial nation was well in advance of its continental competitors. One also sees how Great Britain's lead gradually narrowed, as other European countries and the United States successfully industrialized in the course of the nineteenth century.

Finally, income per person stagnated in the Third World before 1913, in striking contrast to the industrializing regions. Only after 1945, in the era of political independence and decolonization, did Third World countries finally make some real economic progress, beginning in their turn the critical process of industrialization.

The rise of these enormous income disparities, which are poignant indicators of equal disparities in food and clothing, health and education, life expectancy and general material well-being, has generated a great deal of debate. One school of interpretation stresses that the West used science, technology, capitalist organization, and even its critical world-view to create its wealth and greater physical well-being. Another school argues that the West used its political and economic power to steal much of its riches, continuing in the nineteenth (and twentieth) century the rapacious colonialism born of the era of expansion.

These issues are complex, and there are few simple answers. As noted in Chapter 22, the wealth-creating potential of technological improvement and more intensive capitalist organization was indeed great. At the same time, those breakthroughs rested, in part, on Great Britain's having already used political force to dominate the world economy in the nineteenth century. Wealth—unprecedented wealth—was indeed created, but the lion's share of that new wealth flowed to the West and its propertied classes.

Trade and Foreign Investment

Commerce between nations has always been a powerful stimulus to economic development. Never was this more true than in the nineteenth century,

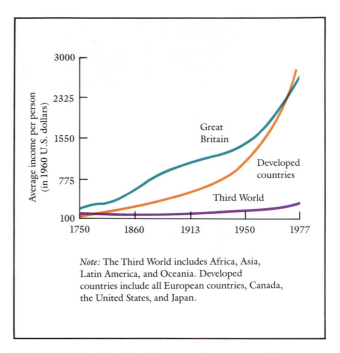

FIGURE 26.1 The Growth of Average Income per Person in the Third World, Developed Countries, and Great Britain, 1750–1970, in 1960 U.S. dollars and prices. *(Source: P. Bairoch and M. Lévy-Leboyer, eds.,* Disparities in Economic Development Since the Industrial Revolution. *New York: St. Martin's Press, 1981, pp. 7–8, 10)*

when world trade grew prodigiously. World trade grew modestly until about 1840, and then it took off. After a slowdown in the last years of the century, another surge lasted until World War One. In 1913 the value of world trade was roughly $38 billion, or about *twenty-five* times what it had been in 1800. (This amount actually understates the growth, since average prices of both manufactured goods and raw materials were lower in 1913 than in 1800.) In a general way, the enormous increase in international commerce summed up the growth of an interlocking world economy, centered in and directed by Europe.

Great Britain played a key role in using trade to tie the world together economically. In 1815 Britain already had a colonial empire, for India, Canada, Australia, and other scattered areas remained British possessions after American independence. The technological breakthroughs of the Industrial Revolution allowed Britain to manufacture cotton textiles, iron, and other goods more cheaply and to far outstrip domestic demand for such products.

Thus British manufacturers sought export markets, first in Europe and then around the world.

Take the case of cotton textiles. By 1820 Britain was exporting half of its production. Europe bought half of these cotton textile exports, while India bought only 6 percent. Then, as European nations and the United States exercised sovereignty to erect protective tariff barriers and promote domestic industry, British cotton textile manufacturers aggressively sought and found other foreign markets in non-Western areas. By 1850 India bought 25 percent and Europe only 16 percent of a much larger total. As a British colony, India could not raise tariffs to protect its ancient cotton textile industry, and thousands of Indian weavers lost their livelihoods.

After the repeal of the Corn Laws in 1846 (see page 741), Britain also became the world's single best market. The decisive argument in the battle against tariffs on imported grain had been, "We must give, if we mean honestly to receive, and buy as well as sell." Until 1914 Britain thus remained the world's emporium, where not only agricultural products and raw materials but also manufactured goods entered freely. Free access to the enormous market of Britain stimulated the development of mines and plantations in many non-Western areas.

The growth of trade was facilitated by the conquest of distance. The earliest railroad construction occurred in Europe (including Russia) and in America north of the Rio Grande; other parts of the globe saw the building of rail lines after 1860. By 1920 more than one-quarter of the world's railroads were in Latin America, Asia, Africa, and Australia. Wherever railroads were built, they drastically reduced transportation costs, opened new economic opportunities, and called forth new skills and attitudes. Moreover, in the areas of massive European settlement—North America and Australia—they were built in advance of the population and provided a means of settling the land.

The power of steam revolutionized transportation by sea as well as by land. In 1807 inhabitants of the Hudson Valley in New York saw the "Devil on the way to Albany in a saw-mill," as Robert Fulton's steamship *Clermont* traveled 150 miles upstream in thirty-two hours. Steam power, long used to drive paddle-wheelers on rivers, particularly in Russia and North America, finally began to supplant sails on the oceans of the world in the late 1860s. Lighter, stronger, cheaper steel replaced iron, which had replaced wood. Screw propellers superseded paddle wheels, while mighty compound steam engines cut fuel consumption by half. Passenger and freight rates tumbled, and the intercontinental shipment of low-priced raw materials became feasible. In addition to the large passenger liners and freighters of the great shipping companies, there were innumerable independent tramp steamers searching endlessly for cargo around the world.

An account of an actual voyage by a typical tramp freighter will highlight nineteenth-century developments in global trade. The ship left England in 1910, carrying rails and general freight to western Australia. From there, it carried lumber to Melbourne in southeastern Australia, where it took on harvester combines for Argentina. In Buenos Aires it loaded wheat for Calcutta, and in Calcutta it took on jute for New York. From New York it carried a variety of industrial products to Australia before returning to England with lead, wool, and wheat after a voyage of approximately 72,000 miles to six continents in seventeen months.

The revolution in land and sea transportation helped European pioneers to open up vast new territories and to produce agricultural products and raw materials there for sale in Europe. Moreover, the development of refrigerated railway cars and, from the 1880s, refrigerator ships enabled first Argentina and then the United States, Australia, and New Zealand to ship mountains of chilled or frozen beef and mutton to European (mainly British) consumers. From Asia, Africa, and Latin America came not only the traditional tropical products—spices, tea, sugar, coffee—but new raw materials for industry, such as jute, rubber, cotton, and coconut oil.

Intercontinental trade was enormously facilitated by the Suez and Panama canals. Of great importance, too, was large and continuous investment in modern port facilities, which made loading and unloading cheaper, faster, and more dependable. Finally, transoceanic telegraph cables inaugurated rapid communications among the financial centers of the world. While a British tramp freighter steamed from Calcutta to New York, a broker in London was arranging by telegram for it to carry an American cargo to Australia. World commodity prices were also instantaneously conveyed by the same network of communications.

The growth of trade and the conquest of distance encouraged the expanding European economy to make massive foreign investments. Begin-

The Suez Canal   Completed in 1869, the hundred-mile canal cut in half the length of the journey between Europe and Asia. This picture from a popular weekly newspaper shows a line of ships passing through the canal on the opening day. *(Source: Giraudon/ Art Resource)*

ning about 1840, European capitalists started to invest large sums in foreign lands. They did not stop until the outbreak of World War One in 1914. By that year, Europeans had invested more than $40 billion abroad. Great Britain, France, and Germany were the principal investing countries, although by 1913 the United States was emerging as a substantial foreign investor. The sums involved were enormous (Map 26.1). In the decade before 1914, Great Britain was investing 7 percent of its annual national income abroad, or slightly more than it was investing in its entire domestic economy. The great gap between rich and poor within Europe meant that the wealthy and moderately well-to-do could and did send great sums abroad in search of interest and dividends.

Most of the capital exported did not go to European colonies or protectorates in Asia and Africa. About three-quarters of total European investment went to other European countries, the United States and Canada, Australia and New Zealand, and Latin America. Europe found its most profitable opportunities for investment in construction of the railroads, ports, and utilities that were necessary to settle and develop the almost-vacant lands in such places as Australia and the Americas. By lending money for a railroad in Argentina or in Canada's prairie provinces, for example, Europeans not only

collected interest but also enabled white settlers to buy European rails and locomotives, developed sources of cheap wheat, and opened still more territory for European settlement. Much of this investment—such as in American railroads, fully a third of whose capital in 1890 was European, or in Russian railroads, which drew heavily on loans from France—was peaceful and mutually beneficial. The victims were native American Indians and Australian aborigines, who were decimated by the diseases, liquor, and weapons of an aggressively expanding Western society.

The Opening of China and Japan

Europe's relatively peaceful development of robust offshoots in sparsely populated North America, Australia, and much of Latin America absorbed huge quantities of goods, investments, and migrants. From a Western point of view, that was the most important aspect of Europe's global thrust. Yet Europe's economic and cultural penetration of old, densely populated civilizations was also profoundly significant, especially for the non-European peoples affected by it. With such civilizations Europeans also increased their trade and profit. Moreover, as had been the case ever since Vasco da

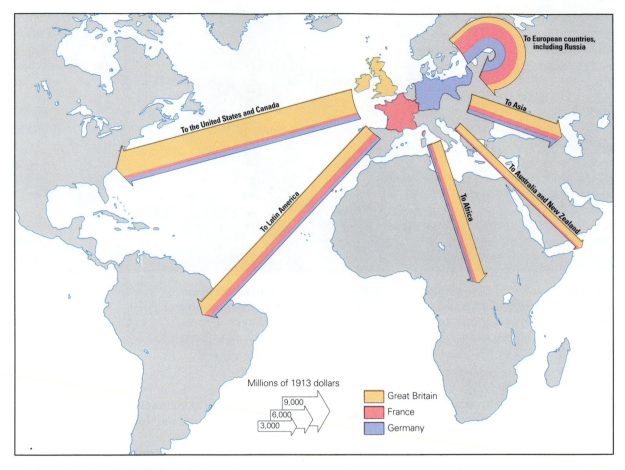

MAP 26.1 European Investment to 1914 Foreign investment grew rapidly after 1850, and Britain, France, and Germany were the major investing nations. As shown above, most European investment was not directed to the area seized by the "new imperialism."

Gama and Christopher Columbus, the expanding Western society was prepared to use force to attain its desires, if necessary. This was what happened in China and Japan, two crucial examples of the general pattern of intrusion into non-Western lands.

Traditional Chinese civilization was self-sufficient. For centuries China had sent more to Europe in the way of goods and inventions than it received, and this was still the case in the eighteenth century. Europeans and the English in particular had developed a taste for Chinese tea, but they had to pay for it with hard silver since China was supremely uninterested in European wares. Trade with Europe was carefully regulated by the Chinese imperial government—the Manchu Dynasty—which was more interested in isolating and controlling the strange "sea barbarians" than in pursuing commercial exchange. The imperial government refused to estab-

lish diplomatic relations with the "inferior" European states, and it required all foreign merchants to live in the southern city of Canton and to buy and sell only from the local merchant monopoly. Practices considered harmful to Chinese interests, such as the sale of opium and the export of silver from China, were strictly forbidden.

For years the little community of foreign merchants in Canton had to accept the Chinese system. By the 1820s, however, the dominant group, the British, were flexing their muscles. Moreover, in the smoking of opium—that "destructive and ensnaring vice" denounced by Chinese decrees—they had found something the Chinese really wanted. Grown legally in British-occupied India, opium was smuggled into China by means of fast ships and bribed officials. The more this rich trade developed, the greedier British merchants became and the more they resented the patriotic attempts of the Chinese government to stem the tide of drug addiction. By 1836 the aggressive goal of the British merchants in Canton was an independent British colony in China and "safe and unrestricted liberty" in trade. They pressured the British government to take decisive action and enlisted the support of British manufacturers with visions of vast Chinese markets to be opened.

At the same time, the Manchu government decided that the opium trade had to be stamped out. It was ruining the people and stripping the empire of its silver, which was going to British merchants to pay for the opium. The government began to prosecute Chinese drug dealers vigorously and in 1839 sent special envoy Lin Tse-hsü to Canton. Lin Tse-hsü ordered the foreign merchants to obey China's laws, "for our great unified Manchu Empire regards itself as responsible for the habits and morals of its subjects and cannot rest content to see any of them become victims of a deadly poison."[1] The British merchants refused and were expelled, whereupon war soon broke out.

Using troops from India and in control of the seas, the British occupied several coastal cities and forced China to surrender. In the Treaty of Nanking in 1842, the imperial government was forced to cede the island of Hong Kong to Britain forever, pay an indemnity of $100 million, and open up four large cities to foreign trade with low tariffs.

Thereafter the opium trade flourished, and Hong Kong developed rapidly as an Anglo-Chinese enclave. China continued to nurture illusions of superiority and isolation, however, and refused to accept foreign diplomats in Peking, the imperial capital. Finally, there was a second round of foreign attack between 1856 and 1860, culminating in the occupation of Peking by seventeen thousand British and French troops and the intentional burning of the emperor's summer palace. Another round of harsh treaties gave European merchants and missionaries greater privileges and protection. Thus did Europeans use military aggression to blow a hole in the wall of Chinese seclusion and open the country to foreign trade and foreign ideas. Blasting away at Chinese sovereignty as well, they forced the Chinese to accept trade and investment on unfavorable terms for the foreseeable future.

China's neighbor, Japan, had its own highly distinctive civilization and even less use for Westerners. European traders and missionaries first arrived in Japan in the sixteenth century. By 1640 Japan had reacted quite negatively to their presence. The government decided to seal off the country from all European influences, in order to preserve traditional Japanese culture and society. Officials ruthlessly persecuted Japanese Christians and expelled all but a few Dutch merchants, who were virtually imprisoned in a single port and rigidly controlled. When American and British whaling ships began to appear off Japanese coasts almost two hundred years later, the policy of exclusion was still in effect. An order of 1825 commanded Japanese officials to "drive away foreign vessels without second thought."[2]

Japan's unbending isolation seemed hostile and barbaric to the West, particularly to the United States. It complicated the practical problems of shipwrecked American sailors and the provisioning of whaling ships and China traders sailing in the eastern Pacific. It also thwarted the hope of trade and profit. Moreover, Americans shared the self-confidence and dynamism of expanding Western society. They had taken California from Mexico in 1848, and Americans felt destined to play a great role in the Pacific. It seemed, therefore, the United States' duty to force the Japanese to share their ports and behave like a "civilized" nation.

After several unsuccessful American attempts to establish commercial relations with Japan, Commodore Matthew Perry steamed into Edo (now Tokyo) Bay in 1853 and demanded diplomatic negotiations with the emperor. Japan entered a grave crisis. Some Japanese warriors urged resistance, but senior officials realized how defenseless their cities were against naval bombardment. Shocked and humiliated, they reluctantly signed a treaty with the United States that opened two ports and permitted trade. Over the next five years, more treaties spelled out the rights and privileges of the Western nations and their merchants in Japan. Japan was "opened." What the British had done in China with war, the Americans had done in Japan with the threat of war.

Western Penetration of Egypt

Egypt's experience illustrates not only the explosive power of the expanding European economy and society but also their seductive appeal in non-Western lands. Of great importance in African and Middle Eastern history, the ancient land of the pharaohs had since 525 B.C. been ruled by a succession of foreigners, most recently by the Ottoman Turks. In 1798 French armies under young General Napoleon Bonaparte invaded the Egyptian part of the Ottoman Empire and occupied the territory for three years. Into the power vacuum left by the French withdrawal stepped an extraordinary Albanian-born Turkish general, Muhammad Ali (1769–1849).

First appointed governor of Egypt by the Turkish sultan, Muhammad Ali soon disposed of his political rivals and set out to build his own state on the strength of a large, powerful army organized along European lines. He drafted for the first time the illiterate, despised peasant masses of Egypt, and he hired French and Italian army officers to train these raw recruits and their Turkish officers. The government was also reformed, new lands were cultivated, and communications were improved. By the time of his death in 1849, Muhammad Ali had established a strong and virtually independent Egyptian state, to be ruled by his family on a hereditary basis within the Turkish empire.

Muhammad Ali's policies of modernization attracted large numbers of Europeans to the banks of the Nile. As one Arab sheik of the Ottoman Empire remarked in the 1830s, "Englishmen are like ants; if one finds a bit of meat, hundreds follow."[3] The port city of Alexandria had more than fifty thousand Europeans by 1864, most of them Italians, Greeks, French, and English. Europeans served not only as army officers but also as engineers, doctors, high government officials, and police officers. Others found their "meat" in trade, finance, and shipping.

To pay for a modern army as well as for European services and manufactured goods, Muhammad Ali encouraged the development of commercial agriculture geared to the European market. This development had profound implications. Egyptian peasants had been poor but largely self-sufficient, growing food for their own consumption on state-owned lands allotted to them by tradition. Faced with the possibility of export agriculture, high-ranking officials and members of Muhammad Ali's family began carving large private landholdings out of the state domain. The new landlords made the peasants their tenants and forced them to grow cash crops for European markets. Borrowing money from European lenders at high rates and still making good profits, Egyptian landowners "modernized" agriculture, but to the detriment of peasant well-being.

East Meets West This painting gives a Japanese view of the first audience of the American Consul and his staff with the shogun, Japan's hereditary military governor, in 1859. The Americans appear strange and ill at ease. *(Source: Laurie Platt Winfrey, Inc.)*

British in Egypt   In this photograph Scottish soldiers pose with the ancient and mysterious Great Sphinx like school children on an outing. *(Source: Bettmann/Hulton)*

These trends continued under Muhammad Ali's grandson Ismail, who in 1863 began his sixteen-year rule as Egypt's *khedive,* or prince. Educated at France's leading military academy, Ismail was a westernizing autocrat. He dreamed of using European technology and capital to modernize Egypt quickly and build a vast empire in northeast Africa. The large irrigation networks he promoted caused cotton production and exports to Europe to boom. Ismail also borrowed large sums to install modern communications, and with his support the Suez Canal was completed by a French company in 1869. The Arabic of the masses rather than the Turkish of the conquerors became the official language, and young Egyptians educated in Europe helped spread new skills and new ideas in the bureaucracy. Cairo acquired modern boulevards, Western hotels, and an opera house. As Ismail proudly declared, "My country is no longer in Africa, we now form part of Europe."[4]

Yet Ismail was too impatient and too reckless. His projects were enormously expensive, and the sale of his stock in the Suez Canal to the British

government did not relieve the situation. By 1876 Egypt owed foreign bondholders a colossal $450 million and could not pay the interest on its debt. Rather than let Egypt go bankrupt and repudiate its loans, as had some Latin American countries and U.S. state governments in the early nineteenth century, the governments of France and Great Britain intervened politically to protect the European bankers who held the Egyptian bonds. They forced Ismail to appoint French and British commissioners to oversee Egyptian finances, in order that the Egyptian debt would be paid in full. This was a momentous decision. It implied direct European political control and was a sharp break with the previous pattern of trade and investment. Throughout most of the nineteenth century, Europeans had used naked military might and political force primarily to make sure that non-Western lands would accept European trade and investment. Now Europeans were going to determine the state budget and effectively rule Egypt.

Foreign financial control evoked a violent nationalistic reaction among Egyptian religious

Ellis Island in New York's harbor was the main entry point into the United States after 1892. For millions of immigrants the first frightening experience in the new land was being inspected and processed through its crowded "pens." *(Source: Culver Pictures)*

leaders, young intellectuals, and army officers. In 1879, under the leadership of Colonel Ahmed Arabi, they formed the Egyptian Nationalist party. Continuing diplomatic pressure, which forced Ismail to abdicate in favor of his weak son Tewfiq (r. 1879–1892), resulted in bloody anti-European riots in Alexandria in 1882. A number of Europeans were killed, and Tewfiq and his court had to flee to British ships for safety. When the British fleet bombarded Alexandria, more riots swept the country, and Colonel Arabi declared that "an irreconcilable war existed between the Egyptians and the English." But a British expeditionary force de-

cimated Arabi's forces and, as a result, occupied all of Egypt.

The British said their occupation was temporary, but British armies remained in Egypt until 1956. They maintained the façade of the khedive's government as an autonomous province of the Ottoman Empire, but the khedive was a mere puppet. The able British consul general Evelyn Baring, later Lord Cromer, ruled the country after 1883. Once a vocal opponent of involvement in Egypt, Baring was a paternalistic reformer who had come to believe that "without European interference and initiative reform is impossible here." Baring's rule did result in tax reforms and better conditions for peasants, while foreign bondholders tranquilly clipped their coupons and Egyptian nationalists nursed their injured pride.

In Egypt, Baring and the British reluctantly but spectacularly provided a new model for European expansion in densely populated lands. Such expansion was based on military force, political domination, and a self-justifying ideology of beneficial reform. This model was to predominate until 1914. Thus did Europe's Industrial Revolution lead to tremendous political as well as economic expansion throughout the world.

THE GREAT MIGRATION

A poignant human drama was interwoven with economic expansion: literally millions of people picked up stakes and left their ancestral lands in the course of history's greatest migration. To millions of ordinary people, for whom the opening of China and the interest on the Egyptian debt had not the slightest significance, this great movement was the central experience in the saga of Western expansion. It was, in part, because of this great migration that the West's impact on the world in the nineteenth century was so powerful and many-sided.

The Pressure of Population

In the early eighteenth century, the growth of European population entered its third and decisive stage, which continued unabated until the twentieth century (see Chapter 19). Birthrates eventually declined in the nineteenth century, but so did death rates, mainly because of the rising standard of living and secondarily because of the medical revolution. Thus the population of Europe (including Asiatic Russia) more than doubled, from approximately 188 million in 1800 to roughly 432 million in 1900.

These figures actually understate Europe's population explosion, for between 1815 and 1932 more than 60 million people left Europe. These migrants went primarily to the "areas of European settlement"—North and South America, Australia, New Zealand, and Siberia—where they contributed to a rapid growth in numbers. The population of North America (the United States and Canada) alone grew from 6 million to 81 million between 1800 and 1900 because of continuous immigration and the high fertility rates of North American women. Since population grew more slowly in Africa and Asia than in Europe, as Figure 26.2 shows, Europeans and people of European origin jumped from about 22 percent of the world's total to about 38 percent on the eve of World War One.

The growing number of Europeans provided further impetus for Western expansion. It was a driving force behind emigration. As in the eighteenth century, the rapid increase in numbers put pressure on the land and led to land hunger and relative overpopulation in area after area. In most countries, migration increased twenty years after a rapid growth in population, as many children of the baby boom grew up, saw little available land and few opportunities, and migrated. This pattern was especially prevalent when rapid population increase predated extensive industrial development, which offered the best long-term hope of creating jobs within the country and reducing poverty. Thus millions of country folk went abroad, as well as to nearby cities, in search of work and economic opportunity. The case of the Irish, who left in large numbers for Britain during the Industrial Revolution and for the United States after the potato famine, was extreme but not unique.

Before looking at the people who migrated, let us consider three facts. First, the number of men and women who left Europe increased rapidly before World War One. As Figure 26.3 shows, more than 11 million left in the first decade of the twentieth century, over five times the number departing in the 1850s. The outflow of migrants was clearly an enduring characteristic of European society for the entire period.

Second, different countries had very different patterns of movement. As Figure 26.3 also shows,

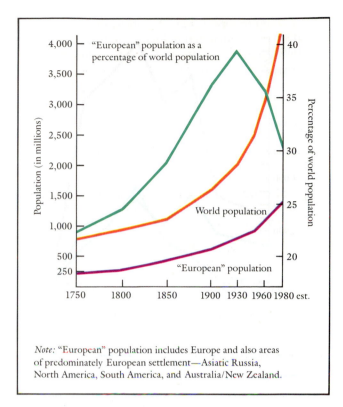

FIGURE 26.2 The Increase of European and World Populations 1750–1980 *(Sources: W. Woodruff,* Impact of Western Man: A Study of Europe's Role in the World Economy. *St. Martin's Press, New York, 1967. p. 103: United Nations.* Statistical Yearbook, *1982, 1985, pp. 2–3.)*

people left Britain and Ireland (which are not distinguished in the British figures) in large numbers from the 1840s on. This emigration reflected not only rural poverty but also the movement of skilled, industrial technicians and the preferences shown to British migrants in the British Empire. Ultimately, about one-third of all European migrants between 1840 and 1920 came from the British Isles. German migration was quite different. It grew irregularly after about 1830, reaching a first peak in the early 1850s and another in the early 1880s. Thereafter it declined rapidly, for Germany's rapid industrialization was providing adequate jobs at home. This pattern contrasted sharply with that of Italy. More and more Italians left the country right up to 1914, reflecting severe problems in Italian villages and relatively slow industrial growth. In sum, migration patterns mirrored social and economic conditions in the various European countries and provinces.

The Jewish Market   on New York's lower East Side was a bustling center of economic and social life in 1900. Jewish immigrants could usually find work with Jewish employers, and New York's Jewish population soared from 73 thousand in 1880 to 1.1 million in 1910. *(Source: The Granger Collection)*

Many landless young European men and women were spurred to leave by a spirit of revolt and independence. In Sweden and in Norway, in Jewish Russia and in Italy, these young people felt frustrated by the small privileged classes, who often controlled both church and government and resisted demands for change and greater opportunity. Many a young Norwegian seconded the passionate cry of Norway's national poet, Bjørnson: "Forth will I! Forth! I will be crushed and consumed if I stay."[5]

Many young Jews wholeheartedly agreed with a spokesman of Kiev's Jewish community in 1882, who declared, "Our human dignity is being trampled upon, our wives and daughters are being dishonored, we are looted and pillaged: either we get decent human rights or else let us go wherever our eyes may lead us."[6] Thus, for many, migration was

a radical way to "get out from under." Migration slowed down when the people won basic political and social reforms, such as the right to vote and social security.

Asian Migrants

Not all migration was from Europe. A substantial number of Chinese, Japanese, Indians, and Filipinos—to name only four key groups—responded to rural hardship with temporary or permanent migration. At least 3 million Asians (as opposed to more than 60 million Europeans) moved abroad before 1920. Most went as indentured laborers to work under incredibly difficult conditions on the plantations or in the gold fields of Latin America, southern Asia, Africa, California, Hawaii, and Australia. White estate owners very often used Asians to replace or supplement blacks after the suppression of the slave trade.

In the 1840s, for example, there was a strong demand for field hands in Cuba, and the Spanish government actively recruited Chinese laborers. They came under eight-year contracts, were paid about twenty-five cents a day, and were fed potatoes and salted beef. Between 1853 and 1873, when such migration was stopped, more than 130,000 Chinese laborers went to Cuba. The majority spent their lives as virtual slaves. The great landlords of Peru also brought in more than 100,000 workers from China in the nineteenth century, and there were similar movements of Asians elsewhere.

Such migration from Asia would undoubtedly have grown to much greater proportions if planters and mine owners in search of cheap labor had had their way. But they did not. Asians fled the plantations and gold fields as soon as possible, seeking greater opportunities in trade and towns. There they came into conflict with other brown-skinned peoples—as in Malaya and East Africa—and with white settlers in areas of European settlement.

These settlers demanded a halt to Asian migration. One Australian brutally summed up the typical view: "The Chinaman knows nothing about Caucasian civilization. . . . It would be less objectionable to drive a flock of sheep to the poll than to allow Chinamen to vote. The sheep at all events would be harmless."[7] By the 1880s Americans and Australians were building "great white walls"—discriminatory laws designed to keep Asians out. Thus a final, crucial factor in the migrations before 1914 was the general policy of "whites only" in the open lands of possible permanent settlement. This, too, was part of Western dominance in the increasingly lopsided world. Largely successful in monopolizing the best overseas opportunities, Europeans and people of European ancestry reaped the main benefits from the great migration. By 1913 people in Australia, Canada, and the United States all had higher average incomes than people in Great Britain, still Europe's wealthiest nation.

The Chinese Exclusion Act   This vicious cartoon from a San Francisco newspaper celebrates American anti-migration laws. Americans and Europeans generally shared the same attitudes regarding the non-Western world. *(Source: Caroline Buckler)*

WESTERN IMPERIALISM

The expansion of Western society reached its apex between about 1880 and 1914. In those years, the leading European nations not only continued to send massive streams of migrants, money, and manufactured goods around the world, but also rushed to create or enlarge vast *political* empires abroad. This political empire building contrasted sharply with the economic penetration of non-Western territories between 1816 and 1880, which had left a China or a Japan "opened" but politically independent. By contrast, the empires of the late nineteenth century recalled the old European colonial empires of the seventeenth and eighteenth centuries and led contemporaries to speak of the new imperialism.

Characterized by a frantic rush to plant the flag over as many people and as much territory as possible, the new imperialism had momentous consequences. It resulted in new tensions among competing European states, and it led to wars and rumors of war with non-European powers. The new imperialism was aimed primarily at Africa and Asia. It put millions of black, brown, and tan peoples directly under the rule of whites. How and why did whites come to rule these peoples?

The Scramble for Africa

The most spectacular manifestation of the new imperialism was the seizure of Africa, which broke sharply with previous patterns and fascinated contemporary Europeans and Americans.

As late as 1880, European nations controlled only 10 percent of the African continent, and their possessions were hardly increasing. The French had begun conquering Algeria in 1830, and within fifty years substantial numbers of French, Italian, and Spanish colonists had settled among the overwhelming Arab majority.

At the other end of the continent, in South Africa, the British had taken possession of the Dutch settlements at Cape Town during the wars with Napoleon I. This takeover had led disgruntled Dutch cattle ranchers and farmers in 1835 to make their so-called Great Trek into the interior, where they fought the Zulu and Xhosa peoples for land. After 1853, while British colonies like Canada and

Australia were beginning to evolve toward self-government, the Boers, or Afrikaners (as the descendants of the Dutch in the Cape Colony were beginning to call themselves), proclaimed their political independence and defended it against British armies. By 1880 Afrikaner and British settlers, who detested each other, had wrested control of much of South Africa from the Zulu, Xhosa, and other African peoples.

European trading posts and forts dating back to the Age of Discovery and the slave trade dotted the coast of West Africa. The Portuguese proudly but ineffectively held their old possessions in Angola and Mozambique. Elsewhere, over the great mass of the continent, Europeans did not rule.

Between 1880 and 1900, the situation changed drastically. Britain, France, Germany, and Italy scrambled for African possessions as if their national livelihood depended on it. By 1900 nearly the whole continent had been carved up and placed under European rule: only Ethiopia in northeast Africa and Liberia on the West African coast remained independent. Even the Dutch settler republics of southern Africa were conquered by the British in the bloody Boer War (1899–1902). In the years before 1914, the European powers tightened their control and established colonial governments to rule their gigantic empires (Map 26.2).

In the complexity of the European seizure of Africa, certain events and individuals stand out. Of enormous importance was the British occupation of Egypt, which established the new model of formal political control. There was also the role of Leopold II of Belgium (r. 1865–1909), an energetic, strong-willed monarch with a lust for distant territory. "The sea bathes our coast, the world lies before us," he had exclaimed in 1861. "Steam and electricity have annihilated distance, and all the non-appropriated lands on the surface of the globe can become the field of our operations and of our success."[8] By 1876 Leopold was focusing on central Africa. Subsequently he formed a financial syndicate under his personal control to send H. M. Stanley, a sensation-seeking journalist and part-time explorer, to the Congo basin. Stanley was able

MAP 26.2 The Partition of Africa European nations carved up Africa after 1880 and built vast political empires.

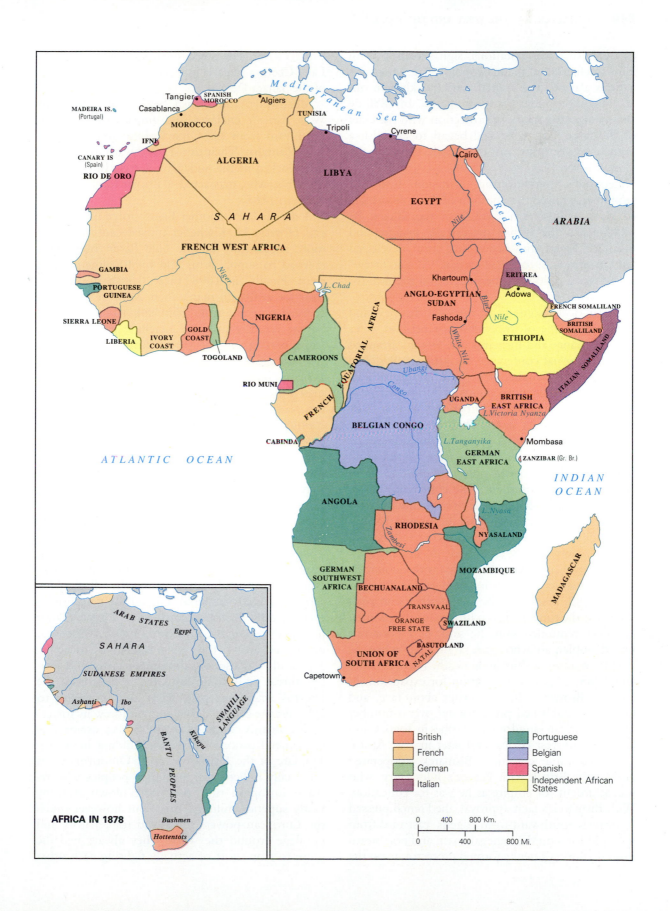

MADEIRA IS. (Portugal)

Tangier
Casablanca
MOROCCO
SPANISH MOROCCO
Algiers
TUNISIA
Tripoli
Cyrene
Cairo

Mediterranean Sea

IFNI
CANARY IS (Spain)
RIO DE ORO

ALGERIA
LIBYA
EGYPT
ARABIA

S A H A R A

Red Sea
Nile

FRENCH WEST AFRICA

GAMBIA
PORTUGUESE GUINEA
SIERRA LEONE
LIBERIA
IVORY COAST
GOLD COAST
TOGOLAND
NIGERIA
CAMEROONS
RIO MUNI

L.Chad
Niger

ERITREA
Khartoum
Adowa
FRENCH SOMALILAND
ANGLO-EGYPTIAN SUDAN
Fashoda
BRITISH SOMALILAND
ETHIOPIA
Blue Nile
Nile
White Nile

FRENCH EQUATORIAL AFRICA

Ubangi
Congo

CABINDA

BELGIAN CONGO

UGANDA
BRITISH EAST AFRICA
L.Victoria Nyanza
L.Tanganyika
Mombasa
ZANZIBAR (Gr. Br.)
GERMAN EAST AFRICA

ATLANTIC OCEAN

INDIAN OCEAN

ANGOLA

L.Nyasa

RHODESIA
NYASALAND
Zambesi
MOZAMBIQUE

GERMAN SOUTHWEST AFRICA
BECHUANALAND
TRANSVAAL
ORANGE FREE STATE
SWAZILAND
MADAGASCAR

BASUTOLAND
NATAL
UNION OF SOUTH AFRICA
Capetown

AFRICA IN 1878

ARAB STATES
Egypt
SAHARA
SUDANESE EMPIRES
Ashanti *Ibo*
SWAHILI LANGUAGE
Kikuyu
BANTU PEOPLES
Bushmen
Hottentots

	British		Portuguese
	French		Belgian
	German		Spanish
	Italian		Independent African States

0   400   800 Km.

0   400   800 Mi.

to establish trading stations, sign "treaties" with African chiefs, and plant Leopold's flag. Leopold's actions alarmed the French, who quickly sent out an expedition under Pierre de Brazza. In 1880 de Brazza signed a treaty of protection with the chief of the large Teke tribe and began to establish a French protectorate on the north bank of the Congo River.

Leopold's buccaneering intrusion into the Congo area raised the question of the political fate of black Africa—Africa south of the Sahara. By 1882, when the British successfully invaded and occupied Egypt, the richest and most developed land in Africa, Europe had caught "African fever." There was a gold-rush mentality, and the race for territory was on.

To lay down some basic rules for this new and dangerous game of imperialist competition, Jules Ferry of France and Bismarck of Germany arranged an international conference on Africa in Berlin in 1884 and 1885. The conference established the principle that European claims to African territory had to rest on "effective occupation" in order to be recognized by other states. This principle was very important. It meant that Europeans would push relentlessly into interior regions from all sides and that no single European power would be able to claim the entire continent. The conference recognized Leopold's personal rule over a neutral Congo Free State and declared all of the Congo basin a free-trade zone. The conference also agreed to work to stop slavery and the slave trade in Africa.

The Berlin conference coincided with Germany's sudden emergence as an imperial power. Prior to about 1880, Bismarck, like many other European leaders at the time, had seen little value in colonies. Colonies reminded him, he said, of a poor but proud nobleman who wore a fur coat when he could not afford a shirt underneath. Then, in 1884 and 1885, as political agitation for expansion increased, Bismarck did an abrupt about-face, and Germany established protectorates over a number of small African kingdoms and tribes in Togo, Cameroon, southwest Africa, and later in East Africa.

In acquiring colonies, Bismarck cooperated against the British with France's Jules Ferry, who was as ardent for empire as he was for education. With Bismarck's tacit approval, the French pressed vigorously southward from Algeria, eastward from their old forts on the Senegal coast, and northward from de Brazza's newly formed protectorate on the

[margin note: nouveau Riches]

Congo River. The object of these three thrusts was Lake Chad, a malaria-infested swamp on the edge of the Sahara Desert.

Meanwhile, the British began enlarging their West African enclaves and impatiently pushing northward from the Cape Colony and westward from Zanzibar. Their thrust southward from Egypt was blocked in the Sudan by fiercely independent Muslims, who massacred a British force at Khartoum in 1885.

A decade later, another British force under General Horatio H. Kitchener moved cautiously and more successfully up the Nile River, building a railroad to supply arms and reinforcements as it went. Finally, in 1898, these British troops met their foe at Omdurman, where Muslim tribesmen charged time and time again only to be cut down by the recently invented machine gun. For one smug participant, the young British officer Winston Churchill, it was "like a pantomime scene" in a play. "These extraordinary foreign figures . . . march up one by one from the darkness of Barbarism to the footlights of civilization . . . and their conquerors, taking their possessions, forget even their names. Nor will history record such trash." For another, more somber English observer, "It was not a battle but an execution. The bodies were not in heaps . . . but they spread evenly over acres and acres."[9] In the end, eleven thousand fanatical Muslim tribesmen lay dead, while only twenty-eight Britons had been killed.

Continuing up the Nile after the Battle of Omdurman, Kitchener's armies found that a small French force had already occupied the village of Fashoda. Locked in imperial competition with Britain ever since the British occupation of Egypt, France had tried to beat the British to one of Africa's last unclaimed areas—the upper reaches of the Nile. The result was a serious diplomatic crisis, and even the threat of war. Eventually, wracked by the Dreyfus affair (see page 813) and unwilling to fight, France backed down and withdrew its forces.

The British conquest of the Sudan exemplifies the general process of empire building in Africa. The fate of the Muslim force at Omdurman was eventually inflicted on all native peoples who resisted European rule: they were blown away by vastly superior military force. But however much the European powers squabbled for territory and privilege around the world, they always had the sense to stop short of actually fighting each other

Omdurman, 1898 European machine guns cut down the charging Muslim tribesmen again and again. "It was not a battle but an execution," said one witness. Thus the Sudan was conquered and one million square miles added to the British empire. *(Source: E. T. Archive)*

for it. Imperial ambitions were not worth a great European war.

Imperialism in Asia

Although the sudden division of Africa was more spectacular, Europeans also extended their political control in Asia. In 1815 the Dutch ruled little more than the island of Java in the East Indies. Thereafter they gradually brought almost all of the 3,000-mile archipelago under their political authority, though—in good imperialist fashion—they had to share some of the spoils with Britain and Germany. In the critical decade of the 1880s, the French under the leadership of Jules Ferry took Indochina. India, Japan, and China also experienced a profound imperialist impact (Map 26.3).

Two other great imperialist powers, Russia and the United States, also acquired rich territories in Asia. Russia, whose history since the later Middle Ages had been marked by almost continuous expansion, moved steadily forward on two fronts throughout the nineteenth century. Russians conquered Muslim areas to the south in the Caucasus and in central Asia and also proceeded to nibble greedily on China's outlying provinces in the Far East, especially in the 1890s.

The United States' great conquest was the Philippines, taken from Spain in 1898 after the Spanish-American War. When it quickly became clear that the United States had no intention of granting independence, Philippine patriots rose in revolt and were suppressed only after long, bitter fighting. (Not until 1934 was a timetable for independence established.) Some Americans protested the taking

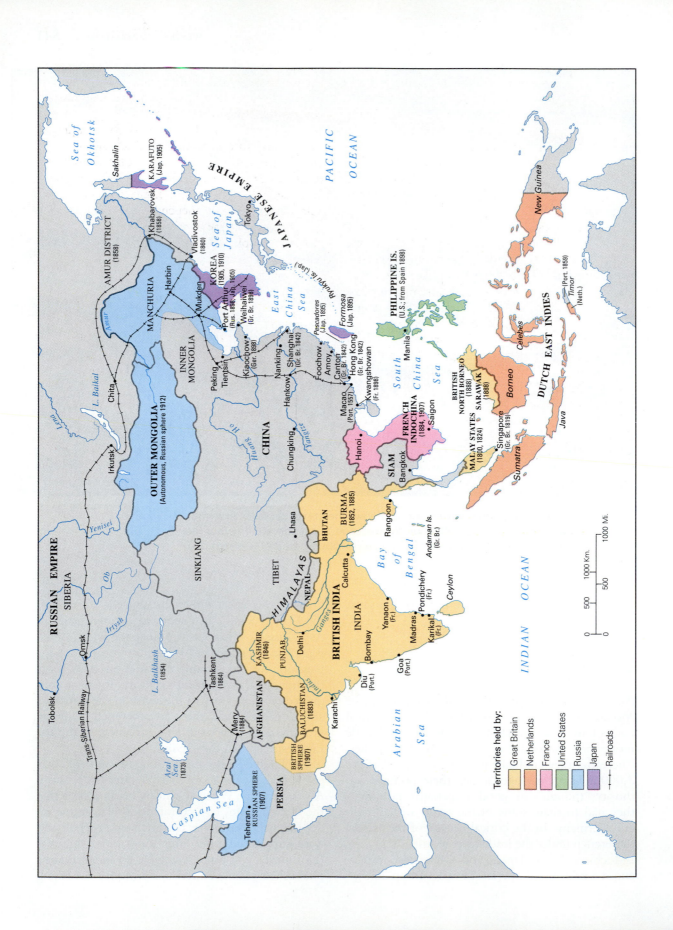

Sea of Okhotsk

Sakhalin

KARAFUTO (Jap. 1905)

JAPANESE EMPIRE

PACIFIC OCEAN

AMUR DISTRICT (1858)

Khabarovsk (1858)

Vladivostok (1860)

Sea of Japan

Tokyo

New Guinea

MANCHURIA

Harbin

Mukden

KOREA (1905, 1910)

Ryukyu Is. (Jap.)

PHILIPPINE IS. (U.S.; from Spain 1898)

DUTCH EAST INDIES

Timor (Port. 1859) (Neth.)

Port Arthur (Rus. 1898; Jap. 1905)

Weihaiwei (Gr. Br. 1898)

East China Sea

Pescadores (Jap. 1895)

Formosa (Jap. 1895)

Manila

Celebes

INNER MONGOLIA

Peking

Tientsin

Kiaochow (Ger.)

Nanking

Shanghai (Gr. Br. 1842)

Hankow

Foochow

Amoy (Gr. Br. 1842)

Canton

Hong Kong (Gr. Br. 1842)

Kwangshowan (Fr. 1898)

South China Sea

BRITISH NORTH BORNEO (1888)

SARAWAK (1888)

Borneo

Java

RUSSIAN EMPIRE

SIBERIA

Tobolsk

Omsk

Trans-Siberian Railway

Irkutsk

Chita

L. Baikal

Lena

Yenisei

Ob

Irtysh

L. Balkhash

Tashkent (1864)

OUTER MONGOLIA (Autonomous, Russian sphere 1912)

Amur

SINKIANG

CHINA

Chungking

Yangtze

Huang Ho

Ho

Macao (Port. 1557)

Hanoi

FRENCH INDOCHINA (1884, 1907)

Saigon

MALAY STATES (1800, 1824)

Singapore (Gr. Br. 1819)

Sumatra

SIAM

Bangkok

TIBET

Lhasa

HIMALAYAS

NEPAL

BHUTAN

BURMA (1852, 1885)

Rangoon

Bay of Bengal

Andaman Is. (Gr. Br.)

KASHMIR (1846)

PUNJAB

Delhi

Ganges

Indus

BRITISH INDIA

INDIA

Bombay

Calcutta

Yanaon (Fr.)

Madras

Pondichéry (Fr.)

Karikal (Fr.)

Ceylon

Goa (Port.)

Diu (Port.)

Arabian Sea

INDIAN OCEAN

AFGHANISTAN

BALUCHISTAN (1883)

Karachi

Merv (1884)

Aral Sea (1873)

BRITISH SPHERE (1907)

RUSSIAN SPHERE (1907)

PERSIA

Teheran

Caspian Sea

Territories held by:

Great Britain	
Netherlands	
France	
United States	
Russia	
Japan	
Railroads	

1000 Mi.

1000 Km.

500

500

0

0

of the Philippines, but to no avail. Thus another great Western power joined the imperialist ranks in Asia.

Causes of the New Imperialism

Many factors contributed to the late-nineteenth-century rush for territory and empire, which was in turn one aspect of Western society's generalized expansion in the age of industry and nationalism. It is little wonder that controversies have raged over interpretation of the new imperialism, especially since authors of every persuasion have often exaggerated particular aspects in an attempt to prove their own theories. Yet despite complexity and controversy, basic causes are clearly identifiable.

Economic motives played an important role in the extension of political empires, especially the British Empire. By the late 1870s, France, Germany, and the United States were industrializing rapidly behind rising tariff barriers. Great Britain was losing its early lead and facing increasingly tough competition in foreign markets. In this new economic situation, Britain came to value old possessions, such as India and Canada, more highly. The days when a leading free-trader like Richard Cobden could denounce the "bloodstained fetish of Empire" and statesman Benjamin Disraeli could call colonies a "millstone round our necks" came to an abrupt end. When continental powers began to grab any and all unclaimed territory in the 1880s, the British followed suit immediately. They feared that France and Germany would seal off their empires with high tariffs and restrictions and that future economic opportunities would be lost forever.

Actually, the overall economic gains of the new imperialism proved quite limited before 1914. The new colonies were simply too poor to buy much, and they offered few immediately profitable investments. Nonetheless, even the poorest, most barren desert was jealously prized, and no territory was ever abandoned. Colonies became important for political and diplomatic reasons. Each leading

country saw colonies as crucial to national security, military power, and international prestige. For instance, safeguarding the Suez Canal played a key role in the British occupation of Egypt, and protecting Egypt in turn led to the bloody conquest of the Sudan. National security was a major factor in the United States' decision to establish firm control over the Panama Canal Zone in 1903. Far-flung possessions guaranteed ever-growing navies the safe havens and the dependable coaling stations they needed in time of crisis or war.

Many people were convinced that colonies were essential to great nations. "There has never been a great power without great colonies," wrote one French publicist in 1877. "Every virile people has established colonial power," echoed the famous nationalist historian of Germany, Heinrich von Treitschke. "All great nations in the fullness of their strength have desired to set their mark upon barbarian lands and those who fail to participate in this great rivalry will play a pitiable role in time to come."[10]

Treitschke's harsh statement reflects not only the increasing aggressiveness of European nationalism after Bismarck's wars of German unification but also Social Darwinian theories of brutal competition among races. As one prominent English economist argued, the "strongest nation has always been conquering the weaker . . . and the strongest tend to be best." Thus European nations, which were seen as racially distinct parts of the dominant white race, had to seize colonies to show they were strong and virile. Moreover, since racial struggle was nature's inescapable law, the conquest of inferior peoples was just. "The path of progress is strewn with the wreck . . . of inferior races," wrote one professor in 1900. "Yet these dead peoples are, in very truth, the stepping stones on which mankind has risen to the higher intellectual and deeper emotional life of to-day."[11] Social Darwinism and racial doctrines fostered imperial expansion.

Finally, certain special-interest groups in each country were powerful agents of expansion. Shipping companies wanted lucrative subsidies. White settlers on dangerous, turbulent frontiers constantly demanded more land and greater protection. Missionaries and humanitarians wanted to spread religion and stop the slave trade. Explorers and adventurers sought knowledge and excitement. Military men and colonial officials, whose role has often been overlooked by those who write

MAP 26.3 Asia in 1914   India remained under British rule while China precariously preserved its political independence.

on imperialism, foresaw rapid advancement and high-paid positions in growing empires. The actions of such groups and the determined individuals who led them thrust the course of empire forward.

Western society did not rest the case for empire solely on naked conquest and a Darwinian racial struggle, or on power politics and the need for naval bases on every ocean. In order to satisfy their consciences and answer their critics, imperialists developed additional arguments.

A favorite idea was that Europeans could and should "civilize" more primitive, nonwhite peoples. According to this view, nonwhites would eventually receive the benefits of modern economies, cities, advanced medicine, and higher standards of living. In time, they might be ready for self-government and Western democracy. Thus the French spoke of their sacred "civilizing mission." Rudyard Kipling (1865–1936), who wrote masterfully of Anglo-Indian life and was perhaps the most

influential writer of the 1890s, exhorted Europeans to unselfish service in distant lands:

Take up the White Man's Burden—
Send forth the best ye breed—
Go bind your sons to exile
To serve your captives' need,
To wait in heavy harness,
On fluttered folk and wild—
Your new-caught, sullen peoples
Half-devil and half-child.[12]

Many Americans accepted the ideology of the white man's burden. It was an important factor in the decision to rule rather than liberate the Philippines after the Spanish-American War. Like their European counterparts, these Americans sincerely believed that their civilization had reached unprecedented heights and that they had unique benefits to bestow on all "less advanced" peoples. Another ar-

"The Administration of Justice"   In this 1895 illustration from a popular magazine, a Belgian official, flanked by native soldiers, settles a tribal dispute in the Congo State. This flattering view of Europe's "civilizing mission" suggests how imperial rule rested on more than just brute force. *(Source: Bettmann/Hulton)*

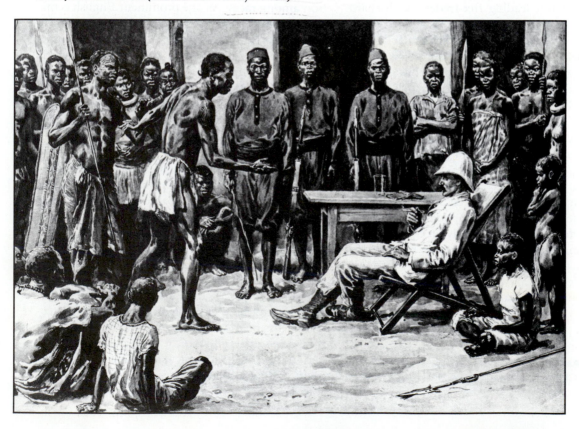

gument was that imperial government protected natives from tribal warfare as well as cruder forms of exploitation by white settlers and business people.

Peace and stability under European control also permitted the spread of Christianity—the "true" religion. In Africa, Catholic and Protestant missionaries competed with Islam south of the Sahara, seeking converts and building schools to spread the Gospel. Many Africans' first real contact with whites was in mission schools. As late as 1942, for example, 97 percent of Nigeria's student population was in mission schools. Some peoples, like the Ibo in Nigeria, became highly Christianized.

Such occasional successes in black Africa contrasted with the general failure of missionary efforts in India, China, and the Islamic world. There, Christians often preached in vain to peoples with ancient, complex religious beliefs. Yet the number of Christian believers around the world did increase substantially in the nineteenth century, and missionary groups kept trying. Unfortunately, "many missionaries had drunk at the well of European racism," and this probably prevented them from doing better.[13]

Critics of Imperialism

The expansion of empire aroused sharp, even bitter, critics. A forceful attack was delivered in 1902, after the unpopular Boer War, by the radical English economist J. A. Hobson (1858–1940) in his *Imperialism,* a work that influenced Lenin and others. Hobson contended that the rush to acquire colonies was due to the economic needs of unregulated capitalism, particularly the need of the rich to find outlets for their surplus capital. Yet, Hobson argued, imperial possessions did not pay off economically for the country as a whole. Only unscrupulous special-interest groups profited from them, at the expense of both the European taxpayer and the natives. Moreover, the quest for empire diverted attention from domestic reform and closing the gap between rich and poor. These and similar arguments were not very persuasive. Most people then (and now) believed that imperialism was economically profitable for the homeland, and a broad and genuine enthusiasm for empire developed among the masses.

Hobson and many other critics struck home, however, with their moral condemnation of whites

imperiously ruling nonwhites. They rebelled against crude Social Darwinian thought. "O Evolution, what crimes are committed in thy name!" cried one foe. Another sardonically coined a new beatitude: "Blessed are the strong, for they shall prey on the weak."[14] Kipling and his kind were lampooned as racist bullies, whose rule rested on brutality, racial contempt, and the Maxim machine gun. Henry Labouchère, a member of Parliament and prominent spokesman for this position, mocked Kipling's famous poem:

Pile on the Brown Man's burden!
And if ye rouse his hate,
Meet his old-fashioned reasons
With Maxims up to date,
With shells and Dum-Dum bullets
A hundred times plain
The Brown Man's loss must never
Imply the White Man's gain.[15]

Similarly, in *Heart of Darkness* the Polish-born novelist Joseph Conrad (1857–1924) castigated the "pure selfishness" of Europeans in "civilizing" Africa; the main character, once a liberal scholar, turns into a savage brute.

Critics charged Europeans with applying a degrading double standard and failing to live up to their own noble ideals. At home, Europeans had won or were winning representative government, individual liberties, and a certain equality of opportunity. In their empires, Europeans imposed military dictatorships on Africans and Asians, forced them to work involuntarily, almost like slaves, and discriminated against them shamelessly. Only by renouncing imperialism, its critics insisted, and giving captive peoples the freedoms Western society had struggled for since the French Revolution, would Europeans be worthy of their traditions. Europeans who denounced the imperialist tide provided colonial peoples with a Western ideology of liberation.

RESPONSES TO WESTERN IMPERIALISM

To peoples in Africa and Asia, Western expansion represented a profoundly disruptive assault. Everywhere it threatened traditional ruling classes, traditional economies, and traditional ways of life. Christian missionaries and European secular ideologies challenged established beliefs and values. Non-Western peoples experienced a crisis of identity, a crisis made all the more painful by the power and arrogance of the white intruders.

The initial response of African and Asian rulers was to try to drive the unwelcome foreigners away. This was the case in China, Japan, and the upper Sudan, as we have seen. Violent antiforeign reactions exploded elsewhere again and again, but the superior military technology of the industrialized West almost invariably prevailed. Beaten in battle, many Africans and Asians concentrated on preserving their cultural traditions at all costs. Others found themselves forced to reconsider their initial hostility. Some (like Ismail of Egypt) concluded that the West was indeed superior in some ways and that it was therefore necessary to reform their societies and copy European achievements. Thus it is possible to think of responses to the Western impact as a spectrum, with "traditionalists" at one end, "westernizers" or "modernizers" at the other, and many shades of opinion in between. Both before and after European domination, the struggle among these groups was often intense. With time, however, the modernizers tended to gain the upper hand.

When the power of both the traditionalists and the modernizers was thoroughly shattered by superior force, the great majority of Asians and Africans accepted imperial rule. Political participation in non-Western lands was historically limited to small elites, and the masses were used to doing what their rulers told them. In these circumstances Europeans, clothed in power and convinced of their righteousness, governed smoothly and effectively. They received considerable support from both traditionalists—local chiefs, landowners, religious leaders—and modernizers—the Western-educated professional classes and civil servants.

Nevertheless, imperial rule was in many ways an imposing edifice built on sand. Support for European rule among the conforming and accepting millions was shallow and weak. Thus the conforming masses followed with greater or lesser enthusiasm a few determined personalities who came to oppose the Europeans. Such leaders always arose, both when Europeans ruled directly and when they manipulated native governments, for at least two basic reasons.

First, the nonconformists—the eventual anti-imperialist leaders—developed a burning desire for human dignity. They came to feel that such dignity was incompatible with foreign rule with its smirks and smiles, its paternalism and condescension. Second, potential leaders found in the Western world the ideologies and justification for their protest. They discovered liberalism with its credo of civil liberty and political self-determination. They echoed the demands of anti-imperialists in Europe and America that the West live up to its own ideals.

More important, they found themselves attracted to modern nationalism, which asserted that every people had the right to control its own destiny. After 1917 anti-imperialist revolt would find another weapon in Lenin's version of Marxian socialism. Thus the anti-imperialist search for dignity drew strength from Western culture, as is apparent in the development of three major Asian countries —India, Japan, and China.

Empire in India

India was the jewel of the British Empire, and no colonial area experienced a more profound British impact. Unlike Japan and China, which maintained a real or precarious independence, and unlike African territories, which were annexed by Europeans only at the end of the nineteenth century, India was ruled more or less absolutely by Britain for a very long time.

Arriving in India on the heels of the Portuguese in the seventeenth century, the British East India Company had conquered the last independent native state by 1848. The last "traditional" response to European rule—the attempt by the established ruling classes to drive the white man out by military force—was broken in India in 1857 and 1858. Those were the years of the Great Rebellion (which the British called a "mutiny"), when an insurrection by Muslim and Hindu mercenaries in the British army spread throughout northern and central India before it was finally crushed, primarily by loyal native troops from southern India. Thereafter Britain ruled India directly. India illustrates, therefore, for better and for worse, what generations of European domination might produce.

After 1858 India was ruled by the British Parliament in London and administered by a tiny, all-white civil service in India. In 1900 this elite consisted of fewer than 3,500 top officials, for a population of 300 million. The white elite, backed by white officers and native troops, was competent and generally well disposed toward the welfare of

The British in India   This photo suggests not only the incredible power and luxury of the British ruling class in India but also its confidence and self-satisfaction. As one British viceroy said, "We are all British gentlemen engaged in the magnificent work of governing an inferior race." *(Source: Bettmann/Hulton)*

the Indian peasant masses. Yet it practiced strict job discrimination and social segregation, and most of its members quite frankly considered the jumble of Indian peoples and castes to be racially inferior. As Lord Kitchener, one of the most distinguished top military commanders of India, stated:

It is this consciousness of the inherent superiority of the European which has won for us India. However well educated and clever a native may be, and however brave he may prove himself, I believe that no rank we can bestow on him would cause him to be considered an equal of the British officer.[16]

When, for example, the British Parliament in 1883 was considering a major bill to allow Indian judges to try white Europeans in India, the British community rose in protest and defeated the measure. The idea that they might be judged by Indians was inconceivable to Europeans, for it was clear to the Europeans that the empire in India rested squarely on racial inequality.

In spite of (perhaps even because of) their strong feelings of racial and cultural superiority, the British acted energetically and introduced many desirable changes to India. Realizing that they needed well-educated Indians to serve as skilled subordinates in the government and army, the British established a modern system of progressive secondary education, in which all instruction was in English. Thus, through education and government service, the British offered some Indians excellent opportunities for both economic and social advancement. High-caste Hindus, particularly quick to respond, emerged as skillful intermediaries between the British rulers and the Indian people, and soon they formed a new elite profoundly influenced by Western thought and culture.

This new bureaucratic elite played a crucial role in modern economic development, which was a second result of British rule. Irrigation projects for agriculture, the world's third largest railroad network for good communications, and large tea and jute plantations geared to the world economy were all developed. Unfortunately, the lot of the Indian masses improved little, for the increase in production was quite literally eaten up by population increase.

Finally, with a well-educated, English-speaking Indian bureaucracy and modern communications, the British created a unified, powerful state. They placed under the same general system of law and administration the different Hindu and Muslim peoples and the vanquished kingdoms of the entire subcontinent—groups that had fought each other for centuries during the Middle Ages and had been repeatedly conquered by Muslim and Mongol invaders. It was as if Europe, with its many states and varieties of Christianity, had been conquered and united in a single great empire.

In spite of these achievements, the decisive reaction to European rule was the rise of nationalism among the Indian elite. No matter how anglicized and necessary a member of the educated classes became, he or she could never become the white ruler's equal. The top jobs, the best clubs, the modern hotels, and even certain railroad compartments were sealed off to brown-skinned men and women. The peasant masses might accept such inequality as the latest version of age-old oppression, but the well-educated, English-speaking elite eventually could not. For the elite, racial discrimination meant not only injured pride but bitter injustice. It flagrantly contradicted those cherished Western concepts of human rights and equality. Moreover, it was based on dictatorship, no matter how benign.

By 1885, when educated Indians came together to found the predominately Hindu Indian National Congress, demands were increasing for the equality and self-government Britain enjoyed and had already granted white-settler colonies, such as Canada and Australia. By 1907, emboldened in part by Japan's success (see the next section), the radicals in the Indian National Congress were calling for complete independence. Even the moderates were demanding home rule for India through an elected parliament. Although there were sharp divisions between Hindus and Muslims, Indians were finding an answer to the foreign challenge. The common heritage of British rule and Western ideals, along with the reform and revitalization of the Hindu religion, had created a genuine movement for national independence.

The Example of Japan

When Commodore Perry arrived in Japan in 1853 with his crude but effective gunboat diplomacy, Japan was a complex feudal society. At the top stood a figurehead emperor; but for more than two hundred years, real power had been in the hands of a hereditary military governor, the *shogun*. With the help of a warrior-nobility known as *samurai*, the shogun governed a country of hard-working, productive peasants and city dwellers. Often poor and restless, the intensely proud samurai were deeply humiliated by the sudden American intrusion and the unequal treaties with Western countries.

When foreign diplomats and merchants began to settle in Yokohama, radical samurai reacted with a wave of antiforeign terrorism and antigovernment assassinations between 1858 and 1863. The imperialist response was swift and unambiguous. An allied fleet of American, British, Dutch, and French warships demolished key forts, further weakening the power and prestige of the shogun's government. Then, in 1867, a coalition led by patriotic samurai seized control of the government with hardly any bloodshed and restored the political power of the emperor. This was the Meiji Restoration, a great turning point in Japanese development.

The immediate, all-important goal of the new government was to meet the foreign threat. The battle cry of the Meiji reformers was "enrich the state and strengthen the armed forces." Yet how was this to be done? In an about-face that was one of history's most remarkable chapters, the young but well-trained, idealistic but flexible, leaders of Meiji Japan dropped their antiforeign attacks. Convinced that Western civilization was indeed superior in its military and industrial aspects, they initiated from above a series of measures to reform Japan along modern lines. They were convinced that "Japan must be reborn with America its mother and France its father."[17] In the broadest sense, the Meiji leaders tried to harness the power inherent in Europe's dual revolution, in order to protect their country and catch up with the West.

In 1871 the new leaders abolished the old feudal structure of aristocratic, decentralized government and formed a strong unified state. Following the example of the French Revolution, they dismantled the four-class legal system and declared social equality. They decreed freedom of movement in a country where traveling abroad had been a most serious crime. They created a free, competitive, government-stimulated economy. Japan began to build railroads and modern factories. Thus the new generation adopted many principles of a free, liberal society; and, as in Europe, such freedom resulted in a tremendously creative release of human energy.

Yet the overriding concern of Japan's political leadership was always a powerful state, and to achieve this, more than liberalism was borrowed from the West. A powerful modern navy was created, and the army was completely reorganized along French and German lines, with three-year military service for all males and a professional officer corps. This army of draftees effectively put down disturbances in the countryside, and in 1877 it was used to crush a major rebellion by feudal elements protesting the loss of their privileges. Japan also borrowed rapidly and adapted skillfully the West's science and modern technology, particularly in industry, medicine, and education. Many Japanese were encouraged to study abroad, and the government paid large salaries to attract foreign experts. These experts were always carefully controlled, though, and replaced by trained Japanese as soon as possible.

By 1890, when the new state was firmly established, the wholesale borrowing of the early restoration had given way to more selective emphasis on those things foreign that were in keeping with Japanese tradition. Following the model of the German Empire, Japan established an authoritarian constitution and rejected democracy. The power of the emperor and his ministers was vast, that of the legislature limited.

Japan successfully copied the imperialism of Western society. Expansion not only proved that Japan was strong; it also cemented the nation together in a great mission. Having "opened" Korea with the gunboat diplomacy of imperialism in 1876, Japan decisively defeated China in a war over Korea in 1894 to 1895 and took Formosa. In the next years, Japan competed aggressively with the leading European powers for influence and terri-

Japanese Industrialization   The famous Tomioka silk reeling factory pioneered with mass-production techniques and women factory workers in the 1870s. The combination shown here of European technology with native dress symbolizes Japan's successful integration of Western practices into the traditional culture of its society. (*Source: Laurie Platt Winfrey, Inc.*)

tory in China, particularly Manchuria. There Japanese and Russian imperialism met and collided. In 1904 Japan attacked Russia without warning, and after a bloody war, Japan emerged with a valuable foothold in China, Russia's former protectorate over Port Arthur (see Map 26.3). By 1910, when it annexed Korea, Japan was a major imperial power, continuously expanding its influence in China in spite of sharp protests from its distant Pacific neighbor, the United States.

Japan became the first non-Western country to use an ancient love of country to transform itself and thereby meet the many-sided challenge of Western expansion. Moreover, Japan demonstrated convincingly that a modern Asian nation could defeat and humble a great Western power. Many Chinese nationalists were fascinated by Japan's achievement. A group of patriots in French-ruled southern Vietnam sent Vietnamese students to Japan to learn the island empire's secret of success. Japan provided patriots in Asia and Africa with an inspiring example of national recovery and liberation.

Toward Revolution in China

In 1860 the two-hundred-year-old Manchu Dynasty in China appeared on the verge of collapse. Efforts to repel the foreigner had failed, and rebellion and chaos wracked the country. Yet the government drew on its traditional strengths and made

The Empress Dowager Tzu Hsi   drew on conservative forces, like the court eunuchs surrounding her here, to maintain her power. Three years after her death in 1908, a revolution broke out and forced the last Chinese emperor, a boy of six, to abdicate. *(Source: Courtesy of the Freer Gallery of Art, Smithsonian Institution, Washington, D.C.)*

a surprising comeback that lasted more than thirty years.

Two factors were crucial in this reversal. First, the traditional ruling groups temporarily produced new and effective leadership. Loyal scholar-statesmen and generals quelled disturbances like the great Tai Ping rebellion. A truly remarkable woman, the empress dowager Tzu Hsi, governed in the name of her young son and combined shrewd insight with vigorous action to revitalize the bureaucracy.

Second, destructive foreign aggression lessened, for the Europeans had obtained their primary goal of commercial and diplomatic relations. Indeed, some Europeans contributed to the dynasty's recovery. A talented Irishman effectively reorganized China's customs office and increased the government tax receipts, while a sympathetic American diplomat represented China in foreign lands and helped strengthen the central government. Such efforts dovetailed with the dynasty's efforts to adopt some aspects of Western government and technology while maintaining traditional Chinese values and beliefs.

The parallel movement toward domestic reform and limited cooperation with the West collapsed under the blows of Japanese imperialism. The Sino-Japanese war of 1894 to 1895 and the subsequent harsh peace treaty revealed China's helplessness in the face of aggression, triggering a rush for foreign concessions and protectorates in China. At the high point of this rush in 1898, it appeared that the European powers might actually divide China among themselves, as they had recently divided Africa. Probably only the jealousy each nation felt toward its imperial competitors saved China from partition, although the United States' Open Door policy, which opposed formal annexation of Chinese territory, may have helped tip the balance. In any event, the tempo and impact of foreign penetration greatly accelerated after 1894.

So, too, did the intensity and radicalism of the Chinese reaction. Like the leaders of the Meiji Restoration, some modernizers saw salvation in Western institutions. In 1898 the government launched a desperate "hundred days of reform" in an attempt to meet the foreign challenge. More radical reformers like the revolutionary Sun Yat-sen (1866–1925), who came from the peasantry and was educated in Hawaii by Christian missionaries, sought to overthrow the dynasty altogether and establish a republic.

On the other side, some traditionalists turned back toward ancient practices, political conservatism, and fanatical hatred of the "foreign devils." "Protect the country, destroy the foreigner" was their simple motto. Such conservative, antiforeign patriots had often clashed with foreign missionaries, whom they charged with undermining reverence for ancestors and thereby threatening the Chinese family and the entire society. In the agony of defeat and unwanted reforms, secret societies like the Boxers rebelled. In northeastern China, more than two hundred foreign missionaries and several thousand Chinese Christians were killed. Once again, the imperialist response was swift and harsh. Peking was occupied and plundered by foreign armies. A heavy indemnity was imposed.

The years after the Boxer Rebellion (1900–1903) were ever more troubled. Anarchy and foreign influence spread, as the power and prestige of the Manchu Dynasty declined still further. Antiforeign, antigovernment revolutionary groups agitated and plotted. Finally, in 1912, a spontaneous uprising toppled the Manchu Dynasty. After thousands of years of emperors and empires, a loose coalition of revolutionaries proclaimed a Western-style republic and called for an elected parliament. The transformation of China under the impact of expanding Western society entered a new phase, and the end was not in sight.

SUMMARY

In the nineteenth century the industrializing West entered the third and most dynamic phase of its centuries-old expansion into non-Western lands. In so doing, Western nations profitably subordinated those lands to their economic interests, sent forth millions of emigrants, and established political influence in Asia and vast political empires in Africa. The reasons for this culminating surge were many, but the economic thrust of robust industrial capitalism, an ever-growing lead in technology, and the competitive pressures of European nationalism were particularly important.

Western expansion had far-reaching consequences. For the first time in human history, the world became in many ways a single unit. Moreover, European expansion diffused the ideas and techniques of a highly developed civilization. Yet the West relied on force to conquer and rule, and

Consequences of the French and Industrial

	Politics	Science and Technology
1800	Napoleonic era, 1799–1815	James Watt's steam engine promotes industrial breakthrough, 1780s
	Congress of Vienna, 1814–1815	
	"Battle of Peterloo," Great Britain, 1819	
1825	Greece wins independence, 1830	First railroad, Great Britain, 1825
	Revolution in France, 1830	Michael Faraday's studies in electromagnetism, 1830–1840s
	Great Britain: Reform Bill of 1832; Poor Law reform, 1834; Chartist movement and repeal of Corn Laws, 1838–1848	
	British complete occupation of India, 1848	
	Revolutions in Europe, 1848	
1850	Second Empire in France, 1852–1870	Modernization of Paris, ca 1850–187
	Crimean War, 1853–1856	Great Exhibition, London, 1851
	Unification of Italy, 1859–1870	Darwin, *Origin of Species,* 1859
	Civil War, United States, 1861–1865	Louis Pasteur develops germ theory o disease, 1860s
	Bismarck in power, Germany, 1862–1890	Suez Canal opened, 1869
	First Socialist International, 1864–1871	Dmitri Mendeleev develops the perio table, 1869
	Unification of Germany, 1866–1871	
	Second Reform Bill, Great Britain, 1867	
	Third Republic in France, 1870–1914	
1875	Congress of Berlin, 1878	Trans-Siberian Railroad, 1890s
	European "scramble for Africa," 1880–1900	Marie Curie, discovery of radium, 18
	Indian National Congress formed, 1883	
	Third Reform Bill, Great Britain, 1884	
	Berlin conference on imperialism, 1884	
	Second Socialist International, 1889–1914	
	Dreyfus affair in France, 1894–1899	
	Spanish-American War, 1898	
	Boer War, 1899–1902	
1900	Russo-Japanese War, 1904–1905	Max Planck develops quantum theory 1900
	Revolution in Russia, 1905	First airplane flight, 1903
	Balkan wars, 1912–1913	Einstein develops relativity theory, 1905–1910

Revolutions, 1800–1914

Economics and Society	Arts and Letters
Jeremy Bentham, 1748–1832	Romantic movement in the arts, ca 1790–1850
Thomas Malthus, *Essay on the Principle of Population,* 1798	Wordsworth, *Lyrical Ballads,* 1798
European economic imperialism, ca 1816–1880	Goya, *The Executions of the Third of May,* 1814
Height of French utopian socialism, 1830s–1840s	Balzac, *The Human Comedy,* 1829–1841
German Zollverein founded, 1834	Delacroix, *Liberty Leading the People,* 1830
European capitalists begin large-scale foreign investment, 1840s	Comte, *System of Positive Philosophy,* 1830–1842
Great Famine in Ireland, 1845–1851	Realism in art and literature, ca 1840–1870
Marx, *Communist Manifesto,* 1848	
Crédit Mobilier founded in France, 1852	Freud, 1856–1939
Japan opened to European influence, 1853	Flaubert, *Madame Bovary,* 1857
Emancipation of the serfs, Russia, 1861	
Marx, *Das Capital,* 1867	
Social welfare legislation, Germany, 1883–1889	Impressionism in art, ca 1870–1900
Witte directs modernization of Russian economy, 1892–1899	Zola, *Germinal,* 1885
Women's suffrage movement, England, ca 1900–1914	Cubism in art, ca 1905–1930
Social welfare legislation, France, 1904, 1910; England, 1906–1914	
Agrarian reforms in Russia, 1907–1912	

it treated non-Western peoples as racial inferiors. Thus non-Western elites, often armed with Western doctrines, gradually responded to the Western challenge. They launched a national, anti-imperialist struggle for dignity, genuine independence, and modernization. This struggle would emerge as a central drama of world history after the great European civil war of 1914 to 1918, which reduced the West's technological advantage and shattered its self-confidence and complacent moral superiority.

NOTES

1. Quoted in A. Waley, *The Opium War Through Chinese Eyes* (New York: Macmillan, 1958), p. 29.
2. Quoted in J. W. Hall, *Japan, from Prehistory to Modern Times* (New York: Delacorte Press, 1970), p. 250.
3. Quoted in R. Hallett, *Africa to 1875* (Ann Arbor: University of Michigan Press, 1970), p. 109.
4. Quoted in Earl of Cromer, *Modern Egypt* (London, 1911), p. 48.
5. Quoted in T. Blegen, *Norwegian Migration to America,* vol. 2 (Northfield, Minn.: Norwegian-American Historical Association, 1940), p. 468.
6. Quoted in I. Howe, *World of Our Fathers* (New York: Harcourt Brace Jovanovich, 1976), p. 25.
7. Quoted in C. A. Price, *The Great White Walls Are Built: Restrictive Immigration to North America and Australia, 1836–1888* (Canberra: Australian National University Press, 1974), p. 175.
8. Quoted in W. L. Langer, *European Alliances and Alignments, 1871–1890* (New York: Vintage Books, 1931), p. 290.
9. Quoted in J. Ellis, *The Social History of the Machine Gun* (New York: Pantheon Books, 1975), pp. 86, 101.
10. Quoted in G. H. Nadel and P. Curtis, eds., *Imperialism and Colonialism* (New York: Macmillan, 1964), p. 94.
11. Quoted in W. L. Langer, *The Diplomacy of Imperialism,* 2d ed. (New York: Alfred A. Knopf, 1951), pp. 86, 88.
12. Rudyard Kipling, *The Five Nations* (London, 1903), quoted by the permission of Mrs. George Bambridge, Methuen & Company, and Doubleday & Company, Inc.
13. E. H. Berman, "African Responses to Christian Mission Education," *African Studies Review* 17 (1974): 530.
14. Quoted in Langer, *Diplomacy of Imperialism,* p. 88.
15. Quoted in Ellis, pp. 99–100.
16. Quoted in K. M. Panikkar, *Asia and Western Dominance: A Survey of the Vasco da Gama Epoch of Asian History* (London: George Allen & Unwin, 1959), p. 116.
17. Quoted in Hall, p. 289.

SUGGESTED READING

General surveys of European expansion in a broad perspective include R. Betts, *Europe Overseas* (1968); A. Thornton, *Imperialism in the Twentieth Century* (1977); T. Smith, *The Patterns of Imperialism* (1981); and W. Woodruff, *Impact of Western Man* (1967), which has an extensive bibliography. D. K. Fieldhouse has also written two fine surveys, *Economics and Empire, 1830–1914* (1970) and *Colonialism, 1870–1945* (1981). G. Barraclough, *An Introduction to Contemporary History* (1964), argues powerfully that Western imperialism and the non-Western reaction to it have been crucial in world history since about 1890. J. A. Hobson's classic *Imperialism* (1902) is readily available, and the Marxist-Leninist case is effectively presented in V. G. Kieran, *Marxism and Imperialism* (1975). Two excellent anthologies on the problem of European expansion are the volume by Nadel and Curtis cited in the Notes and H. Wright, ed., *The "New Imperialism,"* rev. ed. (1975).

Britain's leading position in European imperialism is examined in a lively way by B. Porter, *The Lion's Share* (1976); J. Morris, *Pax Britannica* (1968); and D. Judd, *The Victorian Empire* (1970), a stunning pictorial history. B. Semmel has written widely on the intellectual foundations of English expansion, as in *The Rise of Free Trade Imperialism* (1970). J. Gallegher and R. Robinson, *Africa and the Victorians: The Climax of Imperialism* (1961), is an influential reassessment. H. Brunschwig, *French Colonialism, 1871–1914* (1966), and W. Baumgart, *Imperialism: The Idea and Reality of British and French Colonial Expansion* (1982), are well-balanced studies. A. Moorehead, *The White Nile* (1971), tells the fascinating story of the European exploration of the mysterious upper Nile. Volumes 5 and 6 of K. Latourette, *History of the Expansion of Christianity,* 7 vols. (1937–1945), examine the powerful impulse for missionary work in non-European areas. D. Headrick stresses Western technological superiority in *Tools of Empire* (1981).

Howe and Blegen, cited in the Notes, provide dramatic accounts of Jewish and Norwegian migration to the United States. Most other migrant groups have also found their historians: M. Walker, *Germany and the Emigration, 1816–1885* (1964), and W. Adams, *Ireland and Irish Emigration to the New World* (reissued 1967), are outstanding. Langer's volumes consider the diplomatic aspects of imperialism in exhaustive detail. Ellis's well-illustrated study of the machine gun is fascinating, as is Price on the restriction of Asian migration to Australia. All these works are cited in the Notes.

E. Wolf, *Europe and the People Without History* (1982), considers the impact of imperialism on non-Western peoples with skill and compassion. Two unusual and provocative studies on personal relations between European rulers and non-European subjects are D. Mannoni, *Prospero and Caliban: The Psychology of Colonialization* (1964), and F. Fanon, *Wretched of the Earth* (1965), a bitter attack on white racism by a black psychologist active in the Algerian revolution. Novels also bring the psychological and human dimensions of imperialism alive. H. Rider Haggard, *King Solomon's Mines,* portrays the powerful appeal of adventure in exotic lands, while Rudyard Kipling, the greatest writer of European expansion, is at his stirring best in *Kim* and *Soldiers Three.* Joseph Conrad unforgettably probes European motives in *Heart of Darkness,* while André Gide, *The Immoralist,* closely examines European moral corruption in North Africa.

Hall, cited in the Notes, is an excellent introduction to the history of Japan. Waley, also cited in the Notes, has written extensively and well on China. I. Hsü, *The Rise of Modern China,* 2d ed. (1975), and K. Latourette, *The Chinese: Their History and Culture,* rev. ed. (1964), are fine histories with many suggestions for further reading. E. Reischauer's topical survey, *Japan: The Story of a Nation* (1981), is recommended, as are T. Huber, *The Revolutionary Origins of Modern Japan* (1981), and Y. Fukuzawa, *Autobiography* (1966), the personal account of a leading intellectual who witnessed the emergence of modern Japan.

G. Perry, *The Middle East: Fourteen Islamic Centuries* (1983), concisely surveys nineteenth-century developments and provides up-to-date bibliographies. B. Lewis, *The Middle East and the West* (1963), is a penetrating analysis of the impact of Western ideas on Middle Eastern thought. Hallett, cited in the Notes, and R. July, *A History of the African People* (1970), contain excellent introductions to Africa in the age of imperialism. J. D. Fage, *A History of Africa* (1978), is also recommended. A classic study of Western expansion from an Indian viewpoint is Panikkar's volume mentioned in the Notes. S. Wolpert, *A New History of India,* 2d ed. (1982), incorporates recent scholarship in a wide-ranging study that is highly recommended.

27

The Great Break:
War and Revolution

In the summer of 1914 the nations of Europe went willingly to war. They believed they had no other choice. Moreover, both peoples and governments confidently expected a short war leading to a decisive victory. Such a war, they believed, would "clear the air," and European society would be able to go on as before.

These expectations were almost totally mistaken. The First World War was long, indecisive, and tremendously destructive. To the shell-shocked generation of survivors, it was known simply as the Great War: the war of unprecedented scope and intensity. From today's perspective it is clear that the First World War marked a great break in the course of Western historical development since the French and Industrial revolutions. A noted British political scientist has gone so far as to say that even in victorious and relatively fortunate Great Britain, the First World War was *the* great turning point in government and society, "as in everything else in modern British history. . . . There's a much greater difference between the Britain of 1914 and, say, 1920, than between the Britain of 1920 and today."[1]

This is a strong statement, but it contains a great amount of truth, for all of Europe as well as for Britain. It suggests three questions this chapter will try to answer.

- What caused the Great War?
- How and why did war and revolution have such enormous and destructive consequences?
- And how did the years of trauma and bloodshed form elements of today's world, many of which people now accept and even cherish?

THE FIRST WORLD WAR

The First World War was so long and destructive because it involved all the Great Powers and because it quickly degenerated into a senseless military stalemate. Like evenly matched boxers in a championship bout, the two sides tried to wear each other down. There was no referee to call a draw, only the blind hammering of a life-or-death struggle.

The Bismarckian System of Alliances

The Franco-Prussian War and the foundation of the German Empire opened a new era in international relations. France was decisively defeated in 1871 and forced to pay a large war indemnity and give up Alsace-Lorraine. In ten short years, from 1862 to 1871, Bismarck had made Prussia-Germany—traditionally the weakest of the Great Powers—the most powerful nation in Europe (see pages 797–801). Had Bismarck been a Napoleon I or a Hitler, for whom no gain was ever sufficient, continued expansion would no doubt sooner or later have raised a powerful coalition against the new German Empire. Yet he was not. As Bismarck never tired of repeating after 1871, Germany was a "satisfied" power. Within Europe, Germany had no territorial ambitions and only wanted peace.

But how was peace to be preserved? The most serious threat to peace came from the east, from Austria-Hungary and from Russia. Those two enormous multinational empires had many conflicting interests, particularly in the Balkans, where the Ottoman Empire—the "sick man of Europe"—was ebbing fast. There was a real threat that Germany might be dragged into a great war between the two rival empires. Bismarck's solution was a system of alliances (Figure 27.1) to restrain both Russia and Austria-Hungary, to prevent conflict between them, and to isolate a hostile France.

A first step was the creation in 1873 of the conservative Three Emperors' League, which linked the monarchs of Austria-Hungary, Germany, and Russia in an alliance against radical movements. In 1877 and 1878, when Russia's victories over the Ottoman Empire threatened the balance of Austrian and Russian interests in the Balkans and the balance of British and Russian interests in the Middle East, Bismarck played the role of sincere peacemaker. At the Congress of Berlin in 1878, he saw that Austria obtained the right to "occupy and administer" the Ottoman provinces of Bosnia and Herzegovina to counterbalance Russian gains, while independent Balkan states were also carved from the disintegrating Ottoman Empire.

Bismarck's balancing efforts at the Congress of Berlin infuriated Russian nationalists, and this led Bismarck to conclude a defensive military alliance with Austria against Russia in 1879. Motivated by tensions with France, Italy joined Germany and

The Congress of Berlin, 1878   With the Austrian representative on his right and with other participants looking on, Bismarck the mediator symbolically seals the hard-won agreement by shaking hands with the chief Russian negotiator. The Great Powers often relied on such special conferences to settle their international disputes. *(Source: The Bettmann Archive)*

Austria in 1882, thereby forming what became known as the Triple Alliance.

Bismarck continued to work for peace in eastern Europe, seeking to neutralize tensions between Austria-Hungary and Russia. In 1881 he capitalized on their mutual fears and cajoled them both into a secret alliance with Germany. This Alliance of the Three Emperors lasted until 1887. It established the principle of cooperation among all three powers in any further division of the Ottoman Empire, while each state pledged friendly neutrality in case one of the three found itself at war with a fourth power (except the Ottoman Empire).

Bismarck also maintained good relations with Britain and Italy, while cooperating with France in Africa but keeping France isolated in Europe. In 1887 Russia declined to renew the Alliance of the Three Emperors because of new tensions in the Balkans. Bismarck craftily substituted a Russian-German Reinsurance Treaty, by which both states promised neutrality if the other were attacked.

Bismarck's accomplishments in foreign policy after 1871 were great. For almost a generation, he maintained German leadership in international affairs, and he worked successfully for peace by managing conflicts and by restraining Austria-Hungary and Russia with defensive alliances.

The Rival Blocs

In 1890 the young, impetuous emperor William II dismissed Bismarck, in part because of the chancellor's friendly policy toward Russia since the 1870s. William then adamantly refused to renew the Russian-German Reinsurance Treaty, in spite of Russian willingness to do so. This fateful departure in foreign affairs prompted long-isolated republican

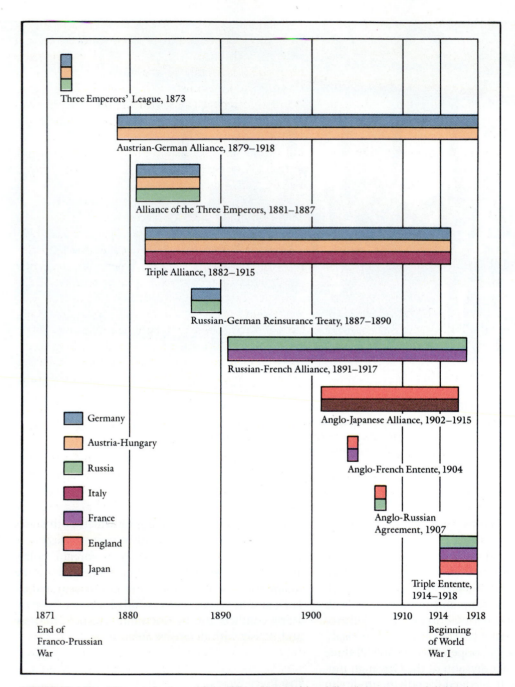

Germany
Austria-Hungary
Russia
Italy
France
England
Japan

Three Emperors' League, 1873

Austrian-German Alliance, 1879–1918

Alliance of the Three Emperors, 1881–1887

Triple Alliance, 1882–1915

Russian-German Reinsurance Treaty, 1887–1890

Russian-French Alliance, 1891–1917

Anglo-Japanese Alliance, 1902–1915

Anglo-French Entente, 1904

Anglo-Russian Agreement, 1907

Triple Entente, 1914–1918

| 1871 | 1880 | 1890 | 1900 | 1910 | 1914 | 1918 |

1871
End of
Franco-Prussian
War

1914
Beginning
of World
War I

FIGURE 27.1 The Alliance System After 1871 Bismarck's subtle diplomacy maintained reasonably good relations among the eastern monarchies—Germany, Russia, and Austria-Hungary—and kept France isolated. The situation changed dramatically in 1891, when the Russian-French Alliance divided the Great Powers into two fairly equal military blocs.

France to court absolutist Russia, offering loans, arms, and friendship. In both countries there were enthusiastic public demonstrations, and in St. Petersburg harbor the autocratic Alexander III stood bareheaded on a French battleship while a band played the *Marseillaise,* the hymn of the Revolution. A preliminary agreement between the two countries was reached in 1891, and in early 1894 France and Russia became military allies. This alliance (see Figure 27.1) was to remain in effect as long as the Triple Alliance of Austria, Germany, and Italy: continental Europe was dangerously divided into two rival blocs.

The policy of Great Britain became increasingly crucial. Long content with "splendid isolation" and no permanent alliances, Britain after 1891 was the only uncommitted Great Power. Could Britain afford to remain isolated, or would it feel compelled to take sides? Alliance with France or Russia certainly seemed highly unlikely. With its vast and rapidly expanding empire, Britain was often in serious conflict with these countries around the world in the heyday of imperialism.

Britain also squabbled with Germany, for Emperor William II was a master of tactless public statements, and Britain found Germany's pursuit of greater world power after about 1897 vaguely disquieting. Nevertheless, many Germans and some Britons believed that their leaders would eventually formalize the "natural alliance" they felt already united the advanced, racially related Germanic and Anglo-Saxon peoples. Alas, such an understanding never materialized. Instead, the generally good relations that had prevailed between Prussia and Great Britain ever since the mid-eighteenth century, and certainly under Bismarck, gave way to a bitter Anglo-German rivalry.

There were several reasons for this tragic development. The hard-fought Boer War (1899–1902) between the British and the tiny Dutch republics of South Africa had a major impact on British policy. British political leaders saw that Britain was overextended around the world. The Boer War also brought into the open widespread anti-British feeling, as editorial writers in many nations denounced the latest manifestation of British imperialism. There was even talk of Germany, Austria, France, and Russia forming a grand alliance against the bloated but insatiable British Empire. Therefore, British leaders prudently set about shoring up their exposed position with alliance and agreements.

Britain improved its often-strained relations with the United States and in 1902 concluded a formal alliance with Japan (see Figure 27.1). Britain then responded favorably to the advances of France's skillful foreign minister, Théophile Delcassé, who wanted better relations with Britain and was willing to accept British rule in Egypt in return for British support of French plans to dominate Morocco. The resulting Anglo-French Entente of 1904 settled all outstanding colonial disputes between Britain and France.

Frustrated by Britain's turn toward France in 1904, Germany decided to test the strength of the entente and drive Britain and France apart. First Germany threatened and bullied France into dismissing Delcassé. However, rather than accept the typical territorial payoff of imperial competition—a slice of French jungle in Africa or a port in Morocco—in return for French primacy in Morocco, the Germans foolishly rattled their swords in 1905. They insisted on an international conference on the whole Moroccan question without presenting precise or reasonable demands. Germany's crude bullying forced France and Britain closer together, and Germany left the Algeciras Conference of 1906 empty-handed and isolated (except for Austria-Hungary).

The result of the Moroccan crisis and the Algeciras Conference was something of a diplomatic revolution. Britain, France, Russia, and even the United States began to see Germany as a potential threat, a would-be intimidator that might seek to dominate all Europe. At the same time, German leaders began to see sinister plots to "encircle" Germany and block its development as a world power. In 1907 Russia, battered by the disastrous war with Japan and the revolution of 1905, agreed to settle its quarrels with Great Britain in Persia and central Asia with a special Anglo-Russian Agreement (see Figure 27.1). As a result of that agreement, Germany's blustering paranoia increased and so did Britain's thinly disguised hostility.

Germany's decision to add a large, enormously expensive fleet of big-gun battleships to its already expanding navy also heightened tensions after 1907. German nationalists, led by the all-too-persuasive Admiral Tirpitz, saw a large navy as the legitimate mark of a great world power. But British leaders like Lloyd George saw it as a detestable military challenge, which forced them to spend the "People's Budget" on battleships rather than social welfare. As Germany's rapid industrial growth allowed it to overcome Britain's early lead, economic rivalry also contributed to distrust and hostility between the two nations. Unscrupulous journalists and special-interest groups in both countries portrayed healthy competition in foreign trade and investment as a form of economic warfare.

Many educated shapers of public opinion and ordinary people in Britain and Germany were increasingly locked in a fateful "love-hate" relationship between the two countries. Proud nationalists in both countries simultaneously admired and feared the power and accomplishments of their nearly equal rival. In 1909 the mass-circulation London *Daily Mail* hysterically informed its readers in a series of reports that "Germany is deliberately preparing to destroy the British Empire."[2] By then, Britain was psychologically, if not officially, in the Franco-Russian camp. The leading nations of Europe were divided into two hostile blocs, both ill prepared to deal with upheaval on Europe's southeastern frontier.

The Outbreak of War

In the early years of this century, war in the Balkans was as inevitable as anything can be in human history. The reason was simple: nationalism was destroying the Ottoman Empire and threatening to break up the Austro-Hungarian Empire. The only questions were what kinds of wars would occur and where they would lead.

Greece had long before led the struggle for national liberation, winning its independence in 1832. In 1875 widespread nationalist rebellion in the Ottoman Empire had resulted in Turkish repression, Russian intervention, and Great Power tensions. Bismarck had helped resolve this crisis at the 1878 Congress of Berlin, which worked out the

German Warships Under Full Steam   As these impressive ships engaged in battle exercises in 1907 suggest, Germany did succeed in building a large modern navy. But Britain was equally determined to maintain its naval superiority, and the spiraling arms race helped poison relations between the two countries. *(Source: Bibliothèque des Arts Décoratifs/Jean-Loup Charmet)*

MAP 27.1 The Balkans After the Congress of Berlin, 1878 The Ottoman Empire suffered large territorial losses but remained a power in the Balkans.

MAP 27.2 The Balkans in 1914 Ethnic boundaries did not follow political boundaries, and Serbian national aspirations threatened Austria-Hungary.

partial division of Turkish possessions in Europe. Austria-Hungary obtained the right to "occupy and administer" Bosnia and Herzegovina. Serbia and Rumania won independence, and a part of Bulgaria won local autonomy. The Ottoman Empire retained important Balkan holdings, for Austria-Hungary and Russia each feared the other's domination of totally independent states in the area (Map 27.1).

After 1878 the siren call of imperialism lured European energies, particularly Russian energies, away from the Balkans. This diversion helped preserve the fragile balance of interests in southeastern Europe. By 1903, however, Balkan nationalism was on the rise once again. Serbia led the way, becoming openly hostile toward both Austria-Hungary and the Ottoman Empire. The Serbs, a Slavic

people, looked to Slavic Russia for support of their national aspirations. To block Serbian expansion and to take advantage of Russia's weakness after the revolution of 1905, Austria in 1908 formally annexed Bosnia and Herzegovina with their predominately Serbian populations. The kingdom of Serbia erupted in rage but could do nothing without Russian support.

Then in 1912, in the First Balkan War, Serbia turned southward. With Greece and Bulgaria it took Macedonia from the Ottoman Empire and then quarreled with its ally Bulgaria over the spoils of victory—a dispute that led in 1913 to the Second Balkan War. Austria intervened in 1913 and forced Serbia to give up Albania. After centuries, nationalism had finally destroyed the Ottoman Empire in Europe (Map 27.2). This sudden but long-awaited event elated the Balkan nationalists and dismayed the leaders of multinational Austria-Hungary. The former hoped and the latter feared that Austria might be next to be broken apart.

Within this tense context, Archduke Francis Ferdinand, heir to the Austrian and Hungarian thrones, and his wife Sophie were assassinated by Bosnian revolutionaries on June 28, 1914, during a state visit to the Bosnian capital of Sarajevo. The assassins were closely connected to the ultranationalist Serbian society The Black Hand. This revolutionary group was secretly supported by members of the Serbian government and was dedicated to uniting all Serbians in a single state. Although the leaders of Austria-Hungary did not and could not know all the details of Serbia's involvement in the assassination plot, they concluded after some hesitation that Serbia had to be severely punished once and for all. After a month of maneuvering, Austria-Hungary presented Serbia with an unconditional ultimatum, on July 23.

The Serbian government had just forty-eight hours in which to agree to cease all subversion in Austria and all anti-Austrian propaganda in Serbia. Moreover, a thorough investigation of all aspects of the assassination at Sarajevo was to be undertaken in Serbia by a joint commission of Serbian and Austrian officials. These demands amounted to control of the Serbian state. When Serbia replied moderately but evasively, Austria began to mobilize and then declared war on Serbia on July 28. Thus a desperate multinational Austria-Hungary deliberately chose war in a last-ditch attempt to stem the rising tide of hostile nationalism. The "Third Balkan War" had begun.

Of prime importance in Austria-Hungary's fateful decision was Germany's unconditional support. Emperor William II and his chancellor Theobald von Bethmann-Hollweg gave Austria-Hungary a "blank check" and urged aggressive measures in early July, even though they realized that war between Austria and Russia was the most probable result. They knew Russian pan-Slavs saw Russia not only as the protector, but also as the eventual liberator, of southern Slavs. As one pan-Slav had said much earlier, "Austria can hold her part of the Slavonian mass as long as Turkey holds hers and vice versa."[3] At the very least a resurgent Russia could not stand by, as in the Bosnian crisis, and simply watch the Serbs be crushed. Yet Bethmann-Hollweg apparently hoped that while Russia (and therefore France) would go to war, Great Britain would remain neutral, unwilling to fight for "Russian aggression" in the distant Balkans. After all, Britain had reached only "friendly understandings" with France and Russia on colonial questions and had no alliance with either power.

In fact, the diplomatic situation was already out of control. Military plans and timetables began to dictate policy. Russia, a vast country, would require much longer to mobilize its armies than Germany and Austria-Hungary. On July 28, as Austrian armies bombarded Belgrade, Tsar Nicholas II ordered a partial mobilization against Austria-Hungary. Almost immediately he found that this was impossible. All the complicated mobilization plans of the Russian general staff had assumed a war with both Austria and Germany: Russia could not mobilize against one without mobilizing against the other. On July 29, therefore, Russia ordered full mobilization and in effect declared general war. For, as the French general Boisdeffre had said to the agreeing Russian tsar when the Franco-Russian military convention was being negotiated in 1892, "mobilization is a declaration of war."[4]

The same tragic subordination of political considerations to military strategy descended on Germany. The German general staff had also thought only in terms of a two-front war. Their plan for war —the Schlieffen plan, the work of Count Alfred von Schlieffen, chief of the German general staff from 1891 to 1906 and a professional military man —called for knocking out France first with a lightning attack through neutral Belgium before turning on Russia.

Thus, on August 2, 1914, General Helmuth von Moltke, "acting under a dictate of self-preservation," demanded that Belgium permit German armies to pass through its territory. Belgium, whose neutrality had been solemnly guaranteed in 1839 by all the great states including Prussia, refused. Germany attacked. Thus Germany's terrible, politically disastrous response to a war in the Balkans was an all-out invasion of France by way of the plains of neutral Belgium on August 3. In the face of this act of aggression, Great Britain joined France and declared war on Germany the following day. The First World War had begun.

Reflections on the Origins of the War

Although few events in history have aroused such interest and controversy as the coming of the First

World War, the question of immediate causes and responsibilities can be answered with considerable certainty. Austria-Hungary deliberately started the "Third Balkan War." A war for the right to survive was Austria-Hungary's desperate, although understandable, response to the aggressive, yet understandable, revolutionary drive of Serbian nationalists to unify their people in a single state. In spite of Russian intervention in the quarrel, it is clear from the beginning of the crisis that Germany not only pushed and goaded Austria-Hungary but was also responsible for turning a little war into the Great War by means of its sledgehammer attack on Belgium and France.

After Bismarck's resignation in 1890, German leaders lost control of the international system. They felt increasingly that Germany's status as a world power was declining while that of Britain, France, Russia, and the United States was growing. Indeed, the powers of what officially became in August 1914 the Triple Entente—Great Britain, France, and Russia—were checking Germany's vague but real aspirations, as well as working to strangle Austria-Hungary, Germany's only real ally. Germany's aggression in 1914 reflected the failure of all European leaders, not just those in Germany, to incorporate Bismarck's mighty empire permanently and peacefully into the international system.

There were other underlying causes. The new overseas expansion—imperialism—did not play a direct role, since the European powers always settled their colonial conflicts peacefully. Yet the easy imperialist victories did contribute to a general European overconfidence and reinforced national rivalries. In this respect imperialism was thought to be influential.

The triumph of nationalism was a crucial underlying precondition of the Great War. Nationalism was at the heart of the Balkan wars, in the form of Serbian aspirations and the grandiose pan-German versus pan-Slavic racism of some fanatics. Nationalism drove the spiraling arms race. More generally, as shown in Chapter 25, the aristocracy and middle classes arrived at nationalistic compromises, while ordinary people looked toward increasingly responsive states for psychological and material well-being.

Broad popular commitment to "my country right or wrong" weakened groups that thought in terms of international communities and consequences. Thus the big international bankers, who

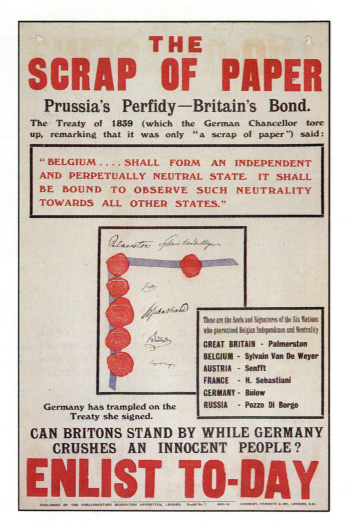

This British Poster shows the signature page of the 1839 treaty guaranteeing the neutrality of Belgium. When German armies invaded Belgium in 1914, Chancellor Bethmann-Hollweg cynically dismissed the treaty as a "scrap of paper"—a perfect line for anti-German propaganda. *(Source: By courtesy of the Trustees of the Imperial War Museum)*

were frightened by the prospect of war in July 1914, and the extreme-left socialists, who believed that the enemy was at home and not abroad, were equally out of step with national feeling.

Finally, the wealthy governing classes underestimated the risk of war in 1914. They had forgotten that great wars and great social revolutions very often go together in history. Metternich's alliance of conservative forces in support of international peace and the domestic status quo had become only a distant memory.

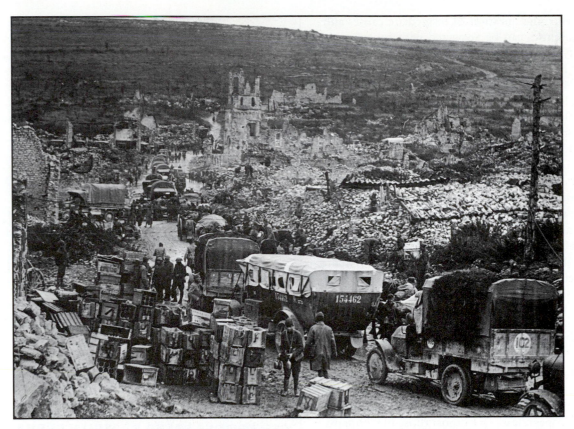

Preparing the Attack The great offenses of the First World War required the mobilization of men and material on an unprecedented scale. This photo shows American troops moving up. *(Source: U.S. Army Signal Corps)*

The First Battle of the Marne

When the Germans invaded Belgium in August 1914, they and everyone else believed that the war would be short, for urban society rested on the food and raw materials of the world economy: "The boys will be home by Christmas." The Belgian army heroically defended its homeland, however, and fell back in good order to join a rapidly landed British army corps near the Franco-Belgian border. This action complicated the original Schlieffen plan of concentrating German armies on the right wing and boldly capturing Paris in a vast encircling movement. Moreover, the German left wing in Lorraine failed to retreat, thwarting the plan to suck French armies into Germany and then annihilate them. Instead, by the end of August, dead-tired German soldiers were advancing along an enormous front in the scorching summer heat. The neatly designed prewar plan to surround Paris

from the north and west had been thrown into confusion.

French armies totaling 1 million, reinforced by more than 100,000 British troops, had retreated in orderly fashion before Germany's 1.5 million men in the field. Under the leadership of the steel-nerved General Joseph Joffre, the French attacked a gap in the German line at the Battle of the Marne on September 6. For three days, France threw everything into the attack. At one point, the French government desperately requisitioned all the taxis of Paris to rush reserves to the troops at the front. Finally, the Germans fell back. Paris and France had been miraculously saved.

Stalemate and Slaughter

The attempts of French and British armies to turn the German retreat into a rout were unsuccessful, and so were moves by both sides to outflank each other in northern France. As a result, both sides began to dig trenches to protect themselves from machine gun fire. By November 1914 an unbroken line of trenches extended from the Belgian ports through northern France past the fortress of Verdun and on to the Swiss frontier.

In the face of this unexpected stalemate, slaughter on the western front began in earnest. The defenders on both sides dug in behind rows of trenches, mines, and barbed wire. For days and even weeks, ceaseless shelling by heavy artillery supposedly "softened up" the enemy in a given area (and also signaled the coming attack). Then young draftees and their junior officers went "over the top" of the trenches in frontal attacks on the enemy's line.

The cost in lives was staggering, the gains in territory minuscule. The massive French and British offensives during 1915 never gained more than three miles of blood-soaked earth from the enemy. In the Battle of the Somme in the summer of 1916, the British and French gained an insignificant 125 square miles at the cost of 600,000 dead or wounded, while the Germans lost half a million men. That same year, the unsuccessful German campaign against Verdun cost 700,000 lives on both sides. The British poet Siegfried Sassoon (1886–1967) wrote of the Somme offensive: "I am staring at a sunlit picture of Hell."

Terrible 1917 saw General Robert Nivelle's French army almost destroyed in a grand spring attack at Champagne, while at Passchendaele in the fall, the British traded 400,000 casualties for 50

The Fruits of War   The extent of carnage, the emotional damage, and the physical destruction were equally unprecedented. Once great cathedrals standing in ruin symbolized the disaster. *(Source: UPI/Bettmann Newsphotos)*

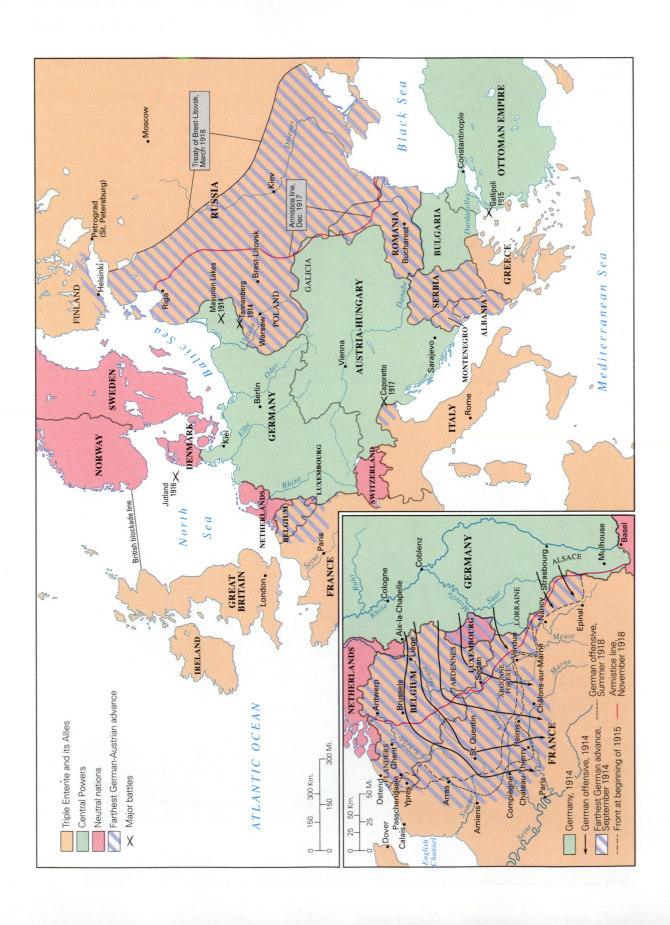

square miles of Belgian Flanders. The hero of Erich Remarque's great novel *All Quiet on the Western Front* (1929) describes one such attack:

We see men living with their skulls blown open; we see soldiers run with their two feet cut off. . . . Still the little piece of convulsed earth in which we lie is held. We have yielded no more than a few hundred yards of it as a prize to the enemy. But on every yard there lies a dead man.

Such was war on the western front.

The war of the trenches shattered an entire generation of young men. Millions who could have provided political creativity and leadership after the war were forever missing. Moreover, those who lived through the holocaust were maimed, shell-shocked, embittered, and profoundly disillusioned. The young soldiers went to war believing in the world of their leaders and elders, the pre-1914 world of order, progress, and patriotism. Then, in Remarque's words, the "first bombardment showed us our mistake, and under it the world as they had taught it to us broke in pieces." For many, the sacrifice and comradeship of the battlefield became life's crucial experience, an experience that "soft" civilians could never understand. A chasm opened up between veterans and civilians, making the difficult postwar reconstruction all the more difficult.

The Widening War

On the eastern front, slaughter did not degenerate into suicidal trench warfare. With the outbreak of the war, the "Russian steamroller" immediately moved into eastern Germany. Very badly damaged by the Germans under Generals Paul von Hindenburg and Erich Ludendorff at the battles of Tannenberg and the Masurian Lakes in August and September 1914, Russia never threatened Germany again. On the Austrian front, enormous armies seesawed back and forth, suffering enormous losses. Austro-Hungarian armies were repulsed twice by little Serbia in bitter fighting. But with the help of German forces, they reversed the Russian advances

MAP 27.3 The First World War in Europe The trench war on the western front was concentrated in Belgium and northern France, while the war in the east encompassed an enormous territory.

of 1914 and forced the Russians to retreat deep into their own territory in the eastern campaign of 1915. A staggering 2.5 million Russians were killed, wounded, or taken prisoner that year.

These changing tides of victory and defeat brought neutral countries into the war (Map 27.3). Italy, a member of the Triple Alliance since 1882, had declared its neutrality in 1914 on the grounds that Austria had launched a war of aggression. Then, in May 1915, Italy joined the Triple Entente of Great Britain, France, and Russia in return for promises of Austrian territory. Bulgaria allied with Austria and Germany, now known as the Central Powers, in September 1915 in order to settle old scores with Serbia.

The entry of Italy and Bulgaria in 1915 was part of a general widening of the war. The Balkans, with the exception of Greece, came to be occupied by the Central Powers, and British forces were badly defeated in 1915 trying to take the Dardanelles from Turkey, Germany's ally. More successful was the entente's attempt to incite Arab nationalists against their Turkish overlords. An enigmatic British colonel, soon known to millions as Lawrence of Arabia, aroused the Arab princes to revolt in early 1917. In 1918 British armies from Egypt smashed the Ottoman Empire once and for all. In their Middle East campaign, the British drew on forces from Australia, New Zealand, and India. Contrary to German hopes, the colonial subjects of the British (and French) did not revolt but loyally supported their foreign masters. The European war extended around the globe as Great Britain, France, and Japan seized Germany's colonies.

A crucial development in the expanding conflict came in April 1917, when the United States declared war on Germany. American intervention grew out of the war at sea, sympathy for the Triple Entente, and the increasing desperation of total war. At the beginning of the war, Britain and France had established a total naval blockade to strangle the Central Powers and prevent deliveries of food and raw materials from overseas. No neutral ship was permitted to sail to Germany with any cargo. The blockade annoyed Americans, but effective propaganda over German atrocities in occupied Belgium, as well as lush profits from selling war supplies to Britain and France, blunted American indignation.

Moreover, in early 1915 Germany launched a counter-blockade using the murderously effective submarine, a new weapon that violated traditional niceties of fair warning under international law. In May 1915, after sinking about ninety ships in the British war zone, a German submarine sank the British passenger liner *Lusitania,* which was also carrying arms and munitions. More than a thousand lives, among them 139 Americans, were lost. President Woodrow Wilson protested vigorously. Germany was forced to relax its submarine warfare for almost two years; the alternative was almost certain war with the United States.

Early in 1917, the German military command—confident that improved submarines could starve their island enemy, Britain, into submission before the United States could come to its rescue—resumed unrestricted submarine warfare. Like the invasion of Belgium, this was a reckless gamble. British shipping losses reached staggering proportions, though by late 1917 naval strategists came up with the inevitable effective response: the convoy system for safe transatlantic shipping. In the meantime, the embattled President Wilson had told a sympathetic Congress and people that the "German submarine warfare against commerce is a warfare against mankind." Thus the last uncommitted great nation, as fresh and enthusiastic as Europe had been in 1914, entered the world war in April 1917, almost three years after it began. Eventually the United States was to tip the balance in favor of the Triple Entente and its allies.

THE HOME FRONT

Before looking at the last year of the Great War, let us turn our attention to the people on the home front. The people behind the lines were tremendously involved in the titanic struggle. War's impact on them was no less massive than on the men crouched in the trenches.

Mobilizing for Total War

In August 1914 most people had greeted the outbreak of hostilities enthusiastically. In every country, the masses believed that their nation was in the right and defending itself from aggression. With the exception of a few extreme left-wingers, even socialists supported the war. Tough standby plans to imprison socialist leaders and break general

strikes protesting the war proved quite unnecessary in 1914. In Germany, for example, the trade unions voted not to strike, and socialists in the parliament voted money for war credits in order to counter the threat of Russian despotism. A German socialist volunteered for the front, explaining to fellow members of the Reichstag that "to shed one's blood for the fatherland is not difficult: it is enveloped in romantic heroism."[5] Everywhere the support of the masses and working class contributed to national unity and an energetic war effort.

By mid-October generals and politicians began to realize that more than patriotism would be needed to win the war, whose end was not in sight. Each country experienced a relentless, desperate demand for men and weapons. In France, for example, the generals found themselves needing 100,000 heavy artillery shells a day, as opposed to the 12,000 they had anticipated using. This enormous quantity had to come from a French steel industry that had lost three-fourths of its iron resources in the first days of the war, when Germany seized the mines of French Lorraine. Each belligerent quickly faced countless shortages, for prewar Europe had depended on foreign trade and a great international division of labor. In each country economic life and organization had to change and change fast to keep the war machine from sputtering to a stop. And change they did.

In each country a government of national unity began to plan and control economic and social life in order to wage "total war." Free-market capitalism was abandoned, at least "for the duration." Instead, government planning boards established priorities and decided what was to be produced and consumed. Rationing, price and wage controls, and even restrictions on workers' freedom of movement were imposed by government. Only through such regimentation could a country make the greatest possible military effort. Thus, though there were national variations, the great nations all moved toward planned economies commanded by the established political leadership.

This revolutionary development would burn deeply into the twentieth-century consciousness. The planned economy of total war released the tremendous energies first harnessed by the French under Robespierre during the French Revolution. Total war, however, was based on tremendously productive industrial economies not confined to a single nation. The result was an effective—and therefore destructive—war effort on all sides.

Waging Total War   A British war plant strains to meet the insatiable demand for trench-smashing heavy artillery shells. Quite typically, many of these defense workers are women. *(Source: By courtesy of the Trustees of the Imperial War Museum)*

Moreover, the economy of total war blurred the old distinction between soldiers on the battlefield and civilians at home. As President Wilson told Americans shortly after the United States entered the war, there were no armies in the struggle in the traditional sense. Rather, "there are entire nations armed. Thus the men [and women] who remain to till the soil and man the factories are not less a part of the army than the men beneath the battle flags."[6] The war was a war of whole peoples and entire populations, and the loser would be the society that cracked first.

Finally, however awful the war was, the ability of governments to manage and control highly complicated economies strengthened the cause of socialism. With the First World War, socialism became for the first time a realistic economic blueprint rather than a utopian program.

Germany illustrates the general trend. It also went furthest in developing a planned economy to wage total war. As soon as war began, Walter Rathenau, the talented, foresighted Jewish industrialist in charge of Germany's largest electrical company, convinced the government to set up a War Raw Materials Board to ration and distribute raw materials. Under Rathenau's direction, every useful material from foreign oil to barnyard manure was inventoried and rationed. Moreover, the board launched successful attempts to produce substitutes, such as synthetic rubber and synthetic nitrates. Without the spectacular double achievement of discovering a way to "fix" nitrogen present in the air and then producing synthetic nitrates in enormous quantity, the blockaded German war machine would have stalled in a matter of months.

Food was also rationed in accordance with physical need. Men and women doing hard manual work were given extra rations. During the last two years of the war, only children and expectant mothers received milk rations. Sometimes mistakes were made that would have been funny if they had not been tragic. In early 1915 German authorities calculated that greedy pigs were eating food that hungry people needed, and they ordered a "hog massacre" only to find that there were too few pigs left to eat an abundant potato crop. Germany also failed to tax the war profits of private firms heavily enough. This contributed to massive deficit financing, inflation, the growth of a black market, and the eventual re-emergence of class conflict.

Following the terrible battles of Verdun and the Somme in 1916, the military leaders Hindenburg and Ludendorff became the real rulers of Germany, and they decreed the ultimate mobilization for total war. Germany, said Hindenburg, could win only "if all the treasures of our soil that agriculture and industry can produce are used exclusively for the conduct of War. . . . All other considerations must come second."[7] This goal, they believed, required that every German man, woman, and child be drafted into the service of the war. Thus, in December 1916, the military leaders rammed through the parliament the Auxiliary Service Law, which required all males between seventeen and sixty to work only at jobs considered critical to the war effort.

Although women and children were not specifically mentioned, this forced-labor law was also aimed at them. Many women already worked in war factories, mines, and steel mills, where they labored like men at the heaviest and most dangerous jobs. With the passage of the Auxiliary Service Law, many more women followed. Children were organized by their teachers into garbage brigades to collect every scrap of useful materials: grease strained from dishwater, coffee grounds, waste paper, tin cans, metal door knockers, bottles, rags, hair, bones, and so forth, as well as acorns, chestnuts, pine cones, and rotting leaves. Potatoes gave way to turnips, and people averaged little more than a thousand calories a day. Thus in Germany total war led to the establishment of history's first "totalitarian" society, and war production increased while some people literally starved to death.

Great Britain mobilized for total war less rapidly and less completely than Germany, for it could import materials from its empire and from the United States. By 1915, however, a serious shortage of shells led to the establishment of a Ministry of Munitions under David Lloyd George. The ministry organized private industry to produce for the war, controlled profits, allocated labor, fixed wage rates, and settled labor disputes. By December 1916, when Lloyd George became prime minister, the British economy was largely planned and regulated. More than two hundred factories and 90 percent of all imports were bought and allocated directly by the state. Subsequently, even food was strictly rationed, while war production continued to soar. Great Britain had followed successfully in Germany's footsteps.

The Social Impact

The social impact of total war was no less profound than the economic, though again there were important national variations. The millions of men at the front and the insatiable needs of the military created a tremendous demand for workers. Jobs were available for everyone. This situation had seldom if ever been seen before 1914, when unemployment and poverty had been facts of urban life. The exceptional demand for labor brought about momentous changes.

One such change was greater power and prestige for labor unions. Having proved their loyalty in August 1914, labor unions became an indispensable partner of government and private industry in the planned war economy. Unions cooperated with war governments on work rules, wages, and production schedules in return for real participation in important decisions. This entry of labor leaders and unions into policy-making councils paralleled the entry of socialist leaders into the war governments.

The role of women changed dramatically. In every country, large numbers of women left home work and domestic service to work in industry, transportation, and offices. By 1917 women formed fully 43 percent of the labor force in Russia. The number of women driving buses and streetcars increased tenfold in Great Britain. Moreover, women became highly visible—not only as munitions workers but as bank tellers, mail carriers, even policewomen.

At first, the male-dominated unions were hostile to women moving into new occupations, believing that their presence would lower wages and change work rules. But government pressure and the principle of equal pay for equal work (at least until the end of the war) overcame these objections. Women also served as nurses and doctors at the front. In general, the war greatly expanded the range of women's activities and changed attitudes toward women. As a direct result of their many-sided war effort, Britain, Germany, and Austria granted women the right to vote immediately after the war. Women also showed a growing spirit of independence during the war, as they started to bob their hair, shorten their skirts, and smoke in public.

War also promoted greater social equality, blurring class distinctions and lessening the gap between rich and poor. This blurring was most apparent in Great Britain, where wartime hardship was never extreme. In fact, the bottom third of the population generally lived *better* than ever before, for the poorest gained most from the severe shortage of labor. The English writer Robert Roberts recalled how his parents' tiny grocery store in the slums of Manchester thrived as never before during the war, when people who had scrimped to buy bread and soup bones were able to afford fancy cakes and thick steaks. In 1924 a British government study revealed that the distribution of income had indeed shifted in favor of the poorest; only half

as many families lived in severe poverty as in 1911, even though total production of goods had not increased. In continental countries greater equality was reflected in full employment, rationing according to physical needs, and a sharing of hardships. There, too, society became more uniform and more egalitarian, in spite of some war profiteering.

Finally, death itself had no respect for traditional social distinctions. It savagely decimated the young aristocratic officers who led the charge, and it fell heavily on the mass of drafted peasants and unskilled workers who followed. Yet death often spared the aristocrats of labor, the skilled workers and foremen. Their lives were too valuable to squander at the front, for they were needed to train

Wartime Propaganda   was skillful and effective. The poster on the left spurred men to volunteer for military service before the draft was introduced in Britain in 1916. The poster on the right appeals to patriotism and the love of family as it urges the French to buy another batch of war bonds. *(Source: By courtesy of the Trustees of the Imperial War Museum)*

the newly recruited women and older unskilled men laboring valiantly in war plants at home.

Growing Political Tensions

During the first two years of war, most soldiers and civilians supported their governments. Even in Austria-Hungary—the most vulnerable of the belligerents, with its competing nationalities—loyalty to the state and monarchy remained astonishingly strong through 1916. Belief in a just cause, patriotic nationalism, the planned economy, and a sharing of burdens united peoples behind their various national leaders. Furthermore, each government did its best to control public opinion to bolster morale. Newspapers, letters, and public addresses were rigorously censored. Good news was overstated; bad news was repressed or distorted.

Each government used both crude and subtle propaganda to maintain popular support. German propaganda hysterically pictured black soldiers from France's African empire raping German women, while German atrocities in Belgium and elsewhere were ceaselessly recounted and exaggerated by the French and British. Patriotic posters and slogans, slanted news and biased editorials inflamed national hatreds and helped sustain superhuman efforts.

By the spring of 1916, however, people were beginning to crack under the strain of total war. In April 1916 Irish nationalists in Dublin tried to take advantage of this situation and rose up against British rule in their great Easter Rebellion. A week of bitter fighting passed before the rebels were crushed and their leaders executed. Strikes and protest marches over inadequate food began to flare up on every home front. Soldiers' morale began to decline. Italian troops mutinied. Numerous French units refused to fight after General Nivelle's disastrous offensive of May 1917. Only tough military justice and a tacit agreement with his troops that there would be no more grand offensives enabled the new general in chief, Henri Philippe Pétain, to restore order. A rising tide of war-weariness and defeatism also swept France's civilian population before Georges Clemenceau emerged as a ruthless and effective wartime leader in November 1917. Clemenceau established a virtual dictatorship, pouncing on strikers and jailing without trial jour-

Irish Nationalists Organized in 1913 to press for Home Rule in Ireland, the unofficial Irish Citizen Army was committed to complete independence from Great Britain. Shown here beneath a defiant pro-republican banner, it fought with other militant groups in the Easter Rebellion. *(Source: Lawrence Collection. National Library of Ireland, Dublin)*

nalists and politicians who dared to suggest a compromise peace with Germany.

The strains were worse for the Central Powers. In October 1916 the chief minister of Austria was assassinated by a young socialist crying, "Down with Absolutism! We want peace!"[8] The following month, when the feeble old Emperor Francis Joseph died sixty-eight years after his mother Sophia had pushed him onto the throne in 1848 (see page 749), a symbol of unity disappeared. In spite of absolute censorship, political dissatisfaction and conflicts among nationalities grew. In April 1917 Austria's chief minister summed up the situation in the gloomiest possible terms. The country and army were exhausted. Another winter of war would bring revolution and disintegration. "If the monarchs of the Central Powers cannot make peace in the coming months," he wrote, "it will be made for them by their peoples."[9] Both Czech and Yugoslav leaders demanded autonomous democratic states for their peoples. The British blockade kept tightening; people were starving.

The strain of total war and the Auxiliary Service Law was also evident in Germany. In the winter of 1916 to 1917, Germany's military position appeared increasingly desperate. Stalemates and losses in the west were matched by temporary Russian advances in the east: hence the military's insistence on the all-or-nothing gamble of unrestricted submarine warfare when the Triple Entente refused in December 1916 to consider peace on terms that were favorable to the Central Powers.

Also, the national political unity of the first two years of war was collapsing as the social conflict of prewar Germany re-emerged. A growing minority of socialists in the parliament began to vote against war credits, calling for a compromise "peace without annexations or reparations." In July 1917 a coalition of socialists and Catholics passed a resolution in the parliament to that effect. Such a peace was unthinkable for conservatives and military leaders. So also was the surge in revolutionary agitation and strikes by war-weary workers that occurred in early 1917. When the bread ration was further reduced in April, more than 200,000 workers struck and demonstrated for a week in Berlin, returning to work only under the threat of prison and military discipline. Thus militaristic Germany, like its ally Austria-Hungary (and its enemy France), was beginning to crack in 1917. Yet it was Russia that collapsed first and saved the Central Powers, for a time.

THE RUSSIAN REVOLUTION

The Russian Revolution of 1917 was one of modern history's most momentous events. Directly related to the growing tensions of World War One, it had a significance far beyond the wartime agonies of a single European nation. The Russian Revolution opened a new era. For some, it was Marx's socialist vision come true; for others, it was the triumph of dictatorship. To all, it presented a radically new prototype of state and society.

The Fall of Imperial Russia

Like its allies and its enemies, Russia embraced war with patriotic enthusiasm in 1914. At the Winter Palace, while throngs of people knelt and sang "God Save the Tsar," Tsar Nicholas II (r. 1894–1917) repeated the oath Alexander I had sworn in 1812 and vowed never to make peace as long as the enemy stood on Russian soil. Russia's lower house, the Duma, voted war credits. Conservatives anticipated expansion in the Balkans, while liberals and most socialists believed alliance with Britain and France would bring democratic reforms. For a moment, Russia was united.

Soon, however, the strains of war began to take their toll. The unprecedented artillery barrages used up Russia's supplies of shells and ammunition, and better-equipped German armies inflicted terrible losses. For a time in 1915, substantial numbers of Russian soldiers were sent to the front without rifles; they were told to find their arms among the dead. There were two million Russian casualties in 1915 alone. Morale declined among soldiers and civilians. Nonetheless, Russia's battered peasant army did not collapse but continued to fight courageously until early 1917.

Under the shock of defeat, Russia moved toward full mobilization on the home front. The Duma and organs of local government took the lead, setting up special committees to coordinate defense, industry, transportation, and agriculture. These efforts improved the military situation, and Russian factories produced more than twice as many shells in 1916 as in 1915. Yet there were many failures, and Russia mobilized less effectively for total war than the other warring nations.

The great problem was leadership. Under the constitution resulting from the revolution of 1905 (see pages 808–809), the tsar had retained complete control over the bureaucracy and the army. Legislation proposed by the Duma, which was weighted in favor of the wealthy and conservative classes, was subject to the tsar's veto. Moreover, Nicholas II fervently wished to maintain the sacred inheritance of supreme royal power, which with the Orthodox church was for him the key to Russia's greatness. A kindly, slightly stupid man, of whom a friend said he "would have been an ideal country gentleman, devoting his life to wife and children, his farms and his sport," Nicholas failed to form a close partnership with his citizens in order to fight the war more effectively. He relied instead on the old bureaucratic apparatus, distrusting the moderate Duma, rejecting popular involvement, and resisting calls to share power.

As a result the Duma, the educated middle classes, and the masses became increasingly critical of the tsar's leadership. Following Nicholas's belated dismissal of the incompetent minister of war, demands for more democratic and responsive government exploded in the Duma in the summer of 1915. "From the beginning of the war," declared one young liberal, "public opinion has understood the character and magnitude of the struggle; it has understood that short of organizing the whole country for war, victory is impossible. But the Government has rejected every offer of help with disdain."[10] In September, parties ranging from conservative to moderate socialist formed the Progressive Bloc, which called for a completely new government responsible to the Duma instead of the tsar. In answer, Nicholas temporarily adjourned the Duma and announced that he was traveling to the front in order to lead and rally Russia's armies.

His departure was a fatal turning point. With the tsar in the field with the troops, control of the government was taken over by the hysterical empress, Tsarina Alexandra, and a debauched adventurer, the monk Rasputin. A minor German princess and granddaughter of England's Queen Victoria, Nicholas's wife was a devoted mother with a sick child, a strong-willed woman with a hatred of parliaments. Having constantly urged her husband to rule absolutely, Alexandra tried to do so herself in his absence. She seated and unseated the top ministers. Her most trusted adviser was "our Friend Grigori," an uneducated Siberian preacher who was appropriately nicknamed Rasputin—the "Degenerate."

Rasputin began his career with a sect noted for mixing sexual orgies with religious ecstasies, and his influence rested on mysterious healing powers. Alexis, Alexandra's fifth child and heir to the throne, suffered from a rare disease, hemophilia. The tiniest cut meant uncontrollable bleeding, terrible pain, and possible death. Medical science could do nothing. Only Rasputin could miraculously stop the bleeding, perhaps through hypnosis. The empress's faith in Rasputin was limitless. "Believe more in our Friend," she wrote her husband in 1916. "He lives for you and Russia." In this atmosphere of unreality, the government slid steadily toward revolution.

In a desperate attempt to right the situation and end unfounded rumors that Rasputin was the empress's lover, three members of the high aristocracy murdered Rasputin in December 1916. The empress went into semipermanent shock, her mind haunted by the dead man's prophecy: "If I die or you desert me, in six months you will lose your son and your throne."[11] Food shortages in the cities worsened, morale declined. On March 8, women calling for bread in Petrograd (formerly St. Petersburg) started riots, which spontaneously spread to the factories and throughout the city. From the front the tsar ordered the troops to restore order, but discipline broke down and the soldiers joined the revolutionary crowd. The Duma responded by declaring a provisional government on March 12, 1917. Three days later, Nicholas abdicated.

The Provisional Government

The March revolution was the result of an unplanned uprising of hungry, angry people in the capital, but it was joyfully accepted throughout the country. The patriotic upper and middle classes rejoiced at the prospect of a more determined and effective war effort, while workers happily anticipated better wages and more food. All classes and political parties called for liberty and democracy. They were not disappointed. As Lenin said, Russia became the freest country in the world. After generations of arbitrary authoritarianism, the provisional government quickly established equality before the law; freedom of religion, speech, and assembly; the right of unions to organize and strike; and the rest of the classic liberal program.

Yet both the liberal and moderate socialist leaders of the provisional government rejected social revolution. The reorganized government formed in May 1917, which included the fiery agrarian socialist Alexander Kerensky, refused to confiscate large landholdings and give them to peasants, fearing that such drastic action in the countryside would only complete the disintegration of Russia's peasant army. For the patriotic Kerensky, as for other moderate socialists, the continuation of war was still the all-important national duty. There would be plenty of time for land reform later, and thus all the government's efforts were directed toward a last offensive in July. Human suffering and war-weariness grew, sapping the limited strength of the provisional government.

From its first day, the provisional government had to share power with a formidable rival—the Petrograd Soviet (or council) of Workers' and Soldiers' Deputies. Modeled on the revolutionary soviets of 1905, the Petrograd Soviet was a huge, fluctuating mass meeting of two to three thousand workers, soldiers, and socialist intellectuals. Seeing itself as a true grassroots revolutionary democracy, this counter- or half-government suspiciously watched the provisional government and issued its own radical orders, further weakening the provisional government. Most famous of these was Army Order No. 1, issued to all Russian military forces as the provisional government was forming.

Order No. 1 stripped officers of their authority and placed power in the hands of elected committees of common soldiers. Designed primarily to protect the revolution from some counter-revolutionary Bonaparte on horseback, Army Order No. 1 instead led to a total collapse of army discipline. Many an officer was hanged for his sins. Meanwhile, following the foolhardy summer offensive, masses of peasant soldiers began "voting with their feet," to use Lenin's graphic phrase. That is, they began returning to their villages to help their families get a share of the land, land that peasants were simply seizing as they settled old scores in a great agrarian upheaval. All across the country, liberty was turning into anarchy in the summer of 1917. It was an unparalleled opportunity for the most radical and most talented of Russia's many socialist leaders, Vladimir Ilyich Lenin (1870–1924).

Lenin and the Bolshevik Revolution

From his youth, Lenin's whole life was dedicated to the cause of revolution. Born into the middle class,

Lenin became an implacable enemy of imperial Russia when his older brother was executed for plotting to kill the tsar in 1887. As a law student he began searching for a revolutionary faith. He found it in Marxian socialism, which began to win converts among radical intellectuals as industrialization surged forward in Russia in the 1890s. Exiled to Siberia for three years because of socialist agitation, Lenin studied Marxian doctrines with religious intensity. After his release, the young priest of socialism joined fellow believers in western Europe. There he lived for seventeen years and developed his own revolutionary interpretations of the body of Marxian thought.

Three interrelated ideas were central for Lenin. First, turning to the early fire-breathing Marx of 1848 and the *Communist Manifesto* for inspiration, Lenin stressed that capitalism could be destroyed only by violent revolution. He tirelessly denounced all revisionist theories of a peaceful evolution to socialism as betraying Marx's message of unending class conflict. Lenin's second, more original, idea was that, under certain conditions, a socialist revolution was possible even in a relatively backward country like Russia. Though capitalism was not fully developed there and the industrial working class was small, the peasants were poor and thus potential revolutionaries.

Lenin believed that at a given moment revolution was determined more by human leadership than by vast historical laws. Thus Lenin's third basic idea: the necessity of a highly disciplined workers' party, strictly controlled by a dedicated elite of intellectuals and full-time revolutionaries like Lenin himself. Unlike ordinary workers and trade-union officials, this elite would never be seduced by short-term gains. It would not stop until revolution brought it to power.

Lenin's theories and methods did not go unchallenged by other Russian Marxists. At the meetings of the Russian Social Democratic Labor party in London in 1903, matters came to a head. Lenin demanded a small, disciplined, elitist party, while his opponents wanted a more democratic party with mass membership. The Russian party of Marxian socialism promptly split into two rival factions. Lenin's camp was called *Bolsheviks*, or "majority group"; his opponents were *Mensheviks*, or "minority group." Lenin's majority did not last, but Lenin did not care. He kept the fine-sounding name Bolshevik and developed the party he wanted: tough, disciplined, revolutionary.

Mass Demonstrations in Petrograd   in June 1917 showed a surge of working-class support for the Bolsheviks. In this photo a few banners of the Mensheviks and other moderate socialists are drowned in a sea of Bolshevik slogans. *(Source: Sovfoto)*

Unlike most other socialists, Lenin did not rally round the national flag in 1914. Observing events from neutral Switzerland, he saw the war as a product of imperialistic rivalries and as a marvelous opportunity for class war and socialist upheaval. The March revolution was, Lenin felt, a step in that direction. Since propaganda and internal subversion were accepted weapons of total war, the German government graciously provided the impatient Lenin, his wife, and about twenty trusted colleagues with safe passage across Germany and back into Russia in April 1917. The Germans hoped that Lenin would undermine the sagging war effort of the world's freest society. They were not disappointed.

Arriving triumphantly at Petrograd's Finland Station on April 3, Lenin attacked at once. To the great astonishment of the local Bolsheviks, he rejected all cooperation with the "bourgeois" provisional government of the liberals and moderate socialists. His slogans were radical in the extreme: "All power to the soviets." "All land to the peasants." "Stop the war now." Never a slave to Marxian determinism, the brilliant but not unduly intellectual Lenin was a superb tactician. The moment was now.

Yet Lenin almost overplayed his hand. An attempt by the Bolsheviks to seize power in July collapsed, and Lenin fled and went into hiding. He was charged with being a German agent, and indeed he and the Bolsheviks were getting money from Germany.[12] But no matter. Intrigue between Kerensky, who became prime minister in July, and his commander in chief General Lavr Kornilov, a popular war hero "with the heart of a lion and the brains of a sheep," resulted in Kornilov's leading a feeble attack against the provisional government in September. In the face of this rightist "counter-revolutionary" threat, the Bolsheviks were rearmed and redeemed. Kornilov's forces disintegrated, but Kerensky lost all credit with the army, the only force that might have saved him and democratic government in Russia.

Trotsky and the Seizure of Power

Throughout the summer, the Bolsheviks had appealed very effectively to the workers and soldiers of Petrograd, markedly increasing their popular support. Party membership had soared from 50,000 to 240,000, and in October the Bolsheviks gained a fragile majority in the Petrograd Soviet. Moreover, Lenin had found a strong right arm—Leon Trotsky, the second most important person in the Russian Revolution.

A spellbinding revolutionary orator and independent radical Marxist, Trotsky (1879–1940) supported Lenin wholeheartedly in 1917. It was he who brilliantly executed the Bolshevik seizure of power. Painting a vivid but untruthful picture of German and counter-revolutionary plots, Trotsky first convinced the Petrograd Soviet to form a special Military-Revolutionary Committee in October and make him its leader. Military power in the capital passed into Bolshevik hands. Trotsky's second master stroke was to insist that the Bolsheviks reduce opposition to their coup by taking power in the name, not of the Bolsheviks, but of the more popular and democratic soviets, which were meeting in Petrograd from all over Russia in early November. On the night of November 6, militants from Trotsky's committee joined with trusty Bolshevik soldiers to seize government buildings and pounce on members of the provisional government. Then on to the congress of soviets! There a Bolshevik majority—roughly 390 of 650 turbulent delegates—declared that all power had passed to the soviets and named Lenin head of the new government.

The Bolsheviks came to power for three key reasons. First, by late 1917 democracy had given way to anarchy: power was there for those who would take it. Second, in Lenin and Trotsky the Bolsheviks had an utterly determined and truly superior leadership, which both the tsarist government and the provisional government lacked. Third, in 1917 the Bolsheviks succeeded in appealing to many soldiers and urban workers, people who were exhausted by war and eager for socialism. With time, many workers would become bitterly disappointed, but for the moment they had good reason to believe they had won what they wanted.

Dictatorship and Civil War

History is full of short-lived coups and unsuccessful revolutions. The truly monumental accomplishment of Lenin, Trotsky, and the rest of the Bolsheviks was not taking power but keeping it. In the next four years, the Bolsheviks went on to conquer the chaos they had helped to create, and they began to build their kind of dictatorial socialist society. The conspirators became conquerors. How was this done?

Lenin had the genius to profit from developments over which he and the Bolsheviks had no control. Since summer, a peasant revolution had been sweeping across Russia, as the tillers of the soil invaded and divided among themselves the great and not-so-great estates of the landlords and the church. Peasant seizure of the land—a Russian 1789—was not very Marxian, but it was quite unstoppable in 1917. Thus Lenin's first law, which supposedly gave land to the peasants, actually merely approved what peasants were already doing. Urban workers' great demand in November was direct control of individual factories by local workers' committees. This, too, Lenin ratified with a decree in November.

Unlike many of his colleagues, Lenin acknowledged that Russia had lost the war with Germany, that the Russian army had ceased to exist, and that the only realistic goal was peace at any price. The price was very high. Germany demanded in December 1917 that the Soviet government give up all its western territories. These areas were inhabited by Poles, Finns, Lithuanians, and other non-Russians—all those peoples who had been conquered by the tsars over three centuries and put into the "prisonhouse of nationalities," as Lenin had earlier called the Russian Empire.

At first, Lenin's fellow Bolsheviks would not accept such great territorial losses. But when German armies resumed their unopposed march into Russia

THE RUSSIAN REVOLUTION

1914	Russia enthusiastically enters the First World War
1915	Two million Russian casualties
	Progressive Bloc calls for a new government responsible to the Duma rather than to the tsar
	Tsar Nicholas adjourns the Duma and departs for the front; control of the government falls to Alexandra and Rasputin
December 1916	Murder of Rasputin
March 8, 1917	Bread riots in Petrograd (St. Petersburg)
March 12, 1917	Duma declares a provisional government
March 15, 1917	Tsar Nicholas abdicates without protest
April 3, 1917	Lenin returns from exile and denounces the provisional government
May 1917	Reorganized provisional government, including Kerensky, continues the war Petrograd Soviet issues Army Order no. 1, granting military power to committees of common soldiers
Summer 1917	Agrarian upheavals: peasants seize estates, peasant soldiers desert the army to participate
October 1917	Bolsheviks gain a majority in the Petrograd Soviet
November 6, 1917	Bolsheviks seize power; Lenin heads the new "provisional workers' and peasants' government"
November 1917	Lenin ratifies peasant seizure of land and worker control of factories; all banks nationalized
January 1918	Lenin permanently disbands the Constituent Assembly
February 1918	Lenin convinces the Bolshevik Central Committee to accept a humiliating peace with Germany in order to pursue the revolution
March 1918	Treaty of Brest-Litovsk: Russia loses one-third of its population
	Trotsky as war commissar begins to rebuild the Russian army
	Government moves from Petrograd to Moscow
1918–1920	Great Civil War
Summer 1918	Eighteen competing regional governments; White armies oppose the Bolshevik revolution
1919	White armies on the offensive but divided politically; they receive little benefit from Allied intervention
1920	Lenin and Red armies victorious, retaking Belorussia and the Ukraine

in February 1918, Lenin had his way in a very close vote in the Central Committee of the party. "Not even his greatest enemy can deny that at this moment Lenin towered like a giant over his Bolshevik colleagues."[13] A third of old Russia's population was sliced away by the German meat ax in the Treaty of Brest-Litovsk in March 1918. With peace, Lenin had escaped the certain disaster of continued war and could uncompromisingly pursue his goal of absolute political power for the Bolsheviks— now renamed Communists—within Russia.

In November 1917 the Bolsheviks had cleverly proclaimed their regime only a "provisional workers' and peasants' government," promising that a freely elected Constituent Assembly would draw up a new constitution. But free elections produced a stunning setback for the Bolsheviks, who won less than one-fourth of the elected delegates. The Socialist Revolutionaries—the peasants' party —had a clear majority. The Constituent Assembly met for only one day, on January 18, 1918. It was then permanently disbanded by Bolshevik soldiers acting under Lenin's orders. Thus, even before the peace with Germany, Lenin was forming a one-party government.

The destruction of the democratically elected Constituent Assembly helped feed the flames of civil war. People who had risen up for self-rule in November saw that once again they were getting dictatorship from the capital. For the next three years, "Long live the [democratic] soviets; down with the Bolsheviks" was to be a popular slogan. The officers of the old army took the lead in organizing the so-called White opposition to the Bolsheviks in southern Russia and the Ukraine, in Siberia, and to the west of Petrograd. The Whites came from many social groups and were united only by their hatred of the Bolsheviks—the Reds.

By the summer of 1918, fully eighteen self-proclaimed regional governments—several of which represented minority nationalities—competed with Lenin's Bolsheviks in Moscow. By the end of the year, White armies were on the attack. In October 1919 it appeared they might triumph, as they closed in on Lenin's government from three sides. Yet they did not. By the spring of 1920, the White armies had been almost completely defeated, and the Bolshevik Red Army had retaken Belorussia and the Ukraine. The following year, the Communists also reconquered the independent nationalist governments of the Caucasus. The civil war was over; Lenin had won.

Lenin and the Bolsheviks won for several reasons. Strategically, they controlled the center, while the Whites were always on the fringes and disunited. Moreover, the poorly defined political program of the Whites was vaguely conservative, and it did not unite all the foes of the Bolsheviks under a progressive, democratic banner. For example, the most gifted of the White generals, the nationalistic General Anton Denikin, refused to call for a democratic republic and a federation of nationalities, although he knew that doing so would help his cause. Most important, the Communists quickly developed a better army, an army for which the divided Whites were no match.

Once again, Trotsky's leadership was decisive. The Bolsheviks had preached democracy in the army and elected officers in 1917. But beginning in March 1918, Trotsky as war commissar re-established the draft and the most drastic discipline for the newly formed Red Army. Soldiers deserting or

Vladimir Lenin Dramatically displaying both his burning determination and his skill as a revolutionary orator, Lenin addresses the victorious May Day celebration of 1918 in Moscow's Red Square. *(Source: Culver Pictures)*

disobeying an order were summarily shot. Moreover, Trotsky made effective use of former tsarist army officers, who were actively recruited and given unprecedented powers of discipline over their troops. In short, Trotsky formed a disciplined and effective fighting force.

The Bolsheviks also mobilized the home front. Establishing "war communism"—the application of the total war concept to a civil conflict—they seized grain from peasants, introduced rationing, nationalized all banks and industry, and required everyone to work. Although these measures contributed to a breakdown of normal economic activity, they also served to maintain labor discipline and to keep the Red Army supplied.

"Revolutionary terror" also contributed to the Communist victory. The old tsarist secret police was re-established as the Cheka, which hunted down and executed thousands of real or supposed foes, such as the tsar and his family and other "class enemies." At one point, shortly after the government moved from Petrograd to Moscow in March 1918, a circus clown in Moscow was making fun of the Bolsheviks to an appreciative audience. Chekists in the crowd quickly pulled out their guns and shot several laughing people. Moreover, people were shot or threatened with being shot for minor nonpolitical failures. The terror caused by the secret police became a tool of the government. The Cheka sowed fear, and fear silenced opposition.

Finally, foreign military intervention in the civil war ended up helping the Communists. After Lenin made peace with Germany, the Allies (the Americans, British, and Japanese) sent troops to Archangel and Vladivostok to prevent war materiel they had sent the provisional government from being captured by the Germans. After the Soviet government nationalized all foreign-owned factories without compensation and refused to pay all of Russia's foreign debts, Western governments and particularly France began to support White armies. Yet these efforts were small and halfhearted. In 1919 Western peoples were sick of war, and few Western politicians believed in a military crusade against the Bolsheviks. Thus Allied intervention in the civil war did not aid the Whites effectively, though it did permit the Communists to appeal to the patriotic nationalism of ethnic Russians, in particular the former tsarist army officers. Allied intervention was both too little and too much.

Together, the Russian Revolution and the Bolshevik triumph were one of the reasons why the First World War was such a great turning point in modern history. A radically new government, based on socialism and one-party dictatorship, came to power in a great European state, maintained power, and eagerly encouraged worldwide revolution. Although halfheartedly constitutional monarchy in Russia was undoubtedly headed for some kind of political crisis before 1914, it is hard to imagine the triumph of the most radical proponents of change and reform except in a situation of total collapse. That was precisely what happened to Russia in the First World War.

THE PEACE SETTLEMENT

Victory over revolutionary Russia boosted sagging German morale, and in the spring of 1918 the Germans launched their last major attack against France. Yet this offensive failed like those before it. With breathtaking rapidity, the United States, Great Britain, and France decisively defeated Germany militarily. The guns of world war finally fell silent. Then, as civil war spread in Russia and as chaos engulfed much of eastern Europe, the victorious Western Allies came together in Paris to establish a lasting peace.

Expectations were high; optimism was almost unlimited. The Allies labored intensively and soon worked out terms for peace with Germany and for the creation of the peace-keeping League of Nations. Nevertheless, the hopes of peoples and politicians were soon disappointed, for the peace settlement of 1919 turned out to be a failure. Rather than creating conditions for peace, it sowed the seeds of another war. Surely this was the ultimate tragedy of the Great War, a war that directly and indirectly cost $332 billion and left 10 million dead and another 20 million wounded. How did it happen? Why was the peace settlement unsuccessful?

The End of the War

In early 1917 the strain of total war was showing everywhere. After the Russian Revolution in March, there were major strikes in Germany. In July a coalition of moderates passed a "peace resolution" in the German parliament, calling for peace without territorial annexations. To counter this moderation born of war-weariness, the German military established a virtual dictatorship. The military also aggressively exploited the collapse of Russian armies after the Bolshevik Revolution. Advancing almost unopposed on the eastern front in early 1918, the German high command won great concessions from Lenin in the Treaty of Brest-Litovsk in March 1918, as we have seen.

With victory in the east quieting German moderates, General Ludendorff and company fell on France once more in the great spring offensive of 1918. For a time, German armies pushed forward, coming within 35 miles of Paris. But Ludendorff's exhausted, overextended forces never broke through. They were decisively stopped in July at the second Battle of the Marne, where 140,000 fresh American soldiers saw action. Adding 2 million men in arms to the war effort by August, the late but massive American intervention decisively tipped the scales in favor of Allied victory.

By September, British, French, and American armies were advancing steadily on all fronts, and a panicky General Ludendorff realized that Germany had lost the war. Yet he insolently insisted that moderate politicians shoulder the shame of defeat, and on October 4 the emperor formed a new, more liberal German government to sue for peace. As negotiations over an armistice dragged on, an angry and frustrated German people finally rose up. On November 3, sailors in Kiel mutinied, and throughout northern Germany soldiers and workers began to establish revolutionary councils on the Russian soviet model. The same day, Austria-Hungary surrendered to the Allies and began breaking apart. Revolution broke out in Germany, and masses of workers demonstrated for peace in Berlin. With army discipline collapsing, the emperor abdicated and fled to Holland. Socialist leaders in Berlin proclaimed a German republic on November 9 and simultaneously agreed to tough Allied terms of surrender. The armistice went into effect on November 11, 1918. The war was over.

Revolution in Germany

Hapsburg Empire ends
①Austria
②Hungary
③Czech
④Yugoslavia

Military defeat brought political revolution to Germany and Austria-Hungary, as it had to Russia. In Austria-Hungary, the revolution was primarily nationalistic and republican in character. Having started the war to preserve an antinationalist dynastic state, the Habsburg empire had perished in the attempt. In its place, independent Austrian, Hungarian, and Czechoslovak republics were proclaimed, while a greatly expanded Serbian monarchy united the south Slavs and took the name of Yugoslavia. The prospect of firmly establishing the new national states overrode class considerations for most people in east central Europe.

The German Revolution of November 1918 resembled the Russian Revolution of March 1917. In both cases, a genuine popular uprising toppled an authoritarian monarchy and established a liberal provisional republic. In both countries, liberals and moderate socialists took control of the central

German revolution

government, while workers' and soldiers' councils formed a counter-government. In Germany, however, the moderate socialists won and the Lenin-like radical revolutionaries in the councils lost. In communist terms, the liberal, republican revolution in Germany in 1918 was only half a revolution: a bourgeois political revolution without a communist second installment. It was Russia without Lenin's Bolshevik triumph.

There were several reasons for the German outcome. The great majority of Marxian socialist leaders in the Social Democratic party were, as before the war, really pink and not red. They wanted to establish real political democracy and civil liberties, and they favored the gradual elimination of capitalism. They were also German nationalists, appalled by the prospect of civil war and revolutionary terror. Moreover, there was much less popular

Rosa Luxemburg A brilliant writer and a leader in the German Social Democratic party, Luxemburg scorned moderate socialism and stressed the revolutionary character of Marxism. Murdered by army officers in 1919, she was canonized by the faithful as a communist saint. *(Source: Courtesy, Centralne Archiwum KCPZPR, Warsaw, Poland)*

Nov 1918 overthrew Weimar Rep

support among workers and soldiers for the extreme radicals than in Russia. Nor did the German peasantry, which already had most of the land, at least in western Germany, provide the elemental force that has driven all great modern revolutions, from the French to the Chinese.

Of crucial importance also was the fact that the moderate German Social Democrats, unlike Kerensky and company, accepted defeat and ended the war the day they took power. This act ended the decline in morale among soldiers and prevented the regular army with its conservative officer corps from disintegrating. When radicals, headed by Karl Liebknecht and Rosa Luxemburg and their supporters in the councils, tried to seize control of the government in Berlin in January, the moderate socialists called on the army to crush the uprising. Liebknecht and Luxemburg were arrested and then brutally murdered by army leaders, an act that caused the radicals in the Social Democratic party to break away in anger and form a pro-Lenin German Communist party shortly thereafter. Finally, even if the moderate socialists had followed Liebknecht and Luxemburg on the Leninist path, it is very unlikely they would have succeeded. Civil war in Germany would certainly have followed, and the Allies, who were already occupying western Germany according to the terms of the armistice, would have marched on to Berlin and ruled Germany directly. Historians have often been unduly hard on Germany's moderate socialists.

The Treaty of Versailles

The peace conference opened in Paris in January 1919 with seventy delegates representing twenty-seven victorious nations. There were great expectations. A young British diplomat later wrote that the victors "were convinced that they would never commit the blunders and iniquities of the Congress of Vienna [of 1815]." Then the "misguided, reactionary, pathetic aristocrats" had cynically shuffled populations; now "we believed in nationalism, we believed in the self-determination of peoples." Indeed, "we were journeying to Paris . . . to found a new order in Europe. We were preparing not Peace only, but Eternal Peace."[14] The general optimism and idealism had been greatly strengthened by President Wilson's January 1918 peace proposal, the Fourteen Points, which stressed national self-determination and the rights of small countries.

The real powers at the conference were the United States, Great Britain, and France, for Germany was not allowed to participate, and Russia was locked in civil war and did not attend. Italy was considered part of the Big Four, but its role was quite limited. Almost immediately the three great allies began to quarrel. President Wilson, who was wildly cheered by European crowds as the spokesman for a new idealistic and democratic international cooperation, was almost obsessed with creating a League of Nations. Wilson insisted that this question come first, for he passionately believed that only a permanent international organization could protect member states from aggression and avert future wars. Wilson had his way, although Lloyd George of Great Britain and especially Clemenceau of France were unenthusiastic. They were primarily concerned with punishing Germany.

Playing on British nationalism, Lloyd George had already won a smashing electoral victory in December on the popular platform of making Germany pay for the war. "We shall," he promised, "squeeze the orange until the pips squeak." Personally inclined to make a somewhat moderate peace with Germany, Lloyd George was to a considerable extent a captive of demands for a total victory worthy of the sacrifices of total war against a totally depraved enemy. As Kipling summed up the general British feeling at the end of the war, the Germans were "a people with the heart of beasts."[15]

France's Georges Clemenceau, "the Tiger" who had broken wartime defeatism and led his country to victory, wholeheartedly agreed. Like most French people, Clemenceau wanted old-fashioned revenge. He also wanted lasting security for France. This, he believed, required the creation of a buffer state between France and Germany, the permanent demilitarization of Germany, and vast German reparations. He feared that sooner or later Germany with its sixty million people would attack France with its forty million, unless the Germans were permanently weakened. Moreover, France had no English Channel (or Atlantic Ocean) as a reassuring barrier against German aggression. Wilson, supported by Lloyd George, would hear none of it. Clemenceau's demands seemed vindictive, violating morality and the principle of national self-determination. By April the conference was deadlocked on the German question, and Wilson packed his bags to go home.

Clemenceau's obsession with security reflected his anxiety about France's long-term weakness. In

The Treaty of Versailles   was signed in the magnificent Hall of Mirrors, part of the vast palace that Louis XIV had built to celebrate his glory. The Allies did not allow Germany to participate in the negotiation of the treaty. *(Source: National Archives, Washington)*

Clemenceau agrees to compromise! ↓

TERMS of the Treaty: ↓

the end, convinced that France should not break with its allies because France could not afford to face Germany alone in the future, he agreed to a compromise. He gave up the French demand for a Rhineland buffer state in return for a formal defensive alliance with the United States and Great Britain. Under the terms of this alliance, both Wilson and Lloyd George promised that their countries would come to France's aid in the event of a German attack. Thus Clemenceau appeared to win his goal of French security, as Wilson had won his of a permanent international organization. The Allies moved quickly to finish the settlement, believing that any adjustments would later be possible within the dual framework of a strong Western alliance and the League of Nations (Map 27.4).

The Treaty of Versailles between the Allies and Germany was the key to the settlement, and the terms were not unreasonable as a first step toward re-establishing international order. (Had Germany won, it seems certain that France and Belgium would have been treated with greater severity, as Russia had been at Brest-Litovsk.) Germany's colonies were given to France, Britain, and Japan as League of Nations mandates. Germany's territorial losses within Europe were minor, thanks to Wilson. Alsace-Lorraine was returned to France. Parts of Germany inhabited primarily by Poles were ceded to the new Polish state, in keeping with the principle of national self-determination. Predominately German Danzig was also placed within the Polish tariff lines, but as a self-governing city under League of Nations protection. Germany had to limit its army to 100,000 men and agree to build no military fortifications in the Rhineland.

More harshly, the Allies declared that Germany (with Austria) was responsible for the war and had therefore to pay reparations equal to all civilian damages caused by the war. This unfortunate and much-criticized clause expressed inescapable popular demands for German blood, but the actual figure was not set, and there was the clear possibility that reparations might be set at a reasonable level in the future, when tempers had cooled.

When presented with the treaty, the German government protested vigorously. But there was no

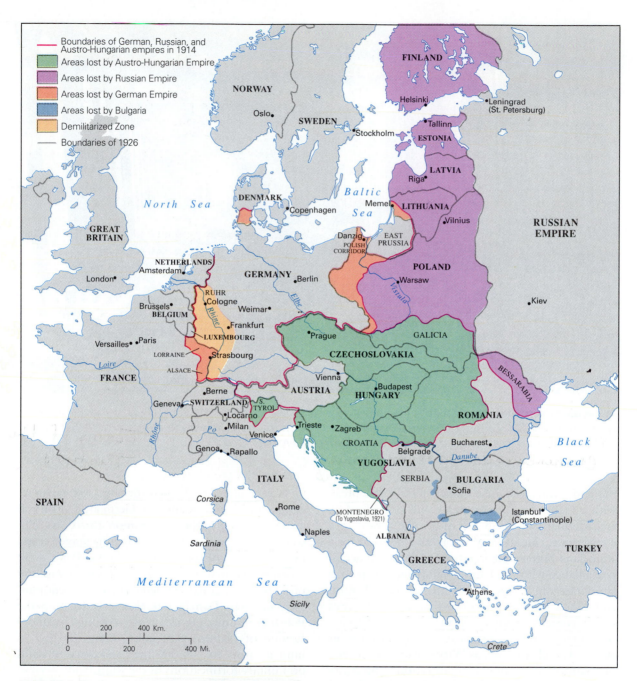

MAP 27.4 Shattered Empires and Territorial Changes After World War One The Great War brought tremendous changes in eastern Europe. New nations were established, and a dangerous power vacuum was created between Germany and Soviet Russia.

Legend:

Boundaries of German, Russian, and Austro-Hungarian empires in 1914

Areas lost by Austro-Hungarian Empire

Areas lost by Russian Empire

Areas lost by German Empire

Areas lost by Bulgaria

Demilitarized Zone

Boundaries of 1926

alternative, especially considering that Germany was still starving because the Allies had not yet lifted their naval blockade. On June 28, 1919, German representatives of the ruling moderate Social Democrats and the Catholic party signed the treaty in the Sun King's Hall of Mirrors at Versailles, where Bismarck's empire had been joyously proclaimed almost fifty years before.

Separate peace treaties were concluded with the other defeated powers—Austria, Hungary, Bulgaria, and Turkey. For the most part, these treaties merely ratified the existing situation in east central Europe following the breakup of the Austro-Hungarian Empire. Like Austria, Hungary was a particularly big loser, as its "captive" nationalities (and some interspersed Hungarians) were ceded to Rumania, Czechoslovakia, Poland, and Yugoslavia. Italy got some Austrian territory. The Turkish empire was broken up. France received Lebanon and Syria, while Britain took Iraq and Palestine, which was to include a Jewish national homeland first promised by Britain in 1917. Officially League of Nations mandates, these acquisitions of the Western powers were one of the more imperialistic elements of the peace settlement. Another was mandating Germany's holdings in China to Japan. The age of Western imperialism lived on. National self-determination remained a reality only for Europeans and their offspring.

American Rejection of the Versailles Treaty

The rapidly concluded peace settlement of early 1919 was not perfect, but within the context of war-shattered Europe it was an acceptable beginning. The principle of national self-determination, which had played such a large role in starting the war, was accepted and served as an organizing framework. Germany had been punished but not dismembered. A new world organization complemented a traditional defensive alliance of satisfied powers. The serious remaining problems could be worked out in the future. Moreover, Allied leaders had seen speed as essential for another reason: they detested Lenin and feared that his Bolshevik Revolution might spread. They realized that their best answer to Lenin's unending calls for worldwide upheaval was peace and tranquility for war-weary peoples.

There were, however, two great interrelated obstacles to such peace: Germany and the United States. Plagued by communist uprisings, reactionary plots, and popular disillusionment with losing the war at the last minute, Germany's moderate socialists and their liberal and Catholic supporters faced an enormous challenge. Like French republicans after 1871, they needed time (and luck) if they were to establish firmly a peaceful and democratic republic. Progress in this direction required understanding yet firm treatment of Germany by the victorious Western Allies, and particularly by the United States.

However, the United States Senate and, to a lesser extent, the American people rejected Wilson's handiwork. Republican senators led by Henry Cabot Lodge refused to ratify the Treaty of Versailles without changes in the articles creating the League of Nations. The key issue was the League's power—more apparent than real—to require member states to take collective action against aggression.

Lodge and others believed that this requirement gave away Congress's constitutional right to declare war. No doubt Wilson would have been wise to accept some reservations. But, in failing health, Wilson with narrow-minded self-righteousness rejected all attempts at compromise. He instructed loyal Democratic senators to vote against any reservations whatsoever to the Treaty of Versailles. In doing so, Wilson assured that the treaty was never ratified by the United States in any form and that the United States never joined the League of Nations. Moreover, the Senate refused to ratify Wilson's defensive alliance with France and Great Britain. America turned its back on Europe.

Perhaps understandable in the light of American traditions and the volatility of mass politics, the Wilson-Lodge fiasco and the new-found gospel of isolationism nevertheless represented a tragic and cowardly renunciation of America's responsibility. Using America's action as an excuse, Great Britain, too, refused to ratify its defensive alliance with France. Bitterly betrayed by its allies, France stood alone. Very shortly, France was to take actions against Germany that would feed the fires of German resentment and seriously undermine democratic forces in the new republic. The great hopes of early 1919 were turning to ashes by the end of the year. The Western alliance had collapsed, and a grandiose plan for permanent peace had given way to a fragile truce. For this and for what came later, the United States must share a large part of the guilt.

SUMMARY

Why did World War One have such revolutionary consequences? Why was it such a great break with the past? World War One was, first of all, a war of committed peoples. In France, Britain, and Germany in particular, governments drew on genuine popular support. This support reflected not only the diplomatic origins of the war but also the way western European society had been effectively unified under the nationalist banner in the later nineteenth century. The relentlessness of total war helps explain why so many died, why so many were crippled physically and psychologically, and why Western civilization would in so many ways never be the same again. More concretely, the war swept away monarchs and multinational empires. National self-determination apparently triumphed, not only in Austria-Hungary but in many of Russia's western borderlands as well. Except in Ireland and parts of Soviet Russia, the revolutionary dream of national unity, born of the French Revolution, had finally come true.

Two other revolutions were products of the war. In Russia, the Bolsheviks established a radical regime, smashed existing capitalist institutions, and stayed in power with a new kind of authoritarian rule. Whether the new Russian regime was truly Marxian or socialist was questionable, but it indisputably posed a powerful, ongoing revolutionary challenge in Europe and Europe's colonial empires.

More subtle, but quite universal in its impact, was an administrative revolution. This revolution, born of the need to mobilize entire societies and economies for total war, greatly increased the power of government. And after the guns grew still, government planning and wholesale involvement in economic and social life did not disappear in Europe. Liberal market capitalism and a well-integrated world economy were among the many casualties of the administrative revolution, and greater social equality was everywhere one of its results. Thus, even in European countries where a communist takeover never came close to occurring, society still experienced a great revolution.

Finally, the "war to end war" did not bring peace but only a fragile truce: in the West the Allies failed to maintain their wartime solidarity. Germany remained unrepentant and would soon have more grievances to nurse. Moreover, the victory of national self-determination in eastern Europe created a power vacuum between a still-powerful Germany and a potentially mighty communist Russia. A vast area lay open to military aggression from two sides.

NOTES

1. M. Beloff, quoted in *U.S. News and World Report,* March 8, 1976, p. 53.
2. Quoted in J. Remak, *The Origins of World War I* (New York: Holt, Rinehart & Winston, 1967), p. 84.
3. Quoted in W. E. Mosse, *Alexander II and the Modernization of Russia* (New York: Collier Books, 1962), pp. 125–126.
4. Quoted in Remak, p. 123.
5. Quoted in J. E. Rodes, *The Quest for Unity: Modern Germany 1848–1970* (New York: Holt, Rinehart & Winston, 1971), p. 178.
6. Quoted in F. P. Chambers, *The War Behind the War, 1914–1918* (London: Faber & Faber, 1939), p. 444.
7. Ibid., p. 168.
8. Quoted in R. O. Paxton, *Europe in the Twentieth Century* (New York: Harcourt Brace Jovanovich, 1975), p. 109.
9. Quoted in Chambers, p. 378.
10. Ibid., p. 110.
11. Ibid., pp. 302, 304.
12. A. B. Ulam, *The Bolsheviks* (New York: Collier Books, 1968), p. 349.
13. Ibid., p. 405.
14. H. Nicolson, *Peacemaking 1919* (New York: Grosset & Dunlap Universal Library, 1965), pp. 8, 31–32.
15. Ibid., p. 24.

SUGGESTED READING

O. Hale, *The Great Illusion,* 1900–1914 (1971), is a thorough account of the prewar era. Both Remak's volume cited in the Notes and L. Lafore, *The Long Fuse* (1971), are highly recommended studies of the causes of the First World War. A. J. P. Taylor, *The Struggle for Mastery in Europe, 1848–1919* (1954), is an outstanding survey of diplomatic developments with an exhaustive bibliography. V. Steiner, *Britain and the Origins of the First World War* (1978), and G. Kennan, *The Decline of Bismarck's European Order: Franco-Russian Relations, 1875–1890* (1979), are also major contributions. K. Jarausch's *The Enigmatic Chancellor* (1973) is an important recent study on Bethmann-Hollweg and German policy in 1914. C. Falls, *The Great War* (1961), is the best brief introduction to military aspects of the war. B. Tuchman, *The Guns of*

August (1962), is a marvelous account of the dramatic first month of the war and the beginning of military stalemate. G. Ritter provides an able study in *The Schlieffen Plan* (1958). J. Winter, *The Experience of World War I* (1988), is a strikingly illustrated history of the war, and A. Horne, *The Price of Glory: Verdun 1916* (1979), is a moving account of the famous siege. J. Ellis, *Eye-Deep in Hell* (1976), is a vivid account of trench warfare. Vera Brittain's *Testament of Youth,* the moving autobiography of a nurse in wartime, shows lives buffeted by new ideas and personal tragedies.

F. L. Carsten, *War Against War* (1982), considers radical movements in Britain and Germany. The best single volume on the home fronts is still the one by Chambers mentioned in the Notes. Chambers drew heavily on the many fine books on the social and economic impact of the war in different countries published by the Carnegie Endowment for International Peace under the general editorship of J. T. Shotwell. A. Marwick, *The Deluge* (1970), is a lively account of war and society in Britain, while G. Feldman, *Army, Industry, and Labor in Germany, 1914–1918* (1966), shows the impact of total war and military dictatorship on Germany. Three excellent collections of essays, R. Wall and J. Winter, eds., *The Upheaval of War: Family, Work, and Welfare in Europe, 1914–1918* (1988), J. Roth, ed., *World War I* (1967), and R. Albrecht-Carrié, ed., *The Meaning of the First World War* (1965), probe the enormous consequences of the war for people and society. The debate over Germany's guilt and aggression, which has been reopened in recent years, may be best approached through G. Feldman, ed., *German Imperialism, 1914–1918* (1972), and A. Hillgruber, *Germany and the Two World Wars* (1981). M. Fainsod, *International Socialism and the World War* (1935), ably discusses the splits between radical and moderate socialists during the conflict. In addition to Erich Maria Remarque's great novel *All Quiet on the Western Front,* Henri Barbusse, *Under Fire* (1917), and Jules Romains, *Verdun* (1939), are highly recommended for their fictional yet realistic re-creations of the war. P. Fussell, *The Great War and Modern Memory* (1975), probes all the powerful literature inspired by the war.

R. Suny and A. Adams, eds., *The Russian Revolution and Bolshevik Victory,* 3d ed. (1990), presents a wide range of old and new interpretations. A. Ulam's work cited in the Notes, which focuses on Lenin, is a masterful introduction to the Russian Revolution, while S. Fitzpatrick, *The Russian Revolution* (1982), provides a provocative reconsideration. B. Wolfe, *Three Who Made a Revolution* (1955), a collective biography of Lenin, Trotsky, and Stalin, and R. Conquest, *V. I. Lenin* (1972), are recommended. Leon Trotsky himself wrote the colorful and exciting *History of the Russian Revolution* (1932), which may be compared with the classic eyewitness account of the young, pro-Bolshevik American John Reed, *Ten Days That Shook the World* (1919). R. Daniels, *Red October* (1969), provides a clear account of the Bolshevik seizure of power, and R. Pipes, *The Formation of the Soviet Union* (1968), is recommended for its excellent treatment of the nationality problem during the revolution. D. Koenker, W. Rosenberg, and R. Suny, eds., *Party, State and Society in the Russian Civil War* (1989), probes the social foundations of Bolshevik victory. A. Wildman, *The End of the Russian Imperial Army* (1980), is a fine account of the soldiers' revolt, and G. Leggett, *The Cheka: Lenin's Secret Police* (1981), shows revolutionary terror in action. Boris Pasternak's justly celebrated *Doctor Zhivago* is a great historical novel of the revolutionary era. R. Massie, *Nicholas and Alexandra* (1971), is a moving popular biography of Russia's last royal family and the terrible health problem of the heir to the throne. H. Nicolson's study listed in the Notes captures the spirit of the Versailles settlement. T. Bailey, *Woodrow Wilson and the Lost Peace* (1963), and W. Widenor, *Henry Cabot Lodge and the Search for an American Foreign Policy* (1981), are also highly recommended. A. Mayer provocatively stresses the influence of domestic social tensions and widespread fear of further communist revolt in *The Politics and Diplomacy of Peacemaking* (1969).

28

The Age of Anxiety

When Allied diplomats met in Paris in early 1919 with their optimistic plans for building a lasting peace, most people looked forward to happier times. They hoped that life would return to normal after the terrible trauma of total war. They hoped that once again life would make sense in the familiar prewar terms of peace, prosperity, and progress. These hopes were in vain. The Great Break—the First World War and the Russian Revolution—had mangled too many things beyond repair. Life would no longer fit neatly into the old molds.

Instead, great numbers of men and women felt themselves increasingly adrift in a strange, uncertain, and uncontrollable world. They saw themselves living in an age of anxiety, an age of continuous crisis, which lasted until at least the early 1950s. In almost every area of human experience, people went searching for ways to put meaning back into life.

- What did the doubts and searching mean for Western thought, art, and culture?
- How did political leaders try to re-establish real peace and prosperity between 1919 and 1939?
- And why did those leaders fail?

These are questions this chapter will explore.

UNCERTAINTY IN MODERN THOUGHT

A complex revolution in thought and ideas was under way before the First World War, but only small, unusual groups were aware of it. After the war, new and upsetting ideas began to spread through the entire population. Western society began to question and even abandon many cherished values and beliefs that had guided it since the eighteenth-century Enlightenment and the nineteenth-century triumph of industrial development, scientific advances, and evolutionary thought.

Before 1914 most people still believed in progress, reason, and the rights of the individual. Progress was a daily reality, apparent in the rising standard of living, the taming of the city, and the steady increase in popular education. Such developments also encouraged the comforting belief in the logical universe of Newtonian physics, as well as faith in the ability of a rational human mind to understand that universe through intellectual investigation. And just as there were laws of science, so were there laws of society that rational human beings could discover and then wisely act on. Finally, the rights of the individual were not just taken for granted, they were actually increasing. Well-established rights were gradually spreading to women and workers, and new "social rights" like old-age pensions were emerging. In short, before World War One, most Europeans had a moderately optimistic view of the world, and with good reason.

From the 1880s on, however, a small band of serious thinkers and creative writers began to attack these well-worn optimistic ideas. These critics rejected the general faith in progress and the power of the rational human mind. Such views were greatly strengthened by the experience of history's most destructive war, which suggested to many that human beings were a pack of violent, irrational animals quite capable of tearing the individual and his or her rights to shreds. There was growing pessimism and a general crisis of the mind, and a growing chorus of thinkers, creative writers, and scientists echoed and enlarged on the themes first expressed by the small group of critics between 1880 and 1914. People did not know what to think. This disorientation was particularly acute in the 1930s, when the rapid rise of harsh dictatorships and the Great Depression transformed old certainties into bitter illusions.

No one expressed this state of uncertainty better than the French poet and critic Paul Valéry (1871–1945) in the early 1920s. Speaking of the "crisis of the mind," Valéry noted that Europe was looking at its future with dark foreboding:

The storm has died away, and still we are restless, uneasy, as if the storm were about to break. Almost all the affairs of men remain in a terrible uncertainty. We think of what has disappeared, and we are almost destroyed by what has been destroyed; we do not know what will be born, and we fear the future, not without reason. . . . Doubt and disorder are in us and with us. There is no thinking man, however shrewd or learned he may be, who can hope to dominate this anxiety, to escape from this impression of darkness.[1]

In the midst of economic, political, and social disruptions Valéry saw the "cruelly injured mind," besieged by doubts and suffering from anxieties. This was the general intellectual crisis of the twentieth century, which touched almost every field of

"The War, as I Saw It"   This was the title of a series of grotesque drawings that appeared in 1920 in *Simplicissimus,* Germany's leading satirical magazine. Nothing shows better the terrible impact of World War One than this profoundly disturbing example of expressionist art. *(Source: Caroline Buckler)*

thought. The implications of new ideas and discoveries in philosophy, physics, psychology, and literature played a central role in this crisis, disturbing "thinking people" everywhere.

Modern Philosophy

Among those thinkers in the late nineteenth century who challenged the belief in progress and the general faith in the rational human mind, the German philosopher Friedrich Nietzsche (1844–1900) was particularly influential. Nietzsche believed that Western civilization had lost its creativity and decayed into mediocrity. Christianity's "slave morality" had glorified weakness and humility. Furthermore, human beings in the West had overstressed rational thinking at the expense of passion and emotion. Nietzsche viewed the pillars of conventional morality—reason, democracy, progress, respectability—as outworn social and psychological constructs whose influence was suffocating any creativity. The only hope of revival was for a few superior individuals to free themselves from the humdrum thinking of the masses and embrace life passionately. Such individuals would become true heroes, supermen capable of leading the dumb herd of inferior men and women. Nietzsche also condemned both political democracy and greater social equality.

The growing dissatisfaction with established ideas before 1914 was apparent in other important thinkers. In the 1890s, the French philosophy professor Henri Bergson (1859–1941) convinced many young people through his writing that immediate experience and intuition are as important as rational and scientific thinking for understanding reality. Indeed, according to Bergson, a religious experience or a mystical poem is often more accessible to human comprehension than a scientific law or a mathematical equation.

Another thinker who agreed about the limits of rational thinking was the French socialist Georges Sorel (1847–1922). Sorel frankly characterized Marxian socialism as an inspiring but unprovable religion rather than a rational scientific truth. Socialism would come to power, he believed, through a great, violent strike of all working people, which would miraculously shatter capitalist society. Sorel rejected democracy and believed that the masses of the new socialist society would have to be tightly controlled by a small revolutionary elite.

The First World War accelerated the revolt against established certainties in philosophy, but that revolt went in two very different directions. In English-speaking countries, the main development was the acceptance of logical empiricism (or logical positivism) in university circles. In continental countries, where esoteric and remote logical empiricism has never won many converts, the primary development in philosophy was existentialism.

Logical empiricism was truly revolutionary. It quite simply rejected most of the concerns of traditional philosophy, from the existence of God to the meaning of happiness, as nonsense and hot air. This outlook began primarily with the Austrian philosopher Ludwig Wittgenstein (1889–1951), who later emigrated to England, where he trained numerous disciples.

Wittgenstein argued in his pugnacious *Tractatus Logico-Philosophicus (Essay on Logical Philosophy)* in 1922 that philosophy is only the logical clarification of thoughts, and therefore it becomes the study of language, which expresses thoughts. The

great philosophical issues of the ages—God, freedom, morality, and so on—are quite literally senseless, a great waste of time, for statements about them can neither be tested by scientific experiments nor demonstrated by the logic of mathematics. Statements about such matters reflect only the personal preferences of a given individual. As Wittgenstein put it in the famous last sentence of his work, "Of what one cannot speak, of that one must keep silent." Logical empiricism, which has remained dominant in England and the United States to this day, drastically reduced the scope of philosophical inquiry. Anxious people could find few if any answers in this direction.

Highly diverse and even contradictory, *existential* thinkers were loosely united in a courageous search for moral values in a world of terror and uncertainty. Theirs were true voices of the age of anxiety.

Most existential thinkers in the twentieth century have been atheists. Like Nietzsche, who had already proclaimed that "God is dead," they did not believe a supreme being had established humanity's fundamental nature and given life its meaning. In the words of the famous French existentialist Jean-Paul Sartre (1905–1980), human beings simply exist: "They turn up, appear on the scene." Only after they "turn up" do they seek to define themselves. Honest human beings are terribly alone, for there is no God to help them. They are hounded by despair and the meaninglessness of life. The crisis of the existential thinker epitomized the modern intellectual crisis—the shattering of traditional beliefs in God, reason, and progress.

Existentialists did recognize that human beings, unless they kill themselves, must act. Indeed, in the words of Sartre, "man is condemned to be free." There is, therefore, the possibility—indeed, the necessity—of giving meaning to life through actions, of defining oneself through choices. To do so, individuals must become "engaged" and choose their own actions courageously, consistently, and in full awareness of their inescapable responsibility for their own behavior. In the end, existentialists argued, human beings can overcome the absurdity that existentialists saw in life.

Modern existentialism developed first in Germany in the 1920s, when the philosophers Martin Heidegger and Karl Jaspers found a sympathetic audience among disillusioned postwar university students. But it was in France during the years immediately after World War Two that existentialism came of age. The terrible conditions of the war reinforced the existential view of life and the existential approach to it. On the one hand, the armies of the German dictator Hitler had conquered most of Europe and unleashed a hideous reign of barbarism. On the other, men and women had more than ever to define themselves by their actions. Specifically, each individual had to choose whether to join the Resistance against Hitler or to accept and even abet tyranny. The writings of Sartre, who along with Albert Camus (1913–1960) was the leading French existentialist, became enormously influential. Himself active in the Resistance, Sartre and his colleagues offered a powerful answer to profound moral issues and the contemporary crisis.

The Revival of Christianity

Christianity and religion in general had been on the defensive in intellectual circles since the Enlightenment, especially during the late nineteenth century. But the loss of faith in human reason and in continual progress now led to a renewed interest in the Christian view of the world in the twentieth century. A number of thinkers and theologians began to revitalize the fundamentals of Christianity, especially after World War One. They had a powerful impact on society. Sometimes described as Christian existentialists because they shared the loneliness and despair of atheistic existentialists, they revived the tradition of Saint Augustine. They stressed human beings' sinful nature, the need for faith, and the mystery of God's forgiveness.

This development was a break with the late nineteenth century. In the years before 1914, some theologians, especially Protestant theologians, had felt the need to interpret Christian doctrine and the Bible so that they did not seem to contradict science, evolution, and common sense. Christ was therefore seen primarily as the greatest moral teacher, and the "supernatural" aspects of his divinity were strenuously played down. An important if extreme example of this tendency was the young Albert Schweitzer's *Quest of the Historical Jesus* (1906). A theologian and later a famous medical missionary and musician of note, Schweitzer (1875–1965) argued that Christ while on earth was a completely natural man whose teachings had been only temporary rules to prepare himself and his disciples for the end of the world, which they were erroneously expecting. In short, some modern theologians were embarrassed by the miraculous, unscientific aspects of Christianity and turned away from them.

The revival of fundamental Christian belief after World War One was fed by rediscovery of the work of the nineteenth-century Danish religious philosopher Søren Kierkegaard (1813–1855), whose ideas became extremely influential. Kierkegaard had rejected formalistic religion and denounced the worldliness of the Danish Lutheran church. He had eventually resolved his personal anguish over his imperfect nature by making a total religious commitment to a remote and majestic God.

Similar ideas were brilliantly developed by the Swiss Protestant theologian Karl Barth (1886–1968), whose many influential writings after 1920 sought to re-create the religious intensity of the Reformation. For Barth, the basic fact about human beings is that they are imperfect, sinful creatures, whose reason and will are hopelessly flawed. Religious truth is therefore made known to human beings only through God's grace. People have to accept God's word and the supernatural revelation of Jesus Christ with awe, trust, and obedience. Lowly mortals should not expect to "reason out" God and his ways.

Among Catholics, the leading existential Christian thinker was Gabriel Marcel (1887–1973). Born into a cultivated French family, where his atheistic father was "gratefully aware of all that . . . art owed to Catholicism but regarded Catholic thought itself as obsolete and tainted with absurd superstitions,"[2] Marcel found in the Catholic church an answer to what he called the postwar "broken world." Catholicism and religious belief provided the hope, humanity, honesty, and piety for which he hungered. Flexible and gentle, Marcel and his countryman Jacques Maritain (1882–1973) denounced anti-Semitism and supported closer ties with non-Catholics.

After 1914 religion became much more relevant and meaningful to thinking people than it was before the war. In addition to Marcel and Maritain, many other illustrious individuals turned to religion between about 1920 and 1950. The poets T. S. Eliot and W. H. Auden, the novelists Evelyn Waugh and Aldous Huxley, the historian Arnold Toynbee, the Oxford professor C. S. Lewis, the psychoanalyst Karl Stern, and the physicist Max Planck were all either converted to religion or attracted to it for the first time. Religion, often of a despairing, existential variety, was one meaningful answer to terror and anxiety. In the words of another famous

Roman Catholic convert, English novelist Graham Greene, "One began to believe in heaven because one believed in hell."[3]

The New Physics

Ever since the Scientific Revolution of the seventeenth century, scientific advances and their implications have greatly influenced the beliefs of thinking people. By the late nineteenth century, science was one of the main pillars supporting Western society's optimistic and rationalistic view of the world. The Darwinian concept of evolution had been accepted and assimilated in most intellectual circles. Progressive minds believed that science, unlike religion and philosophical speculation, was based on hard facts and controlled experiments. Science seemed to have achieved an unerring and almost completed picture of reality. Unchanging natural laws seemed to determine physical processes and permit useful solutions to more and more problems. All this was comforting, especially to people who were no longer committed to traditional religious beliefs. And all this was challenged by the new physics.

An important first step toward the new physics was the discovery at the end of the century that atoms were not like hard, permanent little billiard balls. They were actually composed of many far-smaller, fast-moving particles, such as electrons and protons. The Polish-born physicist Marie Curie (1867–1934) and her French husband discovered that radium constantly emits subatomic particles and thus does not have a constant atomic weight. Building on this and other work in radiation, the German physicist Max Planck (1858–1947) showed in 1900 that subatomic energy is emitted in uneven little spurts, which Planck called "quanta," and not in a steady stream as previously believed. Planck's discovery called into question the old sharp distinction between matter and energy; the implication was that matter and energy might be different forms of the same thing. The old view of atoms as the stable, basic building blocks of nature, with a different kind of unbreakable atom for each of the ninety-two chemical elements, was badly shaken.

In 1905 the German-born Jewish genius Albert Einstein (1879–1955) went further than the Curies and Planck in challenging Newtonian physics. His famous theory of special relativity postulated that time and space are not absolute, but relative to the viewpoint of the observer. To clarify Einstein's idea, consider a person riding on a train. From the viewpoint of an observer outside the train, the passenger's net speed is exactly the same whether the passenger is walking or sitting. From the passenger's viewpoint, walking to the restaurant car is different from sitting in a seat. The closed framework of Newtonian physics was quite limited compared to that of Einsteinian physics,

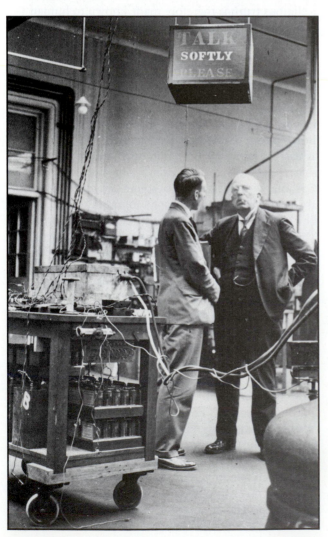

Lord Rutherford The great physicist Ernest Rutherford split the atom in 1919 with a small device he could hold in his hands. Here he is seen with a colleague in Cambridge University's renowned Cavendish Laboratory in 1932, when scientific laboratories engaged in pure research were still relatively small. *(Source: Cavendish Laboratory, Cambridge University / C. E. Wynn-Williams)*

which unified an apparently infinite universe with the incredibly small, fast-moving subatomic world. Moreover, Einstein's theory stated clearly that matter and energy are interchangeable and that all matter contains enormous levels of potential energy.

The 1920s opened the "heroic age of physics," in the apt words of one of its leading pioneers, Ernest Rutherford (1871–1937). Breakthrough followed breakthrough. In 1919 Rutherford showed that the atom could be split. By 1944 seven subatomic particles had been identified, of which the most important was the neutron. The neutron's capacity to pass through other atoms allowed for even more intense experimental bombardment of matter, leading to chain reactions of unbelievable force. This was the road to the atomic bomb.

Although few nonscientists understood the revolution in physics, the implications of the new theories and discoveries, as presented by newspapers and popular writers, were disturbing to millions of men and women in the 1920s and 1930s. The new universe was strange and troubling. It lacked any absolute objective reality. Everything was "relative," that is, dependent on the observer's frame of reference. Moreover, the universe was uncertain and undetermined, without stable building blocks. In 1927 the German physicist Werner Heisenberg (1901–1976) formulated the "principle of uncertainty." Heisenberg's principle postulates that, because it is impossible to know the position and speed of an individual electron, it is therefore impossible to predict its behavior. Instead of Newton's dependable, rational laws, there seemed to be only tendencies and probabilities in an extraordinarily complex and uncertain universe.

Moreover, a universe described by abstract mathematical symbols seemed to have little to do with human experience and human problems. When, for example, Max Planck was asked what science could contribute to resolving conflicts of values, his response was simple: "Science is not qualified to speak to this question." Physics, the queen of the sciences, no longer provided people easy, optimistic answers—nor, for that matter, did it provide any answers at all.

Freudian Psychology

With physics presenting an uncertain universe so unrelated to ordinary human experience, questions regarding the power and potential of the human mind assumed special significance. The findings and speculations of the leading psychologist, Sigmund Freud (see page 781), were particularly disturbing.

Before Freud, poets and mystics had probed the unconscious and irrational aspects of human behavior. But most professional, "scientific" psychologists assumed that a single, unified conscious mind processed sense experiences in a rational and logical way. Human behavior in turn was the result of rational calculation—of "thinking"—by the conscious mind. Basing his insights on the analysis of dreams and of hysteria, Freud developed a very different view of the human psyche beginning in the late 1880s.

According to Freud, human behavior is basically irrational. The key to understanding the mind is the primitive, irrational unconscious, which he called the *id*. The unconscious is driven by sexual, aggressive, and pleasure-seeking desires and is locked in a constant battle with the other parts of the mind: the rationalizing conscious (the *ego*), which mediates what a person *can* do, and ingrained moral values (the *superego*), which tell what a person *should* do. Human behavior is a product of fragile compromise between instinctual drives and the controls of rational thinking and moral values. Since the instinctual drives are extremely powerful, the ever-present danger for individuals and whole societies is that unacknowledged drives will overwhelm the control mechanisms in a violent, distorted way. Yet Freud also agreed with Nietzsche that the mechanisms of rational thinking and traditional moral values can be too strong. They can repress sexual desires too effectively, crippling individuals and entire peoples with guilt and neurotic fears.

Freudian psychology and clinical psychiatry had become an international movement by 1910, but only after 1918 did they receive popular attention, especially in the Protestant countries of northern Europe and in the United States. Many opponents and even some enthusiasts interpreted Freud as saying that the first requirement for mental health is an uninhibited sex life. Thus, after the First World War, the popular interpretation of Freud reflected and encouraged growing sexual experimentation, particularly among middle-class women. For more serious students, the psychology of Freud and his followers drastically undermined the old, easy optimism about the rational and progressive nature of the human mind.

Munch: The Dance of Life   Like his contemporary Sigmund Freud, the expressionist painter Edvard Munch studied the turmoil and fragility of human thought and action. Solitary figures struggling with fear and uncertainty dominate his work. Here the girl in white represents innocence, the tense woman in black stands for mourning and rejection and the woman in red evokes the joy of passing pleasure. *(Source: © Nasjonalgalleriet, Oslo. Photo: Jacques Lathion)*

Twentieth-century Literature

Literature articulated the general intellectual climate of pessimism, relativism, and alienation. Novelists developed new techniques to express new realities. The great nineteenth-century novelists had typically written as all-knowing narrators, describing realistic characters and their relationship to an understandable if sometimes harsh society. In the twentieth century, most major writers adopted the limited, often confused viewpoint of a single individual. Like Freud, these novelists focused their attention on the complexity and irrationality of the human mind, where feelings, memories, and desires are forever scrambled. The great French novelist Marcel Proust (1871–1922), in his semi-autobiographical *Remembrance of Things Past*

(1913–1927), recalled bittersweet memories of childhood and youthful love and tried to discover their innermost meaning. To do so, Proust lived like a hermit in a soundproof Paris apartment for ten years, withdrawing from the present to dwell on the past.

Serious novelists also used the "stream-of-consciousness" technique to explore the psyche. In *Jacob's Room* (1922), Virginia Woolf (1882–1941) turned the novel into a series of internal monologues, in which ideas and emotions from different periods of time bubble up as randomly as from a patient on a psychoanalyst's couch. William Faulkner (1897–1962), perhaps America's greatest twentieth-century novelist, used the same technique in *The Sound and the Fury,* much of whose intense drama is confusedly seen through the eyes of an idiot. The most famous stream-of-consciousness novel—and surely the most disturbing novel of its generation—is *Ulysses,* which the Irish novelist James Joyce (1882–1941) published in 1922. Into *Ulysses'* account of an ordinary day in the life of an ordinary man, Joyce weaves an extended ironic parallel between his hero's aimless wanderings through the streets and pubs of Dublin and the adventures of Homer's hero *Ulysses* on his way home from Troy. Abandoning conventional grammar and blending foreign words, puns, bits of knowledge, and scraps of memory together in bewildering confusion, the language of Ulysses is intended to mirror modern life itself: a gigantic riddle waiting to be unraveled.

As creative writers turned their attention from society to the individual and from realism to psychological relativity, they rejected the idea of progress. Some even described "anti-utopias," nightmare visions of things to come. In 1918 an obscure German high school teacher named Oswald Spengler (1880–1936) published *The Decline of the West,* which quickly became an international sensation. According to Spengler, every culture experiences a life cycle of growth and decline. Western civilization, in Spengler's opinion, was in its old age, and death was approaching in the form of conquest by the yellow race. T. S. Eliot (1888–1965), in his famous poem *The Waste Land* (1922), depicted a world of growing desolation, although after his conversion to Anglo-Catholicism in 1927, Eliot came to hope cautiously for humanity's salvation. No such hope appeared in the work of Franz Kafka (1883–1924), whose novels *The Trial* and *The Castle,* as well as several of his greatest short stories, portray helpless individuals crushed by inexplicably hostile forces. The German-Jewish Kafka died young, at forty-one, and so did not see the world of his nightmares materialize in the Nazi state.

The Englishman George Orwell (1903–1950), however, had seen both that reality and its Stalinist counterpart by 1949 when he wrote perhaps the ultimate in anti-utopian literature: *1984.* Orwell set the action in the future, in 1984. Big Brother—the dictator—and his totalitarian state use a new kind of language, sophisticated technology, and psychological terror to strip a weak individual of his last shred of human dignity. The supremely self-confident chief of the Thought Police tells the tortured, broken, and framed Winston Smith: "If you want a picture of the future, imagine a boot stamping on a human face—forever."[4] A phenomenal best seller, *1984* spoke to millions of people in the closing years of the age of anxiety.

MODERN ART AND MUSIC

Throughout the twentieth century, there has been considerable unity in the arts. The "modernism" of the immediate prewar years and the 1920s is still strikingly modern. Manifestations of modernism in art, architecture, and music have of course been highly varied, just as in physics, psychology, and philosophy; yet there are resemblances, for artists, scientists, and original thinkers partake of the same

Virginia Woolf   Her novels captured sensations like impressionist paintings, and her home attracted a circle of artists and writers known as the Bloomsbury Group. Many of Woolf's essays dealt with women's issues and urged greater opportunity for women's creativity. *(Source: © Gisèle Freund/Photo Researchers)*

culture. Creative artists rejected old forms and old values. Modernism in art and music meant constant experimentation and a search for new kinds of expression. And though many people find the modern visions of the arts strange, disturbing, and even ugly, the twentieth century, so dismal in many respects, will probably stand as one of Western civilization's great artistic eras.

Architecture and Design

Modernism in the arts was loosely unified by a revolution in architecture. The architectural revolution not only gave the other arts striking new settings, it intended nothing less than to transform the physical framework of the urban society according to a new principle: *functionalism*. Buildings, like

Frank Lloyd Wright: The "Falling Water" House Often considered Wright's masterpiece, Falling Water combines modern architectural concepts with close attention to a spectacular site. Anchored to a high rock ledge by means of reinforced concrete, the house soars out over a cascading waterfall at Bear Run in western Pennsylvania. Built in 1937 for a Pittsburgh businessman, Falling Water is now open to the public and attracts 70,000 visitors each year. *(Source: Western Pennsylvania Conservancy/Art Resource)*

industrial products, should be useful and "functional": that is, they should serve, as well as possible, the purpose for which they were made. Thus architects and designers had to work with engineers, town planners, and even sanitation experts. Moreover, they had to throw away useless ornamentation and find beauty and aesthetic pleasure in the clean lines of practical constructions and efficient machinery. The Viennese pioneer Adolf Loos (1870–1933) quite typically equated ornamentation with crime, and the Franco-Swiss genius Le Corbusier (1887–1965) insisted that "a house is a machine for living in."[5]

The United States, with its rapid urban growth and lack of rigid building traditions, pioneered in the new architecture. In the 1890s the Chicago school of architects, led by Louis H. Sullivan (1856–1924), used cheap steel, reinforced concrete, and electric elevators to build skyscrapers and office buildings lacking almost any exterior ornamentation. In the first decade of the twentieth century, Sullivan's student Frank Lloyd Wright (1869–1959) built a series of radically new and truly modern houses featuring low lines, open interiors, and mass-produced building materials. Europeans were inspired by these and other American examples of functional construction as the massive, unadorned grain elevators of the Midwest.

Around 1905, when the first really modern buildings were going up in Europe, architectural leadership shifted to the German-speaking countries and remained there until Hitler took power in 1933. In 1911 the twenty-eight-year-old Walter Gropius (1883–1969) broke sharply with the past in his design of the Fagus shoe factory at Alfeld, Germany. A clean, light, elegant building of glass and iron, Gropius's new factory represented a jump right into the middle of the century.

After the First World War, the new German republic gave Gropius the authority to merge the schools of fine and applied arts at Weimar into a single, interdisciplinary school, the Bauhaus. In spite of intense criticism from conservative politicians and university professors, the Bauhaus brought together many leading modern architects, artists, designers, and theatrical innovators, who worked as an effective, inspired team. Throwing out traditional teaching methods, they combined the study of fine art, such as painting and sculpture, with the study of applied art in the crafts of printing, weaving, and furniture making. Through-

out the 1920s, the Bauhaus, with its stress on functionalism and good design for everyday life, attracted enthusiastic students from all over the world. It had a great and continuing impact.

Along with Gropius, the architect and town planner Le Corbusier had a revolutionary influence on the development of modern architecture. Often drawing his inspiration from industrial forms, such as ocean liners, automobiles, and airplanes, Le Corbusier designed houses with flat roofs, open interior spaces, and clear, clean lines. His famous Savoy Villa at Poissy rested on concrete pillars and seemed to float on air. A true visionary, Le Corbusier sketched plans for a city of the future, with tall buildings surrounded by playgrounds and parks.

Another leader in the modern or "international" style was Ludwig Mies van der Rohe (1886–1969), who followed Gropius as director of the Bauhaus in 1930 and emigrated to the United States in 1937. His classic Lake Shore Apartments in Chicago, built between 1948 and 1951, symbolize the triumph of steel-frame and glass-wall modern architecture, which had grown out of Sullivan's skyscrapers and German functionalism in the great building boom after the Second World War.

Modern Painting

Modern painting grew out of a revolt against French impressionism. The *impressionism* of such French painters as Claude Monet (1840–1926), Pierre Auguste Renoir (1841–1919), and Camille Pissarro (1830–1903) was, in part, a kind of "superrealism." Leaving exact copying of objects to photography, these artists sought to capture the momentary overall feeling, or impression, of light falling on a real-life scene before their eyes. By 1890, when impressionism was finally established, a few artists known as *postimpressionists,* or *expressionists,* were already striking out in new directions. After 1905 art took on the abstract, nonrepresentational character that it generally retains today.

Though individualistic in their styles, postimpressionists were united in their desire to know and depict worlds other than the visible world of fact. Like the early nineteenth-century romantics, they wanted to portray unseen, inner worlds of emotion and imagination. Like modern novelists, they wanted to express a complicated psychological view of reality as well as an overwhelming emotional intensity. In *The Starry Night* (1889), for example, the great Dutch expressionist Vincent van Gogh (1853–1890) painted the vision of his mind's eye. Flaming cypress trees, exploding stars, and a cometlike Milky Way swirl together in one great cosmic rhythm. Paul Gauguin (1848–1903), the French stockbroker-turned-painter, pioneered in expressionist techniques, though he used them to infuse his work with tranquility and mysticism. In 1891 he fled to the South Pacific in search of unspoiled beauty and a primitive way of life. Gauguin believed that the form and design of a picture was important in itself and that the painter need not try to represent objects on canvas as the eye actually saw them.

Fascination with form, as opposed to light, was characteristic of postimpressionism and expressionism. Paul Cézanne (1839–1906), who had a profound influence on twentieth-century painting, was particularly committed to form and ordered design. He told a young painter, "You must see in nature the cylinder, the sphere, and the cone."[6] As Cézanne's later work became increasingly abstract and nonrepresentational, it also moved away from the traditional three-dimensional perspective toward the two-dimensional plane, which has characterized so much of modern art. The expressionism of a group of painters led by Henri Matisse (1869–1954) was so extreme that an exhibition of their work in Paris in 1905 prompted shocked critics to call them *les fauves*—"the wild beasts." Matisse and his followers were primarily concerned, not with real objects, but with the arrangement of color, line, and form as an end in itself.

In 1907 a young Spaniard in Paris, Pablo Picasso (1881–1973), founded another movement—cubism. Cubism concentrated on a complex geometry of zigzagging lines and sharp-angled, overlapping planes. About three years later came the ultimate stage in the development of abstract, nonrepresentational art. Artists such as the Russian-born Wassily Kandinsky (1866–1944) turned away from nature completely. "The observer," said Kandinsky, "must learn to look at [my] pictures . . . as form and color combinations . . . as a representation of mood and not as a representation of *objects*."[7] On the eve of the First World War, extreme expressionism and abstract painting were developing rapidly not only in Paris but also in Russia and Germany. Modern art had become international.

In the 1920s and 1930s, the artistic movements of the prewar years were extended and consolidated. The most notable new developments were *dadaism* and *surrealism*. Dadaism attacked all accepted standards of art and behavior, delighting in outrageous conduct. Its name, from the French word *dada,* meaning "hobbyhorse," is deliberately nonsensical. A famous example of dadaism was a reproduction of Leonardo da Vinci's Mona Lisa in which the famous woman with the mysterious smile sports a mustache and is ridiculed with an obscene inscription. After 1924 many dadaists were attracted to surrealism, which became very influential in art in the late 1920s and 1930s. Surrealism was inspired to a great extent by Freudian psychology. Surrealists painted a fantastic world of wild dreams and complex symbols, where watches melted and giant metronomes beat time in precisely drawn but impossible alien landscapes.

Refusing to depict ordinary visual reality, surrealist painters made powerful statements about the age of anxiety. Picasso's 26-foot-long mural *Guernica* (1937) masterfully unites several powerful strands in twentieth-century art. Inspired by the Spanish Civil War, the painting commemorates the bombing of the ancient Spanish town of Guernica by fascist planes, an attack that took the lives of a thousand people—one out of every eight inhabitants—in a single night of terror. Combining the free distortion of expressionism, the overlapping planes of cubism, and the surrealist fascination with grotesque subject matter, *Guernica* is what Picasso meant it to be: an unforgettable attack on "brutality and darkness."

Modern Music

Developments in modern music were strikingly parallel to those in painting. Composers, too, were attracted by the emotional intensity of expressionism. The ballet *The Rite of Spring* by Igor Stravinsky (1882–1971) practically caused a riot when it was first performed in Paris in 1913 by Sergei Diaghilev's famous Russian dance company. The combination of pulsating, barbaric rhythms from the orchestra pit and an earthy representation of lovemaking by the dancers on the stage seemed a shocking, almost pornographic enactment of a primitive fertility rite.

Picasso: Guernica   In this rich, complex work a shrieking woman falls from a burning house on the far right. On the left a woman holds a dead child, while toward the center are fragments of a warrior and a screaming horse pierced by a spear. Picasso has used only the mournful colors of black, white, and gray. *(Source: Museo del Prado, Madrid. Pablo Picasso, Guernica (1937, May–early June). Oil on canvas.© SPADEM, Paris/VAGA, New York, 1982)*

After the experience of the First World War, when irrationality and violence seemed to pervade the human experience, expressionism in opera and ballet flourished. One of the most famous and powerful examples is the opera *Wozzeck* by Alban Berg (1885–1935), first performed in Berlin in 1925. Blending a half-sung, half-spoken kind of dialogue with harsh, atonal music, *Wozzeck* is a gruesome tale of a soldier driven by Kafka-like inner terrors and vague suspicions of unfaithfulness to murder his mistress.

Some composers turned their backs on long-established musical conventions. As abstract painters arranged lines and color but did not draw identifiable objects, so modern composers arranged sounds without creating recognizable harmonies. Led by the Viennese composer Arnold Schönberg (1874–1951), they abandoned traditional harmony and tonality. The musical notes in a given piece were no longer united and organized by a key; instead they were independent and unrelated. Schönberg's twelve-tone music of the 1920s arranged all twelve notes of the scale in an abstract, mathematical pattern, or "tone row." This pattern sounded like no pattern at all to the ordinary listener and could be detected only by a highly trained eye studying the musical score. Accustomed to the harmonies of classical and romantic music, audiences generally resisted modern atonal music. Only after the Second World War did it begin to win acceptance.

MOVIES AND RADIO

Until after World War Two at the earliest, these revolutionary changes in art and music appealed mainly to a minority of "highbrows" and not to the general public. That public was primarily and enthusiastically wrapped up in movies and radio. The long-declining traditional arts and amusements of people in villages and small towns almost vanished, replaced by standardized, commercial entertainment.

Moving pictures were first shown as a popular novelty in naughty peepshows—"What the Butler Saw"—and penny arcades in the 1890s, especially in Paris. The first movie houses date from an experiment in Los Angeles in 1902. They quickly attracted large audiences and led to the production of short, silent action films like the eight-minute

The Great Dictator   In 1940 the great actor and director, Charlie Chaplin, abandoned the little tramp to satirize the great dictator, Adolph Hitler. Chaplin had strong political views and made a number of films with political themes as the escapist fare of the Great Depression gave way to the reality of the Second World War. *(Source: The Museum of Modern Art/Still Film Archives)*

Great Train Robbery of 1903. American directors and business people then set up "movie factories," at first in the New York area and after 1910 in Los Angeles. These factories churned out two short films each week. On the eve of the First World War, full-length feature films like the Italian *Quo Vadis* and the American *Birth of a Nation,* coupled with improvements in the quality of pictures, suggested the screen's vast possibilities.

During the First World War the United States became the dominant force in the rapidly expanding silent-film industry. In the 1920s, Mack Sennett (1884–1960) and his zany Keystone Cops specialized in short, slapstick comedies noted for frantic automobile chases, custard-pie battles, and gorgeous bathing beauties. Screen stars such as Mary Pickford and Lillian Gish, Douglas Fairbanks and

Rudolph Valentino became household names, with their own "fan clubs." Yet Charlie Chaplin (1889–1978), a funny little Englishman working in Hollywood, was unquestionably the king of the "silver screen" in the 1920s. In his enormously popular role as a lonely tramp, complete with baggy trousers, battered derby, and an awkward, shuffling walk, Chaplin symbolized the "gay spirit of laughter in a cruel, crazy world."[8] Chaplin also demonstrated that, in the hands of a genius, the new medium could combine mass entertainment and artistic accomplishment.

The early 1920s were also the great age of German films. Protected and developed during the war, the large German studios excelled in bizarre expressionist dramas, beginning with *The Cabinet of Dr. Caligari* in 1919. Unfortunately, their period of creativity was short-lived. By 1926 American money was drawing the leading German talents to Hollywood and consolidating America's international domination. Film making was big business, and European theater owners were forced to book whole blocks of American films to get the few pictures they really wanted. This system put European producers at a great disadvantage until "talkies" permitted a revival of national film industries in the 1930s, particularly in France.

Whether foreign or domestic, motion pictures became the main entertainment of the masses until after the Second World War. In Great Britain one in every four adults went to the movies twice a week in the late 1930s, and two in five went at least once a week. Continental countries had similar figures. The greatest appeal of motion pictures was that they offered ordinary people a temporary escape from the hard realities of everyday life. For an hour or two the moviegoer could flee the world of international tensions, uncertainty, unemployment, and personal frustrations. The appeal of escapist entertainment was especially strong during the Great Depression. Millions flocked to musical comedies featuring glittering stars such as Ginger Rogers and Fred Astaire and to the fanciful cartoons of Mickey Mouse and his friends.

Radio became possible with the transatlantic "wireless" communication of Guglielmo Marconi (1874–1937) in 1901 and the development of the vacuum tube in 1904, which permitted the transmission of speech and music. But only in 1920 were the first major public broadcasts of special events made in Great Britain and the United States. Lord Northcliffe, who had pioneered in journalism with the inexpensive, mass-circulation *Daily Mail,* sponsored a broadcast of "only one artist . . . the world's very best, the soprano Nellie Melba."[9] Singing from London in English, Italian, and French, Melba was heard simultaneously all over Europe on June 16, 1920. This historic event captured the public's imagination. The meteoric career of radio was launched.

Every major country quickly established national broadcasting networks. In the United States, such networks were privately owned and financed by advertising. In Great Britain, Parliament set up an independent, high-minded public corporation, the British Broadcasting Corporation (BBC), which was supported by licensing fees. Elsewhere in Europe, the typical pattern was direct control by the government.

Whatever the institutional framework, radio became popular and influential. By the late 1930s, more than three out of every four households in both democratic Great Britain and dictatorial Germany had at least one cheap, mass-produced radio. In other European countries, radio ownership was not quite so widespread, but the new medium was no less important.

Radio in unscrupulous hands was particularly well suited for political propaganda. Dictators like Mussolini and Hitler controlled the airwaves and could reach enormous national audiences with their frequent, dramatic speeches. In democratic countries, politicians such as President Franklin Roosevelt and Prime Minister Stanley Baldwin effectively used informal "fireside chats" to bolster their support.

Motion pictures also became powerful tools of indoctrination, especially in countries with dictatorial regimes. Lenin himself encouraged the development of Soviet film making, believing that the new medium was essential to the social and ideological transformation of the country. Beginning in the mid-1920s, a series of epic films, the most famous of which were directed by Sergei Eisenstein (1898–1948), brilliantly dramatized the communist view of Russian history.

In Germany, Hitler turned to a young and immensely talented woman film maker, Leni Riefenstahl (b. 1902), for a masterpiece of documentary propaganda, *The Triumph of the Will,* based on the Nazi party rally at Nuremberg in 1934. Riefenstahl combined stunning aerial photography, joyful crowds welcoming Hitler, and mass processions of young Nazi fanatics. Her film was a brilliant and all-too-powerful documentary of Germany's "Nazi rebirth." The new media of mass culture were potentially dangerous instruments of political manipulation.

THE SEARCH FOR PEACE AND POLITICAL STABILITY

As established patterns of thought and culture were challenged and mangled by the ferocious impact of World War One, so also was the political fabric stretched and torn by the consequences of the great conflict. The Versailles settlement had established a shaky truce, not a solid peace. Thus politicians and national leaders faced a gigantic task as they struggled to create a stable international order within the general context of intellectual crisis and revolutionary artistic experimentation.

The pursuit of real and lasting peace proved difficult for many reasons. Germany hated the Treaty of Versailles. France was fearful and isolated. Britain was undependable, and the United States had turned its back on European problems. Eastern Europe was in ferment, and no one could predict the future of communist Russia. Moreover, the international economic situation was poor and greatly complicated by war debts and disrupted patterns of trade. Yet for a time, from 1925 to late 1929, it appeared that peace and stability were within reach. When the subsequent collapse of the 1930s mocked these hopes, the disillusionment of liberals in the democracies was intensified.

Germany and the Western Powers

Germany was the key to lasting peace. Only under the pressure of the Allies' naval blockade and threat to extend their military occupation from the Rhineland to the rest of the country had Germany's new republican government signed the Treaty of Versailles in June 1919. To Germans of all political parties, the treaty represented a harsh, dictated peace, to be revised or repudiated as soon as possible. The treaty had neither broken nor reduced Germany, which was potentially still the strongest country in Europe. Thus the treaty had fallen between two stools: too harsh for a peace of reconciliation, too soft for a peace of conquest.

Moreover, with ominous implications for the future, France and Great Britain did not see eye to eye on Germany. By the end of 1919, France wanted to stress the harsh elements in the Treaty of Versailles. Most of the war in the west had been fought on French soil, and much of rich, industrialized northern France had been devastated. The expected costs of reconstruction were staggering; like Great Britain, France had also borrowed large sums from the United States during the war, which had to be repaid. Thus French politicians believed that massive reparations from Germany were a vital economic necessity. Moreover, if the Germans had to suffer to make the payments, the French would not be overly concerned. Having compromised with President Wilson only to be betrayed by America's failure to ratify the treaty, many French leaders saw strict implementation of all provisions of the Treaty of Versailles as France's last best hope. Large reparation payments could hold Germany down indefinitely, and France would realize its goal of security.

The British soon felt differently. Prewar Germany had been Great Britain's second-best market in the entire world, and after the war a healthy, prosperous Germany appeared to be essential to the British economy. Indeed, many English people agreed with the analysis of the young English economist John Maynard Keynes (1883–1946), who eloquently denounced the Treaty of Versailles in his famous *Economic Consequences of the Peace* (1919). According to Keynes's interpretation, astronomical reparations and harsh economic measures would indeed reduce Germany to the position of an impoverished second-rate power, but such impoverishment would increase economic hardship in all countries. Only a complete revision of the foolish treaty could save Germany—and Europe. Keynes's attack exploded like a bombshell and became very influential. It stirred deep guilt feelings about Germany in the English-speaking world, feelings that often paralyzed English and American leaders in their relations with Germany and its leaders between the First and Second World Wars.

The British were also suspicious of France's army —momentarily the largest in Europe—and France's foreign policy. Ever since 1890, France had looked to Russia as a powerful ally against Germany. But with Russia hostile and socialist, and with Britain and the United States unwilling to make any firm commitments, France turned to the newly formed states of eastern Europe for diplomatic support. In 1921 France signed a mutual defense pact with Poland and associated itself closely with the so-called Little Entente, an alliance that joined Czechoslovakia, Rumania, and Yugoslavia against defeated and bitter Hungary. The British and the French were also on cool terms because of conflicts relating to their League of Nations mandates in the Middle East.

While French and British leaders drifted in different directions, the Allied reparations commission completed its work. In April 1921 it announced that Germany had to pay the enormous sum of 132 billion gold marks ($33 billion) in annual installments of 2.5 billion gold marks. Facing possible occupation of more of its territory, the young German republic, which had been founded in Weimar but moved back to Berlin, made its first payment in 1921. Then in 1922, wracked by rapid inflation and political assassinations, and motivated by hostility and arrogance as well, the Weimar Republic announced its inability to pay more. It proposed a moratorium on reparations for three years, with the clear implication that thereafter reparations would either be drastically reduced or eliminated entirely.

The British were willing to accept this offer, but the French were not. Led by their tough-minded, legalistic prime minister, Raymond Poincaré, they decided they either had to call Germany's bluff or see the entire peace settlement dissolve to France's great disadvantage. So, despite strong British protests, France and its ally Belgium decided to pursue a firm policy. In early January 1923, French and Belgian armies began to occupy the Ruhr district, the heartland of industrial Germany, creating the most serious international crisis of the 1920s.

The Occupation of the Ruhr

The strategy of Poincaré and his French supporters was simple. Since Germany would not pay reparations in hard currency or gold, France and Belgium would collect reparations in kind—coal, steel, and machinery. If forcible collection proved impossible, France would use occupation to paralyze Germany and force it to accept the Treaty of Versailles.

Strengthened by a wave of patriotism, the German government ordered the people of the Ruhr to stop working and start resisting—passively—the French occupation. The coal mines and steel mills of the Ruhr grew silent, leaving 10 percent of Germany's total population in need of relief. The

French answer to passive resistance was to seal off, not only the Ruhr, but the entire Rhineland from the rest of Germany, letting in only enough food to prevent starvation. The French also revived plans for a separate state in the Rhineland.

By the summer of 1923, France and Germany were engaged in a great test of wills. As the German government had anticipated, French armies could not collect reparations from striking workers at gunpoint. But French occupation was indeed paralyzing Germany and its economy, for the Ruhr district normally produced 80 percent of Germany's steel and coal. Moreover, the occupation of the Ruhr turned rapid German inflation into runaway inflation. Faced with the need to support the striking Ruhr workers and their employers, the German government began to print money to pay its bills. Prices soared. People went to the store with a big bag of paper money; they returned home with a handful of groceries. German money rapidly lost all value, and so did anything else with a stated fixed value.

Runaway inflation brought about a social revolution. The accumulated savings of many retired and middle-class people were wiped out. The old middle-class virtues of thrift, caution, and self-reliance were cruelly mocked by catastrophic inflation. People told themselves that nothing had real value anymore, not even money. The German middle and lower middle classes, feeling cheated, burned with resentment. Many hated and blamed the Western governments, their own government, big business, the Jews, the workers, the communists for their misfortune. They were psychologically prepared to follow radical leaders in a crisis.

In August 1923, as the mark fell and political unrest grew throughout Germany, Gustav Stresemann assumed leadership of the government. Stresemann adopted a compromising attitude. He called off passive resistance in the Ruhr and in October agreed in principle to pay reparations, but asked for a reexamination of Germany's ability to pay. Poincaré accepted. His hard line was becoming increasingly unpopular with French citizens, and it was hated in Britain and the United States. Moreover, occupation was dreadfully expensive, and France's own currency was beginning to lose value on foreign exchange markets.

More generally, in both Germany and France, power was finally passing to the moderates, who realized that continued confrontation was a destructive, no-win situation. Thus, after five long years of

"Hands Off the Ruhr" The French occupation of the Ruhr to collect reparations payments raised a storm of patriotic protest, including this anti-French poster of 1923. *(Source: Internationaal Instituut voor Sociale Geschiedenis)*

hostility and tension culminating in a kind of undeclared war in the Ruhr in 1923, Germany and France decided to give compromise and cooperation a try. The British, and even the Americans, were willing to help. The first step was a reasonable compromise on the reparations question.

Hope in Foreign Affairs, 1924–1929

The reparations commission appointed an international committee of financial experts headed by an American banker, Charles G. Dawes, to reexamine reparations from a broad perspective. The committee made a series of recommendations known as the Dawes Plan (1924), and the plan was accepted by France, Germany, and Britain. German reparations were reduced and placed on a sliding scale, like an income tax, whereby yearly payments depended on the level of German economic prosperity. The Dawes Plan also recommended large loans to Germany, loans that could come only from the United States. These loans were to help Stresemann's government put its new currency on a firm basis and promote German recovery. In short, Germany would get private loans from the United States and pay reparations to France and Britain, thus enabling those countries to repay the large sums they owed the United States.

This circular flow of international payments was complicated and risky. For a time, though, it worked. The German republic experienced a spectacular economic recovery. By 1929 Germany's

wealth and income were 50 percent greater than in 1913. With prosperity and large, continuous inflows of American capital, Germany easily paid about $1.3 billion in reparations in 1927 and 1928, enabling France and Britain to pay the United States. In 1929 the Young Plan, named after an American businessman, further reduced German reparations and formalized the link between German reparations and French-British debts to the United States. In this way the Americans, who did not have armies but who did have money, belatedly played a part in the general economic settlement, which though far from ideal facilitated the worldwide recovery of the late 1920s.

The economic settlement was matched by a political settlement. In 1925 the leaders of Europe signed a number of agreements at Locarno, Switzerland. Stresemann, who guided Germany's foreign policy until his death in 1929, had suggested a treaty with France's conciliatory Aristide Briand,

The Fruits of Germany's Inflation In the end, currency had value only as waste paper. Here bank notes are being purchased by the bail for paper mills, along with old rags *(Lumpen)* and bones *(Knochen)*. *(Source: Archiv für Kunst u. Geschichte)*

who had returned to office in 1924 after French voters rejected the bellicose Poincaré. By this treaty Germany and France solemnly pledged to accept their common border, and both Britain and Italy agreed to fight either country if it invaded the other. Stresemann also agreed to settle boundary disputes with Poland and Czechoslovakia by peaceful means, and France promised those countries military aid if they were attacked by Germany. For their efforts Stresemann and Briand shared the Nobel Peace Prize in 1926. The effect of the treaties of Locarno was far-reaching. For years, a "spirit of Locarno" gave Europeans a sense of growing security and stability in international affairs.

Hopes were strengthened by other developments. In 1926 Germany joined the League of Nations, where Stresemann continued his "peace offensive." In 1928 fifteen countries signed the Kellogg-Briand Pact, which "condemned and renounced war as an instrument of national policy." The signing states agreed to settle international disputes peacefully. Often seen as idealistic nonsense because it made no provisions for action in case war actually occurred, the pact was nevertheless a hopeful step. It grew out of a suggestion by Briand that France and the United States renounce the possibility of war between their two countries. Briand was gently and subtly trying to draw the United States back into involvement with Europe. When Secretary of State Frank B. Kellogg proposed a multinational pact, Briand appeared close to success. Thus the cautious optimism of the late 1920s also rested on the hope that the United States would accept its responsibilities as a great world power and consequently contribute to European stability.

Hope in Democratic Government

Domestic politics also offered reason to hope. During the occupation of the Ruhr and the great inflation, republican government in Germany had appeared on the verge of collapse. In 1923 Communists momentarily entered provincial governments, and in November an obscure nobody named Adolf Hitler leaped on a table in a beer hall in Munich and proclaimed a "national socialist revolution." But Hitler's plot was poorly organized and easily crushed, and Hitler was sentenced to prison, where he outlined his theories and program

in his book *Mein Kampf (My Struggle)*. Throughout the 1920s, Hitler's National Socialist party attracted support only from a few fanatical anti-Semites, ultranationalists, and disgruntled ex-servicemen. In 1928 his party had an insignificant twelve seats in the national parliament. Indeed, after 1923 democracy seemed to take root in Weimar Germany. A new currency was established, and the economy boomed.

The moderate businessmen who tended to dominate the various German coalition governments were convinced that economic prosperity demanded good relations with the Western powers, and they supported parliamentary government at home. Stresemann himself was a man of this class, and he was the key figure in every government until his death in 1929. Elections were held regularly, and republican democracy appeared to have growing support among a majority of the Germans.

There were, however, sharp political divisions in the country. Many unrepentant nationalists and monarchists populated the right and the army. Germany's Communists were noisy and active on the left. The Communists, directed from Moscow, reserved their greatest hatred and sharpest barbs for their cousins the Social Democrats, whom they endlessly accused of betraying the revolution. The working classes were divided politically, but most supported the nonrevolutionary but socialist Social Democrats.

The situation in France had numerous similarities to that in Germany. Communists and Socialists battled for the support of the workers. After 1924 the democratically elected government rested mainly in the hands of coalitions of moderates, and business interests were well represented. France's great accomplishment was rapid rebuilding of its war-torn northern region. The expense of this undertaking led, however, to a large deficit and substantial inflation. By early 1926 the franc had fallen to 10 percent of its prewar value, causing a severe crisis. Poincaré was recalled to office, while Briand remained minister for foreign affairs. The Poincaré government proceeded to slash spending and raise taxes, restoring confidence in the economy. The franc was "saved," stabilized at about one-fifth of its prewar value. Good times prevailed until 1930.

Despite its political shortcomings, France attracted artists and writers from all over the world in the 1920s. Much of the intellectual and artistic ferment of the times flourished in Paris. As the writer

An American in Paris   The young Josephine Baker suddenly became a star when she brought an exotic African eroticism to French music halls in 1925. American blacks and Africans had a powerful impact on entertainment in Europe in the 1920s and 1930s. *(Source: Bettmann/Hulton)*

Gertrude Stein (1874–1946), a leader of the large colony of American expatriates living in Paris, later recalled, "Paris was where the twentieth century was."[10] More generally, France appealed to foreigners and the French as a harmonious combination of small businesses and family farms, of bold innovation and solid traditions.

Britain, too, faced challenges after 1920. The wartime trend toward greater social equality continued, however, helping to maintain social harmony. The great problem was unemployment. Many of Britain's best markets had been lost dur-ing the war. In June 1921 almost 2.2 million peo-ple—23 percent of the labor force—were out of work, and throughout the 1920s unemployment hovered around 12 percent. Yet the state provided unemployment benefits of equal size to all those without jobs and supplemented those payments with subsidized housing, medical aid, and in-creased old-age pensions. These and other meas-ures kept living standards from seriously declining, defused class tensions, and pointed the way toward the welfare state Britain established after World War Two.

Relative social harmony was accompanied by the rise of the Labour party as a determined champion of the working classes and of greater social equality. Committed to the kind of moderate, "revisionist" socialism that had emerged before World War One (see page 908), the Labour party replaced the Liberal party as the main opposition to the Conservatives. The new prominence of the Labour party reflected the decline of old liberal ideals of competitive capitalism, limited government control, and individual responsibility. In 1924 and 1929, the Labour party under Ramsay MacDonald governed the country with the support of the smaller Liberal party. Yet Labour moved toward socialism gradually and democratically, so that the middle classes were not overly frightened as the working classes won new benefits.

The Conservatives under Stanley Baldwin showed the same compromising spirit on social issues. The last line of Baldwin's greatest speech in March 1925 summarized his international and domestic programs: "Give us peace in our time, O Lord." Thus, in spite of such conflicts as the 1926 strike by hard-pressed coal miners, which ended in an unsuccessful general strike, social unrest in Britain was limited in the 1920s and in the 1930s as well. In 1922 Britain granted southern, Catholic Ireland full autonomy after a bitter guerrilla war, thus removing another source of prewar friction. In summary, developments in both international relations and in the domestic politics of the leading democracies gave cause for cautious optimism in the late 1920s.

THE GREAT DEPRESSION, 1929–1939

Like the Great War, the Great Depression must be spelled with capital letters. Economic depression was nothing new. Depressions occurred throughout the nineteenth century with predictable regularity, as they recur in the form of recessions and slumps to this day. What was new about this depression was its severity and duration. It struck with ever-greater intensity from 1929 to 1933, and recovery was uneven and slow. Only with the Second World War did the depression disappear in much of the world.

The social and political consequences of prolonged economic collapse were enormous. The depression shattered the fragile optimism of political leaders in the late 1920s. Mass unemployment made insecurity a reality for millions of ordinary people, who had paid little attention to the intellectual crisis or to new directions in art and ideas (Map 28.1). In desperation, people looked for leaders who would "do something." They were willing to support radical attempts to deal with the crisis by both democratic leaders and dictators.

The Economic Crisis

There is no agreement among historians and economists about why the Great Depression was so deep and lasted so long. Thus it is best to trace the course of the great collapse before trying to identify what caused it.

Though economic activity was already declining moderately in many countries by early 1929, the crash of the stock market in the United States in October of that year really started the Great Depression. The American stock market boom, which had seen stock prices double between early 1928 and September 1929, was built on borrowed money. Many wealthy investors, speculators, and people of modest means had bought stocks by paying only a small fraction of the total purchase price and borrowing the remainder from their stockbrokers. Such buying "on margin" was extremely dangerous. When prices started falling, the hard-pressed margin buyers either had to put up more money, which was often impossible, or sell their shares to pay off their brokers. Thus thousands of people started selling all at once. The result was a financial panic. Countless investors and speculators were wiped out in a matter of days or weeks.

The general economic consequences were swift and severe. Stripped of their wealth and confidence, battered investors and their fellow citizens started buying fewer goods. Production began to slow down, and unemployment began to rise. Soon the entire American economy was caught in a vicious, spiraling decline.

The financial panic in the United States triggered a worldwide financial crisis, and that crisis resulted in a drastic decline in production in country after country. Throughout the 1920s American bankers and investors had lent large amounts of capital not only to Germany but to many other countries. Many of these loans were short-term, and once

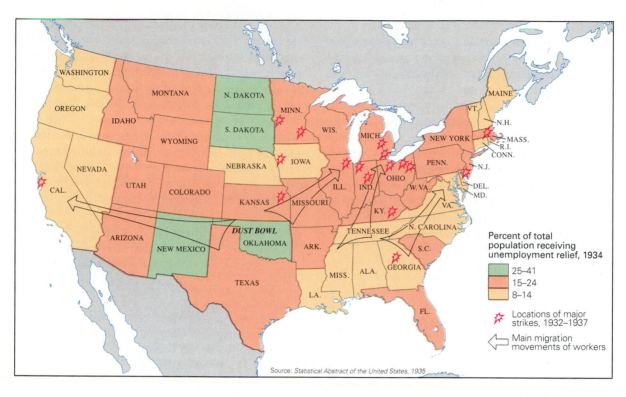

Percent of total
population receiving
unemployment relief, 1934

25–41
15–24
8–14

☆ Locations of major
strikes, 1932–1937

⇦ Main migration
movements of workers

Source: *Statistical Abstract of the United States, 1935*

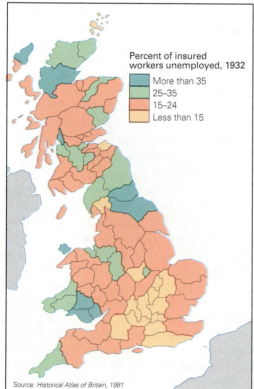

Percent of insured
workers unemployed, 1932

More than 35
25–35
15–24
Less than 15

Source: *Historical Atlas of Britain, 1981*

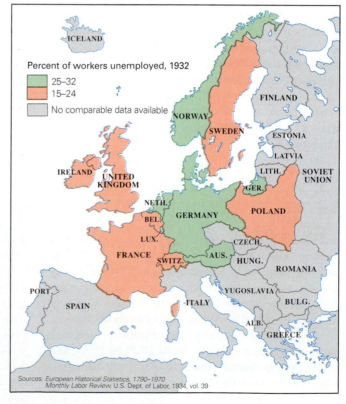

Percent of workers unemployed, 1932

25–32
15–24
No comparable data available

Sources: *European Historical Statistics, 1790–1970*
Monthly Labor Review, U.S. Dept. of Labor, 1934, vol. 39

MAP 28.1 The Great Depression in the United States, Britain, and Europe National
and regional differences were substantial. Germany, industrial northern Britain, and
the American Middle West were particularly hard-hit.

panic broke, New York bankers began recalling them. Gold reserves thus began to flow out of European countries, particularly Germany and Austria, toward the United States. It became very hard for European business people to borrow money, and the panicky public began to withdraw its savings from the banks. These banking problems eventually led to the crash of the largest bank in Austria in 1931 and then to general financial chaos. The recall of private loans by American bankers also accelerated the collapse in world prices, as business people around the world dumped industrial goods and agricultural commodities in a frantic attempt to get cash to pay what they owed.

The financial crisis led to a general crisis of production: between 1929 and 1933, world output of goods fell by an estimated 38 percent. As this happened, each country turned inward and tried to go it alone. In 1931, for example, Britain went off the gold standard, refusing to convert bank notes into gold, and reduced the value of its money. Britain's goal was to make its goods cheaper and therefore more salable in the world market. But because more than twenty nations, including the United States in 1934, also went off the gold standard, no country gained a real advantage. Similarly, country after country followed the example of the United States when it raised protective tariffs to their highest levels ever in 1930 and tried to seal off shrinking national markets for American producers only. Within this context of fragmented and destructive economic nationalism, recovery finally began in 1933.

Although opinions differ, two factors probably best explain the relentless slide to the bottom from 1929 to early 1933. First, the international economy lacked a leadership able to maintain stability when the crisis came. Specifically, as a noted American economic historian concludes, the seriously weakened British, the traditional leaders of the world economy, "couldn't and the United States wouldn't" stabilize the international economic system in 1929.[11] The United States, which had momentarily played a positive role after the occupation of the Ruhr, cut back its international lending and erected high tariffs.

The second factor was poor national economic policy in almost every country. Governments generally cut their budgets and reduced spending when they should have run large deficits in an attempt to stimulate their economies. Since World War Two, such a "counter-cyclical policy," advocated by John Maynard Keynes, has become a well-established weapon against depression. But in the 1930s Keynes's prescription was generally regarded with horror by orthodox economists.

Mass Unemployment

The need for large-scale government spending was tied to mass unemployment. As the financial crisis led to cuts in production, workers lost their jobs and had little money to buy goods. This led to still more cuts in production and still more unemployment, until millions were out of work. In Britain, unemployment had averaged 12 percent in the 1920s; between 1930 and 1935, it averaged more

Middle-Class Unemployment An English office worker's unusual sandwich board poignantly summarizes the bitter despair of the unemployed in the 1930s. *(Source: Bettmann/Hulton)*

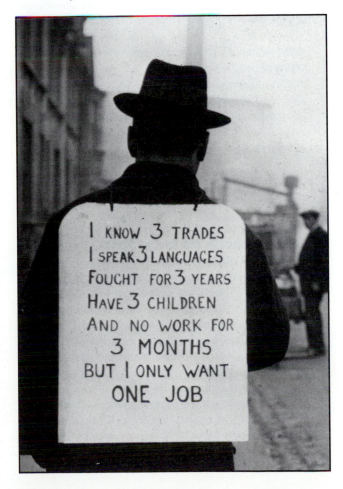

than 18 percent. Far worse was the case of the United States, where unemployment had averaged only 5 percent in the 1920s. In 1932 unemployment soared to about *one-third* of the entire labor force: fourteen million people were out of work (see Map 28.1). Only by pumping new money into the economy could the government increase demand and break the vicious cycle of decline.

Along with its economic effects, mass unemployment posed a great social problem that mere numbers cannot adequately express. Millions of people lost their spirit and dignity in an apparently hopeless search for work. Homes and ways of life were disrupted in millions of personal tragedies. Young people postponed marriages they could not afford, and birthrates fell sharply. There was an increase in suicide and mental illness. Poverty or the threat of poverty became a grinding reality. In 1932 the workers of Manchester, England, appealed to their city officials—a typical appeal echoed throughout the Western world:

We tell you that thousands of people . . . are in desperate straits. We tell you that men, women, and children are going hungry. . . . We tell you that great numbers are being rendered distraught through the stress and worry of trying to exist without work. . . .

If you do not do this—if you do not provide useful work for the unemployed—what, we ask, is your alternative? Do not imagine that this colossal tragedy of unemployment is going on endlessly without some fateful catastrophe. Hungry men are angry men.[12]

Mass unemployment was a terrible time bomb preparing to explode.

The New Deal in the United States

Of all the major industrial countries, only Germany was harder hit by the Great Depression, or reacted more radically to it, than the United States. Depression was so traumatic in the United States because the 1920s had been a period of complacent prosperity. The Great Depression and the response to it marked a major turning point in American history.

President Herbert Hoover and his administration initially reacted to the stock market crash and economic decline with dogged optimism and limited action. In May 1930 Hoover told a group of business and farm leaders, "I am convinced that we

have now passed the worst and with continued unity of effort we shall rapidly recover." When, however, the full force of the financial crisis struck Europe in the summer of 1931 and boomeranged back to the United States, people's worst fears became reality. Banks failed; unemployment soared. In 1932 industrial production fell to about 50 percent of its level in 1929. In these tragic circumstances Franklin Delano Roosevelt, an inspiring wheelchair aristocrat previously crippled by polio, won a landslide electoral victory with grand but vague promises of a "New Deal for the forgotten man."

Roosevelt's basic goal was to reform capitalism in order to preserve it. In his words, "A frank examination of the profit system in the spring of 1933 showed it to be in collapse; but substantially everybody in the United States, in public office and out of public office, from the very rich to the very poor, was as determined as was my Administration to save it."[13] Roosevelt rejected socialism and government ownership of industry in 1933. To right the situation, he chose forceful government intervention in the economy.

In this choice, Roosevelt and his advisers were greatly influenced by American experience in World War One. During the wartime emergency, the American economy had been thoroughly planned and regulated. Roosevelt and his "brain trust" of advisers adopted similar policies to restore prosperity and reduce social inequality. Roosevelt was flexible, pragmatic, and willing to experiment. Government intervention and experimentation were combined in some of the New Deal's most significant measures.

The most ambitious attempt to control and plan the economy was the National Recovery Administration (NRA), established by Congress right after Roosevelt took office. The key idea behind the NRA was to reduce competition and fix prices and wages for everyone's benefit. This goal required government, business, and labor to hammer out detailed regulations for each industry. Along with this kind of national planning in the private sector of the economy, the government believed it could sponsor enough public works projects to assure recovery. Because the NRA broke with the cherished American tradition of free competition and aroused conflicts among business people, consumers, and bureaucrats, it did not work well. By the time the NRA was declared unconstitutional in

President Roosevelt used his famous "fireside chats" to explain his changing policies and to reassure the American people that the New Deal initiatives were working. This photo captures Roosevelt's forceful personality and contagious confidence, which he conveyed over the air waves. *(Source: Brown Brothers)*

1935, Roosevelt and the New Deal were already moving away from government efforts to plan and control the entire economy.

Instead, Roosevelt and his advisers attacked the key problem of mass unemployment directly. The federal government accepted the responsibility of employing directly as many people as financially possible, something Hoover had consistently rejected. Thus, when it became clear in late 1933 that the initial program of public works was too small, new agencies were created to undertake a vast range of projects.

The most famous of these was the Works Progress Administration (WPA), set up in 1935. At its peak in late 1938, this government agency employed more than three million individuals. One-fifth of the entire labor force worked for the WPA at some point in the 1930s. To this day, thousands of public buildings, bridges, and highways built by the WPA stand as monuments to energetic government efforts to provide people with meaningful work. The WPA was enormously popular in a nation long schooled in self-reliance and the work ethic. The hope of a job with the government helped check the threat of social revolution in the United States.

Other social measures aimed in the same direction. Following the path blazed by Germany's Bismarck in the 1880s, the U.S. government in 1935 established a national social security system, with old-age pensions and unemployment benefits, to protect many workers against some of life's uncertainties. The National Labor Relations Act of 1935 gave union organizers the green light by declaring collective bargaining to be the policy of the United States. Following some bitter strikes, such as the sit-down strike at General Motors in early 1937, union membership more than doubled, from four million in 1935 to nine million in 1940. In general, between 1935 and 1938 government rulings and social reforms chipped away at the privileges of the wealthy and tried to help ordinary people.

Yet, despite its undeniable accomplishments in social reform, the New Deal was only partly successful as a response to the Great Depression. At the height of the recovery, in May 1937, seven million workers were still unemployed. The economic situation then worsened seriously in the recession of 1937 and 1938. Production fell sharply, and although unemployment never again reached the fifteen million mark of 1933, it hit eleven million in 1938 and was still a staggering ten million when war broke out in Europe in September 1939.

The New Deal never did pull the United States out of the depression. This failure frustrated Americans then, and it is still puzzling today. Perhaps, as some have claimed, Roosevelt should have used his enormous popularity and prestige in 1933 to nationalize the banks, the railroads, and some heavy industry, so that national economic planning could have been successful. On the other hand, Roosevelt's sharp attack on big business and the wealthy after 1935 had popular appeal but also damaged business confidence and made the great capitalists uncooperative. Given the low level of profit and the underutilization of many factories, however, it is questionable whether business would have behaved much differently even if the New Deal had catered to it.

Finally, it is often argued that the New Deal did not put enough money into the economy through deficit financing. Like his predecessors in the White House, Roosevelt was attached to the ideal of the balanced budget. His largest deficit was only $4.4 billion in 1936. Compare this figure with deficits of $21.5 billion in 1942 and $57.4 billion in 1943, when the nation was prosperously engaged in total war and unemployment had vanished. By 1945 many economists concluded that the New Deal's deficit-financed public works had been too small a step in the right direction. These Keynesian views were to be very influential in economic policy in Europe and America after the Second World War.

The Scandinavian Response to Depression

Of all the Western democracies, the Scandinavian countries under Socialist leadership responded most successfully to the challenge of the Great Depression. Having grown steadily in number in the late nineteenth century, the Socialists became the largest political party in Sweden and then in Norway after the First World War. In the 1920s they passed important social reform legislation for both peasants and workers, gained practical administrative experience, and developed a unique kind of socialism. Flexible and nonrevolutionary, Scandinavian socialism grew out of a strong tradition of cooperative community action. Even before 1900, Scandinavian agricultural cooperatives had shown how individual peasant families could join together for everyone's benefit. Labor leaders and capitalists were also inclined to work together.

When the economic crisis struck in 1929, Socialist governments in Scandinavia built on this pattern of cooperative social action. Sweden in particular pioneered in the use of large-scale deficits to finance public works and thereby maintain production and employment. Scandinavian governments also increased social welfare benefits, from old-age pensions and unemployment insurance to subsidized housing and maternity allowances. All this spending required a large bureaucracy and high taxes, first on the rich and then on practically everyone. Yet both private and cooperative enterprise thrived, as did democracy. Some observers saw Scandinavia's welfare socialism as an appealing "middle way" between sick capitalism and cruel communism or fascism.

Recovery and Reform in Britain and France

In Britain, MacDonald's Labour government and then, after 1931, the Conservative-dominated coalition government followed orthodox economic theory. The budget was balanced, but unemployed workers received barely enough welfare to live. Despite government lethargy, the economy recovered considerably after 1932. By 1937 total production was about 20 percent higher than in 1929. In fact, for Britain the years after 1932 were actually somewhat better than the 1920s had been, quite the opposite of the situation in the United States and France.

This good, but by no means brilliant, performance reflected the gradual reorientation of the British economy. After going off the gold standard in 1931 and establishing protective tariffs in 1932, Britain concentrated increasingly on the national rather than the international market. The old export industries of the Industrial Revolution, such as textiles and coal, continued to decline, but the new industries like automobiles and electrical appliances grew in response to British home demand. Moreover, low interest rates encouraged a housing boom. By the end of the decade there were highly visible differences between the old, depressed industrial areas of the north and the new, growing areas of the south. These developments encouraged Britain to look inward and avoid unpleasant foreign questions.

Because France was relatively less industrialized and more isolated from the world economy, the Great Depression came late. But once the depression hit France, it stayed and stayed. Decline was steady until 1935, and the short-lived recovery never brought production or employment back up to predepression levels. Economic stagnation both reflected and heightened an ongoing political crisis. There was no stability in government. As before 1914, the French parliament was made up of many political parties, which could never cooperate for very long. In 1933, for example, five coalition cabinets formed and fell in rapid succession.

The French lost the underlying unity that had made governmental instability bearable before 1914. Fascist-type organizations agitated against parliamentary democracy and looked to Mussolini's Italy and Hitler's Germany for inspiration. In February 1934, French fascists and semifascists rioted and threatened to overturn the republic. At the same time, the Communist party and many workers opposed to the existing system were looking to Stalin's Russia for guidance. The vital center of moderate republicanism was sapped from both sides.

Frightened by the growing strength of the fascists at home and abroad, the Communists, the Socialists, and the Radicals formed an alliance—the Popular Front—for the national elections of May 1936. Their clear victory reflected the trend toward polarization. The number of Communists in the parliament jumped dramatically from 10 to 72, while the Socialists, led by Léon Blum, became the strongest party in France with 146 seats. The really quite moderate Radicals slipped badly, and the conservatives lost ground to the semifascists.

In the next few months, Blum's Popular Front government made the first and only real attempt to deal with the social and economic problems of the 1930s in France. Inspired by Roosevelt's New Deal, the Popular Front encouraged the union movement and launched a far-reaching program of social reform, complete with paid vacations and a forty-hour workweek. Popular with workers and the lower middle class, these measures were quickly sabotaged by rapid inflation and cries of revolution from fascists and frightened conservatives. Wealthy people sneaked their money out of the country, labor unrest grew, and France entered a severe financial crisis. Blum was forced to announce a "breathing spell" in social reform.

The fires of political dissension were also fanned by civil war in Spain. The Communists demanded that France support the Spanish republicans, while many French conservatives would gladly have joined Hitler and Mussolini in aiding the attack of Spanish fascists. Extremism grew, and France itself was within sight of civil war. Blum was forced to resign in June 1937, and the Popular Front quickly collapsed. An anxious and divided France drifted aimlessly once again, preoccupied by Hitler and German rearmament.

SUMMARY

After the First World War, Western society entered a complex and difficult era—truly an age of anxiety. Intellectual life underwent a crisis marked by pessimism, uncertainty, and fascination with irrational forces. Ceaseless experimentation and rejection of old forms characterized art and music, while motion pictures and radio provided a new, standardized entertainment for the masses. Intellectual and artistic developments that had been confined to small avant-garde groups before 1914 gained wider currency along with the insecure state of mind they expressed.

Politics and economics were similarly disrupted. In the 1920s political leaders groped to create an enduring peace and rebuild the prewar prosperity, and for a brief period late in the decade they even seemed to have succeeded. Then the Great Depression shattered the fragile stability. Uncertainty returned with redoubled force in the 1930s. The international economy collapsed, and unemployment struck millions. The democracies turned inward as they sought to cope with massive domestic problems and widespread disillusionment. Generally speaking, they were not very successful. The old liberal ideals of individual rights and responsibilities, elected government, and economic freedom seemed ineffective and outmoded to many, even when they managed to survive. And in many countries they were abandoned completely.

NOTES

1. P. Valéry, *Variety,* trans. M. Cowley (New York: Harcourt, Brace, 1927), pp. 27–28.
2. G. Marcel, as quoted in S. Hughes, *The Obstructed Path: French Social Thought in the Years of Desperation, 1930–1960* (New York: Harper & Row, 1967), p. 82.
3. G. Greene, *Another Mexico* (New York: Viking Press, 1939), p. 3.
4. G. Orwell, *1984* (New York: New American Library, 1950), p. 220.
5. C. E. Jeanneret-Gris (Le Corbusier), *Towards a New Architecture* (London: J. Rodker, 1931), p. 15.
6. Quoted in A. H. Barr, Jr., *What Is Modern Painting?,* 9th ed. (New York: Museum of Modern Art, 1966), p. 27.
7. Ibid., p. 25.
8. R. Graves and A. Hodge, *The Long Week End: A Social History of Great Britain, 1918–1939* (New York: Macmillan, 1941), p. 131.
9. Quoted in A. Briggs, *The Birth of Broadcasting,* vol. 1 (London: Oxford University Press, 1961), p. 47.
10. Quoted in R. J. Sontag, *A Broken World, 1919–1939* (New York: Harper & Row, 1971), p. 129.
11. C. P. Kindleberger, *The World in Depression, 1929–1939* (Berkeley: University of California Press, 1973), p. 292.
12. Quoted in S. B. Clough et al., eds., *Economic History of Europe: Twentieth Century* (New York: Harper & Row, 1968), pp. 243–245.
13. Quoted in D. Dillard, *Economic Development of the North Atlantic Community* (Englewood Cliffs, N.J.: Prentice-Hall, 1967), p. 591.

SUGGESTED READING

Among general works, E. Wiskemann's, *Europe of the Dictators, 1919–1945* (1966) and Sontag's study cited in the Notes are particularly recommended. The latter has an excellent bibliography. A. Bullock, ed., *The Twentieth Century* (1971), is a lavish visual feast combined with penetrating essays on major developments since 1900. Two excellent accounts of contemporary history—one with a liberal and the other with a conservative point of view—are R. Paxton, *Europe in the Twentieth Century* (1975), and P. Johnson, *Modern Times: The World from the Twenties to the Eighties* (1983). Crucial changes in thought before and after World War One are discussed in three rewarding intellectual histories: G. Masur, *Prophets of Yesterday* (1961); H. S. Hughes, *Consciousness and Society* (1956); and M. Biddiss, *Age of the Masses: Ideas and Society Since 1870* (1977). R. Stromberg, *European Intellectual History Since 1789,* 4th ed. (1986), and F. Baumer, *Modern European Thought: Continuity and Change in Ideas, 1600–1950* (1970), are recommended general surveys.

J. Rewald's, *The History of Impressionism,* rev. ed. (1961) and *Post-Impressionism* (1956) are excellent, as is the work by Barr cited in the Notes. P. Collaer, *A History of Modern Music* (1961), and H. R. Hitchcock, *Architecture: Nineteenth and Twentieth Centuries* (1958), are good introductions, while T. Wolfe, *From Bauhaus to My House* (1981), is a lively critique of modern architecture. L. Barnett, *The Universe and Dr. Einstein* (1952), is a fascinating study of the new physics. A. Storr, *Freud* (1989), and P. Rieff, *Freud* (1956), consider the man and how his theories have stood the test of time. M. White, ed., *The Age of Analysis* (1955), opens up basic questions of twentieth-century psychology and philosophy. H. Liebersohn, *Fate and Utopia in German Sociology* (1988), analyzes developments in German social science, and P. Gay, *Weimar Culture* (1970), is a brilliant exploration of the many-sided artistic renaissance in Germany in the 1920s. M. Marrus, ed., *Emergence of Leisure* (1974), is a pioneering inquiry into an important aspect of mass culture. H. Daniels-Rops, *A Fight for God,* 2 vols. (1966), is a sympathetic history of the Catholic church between 1870 and 1939.

G. Ambrosius and W. Hibbard, *A Social and Economic History of Twentieth-Century Europe* (1989), provides a good survey, while C. Maier, *Recasting Bourgeois Europe* (1975), is an ambitious comparative study of social classes and conflicts in France, Germany, and Italy after World War One. P. Fritzsche, *Rehearsals for Fascism: Populism and Political Mobilization in Weimar Germany* (1990); R. Wohl, *The Generation of 1914* (1979); R. Kuisel, *Capital and State in Modern France: Renovation and Economic Management* (1982); and W. McDougall, *France's Rhineland Diplomacy, 1914–1924* (1978), are four more important studies on aspects of the postwar challenge. M. Childs, *Sweden: The Middle Way* (1961), applauds Sweden's efforts at social reform. W. Neuman, *The Balance of Power in the Interwar Years, 1919–1939* (1968), perceptively examines international politics after the Locarno treaties of 1925. In addition to the contemporary works discussed in the text, the crisis of the interwar period comes alive in R. Crossman, ed., *The God That Failed* (1950), in which famous Western writers tell why they were attracted to and later repelled by communism; J. Ortega y Gasset's renowned *The Revolt of the Masses* (1932); and

F. A. Hayek's *The Road to Serfdom* (1944), a famous warning of the dangers to democratic freedoms.

In addition to Kindleberger's excellent study of the Great Depression cited in the Notes, there is J. Galbraith's very lively and understandable account of the stock market collapse, *The Great Crash* (1955). J. Garraty, *Unemployment in History* (1978), is noteworthy, though novels best portray the human tragedy of economic decline. W. Holtby, *South Riding* (1936), and W. Greenwood, *Love on the Dole* (1933), are moving stories of the Great Depression in England; H. Fallada, *Little Man, What Now?* (1932), is the classic counterpart for Germany. Also highly recommended as commentaries on English life between the wars are R. Graves, *Goodbye to All That,* rev. ed. (1957), and G. Orwell, *The Road to Wigan Pier* (1972). Among French novelists, A. Gide painstakingly examines the French middle class and its values in *The Counterfeiters,* while A. Camus, the greatest of the existential novelists, is at his unforgettable best in *The Stranger* and *The Plague.*

29

Dictatorships and the Second World War

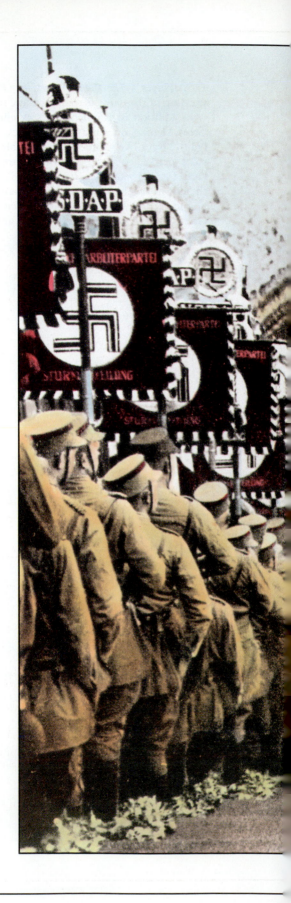

The era of anxiety and economic depression was also a time of growing strength for political dictatorship. Popularly elected governments and basic civil liberties declined drastically in Europe. On the eve of the Second World War, liberal democratic government survived only in Great Britain, France, the Low Countries, the Scandinavian nations, and neutral Switzerland. Elsewhere in Europe, various kinds of "strong men" ruled. Dictatorship seemed the wave of the future. Thus the decline in liberal political institutions and the intellectual crisis were related elements in the general crisis of European civilization.

The era of dictatorship is a highly disturbing chapter in the history of Western civilization. The key development was not simply the resurgence of dictatorship but the rise of a new kind of tyranny—the modern totalitarian state. Modern totalitarianism reached its fullest realization in Communist Russia and Nazi Germany in the 1930s. Stalin and Hitler mobilized their peoples for enormous undertakings and ruled with unprecedented severity. Hitler's mobilization was ultimately directed toward racial aggression and territorial expansion, and his ruthless attack on Poland in 1939 started World War Two.

Nazi armies were defeated by a great coalition, and today we want to believe that the era of totalitarian dictatorship was a terrible accident, that Stalin's slave labor camps and Hitler's gas chambers "can't happen again." Yet the cruel truth is that terrible atrocities continue to plague the world in our time. The Khmer Rouge has inflicted genocide on its people in Kampuchea, and civil wars in the Horn of Africa have brought horrible man-made famines. And there are many other examples. Thus it is all the more vital that we understand Europe's tragic era of totalitarian dictatorship, in order to guard against any future possibility that there would be a recurrence.

- What, then, was the nature of the twentieth-century totalitarian state?
- How did totalitarianism affect ordinary people?
- Finally, how did the rise of totalitarian states result in another world war?

These are the questions this chapter will seek to answer.

AUTHORITARIAN AND TOTALITARIAN STATES

The modern totalitarian state differed from the old-fashioned authoritarian state. Completely rejecting liberal values and drawing on the experience of total war, the totalitarian state exercised much greater control over the masses and mobilized them for constant action. The nature of this control may be examined by comparing the old and new forms of dictatorship in a general way, before entering the strange worlds of Stalin's Russia and Hitler's Germany.

Conservative Authoritarianism

The traditional form of antidemocratic government in European history has been conservative authoritarianism. Like Catherine the Great in Russia and Metternich in Austria, the leaders of such governments have tried to prevent major changes that would undermine the existing social order. To do so, they have relied on obedient bureaucracies, vigilant police departments, and trustworthy armies. Popular participation in government has been forbidden or else severely limited to such natural allies as landlords, bureaucrats, and high church officials. Liberals, democrats, and socialists have been persecuted as radicals, often to find themselves in jail or exile.

Yet old-fashioned authoritarian governments were limited in their power and in their objectives. Lacking modern technology and communications, they did not have the power to control many aspects of their subjects' lives. Nor did they wish to do so. Preoccupied with the goal of mere survival, these governments largely limited their demands to taxes, army recruits, and passive acceptance. As long as the people did not try to change the system, they often had considerable personal independence.

After the First World War, this kind of authoritarian government revived, especially in the less developed eastern part of Europe. There, the parliamentary regimes that had been founded on the wreckage of empires in 1918 fell one by one. By early 1938 only economically and socially advanced Czechoslovakia remained true to liberal political ideals. Conservative dictators also took over in Spain and Portugal.

There were several reasons for this development. These lands lacked a strong tradition of self-government, with its necessary restraint and compromise. Moreover, many of these new states were torn by ethnic conflicts that threatened their very existence. Dictatorship appealed to nationalists and military leaders as a way to repress such tensions and preserve national unity. Large landowners and the church were still powerful forces in these largely agrarian areas, and they often looked to dictators to save them from progressive land reform or communist agrarian upheaval. So did some members of the middle class, which was small and weak in eastern Europe. Finally, though some kind of democracy managed to stagger through the 1920s in Austria, Bulgaria, Rumania, Greece, Estonia, and Latvia, the Great Depression delivered the final blow in those countries in 1936.

Although some of the authoritarian regimes adopted certain Hitlerian and fascist characteristics in the 1930s, their general aims were not totalitarian. They were concerned more with maintaining the status quo than with forcing society into rapid change or war. This tradition has continued in our own time, especially in some of the military dictatorships that ruled in Latin America until quite recently.

Hungary was a good example of conservative authoritarianism. In the chaos of collapse in 1919, Béla Kun formed a Lenin-style government, but communism in Hungary was soon crushed by foreign troops, large landowners, and hostile peasants. Thereafter, a combination of great and medium-sized landowners instituted a semi-authoritarian regime, which maintained the status quo in the 1920s. Hungary had a parliament, but elections were carefully controlled. The peasants did not have the right to vote, and an upper house representing the landed aristocracy was re-established. There was no land reform, no major social change.

Nazi Mass Rally, 1936 This picture captures the spirit of modern totalitarianism. The uniformed members of the Nazi party have willingly merged themselves into a single force and await the command of the godlike leader. *(Source: Wide World Photos)*

In the 1930s the Hungarian government remained conservative and nationalistic. Increasingly, it was opposed by a Nazi-like fascist movement, the Arrow Cross, which demanded radical reform and totalitarian measures.

Another example of conservative authoritarianism was newly independent Poland, where democratic government was overturned in 1926 when General Joseph Pilsudski established a military dictatorship. Sandwiched between Russia and Germany, Poland was torn by bitter party politics. Pilsudski silenced opposition and tried to build a strong state. His principal supporters were the army, major industrialists, and dedicated nationalists.

In Yugoslavia, King Alexander (r. 1921–1934) proclaimed a centralized dictatorship in 1929 to prevent ethnic rivalries among Serbs, Croats, and Slovenes from tearing the country apart. An old-style authoritarian, Alexander crushed democracy, jailed separatists, and ruled through the bureaucracy.

Another example of conservative authoritarianism was Portugal, at the westernmost end of the European peninsula. Constantly shaken by military coups and uprisings after a republican revolution in 1910, very poor and backward Portugal finally got a strong dictator in Antonio de Oliveira Salazar in 1932. A devout Catholic, Salazar gave the church the strongest possible position in the country, while controlling the press and outlawing most political activity. Yet there was no attempt to mobilize the masses or to accomplish great projects. The traditional society was firmly maintained, and that was enough.

Modern Totalitarianism

Although both are dictatorships, modern totalitarianism and conservative authoritarianism differ. They may be thought of as two distinct types of political organization that in practice sometimes share certain elements.

Modern totalitarianism burst on the scene with the revolutionary total war effort of 1914 to 1918. The war called forth a tendency to subordinate all institutions and all classes to one supreme objective: victory. Nothing, absolutely nothing, had equal value. People were called to make ever-greater sacrifices, and their personal freedom was constantly reduced by ever-greater government control. As the outstanding French thinker Elie Halévy put it in 1936, the varieties of modern totalitarian tyranny—fascism, Nazism, and communism—may be thought of as "feuding brothers" with a common father, the nature of modern war.[1]

The crucial experience of World War One was carried further by Lenin and the Bolsheviks during the Russian civil war. Lenin showed how a dedicated minority could make a total effort and achieve victory over a less determined majority. Lenin also demonstrated how institutions and human rights might be subordinated to the needs of a single group—the Communist party—and its leader, Lenin. Thus Lenin provided a model for single-party dictatorship, and he inspired imitators.

Building on its immediate origins in World War One and the Russian civil war, modern totalitarianism reached maturity in the 1930s in Stalinist Russia and Nazi Germany. Both had several fundamental characteristics of modern totalitarianism.

Armed with modern technology and communications, the true totalitarian state began as a dictatorship exercising complete political power, but it did not stop there. Increasingly, the state took over and tried to control just as completely the economic, social, intellectual, and cultural aspects of life. Although such unlimited control could not be fully realized, the individual's freedom of action was greatly reduced. Deviation from the norm even in art or family behavior could become a crime. In theory, nothing was politically neutral, nothing was outside the scope of the state.

This grandiose vision of total state control broke decisively not only with conservative authoritarianism but also with nineteenth-century liberalism and democracy. Indeed, totalitarianism was a radical revolt against liberalism. Liberalism sought to limit the power of the state and protect the sacred rights of the individual. Moreover, liberals stood for rationality, harmony, peaceful progress, and a strong middle class. All of that disgusted totalitarians as sentimental slop. They believed in will power, preached conflict, and worshiped violence. They believed that the individual was infinitely less valuable than the state and that there were no lasting rights, only temporary rewards for loyal and effective service. Only a single powerful leader and a single party, both unrestrained by law or tradition, determined the destiny of the totalitarian state.

Unlike old-fashioned authoritarianism, modern totalitarianism was based not on an elite but on the masses. As in the First World War, the totalitarian state sought and sometimes won the support and even the love of ordinary people. Modern totalitarianism built on politically alert masses, on people who had already become engaged in the political process, most notably through commitment to nationalism and socialism. Its character as a mass movement gave totalitarianism much of its elemental force.

The final shared characteristic of real totalitarian states was their boundless dynamism. The totalitarian society was a fully mobilized society, a society moving toward some goal. It was never content merely to survive, like an old-fashioned military dictatorship or a decaying democracy. Paradoxically, totalitarian regimes never reached their goals. Or, more precisely, as soon as one goal was achieved at the cost of enormous sacrifice, another arose at the leader's command to take its place. Thus totalitarianism was in the end a *permanent* revolution, an *unfinished* revolution, in which rapid, profound change imposed from on high went on forever.

Totalitarianism of the Left and the Right

The two most developed totalitarian states—Stalin's Communist Russia and Hitler's Nazi Germany—shared all the central characteristics of totalitarianism. But although those regimes may seem more alike than not, there were at least two major differences between them.

Communism as practiced in Soviet Russia grew out of Marxian socialism. Nazism in Germany grew out of extreme nationalism and racism. This distinction meant that private property and the middle class received very different treatment in the two states. In Soviet Russia, the socialist program of the radical left was realized: all large holdings of private property were taken over by the state, and the middle class lost its wealth and status. In Germany, big landowners and industrialists on the conservative right were sharply criticized but managed to maintain their private wealth. This difference in property and class relations has led some scholars to speak of "totalitarianism of the left"— Stalinist Russia—and "totalitarianism of the right" —Nazi Germany.

More important were the differing possibilities for regeneration. Socialism, with its concern for social justice and human progress, is linked to the living core of Western civilization and the Judeo-

Vicious Anti-Semitism was visible in all European countries before World War One. This 1898 French cartoon shows the Jewish banker Rothschild worshiping gold and exploiting the whole world. Jews were also denounced as revolutionary socialists intent upon destroying private property and the middle class. *(Source: Historical Pictures Service, Chicago)*

Christian tradition. Stalin's communism was an ugly perversion of socialism, but even in its darkest moments it had the potential for reforming itself and creating a more humane society. Nazism, however, had no such potential. Based on the phobias of anticapitalism, anti-Semitism, and racism, its elements could be found in many a European city before the First World War. Totally negative and devoid of even perverted truth, it promised only destruction and never rebirth.

STALIN'S RUSSIA

Lenin established the basic outlines of a modern totalitarian dictatorship in Russia after the Bolshevik Revolution and during the civil war. Joseph Stalin (1879–1953) finished the job. A master of political infighting, Stalin cautiously consolidated his power and eliminated his enemies in the mid-1920s. Then in 1928, as undisputed leader of the ruling Communist party, he launched the first five-year plan—the "revolution from above," as he so aptly termed it.

The five-year plans were extremely ambitious. Often incorrectly considered a mere set of economic measures to speed up Soviet Russia's industrial development, the five-year plans actually marked the beginning of a renewed attempt to mobilize and transform Soviet society along socialist lines. The goal was to create a new way of life and to generate new attitudes and new loyalties. The means Stalin and the small Communist party elite chose were constant propaganda, enormous sacrifice, and unlimited violence and state control. Thus the Soviet Union in the 1930s became a dynamic, modern totalitarian state.

From Lenin to Stalin

By spring 1921 Lenin and the Bolsheviks had won the civil war, but they ruled a shattered and devastated land. Many farms were in ruins, and food supplies were exhausted. In southern Russia, drought combined with the ravages of war to produce the worst famine in generations. By 1920, according to the government, from 50 to 90 percent of the population in seventeen provinces was starving. Industrial production also broke down completely. In 1921, for example, output of steel and

Lenin and Stalin in 1922. Lenin re-established limited economic freedom throughout Russia in 1921, but he ran the country and the Communist party in an increasingly authoritarian way. Stalin carried the process much further and eventually built a regime based on harsh dictatorship. *(Source: Sovfoto)*

cotton textiles was only about 4 percent of what it had been in 1913. The revolutionary Trotsky later wrote that the "collapse of the productive forces surpassed anything of the kind history had ever seen. The country, and the government with it, were at the very edge of the abyss."[2] The Bolsheviks had destroyed the economy as well as their foes.

In the face of economic disintegration and rioting by peasants and workers, as well as an open rebellion by previously pro-Bolshevik sailors at Kronstadt—a rebellion that had to be quelled with machine guns, the tough but ever-flexible Lenin changed course. In March 1921 he announced the New Economic Policy (NEP), which re-established limited economic freedom in an attempt to rebuild agriculture and industry. During the civil war, the Communists had simply seized grain without payment. Lenin in 1921 substituted a grain tax on the country's peasant producers, who were permitted to sell their surpluses in free markets. Peasants were also encouraged to buy as many goods as they could afford from private traders and small handicraft manufacturers, groups that were now allowed to reappear. Heavy industry, railroads, and banks, however, remained wholly nationalized. Thus NEP saw only a limited restoration of capitalism.

Lenin's New Economic Policy was shrewd and successful, from two points of view. Politically, it was a necessary but temporary compromise with Russia's overwhelming peasant majority. Flushed with victory after their revolutionary gains of 1917, the peasants would have fought to hold onto their land. With fond hopes of immediate worldwide revolution fading by 1921, Lenin realized that his government was not strong enough to take it from them. As he had accepted Germany's harsh terms at Brest-Litovsk in 1918, Lenin made a deal with the only force capable of overturning his government.

Economically, NEP brought rapid recovery. In 1926 industrial output had surpassed the level of 1913, and Russian peasants were producing almost as much grain as before the war. Counting shorter hours and increased social benefits, workers were living somewhat better than they had in the past.

As the economy recovered and the government partially relaxed its censorship and repression, an intense struggle for power began in the inner circles of the Communist party, for Lenin had left no chosen successor when he died in 1924. The principal contenders were the stolid Stalin and the flamboyant Trotsky.

The son of a shoemaker, Joseph Dzhugashvili—later known as Stalin—studied for the priesthood but was expelled from his theological seminary, probably for rude rebelliousness. By 1903 he had joined the Bolsheviks. In the years before the First World War, he engaged in many revolutionary activities in the Transcaucasian area of southern Russia, including a daring bank robbery to get money for the Bolsheviks. This raid gained Lenin's attention and approval. Ethnically a Georgian and not a Russian, Stalin in his early writings focused on the oppression of minority peoples in the Russian Empire. Stalin was a good organizer but a poor speaker and writer, with no experience outside of Russia.

Leon Trotsky, a great and inspiring leader who had planned the 1917 takeover (see page 878) and then created the victorious Red Army, appeared to have all the advantages. Yet it was Stalin who succeeded Lenin. Stalin won because he was more effective at gaining the all-important support of the party, the only genuine source of power in the one-party state. Rising to general secretary of the party's Central Committee just before Lenin's first stroke in 1922, Stalin used his office to win friends and allies with jobs and promises. Stalin also won recognition as commissar of nationalities, a key position in which he governed many of Russia's minorities.

The "practical" Stalin also won because he appeared better able than the brilliant Trotsky to relate Marxist teaching to Russian realities in the 1920s. First, as commissar of nationalities, he built on Lenin's idea of granting minority groups a certain degree of freedom in culture and language while maintaining rigorous political control through carefully selected local Communists. Stalin could loudly claim, therefore, to have found a way to solve the ancient problem of ethnic demands for independence in the multinational state. And of course he did.

Second, Stalin developed a theory of "socialism in one country," which was more appealing to the majority of Communists than Trotsky's doctrine of "permanent revolution." Stalin argued that Russia had the ability to build socialism on its own. Trotsky maintained that socialism in Russia could succeed only if revolution occurred quickly throughout Europe. To many Communists, Trotsky's views seemed to sell Russia short and to promise risky conflicts with capitalist countries by recklessly encouraging revolutionary movements around the world. Stalin's willingness to break with NEP and push socialism at home appealed to young militants. In short, Stalin's theory of socialism in one country provided many in the party with a glimmer of hope in the midst of the capitalist-appearing NEP, which they had come to detest.

With cunning skill Stalin gradually achieved absolute power between 1922 and 1927. First, he allied with Trotsky's personal enemies to crush Trotsky, who was expelled from the Soviet Union in 1929 and eventually was murdered in Mexico in 1940, undoubtedly on Stalin's order. Stalin then aligned with the moderates, who wanted to go slow at home, to suppress Trotsky's radical followers. Finally, having defeated all the radicals, he turned against his allies, the moderates, and destroyed them as well. Stalin's final triumph came at the Party Congress of December 1927, which condemned all "deviation from the general party line" formulated by Stalin. The dictator was then ready to launch his "revolution from above"—the real Russian revolution for millions of ordinary citizens.

The Five-Year Plans

The Party Congress of 1927, which ratified Stalin's seizure of power, marked the end of the New Economic Policy and the beginning of the era of socialist five-year plans. The first five-year plan had staggering economic objectives. In just five years, total industrial output was to increase by 250 percent. Heavy industry, the preferred sector, was to grow even faster; steel production, for example, was to jump almost 300 percent. Agricultural production was slated to increase by 150 percent, and one-fifth of Russia's peasants were scheduled to give up their private plots and join socialist collective farms. In spite of warnings from moderate Communists that these goals were unrealistic, Stalin raised them higher as the plan got under way. By 1930 a whirlwind of economic and social change was sweeping the country.

Stalin unleashed his "second revolution" for a variety of interrelated reasons. There were, first of all, ideological considerations. Like Lenin, Stalin and his militant supporters were deeply committed to socialism as they understood it. Since the country had recovered economically and their rule was secure, they burned to stamp out NEP's private

traders, independent artisans, and few well-to-do peasants. Purely economic motivations were also important. Although the economy had recovered, it seemed to have stalled in 1927 and 1928. A new socialist offensive seemed necessary if industry and agriculture were to grow rapidly.

Political considerations were most important. Internationally, there was the old problem, remaining from prerevolutionary times, of catching up with the advanced and presumably hostile capitalist nations of the West. Stalin said in 1931, when he pressed for ever-greater speed and sacrifice: "We are fifty or a hundred years behind the advanced countries. We must make good this distance in ten years. Either we do it, or we shall go under."[3]

Domestically, there was what Communist writers of the 1920s called the "cursed problem"—the problem of the Russian peasants. For centuries, Russian peasants had wanted to own the land, and finally they had it. Sooner or later, the Communists reasoned, the peasants would become conservative little capitalists and pose a threat to the regime. Therefore, Stalin decided on a preventive war against the peasantry, in order to bring it under the absolute control of the state.

That war was *collectivization*—the forcible consolidation of individual peasant farms into large, state-controlled enterprises. Beginning in 1929, peasants all over the Soviet Union were ordered to give up their land and animals and to become members of collective farms, although they continued to live in their own homes. As for the *kulaks*, the better-off peasants, Stalin instructed party workers to "liquidate them as a class." Stripped of their land and livestock, the kulaks were generally not even permitted to join the collective farms. Many starved or were deported to forced-labor camps for "re-education."

Since almost all peasants were in fact poor, the term *kulak* soon meant any peasant who opposed the new system. Whole villages were often attacked. One conscience-stricken colonel in the secret police confessed to a foreign journalist: "I am an old Bolshevik. I worked in the underground against the Tsar and then I fought in the Civil War. Did I do all that in order that I should now surround villages with machineguns and order my men to fire indiscriminately into crowds of peasants? Oh, no, no!"[4]

Forced collectivization of the peasants led to economic and human disaster. Large numbers of peas-

Plastov: Collective Farm Threshing   This example of socialist realism portrays the results of collectivization in positive terms, but the propaganda message does not seem heavy-handed. These peasants have become employees of a large collective farm and are threshing its wheat crop. Socialist realism was expected to depict—and to glorify—the achievements of the New Soviet society. *(Source: Kiev State Museum of Russian Art)*

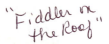

"Fiddler on the Roof"

ants slaughtered their animals and burned their crops in sullen, hopeless protest. Between 1929 and 1933, the number of horses, cattle, sheep, and goats in the Soviet Union fell by at least half. Nor were the state-controlled collective farms more productive. The output of grain barely increased between 1928 and 1938, when it was almost identical to that of 1913. Communist economists had expected collectivized agriculture to pay for new factories. Instead, the state had to invest heavily in agriculture, building thousands of tractors to replace slaughtered draft horses. Collectivized agriculture was unable to make any substantial financial contribution to Soviet industrial development in the first five-year plan. The human dimension of the tragedy was shocking. Collectivization created man-made famine in 1932 and 1933, and many perished. Indeed, Stalin confided to Churchill at Yalta in 1945 that ten million people had died in the course of collectivization.

Yet collectivization was a political victory of sorts. By the end of 1932, fully 60 percent of Rus-

sian peasant families had been herded onto collective farms; by 1938, 93 percent. Regimented and indoctrinated as employees of an all-powerful state, the peasants were no longer even a potential political threat to Stalin and the Communist party. Moreover, the state was assured of grain for bread for urban workers, who were much more important politically than the peasants. Collective farmers had to meet their grain quotas first and worry about feeding themselves second. Many collectivized peasants drew much of their own food from tiny, grudgingly tolerated garden plots that they worked in their off hours. No wonder some peasants joked, with that grim humor peculiar to the totalitarian society, that the initials then used by the Communist party actually stood for "The Second Serfdom, That of the Bolsheviks."

The industrial side of the five-year plans was more successful—indeed, quite spectacular. The output of industry doubled in the first five-year plan and doubled again in the second. Soviet industry produced about four times as much in 1937 as it had in 1928. No other major country had ever achieved such rapid industrial growth. Heavy industry led the way; consumer industry grew quite slowly. Steel production—a near-obsession with Stalin, whose name fittingly meant "man of steel" in Russian—increased roughly 500 percent between 1928 and 1937. A new heavy industrial complex was built almost from scratch in western Siberia. Industrial growth also went hand in hand with urban development. Cities rose where nomadic tribes had grazed their flocks. More than twenty-five million people migrated to cities during the 1930s.

The great industrialization drive, concentrated between 1928 and 1937, was an awe-inspiring achievement purchased at enormous sacrifice. The sudden creation of dozens of new factories required a great increase in investment and a sharp decrease in consumption. Few nations had ever invested more than one-sixth of their yearly net national income. Soviet planners decreed that more than one-third of net income go for investment. This meant that only two-thirds of everything being produced could be consumed by the people *and* the increasingly voracious military. The money was collected from the people by means of heavy, hidden sales taxes.

There was, therefore, no improvement in the average standard of living. Indeed, the most careful studies show that the average nonfarm wage apparently purchased only about *half* as many goods in 1932 as in 1928. After 1932 real wages rose slowly, so that in 1937 workers could buy about 60 percent of what they had bought in 1928. Thus rapid industrial development went with an unprecedented decline in the standard of living for ordinary people.

Two other factors contributed importantly to rapid industrialization: firm labor discipline and foreign engineers. Between 1930 and 1932, trade unions lost most of their power. The government could assign workers to any job anywhere in the country, and individuals could not move without the permission of the police. When factory managers needed more hands, they called on their counterparts on the collective farms, who sent them millions of "unneeded" peasants over the years.

Foreign engineers were hired to plan and construct many of the new factories. Highly skilled American engineers, hungry for work in the depression years, were particularly important until newly trained Soviet experts began to replace them after 1932. The gigantic mills of the new Siberian steel industry were modeled on America's best. Those modern mills were eloquent testimony to the ability of Stalin's planners to harness even the skill and technology of capitalist countries to promote the surge of socialist industry.

Life in Stalinist Society

The aim of Stalin's five-year plans was to create a new kind of society and human personality, as well as a strong industrial economy and a powerful army. Stalin and his helpers were good Marxian economic determinists. Once everything was owned by the state, they believed, a socialist society and a new kind of human being would inevitably emerge. They were by no means totally successful, but they did build a new society, whose broad outlines existed to the early 1980s. For the people, life in Stalinist society had both good and bad aspects.

The most frightening aspect of Stalinist society was brutal, unrestrained police terrorism. First directed primarily against the peasants after 1929, terror was increasingly turned on leading Communists, powerful administrators, and ordinary people for no apparent reason. As one Soviet woman later recalled, "We all trembled because there was no way of getting out of it. Even a Communist himself can be caught. To avoid trouble became an exception."[5] A climate of fear fell on the land.

In the early 1930s, the top members of the party and government were Stalin's obedient servants, but there was some grumbling in the party. At a small gathering in November 1932, even Stalin's wife complained bitterly about the misery of the people. Stalin showered her with insults, and she died that same night, apparently by her own hand. In late 1934 Stalin's number-two man, Sergei Kirov, was suddenly and mysteriously murdered. Although Stalin himself probably ordered Kirov's murder, he used the incident to launch a reign of terror.

In August 1936 sixteen prominent old Bolsheviks confessed to all manner of plots against Stalin in spectacular public trials in Moscow. Then, in 1937, lesser party officials and newer henchmen were arrested. In addition to party members, union officials, managers, intellectuals, army officers, and countless ordinary citizens were struck down. Local units of the secret police were even ordered to arrest a certain percentage of the people in their districts. In all, at least eight million people were probably arrested, and millions never returned from prisons and forced-labor camps.

Stalin's mass purges were truly baffling, and many explanations have been given for them. Possibly Stalin believed that the old Communists, like the peasants under NEP, were a potential threat to be wiped out in a preventive attack. Yet why did leading Communists confess to crimes they could not possibly have committed? Their lives had been devoted to the party and the socialist revolution. In the words of the German novelist Arthur Koestler, they probably confessed "in order to do a last service to the Party," the party they loved even when it was wrong. Some of them were subjected to torture and brainwashing. It has been argued that the purges indicate that Stalin was sadistic or insane, for his blood bath greatly weakened the government and the army. Others see the terror as an aspect of the fully developed totalitarian state, which must by its nature always be fighting real or imaginary enemies. At the least, the mass purges were a message to the people: no one was secure. Everyone had to serve the party and its leader with redoubled devotion.

Another aspect of life in the 1930s was constant propaganda and indoctrination. Party activists lectured workers in factories and peasants on collective farms, while newspapers, films, and radio broadcasts endlessly recounted socialist achievements and capitalist plots. Art and literature became highly political. Whereas the 1920s had seen considerable experimentation in modern art and theater, the intellectual elite were ordered by Stalin to become "engineers of human minds." Writers and artists who could effectively combine genuine creativity and political propaganda became the darlings of the regime. They often lived better than top members of the political elite. It became increasingly important for the successful writer and artist to glorify Russian nationalism. Russian history was rewritten so that early tsars like Ivan the Terrible and Peter the Great became worthy forerunners of the greatest Russian leader of all—Stalin.

Stalin seldom appeared in public, but his presence was everywhere—in portraits, statues, books, and quotations from his "sacred" writings. Although the government persecuted religion and turned churches into "museums of atheism," the state had both an earthly religion and a high priest—Marxian socialism and Joseph Stalin.

Life was hard in Stalin's Soviet Russia. The standard of living declined substantially in the 1930s. The masses of people lived primarily on black bread and wore old, shabby clothing. There were constant shortages in the stores, although very heavily taxed vodka was always readily available. A shortage of housing was a particularly serious problem. Millions were moving into the cities, but the government built few new apartments. In 1940 there were approximately 4 people per room in every urban dwelling, as opposed to 2.7 per room in 1926. A relatively lucky family received one room for all its members and shared both a kitchen and a toilet with others on the floor. Less fortunate workers, kulaks, and class enemies built scrap-lumber shacks or underground dugouts in shantytowns.

Life was hard, but by no means hopeless. Idealism and ideology had real appeal for many Russians, who saw themselves heroically building the world's first socialist society while capitalism crumbled in the West. This optimistic belief in the future of Soviet Russia also attracted many disillusioned Western liberals to communism in the 1930s.

On a more practical level, Soviet workers did receive some important social benefits, such as old-age pensions, free medical services, free education, and day-care centers for children. Unemployment was almost unknown. Finally, there was the possibility of personal advancement.

The keys to improving one's position were specialized skills and technical education. Rapid industrialization required massive numbers of trained experts, such as skilled workers, engineers, and plant managers. Thus the state provided tremendous incentives to those who could serve its needs. It paid the mass of unskilled workers and collective farmers very low wages, but it dangled high salaries and many special privileges before its growing technical and managerial elite. This elite joined with the political and artistic elites in a new upper class, whose members were rich, powerful, and insecure, especially during the purges. Yet the possible gains of moving up outweighed the risks. Millions struggled bravely in universities, institutes, and night schools for the all-important specialized education. One young man summed it up:

Adult Education.   Illiteracy, especially among women, was a serious problem after the Russian Revolution. This early photo shows how adults successfully learned to read and write throughout the Soviet Union. *(Source: Sovfoto)*

"In Soviet Russia there is no capital except education. If a person does not want to become a collective farmer or just a cleaning woman, the only means you have to get something is through education."[6]

Women in Soviet Russia

Women's lives were radically altered by Stalinist society. Marxists had traditionally believed that both capitalism and the middle-class husband exploited women. The Russian Revolution of 1917 immediately proclaimed complete equality of rights for women. In the 1920s divorce and abortion were made very easy, and women were urged to work outside the home and liberate themselves sexually. A prominent and influential Bolshevik feminist,

Alexandra Kollontai, went so far as to declare that the sexual act had no more significance than "drinking a glass of water." This observation drew a sharp rebuke from the rather prudish Lenin, who said that "no sane man would lie down to drink from a puddle in the gutter or even drink from a dirty glass."[7] After Stalin came to power, sexual and familial liberation was played down, and the most lasting changes for women involved work and education.

The changes were truly revolutionary. Young women were constantly told that they must be fully equal to men, that they could and should do anything men could do. Russian peasant women had long experienced the equality of backbreaking physical labor in the countryside, and they continued to enjoy that equality on collective farms. With the advent of the five-year plans, millions of women also began to toil in factories and in heavy construction, building dams, roads, and steel mills in summer heat and winter frost. Yet most of the opportunities open to men through education were also opened to women. Determined women pursued their studies and entered the ranks of the better-paid specialists in industry and science. Medicine practically became a woman's profession. By 1950, 75 percent of all doctors in Soviet Russia were women.

Thus Stalinist society gave women great opportunities but demanded great sacrifices as well. The vast majority of women simply *had* to work outside the home. Wages were so low that it was almost impossible for a family or couple to live only on the husband's earnings. Moreover, the full-time working woman had a heavy burden of household tasks in her off hours, for most Soviet men in the 1930s still considered the home and the children the woman's responsibility. Finally, rapid change and economic hardship led to many broken families, creating further physical, emotional, and mental strains for women. In any event, the often-neglected human resource of women was ruthlessly mobilized in Stalinist society. This, too, was an aspect of the Soviet totalitarian state.

MUSSOLINI'S ITALY

Before turning to Hitler's Germany, it is necessary to look briefly at Mussolini's role in Italy. Like all the other emerging dictators, Mussolini hated liberalism, and he destroyed it in Italy. But that was not all. Mussolini and his supporters were the first to call themselves "fascists"—revolutionaries determined to create a certain kind of totalitarian state. As Mussolini's famous slogan of 1926 put it, "Everything in the state, nothing outside the state, nothing against the state." But Mussolini in power, unlike Stalin and Hitler, did not in fact create a real totalitarian state. His dictatorship was rather an instructive hybrid, a halfway house between conservative authoritarianism and modern totalitarianism.

The Seizure of Power

Before the First World War, Italy was a liberal state moving gradually toward democracy. But there were serious problems. Much of the Italian population was still poor, and class differences were extreme. Many peasants were more attached to their villages and local interests than to the national state. Moreover, the papacy and many devout Catholics, as well as the socialists, were strongly opposed to the heirs of Cavour and Garibaldi, middle-class lawyers and politicians who ran the country largely for their own benefit. Relations between church and state were often tense.

The war worsened the political situation. Having fought on the side of the Allies almost exclusively for purposes of territorial expansion, Italian nationalists were bitterly disappointed with Italy's modest gains at Versailles. Workers and peasants also felt cheated: to win their support during the war, the government had promised social and land reform, which it did not deliver after the war.

Encouraged by the Russian Revolution of 1917, radical workers and peasants began occupying factories and seizing land in 1920. These actions scared and radicalized the property-owning classes. The Italian middle classes were already in an ugly mood, having suffered from inflation during the war. Moreover, after the war, the pope lifted his ban on participation by Catholics in Italian politics, and a strong Catholic party quickly emerged. Thus by 1922 almost all the major groups in Italian society were opposed—though for different reasons—to the liberal parliamentary government.

Into these crosscurrents of unrest and frustration stepped the blustering, bullying Benito Mussolini (1883–1945). Son of a village schoolteacher and a poor blacksmith, Mussolini began his political career as a Socialist leader and radical newspaper editor before World War One. In 1914, powerfully influenced by antiliberal cults of violent action, the young Mussolini urged that Italy join the Allies, a stand for which he was expelled from the Italian Socialist party by its antiwar majority. Later Mussolini fought at the front and was wounded in 1917. Returning home, he began organizing bitter war veterans like himself into a band of Fascists—from the Italian word for "a union of forces."

At first, Mussolini's program was a radical combination of nationalist and socialist demands, including territorial expansion, benefits for workers, and land reform for peasants. As such, it competed with the better-organized Socialist party and failed to get off the ground. When Mussolini saw that his violent verbal assaults on the rival Socialists won him growing support from the frightened middle classes, he shifted gears in 1920. [illegible] only destroying parliamentary government, but forming a strong, dynamic movement that would help the little people against the established interests.

With the government breaking down in 1922, largely because of the chaos created by his direct-action bands, Mussolini stepped forward as the savior of order and property. Striking a conservative note in his speeches and gaining the sympathetic neutrality of army leaders, Mussolini demanded the resignation of the existing government and his own appointment by the king. In October 1922, to force matters, a large group of Fascists marched on Rome to threaten the king and force him to call on Mussolini. The threat worked. Victor Emmanuel III (r. 1900–1946), who had no love for the old liberal politicians, asked Mussolini to form a new cabinet. Thus, after widespread violence and a threat of armed uprising, Mussolini seized power "legally." He was immediately granted dictatorial authority for one year by the king and the parliament.

The Regime in Action

Mussolini became dictator on the strength of Italians' rejection of parliamentary government, coupled with fears of Russian-style revolution. Yet what he intended to do with his power was by no means clear until 1924. Some of his dedicated supporters pressed for a "second revolution." Mussolini's ministers, however, included old conservatives, moderates, and even two reform-minded Socialists. A new electoral law was passed giving two-thirds of the representatives in the parliament to the party that won the most votes, a change that allowed the Fascists and their allies to win an overwhelming majority in 1924. Shortly thereafter, five of Mussolini's Fascist thugs kidnaped and murdered Giacomo Matteotti, the leader of the Socialists in the parliament. In the face of this outrage, the opposition demanded that Mussolini's armed squads be dissolved and all violence be banned.

Although he may or may not have ordered Matteotti's murder, Mussolini stood at the crossroads of a severe political crisis. After some hesitation, he charged forward. Declaring his desire to "make the nation Fascist," he imposed a series of repressive measures. Freedom of the press was abolished, elections were fixed, and the government ruled by decree. Mussolini arrested his political opponents, disbanded all independent labor unions, and put dedicated Fascists in control of Italy's schools. Moreover, he created a Fascist youth movement, Fascist labor unions, and many other Fascist organizations. By the end of 1926, Italy was a one-party dictatorship under Mussolini's unquestioned leadership.

Yet Mussolini did not complete the establishment of a modern totalitarian state. His Fascist party never became all-powerful. It never destroyed the old power structure, as the Communists did in Soviet Russia, or succeeded in dominating it, as the Nazis did in Germany. Membership in the Fascist party was more a sign of an Italian's respectability than a commitment to radical change. Interested primarily in personal power, Mussolini was content to compromise with the old conservative classes that controlled the army, the economy, and the state. He never tried to purge these classes or even move very vigorously against them. He controlled and propagandized labor, but left big business to regulate itself, profitably and securely. There was no land reform.

Mussolini also came to draw on the support of the Catholic church. In the Lateran Agreement of 1929, he recognized the Vatican as a tiny independent state, and he agreed to give the church heavy financial support. The pope expressed his satisfaction and urged Italians to support Mussolini's government.

Nothing better illustrates Mussolini's unwillingness to harness everyone and everything for dynamic action than his treatment of women. He abolished divorce and told women to stay at home

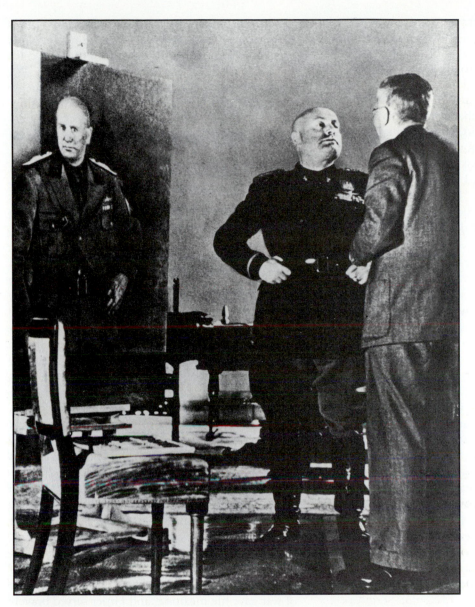

Mussolini   loved to swagger and bully. Here in his office he instinctively strikes his favorite theatrical pose, even as he discusses with its painter a less aggressive portrait of himself. *(Source: Courtesy, Gabriele Stocchi, Rome)*

and produce children. To promote that goal, he decreed a special tax on bachelors in 1934. In 1938 women were limited by law to a maximum of 10 percent of the better-paying jobs in industry and government. Italian women, as women, appear not to have changed their attitudes or behavior in any important way under Fascist rule.

It is also noteworthy that Mussolini's government did not persecute Jews until late in the Second World War, when Italy was under Nazi control. Nor did Mussolini establish a truly ruthless police state. Only twenty-three political prisoners were condemned to death between 1926 and 1944. In spite of much pompous posing by the chauvinist leader and in spite of mass meetings, salutes, and a certain copying of Hitler's aggression in foreign policy after 1933, Mussolini's Italy, though undemocratic, was never really totalitarian.

HITLER'S GERMANY

The most frightening totalitarian state was Nazi Germany. A product of Hitler's evil genius as well as of Germany's social and political situation and the general attack on liberalism and rationality in the age of anxiety, Nazi Germany emerged rapidly after Hitler came to power in 1933. The Nazis quickly smashed or took over most independent organizations, mobilized the economy, and began brutally persecuting the Jewish population. From the start, all major decisions were in the hands of the aggressive dictator Adolf Hitler.

The Roots of Nazism

Nazism grew out of many complex developments, of which the most influential were extreme nationalism and racism. These two ideas captured the mind of the young Hitler, and it was he who dominated Nazism for as long as it lasted.

Born the fourth child of a successful Austrian customs official and an indulgent mother, Adolf Hitler (1889–1945) spent his childhood happily in small towns in Austria. A good student in grade school, Hitler did poorly on reaching high school and dropped out at age fourteen after the death of his father. After four years of unfocused loafing, Hitler finally left for Vienna to become an artist. Denied admission to the Imperial Academy of Fine Arts because he lacked talent, the dejected Hitler stayed on in Vienna. There he lived a comfortable, lazy life on his generous orphan's pension and found most of the perverted beliefs that guided his life.

In Vienna Hitler soaked up extreme German nationalism, which was particularly strong there. Austro-German nationalists, as if to compensate for their declining position in the Austro-Hungarian Empire, believed Germans to be a superior people and the natural rulers of central Europe. They often advocated union with Germany and violent expulsion of "inferior" peoples as the means of maintaining German domination of the Austro-Hungarian Empire.

Hitler was deeply impressed by Vienna's mayor, Karl Lueger, whom he called the "mightiest mayor of all times." Lueger claimed to be a "Christian socialist." With the help of the Catholic trade unions, he had succeeded in winning the support of the little people of Vienna for an attack on capitalism and liberalism, which he held responsible for un-Christian behavior and excessive individualism. A master of mass politics in the urban world, Lueger showed Hitler the enormous potential of anticapitalist and antiliberal propaganda.

From Lueger and others, Hitler eagerly absorbed virulent anti-Semitism, racism, and hatred of Slavs. He was particularly inspired by the racist ravings of an ex-monk named Lanz von Liebenfels. Preaching the crudest, most exaggerated distortions of the Darwinian theory of survival, Liebenfels stressed the superiority of Germanic races, the inevitability of racial conflict, and the inferiority of the Jews. Liebenfels even anticipated the breeding and extermination policies of the Nazi state. He claimed that the master race had to multiply its numbers by means of polygamy and breeding stations, while it systematically sterilized and liquidated inferior races. Anti-Semitism and racism became Hitler's most passionate convictions, his explanation for everything. He believed inferior races—the Slavs and the Jews in particular—were responsible for Austria's woes. The Jews, he claimed, directed an international conspiracy of finance capitalism and Marxian socialism against German culture, German unity, and the German race. Hitler's belief was totally irrational, but he never doubted it.

Although he moved to Munich in 1913 to avoid being drafted in the Austrian army, the lonely Hitler greeted the outbreak of the First World War as a salvation. He later wrote in his autobiography, *Mein Kampf,* that, "overcome by passionate enthusiasm, I fell to my knees and thanked heaven out of an overflowing heart." The struggle and discipline of war gave life meaning, and Hitler served bravely as a dispatch carrier on the western front.

When Germany was suddenly defeated in 1918, Hitler's world was shattered. Not only was he a fanatical nationalist, but war was his reason for living. Convinced that Jews and Marxists had "stabbed Germany in the back," he vowed to fight on. And in the bitterness and uncertainty of postwar Germany, his wild speeches began to attract attention.

In late 1919 Hitler joined a tiny extremist group in Munich called the German Workers' party. In addition to denouncing Jews, Marxists, and democrats, the German Workers' party promised unity under a uniquely German "national socialism," which would abolish the injustices of capitalism and create a mighty "people's community." By 1921 Hitler had gained absolute control of this small but growing party. Moreover, Hitler was already a master of mass propaganda and political showmanship. Party members sported badges and uniforms, gave victory salutes, and marched like robots through the streets of Munich. But Hitler's most effective tool was the mass rally, a kind of political revival meeting. Songs, slogans, and demonstrations built up the tension until Hitler finally arrived. He then often worked his audience into a frenzy with wild, demagogic attacks on the Versailles treaty, the Jews, the war profiteers, and Germany's Weimar Republic.

Party membership multiplied tenfold after early 1922. In late 1923, when the Weimar Republic seemed on the verge of collapse, Hitler decided on an armed uprising in Munich. Inspired by Mussolini's recent easy victory, Hitler had found an ally in General Ludendorff of First World War fame. After Hitler had overthrown the Bavarian government, Ludendorff was supposed to march on Berlin with Hitler's support. The plot was poorly organized, however, and it was crushed by the police, backed up by the army, in less than a day. Hitler was arrested, tried, and sentenced to five years in prison. He had failed for the moment. But Nazism had been born, and it did not die.

Hitler's Road to Power

At his trial, Hitler violently denounced the Weimar Republic and skillfully presented his own program. In doing so he gained enormous publicity and attention. Moreover, he learned from his unsuccessful revolt. Hitler concluded that he had to undermine rather than overthrow the government, that he had to use its tolerant democratic framework to intimidate the opposition and come to power through electoral competition. He forced his more violent supporters to accept his new strategy. Finally, Hitler used his brief prison term—he was released in less than a year—to dictate *Mein Kampf.* There he expounded on his basic themes: "race," with the stress on anti-Semitism; "living space," with a sweeping vision of war and conquered territory; and the leader-dictator (Führer) with unlimited, arbitary power. Hitler's followers had their bible.

In the years of prosperity and relative stability between 1924 and 1929, Hitler concentrated on building his National Socialist German Workers' party, or Nazi party. By 1928 the party had a hundred thousand highly disciplined members under Hitler's absolute control. To appeal to the middle classes, Hitler de-emphasized the anticapitalist elements of national socialism and vowed to fight Bolshevism.

Hitler in Opposition   Hitler returns the salute of his Brown Shirts in this photograph from the third party day rally in Nuremberg in 1927. The Brown Shirts formed a private army within the Nazi movement, and their uniforms, marches, salutes, and vandalism helped keep Hitler in the public eye in the 1920s. *(Source: Courtesy, Bison Books, London)*

"Hitler, Our Last Hope"   So reads the very effective Nazi campaign poster, which is attracting attention with its gaunt and haggard faces. By 1932 almost half of all Germans, like these in Berlin, had come to agree. *(Source: Bildarchiv Preussischer Kulturbesitz. Photo: Herbert Hoffman, 1932)*

The Nazis were still a small splinter group in 1928, when they received only 2.6 percent of the vote in the general elections and twelve Nazis won seats in the parliament. There the Nazi deputies pursued the legal strategy of using democracy to destroy democracy. As Hitler's talented future minister of propaganda Joseph Goebbels (1897–1945) explained in 1928 in the party newspaper, "We become Reichstag deputies in order to paralyze the spirit of Weimar with its own aid. . . . We come as enemies! As the wolf breaks into the sheepfold, so we come."[8]

In 1929 the Great Depression began striking down economic prosperity, one of the barriers that had kept the wolf at bay. Unemployment jumped from 1.3 million in 1929 to 5 million in 1930; that year Germany had almost as many unemployed as

all the other countries of Europe combined. Industrial production fell by one-half between 1929 and 1932. By the end of 1932, an incredible 43 percent of the labor force was unemployed, and it was estimated that only one in every three union members was working full-time. No factor contributed more to Hitler's success than the economic crisis. Never very interested in economics before, Hitler began promising German voters economic as well as political and military salvation.

Hitler focused his promises on the middle and lower middle class—small business people, office workers, artisans, and peasants. Already disillusioned by the great inflation of 1923, these people were seized by panic as bankruptcies increased, unemployment soared, and the dreaded Communists made dramatic election gains. The middle and lower middle classes deserted the conservative and moderate parties for the Nazis in great numbers.

The Nazis also appealed strongly to German youth. Indeed, in some ways the Nazi movement was a mass movement of young Germans. Hitler himself was only forty in 1929, and he and most of his top aides were much younger than other leading German politicians. "National Socialism is the organized will of the youth," proclaimed the official Nazi slogan, and the battle cry of Gregor Strasser, a leading Nazi organizer, was "Make way, you old ones."[9] In 1931 almost 40 percent of Nazi party members were under thirty, compared with 20 percent of Social Democrats. Two-thirds of Nazi members were under forty. National recovery, exciting and rapid change, and personal advancement: these were the appeals of Nazism to millions of German youths.

In the election of 1930, the Nazis won 6.5 million votes and 107 seats, which made them second in strength only to the Social Democrats, the moderate socialists. The economic situation continued to deteriorate, and Hitler kept promising he would bring recovery. In 1932 the Nazi vote leaped to 14.5 million, and the Nazis became the largest party in the Reichstag.

Another reason Hitler came to power was the breakdown of democratic government as early as May 1930. Unable to gain support of a majority in the Reichstag, Chancellor (chief minister) Heinrich Brüning convinced the president, the aging war hero General Hindenburg, to authorize rule by decree. The Weimar Republic's constitution permitted such rule in emergency situations, but the rather authoritarian, self-righteous Brüning intended to use it indefinitely. Moreover, Brüning was determined to overcome the economic crisis by cutting back government spending and ruthlessly forcing down prices and wages. Brüning's ultraorthodox policies not only intensified the economic collapse in Germany, they also convinced the lower middle classes that the country's republican leaders were stupid and corrupt. These classes were pleased rather than dismayed by Hitler's attacks on the republican system. After President Hindenburg forced Brüning to resign in May 1932, the new government headed by Franz von Papen continued to rule by decree.

The continuation of the struggle between the Social Democrats and Communists, right up until the moment Hitler took power, was another aspect of the breakdown of democratic government. The

The Mobilization of Young People was a prime objective of the Nazi leadership. Here boys in a Nazi youth group, some of whom are only children, are disciplined and conditioned to devote themselves to the regime. *(Source: Bettmann/Hulton)*

Communists foolishly refused to cooperate with the Social Democrats, even though the two parties together outnumbered the Nazis in the Reichstag, even after the elections of 1932. German Communists (and the complacent Stalin) were blinded by their ideology and their hatred of the Socialists. They were certain that Hitler's rise represented the last agonies of monopoly capitalism and that a communist revolution would quickly follow his taking power. The Socialist leaders pleaded, even at the Russian embassy, for at least a temporary alliance with the Communists to block Hitler, but to no avail. Perhaps the Weimar Republic was already too far gone, but this disunity on the left was undoubtedly another nail in its coffin.

Finally, there was Hitler's skill as a politician. A master of mass propaganda and psychology, he had written in *Mein Kampf* that the masses were the "driving force of the most important changes in this world" and were themselves driven by hysterical fanaticism and not by knowledge. To arouse such hysterical fanaticism, he believed that all propaganda had to be limited to a few simple, endlessly repeated slogans. Thus, in the terrible economic and political crisis, he harangued vast audiences with passionate, irrational oratory. Men moaned and women cried, seized by emotion. And many uncertain individuals, surrounded by thousands of entranced listeners, found security and a sense of belonging.

At the same time, Hitler excelled at dirty, backroom politics. That, in fact, brought him to power. In 1932 he cleverly succeeded in gaining the support of key people in the army and big business. These people thought they could use Hitler for their own advantage, to get increased military spending, fat contracts, and tough measures against workers. Conservative and nationalistic politicians like Papen thought similarly. They thus accepted Hitler's demand to join the government only if he became chancellor. There would be only two other National Socialists and nine solid Conservatives as ministers, and in such a coalition government, they reasoned, Hitler could be used and controlled. On January 30, 1933, Hitler was legally appointed chancellor by Hindenburg.

The Nazi State and Society

Hitler moved rapidly and skillfully to establish an unshakable dictatorship. His first step was to continue using terror and threats to gain more power while maintaining legal appearances. He immediately called for new elections and applied the enormous power of the government to restrict his opponents. In the midst of a violent electoral campaign, the Reichstag building was partly destroyed by fire. Although the Nazis themselves may have set the fire, Hitler screamed that the Communist party was responsible. On the strength of this accusation, he convinced President Hindenburg to sign dictatorial emergency acts that practically abolished freedom of speech and assembly, in addition to most personal liberties.

When the Nazis won only 44 percent of the vote in the elections, Hitler immediately outlawed the Communist party and arrested its parliamentary representatives. Then, on March 23, 1933, the Nazis pushed through the Reichstag the so-called Enabling Act, which gave Hitler absolute dictatorial power for four years. Only the Social Democrats voted against this bill, for Hitler had successfully blackmailed the Center party by threatening to attack the Catholic church.

Armed with the Enabling Act, Hitler and the Nazis moved to smash or control all independent organizations. Meanwhile, Hitler and his propagandists constantly proclaimed that their revolution was legal and constitutional. This deceitful stress on legality, coupled with the divide-and-conquer technique, disarmed the opposition until it was too late for effective resistance.

The systematic subjugation of independent organizations and the creation of a totalitarian state had massive repercussions. The Social Democratic and Center parties were soon dissolved, and Germany became a one-party state. Only the Nazi party was legal. Elections were farces. The Reichstag was jokingly referred to as the most expensive glee club in the country, for its only function was to sing hymns of praise to the Führer. Hitler and the Nazis took over the government bureaucracy intact, installing many Nazis in top positions. At the same time, they created a series of overlapping Nazi party organizations, responsible solely to Hitler. Thus Hitler had both an established bureaucracy for normal business and a private, personal "party government" for special duties.

In the economic sphere, strikes were forbidden and labor unions were abolished, replaced by a Nazi Labor Front. Professional people—doctors and lawyers, teachers and engineers—also saw their previously independent organizations swallowed up in Nazi associations. Nor did the Nazis neglect cultural and intellectual life. Publishing houses were put under Nazi control, and universities and writers were quickly brought into line. Democratic, socialist, and Jewish literature was put on ever-growing blacklists. Passionate students and pitiful professors burned forbidden books in public squares. Modern art and architecture were ruthlessly prohibited. Life became violently anti-intellectual. As Hitler's cynical minister of propaganda, Joseph Goebbels, put it, "When I hear the word 'culture' I reach for my gun."[10] By 1934 a totalitarian state characterized by frightening dynamism and obedience to Hitler was already largely in place.

By 1934 only the army retained independence, and Hitler moved brutally and skillfully to establish his control there, too. He realized that the army, as well as big business, was suspicious of the Nazi storm troopers (the S.A.), the quasi-military band of three million toughs in brown shirts who had fought Communists and beaten up Jews before the Nazis took power. These unruly storm troopers expected top positions in the army and even talked of a "second revolution" against capitalism. Needing the support of the army and big business, Hitler decided that the S.A. leaders had to be eliminated. On the night of June 30, 1934, he struck.

Hitler's elite personal guard—the S.S.—arrested and shot without trial roughly a thousand S.A. leaders and assorted political enemies. While his propagandists spread lies about S.A. conspiracies, the army leaders and President Hindenburg responded to the purge with congratulatory telegrams. Shortly thereafter, the army leaders swore a binding oath of "unquestioning obedience . . . to the Leader of the German State and People, Adolf Hitler." The purge of the S.A. was another decisive step toward unlimited totalitarian terror. The S.S., the elite guard that had loyally murdered the S.A. leaders, grew rapidly. Under its methodical, inhuman leader, Heinrich Himmler (1900–1945), the S.S. joined with the political police, the Gestapo, to expand its network of special courts and concentration camps. Nobody was safe.

From the beginning, the Jews were a special object of Nazi persecution. By the end of 1934, most Jewish lawyers, doctors, professors, civil servants, and musicians had lost their jobs and the right to practice their professions. In 1935 the infamous Nuremberg Laws classified as Jewish anyone having one or more Jewish grandparents and deprived

Jews of all rights of citizenship. By 1938 roughly one-quarter of Germany's half-million Jews had emigrated, sacrificing almost all their property in order to leave Germany.

Following the assassination of a German diplomat in Paris by a young Jewish boy trying desperately to strike out at persecution, the attack on the Jews accelerated. A well-organized wave of violence destroyed homes, synagogues, and businesses, after which German Jews were rounded up and made to pay for the damage. It became very difficult for Jews to leave Germany. Some Germans privately opposed these outrages, but most went along or looked the other way. Although this lack of response partly reflected the individual's helplessness in the totalitarian state, it was also a sign of the strong popular support Hitler's government enjoyed.

Hitler's Popularity

Hitler had promised the masses economic recovery —"work and bread"—and he delivered. Breaking with Brüning's do-nothing policies, Hitler immediately launched a large public works program to pull Germany out of the depression. Work began on superhighways, offices, gigantic sports stadiums, and public housing. In 1936, as Germany rearmed rapidly, government spending began to concentrate on the military. The result was that unemployment dropped steadily, from six million in January 1933 to about one million in late 1936. By 1938 there was a shortage of workers, and women eventually took many jobs previously denied them by the antifeminist Nazis. Thus everyone had work, and between 1932 and 1938 the standard of living for the average employed worker rose more than 20 percent. The profits of business also increased. For millions of people, economic recovery was tangible evidence in their daily lives that the excitement and dynamism of Nazi rule were based on more than show.

For the masses of ordinary German citizens, who were not Jews, Slavs, Gypsies, Jehovah's Witnesses, or Communists, Hitler's government meant greater equality and exceptional opportunities. It must be remembered that in 1933 the position of the traditional German elites—the landed aristocracy, the wealthy capitalists, and the well-educated professional classes—was still very strong. Barriers between classes were generally high. Hitler's rule

EVENTS LEADING TO WORLD WAR TWO

1919	Treaty of Versailles
	J. M. Keynes, *Economic Consequences of the Peace*
1919–1920	U.S. Senate rejects the Treaty of Versailles
1921	Germany is billed $35 billion in reparations
1922	Mussolini seizes power in Italy
	Germany proposes a moratorium on reparations
January 1923	France and Belgium occupy the Ruhr
	Germany orders passive resistance to the occupation
October 1923	Stresemann agrees to reparations with re-examination of Germany's ability to pay
1924	Dawes Plan: German reparations reduced and put on a sliding scale; large U.S. loans to Germany recommended to promote German recovery; occupation of the Ruhr ends
	Adolf Hitler, *Mein Kampf*
1924–1929	Spectacular German economic recovery; circular flow of international funds enables sizable reparations payments
1925	Treaties of Locarno promote European security and stability
1926	Germany joins the League of Nations
1928	Kellogg-Briand Pact renounces war as an instrument of international affairs
1929	Young Plan further reduces German reparations
	Crash of U.S. stock market
1929–1933	Depths of the Great Depression
1931	Japan invades Manchuria
1932	Nazis become the largest party in the Reichstag
January 1933	Hitler appointed chancellor
March 1933	Reichstag passes the Enabling Act, granting Hitler absolute dictatorial power
October 1933	Germany withdraws from the League of Nations
July 1934	Nazis murder Austrian chancellor
March 1935	Hitler announces German rearmament
June 1935	Anglo-German naval agreement
October 1935	Mussolini invades Ethiopia and receives Hitler's support
1935	Nuremburg Laws deprive Jews of all rights of citizenship
March 1936	German armies move unopposed into the demilitarized Rhineland
July 1936	Outbreak of civil war in Spain
1937	Japan invades China
	Rome-Berlin Axis
March 1938	Germany annexes Austria
September 1938	Munich Conference: Britain and France agree to German seizure of the Sudetenland from Czechoslovakia
March 1939	Germany occupies the rest of Czechoslovakia; the end of appeasement in Britain
August 1939	Russo-German nonaggression pact
September 1, 1939	Germany invades Poland
September 3, 1939	Britain and France declare war on Germany

introduced vast changes in this pattern. For example, stiff educational requirements, which favored the well-to-do, were greatly relaxed. The new Nazi elite was composed largely of young and poorly educated dropouts, rootless lower-middle-class people like Hitler, who rose to the top with breathtaking speed.

More generally, the Nazis, like the Russian Communists, tolerated privilege and wealth only as long as they served the needs of the party. Big business was constantly ordered around, to the point that "probably never in peacetime has an ostensibly capitalist economy been directed as non- and even anticapitalistically as the German economy between 1933 and 1939."[11] Hitler brought about a kind of social revolution, which was enthusiastically embraced by millions of modest middle-class and lower-middle-class people and even by many workers.

Hitler's extreme nationalism, which had helped him gain power, continued to appeal to Germans after 1933. Ever since the wars against Napoleon, many Germans had believed in a special mission for a superior German nation. The successes of Bismarck had furthered such feelings, and near-victory in World War One made nationalists eager for renewed expansion in the 1920s. Thus, when Hitler went from one foreign triumph to another and a great German empire seemed within reach, the majority of the population was delighted and praised the Führer's actions.

By no means all Germans supported Hitler, however, and a number of German groups actively resisted him after 1933. Tens of thousands of political enemies were imprisoned, and thousands were executed. Opponents of the Nazis pursued various goals, and under totalitarian conditions they were never unified, a fact that helps account for their ultimate lack of success. In the first years of Hitler's rule, the principal resisters were the Communists and the Social Democrats in the trade unions. But the expansion of the S.S. system of terror after 1935 smashed most of these leftists. A second group of opponents arose in the Catholic and Protestant churches. However, their efforts were directed primarily at preserving genuine religious life, not at overthrowing Hitler. Finally, in 1938 (and again in 1942 to 1944), some high-ranking army officers, who feared the consequences of Hitler's reckless aggression, plotted against him, unsuccessfully.

NAZI EXPANSION AND THE SECOND WORLD WAR

Although economic recovery and increased opportunities for social advancement won Hitler support, they were only by-products of Nazi totalitarianism. The guiding concepts of Nazism remained space and race—the territorial expansion of the superior German race. As Germany regained its economic strength and as independent organizations were brought under control, Hitler formed alliances with other dictators and began expanding. German expansion was facilitated by the uncertain, divided, pacific Western democracies, which tried to buy off Hitler to avoid war.

Yet war inevitably broke out, in both the West and the East, for Hitler's ambitions were essentially unlimited. On both war fronts the Nazi soldiers scored enormous successes until late 1942, establishing a horrifyingly vast empire of death and destruction. Hitler's reckless aggression also raised a mighty coalition determined to smash the Nazi order. Led by Britain, the United States, and the Soviet Union, the Grand Alliance—to use Winston Churchill's favorite term—functioned quite effectively in military terms. By the summer of 1943, the tide of battle had turned. Two years later, Germany and its allies lay in ruins, utterly defeated. Thus the terrible Nazi empire proved short-lived.

Aggression and Appeasement, 1933–1939

Hitler's tactics in international politics after 1933 strikingly resembled those he used in domestic politics between 1924 and 1933. When Hitler was weak, he righteously proclaimed that he intended to overturn the "unjust system" established by the treaties of Versailles and Locarno—but only by legal means. As he grew stronger, and as other leaders showed their willingness to compromise, he increased his demands and finally began attacking his independent neighbors (Map 29.1).

Hitler realized that his aggressive policies had to be carefully camouflaged at first, for Germany's army was limited by the Treaty of Versailles to only a hundred thousand men. As he told a group of army commanders in February 1933, the early stages of his policy of "conquest of new living space in the East and its ruthless Germanization"

MAP 29.1 The Growth of Nazi Germany, 1933–1939 Until March 1939, Hitler brought ethnic Germans into the Nazi state; then he turned on the Slavic peoples he had always hated.

had serious dangers. If France had real leaders, Hitler said, it would "not give us time but attack us, presumably with its eastern satellites."[12] To avoid such threats to his plans, Hitler loudly proclaimed his peaceful intentions to all the world. Nevertheless, he felt strong enough to walk out of a sixty-nation disarmament conference and withdraw from the League of Nations in October 1933. Stresemann's policy of peaceful cooperation was dead;

the Nazi determination to rearm was out in the open.

Following this action, which met with widespread approval at home, Hitler moved to incorporate independent Austria into a Greater Germany. Austrian Nazis climaxed an attempted overthrow by murdering the Austrian chancellor in July 1934. They were unable to take power, however, because a worried Mussolini, who had initially greeted

Hitler as a fascist little brother, massed his troops on the Brenner Pass and threatened to fight. When, in March 1935, Hitler established a general military draft and declared the "unequal" disarmament clauses of the Treaty of Versailles null and void, other countries appeared to understand the danger. With France taking the lead, Italy and Great Britain protested strongly and warned against future aggressive actions.

Yet the emerging united front against Hitler quickly collapsed. Of crucial importance, Britain adopted a policy of appeasement, granting Hitler everything he could reasonably want (and more) in order to avoid war. The first step was an Anglo-German naval agreement in June 1935, which broke Germany's isolation. The second step came in March 1936, when Hitler suddenly marched his armies into the demilitarized Rhineland, brazenly violating the treaties of Versailles and Locarno. This was the last good chance to stop the Nazis, for Hitler had ordered his troops to retreat if France resisted militarily. But an uncertain France would not move without British support, and the occupation of German soil by German armies seemed right and just to Britain. Its strategic position greatly improved, Germany had handed France a tremendous psychological defeat.

British appeasement, which practically dictated French policy, lasted far into 1939. It was motivated by British feelings of guilt toward Germany and the pacifism of a population still horrified by the memory of the First World War. Like many Germans, British political leaders seriously underestimated Hitler. They believed that they could use him to stop Russian communism. A leading member of Britain's government personally told Hitler in November 1937 that it was his conviction that Hitler "not only had accomplished great things in Germany itself, but that through the total destruction of Communism in his own country . . . Germany rightly had to be considered as a Western bulwark against Communism."[13] Such rigid anticommunist feelings made an alliance between the Western powers and Stalin very unlikely.

Cartoonist David Low's biting criticism of appeasing leaders appeared shortly after Hitler remilitarized the Rhineland. Appeasement also appealed to millions of ordinary citizens, who wanted to avoid at any cost another great war. *(Source: Cartoon by David Low. Reproduced by permission of London Evening Standard/Solo)*

As Britain and France opted for appeasement and Russia watched all developments suspiciously, Hitler found powerful allies. In 1935 the bombastic Mussolini decided that imperial expansion was needed to revitalize fascism. From Italian colonies on the east coast of Africa he attacked the independent African kingdom of Ethiopia. The Western powers and the League of Nations piously condemned Italian aggression—a posture that angered Mussolini—without saving Ethiopia from defeat. Hitler, who had secretly supplied Ethiopia with arms to heat up the conflict, supported Italy energetically and thereby overcame Mussolini's lingering doubts about the Nazis. The result in 1936 was an agreement on close cooperation between Italy and Germany, the so-called Rome-Berlin Axis. Japan, which had been expanding into Manchuria since 1931, soon joined the alliance between Italy and Germany.

At the same time, Germany and Italy intervened in the long, complicated Spanish Civil War, where their support eventually helped General Francisco Franco's fascist movement defeat republican Spain. Spain's only official aid came from Soviet Russia, for public opinion in Britain and especially in France was hopelessly divided on the Spanish question.

By late 1937, as he was proclaiming his peaceful intentions to the British and their gullible prime minister, Neville Chamberlain, Hitler told his generals his real plans. His "unshakable decision" was to crush Austria and Czechoslovakia at the earliest possible moment, as the first step in his long-contemplated drive to the east for "living space." By threatening Austria with invasion, Hitler forced the Austrian chancellor in March 1938 to put local Nazis in control of the government. The next day, German armies moved in unopposed, and Austria became two more provinces of Greater Germany (see Map 29.1).

Simultaneously, Hitler began demanding that the pro-Nazi, German-speaking minority of western Czechoslovakia—the Sudetenland—be turned over to Germany. Yet democratic Czechoslovakia was prepared to defend itself. Moreover, France had been Czechoslovakia's ally since 1924; and if France fought, Soviet Russia was pledged to help. As war appeared inevitable—for Hitler had already told the leader of the Sudeten Germans that "we must always ask so much we cannot be satisfied"—appeasement triumphed again. In September 1938

Chamberlain flew to Germany three times in fourteen days. In these negotiations, to which Russia was deliberately not invited, Chamberlain and the French agreed with Hitler that the Sudetenland should be ceded to Germany immediately. Returning to London from the Munich Conference, Chamberlain told cheering crowds that he had secured "peace with honor . . . peace for our time." Sold out by the Western powers, Czechoslovakia gave in.

Confirmed once again in his opinion of the Western democracies as weak and racially degenerate, Hitler accelerated his aggression. In a shocking violation of his solemn assurances that the Sudetenland was his last territorial demand, Hitler's armies occupied the Czech lands in March 1939, while Slovakia became a puppet state. The effect on Western public opinion was electrifying. For the first time, there was no possible rationale of self-determination for Nazi aggression, since Hitler was seizing Czechs and Slovaks as captive peoples. Thus, when Hitler used the question of German minorities in Danzig as a pretext to confront Poland, a suddenly militant Chamberlain declared that Britain and France would fight if Hitler attacked his eastern neighbor. Hitler did not take these warnings seriously, and thus he decided to press on.

In an about-face that stunned the world, Hitler offered and Stalin signed a ten-year Nazi-Soviet nonaggression pact in August 1939, whereby each dictator promised to remain neutral if the other became involved in war. Even more startling was the attached secret protocol, which ruthlessly divided eastern Europe into German and Russian zones, "in the event of a political territorial reorganization." Although this top-secret protocol sealing the destruction of Poland and the Baltic states became known only after the war, the nonaggression pact itself was enough to make Britain and France cry treachery, for they too had been negotiating with Stalin. But Stalin had remained distrustful of Western intentions. Moreover, Britain and France had offered him military risk without gain, while Hitler had offered territorial gain without risk. For Hitler, everything was set. He told his generals on the day of the nonaggression pact: "My only fear is that at the last moment some dirty dog will come up with a mediation plan." On September 1, 1939, German armies and warplanes smashed into Poland from three sides. Two days later, finally true to their

[margin note, left side: Bismarck: "Germany is satisfied"]

[margin note, center: Something for nothing]

word, Britain and France declared war on Germany. The Second World War had begun.

Hitler's Empire, 1939–1942

Using planes, tanks, and trucks in the first example of the *blitzkrieg,* or "lightning war," Hitler's armies crushed Poland in four weeks. While Soviet Russia quickly took its part of the booty—the eastern half of Poland and the Baltic states of Lithuania, Estonia, and Latvia—French and British armies dug in in the west. They expected another war of attrition and economic blockade.

In spring 1940 the lightning war struck again. After occupying Denmark, Norway, and Holland, German motorized columns broke through southern Belgium, split the Franco-British forces, and trapped the entire British army on the beaches of Dunkirk. By heroic efforts the British withdrew their troops but not their equipment.

France was taken by the Nazis. The aging marshal Henri-Philippe Pétain formed a new French government—the so-called Vichy government—to accept defeat, and German armies occupied most of France. By July 1940 Hitler ruled practically all of western continental Europe; Italy was an ally, and the Soviet Union a friendly neutral. Only Britain, led by the uncompromising Winston Churchill (1874–1965), remained unconquered. Churchill proved to be one of history's greatest wartime leaders, rallying his fellow citizens with stirring speeches, infectious confidence, and bulldog determination.

Germany sought to gain control of the air, the necessary first step for an amphibious invasion of Britain. In the Battle of Britain, up to a thousand German planes attacked British airfields and key factories in a single day, dueling with British defenders high in the skies. Losses were heavy on both sides. Then in September Hitler angrily and foolishly changed his strategy, turning from military objectives to indiscriminate bombing of British cities in an attempt to break British morale. British factories increased production of their excellent fighter planes; antiaircraft defense improved with the help of radar; and the heavily bombed people of London defiantly dug in. In September through October 1940, Britain was beating Germany three to one in the air war. There was no possibility of immediate German invasion of Britain.

In these circumstances, the most reasonable German strategy would have been to attack Britain through the eastern Mediterranean, taking Egypt and the Suez Canal and pinching off Britain's supply of oil. Moreover, Mussolini's early defeats in Greece had drawn Hitler into the Balkans, where Germany quickly conquered Greece and Yugoslavia while forcing Hungary, Romania, and Bulgaria into alliances with Germany by April 1941. This reinforced the logic of a thrust into the eastern Mediterranean. But Hitler was not a reasonable person. His lifetime obsession with a vast eastern European empire for the master race irrationally dictated policy. By late 1940 he had already decided on his next move, and in June 1941 German armies suddenly attacked the Soviet Union along a vast front. With Britain still unconquered, Hitler's decision was a wild, irrational gamble, epitomizing the violent, unlimited ambitions of modern totalitarianism.

Faithfully fulfilling all his obligations under the Nazi-Soviet Pact and even ignoring warnings of impending invasion, Stalin was caught off guard. Nazi armies moved like lightning across the Russian steppe. By October 1941 Leningrad was practically surrounded, Moscow besieged, and most of the Ukraine conquered; yet the Russians did not collapse. When a severe winter struck German armies outfitted in summer uniforms, the invaders were stopped.

While Hitler's armies dramatically expanded the war in Europe, his Japanese allies did the same in Asia. Engaged in a general but undeclared war against China since 1937, Japan's rulers had increasingly come into diplomatic conflict with the Pacific basin's other great power, the United States. When the Japanese occupied French Indochina in July 1941, the United States retaliated by cutting off sales of vital rubber, scrap iron, oil, and aviation fuel. Tension mounted further, and on December 7, 1941, Japan attacked the U.S. naval base at Pearl Harbor in Hawaii. Hitler immediately declared war on the United States, even though his treaty obligations with Japan did not require him to initiate this course of action.

As Japanese forces advanced swiftly into Southeast Asia after the crippling surprise attack at Pearl Harbor, Hitler and his European allies continued the two-front war against the Soviet Union and Great Britain. Not until late 1942 did the Nazis suffer their first major defeats. In the meantime,

Hitler ruled a vast European empire stretching from the outskirts of Moscow to the English Channel. Hitler and the top Nazi leadership began building their "New Order," and they continued their efforts until their final collapse in 1945. In doing so, they showed what Nazi victory would have meant.

Hitler's New Order was based firmly on the guiding principle of Nazi totalitarianism: racial imperialism. Within this New Order, the Nordic peoples—the Dutch, the Norwegians, and the Danes—received preferential treatment, for they were racially related to the Germans. The French, an "inferior" Latin people, occupied the middle position. They were heavily taxed to support the Nazi war effort, but were tolerated as a race. Once Nazi reverses began to mount in late 1942, however, all the occupied territories of western and northern Europe were exploited with increasing intensity. Material shortages and both mental and physical suffering afflicted millions of people.

Slavs in the conquered territories to the east were treated with harsh hatred as "subhumans." At the height of his success in 1941 to 1942, Hitler painted for his intimate circle the fantastic details of a vast eastern colonial empire, where the Poles, Ukrainians, and Russians would be enslaved and forced to die out, while Germanic peasants resettled their abandoned lands. Himmler and the elite corps of S.S. volunteers struggled loyally, sometimes against the German army, to implement part of this general program even before victory was secured. In parts of Poland, the S.S. arrested and evacuated Polish peasants to create a German

Prelude to Murder: This photo captures the terrible inhumanity of Nazi racism. Frightened and bewildered families from the soon-to-be destroyed Warsaw ghetto are being forced out of their homes by German soldiers for deportation to concentration camps. There they face murder in the gas chambers. *(Source: Roger-Viollet)*

"mass settlement space." Polish workers and Russian prisoners of war were transported to Germany, where they did most of the heavy labor and were systematically worked to death. The conditions of Russian slave labor in Germany were so harsh that four out of five Russian prisoners did not survive the war.

Finally, Jews were condemned to extermination, along with Gypsies, Jehovah's Witnesses, and captured Communists. By 1939 German Jews had lost all their civil rights, and after the fall of Warsaw the Nazis began deporting them to Poland. There they and Jews from all over Europe were concentrated in ghettos, compelled to wear the Jewish star, and turned into slave laborers. But by 1941 Himmler's S.S. was carrying out the "final solution of the Jewish question"—the murder of every single Jew. All over Hitler's empire, Jews were arrested, packed like cattle onto freight trains, and dispatched to extermination camps.

There the victims were taken by force or deception to "shower rooms," which were actually gas chambers. These gas chambers, first perfected in the quiet, efficient execution of seventy thousand mentally ill Germans between 1938 and 1941, permitted rapid, hideous, and thoroughly bureaucratized mass murder. For fifteen to twenty minutes came the terrible screams and gasping sobs of men, women, and children choking to death on poison gas. Then, only silence. Special camp workers quickly tore the victims' gold teeth from their jaws and cut off their hair for use as chair stuffing. The bodies were then cremated, or sometimes boiled for oil to make soap, while the bones were crushed to produce fertilizers. At Auschwitz, the most infamous of the Nazi death factories, as many as twelve thousand human beings were slaughtered each day. On the turbulent Russian front, the S.S. death squads forced the Jewish population to dig giant pits, which became mass graves as the victims were lined up on the edge and cut down by machine guns. The extermination of European Jews was the ultimate monstrosity of Nazi racism and racial imperialism. By 1945 six million Jews had been murdered.

The Grand Alliance

While the Nazis built their savage empire, the Allies faced the hard fact that chance, rather than choice, brought them together. Stalin had been cooperating fully with Hitler between August 1939 and June 1941, and only the Japanese attack on Pearl Harbor in December 1941 and Hitler's immediate declaration of war had overwhelmed powerful isolationism in the United States. The Allies' first task was to try to overcome their mutual suspicions and build an unshakable alliance on the quicksand of accident. By means of three interrelated policies they succeeded.

First, President Roosevelt accepted Churchill's contention that the United States should concentrate first on defeating Hitler. Only after victory in Europe would the United States turn toward the Pacific for an all-out attack on Japan, the lesser threat. Therefore, the United States promised and sent large amounts of military aid to Britain and Russia, and American and British forces in each combat zone were tightly integrated under a single commander. America's policy of "Europe first" helped solidify the anti-Hitler coalition.

Second, within the European framework, the Americans and the British put immediate military needs first. They consistently postponed tough political questions relating to the eventual peace settlement and thereby avoided conflicts that might have split the alliance until after the war.

Third, to further encourage mutual trust, the Allies adopted the principle of the "unconditional surrender" of Germany and Japan. The policy of unconditional surrender cemented the Grand Alliance because it denied Hitler any hope of dividing his foes. It probably also discouraged Germans and Japanese who might have tried to overthrow their dictators in order to make a compromise peace. Of great importance for the postwar shape of Europe, it meant that Russian and Anglo-American armies would almost certainly come together to divide all of Germany, and most of the Continent, among themselves.

The military resources of the Grand Alliance were awesome. The strengths of the United States were its mighty industry, its large population, and its national unity. Even before Pearl Harbor, President Roosevelt had called America the "arsenal of democracy" and given military aid to Britain and Russia. Now the United States geared up rapidly for all-out war production and drew heavily on a generally cooperative Latin America for resources. It not only equipped its own armies but eventually gave its allies about $50 billion of arms and equip-

Во имя Родины вперёд богатыри!

For the Motherland's Sake, Go Forward, Heroes

"For the Motherland's Sake, Go Forward, Heroes" Joining the historic Russian warrior and the young Soviet soldier in the common cause, this poster portrays the defense of the nation as a sacred mission and illustrates the way Soviet leaders successfully appealed to Russian nationalism during the war. (*Source: Library of Congress*)

1942 wore on, Britain could increasingly draw on the enormous physical and human resources of its empire and the United States. By early 1943 the Americans and the British combined small aircraft carriers with radar-guided bombers to rid the Atlantic of German submarines. Britain, the impregnable floating fortress, became a gigantic front-line staging area for the decisive blow to the heart of Germany.

As for Soviet Russia, so great was its strength that it might well have defeated Germany without Western help. In the face of the German advance, whole factories and populations were successfully evacuated to eastern Russia and Siberia. There, war production was reorganized and expanded, and the Red Army was increasingly well supplied. The Red Army was also well led, for a new generation of talented military leaders quickly arose to replace those so recently purged. Most important of all, Stalin drew on the massive support and heroic determination of the Soviet people. Broad-based Russian nationalism, as opposed to narrow communist ideology, became the powerful unifying force in what was appropriately called the "Great Patriotic War of the Fatherland."

Finally, the United States, Britain, and Soviet Russia were not alone. They had the resources of much of the world at their command. And, to a greater or lesser extent, they were aided by a growing resistance movement against the Nazis throughout Europe, even in Germany. Thus, although Ukrainian peasants often welcomed the Germans as liberators, the barbaric occupation policies of the Nazis quickly drove them to join and support behind-the-lines guerrilla forces. More generally, after Russia was invaded in June 1941, Communists throughout Europe took the lead in the underground Resistance, joined by a growing number of patriots and Christians. Anti-Nazi leaders from occupied countries established governments-in-exile in London, like that of the "Free French" under the intensely proud General Charles De Gaulle. These governments gathered valuable

ment. Britain received by far the most, but about one-fifth of the total went to Russia in the form of badly needed trucks, planes, and munitions.

Too strong to lose and too weak to win when it stood alone, Britain, too, continued to make a great contribution. The British economy was totally and effectively mobilized, and the sharing of burdens through rationing and heavy taxes on war profits maintained social harmony. Moreover, as

MAP 29.2 World War Two in Europe The map shows the extent of Hitler's empire at its height, before the battle of Stalingrad in late 1942, and the subsequent advances of the Allies until Germany surrendered on May 7, 1945.

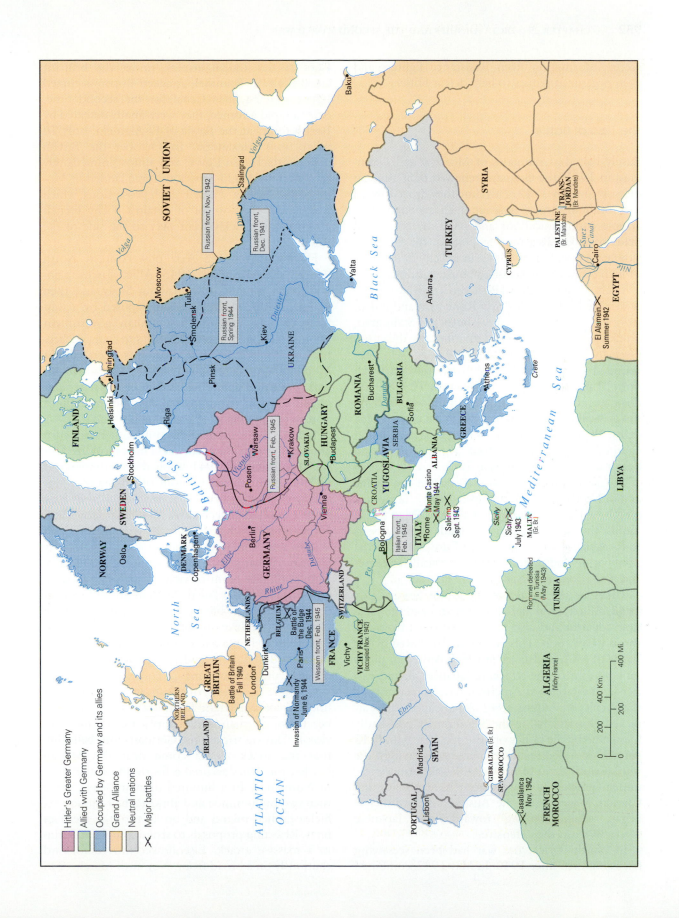

SOVIET UNION

Russian front, Nov. 1942
Stalingrad
Russian front,
Dec. 1941
Russian front,
Spring 1944

Baku

SYRIA

TRANS-
JORDAN
(Br. Mandate)

PALESTINE
(Br. Mandate)

Suez Canal

Cairo

EGYPT

El Alamein
Summer 1942

TURKEY

Ankara

CYPRUS

Black Sea

Yalta

Moscow

Smolensk Tula

Kiev

Dnieper

Dniester

UKRAINE

Pinsk

Riga

FINLAND

Helsinki

Leningrad

Stockholm

SWEDEN

Baltic Sea

Warsaw

Russian front, Feb. 1945

Krakow

Posen

Vistula

SLOVAKIA

HUNGARY

Budapest

Vienna

ROMANIA

Bucharest

Danube

BULGARIA

Sofia

SERBIA

YUGOSLAVIA

CROATIA

ALBANIA

GREECE

Athens

Crete

Mediterranean Sea

LIBYA

NORWAY

Oslo

DENMARK

Copenhagen

Berlin

GERMANY

Elbe

Rhine

Danube

SWITZERLAND

Po

Rome
Monte Casino
May 1944

ITALY

Bologna

Italian front,
Feb. 1945

Salerno
Sept. 1943

Sicily

Sicily
July 1943

MALTA
(Gr. Br.)

Rommel defeated
in Tunisia
(May 1943)

TUNISIA

North Sea

NETHERLANDS

BELGIUM

Battle of
the Bulge
Dec. 1944

Western front, Feb. 1945

FRANCE

Vichy

VICHY FRANCE
(occupied Nov. 1942)

ALGERIA
(Vichy France)

GREAT
BRITAIN

Battle of Britain
Fall 1940

London

Dunkirk

Paris

Invasion of Normandy
June 6, 1944

NORTHERN
IRELAND

IRELAND

ATLANTIC
OCEAN

Ebro

PORTUGAL

Lisbon

Madrid

SPAIN

GIBRALTAR (Gr. Br.)

SP. MOROCCO

Casablanca
Nov. 1942

FRENCH
MOROCCO

Volga

Hitler's Greater Germany
Allied with Germany
Occupied by Germany and its allies
Grand Alliance
Neutral nations
Major battles

400 Km.

400 Mi.

200

200

0

0

secret information from Resistance fighters and even organized armies to help defeat Hitler.

The Tide of Battle

Barely halted at the gates of Moscow and Leningrad in 1941, the Germans renewed their Russian offensive in July 1942. This time they drove toward the southern city of Stalingrad, in an attempt to cripple communications and seize the crucial oil fields of Baku. Reaching Stalingrad, the Germans slowly occupied most of the ruined city in a month of incredibly savage house-to-house fighting.

Then, in November 1942, Soviet armies counterattacked. They rolled over Romanian and Italian troops to the north and south of Stalingrad, quickly closing the trap and surrounding the entire German Sixth Army of 300,000 men. The surrounded Germans were systematically destroyed, until by the end of January 1943 only 123,000 soldiers were left to surrender. Hitler, who had refused to allow a retreat, had suffered a catastrophic defeat. In the summer of 1943, the larger, better-equipped Soviet armies took the offensive and began moving forward (Map 29.2).

In late 1942 the tide also turned in the Pacific and in North Africa. By late spring 1942, Japan had established a great empire in East Asia (Map 29.3). Unlike the Nazis, the Japanese made clever appeals to local nationalists, who hated European imperial domination and preferred Japan's so-called Greater Asian Co-prosperity Sphere.

Then, in the Battle of the Coral Sea in May 1942, Allied naval and air power stopped the Japanese advance and also relieved Australia from the threat of invasion. This victory was followed by the Battle of Midway Island, in which American pilots sank all four of the attacking Japanese aircraft carriers and established American naval superiority in the Pacific. In August 1942, American marines attacked Guadalcanal in the Solomon Islands. Badly hampered by the policy of "Europe first"—only 15 percent of Allied resources were going to fight the war in the Pacific in early 1943—the Americans, under General Douglas MacArthur and Admiral Chester Nimitz, and the Australians nevertheless began "island hopping" toward Japan. Japanese forces were on the defensive.

In North Africa, the war had been seesawing back and forth since 1940. In May 1942, combined German and Italian armies, under the brilliant General Erwin Rommel, attacked British-occupied Egypt and the Suez Canal for the second time. After a rapid advance, they were finally defeated by British forces at the Battle of El Alamein, only 70 miles from Alexandria. In October the British counterattacked in Egypt, and almost immediately thereafter an Anglo-American force landed in Morocco and Algeria. These French possessions, which were under the control of Pétain's Vichy French government, quickly went over to the side of the Allies.

Having driven the Axis powers from North Africa by the spring of 1943, Allied forces maintained the initiative by invading Sicily and then mainland Italy. Mussolini was deposed by a war-weary people, and the new Italian government publicly accepted unconditional surrender in September 1943. Italy, it seemed, was liberated. Yet Mussolini was rescued by German commandos in a daring raid and put at the head of a puppet government. German armies seized Rome and all of northern Italy. Fighting continued in Italy.

Indeed, bitter fighting continued in Europe for almost two years. Germany, less fully mobilized for war than Britain in 1941, applied itself to total war in 1942 and enlisted millions of prisoners of war and slave laborers from all across occupied Europe in that effort. Between early 1942 and July 1944, German war production actually tripled. Although British and American bombing raids killed many German civilians, they were surprisingly ineffective from a military point of view. Also, German resistance against Hitler failed. After an unsuccessful attempt on Hitler's life in July 1944, thousands of Germans were brutally liquidated by S.S. fanatics. Terrorized at home and frightened by the prospect of unconditional surrender, the Germans fought on with suicidal stoicism.

On June 6, 1944, American and British forces under General Dwight Eisenhower landed on the beaches of Normandy in history's greatest naval invasion. Having tricked the Germans into believing that the attack would come near the Belgian border, the Allies secured a foothold on the coast of Normandy. In a hundred dramatic days, more than two million men and almost a half-million vehicles pushed inland and broke through German lines. Rejecting proposals to strike straight at Berlin in a massive attack, Eisenhower moved forward cautiously on a broad front. Not until March 1945

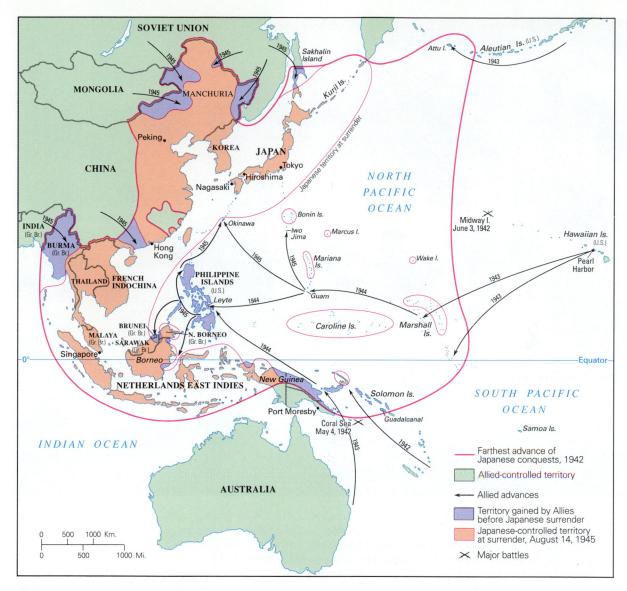

MAP 29.3 World War Two in the Pacific   Japanese forces also overran an enormous territory in 1942, which the Allies slowly recaptured in a long bitter struggle. As this map shows, Japan still held a large Asian empire in August 1945, when the unprecedented devastation of atomic warfare suddenly forced it to surrender.

did American troops cross the Rhine and enter Germany.

The Russians, who had been advancing steadily since July 1943, reached the outskirts of Warsaw by August 1944. For the next six months they moved southward into Romania, Hungary, and Yugoslavia. In January 1945, Red armies again moved westward through Poland, and on April 26 they met American forces on the Elbe River. The Allies

had closed their vise on Nazi Germany and overrun Europe. As Soviet forces fought their way into Berlin, Hitler committed suicide in his bunker, and on May 7 the remaining German commanders capitulated.

Three months later, the United States dropped atomic bombs on Hiroshima and Nagasaki in Japan. Mass bombing of cities and civilians, one of the terrible new practices of World War Two, had

The Normandy Invasion   The first American and British troops hit the beaches at 6:30 A.M. on June 6, 1944. The enemy poured down murderous fire on these Americans at Omaha Beach, but a naval bombardment eventually silenced the German guns. Thousands of Allied planes provided air cover and bombed German troops trying to move up from the interior. *(Source: National Archives, Washington)*

ended in the final nightmare—unprecedented human destruction in a single blinding flash. The Japanese surrendered. The Second World War, which had claimed the lives of more than fifty million soldiers and civilians, was over.

SUMMARY

The Second World War marked the climax of the tremendous practical and spiritual maladies of the age of anxiety, which led in many lands to the rise

of dictatorships. Many of these dictatorships were variations on conservative authoritarianism, but there was also a fateful innovation—the modern totalitarian regime, most fully developed in Communist Russia and Nazi Germany. The totalitarian regimes utterly rejected the liberalism of the nineteenth century. Inspired by the lessons of total war and Lenin's one-party rule, they tried to subordinate everything to the state. Although some areas of life escaped them, state control increased to a staggering, unprecedented degree. The totalitarian regimes trampled on basic human rights with unrestrained brutality and police terror. Moreover, these regimes were armed with the weapons of modern technology, rendering opposition almost impossible.

Both Communist Russia and Nazi Germany tried to gain the *willing* support of their populations. Monopolizing the means of expression and communication, they claimed to represent the masses and to be building new, more equal societies. Many people believed them. Both regimes also won enthusiastic supporters by offering tough, ruthless people from modest backgrounds enormous rewards for loyal and effective service. Thus these totalitarian dictatorships rested on considerable genuine popular support, as well as on police terror. This combination gave them their awesome power and dynamism. That dynamism was, how-

ever, channeled in quite different directions. Stalin and the Communist party aimed at building their kind of socialism and the new socialist personality at home. Hitler and the Nazi elite aimed at unlimited territorial and racial aggression on behalf of a master race; domestic recovery was only a means to that end.

Unlimited Nazi aggression made war inevitable, first with the western European democracies, then with Germany's totalitarian neighbor, and finally with the United States. Plunging Europe into the ultimate nightmare, unlimited aggression unwittingly forged a mighty coalition that smashed the racist Nazi empire and its leader. In the words of the ancient Greeks, he whom the gods would destroy, they first make mad.

The City of Nagasaki   A second atomic bomb struck Nagasaki on August 9, 1945, three days after the first giant fireball incinerated Hiroshima. Approximately 75,000 Japanese were killed or injured at Nagasaki. In this grim photo, taken about a month after the attack, a Japanese survivor pushes his bicycle along a path cleared through the ruins. *(Source: UPI/Bettmann Newsphotos)*

NOTES

1. E. Halévy, *The Era of Tyrannies* (Garden City, N.Y.: Doubleday, 1965), pp. 265–316, esp. p. 300.
2. Quoted in P. C. Roberts, " 'War Communism': A Re-examination," *Slavic Review* 29 (June 1970): 257.
3. Quoted in A. G. Mazour, *Soviet Economic Development: Operation Outstrip, 1921–1965* (Princeton, N.J: Van Nostrand, 1967), p. 130.
4. Quoted in I. Deutscher, *Stalin: A Political Biography,* 2d ed. (New York: Oxford University Press, 1967), p. 325.
5. Quoted in H. K. Geiger, *The Family in Soviet Russia* (Cambridge, Mass.: Harvard University Press, 1968), p. 123.
6. Ibid., p. 156.
7. Quoted in B. Rosenthal, "Women in the Russian Revolution and After," in *Becoming Visible: Women in European History,* ed. R. Bridenthal and C. Koonz (Boston: Houghton Mifflin, 1976), p. 383.
8. Quoted in K. D. Bracher, "The Technique of the National Socialist Seizure of Power," in T. Eschenburg et al., *The Path to Dictatorship, 1918–1933* (Garden City, N.Y.: Doubleday, 1966), p. 117.
9. Quoted in K. D. Bracher, *The German Dictatorship: The Origins, Structure and Effects of National Socialism* (New York: Praeger, 1970), pp. 146–147.
10. Quoted in R. Stromberg, *An Intellectual History of Modern Europe* (New York: Appleton-Century-Crofts, 1966), p. 393.
11. D. Schoenbaum, *Hitler's Social Revolution: Class and Status in Nazi Germany, 1933–1939* (Garden City, N.Y.: Doubleday, 1967), p. 114.
12. Quoted in Bracher, *German Dictatorship,* p. 289.
13. Ibid., p. 306.

SUGGESTED READING

The historical literature on totalitarian dictatorships is rich and fascinating. H. Arendt, *The Origins of Totalitarianism* (1951), is a challenging interpretation. E. Weber, *Varieties of Fascism* (1964), stresses the radical social aspirations of fascist movements all across Europe. F. L. Carsten, *The Rise of Fascism,* rev. ed. (1982), and W. Laqueur, ed., *Fascism* (1976), are also recommended.

R. Stites, *The Women's Liberation Movement in Russia: Feminism, Nihilism, and Bolshevism, 1860–1930* (1978); S. Fitzpatrick, *Cultural Revolution in Russia, 1928–1931* (1978); and the works by Geiger and Deutscher cited in the Notes are all highly recommended, as is Deutscher's sympathetic three-volume study of Trotsky. S. Cohen, *Bukharin and the Bolshevik Revolution* (1973), examines the leading spokesman of moderate communism, who was destroyed by Stalin. R. Conquest, *The Great Terror* (1968), is an excellent account of Stalin's purges of the 1930s. A. Solzhenitsyn, *The Gulag Archipelago* (1964), passionately condemns Soviet police terror, which Solzhenitsyn tracks back to Lenin. A. Koestler, *Darkness at Noon* (1956), is a famous fictional account of Stalin's trials of the Old Bolsheviks. R. Medvedev, *Let History Judge* (1972), is a penetrating and highly recommended history of Stalinism by a Russian dissident. R. Conquest, *The Harvest of Sorrow* (1986), recounts authoritatively Soviet collectivization and the man-made famine. Three other remarkable books are J. Scott, *Behind the Urals* (1942, 1973), an eyewitness account of an American steelworker in Russia in the 1930s; S. Alliluyeva, *Twenty Letters to a Friend* (1967), the amazing reflections of Stalin's daughter, who chose twice to live in the United States before returning home; and M. Fainsod, *Smolensk Under Soviet Rule* (1958), a unique study based on Communist records captured first by the Germans and then by the Americans.

A. De Grand, *Italian Fascism: Its Origins and Development,* 2d ed. (1989), and E. R. Tannebaum, *The Fascist Experience* (1972), are excellent studies of Italy under Mussolini. I. Silone, *Bread and Wine* (1937), is a moving novel by a famous opponent of dictatorship in Italy. Two excellent books on Spain are H. Thomas, *The Spanish Civil War* (1961), and E. Malefakis, *Agrarian Reform and Peasant Revolution in Spain* (1970). In the area of foreign relations, G. Kennan, *Russia and the West Under Lenin and Stalin* (1961), is justly famous, while A. L. Rowse, *Appeasement* (1961), powerfully denounces the policies of the appeasers. R. Paxton, *Vichy France* (1973), tells a controversial story extremely well, and J. Lukac, *The Last European War* (1976), skillfully—and infuriatingly—argues that victory by Hitler could have saved Europe from both Russian and American domination.

On Germany, F. Stern, *The Politics of Cultural Despair* (1963), and G. Mosse, *The Crisis of German Ideology* (1964), are excellent complementary studies on the origins of Nazism. The best single work on Hitler's Germany is Bracher's *The German Dictatorship,* cited in the Notes, while W. Shirer, *The Rise and Fall of the Third Reich* (1960), is the best-selling account of an American journalist who experienced Nazi Germany firsthand. J. Fest, *Hitler* (1974), and A. Bullock, *Hitler* (1953), are engrossing biographies of the Führer. In addition to *Mein Kampf, Hitler's Secret Conversations, 1941–1944* (1953) reveals the dictator's wild dreams and beliefs. Among countless special studies, E. Kogon, *The Theory and Practice of Hell* (1958), is a chilling examination of the concentration camps; M. Mayer, *They Thought They Were Free* (1955), probes the minds of ten ordinary Nazis and why they believed Hitler was their liberator; and A. Speer, *Inside the Third Reich* (1970), contains the fascinating recollections of Hitler's wizard of the armaments industry. G. Mosse, *Toward the Final Solution* (1978), is a powerful history of European racism. A. Mayer, *Why Did the Heavens Not Darken? The "Final Solution" in History* (1989), and L. Dawidowicz, *The War Against the Jews, 1933–1945* (1975), are moving accounts of the Holocaust. Jørgen Haestrup, *Europe Ablaze* (1978), is a monumental account of wartime resistance movements throughout Europe, and *The Diary of Anne Frank* is a remarkable personal account of a young Jewish girl in hiding during the Nazi occupation of Holland.

J. Campbell's *The Experience of World War II* (1989) is attractively illustrated and captures the drama of global conflict. G. Wright, *The Ordeal of Total War, 1939–1945* (1968), is the best comprehensive study on World War Two, while B. H. Liddell Hart, *The History of the Second World War* (1971), is an overview of military developments. Three dramatic studies of special aspects of the war are A. Dallin, *German Rule in Russia, 1941–1945* (1957), which analyzes the effects of Nazi occupation policies on the Soviet population; L. Collins and D. La Pierre, *Is Paris Burning?* (1965), a best-selling account of the liberation of Paris and Hitler's plans to destroy the city; and J. Toland, *The Last Hundred Days* (1966), a lively account of the end of the war.

30

The Recovery of Europe
and the Americas

The total defeat of the Nazis and their allies laid the basis for one of Western civilization's most remarkable recoveries. A battered western Europe dug itself out from under the rubble and experienced a great renaissance in the postwar era, which lasted into the late 1960s.

The western hemisphere, with its strong European heritage, also made exemplary progress. Soviet Russia eventually became more humane and less totalitarian. Yet there was also a tragic setback. The Grand Alliance against Hitler gave way to an apparently endless cold war, in which conflict between East and West threatened world peace and troubled domestic politics.

- What were the causes of the cold war, which was the most disappointing development of the postwar era?

- How and why, in spite of the tragic division of the Continent into two hostile camps, did Europe recover so successfully from the ravages of war and Nazism?

- To what extent did communist eastern Europe and the Americas experience a similar recovery?

- How and why did European empires collapse and Asian and African peoples gain political independence?

These are the questions this chapter will seek to answer.

THE COLD WAR, 1942–1953

In 1945 triumphant American and Russian soldiers came together and embraced on the banks of the Elbe River in the heart of vanquished Germany. At home, in the United States and in the Soviet Union, their loved ones erupted in joyous celebration. Yet victory was flawed. The Allies could not cooperate politically when it came to peacemaking. Motivated by different goals and hounded by misunderstandings, the United States and Soviet Russia soon found themselves at loggerheads. By the end of 1947, Europe was rigidly divided. It was West versus East in the cold war.

The Origins of the Cold War

The most powerful allies in the wartime coalition —Soviet Russia and the United States—began to quarrel almost as soon as the unifying threat of Nazi Germany disappeared. The hostility between the Eastern and Western superpowers was a tragic disappointment for millions of people, but it was not really so surprising. It grew sadly but logically out of military developments, wartime agreements, and long-standing political and ideological differences.

In the early phases of the war, the Americans and the British made military victory their highest priority. They consistently avoided discussion of Stalin's war aims and the shape of the eventual peace settlement. This policy was evident in December 1941 and again in May 1942, when Stalin asked the United States and Britain to agree to Russia's moving its western border of 1938 farther west at the expense of Poland, in effect ratifying the gains Stalin had made from his deal with Hitler in 1939.

Stalin's request ran counter to the moralistic Anglo-American Atlantic Charter of August 1941. In good Wilsonian fashion, the Atlantic Charter had called for peace without territorial expansion or secret agreements, and for free elections and self-determination for all liberated nations. In this spirit, the British and Americans declined to promise Polish territory to Russia; Stalin received only a military alliance and no postwar commitments. Yet the United States and Britain did not try to take advantage of Russia's precarious position in 1942; in fact, they soothed Stalin by promising an invasion of continental Europe as soon as possible. They feared that hard bargaining would anger Stalin and encourage him to consider making a separate peace with Hitler. So they focused on the policy of unconditional surrender to solidify the alliance.

By late 1943, as Allied armies scored major victories, specific issues related to the shape of the postwar world could no longer be postponed. The conference Stalin, Roosevelt, and Churchill held in the Iranian capital of Teheran in November 1943 thus proved of crucial importance in determining subsequent events. There, the Big Three jovially reaffirmed their determination to crush Germany and searched for the appropriate military strategy. Churchill, fearful of the military dangers of a direct attack and anxious to protect Britain's political in-

The Big Three   In 1945 a triumphant Winston Churchill, an ailing Franklin Roosevelt, and a determined Joseph Stalin met at Yalta in southern Russia to plan for peace. Cooperation soon gave way to bitter hostility. *(Source: F.D.R. Library)*

terests in the eastern Mediterranean, argued that American and British forces should follow up their North African and Italian campaigns with an indirect attack on Germany through the Balkans. Roosevelt, however, agreed with Stalin that an American-British frontal assault through France would be better. This agreement was part of Roosevelt's general effort to meet Stalin's wartime demands whenever possible. Roosevelt reportedly told his friend William Bullitt, formerly American ambassador to the Soviet Union, before the Teheran Conference, "I have just a hunch that Stalin doesn't want anything but security for his country, and I think that if I give him everything I possibly

can and ask nothing from him in return, *noblesse oblige,* he won't try to annex anything and will work for a world of democracy and peace."[1]

At Teheran, the Normandy invasion was set for the spring of 1944. Although military considerations probably largely dictated this decision, it had momentous political implications: it meant that the Russian and the American-British armies would come together in defeated Germany along a north-south line and that only Russian troops would liberate eastern Europe. Thus the basic shape of postwar Europe was emerging even as the fighting continued. Real differences over questions like Poland were carefully ignored.

When the Big Three met again at Yalta on the Black Sea in southern Russia in February 1945, rapidly advancing Soviet armies were within a hundred miles of Berlin. The Red Army had occupied not only Poland but also Bulgaria, Romania, Hungary, part of Yugoslavia, and much of Czechoslovakia. The temporarily stalled American-British forces had yet to cross the Rhine into Germany. Moreover, the United States was far from defeating Japan. Indeed, it was believed that the invasion and occupation of Japan would cost a million American casualties—an estimate that led to the subsequent decision to drop atomic bombs in order to save American lives. In short, Russia's position was strong and America's weak.

There was little the increasingly sick and apprehensive Roosevelt could do but double his bet on Stalin's peaceful intentions. It was agreed at Yalta that Germany would be divided into zones of occupation and would pay heavy reparations to the Soviet Union in the form of agricultural and industrial goods, though many details remained unsettled. At American insistence, Stalin agreed to declare war on Japan after Germany was defeated. He also agreed to join the proposed United Nations, which the Americans believed would help preserve peace after the war; it was founded in April 1945 in San Francisco.

For Poland and eastern Europe—"that Pandora's Box of infinite troubles," according to American Secretary of State Cordell Hull—the Big Three struggled to reach an ambiguous compromise at Yalta: eastern European governments were to be freely elected but pro-Russian. As Churchill put it at the time, "The Poles will have their future in their own hands, with the single limitation that they must honestly follow in harmony with their allies, a policy friendly to Russia."[2]

The Yalta compromise over eastern Europe broke down almost immediately. Even before the Yalta Conference, Bulgaria and Poland were in the hands of Communists, who arrived home in the baggage of the Red Army. Minor concessions to noncommunist groups thereafter did not change this situation. Elsewhere in eastern Europe, pro-Russian "coalition" governments of several parties were formed, but the key ministerial posts were reserved for Moscow-trained Communists.

At the postwar Potsdam Conference of July 1945, the long-ignored differences over eastern Europe finally surged to the fore. The compromising Roosevelt had died and been succeeded by the more determined President Harry Truman, who demanded immediate free elections throughout eastern Europe. Stalin refused pointblank. "A freely elected government in any of these East European countries would be anti-Soviet," he admitted simply, "and that we cannot allow."[3]

Here, then, is the key to the much-debated origins of the cold war. American ideals, pumped up by the crusade against Hitler, and American politics, heavily influenced by millions of voters from eastern Europe, demanded free elections in Soviet-occupied eastern Europe. On the other hand, Stalin, who had lived through two enormously destructive German invasions, wanted absolute military security from Germany and its potential Eastern allies, once and for all. Suspicious by nature, he believed that only communist states could truly be devoted allies, and he feared that free elections would result in independent and quite possibly hostile governments on his western border. Moreover, by the middle of 1945 there was no way short of war that the United States and its Western allies could really influence developments in eastern Europe, and war was out of the question. Stalin was bound to have his way.

West versus East

The American response to Stalin's exaggerated conception of security was to "get tough." In May 1945 Truman abruptly cut off all aid to Russia. In October he declared that the United States would never recognize any government established by force against the free will of its people. In March 1946 former British prime minister Churchill ominously informed an American audience that an "iron curtain" had fallen across the Continent, dividing Germany and all of Europe into two antagonistic camps. Soon emotional, moralistic denunciations of Stalin and communist Russia re-emerged as part of American political life. Yet the United States also responded to the popular desire to "bring the boys home" and demobilized with incredible speed. When the war against Japan ended in September 1945, there were 12 million Americans in the armed forces; by 1947 there were only 1.5 million, as opposed to 6 million for Soviet Russia. Some historians have argued that American leaders believed that the atomic bomb gave the

United States all the power it needed; but "getting tough" really meant "talking tough."

Stalin's agents quickly reheated the "ideological struggle against capitalist imperialism." Moreover, the large, well-organized Communist parties of France and Italy obediently started to uncover American plots to take over Europe and aggressively challenged their own governments with violent criticisms and large strikes. The Soviet Union also put pressure on Iran and Turkey, and while Greek Communists battled Greek royalists, another bitter civil war raged in China. By the spring of 1947, it appeared to many Americans that Stalin wanted much more than just puppet regimes in Soviet-occupied eastern Europe. He seemed determined to export communism by subversion throughout Europe and around the world.

The American response to this challenge was the Truman Doctrine, which was aimed at "containing" communism in areas already occupied by the Red Army. Truman told Congress in March 1947: "I believe it must be the policy of the United States to support free people who are resisting attempted subjugation by armed minorities or by outside pressure." To begin, Truman asked Congress for military aid to Greece and Turkey. Then, in June, Secretary of State George C. Marshall offered Europe economic aid—the "Marshall Plan"—to help it rebuild.

Stalin refused Marshall Plan assistance for all of eastern Europe. He purged the last remaining noncommunist elements from the coalition governments of eastern Europe and established Soviet-style, one-party communist dictatorships. The

The Berlin Air Lift   Standing in the rubble of their bombed-out city, a German crowd in the American sector awaits the arrival of a U.S. transport plane flying in over the Soviet blockade in 1948. The crisis over Berlin was a dramatic indication of growing tensions among the Allies, which resulted in the division of Europe into two hostile camps. *(Source: Walter Sanders, LIFE MAGAZINE © Time Inc.)*

seizure of power in Czechoslovakia in February 1948 was particularly brutal and antidemocratic, and it greatly strengthened Western fears of limitless communist expansion, beginning with Germany. Thus, when Stalin blocked all traffic through the Soviet zone of Germany to the former capital of Berlin, which had also been divided into sectors at the end of the war by the occupying powers, the Western Allies responded firmly but not provocatively. Hundreds of planes began flying over the Russian roadblocks around the clock, supplying provisions to the people of West Berlin and thwarting Soviet efforts to swallow them up. After 324 days the Russians backed down: containment seemed to work. In 1949, therefore, the United States formed an anti-Soviet military alliance of Western governments, the North Atlantic Treaty Organization (NATO); in response, Stalin tightened his hold on his satellites, later united in the Warsaw Pact. Europe was divided into two hostile blocs.

In late 1949 the Communists triumphed in China, frightening and infuriating many Americans, who saw an all-powerful worldwide communist conspiracy extending even into the upper reaches of the American government. When the Russian-backed communist forces of northern Korea invaded southern Korea in 1950, President Truman's response was swift. American-led United Nations armies intervened. The cold war had spread around the world and become very hot.

It seems clear that the rapid descent from victorious Grand Alliance to bitter cold war was intimately connected with the tragic fate of eastern Europe. After 1932, when the eastern European power vacuum invited Nazi racist imperialism, the appeasing Western democracies mistakenly did nothing. They did, however, have one telling insight: how, they asked themselves, could they unite with Stalin to stop Hitler without giving Stalin great gains on his western borders? After Hitler's invasion of Soviet Russia, the Western powers preferred to ignore this question and hope for the best. But when Stalin later began to claim the spoils of victory, a helpless but moralistic United States refused to cooperate and professed outrage. One cannot help but feel that Western opposition immediately after the war came too late and quite possibly encouraged even more aggressive measures by the always-suspicious Stalin. And it helped explode the quarrel over eastern Europe into a global confrontation, which became institutionalized and lasted

until the late 1980s despite intermittent periods of relaxation.

THE WESTERN EUROPEAN RENAISSANCE

As the cold war divided Europe into two blocs, the future appeared bleak on both sides of the iron curtain. Economic conditions were the worst in generations, and millions of people lived on the verge of starvation. Politically, Europe was weak and divided, a battleground for cold war ambitions. Moreover, long-cherished European empires were crumbling in the face of Asian and African nationalism. Yet Europe recovered, and the Western nations led the way. In less than a generation, western Europe achieved unprecedented economic prosperity and regained much of its traditional prominence in world affairs. It was an amazing rebirth— a true renaissance.

The Postwar Challenge

After the war, economic conditions in western Europe were terrible. Simply finding enough to eat was a real problem. Runaway inflation and black markets testified to severe shortages and hardship. The bread ration in Paris in 1946 was little more than it had been in 1942 under the Nazi occupation. Rationing of bread had to be introduced in Britain in 1946 for the first time. Both France and Italy produced only about half as much in 1946 as before the war. Many people believed that Europe was quite simply finished. The prominent British historian Arnold Toynbee felt that, at best, western Europeans might seek to civilize the crude but all-powerful Americans, somewhat as the ancient Greeks had civilized their Roman conquerors.

Suffering was most intense in defeated Germany. The major territorial change of the war had moved Soviet Russia's border far to the west. Poland was in turn compensated for this loss to Russia with land taken from Germany (Map 30.1). To solidify these boundary changes, thirteen million people were driven from their homes in eastern Germany (and other countries in eastern Europe) and forced to resettle in a greatly reduced Germany. The Russians were also seizing factories and equipment as reparations, even tearing up railroad tracks and sending the rails to the Soviet Union. The com-

MAP 30.1 Europe After World War Two Both the Soviet Union and Poland took land from Germany, which the Allies partitioned into occupation zones. Those zones subsequently formed the basis of the East and the West German states, as the Iron Curtain fell to divide both Germany and Europe.

mand "Come here, woman," from a Russian soldier was the sound of terror, the prelude to many a rape.

In 1945 and 1946, conditions were not much better in the Western zones. There was the same soul-numbing devastation. Walking through Munich, a survivor wrote that

You could often see for miles, and then you went through canyons, as in the mountains, the rubble towering up on both sides. . . . I wandered like a sleepwalker through this wasteland. . . . There was no city. There was only the ghost, the feeling, the sensation of a devastated, stunned wasteland. The creatures in this wasteland resembled ghosts. . . . Their faces were without expression, their eyes sunken and listless. . . . A huge solitude and despair seized me.[4]

The Western Allies also treated the German population with great severity at first. By February 1946 the average daily diet of a German in the Ruhr had been reduced to two slices of bread, a pat of margarine, a spoonful of porridge, and two small potatoes. Countless Germans sold many of their possessions to American soldiers to buy food. Cigarettes replaced worthless money as currency. The winter of 1946 to 1947 was one of the coldest in memory, and there were widespread signs of actual starvation. By the spring of 1947, refugee-clogged, hungry, prostrate Germany was on the verge of total collapse and threatening to drag down the rest of Europe.

Yet western Europe was not finished. The Nazi occupation and the war had discredited old ideas and old leaders. All over Europe, many people were willing to change and experiment in hopes of building a new and better Europe out of the rubble. New groups and new leaders were coming to the fore to guide these aspirations. Progressive Catholics and revitalized Catholic political parties —the Christian Democrats—were particularly influential.

In Italy the Christian Democrats emerged as the leading party in the first postwar elections in 1946, and in early 1948 they won an absolute majority in the parliament in a landslide victory. Their very able leader was Alcide De Gasperi, a courageous antifascist and former Vatican librarian, firmly committed to political democracy, economic reconstruction, and moderate social reform. In France, too, the Catholic party provided some of the best

postwar leaders, like Robert Schuman. This was particularly true after January 1946, when General De Gaulle, the inspiring wartime leader of the Free French, resigned after having re-established the free and democratic Fourth Republic. As Germany was partitioned by the cold war, a radically purified Federal Republic of Germany found new and able leadership among its Catholics. In 1949 Konrad Adenauer, the former mayor of Cologne and a long-time anti-Nazi, began his long, highly successful democratic rule; the Christian Democrats became West Germany's majority party for a generation. In providing effective leadership for their respective countries, the Christian Democrats were inspired and united by a common Christian and European heritage. They steadfastly rejected totalitarianism and narrow nationalism and placed their faith in democracy and cooperation.

The Socialists and the Communists, active in the Resistance against Hitler, also emerged from the war with increased power and prestige, especially in France and Italy. They, too, provided fresh leadership and pushed for social change and economic reform with considerable success. In the immediate postwar years, welfare measures such as family allowances, health insurance, and increased public housing were enacted throughout much of Europe. In Italy social benefits from the state came to equal a large part of the average worker's wages. In France large banks, insurance companies, public utilities, coal mines, and the Renault auto company were nationalized by the government. Britain followed the same trend. The voters threw out Churchill and the Conservatives in 1945, and the socialist Labour party under Clement Attlee moved toward establishment of the "welfare state." Many industries were nationalized, and the government provided each citizen with free medical service and taxed the middle and upper classes heavily. Thus, all across Europe, social reform complemented political transformation, creating solid foundations for a great European renaissance.

The United States also supplied strong and creative leadership. Frightened by fears of Soviet expansion, the United States provided western Europe with both massive economic aid and ongoing military protection. Economic aid was channeled through the Marshall Plan, which required that the participating countries coordinate their efforts for maximum effectiveness. This requirement led to the establishment of the Organization of European

Economic Cooperation (OEEC). Between early 1948 and late 1952, the United States furnished foreign countries roughly $22.5 billion, of which seven-eighths was in the form of outright gifts rather than loans. Military security was provided through NATO, established as a regional alliance for self-defense and featuring American troops stationed permanently in Europe as well as the protection of the American nuclear umbrella. Thus the United States assumed its international responsibilities after the Second World War, exercising the leadership it had shunned in the tragic years after 1919.

Economic "Miracles"

As Marshall Plan aid poured in, the battered economies of western Europe began to turn the corner in 1948. Impoverished West Germany led the way with a spectacular advance after the Allies permitted Adenauer's government to reform the currency and stimulate private enterprise. Other countries were not far behind. The outbreak of the Korean War in 1950 further stimulated economic activity, and Europe entered a period of rapid, sustained economic progress that lasted into the late 1960s. By 1963 western Europe was producing more than two-and-one-half times as much as it had before the war. Never before had the European economy grown so fast. For politicians and economists, for workers and business leaders, it was a time of astonishing, loudly proclaimed economic "miracles."

There were many reasons for western Europe's brilliant economic performance. American aid helped the process get off to a fast start. Europe received equipment to repair damaged plants and even whole new specialized factories when necessary. Thus critical shortages were quickly overcome. Moreover, since European nations coordinated the distribution of American aid, many barriers to European trade and cooperation were quickly dropped. Aid from the United States helped, therefore, to promote both a resurgence of economic liberalism with its healthy competition and an international division of labor.

As in most of the world, economic growth became a basic objective of all western European governments, for leaders and voters were determined to avoid a return to the dangerous and demoralizing stagnation of the 1930s. Governments gener-

ally accepted Keynesian economics (see Chapter 28) and sought to stimulate their economies, and some also adopted a number of imaginative strategies. Those in Germany and France were particularly successful and influential.

Under Minister of Economy Ludwig Erhard, a roly-poly, cigar-smoking ex-professor, postwar West Germany broke decisively with the totally regulated, strait-jacketed Nazi economy. Erhard bet on the free-market economy, while maintaining the extensive social welfare network inherited from the Hitler era. He and his teachers believed, not only that capitalism was more efficient, but also that political and social freedom could thrive only if there were real economic freedom. Erhard's first step was to reform the currency and abolish rationing and price controls in 1948. He boldly declared, "The only ration coupon is the Mark."[5] At first, profits jumped sharply, prompting business people to employ more people and produce more. By the late 1950s, Germany had a prospering economy and full employment, a strong currency and stable prices. Germany's success aroused renewed respect for free-market capitalism and encouraged freer trade among other European nations.

In France the major innovation was a new kind of planning. Under the guidance of Jean Monnet, an economic pragmatist and apostle of European unity, a planning commission set ambitious but flexible goals for the French economy. It used Marshall aid money and the nationalized banks to funnel money into key industries, several of which were state owned. At the same time, the planning commission and the French bureaucracy encouraged private enterprise to "think big." The often-cautious French business community responded, investing heavily in new equipment and modern factories. Thus France combined flexible planning and a "mixed" state and private economy to achieve the most rapid economic development in its long history. Throughout the 1950s and 1960s, there was hardly any unemployment in France. The average person's standard of living improved dramatically. France, too, was an economic "miracle."

Other factors also contributed to western Europe's economic boom. In most countries after the war, there were large numbers of men and women ready to work hard for low wages and the hope of a better future. Germany had millions of impoverished refugees, while France and Italy still had millions of poor peasants. Expanding industries in

Postwar Reconstruction   The Hamburg apartments on the left were bombed-out shells in 1945, along with 300,000 other housing units in the city. Yet by 1951 these same apartments were replaced, or ingeniously rebuilt (right). In half of the shells, crushed rubble mixed with concrete was poured to provide missing walls and to achieve a quick and economical rehabilitation. *(Source: National Archives, Washington)*

those countries thus had a great asset to draw on. More fully urbanized Britain had no such rural labor pool; this lack, along with a welfare socialism that stressed "fair shares" rather than rapid growth, helps account for its fairly poor postwar economic performance.

In 1945 impoverished Europe was still rich in the sense that it had the human skills of an advanced industrial society. Skilled workers, engineers, managers, and professionals knew what could and should be done, and they did it.

Many consumer products had been invented or perfected since the late 1920s, but few Europeans had been able to buy them during the depression and war. In 1945 the electric refrigerator, the washing machine, and the automobile were rare luxuries. There was, therefore, a great potential demand, which the economic system moved to satisfy.

Finally, ever since 1919 the nations of Europe had suffered from high tariffs and small national markets, which made for small and therefore inefficient factories. In the postwar era, European countries junked many of these economic barriers and gradually created a large unified market—the Common Market. This action, which stimulated the economy, was part of the postwar search for a new European unity.

Toward European Unity

Western Europe's political recovery was spectacular. Republics were re-established in France, West Germany, and Italy. Constitutional monarchs were restored in Belgium, Holland, and Norway. These democratic governments took root once again and thrived. To be sure, only West Germany established a two-party system on the British-American model; states like France and Italy returned to multiparty politics and shifting parliamentary coalitions. Yet the middle-of-the-road parties—primarily the Christian Democrats and the Socialists—dominated and provided continuing leadership. National self-determination was accompanied by civil liberties and great individual freedom. All of this was itself an extraordinary achievement.

Even more remarkable was the still-unfinished, still-continuing movement toward a united Europe. The Christian Democrats with their shared Catholic heritage were particularly committed to "building Europe," and other groups shared their dedication. Many Europeans believed that narrow, exaggerated nationalism had been a fundamental cause of both world wars, and that only through unity could European conflict be avoided in the future. Many western Europeans also realized how very weak their countries were in comparison with the United States and the Soviet Union, the two superpowers that had divided Europe from outside and made it into a cold war battleground. Thus the cold war encouraged some visionaries to seek a new "European nation," a superpower capable of controlling western Europe's destiny and reasserting its influence in world affairs.

The close cooperation among European states required by the Marshall Plan led to the creation of both the OEEC and the Council of Europe in 1948. European federalists hoped that the Council of Europe would quickly evolve into a true European parliament with sovereign rights, but this did not happen. Britain, with its empire and its "special relationship" with the United States, consistently opposed giving any real political power—any sovereignty—to the council. Many old-fashioned continental nationalists and Communists felt similarly. The Council of Europe became little more than a multinational debating society.

Frustrated in the direct political approach, European federalists turned toward economics. As one of them explained, "Politics and economics are closely related. Let us try, then, for progress in economic matters. Let us suppress those obstacles of an economic nature which divide and compartmentalize the nations of Europe."[6] In this they were quite successful.

Two far-seeing French statesmen, the planner Jean Monnet and Foreign Minister Robert Schuman, courageously took the lead in 1950. The Schuman Plan called for a special international organization to control and integrate all European steel and coal production. West Germany, Italy, Belgium, the Netherlands, and Luxembourg accepted the French idea in 1952; the British would have none of it. The immediate economic goal—a single competitive market without national tariffs or quotas—was rapidly realized. By 1958 coal and steel moved as freely among the six nations of the European Coal and Steel Community as among the states of the United States. The more far-reaching political goal was to bind the six member nations so closely together economically that war among them would become unthinkable and virtually impossible. This brilliant strategy did much to reduce tragic old rivalries, particularly that of France and Germany.

The Coal and Steel Community was so successful that it encouraged further technical and economic cooperation among "the Six." In 1957 the same six nations formed Euratom to pursue joint research in atomic energy; they also signed the Treaty of Rome, which created the European Economic Community, generally known as the Common Market (Map 30.2). The first goal of the treaty was gradual reduction of all tariffs among the Six to create a large free trade area. Other goals included the free movement of capital and labor and common economic policies and institutions.

An epoch-making stride toward unity, the Common Market was a tremendous success. Tariffs were rapidly reduced, and the European economy was stimulated. Companies and regions specialized in what they did best. Western Europe was being united in a single market almost as large as that of the United States. Many medium-sized American companies rushed to Europe, for a single modern factory in, say, Belgium or southern Italy had a vast potential market of 170 million customers.

The development of the Common Market fired imaginations and encouraged hopes of rapid progress toward political as well as economic union. In the 1960s, however, these hopes were frustrated by a resurgence of more traditional nationalism. Once again, France took the lead. Mired in a bitter colonial war in Algeria, the country turned in 1958 to General De Gaulle, who established the Fifth French Republic and ruled as its president until 1969. A towering giant both literally and figuratively, De Gaulle was the last of the bigger-than-life wartime leaders. A complex man who aroused a strong and sometimes negative response, especially in the United States, De Gaulle was at heart a romantic nationalist dedicated to reasserting France's greatness and glory. Once he had resolved the Algerian conflict, he labored to re-create a powerful, truly independent France, which would lead and even dictate to the other Common Market states.

De Gaulle personified the political resurgence of the leading nations of western Europe, as well as declining fears of the Soviet Union in the 1960s. Viewing the United States as the main threat to genuine French (and European) independence, he withdrew all French military forces from the "American-controlled" NATO command, which had to move from Paris to Brussels. De Gaulle tried to create financial difficulties for the United States by demanding gold for the American dollars France had accumulated. France also developed its own nuclear weapons. Within the Common Market, De Gaulle in 1963 and again in 1967 vetoed the application of the pro-American British, who were having second thoughts and wanted to join.

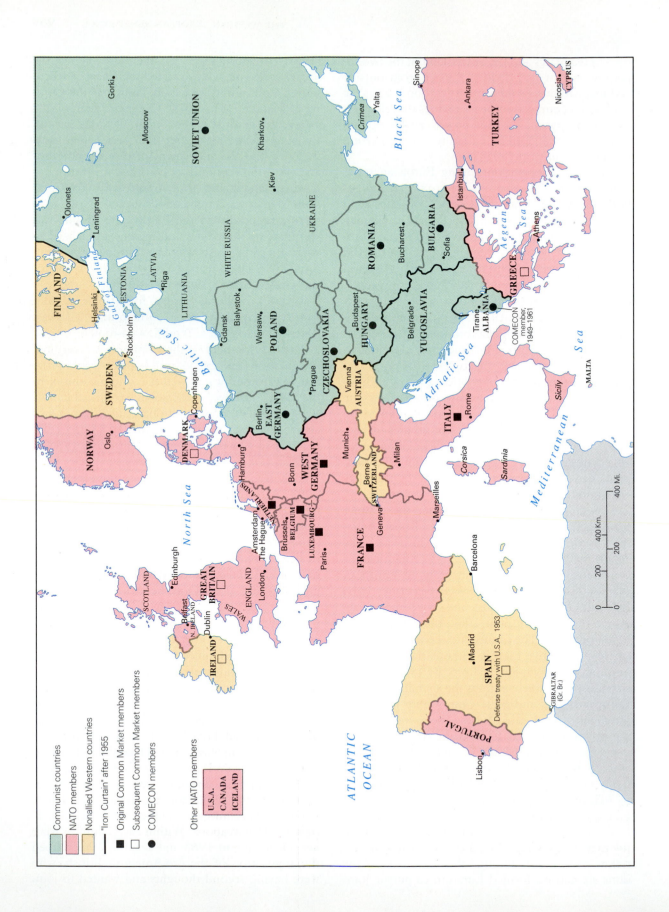

Gorki •

Moscow •

SOVIET UNION

Olonets •
Leningrad •

Kharkov •

Kiev •

UKRAINE

Crimea

Yalta •

Sinope •

Black Sea

Ankara •

TURKEY

CYPRUS
Nicosia •

FINLAND

Helsinki •

Gulf of Finland

ESTONIA
• Riga
LATVIA

LITHUANIA

WHITE RUSSIA

Istanbul •

Aegean Sea

Athens •

GREECE

COMECON member, 1949–1961

SWEDEN

Stockholm •

Baltic Sea

Gdansk •

Bialystok •

Warsaw •

POLAND

Prague •

CZECHOSLOVAKIA

Budapest •

HUNGARY

Vienna •

AUSTRIA

Belgrade •

YUGOSLAVIA

ROMANIA

Bucharest •

BULGARIA

Sofia •

Tirane •
ALBANIA

MALTA

Sicily

Mediterranean Sea

NORWAY

Oslo •

Copenhagen •

DENMARK

Hamburg •

Bonn •

WEST GERMANY

Munich •

Berlin •
EAST GERMANY

Berne •
SWITZERLAND

Milan •

ITALY

Rome •

Corsica

Sardinia

Marseilles •

North Sea

NETHERLANDS

Amsterdam •
The Hague •

Brussels •
BELGIUM

LUXEMBOURG

Paris •

FRANCE

Geneva •

Adriatic Sea

Edinburgh •

SCOTLAND

GREAT BRITAIN

ENGLAND

London •

WALES

Belfast •
N. IRELAND

Dublin •

IRELAND

Barcelona •

Madrid •

SPAIN

Defense treaty with U.S.A., 1953

GIBRALTAR (Gr. Br.)

PORTUGAL

Lisbon •

ATLANTIC OCEAN

400 Mi.

400 Km.

200

200

Legend:

Communist countries

NATO members

Nonallied Western countries

"Iron Curtain" after 1955

Original Common Market members

Subsequent Common Market members

COMECON members

Other NATO members

U.S.A.
CANADA
ICELAND

More generally, he refused to permit the scheduled advent of majority rule within the Common Market, and he forced his partners to accept many of his views. Thus, throughout the 1960s the Common Market thrived economically, but it did not transcend deep-seated nationalism; it remained a union of sovereign states.

Decolonization

The postwar era saw the total collapse of colonial empires. Between 1947 and 1962, almost every colonial territory gained independence. Europe's long expansion, which had reached a high point in the late nineteenth century, was completely reversed (Map 30.3). The spectacular collapse of Western political empires fully reflected old Europe's eclipsed power after 1945. Yet the new nations of Asia and Africa have been so deeply influenced by Western ideas and achievements that the "westernization" of the world has continued to rush forward.

Modern nationalism, with its demands for political self-determination and racial equality, spread from intellectuals to the masses in virtually every colonial territory after the First World War. Economic suffering created bitter popular resentment, and thousands of colonial subjects had been unwillingly drafted into French and British armies. Nationalist leaders stepped up their demands. By 1919 one high-ranking British official mournfully wrote: "A wave of unrest is sweeping over the Empire, as over the rest of the world. Almost every day brings some disturbance or other at our Imperial outposts."[7] The Russian Revolution also encouraged the growth of nationalism, and Soviet Russia verbally and militarily supported nationalist independence movements.

Furthermore, European empires had been based on an enormous power differential between the rulers and the ruled, a difference that had declined

French President De Gaulle and his wife bid farewell to President and Mrs. Kennedy at the presidential palace in Paris in 1961. A proud statesman who never forgot the snubs received from his American and British allies during the war, De Gaulle challenged American leadership in Western Europe. (*Source: Wide World Photos*)

almost to the vanishing point by 1945. Not only was western Europe poor and battered immediately after the war, but Japan had demonstrated that whites were not invincible. With its political power and moral authority in tatters, Europe's only choice was either to submit gracefully or to enter into risky wars of reconquest.

Most Europeans regarded their empires very differently after 1945 than before 1914, or even before 1939. Empire had rested on self-confidence and a sense of righteousness; Europeans had believed their superiority to be not only technical and military but spiritual and moral as well. The horrors of the Second World War and the near-destruction of Western civilization destroyed such complacent arrogance and gave opponents of imperialism the upper hand in Europe. After 1945 most Europeans were willing to let go of their colonies more or less voluntarily and to concentrate on rebuilding at home.

MAP 30.2 European Alliance Systems After the Cold War divided Europe into two hostile military alliances, six Western European countries formed the Common Market in 1957. The Common Market grew later to include most of Western Europe, while the Communist states organized their own economic association— COMECON.

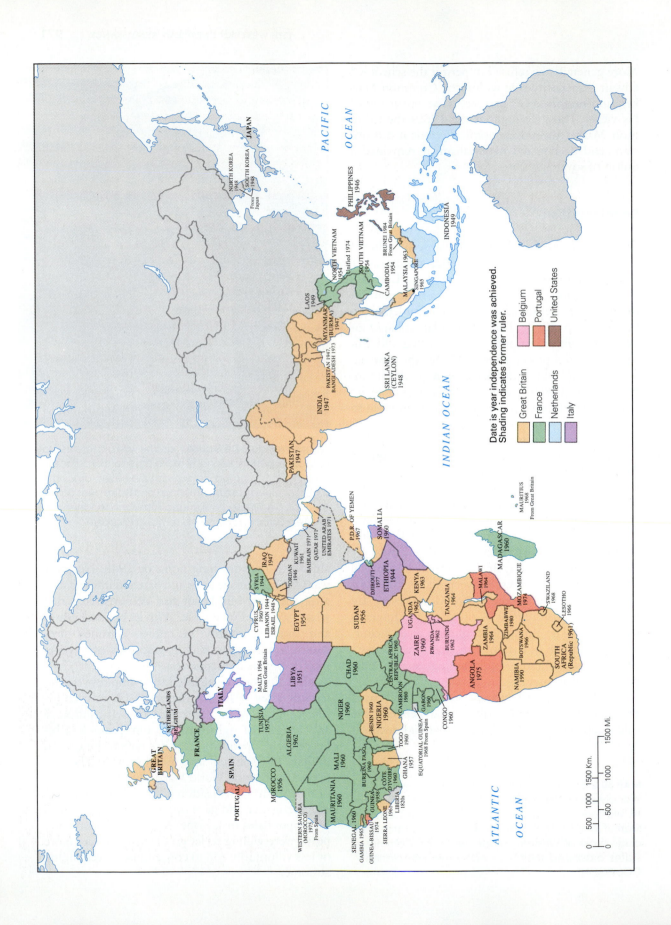

PACIFIC OCEAN

JAPAN

NORTH KOREA
1948

SOUTH KOREA 1948
From Japan

PHILIPPINES
1946

NORTH VIETNAM
1954
Unified 1974

SOUTH VIETNAM
1954

BRUNEI 1984
From Great Britain

CAMBODIA
1954

MALAYSIA 1963

SINGAPORE
1965

INDONESIA
1949

LAOS
1949

MYANMAR
(BURMA)
1947

PAKISTAN 1947,
BANGLADESH 1973

SRI LANKA
(CEYLON)
1948

INDIA
1947

PAKISTAN
1947

INDIAN OCEAN

P.D.R. OF YEMEN
1967

SOMALIA
1960

UNITED ARAB
EMIRATES 1971

QATAR 1971

BAHRAIN 1971

KUWAIT
1961

IRAQ
1947

JORDAN
1946

SYRIA
1944

DJIBOUTI
1977

ETHIOPIA
1944

KENYA
1963

MAURITIUS
1968
From Great Britain

CYPRUS 1960

LEBANON 1944

ISRAEL 1948

EGYPT
1954

SUDAN
1956

UGANDA
1962

TANZANIA
1964

MALAWI
1964

MOZAMBIQUE
1974

SWAZILAND
1968

LESOTHO
1966

MADAGASCAR
1960

MALTA 1964
From Great Britain

ITALY

LIBYA
1951

CHAD
1960

CENTRAL AFRICAN
REPUBLIC 1960

ZAIRE
1960

RWANDA
1962

BURUNDI
1962

ZAMBIA
1964

ZIMBABWE
1980

BOTSWANA
1966

NAMIBIA
1990

ANGOLA
1975

SOUTH
AFRICA
(Republic 1961)

NETHERLANDS

BELGIUM

FRANCE

TUNISIA
1957

NIGER
1960

BENIN 1960

NIGERIA
1960

CAMEROON
1960

GABON
1960

CONGO
1960

GREAT
BRITAIN

SPAIN

PORTUGAL

MOROCCO
1956

ALGERIA
1962

MALI
1960

BURKINA FASO
1960

TOGO
1960

EQUATORIAL GUINEA
1968 From Spain

GHANA
1957

WESTERN SAHARA
(MOROCCO)
1975,
From Spain

MAURITANIA
1960

SENEGAL 1960

GAMBIA 1965

GUINEA-BISSAU
1974

GUINEA
1958

SIERRA LEONE
1961

CÔTE
D'IVOIRE
1960

LIBERIA
1820s

ATLANTIC
OCEAN

Date is year independence was achieved.
Shading indicates former ruler.

Great Britain		Belgium
France		Portugal
Netherlands		United States
Italy		

0   500   1000   1500 Km.

0   500   1000   1500 Mi.

India played a key role in decolonization and the end of empire. India was Britain's oldest, largest, and most lucrative nonwhite possession, and Britain had by far the largest colonial empire. Nationalist opposition to British rule coalesced after the First World War under the leadership of the British-educated lawyer Mahatma Gandhi (1869–1948), who preached nonviolent "noncooperation" with the British. Indian intellectuals effectively argued the old liberal case for equality and self-determination. In response, Britain's rulers gradually introduced political reforms and limited self-government. When the war ended, independence followed very rapidly. The new Labour government was determined to leave India; radicals and socialists had always opposed imperialism, and the heavy cost of governing India had become an intolerable financial burden. The obstacle posed by conflict between India's Hindu and Muslim populations was resolved in 1947 by creating two states, predominantly Hindu India and Muslim Pakistan.

If Indian nationalism drew on Western parliamentary liberalism, Chinese nationalism developed and triumphed in the framework of Marxist-Leninist totalitarianism. In the turbulent early 1920s, a broad alliance of nationalist forces within the Russian-supported *Kuomintang*—the National People's party—was dedicated to unifying China and abolishing European concessions. But in 1927 Chiang Kai-shek (1887–1975), the successor to Sun Yat-sen (see page 851) and the leader of the Kuomintang, broke with his more radical Communist allies, headed by Mao Tse-tung.

In 1931 Mao Tse-tung (1893–1976) led his followers on an incredible 5,000-mile march to remote northern China and dug in. Even war against the Japanese army of occupation could not force Mao and Chiang to cooperate. By late 1945 the long-standing quarrel erupted in civil war. Stalin gave Mao some aid, and the Americans gave Chiang much more. Winning the support of the peasantry by promising to expropriate the big landowners, the tougher, better-organized Communists

forced the Nationalists to withdraw to the island of Taiwan (formerly known as Formosa) in 1949.

Mao and the Communists united China's 550 million inhabitants in a strong centralized state, expelled foreigners, and began building a new society along Soviet lines, with mass arrests, forced-labor camps, and ceaseless propaganda. The peasantry was collectivized, and the inevitable five-year plans concentrated quite successfully on the expansion of heavy industry.

Most Asian countries followed the pattern of either India or China. Britain quickly gave Sri Lanka (Ceylon) and Burma independence in 1948; the Philippines became independent of the United States in 1946. The Dutch attempt to reconquer the Netherlands East Indies was unsuccessful, and in 1949 Indonesia emerged independent.

The French similarly sought to re-establish colonial rule in Indochina, but despite American aid they were defeated in 1954 by forces under the communist and nationalist guerrilla leader Ho Chi Minh (1890–1969), who was supported by Russia and China. At the subsequent international peace conference in Geneva, French Indochina gained

Chinese Red Guards line up before a giant picture of Mao Tse-tung in about 1967. They are waving the "Little Red Book," which contains a collection of Mao's slogans and teachings. *(Source: Wide World Photos)*

MAP 30.3 The New States in Africa and Asia Divided primarily along religious lines into two states, British India led the way to political independence in 1947. Most African territories achieved statehood by the mid-1960s, as European empires passed away, unlamented.

independence. Vietnam was divided into two hostile zones, one communist and one anticommunist, pending unification on the basis of internationally supervised free elections. But the elections were never held, and civil war soon broke out between the North and the South.

In Africa, Arab nationalism was an important factor in the ending of empire. Sharing a common language and culture, Arab nationalists were also loosely united by their opposition to the colonial powers and to the migration of Jewish refugees to Palestine. The British, whose occupation policies in Palestine were condemned by Arabs and Jews, by Russians and Americans, announced their withdrawal from Palestine in 1948. The United Nations voted for the creation of two states, one Arab and one Jewish. The Arab countries immediately attacked the new Jewish nation and suffered a humiliating defeat. In the course of the fighting, thousands of Arab refugees fled from the territory that became the Jewish state of Israel.

Many of these Arab refugees refused to accept defeat. They vowed to fight on, for generations if necessary, until the state of Israel was destroyed or until they established their own independent Palestinian state. The Palestinian refugees also sought the support of existing Arab states, claiming that Israel was the great enemy of Arab interests and Arab nationalism. The Arab-Israeli conflict was destined to outlive the postwar era, enduring to this day.

The Arab defeat in 1948 triggered a nationalist revolution in Egypt in 1952, where a young army officer named Gamal Abdel Nasser (1918–1970) drove out the pro-Western king. In 1956 Nasser abruptly nationalized the Suez Canal, the last symbol and substance of Western power in the Middle East. Infuriated, the British and French, along with the Israelis, invaded Egypt. This was, however, to be the dying gasp of imperial power: the moralistic, anti-imperialist Americans joined with the Russians to force the British, French, and Israelis to withdraw.

The failure of the Western powers to unseat Nasser in 1956 in turn encouraged Arab nationalists in Algeria. Algeria's large French population considered Algeria an integral part of France. It was this feeling that made the ensuing war so bitter and so atypical of decolonization. In the end, General De Gaulle, who had returned to power as part of a movement to keep Algeria French, accepted the principle of Algerian self-determination. In 1962,

after more than a century of French rule, Algeria became independent and the European population quickly fled.

In most of Africa south of the Sahara, decolonization proceeded much more smoothly. Beginning in 1957, Britain's colonies won independence with little or no bloodshed. In 1958 the clever De Gaulle offered the leaders of French black Africa the choice of a total break with France or immediate independence within a kind of French commonwealth. Heavily dependent on France for economic aid and technology, all but one of the new states chose association with France. Throughout the 1960s France (and its western European partners) successfully used economic and cultural ties with former colonies, such as special trading privileges with the Common Market and heavy investment in French-based education, to maintain a powerful European presence in black Africa. Radicals charged France (and Europe generally) with "neocolonialism," designed to perpetuate European economic domination indefinitely. In any event, enduring aid and influence in black Africa was an important manifestation of western Europe's political recovery and even of its possible emergence as a genuine superpower.

SOVIET EASTERN EUROPE

While western Europe surged ahead economically, regaining political independence as American influence gradually waned, eastern Europe followed a different path. Soviet Russia first tightened its grip on the "liberated" nations of eastern Europe under Stalin and then refused to let go. Economic recovery in eastern Europe proceeded, therefore, along Soviet lines, and political and social developments were largely determined by changes in the Soviet Union. Thus one must look primarily at Soviet Russia to understand the achievements and failures of eastern European peoples after the Second World War.

Stalin's Last Years

The unwillingness of the United States to accept what Stalin did to territories occupied by the triumphant Red Army was at least partly responsible for the outbreak and institutionalization of the cold war. Yet Americans were not the only ones who felt disappointed and even betrayed by Stalin's actions.

The Great Patriotic War of the Fatherland—World War Two as seen from the Soviet perspective—had fostered Russian nationalism and a relaxation of totalitarian terror. It also produced a rare but real unity between Soviet rulers and most Russian people. When an American correspondent asked a distinguished sixty-year-old Jewish scientist, who had decided to leave Russia for Israel in 1972, what had been the best period in Russian history, he received a startling answer: the Second World War. The scientist explained: "At that time we all felt closer to our government than at any other time in our lives. It was not *their* country then, but *our* country. . . . It was not *their* war, but *our* war."[8] Having made such a heroic war effort, the vast majority of the Soviet people hoped in 1945 that a grateful party and government would grant greater freedom and democracy. Such hopes were soon crushed.

Even before the war ended, Stalin was moving his country back toward rigid dictatorship. As early as 1944, the leading members of the Communist party were being given a new motivating slogan: "The war on Fascism ends, the war on capitalism begins."[9] By early 1946, Stalin was publicly singing the old tune that war was inevitable as long as capitalism existed. Stalin's invention of a new foreign foe was mainly an excuse for re-establishing totalitarian measures, for the totalitarian state cannot live without enemies. Unfortunately, as dissident Russian historians have argued, Stalin's language at home and his actions in eastern Europe were so crudely extreme that he managed to turn an imaginary threat into a real one, as the cold war took hold.

One of Stalin's first postwar goals was to repress the millions of Soviet citizens who were outside Soviet borders when the war ended. Many had been captured by the Nazis; others were ordinary civilians who had been living abroad. Many were opposed to Stalin; some had fought for the Germans. Determined to hush up the fact that large numbers of Soviet citizens hated his regime so much that they had willingly supported the Germans and refused to go home, Stalin demanded that all these "traitors" be returned to him. At Yalta, Roosevelt and Churchill agreed, and they kept their word. American and British military commanders refused to recognize the right of political asylum under any circumstances.

Roughly two million people were delivered to Stalin against their will. Most were immediately arrested and sent to forced-labor camps, where about 50 percent perished. The revival of many forced-labor camps, which had accounted for roughly one-sixth of all new construction in Soviet Russia before the war, was further stimulated by large-scale purges, particularly in 1945 and 1946, of many people who had never left the Soviet Union.

Culture and art were also purged. Rigid anti-Western ideological conformity was reimposed in violent campaigns led by Stalin's trusted henchman, Andrei Zhdanov. Zhdanov denounced many artists, including the composers Sergei Prokofiev and Dimitri Shostakovich and the outstanding film director Sergei Eisenstein. The great poet Anna Akhmatova was condemned as "a harlot and nun who mixes harlotry and prayer" and, like many others, was driven out of the writers' union, thus practically ensuring that her work would not be published. In 1949 Stalin launched a savage verbal attack on Soviet Jews, who were accused of being pro-Western and antisocialist.

In the political realm, Stalin reasserted the Communist party's complete control of the government and his absolute mastery of the party. Five-year plans were reintroduced to cope with the enormous task of economic reconstruction. Once again, heavy and military industry were given top priority, and consumer goods, housing, and still-collectivized agriculture were neglected. Everyday life was very hard: in 1952 the wages of ordinary people still bought 25 to 40 percent *less* than in 1928. In short, it was the 1930s all over again in Soviet Russia, although police terror was less intense than during that era's purges.

Stalin's prime postwar innovation was to export the Stalinist system to the countries of eastern Europe. The Communist parties of eastern Europe had established one-party states by 1948, thanks to the help of the Red Army and the Russian secret police. Rigid ideological indoctrination, attacks on religion, and a lack of civil liberties were soon facts of life. Industry was nationalized, and the middle class was stripped of its possessions. Economic life was then faithfully recast in the Stalinist mold. Forced industrialization, with five-year plans and a stress on heavy industry, lurched forward without regard for human costs. For the sake of ideological uniformity, agriculture had to be collectivized; this process went much faster in Bulgaria and Czechoslovakia than in Hungary and Poland. Finally, the

Frenz: Pink Snow   This light-hearted, fanciful rendition of traditional Russian themes hardly seems a threat to the Stalinist state. Yet it failed to conform to the official style of socialist realism and thus was suppressed with a host of other works during Zhdanov's brutal cultural purge. *(Source: Sovfoto)*

satellite countries were forced to trade heavily with Soviet Russia on very unfavorable terms, as traditional economic ties with western Europe were forcibly severed.

Only Josip Tito (1892–1980), the popular Resistance leader and Communist chief of Yugoslavia, was able to resist Russian economic exploitation successfully. Tito openly broke with Stalin in 1948, and since there was no Russian army in Yugoslavia, he got away with it. Tito's successful proclamation of Communist independence led the infuriated and humiliated Stalin to purge the Communist parties of eastern Europe. Hundreds of thousands who had joined the party after the war were expelled. Popular Communist leaders who, like Tito, had led the Resistance against Germany, were made to star in reruns of the great show trials of the 1930s, complete with charges of treason, unbelievable confessions, and merciless executions. Thus did history repeat itself as Stalin sought to create absolutely obedient instruments of domination in eastern Europe.

Reform and De-Stalinization

In 1953 the aging Stalin finally died, and a new era slowly began in Soviet eastern Europe. Even as they struggled for power, Stalin's heirs realized that change and reform were necessary. There was, first of all, widespread fear and hatred of Stalin's political terrorism, which had struck both high and low with its endless purges and unjust arrests. Even Stalin's secret-police chief, Lavrenti Beria, publicly advocated a relaxation of controls in an unsuccessful attempt to seize power. Beria was arrested and shot, after which the power of the secret police was curbed and many of its infamous forced-labor camps were gradually closed. Change was also necessary for economic reasons. Agriculture was in bad shape, and shortages of consumer goods were discouraging hard work and initiative. Finally, Stalin's aggressive foreign policy had led directly to an ongoing American commitment to western Europe and a strong Western alliance. Soviet Russia was isolated and contained.

On the question of just how much change should be permitted, the Communist leadership was badly split. The conservatives, led by Stalin's long-time foreign minister, the stone-faced Vyacheslav Molotov, wanted to make as few changes as possible. The reformers, led by Nikita Khrushchev, argued for major innovations. Khrushchev (1894–1971), who had joined the party as an uneducated coal miner in 1918 at twenty-four and had risen steadily to a high-level position in the 1930s, was emerging as the new ruler by 1955.

To strengthen his position and that of his fellow reformers within the party, Khrushchev launched an all-out attack on Stalin and his crimes at a closed session of the Twentieth Party Congress in 1956. In gory detail he described to the startled Communist delegates how Stalin had tortured and murdered thousands of loyal Communists, how he had trusted Hitler completely and bungled the country's defense, and how he had "supported the glorification of his own person with all conceivable methods." For hours Soviet Russia's top leader delivered an attack whose content would previously have been dismissed as "anticommunist hysteria" in many circles throughout the Western world.

Khrushchev's "secret speech," read to Communist party meetings throughout the country, strengthened the reform movement. The liberalization—or "de-Stalinization," as it was called in the West—of Soviet Russia was genuine. The Communist party jealously maintained its monopoly on political power, but Khrushchev shook it up and brought in new blood. The economy was made more responsive to the needs and even some of the desires of the people, as some resources were shifted from heavy industry and the military toward consumer goods and agriculture. Stalinist controls over workers were relaxed, and independent courts rather than the secret police judged and punished nonpolitical crimes.

Russia's very low standard of living finally began to improve and continued to rise throughout the 1960s. By 1970 Russians were able to buy twice as much food, three times as much clothing, and twelve times as many appliances as in 1950. (Even so, the standard of living in Soviet Russia was only about half that of the wealthier western European countries in 1970 and well below that of eastern European countries as well.)

De-Stalinization created great ferment among writers and intellectuals, who hungered for cultural freedom. The poet Boris Pasternak (1890–1960), who survived the Stalinist years by turning his talents to translating Shakespeare, finished his great novel *Doctor Zhivago* in 1956. Published in the West but not in Russia, *Doctor Zhivago* is both a literary masterpiece and a powerful challenge to communism. It tells the story of a prerevolutionary intellectual who rejects the violence and brutality of the revolution of 1917 and the Stalinist years. Even as he is destroyed, he triumphs because of his humanity and Christian spirit. Pasternak was forced by Khrushchev himself to refuse the Nobel Prize in 1958—but he was not shot. Other talented writers followed Pasternak's lead, and courageous editors let the sparks fly.

The writer Alexander Solzhenitsyn (b. 1918) created a sensation when his *One Day in the Life of Ivan Denisovich* was published in Russia in 1962. Solzhenitsyn's novel portrays in grim detail life in a Stalinist concentration camp—a life to which Solzhenitsyn himself had been unjustly condemned—and is a damning indictment of the Stalinist past.

Khrushchev also de-Stalinized Soviet foreign policy. "Peaceful coexistence" with capitalism was possible, he argued, and great wars were not inevitable. Khrushchev made positive concessions: he met with U.S. President Dwight Eisenhower at the first summit meeting since Potsdam, and he agreed in 1955 to real independence for a neutral Austria after ten long years of Allied occupation. Thus there was considerable relaxation of cold war tensions between 1955 and 1957. At the same time, Khrushchev began wooing the new nations of Asia and Africa—even if they were not communist—with promises and aid. He also proclaimed that there could be different paths to socialism, thus calling a halt to the little cold war with Tito's Yugoslavia.

De-Stalinization stimulated rebelliousness in the eastern European satellites. Having suffered in silence under Stalin, Communist reformers and the masses were quickly emboldened to seek much greater liberty and national independence. Poland took the lead in March 1956: riots there resulted in the release of more than nine thousand political prisoners, including the previously purged Wladyslaw Gomulka. Taking charge of the government, Gomulka skillfully managed to win greater autonomy for Poland while calming anti-Russian feeling.

Hungary experienced a real and very tragic revolution. Led by students and workers—the classic urban revolutionaries—the people of Budapest installed a liberal Communist reformer as their new chief in October 1956. Soviet troops were forced to leave the country. One-party rule was abolished, and the new government promised free elections, freedom of expression, and massive social changes. Worst of all from the Russian point of view, the new government declared Hungarian neutrality and renounced Hungary's military alliance with Moscow. As in 1849, the Russian answer was to invade Hungary with a large army and to crush, once again, a national, democratic revolution.

Fighting was bitter until the end, for the Hungarians hoped that the United States would fulfill its earlier propaganda promises and come to their aid. When this did not occur because of American unwillingness to risk a general war, the people of eastern Europe realized that their only hope was to strive for small domestic gains while following Russia obediently in foreign affairs. This cautious approach produced some results. In Poland, for example, the peasants were not collectivized, and Catholics were allowed to practice their faith. Thus eastern Europe profited, however modestly, from Khrushchev's policy of de-Stalinization and could hope for still greater freedom in the future.

The Fall of Khrushchev

In October 1962 a remarkable poem entitled "Stalin's Heirs," by the popular young poet Yevgeny Yevtushenko (b. 1933), appeared in *Pravda*, the official newspaper of the Communist party and the most important one in Soviet Russia. Yevtushenko wrote:

Some of his heirs are in retirement pruning their
  rosebushes,
  and secretly thinking that their time will come again.
Others even attack Stalin from the rostrum but at
  home, at night-time, think back to bygone days.[10]

Like Solzhenitsyn's novel about Stalin's concentration camps, published a month later, this very political poem was authorized by Communist party boss Khrushchev himself. It was part of his last, desperate offensive against the many well-entrenched conservative Stalinists in the party and government, who were indeed "secretly thinking that their time will come again." And it did.

Within two years Khrushchev had fallen in a bloodless palace revolution. Under Leonid Brezhnev (1906–1982), Soviet Russia began a period of limited "re-Stalinization." The basic reason for this development was that Khrushchev's Communist colleagues saw de-Stalinization as a dangerous, two-sided threat. How could Khrushchev denounce the dead dictator without eventually denouncing and perhaps even arresting his still-powerful henchmen? In a heated secret debate in 1957, when the conservatives had tried without success to depose the menacing reformer, Khrushchev had pointed at two of Stalin's most devoted followers, Molotov and Kaganovich, and exclaimed: "Your hands are stained with the blood of our party leaders and of innumerable innocent Bolsheviks!" "So are yours!" Molotov and Kaganovich shouted back at him. "Yes, so are mine," Khrushchev replied. "I admit this. But during the purges I was merely carrying out your order. . . . I was not responsible. You were."[11] Moreover, the widening campaign of de-Stalinization posed a clear threat to the dictatorial authority of the party. It was producing growing, perhaps uncontrollable, criticism of the whole communist system. The party had to tighten up while there was still time. It was clear that Khrushchev had to go.

Another reason for conservative opposition was Khrushchev's foreign policy. Although he scored some diplomatic victories, notably with Egypt and India, Khrushchev's policy toward the West was highly erratic and ultimately unsuccessful. In 1958 he ordered the Western Allies to evacuate West Berlin within six months, which led only to a reaffirmation of Allied unity and to Khrushchev's backing down. Then in 1961, as relations with Communist China deteriorated dramatically, Khrushchev ordered the East Germans to build a wall between East and West Berlin, thereby sealing off West Berlin in clear violation of existing access agreements among the Great Powers. The recently elected U.S. president, John F. Kennedy, acquiesced. Emboldened and seeing a chance to change the balance of military power decisively,

Khrushchev ordered missiles with nuclear warheads installed in Fidel Castro's communist Cuba. President Kennedy countered with a naval blockade of Cuba, and after a tense diplomatic crisis, Khrushchev was forced to remove the Russian missiles in return for American pledges not to disturb Castro's regime. Khrushchev looked like a bumbling buffoon; his influence, already slipping, declined rapidly after the Cuban fiasco, and in October 1964 he was forced to resign by the Communist party's Central Committee.

After Brezhnev and his supporters took over in 1964, they started talking cautiously of Stalin's "good points" and ignoring his crimes. Their praise of the whole Stalinist era, with its rapid industrialization and wartime victories, informed Soviet citizens that no fundamental break with the past had occurred at home. Russian leaders also launched a massive arms buildup, determined never to suffer Khrushchev's humiliation in the face of American nuclear superiority. And they began building the large navy and air force necessary for intervention in faraway places, like Cuba, around the globe. Yet Brezhnev and company proceeded cautiously in the mid-1960s. They avoided direct confrontation with the United States and seemed more solidly committed to peaceful coexistence than the deposed Khrushchev—to the great relief of people in the West.

THE WESTERN HEMISPHERE

One way to think of what historians used to call the New World is as a vigorous offshoot of Western civilization, an offshoot that has gradually developed its own characteristics while retaining European roots. From this perspective, one can see many illuminating parallels and divergences in the histories of Europe and the Americas. So it was after the Second World War. The western hemisphere experienced a many-faceted postwar recovery, somewhat similar to that of Europe, though it began earlier, especially in Latin America.

Postwar Prosperity in the United States

The Second World War cured the depression in the United States and brought about the greatest boom in American history. Unemployment practically vanished, as millions of new workers, half of them women, found jobs. Personal income doubled, and the well-being of Americans increased dramatically. Yet the experience of the 1930s weighed heavily on people's minds, feeding fears that peace would bring renewed depression.

In fact, conversion to a peacetime economy went smoothly, marred only by a spurt of inflation accompanying the removal of government controls. Moreover, the U.S. economy continued to advance fairly steadily for a long generation. Though cold war fears marked American relations with the rest of the world, economic prosperity kept the public generally satisfied at home.

This helps explain why postwar domestic politics consisted largely of modest adjustments to the status quo until the 1960s. After a flurry of unpopular postwar strikes, a conservative Republican Congress chopped away at the power of labor unions by means of the Taft-Hartley Act of 1947. But Truman's upset victory in 1948 demonstrated that Americans had no interest in undoing Roosevelt's social and economic reforms. The Congress proceeded to increase social security benefits, subsidize middle- and lower-class housing, and raise the minimum wage. These and other liberal measures consolidated the New Deal. But true innovations, whether in health or civil rights, were rejected, and in 1952 the Republican party and the voters turned to General Eisenhower, a national hero and self-described moderate.

The federal government's only major new undertaking during the "Eisenhower years" was the interstate highway system, a suitable symbol of the basic satisfaction of the vast majority. Some Americans feared that the United States was becoming a "blocked society," obsessed with stability and incapable of wholesome change. This feeling contributed in 1960 to the election of the young, attractive John F. Kennedy, who promised to "get the country moving again." President Kennedy captured the popular imagination with his flair and rhetoric, revitalized the old Roosevelt coalition, and modestly expanded existing liberal legislation before he was struck down by an assassin's bullet in 1963.

The Civil Rights Revolution

Belatedly and reluctantly, complacent postwar America experienced a genuine social revolution:

after a long and sometimes bloody struggle, blacks (and their white supporters) threw off a deeply entrenched system of segregation, discrimination, and repression. This movement for civil rights advanced on several fronts. Eloquent lawyers from the National Association for the Advancement of Colored People (NAACP) challenged school segregation in the courts and in 1954 won a landmark decision in the Supreme Court that "separate educational facilities are inherently unequal."

While state and local governments in the South were refusing to comply, blacks were effectively challenging institutionalized inequality with bus boycotts, sit-ins, and demonstrations. As Martin Luther King told the white power structure, "We will not hate you, but we will not obey your evil laws."[12]

Blacks also used their growing political power in key northern states to gain the support of the liberal wing of the Democratic party. All these efforts culminated after the liberal landslide that elected Lyndon Johnson in 1964. The Civil Rights Act of 1964 categorically prohibited discrimination in public services and on the job. In the follow-up Voting Rights Act of 1965, the federal government firmly guaranteed all blacks the right to vote. By the 1970s, substantial numbers of blacks had been elected to public and private office throughout the southern states, showing proof positive that dramatic changes had occurred in American race relations.

Black voters and political leaders enthusiastically supported the accompanying surge of new liberal social legislation in the mid-1960s. President Johnson, reviving the New Deal approach of his early congressional years, solemnly declared "unconditional war on poverty." Congress and the administration created a host of antipoverty projects, such as the domestic peace corps, free preschools for slum children, and community-action programs. Although these programs were directed to all poor Americans—the majority of whom are white—they were also intended to extend greater equality for blacks to the realm of economics. More generally, the United States promoted in the mid-1960s the kind of fundamental social reform that western Europe had embraced immediately after World War Two. The United States became much more of a welfare state, as government spending for social benefits rose dramatically and approached European levels.

Economic Nationalism in Latin America

Although the countries of Latin America share a European heritage, specifically a Spanish-Portuguese heritage, their striking differences make it difficult to generalize meaningfully about modern Latin American history. Yet a growing economic nationalism seems unmistakable. As the early nineteenth century saw Spanish and Portuguese colonies win wars of political independence, recent history has been an ongoing quest for genuine economic independence through local control and industrialization, which has sometimes brought Latin American countries into sharp conflict with Europe and the United States.

To understand the rise of economic nationalism, one must remember that Latin American countries developed as producers of foodstuffs and raw materials, which were exported to Europe and the United States in return for manufactured goods and capital investment. This exchange was mutually beneficial, especially in the later nineteenth century, and the countries that participated most actively, like Argentina and southern Brazil, became the wealthiest and most advanced. There was, however, a heavy price to pay. Latin America became very dependent on foreign markets, products, and investments. Industry did not develop, and large landowners profited most, further enhancing their social and political power.

The old international division of labor, disrupted by the First World War but re-established in the 1920s, was finally destroyed by the Great Depression—a historical turning point as critical for Latin America as for the United States. Prices and exports of Latin American commodities collapsed as Europe and the United States drastically reduced their purchases and raised tariffs to protect domestic producers. With foreign sales plummeting, Latin American countries could not buy industrial goods abroad. Latin America suffered the full force of the global economic crisis.

The result in the larger, more important Latin American countries was a profound shift in the direction of economic nationalism after 1930. The more popularly based governments worked to reduce foreign influence and gain control of their own economies and natural resources. They energetically promoted national industry by means of high tariffs, government grants, and even state enterprise. They favored the lower middle and urban

The March on Washington   in August 1963 marked a dramatic climax in the civil rights struggle. More than 200,000 people gathered at the Lincoln Memorial to hear the young Martin Luther King deliver his greatest address, his ''I have a dream'' speech. *(Source: Francis Miller, LIFE MAGAZINE © Time Warner Inc.)*

working classes with social benefits and higher wages in order to increase their purchasing power and gain their support. These efforts at recovery were fairly successful. By the late 1940s, the factories of Argentina, Brazil, and Chile could generally satisfy domestic consumer demand for the products of light industry. In the 1950s, some countries began moving into heavy industry. Economic nationalism and the rise of industry are particularly striking in the two largest and most influential countries, Mexico and Brazil, which together account for half the population of Latin America.

Mexico   Overthrowing the elitist, upper-class rule of the tyrant Porfirio Díaz, the spasmodic, often-chaotic Mexican Revolution of 1910 culminated in 1917 in a new constitution. This radical nationalistic document called for universal suffrage, massive land reform, benefits for labor, and strict control of foreign capital. Actual progress was quite modest until 1934, when a charismatic young Indian from a poor family, Lázaro Cárdenas, became president and dramatically revived the languishing revolution. Under Cárdenas, many large estates were divided up among small farmers or returned undivided to Indian communities.

Meanwhile, because foreign capitalists were being discouraged, Mexican business people built many small factories and managed to thrive. The government also championed the cause of industrial workers. In 1938, when Mexican workers became locked in a bitter dispute with British and American oil companies, Cárdenas nationalized the petroleum industry—to the astonishment of a world unaccustomed to such actions. Finally, the 1930s saw the flowering of a distinctive Mexican culture, which proudly embraced its Indian past and gloried in the modern national revolution.

Diego Rivera (1886–1957) was one of the great and committed painters of the Mexican Revolution. Rivera believed that art should reflect the "new order of things" and inspire the common people—the workers and the peasants. One of Rivera's many wall paintings, this vibrant central mural in the National Palace in Mexico City, depicts a brutal Spanish conquest and a liberating revolution. *(Source: Robert Frerck/Odyssey Productions)*

In 1940 the official, semi-authoritarian party that has governed Mexico continuously since the revolution selected the first of a series of more moderate presidents. Steadfast in their radical, occasionally anti-American rhetoric, these presidents used the full power of the state to promote industrialization through a judicious mixture of public, private, and even foreign enterprise. The Mexican economy grew rapidly, at about 6 percent per year from the early 1940s to the late 1960s, with the upper and middle classes reaping the lion's share of the benefits.

Brazil After the fall of the monarchy in 1889, politics had largely been dominated by the coffee barons and by regional rivalries. These rivalries and deteriorating economic conditions allowed a military revolt led by Getulio Vargas, governor of one of Brazil's larger states, to seize control of the federal government in 1930. Vargas, who proved to be a consummate politician, fragmented the opposition and established a mild dictatorship that lasted until 1945. Vargas's rule was generally popular, combining as it did effective economic nationalism and moderate social reform.

Somewhat like President Franklin Roosevelt in the United States, Vargas decisively tipped the balance of political power away from the Brazilian states to the ever-expanding federal government, which became a truly national government for the first time. Vargas and his allies also set out to industrialize Brazil and gain economic independence. While the national coffee board used mountains of surplus coffee beans to fire railroad locomotives, the government supported Brazilian manufacturers with high tariffs, generous loans, and labor peace. This probusiness policy did not prevent new social legislation: workers received shorter hours, pensions, health and accident insurance, paid vacations, and other benefits. Finally, Vargas shrewdly upheld the nationalist cause in his relations with the giant to the north. Early in the Second World War, for example, he traded acceptance of U.S. military bases in Brazil for American construction of Brazil's first huge steel-making complex. By 1945, when the authoritarian Vargas fell in a bloodless military coup that called for greater political liberty, Brazil was modernizing rapidly.

Modernization continued for the next fifteen years. The economy boomed. Presidential politics were re-established, while the military kept a watchful eye for extremism among the civilian politicians. Economic nationalism was especially vigorous under the flamboyant President Kubitschek (1956–1960), a doctor of German-Czech descent. The government borrowed heavily from international bankers to promote industry and built the extravagant new capital of Brasília in the midst of a wilderness. When Brazil's creditors demanded more conservative policies to stem inflation, Kubitschek delighted the nationalists with his firm and successful refusal. His slogan was "Fifty Years' Progress in Five," and he seemed to mean it.

The Brazilian and Mexican formula of national economic development, varying degrees of electoral competition, and social reform was shared by some other Latin American countries, notably Argentina and Chile. By the late 1950s, optimism was widespread, if cautious. Economic and social progress seemed to promise less violent, more democratic politics. These expectations were profoundly shaken by the Cuban Revolution.

The Cuban Revolution

Although many aspects of the Cuban Revolution are obscured by controversy, certain background conditions are clear. First, after achieving independence in 1898, Cuba was for many years virtually an American protectorate. The Cuban constitution gave the United States the legal right to intervene in Cuban affairs, a right that was frequently exercised until Roosevelt renounced it in 1934. Second, and partly because the American army had often been the real power, Cuba's political institutions were weak and its politicians were extraordinarily corrupt. Under the strongman Fulgencio Batista, an opportunistic ex-sergeant who controlled the government almost continually from 1933 to 1958, graft and outright looting were a way of life. Third, Cuba was one of Latin America's most prosperous and advanced countries by the 1950s, but its sugar-and-tourist economy was dependent on the United States. Finally, the enormous differences between rich and poor in Cuba were typical of Latin America. But Cuba also had a strong Communist party, which was highly unusual.

Fidel Castro, a magnetic leader with the gift of oratory and a flair for propaganda, managed to unify anti-Batista elements in a revolutionary front. When Castro's guerrilla forces triumphed in late 1958, the new government's goals were unclear.

Castro had promised a "real" revolution but had always laughed at charges that he was a communist. As the regime consolidated its power in 1959 and 1960, it became increasingly clear that "real" meant "communist" in Castro's mind. Wealthy Cubans, who owned three-quarters of the sugar industry and many profitable businesses, fled to Miami. Soon the middle class began to follow.

Meanwhile, relations with the Eisenhower administration—which had indirectly supported Castro by refusing to sell arms to Batista after March 1958—deteriorated rapidly. Thus, in April 1961, newly elected President Kennedy went ahead with a pre-existing CIA plan to use Cuban exiles to topple Castro. But the Kennedy administration lost its nerve and abandoned the exiles as soon as they were put ashore at the Bay of Pigs. This doomed the invasion, and the exiles were quickly captured, to be ransomed later for $60 million.

The Bay of Pigs invasion—a triumph for Castro and a humiliating, roundly criticized fiasco for the United States—had significant consequences. It freed Castro to build his version of a communist society, and he did. Political life in Cuba featured "anti-imperialism," an alliance with the Soviet bloc, the dictatorship of the party, and a vigorously promoted Castro cult. Revolutionary enthusiasm was genuine among party activists, much of Cuba's youth, and some of the masses some of the time. Prisons and emigration silenced opposition. The economy was characterized by all-pervasive state ownership, collective farms, and Soviet trade and aid. Early efforts to industrialize ran aground, and sugar production at pre-Castro levels continued to dominate the economy. Socially, the regime pursued equality and the creation of a new socialist personality. In short, revolutionary totalitarianism came to the Americas.

The failure of the United States' halfhearted effort to derail Castro probably encouraged Khrushchev to start putting nuclear missiles in Cuba, leading directly to the most serious East-West crisis since the Korean War. And, although the Russians backed down (see page 979), Castro's survival heightened both hopes and fears that the Cuban Revolution could spread throughout Latin America. As leftists were emboldened to try guerrilla warfare, conservatives became more rigid and suspicious of calls for change. In the United States, fear of communism aroused heightened cold war–style interest in Latin America. Using the Organization of American States to isolate Cuba, the United States in 1961 pledged $10 billion in aid over ten years to a new hemispheric "Alliance for Progress." The alliance was intended to promote long-term economic development and social reform, which American liberals hoped would immunize Latin America from the Cuban disease.

U.S. aid did contribute modestly to continued Latin America economic development in the 1960s, although population growth canceled out two-thirds of the increase on a per capita basis. Democratic social reforms—the other half of the Alliance for Progress formula—proceeded slowly, however. Instead, the period following the Cuban Revolution saw the rise of extremism and a revival of conservative authoritarianism in Latin America. These developments marked the turbulent beginnings of a new era in the late 1960s.

SUMMARY

The recovery of Europe and the Americas after World War Two is one of the most striking chapters in the long, uneven course of Western civilization. Although the dangerous tensions of the cold war frustrated fond hopes for a truly peaceful international order, the transition from imperialism to decolonization proceeded rapidly, surprisingly smoothly, and without serious damage to western Europe. Instead, as eastern Europe fell under harsh one-party Communist rule, genuine political democracy gained unprecedented strength in the West, and economic progress quickened the pace of ongoing social and cultural transformation. Thus the tremendous promise inherent in Western society's fateful embrace of the "dual revolution," which had begun in France and England in the late eighteenth century and which had been momentarily halted by the agonies of the Great Depression and the horrors of Nazi totalitarianism, was largely if perhaps only temporarily realized in the shining achievements of the postwar era.

NOTES

1. W. Bullitt, "How We Won the War and Lost the Peace," *Life*, August 30, 1948, p. 94.
2. Quoted in N. Graebner, *Cold War Diplomacy, 1945–1960* (Princeton, N.J.: Van Nostrand, 1962), p. 17.
3. Ibid.

4. Quoted in F. Prinz, ed., *Trümmerzeit in München* (Munich: Münchner Stadtmuseum, 1984), p. 273; trans. J. Buckler.

5. Quoted in J. Hennessy, *Economic "Miracles"* (London: André Deutsch, 1964), p. 5.

6. P. Van Zeeland, in *European Integration,* ed. C. G. Haines (Baltimore: Johns Hopkins Press, 1957), Preface, p. xi.

7. Lord Milner, quoted in R. von Albertini, "The Impact of Two World Wars on the Decline of Colonialism," *Journal of Contemporary History* 4 (January 1969): 17.

8. Quoted in H. Smith, *The Russians* (New York: Quadrangle Books/New York Times, 1976), p. 303.

9. Quoted in D. Treadgold, *Twentieth Century Russia,* 5th ed. (Boston: Houghton Mifflin, 1981), p. 442.

10. Quoted in M. Tatu, *Power in the Kremlin: From Khrushchev to Kosygin* (New York: Viking Press, 1968), p. 248.

11. Quoted in I. Deutscher, "The U.S.S.R. Under Khrushchev," in *Soviet Society,* ed. A. Inkeles and K. Geiger (Boston: Houghton Mifflin, 1961), p. 41.

12. Quoted in S. E. Morison et al., *A Concise History of the American Republic* (New York: Oxford University Press, 1977), p. 697.

SUGGESTED READING

An excellent way to approach wartime diplomacy is through the accounts of the statesmen involved. Great leaders and matchless stylists, Winston Churchill and Charles De Gaulle have both written histories of the war in the form of memoirs. Other interesting memoirs are those of Harry Truman (1958); Dwight Eisenhower, *Crusade in Europe* (1948); and Dean Acheson, *Present at the Creation* (1969), a beautifully written defense of American foreign policy in the early cold war. W. A. Williams, *The Tragedy of American Diplomacy* (1962), and W. La Feber, *America, Russia, and the Cold War* (1967), claim, on the contrary, that the United States was primarily responsible for the conflict with the Soviet Union. Two other important studies focusing on American policy are J. Gaddis, *The United States and the Origins of the Cold War* (1972), and D. Yergin, *Shattered Peace: The Origins of the Cold War and the National Security Council* (1977). A. Fontaine, a French journalist, provides a balanced general approach in his *History of the Cold War,* 2 vols. (1968). V. Mastny's thorough investigation of Stalin's war aims, *Russia's Road to the Cold War* (1979), is highly recommended.

R. Mayne, *The Recovery of Europe, 1945–1973,* rev. ed. (1973), and N. Luxenburg, *Europe Since World War II,* rev. ed. (1979), are recommended general surveys, as are two important works: W. Laqueur, *Europe Since Hitler,* rev. ed. (1982), and P. Johnson, *Modern Times: The World from the Twenties to the Eighties* (1983). T. White, *Fire in the Ashes* (1953), is a vivid view of European resurgence and Marshall Plan aid by an outstanding journalist. I. and D. Unger, *Postwar America: The United States Since 1945* (1989), and W. Leuchtenberg, *In the Shadow of FDR: From Harry Truman to Ronald Reagan,* rev. ed. (1989), ably discuss developments in the United States. Postwar economic and technological developments are analyzed in G. Ambrosius and W. Hibbard, *A Social and Economic History of Twentieth-Century Europe* (1989). A. Shonfield, *Modern Capitalism* (1965), provides an engaging, optimistic assessment of the growing importance of government investment and planning in European economic life. F. R. Willis, *France, Germany, and the New Europe, 1945–1967* (1968), is useful for postwar European diplomacy. Three outstanding works on France are J. Ardagh, *The New French Revolution* (1969), which puts the momentous social changes since 1945 in human terms; G. Wright, *Rural Revolution in France: The Peasantry in the Twentieth Century* (1964); and D. L. Hanley et al., eds., *France: Politics and Society Since 1945* (1979). R. Dahrendorf, *Society and Democracy in Germany* (1971), and H. S. Hughes, *The United States and Italy* (1968), are excellent introductions to modern German and Italian history. A. Marwick, *British Society Since 1945* (1982), and A. H. Halsey, *Change in British Society,* 2d ed. (1981), are good on postwar developments.

H. Seton-Watson, *The East European Revolution* (1965), is a good history of the communization of eastern Europe, and S. Fischer-Galati, ed., *Eastern Europe in the Sixties* (1963), discusses major developments. P. Zinner's, *National Communism and Popular Revolt in Eastern Europe* (1956) and *Revolution in Hungary* (1962) are excellent on the tragic events of 1956. Z. Brzezinski, *The Soviet Bloc: Unity and Conflict* (1967), is a major inquiry. W. Connor, *Socialism, Politics and Equality: Hierarchy and Change in Eastern Europe and the USSR* (1979), and J. Hough and M. Fainsod, *How the Soviet Union Is Governed* (1978), are important general studies. A. Amalrik, *Will the Soviet Union Survive Until 1984?* (1970), is a fascinating interpretation of Soviet society and politics in the 1960s by a Russian who paid for his criticism with prison and exile. A. Lee, *Russian Journal* (1981), and H. Smith's, *The Russians,* cited in the Notes, are excellent journalistic yet comprehensive reports by perceptive American observers.

R. von Albertini, *Decolonialization* (1971), is a good history of the decline and fall of European empires. The tremendous economic problems of the newly independent countries of Asia and Africa are discussed sympathetically by B. Ward, *Rich Nations and Poor Nations* (1962), and R. Heilbroner, *The Great Ascent* (1953). Two excellent general studies on Latin America are J. E. Fagg, *Latin America: A General History,* 3d ed. (1977), and R. J. Shafer, *A History of Latin America* (1978). Both contain detailed suggestions for further reading.

31

Life in the Postwar Era

While Europe staged its astonishing political and economic recovery from the Nazi nightmare, the patterns of everyday life and the structure of Western society were changing no less rapidly and remarkably. Epoch-making inventions and new technologies—the atomic bomb, television, computers, jet planes, and contraceptive pills, to name only a few—profoundly affected human existence. Important groups in society formulated new attitudes and demands, which were reflected in such diverse phenomena as the ever-expanding role of government, the revolt of youth in the late 1960s, and the women's movement. Rapid social change was clearly a fact of life in the Western world.

It was by no means easy to make sense out of all these changes while they were happening. Many "revolutions" and "crises" proved to be merely passing fads, sensationally ballyhooed by the media one day and forgotten the next. Some genuinely critical developments, such as those involving the family, were complex and contradictory, making it hard to understand what was really happening, much less explain why. Yet, by the 1980s, the great changes in social structure and everyday life that took place after the Second World War were coming into sharper focus. Above all, the historian was gaining vital perspective, for it became increasingly clear that the years from about 1968 to 1974 marked the end of the postwar period, as shall be seen in Chapter 32. Thus the startling postwar renaissance emerged in its turn as a separate era in the long evolution of the West, an era with its own distinctive social characteristics but still linked to what came before and after.

- How, then, did Western society and everyday life change in the postwar era, and why?
- What did these changes mean to people?

These are the questions this chapter will seek to answer.

SCIENCE AND TECHNOLOGY

Ever since the Scientific Revolution of the seventeenth century and the Industrial Revolution at the end of the eighteenth century, scientific and techni-

cal developments have powerfully influenced attitudes, society, and everyday life. Never was this influence stronger than after about 1940. Fantastic pipe dreams of science fiction a brief century ago became realities. Submarines passed under the North Pole, and astronauts walked on the moon. Skilled surgeons replaced their patients' failing arteries with plastic tubing. Millions of people around the world simultaneously watched a historic event on television. The list of wonders seemed endless.

The reason science and technology proved so productive and influential was that, for the first time in history, they were effectively joined together on a massive scale. This union of "pure theoretical" science with "applied" science or "practical" technology had already made possible striking achievements in the late nineteenth century in some select fields, most notably organic chemistry, electricity, and preventive medicine. Generally, however, the separation of science and technology still predominated in the late 1930s. Most scientists were university professors, who were little interested in such practical matters as building better machines and inventing new products. Such problems were the concern of tinkering technicians and engineers, who were to a large extent trained on the job. Their accomplishments and discoveries owed more to careful observation and trial-and-error experimentation than to theoretical science.

During World War Two, however, scientists and technicians increasingly marched to the sound of the same drummer. Both scientific research and technical expertise began to be directed at difficult but highly practical military problems. The result was a number of spectacular breakthroughs, such as radar and the atomic bomb, which had immediate wartime applications. After the war, this close cooperation between pure science and applied technology continued with equal success. Indeed, the line between science and technology became harder and harder to draw.

The consequences of the new, intimate link between science and technology were enormous. Seventeenth-century propagandists for science, such as Francis Bacon, had predicted that scientific knowledge of nature would give human beings the power to control the physical world. With such control, they believed, it would be possible to create material abundance and genuine well-being. The successful union of science and technology created new industries and spurred rapid economic growth after 1945, making this prediction finally come true for the great majority of people in Europe and North America in the postwar era.

At the same time, however, the unprecedented success of science in controlling and changing the physical environment produced unexpected and unwanted side effects. Chemical fertilizers poisoned rivers in addition to producing bumper crops. A great good like the virtual elimination of malaria-carrying mosquitoes by DDT dramatically lowered the death rate in tropical lands, but it also contributed to a population explosion in those areas. The list of such unwelcome side effects became very long. By the late 1960s, concern about the undesirable results of technological change had brought into being a vigorous environmental movement. The ability of science and technology to control and alter nature was increasingly seen as a two-edged sword, which had to be wielded with great care and responsibility.

The Stimulus of World War Two

Just before the outbreak of World War Two, a young Irish scientist and Communist named John Desmond Bernal wrote a book entitled *The Social Function of Science.* Bernal argued that the central government should be the source of funds for scientific research and that these funds should be granted on the basis of the expected social and political benefits. Most scientists were horrified by Bernal's proposals, which were contradictory to their cherished ideals. Scientists were committed to designing their own research without regard for its immediate usefulness. As late as 1937, the great physicist Ernest Rutherford could state that the work he and his colleagues were doing in nuclear physics at Cambridge University had no conceivable practical value for anyone, and he expressed delight that such was the case. Nor did university scientists concern themselves with government grants, since many had independent incomes to help finance their still-inexpensive experiments.

The First Jet Engine The marriage of pure science and technology produced inventions like the jet engine. The inventor, Frank Whittle, shows the engine to Dr. Alexander Wetmore, Secretary of the Smithsonian (left), as he accepts the gift from British Ambassador Sir Oliver Franks (right). *(Source: Bettmann/Hulton)*

Atomic Weapons   were the ultimate in state-directed scientific research. In this photo the awesome mushroom cloud of an American atomic bomb rises over the Pacific island of Bikini. *(Source: U.S. Dept. of Energy)*

The Second World War changed this pattern. Pure science lost its impractical innocence. Most leading university scientists went to work on top-secret projects to help their governments fight the war. The development of radar by British scientists was a particularly important outcome of this new kind of sharply focused research.

As early as 1934, the British Air Ministry set up a committee of scientists and engineers to study the problem of air defense systematically. A leading British expert's calculations on radio waves suggested that the idea of a "death ray" so powerful it could destroy an attacking enemy aircraft was nonsense, but that detection of enemy aircraft by radio waves was theoretically possible. Radio waves emitted at intervals by a transmitter on the ground would bounce off flying aircraft, and a companion receiver on the ground would hear this echo and detect the approaching plane. Experiments went forward, and by 1939 the British had installed a very primitive radar system along the southern and eastern coasts of England.

Immediately after the outbreak of war with Germany in September 1939, the British military enlisted leading academic scientists in an all-out effort to improve the radar system. The basic problem was developing a high-powered transmitter capable of sending very short wavelengths, which could be precisely focused in a beam sweeping the sky like a searchlight. In the summer of 1940, British physicists made the dramatic technical breakthrough that solved this problem of short-wave transmission. The new and radically improved radar system, which was quickly installed, played a key role in Britain's victory in the battle for air supremacy in the fall of 1940. During the war, many different types of radar were developed—for fighter planes, for bombers, for detection of submarines.

After 1945, war-born microwave technology generated endless applications, especially in telecommunications. Microwave transmission carried long-distance conversations, television programs, and messages to and from satellites.

The air war also greatly stimulated the development of jet aircraft and computers. Although the first jet engines were built in the mid-1930s, large-scale government-directed research did not begin until immediately before the war. The challenge was to build a new kind of engine—a jet engine—capable of burning the low-grade "leftovers" of petroleum refining, thereby helping to overcome the desperate shortage of aviation fuel. The task proved extremely difficult and expensive. Only toward the end of the war did fast, high-flying jet fighters become a reality. Quickly adopted for both military and peacetime purposes after the war, jet airplanes contributed to the enormous expansion of commercial aviation in the 1950s.

The problems of air defense also spurred further research on electronic computers, which had barely come into existence before 1939. Computers calculated the complex mathematical relationships between fast-moving planes and antiaircraft shells, to increase the likelihood of a hit.

Wartime needs led to many other major technical breakthroughs. Germany had little oil and was almost completely cut off from foreign supplies. But Germany's scientists and engineers found ways to turn coal into gasoline so that the German war machine did not sputter to a halt.

The most spectacular result of directed scientific research during the war was the atomic bomb. In August 1939, Albert Einstein wrote to President Franklin Roosevelt, stating that recent work in physics suggested that

it may become possible to set up a nuclear chain reaction in a large mass of uranium, by which vast amounts of power and large quantities of new radium-like elements would be generated.... This new phenomenon would also lead to the construction of bombs, and it is conceivable—though much less certain—that extremely powerful bombs of a new type may thus be constructed.[1]

This letter and ongoing experiments by nuclear physicists led to the top-secret Manhattan Project and the decision to build the atomic bomb.

The American government spared no expense to turn a theoretical possibility into a practical reality. A mammoth crash program went forward in several universities and special laboratories, the most important of which was the newly created laboratory at Los Alamos in the wilds of New Mexico. The Los Alamos laboratory was masterfully directed from 1942 by J. Robert Oppenheimer (1904–1967), a professor and theoretical physicist. Its sole objective was to design and build an atomic bomb. Toward that end Oppenheimer assembled a team of brilliant American and European scientists and managed to get them to cooperate effectively. After three years of intensive effort, the first atomic bomb was successfully tested in July 1945. In August 1945, two bombs were dropped on Hiroshima and Nagasaki, ending the war with Japan.

The atomic bomb showed the world both the awesome power and the heavy moral responsibilities of modern science and its high priests. As one of Oppenheimer's troubled colleagues exclaimed while he watched the first mushroom cloud rise over the American desert, "We are all sons-of-bitches now!"[2]

The Rise of Big Science

The spectacular results of directed research during World War Two inspired a new model for science—"Big Science." By combining theoretical work with sophisticated engineering in a large organization, Big Science could attack extremely difficult problems. Solution of these problems led to new and better products for consumers and to new and better weapons for the military. In any event, the assumption was that almost any conceivable technical goal might be attained. Big Science was extremely expensive. Indeed, its appetite for funds was so great that it could be financed only by governments and large corporations. Thus the ties between science and tax-paying society grew very close.

Science became so "big" largely because its equipment grew ever more complex and expensive.

The Apollo Program Astronauts Neil Armstrong, Michael Collins, and Edwin Aldrin, Jr., took off from Florida on July 16, 1969 in the Apollo spacecraft. Astronaut Armstrong was the first man to set foot on the moon, four days later, on July 20. The astronauts splashed down in the Pacific Ocean, and recovery was made by the U.S.S. *Hornet* on July 24. *(Source: National Aeronautics and Space Administration)*

Because many advances depended directly on better instruments, the trend toward bigness went on unabated. This trend was particularly pronounced in atomic physics, perhaps the most prestigious and influential area of modern science. When Rutherford first "split the atom" in 1919, his equipment cost only a few dollars. In the 1930s the price of an accelerator, or "atom smasher," reached $10,000, and the accelerators used in high-energy experiments while the atomic bomb was being built were in the $100,000 range. By 1960, however, when the western European nations pooled their resources in the European Council for Nuclear Research (CERN) to build an accelerator outside of Geneva—an accelerator with power in billions rather than millions of electron volts—the cost had jumped to $30 million. These big accelerators did an amazingly good job of prying atoms apart, and over two hundred different particles have been identified so far. Yet new answers produced new questions, and the logic of ever-more-sophisticated observations demanded ever-more-powerful and ever-more-costly accelerators in the postwar period.

Astronomers followed physicists in the ways of Big Science. Their new eye was the radio telescope, which picked up radio emissions rather than light. In the 1960s the largest of these costly radio telescopes sat atop a mountain and had a bowl a thousand feet wide to focus the radio signals from space. Aeronautical research and development also attained mammoth proportions. The cost of the Anglo-French *Concorde,* the first supersonic passenger airliner, went into the billions. Even ordinary science became big and expensive by historical standards. The least costly laboratory capable of doing useful research in either pure or applied science required around $200,000 a year in the 1960s.

Populous, victorious, and wealthy, the United States took the lead in Big Science after World War Two. Between 1945 and 1965, spending on scientific research and development in the United States grew five times as fast as the national income. By 1965 fully 3 percent of all income in the United States was spent on science. While large American corporations maintained impressive research laboratories, fully three-quarters of all funds spent on scientific research and development in the United States were coming from the government by 1965. It was generally accepted that government should finance science heavily. One wit pointed out that by the mid-1960s the "science policy" of the supposedly conservative Republican party in the

United States was almost identical to that of the supposedly revolutionary Communist party of the Soviet Union.

One of the reasons for the similarity was that science was not demobilized in either country after the war. Indeed, scientists remained a critical part of every major military establishment and, after 1945 as during World War Two, a large portion of all scientific research went for "defense." Jet bombers gave way to rockets, battleships were overtaken by submarines with nuclear warheads, and spy planes were replaced with spy satellites. All such new weapons demanded breakthroughs no less remarkable than those of radar and the first atomic bomb. After 1945 roughly one-quarter of all men and women trained in science and engineering in the West—and perhaps more in the Soviet Union—were employed full-time in the production of weapons to kill other humans.

Sophisticated science, lavish government spending, and military needs all came together in the space race of the 1960s—the most sensational example of Big Science in action after the creation of the atomic bomb. In 1957 the Russians used long-range rockets developed in their nuclear weapons program to put a satellite in orbit. In 1961 they sent the world's first cosmonaut circling the globe. Breaking with President Eisenhower's opposition to an expensive space program, President Kennedy made an all-out U.S. commitment to catch up with the Russians and land a manned spacecraft on the moon "before the decade was out." Harnessing pure science, applied technology, and up to $5 billion a year, the Apollo Program achieved its ambitious objective in 1969. Four more moon landings followed by 1972.

The rapid expansion of government-financed research in the United States attracted many of Europe's best scientists during the 1950s and 1960s. Thoughtful Europeans lamented this "brain drain." In his best seller *The American Challenge* (1967), the French journalist Jean-Jacques Servan-Schreiber warned that Europe was falling hopelessly behind the United States in science and technology. The only hope was to copy American patterns of research before the United States achieved an absolute stranglehold on computers, jet aircraft, atomic energy, and indeed most of the vital dynamic sectors of the late-twentieth-century economy.

In fact, a revitalized Europe was already responding to the American challenge. European countries

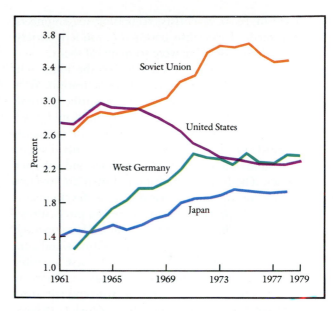

FIGURE 31.1 Research and Development Expenditures as a Percentage of GNP in the United States, Soviet Union, West Germany, and Japan, 1961–1979 While the United States spent less of its national income on research and development after the early 1960s, European nations and Japan spent more. This helped Europe and Japan narrow or even close the technological gap that had existed after the end of World War Two. (*Source: Data Resources, Inc.*)

were beginning to pool their efforts and spend more on science and engineering, as they concentrated on big projects like the *Concorde* supersonic passenger airliner and the peaceful uses of atomic energy. Thus European countries created their own Big Science. By 1974 many European nations were devoting a substantial percentage of their income to research and development and were in the process of achieving equality with the United States in many fields of scientific endeavor (Figure 31.1).

The Life of Scientists and Technologists

The rise of Big Science and of close ties between science and technology greatly altered the lives of scientists. The scientific community grew much larger than ever before: of all the scientists who have ever lived, nine out of ten are still alive today. The astonishing fact is that the number of scientists has been doubling every fifteen years for the past three centuries. There were, therefore, about four times as many scientists in 1975 as in 1945, just as there were a *million* times as many scientists as there were in 1670. Scientists, technologists, engineers, and medical specialists counted in modern society, in part because there were so many of them.

One important consequence of the bigness of science was its high degree of specialization. With close to a hundred thousand scientific journals being published by the 1970s, no one could possibly master a broad field like physics or medicine. Instead, a field like physics was constantly dividing and subdividing into new specialties and subdisciplines. The fifty or one hundred men and women who were truly abreast of the latest developments in a highly specialized field formed an international "invisible college." Cooperating and competing, communicating through special journals and conferences, the leading members of these invisible colleges kept the problems of the subdiscipline under constant attack. Thus intense specialization undoubtedly increased the rates at which both basic knowledge was acquired and practical applications were made.

Highly specialized modern scientists and technologists normally had to work as members of a team. The problems and equipment of Big Science were simply too complicated and expensive for a person to work effectively as an individual researcher. The collaborative "team" character of much of modern scientific research—members of invisible colleges were typically the leaders of such teams—completely changed the work and lifestyle of modern scientists. Old-fashioned, prewar scientists were like professional golfers—lonely individuals who had to make all the shots themselves. Modern scientists and technologists were more like players on American professional football teams. There were owners and directors, coaches and assistant coaches, overpaid stars and unsung heroes, veterans and rookies, kickoff specialists and substitutes, trainers and water boys.

If this parallel seems fanciful, consider the research group of Luis Alvarez at the high-energy physics Radiation Laboratory of the University of California at Berkeley in the late 1960s. This group consisted of more than two hundred people. At the top were Alvarez and about twenty Ph.D.'s, followed by twenty graduate research assistants and fourteen full-time engineers. Almost fifty people were categorized as "technical leadership"—computer programmers, equipment operators, and so on. Finally, there were more than a hundred "technical assistants"—primarily scanners who analyzed photographs showing the tracks of particles after various collisions. A laboratory like that of CERN outside Geneva resembled a small city of several thousand people—scientists, technicians, and every kind of support personnel. A great deal of modern science and technology went on, therefore, in large, well-defined bureaucratic organizations. The individual was very often a small cog in a great machine, a member of a scientific army.

The advent of large-scale scientific bureaucracies led to the emergence of a new group, science managers and research administrators. Such managers generally had scientific backgrounds, but their main tasks were scheduling research, managing people, and seeking money from politicians or financial committees of large corporations. This last function was particularly important, for there were limits to what even the wealthiest governments and corporations would spend for research. Competition for funds was always intense, even in the fat 1960s.

Many science managers were government bureaucrats. These managers doled out funds and "refereed" the scientific teams that were actually playing on the field. Was the *Concorde* supersonic jet too noisy to land in New York City? Did saccharin cause cancer, and should it be banned? The list of potential questions was endless. Beginning in the late 1960s, the number of such referees and the penalties they were imposing seemed to explode, driven forward by public alarm about undesirable side effects of technological advance. More generally, the growth of the scientific bureaucracy suggested how scientists and technologists permeated the entire society and many aspects of life.

Two other changes in the lives of scientists should be noted briefly. One was the difficulty of appraising an individual's contribution to a collaborative team effort. Who deserved the real credit (or blame) for a paper that listed twenty-five physicists as coauthors? Even in a field like chemistry, which remained relatively "small" in its research techniques, more than two-thirds of all papers had two or more authors by the 1970s. Questions of proper recognition within the team effort were thus very complicated and preoccupying to modern scientists.

A second, related change was that modern science became highly, even brutally, competitive. This competitiveness is well depicted in Nobel Prize winner James Watson's fascinating book *The Double Helix,* which tells how in 1953 Watson and an Englishman, Francis Crick, discovered the structure of DNA, the molecule of heredity. A brash young American Ph.D. in his twenties, Watson seemed almost obsessed by the idea that some other research team would find the solution first and thereby deprive him of the fame and fortune he desperately wanted. With so many thousands of like-minded researchers in the wealthy countries of the world, it was hardly surprising that scientific and technical knowledge rushed forward in the postwar era.

TOWARD A NEW SOCIETY

The prodigious expansion of science and technology greatly affected the peoples of the Western world. By creating new products and vastly improved methods of manufacturing and farming, it fueled rapid economic growth and rising standards of living. Moreover, especially in Europe, scientific and technological progress, combined with economic prosperity, went a long way toward creating a whole new society after World War Two.

This new society was given many catchy titles. Some called it the "technocratic society," a society of highly trained specialists and experts. For others, fascinated by the great increase in personal wealth, it was the "affluent society" or the "consumer society." For those struck by the profusion of government-provided social services, it was simply the "welfare state." For still others, it was the "permissive society," where established codes of conduct no longer prevailed. In fact, Western society in the postwar era was all of these: technocratic, affluent, welfare-oriented, and permissive. These characteristics reflected changes in the class structure and indicated undeniable social progress.

The Changing Class Structure

After 1945 European society became more mobile and more democratic. Old class barriers relaxed, and class distinctions became fuzzier.

Changes in the structure of the middle class, directly related to the expansion of science and technology, were particularly influential in the general drift toward a less rigid class structure. The model for the middle class in the nineteenth and early twentieth centuries was the independent, self-employed individual who owned a business or prac-

ticed a liberal profession like law or medicine. Many businesses and professional partnerships were tightly held family firms. Marriage into such a family often provided the best opportunity for an outsider to rise to the top. Ownership of property —usually inherited property—and strong family ties were often the keys to wealth and standing within the middle class.

This traditional pattern, which first changed in the United States and the Soviet Union (for very different reasons) before the Second World War, declined drastically in western Europe after 1945. A new breed of managers and experts rose to replace traditional property owners as the leaders of the middle class. Within large bureaucratic corporations and government, men and women increasingly advanced as individuals and on the basis of merit (and luck). Ability to serve the needs of a

The Double Helix   The giant DNA molecule, which governs heredity in living things, has the form of a double helix, a kind of spiraling ladder with alternating sides of phosphate and sugar. James Watson and Francis Crick discovered the double helix structure of DNA, represented here by the model they are examining. *(Source: MRC Laboratory of Molecular Biology, University of Cambridge)*

A Modern Manager Despite considerable discrimination, women were increasingly found in the expanding middle class of salaried experts after World War Two, working in business, science, and technology. *(Source: Niépce-Rapho/Photo Researchers)*

large organization, which usually depended on special expertise, largely replaced inherited property and family connections in determining an individual's social position in the middle and upper middle class. Social mobility, both upward and downward, increased. At the same time, the middle class grew massively and became harder to define.

There were a number of reasons for these developments. Rapid industrial and technological expansion created in large corporations and government agencies a powerful demand for technologists and managers capable of responding effectively to an ever-more-complicated world. This growing army of specialists—the backbone of the new middle class—could be led effectively only by like-minded individuals, of whom only a few at best could come from the old property-owning families.

Second, the old propertied middle class lost control of many of its formerly family-owned businesses. Even very wealthy families had to call on the general investing public for capital, and heavy inheritance taxes forced sales of stock, further diluting family influence. Many small businesses (including family farms) simply passed out of existence, and their ex-owners joined the ranks of salaried employees. In Germany in 1950, for example, self-employed people formed 33 percent of the labor force, and white-collar workers constituted 20 percent. By 1962 the percentages for these two groups were exactly reversed. Moreover, the wave of nationalization in western and eastern Europe after the Second World War automatically replaced capitalist owners with salaried managers and civil servants in state-owned companies.

Top managers and ranking civil servants therefore represented the model for a new middle class of salaried specialists. Well paid and highly trained, often with backgrounds in science or engineering or accounting, these experts increasingly came from all social classes, even the working class. Pragmatic and realistic, they were primarily concerned with efficiency and practical solutions to concrete problems. Generally, they were not very interested in the old ideological debates about capitalism and socialism, confidently assuming that their skills were indispensable in either system or any combination of the two.

Indeed, the new middle class of experts and managers was an international class, not much different in socialist eastern Europe than in capitalist western Europe and North America. Everywhere successful managers and technocrats passed on the opportunity for all-important advanced education to their children, but only in rare instances could they pass on the positions they had attained. Thus the new middle class, which was based largely on specialized skills and high levels of education, was more open, democratic, and insecure than the old propertied middle class.

The structure of the traditional lower classes also became more flexible and open. There was a mass exodus from farms and the countryside. One of the most traditional and least mobile groups in European society drastically declined: after 1945 the number of peasants declined by more than 50 percent in almost every European country. Meanwhile, because of rapid technological change, the industrial working class ceased to expand, stabilizing at slightly less than one-half of the labor force in wealthy advanced countries. Job opportunities for white-collar and service employees, however, expanded rapidly. Such employees bore a greater resemblance to the new middle class of salaried specialists than to industrial workers, who were better educated and more specialized. Developments within the lower classes contributed, therefore, to the breakdown of rigid social divisions.

Social Security Reforms and Rising Affluence

While the demands of modern technology and big bureaucracies broke down rigid class divisions, European governments, with their new and revitalized political leadership (see page 966), reduced class tensions with a series of social security reforms. Many of these reforms simply strengthened social security measures first pioneered in Bismarck's Germany before World War One. Unemployment and sickness benefits were increased and extended, as were retirement benefits and old-age pensions. Other programs were new.

Britain's Labour government took the lead immediately after the Second World War in establishing a comprehensive national health system; other European governments followed the British example. Depending on the system, patients either received completely free medical care or paid only a very small portion of the total cost.

Most countries also introduced family allowances—direct government grants to parents to help them raise their children. Lower-paid workers generally received the largest allowances, and the rate per child often kept increasing until the third or fourth child. These allowances helped many poor families make ends meet. Most European governments also gave maternity grants and built inexpensive public housing for low-income families and individuals. Other social welfare programs ranged from cash bonuses for getting married in Belgium and Switzerland to subsidized vacations for housewives in Sweden.

It would be wrong to think that the expansion of social security services after World War Two provided for every human need "from cradle to grave," as early advocates of the welfare state hoped and its critics feared. But these social reforms did provide a humane floor of well-being, below which very few individuals could fall in the advanced countries of northern and western Europe. (Social benefits were greatest in the wealthiest nations, such as Sweden, West Germany, and Britain, and less in poorer areas of southern and eastern Europe.)

These reforms also promoted greater social and economic equality. They were expensive, paid for in part by high taxes on the rich. In Britain, for example, where social security benefits for the population at large and taxes on the rich both became quite high, the top 5 percent of the population received about 14 percent of national income after taxes in 1957, as opposed to fully 43 percent in 1913. Thus extensive welfare measures leveled society both by raising the floor and by lowering the ceiling.

The rising standard of living and the spread of standardized, mass-produced consumer goods also worked to level Western society. A hundred years ago, food and drink cost roughly two-thirds of the average family's income in western and northern Europe; by the mid-1960s, they took only about one-third to two-fifths of that family's income. Consumption of traditional staples like bread and potatoes actually declined almost everywhere in Europe after 1945; yet because incomes have risen rapidly, people eat more meat, fish, and dairy products. The goal of adequate and good food was attained almost universally in advanced countries.

But progress introduced new problems. People in Europe and North America were eating too much rather than too little, giving rise to an endless proliferation of diet foods and diet fads. Another problem was that modern consumers often appeared remarkably ignorant of basic nutrition. They stuffed themselves with candy, soft drinks, French fries, and spongy white bread, and frequently got poor value for their money. Finally, the traditional pleasures of eating good food well prepared suffered major declines in the postwar age of fast-food franchises and mass-produced burgers and standardized buns.

The phenomenal expansion of the automobile industry exemplified even more strikingly the emergence of the consumer society. In the United States, automobile ownership was commonplace far down the social scale by the mid-1920s, whereas only the rich could generally afford cars in Europe before the Second World War. In 1948 there were only five million cars in western Europe, and most ordinary people dreamed at most of stepping up from a bicycle to a motorcycle. With the development of cheaper, mass-produced cars, this situation changed rapidly. By 1957 the number of cars had increased to fifteen million, and automobiles had become a standard item of middle-class consumption. By 1965 the number of cars in western Europe had tripled again to forty-four million, and car ownership had come well within the range of better-paid workers.

Europeans took great pleasure in the products of the "gadget revolution" as well. Like Americans,

Sports Fans developed fierce tribal loyalties, finding comradeship and a sense of belonging cheering for their teams. Here Liverpool's famous rooting section goes wild with delight after its team clinches the English soccer championship in 1977. Soccer matches have occasionally degenerated into pitched battles between rival fans. *(Source: Wide World Photos)*

Europeans filled their houses and apartments with washing machines, vacuum cleaners, refrigerators, dishwashers, radios, TVs, and stereos. The purchase of these and other consumer goods was greatly facilitated by installment purchasing, which allowed people to buy on credit. Before World War Two, Europeans had rarely bought "on time." But with the expansion of social security safeguards, reducing the need to accumulate savings for hard times, ordinary people were increasingly willing to take on debt. This change had far-reaching consequences.

Household appliances became necessities for most families. Middle-class women had to do much of their own housework, for young girls avoided domestic service like the plague. Moreover, more women than ever before worked outside the home, and they needed machines to help do household chores as quickly as possible. The power tools of "do-it-yourself" work also became something of a necessity, for few dependable artisans were available for household repairs.

Leisure and recreation occupied an important place in consumer societies. Indeed, with incomes rising and the workweek shrinking from roughly forty-eight hours right after the war to about forty-one hours by the early 1970s, leisure became big business. In addition to ever-popular soccer matches and horse races, movies, and a growing addiction to television, individuals had at their disposal a vast range of commercialized hobbies, most of which could soak up a lot of cash. Newsstands were full of specialized magazines about everything from hunting and photography to knitting and antique collecting. Interest in "culture," as measured by attendance at concerts and exhibitions, also increased. Even so, the commercialization of leisure through standardized manufactured products was striking.

The most astonishing leisure-time development in the consumer society was the blossoming of mass travel and tourism. Before the Second World War, travel for pleasure and relaxation remained a rather aristocratic pastime. Most people had neither the time nor the money for it. But with month-long paid vacations required by law in most European countries, and widespread automobile ownership, beaches and ski resorts came within the reach of the middle class and many workers. At certain times of year, hordes of Europeans surged to the sea or the mountains, and woe to the traveler who had not made arrangements well in advance.

By the late 1960s packaged tours with cheap group flights and bargain hotel accommodations had made even distant lands easily accessible. One-fifth of West Germany's population traveled abroad each year. A French company, the Club Méditerranée, grew rich building imitation Tahitian paradises around the world. At Swedish nudist colonies on secluded West African beaches, secretaries and salespersons from Stockholm fleetingly worshiped the sun in the middle of the long northern winter. Truly, consumerism had come of age.

Renewed Discontent and the Student Revolt

For twenty years after 1945, Europeans were largely preoccupied with the possibilities of economic progress and consumerism. The more democratic class structure also helped to reduce social tension, and ideological conflict went out of style. In the late 1960s, however, sharp criticism and discontent re-emerged. It was a common complaint that Europeans were richer but neither happier nor better. Social conflicts began to appear once more.

Simmering discontent in eastern Europe was not hard to understand. The gradual improvement in the standard of living stood in stark contrast to the ongoing lack of freedom in political and intellectual life and made that lack of freedom all the more distasteful. As will be shown in the next chapter, such dissatisfaction found eloquent expression once again, despite the refinement of techniques of repression in eastern Europe and the willingness of the Soviet Union to crush reform efforts in Czechoslovakia with military might in 1968.

The reappearance of discontent in western Europe was not so easily explained. From the mid-1950s on, western European society was prosperous, democratic, and permissive. Yet this did not prevent growing hostility to the existing order among some children of the new society. Radical students in particular rejected the materialism of their parents and claimed that the new society was repressive and badly flawed. Though these criticisms and the movements they sparked were often ridiculed by the older generation, they reflected some real problems of youth, education, and a society of specialists. They deserve closer attention.

In contrast to the United States, high school and university educations in Europe were limited for centuries to a small elite. That elite consisted mainly of young men and women from the well-to-do classes, along with a sprinkling of scholarship students from humble origins. Whereas 22 percent of the American population was going on to some form of higher education in 1950, only 3 to 4 percent of western European youths were doing so. Moreover, European education was still directed toward traditional fields: literature, law, medicine, and pure science. Its basic goal was to pass on culture and pure science to an elite, and with the exception of law and medicine, applied training for specialists was not considered very important.

After World War Two, public education in western Europe began to change dramatically. Enrollments skyrocketed. By 1960 there were at least three times as many students going to some kind of university as there had been before the war, and the number continued to rise sharply until the 1970s. Holland had ten thousand university students in 1938 and a hundred thousand in 1960. In France 14 percent of young people went to a university in 1965, as opposed to 4.5 percent in 1950. With an increase in scholarships and a growing awareness that higher education was the key to success, European universities became more democratic, opening their doors to more students from the lower middle and lower classes. Finally, in response to the prodigious expansion of science and technology, the curriculum gradually changed. All sorts of new, "practical" fields—from computer science to business administration—appeared alongside the traditional liberal arts and sciences.

The rapid expansion of higher education created problems as well as opportunities for students. Classes were badly overcrowded, and there was little contact with professors. Competition for grades became intense. Moreover, although more "practical" areas of study were added, they were added less quickly than many students wanted. Thus many students felt that they were not getting the kind of education they needed for the modern world and that basic university reforms were absolutely necessary. The emergence of a distinctive "youth culture" also brought students into conflict with those symbols of the older generation and parental authority—professors and school officials.

These tensions within the exploding university population came to a head in the late 1960s and early 1970s. Following in the footsteps of their American counterparts, who pioneered with large-scale student protests in the mid-1960s, European university students rose to challenge their university administrations and even their governments.

The most far-reaching of these revolts occurred in France in 1968. It began at the stark new University of Nanterre in the gloomy industrial suburbs of Paris. Students demanded both changes in the curriculum and a real voice in running the university. The movement spread to the hallowed halls of the medieval Sorbonne in the heart of Paris. Students occupied buildings and took over the university. This takeover led to violent clashes with police, who were ordered in to break up a demonstration that was fast becoming an uprising.

The student radicals appealed to France's industrial workers for help. Rank-and-file workers ignored the advice of their cautious union officials, and a more or less spontaneous general strike spread across France in May 1968. It seemed certain that President De Gaulle's Fifth Republic would collapse. In fact, De Gaulle stiffened, declaring he was in favor of reforms but would oppose

"bedwetting." Securing the firm support of French army commanders in West Germany, he moved troops toward Paris and called for new elections. Thoroughly frightened by the protest-turned-upheaval and fearful that a successful revolution could lead only to an eventual Communist takeover, the masses of France voted for a return to law and order. De Gaulle and his party scored the biggest electoral victory in modern French history, and the mini-revolution collapsed.

Yet the proud De Gaulle and the confident, if old-fashioned, national political revival he represented had been cruelly mocked. In 1969 a tired and discouraged President De Gaulle resigned over a minor issue, and within a year he was dead. For much of the older generation in France, and indeed throughout western Europe, the student revolution of 1968 signaled the end of illusions and the end of an era. Social stability and material progress

Student Protest in Paris   These rock-throwing students in the Latin Quarter of Paris are trying to force education reforms or even to topple De Gaulle's government. Throughout May 1968 students clashed repeatedly with France's tough riot police in bloody street fighting. *(Source: Bruno Barbey/Magnum)*

had resulted in conflict and uncertainty. Under such conditions, all schemes for western European equality with the external superpowers—the United States and the Soviet Union—would have an air of unreality.

The student protest of the 1960s, which peaked in 1968 but echoed well into the 1970s, was due to more than overcrowded classrooms and outdated courses. It reflected a rebirth of romantic revolutionary idealism, which repudiated the quest for ever more consumer goods as stupid and destructive. Student radicalism was also related to the Vietnam War, which led many students in Europe and America to convince themselves that Western civilization was immoral and imperialistic. Finally, the students of the late 1960s were a completely new generation: they had never known anything but prosperity and tranquility, and they had grown bored with both.

The student revolt was also motivated by new perceptions about the new society of highly trained experts. Some reflective young people feared that universities would soon do nothing but turn out docile technocrats both to stock and to serve "the establishment." Others saw the class of highly trained specialists they expected to enter as the new exploited class in society. The remedy to this situation, both groups believed, was "participation"— the democratization of decision making *within* large, specialized bureaucratic organizations. Only in this way would such organizations serve real human needs and not merely exploit the individual and the environment. Thus the often unrealistic and undisciplined student radicals tried to answer a vital question: how was the complex new society of specialized experts to be made humane and responsive?

WOMEN AND THE FAMILY

The growing emancipation of women in Europe and North America was unquestionably one of the most important developments after the Second World War. This development gathered speed in the 1960s and reached a climax in the mid-1970s. Women demanded and won new rights. Having shared fully in the postwar education revolution, women were better educated than ever before. They took advantage of the need for trained experts in a more fluid society and moved into areas of employment formerly closed to them. Married women in particular became much more likely to work outside the home than they had been a few short years earlier. Women no longer had to fatalistically accept child bearing and child rearing, for if they wished they could use modern techniques of contraception to control the number and spacing of their offspring. In short, women became more equal and independent, less confined and stereotyped. A major transformation was in process.

The changing position of women altered the modern family. Since the emancipation of women is still incomplete, it is impossible to say for certain whether some major revolution has occurred within the family. Nevertheless, as women today consolidate and expand the breakthroughs of the 1960s and early 1970s, it seems clear that the family has experienced some fundamental reorientations. This becomes apparent if we examine women's traditional role in the home and then women's new roles outside the home in the postwar era.

Marriage and Motherhood

Before the Industrial Revolution, most men and women married late, and substantial numbers never married at all. Once a woman was married, though, she normally bore several children, of whom a third to a half would not survive to adulthood. Moreover, many women died in childbirth. With the growth of industry and urban society, people began to marry earlier, and fewer remained unmarried. As industrial development led to higher incomes and better diets, more children survived to adulthood, and population grew rapidly in the nineteenth century. By the late nineteenth century, contraception within marriage was spreading.

In the twentieth century, and especially after World War Two, these trends continued. In the postwar era, women continued to marry earlier. In Sweden, for example, the average age of first marriage dropped steadily from twenty-six in the early 1940s to twenty-three in the late 1960s. Moreover, more than nine out of ten women were marrying at least once, usually in their early twenties. Marriage was never more in vogue than in the generation after the Second World War. The triumph of romantic attraction over financial calculation seemed complete, and perhaps never before had young couples expected so much emotional satisfaction from matrimony.

After marrying early, the typical woman in Europe, the United States, and Canada had her children quickly. Whereas women in the more distant past very often had children as long as they were fertile, women in Europe and North America were having about 80 percent of their children before they were thirty. As for family size, the "baby boom" that lasted until the early 1960s made for fairly rapid population growth of 1 to 1.5 percent per year in many European countries. In the 1960s, however, the long-term decline in birthrates resumed. Surveys in northern and western Europe began to reveal that most women believed that two instead of three children were ideal.

Women must have 2.1 children on the average if total population is to remain constant over the long term. Indeed, the number of births fell so sharply in the 1960s that total population practically stopped growing in many European countries. By the mid-1970s more people were dying each year than were being born in Austria, East Germany, West Germany, and Luxembourg, where total numbers actually declined. The United States followed the same trend; the birthrate declined from twenty-five per thousand in 1957 to fifteen per thousand in 1973, and it recovered slightly thereafter only because the baby boomers were reaching child-bearing age, not because individual women were having more children. Since the American death rate has remained practically unchanged, the rate of population growth from natural increase (that is, excluding immigration) dropped by two-thirds, from 1.5 percent to 0.6 percent per year between the 1950s and the 1970s. The population of Africa, Asia, and Latin America was still growing very rapidly from natural increase, but that was certainly not true for most European countries and countries of predominately European ancestry.

The culmination of the trends toward early, almost-universal marriage and small family size in wealthy societies had revolutionary implications for women. An examination of these implications suggests why the emancipation of women—sooner or later—was almost assuredly built into the structure of modern life.

The main point is that motherhood occupied a much smaller portion of a woman's life than at the beginning of this century. The average woman's life expectancy at birth increased from about fifty years in 1900 to about seventy-five years in 1970. At the same time, women were increasingly compressing childbearing into the decade between their twentieth and thirtieth birthdays, instead of bearing children until they were in their late thirties. By the early 1970s about half of Western women, and more than half in some nations, were having their last baby by the age of twenty-six or twenty-seven. When the youngest child trooped off to kindergarten, the average mother still had more than forty years of life in front of her.

This was a momentous change. Throughout history, most married women had been defined to a considerable extent as mothers. Motherhood was very demanding: pregnancy followed pregnancy, and there were many children to nurse, guide, and bury. Now, however, the years devoted to having babies and caring for young children represented at most a seventh of the average woman's life. Motherhood had become a relatively short phase in most women's total life span. Perhaps a good deal of the frustration that many women felt in the 1960s and 1970s was due to the fact that their traditional role as mothers no longer absorbed the energies of a lifetime, and new roles in the male-dominated world outside the family were opening up slowly.

A related revolutionary change for women was that the age-old biological link between sexual intercourse and motherhood was severed. As is well known, beginning in the early 1960s many women chose to gain effective control over pregnancy with oral contraceptives and intrauterine devices. They no longer relied on undependable males and their undependable methods. Less well known are certain physiological facts, which help explain why many women in the advanced countries did elect to practice birth control at some point in their lives.

Women in the postwar era were capable of having children for many more years than their forebears. The age of *menarche*—the age at which girls begin to menstruate and become fertile—had dropped from about seventeen years in the early nineteenth century to about thirteen years by the 1970s. At the same time, the age at onset of menopause rose. At the beginning of the eighteenth century, menopause occurred at about age thirty-six, on average; it now occurred at about fifty. These physiological changes over time are poorly understood, but they were apparently due to better diets and living standards, which also substantially increased people's height and size. In any event, many modern women chose to separate their sexual lives from their awesome reproductive power, which had increased with the lengthening of the

Britain's Women on the March   After World War Two, more and more women entered the labor market as full-time workers. Although most Western women had full political rights by this time, they continued to struggle for economic rights, as these marchers through London's Piccadilly demonstrate. *(Source: Globe Photos)*

time in which they were capable of bearing children. In doing so, these women became free to pursue sensual pleasure for its own sake. The consequences of this revolutionary development will continue to work themselves out for a long time.

Women at Work

For centuries before the Industrial Revolution, ordinary women were highly productive members of society. They often labored for years before marriage to accumulate the necessary dowry. Once married, women worked hard on farms and in home industries while bearing and caring for their large families. With the growth of modern industry and large cities, young women continued to work as wage earners. But once a poor woman married, she typically stopped working in a factory or a

shop, struggling instead to earn money at home by practicing some low-paid craft as she looked after her children. In the middle classes, it was a rare and tough-minded woman who worked outside the home for wages, although charity work was socially acceptable.

Since the beginning of the twentieth century and especially after World War Two, the situation has changed dramatically once again. Opportunities for women of modest means to earn cash income within the home practically disappeared. Piano teachers, novelists, and part-time typists still worked at home as independent contractors, but the ever-greater complexity of the modern wage-based economy and its sophisticated technology meant that almost all would-be wage earners had to turn elsewhere. Moreover, motherhood took less and less time, so that the full-time mother-housewife had less and less economic value for families.

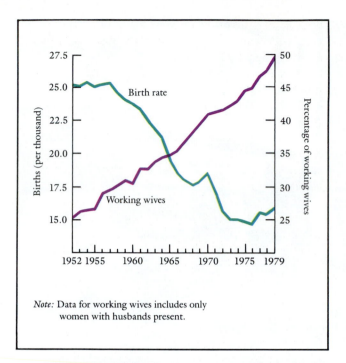

FIGURE 31.2 The Decline of the Birthrate and the Increase of Working Wives in the United States, 1952–1979 The challenge of working away from home encouraged American wives to prefer fewer children and helped to lower the birthrate.

Thus the reduction of home-centered work and child care resulted in a sharp rise across Europe and North America in the number of married women who were full-time wage earners.

In communist countries, the trend went the furthest. In the Soviet Union, most married women worked outside the home; there women accounted for almost half of all employed persons in the postwar era. In noncommunist western Europe and North America, there was a good deal of variety, depending on whether married women had traditionally worked outside the home, as in France or Sweden, or stayed at home, as in Belgium and Switzerland. Nevertheless, the percentage of married women who worked rose sharply in all countries, from a range of roughly 20 to 25 percent in 1950 to a range of 35 to 60 percent in the 1970s. This rise was particularly dramatic in the United States, where married women were twice as likely to be employed in 1979 as they were in 1952.

The dramatic growth of employment among married women was a development whose ultimate effects are still unknown. Nevertheless, it seems clear that the rising employment of married women was a powerful force in the drive for women's equality and emancipation. Take the critical matter of widespread discrimination between men and women in pay, occupation, and advancement. The young unmarried woman of eighty years ago generally accepted such injustices. She thought of them as temporary nuisances and looked forward to marriage and motherhood for fulfillment. In the postwar era, a married wage earner in her thirties developed a totally different perspective. Employment became a permanent condition within which she, like her male counterpart, sought not only income but psychological satisfaction as well. Sexism and discrimination quickly became increasingly loathsome and evoked that sense of injustice that drives revolutions and reforms. The "movement" spread, winning converts among the young and newly awakened.

Rising employment for married women was a factor in the decline of the birthrate (Figure 31.2). Women who worked had significantly fewer children than women of the same age who did not. Moreover, survey research showed that young women who had worked and intended to work again revised downward the number of children they expected to have after the first lovable but time-consuming baby was born. One reason was obvious: raising a family while holding down a full-time job was a tremendous challenge and often resulted in the woman's being grossly overworked. The fatiguing, often frustrating multiple demands of job, motherhood, and marriage simply became more manageable with fewer children.

Another reason for the decline of the birthrate was that motherhood interrupted a woman's career. The majority of women in Western countries preferred or were forced to accept—interpretations varied—staying at home for a minimum of two or three years while their children were small. The longer the break in employment, the more a woman's career suffered. Women consistently earned less than men partly because they were employed less continuously and thus did not keep moving steadily up the bureaucratic ladders of large organizations.

Because most Western countries did little to help women in the problem of re-employment after their children were a little older, some women came to advocate the pattern of career and family typically found in communist eastern Europe. There, women were usually employed continuously until they retired. There were no career-complicating interruptions for extended mothering. Instead, a woman in a communist country received as her right up to three months of maternity leave to care for her newborn infant and recover her strength. Then she returned to her job, leaving her baby in the care of a state-run nursery or, more frequently, a retired relative or neighbor. By the 1970s some western European countries were beginning to provide well-defined maternity leaves as part of their social security systems. The United States lagged far behind in this area.

What the increasing numbers of career-minded women with independent, self-assertive spirits meant for marriage and relations between the sexes was by no means clear. As we have seen, marriage remained an almost universal experience. More-over, the decline of informal village and neighborhood socializing with the advent of the automobile and suburban living made most wives and husbands more dependent than ever on their mates (and their children) for their emotional needs. Never had more been demanded from hearth and home.

The great increase in life expectancy for males and females by itself made marriage more stable, at least in one sense. The average couple was living together for forty years before the death of one dissolved the union, as opposed to less than twenty years together at the beginning of the century. And husbands were slowly getting the message that the old rule of leaving the dishes and diapers exclusively to wives needed rewriting, especially in two-income families. In short, the nuclear family

A Working Mother waves good-bye to her child in this scene from contemporary American life. Young couples seeking to own a large, elegant house, like the one shown here, almost always need the combined income of two wage earners. *(Source: Richard Hutchings/Photo Researchers)*

showed great strength, adapting itself once again to changing values and changing conditions.

At the same time, contrary trends clearly emerged in the late 1960s and carried over strongly into the 1970s and 1980s. Everywhere the divorce rate kept moving up: it doubled in the United States, for example, between 1970 and 1980. Nearly everywhere in Western countries, except in southern Europe, over one-quarter of marriages ended in divorce by the early 1980s; in Sweden the proportion was one in two. Studies of marriage showed that working women were considerably more likely to get divorced than nonworking women. The independent working woman could more easily afford to leave if dissatisfied, while the no-income career housewife was more nearly locked into her situation.

Beginning in the very late 1960s, the marriage rate also began to plunge in a number of Western countries, and it continued to decline throughout the 1970s before stabilizing in the 1980s. Both women and men married progressively later, and those who never married increased as a portion of the population. As the number of singles grew, there was also a considerable increase in the number of unmarried couples living together, reminiscent of patterns among the European working classes in the early days of industrialization. Some observers argued that young women and men were only postponing marriage because of less robust economic conditions. Others contended that marriage, after its long rise, was finally in retreat in the face of growing careerism and acceptance of new, less structured relations between (and within) the sexes. More fundamentally, falling birthrates, more married women in the workplace, later marriage, and increased divorce (and remarriage) rates were all related to the growing emancipation of women. They were all part of a complicated constellation of striking changes, which strongly suggested that a major break with the past had taken place in marriage patterns and family relationships.

SUMMARY

This chapter has examined the major postwar social changes that accompanied the political recovery and economic expansion discussed in Chapter 30. These social changes were profound. Science combined with technology, often under government

direction, to fulfill the loftiest hopes of its enthusiasts and achieve amazing success. The triumphs of applied science contributed not only to economic expansion but also to a more fluid, less antagonistic class structure, in which specialized education was the high road to advancement, regardless of the political system. Within the prosperous, increasingly technocratic society, women asserted themselves. Beginning in the 1960s, they moved increasingly into the labor market and gave birth to fewer children. In doing so, women began striking off in a new direction, a trend that has continued to this day. Their greater commitment to employment and their decision to raise fewer children—a social pattern in sharp contrast to that of the late 1940s and 1950s—foretold the more general break in Western history that occurred shortly thereafter, as will be shown in Chapter 32.

NOTES

1. Quoted in J. Ziman, *The Force of Knowledge: The Scientific Dimension of Society* (Cambridge: Cambridge University Press, 1976), p. 128.
2. Quoted in S. Toulmin, *The Twentieth Century: A Promethean Age,* ed. A. Bullock (London: Thames & Hudson, 1971), p. 294.

SUGGESTED READING

Ziman's volume cited in the Notes, which has an excellent bibliography, is a penetrating look at science by a leading physicist. C. P. Snow's widely discussed book, *The Two Cultures and the Scientific Revolution,* rev. ed. (1963), explores the gap between scientists and nonscientists. A. Toffler, *Future Shock* (1970), is an interesting but exaggerated best seller, which claims that many contemporary psychological problems are due to overly rapid technical and scientific development. J. Ellul, *The Technological Society* (1964), is also highly critical of technical progress, while D. S. Landes, *The Unbound Prometheus: Technological Change and Industrial Development in Western Europe from 1750 to the Present* (1969), remains enthusiastic. Two more stimulating works on technology are J. J. Servan-Schreiber, *The World Challenge* (1981), and H. Jacoby, *The Bureaucratization of the World* (1973). A. Bramwell, *Ecology in the Twentieth Century: A History* (1989), examines negative aspects of technical and industrial development.

In addition to studies cited in the Suggested Reading for Chapter 30, A. Simpson, *The New Europeans* (1968), is a good guide to contemporary Western society. Two engaging books on recent intellectual developments are J. Barzun, *The House of Intellect* (1959), and R. Stromberg, *After Everything: Western Intellectual History Since 1945* (1970). L. Wylie, *Village in the Vauclause,* rev. ed. (1964), and P. J. Hélias, *The Horse of Pride* (1980), provide fascinating pictures of life in the French village. A. Kriegel's *The French Communists* (1972) and *Eurocommunism* (1978) are also recommended. A. Touraine, *The May Movement* (1971), is sympathetic toward the French student revolt, while the noted sociologist R. Aron, in *The Elusive Revolution* (1969), is highly critical. F. Zweig, *The Worker in an Affluent Society* (1961), probes family life and economic circumstances in the British working class on the basis of extensive interviews. R. E. Tyrrell, ed., *The Future That Doesn't Work* (1977), is a polemical but absorbing attack on British socialism. W. Hollstein, *Europe in the Making* (1973), is a fervent plea to integrate Europe by a former top official of the Common Market. The magazines *Encounter, Commentary,* and *The Economist* often carry interesting articles on major social and political trends, as do *Time* and *Newsweek.*

E. Sullerot, *Women, Society and Change* (1971), is an outstanding introduction to women's evolving role. R. Patia, ed., *Women in the Modern World* (1967), compares women's situations in many countries. Two other influential books on women and their new awareness are S. de Beauvoir, *The Second Sex* (1962), and B. Friedan, *The Feminine Mystique* (1963). These may be compared with C. Lasch, *Haven in a Heartless World* (1977), and A. Cherlin, *Marriage, Divorce, Remarriage* (1981), which interpret changes in the American family. P. Robinson, *The Modernization of Sex* (1976), tells the fascinating story of the American investigators who helped change public attitudes by studying human sexual relations "scientifically."

On feminism in general, see B. Smith, *Changing Lives: Women in European History Since 1700* (1989), which provides a good overview and a current bibliography, and N. Cott, *The Grounding of Modern Feminism* (1987). The women's movement in Italy is considered in L. Birnbaum, *Liberazione de la Donna* (1986), which is written in English despite the Italian title. C. Duchen, *Feminism in France: From May '68 to Mitterrand* (1986), is also recommended. Good studies on British women include E. Wilson, *Only Halfway to Paradise: Women in Postwar Britain, 1945–1968* (1980), and M. Barrett, *Women's Opposition Today* (1980). C. Goldin, *Understanding the Gender Gap: An Economic History of American Women* (1989), provides a provocative economic analysis of women's issues.

32

The Recent Past, 1968 to the Present

*S*ometime during the late 1960s or early 1970s, the postwar era came to an end. With fits and starts, a new age opened, as postwar certitudes like domestic political stability, social harmony, and continuous economic improvement evaporated. In any event, that is how this historian reads the most recent past. Others may form different judgments, for we are simply too close to the postwar era to gain vital perspective on the period that has succeeded it. As Voltaire once said, "The man who ventures to write contemporary history must expect to be attacked for everything he has said and everything he has not said."[1]

Yet the historian must take a stand. We have already examined some indications of the end of the postwar era. Fundamental changes within the family, featuring new roles for women, gathered momentum in the late 1960s. The mini-revolution of 1968 was a fundamental turning point in recent French history, symptomatic of a general rebirth of political instability and even crisis in several leading nations. Above all, the astonishing postwar economic advance, unparalleled in its rapidity and consistency, came to an abrupt halt. Old, almost forgotten, problems like high unemployment, expensive energy, and international monetary instability suddenly re-emerged, and the buoyant self-confidence of the postwar era disappeared.

Finally, the end of the postwar era saw a gradual, groping march toward a new era in East-West relations, as renewed efforts to reduce cold war tensions and to liberalize Communist eastern Europe often dominated the headlines. These efforts achieved some success in the 1970s, and after renewed cold war competition in the early 1980s they reached fruition as the Soviet Union entered a period of sweeping change and communist rule collapsed in the satellite states of eastern Europe. The tremendous improvement in East-West relations provided a spectacular counterbalance to the long years of economic difficulties, which remained serious in the late 1980s, especially in eastern Europe.

In an attempt to make sense out of a turbulent recent past, which merges with an uncertain present, this chapter will focus on three questions of fundamental importance.

- First, why, after a generation, did the world economy shift into reverse gear, and what were some of the social consequences of that shift?
- Second, what were the most striking political developments within the nations of the Atlantic alliance? Specifically, how did West Germany take the initiative in trying to negotiate an enduring reconciliation with its communist neighbors, and why did the United States enter into a time of troubles before seeking to reassert its strength and leadership in the 1980s?
- Third, how did these changes interact with the evolution of the Soviet bloc?

Finally, the chapter will close with the astonishing changes of the Gorbachev era and with some reflections on the future.

THE TROUBLED ECONOMY

The energy crisis looms large in the sudden transition from almost automatic postwar growth to serious economic difficulties in the 1970s and 1980s. The first surge in oil prices in 1973 stunned the international economy, and the second surge in 1979 led to the deepest recession since the 1930s. The collapse of the postwar monetary system in 1971 and the rapid accumulation of international debts also caused heavy long-term damage. The social consequences of harder times were profound and many-sided.

Money and Oil

During the Second World War, British and American leaders were convinced that international financial disorder after 1918 had contributed mightily to economic problems, the Great Depression, and renewed global warfare. They were determined not to repeat their mistakes, and in the Bretton Woods Agreement of 1944 they laid the foundations for a new international monetary system, which proved instrumental in the unprecedented postwar boom.

The new system, operating through the World Bank and the International Monetary Fund, was based on the American dollar, which was supposed to be "as good as gold" because foreign governments could always exchange dollars for gold at $35 an ounce. The United States proceeded to make needed dollars readily available to the rest of the world, so readily that by early 1971 it had only $11 billion in gold left in Fort Knox and Europe had accumulated 50 billion American dollars. The result was a classic, long-overdue "run on the bank" in 1971, as foreigners panicked and raced to exchange their dollars for gold. President Richard Nixon was forced to stop the sale of American gold. The price of gold then soared on world markets, and the value of the dollar declined. Fixed rates of exchange were abandoned, and great uncertainty replaced postwar predictability in international trade and finance.

Even more serious was the dramatic reversal in the price and availability of energy. As described in Chapter 22, coal-fired steam engines broke the bottleneck of chronically inadequate energy in the late-eighteenth-century economy, making possible the Industrial Revolution and improved living standards in the nineteenth century. In the twentieth century, petroleum proved its worth, and the great postwar boom was fueled by cheap oil, especially in western Europe. Cheap oil from the Middle East permitted energy-intensive industries—automobiles, chemicals, and electric power—to expand rapidly and lead other sectors of the economy forward. More generally, cheap oil and cheap energy encouraged businesses to invest massively in machinery and improved technology. This investment enabled workers to produce more and allowed a steady rise in the standard of living without much inflation.

Saudi Riches   Saudi Arabia has enormous oil reserves, making it one of the most influential members of the Organization of Petroleum Exporting Countries and giving it one of the world's highest per capita incomes. Oil has also made rich men of Prince Fahd and King Khalid, shown here. *(Source: Robert Azzi/Woodfin Camp & Associates)*

In the 1950s and 1960s, the main oil-exporting countries, grouped together in the Arab-dominated Organization of Petroleum Exporting Countries (OPEC), had watched the price of crude oil decline consistently compared to the price of manufactured goods, as the Western oil companies vigorously expanded production and kept prices low to win users of coal to petroleum (Map 32.1). The Egyptian leader Nasser argued that Arab countries should manipulate oil prices to increase their revenues and also to strike at Israel and its Western allies. But Egypt lacked oil and Nasser failed. Colonel Muammar Khadafy of Libya proved more successful. He won important concessions from Western nations and oil companies in the early 1970s, and his example activated the OPEC countries. In 1971 OPEC for the first time presented a united front against the oil companies and obtained a solid price increase. The stage was set for the revolution in energy prices during the fourth Arab-Israeli war in October 1973.

The war began on the solemn Sabbath celebration of Yom Kippur, or the Day of Atonement, the holiest day in the Jewish calendar. Egypt and Syria launched a surprise attack on an unsuspecting Israel, breaking through defense positions and destroying a large part of the Israeli air force. In response to urgent pleas, the United States airlifted $2.2 billion of its most sophisticated weapons to Israel, which accepted a cease-fire after its successful counterattack had encircled much of the Egyptian army. Surprisingly, the Yom Kippur War eventually led to peace between Egypt and Israel. Egypt's initial military victories greatly enhanced the power and prestige of General Anwar Sadat (1918–1981), Nasser's successor. This advantage enabled the realistic Sadat to achieve in 1979 the negotiated settlement with Israel that he had long desired.

In the first days of the war, the Arab (and non-Arab) oil producers in OPEC placed an embargo on oil shipments to the United States and the Netherlands, in retaliation for their support of Israel. They also cut production and raised prices by 70 percent, ostensibly to prevent Europe from sharing oil with the United States. In reality, greed and a

MAP 32.1 OPEC and the World Oil Trade   Though much of the world depends on imported oil, Western Europe and Japan are OPEC's biggest customers. What major oil exporters remain outside of OPEC?

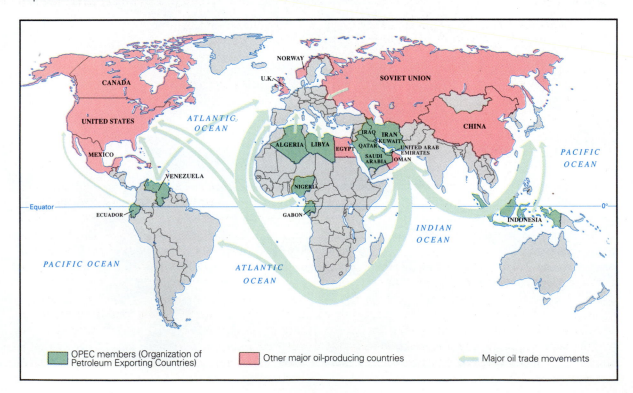

The Egyptian-Israeli Peace Treaty   of 1979 is celebrated by the men who made it possible: Egypt's President Anwar al-Sadat, U.S. President Jimmy Carter, and Israeli Prime Minister Menachem Begin. Egypt recognized Israel's right to exist and established normal diplomatic relations, while Israel agreed to withdraw from Egyptian territory occupied in the Six-Day War of 1967. *(Source: National Archives and Records Administration)*

desire for revenge against the West took over: a second increase in December, after the cease-fire, meant that crude oil prices quadrupled in less than a year. It was widely realized that OPEC's brutal action was economically destructive, but the world's major powers did nothing. The Soviet Union was a great oil exporter and benefited directly, while a cautious western Europe looked to the United States for leadership. But the United States was immobilized, its attention absorbed by the Watergate crisis (see page 1020). Thus governments, companies, and individuals were left to deal piecemeal and manage as best they could with the so-called oil shock—a "shock" that really turned out to be an earthquake.

Inflation, Debt, and Unemployment

Coming close on the heels of upheaval in the international monetary system, the price revolution in energy sources plunged the world into its worst economic decline since the 1930s. The energy-intensive industries that had driven the economy up in the 1950s and 1960s now dragged it down in the mid-1970s. Yet, while industrial output fell, soaring energy costs sent prices surging. "Stagflation"—the unexpected combination of economic stagnation and rapid inflation—developed to bedevil the public and baffle economists. Unemployment rose, while productivity and living standards declined.

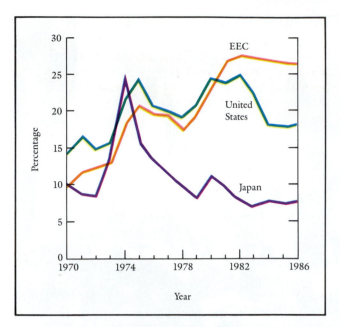

FIGURE 32.1 The Misery Index, 1970–1985 Combining rates of unemployment and inflation provided a simple but effective measure of economic hardship. This particular index represents the sum of two times the unemployment rate plus the inflation rate, reflecting the widespread belief that joblessness causes more suffering than higher prices. EEC = European Economic Community, or Common Market countries. *(Source: OECD data, as given in* The Economist, *June 15, 1985, p. 69.)*

But no cycle lasts forever, and by 1976 a modest recovery was in progress. People were learning to save energy, turning down thermostats, and buying smaller cars. Optimists argued that the challenge of redesigning lifestyles to cope with expensive energy actually represented a great opportunity.

Iran's Islamic revolution in 1978 and 1979 confounded these hopes, at least in the short run. Iranian oil production collapsed, OPEC again doubled the price of crude oil, and the world economy succumbed to its second oil shock. Once again, unemployment and inflation rose dramatically before another recovery began in 1982, driven by a reversal in oil prices, falling interest rates, and large U.S. trade and budget deficits. But the recovery was very uneven. In the summer of 1985, the unemployment rate in western Europe rose to its highest levels since the Great Depression. Fully nineteen million people were unemployed. Although unemployment declined somewhat in the late 1980s, large numbers of people remained out of work.

Many means were devised in the 1970s to measure the troubled economy, but perhaps none was more telling than the "misery index." First used with considerable effect by candidate Jimmy Carter in the 1976 U.S. presidential debates, the misery index combined rates of inflation and unemployment in a single, powerfully emotional number. Figure 32.1 presents a comparison of misery indexes for the United States and the Common Market countries between 1970 and 1986. As may be seen, "misery" increased on both sides of the Atlantic, but the increase was substantially greater in western Europe. This helps explain why these hard times—often referred to by Europeans simply as "the crisis"—probably had an even greater psychological impact on Europeans than on Americans.

Nor was the Soviet bloc spared. Both the Soviet Union and the satellite states of its eastern European empire did less and less well: annual rates of economic growth fell from 6 to 7 percent in the late 1960s to 2 to 3 percent in 1980. This performance was no worse than that of most Western countries, but it mocked the long-standing propaganda boast that communist countries would "catch and surpass the capitalistic West," a phrase that was quietly dropped in favor of less humorous slogans.

Debts and deficits piled up quickly in the troubled economy of the 1970s and 1980s. In the first place, the price hikes of 1973 required a massive global transfer of wealth to the OPEC countries from both rich and poor nations. Like individual consumers suddenly faced with a financial emergency, countries scrambled to borrow to pay their greatly increased fuel bills. Poor countries, especially, turned to the big private international banks. These banks received deposits—the so-called petrodollars—from OPEC members and lent them back out to poor countries so that these nations could pay their oil bills. This circular flow averted total collapse, but there was a high price to pay in the form of a rapid expansion of international debt.

Rich nations also went on a borrowing binge. Almost everywhere they ran up big debts to pay for imported oil and also to maintain social welfare services, as their economies declined and tax receipts fell. Western consumers also joined the race for ever-higher levels of debt. Borrowing to buy before prices rose seemed smart in the 1970s, and that attitude carried over into the 1980s. Like burgeoning government debt, a record-high level of consumer debt was a two-edged sword. It sustained current economic activity but quite possibly posed serious repayment problems, an appropriately ambiguous reflection of the troubled economy.

Some Social Consequences

The most pervasive consequences of recent economic stagnation were probably psychological and attitudinal. Optimism gave way to pessimism; romantic utopianism yielded to sober realism. This drastic change in mood—a complete surprise only to those who had never studied history—affected states, institutions, and individuals in countless ways.

To be sure, there were heartbreaking human tragedies—lost jobs, bankruptcies, and mental breakdowns. But, on the whole, the welfare system fashioned in the postwar era prevented mass suffering and degradation. Extended benefits for the unemployed, pensions for the aged, free medical care for the needy, surplus food and special allowances for parents with children—all these and a host of lesser supports did their part. The responsive, socially concerned national state undoubtedly contributed to the preservation of political stability and democracy in the face of economic difficulties, difficulties that might have brought revolution and dictatorship in earlier times.

The energetic response of governments to social needs helps explain the sharp increase in total government spending in most countries during the 1970s and 1980s. In 1982 western European governments spent an average of more than one-half of gross national income, as compared to only 37 percent fifteen years earlier. In the United States, the combined share of federal, state, and local government expenditures rose from 31 to 35 percent in the same years. The role of government in everyday life became more important.

In all countries, people were much more willing to see their governments increase spending than raise taxes. This imbalance contributed to the rapid growth of budget deficits, national debts, and inflation. By the late 1970s a powerful reaction to government's ever-increasing role set in, and Western governments were gradually forced to introduce austerity measures to slow the seemingly inexorable growth of public spending and the welfare state. The partially successful efforts of Margaret Thatcher in Britain and Ronald Reagan in the United States to limit the growth of social programs absorbed the attention of the English-speaking world, but François Mitterrand of France was the temporary exception who proved the general rule. After his election as president in 1981, Mitterrand led his Socialist party and Communist allies on a vast program of nationalization and public investment designed to spend France out of economic stagnation. By 1983 this attempt had clearly failed. Mitterrand's Socialist government was then compelled to impose a wide variety of austerity measures and to maintain those policies for the rest of the decade. The success of Thatcher, Reagan, and then Mitterrand in imposing antispending, antiwelfare policies led some observers to conclude, no doubt prematurely, that socialism had simply died in the West in the 1980s.

When governments were eventually forced to restrain spending, Big Science was often singled out for cuts, unless its ties to the military were very direct. The problems of CERN were a good example. Formed to pool western European efforts in high-energy particle physics (see page 992), CERN succeeded admirably in stealing the lead from the United States in this exciting but esoteric and uncommercial field. But the costs were truly enormous. In the 1980s CERN was increasingly attacked as an extravagant misallocation of scarce resources at a time when new fields, such as computers and genetic research, were bursting with scientific opportunities that offered mouth-watering commercial applications. More generally, tighter funding for Big Science accelerated the ongoing computer revolution. That revolution thrived on the diffusion of unprecedented computational and informational capacity to small research groups and private businesses, which were both cause and effect of the revolution itself.

Individuals felt the impact of austerity even earlier, for unlike governments they could not pay their bills by printing money and going ever further into debt. The energy crisis forced them to reexamine not only their fuel bills, but the whole pattern of self-indulgent materialism in the postwar era as well. The result was a leaner, tougher lifestyle, featuring more attention to nutrition and a passion for exercise. Correspondingly, there was less blind reliance on medical science for good health and a growing awareness that individuals must accept a large portion of the responsibility for illness and disease. More people began to realize that they could substantially increase their life spans simply by eating regular meals, sleeping seven or eight hours each night, exercising two or three times a week, maintaining moderate weight, forgoing smoking, and using alcohol only in moderation. A forty-five-year-old American male who practiced three or fewer of these habits could expect to live to be sixty-seven; one who adhered to five or six could expect to live eleven more years.

Economic troubles also strengthened existing trends within the family. Both men and women were encouraged to postpone marriage until they had put their careers on a firm foundation, so the age of marriage rose sharply for both sexes in many Western countries. Indeed, the very real threat of unemployment—or "underemployment" in a dead-end job—seemed to shape the outlook of a whole generation. The students of the 1980s were serious, practical, and often conservative. As one young woman at a French university told a reporter in 1985, "Jobs are the big worry now, so everyone wants to learn something practical."[2] In France, as elsewhere, it was an astonishing shift from the romantic visions and political activism of the late 1960s.

Harder times meant that ever-more women did work after they married. In the United States, 66 percent of all married women held jobs in 1986, as opposed to 55 percent in 1979 and 46 percent in 1973. New attitudes related to personal fulfillment were one reason for the continuing increase, especially for well-educated, upper-middle-class women. But for the vast majority of married women—the four-fifths who fell below the top 20 percent—economic necessity also played a major role.

Many wives in poor and middle-class families simply had to work, because after 1973 the average husband was earning less after the effects of continuous inflation were taken into account. The average inflation-adjusted wage for men in the United States declined to $26,000 in 1986, as opposed to $26,700 in 1979 and $28,600 in 1973. The per-

"The New Poor" Economic crisis and prolonged unemployment in the early 1980s reduced many from modest affluence to harsh poverty, creating a class of new poor. This photograph captures that human tragedy. After two years of unemployment, this homeless French office worker must sleep each night in a makeshift shelter for the destitute. *(Source: Dennis Stock/Magnum)*

centage decline for the large group of American men with a high school degree or less education was substantially greater in these years.[3] As in the preindustrial era, the wife's labor provided the margin of survival for millions of hard-pressed families.

THE ATLANTIC ALLIANCE

Forged in the late 1940s to rebuild Europe and prevent possible Soviet expansion beyond the iron curtain, the Atlantic alliance—formally expressed in the North Atlantic Treaty Organization (NATO)—remained an enduring reality in the face of economic difficulties. But the alliance was neither static nor monolithic, and its evolution reflected major developments within the member states. Those in West Germany and the United States were of critical importance.

Germany's Eastern Initiative

The turning points of history are sometimes captured in dramatic moments rich in symbolism. So it was in December 1970, when West German Chancellor Willy Brandt flew to Poland for the signing of a historic treaty of reconciliation. Brandt laid a wreath at the tomb of the Polish unknown soldier and another at the monument commemorating the armed uprising of Warsaw's Jewish ghetto against occupying Nazi armies, after which the ghetto was totally destroyed and the Jewish survivors sent to the gas chambers. Standing before the ghetto memorial, a somber Brandt fell to his knees and knelt as if in prayer. "I wanted," Brandt said later, "to ask pardon in the name of our people for a million-fold crime which was committed in the misused name of the Germans."[4]

Brandt's gesture at the Warsaw ghetto memorial and the treaty with Poland were part of his policy of reconciliation with eastern Europe, which aimed at nothing less than a comprehensive peace settlement for central Europe and a new resolution of the "German question." That weighty question had first burst on the European scene with the modern nationalism of the French Revolution. How could fragmented Germany achieve political unity, and what role would a powerful, unified Germany play in the international order? "Resolved" in a certain fashion by Bismarck's wars of

unification, the question was posed again in the twentieth century when an aggressive Germany tried twice to conquer Europe. Agreed on crushing Hitler and de-Nazifying Germany during the Second World War, the wartime Allies then found themselves incapable of working together and imposing a general peace treaty on defeated Germany (see pages 960–962). Instead, Germany was divided into two antagonistic states by 1949, and the German question continued to fester as national unity disappeared.

The Federal Republic of Germany—commonly known as West Germany—was the larger of the two, with forty-five million inhabitants as opposed to eighteen million in East Germany. Formed out of the American, British, and French zones of occupation and based on freely expressed popular sovereignty, the Federal Republic claimed that the communist dictatorship installed by the Russians lacked free elections and hence all legal basis. While concentrating on completing its metamorphosis from defeated enemy to invaluable ally within NATO and the Common Market, West Germany also sought with some success to undermine the East German communist regime. Between 1949 and 1954, it welcomed with open arms 2.3 million East German refugees seeking political freedom and economic opportunity, and East Germany limped along while the Federal Republic boomed. But the building of the Berlin Wall in 1961 (see page 978) changed all that. It sealed the refugees' last escape route through West Berlin and allowed East Germany to stabilize and eventually become the world's most prosperous communist country.

As the popular socialist major of West Berlin, Willy Brandt understood the significance of the Berlin Wall and the lack of an energetic U.S. response to its construction. He saw the painful limitations of West Germany's official hard line when the Allies had, in fact, accepted the postwar status quo. Thus Brandt became convinced that a revitalized West Germany needed a new foreign policy, just as the German Social Democratic party he headed had abandoned doctrinaire Marxian socialism to become a broad-based opposition party after the Second World War. After a long battle and two bitter electoral defeats in the 1960s, Brandt became foreign minister in a coalition government in 1966 and won the chancellorship in 1969.

Brandt's victory marked the Federal Republic's political coming of age. First, it brought the Social Democrats to national power for the first time

Willy Brandt in Poland, 1970   Chancellor Brandt's gesture at the Warsaw memorial to the Jewish victims of Nazi terrorism was criticized by some West Germans but praised by many more. This picture reached an enormous audience, appearing in hundreds of newspapers in both the East and the West. *(Source: Bilderdienst Süddeutscher Verlag)*

since the 1920s and showed that genuine two-party political democracy had taken firm hold. Second, it was a graphic indication of West Germany's new-found liberalism and political tolerance, for the gravel-voiced Brandt was a very unconventional German. Illegitimate son of a poor, unwed shop-girl, and a fire-breathing socialist in his youth, Brandt had fled to Norway in the 1930s and had fought against Nazi Germany in the Second World War. Yet the electorate judged the man himself, turning a deaf ear to smears and innuendoes about treason and low birth. Third, Brandt showed that West Germany, postwar Europe's economic giant and political dwarf, was now both prepared and willing to launch major initiatives in European affairs.

The essence of Brandt's policy was to seek genuine peace and reconciliation with the communist East, as Adenauer had already done with France and the West. He negotiated treaties with the Soviet Union, Poland, and Czechoslovakia, which finally accepted existing state boundaries and the loss of eastern territory to Poland and the Soviet Union (see Map 30.1), in return for a mutual renunciation of force or the threat of force. Using the imaginative formula of "two German states within one German nation," Brandt's government also broke decisively with the past and entered into direct relations with East Germany, aiming for modest practical improvements rather than reunification, which at that point remained impractical.

Brandt constantly reiterated that none of these changes affected the respective military alliances of NATO and the Warsaw Pact. Yet, by boldly establishing "normal relations" with the communist East, West Germany seemed to turn another page not only on its ever-more-distant Nazi past, but on many cold war conflicts as well. Thus West Germany's eastern peace settlement contributed to a general reduction in East-West tensions, which included a limited agreement on nuclear arms control between the United States and the Soviet Union in 1972. And with the German question apparently resolved, West Germany had freed itself to assume without reservations a leading role in Europe.

Political Crisis in the United States

The late 1960s and early 1970s also marked the end of the postwar era in the United States. The natural leader of the Atlantic alliance fell into a long and self-destructive political crisis, which weakened the nation at home and abroad and echoed throughout the 1970s.

The crisis in the United States had numerous manifestations, ranging from apparently uncontrollable annual summer riots to brutal political assassinations, which struck down Martin Luther King and both President John F. Kennedy and his younger brother Robert. But the crisis first reached vast proportions in connection with President Johnson's leadership during the undeclared Vietnam War. Thus President Johnson, who wanted to go down in history as a master reformer and healer of old wounds (see page 980), left new ones as his most enduring legacy.

American involvement in Vietnam had its origins in the cold war and the ideology of containment (see page 963). From the late 1940s on, most Americans and their leaders viewed the world in terms of a constant struggle to stop the spread of communism, although they were not prepared to try to roll back communism where it already existed. As Europe began to revive and China established a communist government in 1949, efforts to contain communism shifted to Asia. The bloody Korean War (1950–1953) ended in stalemate, but the United States did succeed in preventing a communist government in South Korea. After the defeat of the French in Indochina in 1954, the Eisenhower administration refused to sign the Geneva accords that temporarily divided the country into two zones pending national unification by means of free elections. President Eisenhower then proceeded to acquiesce in the refusal of the anticommunist South Vietnamese government to accept the verdict of elections and provided it with military aid. President Kennedy greatly increased the number of American "military advisers," to sixteen thousand, and had the existing South Vietnamese leader deposed in 1963 when he refused to follow American directives.

After successfully portraying his opponent, Barry Goldwater, as a trigger-happy extremist in a nuclear age and resoundingly winning the 1964 election on a peace platform, President Johnson proceeded to expand the American role in the Vietnam conflict. As Johnson explained to his ambassador in Saigon, "I am not going to lose Vietnam. I am not going to be the President who saw Southeast Asia go the way China went."[5] American strategy was to "escalate" the war sufficiently to break the will of the North Vietnamese and their southern allies, the Vietcong, without resorting to "overkill" that might risk war with the entire communist bloc. Thus the South received massive military aid, American forces in South Vietnam gradually grew to a half-million men, and the United States bombed North Vietnam with ever-greater intensity. But there was no invasion of the North, nor were essential seaborne military supplies from the Soviet Union ever disrupted. In the end, the strategy of limited war backfired. It was the Americans themselves who grew weary, and the American leadership that cracked.

The undeclared war in Vietnam, fought nightly on American television, eventually divided the nation. Initial support was strong. The politicians, the media, and the population as a whole saw the war as part of a legitimate defense against communist totalitarianism in all poor countries. But in 1966 and 1967 influential opinion leaders like the *New York Times* and the *Washington Post* turned hostile, and the television networks soon followed. A growing number of critics denounced the war as an immoral and unsuccessful intrusion into a complex and distant civil war. There were major protests, often led by college students. Criticism reached a crescendo after the Vietcong "Tet Offensive" in January 1968. This, the Communists' first major attack with conventional weapons on major cities, failed militarily: the Vietcong suffered heavy losses and the attack did not spark a mass uprising. But U.S. critics of the Vietnam War interpreted the bloody combat as a decisive American defeat, clear proof that a Vietcong victory was inevitable. And although public opinion polls never showed more than 20 percent of the people supporting American withdrawal before that became the announced policy after the November 1968 elections, America's leaders now lost all heart. After an ambiguous defeat in the New Hampshire primary, President Johnson tacitly admitted defeat: he called for negotiations with North Vietnam and announced that he would not stand for re-election.

Elected by a razor-slim margin in 1968, President Richard Nixon sought to gradually disengage America from Vietnam and the accompanying national crisis. He restated the long-standing American objective of containment in Vietnam, of aiding the "South Vietnamese people to determine their own political future without outside interfer-

Nixon in China, 1972   Shown here toasting U.S.–China friendship with Chinese Premier Chou En-lai in Peking in February 1972, President Nixon took advantage of Chinese fears of the Soviet Union to establish good relations with Asia's Communist giant. Arriving after twenty-five years of mutual hostility, reconciliation with China was Nixon's finest achievement. *(Source: John Dominis, LIFE MAGAZINE © Time Inc. 1972)*

ence."[6] Using American military power more effectively, while simultaneously pursuing peace talks with the North Vietnamese, Nixon cut American forces in Vietnam from 550,000 to 24,000 in four years. The cost of the war dropped from $25 billion a year under Johnson to $3 billion under Nixon. Moreover, President Nixon launched a daring flank attack in diplomacy. He journeyed to China in 1972 and reached a spectacular if limited reconciliation with Communist China, which took advantage of China's growing fears of the Soviet Union and undermined North Vietnam's position. In January 1973, fortified by the overwhelming endorsement of the people in his 1972 electoral triumph, President Nixon and Secretary of State Henry Kissinger finally reached a peace agreement with North Vietnam. The agreement allowed remaining American forces to complete their withdrawal, while the United States reserved the right to resume bombing if the accords were broken. South Vietnamese forces seemed to hold their own, and the storm of crisis seemed past.

Instead, as the Arab oil embargo unhinged the international economy, the United States reaped the Watergate whirlwind. Like some other recent American presidents, Nixon authorized spying activities that went beyond the law. But in an atmosphere in which a huge series of secret government documents—later known as the "Pentagon Papers"—could be stolen and then given to the country's most influential newspaper for publication as part of its anti-Vietnam War campaign, Nixon went further than his predecessors. He authorized special units to use various illegal means to stop the leaking of government secrets to the press. One such group broke into the Democratic party headquarters in Washington's Watergate complex in June 1972 and was promptly arrested. Eventually, the media and the machinery of congressional investigation turned the break-in and later efforts to hush up the bungled job into a great moral issue. In 1974 a beleaguered Nixon was forced to resign in disgrace, as the political crisis in the United States reached its culmination.

The consequences of renewed political crisis during the Watergate affair were profound. First, the scandal resulted in a major shift of power away from the presidency toward Congress, especially in foreign affairs. Therefore, as American aid to South Vietnam diminished in 1973 and as an emboldened North Vietnam launched a general invasion against South Vietnamese armies in early 1974, first President Nixon and then President Gerald Ford stood by because Congress refused to permit any American response. After more than thirty-five years of battle, the Vietnamese Communists unified their country in 1975 as a totalitarian state—a second consequence of the U.S. crisis. Third, the belated fall of South Vietnam in the wake of Watergate shook America's postwar pride and confidence. Generally interpreted as a disastrous American military defeat, the Vietnam experience left the United States divided and uncertain. Only gradually did the country recover a sense of purpose in world affairs.

Détente or Cold War?

Brandt's Eastern initiatives and Nixon's phased withdrawal from Vietnam were part of many-sided Western efforts to reduce East-West tensions in the early 1970s. This policy of *détente,* or progressive relaxation of cold war tensions, reached its apogee with the Conference on Security and Cooperation in Europe, a thirty-five-nation summit that opened negotiations in Helsinki, Finland, in 1973 and concluded a final agreement in 1975. The Helsinki Conference included all European nations (except isolationist Albania), the United States, and Canada, and its Final Act contained certain elements of a general European peace treaty, like those signed at Vienna in 1815 and at Versailles in 1919. The Final Act formally stated that Europe's existing political frontiers, including those separating the two Germanies, could not be changed by force, and it provided for increased East-West economic and cultural relations as well. Thus the Atlantic alliance solemnly accepted the territorial status quo in eastern Europe, as well as the Soviet Union's gains from World War Two. In return for this major concession, the Soviet Union and its allies agreed to numerous provisions guaranteeing the human rights and political freedoms of their peoples. The Final Act was a compromise embodying Western concerns for human rights and Soviet preoccupations with military security and control of eastern Europe. Optimists saw a bright new day breaking in international relations.

These hopes gradually faded in the later 1970s. The Soviet Union and its allies often ignored the human rights provisions of the Helsinki agreement. Moreover, East-West political competition remained very much alive outside Europe. Many

Americans became convinced that the Soviet Union was taking advantage of détente, steadily building up its military might and pushing for political gains in Africa, Asia, and Latin America. Having been expelled from Egypt by Anwar Sadat after the 1973 war with Israel, the Soviets sought and won toeholds in South Yemen, Somalia, and later Ethiopia. Supporting guerrilla wars against the Portuguese in Angola and Mozambique, the Soviet Union was rewarded with Marxian regimes in both countries.

But it was in Afghanistan that Soviet action seemed most contrary to the spirit of détente. The Soviet Union had long been interested in its Islamic neighbor, and in April 1978 a pro-Soviet coup established a Marxian regime there. This new government soon made itself unpopular, and rebellion spread through the countryside. To preserve Communist rule, the Soviet Union in December 1979 suddenly airlifted crack troops to Kabul, the capital, and occupied Afghanistan with 100,000 men. Alarmed by the scale and precision of the Soviet invasion, many Americans feared that the oil-rich states of the Persian Gulf would be next and searched for an appropriate response.

President Carter tried to lead the Atlantic alliance beyond verbal condemnation, but among the European allies only Great Britain supported the American policy of economic sanctions. France, and especially West Germany, argued that the Soviets' deplorable action in Afghanistan should not be turned into an East-West confrontation and tried to salvage as much as possible of détente within Europe.

The alliance showed the same lack of concerted action when an independent trade union rose in Poland (see page 1027). After the declaration of martial law in Poland in December 1981, western Europe refused to follow the United States in imposing economic sanctions against Poland and the Soviet Union. Some observers concluded that the alliance had lost the will to think and act decisively in relations with the Soviet bloc. Others noted that occasional dramatic differences within the alliance reflected the fact that the Common Market and the United States had drifted apart and become economic rivals.

Yet, despite its very real difficulties, the Atlantic alliance, formed in the late 1940s to check Soviet expansion in Europe, endured and remained true to its original purpose in the 1980s. The U.S. military buildup launched by Jimmy Carter in his last years in office was accelerated by President Ronald Reagan, who was swept into office in the 1980 election by the wave of patriotism following an agonizing hostage crisis in Iran. The new American leadership was convinced that the military balance had tipped in favor of the Soviet Union. Increasing defense spending rapidly, the Reagan administration concentrated especially on nuclear arms and an expanded navy as keys to a resurgence of American power in the post-Vietnam era. Somewhat reluctantly, and in the face of large protest demonstrations, European governments agreed that NATO's forces had to be strengthened and that medium-range American cruise missiles with nuclear warheads should be installed on their soil, in response to the Soviet Union's vast arsenal of missiles targeted to destroy western Europe.

Thus the Atlantic alliance bent, but it did not break. In doing so, Western society gave indirect support to ongoing efforts to liberalize authoritarian communist states in eastern Europe, efforts that after repeated defeats finally burst through in spectacular fashion in the late 1980s. It is to this remarkable movement, which culminated in 1989 in the most promising achievement of the recent past, that we now turn.

THE SOVIET BLOC

Occasional differences within the NATO alliance on how to treat the Soviet bloc reflected not only shifts in Soviet conduct in foreign affairs, but also ambiguities in the course of developments within eastern Europe itself. On the one hand, attempts to liberalize the system had arisen in the 1950s, and the brutal totalitarianism of the Stalinist era was not re-established after Nikita Khrushchev fell from power in 1964. These changes encouraged Western hopes of gradual liberalization and of a more democratic, less threatening Soviet eastern Europe.

On the other hand, hard facts frequently intervened. The Soviet Union repeatedly demonstrated that it remained a harsh and aggressive dictatorship, a dictatorship that paid only lip service to egalitarian ideology and that was determined to uphold its rule throughout eastern Europe. Periodic efforts to achieve fundamental political change were inevitably doomed to failure, sooner or later. Or so it seemed to most Western experts into the middle of the 1980s.

And then Mikhail Gorbachev burst upon the scene. The new Soviet leader opened an era of reform that was as sweeping as it was unexpected. Many believed that Gorbachev would fall from power and that his reforms would fail in the Soviet Union. Such an outcome is clearly possible. Yet the scope of reform and then revolution in eastern Europe suggests that peoples there have indeed made a decisive breakthrough toward greater personal freedom and political democracy. Above all, reform in eastern Europe is based on powerful historical forces. It is not just the work of a single imaginative leader. It is also the result of long-standing campaigns to humanize communism and of a social transformation in the Soviet Union that has made rigid one-party dictatorship counterproductive and probably obsolete, as we shall now see.

The Czechoslovak Experiment

In the wake of Khrushchev's reforms in the Soviet Union (see pages 976–978), the 1960s brought modest liberalization and more consumer goods to eastern Europe, as well as somewhat greater national autonomy, especially in Poland and Rumania. Czechoslovakia moved more slowly, but in January 1968 it began making up for lost time. The reform elements in the Czechoslovak Communist party gained a majority and voted out the longtime Stalinist leader in favor of Alexander Dubček. The new government launched a series of major economic and political initiatives that fascinated observers around the world.

Educated in Moscow, Dubček was a dedicated Communist. But he and his allies within the party were also idealists who believed that they could reconcile genuine socialism with personal freedom and internal party democracy. Thus local decision making by trade unions, managers, and consumers replaced rigid bureaucratic planning. Censorship was relaxed, and mindless ideological conformity gave way to exciting free expression. People responded enthusiastically, and the reform program proved enormously popular. Czechoslovakia had been eastern Europe's only advanced industrial state before the Second World War, and Dubček was reviving traditions that were still deeply cherished.

Although Dubček remembered the lesson of Russian troops crushing the Hungarian revolution (see page 978) and constantly proclaimed his loy-

The End of Reform   In August 1968 Soviet tanks rumbled into Prague to extinguish Czechoslovakian efforts to build a humane socialism. Here people watch the massive invasion from the sidewalks, knowing full well the suicidal danger of armed resistance. *(Source: Joseph Koudelka PP/Magnum)*

alty to the Warsaw Pact of communist states, the determination of the Czech reformers to build "socialism with a human face" frightened hard-line Communists. These fears were particularly strong in Poland and East Germany, where the leaders knew full well that they lacked popular support. Moreover, the Soviet Union feared that a liberalized Czechoslovakia would eventually be drawn to neutralism, or even to the democratic West. Thus the Eastern bloc countries launched a concerted campaign of intimidation against the Czech leaders, but Dubček's regime refused to knuckle under. The Soviet response was brutal. In August 1968, 500,000 Russian and allied eastern European troops suddenly occupied Czechoslovakia.

The Czechs made no attempt to resist militarily. The Soviets immediately arrested Dubček and the other top leaders and flew them to Moscow, where they were forced to surrender to Soviet demands. Gradually but inexorably, the reform program was abandoned and its supporters removed from office. Thus the Czechoslovak experiment in humanizing communism and making it serve the needs of ordinary citizens failed.

Shortly after the Czechoslovak invasion, Brezhnev declared the so-called Brezhnev Doctrine, according to which Soviet Russia and its allies had the right to intervene in any socialist country whenever they saw the need. Predictably, the occupation of Czechoslovakia raised a storm of protest. Many Communist parties in western Europe were harshly critical, partly out of conviction and partly to limit their electoral losses. But the occupation did not seriously alter ongoing Western efforts—most notably, those of West Germany's Willy Brandt—to secure better relations with the Eastern bloc countries. The reason was simple. The West considered Czechoslovakia to be part of Russia's sphere of influence, for better or worse. Thus the empire that Stalin had built remained solidly in place, and permanent changes in eastern Europe depended on developments in the Soviet Union.

The Soviet Union to 1985

The 1968 invasion of Czechoslovakia was the crucial event of the Brezhnev era, which really lasted beyond the aging leader's death in 1982, until the emergence in 1985 of Mikhail Gorbachev. The invasion demonstrated unmistakably the intense conservatism of Russia's ruling elite and its determination to maintain the status quo in the Soviet bloc.

Indeed, the aftermath of intervention in Czechoslovakia also brought a certain re-Stalinization of Soviet Russia. But now dictatorship was collective rather than personal, and coercion replaced uncontrolled terror. This compromise seemed to suit the leaders and a majority of the people, and the Soviet Union appeared stable in the 1970s and early 1980s.

A slowly rising standard of living for ordinary people contributed to stability, although the economic crisis of the 1970s markedly slowed the rate of improvement, and long lines and innumerable shortages persisted. The enduring differences between the life of the elite and the life of ordinary people also reinforced the system. Ambitious individuals still had tremendous incentive to do as the state wished, in order to gain access to special, well-stocked stores, attend special schools, and travel abroad.

Another source of stability was that ordinary Great Russians remained intensely nationalistic. Party leaders successfully identified themselves with this patriotism, stressing their role in saving the country during the Second World War and protecting it now from foreign foes, including eastern European "counter-revolutionaries." Moreover, the politically dominant Great Russians, who are concentrated in the central Russian heartland and in Siberia—formally designated as the Russian Federation—and who also hold through the Communist Party the commanding leadership positions in the non-Russian republics, constitute less than half of the total Soviet population. The Great Russians generally feared that greater freedom and open political competition might therefore result in demands for autonomy and even independence, not only by eastern European nationalities, but by the non-Russian nationalities of the smaller republics and the autonomous regions within the Soviet Union itself (Map 32.2). Thus liberalism and democracy generally appeared as alien political philosophies designed to undermine Russia's power and greatness.

The strength of the government was expressed in the re-Stalinization of culture and art. Free expression and open protest disappeared. In 1968, when a small group of dissenters appeared in Red Square

to protest the invasion of Czechoslovakia, they were arrested before they could unfurl their banners. This proved to be the high point of dissent, for in the 1970s Brezhnev and company made certain that Soviet intellectuals did not engage in public protest. Acts of open nonconformity and protest were severely punished, but with sophisticated, cunning methods.

Most frequently, dissidents were blacklisted and thus rendered unable to find a decent job, since the government was the only employer. This fate was enough to keep most in line. More determined but unrenowned protesters were quietly imprisoned in jails or mental institutions. Celebrated nonconformists such as Solzhenitsyn were permanently expelled from the country. Once again, Jews were persecuted as a "foreign" element, though some were eventually permitted to emigrate to Israel. As the distinguished Russian dissident historian Roy Medvedev explained in the mid-1970s,

The technology of repression has become more refined in recent years. Before, repression always went much farther than necessary. Stalin killed millions of people when arresting 1000 would have enabled him to control the people. Our leaders . . . found out eventually that you don't have to put people in prison or in a psychiatric hospital to silence them. There are other ways.[7]

Eliminating the worst aspects of Stalin's totalitarianism strengthened the regime, and rule by a self-perpetuating Communist elite in the Soviet Union appeared to be quite solid in the 1970s and early 1980s.

Yet beneath the dreary immobility of political life in the Brezhnev era the Soviet Union experienced profound changes. As a perceptive British journalist put it in 1986, "The country went through a social revolution while Brezhnev slept."[8] Three aspects of this revolution, which was seldom appreciated by Western observers at the time, were particularly significant.

First, the growth of the urban population, which had raced forward at breakneck speed in the Stalin years, continued rapidly in the 1960s and 1970s. In 1985 two-thirds of all Soviet citizens lived in cities, and a quarter lived in big cities (see Map 32.2). Of great significance, this expanding urban population lost its old peasant ways. As a result, it acquired more education, better job skills, and greater sophistication.

Second, the number of highly trained scientists,

MAP 32.2 Russian Republics One of the biggest challenges faced by Soviet leaders stems from the sheer size and diversity of the Soviet Union. Although the Great Russians dominate the Soviet Union and the Communist Party, they represent less than half the population. This map illustrates the potential for civic unrest spurred by resurgent nationalism.

managers, and specialists expanded prodigiously, jumping fourfold between 1960 and 1985. Thus the class of well-educated, pragmatic, and self-confident experts, which played such an important role in restructuring industrial societies after World War Two (see pages 995–997), developed rapidly in the Soviet Union. Moreover, leading Soviet scientists and technologists sought membership in the international "invisible college" of their disciplines, like their colleagues in the West. Correspondingly, they sought the intellectual freedom necessary to do significant work, and they often obtained it because their research had practical (and military) value.

Finally, education and freedom for experts in their special areas helped foster the growth of Soviet public opinion. Educated people read, discussed, and formed definite ideas about social questions. And if caution dictated conventional ideas (at least in public), many important issues could be approached and debated in "nonpolitical" terms. Developing definite ideas on such things as environmental pollution or urban transportation, educated urban people increasingly saw themselves as worthy of having a voice in society's decisions, even its political decisions. This, too, was part of the quiet transformation that set the stage for the reforms of the Gorbachev era.

The Rise of Solidarity   This photograph shows the determination and mass action that allowed Polish workers to triumph in August 1980. Backed by a crowd of enthusiastic supporters, leader Lech Walesa announces the historic Gdansk Agreement to striking workers at the main gate of the Lenin Shipyards. *(Source: Jean Gaumy/Magnum)*

Solidarity in Poland

Before turning to those recent Soviet developments, we need to look at the growth of popular protest in the Soviet Union's satellite empire. In Poland, workers joined together en masse to fight peacefully for freedom and self-determination, while the world watched in amazement. Crushed in the short run but refusing to admit defeat, the Polish workers waged a long campaign that inspired and reflected a powerful reform current in eastern Europe.

Poland was an unruly satellite from the beginning. Stalin said that introducing communism to Poland was like putting a saddle on a cow. Efforts to saddle the cow—really a spirited stallion—led to widespread riots in 1956 (see pages 977–978). As a result, the Polish Communists dropped efforts to impose Soviet-style collectivization on the peasants and to break the Roman Catholic church. Most agricultural land remained in private hands as the Catholic church thrived. With an independent agriculture and a vigorous church, the Communists failed to monopolize society.

They also failed to manage the economy effectively. The 1960s saw little economic improvement. When the government suddenly announced large price increases right before Christmas in 1970, Poland's working class rose again in angry protest. Factories were occupied and strikers were shot, but a new Communist leader came to power nevertheless. The government then wagered that massive inflows of Western capital and technology, especially from a now-friendly West Germany, could produce a Polish "economic miracle" that would win popular support for the regime. Instead, bureaucratic incompetence coupled with worldwide recession put the economy into a nose dive by the mid-1970s. Workers, intellectuals, and the church became increasingly restive. Then the real "Polish miracle" occurred: Cardinal Karol Wojtyla, archbishop of Cracow, was elected pope in 1978. In June 1979 he returned for an astonishing pilgrimage across his native land. Preaching love of Christ and country and the "inalienable rights of man," Pope John Paul II electrified the Polish nation. The economic crisis became a spiritual crisis as well.

In August 1980, as scattered strikes to protest higher meat prices spread, the sixteen thousand workers at the gigantic Lenin Shipyards in Gdansk (formerly known as Danzig) laid down their tools and occupied the showpiece plant. As other workers along the Baltic coast joined "in solidarity," the strikers advanced truly revolutionary demands: the right to form free trade unions, the right to strike, freedom of speech, release of political prisoners, and economic reforms. After eighteen days of shipyard occupation, as families brought food to the gates and priests said mass daily amid huge overhead cranes, the government gave in and accepted the workers' demands in the Gdansk Agreement. In a state where the Communist party claimed to rule on behalf of the proletariat, a working-class revolt had won an unprecedented victory.

Led by a feisty Lenin Shipyards electrician and devout Catholic named Lech Walesa, the workers proceeded to organize their free and democratic trade union. They called it "Solidarity." Joined by intellectuals and supported by the Catholic church, Solidarity became the union of a nation. By March 1981 it had a membership of 9.5 million, of 12.5 million who were theoretically eligible. A full-time staff of forty thousand linked the union members together, as Solidarity published its own newspapers and cultural and intellectual freedom blossomed in Poland. Solidarity's leaders had tremendous well-organized support, and the threat of calling a nationwide strike gave them real power in ongoing negotiations with the Communist bosses.

But if Solidarity had power, it did not try to take power in 1981. History, the Brezhnev Doctrine, and virulent attacks from communist neighbors all guaranteed the intervention of the Red Army and a terrible blood bath if Polish Communists "lost control." Thus the Solidarity revolution remained a "self-limiting revolution," aiming at defending the cultural and trade-union freedoms won in the Gdansk Agreement without directly challenging the Communist monopoly of political power.

Solidarity's combination of strength and moderation postponed a showdown. The Soviet Union, already condemned worldwide for its invasion of Afghanistan, played a waiting game of threats and pressure. After a crisis in March 1981 that followed police beatings of Solidarity activists, Walesa settled for minor government concessions, and Solidarity again dropped plans for a massive general strike. It was a turning point. Criticism of Walesa's moderate leadership and calls for local self-government in unions and factories grew. Solidarity lost its cohesiveness. The worsening economic crisis also encouraged grassroots radicalism and frustration: a hunger-march banner proclaimed that "A hungry nation can eat its rulers."[9] With an eye on Western public opinion, the Polish Communist leadership shrewdly denounced Solidarity for promoting economic collapse and provoking Russian invasion. In December 1981 the Communist leader General Jaruzelski suddenly struck in the dead of subfreezing night, proclaiming martial law and cutting all communications, arresting Solidarity's leaders and "saving" the nation.

Outlawed and driven underground, Solidarity fought successfully to maintain its organization and to voice the aspirations of the Polish masses after 1981. Part of the reason for the union's survival was the government's unwillingness (and probably its inability) to impose full-scale terror. Moreover, in schools and shops, in factories and offices, millions decided to continue acting as if they were free, even though they were not. Therefore, cultural and intellectual life remained extremely vigorous in spite of renewed repression. At the same time, the faltering Polish economy, battered by the global stagnation of the early 1980s and crippled by a disastrous brain drain after 1981, continued to deteriorate. Thus popular support for outlawed Solidarity remained strong and deep under martial law in the 1980s, preparing the way for its resurgence at the end of the decade.

The rise and survival of Solidarity showed again the fierce desire of millions of eastern Europeans for greater political liberty. The union's strength also demonstrated the enduring appeal of cultural freedom, trade-union rights, patriotic nationalism, and religious feeling. Not least, Solidarity's challenge encouraged fresh thinking in the Soviet Union, ever the key to lasting change in the Eastern bloc.

Reform in the Soviet Union

Fundamental change in Russian history has often come in short, intensive spurts, which contrast vividly with long periods of immobility. We have studied four of these spurts: the ambitious "westernization" of Peter the Great in the early eighteenth century (see pages 552–554), the Great Reforms connected with the freeing of the serfs in the mid-nineteenth century (see pages 806–808), the Russian Revolution of 1917 (see pages 875–882), and Stalin's wrenching "revolution from above" in the 1930s (see pages 925–933). To this select list of decisive transformations, we must now add the era of fundamental reforms launched by Mikhail Gorbachev in 1985. The ultimate fate of these ongoing reforms is still unclear. But they have already had a profound, probably irreversible impact. They have brought political and cultural liberalization in the Soviet Union, and they have permitted democracy and national self-determination to triumph spectacularly in the old satellite empire.

As we have seen, the Soviet Union's Communist elite seemed secure in the early 1980s, as far as any challenge from below was concerned. The long-established system of administrative controls continued to stretch downward from the central ministries and state committees to provincial cities, and from there to factories, neighborhoods, and villages. At each level of this massive state bureaucracy, the overlapping hierarchy of the Communist party, with its 17.5 million members, continued to watch over all decisions and manipulate every aspect of national life. Organized opposition was impossible, and average people simply left politics to the bosses.

Yet the massive state and party bureaucracy was a mixed blessing. It safeguarded the elite, but it also promoted apathy in the masses. Discouraging personal initiative and economic efficiency, it was also ill suited to secure the effective cooperation of the rapidly growing class of well-educated urban experts. Therefore, when the ailing Brezhnev finally died in 1982, his successor, the long-time chief of the secret police, Yuri Andropov, tried to invigorate the system. Andropov introduced modest reforms to improve economic performance and campaigned against worker absenteeism and high-level corruption. Relatively little came of these efforts, but they combined with a worsening economic situation to set the stage for the emergence in 1985 of Mikhail Gorbachev, the most vigorous Soviet leader in a generation.

Gorbachev was smart, charming, and tough. As long-time Soviet foreign minister Andrei Gromyko reportedly said, "This man has a nice smile, but he has got iron teeth."[10] In his first year in office, Gorbachev attacked corruption and incompetence in the upper reaches of the bureaucracy, and he consolidated his power by packing the top level of the party with his supporters. He attacked alcoholism and drunkenness, which were deadly scourges of Soviet society. More basically, he elaborated a whole series of reform policies designed to revive and even remake the vast Soviet Union.

The first set of reform policies was designed to transform and restructure the economy, which was falling ever further behind that of the West in the 1980s and failing to provide for the very real needs of the Soviet population. To accomplish this economic restructuring—this *perestroika*—Gorbachev and his supporters permitted freer prices, more independence for state enterprises, and the setting up of profit-seeking private cooperatives to provide personal services. These reforms initially produced some improvements, but shortages then grew as the economy stalled at an intermediate point between central planning and free-market mechanisms. By 1990 Gorbachev's timid economic initiatives had met with very little success, posing a serious threat to his leadership and the entire reform program.

Gorbachev's bold and far-reaching campaign "to tell it like it is" was much more successful. Very popular in a country where censorship, dull uniformity, and outright lies had long characterized public discourse, the newfound openness—the *glasnost*—of the government and the media marked an astonishing break with the past. A disaster like the Chernobyl nuclear accident, which devastated part of the Ukraine and showered Europe with radioactive fallout, was investigated and reported with honesty and painstaking thoroughness. The works of long-banned and vilified Russian émigré writers sold millions of copies in new editions, while denunciations of Stalin and his terror became standard fare in plays and movies. Thus openness in government pronouncements led rather quickly to something approaching free speech and free expression, a veritable cultural revolution.

Democratization was the third element of reform. Beginning as an attack on corruption in the Communist party and as an attempt to bring the class of educated experts into the decision-making process, it led to the first free elections in the Soviet Union since 1917. Gorbachev and the party remained in control, but a minority of critical independents were elected in April 1989 to a revitalized Congress of People's Deputies. Many top-ranking communists who ran unopposed saw themselves defeated as a majority of angry voters struck their names from the ballot. Millions of Soviets then watched the new congress for hours on television, as Gorbachev and his ministers saw their proposals debated and even rejected.

Democratization also encouraged demands for greater autonomy by non-Russian minorities, especially in the Baltic region and in the Caucasus. These demands certainly went beyond what Gorbachev had envisaged. In April 1989 troops with sharpened shovels charged into a rally of Georgian separatists in Tbilisi and left twenty dead. But whereas China's Communist leaders brutally massacred similar prodemocracy demonstrators in Beijing in June 1989 and reimposed rigid authoritarian rule, Gorbachev drew back from repression. Thus nationalist demands continued to grow in the non-Russian Soviet republics, an unexpected consequence of democratization.

Finally, the Soviet leader brought "new political thinking" to the field of foreign affairs. And he acted on it. He withdrew Soviet troops from Afghanistan, encouraged reform movements in Poland and Hungary, and sought to reduce East-West tensions. Of enormous historical importance, Gorbachev pledged to respect the political choices of the peoples of eastern Europe, and he thereby repudiated the Brezhnev Doctrine, which had arrogantly proclaimed the right of the Soviet Union and its allies to intervene at will in eastern Europe. By 1989 it seemed that, if Gorbachev held to his word, the tragic Soviet occupation of eastern Europe might well wither away, taking the long cold war with it.

THE REVOLUTIONS OF 1989

Instead, history accelerated, and 1989 brought a series of largely peaceful revolutions throughout eastern Europe (Map 32.3). These revolutions overturned existing communist regimes and ended the Communist party's monopoly of power. Revolutionary mass demonstrations led to the formation of provisional governments dedicated to democratic elections, human rights, and national rejuvenation. Watched on television in the Soviet Union and around the world, these stirring events marked the triumph and the transformation of the long-standing reform movement we have been considering in this chapter.

Solidarity and the Polish people again led the way. In 1988 widespread labor unrest, raging inflation, and the outlawed Solidarity's refusal to coop-

erate with the military government had brought Poland to the brink of economic collapse. Profiting from Gorbachev's tolerant attitude and skillfully mobilizing its forces, Solidarity pressured Poland's frustrated Communist leaders into another round of negotiations that might work out a sharing of power to resolve the political stalemate and the

Newly Elected President Mikhail Gorbachev vowed in his acceptance speech before the Supreme Soviet, the U.S.S.R.'s parliament, to assume "all responsibility" for the success or failure of perestroika. Previous parliaments were no more than tools of the Communist party, but this one has actively debated and sometimes opposed government programs. *(Source: Vlastimir Shone/Gamma-Liaison)*

economic crisis. The subsequent agreement legalized Solidarity again after eight long years. The agreement also declared that a large minority of representatives to the Polish parliament would be chosen by free elections in June 1989. The Communist party was still guaranteed a majority, but Solidarity won every single contested seat in an overwhelming victory. On July 4, 1989, Solidarity members jubilantly entered the 460-member Polish parliament, the first freely elected opposition in a communist country. A month later the editor of Solidarity's weekly newspaper was sworn in as the first noncommunist leader in eastern Europe since

Stalin used Soviet armies to impose his system there after the Second World War.

Hungary followed Poland. Hungary's Communist boss, János Kádár, had permitted liberalization of the rigid planned economy after the 1956 uprising, in exchange for political obedience and continued Communist control. In May 1988, in an effort to hang on to power by granting modest political concessions, the party replaced Kádár with a reform Communist. But growing popular resistance rejected piecemeal progress, forcing the Communist party to renounce one-party rule and schedule free elections for early 1990. Welcoming Western in-

MAP 32.3 Democratic Movements in Eastern Europe, 1989   With Gorbachev's repudiation of the Brezhnev Doctrine, the desire for freedom and democracy spread throughout Eastern Europe. Countries that had been satellites in the orbit of the Soviet Union began to set themselves free to establish their own place in the universe of free nations.

Celebrating on the Berlin Wall   In a year filled with powerful images, none was more dramatic or more hopeful than the opening of the Berlin Wall, symbol of the harsh division between Eastern and Western Europe. *(Source: Tom Haley/SIPA-PRESS)*

vestment and moving rapidly toward multiparty democracy, Hungarians gleefully tore down the barbed-wire "iron curtain" with Austria and opened their border to East German refugees.

As thousands of dissatisfied East Germans began pouring into Hungary, before going on to immediate resettlement in thriving West Germany, growing economic dislocation and huge candlelight demonstrations brought revolution in East Berlin. The Berlin Wall was opened, and people danced for joy atop that grim symbol of the prison state. East Germany's aging Communist leaders were swept aside and in some case arrested, as general elections were scheduled for March 1990. Subsequently, a conservative-liberal "Alliance for Germany," which was closely tied to West German Chancellor Helmut Kohl's Christian Democrats, defeated the East German Social Democrats in these elections. The Alliance for Germany quickly negotiated an economic union on favorable terms with Chancellor

Kohl, and by the summer of 1990 only certain political and military aspects of German unification remained unresolved, for these questions affected the security of the Soviet Union and the general balance of power in Europe. Communism also died in Czechoslovakia in December 1989, in an almost good-humored ousting of Communist bosses in ten short days.

Only in Romania was revolution violent and bloody. There the iron-fisted Communist dictator, Nicolae Ceauşescu, had long combined Stalinist brutality with stubborn independence from Moscow. Faced with mass protests, Ceauşescu, alone among eastern European bosses, ordered his ruthless security forces to slaughter thousands, thereby sparking a classic armed uprising. After Ceauşescu's forces were defeated, the tyrant and his wife were captured and executed by a military court. A coalition government emerged from the fighting, although the legacy of Ceauşescu's oppression left

In Bucharest's Palace Square, cranes remove the statue of Stalin that dominated the square during the dictatorship of Nicolae Ceauşescu. Despite Ceauşescu's vow that democratic reform would come to Romania "when pears grow on poplar trees," citizens joined in a mass revolt to topple the despot and his oppressive regime. *(Source: BI/Gamma-Liaison)*

a troubled country with an uncertain political future.

As the 1990s began, the revolutionary changes that Gorbachev had permitted, and even encouraged, had triumphed in all but two eastern European states—tiny Albania and the vast Soviet Union. The great question now became whether the Soviet Union would follow its former satellites, and whether reform communism would give way there to a popular anticommunist revolution. Near civil war between Armenians and Azerbaijanis in the Caucasus, assertions of independence in the Baltic states, including Lithuania's bold declaration of national sovereignty, and growing dissatisfaction among the Great Russian masses were all parts of a fluid, unstable political situation. Increasingly, the reform-minded Gorbachev, the most creative world leader of the late twentieth century, stood as a besieged moderate, assailed by those who wanted revolutionary changes and by hard-line Communists who longed to reverse course and clamp down. Only time would tell how Gorbachev would meet this two-sided challenge and how far he would go in his reforms. Yet it seems probable that the Soviet Union, like the nations of eastern Europe, has already experienced irreversible movement in the direction of personal freedom and political democracy, a most surprising development that accords magnificently with the noblest traditions of Western society.

THE FUTURE IN PERSPECTIVE

What about the future? For centuries, astrologers and scientists, experts and ordinary people, have been trying to answer this question. Although it may seem that the study of what has been has little to say about what will be, the study of history over a long period is actually very useful in this regard. It helps put the future in perspective.

In 1931 a distinguished Harvard professor of genetics examined the prospects for the human race in an article read by millions. Among his predictions was that "in the year 2500 the population of the world should be about 3,500 millions, or about twice the figures of today."[11] In fact, the population of the world reached five billion in the 1980s and, outside the highly developed countries of Europe and North America, is still growing rapidly. The six-century projection of the learned expert was proved dead wrong in less than fifty years.

History is full of such erroneous predictions, a few of which we have mentioned in this book. Yet lack of success has not diminished the age-old desire to look into the future. Self-proclaimed experts even pretend that they have created a new science of futurology. With great pomposity they often act as if their hunches and guesses about future human developments are inescapable realities. Yet the study of history teaches healthy skepticism regarding such predictions, however scientific they may appear. Past results suggest that most such predictions will simply not come true, or not in the anticipated way. Thus history provides some psychological protection from the fantastic visions of modern astrologers.

This protection has been particularly valuable in recent years, because many recent projections into the future have been quite pessimistic, just as they were very optimistic in the 1950s and 1960s. Many people in the Western world have feared that conditions are going to get worse rather than better. For example, there have been fears that trade wars will permanently cripple the world economy, that pollution will destroy the environment, and that the traditional family will disappear. Until recently, many experts and politicians were predicting that the energy crisis—in the form of skyrocketing oil prices—meant disaster, in the form of lower standards of living at best and the collapse of civilization at worst. Then some of these same experts worried that the unexpected sharp decline in oil prices in the early 1980s would bankrupt both Third World oil producers, such as Mexico, and the large American banks that have lent them so much money. In fact, both the oil producers and the big banks muddled through and show few signs of collapsing. It is heartening to know that most such dire predictions do not prove true, just as the same knowledge of likely error is sobering in times of optimistic expectations.

One of the more frightening and pessimistic predictions recently in vogue has been that the northern nations of Europe and North America will increasingly find themselves locked in a life-and-death struggle with the poor, overpopulated southern nations of Africa, Asia, and South America. This North-South conflict, it has been predicted, will replace the old cold war struggle of East and West with a much more dangerous international class and race conflict of rich versus poor, white versus colored. Such, it is said, is the bitter legacy of Western imperialism.

As Map 32.4 shows, there is indeed an enormous gap between the very wealthy nations of noncommunist western Europe and North America and the very poor nations of much of Africa and Asia. Yet closer examination does not reveal a growing split between two sharply defined economic camps. On the contrary, there are five or six distinct categories of nations in terms of income level. The countries of eastern Europe form something of a middle-income group, despite their serious economic problems and long decades of communist dictatorship and mismanagement. So do the major oil-exporting states, which are still behind the wealthier

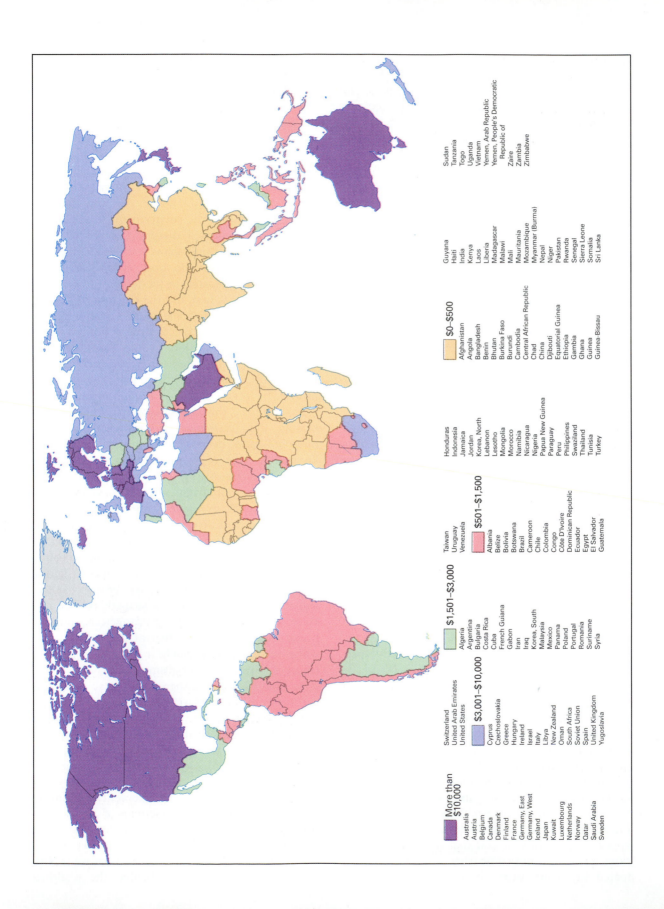

countries of western Europe. Poverty in parts of Latin America is severe, but as the map shows, standards of living are substantially higher there than in much of Africa and Asia, both of which encompass considerable variation.

When one considers differences in culture, religion, politics, and historical development, the supposed split between "rich" and "poor" nations breaks down still further. Thus a global class war between rich and poor appears unlikely in the foreseeable future. A more reasonable expectation is continuing pressure to reduce international economic differences through taxation and welfare measures, as has already occurred domestically in the wealthy nations. Such pressure may well bring at least modest success, for the wealthy nations generally realize that an exclusively Western (or "Northern") viewpoint on global issues is unrealistic and self-defeating. The true legacy of Western imperialism is one small world.

It is this that has made the nuclear arms race so ominous. Not only do the United States and the Soviet Union possess unbelievably destructive, ever-expanding nuclear arsenals, but Great Britain, France, China, and India all have "the bomb," and probably Israel and South Africa do as well. Other countries are equipped or desire to "go nuclear." Thus some gloomy experts have predicted that twenty or thirty states may have nuclear weapons in the near future. In a world plagued by local wars and ferocious regional conflicts, these experts have concluded that nuclear war is almost inevitable and have speculated that the human race is an "endangered species."

Such predictions and the undeniable seriousness of the arms race appear to have jolted Western populations out of their customary fatalism regarding nuclear weapons. Recent efforts to reduce or even halt the nuclear buildup in the Soviet Union and the NATO alliance have made some real progress. Above all, the Gorbachev era in the Soviet Union has opened the way to new thinking and genuine superpower cooperation on nuclear arms questions. An optimist can hope that comparable concern in non-Western areas may yet develop to help create the global political will necessary to control nuclear proliferation before it is too late.

MAP 32.4 Estimated GNP per Capita Income in the Early 1980s

Whatever does or does not happen, the study of history puts the future in perspective in other ways. We have seen that every age has its problems and challenges. Others before us have trod these paths of crisis and uncertainty. This knowledge helps save us from exaggerated self-pity in the face of our own predicaments.

Perhaps our Western heritage may even inspire us with pride and measured self-confidence. We stand, momentarily, at the end of the long procession of Western civilization winding through the ages. Sometimes the procession has wandered, or backtracked, or done terrible things. But it has also carried the efforts and sacrifices of generations of toiling, struggling ancestors. Through no effort of our own, we are the beneficiaries of those sacrifices and achievements. Now that it is our turn to carry the torch onward, we may remember these ties with our forebears.

To change the metaphor, we in the West are like a card player who has been dealt many good cards. Some of them are obvious, like our technical and scientific heritage or our commitments to human rights and the individual. Others are not so obvious, sometimes half-forgotten or even hidden up the sleeve. One thinks, for example, of the Christian Democrats, the moderate Catholic party, which emerged after World War Two to play such an important role in the western European renaissance. And in the almost miraculous victory of peaceful revolution in eastern Europe in 1989—in what the Czech playwright-turned-president Václav Havel called "the power of the powerless"—we see again the regenerative strength of the Western ideals of individual rights, representative government, and nationhood in the European homeland. We hold a good hand.

Our study of history, of mighty struggles and fearsome challenges, of shining achievements and tragic failures, gives a sense of what is the essence of life itself: the process of change over time. Again and again we have seen how peoples and societies evolve, influenced by ideas, human passions, and material conditions. As sure as anything is sure, this process of change over time will continue, as the future becomes the present and then the past. And students of history are better prepared to make sense of this unfolding process because they have already observed it. They know how change goes forward, on the basis of existing historical forces, and their projections will probably be as good as

The World in Modern Times, 1914 to the Present

	Politics	Science and Technology
1914	World War One, 1914–1918 *Lusitania* sunk, 1915 Easter Rebellion, 1916 U.S. declares war on Germany, 1917 Bolshevik Revolution, 1917–1918 Treaty of Versailles, 1919	Submarine warfare, 1915 Ernest Rutherford split the atom, 1919
1920	Mussolini seizes power, 1922 Forced collectivization in the Soviet Union, 1929 Stalin orders mass purges, ca 1929–1939 Hitler becomes chancellor of Germany, 1933 Rome-Berlin Axis, 1936 Nazi–Soviet Non-Agression Pact, 1939 World War Two begins, 1939	"Heroic age of physics," 1920s First major public broadcasts in Great Britain and the United States, 1920 Werner Heisenberg, "principle of uncertainty," 1927 Talking movies, 1930 First jet engines, ca 1935 Radar system in England, 1939
1940	Japan bombs Pearl Harbor, 1941 War in Europe ends, 1945 U.S. drops atomic bombs on Japan, 1945 United Nations, 1945 Cold war era begins, 1947 Collapse of colonial empires, 1947–1962 Israel established, 1948 Communist government in China, 1949 Korean War, 1950–1953 Civil war in Vietnam, 1954 "Peaceful coexistence," ca 1955–1957	J. Robert Oppenheimer, 1904–1967 First atomic bomb tested, 1945 James Watson and Francis Crick discover structure of DNA molecule, 1953 Russian satellite in orbit, 1957
1960	The Berlin Wall, 1961 United States in Vietnam, ca 1961–1973 *Détente,* 1970s Islamic Revolution in Iran, 1978–1979	European Council for Nuclear Research, 1960 Space race, 1960s Russian cosmonaut first to orbit globe, 1961 American astronaut first person on the moon, 1969
1980	Solidarity in Poland, 1980 *Glasnost* in the Soviet Union, 1985 Prodemocracy demonstrations in Beijing, 1989 Revolutions in Eastern Europe, 1989–1990 Berlin Wall opened, 1990	

Economics and Society	Arts and Letters
Planned economies in Europe, 1914	Marcel Proust, *Remembrance of Things Past,* 1913–1927
Bread riots in Russia, 1917	"Modernism," ca 1905–1929
	Oswald Spengler, *The Decline of the West,* 1918
	Walter Gropius, the Bauhaus, ca 1919–1921
New Economic Policy in the Soviet Union, 1921	Modern existentialism, 1920s
American stock market boom, 1928–1929	Dadaism in art, 1920s
	Virginia Woolf, *Jacob's Room,* 1922
The Great Depression, 1929–1933	James Joyce, *Ulysses,* 1922
Roosevelt's "New Deal," 1933	T. S. Eliot, *The Waste Land,* 1922
National Recovery Administration, 1935	Surrealism in art, ca 1925
Mexico nationalizes petroleum industry, 1938	Erich Remarque, *All Quiet on the Western Front,* 1929
	Pablo Picasso, *Guernica,* 1937
Bretton Woods Agreement, 1944	Ludwig Mies van der Rohe, Lake Shore Apartments, 1948–1951
Marshall Plan, 1947	George Orwell, *1984,* 1949
Organization of European Economic Cooperation, 1948	Boris Pasternak, *Doctor Zhivago,* 1956
European economic progress, ca 1950–1969	
European Coal and Steel Community, 1952	
European Economic Community, 1957	
Collapse of postwar monetary system, 1971	Alexander Solzhenitsyn, *One Day in the Life of Ivan Denisovitch,* 1962
OPEC oil price increase, 1973	
Stagflation, 1970s	
Gorbachev implements perestroika, 1985	
Economic crisis in Poland, 1988	
Economic union between East and West Germany, 1989	

those of the futurologists. Students of history are also prepared for the new and unexpected in human development, for they have already seen great breakthroughs and revolutions. They have an understanding of how things really happen.

NOTES

1. Quoted in W. Laqueur, *Europe Since Hitler* (Baltimore: Penguin Books, 1972), p. 9.
2. *Wall Street Journal*, June 25, 1985, p. 1.
3. S. Rose and D. Fasenfest, *Family Income in the 1980s: New Pressures on Wives, Husbands and Young Adults* (Washington, D.C.: Economic Policy Institute, 1988), Working Paper No. 103, pp. 5–8.
4. Quoted in Kessing's Research Report, *Germany and East Europe Since 1945: From the Potsdam Agreement to Chancellor Brandt's "Ostpolitik"* (New York: Charles Scribner's Sons, 1973), pp. 284–285.
5. Quoted in S. E. Morison et al., *A Concise History of the American Republic* (New York: Oxford University Press, 1977), p. 735.
6. Richard Nixon, *Public Papers, 1969* (Washington, D.C.: U.S. Government Printing Office, 1971), p. 371.
7. Quoted in H. Smith, *The Russians* (New York: Quadrangle Books/New York Times, 1976), pp. 455–456.
8. M. Walker, *The Waking Giant: Gorbachev's Russia* (New York, Pantheon Books, 1987), p. 175.
9. T. G. Ash, *The Polish Revolution: Solidarity* (New York: Charles Scribner's Sons, 1983), p. 186.
10. Quoted in *Time*, January 6, 1986, p. 66.
11. E. M. East, in *Scientific Monthly*, April 1931; also in *Reader's Digest* 19 (May 1931): 151.

SUGGESTED READING

Many of the studies cited in the Suggested Reading for Chapters 30 and 31 are of value for the years since 1968 as well. Journalistic accounts in major newspapers and magazines are also invaluable tools for an understanding of recent developments. Among general works, W. Laqueur, *Europe Since Hitler*, rev. ed. (1982), and W. Keylor, *The Twentieth Century: An International History* (1984), are particularly helpful with their extensive, up-to-date bibliographies. The culture and politics of protest are provocatively analyzed in H. Hughes, *Sophisticated Rebels: The Political Culture of European Dissent, 1968–1987* (1988), and W. Hampton, *Guerrilla Minstrels:*

John Lennon, Joe Hill, Woodie Guthrie, Bob Dylan (1986). B. Jones, *The Making of Contemporary Europe* (1980), is a good brief account, while G. Parker, *The Logic of Unity* (1975), analyzes the forces working for and against European integration. D. Swann, *The Economics of the Common Market,* 5th ed. (1984), carries developments into the 1980s. L. Barzini, *The Europeans* (1983), draws engaging group portraits of the different European peoples today and is strongly recommended. On West Germany, H. Turner, *The Two Germanies Since 1945: East and West* (1987); L. Whetten, *Germany's Ostpolitik* (1971); and W. Patterson and G. Smith, eds., *The West German Model: Perspectives on a Stable State* (1981), are good introductions. Willy Brandt eloquently states his case for reconciliation with the East in *A Peace Policy for Europe* (1969). The spiritual dimension of West German recovery is probed by G. Grass in his world-famous novel *The Tin Drum* (1963), as well as in the novels of H. Böll. W. Laqueur, *The Germans* (1985), is a highly recommended contemporary report by a famous historian doubling as a journalist. P. Jenkins, *Mrs Thatcher's Revolution: The End of the Socialist Era* (1988), and D. Singer, *Is Socialism Doomed? The Meaning of Mitterrand* (1988), are provocative studies on Great Britain and France in the 1980s. Two outstanding works on the Vietnam War are N. Sheehan, *A Bright and Shining Lie: John Paul Vann and America in Vietnam* (1988), and A. Short, *The Origins of the Vietnam War* (1989).

Among the many books to come out of the Czechoslovak experience in 1968, three are particularly recommended: H. Schwartz, *Prague's 200 Days: The Struggle for Democracy in Czechoslovakia* (1969); I. Svitak, *The Czechoslovak Experiment, 1968–1969* (1971); and Z. Zeman, *Prague Spring* (1969). M. Kaufman, *Mad Dreams, Saving Graces: Poland, a Nation in Conspiracy* (1989), carries developments through the summer of 1989, while R. Leslie, *The History of Poland Since 1863* (1981), provides long-term perspective. T. Ash's book cited in the Notes is the best early study of Solidarity and it and more recent articles by Ash are highly recommended. It may be compared with a less sympathetic account by N. Ascherson, *The Polish August: The Self-limiting Revolution* (1982). A. Bramberg, ed., *Poland: Genesis of a Revolution* (1983), is a valuable collection of documents with extensive commentary.

On the Soviet Union, in addition to works cited in Chapter 30, D. Shipler, *Russia: Broken Idols, Solemn Dreams* (1983), is a solid report by an American journalist, while A. Shevchenko, *Breaking with Moscow* (1985), is the altogether fascinating autobiography of a top Russian diplomat who defected to the United States. A. De Porte, *Europe Between the Superpowers: The Enduring Balance* (1979), and J. Hough and M. Fainsod, *How the Soviet Union Is Governed* (1979), are major scholarly studies. M. Lewin, *The Gorbachev Phenomenon: A Historical Inter-*

pretation (1988), is excellent on the origins of the ongoing reforms, while Walker's *The Waking Giant,* cited in the Notes, is a fascinating eyewitness account of Soviet life in the mid-1980s. B. Eklof, *Soviet Briefing: Gorbachev and the Reform Period* (1989), focuses on 1987, a critical year. *The New York Times,* a great newspaper, provides excellent coverage of the revolutions of 1989 and of fast-breaking developments in eastern Europe and in the Soviet Union.

Among innumerable works on recent economic developments, L. Thurow, *The Zero-Sum Society* (1981), is an interesting example of early 1980s pessimism in the United States, and it may be compared with the engaging and informative work by J. Eatwell, *Whatever Happened to Britain? The Economics of Decline* (1982). W. Rostow, *The World Economy: History and Prospect* (1977), is a massive scholarly tome by a perennial optimist, and P. Hawkins, *The Next Economy* (1983), contains intelligent insights that merit consideration by the ordinary citizen. Three major intellectual works, which are rather somber in their projections, are R. Heilbroner, *An Inquiry into the Human Prospect* (1974), and J. Revel, *The Totalitarian Temptation* (1977) and *How Democracies Perish* (1983).

Chapter Opener Credits

Chapter 1: *Courtesy of the Trustees of the British Museum.* The Royal Standard of Ur, peace panel.

Chapter 2: *Ronny Jaques/Photo Researchers.* Audience hall of King Darius, Persepolis.

Chapter 3: *John Veltri/Photo Researchers.* The Erechtheum, Parthenon.

Chapter 4: *Robert Harding Picture Library.* (Detail) Panel from Alexander Sarcophagus.

Chapter 5: *Michael Holford.* The Pont du Gard, a Roman aqueduct at Nîmes in southern France.

Chapter 6: *TSW/CLICK/Chicago Ltd.* Hadrian's Wall, Cuddy's Crag, Northumberland.

Chapter 7: *Scala/Art Resource.* Apse mosaic of S. Apollinare in Classe, Ravenna.

Chapter 8: *Stiftsbibliothek St. Gallen.* Carolingian soldiers laying siege to a town.

Chapter 9: *Giraudon/Art Resource.* St. Bernard, Abbot of Clairvaux, preaching to his fellow Cistercians.

Chapter 10: *The Pierpont Morgan Library.* "April," from *Hours of the Virgin.*

Chapter 11: *Jonathan Blair/Woodfin Camp & Associates.* Carcassonne, southern France.

Chapter 12: *Bibliothèque royale Albert 1er, Brussels.* Burying the victims of the plague, Tournai.

Chapter 13: *Scala/Art Resource.* The family and court of Lodovico II Gonzaga, of Mantua.

Chapter 14: *Courtesy, Dr. Henning Schleifenbaum.* Frederick the Wise of Saxony had a dream of Luther posting his theses with a gigantic quill.

Chapter 15: *Reproduced by courtesy of the Trustees, The National Gallery, London.* Jean de Dinteville and Bishop Georges de Selve, the French ambassadors, 1533.

Chapter 16: *Courtesy of the Board of Trustees of the Victoria & Albert Museum.* A tapestry depicting Louis XIV and his courtiers hunting in the grounds of Vincennes.

Chapter 17: *Robert Harding Picture Library.* Peter the Great's Summer Palace at Peterhof.

Chapter 18: *The British Library.* An early library in a British coastal town, 18th century.

Chapter 19: *The Bridgeman Art Library. Reproduced by courtesy of the City of Bristol and Art Gallery.* Broad Quay, Bristol, early 18th century.

Chapter 20: *Musée Carnavalet/Bulloz.* People in the Paris marketplace celebrating the news of the birth of the Dauphin, 1792.

Chapter 21: *Musée Carnavalet/Bulloz.* Locked out of their meeting hall, members of the Third Estate meet at an indoor tennis court, June 20, 1789.

Chapter 22: *The Bridgeman Art Library. Reproduced by courtesy of the Royal Holloway & Bedford New College, Surrey.* Paddington Station, London, 1862, bustling with middle-class travellers.

Chapter 23: *Historisches Museen der Stadt Wien.* Citizens of Vienna astride the barricades during the revolution of 1848.

Chapter 24: *Museum of London.* Urban growth, 19th-century London.

Chapter 25: *Fabio Lensini/Madeline Grimoldi.* The meeting of Garibaldi and Victor Emmanuel.

Chapter 26: *Peabody Museum of Salem. Photo: Mark Sexton.* Flags of various countries flying in front of factories at Canton Harbor.

Chapter 27: *Trustees of the Imperial War Museum.* World War One trench warfare.

Chapter 28: *Collection of Whitney Museum of American Art.* The unemployed seeking jobs during the 1930s Depression in the United States.

Chapter 29: *Archiv/Photo Researchers. Cindy Pardy, Artist.* Adolf Hitler at Bueckeberg (Westfalia).

Chapter 30: *Leonard Freed/Magnum.* A young *Grepo,* an East German border guard, manning the Berlin Wall in the 1960s.

Chapter 31: *Bill Ray, LIFE MAGAZINE, © Time Warner Inc.* Paris students riot, 1968.

Chapter 32: *Nicolas/Sipa-Press.* French nuclear reactor at St. Laurent des Eaux, France.

Notes on the Illustrations

Pages 2–3: Peace panel of the Royal Standard of Ur, mosaic, ca 2500 B.C. The "standard," a rectangular wooden box 18 inches long, was probably a sounding board of a musical instrument used on ceremonial occasions.

Page 7: Paintings by Stone Age hunters, from Lascaux caves in southern France, 15,000–10,000 B.C.

Page 15: Commemorative stele from Susa of the victory of Naramsin, after the Babylonian conquest of Sippar and other cities, ca 2389–2353 B.C. Pink sandstone; 78⅘ x 41⅓ in.

Page 19: Detail from an inlaid panel from a harp found in the Royal Cemetery at Ur, ca 2500 B.C.

Page 20: The judgments of Hammurabi were inscribed in 3600 lines of cuneiform writing on the 8 ft. high black basalt pillar. Late Larsa period, 1930–1888 B.C.

Page 23: The Narmer Palette was found in the ruins of a temple at Nekhen, ca 3100 B.C. Made of carved schist, h. 29¼ in., it is the earliest example of the Egyptians' hieroglyphic writing. From the Egyptian Museum, Cairo.

Page 26: Detail from a wall painting from an Old Kingdom tomb, ca 2300 B.C.

Page 28: This statue of the Goddess Selket is of gilded and painted wood, h. 90 cm., from the tomb of Tutankhamon, Valley of the Kings, Thebes. New Kingdom, 18th dynasty, 1347–1337 B.C..

Page 31: These four seated figures of Ramses II, h. 67 ft., each weighing 1,200 tons, are part of the façade fronting Ramses' Great Temple at Abu Simbel, 3200 B.C.

Page 34–35: At Persepolis Persians and delegations of subject peoples mounted the wide apadana steps with tributes for King Darius I, climbing past the figures of royal guards.

Page 38: A stone relief from Sargon II's palace at Dur-Sharrukin (modern Khorsabad), 8th century B.C.

Page 39: Fresco from a tomb at Beni-Hassan in Upper Egypt, ca 1890 B.C. From the Kunsthistorisches Museum, Vienna.

Page 45: Detail from the mosaic floor of the ancient Beth Alpha Synagogue, Israel.

Pages 46 and 49: Alabaster reliefs from the center palace, Nimrud, ca 745–727 B.C.

Page 51: From the Teheran Bastan Museum, Iran.

Page 52: Cyrus the Great's tomb at Pasargadae, Iran, is of limestone; from the Achaemenid Period, ca 530 B.C. From the Iranian Expedition of The Oriental Institute of The University of Chicago, 1932.

Page 53: Attributed to the "painter of Myson," ca 500 B.C.

Page 56: Closeup of relief on the southern wall, Persepolis, ca 500 B.C., from Achaemenid Period.

Pages 63–64: The Erechtheum, built during the reconstruction of the Acropolis by Pericles after its devastation by the Persians, is unique among Greek buildings; it has porches on three sides, each quite different in size and rising from different levels. It was constructed as a shrine enclosing the site where the city of Athens had its beginnings.

Page 67: One of the best-preserved of the lavish wall paintings that were covered by a thick layer of ash and pumice when a volcanic explosion tore apart half of the island of Santorini, or Thera, ca 1500 B.C.

Page 68: Funeral games of Patrochus: A fragment of an Athenian bowl from Pharsalus (Thessaly), 6th century B.C., signed by the painter Sophilus.

Page 75: This painting from the "Chigi" vase is the earliest surviving picture of the new style of close-order, heavily-armed infantry adopted by the Greeks, ca end of 8th century B.C. Found at Formello, near Rome; h. 10¼ in.

Page 86: This 5th century B.C. bronze, dredged from the sea near Cape Artemisium, in Attica, is thought to represent Poseidon or Zeus.

Page 90: Black-figured amphora, *Women working wool,* from Lekythos, ca 560 B.C., h. 6¾ in.

Pages 100–101: Detail from the Alexander Sarcophagus, ca 325–300 B.C.; h. of Frieze 69 cm; found in the royal cemetery at Sidon, Phoenicia, late 4th century B.C. Alexander, wearing the heroic lion's-scalp helmet, is on horseback at the left. From the Archaeological Museum, Istanbul.

Page 104: This mosaic, found at Pompeii, is thought to be a copy of an original painting of ca 330 B.C.

Page 116: Deities of Palmyrene in bas-relief, gypsum. Selukos Nikator crowning the Tyche of Dura.

Page 117: The Tyche (or Fortune) of Antioch; the original probably executed by Eutychides of Sikyon, ca 300 B.C. Marble; h. 37¾ in. Vatican, Galleria Candelabri: Scomparto IV, 48 inv. 2672.

Page 120: Life-size marble genre statue, probably created as a garden sculpture, ca 180 B.C. From the Palazzo dei Conservatori, Rome.

Page 122: The celestial globe of the Farnese Atlas is one of the finest representations of stars to appear in the antique world. The Farnese Atlas dates to the 1st–2nd century A.D. and is a marble copy of the Hellenistic original.

Pages 129–130: The Pont du Gard, at Nîmes in southern France, is the finest example of Roman practical engineering. This great aqueduct, 885 ft. long and made of unadorned stone blocks, was built ca A.D. 14 to bring water to Nîmes from higher ground to the north.

Page 133: This terracotta statue of the Sun god Aplu—known as Apollo to the Greeks—stood on a temple ridgepole in Veii. It was probably made by the sculptor Vulca, or his school, ca 500 B.C.

Page 142: Roman bronze decoration forming part of a horse harness, 3rd century B.C.

Page 150: Stone bas-relief, found in Saint Remy, Provence; 59 x 83 cm. From the Musée de la Civilisation Gallo-Romaine, Lyon.

Pages 156–157: A section of Hadrian's Wall at Cuddy's Crag, Northumberland. Hadrian's Wall was the formidable barrier that wound across northern Britain, 2nd century A.D.

Page 159: From the Museo della Terme, Rome.

Page 160: Detail, the onyx Chalcedony gem (cameo) of Augustus and Roma, early 1st century A.D. From the Kunsthistorisches Museum, Vienna.

Page 163: In this mosaic Virgil is seated between the muses of Epic and Tragedy, and reading from his *Aeneid.* From the Bardo Museum, Tunis.

Page 164: The reliefs adorning the Ara Pacis, the altar of Augustan peace, are among the greatest works of art of the early Roman empire. The Roman Senate had the altar erected on the Campus Martius to commemorate Augustus' return from Gaul, where he had been living for three years.

Page 167: Mosaic from the Sant'Apollinare Nuovo, Ravenna, 6th century A.D.

Page 170: Bas-relief of spoils being carried from the temple in Jerusalem. From the Arch of Titus, Rome, 80–85 A.D.

Page 174: The port of Ostia had been pillaged by pirates in 68 B.C. Augustus made it one of his many rebuilding projects. By A.D. 150 this large cosmopolitan city boasted new harbors, fine public buildings, airy apartments, and had become the largest receiving port in Italy.

Page 179: This 4th century porphyry group shows Diocletian and Maximian with their respective caesars, their sons-in-law. From the Basilica of San Marco, Venice.

Page 182: Roman mosaic of a North African villa, from the Bardo Museum, Tunis, 3rd or 4th century A.D.

Pages 190–191: Apse mosaic, S. Apollinare in Classe, Ravenna; ca A.D. 533–549.

Page 194: This uncolored pen and ink drawing is from the *Utrecht Psalter,* an outstanding example of a new mode of Carolingian illustration developed from a fusion of Anglo-Saxon, Irish, and Frankish techniques, 9th century. MS 32, fol. 90v.

Page 207: Miniature of St. Benedict, founder of the Abbey of Monte Cassino, blessing the Abbot Desiderius, who rebuilt the Abbey and founded a school of Byzantine-influenced mosaicists and painters.

Page 212: Fashioned in gilt bronze, this figure of a mounted warrior is part of the ornamentation on a Lombard chief's shield made about A.D. 700, found Stabio in Switzerland.

Page 215: Mosaic from Carthage, ca 500 A.D.

Page 218: Emperor Justinian and his court, A.D. 546–548, in mosaic at San Vitale, Ravenna, Italy.

Page 223: From Al-Biruni, *Chronology of Ancient Nations,* ca 1307 A.D., folio 10v.

Page 226: Detail of an ivory casket of Al Mughira, son of the caliph Abd-el-Rahman III, who was assassinated in 176 A.D.

Pages 230–231: Miniature from the St. Gallen "Golden Psalter," Cod. 22, p. 141.

Page 235: This bronze statue of the Emperor Charlemagne shows him carrying an orb to symbolize worldly peace. He was the first Christian monarch to be sculpted in an equestrian statue. 9th–10th century A.D.; h. 24 cm. (Louvre)

Page 245: Wellcome Institute Western MS 290, ps.-Galen, *Anatomy,* 15th century, fol. 53v.

Page 246: Wellcome Institute MS 544, *Miscellanea medica XVII,* early 14th century, fol. 65r.

Page 248: Cod. Pal. Germ. 164, fol. 6v (Heidelberger Sachsenspiegel)

Page 253: The invasion of Danes under Hinguar (Ingrar) and Bubba: Seven shiploads of men in three tiers. From *Life, Passion and Miracles of St. Edmund,*

King and Martyr in Latin, Bury St. Edmund's, ca 1130. Ms. 736, f. 9v.

Pages 258–259: Miniature from Jean Fouquet, *Les Heures d'Etienne Chevalier,* ca 1460. From Musée Conde, Chantilly.

Page 261: This plaque is one from a series of nineteen, known as the Magdeburg ivories (German or Northern Italian), 10th century; 5 x 4½ in. (41.100.157)

Page 263: From *Hadith of Bayad and Riyad,* Arab ms. 368, 13th century.

Page 264: Benedictine Abbey of Mont-Saint-Michel, founded in 708 in the Department of the Manche in northwestern France, a mile off the French coast in the English Channel and formerly an island at high tide. Heavily fortified.

Page 265: The third and greatest of the abbey churches of Cluny was begun by St. Hugh in 1088. By 1095 the east end was finished, and was consecrated by Pope Urban II, himself a former Cluniac monk. LAT 177 16, f. 91. Bibliothèque Nationale.

Page 266: Rievaulx Abbey was founded in Yorkshire, England, as a Cistercian house in 1130. By 1175 all of its monastic buildings were complete. The nave of Rievaulx Abbey, dating to 1135–1140, is today the oldest remaining Cistercian structure in the world.

Page 272: Crusaders fighting the Saracens. *Roman de Godefroi de Bouillon,* fol. 19r. Paris, 1337. Bibliothèque Nationale.

Page 273: FR 352, f. 62. Bibliothèque Nationale.

Pages 278–279: "April" miniature from the *Hours of the Virgin,* MS 399 fol. 5v. Flanders, ca 1515.

Page 281: From MS Sloane 2435, fol. 85, British Library.

Page 285: From *Piers Plowman,* MS. R.3, fol. 3v.

Page 287: From Rene I, d'Anjoy, *Le Mortifiement de vaine plaisance.* MS 705, f. 38v. French, 15th century.

Page 290: Miniature from the *Winchester Psalter;* English, painted at Winchester for the Bishop, Henry of Bois, ca 1150–1160. Cott. Ner. CIV, fol. 39r, British Library.

Page 292: From MS. 93, fol. 102, Pseudo-Apuleius, Herbarium C 111, 2.

Page 293: From MS Bodley 270b, fol. 176, Bodleian Library, Oxford.

Page 296: This is one of the most famous of a group of finely carved Parisian Caskets for jewels or other precious objects, probably all made in the same workshop. French, first half of the 14th century. L. 9¾ in.

Page 299: Miniature from Jean de Wavrin's *Chronique d'Angleterre,* siege of the castle of Mortagne. Flemish, late fifteenth century. MS. Roy. 14. E.IV, fol. 23r. British Library.

Page 301: From MS 13 321, Wiesbaden, Codex B, f lr. Museum of the City of Cologne.

Page 302: Frontispiece of Moralized Bible, thirteenth century.

Page 305: From the Exultet Roll (Burberini lat. 592), ca A.D. 1075; w. 11⅜ in.

Page 306: From Kenneth John Conant, *Cluny: Les églises et la maison du chef d'ordre.* The Mediaeval Academy of America Publication No. 77. Cambridge, Mass., 1968.

Pages 310–311: Carcassonne, in south-western France, is the most complete example today of a medieval fortified town. Parts of the walls go back to the Visigothic period, but most of the inner wall, with the citadel, dates from the 11th and 12th centuries, and the outer from the end of the 13th century. Extensive restoration was carried out in the 19th century.

Page 313: Presumed to be the work of Matilda, queen of William the Conqueror, the original tapestry (ca 1100) can be seen in the city of Bayeux, France. A replica is in the Victoria and Albert Museum, London.

Page 320: From Petro d'Eboli, *De Rebus siclis carmen,* Italian, ca 1200. Codex 120, f. 101.

Page 322: Head of a king, limestone, from front façade of Abbey of St. Denis. French, ca 1140. Founded as a royal abbey ca 630 by the Merovingian king Dagobert I, St. Denis was rebuilt by Suger 1137–1144. In its east end the transcendental quality of Gothic architecture was first expressed.

Page 323: Carrow Psalter MS., fol. 15v. Thirteenth century.

Page 325: Ms. Rh. 15 f. 54 recto.

Page 327: From Jacques de Guisis, *Chroniques de Hainaut,* Flemish, 1448. Ms 9242, fol. 48 verso.

Pages 331 and 335: Miniatures from the town laws of Hamburg, 1497.

Page 344: This tapestry, now in the Isabella Stewart Gardner Museum, Boston, was purchased from Bachereau, Paris, in 1897. It is 12 feet, 3 inches high and 14 feet, 10 inches wide, and may be part of a series of which another panel is in the Saragossa Cathedral.

Page 347: Pedro Berruguete (Spanish, 1477–1504), *St. Dominick presiding over an Auto da Fé.* Tempera on panel; 5′ ½″ x 3′ ¼″. From the sacristy of Santo Tomás of Avila, where there was a companion panel now believed to be in a private collection in London.

Pages 354–355: Miniature from the *Annales* of Gilles li Muisis, Flemish, 1352. MS 13076–7, fol. 24v.

Page 358: *St. Sebastian Interceding for the Plague-Stricken* by Josse Lieferinxe.

Page 361: From the *2nd Chronique* of Gilles li Muisis, Flemish, 1349, fol. 14v.

Page 366: From Sir Jean Froissart's *Chronicles of England, France and Spain,* 14th century. MS Fr. 2643, fol. 312v. Bibliothèque Nationale.

Page 367: This is the only known contemporary picture of Joan of Arc. AE^II 447, f. 27.

Page 368: From MS Roy 20 CVII, fol 41v, British Library.

Page 371: Detail, fresco by Domenico di Michelino, *Allegory of the Divine Comedy,* of Dante with *La Divina Commedia* 1465. Florence Cathedral.

Page 375: From MS Bodley 264, fol. 245v, Bodleian Library, Oxford.

Page 376: Misericord from Henry VII's Chapel, Westminster Abbey.

Page 379: During the French peasant rebellion of the 14th century, the most famous uprising was the *Jacquerie,* which began in the Beqauvais region in 1358, when men were killed if they didn't have worker's hands. From Sir Jean Froissart's *Chronicles,* MS Fr. 2643, fol. 226v. Bibliothèque Nationale.

Page 382: *The Four Horsemen of the Apocalypse,* woodcut ca 1498, by Albrecht Dürer, German painter and engraver (1471–1528) regarded as leader of the German Renaissance school of painting.

Pages 386–387: Andrea Mantegna (Italian, 1431–1506), *The Court of the Gonzaga Family,* 1473–1474. Fresco, w. ca 19′ 8″. From the Palazzo Ducale, Mantua. The Gonzaga family, who reigned over Mantua from 1328 to 1627, invited Mantegna to their court in 1460. He continued to paint there until his death. In this fresco, from the walls of the Camera degli Sposi, Mantegna shows an intimate family festivity, the visit paid by Cardinal Francesco Gonzaga to his parents in Mantua.

Page 389: Woodcut, Italian (Florence), probably late 15th century.

Page 392: The Palazzo Vecchio (1298–1314) is attributed to Arnolfo di Cambio and was built as the seat of the Signoria, the government of the Florentine republic. This fortified palace is also known as the Palazzo della Signoria.

Page 394: Filippo Brunelleschi (1377–1440), *Sacrifice of Isaac,* from the competition to design the north doors of the Baptistery of S. Giovanni, Florence, 1401–1402. Gilded bronze relief, 21 x 17½ in. (inside molding). From the Museo Nazionale del Bargello, Florence. Brunelleschi, trained as a sculptor, was the founder of the Renaissance style in architecture.

Page 395: Quentin Metsys (Dutch, 1466–1530), *The Moneychanger* (Goldweigher) *and His Wife,* 1514. Panel; 28 x 26¾ in.

Page 397: Benozzo Gozzolli (Italian), *Journey of the Magi,* ca 1459. From the Medici Riccardi Palace, Florence. Nominally of the journey of the Magi, this painting in fact shows the magnificence of the Florentine Renaissance Court, with Lorenzo de' Medici on a hunting expedition in the foreground. The fresco was commissioned by Piero de' Medici, seen in profile riding behind his son Lorenzo.

Page 398: Michelangelo Buonarroti (1475–1564), *David,* 1501–1504. Marble; h. 13′ 6″. Galleria dell'Accademia, Florence. Michelangelo was a Florentine painter, sculptor, and architect of the High Renaissance.

Page 401: Engraving by Johannes Stradanus (J. van der Straet), Belgian painter (1523–1605).

Page 403: Sofonisba Anguissola (Italian, 1532/35–1625), *Portrait of the Artist's Sister,* ca 1559. Oil on canvas; 33½ x 26 in. This prolific artist was the first of Renaissance women artists to establish an international reputation, and the first for whom a substantial body of work exists. In this portrait, her sister Minerva wears a medallion that depicts another Minerva, the ancient Roman goddess of wisdom and the arts.

Page 405: *The Adoration,* 1507, by Hans Baldung (also called Hans Grien or Grün), German painter, engraver, and designer of woodcuts and glass painting (1476?–1545).

Page 406: Engraving by Galle after Stradan.

Page 408: Jan van Eyck (Flemish, 1422–1441), *Madonna of Chancellor Rodin,* ca 1435.

Page 409: Hieronymus Bosch (Hieronymus van Aeken), Dutch painter (ca 1450–1516), *Death and the Miser.*

Page 411: From *Ethique d'Aristotle,* French, 15th century. MS I.2 (927), fol. 145r. Bibliothèque de la Ville, Rouen.

Page 415: From *Barcelona Haggadah,* Add MS 1476f, f. 28v., British Library.

Pages 418–419: Lucas Cranach the Elder (?) (1472–1553), *Traum zu Schwinitz,* an allegorical painting.

Page 422: Lucas Cranach the Elder (1472–1553), *Passional Christi und Antichristi,* Wittenberg, 1521.

Page 424: Lucas Cranach the Younger (German, 1515–1586), *Martin Luther and the Wittenberg Reformers,* ca 1543. Oil on panel; 27⅝ x 15⅝ in.

Page 425: Attributed to Hieronymus Bosch (Dutch, ca 1450–1516), *Christ Before Pilate.* Oil on panel, 80 by 100 cm.

Page 426: *The Small Crucifixion,* ca 1510, by Matthias Grünewald, German painter (ca 1465–1528). Wood; 24¼ x 18⅛ in. (1961.9.19)

Page 429: Matthias Gerung (Geron) (German, 1500–1569), *Satire on Indulgences,* before 1536. Coburg (I.349.11)

Page 430: Detail from the 1528 escutcheon of the town of Überlingen; in the Überlingen town hall.

Page 435: Titian (Tiziano Vecellio, 1487–1577), *Charles V on Horseback,* 1548. Oil on canvas; 10′ 10½″ x 9′ 2″. The colors of this portrait are dark, perhaps emphasized by restorations that followed damage incurred in a fire in the eighteenth century.

Page 439: Attributed to Jean Perrissin (ca 1530–1611), *Temple de Lyon, nommé Paradis,* 1565.

Page 442: Woodcut from Foxe, 1569 edition, British Library.

Page 443: *Sir Thomas More* (1478–1535), painted in 1527 by Hans Holbein the Younger, German painter (1497?–1543) and court painter to Henry VIII.

Page 447: Raphael, *Leo X with Cardinals Ludovico de' Rossi and Giuliano de' Medici,* commissioned between 1517–1519. Florence: Pitti Palace.

Page 448: Council of Trent by an unknown artist; detached fresco, Secretariat of State, Vatican.

Pages 456–457: Hans Holbein the Younger (1497?–1543), *Jean de Dinteville and Georges de Seluc (The Ambassadors),* 1533. 81¼ x 82½ in.

Page 459: *Cantino Planisphere,* Portuguese, color on parchment, ca 1502.

Page 469: Long the site of a royal residence and hunting lodge, Fontainebleau was expanded and transformed by Francis I in 1530–1540. Il Rosso (Giovanni Battista de'Rossi, 1494–1540), Florentine painter; Francesco Primaticcio, Italian painter and architect (1504–1570); and Sebastiano Serlio, Italian architect and writer on art (1475–1554) were called by Francis I from Italy to build and decorate the palace. The gallery of Francis I set a fashion in decoration imitated throughout Europe.

Page 470: School of Fontainebleau (French, 16th century), *Triple Profile Portrait;* oil on slate, ca 1560–1580; 22½ x 22½ in. (Acc. no. M1965.55)

Page 479: Jan Asselyn, *Gustav Adolf at the Battle of Lutzen,* 1632. 89.4 x 121.8 cm.

Page 481: David Vinckboons (Flemish-Dutch, 1576/1578–1632), *The Peasant's Misfortune.*

Page 484: MS Rawl. D 410, fol. 1, Bodleian Library, Oxford.

Page 492: Paulo Veronese (Paulo Caliari: 1528?–1588), *Mars and Venus United by Love.* Oil on canvas; 81 x 63⅜ in.

Page 493 Diego Rodriguez de Silva y Velázquez (1599–1660), *Juan de Pareja,* ca 1610–1670. Oil on canvas; h. 32 in.; w. 27½ in. The Metropolitan Museum of Art, Fletcher Fund, Rogers Fund, and Bequest of Miss Adelaide Milton de Groot (1876–1967), by exchange, supplemented by gifts from friends of the Museum, 1971.

Pages 498–499: Charles Lebrun (1619–1690), who conceived and designed the series from which this tapestry—the July Tapestry—comes, was very influential in the arts in France during Louis XIV's reign. He became director of the Gobelins factory, where this tapestry was made in the late 17th century.

Page 503: Philippe de Champaigne (French, 1602–1674), *Cardinal Richelieu Swearing the Order of the Holy Ghost.*

Page 504: Antoine Coysevox (French, 1640–1730), *Louis XIV,* statue for the Town Hall of Paris, 1687–1689.

Page 508: "The Noble Is the Spider," from Jacques Lagniet, *Receuil des Proverbes,* 1657–1663.

Page 510: Nicholas Poussin (French, 1594–1665), *The Rape of the Sabine Women,* ca 1636–1637. Oil on canvas; 60⅞ x 82⅝ in. (46.160)

Page 517: Velazquez, *The Fable of Arachne (The Tapestry Weavers),* 1644–1648. Oil on canvas; 7′ 3″ x 9′ 6″. This painting represents a scene in Juan Alvarez's tapestry and carpet workshop in Madrid.

Page 525: Johannes Vermeer, known as Jan Vermeer van Delft (Dutch, 1632–1675), *Woman Holding a Balance,* ca 1664. Canvas; 16¾ x 15 in.

Page 527: Hiob Adriaensz Berckheyde, *The Old Stock Exchange, Amsterdam.* Canvas; 85 x 105 cm. (Inv. no. 1043)

Page 528: Pieter Claesz (Dutch, 1597–1660), *Still Life with Musical Instruments.*

Pages 532–533: Peter the Great brought architects and

artists from the West to design and build his Summer Palace at Peterhof.

Page 544: J.C. Merk (or Merck) (d. 1730), *Prussian Riesengrenadier*, ca 1730. Plate 9 (Windsor 1260). Oil on canvas; 79½ x 39½ in.

Page 550: The Church of St. Basil (formerly the Cathedral of the Intercession), Moscow, 1555–1560, with 17th century additions.

Page 553: Etienne Falconnet (1716–1791), *The Bronze Horseman, St. Petersburg* (Leningrad), completed in 1783.

Page 555: The grand stairway of the Residenz at Würzburg (built by the powerful Schönborn family) was intended by its architect Balthasar Neumann (1678–1753) to allow a slow ascent to be able to take in gradually the ceiling painting by Giovanni Battista Tiepolo glorifying Bishop Schönborn, 1750–1753.

Pages 562–563: T. Malton, *Hall's Library at Margate*, aquatint, 1789.

Page 571: Louis XIV and Colbert visiting the Académie des Sciences, from C. Perrault's *Mémoires pour servir à l'histoire naturelle des animaux*, 1671.

Page 572: Frans Hals (Dutch, 1581/85–1666), *René Descartes*, 1649. Oil on panel, 19 x 14 cm.

Page 578: "Die Tafelrunde" is a copy by Joachim Tietze, Berlin, of the painting by Adolph von Menzel, 1850. The original belonged to the National Gallery, Berlin, and was destroyed in 1945.

Page 582: *Une Soirée chez Madame Geoffrin* by Anicet-Charles-Gabriel Lemonnier, (French, 1793–1824), depicts the first reading of Voltaire's "L'Orpheline de Chine" in 1755.

Page 586: V. Eriksen, *Catherine II on Horseback*, 1762.

Page 590: Marten Meytens (alternate spelling: Mijtens; Swedish-Austrian, 1695–1770), *Kaiseria Maria Theresie mit Familie*. Meytens was an active court painter; in 1759 he was made director of the Vienna Academy of Art.

Page 599: *Les Glaneuses* by Jean-François Millet (1814–1875), French genre and landscape painter of the Barbizon school. Oil on canvas, 21¼ x 26 in.

Page 604: Painting by Thomas Weaver, engraved by William Ward and published July 21, 1812. Mezzotint, 23⁷⁄₁₀ x 17⅘ in.

Page 615: Samuel Scott (English, 1702–1772), *Old East India Quay, London*, Victoria and Albert Museum. Samuel Scott was the most distinguished native English topographical view painter in the eighteenth century. Such painting was popularized in England by Canaletto during his residence there from 1746–1755.

Page 620: Frontispiece from a map of "the most Inhabited part of Virginia containing the whole province of Maryland with part of Pennsylvania, New Jersey and North Carolina drawn by Joshua Fry and Peter Jefferson in 1775," in Thomas Jeffrey's *America Atlas*, 1776, The British Library.

Page 622: Charles Willson Peale (American, 1741–1827), *General John Cadwalader, His First Wife Elizabeth and Their Daughter Anne*, 1772. Philadelphia Museum of Art: The Cadwalader Collection, purchased with funds contributed by the Pew Memorial Trust and gift of the Cadwalader Family. Peale was primarily an artist, yet also a naturalist and inventor. He enjoyed the generous patronage of John Cadwalader.

Pages 626–627: P. Debucourt, *Celebrations in Les Halls on the Birth of Dauphin, 21st January, 1782*.

Page 630: Jean-Baptiste Siméon Chardin (French, 1699–1779), *The Kitchen Maid*, ca 1738. Canvas; 18¼ x 14¾ in. (1952.5.38(117)) Chardin is now considered to be the most popular eighteenth century French artist. He was a realist in the manner of seventeenth-century Dutch masters.

Page 633: Attr. to Master of the Beguins (French, active ca 1650–1660), *Beggars at a Doorway*.

Page 640: Louis (or Antoine?) Le Nain (French, 1593–1648), *Famille de paysans dans un interieur*, ca 1640.

Page 647: "The Remarkable Effects of Vaccination," an anonymous nineteenth-century Russian cartoon in the Clements C. Fry Collection of Medical Prints and Drawings, Yale Medical Library.

Page 650: After M.E. Guignes, *Planting Crosses at Embrun in May*. From *L'Illustration*, 1855 (1ᵉ semester), p. 309.

Page 651: W.W. Wheatley, "Dancing around the Church," 1848.

Page 653: From the City Temple, London.

Pages 658–659: After David, and probably the work of a collaborator of David, *The Tennis Court Oath*. This is a slightly smaller painting than the famous pen drawing with sepia wash by David, 1791. It gives some idea of the intended color scheme of David's great project, which only remains as the famous drawing.

Page 664: John Trumbell (American, 1756–1843), *Signing of the Declaration of Independence*, 1786. Oil on canvas; 21⅛ x 31½ in. John Trumbell was considered to be one of the most significant American artists of his time.

Page 667: *Louis XVI and Benjamin Franklin*, France (Niderville, Lorraine). Probably by Charles Gabriel Sauvage, called Lemire (1741–1827). Biscuit porcelain, ca 1783–1785. H. 12⅝ in.

Page 672: A primitive but contemporary representation of the taking of the Bastille, by "Cholet" who was a participant in the attack.

Page 675: This was the first portrait of Mary Wollstonecraft, by an unknown artist, commissioned by William Roscoe.

Page 679: "Un Comité révolutionnaire sous la Terreur," after Alexandre Évariste Fragonard, French historical painter (1780–1850).

Page 682: Jacques-Louis David (French, 1748–1825), *Napoleon Crossing the Alps*. Oil on canvas.

Page 684: Francisco de Goya y Lucientes, *The Third of May, 1808* (1814–1815). Oil on canvas; 8 ft. 9 in. x 11 ft. 3½ in. Goya was known in the Spain of his day as a portraitist, history painter, and church painter.

Pages 690–691: William-Powell Frith (British, 1819–1909), *The Railway Station* (detail), completed 1862. Oil on canvas; 45¼ x 98¼ in.

Page 698: Engraving by Henry Beighton, 1717, of the atmospheric steam engine invented about 1705 by Thomas Newcomen, English blacksmith (1663–1729).

Page 701: Honoré Daumier (French, 1808–1879), *The Third-Class Carriage.* Oil on canvas. Daumier was both a caricaturist and a serious painter.

Page 712: From *Parliamentary Papers,* 1842, vol. XV.

Pages 718–719: Anton Ziegler, *Barricade in the Michaeler Square on the Night of 26 to 27 May 1848.* Oil on canvas; 68 x 55 cm.

Page 721: Isabey, *Congress of Vienna.* Royal Library, Windsor Castle, RL.21539.

Page 725: *Count Clemens von Metternich* (1773–1859) by Sir Thomas Lawrence, English painter (1769–1830).

Page 732: Left to right: K. Marx, F. Engels (rear), with Marx's daughters: Jenny, Eleanor, and Laura, photographed in the 1860s.

Page 734: John Constable (English, 1776–1837), *The Hay Wain.* Constable was one of the two great romantic painters of the period (Joseph Turner being the other), and was the first artist of importance to paint outdoors.

Page 737: Josef Danhauser (German, 1805–1845), *Liszt am Klavier,* 1840.

Page 739: Eugene Delacroix (French, 1798–1863), *Les Massacres de Scio.* Delacroix was leader of the Romantic school. This dramatic interpretation of a contemporary event scandalized Paris Salon visitors in 1824.

Page 743: Eugene Delacroix (French, 1798–1863), *Liberty Leading the People,* 1830. Oil on canvas; 10½ x 128 in. Exhibited at the Paris Salon of 1831, the painting was acquired by the French Government.

Page 745: Honoré Daumier (French, 1808–1879), *Legislative Belly,* lithograph, 1834, 42 x 52.5 cm. Charles Deering Collection (1941.1258)

Pages 754–755: John O'Connor, *St. Pancras Hotel and Station from Pentonville Road.*

Page 758: "The Court for King Cholera," cartoon from *Punch,* XXIII (1852), 139.

Page 759: From Mayhew's *London Labour and the London Poor;* after a daguerrotype Beard.

Page 762: Cross-section of a Parisian house, about 1850, from Edmund Texier, *Tableauade Paris,* Paris, 1852, vol. I, p. 65.

Page 768: Paul-Emile Chabas (French, 1869–1937), *Un Coin de Table,* 1904. Oil on canvas. Bibliotheque des Arts Decoratifs.

Page 772: Pierre-Auguste Renoir (French, 1841–1919), *Le Moulin de la Galette a Montmartre,* 1876. 4 ft 3½ in x 5 ft 9 in. Bequest of Gustave Caillabotte, 1894.

Page 775: Henri de Toulouse-Lautrec (French, 1864–1901), *At "A La Mie."* Oil on cardboard; 21 x 26¾ in. Purchased by S.A. Denio Fund and General Income for 1940.

Page 777: After a drawing by C. Koch, 1890.

Page 785: Hilaire Germain Edgar Degas (French, 1834–1917), *Les Repasseuses,*

Pages 788–789: Wall painting from the Town Hall and Civic Museum, Siena.

Page 792: Demolition of part of the Latin Quarter in 1860. Engraving from a drawing by Félix Thorigny.

Page 795: R. Legat, *Battle of Calatafim,* 1860.

Page 804: Thure de Thulstrup, *The Battle of Gettysburg,* from the *CIVIL WAR, Gettysburg* (Time-Life Books, Inc.). Courtesy, The Seventh Regiment Fund, Inc.

Page 807: Merchants of Nijni-Novgorod drinking tea. From *L'Illustration,* 29 August 1905.

Page 816: After Franz Schlegel, *Hussars of the 15th Regiment Dispersing Demonstrators in front of the Vienna Parliament Building, November 28, 1897.* Engraving.

Pages 822–823: Oil painting on glass, post 1780, by unknown Chinese artist.

Page 830: Townsend Harris, the American Consul, meeting with representatives of the Tokugawa Shogunate. Color on paper, 1857. Artist unknown. Tsuneo Tamba Collection, Yokohama.

Page 831: Scottish troops at the Great Sphinx at Giza, after helping to defeat Tarabi Pasha at the battle of Tel-el-Kebir, 1882.

Page 836: The intersection of Orchard and Hester Streets on New York City's Lower East Side, ca 1905. Oil over a photograph.

Page 841: A. Sutherland, *Battle of Omdurman,* September 2, 1898. Colored lithograph.

Page 844: From "The Graphic," November 9, 1895.

Page 849: Ichiyosai Kuniteru, *Tomioka raw-silk reeling factory,* ca 1875. Painted wood block. Tsuneo Tamba Collection, Yokohama.

Page 856–857: John Nash (English), *Over the Top.*

Page 859: Anton von Werner (German, 1843–1915), *The Congress of Berlin,* 1878.

Page 862: After a watercolor by Willy Stöwer (German), *The German Fleet,* 1907.

Pages 890–891: Isaac Soyer (American, 1907–   ), *Employment Agency,* 1937. Oil on canvas; 34¼ × 45 in. Whitney Museum of American Art (Purchase 37.44). Photo: Geoffrey Clements, New York.

Page 898: Edvard Munch (Norwegian, 1863–1944), *The Dance of Life,* 1899.

Page 900: Frank Lloyd Wright (American architect, 1869–1959), Falling Water, Bear Run, Pennsylvania —perhaps the greatest modern house in America, 1936. The largely self-taught Wright was an exponent of what he called "organic architecture": the idea that a building should blend in with its setting and be harmonious with nature.

Page 903: Pablo Picasso (Spanish, 1881–1973), *Guernica,* 1937. The original oil on canvas, 11 ft. 5½ in x 25 ft. 5¾ in., is in the Museo del Prado, Madrid.

Page 925: French caricature by C. Leavdre, 1898.

Page 929: Arkady Aleksandrovich Plastov (Russian 1893–1972) *Collective Farm Threshing,* 1949. Oil on canvas, 200 x 382 cm. Plastov's career was entirely in the Soviet era; his great paintings were calls to action—icons of socialism.

Page 945: The cartoon "Stepping Stones to Glory" by Sir David Low (1891–1963) appeared in the London *Evening Standard* on 8 July 1936.

Page 950: I. Toidze (Russian), *For the Motherland's Sake, Go Forward, Heroes,* 1942 poster.

Page 982: Detail from Diego Rivera's monumental fresco painting (8.59 x 12.87 m), *History of Mexico: From the Conquest to the Future,* 1929–1930. From the West Wall, Stairway of the Palacio Nacional, Mexico City. In this detail, the priest Hidalgo presides over the cause of independence. In the center the Mexican eagle, symbol of nationality, holds the Aztec emblem of ceremonial war. Rivera was a painter, printmaker, sculptor, book illustrator, as well as a political activist.

Index